CONTRACTS:

CASES AND COMMENTARIES

SEVENTH EDITION

Edited by

CHRISTINE BOYLE

Professor of Law,
University of British Columbia

and

DAVID R. PERCY, Q.C.

Dean of Law,
University of Alberta

THOMSON

CARSWELL

Library and Archives Canada Cataloguing in Publication Data

    Contracts: cases and commentaries / edited by Christine Boyle and David R. Percy. — 7th ed.

ISBN 0-459-24155-9

    1. Contracts—Canada—Cases. I. Boyle, Christine, 1949- II. Percy, David R., 1946-

KE850.A7C65 2004   346.7102   C2004-903589-4
KF801.A7C65 2004

Composition: Computer Composition of Canada Inc.

One Corporate Plaza
2075 Kennedy Road
Toronto, Ontario   M1T 3V4

Customer Relations:
Toronto 1-416-609-3800
Elsewhere in Canada/U.S. 1-800-387-5164
Fax 1-800-298-5094
www.carswell.com
E-mail: carswell.orders@thomson.com

CONTRIBUTORS

Janet K. Baldwin

of the Faculty of Law, University of Manitoba   Chapters 2 and 4

Christine L. M. Boyle

of the Faculty of Law, University of British Columbia   Chapters 1 and 13

Tamara Buckwold

of the Faculty of Law, University of Saskatchewan   Chapters 3 and 6

Richard F. Devlin

of the Faculty of Law, Dalhousie University   Chapter 10

Robert D. Flannigan

of the Faculty of Law, University of Saskatchewan   Chapters 5 and 12

John D. McCamus

of Osgoode Hall Law School   Chapter 7

David J. Mullan

of the Faculty of Law, Queen's University   Chapter 14

David R. Percy

of the Faculty of Law, University of Alberta   Chapters 4, 9 and 11

Nicholas S. Rafferty

of the Faculty of Law, University of Calgary   Chapter 8

James A. Rendall

of the Faculty of Law, University of Calgary   Chapter 8

Linda J. Vincent

of the Faculty of Law, University of Manitoba   Chapters 2 and 4

Robert Wai

of Osgoode Hall Law School   Chapter 2

PREFACE

This casebook had its genesis during the mid-1970s in a number of gatherings of contracts teachers at annual meetings of the Canadian Association of Law Teachers. It was inspired by a widely-held feeling that there was a need for a national book which might command acceptance across the common law provinces. Initially, Janet Baldwin of the University of Manitoba gathered materials from a number of teachers and these were used, in whole or in part, at several law schools in different parts of the country. These materials met with a favourable response and, at the C.A.L.T. meeting in Fredericton in 1977, the present editors were charged with the task of organizing the existing materials for publication.

The resulting book (of which this is the seventh edition) has therefore been produced by a number of law teachers. There have been a number of changes in the responsibility for individual chapters in this edition. We are pleased to welcome two new contributors, Professor Tamara Buckwold of the University of Saskatchewan, who has taken over responsibility for the chapters on Certainty and Contingent Agreements, and Professor Robert Wai of Osgoode Hall Law School, who has taken over responsibility for the chapter on Formation of the Agreement: Offer and Acceptance. We extend our thanks and best wishes to departing contributors, Professors Janet Baldwin and Linda Vincent of the University of Manitoba and Professor Don Clark of the University of Saskatchewan.

As editors, we have played two roles. As in the past, we have attempted to introduce a degree of uniformity to the various sections of the book without affecting the flavour of each individual contribution. We have also added commentaries and questions and notes throughout, when they appeared necessary, and have edited sections, sometimes drastically, in order to keep the size of the book within reasonable bounds. Nevertheless, one of the beneficial results of this type of co-operative casebook may be that students will be exposed to slightly different approaches to contracts problems.

In addition to our traditional role, in recent editions we have allowed our own views about teaching contracts and the nature of the subject to emerge more directly than in the past. We hope that we have succeeded in doing so in a manner that does not impose our views on those teachers who take a different approach.

This role was thrust upon us by two needs. First, it is difficult in a collaborative book to reflect some of the broader themes of contracts without intruding on the approach of an individual contributor. In the past, Christine Boyle addressed this need in a lengthy Student Introduction. However, this portion of the book was more than a conventional Introduction and, in the opinion of Christine's co-editor, raised important themes which deserved to be recognized as a regular part of a course in Contracts. Christine's reworked material was therefore elevated to the status of a chapter. Although it is found in Chapter One, it can be read and discussed at either, or both of, the beginning and end of the course. Under the former possibility, students will be alerted to the context of the materials which they are about to study. Under the latter possibility, students will have absorbed the details of the course and be in a position to reflect on their implications.

Second, if there is a dominant theme that has emerged over the life of this book, it concerns the place of Contracts in the law of civil obligations. At the time of the first edition, Canadian courts were still wrestling with the relationship between Torts and Contracts. Over the past decade, a similar debate has taken place over the interaction between fiduciary obligations and Contracts. Both of these developments cut across the individual categories of the subject in a manner that was difficult to accommodate in the traditional structure of a course in Contracts. Over the same time period, the courts began to explore the existence of a duty of good faith in Contracts and, partly because of the influential work of Professor Waddams, to rely increasingly on the principle of unconscionability. Most of these developments are concerned with the protection of people in vulnerable positions or with the imposition of limits on the ability of contracting parties to pursue their self interest. David Percy has therefore prepared in Chapter 11 some materials which explore briefly the inter-relationship between these currents and the different limits which some of them impose on the parties' pursuit of their own interests at the expense of their contracting partner.

We felt that it was unfair to place these materials in chapters that were the prime responsibility of other contributors and recognized that our own views are personal and might be tendentious. We have accordingly labelled the chapters "An Editor's Comment."

In this edition, we have retained the structural changes that were implemented in the sixth edition. As always, a considerable amount of new and topical material has been added. In Chapter 2, Professor Wai has dealt with the challenges of contract formation in electronic commerce (e-commerce) by including *ProCD v. Matthew Zeidenberg and Silken Mountain Web Services, Inc.* (1996), 86 F.3d 1447 (U.S. Court of Appeals, Seventh Circuit) and *Rudder v. Microsoft Corp.* (1999), 2 C.P.R. (4th) 474, 40 C.P.C. (4th) 394 (Ont. S.C.J.), as well as a note on e-commerce legislation. The chapter also notes continuing developments in the law of tenders.

Professor Buckwold has substantially re-written chapters 3 and 6. Chapter 3, on certainty of terms, contains an expanded discussion of good faith in contractual negotiations in the context of the decisions of the Courts of Appeal of British Columbia and New Zealand in *Mannpar Enterprises Ltd. v. Canada* (1999), 173 D.L.R. (4th) 243 (B.C. C.A.) and *Wellington City Council v. Body Corporate 51702 (Wellington)*, [2002] 3 N.Z.L.R. 486 (C.A.) respectively. The section on Anticipation of Formalization now includes *Bawitko Investments Ltd. v. Kernels Popcorn Ltd.* (1991), 79 D.L.R. (4th) 97 (Ont. C.A.). In Chapter 6, the remedial problem that occurs where there is a breach of a subsidiary obligation in a contingent agreement is now illustrated by *Eastwalsh Homes Ltd. v. Anatal Developments Ltd.* (1993), 12 O.R. (3d) 675 (Ont. C.A.).

The discussion of the different theoretical approaches to the enforcement of promises in Chapter 4 is now bolstered by the classic American decision of *Wood v. Lucy, Lady Duff-Gordon*, 118 N.E. 214 (1917). The debate on the direction of promissory estoppel in Canada and the distinction between the shield and the sword is illustrated by *M. (N.) v. A. (A.T.)* (2003), 13 B.C.L.R. 73 (B.C. C.A.).

Professor Flannigan's chapter on Privity now includes the Supreme Court of Canada decision in *Fraser River Pile & Dredge Ltd. v. Can-Dive Services Ltd.* [1999] 3 S.C.R. 108, which emerged just too late for the sixth edition. He includes in Chapter 12 the House of Lords decision in *Royal Bank of Scotland plc v. Etridge (No. 2)*, [2001] 3 W.L.R. 1021 (H.L.).

In Chapter 7, Professor McCamus has replaced the Ontario Business Practices Act with the Alberta Fair Trading Act, R.S.A. 2000, c. F.-2 as an example of the new generation of consumer protection legislation and has included notes on *978011 Ontario Limited v. Cornell Engineering Co.* (2001), 198 D.L.R. (4th) 615 (Ont. C.A.) and 968703 Ontario Ltd. v. Vernon (2002), 58 O.R. (3d) 215 (C.A.).

The *Cornell* case is also noted by Professor Rafferty in the chapter on Standard Forms and Exclusion Clauses, as well as *Guarantee Co. of North America v. Gordon Capital Corp.* (1999), 178 D.L.R. (4th) 1 (S.C.C.) and *Shelanu Inc. v. Print Three Franchising Corp.* (2003), 226 D.L.R. (4th) 577 (Ont. C.A.). He includes, on the application of exclusion clauses, the important case of *Solway v. Davis Moving & Storage Inc.* (2002), 62 O.R. (3d) 522 (C.A.), leave to appeal to S.C.C. dismissed May 29, 2003.

Chapter 9 on Mistake changed little through the first six editions of this book. The new chapter is considerably revamped by the inclusion of the English Court of Appeal decision in *The Great Peace*, [2002] 4 All E.R. 689 (C.A.), which has started a debate on the future of equitable mistake in Canada. The House of Lords re-cast the old chestnut of mistaken identity by its controversial examination of how the law of contracts might respond to identity theft in *Shogun Finance Ltd. v. Hudson* [2003] UKHL 62 and the Supreme Court of Canada has provided a new starting point for the analysis of rectification in *Performance Industries Ltd. v. Sylvan Lake & Tennis Club Ltd.* [2002] 1 S.C.R. 1.

Professor Devlin's chapter on frustration now includes *KBK No. 138 Ventures Ltd. v. Canada Safeway Ltd.* (2000), 185 D.L.R. (4th) 650 (B.C. C.A.).

The chapter on Illegality and Public Policy includes notes on *M. v. H.*, [1999] 2 S.C.R. 3 and *Transport North American Express Ltd. v. New Solutions Financial Corp.* (2004), 235 D.L.R. (4th) 385 (S.C.C.).

Chapter 14 now contains *Attorney-General v. Blake*, [2001] 1 A.C. 268 (H.L.), dealing with disgorgement of profits and the important S.C.C. decision on punitive damages in *Whiten v. Pilot Insurance*, [2002] 1 S.C.R. 595. The material on specific performance includes *John E. Dodge Holdings Ltd. v. 805062 Ontario Ltd.* (2003), 63 O.R. (3d) 304 (C.A.).

The book continues to be designed primarily as a teaching tool rather than a reference work. Accordingly, we have generally given limited citations in the body of the text, with more extensive correlative citations in the Table of Cases.

The materials and their organization are somewhat traditional, for they are designed to constitute the basis of a core course in contracts. We do not attempt to imbue the reader with a particular philosophy of the law of contracts and indeed any attempt to do so would be fruitless given the number and variety of our contributors. Rather we try to note a number of different approaches to contracts throughout and to leave scope for individual teachers to pursue their own themes with these materials as a solid base. The book is, of course, designed for use in all common law courses and as a result we include from different jurisdictions statutory references where appropriate and try to avoid concentration upon a particular province when excerpts from statutes are included in the materials. It is hoped that this will awaken students to the increasingly different legislative trends which have been adopted across the country and create an awareness of the approaches of jurisdictions other than the one in which they are studying.

In reflecting these important developments, we hope that we have retained the features of earlier editions, which have commanded broad acceptance at law schools which focus on the common law. Christine Boyle wishes to acknowledge the financial support of the University of British Columbia and the intelligent and reliable contribution of her research assistant, Jesse Nyman. David Percy very much appreciates the contribution of his assistant, Patricia Curtis, the many thoughtful comments of his colleague, Shannon O'Byrne, and valuable discussions with Richard Bauman and Moin Yahya. On behalf of David Mullan, we express appreciation to Martha Boyle for research assistance. Finally, we both appreciate the continued support of our publishers, who do an outstanding editing job.

Christine Boyle
David R. Percy
Vancouver and Edmonton
April 30, 2004

ACKNOWLEDGMENTS

The Editors are grateful to the following persons and organizations for permission to reproduce the materials or excerpts indicated below.

Alberta Reports
Maritime Law Book Ltd.
Fredericton, New Brunswick

All England Law Reports
Butterworth & Co. (Publishers) Ltd.
London, England

American Law Institute's Restatement of the Law, Second: Contracts
The American Law Institute
Philadelphia, Pennsylvania
© 1979 by The American Law Institute. Reproduced with permission.

Atlantic Provinces Reports
Maritime Law Book Ltd.
Fredericton, New Brunswick

Canadian Insurance Law Reporter
C.C.H. Canadian Limited
North York, Ontario

Cheshire, Fifoot & Furmston Law of Contract, 12th edition (1991)
M.P. Furmston
The Butterworths Division of Reed Elsevier (UK) Limited
London, England

Commercial Fiduciary Obligation
R. Flannigan
Alberta Law Review
Faculty of Law, University of Alberta
Edmonton, Alberta

Commonwealth Law Reports
The Law Book Company Limited
New South Wales, Australia

A Contract
William E. Conklin
in Richard F. Devlin ed. Canadian Perspectives on Legal Theory (1991)
Emond Montgomery
Toronto, Ontario

Contracts — Innominate Terms: Contractual Encounters of the Third Kind
Allan C. Hutchinson and John N. Wakefield
Canadian Bar Review
University of New Brunswick, Faculty of Law
Fredericton, New Brunswick

Developments in Contract Law
B. Reiter and K. Swan
Supreme Court Law Review 1978-79 Term
Butterworths Canada Ltd.
Markham, Ontario
Reprinted with permission of Butterworths Canada Ltd. 1980

Do We Need a Parol Evidence Rule?
Stephen M. Waddams
Canadian Business Law Journal
Toronto, Ontario

Dominion Law Reports
Canada Law Book
Aurora, Ontario

Donor Insemination Agreement
barbara j. findlay
Dahl findlay Connors
Vancouver, British Columbia

Economic Analysis of Law
Richard A. Posner
Little, Brown
Toronto, Ontario

English Reports
Sweet & Maxwell Ltd.
London, England

Good Faith in Contractual Performance: Recent Developments
Shannon Kathleen O'Byrne
Canadian Bar Review
University of New Brunswick, Faculty of Law
Fredericton, New Brunswick

An Introduction to The Law of Contract 5th edition (1995)
P.S. Atiyah
Oxford University Press
Oxford, England
© Patrick Selim Atiyah 1995
Reprinted by permission of Oxford University Press

The Judicial Control of Contractual Unfairness
David Tiplady and Modern Law Review
Blackwell Publishers
Oxford, England

The Law of Contract, 2nd edition (1993) and 3rd edition (1997)
Hugh Collins
The Butterworths Division of Reed Elsevier (UK) Limited
London, England

The Law of Contract 9th edition (1995)
G.H. Treitel
Sweet & Maxwell Ltd.
London, England

The Law of Contracts, 1977 edition and 4th edition (1999)
Stephen M. Waddams
Canada Law Book Inc.
240 Edward Street,
Aurora, Ontario
L4G 3S9 Canada

The Law Reports
The Incorporated Council of Law Reporting for England and Wales
London, England

Legal Essays and Addresses (1939)
Lord Wright of Durley
Cambridge University Press

North American Branch
New York, New York
Reprinted with the permission of Cambridge University Press.

The Limits of Freedom of Contract (1993)
Michael J. Trebilcock
Harvard University Press
Cambridge, Massachusetts

Lloyd's List Reports
Lloyd's of London Press
London, England

Mistake in Equity: Solle v. Butcher Re-examined
Davies
Manitoba Law Journal
University of Manitoba
Winnipeg, Manitoba

National Reporter

New Brunswick Reports (Second Series)

Newfoundland and Prince Edward Island Reports

Nova Scotia Reports (Second Series)
Maritime Law Book Ltd.
Fredericton, New Brunswick

Ontario Reports
Law Society of Upper Canada
Toronto, Ontario

Pacific Reporter 2d

North Western Reporter
West Publishing Company
Eagan, Minnesota

The Parol Evidence Rule (1976)

McLauchlan
Professional Publications Ltd.
Wellington, New Zealand

The Path of the Law
Oliver Wendell Holmes
Harvard Law Review
Cambridge, Massachusetts
Copyright © 1897 by The Harvard Law Review Association

Penzoil v. Texaco
M.G. Yudof and J.L. Jeffers
Alberta Law Review
Faculty of Law, University of Alberta
Edmonton, Alberta

Privity of Contract: Contracts for the Benefit of Third Parties (1996)
Law Com. No. 242, Cm 3329
The Law Commission for England and Wales
Norwich, England
Crown copyright material is reproduced with the permission of the Controller
of Her Majesty's Stationery Office

The Reliance Interest in Contract Damages
L.L. Fuller and William R. Perdue, Jr.
Yale Law Journal
New Haven, Connecticut
Reprinted by permission of The Yale Law Journal Company and Fred B.
Rothman & Company from *The Yale Journal*, Vol. 46, at pp. 52-63

Report on Amendment of the Law of Contract (1987)
Ontario Law Reform Commission
© Queen's Printer for Ontario

Report on Sale of Goods (1979)
Ontario Law Reform Commission
© Queen's Printer for Ontario

**Restitutionary Recovery of Benefits Conferred Under Contracts in Conflict
with Statutory Policy — The New Golden Rule**
John D. McCamus
Osgoode Hall Law Journal

Osgoode Hall Law School
North York, Ontario

The Right to Procreate: When Rights Claims Have Gone Wrong
L. Shanner
McGill Law Journal
Revue de droit de McGill inc.
Montreal, Quebec

Social Force Majeure — A New Concept in Nordic Consumer Law
Thomas Wilhelmsson
Journal of Consumer Policy
Kluwer Academic Publishers
Norwell, Massachusetts

Sourcebook on French Law (1996)
D. Pollard
Cavendish Publishing Limited
London, England

Supreme Court Reports (Canada)
Supply and Services Canada
Hull, Quebec

Winfield and Jolowicz on Tort 13th edition (1989)
W.V.H. Rogers
Sweet & Maxwell Ltd.
London, England

A Note Regarding Case Citations

As part of Carswell's commitment to provide you with convenient and current legal information, case references added to this service also include Westlaw*e*CARSWELL citations.

Carswell is pleased to provide Westlaw*e*CARSWELL to law faculty and students attending a Canadian law school. Contact your Law Library Director to obtain a complientary password.

The following is an example of the Westlaw*e*CARSWELL citation format used on Westlaw*e*CARSWELL and in this service:

2004 CarswellOnt 1234

- **"2004"** is the year of the decision.
- **"CarswellOnt"** indicates that this is a decision from the Province of Ontario added to Westlaw*e*CARSWELL. Similarly, **"CarswellBC"** indicates a decision from the Province of British Columbia added to Westlaw*e*CARSWELL, and so on. Cases originating in Federal Courts have **"CarswellNat"** citations, while a decision from the Supreme Court of Canada will have a cite based on the jurisdiction in which it originated. Thousands of judicial decisions from every jurisdiction across Canada are available on Westlaw*e*CARSWELL.
- **"1234"** indicates that this was the 1, 234th decision added to Westlaw*e*CARSWELL in 2001.

The addition of Westlaw*e*CARSWELL cites will provide a convenient point of reference for those who use Westlaw*e*CARSWELL. Please note, however, that case citations previously added to this service may not necessarily contain Westlaw*e*CARSWELL cases.

Westlaw*e*CARSWELL is a leading, Internet-based legal research service which combines the Internet's simplicity with state-of-the-art searching capabilities. If you would like to learn more about Westlaw*e*CARSWELL or are interested in seeing this valuable product, we invite you to call Customer Relations at 416-298-5140 (Toronto) or 1-800-387-5164 (North America) or visit our website at http://www.carswell.com/.

CONTENTS

TABLE OF CASES

(Page references to primary cases appear in bold.)

Chapter 1

AN INTRODUCTION TO THE STUDY OF THE LAW OF CONTRACTS: AN EDITOR'S COMMENT

The law of contracts has been called "an affirmation of the human will to affect the future" through the "extraordinarily powerful mechanism [of] protecting exchange into the future." Macneil, *The New Social Contract* (1980), at 6-7. Its study should be valuable to you for a number of reasons. You will gain a familiarity with the substantive law, that is, the law relating to the formation of contracts, factors affecting the validity of contracts, and remedies for breach of contract. This is important in itself and provides a useful stepping-stone to courses drawing on the general principles of contract law, such as sale of goods, consumer protection, insurance, real estate transactions, and labour law. In terms of the basic values underlying legal systems generally, reflection on a value fundamental to the law of contracts, namely freedom of contract, will equip you to engage in analysis of areas of law where overlapping or conflicting values are at stake, such as human rights law and property law.

On a different level, you will also acquire a variety of basic skills associated with the analysis and use of case law and, to a rather lesser extent, legislation. This book is designed as an aid to the acquisition of these essential skills, via the study and discussion of the decisions of the courts as well as statutory law and academic comment. You will notice a continuing emphasis on the application of rules and principles to hypothetical fact situations, as well as notes and questions designed to encourage you to consider the direction of possible law reform.

An understanding of principles and the acquisition of legal techniques and skills are not all that is important to the person who wishes to have a legal education. The law should not be studied in a philosophical vacuum, without consideration of its function in society and without discussion of the value judgments inherent in any judicial decision or legislative rule. Since values change and since the common law is made up of a large number of decisions based on particular fact situations, the law is constantly evolving, at some times more rapidly than at others, and is not made up of a static body of rules, simply awaiting discovery by the conscientious student.

However, the urge to find the reassuring certainty of a settled and coherent body of doctrine with its own internal logic is an understandable one and is in fact reflected in some of the enormously rich academic writing about the law of contracts. No one approach to the study of this area of law is emphasized here, as this book is intended to contain what the contributors feel to be core materials for a basic course in the principles of contract law. Your own instructor will direct you to and discuss with you the writings that he or she feels will best promote critical reflection on the basic material reproduced here. However, it may be useful at this point to consider some broad themes.

1. The Classical Theory of Contract

There is academic debate about the point at which it was possible to say that a body of law containing general principles relevant to all contracts had emerged, but there is some agreement that what is often called the "classical" theory of contract, consistent with the ideology of *laissez faire* liberalism, flourished in the 19th century. This is a shorthand way of referring to a number of ideas—that the law could be reduced to statements of rules, and conflicting cases labelled as "wrong"; that the law was concerned with the objective manifestation of agreement, not the parties' private thoughts; that freedom existed for people to contract as they chose; that the law should leave individuals free to maximize their private advantage; and that contractual liability was strict once a bargain that the law recognized as a contract had been struck. These ideas retain great power, and some academic writing still gives the impression of a rather stable body of rules relating to such familiar headings as Offer, Acceptance, and Consideration. The roots of contract law in English sources are still evident, and statutory changes have tended to be concentrated in areas that have acquired the status of subjects to be studied in their own right, such as sale of goods and human rights, mentioned earlier.

The idea that there is a stable body of doctrine has been confronted with cogent arguments that we must pay attention to what the courts are actually doing. In one controversial and stimulating book, *The Death of Contract* (1974), Gilmore concludes, at 102:

> I have one final thought. We have become used to the idea that, in literature and the arts, there are alternating rhythms of classicism and romanticism. During classical periods, which are, typically, of brief duration, everything is neat, tidy and logical; theorists and critics reign supreme; formal rules of structure and composition are stated to the general acclaim. During classical periods, which are, among other things, extremely dull, it seems that nothing interesting is ever going to happen again. But the classical aesthetic, once it has been formulated, regularly breaks down in a protracted romantic agony. The romantics spurn the exquisitely stated rules of the preceding period; they experiment, they improvise; they deny the existence of any rules; they churn around in an ecstasy of self-expression. At the height of a romantic period, everything is confused, sprawling, formless and chaotic—as well as, frequently, extremely interesting.

When reading the cases in this book consider to what extent Canadian judges adhere rigidly to what they conceive to be established doctrine, particularly in the form of English case law, and the extent to which you can find traces of experimentation (whether stated or not) with "romantic" ideals relating to the purposes of contract law.

Law is a social construct and so for various societal reasons, including economic, technological, and social, the law must change and adapt over time.

Examples include the creation of a body of labour law in response to the industrial revolution and the modern law of negligence in response to the increasing complexity of social interaction. The law of contracts is no different. As new technologies emerge that allow parties to contract in a multiplicity of fashions, the law of contracts must adapt to meet these developments. The recent widespread use of the Internet and e-mail has presented one such challenge. As Michael Geist writes in *Internet Law in Canada*, 3rd ed. (2002), at 598:

> In certain respects, the introduction of new technologies has not disrupted the "ebb and flow" of contract law. It has adequately adapted to the internet predecessors such as post mail, telex machines and fax machines. E-mail and the World Wide Web are simply the newest incarnations along this evolutionary path.
>
> The Internet does, however, present some novel issues . . . contracts consummated "on the fly" without an underlying relationship . . . clickwrap agreements. . . . a contract that is assented to by clicking "I Agree" . . . [and] can parties be bound to new terms after the exchange of consideration?

In this edition, increased attention is paid to issues of how the law is developing to confront such novel issues.

2. The Intersection of "Private" and "Public" Law

It would be a mistake to think of the law of contracts as exclusively concerned with private exchanges. There are many ways in which the private or free market presupposes, overlaps or exists in tension with public regulation.

First, as Trebilcock, a law and economics scholar, graphically writes in *The Limits of Freedom of Contract* (1993), at 23:

> [I]f political, bureaucratic, regulatory, judicial, or law enforcement offices were auctioned off to the highest bidder, or police officers, prosecutors, bureaucrats, regulators, or judges could be freely bribed in individual cases, or votes could be freely bought and sold, a system of private property and private exchange would be massively destabilized.

Indeed, it has been said, for instance, by Hutchinson, a critical legal scholar (in his comment on Trebilcock's book, "Michael and Me: A Post-Modern Friendship" (1995), 33 Osgoode Hall L.J. 237 at 244), that the free market is a form of government regulation in itself.

Second, markets are not simply left to operate untouched by democratic decisions about how to promote such things as equality, a healthy environment, safe and fair working and housing conditions, and the public welfare in general. Debates about the appropriate balance between private ordering and public regulation, for instance, in relation to such areas as rent control and minimum wage laws, are commonplace with respect to the law of contracts. Such debates about the relative value that should be placed on autonomy and welfare considerations take place most dramatically in relation to such areas as preconception contracts (surrogacy) and sexuality, discussed in Chapter 13 on Illegality and Public Policy, although it seems to be relatively uncontroversial in Canada at the moment that some things, such as blood and human organs, should not be commodified. You will find that thinking about such issues makes it clear that, as Trebilcock also notes, *supra*, at *v*, "[b]ehind the law of contracts lies a much broader set of economic, social, and political values that define the role of markets in our lives."

3. "Freedom of Contract"

There are signs of judicial as well as legislative moves away from a rigid insistence on the idea that people are *free* to contract as they wish (which has, of course, never been true to more than a limited extent), and that therefore contracts are sacred, towards a recognition of the economic and psychological realities of contracting. You can draw on your own experience as to the degree to which freedom of contract is a reality. On a trivial level, have you ever tried to negotiate a dry cleaning contract? On a much more fundamental level, do you believe that anyone has refused to contract with you, for instance, by refusing to rent you an apartment because of your race or because you were on welfare? Might a contract have been terminated because of the discovery of your sexual identity, as in *Vriend v. Alberta*, [1998] 1 S.C.R. 493? For an example of drawing on experience of discrimination rather than freedom, see Grider, "Hair Salons and Racial Stereotypes: The Impermissible Use of Racially Discriminatory Pricing Schemes" (1989), 12 Harv. Women's L.J. 75. One can turn as well to empirical research into how freedom may be affected by social location. One well-known investigation was into the price paid for cars in Chicago. See Ayres, "Fair Driving: Gender and Race Discrimination in Retail Car Negotiations" (1991), 104 Harv. L.R. 817. Ayres found that retail car dealerships systemically offered significantly better final prices on identical cars to white men than they did to black people and women. Moreover, he notes at 829, race and gender discrimination were synergistic or "superadditive": the discrimination against the black female tester was greater than the combined discrimination against both the white female and the black male tester." See also Ayres, "Further Evidence of Discrimination in New Car Negotiations and Estimates of its Cause" (1995), 94 Mich. L. Rev. 109. More recent research has focused on insurance contracts, raising concerns about availability, service, cost and coverage linked to social location. See, for instance, Glenn, "The Shifting Rhetoric of Insurance Denial" (2000), 34 Law and Society Rev. 779, and Tarr, "Civil Orders for Protection: Freedom or Entrapment?" (2003), 11 Wash. U. J.L. & Pol'y 157 (re insurance for battered women) at 177.

There are legal as well as empirical limits on freedom of contract, some of which are the subject of debate. For instance, the Trillium Gift of Life Network Act, S.O. 1990, c. H.20, s. 10, states:

> No person shall buy, sell or otherwise deal in, directly or indirectly, for a valuable consideration, any tissue for a transplant, or any body or part or parts thereof other than blood or a blood constituent, for therapeutic purposes, medical education or scientific research, and any such dealing is invalid as being contrary to public policy.

Furthermore, the law has responded to experiences that freedom of contract includes freedom to discriminate in various ways. While the primary focus of these materials is on the common law principles of contract law, you should be aware that there is legislation dealing with such matters as consumer protection, employment standards and residential tenancies. As mentioned above, an important body of law which interacts with contract law relates to human rights, leg-islative efforts to combat such evils as racism and sexism in the market. Indeed concerns about freedom of contract and freedom from discrimination are signif-icantly intertwined. For instance, the Human Rights Code, R.S.B.C. 1996, c. 210, s. 13, prohibits, among other things, discrimination in employment.

While debates about the freedom of contract and discrimination are closest to the surface in relation to government regulation, there are similar tensions in the common law itself. While the common law of contract has not developed a principle of non-discrimination, it has become more activist in protecting vulner-able people. This can be seen in a number of doctrines. For example, the doctrine of unconscionability offers some protection from unfair bargains. Here the law insists on individual responsibility to avoid taking advantage of inequality. An-other area where arguments can be made about the appropriate mix of self-interest and responsibility toward others is the evolving doctrine of good faith. This doctrine is evolving, although it is not yet possible to say that there is a general obligation to act in good faith in negotiation and performance. See generally, Beatson and Friedman, *Good Faith and Fault in Contract Law* (1995) and Burton and Anderson, *Contractual Good Faith* (1995). As you study these materials, try to identify areas where there is an explicit or implicit imposition of a duty to act in good faith and consider what the content of such a duty might be. For instance, is there a duty to negotiate the renewal of a lease in good faith? To what extent are aggrieved parties likely to be denied remedies where they have failed to act in good faith? A further discussion of this concept, which transcends basic con-tractual doctrine relating to formation and performance of contracts, will be postponed until later in this book.

Finally, there is a tendency to present freedom of contract (the emphasis on individual autonomy) and freedom from economic oppression (the emphasis on both collective responsibility and individual responsibility for others) as compet-ing sets of values. For an argument that each principle needs the other for its own coherence, see Brudner, "Reconstructing Contracts" (1993), 43 U.T.L.J. 1, at 7:

> On the one hand, without any restraint in the name of equality, freedom of contract contradicts itself, for it collapses into the right of the stronger. On the other hand, the absolutization of equality destroys freedom of contract and thereby contradicts itself as a realization of equal *autonomy*.

Given such debates, some writers find it useful to refer to modern contract law as neoclassical. Thus:

> [A]s a matter of substantive principle neoclassical contract law attempts to balance the indi-vidualist ideals of classical contract with communal standards of responsibility to others.

Feinman, "The Significance of Contract Theory" (1990), 58 U. of Cinn. L.R. 1283, at 1287-88. (This article contains a useful overview of the principal theories of contract outside the neoclassical mainstream.)

4.   What Promises are Enforceable?

Not all promises are legally enforceable, so a central question for the contracts lawyer concerns the identification of those which are. Expectations, reasonable and otherwise, can be aroused by a number of things, so that the initial
chapters of this book are devoted to materials relating to the creation of the
obligation—the issue of what it is that people do to attract the enforcement
machinery of the law with respect to their commitments. The traditional view has
been that expectations are only protected where they have been aroused by an
exchange, or by the promise of an exchange. Contracts lawyers use the term of
art "consideration" to refer to the idea that a promise must usually be bought in
some way to be enforceable. Thus, if someone had been promised a gift of $1,000
and, as a result, had at least some expectation of receiving that amount, the law
would not normally enforce the promise because it lacked "consideration". The
law might have been influenced to a greater extent by morality and developed a
rule that *all* promises should be kept (although there might be economic objections
to this). One alternative that is already having some impact on the law is that
promises which have been reasonably relied upon should be kept. See, *e.g.*,
Atiyah, "Contracts, Promises and the Law of Obligations" (1978), 94 L.Q.R. 193.
He argues, at 207, that there is an "increased emphasis on reliance and [a] declining
stress on free choice" and states these ideas more fully in his book, *The Rise and
Fall of Freedom of Contract* (1979).

You will start to develop your own ideas soon about which obligations are
(and should be) legally enforceable—when an expectation by one individual is
sufficient justification for imposing a legal obligation on another. In doing this it
will be necessary to look behind the words of the judges who decide cases, and
who often still find the justifications for their decisions in discovering the "intentions" of the parties. When you encounter this type of language consider to what
extent the judge tries to discover the "intention" of the parties and to carry out
that intention, or whether in some cases this is simply a convenient way of saying,
without appearing too paternalistic, that the judge is satisfied that the result
reached is a fair one.

5.   What Remedy for Breach?

The language of "expectation" and "reliance" is also used with respect to
another fundamental issue. Once it is established that an enforceable promise
exists, and there is a breach of that promise, the question becomes one of the
appropriate remedy. Of course it must be remembered that in the vast majority of
cases contracts are performed and any disputes are settled without recourse to the
courts. It is an assumption that perhaps can be said to form part of the classical
theory of contract law that legal remedies have an impact on human behaviour.
That cannot be demonstrated without empirical research into what contracting
parties actually do and think, and there is at least one school of thought which
minimizes the significance of the law as a mechanism for dispute settlement.
Macauley, in his article, "Elegant Models, Empirical Pictures and the Complex-

ities of Contract" (1977), 11 Law and Soc. R. 507, at 510, states that "other techniques of dispute avoidance and settlement are usually available that will produce acceptable results, allow relationships to continue and cost much less than litigation". The law and lawyers are supposed to be providing a service for consumers. If the law is too complex and unpredictable, as well as being destructive rather than supportive of continuing relationships, then it is surely not living up to the reasonable expectations of those consumers.

The usual remedy for breach is the award of damages, although in some cases the aggrieved party (the plaintiff) will be entitled to the remedy of specific performance—an order to the party in breach (the defendant) to carry out his or her promise—or an injunction—an order to the defendant not to act in breach of contract. These remedies are available where monetary damages are not a sufficient remedy. The amount of money that the plaintiff should get as compensation often poses difficult problems for the courts. Should the plaintiff get his or her out-of-pocket or reliance losses or should there be an entitlement to the amount of profit that the plaintiff expected to make out of the contract? Will there necessarily be a clear distinction between the two? Clearly the answer will not always be the same and the answer is intimately bound up with the rationale for the decision to enforce the promise in the first place. In some cases neither expectation nor reliance losses will be appropriate or even sought by the plaintiff, who may simply want out of the contract and therefore ask for the remedy of rescission, with restitution of any benefits that have already passed. While you are thinking about which promises should be enforced, it is useful to bear in mind that you can make an argument for enforceability which takes into account the amount of damages that the plaintiff should get in case of breach. Flexibility of approach to the award of damages is an aid to creative argument as to which promises should be enforced.

6.   Theories of Contract Law

Material that throws light on these issues and that has become increasingly influential in recent years relates to the study of law in its economic context. Although enthusiasts of the analysis of law from an economic standpoint do not claim that this approach answers all our questions about contract law, the growing body of literature does help to provide a stimulating perspective. There would probably be general agreement (though not necessarily agreement on its contents) that the classic text in this area is Posner, *Economic Analysis of Law*, 6th ed. (2003), which contains a section on contracts, with discussion of such matters as the economic reasons why the law enforces some promises and not others, and recognizes some excuses for non-performance. For a critique of such economic analysis see Atiyah, "Executory Contracts, Expectation Damages, and the Economic Analysis of Contract", in *Essays on Contract* (1986), at 150-78. A major Canadian contribution to this literature is Trebilcock, *The Common Law of Restraint of Trade* (1986). Professor Trebilcock argues that the common law is not particularly efficient in this area of contract law and an extract from this work is used to illustrate some problems with judicial assumptions relating to standard form contracts in Chapter 8. In the following materials you are referred from time to time to writings which utilize an economic perspective in a particular context.

A body of scholarship, often referred to as "critical legal studies", has built upon realist insights, which focus on how law functions in practice. See *e.g.*, Cohen, "The Basis of Contract" (1933), 46 Harv. L. Rev. 553. Critical scholars take issue with the conventional presumption about law as being true, valid, and useful in a non-ideological way, suggesting that law actually is a constructed reality, the form, substance, and method of which conceals its problematic, controversial, and ideological nature. See *e.g.*, Gabel and Feinman, "Contract Law as Ideology" in Kairys (ed.), *The Politics of Law* (1982), at 181.

As well, there is now a body of feminist analysis of this area of law. It may be useful to approach such analyses from a fundamental theoretical perspective, focusing on the concept of social contract. Such a perspective draws on contract theory to suggest how human political organization should be understood. While treaties with aboriginal peoples could provide legitimacy for the Canadian state in its exercise of power over aboriginal peoples, and marriages still, for some, provide legitimacy for some sexual relations, the theory of the social contract attempts to provide legitimacy for the exercise of power in itself. Pateman describes the social contract in her book, *The Sexual Contract* (1988), as follows, at 2:

> Social contract theory is conventionally presented as a story about freedom. One interpretation of the original contract is that the inhabitants of the state of nature exchange the insecurities of natural freedom for equal, civil freedom which is protected by the state. In civil society freedom is universal; all adults enjoy the same civil standing and can exercise their freedom by, as it were, replicating the original contract when, for example, they enter into the employment contract or the marriage contract.

As a theory it was chiefly used to criticize traditional forms of authority, but it largely neglected the exclusion of women from the status of equal, civil freedom. Pateman states, at 6:

> In the natural condition 'all men are born free' and are equal to each other; they are 'individuals' . . . how in such a condition can the government of one man by another ever be legitimate; how can political right exist? Only one answer is possible without denying the initial assumption of freedom and equality. The relationship must arise through agreement. . . . But women are not born free; women have no natural freedom. The classic pictures of the state of nature also contain an order of subjection—between men and women. With the exception of Hobbes, the classic theorists claim that women naturally lack the attributes and capacities of 'individuals'. Sexual difference is political difference. . . . Women are not party to the original contract through which men transform their natural freedom into the security of civil freedom.

The story of how exclusion was given concrete social and legal form is now familiar. Until relatively recently women lacked the vote, and achieved it in stages reflecting variations in their status. There were barriers to employment, and married women lacked capacity to enter into contracts. In general the state collaborated in the subjection of women rather than protecting their equality and civil freedom. Privacy ideology was a powerful force in justifying the exclusion of women from public life and denying them the protection of the state in their private life. See, *e.g.*, O'Donovan, *Sexual Divisions in Law* (1985).

But does this exclusion of women from the social contract until relatively recently have any implications for current contract law? Thready has noted that, historically, "contract pertained to market transactions, which generally excluded inter-familial bargaining; and . . . women were barred by law and custom from engaging in market transactions." ("Feminists and Contract Doctrine" (1999), 32 Ind. L.Rev. 1247.) It would be surprising if modern law did not bear at least traces of this history.

Some commentators reject this idea. Thus, Madame Justice Wilson, in her famous lecture on "Will Women Judges Really Make a Difference?", expressed the view that there were whole areas of law in which there is no uniquely feminine perspective, and gave the law of contracts as an example.

> Taking from my own experience as a judge of fourteen years' standing . . . there are probably whole areas of law on which there is no uniquely feminine perspective. This is not to say that the development of the law in these areas has not been influenced by the fact that lawyers and judges have all been men. Rather, the principles and the underlying premises are so firmly entrenched and so fundamentally sound that no good would be achieved by attempting to re-invent the wheel, even if the revised version did have a few more spokes in it. I have in mind areas such as the law of contract, the law of real property, and the law applicable to corporations.

((1990), 28 Osgoode Hall L.J. 507, at 515)

As you study various contractual doctrines, such as intention to create legal relations, unconscionability or public policy, you may wish to test that view. For instance, feminist scholars have tended to be critical of contract law's emphasis on the notion of exchange, fundamental to the doctrine of consideration. See, *e.g.*, Williams, "On Being the Object of Property" (1988), 14 Signs 8. "Contract's role in fueling a market-based economy has rendered it suspect . . . garnering it criticism for encouraging unadulterated self-interest and commodification" (Testy, "An Unlikely Resurrection" (1995), 90 Northwestern U.L.R. 219, at 222). Feminist analyses have been critiqued in their turn, for instance for failing to include perspectives drawn from lesbian legal theory. Indeed, Testy argues that lesbian theory is resurrecting contracts by recognizing its complexities and its potential to empower women.

Students who have an interest in feminist legal debates, and who may wish to critique *these* materials from a feminist perspective should consult Frug, "Re-Reading Contracts: A Feminist Analysis of a Contracts Casebook" (1985), American Univ. L. Rev. 1065.

Much of the feminist work that has been published focuses on particular issues of public policy taken up in Chapter 13, Illegality and Public Policy, such as preconception contracts. See, *e.g.*, Devlin, "Baby M.: The Contractual Legitimation of Misogyny" (1988), 10 R.F.L. (3d) 4. Such work raises questions of general importance since it draws attention to the taken-for-granted assumptions about the boundaries of contract law. In reading the materials, you may wish to consider the implications of the focus on the commercial rather than the family context:

> Present law, like the society it reflects, assumes that the family is and should remain primarily, a universe defined in status terms, a universe of love, not money, of commitment, not negotiation, of relationship, not autonomy.

(Dolgin, "Status and Contract in Feminist Legal Theory of the Family: A Reply to Bartlett" (1990-91), 12 Women's Rights Law Reporter 103, at 107.)

Questions about boundaries, and indeed the fundamental value of contract law, will arise with respect to the doctrine of Intention to Create Legal Relations, in Chapter 4.

There is also a significant body of feminist literature on specialized legislative topics, such as pay equity, domestic work, affirmative action and human rights, which are largely beyond the scope of this book. But see, *e.g.*, Macklin, "Foreign Domestic Worker: Surrogate Housewife or Mail Order Servant?" (1992), 37 McGill L.J. 681.

7.   Relational Contracts

Other perspectives deal with issues which underlie a great deal of thinking about contracts, such as whether traditional doctrine is adequate to deal with the enormous variety of types of contract. One influential commentator has pointed out that there is an unwarranted focus on one-time exchanges rather than on ongoing relationships. The work of Ian Macneil is well known as pointing out the importance and ubiquitousness of relational transactions, such as employment contracts and long-term supply and service agreements.

> Modern contractional relations too tend to involve large numbers of people, often huge numbers of people. Even the family and small enterprises of various kinds usually involve more than the two parties of the paradigm discrete transaction.

(Macneil, *The New Social Contract* (1980), at 21.)

His work contains a powerful critique of the law relating to the paradigm contract as not being responsive to relational transactions, which should be examined in their context. See most recently Macneil, "Relational Contract Theory: Challenges and Queries" (2000), 94 Nw.U.L.Rev. 877, in "Relational Contract Theory: Unanswered Questions A Symposium in Honor of Ian R. Macneil", *ibid.*

Relational contract theory recognizes that parties may not be able to fix all terms at the moment of contracting (even supposing that moment can be identified, as the material on the Battle of the Forms in Chapter 2, section 4 will illustrate). As well, parties in a long-term relationship may not wish to be confrontational or maximize their short-term advantage. Law that may be appropriate to, *e.g.*, a contract for the purchase of a car, may not be as useful to the parties to a long-term contract for the sale of natural gas. Such variation presents a challenge to contract doctrine, but so does the development of separate rules for relational contracts. See Eisenberg, "Why There is No Law of Relational Contracts", *ibid.*

On the other hand, people with good reason to lack confidence in how they will be treated by others in the future may try to insist on detail agreed in advance and may see law as some protection from exploitation. For a powerful account of how the author, an African American woman, insisted on a detailed lease, see Williams, "Alchemical Notes: Reconstructing Ideals from Deconstructed Rights" (1987), 22 Harv. C.R.-C.L. L. Rev. 401. For a discussion of Macneil's work in the context of "intimate private ordering—the quintessential relational contract", see Christensen, "Legal Ordering of Family Values: The Case of Gay and Lesbian Families" (1997), 18 Cardozo L.R. 1299. He argues at 1336-37 that acceptance of Macneil's critique "may hold out the best hope available for the development of a gay-friendly contract law".

For a discussion of relational theory linked to a feminist approach, see Tidwell and Linzer, "The Flesh-Colored Band Aid—Contracts, Feminism, Dialogue, and Norms" (1991), 28 Hous. L.R. 791, and for a response, Dow, "Law School Feminist Chic and Respect for Persons: Comments on Contract Theory and Feminism in 'The Flesh-Colored Band Aid'", ibid., at 819.

8.   First Nations and Treaties

Questions about boundaries and appropriateness of contract analysis also arise with respect to treaties between the Crown and First Nations peoples. While issues of how such treaties should be analyzed are too specialized to be more than touched on in a book of this nature, students should be aware that contract law and theory may be drawn upon in cases ranging from a simple sale of goods to complex agreements between peoples. Treaties are not of course simply contracts in the ordinary sense — they could be seen as resembling international agreements and as having a constitutional quality, reflecting fundamental commitments. See, for instance, Cardinal, *The Unjust Society* (1969), at 28, "to the Indians of Canada, the treaties represent an Indian Magna Carta". Even if contract analysis, which may not capture such contested international/constitutional qualities, were appropriate, it is not yet clear that, in Canadian law, treaties are accorded the status of contract, with the connotations of sanctity that implies.

In *Pawis v. R.* (1979), 102 D.L.R. (3d) 602 (Fed. T.D.) the Ojibway plaintiffs sued the Crown for, among other things, breach of contract. They argued that, by enacting the Ontario Fishery Regulations under the Fisheries Act without exempting the Ojibway people from their application, the Crown breached the contractual obligations it had undertaken in the Lake Huron Treaty of 1850. The court, while saying that it was obvious that the Treaty was not a treaty in the international law sense, agreed that it was "tantamount to a contract". However, the plaintiffs lost, the court implying a term that the treaty was subject to possible future regulations, that the regulations could not at the same time be legal and a breach of contract, and that the plaintiffs did not have the status to sue as individuals. It should be noted, however, that it is possible to find treaties binding as treaties without engaging in contract analysis, depending on what remedy is being sought. See *R. v. Simon* (1985), 23 C.C.C. (3d) 238 (S.C.C.) in which the court held that the appellant, a Mi'kmaq, had a treaty right to hunt that could not be restricted by provincial legislation. See generally, Miller (ed.), *Sweet Promises: A Reader on Indian-White Relations in Canada* (1991).

Treaties, or any contracts between governments and aboriginal peoples, or between governments acting on behalf of aboriginal peoples and other parties, are different from most contracts in that the Crown has a fiduciary obligation to aboriginal peoples, so that the normal assumptions about the social utility of the pursuit of self-interest are not applicable.

[T]he government has the responsibility to act in a fiduciary capacity with respect to aboriginal peoples. The relationship between the Government and aboriginals is trust-like, rather than adversarial, and contemporary recognition and affirmation of aboriginal rights must be defined in light of this historic relationship.

R. v. Sparrow, [1990] 1 S.C.R. 1075, at 1110. The fact that "the honour of the Crown" is at stake with respect to treaties makes them stand out, as a form of contract, in sharp relief against the general law of contracts, where fiduciary duties are exceptional, albeit now supplemented by the fledging doctrine of good faith, mentioned earlier. Nevertheless a study of contract law will alert you to many questions relevant to issues of pre-contract obligations, interpretation and enforcement. For instance, is there an obligation to negotiate in good faith? Is there is a difference between treaties and modern commercial transactions between two parties of relatively equal bargaining power? Is interpretation strict or generous, and how do the courts reconcile different perspectives? When can terms be implied? When can evidence be offered that treaties were partly oral and partly written? See generally *Marshall v. Canada* (1999), 177 D.L.R. (4th) 513, [1999] S.C.J. No. 55 (S.C.C.).

Attention to treaties also illustrates the point that contracting takes place in many different contexts, thus creating a need for doctrinal flexibility.

9. Transcending Conceptual Boundaries

A further point flowing from the fact that there are many different ways of thinking about contract law and its response to changing social realities, is, obviously, that you should try and develop your own ideas about the law. It may be helpful to that effort to avoid thinking of contracts, or any of your courses, in "pigeonholes". The law of contracts does not occupy a well-defined conceptual territory of its own. It obviously overlaps with other areas of law such as property, criminal law and, particularly, torts. Indeed there is no reason why a breach of contract should not be regarded as simply another species of tort, as indeed it once was, especially if the law develops in the direction of the enforcement of promises inducing reasonable reliance, as Gilmore argues in *The Death of Contract*. Torts and contract law, however, have tended to evolve separately, at least since the nineteenth century, although it is still important not to draw a rigid line of demarcation between the two subjects. It is increasingly common, for example, to find a single case involving potential liability in both areas, so that the student and the practitioner must consider all possible remedies. The law relating to the overlap between torts and contracts is discussed in Chapter 7 of this book.

A significant example of an overlap is, as mentioned above, that between the law relating to aboriginal rights, treaties and contracts, streams of law which often are considered in isolation. See Bell and Buss, "The Promise of Marshall on the Prairies: A Framework for Analyzing Unfulfilled Treaty Promises" (2000), 63 Sask. L. Rev. 667 at 673. Another important overlap, is with the developing law of restitution or quasi-contract, which provides a remedy in many cases of "unjust enrichment", outside the purview of contract and tort remedies.

Canadian law recognized unjust enrichment as a distinct legal doctrine in a series of cases starting with *Deglman v. Guaranty Trust Co.* [[1954] S.C.R. 725], part of which is set out in Chapter 4, section 8(c)(iii). Restitution is particularly important where the contract fails for some reason such as uncertainty, mistake, or frustration, and will be considered in the chapters dealing with these topics, as well as in Chapter 7. For a useful, brief survey, see Justice McLachlin, "Restitution in Canada" in Cornish, Nolan, O'Sullivan and Virgo (eds.), *Restitution Past, Present and Future* (1998), 275 and generally, Maddaugh and McCamus, *The Law of Restitution*, 2nd ed. (2004).

Therefore, although it is essential to classify the law temporarily in order to analyze it, the student is urged to retain an awareness of such vital interrelationships.

10. A Final Word of Caution

Perhaps a more important warning, however, relates to the need to keep these materials in perspective. The student should realize that the emphasis on case law, especially appellate case law, is not the only way to study "law" and represents a particular focus which not all would accept as useful. One alternative would be to discover empirically-recurring problems for contracting parties and examine the impact of the law on these problems, rather than allowing the choice of appropriate areas of study to be dictated by the lottery of litigation. Such an approach would concentrate on the total functioning of the law, that is, on the sociology of the law as a means of social control and as a mechanism for dispute settlement. Although this approach is not adopted here, our contributors preferring to concentrate on the inculcation of skills associated with more traditional materials, it is important to remember that this has significant limitations, dictated by the objectives chosen. Nevertheless, it is vital to bear in mind, while studying the following materials, that judicial decisions and legislative choices must be tested against the values of providing a body of law which meets the needs of people who enter into contracts and of creating an efficient decision-making process.

Chapter 2

FORMATION OF THE AGREEMENT: OFFER AND ACCEPTANCE

1. Introduction

The classification of private obligations in common law systems has traditionally depended upon a distinction between obligations based on consent to an exchange (often to take place in the future), which are the province of the law of contracts, and obligations created by the general law, which are considered under the headings of torts and restitution. The distinction has been increasingly criticized in recent times and students will notice at a number of points during first year courses in Contracts and Torts that it has become relatively blurred. Nevertheless, some classification is necessary simply in order to introduce manageability into the field of private obligation and the traditional approach at least fulfils this function.

The first prerequisite to contractual liability based on consent is that the parties must have reached an agreement. The enforcement by common law courts of contracts under the "classical" theory of contract is supported by the claim that courts are simply enforcing a mutual agreement freely consented to by each party to the contract. The idea of agreement also supports the view of contracts as a vehicle agreed to in advance for the planning of social relations among parties, including the facilitation of economic relationships important to a market economy. Requiring an agreement for contractual liability, however, opens up a series of further issues to be resolved. For example, to what extent need there be a single moment when the minds of the parties to the agreement should be in exact convergence, expressed in the notion of a *consensus ad idem*? How should parties manifest their consent to each other and to outsiders including the courts? In addressing whether an agreement exists, should courts address concerns about imperfect or incorrect information and unequal bargaining power? As Hugh Collins, *The Law of Contract*, 4th ed. (2003), at 59, has observed:

> To decide when consent has been given by both parties to a contract, the authors of traditional contract textbooks devised an intricate set of rules employing the concepts 'offer and acceptance' to fix the moment of responsibility. These rules typify the formalist qualities of classical law: they are detailed, technical, and mysterious, yet claim logical derivation from the idea of agreement. Judges quickly appreciated the rigour of this analytical framework, and in the nineteenth century they adopted most of the terminology from the textbooks.

The formal framework of offer and acceptance rules determines the existence of contractual agreement through a stylized sequence of actions. Ideally, agreement would unfold through a sequence of events that match up to the formal categories of an offer, communication of the offer, an acceptance on the terms of the offer, and communication of the acceptance. Through these stylized requirements, contract law analysis determines that party behavior has crystallized in an agreement that could be the basis for a contract. However, commentators have often warned that the "rules" of offer and acceptance are merely tools of analysis to assist in defining the "moment of responsibility" rather than *a priori* statements to be blindly applied in a broad variety of circumstances. The recognition that the rules are merely tools should cause you to ask "tools to what ends?" How do the particular rules of offer and acceptance protect defensible policies, such as the freedom of contract of the offeror and the reliance and expectation interests of the offeree?

Courts increasingly acknowledge that a more flexible approach to determining when an agreement exists is required in practice to address the wide range of contracting situations and the varying policies raised by different situations. Some of the difficulties caused by moulding the principles of offer and acceptance in cases to which they do not readily apply are discussed by Fridman, "Making a Contract" (1988-89), Pitblado Lect. 2. In *New Zealand Shipping Co. Ltd. v. A.M. Satterthwaite & Co.*, [1975] A.C. 154 at 167 (P.C.), Lord Wilberforce observed:

> It is only the precise analysis of this complex of relations into the classical offer and acceptance, with identifiable consideration, that seems to present difficulty, but this same difficulty exists in many situations of daily life, *e.g.*, sales at auction; supermarket purchases; boarding an omnibus; purchasing a train ticket; tenders for the supply of goods; offers of rewards; acceptance by post; warranties of authority by agents; manufacturers' guarantees; gratuitous bailments; bankers' commercial credits. These are all examples which show that English law, having committed itself to a rather technical and schematic doctrine of contract, in application takes a practical approach, often at the cost of forcing the facts to fit uneasily into the slots of offer, acceptance and consideration.

These comments are equally applicable to modern Canadian law. Many of the rules of offer and acceptance are highly contextual, depending on an assessment of the language, conduct, and circumstances of the particular case. For example, a context of previous business and legal relations between parties might impact on the interpretation of whether the behavior of parties constitutes offer and acceptance; see the material on the "Battle of the Forms" as well as the decision in *Saint John Tug Boat Co. v. Irving Refinery Ltd., infra*, in section 4 of this chapter. Furthermore, courts may stretch concepts of offer and acceptance to the point where a new rule arguably is created. In this respect, consider the rules for formation of unilateral contracts, such as in *Carlill v. Carbolic Smoke Ball Co.*, and the development of "two-contract" analysis in the Canadian law on tendering, as in *R. v. Ron Engineering & Construction (Eastern) Ltd.*, both *infra*, in section 2 of this chapter. Cases such as these stand as a warning against an excessive reliance on rigid formulations of the "rules" of contract formation.

The differences between formalist approaches and more contextual approaches are illustrated throughout this chapter. Consider the new scenarios that are presented for Canadian contract law by changing social and economic conditions. For example, do changing Canadian social values related to freedom to discriminate based on race or class impact on the rules or application of the rules of offer and acceptance: *Christie v. York, infra*, in section 2 of this chapter?

Another context for Canadian contract law is the impact of increasing numbers of cross-border transactions to which Canadians may be parties. Judgments from Canadian, Commonwealth and U.S. courts are included throughout this book to illustrate rules or debates that are relevant in all common law Canadian jurisdictions. However, there are some differences in rules of offer and acceptance among different Canadian legal jurisdictions, as well as between Canadian and non-Canadian jurisdictions. For example, various notes in the chapter contrast common law contract principles with provisions of the Québec Civil Code, such as the rules with respect to revocation of "firm" offers. Such comparisons show that current common law rules on offer and acceptance are not the only options among a range of reasonable alternatives. Furthermore, such contrasting comparative laws hint at the complexity of contractual situations with connections to more than one legal jurisdiction. Efforts to find some common international rules through international treaties are evidenced with respect to some kinds of contracts in the United Nations Convention on Contracts for the International Sale of Goods, referred to in the notes and implemented in all Canadian jurisdictions. Often, however, common international rules are lacking, and determination of the applicable rules of contract and the relevant courts to resolve contractual disputes depend on navigating the often challenging rules of private international law; see section 5 of this chapter.

Lastly, consider the impact on contract formation of the changing technological setting for modern transactions. In light of the enormous amount of trade now conducted by almost instantaneous means of communication such as facsimiles, e-mail and the Internet and World Wide Web, contrast the approach to the time and place of formation of contract that the common law courts adopt in *Brinkibon Ltd.* and *Rudder v. Microsoft Corp., infra*, section 5(a) of this chapter, with the approach taken towards contracts formed by correspondence in the 19th century cases in sections 5(b) and 6. Various notes in this chapter also consider the legislative response towards contract formation found in e-commerce legislation in Canadian jurisdictions.

2.   Offer and Invitation to Treat

CANADIAN DYERS ASSOCIATION LTD. v. BURTON

(1920), 47 O.L.R. 259 (H.C.)

MIDDLETON J. The question argued was whether, upon the correspondence discussed, a contract had been made out.

There can be no doubt of the elementary principle that there can be no contract of sale unless there can be found an offer to sell and an acceptance of the offer or an offer to purchase and an acceptance of that offer. A mere quotation of price does not constitute an offer to sell to the person to whom the quotation is addressed. It is no more than an invitation to him to make an offer to buy at that price or any price he may see fit to offer, calling for an acceptance on the part of the vendor before there is a completed contract.

In each case of this type it is a question to be determined upon the language used, in the light of the circumstances in which it is used, whether what is said by the vendor is a mere quotation of price or in truth an offer to sell.

Harvey v. Facey, [1893] A.C. 552, does not determine any new law, but is an illustration of the application of the principle involved. The would-be purchasers sent a telegram in which they asked two questions: "Will you sell us B.H.P.? Telegraph lowest cash price." The reply was: "Lowest cash price for B.H.P. £900." Assuming this to be an offer, the plaintiffs wired acceptance. Their Lordships held that there was no contract. The defendant "replied to the second question only, and gives his lowest price . . . the appellants treat the answer . . . stating his lowest price as an unconditional offer to sell to them at the price named" (p. 555). In the view of their Lordships, an affirmative answer to the first question was not implied, and the defendant had made no offer to sell, but stated only his price. If the decision does more than illustrate the undoubted principle, it may be taken as establishing that "the mere statement of the lowest price at which the vendor would sell contains no implied contract to sell at that price to the persons making the inquiry" (p. 556).

The true principle is well stated in 35 Cyc., p. 50, citing American cases: "The question is one of intention; and whether a proposal is to be construed as an invitation to deal or as an offer which can be turned into a binding agreement by acceptance depends upon the language used and the circumstances of the particular case."

In *Johnston v. Rogers* (1899), 30 O.R. 150, the vendors sent a circular letter: "We quote you," etc. This was held not to be an offer to sell, but a mere invitation to make an offer to purchase.

In *Harty v. Gooderham* (1871), 31 U.C.R. 18, a quotation of prices, followed by the statement, "Shall be happy to have an order from you, to which we will give prompt attention," was held to be an offer which became a contract upon the plaintiffs' acceptance.

Attempting now to apply this law to the case in hand, we find that in May, 1918, the plaintiffs wrote the defendant: "With reference to purchasing this property (25 Hanna avenue), kindly state your lowest price. We will then give the same our best consideration."

On the 6th June, the defendant answered: "Re house 25 Hanna. The lowest price I would care to sell at for cash would be $1,650, as anything less would not bring me in as good a return on my money as my present rental. I would have sold before, but, being a director of the company then, I did not, for obvious reasons. This is the last link between me and my old associations."

This can be understood better when it is known that the house in question is next door to the factory of the plaintiffs, and that the defendant had been a director of the company.

Matters then stood for a year and a half, when the plaintiffs wrote, on the 16th October, 1919: "We would be pleased to have your very lowest price for 25

Hanna avenue. Perhaps we could get closer together than the last figure given us."

On the 21st October the defendant wrote: "I beg to acknowledge receipt of your favour of the 16th instant, and in reply would say that the last price I gave you is the lowest I am prepared to accept. In fact I feel that under present conditions that this is exceptionally low and if it were to any other party I would ask more."

This was treated as an offer and . . . accepted. A cheque for $500 was sent, and the defendant was asked to have a deed prepared. This was on the 23rd October. On the 27th, the defendant's solicitor sent a draft deed and said he would be ready to close on the 1st. Some correspondence took place about the deed and title, but no trouble developed until the 5th November, when the defendant's solicitor wrote that there was no contract, and returned the cheque for $500.

It might suffice to say that, in my opinion, there was here far more than a mere quotation of price. Read in connection with the earlier letters of 1918, the letter of the 16th October, 1919, was in effect a request for a price at which the defendant was willing to sell to the plaintiffs, and the reply of the 21st, the vital matter, was more than a quotation of price, and was a statement of readiness to sell to the plaintiffs at the price already named. I attach importance to the words, "the price . . . is the lowest I am prepared to accept . . . if it were to any other party I would ask more". Surely, unless language is used to conceal thought, this is an offer.

In other cases that I have read, the conduct of the defendant has been consistent with his view that an offer has not been made. He has at once disavowed the idea of a contract without further action on his part. If the language here is ambiguous, then it is fair to see how the defendant himself viewed the situation. When the letter of the 23rd reached him, he did not say: "There is no contract. Your letter is an offer which I do not accept;" but he submits a deed and suggests an immediate search of his title, and names an early date for closing—in the meantime retaining the cheque sent. His actions show that he regarded his letter as an offer and the letter of the 23rd as making a contract. . . .

NOTE and QUESTIONS

1.(a) What major details were still left to be settled at the time of offer and acceptance? Does the absence of agreement on these details reveal anything about the parties' intentions? The issue of certainty of terms is discussed in Chapter 3, *infra*.

(b) How far should the defendant's subsequent conduct be relevant to the question whether he made an offer in the first place?

2. In what sense did the court use an "objective" approach to interpretation of the words and conduct in *Canadian Dyers*?

3. In *Hongkong Bank of Canada v. Richardson Greenshields of Canada Ltd.*, [1989] B.C.W.L.D. 638 (S.C.), the bank wished to dispose of Government of Canada Bonds with a face value of $15 million, due to a "free fall in the market". Two of the bank's senior dealers requested quotes on these bonds from various brokerage houses, including Richardson Greenshields, *via* direct telephone lines. "It should be noted that a quote is a general level of the marketplace, while a price may be acted upon." Later, one of these dealers saw the Richardson Greenshields light come on her telephone and testified as follows:

Q. All right. And what did you do?

A. I picked up the receiver, pushed the line and the trader on the other end said that the [bonds] were 97 and 5/8-7/8.

Q. Yes.

A. I repeated the price to him, 97 5/8-7/8. He said, "that is correct". And I sell you 10 million at 97 and 5/8. There was a pause on the line, he says, "that's done" and that was the end of the phone conversation.

Neither party identified themselves. The dealer then made a notation on a "deal sheet", which is an "internal document upon which a buyer or seller confirms the subject matter of a transaction. The sheet is not sent to the brokerage house." Richardson Greenshields refused to accept delivery of the bonds, denying any knowledge of the transaction. The court found that an agreement to sell the bonds existed. This case was appealed on the question of damages only: (1990), 48 B.C.L.R. (2d) 139 (C.A.).

PHARMACEUTICAL SOCIETY OF GREAT BRITAIN v. BOOTS CASH CHEMISTS (SOUTHERN) LTD.

[1953] 1 Q.B. 401, [1953] 1 All E.R. 482 (C.A.)

The defendants, Boots, operated a self-service pharmacy. One part of the store was called the "Toilet Dept.," and another the "Chemists' Dept." Proprietary medicines were displayed in the Chemists' Dept. with an indication of the price of each. One section of that department was devoted exclusively to drugs which were included in, or which contained substances included in, Part I of the Poisons List referred to in section 17 (1) of the Pharmacy and Poisons Act, 1933.

When the pharmacy was open for the sale of drugs the manager, the registered pharmacist, and one or more of the assistants were present in the room. In order to leave the customer had to pass by one of two exits, at each of which was a cash desk where a cashier was stationed who scrutinized the articles selected by the customer, assessed the value and accepted payment. The Chemists' Dept. was under the personal control of the registered pharmacist, who carried out all his duties subject to the directions of a superintendent in accordance with the provisions of section 9 of the Act.

The pharmacist was stationed near the poisons section, where his certificate of registration was conspicuously displayed, and was in view of the cash desks. In every case involving the sale of a drug the pharmacist supervised that part of the transaction which took place at the cash desk and was authorized by the defendants to prevent at that stage of the transaction, if he thought fit, any customer from removing any drug from the premises. No steps were taken by the defendants to inform the customers, before they selected any article which they wished to purchase, of the pharmacist's authorization.

Two customers, following the procedure outlined above, respectively purchased a bottle containing a medicine known as compound syrup of hypophosphites, containing 0.01% W/V strychnine, and a bottle containing medicine known as famel syrup, containing 0.23% W/V codeine, both of which substances are poisons included in Part I of the Poisons List.

The issue was whether these sales were effected by or under the supervision of a registered pharmacist, in accordance with section 18(1)(a)(iii) of the Pharmacy and Poisons Act, 1933.

The Lord Chief Justice decided that they were. The Pharmaceutical Society appealed.

SOMERVELL L.J. . . . . The plaintiffs are the Pharmaceutical Society, incorporated by Royal charter. One of their duties is to take all reasonable steps to enforce the provisions of the Act. The provision in question is contained in section 18. . . . It is not disputed that in a chemist's shop where this self-service system does not prevail a customer may go in and ask a young woman assistant, who will not herself be a registered pharmacist, for one of these articles on the list, and the transaction may be completed and the article paid for, although the registered pharmacist, who will no doubt be on the premises, will not know anything himself of the transaction, unless the assistant serving the customer, or the customer, requires to put a question to him. It is right that I should emphasize, as did the Lord Chief Justice, that these are not dangerous drugs. They are substances which contain very small proportions of poison, and I imagine that many of them are the type of drug which has a warning as to what doses are to be taken. They are drugs which can be obtained, under the law, without a doctor's prescription.

The point taken by the plaintiffs is this: it is said that the purchase is complete if and when a customer going round the shelves takes an article and puts it in the receptacle which he or she is carrying, and that therefore, if that is right, when the customer comes to the pay desk, having completed the tour of the premises, the registered pharmacist, if so minded, has no power to say: "This drug ought not to be sold to this customer." Whether and in what circumstances he would have that power we need not inquire, but one can, of course, see that there is a difference if supervision can only be exercised at a time when the contract is completed.

I agree with the Lord Chief Justice in everything that he said, but I will put the matter shortly in my own words. Whether the view contended for by the plaintiffs is a right view depends on what are the legal implications of this layout—the invitation to the customer. Is a contract to be regarded as being completed when the article is put into the receptacle, or is this to be regarded as a more organized way of doing what is done already in many types of shops—and a bookseller is perhaps the best example—namely, enabling customers to have free access to what is in the shop, to look at the different articles, and then, ultimately, having got the ones which they wish to buy, to come up to the assistant saying "I want this"? The assistant in 999 times out of 1,000 says "That is all right," and the money passes and the transaction is completed. I agree . . . that in the case of an ordinary shop, although goods are displayed and it is intended that customers should go and choose what they want, the contract is not completed until, the customer having indicated the articles which he needs, the shopkeeper, or someone on his behalf, accepts that offer. Then the contract is completed. I can see no reason at all, that being clearly the normal position, for drawing any different implication as a result of this layout.

The Lord Chief Justice, I think, expressed one of the most formidable difficulties in the way of the plaintiffs' contention when he pointed out that, if the plaintiffs are right, once an article has been placed in the receptacle the customer himself is bound and would have no right, without paying for the first article, to substitute an article which he saw later of a similar kind and which he perhaps preferred. I can see no reason for implying from this self-service arrangement any implication other than . . . that it is a convenient method of enabling customers to see what there is and choose, and possibly put back and substitute, articles which they wish to have, and then to go up to the cashier and offer to buy what they have so far chosen. On that conclusion the case fails, because it is admitted that there was supervision in the sense required by the Act and at the appropriate moment of time. For these reasons, in my opinion, the appeal should be dismissed.

BIRKETT L.J. . . . The two women customers in this case each took a particular package containing poison from the particular shelf, put it into her basket, came to the exit and there paid. It is said, on the one hand, that when the customer takes the package from the poison section and puts it into her basket the sale there and then takes place. On the other hand, it is said the sale does not take place until that customer, who has placed that package in the basket, comes to the exit.

The Lord Chief Justice dealt with the matter in this way, and I would like to adopt his words [[1952] 2 Q.B. 795 at 802]:

> It seems to me, therefore, that the transaction is in no way different from the normal transaction in a shop in which there is no self-service scheme. I am quite satisfied it would be wrong to say that the shopkeeper is making an offer to sell every article in the shop to any person who might come in and that that person can insist on buying any article by saying "I accept your offer."

Then he went on to deal with the illustration of the bookshop, and continued:

> Therefore, in my opinion, the mere fact that a customer picks up a bottle of medicine from the shelves in this case does not amount to an acceptance of an offer to sell. It is an offer by the customer to buy and there is no sale effected until the buyer's offer to buy is accepted by the acceptance of the price. The offer, the acceptance of the price, and therefore the sale take place under the supervision of the pharmacist. That is sufficient to satisfy the requirements of the section for by using the words "the sale is effected by, or under the supervision of, a registered pharmacist" the Act envisages that the sale may be effected by someone not a pharmacist. I think, too, that the sale is effected under his supervision if he is in a position to say "You must not have that: that contains poison," so that in any case, even if I were wrong in the view that I have taken on the question as to when the sale was completed, and it was completed when the customer took the article from the shelf, it would still be effected under the supervision of the pharmacist within the meaning of section 18.

I agree with that, and I agree that this appeal ought to be dismissed.

[Romer L.J. delivered a concurring judgment.]

NOTE and QUESTIONS

1. *Pharmaceutical Society v. Boots* is concerned with a breach of a regulatory statute. Is there any reason for using the same rules of offer and acceptance for deciding private law contractual liability, for example of a person who discovers that he or she does not have sufficient money to pay for the price of the goods that the cashier has entered into the cash register, and for determining criminal liability, for example of a person charged with theft for changing price tags of goods for sale? See *R. v. Dawood* (1975), [1976] 1 W.W.R. 262 (Alta. C.A.); *R. v. Milne*, [1992] 1 S.C.R. 697.

2. If the display of goods had been held to be an offer in the *Boots* case, (a) when would acceptance be made; and (b) would the defendant have been in violation of the Act? See also *R. v. Steinberg's Ltd.* (1976), 70 D.L.R. (3d) 624 (Ont. C.A.) at 630-31. Is the finding in the *Boots* case with respect to offer necessary to protect the freedom of a potential purchaser to change her or his mind?

3. Why is a display of goods in a shop window or a store not traditionally regarded as an offer? What practical consequences flow from this? In "Some Aspects of Offer and Acceptance" (1939), 55 L.Q.R. 499, Winfield comments, at 518:

> If the display of such goods were an offer, then the shopkeeper might be forced to contract with his worst enemy, his greatest trade rival, a reeling drunkard, or a ragged and verminous tramp.

The implication of Winfield's justification is that the formation of contracts in stores (and other venues apparently open to the public, such as restaurants or sporting facilities) is a purely private matter and that the law of contracts has no right to interfere with the decisions of the operator of the venue as long as they do not breach any contract. A vivid illustration of the consequences of this view is provided by *Christie v. York Corporation*, [1940] S.C.R. 139, in which the plaintiff, who had originally come from Jamaica but who had been a permanent resident of Québec for 20 years, held season tickets at the Montreal Forum. He had often dropped into the tavern at the Forum, operated by the defendant, for a beer while attending hockey games. On the evening in question, he entered the tavern with 2 friends and ordered 3 beers. In the words of Davis J. (dissenting, at 146), "the waiter declined to fill the order, stating that he was instructed not to serve coloured people." The plaintiff sued in breach of contract and tort for $200 for the humiliation he had suffered. Neither the majority nor the dissenting judge considered the claim for breach of contract.

The case nonetheless demonstrates the influence of the policy value of freedom of contract. The majority found, at 142, that the innkeeper was not liable because the underlying principle for interpretation of the relevant Québec statutes was that of "complete freedom of commerce. Any merchant is free to deal as he may choose with any individual member of the public."

In a case comment, former Chief Justice Laskin criticized *Christie v. York*: "The principle of freedom of commerce enforced by the Court majority is itself merely the reading of social and economic doctrine into law, and doctrine no longer possessing its nineteenth century validity." ((1940), 18 Can. Bar Rev. 314 at 316).

Without considering the impact of legislation, should the law of contract respond to cases such as *Christie v. York*? Were the existing rules of offer flexible enough that a different result in *Christie v. York* could have been reached, or did a new rule or exception need to be created?

Consider the potential conflict between the freedom of contract of some parties, in particular those offering important goods and services, and the availability of contracting opportunities for other parties. In *The Alchemy of Rights and Race* (1991), at 146-148, Patricia Williams notes several ways in which contracting possibilities, while hardly the only requirement of human dignity, are important to the realization of individuals in modern society of

> . . . that creative commerce by which I may be recognized as whole, by which I may feed and clothe and shelter myself, by which I may be seen as equal – even if I am a stranger. For me, stranger-stranger relations are better than stranger-chattel.

Human rights legislation now addresses the tension between freedom of contract and freedom from discrimination. See the following statutes (and their relevant amendments). Human Rights, Citizenship and Multiculturalism Act, R.S.A. 2000, c. H-14; Human Rights Code, R.S.B.C. 1996, c. 210; Human Rights Code, C.C.S.M., c. H175; Human Rights Act, R.S.N.B. 1973, c. H-11; Human Rights Code, R.S.N.L. 1990, c. H-14; Fair Practices Act, R.S.N.W.T. 1988, c. F-2; Human Rights Act, R.S.N.S. 1989, c. 214; Human Rights Code, R.S.O. 1990, c. H.19; Human Rights Act, R.S.P.E.I. 1988, c. H-12; Saskatchewan Human Rights Code, S.S. 1979, c. S-24.1; Fair Practices Act, R.S.Y. 1986, c. 62.

What happens when human rights legislation fails to deal effectively with the discrimination in question, for example due to lack of effective enforcement?

4. How might courts deal with the question of offer and invitation to treat in the following circumstances?

    (a) A display of cars on a used car lot. See *R. v. Bermuda Holdg. Ltd.* (1969), 9 D.L.R. (3d) 595 (B.C. S.C.).

    (b) A department store catalogue. See *Assn. Pharmaceutique v. T. Eaton Co.* (1931), 50 B.R. 482; in *Québec (Sous-Ministre du Revenu) c. Simpsons-Sears Ltd.*, [1986] R.L. 37 (Que. C.A.) the court assumed that the catalogues were offers.

    (c) A display of goods on a home shopping television network.

    (d) A web site listing of a company's products or services. If this were held to be an offer, what would be the acceptance?

    (e) A classified advertisement such as the following:

HERITAGE PARK
4 BEDROOMS

Original owner offers this fine family bungalow located in a choice residential area. 1440 sq. ft. with centre hall plan. Kitchen includes built-in stove. Nicely landscaped including enclosed patio and side drive. Existing mortgage at 5 per cent available. A pleasure to see. Asking $204,900. Call Harvey Foster at 832-6485.

    (f) a renewal package sent to season ticket holders. See *Stern v. Cleveland Browns Football Club Inc.*, W.L. 761163 (Ohio App., 1996).

5. Does the erroneous continuation of automatic debits of a bank account of an insured, even after termination of the policy because of age, amount to a continuance of an insurance policy? In *McCunn Estate v. Canadian Imperial Bank of Commerce* (2001), 53 O.R. (3d) 304 (C.A.), the Ontario Court of Appeal reversed the trial judge's determination that there was a continuance of the insurance contract. For the majority, Borins J.A., at para.18, held that to find a continuance "it was necessary that the bank, with the requisite knowledge and intent, make an offer to provide insurance, and that Mrs. McCunn, with the requisite knowledge and intent, accept the offer." In dissent, Feldman J.A., at para. 50, found that "the offer is the Bank's deduction of premiums and sending of statements, while acceptance is demonstrated by Mrs. McCunn's lack of objection to the continuation of her life insurance policy regime by continuing to allow the deduction of premiums from her account."

6. Harvey Foster went to his local supermarket to purchase a bottle of soda water. As he took it off the shelf, the bottle exploded causing him personal injury. Advise Harvey if it would make any difference if the bottle exploded:

    (i)   when he had already placed it in the wire basket?

    (ii) when he removed it from the wire basket to hand to the cashier?

    (iii) when the clerk requested the purchase price?

    (iv) when he paid the price and took the bottle?

    (v)   when he was picking up a bottle, perhaps left by an earlier customer, to separate it from his own purchases at the checkout?

See *Barker v. Allied Supermarket* (1979), 596 P. 2d 870 (Okla. S.C.); *Fender v. Colonial Stores Inc.* (1976), 225 S.E. 691 (Ga. C.A.); *Giant Food v. Washington Coca-Cola Bottling Co. Inc.* (1975), 332 A. (2d) 1, affirming 318 A. (2d) 874; *Gillespie v. Great Atl. and Pac. Tea Co.* (1972), 187 S.E. (2d) 441; *Sanchez-Lopez v. Fedco Food Corpn.* (1961), 211 N.Y.S. (2d) 953. See also *Hart v. Bell Tel. Co. of Can.* (1979), 102 D.L.R. (3d) 465 (Ont. C.A.), and Willhoft, "Exploding Carbonated Beverage Bottles", [1986] The Law Society's Gazette 1964.

The Queensland Court of Appeal in *Cottee v. Franklin Self-Serve Pty Ltd.*, [1997] 1 Qd.R. 469, found a contractual bailment of a shopping trolley which collapsed while it was being pushed from the store to the car park injuring the plaintiff shopper. This contract formed part of the contract for the purchase of goods even though there was no communication or separate consideration in regard to the trolley. What might have been the result if the injury had arisen from the use of a defective trolley within the store prior to making a purchase?

What are the advantages of a finding of contractual liability in personal injury cases? See Kapnoullas, "The Contractual Liability of Supermarkets for Defective Trolleys" (1997), 11 Journal of Contract Law 259.

7. In *City Parking Services v. Murray* (1992), 99 Nfld. & P.E.I.R. 11 (Nfld. T.D.) the plaintiff ran a parking lot. "There is no attendant at the site. Neither is there an automated system regulating admission to the lot or collecting a fee. There are two four foot by four foot signs which I find would have been visible to drivers entering the parking lot. Written in red letters are the words:

COMMERCIAL CAR PARK OPERATING 24 HOURS A DAY

Parking Terms for those *without* Monthly Permits are as follows:

(1) $45.00 per use of parking space (maximum 24 hours before recharge).

(2) $45.00 Parking Fee is for use of space only. The owner or his agents accept no responsibility or liability whatsoever for damage or injury to vehicle, contents or persons however caused. Parking is solely and entirely at your own risk.

.....

(4) Parking a vehicle on this lot constitutes acceptance and agreement with the above contract terms."

The court declared "that the signs constitute[d] an offer capable of acceptance by the driver of a motor vehicle by parking on the lot . . . without further communication with the owner".

City Parking was followed in *A.P. Parking Garage Inc. v. Pitcher* (1996), 138 Nfld. & P.E.I.R. 123 (Nfld. Prov. Ct.) which held that a parking meter offered parking for 75¢ per hour which was accepted by the motorist parking and depositing money in the meter. A later notice charging a "violation fee of $10.00" when the parking meter was expired was, therefore, invalid.

Would the result be the same if this were the sign? "Illegally parked vehicles towed away by Tag N Tow Inc. By parking on these premises you are deemed to have consented to the removal of any unauthorized or illegally parked vehicle and agreed to reimburse Tag N Tow Inc. for all removal and/or storage expenses."

See *Tag N Tow v. Parker* (1996), 190 A.R. 230 at 231 (Alta. Prov. Ct.). Compare *Arthur v. Anker*, [1996] 3 All E.R. 783 (C.A.) on the issue of consent in tort.

CARLILL v. CARBOLIC SMOKE BALL CO.

[1893] 1 Q.B. 256 (C.A.)

The defendants, who were the proprietors and vendors of a medical preparation called "The Carbolic Smoke Ball," inserted in the *Pall Mall Gazette* of November 13, 1891, and in other newspapers, the following advertisement:

100*l* reward will be paid by the Carbolic Smoke Ball Company to any person who contracts the increasing epidemic influenza, colds, or any disease caused by taking cold, after having used the ball three times daily for two weeks according to the printed directions supplied with each ball. 1000*l* is deposited with the Alliance Bank, Regent Street, shewing our sincerity in the matter.

During the last epidemic of influenza many thousand carbolic smoke balls were sold as preventives against the disease, and in no ascertained case was the disease contracted by those using the carbolic smoke ball.

One carbolic smoke ball will last a family several months, making it the cheapest remedy in the world at the price, 10s., post free. The ball can be refilled at a cost of 5s. Address, Carbolic Smoke Ball Company, 27, Princes Street, Hanover Square, London.

The plaintiff on the faith of this advertisement, bought one of the balls at a chemist's and used it as directed, three times a day, from November 20, 1891.

On January 17, 1892, she caught influenza. Hawkins J. held that she was entitled to recover the £100. The defendants appealed. . . .

BOWEN L.J. . . . We were asked to say that this document was a contract too vague to be enforced.

The first observation which arises is that the document itself is not a contract at all, it is only an offer made to the public. The defendants contend next, that it is an offer the terms of which are too vague to be treated as a definite offer, inasmuch as there is no limit of time fixed for the catching of the influenza, and it cannot be supposed that the advertisers seriously meant to promise to pay money to every person who catches the influenza at any time after the inhaling of the smoke ball. It was urged also, that if you look at this document you will find much vagueness as to the persons with whom the contract was intended to be made—that, in the first place, its terms are wide enough to include persons who may have used the smoke ball before the advertisement was issued; at all events, that it is an offer to the world in general, and, also, that it is unreasonable to suppose it to be a definite offer, because nobody in their senses would contract themselves out of the opportunity of checking the experiment which was going to be made at their own expense. It is also contended that the advertisement is rather in the nature of a puff or a proclamation than a promise or offer intended to mature into a contract when accepted. But the main point seems to be that the vagueness of the document shews that no contract whatever was intended. It seems to me that in order to arrive at a right conclusion we must read this advertisement in its plain meaning, as the public would understand it. It was intended to be issued to the public and to be read by the public. How would an ordinary person reading this document construe it? It was intended unquestionably to have some effect, and I think the effect which it was intended to have, was to make people use the smoke ball, because the suggestions and allegations which it contains are directed immediately to the use of the smoke ball as distinct from the purchase of it. It did not follow that the smoke ball was to be purchased from the defendants directly, or even from agents of theirs directly. The intention was that the circulation of the smoke ball should be promoted, and that the use of it should be increased. The advertisement begins by saying that a reward will be paid by the Carbolic Smoke Ball Company to any person who contracts the increasing epidemic after using the ball. It has been said that the words do not apply only to persons who contract the epidemic after the publication of the advertisement, but include persons who had previously contracted the influenza. I cannot so read the advertisement. It is written in colloquial and popular language, and I think that it is equivalent to this: "100*l* will be paid to any persons who shall contract the increasing epidemic after having used the carbolic smoke ball three times daily for two weeks." And it seems to me that the way in which the public would read it would be this, that if anybody, after the advertisement was published, used three times daily for two weeks the carbolic smoke ball, and then caught cold, he would be entitled to the reward. Then again it was said: "How long is this protection to endure? Is it to go on for ever, or for what limit of time?" I think that there are two constructions of this document, each of which is good sense, and each of which seems to me to satisfy the exigencies of the present action. It may mean that the protection is warranted to last during the epidemic, and it was during the epidemic that the plaintiff contracted the disease. I think, more probably, it means that the smoke ball will be a protection while it is in use. That seems to me the way in which an ordinary person would understand an advertisement about medicine, and about a specific against influenza. It could not be supposed that after you have left off using it you are still to be protected for ever, as if there was to be a stamp set upon your forehead that you were never to catch influenza because you had once used the carbolic smoke ball. I think the immunity is to last during the use of the ball. That is the way in which I should naturally read it, and it seems to me that the subsequent language of the advertisement supports that construction. It says: "During the last epidemic of influenza many thousand carbolic smoke balls were sold, and in no ascertained case was the disease contracted by those using" (not "who had used") "the carbolic smoke ball," and it concludes with saying that one smoke ball will last a family several months (which imports that it is to be efficacious while it is being used), and that the ball can be refilled at a cost of 5s. I, therefore, have myself no hesitation in saying that I think, on the construction of this advertisement, the protection was to endure during the time that the carbolic smoke ball was being used. My brother, the Lord Justice who preceded me, thinks that the contract would be sufficiently definite if you were to read it in the sense that the protection was to be warranted during a reasonable period after use. I have some difficulty myself on that point; but it is not necessary for me to consider it further, because the disease here was contracted during the use of the carbolic smoke ball.

Was it intended that the 100*l* should, if the conditions were fulfilled, be paid? The advertisement says that 1000*l* is lodged at the bank for the purpose. Therefore, it cannot be said that the statement that 100*l* would be paid was intended to be a mere puff. I think it was intended to be understood by the public as an offer which was to be acted upon.

But it was said there was no check on the part of the persons who issued the advertisement, and that it would be an insensate thing to promise 100*l* to a person who used the smoke ball unless you could check or superintend his manner of using it. The answer to that argument seems to me to be that if a person chooses to make extravagant promises of this kind he probably does so because it pays him to make them, and, if he has made them, the extravagance of the promises is no reason in law why he should not be bound by them.

It was also said that the contract is made with all the world—that is, with everybody; and that you cannot contract with everybody. It is not a contract made with all the world. There is the fallacy of the argument. It is an offer made to all the world; and why should not an offer be made to all the world which is to ripen into a contract with anybody who comes forward and performs the condition? It is an offer to become liable to any one who, before it is retracted, performs the condition, and, although the offer is made to the world, the contract is made with that limited portion of the public who come forward and perform the condition on the faith of the advertisement. It is not like cases in which you offer to negotiate, or you issue advertisements that you have got a stock of books to sell, or houses to let, in which case there is no offer to be bound by any contract. Such advertisements are offers to negotiate—offers to receive offers—offers to chaffer, as, I think, some learned judge in one of the cases has said. If this is an offer to be bound, then it is a contract the moment the person fulfils the condition. . . .

Then it was said that there was no notification of the acceptance of the contract. One cannot doubt that, as an ordinary rule of law, an acceptance of an offer made ought to be notified to the person who makes the offer, in order that the two minds may come together. Unless this is done the two minds may be apart, and there is not that consensus which is necessary according to the English law—I say nothing about the laws of other countries—to make a contract. But there is this clear gloss to be made upon that doctrine, that as notification of acceptance is required for the benefit of the person who makes the offer, the person who makes the offer may dispense with notice to himself if he thinks it desirable to do so, and I suppose there can be no doubt that where a person in an offer made by him to another person, expressly or impliedly intimates a particular mode of acceptance as sufficient to make the bargain binding, it is only necessary for the other person to whom such offer is made to follow the indicated method of acceptance; and if the person making the offer, expressly or impliedly intimates in his offer that it will be sufficient to act on the proposal without communicating acceptance of it to himself, performance of the condition is a sufficient acceptance without notification. . . .

Now, if that is the law, how are we to find out whether the person who makes the offer does intimate that notification of acceptance will not be necessary in order to constitute a binding bargain? In many cases you look to the offer itself. In many cases you extract from the character of the transaction that notification is not required, and in the advertisement cases it seems to me to follow as an inference to be drawn from the transaction itself that a person is not to notify his acceptance of the offer before he performs the condition, but that if he performs the condition notification is dispensed with. It seems to me that from the point of view of common sense no other idea could be entertained. If I advertise to the world that my dog is lost, and that anybody who brings the dog to a particular place will be paid some money, are all the police or other persons whose business it is to find lost dogs to be expected to sit down and write me a note saying that they have accepted my proposal? Why, of course, they at once look after the dog, and as soon as they find the dog they have performed the condition. The essence of the transaction is that the dog should be found, and it is not necessary under such circumstances, as it seems to me, that in order to make the contract binding there should be any notification of acceptance. It follows from the nature of the thing that the performance of the condition is sufficient acceptance without the notification of it, and a person who makes an offer in an advertisement of that kind makes an offer which must be read by the light of that common sense reflection. He does, therefore, in his offer impliedly indicate that he does not require notification of the acceptance of the offer.

A further argument for the defendants was that this was a nudum pactum—that there was no consideration for the promise—that taking the influenza was only a condition, and that the using the smoke ball was only a condition, and that there was no consideration at all; in fact, that there was no request, express or implied, to use the smoke ball. Now, I will not enter into an elaborate discussion upon the law as to requests in this kind of contract. . . . The short answer [is] that there is here [a] request to use involved in the offer. Then as to the alleged want of consideration. The definition of "consideration" given in Selwyn's Nisi Prius, 8th ed., p. 47, . . . is this: "Any act of the plaintiff from which the defendant derives a benefit or advantage, or any labour, detriment, or inconvenience sustained by the plaintiff, provided such act is performed or such inconvenience suffered by the plaintiff, with the consent, either express or implied, of the defendant." Can it be said here that if the person who reads this advertisement applies thrice daily, for such time as may seem to him tolerable, the carbolic smoke ball to his nostrils for a whole fortnight, he is doing nothing at all—that it is a mere act which is not to count towards consideration to support a promise (for the law does not require us to measure the adequacy of the consideration). Inconvenience sustained by one party at the request of the other is enough to create a consideration. I think, therefore, that it is consideration enough that the plaintiff took the trouble of using the smoke ball. But I think also that the defendants received a benefit from this user, for the use of the smoke ball was contemplated by the defendants as being indirectly a benefit to them, because the use of the smoke balls would promote their sale. . . .

LINDLEY M.R. [whose judgment preceded that of Bowen L.J. in the original case report, added the following rebuttal to counsel's argument that there was no contract because acceptance had not been communicated]

But then it is said, "Supposing that the performance of the conditions is an acceptance of the offer, that acceptance ought to have been notified." Unquestionably, as a general proposition, when an offer is made, it is necessary in order to make a binding contract, not only that it should be accepted, but that the acceptance should be notified. But is that so in cases of this kind? I apprehend that they are an exception to that rule, or, if not an exception, they are open to the observation that the notification of the acceptance need not precede the performance. This offer is a continuing offer. It was never revoked, and if notice of acceptance is required—which I doubt very much, for I rather think the true view is that which was expressed and explained by Lord Blackburn in the case of *Brogden v. Metropolitan Ry. Co.* [(1877), 2 App. Cas. 666 (H.L.)]—if notice of acceptance is required, the person who makes the offer gets the notice of acceptance contemporaneously with his notice of the performance of the condition. If he gets notice of the acceptance before his offer is revoked, that in principle is all you want. I, however, think that the true view, in a case of this kind, is that the person who makes the offer shows by his language and from the nature of the transaction that he does not expect and does not require notice of the acceptance apart from notice of the performance.

[A.L. Smith L.J. delivered a concurring judgment. Appeal dismissed.]

NOTE and QUESTIONS

1. This case and its historical context are fully discussed by Simpson in "Quackery and Contract Law: The Case of The Carbolic Smoke Ball" (1985), 14 J. of Legal Studies 345.

2. Suppose that Mrs. Carlill bought the smoke ball and used it as directed from 20th November 1891. On 10th December 1891, however, the defendant revoked its offer. On 11th December, Mrs. Carlill caught influenza. Could she recover £100?

3. It may be difficult to fit this case into a traditional model of offer and acceptance. Although acceptance is not fully discussed until section 4 of this chapter, when do you consider that acceptance of the Smoke Ball Company's offer might have occurred?

For how long should the offeror be able to withdraw the offer? A consideration of the revocation of an offer of a unilateral contract can be found in section 6(a) of this chapter. See Tiersma, "Reassessing Unilateral Contracts: The Role of Offer, Acceptance and Promise" (1992-93), 26 U.C. Davis L. Rev. 1 for an argument that a unilateral "promise" should be binding from the time it is made, subject to performance of the condition(s). He also points out that unilateral contracts are more important than commonly thought, arising, for example, in relation to employee benefits, real estate agents' commissions and manufacturers' guarantees.

GOLDTHORPE v. LOGAN

[1943] O.W.N. 215, [1943] 2 D.L.R. 519 (C.A.)

LAIDLAW J.A. [delivering the judgment of the court] This is an appeal by the plaintiffs from a judgment of Hope J. . . . The female appellant had some hairs on her face and wanted to have them removed. She saw advertisements published in a newspaper by the defendant Anne Graham Logan. She went to the place of business stated in the advertisement and consulted the defendant Kathleen Fitzpatrick, a registered nurse, who was an employee of the defendant Logan. She was told that her face could be definitely "cleared," that the hair could be removed permanently, and the result was guaranteed. She then submitted to a number of "treatments" by electrolysis for the purpose of removing the hairs but the result was not satisfactory. Hairs continued to grow on her face in the same way as before and in spite of the efforts of the defendants to remedy the condition. She claims in this action that the treatments by or on behalf of the defendants were unskilfully or negligently administered or should not have been administered at all, and that as a result thereof she has suffered damages. Her husband alleges that he has had great worry and suffering as a result of his wife's condition: that he has suffered loss and expense, and therefore he also claims damages from the defendants. When the matter came to trial the plaintiffs by leave of the Court amended the statement of claim. The amendment in part is "In the alternative the plaintiffs claim the defendants were under a contract to remove safely and permanently the superfluous hairs in existence when the treatment was given, and guaranteed satisfactory results, and failed to carry out the contract and the plaintiffs allege that the results were not satisfactory."

There are three questions to be determined: (1) Was there any negligence on the part of the defendants which caused loss or damages to the plaintiffs? (2) Was there a contract between the defendant Logan and the plaintiff Pearl Elizabeth Goldthorpe? (3) If so, what is the result in law of a breach thereof on the part of the defendant?

The learned trial Judge was unable to find that the plaintiff has established either in tort or in contract the case which is alleged against the defendants. He does not find that there was any stimulation of growth of hairs by reason of the treatments administered by the defendants and says that any such stimulation of growth can more reasonably be attributed to a different cause. It is my opinion that the plaintiffs have not adduced evidence from which the Court might reasonably make a finding of negligence on the part of the defendants or either of them. . . . But the alternative allegation to the effect that the defendant Logan is responsible in law by reason of a breach of contract made by or on her behalf with the female plaintiff requires careful consideration. The elements of a valid contract are well known, and it is only necessary to analyze the evidence to determine whether or not they exist in this case. I at once examined the advertisement published by the defendant Logan. It appears in two forms, but the portions relevant to the question now studied are the same. I excerpt the contents as follows: "HAIRS . . . removed safely and permanently by ELECTROLYSIS . . . No marks, No scars, Results Guaranteed. ANNE GRAHAM LOGAN . . . 140 Carlton St." What is the true nature and construction of this advertisement? It is a distinct communication by the defendant Logan to each and every member of the public. What intention did she possess and convey to such persons by the words she used? To ascertain that intention we may in this instance look at the surrounding circumstances. She was carrying on a business in which she appealed for public support and patronage. She required customers to buy services she desired to sell. She was a vendor seeking a purchaser. What she meant to say, and the sensible interpretation of her words is this: "If you will submit yourself to my treatment and pay me (certain charges) I undertake to remove hairs safely and permanently by electrolysis and I promise to obtain a satisfactory result." The effect in law of such a statement is to create an offer from the person by whom it is made to every person who is willing to accept the terms and conditions of it. It may, perhaps, be suggested that this meaning and effect of the advertisement is strained and unfair. I think it is not. On the contrary, I read it in its plain meaning as the public would understand it. Moreover, after Mrs. Goldthorpe was persuaded by this public offer to attend at the defendant's place of business she was given further assurance that the hairs on her face could be successfully and permanently removed without stimulation, without risk, and without pain. The defendants again "guaranteed results." They did not ask for nor suggest any exemption, exception, or qualification of any kind, but on the contrary they made promises which were absolute and unlimited. They were reckless and rash without any regard whatever to the particular circumstances of the case. No physical examination of Mrs. Goldthorpe was required nor suggested. No inquiry was made for the purpose of disclosing any organic trouble or cause of the excessive hair. The defendants simply were content to take the risk of failure irrespective of any underlying causes of the unfortunate ailment, and they exposed themselves to just such an action as this. If the vendor's self-confidence had persuaded her into an excessive, extravagant promise, she cannot now escape a complaint from a credulous and distressed person to whom she gave assurance of future excellence and relief from her burden. The strong cannot disregard any undertaking binding in law, however lightly given, and the weak unfortunate person, however gullible, can be sure that the Courts of this country will not permit anyone to escape the responsibility arising from an enforceable promise. The words of Hawkins J., are fitting and applicable. He says:

> Such advertisements do not appeal so much to the wise and thoughtful as to the credulous and weak portions of the community; and if the vendor of an article, whether it be medicine smoke or anything else, with a view to increase its sale and use, thinks fit publicly to promise to all who buy or use it that, to those who shall not find it as surely efficacious as it is represented by him to be he will pay a substantial sum of money, he must not be surprised if occasionally he is held to his promise: *Carlill v. Carbolic Smoke Ball Co.* [*supra*].

I now consider whether there was acceptance in law of the offer made by the defendant. The offer was made to the public. Any member was free to lend oneself to the terms and conditions and assent thereto.

The female plaintiff accordingly accepted the offer, and her acceptance was communicated to the defendant Logan by her conduct. These parties had a common intention, and there was good consideration present. It was constituted by the detriment or inconvenience sustained by the female plaintiff. Her submission to the treatments, in accordance with advertisement, was a benefit sought by the advertiser. . . . The adequacy of such consideration is not for the Court [to judge] . . . I hold that there was an agreement made between the plaintiff, Pearl Elizabeth Goldthorpe and the defendant, Ann Graham Logan, and that such agreement is enforceable at law by the female plaintiff. It is apparent from what I have said that, in my opinion there was a breach of such agreement on the part of the defendant Logan.

I therefore examine the evidence and law to ascertain what result must follow. Mrs. Goldthorpe paid various amounts from time to time, and the total is not agreed upon nor clearly established by evidence. I would settle all difference between the parties by a finding that the total sum paid was $13.25. She received no benefit whatever from the treatments, and the defendant Logan must repay to her the sum as settled. In addition she sustained further loss and damage, and she is entitled to be put in the same situation, so far as money can do so, as she would have been if the contract had been fully performed. She does not now complain of scars on her face but only of the continued existence of hairs. If there be a greater growth of hair than before the treatments were administered, that unfortunate condition is not caused by a breach of the contract, but, as found by the learned trial Judge, is attributable to another cause. It is not easy to determine the amount of such damage sustained under the particular circumstances, but I think $100 would be reasonable and fair. . . . Her action against the defendant Kathleen Fitzpatrick, and the action on behalf of the plaintiff J. Thomas Goldthorpe, against both defendants, should be dismissed without costs. . . .

[Appeal allowed in part.]

NOTES and QUESTIONS

1. Was it necessary for the court to find that the advertisement was an offer to enable Mrs. Goldthorpe to recover?

2. Cases such as *Goldthorpe v. Logan* are now often affected by legislation, see, *e.g.*, the Consumer Protection Act, C.C.S.M., c. C200, s. 58(8), the Business Practices Act, C.C.S.M., c. B120 and similar legislation discussed in Chapter 7, section 4.

3. In *Bowerman v. Association of British Travel Agents Ltd.*, [1996] C.L.C. 451 (C.A.) Hobhouse L.J. (Waite L.J. concurring) applied *Carlill* to a notice describing ABTA's scheme of protection against the financial failure of ABTA members; ". . . this document is intended to be read and would reasonably be read by a member of the public as containing an offer of a promise which the customer is entitled to accept by choosing to do business with an ABTA member." Why could it be important to find that the notice was an offer?

4. If a law school bulletin indicated that applicants would be admitted on the basis of university grade point averages and LSAT scores only, would a rejected applicant have a contractual claim if the school used unpublished non-academic criteria? Compare *Acadia University v. Sutcliffe* (1978), 85 D.L.R. (3d) 115 (N.S. Co. Ct.) and *Wong v. Lakehead University*, [1991] O.J. No. 1901 (Ont. Gen. Div.) with *Steinberg v. Chicago Medical School*, 371 N.E. 2d 634 (Ill. S.C., 1977).

5.(a) When might it be argued that a contract is complete at an auction sale? See the Sale of Goods Act, R.S.A. 2000, c. S-2, s. 57; R.S.B.C. 1996, c. 410, s. 72; C.C.S.M., c. S10, s. 59; R.S.N.B. 1973, c. S-1, s. 55; R.S.N.L. 1990, c. S-6, s. 59; R.S.N.S. 1989, c. 408, s. 59; R.S.O. 1990, c. S.1, s. 56; R.S.P.E.I. 1988, c. S-1, s. 58; R.S.S. 1978, c. S-1, s. 57. Section 56(b) of the Ontario statute provides that in sale by auction, "a sale is complete when the auctioneer announces its completion by the fall of a hammer or in any other customary manner, and until such announcement is made any bidder may retract his, her or its bid." Do these rules accord with the expectations of sellers and buyers? How much risk is there of detrimental reliance on the part of potential buyers in the auction context? The Ontario Law Reform Commission (O.L.R.C.) has recommended clarifications and changes to these sections in the *Report on Sale of Goods* (1979), vol. I, at 86-90.

(b) What does it mean to say that an auction sale is "without reserve" or "unreserved"? *Proctor v. Almansask Dist. Ltd.* (1984), 37 Alta. L.R. (2d) 164 (Prov. Ct.). Cf. *McManus v. Nova Scotia* (1995), 144 N.S.R. (2d) 182 (S.C.), affirmed (1996), 156 N.S.R. (2d) 159 (C.A.) although in *McManus* the advertised term was changed before the auctioneer put up the assets of a company for auction and called for bids. See also Hickling, "Auctions Without Reserve" (1970), 5 U.B.C.L. Rev. 187.

HARVELA INVESTMENTS LTD. v. ROYAL TRUST CO. OF CANADA (C.I.) LTD.

[1986] A.C. 207, [1985] 3 W.L.R. 276, [1985] 2 All E.R. 966 (H.L.)

LORD TEMPLEMAN My Lords, by telex messages (the invitation) dispatched on 15 September 1981 the respondent vendors, Royal Trust Co. of Canada (CI) Ltd, invited the appellant, Harvela Investments Ltd (Harvela), and Sir Leonard Outerbridge (Sir Leonard), to make offers to purchase the vendors' shares in A Harvey & Co. Ltd (the shares). The invitation stipulated that offers must be made by sealed tender or confidential telex which would not be divulged by the vendors before the invitation expired at 3 p.m. on 16 September 1981 when the vendors would accept 'the highest offer'. Completion of the purchase was to take place within 30 days of 16 September 1981 in Canadian dollars.

Harvela offered $2,175,000. Sir Leonard offered $2,100,000 'or C$101,000 in excess of any other offer which you may receive which is expressed as a fixed monetary amount, whichever is the higher'. Harvela claim the shares at the price of $2,175,000. Sir Leonard claims the shares at the price of $2,276,000 as a result of his referential offer of $101,000 more than Harvela's fixed offer. [The trial judge] found in favour of Harvela. . . . The Court of Appeal . . . found in favour of Sir Leonard. . . . This appeal is brought by Harvela. . . .

Where a vendor undertakes to sell to the highest bidder the vendor may conduct the sale by auction or by fixed bidding. In an auction sale each bidder may adjust his bid by reference to rival bids. In an auction sale the purchaser pays more than any other bidder is prepared to pay to secure the property. The purchaser does not necessarily pay as much as the purchaser was prepared to pay to secure the property. In an auction a purchaser who is prepared to pay $2.5m to secure a property will be able to purchase for $2.2m if no other bidder is prepared to offer as much as $2.2m.

In a fixed bidding sale a bidder may not adjust his bid. Each bidder specifies a fixed amount which he hopes will be sufficient, but not more than sufficient, to exceed any other bid. The purchaser in a fixed bidding sale does not necessarily pay as much as the purchaser was prepared to pay to secure the property. But any bidder who specifies less than his best price knowingly takes a risk of being outbid. In a fixed bidding sale a purchaser who is prepared to pay $2.5m to secure the property may be able to purchase for $2.2m if the purchaser offers $2.2m and no other bidder offers as much as $2.2m. But if a bidder prepared to pay $2.5m only offers $2.2m he will run the risk of losing the property and will be mortified to lose the property if another bidder offers $2.3m. Where there are two bidders with ample resources, each determined to secure the property and to prevent the other bidder from acquiring the property, the stronger will prevail in the fixed bidding sale and may pay more than in an auction which is decided not by the strength of the stronger but by the weakness of the weaker of the two bidders. On the other hand, an open auction provides the stimulus of perceived bidding and compels each bidder, except the purchaser, to bid up to his maximum.

Thus auction sales and fixed bidding sales are liable to affect vendors and purchasers in different ways and to produce different results. The first question raised by this appeal, therefore, is whether Harvela and Sir Leonard were invited to participate in a fixed bidding sale, which only invited fixed bids, or were invited to participate in an auction sale, which enabled the bid of each bidder to be adjusted by reference to the other bid. A vendor chooses between a fixed bidding sale and an auction sale. A bidder can only choose to participate in the sale or to abstain from the sale. The ascertainment of the choice of the vendors in the present case between a fixed bidding sale and an auction sale by means of referential bids depends on the presumed intention of the vendors. That presumed intention must be deduced from the terms of the invitation read as a whole. . . .

[Lord Templeman found that the invitation was designed to provoke the best price that Harvela and Sir Leonard were each prepared to offer in ignorance of the rival bid and continued.]

To constitute a fixed bidding sale all that was necessary was that the vendors should invite confidential offers and should undertake to accept the highest offer. Such was the form of the invitation. It follows that the invitation on its true construction created a fixed bidding sale and that Sir Leonard was not entitled to submit and the vendors were not entitled to accept a referential bid.

The argument put forward by counsel for Sir Leonard was that the referential bid was an 'offer' and therefore Sir Leonard was entitled to submit a referential bid. In acceding to this argument, the Court of Appeal recognized that the consequences could be unfortunate and would be unforeseeable; the Court of Appeal was inclined to blame such unfortunate and unforeseeable consequences on the vendors for binding themselves to accept the highest bid or for not expressly forbidding the submission of a referential bid. My Lords, in my opinion the argument based on the possible meaning of the word 'offer' confuses definition with construction and the procedure adopted by the vendors is not open to justifiable criticism because the invitation was clear and unambiguous. The court is not concerned to define the word 'offer' in isolation without regard to its context and by reference to the widest possible meaning which can be culled from the weightiest available dictionary. The mere use by the vendors of the word 'offer' was not sufficient to invoke all the frustrating dangers and uncertainties which inevitably follow from uncontrolled referential bids. The task of the court is to construe the invitation and to ascertain whether the provisions of the invitation, read as a whole, create a fixed bidding sale or an auction sale. I am content to reach a conclusion which reeks of simplicity, which does not require a draftsman to indulge in prohibitions, but which obliges a vendor to specify and control any form of auction which he seeks to combine with confidential bidding. The invitation required Sir Leonard to name his price and required Harvela to name its price and bound the vendors to accept the higher price. The invitation was not difficult to understand and the result was bound to be certain and to accord with the presumed intentions of the vendors discernible from the express provisions of the invitation. Harvela named the price of $2,175,000; Sir Leonard failed to name any price except $2,100,000, which was less than the price named by Harvela. The vendors were bound to accept Harvela's offer. . . .

[Lord Fraser of Tullybelton, Lord Diplock, Lord Edmund-Davies, and Lord Bridge of Harwich concurred. Appeal allowed.]

NOTE

Re Multi-Pêches Inc., [1989] R.J.Q. 401 (C.S.) was the first Canadian case to consider the validity of referential bids. It followed the reasoning of the *Harvela* decision but, in a specialized context involving the sale of the assets of an insolvent company, it annulled the acceptance of the referential bid without requiring the vendor to accept the only other bid.

R. v. RON ENGINEERING & CONSTRUCTION (EASTERN) LTD.

[1981] 1 S.C.R. 111, 13 B.L.R. 72, 119 D.L.R. (3d) 267, 35 N.R. 40

The contractor submitted a tender to build a project for a price of $2,748,000. In accordance with the Information for Tenderers, the contractor also submitted as a tender deposit a certified cheque in the amount of $150,000. Paragraph 13 of the Information for Tenderers supplied by the owner stated:

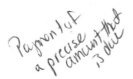
Payment of a precise amount is due

> Except as otherwise herein provided the tenderer guarantees that if his tender is withdrawn before the Commission shall have considered the tenders or before or after he has been notified that his tender has been recommended to the Commission for acceptance or that if the Commission does not for any reason receive within the period of seven days as stipulated and as required herein, the Agreement executed by the tenderer, the Performance Bond and the Payment Bond executed by the tenderer and the surety company and the other documents required herein, the Commission may retain the tender deposit for the use of the Commission and may accept any tender, advertise for new tenders, negotiate a contract or not accept any tender as the Commission may deem advisable.

Tenders for the construction project closed at 3:00 p.m. on July 4, 1972. The contractor's employee who filed the tender remained for the opening of tenders and learned that its tender was $632,000 lower than the next lowest tender. The representative contacted the president of the company immediately and, at 4:12 p.m. on July 4, 1972, the contractor sent a telex which read in part as follows:

> Today we submitted our tender for the above project and unfortunately due to the rush of compiling our last figures we omitted to add to our total the sum for our own forces work and general condition in the amount of $750,058.00 which actually should have been added to our lump sum tender amount for a total of 3,498,058.00 dollars.

> Due to this unfortunate error we would appreciate being given the opportunity to show to you our estimate indicating the error and to hereby request to withdraw our tender. . . .

In subsequent correspondence and in the proceedings the contractor maintained that it had not withdrawn its tender, but that it was incapable of being accepted.

In the course of its judgment, the court considered whether, under these circumstances, the contractor would have been entitled to withdraw its tender and recover its deposit.

ESTEY J. [delivering the judgment of the court]

. . . The revocability of the offer must, in my view, be determined in accordance with the "General Conditions" and "Information for Tenderers" and the related documents upon which the tender was submitted. There is no question when one reviews the terms and conditions under which the tender was made that a contract arose upon the submission of a tender between the contractor and the owner whereby the tenderer could not withdraw the tender for a period of sixty days after the date of the opening of the tenders. Later in these reasons this initial contract is referred to as contract A to distinguish it from the construction contract itself which would arise on the acceptance of a tender, and which I refer to as contract B. Other terms and conditions of this unilateral contract which arose by the filing of a tender in response to the call therefor under the aforementioned terms and conditions, included the right to recover the tender deposit sixty days after the opening of tenders if the tender was not accepted by the owner. This contract is brought into being automatically upon the submission of a tender. The terms and conditions specified in the tender documents and which become part of the terms of contract A between the owner and the contractor included the following provision:

> 6. *Withdrawal or Qualifying of Tenders*

>> A tenderer who has already submitted a tender may submit a further tender at any time up to the official closing time. The last tender received shall supersede and invalidate all tenders previously submitted by that tenderer for this contract.

A tenderer may withdraw or qualify his tender at any time up to the official closing time by submitting a letter bearing his signature and seal as in his tender to the Commission Secretary or his authorized representative in his office who will mark thereon the time and date of receipt and will place the letter in the tender box. No telegrams or telephone calls will be considered.

.....

[Paragraph 13 of the Information for Tenderers also provided for the return of the tender deposit on the execution of the construction contract. The court continued its analysis as follows.]

Here the contractor expressly avoided employing any terminology indicating a withdrawal of the tender, and indeed affirmatively asserted the position through-out that the offer had not been revoked. The owner did proffer a construction agreement and this agreement was not executed by the tenderer within the seven day period. . . .

The tender submitted by the respondent brought contract A into life. This is sometimes described in law as a unilateral contract, that is to say a contract which results from an act made in response to an offer, as for example in the simplest terms, "I will pay you a dollar if you will cut my lawn". No obligation to cut the lawn exists in law and the obligation to pay the dollar comes into being upon the performance of the invited act. Here the call for tenders created no obligation in the respondent or in anyone else in or out of the construction world. When a member of the construction industry responds to the call for tenders, as the respondent has done here, that response takes the form of the submission of a tender, or a bid as it is sometimes called. The significance of the bid in law is that it at once becomes irrevocable if filed in conformity with the terms and conditions under which the call for tenders was made and if such terms so provide. There is no disagreement between the parties here about the form and procedure in which the tender was submitted by the respondent and that it complied with the terms and conditions of the call for tenders. Consequently, contract A came into being. The principal term of contract A is the irrevocability of the bid, and the corollary term is the obligation in both parties to enter into a contract (contract B) upon the acceptance of the tender. Other terms include the qualified obligations of the owner to accept the lowest tender, and the degree of this obligation is controlled by the terms and conditions established in the call for tenders.

The role of the deposit under contract A is clear and simple. The deposit was required in order to ensure the performance by the contractor-tenderer of its obligations under contract A. The deposit was recoverable by the contractor under certain conditions, none of which were met; and also was subject to forfeiture under another term of the contract, the provisions of which in my view have been met. . . .

[On this basis, the Supreme Court of Canada confirmed the dismissal by the trial judge of the contractor's claim for the return of the tender deposit. Appeal allowed.]

NOTES

1. The consequences of the contractor's mistake in the *Ron Engineering* case are considered *infra* in Chapter 9, section 2(b). The question of whether a promise not to withdraw an offer is legally binding is discussed later in section 6 of this chapter.

2. The traditional analysis of tenders is described as follows:

> [A] statement inviting tenders for the supply of goods or for the execution of works is not normally an offer. The offer comes from the person who submits the tender and there is no contract until the person asking for the tenders accepts one of them.

Treitel, *The Law of Contract*, 11th ed. (2003) at 15 (notes omitted). See, generally, Fridman, "Tendering Problems" (1987), 66 Can Bar Rev. 582.

3. The two-contract analysis of Estey J. in *Ron Engineering* has significantly reformed the law of tenders in Canada by developing a legal basis to protect the integrity of the tendering process, particularly in the awarding of government contracts. It similarly affects the relationship that is created when a subcontractor submits a bid to the general contractor, as can be seen in *Northern Construction Ltd. v. Gloge Heating & Plumbing Ltd.*, [1986] 2 W.W.R. 649 (Alta. C.A.) and *Fred Welsh Ltd. v. B.G.M. Construction Ltd.*, [1996] 10 W.W.R. 400 at 410 (B.C. S.C.).

Nevertheless, the analysis left many questions unanswered. Many inconsistencies related to the obligations of the person who invites tenders and who, in Construction Law, is usually described as the owner. The most important of these inconsistencies are described in Note 4.

4. In the contract A analysis, the owner can impose obligations on tenderers through the provisions of the Invitation to Tender. The Invitation to Tender amounts to an offer of contract A, which each contractor accepts by submitting a tender. In contrast to the unilateral contract analysis of contract A in *Ron Engineering*, subsequent cases have usually found that contract A is a bilateral contract involving immediate contractual obligations on both the bidder and the owner. By this mechanism, rules set out in the Invitation to Tender can also become contractual obligations which bind the owner.

Zutphen Brothers Construction Ltd. v. Nova Scotia (1994), 12 C.L.R. (2d) 111 (N.S. S.C.) provides a simple example of how the Invitation to Tender imposes obligations on the owner. The Government of Nova Scotia invited tenders to construct a concrete bridge in Cape Breton. The tender documents advised tenderers that they could submit an alternate bid for a bridge to be built of structural steel and added "To be acceptable, a structural steel alternative must show a substantial saving" over the concrete design. The plaintiff submitted the lowest tender for a concrete bridge, but the owner accepted the bid of another company to build a bridge of structural steel, despite the fact that, rather than showing a substantial saving, the steel bridge was more costly than a concrete bridge. The court found that the owner's award of the contract constituted a breach of a term of contract A.

Despite cases such as this, the owner, who is normally responsible for the preparation of the Invitation to Tender, appears to remain in control of the extent of the obligations which it is willing to assume. Virtually all Invitations to Tender contain a device often known as the "privilege clause", which essentially states that the owner may not accept the lowest tender received and need not accept any tender for the project.

The first set of problems in relation to the obligations of the owner under contract A arose when the courts considered the relationship between the specific rules of the Invitation to Tender and the privilege clause. For example, in *R. v. Canamerican Auto Lease & Rental Ltd.*, [1987] 3 F.C. 144 (C.A.), the court refused to allow a general privilege clause to nullify liability for breach of a specific award procedure clause contained in the Invitation to Tender, noting at 157-158, "that to give paramountcy to this clause of the Specifications would be to render nugatory and completely meaningless the award procedure clause of the Specifications". However, other courts treated the privilege clause as paramount and allowed the clause to nullify any other obligation which the owner might otherwise have assumed as a result of the Invitation to Tender, as in *M.J.B. Enterprises Ltd. v. Defence Construction (1951) Ltd.* (1997), 196 A.R. 124 (C.A.). The decision of the Supreme Court of Canada in this case is set out in the next extract.

The second set of problems arose when courts found that contract A contained certain implied obligations of the owner which at first sight appeared to be contradicted by the privilege clause. These cases often involved an owner who rejected the lowest tender and awarded the contract to another bidder on the basis of a preference in favour of local contractors which was not disclosed in the tender documents. For example in *Chinook Aggregates Ltd. v. Abbotsford*, [1990] 1 W.W.R. 624, referred to in *M.J.B. Enterprises, infra*, the British Columbia Court of Appeal, notwithstanding the presence of a privilege clause, affirmed, at 630, the finding of a trial judge that where "there was a custom and usage in the construction industry . . . that in the absence of notice from the owner of preferential rules or criteria for the award of a contract, then all the participants in the industry acted on the principle that the low qualified bidder got the job." On this basis, the owner was found liable to the lowest bidder whose tender had been rejected in favour of a local contractor.

Many of the difficulties created in these decisions are addressed in the following case.

M.J.B. ENTERPRISES LTD. v. DEFENCE CONSTRUCTION (1951) LTD.

[1999] 1 S.C.R. 619, 170 D.L.R. (4th) 577

IACOBUCCI J. [delivering the judgment of the court]

INTRODUCTION

The central issue in this appeal is whether the inclusion of a "privilege clause" in the tender documents allows the person calling for tenders (the "owner") to disregard the lowest bid in favour of any other tender, including a non-compliant one. The leading Canadian case on the law of tenders is *R. in Right of Ontario v. Ron Engineering & Construction (Eastern) Ltd.*, *supra*, which concerned the obligations of a contractor who submitted a bid in response to a call for tenders. This Court held that, upon the submission of this tender, a contract arose between the contractor and the owner in that case and imposed certain obligations upon the contractor. The contract, referred to as "Contract A", was distinguished from the construction contract, "Contract B", to be entered into if the tender was accepted, Contract A imposed certain obligations upon the contractor. The present appeal instead asks whether Contract A arose in this case and what obligations, if any, it imposes on the *owner*. It is the contention of M.J.B. Enterprises Ltd. (the "appellant") that in the circumstances of this case Defence Construction (1951) Limited (the "respondent") was obligated to accept the lowest valid tender. The respondent argues that the privilege clause precludes the finding of such an obligation.

FACTUAL BACKGROUND

The respondent invited tenders for the construction of a pump house, the installation of a water distribution system and the dismantling of a water tank on the Canadian Forces Base in Suffield, Alberta. Four tenders were received, including one from the appellant. The contract was awarded to Sorochan Enterprises Ltd. ("Sorochan"), the lowest tenderer, and the work was carried out. The appellant was the second lowest tenderer.

The respondent had issued detailed directions to tenderers in the 11 documents which, according to the Tender Form, comprised the Tender Documents.

One of these documents was the Instructions to Tenderers, paragraph 13 of which stated: "The lowest or any tender shall not necessarily be accepted". The parties have referred to this as the "privilege clause". In addition, prior to the close of tenders, the respondent issued two amendments to the Tender Documents.

The original specifications in the Tender Documents contemplated that the tenderers would provide a lump sum price for the construction of the pump house and demolition of the water tank, but would submit a per lineal metre price for construction of the water system. There were three different types of material in which water pipe might be laid and with which the trenches for the pipes might be backfilled: Type 2 (essentially a large gravel fill), Type 3 (native backfill) or Type 4 (a lean slurry concrete). The site engineer would determine the type of material required at various parts of the distribution system. Since the lineal costs of these different fills varied widely, the specifications originally included a schedule of quantities which allowed the tenderers to submit their bids on a basis which would make the final cost contingent upon the amount of the different fills required, i.e., the tenderer could set out different amounts per lineal metre for each of Types 2, 3 and 4 fill. However, the amendments to the Tender Documents deleted the schedule of quantities. The effect of this was to require the tenderers to submit only one price per lineal metre for the water distribution system regardless of the type of fill which would ultimately be designated by the engineer during construction. The appellant interpreted this to assign the risk of knowing how much of Type 2, Type 3, and Type 4 fill would be required to the successful contractor, as the contractor would receive the same cent unit price per lineal metre of measurement regardless of the actual costs incurred by the contractor.

The tender submitted by Sorochan included a handwritten note stating:

Please note:

Unit Prices per metre are based on native backfill (Type 3). If Type 2 material is required from top of pipe zone to bottom of sub-base material for gravel or paved areas, add $60.00 per metre.

Despite complaints by the appellant, and other tenderers, that this note constituted a qualification by Sorochan that invalidated its tender, the respondent determined the note was merely a clarification and accepted Sorochan's bid. The appellant brought an action for breach of contract, claiming that Sorochan's bid should have been disqualified and that its tender should have been accepted as the lowest valid bid.

Prior to trial, the parties agreed on damages of $398,121.27, subject to the determination of liability. However, there were two issues they did not agree on, the cost of a supervisor and the cost of Type 2 backfill that was included in the appellant's tender that, had the appellant been awarded the construction contract, would not have been required by the engineer. The amount in dispute totals $251,056.89.

The trial judge found that the note was a qualification but held that, given the presence of the privilege clause, the respondent was under no obligation to award the contract to the appellant as the next lowest bidder. The Alberta Court of Appeal dismissed the appeal. . . .

THE COURTS BELOW

.....

[In the Court of Appeal] McClung J.A. held that the meaning of the privilege clause was not ambiguous, and was placed in the bidding process to protect the expenditure of public funds which are a common property resource of the people of Canada. Although the Alberta Guide to Construction Procedures provides that the construction contract should be awarded to the contractor submitting the lowest proper tender, those rules only apply where they are not inconsistent with the terms of the federal bidding package. In this case, "the privilege clause, section 13, is a complete answer to M.J.B.'s action" (p. 127).

ISSUES

The major issue in this appeal comes down to the following: does the respondent's inclusion of a "privilege clause" in the tender documents at issue in this case allow the respondent to disregard the lowest bid in favour of any other tender, including a non-compliant one?

ANALYSIS

A. *General Principles*

As I have already indicated, any discussion of contractual obligations and the law of tendering must begin with this Court's decision in *Ron Engineering*, *supra*.

.....

I . . . do not wish to be taken to endorse Estey J's characterization of Contract A as a unilateral contract in *Ron Engineering*. His analysis has been strongly criticized: see R. S. Nozick, Comment on *The Province of Ontario and the Water Resources Commission v. Ron Engineering and Construction (Eastern) Ltd. (S.C.C.)* (1982), 60 Can. Bar Rev. 345, at p. 350; J. Swan, *Comment on The Queen v. Ron Engineering & Construction (Eastern) Ltd.* (1981), 15 U.B.C. L. Rev. 447 at p. 455. . . . However, each case turns on its facts and since the revocability of the tender is not at issue in the present appeal, I see no reason to revisit the analysis of the facts in *Ron Engineering*.

What is important, therefore, is that the submission of a tender in response to an invitation to tender may give rise to contractual obligations, quite apart from the obligations associated with the construction contract to be entered into upon the acceptance of a tender, depending upon whether the parties intend to initiate contractual relations by the submission of a bid. If such a contract arises, its terms are governed by the terms and conditions of the tender call.

I note that the jurisprudence in other common law jurisdictions supports the approach that, depending upon the intentions of the parties, an invitation to tender can give rise to contractual obligations upon the submission of a bid: see *Blackpool and Fylde Aero Club Ltd. v. Blackpool Borough Council*, [1990] 3 All E.R. 24 (C.A.); *Hughes Aircraft Systems International v. Airservices Australia* (1997),

146 A.L.R. 1 (F.C.); and *Pratt Contractors Ltd. v. Palmerston North City Council*, [1995] 1 N.Z.L.R. 469 (H.C.).

So this brings us to ask whether Contract A arose in this case and, if so, what were its terms?

B. *Contract A*

Both parties in the present appeal agree with the Contract A/Contract B analysis outlined in *Ron Engineering* and that the terms of Contract A, if any, are to be determined through an examination of the terms and conditions of the tender call. In particular, they agree that Contract A arose, but disagree as to its terms.

.....

[W]hether or not Contract A arose depends upon whether the parties intended to initiate contractual relations by the submission of a bid in response to the invitation to tender. In the present case I am persuaded that this was the intention of the parties. At a minimum, the respondent offered, in inviting tenders through a formal tendering process involving complex documentation and terms, to consider bids for Contract B. In submitting its tender, the appellant accepted this offer. The submission of the tender is good consideration for the respondent's promise, as the tender was a benefit to the respondent, prepared at a not insignificant cost to the appellant, and accompanied by the Bid Security. The question to be answered next is the precise nature of the respondent's contractual obligations.

The main contention of the appellant is that the respondent was under an obligation to award Contract B to the lowest compliant tender. As the Sorochan bid was invalid, Contract B should have been awarded to the appellant. . . .

[The appellant argued] that there is an implied term in Contract A such that the lowest compliant bid must be accepted. The general principles for finding an implied contractual term were outlined by this Court in *Canadian Pacific Hotels Ltd. v. Bank of Montreal*, [1987] 1 S.C.R. 711. Le Dain J., for the majority, held that terms may be implied in a contract: (1) based on custom or usage; (2) as the legal incidents of a particular class or kind of contract; or (3) based on the presumed intention of the parties where the implied term must be necessary "to give business efficacy to a contract or as otherwise meeting the 'officious bystander' test as a term which the parties would say, if questioned, that they had obviously assumed" (p. 775). . . .

While in the case of a contract arising in the context of a standardized tendering process there may be substantial overlap involving custom or usage, the requirements of the tendering process, and the presumed intentions of the party, I conclude that, in the circumstances of the present case, it is appropriate to find an implied term according to the presumed intentions of the parties.

As mentioned, Le Dain J. stated in *Canadian Pacific Hotels Ltd.*, *supra*, that a contractual term may be implied on the basis of presumed intentions of the parties where necessary to give business efficacy to the contract or where it meets the "officious bystander" test. It is unclear whether these are to be understood as two separate tests but I need not determine that here. What is important in both formulations is a focus on the intentions of the *actual* parties. A court, when dealing with terms implied in fact, must be careful not to slide into determining the intentions of *reasonable* parties. This is why the implication of the term must have a certain degree of obviousness to it, and why, if there is evidence of a contrary intention, on the part of either party, an implied term may not be found on this basis. As G. H. L. Fridman states in *The Law of Contract in Canada*, 3rd ed. (1994), at p. 476:

> In determining the intention of the parties, attention must be paid to the express terms of the contract in order to see whether the suggested implication is necessary and fits in with what has clearly been agreed upon, and the precise nature of what, if anything, should be implied.

In this respect, I find it difficult to accept that the appellant, or any of the other contractors, would have submitted a tender unless it was understood by all involved that only a compliant tender would be accepted. However, I find no support for the proposition that, in the face of a privilege clause such as the one at issue in this case, the *lowest* compliant tender was to be accepted. A review of the Tender Documents, including the privilege clause, and the testimony of the respondent's witnesses at trial, indicates that, on the basis of the presumed intentions of the parties, it is reasonable to find an implied obligation to accept only a compliant tender. . . .

It is clear from the foregoing description of the Instructions to Tenderers and the Tender Form that the invitation for tenders may be characterized as an offer to consider a tender *if that tender is valid*. An invalid tender would be, as outlined in these documents, one that either was submitted too late, was not submitted on the required Tender Form, altered the Tender Form or did not provide the information requested, did not include the required Bid Security, had an imbalance in prices, did not comply with the Rules of Practice for sub-trades, or did not conform to the plans and specifications.

A tender, in addition to responding to an invitation for tenders, is also an offer to perform the work outlined in the plans and specifications for a particular price. The invitation for tenders is therefore an invitation for offers to enter into Contract B on the terms specified by the owner and for a price specified by the contractor. The goal for contractors is to make their bid as competitive as possible while still complying with the plans and specifications outlined in the Tender Documents.

In this regard, it is important to note that the respondent did not invite negotiations over the terms of either Contract A or Contract B. The only items to be added to the Tender Form by the tenderer, in addition to the tenderer's name and its prices are: GST registration number, the names of sub-contractors, its structural steel fabricator and erector, the number of days it will start work within after notification of the contract award, signature, witness to signature and address, date, telephone and fax number. . . .

Therefore, according to the Instructions to Tenderers and the Tender Form, a contractor submitting a tender must submit a valid tender and, in submitting its tender, is not at liberty to negotiate over the terms of the Tender Documents. Given this, it is reasonable to infer that the respondent would *only* consider valid tenders. For the respondent to accept a non-compliant bid would be contrary to the express indication in the Instructions to Tenderers that any negotiation of an amendment would have to take place according to the provisions of paragraph 12(b) [of the Instructions to Tenderers, which provided that any request for amendments to the tender documents should be received at least 14 days before the tender closing time.] It is also contrary to the entire tenor of the Tender Form, which was the only form required to be submitted in addition to the Bid Security, and which does not allow for any modification of the plans and specifications in the Tender Documents.

The rationale for the tendering process, as can be seen from these documents, is to replace negotiation with competition. This competition entails certain risks for the appellant. The appellant must expend effort and incur expense in preparing its tender in accordance with strict specifications and may nonetheless not be awarded Contract B. It must submit its Bid Security which, although it is returned if the tender is not accepted, is a significant amount of money to raise and have tied up for the period of time between the submission of the tender and the decision regarding Contract B. As Bingham L.J. stated in *Blackpool & Fylde Aero Club Ltd.*, with respect to a similar tendering process, this procedure is "heavily weighted in favour of the invitor". It appears obvious to me that exposing oneself to such risks makes little sense if the respondent is allowed, in effect, to circumscribe this process and accept a non-compliant bid. Therefore I find it reasonable, on the basis of the presumed intentions of the parties, to find an implied term that only a compliant bid would be accepted.

Having found that there was an implied term in Contract A that the respondent was to accept only compliant bids, I must now deal with the argument that the privilege clause overrode this implied term. . . .

Although the respondent has not disputed the trial judge's finding that the Sorochan tender was non-compliant, the respondent argues that the privilege clause gave it the discretion to award the contract to anyone, including a non-compliant bid, or to not award the contract at all, subject only to a duty to treat all tenderers fairly. It argues that because it accepted the Sorochan tender with the good faith belief that it was a compliant bid, it did not breach its duty of fairness.

The words of the privilege clause are clear and unambiguous. As this Court stated in *Cartwright & Crickmore, Ltd. v. MacInnes*, [1931] S.C.R. 425, at p. 431, "there can be no recognized custom in opposition to an actual contract, and the special agreement of the parties must prevail". However, the privilege clause is only one term of Contract A and must be read in harmony with the rest of the Tender Documents. To do otherwise would undermine the rest of the agreement between the parties.

I do not find that the privilege clause overrode the obligation to accept only compliant bids, because on the contrary, there is a compatibility between the privilege clause and this obligation. I believe that the comments of I. Goldsmith, in *Goldsmith on Canadian Building Contracts*, 4th ed. (1988 (looseleaf)), at p. 1-20, regarding the importance of discretion in accepting a tender are particularly helpful in elucidating this compatibility:

> The purpose of the [tender] system is to provide competition, and thereby to reduce costs, although it by no means follows that the lowest tender will necessarily result in the cheapest job. Many a "low" bidder has found that his prices have been too low and has ended up in financial difficulties, which have inevitably resulted in additional costs to the owner, whose right to recover them from the defaulting contractor is usually academic. Accordingly, the prudent owner will consider not only the amount of the bid, but also the experience and capability of the contractor, and whether the bid is realistic in the circumstances of the case. In order to eliminate unrealistic tenders, some public authorities and corporate owners require tenderers to be prequalified.

In other words, the decision to reject the "low" bid may in fact be governed by the consideration of factors that impact upon the ultimate cost of the project.

Therefore even where, as in this case, almost nothing separates the tenderers except the different prices they submit, the rejection of the lowest bid would not imply that a tender could be accepted on the basis of some undisclosed criterion. The discretion to accept not necessarily the lowest bid, retained by the owner through the privilege clause, is a discretion to take a more nuanced view of "cost" than the prices quoted in the tenders. In this respect, I agree with the result in *Acme Building & Construction Ltd. v. Newcastle (Town)* (1992), 2 C.L.R. (2d) 308 (Ont. C.A.). In that case Contract B was awarded to the second lowest bidder because it would complete the project in a shorter period than the lowest bid, resulting in a large cost saving and less disruption to business, and all tendering contractors had been asked to stipulate a completion date in their bids. It may also be the case that the owner may include other criteria in the tender package that will be weighed in addition to cost. However, needing to consider "cost" in this manner does not require or indicate that there needs to be a discretion to accept a non-compliant bid.

The additional discretion not to award a contract is presumably important to cover unforseen [*sic*] circumstances, which is not at issue in this appeal. For example, *Glenview Corp. v. Canada (Minister of Public Works)* (1990), 34 F.T.R. 292, concerned an invitation to tender whose specifications were found to be inadequate after the bids were submitted and opened by the department of public works. Instead of awarding a contract on the basis of inadequate specifications, the department re-tendered on the basis of improved specifications. Nonetheless, this discretion is not affected by holding that, in so far as the respondent decides to accept a tender, it must accept a *compliant tender*.

Therefore I conclude that the privilege clause is compatible with the obligation to accept only a compliant bid. As should be clear from this discussion, however, the privilege clause is incompatible with an obligation to accept only the *lowest* compliant bid. With respect to this latter proposition, the privilege clause must prevail.

The appellant disagrees with this conclusion and submits that the majority of Canadian jurisprudence supports the proposition that the person calling for tenders should award Contract B to the lowest valid tender despite the presence of a privilege clause like the one in issue in this appeal. To the extent that these decisions are incompatible with the analysis just outlined, I decline to follow them. Nonetheless, I have reviewed the cases submitted to this Court and find that they do not stand for the proposition that the lowest valid tender must be accepted. Those cases that in fact deal with the interpretation of the privilege clause in the context of a finding that Contract A arose between the parties are instead generally consistent with the analysis outlined above.

For example, a number of lower court decisions have held that an owner cannot rely on a privilege clause when it has not made express all the operative terms of the invitation to tender: see *Chinook Aggregates Ltd. v. Abbotsford (Municipal District)* (1987), 28 C.L.R. 290 (B.C. Co. Ct.), aff'd (1989), 35 C.L.R. 241 (B.C. C.A.); *Kencor Holdings Ltd. v. Saskatchewan*, [1991] 6 W.W.R. 717 (Sask. Q.B.); *Fred Welsh Ltd. v. B.G.M. Construction Ltd.*, [1996] 10 W.W.R. 400 (B.C. S.C.); *George Wimpey Canada Ltd. v. Hamilton Wentworth (Regional Municipality)* (1987), 34 C.L.R. (2d) 123 (Ont. H.C.); *Martselos Services Ltd. v. Arctic College*, [1994] 3 W.W.R. 73 (N.W.T. C.A.), leave to appeal denied, [1996] 3 S.C.R. (viii). Similarly, a privilege clause has been held not to allow bid shopping or procedures akin to bid shopping: see *Twin City Mechanical v. Bradsil (1967) Ltd.*, (1996), 31 C.L.R. (2d) 210 (Ont. H.C.), and *Thompson Bros. (Const.) Ltd. v. Wetaskiwin City* (1997), 34 C.L.R. (2d) 197 (Alta. Q.B.). . . .

C. *Breach of Contract A*

Applying the foregoing analysis to the case at bar, I find that the respondent was under no contractual obligation to award the contract to the appellant, who the parties agree was the lowest compliant bid. However, this does not mean that Contract A was not breached.

Sorochan was only the lowest bidder because it failed to accept, and incorporate into its bid, the risk of knowing how much of Type 2, Type 3, and Type 4 fill would be required. As the Court of Appeal outlined, this risk was assigned to the contractor. Therefore Sorochan's bid was based upon different specifications. Indeed, it is conceded that the Sorochan bid was non-compliant. Therefore, in awarding the contract to Sorochan, the respondent breached its obligation to the appellant, and the other tenderers, that it would accept only a compliant tender.

The respondent's argument of good faith in considering the Sorochan bid to be compliant is no defence to a claim for breach of contract: it amounts to an argument that because it thought it had interpreted the contract properly it cannot be in breach. Acting in good faith or thinking that one has interpreted the contract correctly are not valid defences to an action for breach of contract.

D. *Damages*

Given that Contract A was breached, the next question for the Court to determine is the question of damages. The general measure of damages for breach of contract is, of course, expectation damages. In the present appeal, we know that the respondent intended to award Contract B, as it in fact awarded this contract, albeit improperly, to Sorochan. Therefore there is no uncertainty as to whether the respondent would have exercised its discretion not to award Contract B. Moreover, the award of the contract to Sorochan was made on the basis that it was the lowest bid. The question is whether the appellant can claim that, had

Contract B not been awarded to Sorochan, it would have been awarded to the appellant for submitting the lowest valid bid.

In my opinion, on a balance of probabilities, the record supports the appellant's contention that as a matter of fact it would have been awarded Contract B had the Sorochan bid been disqualified. . . .

[The appellant was awarded damages in the amount of $398,121.27, which had been agreed by the parties subject to the determination of liability. Two disputed items of damages were referred to the Alberta Court of Queen's Bench for assessment. Appeal allowed.]

NOTES

1. The approach to tenders adopted by the Supreme Court of Canada is often justified as being in accordance with the practical requirements of the tendering process. However, consider the range of further issues that the contract A approach raises. For example, how far should the analysis apply to earlier stages of a tendering process? In construction bidding processes, the call for tenders may be preceded by a request for information ("RFI") and a request for proposals ("RFP"). What rules should apply to these earlier stages? In *Buttcon Ltd. v. Toronto Electronic Commissioners* (2003), 65 O.R. (3d) 601 (S.C.J.), the court concluded that the RFP did not create a contract A, while in *WindPower Inc. et al. v. Saskatchewan Power Corp.* (2002), 217 Sask. R. 193 (C.A.), the court assumed that an RFP was governed by a contract A analysis.

2. The two-contract analysis from *Ron Engineering* has generated significant litigation, particularly in interpreting the scope of the obligations of parties under contract A. In *Martel Building Ltd. v. R.*, [2000] 2 S.C.R. 860 the Supreme Court of Canada considered, among other issues, the duties of the federal Department of Public Works in a call for tenders to lease office space for a governmental agency. Martel, which had been the agency's existing landlord, submitted a bid that, while originally the lowest, was not successful, partly because of adjustments made by the Department to take into account improvements required by the tenant or "fit up costs", contiguous space requirements, and costs for a secured-card access system. Justices Iacobucci and Major, writing for the court, noted, at para. 81, that contract A could include implied terms, and found, at para. 88, that given the circumstances of the case, "a term to be fair and consistent in the assessment of the tender bids is justified based on the presumed intentions of the parties. Such implication is necessary to give business efficacy to the tendering process." The court noted, at para. 89, however, that the implied duty of fair and equal treatment had to be understood only after close examination of the tender documents: "[I]n order to respect the parties' intentions and reasonable expectations, such a duty must be defined with due consideration to the express contractual terms of the tender." In this case, the court noted a privilege clause as well as other express terms giving the Department significant discretion with respect to disputed factors in the bid evaluation such as "fit-up costs" and the amount of contiguous space required. In the result, the court found that the owner's action of adjusting Martel's tender (but not those of the other bidders) for the cost of a secured-card access system was a breach of the implied term. However, this breach did not result in any contractual damages, as Martel's tender would not have been successful even if it had not been adjusted to make provision for a secured-card access system.

Whether there were any implied terms and whether any were breached seems highly specific to the facts of the particular bidding process. Is this unsettled situation with respect to the scope of implied terms in contract A truly in accord with the commercial reality of tendering practice? Are these temporary problems of clarification or inevitable problems of interpretation and application?

3. In a variation of the implied term approach, some courts, particularly in discussing government tenders, have been inclined to describe the owner's obligations in terms of a duty to act fairly and in good faith. See, *e.g.*, *Thomas C. Assaly Corp. v. R.* (1990), 34 F.T.R. 156 (T.D.) at 158, *Glenview Corp. v. Canada (Minister of Public Works)* (1990), 34 F.T.R. 292 (T.D.) at 296 and *Martselos Services Ltd. v. Arctic College* (1992), 5 B.L.R. (2d) 204 (N.W.T. S.C.), reversed on other grounds, [1994] 3 W.W.R. 73 (N.W.T. C.A.), leave to appeal refused [1994] 8 W.W.R. lxvi (S.C.C.).

In *Martel, supra* note 2, however, the Supreme Court of Canada rejected an analysis of business negotiations in the tendering context as involving a general duty of good faith. Related issues are discussed in Chapter 11 of this book.

4. In the tendering process in the construction industry, general contractors build their own tenders on the basis of bids submitted to them by sub-contractors. It is now clear that the relationship between the general contractor, which receives sub-trade bids, and sub-contractors, is also governed by the rules of contract A. See *Naylor Group Inc. v. Ellis-Don Construction Ltd.*, [2001] 2 S.C.R. 943.

3.   Communication of Offer

BLAIR v. WESTERN MUTUAL BENEFIT ASSN.
[1972] 4 W.W.R. 284 (B.C. C.A.)

BULL J.A. (orally) This is an appeal from a portion of a judgment made on a motion for directions by the liquidator of the respondent society in voluntary liquidation . . . in which a former employee, a Miss Blair, was held not to be entitled to retirement pay of $8,000. The basis of the claim is a resolution of the board of directors of the respondent passed on 8th March 1969 in the following terms:

> Mr. Fedyk then said he would like to make a suggestion if Miss Blair decided to relinquish her position with the Association at any time in the future, in view of the fact that she had given her life to the Association for almost thirty years, that she be given a grant of at least two years' salary, as retirement pay. Mr. Fedyk said he would like to make such a motion, seconded by Mr. Charlesworth. Carried unanimously.

The appellant, Miss Blair, was a secretary and stenographer in the employ of the respondent and she retired in June 1969. In due course she claimed $8,000 (which represents approximately two years' salary) as retirement pay pursuant to the resolution that I have just read. She filed an affidavit in which she said that, although she was not present at the time the resolution was passed, when the meeting was over the president or another director (she could not be sure which) dictated the minutes of the meeting to her. She transcribed them and delivered them to the president, who, about two weeks later, signed them. She did not suggest that the content of the resolution or the grant of the retirement pay was in any way communicated to her as an act or offer or promise of the company or that her knowledge of its existence was other than that so received as a stenographer, which I have just set out, of taking and transcribing dictation. I must also point out that there is no evidence at all that Miss Blair, when she did resign, did so because of the existence of the resolution in question or because of any obligation which she felt the society had to her under that resolution. . . .

The reasons of the Judge below for his refusal to find the respondent bound to pay the retirement pay to Miss Blair can be summed up that he found there was: (a) no promise made and accepted for valid consideration; (b) no change in the existing relationships between the parties; and (c) no evidence of any intention to change those relationships to create legal obligations.

The appellant's main submissions to this Court are that the resolution constituted an offer to pay on retirement and that Miss Blair's act of retirement at a later date constituted an acceptance and, hence, a binding legal contractual obligation arose.

The second principal submission was that, even if a binding contract had not ensued by reason of lack of consideration or otherwise, in equity the respondent, having made a promise or representations of fact that Miss Blair would get retirement pay, expecting her to act upon it, and she did, cannot now be heard to say that it is not so bound. Many well-known authorities were cited to support both propositions.

However, in my view this appeal must be decided on the very threshold of those submissions. In my opinion a bare resolution such as here, but without advice, formal or otherwise, to the appellant to indicate that the intention expressed in the resolution was being carried out or implemented and the terms of her engagement or employment varied or altered thereby, cannot be considered ipso facto to create or indicate an intention to create a legal obligation capable of acceptance.

As I have indicated, all that was done was an internal act of the minutes of a meeting being dictated to a stenographer in order that they be transcribed for entry into the minute book. I cannot think that under such circumstances the resolution should create a binding obligation without any attempt, by communication or offer, to make it such. The use of the appellant's technical services for which she was apparently employed surely cannot convert what was not in itself an offer into one unless there was something to show that the respondent so intended.

In my view there is nothing here to show any such intention. I am of the opinion that it was not shown that the intention of the respondent reflected in its resolution was implemented by communication or otherwise in any other way to constitute it or to be interpreted or construed as an offer capable of acceptance or as an indication that it intended to be legally bound thereby.

Further, even if I be wrong in that, there is nothing whatsoever to show that Miss Blair relied on or retired by virtue of the resolution. She swore to nothing on that score except that she had no knowledge at any time of the resolution having been varied or modified or reconsidered. That does not meet the point I make.

The reasoning as above applies equally to the other submissions based in equity and estoppel; but, more important, I can find no evidence, as I have indicated, of any promise or of any representations of fact made to the appellant upon which she was expected to act or upon which she did act. The evidence was simply not there. It follows that that submission must fail. . . .

McFARLANE J.A. (orally) . . . I do not wish to base my decision in this case upon the somewhat informal manner in which that resolution—which concerned her alone, not other employees of the Association—was communicated to her. It does seem to me that whether the communication was in her capacity simply as that of an amanuensis or whether it was in her capacity as general agent (and one might also say acting secretary-treasurer), on the rather vague evidence which is before us I would not like to base my decision upon the conclusion that, assuming the resolution to be an offer intended to be accepted, it was not communicated in a way which would justify Miss Blair in treating it as an offer and accepting it.

The next problem is the one which causes difficulty for me and that is whether or not there is evidence here that Miss Blair did accept the offer and did consider it an offer and accept it. In that respect the only evidence we have from her affidavit is that in, I believe it was April, she in fact resigned; as she put it, "I resigned my salary as an employee". She does not say that the resolution of which she had knowledge was the inducing factor or that she in any way regarded the resolution as an offer to her which she accepted. It seems to me that the closest she came to this in the affidavit which she filed was when she said this:

> When I left the Association I had no reason to doubt the intention or the ability of the said Association to carry out its promise to pay me retirement pay in the amount recorded in the original minute.

> .....

Having regard to that, I think that the evidence . . . fails to establish the necessary connection between the resolution and the retirement in order to support either of Mr. Johnson's arguments. . . .

It is for that reason that I cannot accede to the appellant's arguments presented here. . . .

ROBERTSON J.A. (orally) I would dismiss the appeal for the reasons given by my brother Bull, in which I concur.

With reference to the first ground upon which he based his decision, I shall add a reference to a case in the Court of Appeal in Southern Ireland. It is *Wilson v. Belfast Corpn.* (1921), 55 I.L.T. 205. The headnote reads, in part, as follows:

> Belfast city council passed a resolution on 1st September, 1914, to the effect that half wages would be paid to employees who joined the forces. Without the council's authority this resolution was published in the Press. Later, on 1st October, a second resolution was passed limiting offer of half pay to such persons as were in the council's service on 5th August, 1914. Subsequent to this second resolution, the plaintiff entered the service of the corporation, and later joined the army. He was killed in action. His widow and infant son alleged a contract between the council and the deceased, and they brought an action to recover 89 pounds, the amount claimed to be due as half pay from date of enlistment to date of death.

> The Judge of Assize gave plaintiffs a decree for this amount. This decree was unanimously reversed by the King's Bench Division on a new trial motion. On appeal in Court of Appeal in Southern Ireland:

> HELD, by O'Connor, L.J. (affirming the decision of the King's Bench Division), that there was no contract; that the council's resolution was not intended as an offer; that unauthorised publication in the Press did not constitute communication. . . .

In my opinion the passing of the resolution upon which the claim here is based was not intended as an offer and the communication of the existence of that resolution by way of dictating it to the claimant in her capacity as a stenographer was no more the making of an offer than was the publication of the offer in the press in the case that I have just cited. . . .

[Appeal dismissed.]

NOTES and QUESTIONS

1. Would it make any difference to the result in *Blair v. West. Mut. Benefit Assn.* if the offer were held to have been properly communicated?

2. A corporation, such as Western Mutual Benefit Association, is for most purposes considered a legal person, separate and distinct at law from any of its owners, directors or employees. This places limits on the capacity of business associations to make decisions such as entering into contracts. This situation can be compared to that of various public entities. In *Campbell v. Inverness (County)* (1990), 98 N.S.R. (2d) 330 at 342 and 344 (T.D.) the court stated ". . . that a minimum requirement for the exercise by a municipality of its capacity to contract is the passage of a resolution by the municipal council". While "[a] municipal resolution can be interpreted as constituting or as author-izing a contract . . . [it] has not traditionally been considered to be an effective means of assumption of legal contractual obligation; since it can be reconsidered, amended or rescinded at any time, it is little more than a political promise, which is beyond the scope of the law of enforceable contract". See also *Leger v. Edmonton (City)* (1989), 63 D.L.R. (4th) 279 (Alta. Q.B.).

3. In *Fred Welsh Ltd. v. BGM Construction Ltd.*, [1996] 10 W.W.R. (B.C. S.C.) the court held "that the plaintiff's procedure of using the phone with confirming fax immediately prior to the deadline was accepted and necessary practice" and satisfied the requirement of a bid in writing by the deadline.

WILLIAMS v. CARWARDINE

(1833), 4 B. & Ad. 621, 110 E.R. 590 (K.B.)

. . . At the trial before Parke J., at the last Spring Assizes for the county of Hereford, the following appeared to be the facts of the case:—One Walter Car-wardine, the brother of the defendant, was seen on the evening of the 24th of March 1831, at a public-house at Hereford, and was not heard of again till his body was found on the 12th of April in the river Wye, about two miles from the city. An inquest was held on the body on the 13th of April and the following days till the 19th; and it appearing that the plaintiff [Mary Anne Williams] was at a house with the deceased [whom the plaintiff described as a "lusty man"] on the night he was supposed to have been murdered, she was examined before the magistrates, but did not then give any information which led to the apprehension of the real offender. On the 25th of April the defendant caused a handbill to be published, stating that whoever would give such information as should lead to a discovery of the murderer of Walter Carwardine should, on conviction, receive a reward of 20*l*; and any person concerned therein, or privy thereto, (except the party who actually committed the offence) should be entitled to such reward, and every exertion used to procure a pardon; and it then added, that information was to be given, and application for the above reward was to be made to Mr. William Carwardine, Holmer, near Hereford. Two persons were tried for the murder at the Summer Assizes 1831, but acquitted. Soon after this, the plaintiff was severely beaten and bruised by one . . . [William Williams, who was apparently aware that Mary Williams had witnessed the murder] and on the 23d of August 1831, believing she had not long to live, and to ease her conscience, she made a voluntary statement, containing information which led to the subsequent conviction of Williams [for the murder of Walter Carwardine]. Upon this evidence it was contended, that as the plaintiff was not induced by the reward promised by the defendant, to give evidence, the law would not imply a contract by the defendant to pay her the 20*l*. The learned Judge was of the opinion, that the plaintiff, having given the information which led to the conviction of the murderer, had performed the condition on which the 20*l* was to become payable, and was therefore entitled to recover it; and he directed the jury to find a verdict for the plaintiff, but desired them to find specially whether she was induced to give the information by the offer of the promised reward. The jury found that she was not induced by the offer of the reward, but by other motives. . . .

[A different report of this case (172 E.R. 1101 at 1104) shows the following exchange between Denman C.J. and Curwood, one of the counsel in the case, prior to the giving of judgment on the appeal by the defendant.

> DENMAN C.J. Was any doubt suggested as to whether the plaintiff knew of the handbill at the time of her making the disclosure?
> CURWOOD. She must have known of it, as it was placarded all over Hereford, the place at which she lived.]
> DENMAN C.J. The plaintiff, by having given information which led to the conviction of the murderer of Walter Carwardine, has brought herself within the terms of the advertisement, and therefore is entitled to recover.
> LITTLEDALE J. The advertisement amounts to a general promise, to give a sum of money to any person who shall give information which might lead to the discovery of the offender. The plaintiff gave that information.
> PARKE J. There was a contract with any person who performed the condition mentioned in the advertisement.
> PATTESON J. I am of the same opinion. We cannot go into the plaintiff's motives.

Rule refused.

R. v. CLARKE

(1927), 40 C.L.R. 227 (Aust. H.C.)

HIGGINS J. In my opinion, this appeal should be allowed.

It must be clearly understood, however, that we, as a Court, have no responsibility for the policy of the Government in resisting this claim. As the Chief Justice of the Supreme Court has said, Clarke gave evidence which was of the greatest value to the Crown in the prosecution of Coulter and Treffene, and without that evidence there would have been no case which could have been left to the jury against them. The refusal of the Crown to pay the reward in this case is likely to weaken the efficacy of such a bait when the Crown seeks information from accessories to crimes hereafter.

Clarke cannot succeed in this action unless he can establish a contract between the Crown and himself. I think that there was no contract. I prefer to deal with this main issue, the issue to which the learned Judges of the Supreme Court have mainly addressed themselves, involving, as it does, the very roots of the English law as to contract; and I shall assume, at present, that Clarke strictly fulfilled all the conditions of the promise held out by the proclamation. Considering the present state of the English authorities, it is not at all surprising that the Chief Justice and Northmore J. on the one side and Burnside and Draper JJ. on the other should differ in their conclusions, after their closely reasoned judgments.

The murders were committed towards the end of April 1926; the proclamation of reward was issued on 21st May; the information was given by Clarke
on 10th June and at the trial. One of the murderers, Treffene, was arrested on 6th
June, with Clarke; the other, Coulter, was arrested on 10th June; both were indicted
in August and convicted in September of the murder of Walsh; there was an
appeal to the Court of Criminal Appeal, which failed; and, after the failure of the
appeal, Clarke, on the suggestion of Inspector Condon, for the first time thought
of the reward and decided to claim it. But he had seen the proclamation in May.
On 6th June, Clarke gave false information in order to screen the murderers; and,
as he says,

> I had no intention then of doing anything to earn the reward. . . . On 10th June, I began
> to break down under the strain. Manning took down my statement on 10th June at my request.
> I had no thought whatever then of the reward that had been offered. My object was my own
> protection against a false charge of murder. . . . Up to 10th June I had no intention of doing
> anything to earn the reward. At the inquest . . . I was committed for trial as an accessory. . . .
> *When I gave evidence in the Criminal Court I had no intention of claiming the reward. I first
> decided to claim the reward a few days after the appeal had been dealt with.* Inspector Condon
> told me to make application. *I had not intended to apply for the reward up to that date.* I did
> not know exactly the position I was in. Up to that time I had not considered the position. . . .
> *I had not given the matter consideration at all.* My motive was to clear myself of the charge
> of murder. *I gave no consideration and formed no intention with regard to the reward.*

These statements of Clarke show clearly that he did not intend to accept the offer
of the Crown, did not give the information on the faith of, or relying on, the
proclamation. He did not mentally assent to the Crown's offer; there was no
moment of time at which there was, till after the information was given, as between
Clarke and the Crown, a *consensus* of mind. Most of the cases turn on the
communication of assent, from the "offeree" to the "offeror"; communication is
necessary, and it may be by act as well as by words; but there can be no *communication* of assent until there be assent. If the case so much relied on for Clarke,
the case of *Williams v. Carwardine* [*supra*], can be taken as deciding that mutual
consent to the terms is not necessary, as well as communication of assent by the
offeree, I can only point to higher and more recent authority [for the view that an
offer does not bind the person who makes it until it has been accepted, and its
acceptance has been communicated].

But I do not regard *Williams v. Carwardine* as deciding anything to the
contrary of this doctrine. That case seems to me not to deal with the essential
elements for a contract at all: it shows merely that the *motive* of the informer in
accepting the contract offered (and the performing the conditions is usually sufficient evidence of acceptance) has nothing to do with his right to recover under
the contract. The reports show (as it was assumed by the Judges after the verdict
of the jury in favour of the informer), that the informer *knew* of the offer when
giving the information, and meant to accept the offer though she had also a *motive*
in her guilty conscience. The distinguished jurist, Sir Frederick Pollock, in his
preface to vol. 38 of the Revised Reports, makes comments adverse to the case;
but I concur with Burnside J. in his view that we cannot treat such comments as
equivalent to an overruling of a clear decision. The case of *Gibbons v. Proctor*
[(1891), 64 L.T. 594] is much more difficult to explain. There a policeman was

held entitled to recover a reward offered by handbills, for information given to the superintendent of police which led to arrest and conviction, although the policeman did not know of the handbills before he sent the information by his agents, or before the handbills reached the superintendent. This would seem to mean that a man can accept an offered contract before he knows that there is an offer—that knowledge of the offer before the informer supplies the information is immaterial to the existence of the contract. *Anson on Contracts* (16th ed.), p. 55, thinks that this decision must be wrong. I venture to think so too; and, though we cannot well overrule it, we ought not to follow it for the purposes of this Court. . . . The reasoning of Woodruff J. in *Fitch v. Snedaker* [(1868), 38 N.Y. 248], seems to me to be faultless; and the decision is spoken of in Anson (p. 24) as being undoubtedly correct in principle:—"The motive inducing consent may be immaterial, but the consent is vital. Without that there is no contract. How then can there be consent or assent to that of which the party has never heard?" Clarke had seen the offer, indeed; but it was not present to his mind—he had forgotten it, and gave no consideration to it, in his intense excitement as to his own danger. There cannot be assent without knowledge of the offer; and ignorance of the offer is the same thing whether it is due to never hearing of it or to forgetting it after hearing. But for this candid confession of Clarke's it might fairly be presumed that Clarke, having once seen the offer, acted on the faith of it, in reliance on it; but he has himself rebutted that presumption.

I have been struck by the resemblance of the position to that of an action based on misrepresentation. The statement of claim must allege and show that the plaintiff acted in reliance on the misrepresentation. If the defendant can establish that the plaintiff did not rely on the misrepresentation, the plaintiff fails. . . .

I need not dilate at length on the now classic case of *Carlill v. Carbolic Smoke Ball Co.* [*supra*]. It is quite consistent with the view which I have stated. The facts were not in dispute and one of the facts was that the plaintiff had bought the smoke balls *on the faith of* the advertisement. This important fact is stated again in the report on appeal; and it is just the fact which is not, and could not be, found under the circumstances of this case. My view is that Clarke did not act *on the faith of, in reliance upon*, the proclamation; and that although the exact fulfilment of the conditions stated in the proclamation would raise a presumption that Clarke was acting on the faith of, in reliance upon, the proclamation, that presumption is rebutted by his own express admission.

For these reasons, I am of opinion that the judgment of the Chief Justice was right, and that this appeal ought to be allowed.

As for the argument of the Crown to the effect that the conditions of the offer have not been fulfilled by Clarke, the point becomes unnecessary to decide if Clarke has failed to establish the contract; but, if it should become necessary to express an opinion on these points, I have come to the conclusion that the Crown is right. The promise of the Crown was to pay the reward for "such information as *shall lead to the arrest and conviction of the person or persons who committed the murders*." The information given did not lead to the arrest of Treffene, for he was arrested on 6th June *before* the information was given. Nor did the information given lead to the conviction of the persons who committed the murders—both murders: it led only to the conviction of the persons who committed one murder, the murder of Walsh. It is no answer to say that the Crown could have had the men tried for the murder of Pitman if it chose. The proclamation here differs from the advertisement in *Williams v. Carwardine*, in that the words here are "such information as *shall* lead" etc., not "such information as *may* lead" etc., and the information did not in fact lead to convictions for the two murders. This argument may involve the result that the proclamation was misleading and illusory; but that is no answer if the argument is sound.

[Appeal allowed.]

NOTES and QUESTIONS

1. The judgments of Starke and Isaacs JJ. in favour of the appellant are omitted. Isaacs J. said, "It is true that without his information and evidence no conviction was probable, but it is also abundantly clear that he was not acting for the sake of justice or from any impulse of conscience or because he was asked to do so, but simply and solely on his own initiative, to secure his own safety from the hand of the law and altogether irrespective of the proclamation. He has, in my opinion, neither a legal nor a moral claim to the reward"; and later, "An offer of £100 to any person who should swim a hundred yards in the harbour on the first day of the year, would be met by voluntarily performing the feat with reference to the offer, but would not in my opinion be satisfied by a person who was accidentally or maliciously thrown overboard on that day and swam the distance simply to save his life, without any thought of the offer."

Do you agree?

2. How would you distinguish *Williams v. Carwardine* and *R. v. Clarke*? Which approach would *Blair v. West. Mut. Benefit Assn.*, *supra*, tend to favour?

3. In *Simmons v. U.S.* (1962), 308 F. 2d 160, the U.S. Court of Appeals (4th Cir.) considered the relationship that must exist between an offer of a unilateral contract and its acceptance in the course of a tax decision as to whether a prize awarded in a fishing derby amounted to a non-taxable gift or a taxable sum which the winner had a legal right to claim.

SOBELOFF C.J. Diamond Jim III, a rock fish, was one of millions of his species swimming in the Chesapeake Bay, but he was a very special fish, and he occasions some nice legal questions. Wearing a valuable identification tag, he was placed on June 19, 1958 in the waters of the Bay by employees of the American Brewery, Inc., with the cooperation of Maryland state game officials. According to the well-publicized rules governing the brewery-sponsored Third Annual American Beer Fishing Derby, anybody who caught Diamond Jim III and presented him to the company, together with the identification tag and an affidavit that he had been caught on hook and line, would be entitled to a cash prize of $25,000.00. The company also placed other tagged fish in the Chesapeake, carrying lesser prizes.

Fishing on the morning of August 6, 1958, William Simmons caught Diamond Jim III. At first, he took little notice of the tag, but upon re-examining it a half hour later, he realized that he had caught the $25,000 prize fish. After Simmons and his fishing companions appropriately marked the happy event, he hastened to comply with the conditions of the contest. Soon thereafter, in the course of a television appearance arranged by the brewery, he received the cash prize. The record shows that Simmons knew about the contest, but, as an experienced fisherman, he also knew that his chances of landing that fish were minuscule, and he did not have Diamond Jim III in mind when he set out that morning.

Thereupon, an alert District Director of the Internal Revenue Service came forward with the assertion that the cash prize was includable in Simmons' gross income under section 61(a) and section 74(a) of the Internal Revenue Code, 26 U.S.C.A. 61(a), 74(a) and assessed a tax deficiency of $5,230.00. . . .

Moreover, under accepted principles of contract law on which we may rely in the absence of pertinent Maryland cases, the company was legally obligated to award the prize once Simmons had caught the fish and complied with the remaining conditions precedent. The offer of a prize or reward for doing a specified act, like catching a criminal, is an offer for a unilateral contract. For the offer to be accepted and the contract to become binding, the desired act must be performed with the knowledge of the offer. The evidence is clear that Simmons knew about the Fishing Derby the morning he caught Diamond Jim III. It is not fatal to his claim for refund that he did not go fishing for the express purpose of catching one of the prize fish. So long as the outstanding offer was known to him, a person may accept an offer for a unilateral contract by rendering performance, even if he does so primarily for reasons unrelated to the offer. Consequently, since Simmons could require the company to pay him the prize, the case is governed by *Robertson v. U.S.* (1952), 343 U.S. 711 at 713-14. There, the Supreme Court held that, since the sponsor of a contest for the best symphonies submitted was legally obligated to award prizes in accordance with his offer, the payment made was not a gift to the recipient.

4. Suppose that Mr. Simmons in *Simmons v. U.S.*, *supra*, was a commercial fisherman on Chesapeake Bay. Angry at the intrusion of weekend fisherman, he said on the day of the fishing Derby "I hate these giveaway contests. If I catch the prize fish, I will throw him back". Mr. Simmons subsequently catches the prize fish and has a sudden change of heart. Can he claim the prize?

5. In *"Industrial America" Inc. v. Fulton Industries Inc.* (1971), 285 A. 2d 412 (Del. S.C.), the court commented that the act of accepting an offer of a unilateral contract provides the "requisite overt manifestation of assent if the act is done intentionally; *i.e.* if there is a 'conscious will' to do it. . . . But 'it is not material what induces the will', Restatement of the Law of Contracts, 20, Comment (a). Otherwise stated, motive in the manifestation of assent is immaterial. There may be primary and secondary reasons or motives for a performance constituting manifestation of assent to an offer inviting acceptance by performance; and the 'chief reason' or the prevailing motive need not necessarily be the offer itself. A unilateral contract may be enforceable when the promisor has received the desired service even though the service was primarily motivated by a reason other than the offer." The court noted a proposed change in section 55 of the Restatement of the Law of Contracts shifting "the emphasis away from a manifestation of intent to accept to a manifestation of intent not to accept; thereby establishing, it would appear, a rebuttable presumption of acceptance arising from performance when the offer invites acceptance by performance."

6. Gloria Greer placed the following advertisement in the *Free Tribune*: "Reward of $100.00 to the finder of my dearly beloved dog, Kate." Harvey Foster is not a reader of the *Free Tribune* and does not know of this generous reward. He does, however, find Kate, identifies her owner from her collar and being an honest citizen returns her to Gloria. Advise Harvey. Would it make any difference if Harvey had heard of the offer from a neighbour? See Hudson, *"Gibbons v. Proctor* Revisited" (1968), 84 L.Q.R. 503.

7. The Civil Code of Québec, Book 5, Obligations, Ch. II, Contracts, s. III, provides:

Art. 1395. The offer of a reward made to anyone who performs a particular act is deemed to be accepted and is binding on the offeror when the act is performed, even if the person who performs the act does not know of the offer, unless, in cases which admit of it, the offer was previously revoked expressly and adequately by the offeror.

8. On 15th October Harvey Foster mailed a letter from Dauphin to Gloria Greer in Winnipeg offering to purchase her car for $1500. On 17th October Gloria Greer mailed an offer to Harvey offering to sell the same car for $1500. Harvey's letter arrived on 19th October and Gloria's on 20th October. Is there a contract and if so, when? See *Tinn v. Hoffman* (1873), 29 L.T. 271.

4. Acceptance

LIVINGSTONE v. EVANS

[1925] 3 W.W.R. 453, [1925] 4 D.L.R. 769 (Alta. S.C.)

WALSH J. The defendant, T.J. Evans, through his agent, wrote to the plaintiff offering to sell him the land in question for $1800 on terms. On the day that he received his offer the plaintiff wired this agent as follows:—"Send lowest cash price. Will give $1600 cash. Wire." The agent replied to this by telegram as follows "Cannot reduce price." Immediately upon the receipt of this telegram the plaintiff wrote accepting the offer. It is admitted by the defendants that this offer and the plaintiff's acceptance of it constitute a contract for the sale of this land to the plaintiff by which he is bound unless the intervening telegrams above set out put an end to his offer so that the plaintiff could not thereafter bind him to it by his acceptance of it.

It is quite clear that when an offer has been rejected it is thereby ended and it cannot be afterwards accepted without the consent of him who made it. The simple question and the only one argued before me is whether the plaintiff's counter-offer was in law a rejection of the defendants' offer which freed them from it. *Hyde v. Wrench* (1840), 49 E.R. 132, a judgment of Lord Langdale, M.R., pronounced in 1840, is the authority for the contention that it was. The defendant offered to sell for £1000. The plaintiff met that with an offer to pay £950 and (to quote from the judgment, [at p. 133])

> he thereby rejected the offer previously made by the Defendant. I think that it was not competent for him to revive the proposal of the Defendant, by tendering an acceptance of it.

Stevenson, Jaques & Co. v. McLean (1880), 5 Q.B.D. 346, a later case relied upon by Mr. Grant is easily distinguishable from *Hyde v. Wrench*, as it is in fact distinguished by Lush, J., who decided it. He held (p. 350) that the letter there relied upon as constituting a rejection of the offer was not a new proposal "but a mere inquiry, which should have been answered and not treated as a rejection" but the Judge said that if it had contained an offer it would have likened the case to *Hyde v. Wrench*.

Hyde v. Wrench has stood without question for 85 years. It is adopted by the text writers as a correct exposition of the law and is generally accepted and recognized as such. I think it not too much to say that it has firmly established it as a part of the law of contracts that the making of a counter-offer is a rejection of the original offer.

The plaintiff's telegram was undoubtedly a counter-offer. True, it contained an inquiry as well but that clearly was one which called for an answer only if the counter-offer was rejected. In substance it said:—"I will give you $1600 cash. If you won't take that wire your lowest cash price." In my opinion it put an end to the defendants' liability under their offer unless it was revived by the telegram in reply to it.

The real difficulty in the case, to my mind, arises out of the defendants' telegram "cannot reduce price." If this was simply a rejection of the plaintiff's counter-offer it amounts to nothing. If, however, it was a renewal of the original offer it gave the plaintiff the right to bind the defendants to it by his subsequent acceptance of it.

With some doubt I think that it was a renewal of the original offer or at any rate an intimation to the plaintiff that he was still willing to treat on the basis of it. It was, of course, a reply to the counter-offer and to the inquiry in the plaintiff's telegram, but it was more than that. The price referred to in it was unquestionably that mentioned in his letter. His statement that he could not reduce that price strikes me as having but one meaning, namely, that he was still standing by it and, therefore, still open to accept it.

There is support for this view in a judgment of the Ontario Appellate Division which I have found in *Cowan v. Boyd* (1921), 61 D.L.R. 497. That was a landlord and tenant matter. The landlord wrote the tenant offering a renewal lease at an increased rent. The tenant replied that he was paying as high a rent as he should and if the landlord would not renew at the present rental he would like an early reply as he purposed buying a house. To this the landlord replied simply saying that he would call on the tenant between two certain named dates. Before he called and without any further communication between them the tenant wrote accepting the landlord's original offer. Widdifield, Co. Ct. J., before whom the matter first came held that the tenant's reply to the landlord's offer was not a counter-offer but a mere request to modify its terms. The Appellate Division did not decide that question though from the ground on which it put its judgment it must have disagreed with the Judge below. It sustained his judgment, however, *per* Meredith, C.J.O., at p. 500, on the ground that the landlord's letter promising to call on the tenant left open the original offer for further discussion so that the tenant had the right thereafter to accept it as he did.

The landlord's letter in that case was, to my mind, much more unconvincing evidence of his willingness to stand by his original offer in the face of the tenant's rejection of it than is the telegram of the defendants in this case. That is the judgment of a very strong Court, the reasons for which were written by the late Chief Justice Meredith. If it is sound and it is not for me to question it, *a fortiori* must I be right in the conclusion to which I have come.

I am, therefore, of the opinion that there was a binding contract for the sale of this land to the plaintiff of which he is entitled to specific performance. It was admitted by his counsel that if I reached this conclusion his subsequent agreement to sell the land to the defendant Williams would be of no avail as against the plaintiff's contract.

There will, therefore, be judgment for specific performance with a declaration that the plaintiff's rights under his contract have priority over those of the defendant Williams under his. The plaintiff will have his costs as agreed by the case. . . .

NOTE and QUESTIONS

1.(a) Suppose, in reply to an offer by A, B writes, "I shall want to consider your offer for more than the time which you have allowed me for that purpose because I am so situated now that I cannot return an immediate answer. However, the situation is such that if you want to settle the matter at once, I will close with you now at 5% less than the price you name." Can B still accept A's offer?

(b) Suppose the offeror says when making the offer, "I expect you to reject this offer upon first consideration, but I want you to consider it further, because I think you will accept when you have thought about it a while." The offeree immediately sends a rejection which the offeror ignores. On further thought, the offeree sends an acceptance. Is there a contract? See Oliphant, "The Duration and Termination of an Offer" (1920), 18 Mich. L.R. 201 at 209.

2. The Civil Code of Québec, Book 5, Obligations, Ch. II, Contracts, s. III provides:

> **Art. 1393**. Acceptance which does not correspond substantially to the offer or which is received by the offeror after the offer has lapsed does not constitute acceptance.

It may, however, constitute a new offer.

BUTLER MACHINE TOOL CO. v. EX-CELL-O CORP.

[1979] 1 W.L.R. 401, [1979] 1 All E.R. 965 (C.A.)

On 23rd May 1969, in response to an inquiry by the buyers, the sellers quoted a price for a machine tool for £75,535, with delivery to be given in 10 months. On the back of their offer were a number of terms and conditions, which stipulated that they were to "prevail over any terms and conditions in the buyer's order". One of the conditions purported to allow the seller to charge the buyers the price for the machine prevailing at the time of delivery. The buyers replied by placing an order for the purchase of the machine. Their document stipulated that the order was subject to a number of terms and conditions which differed from those put forward by the sellers and which, in particular, made no provision for any increase in price.

At the foot of the buyer's order form, there was a tear-off slip upon which the sellers were invited to accept the order "on the terms and conditions stated thereon". On 5th June 1969, the sellers completed and returned this slip to the buyers with a letter stating that the buyers' order was being entered in accordance with the sellers' quotation of 23rd May 1969. When the sellers ultimately came to deliver the machine, they claimed to be entitled to an additional £2,892, under the price formula of their original offer. The buyers took the position that their order prevailed and that there was accordingly a fixed price contract. The sellers' action for damages succeeded at trial on the ground that the price variation clause in the sellers' offer was a term which was intended to prevail.

LORD DENNING M.R. . . . . No doubt a contract was . . . concluded. But on what terms? The sellers rely on their general conditions and on their last letter which said 'in accordance with our revised quotation of 23rd May' (which had on the back the price variation clause). The buyers rely on the acknowledgment signed by the sellers which accepted the buyers' order 'on the terms and conditions stated thereon' (which did not include a price variation clause).

If those documents are analysed in our traditional method, the result would seem to me to be this: the quotation of 23rd May 1969 was an offer by the sellers to the buyers containing the terms and conditions on the back. The order of 27th May 1969 purported to be an acceptance of that offer in that it was for the same machine at the same price, but it contained such additions as to cost of installation, date of delivery and so forth, that it was in law a rejection of the offer and constituted a counter-offer. That is clear from *Hyde v. Wrench* [(1840), 49 E.R. 132 (Rolls Ct.)]. As Megaw J. said in *Trollope & Colls v. Atomic Power Constructions* [[1962] 3 All E.R. 1035 at 1038] '. . . the counter-offer kills the original offer'. The letter of the sellers of 5th June 1969 was an acceptance of that counter-offer, as is shown by the acknowledgment which the sellers signed and returned to the buyers. The reference to the quotation of 23rd May 1969 referred only to the price and identity of the machine. . . .

The better way is to look at all the documents passing between the parties and glean from them, or from the conduct of the parties, whether they have reached agreement on all material points, even though there may be differences between the forms and conditions printed on the back of them. As Lord Cairns LC said in *Brogden v. Metropolitan Railway Co.* [(1877), 2 App. Cas. 666 at 672]:

> . . . there may be a *consensus* between the parties far short of a complete mode of expressing it, and that *consensus* may be discovered from letters or from other documents of an imperfect and incomplete description.

Applying this guide, it will be found that in most cases when there is a 'battle of forms' there is a contract as soon as the last of the forms is sent and received without objection being taken to it. That is well observed in Benjamin on Sale [9th ed. (1974), 84-85]. The difficulty is to decide which form, or which part of which form, is a term or condition of the contract. In some cases the battle is won by the man who fires the last shot. He is the man who puts forward the latest term and conditions: and, if they are not objected to by the other party, he may be taken to have agreed to them. [See] . . . Professor Guest in Anson's Law of Contract [24th ed. (1975), at 37-38] where he says that 'the terms of the contract consist of the terms of the offer subject to the modifications contained in the acceptance'. That may however go too far. In some cases, however, the battle is won by the man who gets the blow in first. If he offers to sell at a named price on the terms and conditions stated on the back and the buyer orders the goods purporting to accept the offer on an order form with his own different terms and conditions on the back, then, if the difference is so material that it would affect the price, the buyer ought not to be allowed to take advantage of the difference unless he draws it specifically to the attention of the seller. There are yet other cases where the battle depends on the shots fired on both sides. There is a concluded contract but the forms vary. The terms and conditions of both parties are to be construed together. If they can be reconciled so as to give a harmonious result, all well and good. If differences are irreconcilable, so that they are mutually contradictory, then the conflicting terms may have to be scrapped and replaced by a reasonable implication.

In the present case the judge thought that the sellers in their original quotation got their blow in first; especially by the provision that 'These terms and conditions shall prevail over any terms and conditions in the Buyer's order'. It was so emphatic that the price variation clause continued through all the subsequent dealings and that the buyer must be taken to have agreed to it. I can understand that point of view. But I think that the documents have to be considered as a whole. And, as a matter of construction, I think the acknowledgment of 5th June 1969 is the decisive document. It makes it clear that the contract was on the buyers' terms and not on the sellers' terms: and the buyers' terms did not include a price variation clause.

I would therefore allow the appeal and enter judgment for the buyers.

[Lawton and Bridge L.JJ. delivered concurring judgments.]

QUESTION

What might have been the result in the *Butler Machine Tool* case if the sellers had not returned the completed tear-off slip, but had merely ignored it and supplied the machine tool? If there were a binding contract, when would it be formed and on what terms?

TYWOOD INDUSTRIES LTD. v. ST. ANNE-NACKAWIC PULP & PAPER CO. LTD.

(1979), 100 D.L.R. (3d) 374 (Ont. H.C.)

GRANGE J. The plaintiff's action is for the price of goods sold. The defendant has moved to stay the action under s. 7 of the *Arbitrations Act*, R.S.O. 1970, c. 25, upon the ground that the agreement of sale contained a clause for submission to arbitration. . . .

The defendant's invitation to tender was dated September 19, 1977. The document on its face was entitled "A Request for Quotation" and set forth the goods required. On the reverse side were set forth the "Terms and Conditions". There were 13 of these, none of which dealt with arbitration. On September 26, 1977, the plaintiff replied with a quotation in a letter form, but the reverse side of the letter contained a list of 12 "Terms and Conditions of Sale", none of which made reference to arbitration. Condition 12 read as follows:

> 12. No modification of the above Conditions of Sale shall be effected by our receipt or acknowledgment of a purchase order containing additional or different conditions.

There followed some telephone and telex communications between the parties and a revised proposal was submitted by the plaintiff under date of November 7, 1977, with the same 12 "Terms and Conditions of Sale" on the reverse side. Then came two purchase orders from the defendant dated January 6, 1978 and July 3, 1978, each of which contained on the reverse "Terms and Conditions" of which the nineteenth and last read as follows:

> 19. This Contract shall be governed by and construed according to the laws of the Province of New Brunswick. Any controversy arising out of or relating to this Order, or the breach thereof, shall be settled by arbitration in Fredericton in accordance with the Arbitration Act of the Province of New Brunswick.

The plaintiff's copy was not produced but it is alleged to have printed thereon: "This order is accepted by the vendor subject to the terms and conditions on the face and reverse side of this order." It is also alleged to have printed thereon the instructions (to the vendor): "Mail acceptance copy of this order promptly giving definite shipment date." It appears to be common ground that neither the purchase order was signed by the plaintiff nor returned to the defendant. The goods were then delivered. . . .

While the parties may have agreed to arbitration I am certainly not satisfied that this is so. I have the greatest doubt that the plaintiff put its mind to the question at all. Certainly it tried (perhaps not consciously) to impose its non-arbitrable condition upon the defendant when it quoted its price originally. It at no time acknowledged the supremacy of the defendant's terms. On the other hand, the defendant (again perhaps not consciously) did try to impose the arbitration term in the purchase orders, but it drew no particular attention to that term. Nor did it complain when the plaintiff failed to return the vendor's copy of the purchase orders with an acknowledgement of the terms sought to be imposed. This was a commercial transaction and terms might well have been expected, but the conduct of both parties seems to me to indicate that neither party considered any terms other than those found on the face of the documents (*i.e.*, the specifications and the price) important. What was important to both was the consummation of the business deal that had been arranged between them. . . .

[Defendant's application for stay dismissed.]

ONTARIO LAW REFORM COMMISSION, REPORT ON SALE OF GOODS: THE BATTLE OF THE FORMS

(1979), vol. I, at 81

Few formational problems are more difficult to resolve than the conflict that arises when a buyer and a seller use different forms to record the terms upon which they are willing to enter into a bargain. That the use of conflicting purchase order and acknowledgment forms is as common in Ontario as it is in the U.S., emerges clearly from the Research Team's analysis of contractual forms and the replies to the Canadian Manufacturers' Association Questionnaire. In a typical case the buyer forwards his printed purchase order form, which is made "subject" to the terms and conditions appearing in the same document. The seller responds by sending his acknowledgment or confirmation form, which also contains its own terms and conditions; however, these often differ in material respects from those in the buyer's form. Into this basic scenario many variants may be injected. A few examples will suffice: the exchange of forms may have been preceded, or be accompanied, by oral communications; one or other form may reject in advance any modifications to the terms in the form not expressly assented to in writing; or, one form may state a term that is not reproduced in the document of the other party. Most importantly, the parties may proceed with performance on the assumption that a binding agreement has been concluded and only "discover" the disparity in the documentary exchanges when the parties are locked in conflict. How should the law resolve this apparent impasse?

Anglo-Canadian contract law has traditionally approached the problem by holding that, to constitute a completed contract, the forms exchanged must contain no variant terms [the "mirror image" rule]. When this condition is not satisfied, the document later in time, which could be the seller's confirmation or the buyer's purchase order, is not a true acceptance but constitutes a counter-offer; that is, unless the additional terms can be treated as proposals that were not intended to be mandatory in nature. There is, therefore, no binding contract and either party may refuse to continue with performance. But if performance has been tendered to and accepted by the buyer after the buyer has received the seller's confirmation, the buyer is deemed to have accepted the seller's counter-offer, at any rate where the seller's confirmation followed receipt of the buyer's order. This proposition is sometimes referred to as "the performance rule" [also known as the "last shot" or the "last past the post" rule].

[Footnotes omitted.]

NOTES and QUESTIONS

1. The O.L.R.C. questioned the relevance of these rules to commercial reality. The Report cited two contrasting businesspersons' views about the value of such forms:

The first was expressed by a CMA respondent in the following language:

It has been my experience that the mechanics of buying and selling in the private sector in inter-company commerce are much the same the country over. The basis of the system is the exchange of printed Purchase Order Forms and Sales Order Forms. The creation of both forms follows a predictable pattern.

The buyer's system engineer designs the front of the P.O. form such that all information required to communicate his needs are stated. His lawyer then fills up the back of the form.

The seller's systems engineer designs the front of the S.O. form such that effect may be given the buyer's wishes. His lawyer also fills up the back of the form.

The front of the forms is a manifestation of good communications; the back of the forms is a manifestation of what your profession calls the adversary system, I believe.

Fortunately, a conspiracy developed many years ago between Purchasing Agents and Sales Managers under which both agreed not to read the backsides of the other's form. Were it not for this layman's conspiracy, the economy of Ontario would doubtless be destroyed.

A second, and less sceptical, view appears in a manual prepared by another respondent for the guidance of its staff. This describes the use of standard forms as "a practical way of handling thousands of orders per month for standard commercial items not involving systems or other special applications".

The O.L.R.C. recommended only the adoption of a provision similar to the United States Uniform Commercial Code, Art. 2-207 (3), reading as follows:

Conduct by both parties which assumes the existence of a contract is sufficient to establish a contract of sale although the writings or other communications of the parties do not otherwise establish a contract, and in such a case the terms of the contract consist of those terms on which the parties have agreed together with any supplementary terms incorporated under any provision of this Act.

(O.L.R.C., *Report on Sale of Goods* (1979), vol. III, "A Draft to Revise The Sale of Goods Act", s. 4.2 (3).)

2. The United Nations Convention on Contracts for the International Sale of Goods, commonly known as the Vienna Convention or C.I.S.G., came into force on 1st January, 1988 and has now been ratified by 63 states on all 5 continents. The member states include Canada, the United States, a substantial number of Latin American countries, most of western Europe (but not the United Kingdom or Eire), Russia and many eastern European countries, Australia and New Zealand, China and other

Asian countries (but not India or Japan). Canada acceded to the Convention in 1991 and it came into force in Canada a year later. By January, 1993, federal and provincial implementing statutes were in place in all jurisdictions.

Article 1(1) of the Convention states: "This Convention applies to contracts of sale of goods between parties whose places of business are in different states: (a) when the states are Contracting States; or (b) when the rules of private international law lead to the application of the law of a Contracting State." It may, however, be expressly excluded by the parties.

The rules relating to formation of the contract are in Part II. Article 19 provides:

(1) A reply to an offer which purports to be an acceptance but contains additions, limitations or other modifications is a rejection of the offer and constitutes a counter-offer.

(2) However, a reply to an offer which purports to be an acceptance but contains additional or different terms which do not materially alter the terms of the offer constitutes an acceptance, unless the offeror, without undue delay, objects orally to the discrepancy or dispatches a notice to that effect. If he does not so object, the terms of the contract are the terms of the offer with the modifications contained in the acceptance.

(3) Additional or different terms relating, among other things, to the price, payment, quality and quantity of the goods, place and time of delivery, extent of one party's liability to the other or the settlement of disputes are considered to alter the terms of the offer materially.

3. For further discussion of the "Battle of the Forms" see, *e.g.*, Panel Discussion (1980), 4 Can. Bus. L.J. 263; Adams, "The Battle of the Forms" (1979), 95 L.Q.R. 481 and Jacobs, "The Battle of the Forms: Standard Term Contracts in Comparative Perspective" (1985), 34 Int. & Comp. L.Q. 297.

4. If there is no contract, how might the law adjust the positions of the parties? See McKendrick, "The Battle of the Forms and the Law of Restitution" (1988), 8 Oxford Jl. of L.S. 197 at 220.

5. All Canadian jurisdictions now have legislation addressing issues, including contract issues, with respect to e-commerce. The legislation is aimed at the facilitation of contracting in electronic form either between persons directly or between persons and an agent or server, and is based on the Uniform Electronic Commerce Act, which was developed by the Uniform Law Conference of Canada, which in turn considered the Model Law on Electronic Commerce adopted in 1996 by the United Nations Commission on International Trade (UNCITRAL). Canadian e-commerce legislation provides, *inter alia*, that offer and acceptance are permitted though electronic means. For example, the Ontario Electronic Commerce Act 2000, S.O. 2000, c. 17, provides that:

19. (1) An offer, the acceptance of an offer or any other matter that is material to the formation or operation of contract may be expressed,

(a) by means of electronic information or an electronic document; or

(b) by an act that is intended to result in an electronic communication, such as,

(i) touching or clicking on an appropriate icon or other place on a computer screen, or

(ii) speaking.

(2) Subsection (1) applies unless the parties agree otherwise.

(3) A contract is not invalid or unenforceable by reason only of being in electronic form.

20. A contract may be formed by the interaction of an electronic agent and an individual or by the interaction of electronic agents.

21. An electronic transaction between an individual and another person's electronic agent is not enforceable by the other person if,

(a) the individual makes a material error in electronic information or an electronic document used in the transaction;

(b) the electronic agent does not give the individual an opportunity to prevent or correct the error;

(c) on becoming aware of the error, the individual promptly notifies the other person; and

(d) in a case where consideration is received as a result of the error, the individual,

    (i) returns or destroys the consideration in accordance with the other person's instructions or, if there are no instructions, deals with the consideration in a reasonable manner, and

    (ii) does not benefit materially by receiving the consideration.

See also, *e.g.* Electronic Commerce Act, S.N.S. 2000, c. 26; Electronic Information and Documents Act, S.S. 2000, c. E-7.22; Electronic Transactions Act, S.B.C. 2001, c. 10; Electronic Transactions Act, S.A. 2001, c. E-5.5.

It is argued that the extension of normal contracting principles to electronic means is important to facilitating the growth and achieving the benefits of e-commerce. However, do offer and acceptance by electronic means involve the need for modified rules or greater restrictions in application of the rules? For example, do consumers fully understand that clicking on a computer icon means that they have accepted a binding legal contract, together with all the terms of that contract? See, *e.g.*, Gleick, "Click to Agree", *New York Times Magazine*, 10 May 1998. See more generally on matters of contract formation and e-commerce, Gregory, "Solving Legal Issues in Electronic Commerce" (1999), 32 Can. Bus. L.J. 84; Takach, *Computer Law*, 2nd ed. (2003), Chapter 6. Further issues arise with respect to the time and place of acceptance, and the relevant governing rules of electronic contracts that cross national and provincial boundaries; see section 5, *infra*. The following case raises, in a pronounced way, the policy issues involved in extending simple rules of offer and acceptance to the electronic context.

ProCD v. MATTHEW ZEIDENBERG AND SILKEN MOUNTAIN WEB SERVICES, INC.

86 F.3d 1447 (U.S. C.A. 7th Cir., 1996)

EASTERBROOK, Circuit Judge [delivering the opinion of the court] Must buyers of computer software obey the terms of shrinkwrap licenses? The district court held not . . . they are not contracts because the licenses are inside the box rather than printed on the outside. . . . [W]e disagree with the district judge's conclusion. . . . Shrinkwrap licenses are enforceable unless their terms are objectionable on grounds applicable to contracts in general (for example, if they violate a rule of positive law, or if they are unconscionable). Because no one argues that the terms of the license at issue here are troublesome, we remand with instructions to enter judgment for the plaintiff.

I

ProCD, the plaintiff, has compiled information from more than 3,000 telephone directories into a computer database. We may assume that this database cannot be copyrighted, although it is more complex, contains more information (nine-digit zip codes and census industrial codes), is organized differently, and therefore is more original than the single alphabetical directory. . . . ProCD sells a version of the database, called SelectPhone (trademark), on CD-ROM discs. . . . The "shrinkwrap license" gets its name from the fact that retail software packages are covered in plastic or cellophane "shrinkwrap," and some vendors, though not ProCD, have written licenses that become effective as soon as the customer tears the wrapping from the package. Vendors prefer "end user license," but we use the more common term. . . . A proprietary method of compressing the data serves as effective encryption too. Customers decrypt and use the data with the aid of an application program that ProCD has written. This program, which is copyrighted, searches the database in response to users' criteria (such as "find all people named Tatum in Tennessee, plus all firms with 'Door Systems' in the corporate name"). The resulting lists (or, as ProCD prefers, "listings") can be read and manipulated by other software, such as word processing programs.

The database in SelectPhone (trademark) cost more than $10 million to compile and is expensive to keep current. It is much more valuable to some users than to others. The combination of names, addresses, and . . . codes enables manufacturers to compile lists of potential customers. Manufacturers and retailers pay high prices to specialized information intermediaries for such mailing lists; ProCD offers a potentially cheaper alternative. People with nothing to sell could use the database as a substitute for calling long distance information, or as a way to look up old friends who have moved to unknown towns, or just as an electronic substitute for the local phone book. ProCD decided to engage in price discrimination, selling its database to the general public for personal use at a low price (approximately $150 for the set of five discs) while selling information to the trade for a higher price.

If ProCD had to recover all of its costs and make a profit by charging a single price—that is, if it could not charge more to commercial users than to the general public—it would have to raise the price substantially over $150. The ensuing reduction in sales would harm consumers who value the information at, say, $200. They get consumer surplus of $50 under the current arrangement but would cease to buy if the price rose substantially. If because of high elasticity of demand in the consumer segment of the market the only way to make a profit turned out to be a price attractive to commercial users alone, then all consumers would lose out—and so would the commercial clients, who would have to pay more for the listings because ProCD could not obtain any contribution toward costs from the consumer market.

To make price discrimination work, however, the seller must be able to control arbitrage [profiting from different prices in different markets]. An air carrier sells tickets for less to vacationers than to business travelers, using advance purchase and Saturday-night-stay requirements to distinguish the categories. A producer of movies segments the market by time, releasing first to theaters, then to pay-per-view services, next to the videotape and laserdisc market, and finally to cable and commercial tv. Vendors of computer software have a harder task. Anyone can walk into a retail store and buy a box. Customers do not wear tags saying "commercial user" or "consumer user." Anyway, even a commercial-user-detector at the door would not work, because a consumer could buy the software and resell to a commercial user. That arbitrage would break down the price discrimination and drive up the minimum price at which ProCD would sell to anyone.

Instead of tinkering with the product and letting users sort themselves—for example, furnishing current data at a high price that would be attractive only to commercial customers, and two-year-old data at a low price—ProCD turned to the institution of contract. Every box containing its consumer product declares that the software comes with restrictions stated in an enclosed license. This license, which is encoded on the CD-ROM disks as well as printed in the manual, and which appears on a user's screen every time the software runs, limits use of the application program and listings to non- commercial purposes.

Matthew Zeidenberg bought a consumer package of SelectPhone (trademark) in 1994 from a retail outlet in Madison, Wisconsin, but decided to ignore the license. He formed Silken Mountain Web Services, Inc., to resell the information in the SelectPhone (trademark) database. The corporation makes the database available on the Internet to anyone willing to pay its price—which, needless to say, is less than ProCD charges its commercial customers. Zeidenberg has purchased two additional SelectPhone (trademark) packages, each with an updated version of the database, and made the latest information available over the World Wide Web, for a price, through his corporation. ProCD filed this suit seeking an injunction against further dissemination that exceeds the rights specified in the licenses (identical in each of the three packages Zeidenberg purchased). The district court held the licenses ineffectual because their terms do not appear on the outside of the packages. The court added that the second and third licenses stand no different from the first, even though they are identical, because they might have been different, and a purchaser does not agree to—and cannot be bound by—terms that were secret at the time of purchase. . . .

II

Following the district court, we treat the licenses as ordinary contracts accompanying the sale of products, and therefore as governed by the common law of contracts and the Uniform Commercial Code . . . Zeidenberg does not argue that Silken Mountain Web Services is free of any restrictions that apply to Zeidenberg himself, because any effort to treat the two parties as distinct would put Silken Mountain behind the eight ball on ProCD's argument that copying the application program onto its hard disk violates the copyright laws. Zeidenberg does argue, and the district court held, that placing the package of software on the shelf is an "offer," which the customer "accepts" by paying the asking price and leaving the store with the goods . . . In Wisconsin, as elsewhere, a contract includes only the terms on which the parties have agreed. One cannot agree to hidden terms, the judge concluded. So far, so good—but one of the terms to which Zeidenberg agreed by purchasing the software is that the transaction was subject to a license. Zeidenberg's position therefore must be that the printed terms on the outside of a box are the parties' contract—except for printed terms that refer to or incorporate other terms. But why would Wisconsin fetter the parties' choice in this way? Vendors can put the entire terms of a contract on the outside of a box only by using microscopic type, removing other information that buyers might find more useful (such as what the software does, and on which computers it works), or both. The "Read Me" file included with most software, describing system requirements and potential incompatibilities, may be equivalent to ten pages of type; warranties and license restrictions take still more space. Notice on the outside, terms on the inside, and a right to return the software for a refund if the terms are unacceptable (a right that the license expressly extends), may be a means of doing business valuable to buyers and sellers alike. See E. Allan Farnsworth, 1 Farnsworth on Contracts § 4.26 (1990); Restatement (2d) of Contracts § 211 comment a (1981) ("Standardization of agreements serves many of the same functions as standardization of goods and services; both are essential to a system of mass production and distribution. Scarce and costly time and skill can be devoted to a class of transactions rather than the details of individual transactions."). Doubtless a state could forbid the use of standard contracts in the software business, but we do not think that Wisconsin has done so. [For discussion of standard form contracts more generally see Chapter 8, section 3.]

Transactions in which the exchange of money precedes the communication of detailed terms are common. Consider the purchase of insurance. The buyer goes to an agent, who explains the essentials (amount of coverage, number of years) and remits the premium to the home office, which sends back a policy. On the district judge's understanding, the terms of the policy are irrelevant because the insured paid before receiving them. Yet the device of payment, often with a "binder" (so that the insurance takes effect immediately even though the home office reserves the right to withdraw coverage later), in advance of the policy, serves buyers' interests by accelerating effectiveness and reducing transactions costs. Or consider the purchase of an airline ticket. The traveler calls the carrier or an agent, is quoted a price, reserves a seat, pays, and gets a ticket, in that order. The ticket contains elaborate terms, which the traveler can reject by canceling the reservation. To use the ticket is to accept the terms, even terms that in retrospect are disadvantageous. See *Carnival Cruise Lines, Inc. v. Shute*, 499 U.S. 585 . . . (1991). . . . Just so with a ticket to a concert. The back of the ticket states that the patron promises not to record the concert; to attend is to agree. A theater that detects a violation will confiscate the tape and escort the violator to the exit. One could arrange things so that every concertgoer signs this promise before forking over the money, but that cumbersome way of doing things not only would lengthen queues and raise prices but also would scotch the sale of tickets by phone or electronic data service.

Consumer goods work the same way. Someone who wants to buy a radio set visits a store, pays, and walks out with a box. Inside the box is a leaflet containing some terms, the most important of which usually is the warranty, read for the first time in the comfort of home. By Zeidenberg's lights, the warranty in the box is irrelevant; every consumer gets the standard warranty implied by the UCC in the event the contract is silent; yet so far as we are aware no state disregards warranties furnished with consumer products. Drugs come with a list of ingredients on the outside and an elaborate package insert on the inside. The package insert describes drug interactions, contraindications, and other vital information—but, if Zeidenberg is right, the purchaser need not read the package insert, because it is not part of the contract.

Next consider the software industry itself. Only a minority of sales take place over the counter, where there are boxes to peruse. A customer may place an order by phone in response to a line item in a catalog or a review in a magazine. Much software is ordered over the Internet by purchasers who have never seen a box.

Increasingly software arrives by wire. There is no box; there is only a stream of electrons, a collection of information that includes data, an application program, instructions, many limitations ("MegaPixel 3.14159 cannot be used with Byte-Pusher 2.718"), and the terms of sale. The user purchases a serial number, which activates the software's features. On Zeidenberg's arguments, these unboxed sales are unfettered by terms—so the seller has made a broad warranty and must pay consequential damages for any shortfalls in performance, two "promises" that if taken seriously would drive prices through the ceiling or return transactions to the horse-and-buggy age. [For discussion of the incorporation of exclusion clauses, see Chapter 8, section 3(d)(ii).]

[The judge reviewed a number of U.S. court decisions and continued:] What then does the current version of the UCC have to say? We think that the place to start is § 2-204(1): "A contract for sale of goods may be made in any manner sufficient to show agreement, including conduct by both parties which recognizes the existence of such a contract." A vendor, as master of the offer, may invite acceptance by conduct, and may propose limitations on the kind of conduct that constitutes acceptance. A buyer may accept by performing the acts the vendor proposes to treat as acceptance. And that is what happened. ProCD proposed a contract that a buyer would accept by using the software after having an opportunity to read the license at leisure. This Zeidenberg did. He had no choice, because the software splashed the license on the screen and would not let him proceed without indicating acceptance. So although the district judge was right to say that a contract can be, and often is, formed simply by paying the price and walking out of the store, the UCC permits contracts to be formed in other ways. ProCD proposed such a different way, and without protest Zeidenberg agreed. Ours is not a case in which a consumer opens a package to find an insert saying "you owe us an extra $10,000" and the seller files suit to collect. Any buyer finding such a demand can prevent formation of the contract by returning the package, as can any consumer who concludes that the terms of the license make the software worth less than the purchase price. Nothing in the UCC requires a seller to maximize the buyer's net gains.

Section 2-606, which defines "acceptance of goods", reinforces this understanding. A buyer accepts goods under § 2-606(1)(b) when, after an opportunity to inspect, he fails to make an effective rejection under § 2-602(1). ProCD extended an opportunity to reject if a buyer should find the license terms unsatisfactory; Zeidenberg inspected the package, tried out the software, learned of the license, and did not reject the goods. We refer to § 2-606 only to show that the opportunity to return goods can be important; acceptance of an offer differs from acceptance of goods after delivery . . .; but the UCC consistently permits the parties to structure their relations so that the buyer has a chance to make a final decision after a detailed review. [Discussion of the concept of acceptance and in particular the issue of acceptance by silence in *Felthouse v. Bindley* can be found later in this chapter in section 4.]

Some portions of the UCC impose additional requirements on the way parties agree on terms. A disclaimer of the implied warranty of merchantability must be "conspicuous." UCC § 2-316(2), incorporating UCC § 1-201(10). Promises to make firm offers, or to negate oral modifications, must be "separately signed." UCC §§ 2-205, 2-209(2). These special provisos reinforce the impression that, so far as the UCC is concerned, other terms may be as inconspicuous as the forum-selection clause on the back of the cruise ship ticket in *Carnival Lines* [*supra*]. Zeidenberg has not located any Wisconsin case—for that matter, any case in any state—holding that under the UCC the ordinary terms found in shrinkwrap licenses require any special prominence, or otherwise are to be undercut rather than enforced. In the end, the terms of the license are conceptually identical to the contents of the package. Just as no court would dream of saying that SelectPhone (trademark) must contain 3,100 phone books rather than 3,000, or must have data no more than 30 days old, or must sell for $100 rather than $150—although any of these changes would be welcomed by the customer, if all other things were held constant—so, we believe, Wisconsin would not let the buyer pick and choose among terms. Terms of use are no less a part of "the product" than are the size of the database and the speed with which the software compiles listings. Competition among vendors, not judicial revision of a package's contents, is how consumers are protected in a market economy . . . ProCD has rivals, which may elect to compete by offering superior software, monthly updates, improved terms of use, lower price, or a better compromise among these elements. As we stressed above, adjusting terms in buyers' favor might help Matthew Zeidenberg today (he already has the software) but would lead to a response, such as a higher price, that might make consumers as a whole worse off.

[Easterbrook J. also held for ProCD on the issue of copyright. Appeal allowed.]

NOTE

Does this decision accord with the expectations of purchasers conducting e-commerce? Legislation in a number of jurisdictions has made an effort to extend and to some extent tailor consumer protection for e-commerce transactions in order to protect consumers acting for personal, family or household purposes. For example, federal and provincial ministers of consumer affairs in Canada developed the Internet Sales Contract Template for consumer transactions "formed by text-based Internet communications." See: <http://strategis.ic.gc.ca/epic/internet/inoca-bc.nsf/vwGenerated-InterE/ca01642e.html>. Similar provisions have been enacted in provincial legislation. See Fair Trading Act, R.S.A. 2000, c. F-2, s. 42 and Internet Sales Contract Regulation, Alta. Reg. 81/2001; The Consumer Protection Act, C.C.S.M., c. C200, ss. 127-135; Consumer Protection Act, 2002, S.O. 2002, c. 30, Sched. A, ss. 37-40.

DAWSON v. HELICOPTER EXPLORATION CO.

[1955] S.C.R. 868, [1955] 5 D.L.R. 404

In 1931, Dawson had discovered and staked a mineral deposit in a remote area at the head of the Leduc River in British Columbia and a report of his discovery had been made to the B.C. Mines Department. He filed claims, which subsequently lapsed. In 1951, Dawson, who was then an officer in the U.S. Naval Reserve Engineering Corps and stationed in Utah, communicated several times with the respondent concerning the exploitation of this property.

In January 1951, Dawson received the following proposal from Mr. Springer of the respondent:

> I would be interested in making some arrangements next summer to finance you in staking the claims for which we would give you an interest. I would suggest that we should pay for your time and expenses and carry you for a 10% non-assessable interest in the claims.

To this Dawson replied:

> Your proposition as stated in your letter appeals to me as being a fair one. I would be pleased to meet you in Ogden.

In February 1951, Dawson was sent overseas on active duty. However, he wrote to the respondent that this change in circumstances "need not necessarily interrupt our plans regarding the Leduc River plans" and pointed out that he might be able to obtain a leave to show the properties to the respondent.

On March 5, 1951, the respondent wrote:

> I agree with you that the best arrangements would be to have you take us into the property, as you know definitely where your showings are.
>
> I am expecting to operate the helicopter in that country this year. It would depend upon whether I get a pilot or not. If I am operating it, it will be a simple matter to go into this country, probably from Stewart or Summit Lake, north of the Premier [sic].
>
> I hereby agree that, if you take us in to the showings and we think they warrant staking, that we will stake the claims and give you a 10% non-assessable interest. The claims would be recorded in our name and we will have full discretion in dealing with them—you to get 10% of the vendor interest.
>
> I do not think one should attempt to go into this country until about the first day of August, so any time during August would do. You can keep me advised as to your movements and when you could get away during the month. If it is impossible to get away in August, the last half of July and all September would be alright.

On April 12, 1951 Dawson replied:

> Your recent letter regarding the Leduc R. properties was forwarded by my wife.
>
> August or Sept. is the proper time to inspect this locality. The most ground can then be seen.
>
> If you will inform me, if and when you obtain a pilot for your 'copter, I will immediately take steps for a temporary release in order to be on hand.
>
> Should it appear that you will not be able to get a pilot I would appreciate it if you would so inform me.

Dawson heard no more until June 7, 1951, when the respondent wrote:

> Up to a little over a week ago it did not look as though we would be able to secure a pilot for our helicopter. However, we have a man now who we hope will be satisfactory.
>
> I was talking to Tom McQuillan, who is prospecting for us this year; he said he had been over your showings at the head of the Leduc River, and in his opinion it would be practically impossible to operate there, as the showings were in behind ice fields, which along with the extreme snow falls made it very doubtful if an economic operation could be carried on.
>
> We have also been delayed in getting away this year, due to pilot trouble, and have so much work lined up that I am doubtful whether we will have time to visit your showings, also I do not think we would be warranted in making the effort to get in there due to the unfavorable conditions. I must advise you therefore, not to depend on our making this trip, and suggest if you are still determined to go in, to make other arrangements.

To this no reply was sent by Dawson. On August 1 an exploration party of the respondent investigated the Leduc River area and located showings reported in 1931 by Dawson. This did not become known to Dawson until some time in 1952. In 1953 the respondent made arrangements to enter upon the development of the claims by a new company to which the claims were sold in exchange for paid-up shares of the capital stock. Later on Dawson took legal advice and the action was launched on November 23, 1953.

RAND J. The substantial contention of the respondent is that any offer contained in the correspondence and in particular the letter of March 5 called for an acceptance not by promise but by the performance of an act, the location of the claims by Dawson for the respondent. It is based upon the well known conception which in its simplest form is illustrated by the case of a reward offered for some act to be done. To put it in other words, no intention was conveyed by Springer when he said "I hereby agree" that Dawson, if agreeable, should have replied "I hereby accept" or words to that effect: the offer called for and awaited only the act to be done and would remain revocable at any time until every element of that act had been completed.

The error in this reasoning is that such an offer contemplates acts to be performed by the person only to whom it is made and in respect of which the offeror remains passive, and that is not so here. What Dawson was to do was to proceed to the area with Springer or persons acting for him by means of the respondent's helicopter and to locate the showings. It was necessarily implied by Springer that he would participate in his own proposal. This involved his promise that he would do so and that the answer to the proposal would be either a refusal or a promise on the part of Dawson to a like participation. The offer was unconditional but contemplated a performance subject to the condition that a pilot could be obtained by the respondent.

Dawson's answer of April 12 was, as I construe it, similarly an unqualified promissory acceptance, subject as to performance to his being able to obtain the necessary leave. It was the clear implication that Springer, controlling the means of making the trip, should fix the time and should notify Dawson accordingly. As the earlier letters show, Dawson was anxious to conclude some arrangement and if he could not make it with Springer he would seek it in other quarters.

Although in the circumstances, because the terms proposed involve such complementary action on the part of both parties as to put the implication beyond doubt, the precept is not required, this interpretation of the correspondence follows the tendency of courts to treat offers as calling for bilateral rather than unilateral action when the language can be fairly so construed, in order that the transaction shall have such "business efficacy as both parties much have intended that at all events it should have": Bowen L.J. in *The Moorcock* [(1889), 14 P.D. 64 at 68]. In theory . . . an offer in the unilateral sense can be revoked up to the last moment before complete performance. At such a consequence many courts have balked; and it is in part that fact that has led to a promissory construction where that can be reasonably given. What is effectuated is the real intention of both parties to close a business bargain on the strength of which they may, thereafter, plan their courses.

This question is considered in Williston on Contracts, 1936 Ed., Vol. 1, pp. 76 and 77, in which the author observes:—

> Doubtless wherever possible, as matter of interpretation, a court would and should interpret an offer as contemplating a bilateral rather than a unilateral contract, since in a bilateral contract both parties are protected from a period prior to the beginning of performance on either side—that is from the making of the mutual promises.
>
> At the opening of the present century the courts were still looking for a clear promise on each side in bilateral contracts. A bargain which lacked such a promise by one of the parties was held to lack mutuality and, therefore, to be unenforceable. Courts are now more ready to recognize fair implications as effective: "A promise may be lacking, and yet the whole writing may be 'instinct with an obligation,' imperfectly expressed," which the courts will regard as supplying the necessary reciprocal promise.

The expression "instinct with an obligation" . . ., is employed by Cardozo J. in *Wood v. Lady Lucy Duff Gordon* [(1917), 222 N.Y. 88 at 98], in the following passage:—

> It is true that he does not promise in so many words that he will use reasonable efforts to place the defendant's indorsements and market her designs. We think, however, that such a promise is fairly to be implied. *The law has outgrown its primitive stage of formalism when the precise word was the sovereign talisman, and every slip was fatal.* A promise may be lacking and yet the whole writing may be "instinct with an obligation" imperfectly expressed.

These observations apply obviously and equally to both offer and acceptance.

The question of an anticipatory breach by the letter of June 7 was raised, but that was superseded by the subsequent events. Dawson was bound to remain ready during a reasonable time prior to that mentioned for the trip to endeavour, upon notice from Springer, to obtain leave of absence. But in promising Dawson that the company would co-operate, Springer impliedly agreed that the company would not, by its own act, prevent the complementary performance by Dawson. In doing what it did, the company not only violated its engagement, but brought to an end the subject matter of the contract. By that act it dispensed with any further duty of readiness on the part of Dawson whether or not he was aware of what had taken place. Even assuming the technical continuance of the obligations and the necessity of an affirmative step in order to treat an anticipatory breach as a repudiation, the action was not brought until long after the time for performance had passed. Being thus excused, Dawson's obtaining leave, apart from any pertinency to damages, became irrelevant to the cause of action arising from the final breach.

I would, therefore, allow the appeal and remit the cause to the Supreme Court of British Columbia for the assessment of damages. The appellant will have his costs throughout.

ESTEY J. . . . The letter of March 5, 1951, was an offer on the part of the respondent made in response to appellant's request for "a definite arrangement" and, with great respect to those who hold a contrary view, the appellant's letter of April 12 constitutes an acceptance of that offer, more particularly as every portion thereof is consistent only with the appellant's intention that he was accepting and holding himself in readiness to perform his part. While it has been repeatedly held that an acceptance must be absolute and unequivocal . . . it is equally clear that such an acceptance need not be in express terms and may be found in the language and conduct of the acceptor. The learned author of *Pollock on Contracts*, 13th ed., in discussing the rule that "the acceptance must be absolute and unqualified," states at 30:

> Simple and obvious as the rule is in itself, the application to a given set of facts is not always obvious, inasmuch as contracting parties often use loose and inexact language, even when their communications are in writing and on important matters. The question whether the language used on a particular occasion does or does not amount to an acceptance is wholly a question of construction, and generally though not necessarily the construction of a written instrument. . . .

The respondent's undertaking would require that it make reasonable efforts to locate a pilot and, having done so, that it would convey the appellant into the area in August or September of 1951 and if, when relocated, the respondent staked the claims it would give to the appellant a 10% non-assessable interest. If, under this contract, the respondent did not obtain a pilot, the contract would be at an end. Moreover, if the claims were relocated and, in the opinion of the respondent, were not worth staking, the appellant would not receive the 10%. These terms were agreed upon and may be described as conditions subsequent.

> A contract may contain within itself the elements of its own discharge, in the form of provisions, express or implied, for its determination in certain circumstances. These circumstances may be the non-fulfilment of a condition precedent; the occurrence of a condition subsequent; or the exercise of an option to determine the contract, reserved to one of the parties by its terms.
>
>   .....
>
> In the second case the parties introduce a provision that the fulfilment of a condition or the occurrence of an event shall discharge either one of them or both from further liabilities under the contract. *Anson's Law of Contract*, 20th ed., 310-11.

Moreover, when this correspondence is read as a whole, respondent's letter of repudiation dated June 7, 1951 . . . appears to be written on the basis that the parties had agreed with respect to taking the appellant into the area. It is not suggested that there was any term or item left in abeyance or to be subsequently agreed upon. The suggestion is rather that, because of the additional information, the project did not commend itself from an economic point of view, and, in any event, the respondent had not time to undertake it, and the letter concludes with the sentence:

> I must advise you therefore, not to depend on our making this trip, and suggest if you are still determined to go in, to make other arrangements.

The word "arrangements" is rather a general term with no precise meaning, but it is of some significance that the appellant, in his letter of February 28, 1951, asked for "a definite arrangement," which was concluded, and the respondent now suggests that appellant make other arrangements. A reading of this letter as a whole appears to corroborate that the parties had concluded a contract.

The learned trial judge further held:

> Alternatively if the correspondence establishes a contract, then there was a termination of it by Springer, accepted by the plaintiff, and a mutual abandonment of it by the parties.

The repudiation referred to is contained in respondent's letter to appellant dated June 7, 1951. . . .

The appellant made no reply to this letter and nothing passed between himself and the respondent until he called at the latter's office in Vancouver about December 15, 1952, when he and Springer had a conversation, during which, as the appellant deposes, Springer, in referring to the correspondence in 1951, said: "... it was not their original intention to go in but that Kvale [a prospector employed by Springer] had made an independent discovery of the copper back in 1948 and they decided to go back and check up on that." This statement is largely corroborated by Kvale and is not referred to by Springer. About April 4, 1953, appellant again interviewed Springer at the respondent's office in Vancouver, when Springer made it clear that he would neither pay any amount to the appellant nor further discuss this matter. Appellant, in November of that year, put the matter in the hands of his solicitor.

It is contended that the appellant's silence, after his receipt of the letter of June 7, 1951, until his interview in December, 1952, constituted an abandonment of the contract. No authority was cited where silence alone has been held to constitute an abandonment. . . .

As already stated, Springer, at the outset of the correspondence, expressed his interest in appellant's claims and the respondent's financing him upon a percentage basis. In February, 1950, the respondent corporation was incorporated and Springer became President and General Manager. Both McQuillan and Kvale were employed by the respondent in 1951 and Kvale's contract is dated April 20 of that year. Springer, in the course of his evidence and in discussing the letter of June 7, 1951, stated:

> McQuillan was going out for us, and I had heard of these showings . . . I knew that McQuillan and Kvale had been up for another of my companies in that area and had looked over the showings, made discoveries. So I inquired of McQuillan about what he thought of Dawson's showings, and he said he didn't think they were of importance, and discouraged—and his report was quite discouraging.

The letter of repudiation is dated June 7, 1951, and during the next month Kvale and McQuillan were taken into the area by helicopter. They were again taken into the area where, on August 2 of that year, they staked a number of claims which were duly recorded. The record does not indicate when respondent changed its mind as indicated by Springer's remark to appellant at its office in December, 1952, but it is apparent that many of the difficulties emphasized in the letter of June 7 had either disappeared or been overcome by the following month. Upon this record it rather appears that the respondent concluded it could continue without assistance from the appellant and, therefore, wrote the letter of repudiation.

The respondent, in this letter of repudiation, set forth its reasons therefore which it would be difficult for the appellant, stationed as he was in the Marshall Islands, to effectively appraise. I do not think that under such circumstances a conclusion adverse to the appellant can be drawn from his failure to further press the respondent at that time. Immediately upon his return in December 1950, [sic] he "wrote to the Mining Recorder at Prince Rupert" and apparently continued his examination to ascertain what had, in fact, taken place. He visited the premises in June and July, 1950 [sic] and relocated the three claims which he had found in

1931. When he had ascertained, at least in part, what had taken place, he made his position known to the respondent in December of 1952. Moreover, while silence may be evidence of repudiation, its weight must depend upon the circumstances and here I do not think his silence, coupled with the steps he took immediately upon his return from the Marshall Islands, sufficiently supports a conclusion that he, at any time, intended to abandon his rights under the contract.

Upon receipt of the letter of repudiation dated June 7, 1951, the appellant might have accepted it and forthwith claimed damages. Since, however, he did not accept it, the contract remained in force and binding upon both parties. It, therefore, remained the duty of the respondent, having obtained a pilot, to take the appellant into the area in August or September. Not only did the respondent not do so, but, notwithstanding the terms of its letter of repudiation, it, in fact, took Kvale and McQuillan into the area where they staked claims on behalf of the respondent. This conduct constituted a breach of its contract.

The appeal should be allowed with costs throughout and the matter referred back to the Supreme Court of British Columbia to determine the damages.

[Fauteux J. concurred with Rand J., Cartwright J. concurred with Estey J. and Kerwin C.J.C. delivered a dissenting judgment.]

FELTHOUSE v. BINDLEY

(1862), 11 C.B. (N.S.) 869, 142 E.R. 1037 (Ex. Ch.)

The plaintiff, Paul Felthouse, had discussed with his nephew, John Felthouse, the purchase of a horse belonging to the nephew. However, owing to a misunderstanding, the uncle considered that he had purchased the horse for £30, whereas the nephew thought that the price was 30 guineas [a guinea was worth slightly more than £1].

As a result, the uncle wrote to the nephew on January 2nd offering to split the difference and adding:

> You can send him at your convenience, between now and the 25th of March. If I hear no more about him, I consider the horse mine at 30 pounds and 15 shillings.

To this letter the nephew sent no reply. On February 25th, an auction sale was held of the nephew's farming stock. Bindley, the auctioneer, was instructed to reserve the horse in question from the sale, but he forgot to do so and the horse was sold for £33.

On February 27th, the nephew wrote to the uncle that, at the time when the auctioneer was taking an inventory of the nephew's stock, he had said that:

> That horse (meaning the one I sold to you) is sold.

The auctioneer also wrote to the uncle admitting:

> Instructions were given to me to reserve the horse: but the lapse of time, and a multiplicity of business pressing upon me caused me to forget my previous promise.

On these facts, the uncle brought an action against the auctioneer for the conversion of the horse. At trial, the defendant objected that the property in the horse was not vested in the plaintiff at the time of the sale by the defendant.

A verdict was found for the plaintiff, damages were fixed at £33, leave being reserved to the defendant to move to enter a nonsuit, if the Court should be of opinion that the objection was well founded.

WILLES J. I am of the opinion that the rule to enter a nonsuit should be made absolute [with the result that the defendant's appeal was successful] . . .

It is clear that there was no complete bargain on the 2nd of January: and it is also clear that the uncle had no right to impose upon the nephew a sale of his horse for £30.15s. unless he chose to comply with the conditions of writing to repudiate the offer. The nephew might, no doubt, have bound his uncle to the bargain by writing to him: the uncle might also have retracted his offer at any time before acceptance. It stood an open offer: and so things remained until the 25th of February, when the nephew was about to sell his farming stock by auction. The horse in question being catalogued with the rest of the stock, the auctioneer (the defendant) was told that it was already sold. It is clear, therefore, that the nephew in his own mind intended his uncle to have the horse at the price which he (the uncle) had named,—£30.15s.: but he had not communicated such his intention to his uncle, or done anything to bind himself. Nothing, therefore, had been done to vest the property in the horse in the plaintiff down to the 25th of February, when the horse was sold by the defendant. It appears to me that, independently of the subsequent letters, there had been no bargain to pass the property in the horse to the plaintiff, and therefore that he had no right to complain of the sale. Then, what is the effect of the subsequent correspondence? The letter of the auctioneer amounts to nothing. The more important letter is that of the nephew, of the 27th of February, which is relied on as shewing that he intended to accept and did accept the terms offered by his uncle's letter of the 2nd of January. That letter, however, may be treated either as an acceptance then for the first time made by him, or as a memorandum of a bargain complete before the 25th of February, sufficient within the Statute of Frauds. It seems to me that the former is the more likely construction: and, if so, it is clear that the plaintiff cannot recover. But, assuming that there had been a complete parol bargain before the 25th of February, and that the letter of the 27th was a mere expression of the terms of that prior bargain, and not a bargain then for the first time concluded, it would be directly contrary to the decision of the court of Exchequer in *Stockdale v. Dunlop*, [(1840), 151 E.R. 391], to hold that that acceptance had relation back to the previous offer so as to bind third persons in respect of a dealing with the property by them in the interim. . . .

[Byles and Keating JJ. concurred in making the rule absolute.]

NOTES and QUESTIONS

1. Could the nephew have sued the uncle, if the horse had been reserved from the sale but the uncle had then changed his mind? See *Fairline Shipping Corp. v. Adamson*, [1975] Q.B. 180, and Miller, "*Felthouse v. Bindley* Revisited" (1972), 35 Mod. L. Rev. 489.

2. The problem of unsolicited goods has been dealt with by legislation in a number of jurisdictions. Ontario, Nova Scotia, British Columbia, Newfoundland and Saskatchewan provide that payment for unsolicited goods is not required, even if the recipient uses them, and limits the liability of recipients of unsolicited credit cards. See Consumer Protection Act, R.S.O. 1990, c. C.31, s. 36;

R.S.N.S. 1989, c. 92, s. 23; R.S.B.C. 1996, c. 69, s. 47, Unsolicited Goods and Credit Cards Act, R.S.N. 1990, c. U-6, ss. 3, 4, 5; Consumer Protection Act, S.S. 1996, c. C-30.1, ss. 72-75.

Prince Edward Island simply prohibits the delivery of unsolicited goods and the issuing of unsolicited credit cards, with an appropriate penalty. See Consumer Protection Act, R.S.P.E.I. 1988, c. C-19, s. 17(1). Other provinces, such as Manitoba and Alberta, in contrast, prohibit the issue of unsolicited credit cards. See Consumer Protection Act, C.C.S.M., c. C200, s. 114; Fair Trading Act, R.S.A. 2000, c. F-2, s. 86.

3. If a person orders goods for a trial period, then decides not to purchase but does nothing, is he or she liable to pay for the goods? See Sale of Goods Act, C.C.S.M., c. S10, s. 20, R. 4. The case of *Atari Corp. v. Electronics Boutique Stores (U.K.) Ltd.*, [1998] 1 All E.R. 1010 (C.A.) deals with the question of what a buyer must do to exercise its right of rejection in a sale or return transaction.

Would it make any difference if the person who orders the goods has already paid for them?

If the buyer rejects the offer to sell but uses the goods anyway, would the buyer have to pay for this use?

Compare *Silver's Garage Ltd. v. Bridgewater*, [1971] S.C.R. 577, with *Manco Ltd. v. Atl. Forest Products Ltd.* (1971), 24 D.L.R. (3d) 194 (N.B. C.A.). Are traditional contract law rules appropriate in such cases?

4. Gloria Greer joined the Readers' Club by filling in and returning a membership card entitling new members to a special introductory bonus of five books for $12.50. The circular containing the card advertised the following features of membership:

> You receive the *Reader's Club Newsletter* 12 times a year. Each issue reviews the Club Selection plus 100 Alternates.—If you want the Club selection, do nothing. It will be shipped to you automatically. If you want one or more of the Alternates, or no book at all, indicate your decision on our reply form and return it in the postage-paid envelope provided, by the date specified. A shipping and handling charge is added to each shipment.—*Introductory Membership Offer*. Choose any five books from the accompanying brochure for only $12.50 (plus shipping and handling charges). During the next three years you simply agree to buy only five Club Selections or Alternates from the hundreds offered.—*Return Privilege*. If the *Newsletter* is delayed and you receive the Club Selection without having had 10 days to notify us, you may return it for credit at our expense.—*Cancellations*. Membership may be terminated by you or by the Club, at any time after you have bought five additional books.

Gloria chose her five books for $12.50 and duly received them. The next newsletter, however, contained a club selection "Contracts for the Layperson," and 100 alternates which were all unattractive to her and so she ignored it. When the club selection was delivered, Gloria wrote to the Reader's Club saying she had changed her mind and did not wish to be part of an organization that involved such boring books. What is Gloria's legal position?

The Consumer Protection Act, R.S.B.C. 1996, c. 69, Part 4, s. 54(2) provides that in such a situation "the buyer has no legal obligation to the seller with respect to the goods, unless the buyer has received or is deemed to have received the notice or the goods at least 15 days before the date on which the buyer must (a) notify the seller of the buyer's decision not to receive the goods, or (b) return the goods".

5. The Civil Code of Québec, Book 5, Obligations, Ch. II, Contracts, s. III, provides:

> **Art. 1394.** Silence does not imply acceptance of an offer, subject only to the will of the parties, the law or special circumstances, such as usage or a prior business relationship.

6. Article 18(1) of the Vienna Convention states "Silence or inactivity does not in itself amount to acceptance". Article 9, however, may leave room for silence to be effective due to usage or established practice.

7. In the late 1990s, cable companies provided their subscribers with free access to a large number of exciting new channels for a trial period. After this initial period, subscribers were billed for continuing access, unless they had indicated to the company that they did not wish to continue to receive these channels (negative option selling).

Harvey Foster was only a viewer of CBC television and was not interested in any of these new channels, but omitted to send in the card rejecting the expanded service. Is he liable to pay for the new channels?

The Consumer Protection Act, R.S.B.C. 1996 c. 69, Part 4, s. 55 provides:

(2) A contract for an unsolicited service sold by means of a negative option offer is not enforceable by the seller against an individual . . .

(5) Consent [either orally or in writing] cannot be inferred from the individual's

(a) inaction,
(b) use of the service,
(c) consent to purchase another similar service, or
(d) payment for the service.

(6) Subsection (2) applies to a change to an individual's existing service only if

(a) the change is made pursuant to a negative option offer and,
(b) without the consent of the individual, the change

(i) provides a new, unsolicited service for which an extra charge is made or
(ii) reduces an existing service without reducing the price proportionately.

(7) Subsection (2) does not apply to

(a) a change to the price of an existing service, or
(b) a renewal of an existing service if the service is not otherwise changed.

Nova Scotia has also introduced legislation banning negative option strategies in respect of services. See s. 24A of Consumer Protection Act, R.S.N.S 1989, c. 92, as amended by S.N.S. 1994, c. 16, s. 2.

There have also been proposed bills to amend the federal Competition Act to restrict the use of negative option marketing. See, for example, An Act to Amend the Competition Act (Negative Option Marketing), Bill C-276, which was passed by the House of Commons on May 17, 2000 but died on the Order Paper October 22, 2000.

SAINT JOHN TUG BOAT CO. v. IRVING REFINERY LTD.

[1964] S.C.R. 614, 49 M.P.R. 284, 46 D.L.R. (2d) 1

RITCHIE J. [delivering the judgment of the court] . . . Since early in 1960, the respondent has operated an oil refinery bordering on the harbour of Saint John, New Brunswick, at Courtenay Bay, and as a necessary incident of this operation it is supplied with crude oil brought by large tankers which are owned or chartered by the California Shipping Company, a corporation with its head office in the United States of America, which was, at all times material hereto, represented at Saint John by Kent Lines Limited, a shipping firm which was owned or controlled by the same interests as the respondent company.

It was important to the respondent that tugs should be available when required to guide the incoming tankers into the harbour as any delay whilst they waited in the harbour approaches involved demurrage charges and to meet this situation, Mr. K.C. Irving, the chairman of the board of directors of the respondent company and president of Kent Lines Limited, had one of the other companies in which he was interested purchase tugs to do this work. Unfortunately, however, from the time when the large tankers first started servicing the refinery in April 1960, up to and including the date of the trial, difficulty was encountered in having these tugs used by the Saint John Harbour pilots and it accordingly became necessary to employ the services of the appellant's tug boats which were the only other such boats available in the harbour.

On March 24, 1961, no firm arrangements having been made as to the employment of these tugs by the respondent during the forthcoming months, the Saint John Tug Boat Company Limited wrote to Kent Lines Limited in the following terms:

Dear Sirs:

This is to advise you that unless some special arrangement is made, on or after early in April when the winter port season closes here, we will only have two tug boats available for assisting in docking and undocking ships in St. John Harbour.

If we do not hear from you we will assume that you are making arrangements elsewhere for any additional tugs that you may require.

On the same day, C.N. Wilson, the president of the appellant company, wrote to Mr. Irving, in part, as follows:

My dear Kenneth:

I am enclosing herewith copy of letter which we are sending to Kent Line Ltd. concerning tug services in St. John Harbour this coming summer.

.....

We do appreciate the work we have received from Kent Line Ltd. and thought it was only fair to advise both them and you of our plans for this coming summer. If more than two tugs are required from us during the coming season, we feel that we could arrange to provide them if we are advised to this effect now. However special rates will need to be agreed upon as it would be absolutely impossible for us to provide them at the present tariff rates.

This was followed by a letter of March 27 addressed to Kent Lines Limited which was also brought to the attention of K.C. Irving and which is now claimed as containing the terms under which the appellant's tug *Ocean Rockswift* was made available to the respondent during the period covered by the statement of claim. That letter reads:

Gentlemen:

With further reference to our letter of the 24th inst. and our telephone conversation of this morning, we would say that as it looks now, we will probably be keeping available for assisting in docking and undocking ships in St. John Harbour this coming summer, the tugs "OCEAN HAWK II", 900 h.p. Diesel; and the "OCEAN WEKA", 400 h.p. Diesel.

We could make either the tug "OCEAN ROCKSWIFT", Steam, 1,000 h.p. and/or the tug "OCEAN OSPREY", Steam, 1,000 h.p. available for your large tankers at a cost per day each of $450.00. This of course would take in Sundays and holidays as well as the ordinary working day and would be for all days during the month regardless of whether the tug was working or not.

If at any time, more than two tugs were required and the "ROCKSWIFT" and/or the "OSPREY" were used on work other than large tankers, we would give you credit at the tariff rate on the earnings of this tug, less 10% for handling.

As we have other enquiries concerning the "OCEAN OSPREY" and the "OCEAN ROCK-SWIFT", we would appreciate your early decision as to whether or not the above is of interest to you.

There was no written acceptance of this offer, but it is not disputed that the respondent made verbal arrangements for the rental of the *Ocean Rockswift* for a period of one month commencing June 13, 1961, for the services and at the rates set out in the letter of March 27, nor is it disputed that this arrangement was expressly extended twice, each time for a period of two weeks and it appears to be agreed also that these extensions were intended to cover the time until the arrival of an Irving tug which was expected to be available sometime in the month of August. There is evidence also that Mr. L.L. Henning, the president of the respondent company, was succeeded in this position by a Mr. W.R. Forsythe in August 1961, and that before leaving Saint John he had told the president of the appellant company "that he should for any further extensions contact Mr. Forsythe".

Neither Mr. Forsythe nor any other officer of the respondent formally authorized any further extension of the agreement but the services of the *Ocean Rockswift* continued to be employed by the respondent until late in February 1962, and accounts for these services were rendered by the appellant to the respondent each month, up to and including February 28, 1962. Each of these accounts carried the heading: "To Rental '*Ocean Rockswift*' As Per our letter of March 27th, 1961" and disclosed that the rental was $450 per day "Less Credit Note Attached".

The effect of this method of billing was that the respondent company was charged $450 per day for the privilege of having this tug "standing by" and that the normal tariff rate paid by other companies for the tug's services was deducted from the $450, but this deduction was reduced by 10 per cent to defray the appellant's "handling charges". The way this worked out in respect of the larger tankers which were escorted to the refinery was that the normal tariff rate for each such tanker was paid by Kent Lines Limited, and this amount was duly deducted from the $450 daily "stand-by" charge which was billed to the respondent. When the respondent found that the appellant was deducting the 10 per cent for handling charges in respect of these tankers, it protested and in giving judgment at the trial the learned trial judge, in my opinion quite rightly, excluded this charge in respect of such tankers from the total bill.

There does not appear to have been any difference in the use which the respondent made of the *Ocean Rockswift* after July 31, 1961, nor, apart from its complaint about the 10 per cent handling charge, did the respondent give any indication to the appellant as to any change in the arrangements for the tug's employment or the *per diem* charges being made for its services until late in February 1962, but all the appellant's invoices for the services of the tug since July 1961, remain unpaid, and the respondent now denies liability for all charges after the middle of August in that year.

In finding the respondent liable for payment of these invoices up to and including February 28 (less the 10 per cent adjustment above referred to) the learned trial judge stated:

> Although the plaintiff over the period in question was pressing Mr. Forsythe for payment, there was no written or verbal notification to it that the defendant refused to accept liability as invoiced for the rental of the *Rockswift*. Even in the latter part of February, 1962, when Mr. Forsythe was invited by Mr. Keith Wilson "to take her off charter", Mr. Forsythe said he would have to talk to Mr. Irving first.

> I find that the defendant knew that the *Ocean Rockswift* continued after August 1, 1961, in commission on call to assist and did assist the large tankers during the period in question, and that the plaintiff expected payment on a rental basis for its being kept in commission. The defendant had ample opportunity to notify the plaintiff that it did not accept any liability on that basis, but did not do so. The defendant acquiesced in the tug being so employed. It had and took the benefit of such stand-by service and the probable avoidance of demurrage charges.

> .....

If it were assumed, as respondent's counsel contends, that it was the intention and understanding of both parties that the offer of hire should come to an end on August 15, 1961, or that its life was in any event limited to September 21 of that year, then it would appear to follow that in making the "stand-by" services of the tug available after that date the appellant was making a new offer and the invoices make it clear that it was an offer for the same services at the same rate. The same considerations would apply with equal force to the services rendered after December 15 if it were assumed, as the Appeal Division found, that the original offer did not extend beyond that date.

The question to be determined on this appeal is whether or not the respondent's course of conduct during the months in question constituted a continuing acceptance of these offers so as to give rise to a binding contract to pay for the "stand-by" services of the tug at the rate specified in the invoices furnished by the appellant.

The test of whether conduct, unaccompanied by any verbal or written undertaking, can constitute an acceptance of an offer so as to bind the acceptor to the fulfilment of the contract, is made the subject of comment in Anson on Contracts, 21st ed., p. 28, where it is said:

> The test of such a contract is an objective and not a subjective one, that is to say, the intention which the law will attribute to a man is always that which his conduct bears when reasonably construed, and not that which was present in his own mind. So if A allows B to work for him under such circumstances that no reasonable man would suppose that B meant to do the work for nothing, A will be liable to pay for it. The doing of the work is the offer; the permission to do it, or the acquiescence in its being done, constitutes the acceptance.

In this connection reference is frequently made to the following statement contained in the judgment of Lord Blackburn in *Smith v. Hughes* [(1871), L.R. 6 Q.B. 597 at 607], which I adopt as a proper test under the present circumstances:

> If, whatever a man's real intention may be he so conducts himself that a reasonable man would believe that he was consenting to the terms proposed by the other party and that other party upon that belief enters into a contract with him, the man thus conducting himself would be equally bound as if he had intended to agree to the other party's terms.

The American authorities on the same subject are well summarized in Williston on Contracts, 3rd ed., vol. I, para. 91A where it is said:

> Silence may be so deceptive that it may become necessary for one who receives beneficial services to speak in order to escape the inference of a promise to pay for them. It is immaterial in this connection whether the services are requested and the silence relates merely to an undertaking to pay for them, or whether the services are rendered without a preliminary request but with knowledge on the part of the person receiving them that they are rendered with the expectation of payment. In either case, the ordinary implication is that the services are to be

paid for at their fair value, or at the offered price, if that is known to the offeree before he accepts them.

It must be appreciated that mere failure to disown responsibility to pay compensation for services rendered is not of itself always enough to bind the person who has had the benefit of those services. The circumstances must be such as to give rise to an inference that the alleged acceptor has consented to the work being done on the terms upon which it was offered before a binding contract will be implied.

As was observed by Bowen L.J. in *Falcke v. Scottish Imperial Ins. Co.* [(1886), 34 Ch. D. 234 at 248]:

> Liabilities are not to be forced upon people behind their backs any more than you can confer a benefit upon a man against his will.

Like the learned trial judge, however, I would adopt the following excerpt from Smith's Leading Cases, 13th ed. at p. 156 where it is said:

> But if a person knows that the consideration is being rendered for his benefit with an expectation that he will pay for it, then if he acquiesces in its being done, taking the benefit of it when done, he will be taken impliedly to have requested its being done: and that will import a promise to pay for it.

In the present case the ordinary tariff rates for the tug's normal services were being paid by Kent Lines Limited, a company closely associated with the respondent, and it is perhaps for this reason that, in the absence of any formal agreement fixing any additional rate, the respondent took no steps to either pay for or dispense with the "stand-by" services which continued to be rendered for its benefit until February 1962. . . .

Neither the absence of an express agreement nor the fact that the respondent did not consider itself liable to pay for the "stand-by" services after July 31 can, however, be treated as determining the issue raised by this appeal. The question is not whether the appellant is entitled to recover from the respondent under the terms of an express or recorded agreement, but rather whether an agreement is to be implied from the respondent's acquiescence in the tug's services being supplied for its benefit during the period for which the claim is now made.

In my view the respondent must be taken to have known that the *Ocean Rockswift* was being kept "standing by" for its use until the end of February 1962, and to have known also that the appellant expected to be paid for this special service at the *per diem* rate specified in the monthly invoices which were furnished to it, but the matter drifted from day to day without any move being made on the respondent's behalf to either dispense with the service or complain about the charge. I do not think it was unreasonable to draw the conclusion from this course of conduct that the respondent was accepting the continuing special services on the terms proposed in the March letters and the appellant is accordingly entitled to recover the sums charged in the invoices up to and including the month of February 1962 (subject to the adjustment as to handling charges) as being money due pursuant to a contract which was concluded by the respondent's own acquiescence.

[The judgment of the trial judge was accordingly restored and damages of $79,639.00 were awarded, representing charges until February 28, 1962.]

ELIASON v. HENSHAW

(1819), 4 Wheaton 225, 4 U.S. (L. Ed.) 556

WASHINGTON J. This is an action, brought by the defendant in error [plaintiff in the court below and sellers], to recover damages for the non-performance of an agreement, alleged to have been entered into by the plaintiffs in error [defendants in the court below and alleged buyers], for the purchase of a quantity of flour at a stipulated price. The evidence of this contract given in the Court below, . . . is to the following effect: A letter from the plaintiffs . . . to the defendant, dated the 10th of February, 1813, in which they say:

> Capt. Conn informs us that you have a quantity of flour to dispose of. We are in the practice of purchasing flour at all times, in Georgetown, and will be glad to serve you, either in receiving your flour in store, when the markets are dull, and disposing of it when the markets will answer to advantage, or we will purchase at market price when delivered; if you are disposed to engage two or three hundred barrels at present, we will give you 9 dollars 50 cents per barrel, deliverable the first water in Georgetown, or any service we can. If you should want an advance, please write us by mail, and will send you part of the money in advance.

In a postscript they add, "Please write by return of wagon whether you accept our offer." This letter was sent from the house at which the writer then was, about two miles from Harper's Ferry, to the defendant in error at his mill, at Mill Creek, distant about 20 miles from Harper's Ferry, by a wagoner then employed by the defendant to haul flour from his mill to Harper's Ferry, and then about to return home with his wagon. He delivered the letter to the defendant on the 14th of the same month, to which an answer, dated the succeeding day, was written by the defendant, addressed to the plaintiffs at Georgetown, and despatched by a mail which left Mill Creek on the 19th, being the first regular mail from that place to Georgetown. In this letter the writer says,

> Your favour of the 10th inst. was handed me by Mr. Chenoweth last evening. I take the earliest opportunity to answer it by post. Your proposal to engage 300 barrels of flour, delivered in Georgetown, by the first water, at 9 dollars 50 cents per barrel, I accept, and shall send on the flour by the first boats that pass down from where my flour is stored on the river; as to any advance, will be unnecessary—payment on delivery is all that is required.

On the 25th of the same month, the plaintiffs addressed to the defendant an answer to the above, dated at Georgetown, in which they acknowledge receipt of it, and add,

> Not having heard from you before, had quite given over the expectation of getting your flour, more particularly as we requested an answer by return of wagon the next day, and as we did not get it, had bought all we wanted.

The wagoner, by whom the plaintiff's first letter was sent, informed them, when he received it, that he should not probably return to Harper's Ferry, and he did not in fact return in the defendant's employ. The flour was sent down to Georgetown some time in March, and the delivery of it to the plaintiffs was regularly tendered and refused. . . .

It is an undeniable principle of the law of contracts, that an offer of a bargain by one person to another, imposes no obligation upon the former, until it is accepted by the latter, according to the terms in which the offer was made. Any qualification of, or departure from, those terms, invalidates the offer, unless the same be agreed to by the person who made it. Until the terms of the agreement have received the assent of both parties, the negotiation is open, and imposes no obligation upon either.

In this case, the plaintiffs in error offered to purchase from the defendant two or three hundred barrels of flour, to be delivered at Georgetown, by the first water, and to pay for the same 9 dollars 50 cents per barrel. To the letter containing this offer, they required an answer by the return of the wagon, by which the letter was despatched. This wagon was, at that time, in the service of the defendant, and employed by him in hauling flour from his mill to Harper's Ferry, near to which place the plaintiffs then were. The meaning of the writers was obvious. They could easily calculate by the usual length of time which was employed by this wagon, in travelling from Harper's Ferry to Mill Creek, and back again with a load of flour, about what time they should receive the desired answer, and, therefore, it was entirely unimportant, whether it was sent by that, or another wagon, or in any other manner, provided it was sent to *Harper's Ferry*, and was not delayed beyond the time which was ordinarily employed by wagons engaged in hauling flour from the defendant's mill to Harper's Ferry. Whatever uncertainty there might have been as to the *time* when the answer would be received, there was none as to the *place* to which it was to be sent; this was distinctly indicated by the mode pointed out for the conveyance of the answer. The place, therefore, to which the answer was to be sent, constituted an essential part of the plaintiff's offer.

It appears, however, . . . that no answer to this letter was at any time sent to the plaintiffs, at Harper's Ferry. Their offer, it is true, was accepted by the terms of a letter addressed Georgetown, and received by the plaintiffs at that place; but an acceptance communicated at a place different from that pointed out by the plaintiffs, and forming a part of their proposal, imposed no obligation binding upon them, unless they had acquiesced in it, which they declined doing.

It is no argument, that an answer was received at Georgetown; the plaintiffs in error had a right to dictate the terms upon which they would purchase the flour, and, unless they were complied with, they were not bound by them. All their arrangements may have been made with a view to the circumstance of place, and they were the only judges of its importance. There was, therefore, no contract concluded between these parties. . . .

NOTE and QUESTION

1. Could the seller have accepted by dispatching a rider who arrived at Harper's Ferry before the wagon? If so, when would the acceptance be effective?

2. The cases in this section involve bilateral contracts. Compare the results in cases of unilateral contracts, where the acceptance must be strictly in accordance with the terms prescribed in the offer, unless this is waived by the offeror. See *Baughman v. Rampart Resources Ltd.*, [1995] 6 W.W.R. 99 (B.C. C.A.).

CARMICHAEL v. BANK OF MONTREAL

[1972] 3 W.W.R. 175, 25 D.L.R. (3d) 570 (Man. Q.B.)

HAMILTON J. The plaintiff seeks specific performance of an offer to purchase the house owned by the defendant at Portage la Prairie, or damages in the alternative.

The local manager of the defendant, on instructions, listed the house with a real estate broker, Cuthbert-Lyon Ltd. (hereinafter called Cuthbert), on a multiple listing basis for sale at $28,900. The listing agreement permitted all members of the Manitoba Real Estate Association to act as agents for the bank in attempting to sell the house. Cuthbert became the listing agent and all other agents became sub-agents. . . .

[The plaintiff made an offer to purchase the house for $26,000 through Tilley, a sub-agent, who sent the offer to Cuthbert. Cuthbert in turn forwarded this offer to the defendant's manager.]

On September 2, 1971, defendant's manager received instructions to extend an offer giving plaintiff until September 3, 1971, to purchase the house for $27,500. No particular time of day was specified in the instructions from the manager's superiors, however, the manager and Cuthbert agreed that plaintiff would have until 6:00 p.m. on September 3rd to accept this offer (referred to by the witnesses as a counter-offer). Cuthbert was instructed to advise plaintiff of the bank's offer. This request by the bank was confirmed by letter of September 2nd from the defendant to Cuthbert. The letter reads:

> Referring to your letter of 31st August and our telephone conversation of today, this letter is to confirm our request to you to make a counter-offer to Mr. Carmichael in the amount of $27,500.00 cash. This counter-offer is to expire on the 3rd day of September, 1971.

On September 2nd, Cuthbert wrote Tilley confirming the terms of the defendant's letter and adding the time of expiry, "to expire Friday, September 3, 1971, at 6 p.m.".

Although Cuthbert, in his letter, asked Tilley to "please advise our firm directly in correspondence when you have reached a decision with Mr. Carmichael", this method of acceptance was not referred to in the defendant's letter to Cuthbert nor in the *viva voce* evidence of the bank manager or of Mr. Cuthbert.

Tilley was unable to contact the plaintiff until just before noon on September 3rd. The plaintiff was undecided whether or not to accept the bank's offer to sell to him at $27,500 and wished to view the property again with his wife. By the time Mrs. Carmichael was free and the keys could be obtained from Cuthbert, it was 5:00 p.m. A decision was made after a 10-minute view of the house to accept the offer of $27,500. I find that it was the effort of Tilley that finally closed the sale and persuaded the plaintiff to accept the bank's offer. . . .

[The plaintiff then returned to Tilley's office and at 5:30 p.m. signed the following document, which Tilley had prepared.]

> We hereby wish to confirm that Mr. W. Carmichael (spelling not clear) agrees to meet your counter offer in the amount of $27,500 cash.
>
> Counter offer in the amount of $27,500 accepted by Purchaser.

Tilley testified that the time of 5:45 p.m. was placed on the document after it was signed and I accept that evidence.

Tilley telephoned Cuthbert's office but received no answer. He then telephoned defendant's bank and asked for the manager. On being advised that the manager had left for the day he asked for the assistant manager and advised the person he thought to be the assistant manager that Mr. Carmichael had accepted the counter-offer. On being told by this person that he did not have authority to accept the offer, Tilley requested a note be made of the time of his call and placed on the manager's desk.

Tilley then telephoned the bank manager's home and on being advised he was not in, left a message for the manager to call. He then telephoned Cuthbert's home, was advised that he was not at home, but asked if he might deliver a letter to the home. Being told that he might, Tilley went to the Cuthbert home and at approximately 6:15 p.m. left the letter of acceptance there.

In the meantime the manager had returned to the bank "either at one minute before or one minute after six" and was advised of the nature of Tilley's call. When he returned to his home he received the message and telephoned Tilley. Tilley told him that the bank's offer to sell to Mr. Carmichael at $27,500 had been accepted. The bank manager told Tilley the acceptance was too late and that the offer could only have been accepted if it had been in writing and delivered to Cuthbert's office. . . .

Tilley being an agent of the defendant was therefore authorized, in fact required, to place all reasonable offers before the vendor. He had the same authority as Cuthbert to pass on to plaintiff the counter-offer. It was defendant who was offering to sell to plaintiff. Plaintiff accepted defendant's offer and that acceptance was conveyed to defendant through its agent, Tilley.

To complete the chain of binding contract there must be the extension of an offer, its acceptance and the communication of that acceptance to the offeror, in this case the vendor. I find there was effective communication of plaintiff's acceptance of defendant's counter-offer.

There is no doubt that Tilley, initially the vendor's agent, was still clothed with authority to deal with prospective purchasers and to pass on communications between the vendor and the purchaser. His telephone call to the defendant's branch before 6:00 p.m. was an act relating to his agency relationship. His advising defendant's employee on the telephone that the counter-offer had been accepted by plaintiff effectively constituted the plaintiff's communication of his acceptance to defendant.

Defendant takes the position that this telephone call was not an effective acceptance because (1) it was not in writing, and (2) because the employee at the bank was not an official authorized to receive the acceptance. The evidence showed, however, that the manager returned to the bank office about 6:00 p.m. and was informed of the telephone call and acceptance of the counter-offer. Although this acceptance passed through several hands it was received by the bank manager who without question had the right to receive that notice on behalf of the defendant. The bank manager, in cross-examination, said he returned to the bank at about 6:00 p.m. but could not say if it was then one minute before or one minute after six. I was not impressed by the bank manager when he discussed details of this nature and find that he was aware of the acceptance of the counter-offer prior to the 6:00 p.m. deadline.

The manager of the defendant bank took the position that the offer could not be accepted other than in writing. He said in evidence written notice should have been delivered prior to the 6:00 p.m. deadline, either to the agent Cuthbert or to the bank. The law appears clear that an offer made in writing may be accepted by parole [*sic*] or in fact by the conduct of the parties. To establish a contract there must be an offer, its acceptance, and the communication of that acceptance to the offeror. . . .

The verbal communication of the acceptance of the counter-offer to a responsible person in charge at the defendant's bank was, in my opinion, sufficient acceptance of the offer. In any event the communication went further than this and came to the attention of the manager of the defendant prior to the 6:00 p.m. deadline.

Even if this communication had not been made I would have held that the delivery of the written acceptance to the residence of Cuthbert at 6:15 p.m. constituted sufficient compliance with the terms of the counter-offer. The Cuthbert office had closed at 5:30 p.m. and the bank manager was absent from the bank between 4:00 p.m. and 6:00 p.m. (and was not expected back) making it impossible for Tilley or the plaintiff to accept the counter-offer in the way Cuthbert and the bank manager say it should have been accepted—by delivery of a written acceptance to one of them.

He who seeks equity must do equity.

It is surely to be presumed that if one party makes an offer to another, giving a period of time for acceptance, the offeror must make it possible for the offer to be accepted. One cannot as here, intentionally or otherwise, give until 6:00 p.m. for acceptance, then absent himself so that he cannot be reached. It was an implied term of the offer standing open until 6:00 p.m. that there would be some person available until that time to whom acceptance could be given. . . .

If I am wrong in finding that the acceptance was communicated orally but effectively to the manager at the bank by 6:00 p.m. then I am of the opinion that delivery of the written acceptance of the bank's counter-offer to Mrs. Cuthbert, who we found later was an officer of Cuthbert, was made within a reasonable time and that this constituted substantial and sufficient compliance with the terms of the counter-offer.

In the result, I find a binding offer and acceptance.

[It appears that on September 8, 1971, the bank had accepted an offer from another prospective purchaser. Nevertheless, Hamilton J. held that the plaintiff was entitled to an order for specific performance of his contract of sale.]

NOTE and QUESTIONS

1. Would there have been a sufficient acceptance if one of the bank tellers had taken Tilley's telephone call before 6 p.m.?

2. On what basis could a term be implied that the offeror must not make it impossible to accept the offer in time?

3. Why was communication of the written acceptance to Tilley not sufficient? Compare *Struthmann v. Routly*, [1994] O.J. No. 1535 (Gen. Div.).

4. In *Whitehall Estates Ltd. v. McCallum* (1975), 63 D.L.R. (3d) 320 (B.C. C.A.), Taggart J.A. found a telephoned acceptance to the realtor of a counter-offer to sell property to be binding. A similar approach was taken in *Humble Invt. Ltd. v. N.M. Skalbania Ltd.* (1983), 22 Sask. R. 81 (C.A.). In contrast, the Manitoba Court of Appeal, while approving *Whitehall Estates* in principle, has taken a stricter position in practice. See *Jen-Den Investments Ltd. v. Northwest Farms Ltd.*, [1978] 1 W.W.R. 290 (Man. C.A.). The court reiterated its position in *Megill-Stephenson Co v. Woo* (1989), 59 D.L.R. (4th) 146 (Man. C.A.), in which it commented, at 150-51:

> In spite of the repeal of the *Statute of Frauds*, [in 1983 in Manitoba only] the practice in dealing with the purchase and sale of land is to have the contracts in written form, and that was the obvious expectation between the parties in this dispute.

The requirements of the Statute of Frauds are discussed in Chapter 4, and in particular section 8, *infra*.

5. Communication of Acceptance

(a) INSTANTANEOUS METHODS OF COMMUNICATION

BRINKIBON LTD. v. STAHAG STAHL UND STAHLWARENHANDELSGESELLSCHAFT mbH

[1983] 2 A.C. 34, [1982] 2 W.L.R. 264, [1982] 1 All E.R. 293 (H.L.)

LORD WILBERFORCE My Lords, the appellants (the buyers) desire to sue in this country the respondents (the sellers), an Austrian company, for breach of an alleged contract for the supply of steel. In order to do so, they must obtain leave to serve notice of their writ on the sellers under one or other of the provisions of RSC Ord II, rI(I). Those relied on are paras (*f*) and (*g*). To satisfy para (*f*), the buyers must show that the contract was 'made within the jurisdiction'; . . .

The question whether a contract was made within the jurisdiction will often admit of a simple answer: if both parties are in England at the time of making it, or if it is contained in a single document signed by both parties in England, there is no difficulty. But in the case of contracts involving negotiations, where one party is abroad, the answer may be difficult to find. Sophisticated analysis may be required to decide when the last counter-offer was made into a contract by acceptance, or at what point a clear consensus was reached and by virtue of what words spoken or of what conduct. In the case of successive telephone conversations it may indeed be most artificial to ask where the contract was made; if one asked the parties, they might say they did not know, or care. The place of making a contract is usually irrelevant as regards validity, or interpretation, or enforcement. Unfortunately it remains in Ord II as a test for purposes of jurisdiction, and courts have to do their best with it.

In the present case it seems that if there was a contract (a question which can only be decided at the trial), it was preceded by and possibly formed by a number of telephone conversations and telexes between London and Vienna, and there are a number of possible combinations on which reliance can be placed. At this stage we must take the alternatives which provide reasonable evidence of a contract in order to see if the test is satisfied. There are two. (i) A telex dated 3 May 1979 from the sellers in Vienna, said to amount to a counter-offer, followed by a telex from the buyers in London to the sellers in Vienna dated 4 May 1979, said to amount to an acceptance. (ii) The above telex dated 3 May 1979 from the sellers followed by action, by way of opening a letter of credit, said to have amounted to an acceptance by conduct.

The first of these alternatives neatly raises the question whether an acceptance by telex as sent from London but received in Vienna causes a contract to be made in London or Vienna. If the acceptance had been sent by post, or by telegram, then, on existing authorities, it would have been complete when put into the hands of the Post Office, in London. If on the other hand it had been telephoned, it would have been complete when heard by the offeror, in Vienna. So in which category is a telex communication to be placed? Existing authority of the Court of Appeal decides in favour of the latter category, i.e. a telex is to be assimilated to other methods of instantaneous communications: see *Entores Ltd. v. Miles Far East Corp.*, [1955] 2 Q.B. 327. . . . The buyers ask that this case, which has stood for 30 years, should now be reviewed.

Now such review as is necessary must be made against the background of the law as to the making of contracts. The general rule, it is hardly necessary to state, is that a contract is formed *when* acceptance of an offer is communicated by the offeree to the offeror. And if it is necessary to determine *where* a contract is formed (as to which I have already commented) it appears logical that this should be at the place where acceptance is communicated to the offeror. In the common case of contracts, whether oral or in writing inter praesentes, there is no difficulty; and again logic demands that even where there is not mutual presence at the same place and at the same time, if communication is instantaneous, for example by telephone or radio communication, the same result should follow.

Then there is the case (very common) of communication at a distance, to meet which the so-called 'postal rule' has developed. . . . In these cases too it seems logical to say that the place, as well as the time, of acceptance should be *where* (as *when*) the acceptance is put into the charge of the post office.

In this situation, with a general rule covering instantaneous communication inter praesentes, or at a distance, with an exception applying to non-instantaneous communication at a distance, how should communications by telex be categorised? In *Entores Ltd. v. Miles Far East Corp.* the Court of Appeal classified them with instantaneous communications. Their ruling, which has passed into the textbooks, including *Williston on Contracts*, appears not to have caused either adverse comment, or any difficulty to businessmen. I would accept it as a general rule. Where the condition of simultaneity is met, and where it appears to be within the mutual intention of the parties that contractual exchanges should take place in this way, I think it a sound rule, but not necessarily a universal rule.

Since 1955 the use of telex communication has been greatly expanded, and there are many variants on it. The senders and recipients may not be the principals to the contemplated contract. They may be servants or agents with limited authority. The message may not reach, or be intended to reach, the designated recipient immediately: messages may be sent out of office hours, or at night, with the intention, or on the assumption, that they will be read at a later time. There may be some error or default at the recipient's end which prevents receipt at the time contemplated and believed in by the sender. The message may have been sent and/or received through machines operated by third persons. And many other variations may occur. No universal rule can cover all such cases; they must be resolved by reference to the intentions of the parties, by sound business practice and in some cases by a judgment where the risks should lie. . . .

The present case is, as *Entores Ltd. v. Miles Far East Corp.* itself, the simple case of instantaneous communication between principals, and, in accordance with the general rule, involves that the contract (if any) was made when and where the acceptance was received. This was on 4 May 1979 in Vienna.

The alternative argument under this head was that the contract was made by an offer made from Vienna (as above, on 3 May 1979) and an acceptance by conduct in the United Kingdom. The conduct relied on was the giving of instructions by the buyers to set up a letter of credit, as requested in the sellers' telex of 3 May 1979. The buyers' telex of 4 May 1979 opened with the words: 'confirm having opened our irrevocable letter of credit no: 0761/79 on account of midestrade est., chiasso, switzerland . . . 'Midestrade Est is, it appears, the company behind the buyers, a fact which raises the question whether a letter of credit on their account satisfied the terms of the sellers' request. I need not come to a conclusion on this point because I am satisfied that the letter of credit was not opened in the United Kingdom. Instructions were indeed given by the buyers to their bank in the United Kingdom to open it, and the bank gave instructions on 4 May 1979 to their correspondent in Vienna, but these steps were between the buyers and their agents only. They could not amount, in my opinion, to an acceptance of the offer of 3 May 1979. This took place, if at all, when the correspondent bank in Vienna notified the sellers; this they did in Vienna. On neither ground, therefore, can it be said that the contract was made within the jurisdiction and the case under para (*f*) of rI(I) must fail. . . .

LORD FRASER OF TULLYBELTON [who concurred in the speech of Lord Wilberforce, added the following reasons for treating an acceptance by telex as effective on receipt.] Secondly, once the message has been received on the offeror's telex machine, it is not unreasonable to treat it as delivered to the principal offeror, because it is his responsibility to arrange for prompt handling of messages within his own office. Thirdly, a party (the acceptor) who tries to send a message by telex can generally tell if his message has not been received on the other party's (the offeror's) machine, whereas the offeror, of course, will not know if an unsuccessful attempt has been made to send an acceptance to him. It is therefore convenient that the acceptor, being in the better position, should have the responsibility of ensuring that his message is received. For these reasons I think it is right that in the ordinary simple case, such as I take this to be, the general rule and not the postal rule should apply. But I agree with both my noble and learned friends that the general rule will not cover all the many variations that may occur with telex messages.

[The concurring speeches of Lord Brandon of Oakbrook, Lord Russell of Killowen and Lord Bridge of Harwich are omitted.]

NOTES and QUESTIONS

1. Determination of when and where a contract is made is relevant to a number of issues, of which the jurisdictional question in *Brinkibon* is only one. For example, determination of when an offer has been accepted is obviously important to efforts by the offeree to revoke the offer; see *infra*, section 6. Note that rules for determining the jurisdiction of courts need not necessarily follow the substantive rules of contract formation. Where contracts are concluded by instantaneous means of communication, modern Canadian cases have, as in *Brinkibon*, usually held that, at least for jurisdictional purposes, the contract is formed where the acceptance is received. See *Re Viscount Supply Co.* (1963), 40 D.L.R. (2d) 501 (Ont. H.C.); *Re Modern Fashions Ltd.*; *Sennett v. Tape Estate* (1986), 45 Sask. R. 314 (Q.B.) and *National Bank of Can. v. Cedar Dale Industries Inc.* (1989), 97 N.B.R. (2d) 352 (C.A.), affirming (1988), 92 N.B.R. (2d) 199 (Q.B.); *McDonald & Sons Ltd. v. Export Packers Co.* (1979), 95 D.L.R. (3d) 174 (B.C. S.C.).

The Civil Code of Québec, Book 5, Obligations, Ch. II, Contracts, s. III, provides:

> **Art. 1387.** A contract is formed when and where acceptance is received by the offeror, regardless of the method of communication used, and even though the parties have agreed to reserve agreement as to secondary terms.

2. In *Eastern Power Ltd. v. Azienda Comunale Energia & Ambiente* (1999), 178 D.L.R. (4th) 409 (Ont. C.A.), the court in deciding on jurisdiction applied the instantaneous rule with respect to an acceptance by fax, at 418. A similar approach to faxed acceptance was found outside the jurisdictional context, in *John Balcom Sales Inc. v. Poirier* (1991), 49 C.P.C. (2d) 180 (N.S. Co. Ct.), where an offer to purchase incorporating an agreement to pay the realtor's commission was transmitted to the vendors in Ottawa by fax from Berwick, King's County, Nova Scotia. On the same day the document was signed by the vendors and transmitted back to the realtor at Berwick by fax. The court held, contrary to the Small Claims Court, that the "mail box doctrine" did not apply to facsimile transmissions. At 187 it stated: "The considerations which made it highly practical, if not imperative, in the interests of commerce, for the offeree to have knowledge in a timely fashion that he had a firm contract do not apply to facsimile transmissions. The communication is instantaneous. The offeree could easily have confirmed within minutes that they had a binding contract. I, therefore, find that the contract was executed at Berwick." This appears to reflect the position in Australia; see Young, "Current Topics" (1992), 66 Aust. L.J. 326.

3. At 4 p.m. EDT, A in Toronto sent an offer by e-mail to B in Fort McMurray, Alberta to sell certain earth-moving equipment. B sent an acceptance by e-mail from Fort McMurray at 3:30 p.m. MDT, but when it was received in A's office everyone had left for the night. Although A's office opened at 8:30 a.m. EDT the following morning, A only read B's acceptance at 10:00 a.m. When was the contract formed? Consider *The Brimnes*, [1975] Q.B. 929 (C.A.).

4. Many academics (*e.g.*, Farnsworth, *Contracts*, s. 3.22 at 317 (2nd ed. 1998)), feel that the receipt rule should apply to all substantially instantaneous means of communication, such as the telephone, fax and e-mail. Fasciano argues, however, that the receipt rule should only apply where the method of communication is substantially instantaneous and two-way. Thus, it should apply to telephone, fax and electronic data interchange, if the offeror's machine can acknowledge accurate receipt. It should not, however, apply to e-mail acceptances sent via the Internet as these are not necessarily substantially instantaneous or two-way. Internet e-mail acceptances should be effective on dispatch when the offeree successfully sends the message using an independent service provider or the offeree's own server passes the message onto the Internet. "Internet Electronic Mail: A Last Bastion for the Mailbox Rule" (1997), 25 Hofstra L. Rev. 971. For a general discussion of the law in this area, see Coote "The Instantaneous Transmission of Acceptances" (1971), 4 N.Z.U.L. Rev 331, and see also Dickie, "When and Where are Electronic Contracts Concluded?" (1998), 49 N.I.L.Q. 332.

5. The globalization of markets suggests a need for a unified approach to these issues. Compare the following approaches:

(a) The Vienna Convention (*supra*) provides in Art. 18(2) that: "An acceptance of an offer becomes effective at the moment the indication of assent reaches the offeror." It defines "reaches" in Art. 24: "For the purposes of this Part of the Convention, an offer, declaration of acceptance or any other indication of intention "reaches" the addressee when it is made orally to him or delivered by any other means to him personally, to his place of business or mailing address or, if he does not have a place of business or mailing address, to his habitual residence." The Convention also provides in Art. 18(3): "However, if, by virtue of the offer or as a result of practices which the parties have established between themselves or of usage, the offeree may indicate assent by performing an act, such as one relating to the dispatch of the goods or payment of the price, without notice to the offeror, the acceptance is effective at the moment the act is performed. . . ."

(b) Electronic commerce is an increasingly important component of international trade. The UNCITRAL Model Law on Electronic Commerce provides *inter alia*:

Article 2(a) 'Data message' means information generated, sent, received or stored by electronic, optical or similar means including, but not limited to, electronic data interchange (EDI), electronic mail, telegram, telex or telecopy;

Article 11(1) In the context of contract formation, unless otherwise agreed by the parties, an offer and the acceptance of an offer may be expressed by means of data messages. Where a data message is used in the formation of a contract, that contract shall not be denied validity or enforceability on the sole ground that a data message was used for that purpose.

Article 15(1) Unless otherwise agreed between the originator and the addressee, the dispatch of a data message occurs when it enters an information system outside the control of the originator or of the person who sent the data message on behalf of the originator.

(2) Unless otherwise agreed between the originator and the addressee, the time of receipt of a data message is determined as follows:

(a) if the addressee has designated an information system for the purpose of receiving data messages, receipt occurs:

(i) at the time when the data message enters the designated information system; or

(ii) if the data message is sent to an information system of the addressee that is not the designated information system, at the time when the data message is retrieved by the addressee;

(b) if the addressee has not designated an information system, receipt occurs when the data message enters an information system of the addressee.

(3) Paragraph (2) applies notwithstanding that the place where the information system is located may be different from the place where the data message is deemed to be received under paragraph (4).

(4) Unless otherwise agreed between the originator and the addressee, a data message is deemed to be dispatched at the place where the originator has its place of business, and is deemed to be received at the place where the addressee has its place of business. For the purposes of this paragraph:

(a) if the originator or the addressee has more than one place of business, the place of business is that which has the closest relationship to the underlying transaction or, where there is no underlying transaction, the principal place of business;

(b) if the originator or the addressee does not have a place of business, reference is to be made to its habitual residence.

The Model Law does not, however, opt for either the dispatch or receipt rule, leaving this to national law on contract formation.

6. In Canada, the federal Uniform Electronic Commerce Act and various provincial statutes such as the Electronic Commerce Act, 2000, S.O. 2000, c. 17, contain provisions based on the UNCITRAL Model Law. There are some distinctions. For example, in contrast to the Model Law, the Canadian legislation provides presumptive rules which deem receipt to occur when the electronic document both enters the information system designated by the addressee and is capable of being retrieved and processed by the addressee. In the case where no information system has been designated, receipt is deemed to occur when the addressee becomes aware of the electronic document in its information system and it becomes capable of being retrieved and processed by the addressee. Section 22(1) of the Ontario Electronic Commerce Act, 2000, for example, provides that the time of the sending of electronic information or an electronic document is when it enters an information system outside of the sender's control, or if the sender and addressee use the same information system, when it is capable of being retrieved and processed by the addressee.

Consumer protection legislation has been extended to include online sales. For example, the Ontario Consumer Protection Act, 2000 requires that suppliers in consumer agreements that are Internet agreements shall provide an express opportunity to accept or decline the agreement or to correct errors immediately after entering into it (s. 38(2)), and shall deliver a copy of the agreement in writing containing prescribed information within a prescribed period (s. 39).

See more generally on matters of consumer protection and electronic commerce, Waite, "Consumer Protection Issues in Internet Commerce" (1999), 32 Can. Bus. L.J. 132; Brownsword and Howells, "When Surfers Start to Shop: Internet Commerce and Contract Law" (1999), 19 Legal Studies 287; and Takach, *Computer Law*, 2nd ed. (2003), Chapter 5.

7. The determination in *Brinkibon* of where acceptance occurred and where the contract was formed was important to the particular English procedural rules concerning whether the English court had jurisdiction over the dispute. Some care is required as the rules of different jurisdictions may vary. Many jurisdictions pay close attention to any express choice by the parties to a contract of the jurisdiction where disputes will be heard, through "forum selection" clauses. Consider how issues of forum selection are related to issues of offer and acceptance in the electronic commerce context in the following case.

RUDDER v. MICROSOFT CORP.

(1999), 2 C.P.R. (4th) 474, 40 C.P.C. (4th) 394 (Ont. S.C.J.)

WINKLER J. This is a motion by the defendant Microsoft for a permanent stay of this intended class proceeding. The motion is based on two alternative grounds, first that the parties have agreed to the exclusive jurisdiction, and venue, of the courts, in King County in the State of Washington in respect of any litigation between them, and secondly, that in any event, Ontario is not the appropriate forum for the conduct of this proceeding and that the service *ex juris* of the Statement of Claim ought to be set aside.

The Microsoft Network ("MSN"), is an online service, providing, *inter alia*, information and services including Internet access to its members. The service is provided to members, around the world, from a "gateway" located in the State of Washington through computer connections most often made over standard telephone lines.

The proposed representative plaintiffs in this action were subscriber members of MSN. Both are law school graduates, one of whom is admitted to the Bar in Ontario while the other worked as a legal researcher. They were associated with the law firm which originally represented the intended class. The plaintiffs claim under the Class Proceedings Act, 1992, S.O., c. 6 on behalf of a Canada-wide class defined as:

> All persons resident in Canada who subscribed for the provision of Internet access or information or services from or through MSN, The Microsoft Network, since September 1, 1995.

This class is estimated to contain some 89,000 MSN members across Canada.

The plaintiffs claim damages for breach of contract, breach of fiduciary duty, misappropriation and punitive damages in the total amount of $75,000,000.00 together with an accounting and injunctive relief. The plaintiffs allege that Microsoft has charged members of MSN and taken payment from their credit cards in breach of contract and that Microsoft has failed to provide reasonable or accurate information concerning accounts. The Statement of Claim was served on Microsoft at its offices in Redmond, Washington on January 5, 1998.

The contract which the plaintiffs allege to have been breached is identified by MSN as a "Member Agreement". Potential members of MSN are required to electronically execute this agreement prior to receiving the services provided by the company. Each Member Agreement contains the following provision:

> 15.1 This Agreement is governed by the laws of the State of Washington, U.S.A., and you consent to the exclusive jurisdiction and venue of courts in King County, Washington, in all disputes arising out of or relating to your use of MSN or your MSN membership.

The defendant relies on this clause in support of its assertion that the intended class proceeding should be permanently stayed.

Although the plaintiffs rely on the contract as the basis for their causes of action, they submit that the court ought not to give credence to the "forum selection clause" contained within. It is stated in support of this contention that the representative plaintiffs read only portions of the Member Agreement and thus had no notice of the forum selection clause. . . .

I cannot accede to these submissions. In my view, the forum selection clause is dispositive and there is nothing in the factual record which persuades me that I should exercise my discretion so as to permit the plaintiffs to avoid the effect of the contractual provision. Accordingly, an order will go granting the relief sought by the defendant. My reasons follow.

Analysis and Disposition

Forum selection clauses are generally treated with a measure of deference by Canadian courts. Madam Justice Huddart, writing for the court in *Sarabia v. "Oceanic Mindoro"* (1996), 4 C.P.C. (4th) 11 (B.C. C.A.), leave to appeal denied [1997] S.C.C.A. No. 69, adopts the view that forum selection clauses should be treated the same as arbitration agreements. She states at 20:

> Since forum selection clauses are fundamentally similar to arbitration agreements, . . . there is no reason for forum selection clauses not to be treated in a manner consistent with the deference shown to arbitration agreements. *Such deference to forum selection clauses achieves greater international commercial certainty, shows respect for the agreements that the parties have signed, and is consistent with the principle of international comity.* (Emphasis added.)

Huddart J.A. further states at 21 that "a court is not bound to give effect to an exclusive jurisdiction clause" but that the choice of the parties should be respected unless "there is strong cause to override the agreement." The burden for a showing of a "strong cause" rests with the plaintiff and the threshold to be surpassed is beyond the mere "balance of convenience". The approach taken by Huddart J.A. is consistent with that adopted by courts in Ontario . . . .

The plaintiffs contend, first, that regardless of the deference to be shown to forum selection clauses, no effect should be given to the particular clause at issue in this case because it does not represent the true agreement of the parties. It is the plaintiffs' submission that the form in which the Member Agreement is provided to potential members of MSN is such that it obscures the forum selection clause. Therefore, the plaintiffs argue, the clause should be treated as if it were the fine print in a contract which must be brought specifically to the attention of the party accepting the terms. Since there was no specific notice given, in the plaintiffs' view, the forum selection clause should be severed from the Agreement which they otherwise seek to enforce.

The argument advanced by the plaintiffs relies heavily on the alleged deficiencies in the technological aspects of electronic formats for presenting the terms of agreements. In other words, the plaintiffs contend that because only a portion of the Agreement was presented on the screen at one time, the terms of the Agreement which were not on the screen are essentially "fine print".

I disagree. The Member Agreement is provided to potential members of MSN in a computer readable form through either individual computer disks or via the Internet at the MSN website. In this case, the plaintiff Rudder . . . received a computer disk as part of a promotion by MSN. The disk contained the operating software for MSN and included a multi-media sign up procedure for persons who wished to obtain the MSN service. As part of the sign-up routine, potential members of MSN were required to acknowledge their acceptance of the terms of the Member Agreement by clicking on an "I Agree" button presented on the computer screen at the same time as the terms of the Member Agreement were displayed.

Rudder admitted . . . that the entire agreement was readily viewable by using the scrolling function on the portion of the computer screen where the Membership Agreement was presented. Moreover, Rudder acknowledged that he "scanned" through part of the Agreement looking for "costs" that would be charged by MSN. He further admitted that once he had found the provisions relating to costs, he did not read the rest of the Agreement. An excerpt from the transcript of Rudder's cross-examination is illustrative:

> Q. 314. I will now take you down to another section. I am now looking at heading 15, which is entitled "General", and immediately underneath that is subsection 15.1. Now, do I take it, when you were scanning, you would have actually scanned past this, and you would have at least seen there was a heading that said "General"? Is that fair? Or did you not even scan all the way through?
>
> A. I did not go all the way down, I can honestly say. Once I found out what it would cost me, that is where I would stop.
>
> Q. 315. So, I take it that you did not read 15.1?
>
> A. No, I definitely did not read this, no.
>
> Q. 316. I now have 15.4 on the screen, and presumably you did not read that either?
>
> A. No, I did not.

Q. 317. I take it, during the whole signup process that you did, you did the whole thing online on the computer . . .

A. Yes.

Q. 318. . . . using the disk? And we will come to the connection. You did not have any voice communication with MSN?

A. No.

Q. 319. Or with Microsoft Corporation?

A. No.

Q. 320. You did not have any written correspondence with them at the time of signup?

A. No.

Q. 321. All right. Now, I take it that, after doing the review of this that you did do, you clicked, "I agree"? Is that what you did?

A. *After I was satisfied with what it was going to cost me, I agreed.* (Emphasis added.)

I have viewed the Member Agreement as it was presented to Rudder during the sign up procedure. All of the terms of the Agreement are displayed in the same format. Although, there are certain terms of the Agreement displayed entirely in upper-case letters, there are no physical differences which make a particular term of the agreement more difficult to read than any other term. In other words, there is no fine print as that term would be defined in a written document. The terms are set out in plain language, absent words that are commonly referred to as "legalese". Admittedly, the entire Agreement cannot be displayed at once on the computer screen, but this is not materially different from a multi-page written document which requires a party to turn the pages. Furthermore, the structure of the sign-up procedure is such that the potential member is presented with the terms of membership twice during the process and must signify acceptance each time. Each time the potential member is provided with the option of disagreeing which terminates the process. The second time the terms are displayed occurs during the online portion of the process and at that time, the potential member is advised via a clear notice on the computer screen of the following:

> . . . The membership agreement includes terms that govern how information about you and your membership may be used. To become a MSN Premier member, you must select "I Agree" to acknowledge your consent to the terms of the membership agreement. If you click "I Agree" without reading the membership agreement, you are still agreeing to be bound by all of the terms of the membership agreement, without limitation. . . ."

On cross-examination, Rudder admitted to having seen the screen containing the notice . . . . [He was then asked the following question.]

Q. 375. Did you understand, when you clicked "I Agree" on this occasion, that you were agreeing to was something that was going to govern your legal relationship surrounding your use of MSN?

A. If you are asking me if I made a mental note, or if I had knowledge of that, no, I did not really pay attention to that. That is a common practice when I sign up on anything. Like I said, my main concern is what the costs are.

It is plain and obvious that there is no factual foundation for the plaintiffs' assertion that any term of the Membership Agreement was analogous to "fine print" in a written contract. What is equally clear is that the plaintiffs seek to avoid the consequences of specific terms of their agreement while at the same time seeking to have others enforced. Neither the form of this contract nor its manner of presentation to potential members are so aberrant as to lead to such an anomalous result. To give effect to the plaintiffs' argument would, rather than advancing the goal of "commercial certainty" . . . move this type of electronic transaction into the realm of commercial absurdity. It would lead to chaos in the marketplace, render ineffectual electronic commerce and undermine the integrity of any agreement entered into through this medium.

On the present facts, the Membership Agreement must be afforded the sanctity that must be given to any agreement in writing . . . . Moreover, given that both of the representative plaintiffs are graduates of law schools and have a professed familiarity with Internet services, their position is particularly indefensible.

[The action brought by the plaintiffs in Ontario was permanently stayed.]

NOTES

1. Contractual parties may expressly agree to resolve their disputes through arbitration rather than pursuant to a forum selection clause. In *Kanitz v. Rogers Cable Inc.* (2002), 58 O.R. (3d) 299 (S.C.J.), Rogers Cable brought a motion for stay of action of class action litigation commenced by various Rogers subscribers for difficulties in their Internet cable service. The stay was granted because of the presence of an arbitration clause, posted by Rogers Cable, on its website as an amendment to the subscribers' user agreements between Rogers and its subscribers, including the plaintiff. The original user agreement provided that amendments to the agreement could be done by regular mail, e-mail, or by posting notice of amendments to the Rogers website. Nordheimer J. used similar reasoning to that in *Rudder* to justify enforcement of the arbitration clause.

2. Even if a court decides it has jurisdiction, it still must determine which set of contract rules should apply to the dispute; that is, the court must decide the "choice of law" or "governing law" issue. Under the conflict of law (or private international law) rules of most jurisdictions, the governing law for a contractual relation is significantly dependent on any express choice selected by the parties in a "choice of law" clause. Clause 15.1 of the contract in *Rudder* contains both a forum selection clause and a choice of law clause.

3. The *Rudder* decision raises a number of questions in relation to forum selection that are also important in the law of exclusion clauses. On the issues relating to notice of clauses in written documents and the effect of a failure to read a document, see *infra*, Chapter 8, section 3(d).

(b)   MAILED ACCEPTANCES

HOUSEHOLD FIRE & CARRIAGE ACCIDENT INSURANCE CO. v. GRANT

(1879), 4 Ex. D. 216 (C.A.)

In 1874 Kendrick was acting in Glamorganshire as the agent of the company for the placing of their shares. On the 30th of September the defendant handed to Kendrick an application in writing for shares in the plaintiffs' company, which stated that the defendant had paid to the bankers of the company £5, being a deposit of 1s. per share, and requesting an allotment of 100 shares, and agreeing to pay the further sum of 19s. per share within twelve months of the date of the allotment. Kendrick duly forwarded this application to the plaintiffs in London, and the secretary of the company on the 20th of October, 1874, made out the letter of allotment in favour of the defendant, which was posted addressed to the defendant at his residence; his name was then entered on the register of share-holders. This letter of allotment never reached the defendant. The defendant never paid the £5 mentioned in his application, but the plaintiff's company being in-debted to the defendant in the sum of £5 for commission, that sum was duly credited to his account in their books. In July, 1875, a dividend at the rate of 2-1/2 per cent. was declared on the shares, and in February, 1876, a further dividend was declared at the same rate; these dividends, amounting altogether to the sum of 5s., were also credited to the defendant's account in the books of the plaintiffs' company. Afterwards the company went into liquidation, and on the 7th of December, 1877, the official liquidator applied for the sum sued for from the defendant; the defendant declined to pay on the ground that he was not a share-holder.

On these facts the learned judge left two questions to the jury. 1. Was the letter of allotment of the 20th of October in fact posted? 2. Was the letter of allotment received by the defendant? The jury found the first question in the affirmative and the last in the negative.

At trial, judgment was entered for the plaintiffs. The defendant appealed.

THESIGER L.J. In this case the defendant made an application for shares in the plaintiffs' company under circumstances from which we must imply that he authorized the company, in the event of their allotting to him the shares applied for, to send the notice of allotment by post. The company did allot him the shares, and duly addressed to him and posted a letter containing the notice of allotment, but upon the finding of the jury it must be taken that the letter never reached its destination. In this state of circumstances Lopes, J. has decided that the defendant is liable as a shareholder. He based his decision mainly upon the ground that the point for his consideration was covered by authority binding upon him, and I am of opinion that he did so rightly, and that it is covered by authority equally binding upon this Court. . . .

Now, whatever in abstract discussion may be said as to the legal notion of its being necessary, in order to the effecting of a valid and binding contract, that the minds of the parties should be brought together at one and the same moment, that notion is practically the foundation of English law upon the subject of the formation of contracts. Unless therefore a contract constituted by correspondence is absolutely concluded at the moment that the continuing offer is accepted by the person to whom the offer is addressed, it is difficult to see how the two minds are ever to be brought together at one and the same moment. . . . But on the other hand it is a principle of law, as well established as the legal notion to which I have referred, that the minds of the two parties must be brought together by mutual communication. An acceptance, which only remains in the breast of the acceptor without being actually and by legal implication communicated to the offerer, is no binding acceptance. How then are these elements of law to be harmonised in the case of contracts formed by correspondence through the post? I see no better mode than that of treating the post office as the agent of both parties, . . . [I]f the post office be such common agent, then it seems to me to follow that, as soon as the letter of acceptance is delivered to the post office, the contract is made as complete and final and absolutely binding as if the acceptor had put his letter into the hands of a messenger sent by the offerer himself as his agent to deliver the offer and receive the acceptance. What other principle can be adopted short of holding that the contract is not complete by acceptance until and except from the time that the letter containing the acceptance is delivered to the offerer, a principle which has been distinctly negatived? . . .

There is no doubt that the implication of a complete, final, and absolutely binding contract being formed, as soon as the acceptance of an offer is posted, may in some cases lead to inconvenience and hardship. But such there must be at times in every view of the law. It is impossible in transactions which pass between parties at a distance, and have to be carried on through the medium of correspondence, to adjust conflicting rights between innocent parties, so as to make the consequences of mistake on the part of a mutual agent fall equally upon the shoulders of both. At the same time I am not prepared to admit that the implication in question will lead to any great or general inconvenience or hardship. An offerer, if he chooses, may always make the formation of the contract which he proposes dependent upon the actual communication to himself of the acceptance. If he trusts to the post he trusts to a means of communication which, as a rule, does not fail, and if no answer to his offer is received by him, and the matter is of importance to him, he can make inquiries of the person to whom his offer was addressed. On the other hand, if the contract is not finally concluded, except in the event of the acceptance actually reaching the offerer, the door would be opened to the perpetration of much fraud, and, putting aside this consideration, considerable delay in commercial transactions, in which despatch is, as a rule, of the greatest consequence, would be occasioned; for the acceptor would never be entirely safe in acting upon his acceptance until he had received notice that his letter of acceptance had reached its destination.

Upon balance of conveniences and inconveniences it seems to me . . . more consistent with the acts and declarations of the parties in this case to consider the contract complete and absolutely binding on the transmission of the notice of allotment through the post, as the medium of communication that the parties themselves contemplated, instead of postponing its completion until the notice had been received by the defendant.

BRAMWELL L.J. [dissenting] . . . Where a proposition to enter into a contract is made and accepted, it is necessary, as a rule, to constitute the contract that there should be a communication of that acceptance to the proposer. . . .

That if there is a difference where the acceptance is by a letter sent through the post which does not reach the offerer, it must be by virtue of some general rule or some particular agreement of the parties. As, for instance, there might be an agreement that the acceptance of the proposal may be by sending the article offered by the proposer to be bought, or hanging out a flag or sign to be seen by the offerer as he goes by, or leaving a letter at a certain place, or any other agreed mode, and in the same way there might be an agreement that dropping a letter in a post pillar box or other place of reception should suffice.

That as there is no such special agreement in this case, the defendant, if bound, must be bound by some general rule which makes a difference when the post office is employed as the means of communication.

That if there is any such general rule applicable to the communication of the acceptance of offers, it is equally to all communications that may be made by post. Because, as I have said, the question is not whether this communication may be made by post. If, therefore, posting a letter which does not reach is a sufficient communication of acceptance of an offer, it is equally a communication of everything else which may be communicated by post . . . The question then is, is posting a letter which is never received a communication to the person addressed, or an equivalent, or something which dispenses with it? It is for those who say it is to make good their contention, I ask why is it? My answer beforehand to any argument that may be urged is, that it is not a communication, and that there is no agreement to take it as an equivalent for or to dispense with a communication. That those who affirm the contrary say the thing which is not. . . . That because a man, who may send a communication by post or otherwise, sends it by post, he should bind the person addressed, though the communication never reaches him, while he would not so bind him if he had sent it by hand, is impossible. There is no reason in it; it is simply arbitrary. I ask whether any one who thinks so is prepared to follow that opinion to its consequence; suppose the offer is to sell a particular chattel, and the letter accepting it never arrives, is the property in the chattel transferred?

It is said that a contrary rule would be hard on the would-be acceptor, who may have made his arrangements on the footing that the bargain was concluded. But to hold as contended would be equally hard on the offerer, who may have made his arrangements on the footing that his offer was not accepted; his non-receipt of any communication may be attributable to the person to whom it was made being absent. What is he to do but to act on the negative, that no communication has been made to him? Further, the use of the post office is no more authorized by the offerer than the sending an answer by hand, and all these hardships would befall the person posting the letter if he sent it by hand. Doubtless in that case he would be the person to suffer if the letter did not reach its destination. Why should his sending it by post relieve him of the loss and cast it on the other party. It was said, if he sends it by hand it is revocable, but not if he sends it by post, which makes the difference. But it is revocable when sent by post, not that the letter can be got back, but its arrival might be anticipated by a letter by hand or telegram, and there is no case to show that such anticipation would not prevent the letter from binding. It would be a most alarming thing to say that it would. That a letter honestly but mistakenly written and posted must bind the writer if hours before its arrival he informed the person addressed that it was coming, but was wrong and recalled . . .

Further, it seems admitted that if the proposer said, "unless I hear from you by return of post the offer is withdrawn," that the letter accepting it much reach him to bind him . . . If it is admitted, is it not what every letter says? Are there to be fine distinctions, such as, if the words are "unless I hear from you by return of post, &c.," it is necessary the letter should reach him, but "let me know by return of post," it is not; or if in that case it is, yet it is not where there is an offer without those words. Lord Blackburn says that Mellish L.J. accurately stated that where it is expressly or impliedly stated in the offer, "you may accept the offer by posting a letter," the moment you post this letter the offer is accepted. I agree; and the same thing is true of any other mode of acceptance offered with the offer and acted on—as firing a cannon, sending off a rocket, give your answer to my servant the bearer. Lord Blackburn was not dealing with the question before us; there was not doubt in the case before him that the letter had reached. . . .

The only other authority is the expression of opinion by Lopes J. in the present case. He says the proposer may guard himself against hardship by making the proposal expressly conditioned on the arrival of the answer within a definite time. But it need not be express nor within a definite time. It is enough that it is to be inferred that it is to be, and if it is to be it must be within a reasonable time. The mischievous consequences he points out do not follow from that which I am contending for. I am at a loss to see how the post office is the agent for both parties. What is the agency as to the sender? merely to receive? But suppose it is not an answer, but an original communication. What then? Does the extent of the agency of the post office depend on the contents of the letter? But if the post office is the agent of both parties, then the agent of both parties has failed in his duty, and to both. Suppose the offerer says, "My offer is conditional on your answer reaching me." Whose agent is the post office then? But how does an offerer make the post office his agent, because he gives the offeree an option of using that or any other means of communication.

I am of opinion that this judgment should be reversed. I am of opinion that there was no bargain between these parties to allot and take shares, that to make such bargain there should have been an acceptance of the defendant's offer and a communication to him of that acceptance. That there was no such communication. That posting a letter does not differ from other attempts at communication in any of its consequences, save that it is irrevocable as between the poster and post office. The difficulty has arisen . . . from supposing that because there is a right to have recourse to the post as a means of communication, that right is attended with some peculiar consequences, and also from supposing that because if the letter reaches it binds from the time of posting, it also binds though it never reaches. . . .

[The judgment of Baggallay L.J., who agreed with Thesiger L.J., is omitted. Judgment affirmed.]

NOTES and QUESTIONS

1. In "Trashing with Trollope: A Deconstruction of the Postal Rules in Contract" (1992), 12 Oxford Jl. L.S. 170, Simon Gardner looks at various justifications for the different postal rules in regard to acceptance and revocation and offers some alternative historical explanations.

2. Canadian cases have tended to follow the approach of *Household Fire and Carriage Accident Ins. Co. v. Grant* to the postal acceptance rule. For example, in *Sibtac Corp. v. Soo* (1978), 83 D.L.R. (3d) 116 (Ont. H.C.), an option to renew a lease, contained in a letter and requiring "Notication [*sic*]

of . . . the exercising of option sixty days prior to Nov. 1/73", was handed to the plaintiff lessee. Notice was mailed on the 11th or 12th July 1973, but there was no evidence of receipt. The judge applied the postal acceptance rule as it was not "unreasonable for the plaintiff to have exercised the option as it did".

Some earlier Canadian cases, particularly from Québec, such as *Charlebois v. Baril*, [1928] S.C.R. 88, seemed to restrict the application of the postal acceptance rule to contracts formed wholly by correspondence. The Civil Code of Québec, Art. 1387, has adopted a general requirement of receipt. Should there be a general rule and, if so, should the acceptance be effective on receipt or dispatch? If on receipt, does this mean that the offeror must be informed or merely that the acceptance must be delivered?

3. *Smith & Osberg Ltd. v. Hollenbeck*, [1938] 3 W.W.R. 704 (B.C. S.C.), suggested that the rule might apply to telegrams where the circumstances were "such as to warrant the conclusion that an acceptance by telegram was impliedly authorized". In *R. v. Commercial Credit Corp.* (1983), 4 D.L.R. (4th) 314 (N.S. C.A.), the mailed acceptance rule was applied where an acceptance was delivered to a courier in St. Cloud, Minnesota and transmitted to Dartmouth, Nova Scotia.

HOLWELL SECURITIES v. HUGHES

[1974] 1 W.L.R. 155, [1974] 1 All E.R. 161 (C.A.)

LAWTON L.J. The issue in this appeal was clear. Did the plaintiffs exercise an option to purchase the premises known as 571 High Road, Wembley, by posting a letter to the defendant which he never received? The answer to this problem can be reached by two paths: the short one and the roundabout one. Both, in my judgment, are satisfactory but the roundabout one has some paths leading off it which can lead the traveller after legal truth astray. The plaintiffs, I think, took one of these paths. I propose in this judgment to start by taking the short path and then to survey the other.

It is a truism of the law relating to options that the grantee must comply strictly with the conditions stipulated for exercise. It follows that the first task of the court is to find out what was stipulated: the instrument of grant has to be construed. It is a formal document which must have been drafted by someone familiar with conveyancing practice. From its layout and content it is likely to have been based on a precedent in the Encyclopaedia of Forms and Precedents. It follows, so it seems to me, that the words and phrases in it should be given precise meanings whenever possible and that words which are in common use amongst conveyancers should be construed in the way they use such words.

The material parts of the option clause are as follows: 'The said option shall be exercisable by notice in writing to the Intending Vendor at any time within six months from the date hereof . . .' In my judgment, the phrase 'notice in writing' is of importance in this context. Conveyancers are familiar with it and frequently use it. . . . In the option clauses under consideration the draftsman used the phrase in connection with the exercise of the option but in other parts of the agreement he was content to use such phrases as 'agreed in writing' (see cl 4) and 'if required in writing' (see cl 8 (a)). Should any inference be drawn from the use of the word 'notice'? In my judgment, Yes. Its derivation is from the Latin word for knowing. A notice is a means of making something known. The Shorter Oxford English Dictionary gives as the primary meaning of the word: 'Intimation, information, intelligence, warning . . . formal intimation or warning of something.' If a notice is to be of any value it must be an intimation to someone. A notice which cannot impinge on anyone's mind is not functioning as such.

Now in this case, the 'notice in writing' was to be one 'to the Intending Vendor'. It was to be an intimation to him that the grantee had exercised the option: he was the one who was to be fixed with the information contained in the writing. He never was, because the letter carrying the information went astray. The plaintiffs were unable to do what the agreement said they were to do, namely, fix the defendant with knowledge that they had decided to buy his property. If this construction of the option clause is correct, there is no room for the application of any rule of law relating to the acceptance of offers by posting letters since the option agreement stipulated what had to be done to exercise the option. On this ground alone I would dismiss the appeal.

I turn now to what I have called the roundabout path to the same result. Counsel for the plaintiffs submitted that the option was exercised when the letter was posted, as the rule relating to the acceptance of offers by post did apply. The foundation of his argument was that the parties to this agreement must have contemplated that the option might be, and probably would be, exercised by means of a letter sent through the post. I agree. This, submitted counsel, was enough to bring the rule into operation. I do not agree. In *Henthorn v. Fraser* [[1892] 2 Ch. 27] Lord Herschell stated the rule as follows:

> Where the circumstances are such that it must have been within the contemplation of the parties that, according to the ordinary usages of mankind, the post might be used as a means of communicating the acceptance of an offer, the acceptance is complete as soon as it is posted.

It was applied by Farwell J. in *Bruner v. Moore* [[1904] 1 Ch. 305] to an option to purchase patent rights. The option agreement, which was in writing, was silent as to the manner in which it was to be exercised. The grantee purported to do so by a letter and a telegram.

Does the rule apply in *all* cases where one party makes an offer which both he and the person with whom he was dealing must have expected the post to be used as a means of accepting it? In my judgment, it does not. First, it does not apply when the express terms of the offer specify that the acceptance must reach the offeror. . . . Secondly, it probably does not operate if its application would produce manifest inconvenience and absurdity. This is the opinion set out in Cheshire and Fifoot's Law of Contract [8th. ed. (1972), p. 43]. It was the opinion of Bramwell B as is seen by his judgment in *British & American Telegraph Co. v. Colson* [(1871), L.R. 6 Exch. 108] and his opinion is worthy of consideration even though the decision in that case was overruled by this court in *Household Fire and Carriage Accident Insurance Co. Ltd. v. Grant* [*supra*]. The illustrations of inconvenience and absurdity which Bramwell B gave are as apt today as they were then. Is a stockbroker who is holding shares to the orders of his client liable in damages because he did not sell in a falling market in accordance with the instructions in a letter which was posted but never received? Before the passing of the Law Reform (Miscellaneous Provisions) Act 1970 (which abolished actions for breach of promise of marriage), would a young soldier ordered overseas have been bound in contract to marry a girl to whom he had proposed by letter, asking her to let him have an answer before he left and she had replied affirmatively in good time but the letter had never reached him? In my judgment, the factors of inconvenience and absurdity are but illustrations of a wider principle, namely, that the rule does not apply if, having regard to all the circumstances, including the nature of the subject-matter under consideration, the negotiating parties cannot have intended that there should be a binding agreement until the party accepting an offer or exercising an option had in fact communicated the acceptance or exercise to the other. In my judgment, when this principle is applied to the facts of this case it becomes clear that the parties cannot have intended that the posting of a letter should constitute the exercise of the option. . . .

RUSSELL L.J. . . . This leaves an alternative contention for the plaintiffs which Templeman J. dismissed with brevity. When the defendant's solicitors received the plaintiffs' solicitors' letter dated 14th April, they communicated by telephone with the defendant. The defendant's evidence was as follows:

Q. Did you then, as a result of that, ring Messrs Bulcraig & Davis?

A. As a result of that, I did, yes.

Q. And to whom did you speak there?

A. I spoke to Mr. Wade.

Q. Do you remember what he told you?

A. Yes.

Q. Not the exact words?

A. No. He asked me if I had heard from Messrs Brecher, the other people's solicitors, and I said "No". He said "Well, I have had a letter from them delivered to me today and I understand that you will be getting a letter as well, or a copy of this". My recollection is that he said "a letter" but later I understood that what was meant was a copy. And he said: "I don't think this option is exercised properly until notice is served on you", or "until you receive a letter", and I said "Oh, dear, I had intended to go to Ireland this evening. Will it be all right if I do?" and he said "Yes, it would". My recollection is that he said "Your presence does not have to be there" or "You don't have to be there yourself, if the letter is delivered, or posted to you".

Counsel for the plaintiffs argued that since the defendant knew that the plaintiffs were anxious to exercise the option, and there was in existence a written notice exercising it, therefore there was a 'notice in writing to the defendant'. I consider this argument to be fallacious. A person does not give notice in writing to another person by sitting down and writing it out and then telephoning to that other saying, 'Listen to what I have just written'. Moreover, the defendant did not have knowledge of the existence of the combination of two letters which alone could be said to be an exercise of the option. *Dickinson v. Dodds*, [*infra*, section 6(a)] which was referred to, does not assist on this point: all it does is to show that an offeree cannot accept a withdrawable offer after he has learnt, by whatever means, that it has been withdrawn.

[Buckley L.J. agreed with Russell L.J. Appeal dismissed.]

NOTES and QUESTIONS

1. For an overview of the implications of this decision and also of *Brinkibon*, see Jacobs, "Communication of Acceptance" (1983), Lloyd's Mar. and Comm. Law 663.

2. Are there any rational grounds for distinguishing *Holwell Securities v. Hughes* from *Carmichael v. Bank of Montreal, supra*, section 4?

3. In *Island Properties Ltd. v. Entertainment Ent. Ltd.* (1983), 146 D.L.R. (3d) 505, varied in part 26 D.L.R. (4th) 347 (Nfld. C.A.), the counter-offer for the sale of land provided that:

> This Counter Offer shall be irrevocable by the Vendor until 11:59 p.m. July 9 1980 after which time, if not accepted by the Purchaser and the copy *delivered* to the Vendor or his Agent, this Counter Offer shall be null and void. [Emphasis added.]

The counter-offer was sent from St. John's, Newfoundland to the plaintiff in Leduc, Alberta, by special delivery post on 3rd July 1980, but was not received by the plaintiff's office until 8th July 1980. The court commented, at 515:

> it would be the height of unreasonableness, bordering on the incredible, to suggest that the plaintiff should have delivered the executed acceptance of the counter-offer 'to the Vendor or his Agent', in person, before 11:59 p.m. on July 9, 1980. The mailing of the counter-offer within the time prescribed therein, constituted a valid delivery of the plaintiff's acceptance of same.

The court was fortified in this conclusion by the fact that the plaintiff had, in addition, sent a telegram to the agent, which was read over the telephone to the agent on 9th July and had telephoned an acceptance to the agent on 9th July. These actions were also held to constitute acceptance by the plaintiff.

4. On 15th October, A mails an offer to B to sell a specified quantity of wool and requests an answer "by return". The letter is dated 15th October and the postmark bears the same date. A misdirects the letter, with the result that it does not reach B until 27th October. On receipt of the offer, B immediately mails a letter of acceptance, which A receives on 30th October. On 25th October, A, assuming that B had not accepted the offer, sold the wool to T. Is A liable to B in damages for breach of contract? See *Adams v. Lindsell* (1818), 106 E.R. 250.

6. Termination of Offer

(a) REVOCATION

BYRNE v. VAN TIENHOVEN

(1880), 5 C.P.D. 344

On 1st October, the defendants, from Cardiff, mailed an offer to sell to the plaintiffs in New York 1,000 boxes of tin plates at a fixed price. The offer was received on 11th October and the plaintiffs immediately accepted by telegram on 11th October and confirmed by letter on 15th October.

On 8th October, the defendant mailed a revocation of the offer which was received on 20th October. The plaintiffs, on the assumption that they had purchased the tin plates, had already sold them to a third party. Consequently, they brought an action for breach of contract for failure to deliver.

LINDLEY J. . . . . There is no doubt that an offer can be withdrawn before it is accepted, and it is immaterial whether the offer is expressed to be open for acceptance for a given time or not. For the decision of the present case, however, it is necessary to consider two other questions, viz.: 1. Whether a withdrawal of an offer has any effect until it is communicated to the person to whom the offer has been sent? 2. Whether posting a letter of withdrawal is a communication to the person to whom the letter is sent?

It is curious that neither of these questions appears to have been actually decided in this country. As regards the first question, I am aware that Pothier and some other writers of celebrity are of opinion that there can be no contract if an offer is withdrawn before it is accepted, although the withdrawal is not communicated to the person to whom the offer has been made. The reason for this opinion is that there is not in fact any such consent by both parties as is essential to constitute a contract between them. Against this view, however, it has been urged that a state of mind not notified cannot be regarded in dealings between man and man; and that an uncommunicated revocation is for all practical purposes and in point of law no revocation at all. . . . This view, moreover, appears to me much more in accordance with the general principles of English law than the view maintained by Pothier. I pass, therefore, to the next question, viz., whether posting the letter of revocation was a sufficient communication of it to the plaintiff. . . . It may be taken as now settled that where an offer is made and accepted by letters sent through the post, the contract is completed the moment the letter accepting the offer is posted, even although it never reaches its destination. When, however, these authorities are looked at, it will be seen that they are based upon the principle that the writer of the offer has expressly or impliedly assented to treat an answer to him by a letter duly posted as a sufficient acceptance and notification to himself, or in other words, he has made the post office his agent to receive the acceptance and notification of it. But this principle appears to me to be inapplicable to the case of the withdrawal of an offer. In this particular case I can find no evidence of any authority in fact given by the plaintiffs to the defendants to notify a withdrawal of their offer by merely posting a letter; and there is no legal principle or decision which compels me to hold, contrary to the fact, that the letter of the 8th of October is to be treated as communicated to the plaintiff on that day or on any day before the 20th, when the letter reached them. But before that letter had reached the plaintiffs they had accepted the offer, both by telegram and by post, and they had themselves resold the tinplates at a profit. In my opinion the withdrawal by the defendants on the 8th of October of their offer of the 1st was inoperative; and a complete contract binding on both parties was entered into on the 11th of October, when the plaintiffs accepted the offer of the 1st, which they had no reason to suppose had been withdrawn. Before leaving this part of the case it may be as well to point out the extreme injustice and inconvenience which any other conclusion would produce. If the defendants' contention were to prevail no person who had received an offer by post and had accepted it would know his position until he had waited such a time as to be quite sure that a letter withdrawing the offer had not been posted before his acceptance of it. It appears to me that both legal principles, and practical convenience require that a person who has accepted an offer not known to him to have been revoked, shall be in a position safely to act upon the footing that the offer and acceptance constitute a contract binding on both parties. . . .

[Part of the reasons for judgment of Lindley J. is omitted. Judgment for plaintiffs.]

NOTE

On the question of withdrawal of letters of acceptance, see *Countess of Dunmore v. Alexander* (1830), 9 Sh. (Ct. of Sess.) 190 (Scot.); *Wenkheim v. Arndt* (1873), 1 Jur. 73 (N.Z.); Hudson, "Retractation of Letters of Acceptance" (1966), 82 L.Q.R. 169. Article 22 of the Vienna Convention, *supra* provides: "An acceptance may be withdrawn if the withdrawal reaches the offeror before or at the same time as the acceptance would have become effective."

DICKINSON v. DODDS

(1876), 2 Ch. D. 463 (C.A.)

On Wednesday, June 10th the defendant Dodds gave to the plaintiff the following offer:

I hereby agree to sell to Mr. George Dickinson the whole of the dwelling-houses, garden ground, stabling, and outbuildings thereto belonging, situate at Croft, belonging to me, for the sum of £800.

As witness my hand this tenth day of June, 1874.

£800. (Signed) John Dodds.

P.S.—This offer to be left over until Friday, 9 o'clock, A.M.J.D. (the twelfth), 12th June, 1874.

(Signed) J. Dodds.

In the afternoon of the Thursday the plaintiff was informed by a Mr. Berry that Dodds had been offering or agreeing to sell the property to Thomas Allan, the other defendant. Thereupon the plaintiff, at about half-past seven in the evening, went to the house of Mrs. Burgess, the mother-in-law of Dodds, where he was then staying, and left with her a formal acceptance in writing of the offer to sell the property. According to the evidence of Mrs. Burgess this document never in fact reached Dodds, she having forgotten to give it to him.

On the following (Friday) morning, at about seven o'clock, Berry, who was acting as agent for Dickinson, found Dodds at the Darlington railway station, and handed to him a duplicate of the acceptance by Dickinson, and explained to Dodds its purport. He replied that it was too late, as he had sold the property. A few minutes later Dickinson himself found Dodds entering a railway carriage, and handed him another duplicate of the notice of acceptance, but Dodds declined to receive it, saying, "You are too late. I have sold the property."

It appeared that on the day before, Thursday, the 11th of June, Dodds had signed a formal contract for the sale of the property to the defendant Allan for £800, and had received from him a deposit of £40.

Dickinson accordingly brought an action of specific performance against Dodds.

MELLISH L.J. [having construed the defendant's letter of 10th June as an offer.] . . . Well, then, this being only an offer, the law says—and it is a perfectly clear rule of law—that, although it is said that the offer is to be left open until Friday morning at 9 o'clock, that did not bind Dodds. He was not in point of law bound to hold the offer over until 9 o'clock on Friday morning. He was not so bound either in law or in equity. Well, that being so, when on the next day he made an agreement with Allan to sell the property to him, I am not aware of any ground on which it can be said that the contract with Allan was not as good and binding a contract as ever was made. Assuming Allan to have known (there is some dispute about it, and Allan does not admit that he knew of it, but I will assume that he did) that Dodds had made the offer to Dickinson, and had given him till Friday morning at 9 o'clock to accept it, still in point of law that could not prevent Allan from making a more favourable offer than Dickinson, and entering at once into a binding agreement with Dodds.

Then Dickinson is informed by Berry that the property has been sold by Dodds to Allan. Berry does not tell us from whom he heard it, but he says that he did hear it, that he knew it, and that he informed Dickinson of it. Now, stopping there, the question which arises is this—If an offer has been made for the sale of property, and before that offer is accepted, the person who has made the offer enters into a binding agreement to sell the property to somebody else, and the person to whom the offer was first made receives notice in some way that the property has been sold to another person, can he after that make a binding contract by the acceptance of the offer? I am of opinion that he cannot. The law may be right or wrong in saying that a person who has given to another a certain time within which to accept an offer is not bound by his promise to give that time; but, if he is not bound by that promise, and may still sell the property to some one else, and if it be the law that, in order to make a contract, the two minds must be in agreement at some one time, that is, at the time of the acceptance, how is it possible that when the person to whom the offer has been made knows that the person who has made the offer has sold the property to someone else, and that, in fact, he has not remained in the same mind to sell it to him, he can be at liberty to accept the offer and thereby make a binding contract? It seems to me that would be simply absurd. If a man makes an offer to sell a particular horse in his stable, and says, "I will give you until the day after to-morrow to accept the offer," and the next day goes and sells the horse to somebody else, and receives the purchase money from him, can the person to whom the offer was originally made then come and say, "I accept," so as to make a binding contract, and so as to be entitled to recover damages for the non-delivery of the horse? If the rule of law is that a mere offer to sell property, which can be withdrawn at any time, and which is made dependent on the acceptance of the person to whom it is made, is a mere *nudum pactum*, how is it possible that the person to whom the offer has been made can by acceptance make a binding contract after he knows that the person who has made the offer has sold the property to some one else? It is admitted law that, if a man who makes an offer dies, the offer cannot be accepted after he is dead, and parting with the property has very much the same effect as the death of the owner, for it makes the performance of the offer impossible. I am clearly of opinion that, just as when a man who has made an offer dies before it is accepted it is impossible that it can then be accepted, so when once the person to whom the offer was made knows that the property has been sold to some one else, it is too late for him to accept the offer, and on that ground I am clearly of opinion that ~~there was no binding contract for the sale of this property by Dodds to Dickinson~~, and even if there had been, it seems to me that the sale of the property to Allan was first in point of time. However, it is not necessary to consider, if there had been two binding contracts, which of them would be entitled to priority in equity, because there is no binding contract between Dodds and Dickinson.

[Baggally J.A. concurred. The concurring judgment of James L.J. is omitted.]

NOTES and QUESTIONS

1. The headnote in *Dickinson v. Dodds* reads, in part:

> An offer to sell property may be withdrawn before acceptance without any formal notice to the person to whom the offer is made. It is sufficient if that person has actual knowledge that the person who made the offer has done some act inconsistent with the continuance of the offer, such as selling the property to a third person.
>
> *Semble*, that the sale of the property to a third person would of itself amount to a withdrawal of the offer, even although the person to whom the offer was first made had no knowledge of the sale.

Do you agree? What theory of agreement was apparently in the mind of the writer of the headnote (and to some extent in the mind of Mellish L.J.)?

2. Does it make any difference who Berry is?

3. Would it make any difference if Berry had not passed the information on to Dickinson?

4. Harvey Foster has made an offer to buy property from Gloria Greer. Before Gloria accepts the offer she hears from a reliable source that Harvey has purchased another similar property since the offer was made to her. Can Gloria still accept?

5. The O.L.R.C.'s *Report on Amendment of the Law of Contract* considers that the common law approach to firm offers, that is, offers which are stated to be irrevocable, "gives rise to many difficulties and does not reflect the business community's understanding of the significance of firm offers". The Commission recommends, at 25:

> [A]n offer, made by a person in the course of a business, which expressly provides that it will be held open should not be revocable for lack of consideration during the time stated or, if no time is stated, for a reasonable time not to exceed three months. . . . [T]here should be no change in the law relating to firm offers not made in the course of business . . . [unless they fall within the scope of their general recommendations in regard to formal contracts or injurious reliance].

6. The Civil Code of Québec, Book 5, Obligations, Ch. II, Contracts, s. III provides:

> **Art. 1390.** An offer to contract may be made to a determinate or indeterminate person, and a term for acceptance may or may not be attached to it.
>
> Where a term is attached, the offer may not be revoked before the term expires; if none is attached, the offer may be revoked at any time before acceptance is received by the offeror.

> **Art. 1391.** Where the offeree receives a revocation before the offer, the offer lapses, even though a term is attached to it.

7. The Vienna Convention, *supra*, provides in Art. 15(2) that:

> An offer, even if it is irrevocable, may be withdrawn if the withdrawal reaches the offeree before or at the same time as the offer.

> Art. 16(1) Until a contract is concluded an offer may be revoked if the revocation reaches the offeree before he has dispatched an acceptance.

> (2) However, an offer cannot be revoked:

(a) if it indicates, whether by stating a fixed time for acceptance or otherwise, that it is irrevocable; or

(b) if it was reasonable for the offeree to rely on the offer as being irrevocable and the offeree has acted in reliance on the offer.

How can these sections mesh with the provision in Art. 18(2): "An acceptance of an offer becomes effective at the moment the indication of assent reaches the offeror . . ."?

8. In the *Ron Engineering* decision, *supra*, section 2, the Supreme Court of Canada adopted the contract A analysis to ensure that a provision in a tender, which stipulated that the tender was irrevocable for a fixed period, bound the contractor.

Is there any reason why this analysis should be restricted to tenders and not applied to other offers that are expressed to be irrevocable for a certain period, such as that found in *Dickinson v. Dodds*?

9. The primary means in the common law of contract to enforce a promise to keep an offer open is through an option contract; see *Holwell Securities v. Hughes, supra*, section 5 of this chapter. An option contract usually requires that consideration be provided by the offeree in exchange for the promise to keep the offer open. Consideration is the subject of Chapter 4 of this book. In *Baughman v. Rampart Resources Ltd.* (1995), 124 D.L.R. (4th) 252 (B.C. C.A.), at paras. 31 and 41, Southin J.A. summarized the nature of an option contract to keep an offer open as follows:

> An option is simply an offer supported by consideration. It gives the offeree a choice to accept or not accept in accordance with its requirements. He may only accept it in accordance with its requirements. . . . [Southin J.A. then noted three propositions in relation to option contracts:]
>
> 1. An attempted revocation of an irrevocable offer cannot deprive the offeree of his right to accept the offer according to its terms.
>
> 2. If he does accept the offer, there is then a binding contract by which the usual rights and obligations of any bilateral contract come into operation.
>
> 3. If the offeree does not perform the requirements for acceptance of the offer, he has no contract of, for instance, purchase and sale, if that is what the option is about, and thus no remedy on that contract, but he may have an action for damages for breach of the promise to keep the offer open. In other words, the breach of the promise to keep the offer open cannot necessarily be equated in matter of remedy with breach of a contract made by acceptance of the offer.

To seek a remedy under the option contract, a party must act in compliance with the terms of the option. For example, if the option contract sets a deadline or a means through which the offer to purchase a piece of property is to be made, then the offeree must comply with such terms in order to seek a remedy for breach of the option contract. See, *e.g. Holwell Securities, supra*, and *Fraresso v. Wanczyk* (2000), [2000] B.C.J. No. 961 (C.A.), reversed on reconsideration, [2000] B.C.J. No. 2285 (C.A.) (with respect to further findings of fact), leave to appeal refused, [2000] S.C.C.A. No. 644. See also *Mitsui & Co. (Canada) v. Royal Bank*, [1995] 2 S.C.R. 187.

In *Sail Labrador Ltd. v. Navimar Corp.* (1998), [1999] 1 S.C.R. 265, the Supreme Court of Canada confirmed that option contracts are often unilateral contracts, but may also take the form of bilateral contracts. Justice Bastarache notes, at para.36, that: "Upon granting the option, the optioner undertakes the promise to honour its terms if it is exercised by the optionee. The optionee, on the other hand, is under no corresponding obligation to exercise the option. However, if the optionee chooses to exercise the option, it can do so simply by performing the required conditions precedent."

10. In the U.S. case of *Petterson v. Pattberg* (1928), 248 N.Y. 86, a mortgagee offered to allow a mortgagor to discharge a mortgage by paying the outstanding balance before a certain date. The mortgagor arrived at the mortgagee's residence before the appointed day and knocked at the door. The defendant mortgagee demanded the name of the caller. Petterson replied: "It is Mr. Petterson. I have come to pay off the mortgage." The defendant answered that he had sold the mortgage. Petterson stated that he would like to talk to the mortgagee, so the defendant partly opened the door. Thereupon

Petterson exhibited the cash and said he was ready to pay off the mortgage according to the agreement. The defendant refused to take the money.

The New York Court of Appeals interpreted the mortgagee's offer as an offer of a unilateral contract and held that no contract had been created, as the offer had been revoked before the act of acceptance had been performed. See also *Beer v. Lea* (1912), 7 D.L.R. 434, affirmed 14 D.L.R. 236 (Ont. H.C.).

ERRINGTON v. ERRINGTON AND WOODS

[1952] 1 K.B. 290, [1952] 1 All E.R. 149 (C.A.)

DENNING L.J. The facts are reasonably clear. In 1930 the father bought the house for his son and daughter-in-law to live in. The father put down £250 in cash and borrowed £500 from a building society on the security of the house, repayable with interest by instalments of 15s. 0d. a week. He took the house in his own name and made himself responsible for the instalments. The father told the daughter-in-law that the £250 was a present for them, but he left them to pay the building society instalments of 15s. 0d. a week themselves. He handed the building society book to the daughter-in-law and said to her: "Don't part with this book. The house will be your property when the mortgage is paid." He said that when he retired he would transfer it into their names. She has in fact paid the building society instalments regularly from that day to this with the result that much of the mortgage has been repaid, but there is a good deal yet to be paid. The rates on the house came to 10s. 0d. a week. The couple found that they could not pay those as well as the building society instalments, so the father said he would pay them and did so.

It is to be noted that the couple never bound themselves to pay the instalments to the building society; and I see no reason why any such obligation should be implied. It is clear law that the court is not to imply a term unless it is necessary; and I do not see that it is necessary here. Ample content is given to the whole arrangement by holding that the father promised that the house should belong to the couple as soon as they paid off the mortgage. The parties did not discuss what was to happen if the couple failed to pay the instalments to the building society, but I should have thought it clear that, if they did fail to pay the instalments, the father would not be bound to transfer the house to them. The father's promise was a unilateral contract—a promise of the house in return for their act of paying the instalments. It could not be revoked by him once the couple entered on performance of the act, but it would cease to bind him if they left it incomplete and unperformed, which they have not done. If that was the position during the father's lifetime, so it must be after his death. If the daughter-in-law continues to pay all the building society instalments, the couple will be entitled to have the property transferred to them as soon as the mortgage is paid off; but if she does not do so, then the building society will claim the instalments from the father's estate and the estate will have to pay them. I cannot think that in those circumstances the estate would be bound to transfer the house to them, any more than the father himself would have been ... the couple were licensees, having a permissive occupation short of a tenancy, but with a contractual right, or at any rate, an equitable right to remain so long as they paid the instalments, which would grow into a good equitable title to the house itself as soon as the mortgage was paid. This is, I think, the right view of the relationship of the parties. . . .

In the present case it is clear that the father expressly promised the couple that the property should belong to them as soon as the mortgage was paid, and impliedly promised that so long as they paid the instalments to the building society they should be allowed to remain in possession. They were not purchasers because they never bound themselves to pay the instalments, but nevertheless they were in a position analogous to purchasers. They have acted on the promise, and neither the father nor his widow, his successor in title, can eject them in disregard of it. The result is that in my opinion the appeal should be dismissed and no order for possession should be made. . . .

[Part of the reasons for judgment of Denning L.J. and the concurring judgments of Somervell and Hodson L.JJ. are omitted.]

NOTES and QUESTIONS

1. The O.L.R.C. in its *Report on Sale of Goods* recommends that an offer shall be construed as inviting acceptance in any manner and by any medium reasonable in the circumstances, including either a promise to perform or performance of the requested act, where the offeror does not specify an exclusive manner. For example, A forwards an order for goods to B and adds "Please ship as soon as possible". B may either promise to ship or ship the goods unless the offeror has shown a contrary intention. Thus, the rigid classification of contracts as bilateral *or* unilateral is blurred. Is this desirable?

In this context, the tender or beginning of the invited performance is an acceptance by performance and binds the offeree to render complete performance. *Quaere* whether this would affect the situation where only acceptance by performance is contemplated.

(The Commission also discusses the question of notification of acceptance by performance. See *Report on Sale of Goods*, vol. I, 76-80.)

2. How can an offeror revoke an offer made to the world at large, such as that in *Carlill v. Carbolic Smoke Ball Co.*, *supra*, section 2? See *Shuey v. U.S.* (1875), 92 U.S. 73. If not revoked how long would such an offer remain open? See *"Industrial America" Inc. v. Fulton Industries Inc.* (*supra*, note 5 following *R. v. Clarke*).

3. Gloria Greer is a long-distance swimmer. The Manitoba Department of Tourism offers a prize of $50,000 and the Harvey Foster Sr. memorial cup to anyone swimming Lake Winnipeg on Queen Victoria's birthday. Gloria, excited by this prospect, spends the winter months training in Florida. On Queen Victoria's birthday, Gloria begins to swim Lake Winnipeg. When she is 100 yards from the other shore, the patrol boat receives a message that the prize offer has been withdrawn, which it immediately relays to Gloria. Gloria, however, continues to the other shore. Advise Gloria.

(a) Would it make any difference if the offer had been withdrawn when she was 100 yards into the lake?

(b) Would it make any difference if the offer had been withdrawn just before she entered the lake?

(b) LAPSE

BARRICK v. CLARK

[1951] S.C.R. 177, [1950] 4 D.L.R. 529

The appellants, executors of the estate of one E.J. Barrick, had been negotiating for about seven weeks for the sale of three quarter-sections of the late Mr. Barrick's land to the respondent, Clark, who resided in Luseland, Saskatchewan. The appellants were represented in negotiations by R.N. Barrick of Toronto. On October 30, 1947, Clark offered to purchase the land in question for $14,500.00, with a possession date anytime between January 1st and March 1st, 1948, and asked Barrick to reply to his offer by telegram. Barrick did not reply by telegram, but wrote to Clark on November 15:

> We are prepared to sell this land for $15,000 cash. If this price is satisfactory to you, the deal could be closed immediately, by preparing an agreement for sale to be given you on receipt of initial payment of $2,000—transfer of clear title to be given you on Jan. 1st, 1948, on receipt of balance of purchase price $13,000. The present tenant Kostrosky's lease expires March 1st, 1948. Trusting to hear from you as soon as possible.

This letter was delivered in Luseland on November 20, when Clark was absent on a hunting trip in Alberta.

Mrs. Clark opened the letter and wrote to Barrick that her husband was out of town, but expected back in about 10 days, that she would "endeavour to locate him", and requested "that you hold the deal open until you hear from him". Barrick made no reply to this letter from Mrs. Clark.

Clark returned on December 10, when he wrote in part:

> Owing to various circumstances I am not going to ask the Estate to split the difference between my offer and their figure though I think $14,750 would be a fair compromise. I am enclosing a cheque for $2,000 drawn on my account at the National Trust Co. Edmonton. The transfer and necessary papers I wish made out in the name of Frank J. Clark. I agree to pay the balance of the purchase price on or before Jan. 1st upon production by the Estate of evidence of a clear title and a properly completed transfer. . . .
> Kindly acknowledge receipt of this letter by return mail.

In the meantime the appellant William Hohmann, also of Luseland, without knowledge of Clark's correspondence, on November 28th inquired of Barrick with regard to this land and Barrick, on November 30th, offered him the land for $15,000 cash. Hohmann accepted this offer on December 3rd and both Hohmann and Barrick desired that this contract be carried out.

The day after writing his letter of December 10th respondent Clark heard of Hohmann's purchase and on that date wired Barrick as follows:

> RETURNED HERE YESTERDAY MORNING FROM BIG GAME HUNTING TRIP AIR-MAILED LETTER TO YOU LAST NIGHT ENCLOSING TWO THOUSAND DOLLARS THIS MORNING TOWN GOSSIP CLAIMS WILLIAM HOHMANN HAS BOUGHT THE THREE QUARTERS PRESUME YOU RECEIVED MRS. CLARKS LETTER NOVEMBER TWENTIETH TRUST THAT REPORT IS NOT CORRECT WOULD APPRECIATE REPLY BY WIRE

Barrick received this wire on December 12th and on that date wrote Clark as follows:

> I received your wire to-day. I received Mrs. Clark [*sic*] letter of Nov. 20th in reply to mine of Nov. 15. Mrs. Clark informed me that as you would be away for ten days and requested me to hold the deal open until your return. I held the deal open for you until Dec. 6th when I received an offer from Wm. Hohmann of $15,000 all cash which I accepted having had no reply from you. My solicitor is preparing Transfer of title to Mr. Hohmann and if he comes across with $15,000 he will be given same. If he fails to do so, I shall be at liberty to sell to some one else.
>
> I am very sorry this hitch has occurred and I shall return your $2000 immediately on receipt of same.

[Kellock J. found the reference to Dec. 6th to be in error.]

Clark sought a decree of specific performance of the alleged contract between himself and Barrick. His action was dismissed by McKercher J. However, this judgment was reversed in the Saskatchewan Court of Appeal, where MacDonald J.A. commented ([1949] 2 W.W.R. 1009):

> The first argument advanced by the defendants Barrick is based on the ground alleged in the amended par. 4 of the defence, namely, that the plaintiff by his delay in accepting the offer in the letter dated November 15, 1947, induced these defendants to believe that the offer was not accepted but was rejected by the plaintiff. The defendant Hohmann pleads that the offer of November 15, 1947, "elapsed and was abandoned, rejected or repudiated by plaintiff's failure to accept the same within a reasonable time."
>
> No doubt an offer remains open only for the time stated in the offer or, if no time is mentioned, for a reasonable time having regard to the nature and circumstances of the offer provided that it has not in the meantime been withdrawn.
>
> The learned trial Judge finds that it did elapse. He also appears to hold that there was a time limited within which the offer had to be accepted.
>
> As to the latter ground, it is sufficient to say that the correspondence does not set any date before which the offer must be accepted. In my opinion the offer did not elapse by effluxion of time. . . .
>
> So, in this case, the defendants Barrick, not having withdrawn their offer, must in law be considered as making it until it was received by the plaintiff. It was then accepted. . . .
>
> So I conclude that the offer of November 15, 1947, did not elapse by effluxion of time.

In the Supreme Court of Canada, the following judgments were delivered.

ESTEY J. Upon the assumption that Clark's letter of December 10th otherwise constituted an acceptance of Barrick's counter-offer of November 15th, the question arises: Was it within a reasonable time? The parties had throughout conducted their negotiations by letters and, as Barrick's counter-offer did not specify a time for an acceptance other than a suggestion of a reply as soon as possible, Clark had a reasonable time within which to make his acceptance by the posting of a letter to that effect. . . . What will constitute a reasonable time depends upon the nature and character and the normal or usual course of business in negotiations leading to a sale, as well as the circumstances of the offer including the conduct of the parties in the course of negotiations. . . .

Farm lands, apart from evidence to the contrary (not here adduced), are not subject to frequent or sudden changes or fluctuations in price and, therefore, in the ordinary course of business a reasonable time for the acceptance of an offer would be longer than that with respect to such commodities as shares of stock upon an established trading market. It would also be longer than in respect to goods of a perishable character. With this in mind the fact, therefore, that it was land would tend to lengthen what would be concluded as a reasonable time, which, however, must be determined in relation to the other circumstances.

While the correspondence between Clark and Barrick commenced with the letter of September 8th, much of the time was spent by Barrick in ascertaining the current selling value of the land. Even in his letter which induced Clark to make his offer of October 30th, Barrick indicated that he had not satisfied himself as to the current selling value. Clark himself, in his offer of October 30th, asked "for the estate's decision as fast as possible" and, if Barrick had decided to recommend his offer, to wire accordingly. Barrick, apparently appreciating Clark's desire to conclude this matter, as he explained in his counter-offer, consulted with those interested in the estate and made a concrete reply in the nature of a counter-offer. Clark had obviously made up his mind at least on October 30th as to the current selling value of the land. This is not only evidenced by his offer of that date, but when he returned upon December 10th he immediately accepted the counter-offer.

Under the circumstances of this case, the offer must be taken to have been received by Clark on November 20. It was addressed to him and received at this usual address and opened by his wife who, though she did not care to take the responsibility to deal with the counter-offer, had been apprised of these negotiations and, upon his own evidence, she had at least authority to receive the offer, if not to deal therewith. . . .

The offer of Barrick remained open for acceptance and in that sense as being renewed every moment until a reasonable time elapsed. While this time may be expressly enlarged by an act on the part of the offeror, a letter to him asking that the offer be kept open does not enlarge this reasonable time if the offeror elects, as he did, to not make reply. In that event the rights of the parties remain unchanged.

The offeree has the right, within a reasonable time, to accept and it is only by such an acceptance that he is given any rights against the offeror. What Barrick did or intended to do does not alter that time. If, when he accepted Hohmann's offer, a reasonable time had not elapsed, it would only be in the event that Clark's acceptance was within a reasonable time that the latter would have any right to take exception thereto.

It was particularly pointed out that there had been no sale for this land over a period of years. Possession could not be had until March 1st and, in any event, no farming operations could take place until spring conditions permitted. These are factors to be considered. However, there was, at the time material to these negotiations, a demand for this land. The owner, desiring to sell, would wish to avail himself of these conditions and those negotiating, other than the successful purchaser, would, no doubt, desire to consider other land or other possible courses that might be open to them. Clark, by his offer of October 30th, because of his insistence upon reply by wire, must have had these latter considerations in mind rather than the date of possession or spring operations on the farm. Barrick, while he did not perhaps evidence as much concern as to the date of concluding the transaction, did, in his offer of November 15th, in appreciation of Clark's desire, intimate that "the deal could be closed immediately" and concluded with what might be accepted as the expression of a hope that Clarke would reply "as soon as possible". A review of all the authorities submitted as well as others reviewed leads me to conclude, with great respect to those learned Judges who hold a contrary opinion, that Clark did not accept Barrick's offer within a reasonable time.

KELLOCK J. . . . Treating this letter [of November 15th] as an offer, there are, I think, three indications in the letter itself which show that December 10th was beyond a reasonable time for acceptance. In the first place, the appellant states that if respondent were satisfied with the price, the transaction could be *immediately* closed by the preparation and delivery of an agreement of sale in exchange for $2,000 to be paid by the respondent. It is true that the word "immediately" does not directly relate to the acceptance of the offer, but it indicates that, as regards the closing of the transaction which would follow acceptance of the offer, there should be no delay.

In the second place, the respondent is asked to give his answer "as soon as possible". It is true that this phrase is not an unusual one, but it is a circumstance indicating that promptness and not dilatoriness was expected.

The clearest indication in the letter, however, as to the time for acceptance is the provision that after acceptance of the offer, a formal agreement of sale would be executed and exchanged for a payment of $2,000, and that the balance of the purchase-price would be paid on January 1, 1948, when a conveyance would be given. I think it would be absurd to say that the appellant expected that the respondent could accept the offer as late as December 10th (of which the appellant would not learn until the 13th or 15th) and that thereafter an agreement would be prepared and sent out to the respondent to be exchanged for the $2,000 payment. This would use up most of the little more than 2 weeks intervening between the receipt of the acceptance by the appellant and January 1. In my opinion, the letter clearly indicates by its own terms that acceptance was to be made promptly if at all, and that December 10th was entirely outside the contemplation of the offerer. The only reason the offer was not in fact dealt with promptly was because the respondent was absent on a hunting expedition.

[Rinfret C.J.C. concurred with Kellock J. The concurring judgments of Taschereau and Locke JJ. are omitted. Appeal allowed.]

NOTES and QUESTION

1. In *Beer v. Townsgate I Ltd.* (1997), 152 D.L.R. (4th) 671 (Ont. C.A.), a number of purchasers signed offers to buy luxury condominiums from a developer in February 1989 in an inflated market. Each offer stated that it was "irrevocable by the Purchaser until one minute before midnight on the fifteenth day after its date, after which time if not accepted, this offer shall be null and void and the deposit returned to the Purchaser without interest . . . This offer when accepted shall constitute a binding contract of purchase and sale". The offers provided for closing in May, 1991, but by the end of 1989, the condominium market fell into a rapid decline. The offers were apparently signed by the vendor "within a week", but six of the purchasers did not receive their accepted agreements within fifteen days. The Court of Appeal held that on the wording of these agreements it was not sufficient that the acceptance was merely signed but that communication was required. The court then discussed what would amount to acquiescence to late acceptance: "I think that something more than passive acceptance of documents may be required. Basing acquiescence or affirmation on passive conduct

would place an unfair burden on purchasers to actually repudiate the contract when . . . there would seem to be no reason for them to do so. However, when purchasers actively continue to 'assert their rights' under the contract, it is evident that they have affirmed its existence. In addition, permitting the deposit cheques to be cashed is compelling evidence. This accords with common sense and reasonable commercial expectations". In any event, the court found that the purchasers were estopped from denying the existence of the contracts. See Chapter 4, section 5.

2. The Civil Code of Québec, Book 5, Obligations, Ch. II, Contracts, s. III provides:

> **Art. 1392.** An offer lapses if no acceptance is received by the offeror before the expiry of the specified term or, where no term is specified, before the expiry of a reasonable time; it also lapses in respect of the offeree if he has rejected it.
>
> The death or bankruptcy of the offeror or the offeree, whether or not a term is attached to the offer, or the institution of protective supervision in respect of either of them also causes the offer to lapse, if that event occurs before acceptance is received by the offeror.

3. The Vienna Convention, *supra*, provides in articles 20 and 21:

> 20(1) A period of time for acceptance fixed by the offeror in a telegram or a letter begins to run from the moment the telegram is handed in for dispatch or from the date shown on the letter or, if no such date is shown, from the date shown on the envelope. A period of time for acceptance fixed by the offeror by telephone, telex or other means of instantaneous communication, begins to run from the moment that the offer reaches the offeree.
>
> .....
>
> 21(1) A late acceptance is nevertheless effective as an acceptance if without delay the offeror orally so informs the offeree or dispatches a notice to that effect.
>
> (2) If a letter or other writing containing a late acceptance shows that it has been sent in such circumstances that if its transmission had been normal it would have reached the offeror in due time, the late acceptance is effective as an acceptance unless, without delay, the offeror orally informs the offeree that he considers his offer as having lapsed or dispatches a notice to that effect.

To what extent does the Convention retain some of the features of the postal acceptance rule?

MANCHESTER DIOCESAN COUNCIL OF EDUCATION v. COMMERCIAL AND GENERAL INVESTMENTS LTD.

[1970] 1 W.L.R. 241, [1969] 3 All E.R. 1593 (Ch.D.)

BUCKLEY J. The plaintiff, Manchester Diocesan Council for Education, is a corporate body in which there is vested a freehold property known as the Hesketh Fletcher Senior Church of England School, which, as its name indicates, was formerly used for the purposes of a school. Part of this property was vested in the plaintiff by a scheme framed by the Minister of Education in 1962 under the Endowed Schools Acts 1869 to 1948. Clause 4 of the scheme is in the following terms:

> The Governing Body [that is the plaintiff] is hereby authorised to sell any of the premises of the Foundations, the Schools of which have been, or are about to be, closed, subject in each case to the approval of the purchase price by the Minister of Education . . . [now the Secretary of State for Education and Science].

The Hesketh Fletcher school was closed in August 1967. In February 1963 in anticipation of this closure, negotiations were opened between the plaintiff's surveyor and a surveyor acting for the defendant company, which is a property development company.

[About October, 1963] the plaintiff decided to sell the property by tender. For this purpose it caused particulars and conditions of sale to be prepared. These incorporated a form of tender. The conditions required tenders to be sent to the plaintiff's surveyor on or before 27th of August 1964 and stipulated that the sale was subject to approval of the purchase price by the Secretary of State for Education and Science. Condition 4 was in the following terms:

> The person whose tender is accepted shall be the purchaser and shall be informed of the acceptance of his tender by letter sent to him by post addressed to the address given in his tender and every letter shall be deemed to have been received in due course of post. . . .

On 25th August 1964 the defendant company completed the form of tender, offering a sum of £28,500 in the following terms:

> We Commercial and General Investments Limited of 15 Berkeley Street, London, W. 1 hereby offer to buy from the [plaintiff] the property described in the foregoing particulars for the sum of £28,500 . . . And we agree that in the event of this offer being accepted in accordance with the above conditions on or before the day named in the conditions for this purpose we will pay the said purchase money and carry out and complete the purchase in accordance with the said conditions: dated this 25th day of August, 1964.

Then it is signed on behalf of the defendant company by, I suppose one of the directors, and the address is given, no. 15 Berkeley Street, London, W.1. No day was in fact named in the conditions as the day on or before which any offer should be accepted. This part of the form of tender was presumably included as the result of an oversight. This tender was despatched to the plaintiff's surveyor on the 26th of August, 1964, and was presumably received on the following day.

On 1st September 1964 the plaintiff's surveyor informed the defendant company's surveyor that the defendant company's offer was the highest one received and that the plaintiff's surveyor had recommended its acceptance. In this letter the plaintiff's surveyor wrote: "We shall write to you again as soon as we receive formal instructions." On the 14th September the defendant company's surveyor replied in a letter which he wrote: " . . . I look forward to receiving formal acceptance in early course", and in the same letter named the defendant company's solicitors to whom a contract could be sent. This letter was acknowledged by the plaintiff's surveyor on 15th September who then wrote:

> The sale has now been approved by the [plaintiff], the Incumbent and the Board of School Governors. Mr. L.H. Orford, Diocesan Registrar, of this address has been instructed to obtain the approval of the Secretary of State for Education. As soon as this is given he will be getting in touch with Messrs. D.J. Freeman & Company [the defendant company's] solicitors.

The plaintiff relies on this letter as an acceptance of the defendant company's offer, notwithstanding that the procedure envisaged by condition 4 was not followed. . . .

 . . . [O]n 18th November 1964, the Secretary of State approved the sale . . . On 23rd December 1964 the plaintiff's solicitors wrote to the defendant company's solicitors:

> We act for the [plaintiff] and understand that you act for the [defendant company] who submitted an offer by tender of £28,500 to purchase the above site, and which was accepted by [the plaintiff] subject to the consent of the Department of Education and Science. We are

writing to inform you that this consent has now been obtained and we conclude that the Contract is therefore binding on both parties. Kindly confirm.

The defendant company's solicitors replied on 5th January 1965:

We acknowledge receipt of your letter of 23rd ultimo upon which we have obtained [the defendant company's] instructions and regret that we cannot confirm that there is a binding contract between the parties in the matter.

On 6th January 1965 the plaintiff's solicitors wrote:

We acknowledge receipt of your letter of yesterday's date and are surprised to hear that [the defendant company] do not consider themselves bound. So far as we are concerned they put in the highest tender and its acceptance was communicated to them, subject only to the approval of the Church Commissioners which has now been obtained, and we consider a binding Contract is in existence. We shall be glad to know, however, if there is any reason for [the defendant company's] attitude, as any further Contract would only contain exactly the same terms as those contained in the tender submitted by them.

On the following day they wrote to the defendant company at no. 15, Berkeley Street (the address of the defendant company given in the form of tender) giving formal notice of acceptance of the defendant company's tender. On the same day the defendant company's solicitors wrote to the plaintiff's solicitors that the defendant company no longer wished to proceed with the purchase.

It is common ground that, if it was still open to the plaintiff to accept the tender on 7th January, the plaintiff's solicitors' letter of that date was an effective acceptance which took effect when the letter was posted, and that in that event the defendant company's withdrawal of their offer was too late. It is said, however, that because of the lapse of time between 25th August 1964 and 7th January 1965, the offer contained in the tender must be regarded as having lapsed before 7th January 1965. On either footing the withdrawal of the offer on 7th January is irrelevant. The writ was issued on 24th August 1965. The plaintiff claims a declaration that the tender and either the letter of 15th September 1964 or that of 7th January 1965 constituted a binding contract and consequential relief.

The first question is whether the plaintiff can rely on the letter of 15th September 1964 as an acceptance of the offer constituted by the tender. . . . Apart from any effect condition 4 may have on the position, I feel no doubt that the letter of 15th September should be read as a communication to the defendant company through its surveyor of the fact that the plaintiff had approved the sale of the property to the defendant company, that is to say, had accepted the defendant company's offer. It was a statement of the formal instructions received by the plaintiff's surveyor which were foreshadowed in the letter of 1st September and was in reply to the defendant company's surveyor's letter saying that he looked forward to receiving a formal acceptance.

The offer contained in the tender was to the effect that in the event of its being accepted in accordance with the condition of sale on or before the day named therein for that purpose (and none was so named) the defendant company would pay the price and complete the purchase. An offeror may by the terms of this offer indicate that it may be accepted in a particular manner. In the present case the conditions included condition 4 which I have read. It is said on the defendant company's behalf that the condition was not complied with until 7th

January 1965; that until that date the offer was never accepted in accordance with its terms; and that consequently nothing earlier than that date can be relied on as an acceptance resulting in a binding contract. If an offeror stipulates by the terms of his offer that it may, or that it shall, be accepted in a particular manner a contract results as soon as the offeree does the stipulated act, whether it has come to the notice of the offeror or not. In such a case the offeror conditionally waives either expressly or by implication the normal requirement that acceptance must be communicated to the offeror to conclude a contract. There can be no doubt that in the present case, if the plaintiff or its authorised agent had posted a letter addressed to the defendant company at no. 15, Berkeley Street, on or about 15th September informing the defendant company of the acceptance of its tender, the contract would have been complete at the moment when such letter was posted, but that of [*sic*] course was not taken. Condition 4, however, does not say that that shall be the sole permitted method of communicating an acceptance. It may be that an offeror, who by the terms of his offer insists on acceptance in a particular manner, is entitled to insist that he is not bound unless acceptance is effected or communicated in that precise way, although it seems probable that, even so, if the other party communicates his acceptance in some other way, the offeror may by conduct or otherwise waive his right to insist on the prescribed method of acceptance. Where, however, the offeror has prescribed a particular method of acceptance, but not in terms insisting that only acceptance in that mode shall be binding, I am of opinion that acceptance communicated to the offeror by any other mode which is no less advantageous to him will conclude the contract. Thus in *Tinn v. Hoffman & Co.* [(1873), 29 L.T. 271 (Ex. Ch.)], where acceptance was requested by return of post, Honeyman J. said:

> That does not mean exclusively a reply by letter by return of post, but you may reply by telegram or by verbal message, or by any means not later than a letter written and sent by return of post. . . .

If an offeror intends that he shall be bound only if his offer is accepted in some particular manner, it must be for him to make this clear. Condition 4 in the present case had not, in my judgment, this effect.

Moreover, the inclusion of condition 4 in the defendant company's offer was at the instance of the plaintiff, who framed the conditions and the form of tender. It should not, I think, be regarded as a condition or stipulation imposed by the defendant company as offeror on the plaintiff as offeree, but as a term introduced into the bargain by the plaintiff and presumably considered by the plaintiff as being in some way for the protection or benefit of the plaintiff. It would consequently be a term strict compliance with which the plaintiff could waive, provided the defendant company was not adversely affected. The plaintiff did not take advantage of the condition which would have resulted in a contract being formed as soon as a letter of acceptance complying with the condition was posted, but adopted another course, which could only result in a contract when the plaintiff's acceptance was actually communicated to the defendant company.

For these reasons, I have reached the conclusion that in accordance with the terms of the tender it was open to the plaintiff to conclude a contract by acceptance actually communicated to the defendant company in any way; and, in my judgment, the letter of 15th September constituted such an acceptance. . . .

But it is said that cl. 4 of the 1962 scheme conferred only a conditional power of sale and that ministerial approval was necessary before a contract of sale could be made. . . . By that clause the governing body is authorised to sell property comprised in the scheme but any sale—i.e., any contract for sale—is required to be conditional on ministerial approval of the price being obtained. The power to complete a sale is conditional on prior approval, but not the power to contract. The fact that ministerial approval was not obtained until 18th November 1964 does not, in my judgment, invalidate the contract, if any, made on 15th September.

If I am right in thinking that there was a contract on 15th September 1964 that disposes of the case but, in case I should be held to be wrong in that view, I will now consider the other point in the case and will for this purpose assume that no contract was made at that date. On this basis no contract can have been concluded before 7th January 1965. The defendant company contend that, as the tender stipulated no time within which it must be accepted, it was an implied term of the offer that it must be accepted, if at all, within a reasonable time. It is said that acceptance on 7th January was not within a reasonable time.

It has long been recognised as being the law that, where an offer is made in terms which fix no time limit for acceptance, the offer must be accepted within a reasonable time to make a contract. . . . There seems, however, to be no reported case in which the reason for this is explained.

There appear to me to be two possible views on methods of approaching the problem. First, it may be said that by implication the offer is made on terms that, if it is not accepted within a reasonable time, it must be treated as withdrawn. Alternatively, it may be said that, if the offeree does not accept the offer within a reasonable time, he must be treated as having refused it. On either view the offer would cease to be a live one on the expiration of what in the circumstances of the particular case should be regarded as a reasonable time for acceptance. The first of these alternatives involves implying a term that if the offer is not accepted within a reasonable time, it shall be treated as withdrawn or lapsing at the end of that period if it has not been accepted; the second is based on an inference to be drawn from the conduct of the offeree, that is, that having failed to accept the offer within a reasonable time he has manifested an intention to refuse it. If, in the first alternative, the time which the offeror is to be treated as having set for acceptance is to be such a time as is reasonable at the date of the offer, what is reasonable must depend on circumstances then existing and reasonably likely to arise during the continuance of the offer; but it would be not unlikely that the offeror and offeree would make different assessments of what would be reasonable even if, as might quite possibly not be the case, they based those judgments on identical known and anticipated circumstances. No doubt a court could resolve any dispute about this, but this approach clearly involves a certain degree of uncertainty about the precise terms of the offer. If on the other hand the time which the offeror is to be treated as having set for acceptance is to be such a time as turns out to be reasonable in the light of circumstances then existing and of circumstances arising thereafter during the continuance of the offer, whether foreseeable or not, an additional element of uncertainty is introduced. The second alternative on the other hand involves simply an objective assessment of facts and the determination of the question whether on the facts the offeree should in fairness to both parties be regarded as having refused the offer.

It does not seem to me that either party is in greater need of protection by the law in this respect than the other. Until his offer has been accepted, it is open to the offeror at any time to withdraw it or to put a limit on the time for acceptance. On the other hand, the offeree can at any time refuse the offer or, unless he has been guilty of unreasonable delay, accept it. Neither party is at a disadvantage. Unless authority constrains me to do otherwise, I am strongly disposed to prefer the second alternative to the first. . . .

I have dealt with this part of the case at some length because, if the first alternative were the correct view of the law and if what is reasonable had to be ascertained as at the time of the offer, the subsequent conduct of the parties would be irrelevant to the question how long the offer should be treated as remaining open. In my opinion, however, the subsequent conduct of the parties is relevant to the question, which I think is the right test, whether the offeree should be held to have refused the offer by his conduct.

In my judgment the letter of 15th September 1964 excludes the possibility of imputing to the plaintiff a refusal of the offer. If that letter does not itself constitute an effective acceptance, it clearly discloses an intention to accept from which there is nothing to suggest a departure before 7th January 1965. Accordingly, if no contract was formed earlier, I am of opinion that it was open to the plaintiff to accept it on 7th January and that the plaintiff's letter of that date was effectual to bind the defendant company contractually. . . .

[An order for specific performance was granted.]

NOTES and QUESTIONS

1. Buckley J. states two theoretical bases for the rule that an offer is open for acceptance only for a reasonable time. Which basis was used by (a) the Saskatchewan Court of Appeal (b) the Supreme Court of Canada in *Barrick v. Clark*, [1951] S.C.R. 177, *supra*? What effect would the different theories have on the result in that case?

2. An offer can on its terms set an event or condition that would limit the possibility of its acceptance. This could apply as well to situations where the subject matter of the offer is destroyed before the acceptance has occurred. Courts have found that such events mean that the offer is not capable of being accepted. See *Reitzel v. Rej-Cap Manufacturing Ltd.* (1985), 53 O.R. (2d) 116 (H.C.) This can be contrasted with the situation where subject matter is destroyed after the formation of the contract, a situation which may result in frustration of contract, *infra*, Chapter 10.

3. In *Financings Ltd. v. Stimson*, [1962] 1 W.L.R. 1184 (C.A.) on 16th March 1961, the defendant signed an offer to enter into a hire-purchase agreement with the plaintiffs for the purchase of a car for £350, the agreement to "become binding . . . [on the plaintiffs] only upon acceptance by signature . . .". On 18th March the defendant paid the first installment and was allowed to take the car away but, dissatisfied, returned it to the dealer two days later and cancelled his insurance. On the night of 24th March the car dealer's premises were broken into, and the car was stolen and severely damaged. When it was recovered, it was sold by the plaintiffs for £240. On 25th March the plaintiffs signed the acceptance. In an action on the hire-purchase agreement, the court held that if the offer had not been revoked by the return of the car to the dealer, it was conditional on the car remaining in substantially the same condition as it was when the offer was made until the moment of acceptance.

This case was followed in *Clark Agri Service Ltd. v. 705680 Ontario Ltd. (c.o.b. Glen Elevators)* (1996), 2 C.P.C. (4th) 78 (Ont. Gen. Div.), in which an offer to settle a property dispute, if not revoked by being replaced with a second offer, was terminated when a tornado damaged the property.

Chapter 3

FORMATION OF THE AGREEMENT: CERTAINTY OF TERMS

1. Introduction

The theory that the existence of a contract is based upon the mutual acceptance of reciprocal obligations is premised on the assumption that it is possible to determine what those obligations are. Hence one of the requirements of a contract's formation is that its terms define the parties' obligations with certainty. The theme that underlies the body of law associated with the requirement of certainty is fundamentally the same as that underlying the principles of offer and acceptance. Both address the question of whether the parties are truly in agreement; that is, whether they share an unambiguous understanding of their respective rights and obligations. To express the point in more elegant and traditional terms, the question is whether the parties have achieved *consensus ad idem*. If the answer is no, the parties may have made an agreement, but it is not a contract.

As we saw in the last chapter, a purported acceptance of an offer to contract that departs materially from the terms of the offer is not effective; no contract arises from the parties' exchange. That is so because the offeror has expressed a willingness to proceed under one set of right and obligations, but the offeree has expressed a willingness to accept rights and obligations that differ in one or more respects from those contemplated by the offeror. They have not agreed to the same thing.

Frequently, however, the parties' respective positions as to the terms of their agreement are not manifested by the sequential sort of exchange generally associated with issues of offer and acceptance. Rather, we are presented with what purports to be a complete agreement, but one in which the obligations the parties have mutually accepted as comprising its content are not in all respects clear. The difficulty is not that the parties have apparently agreed to different things, but that they have not reached agreement at all on one or more material points of the contemplated transaction or relationship or, in some instances, that it is not possible to determine from the words used what they have agreed. Of course, if the matter becomes the subject of litigation, one of the parties will invariably assert that agreement *has* been reached, on the basis of a proffered explanation of what the words used were intended to mean. The party resisting enforcement of the agreement will argue not only that the words as interpreted by the other party do not represent what the parties agreed, but that it is impossible to draw from them *any* conclusion about the basis upon which the matter in issue is to proceed. If it is not possible to identify the terms upon which the parties have agreed, there can be no contract.

The terminology employed in connection with problems of uncertainty in the context of contract formation can be deceptive. Lawyers, judges and commentators often discuss the issue in terms of whether there is an "enforceable" contract between the parties, or whether a contract is "void" for uncertainty. That language is misleading, since it suggests that a contract exists, but that it cannot be enforced because its terms are not certain. Notwithstanding such language, the real subject of discussion is whether a contract has come into existence at all. The question is not one of contract enforcement, but one of contract formation.

Although the problem of uncertainty relates to contract formation rather than contract enforcement, it is helpful to keep in mind the relationship between these two dimensions of contract doctrine when considering cases that raise this issue. The conclusion that a contract is "enforceable" means that if one of the parties "breaches" the contract by failing to perform the obligation imposed by the term breached, the law offers a "remedy" to the other party or parties. The remedy awarded by the court is ordinarily a directive that the party in breach pay monetary compensation for the breach (an award of "damages"). In limited circumstances the court may direct that the party in breach actually perform the contractual obligation in question (an award of "specific performance"). The sum of money to which a party seeking enforcement is entitled by way of damages is designed to put him or her in the position he or she would have been in had the other party's contractual obligations been fulfilled. Therefore, in order to grant a remedy, it must be possible to define precisely what it is that the party in breach was obliged to do under the contract. If it is not possible to determine that question by reference to the terms of the parties' agreement, no basis exists for the award of a remedy for breach of contract; hence it may be untenable to maintain that there *is* a contract. Accordingly, a court is likely to be influenced in deciding whether an agreement is sufficiently certain to be regarded as a contract by the question of whether its terms allow for determination of the sum of money that appropriately compensates for non-performance by one of the parties. The subject of contract remedies is discussed in Chapter 14.

The intention of parties to an agreement is relevant to the question of whether the terms used are sufficiently certain to support a contract in two respects. If there is a degree of uncertainty in the terms of an agreement, the court will not attempt to resolve that uncertainty in aid of the conclusion that the agreement is a contract unless it is clear that the parties intended to contract; that is, that they intended to create mutually binding and enforceable obligations. Secondly, the exercise of determining whether the terms of the agreement define the parties' obligations with sufficient certainty depends upon ascertaining the parties' intention as to the meaning of the language used. In the law of contract, the determination of intention is ordinarily approached objectively. The issue is not what each of the parties actually intended (a subjective approach), but rather what they must reasonably be viewed as having intended given the language used and the circumstances and aim of the transaction (an objective approach). As you read the cases in this chapter, consider whether the courts have used an objective or a subjective approach in determining whether the terms of an agreement clearly establish the parties' shared intention as to their respective obligations.

The use of an objective standard to give content to the language of agreement facilitates the contracting process, in that it allows for determination of the parties' reciprocal obligations notwithstanding a certain degree of ambiguity in the words through which they have expressed their intention. The fact that one party denies the view advanced by the other as to the meaning and clarity of the terms used does not preclude a finding that agreement was reached. However, the courts are ordinarily anxious to ensure that they do not improperly impose obligations that the parties did not intend to assume by finding an agreement on terms to which they did not assent. The judicial "filling in of the blanks" in the language of agreement based on what the parties must reasonably be presumed to have intended may facilitate the conclusion of a contemplated transaction. However, if carried too far, it may impose a contractual liability to which one or both of the parties had no intention of being exposed. Accordingly, there is a tension between fulfilling the reasonable expectations of parties by giving effect to their agreement, notwithstanding deficiencies in its expression, and defeating their reasonable expectations by imposing an agreement that was not intended.

The headings below loosely categorize the various objections to enforcement. The common theme is the argument that, because the terms fail to define the essential obligations of the parties, a contract has not been formed. Though categorization assists in the analysis of these cases, there is no bright line between them. This is particularly true in connection with the cases considered in sections 3 through 5, in which the question raised is whether parties whose agreement contemplates a further course of negotiation to finalize identified terms of a transaction have succeeded in creating enforceable obligations through the vehicle of a contract.

2.   Vagueness

R. v. CAE INDUSTRIES LTD.

[1986] 1 F.C. 129, [1985] 5 W.W.R. 481, 30 B.L.R. 236, 20 D.L.R. (4th) 347, 61 N.R. 19 (C.A.), leave to appeal to S.C.C. refused (1985), 20 D.L.R. (4th) 347n

Negotiations took place between the Government of Canada and the respondent about the possibility of the respondent taking over and running an aircraft maintenance base no longer required by Air Canada. In March 1969, the following letter was written and signed by three ministers:

THE MINISTER OF TRANSPORT

OTTAWA, March 26, 1969.

Mr. C.D. Reekie,
President,
CAE Industries Ltd.
P.O. Box 6166,
Montreal 3, P.Q.

Dear Mr. Reekie:

On February 28, 1969, you wrote to Mr. E.L. Hewson of the Department of Transport asking for certain assurances in connection with the proposed purchase of Air Canada's Winnipeg Maintenance Base by Northwest Industries Ltd., a subsidiary of CAE Industries Ltd. On the basis of an agreement having been signed by your firm and by Air Canada, the undersigned have been authorized to provide the following assurances in this matter.

(a) The Government of Canada agrees with the objective that present employment levels should be maintained and that every possible effort should be made to assist in the development of a viable and continuing aerospace industry in Winnipeg.

(b) It also agrees that 700,000 manhours of direct labour per annum is a realistic target for the operation of a viable enterprise in these facilities and that current estimates of future workload suggest a potential gap between actual and minimum levels in the years 1971 to 1976 unless new repair and overhaul work or aerospace manufacturing contracts can be obtained.

(c) The Department of Defence Production can guarantee no more than 40,000 to 50,000 direct labour manhours per year in the period 1971-1976 as "set-aside" repair and overhaul work, but the Government of Canada will employ its best efforts to secure the additional work required from other government departments and crown corporations to meet the target level of 700,000 direct labour manhours.

(d) In fulfilling the commitment set out in (c) above, the Government of Canada agrees that any additional work allocated to the Winnipeg Maintenance Base will not be taken from government contract work presently carried out by Northwest Industries in Edmonton.

(e) It further agrees that the existing Air Canada lease from the Department of Transport will be assigned to NWI under present financial terms and conditions for a period of ten years.

Yours sincerely,

Paul T. Hellyer

Concurred in by:
Hon. J.L. Pépin,
Minister of Trade and Commerce
Hon. D.C. Jamieson,
Minister of Defence Production

The respondent then arranged for the purchase of the base by a subsidiary company. In 1971, the workload at the maintenance base diminished and the respondent sued for breach of contract.

STONE J.: . . .

Was a contract intended?

[The topic of Intention to Create Legal Relations is addressed in Chapter 4, section 6.]

The appellant contends that in the circumstances the letter of March 26, 1969 was never intended to become a binding legal contract . . . .

I share the view expressed by Mr. Justice Pratte that the circumstances in which the letter was written do not disclose an intention to enter into a purely political arrangement rather than a contract. Intention to enter a contract may be gathered from the surrounding circumstances, as was pointed out by Middleton J. in *Lindsey v. Heron & Co.* [*infra*, Chapter 9, section 2], quoting from *Corpus Juris*, vol. 13, at 265:

> The apparent mutual consent of parties essential to the formation of a contract, must be gathered from the language employed by them, and the law implies to a person an intention corresponding to the reasonable meaning of his words and acts. It judges his intention from his outward expression and excludes all questions in regard to his unexpressed intention.

The government of the day was faced with a decision by Air Canada to phase out its aircraft maintenance base at Winnipeg. The initiative to find a buyer in the private sector was taken by the government itself and it was the government that approached the respondent as a potential buyer. It was seeking through the respondent a solution for a particular problem. It was eager and anxious to find a buyer so that the maintenance base and associated employment in Winnipeg could be preserved.

In my view the circumstances in which the letter was written distinguishes this case from others where it has been found that no intention to contract was present: see, *e.g.*, *Joy Oil Co. Ltd. v. The King*, [1951] 3 D.L.R. 582, [1951] S.C.R. 624, and *Meates v. Attorney-General*, [1979] 1 N.Z.L.R. 415 (S.C.). It is clear from the evidence that the parties treated the document as a binding contract to the extent that it was partly performed. Moreover, as has been pointed out, the onus of proof in a case of this kind "is on the person who asserts that no legal effect is intended, and the onus is a heavy one": *Edwards v. Skyways Ltd.*, [1964] 1 W.L.R. 349 (Q.B.) at p. 355; and see also *Bahamas Oil Refining Co. v. Kristiansands Tankrederei A/S (The "Polyduke")*, [1978] 1 Lloyd's Rep. 211 (Q.B.). It is my view that the burden has not been discharged. I have concluded on the basis of evidence and the findings of the judge below that there was an intention on the part of both parties to enter into a binding legal contract.

Is the contract vague and uncertain or incomplete?

My conclusion that the parties intended to enter into a binding legal contract does not mean that they succeeded in doing so. The appellant strenuously contends that the language used by the parties is so vague and uncertain or the document is so incomplete as to render the contract unenforceable. The learned judge below disagreed.

No doubt the parties chose to cast their agreement, arrived at after lengthy negotiations, in a somewhat unusual form and style. But that, in itself, ought not to deter us from giving it effect if the parties have expressed themselves in language sufficiently clear as to have created rights and obligations enforceable in a Court of law. This is especially so where, as already noted, the contract has been partly performed for then, as Mignault J. said in *Kelly v. Watson* (1921), 57 D.L.R. 363 at p. 369, 61 S.C.R. 482 at 490, [1921] 1 W.W.R. 958, unless it be incomplete "the Court . . . will struggle against the difficulty ensuing from the vagueness of the contract". As in *Hillas & Co. Ltd. v. Arcos Ltd.* [*infra*, section 3], we are dealing here with a commercial contract. . . . I am of the view that we should make every effort to find a meaning in the words actually used by the parties in deciding whether an enforceable contract exists. That, it seems to me, is called for by the cases. Thus, in *Marquest Industries Ltd. v. Willows Poultry Farms Ltd.* (1968), 1 D.L.R. (3d) 513 at 517-8, . . . (B.C. C.A.), it was stated:

In the first place, consideration must be given to the duty of a Court and the rules it should apply, where a claim is made that a portion of a commercial agreement between two contracting parties is void for uncertainty or, to put it another way, is meaningless. The primary rule of construction has been expressed by the maxim, *ut res magis valeat quam pereat* or as paraphrased in English, "a deed shall never be void where the words may be applied to any extent to make it good". The maxim . . . [establishes] that every effort should be made by a Court to find a meaning, looking at substance and not mere form, and that difficulties in interpretation do not make a clause bad as not being capable of interpretation, so long as a definite meaning can properly be extracted. In other words, every clause in a contract must, if possible, be given effect to. Also, as stated as early as 1868 in *Gwyn v. Neath Canal Navigation Co.* (1868), L.R. 3 Ex. 209, that if the real intentions of the parties can be collected from the language within the four corners of the instrument, the Court must give effect to such intentions by supplying anything necessarily to be inferred and rejecting whatever is repugnant to such real intentions so ascertained.

On the other hand, I would also agree that the contract before us would not be good if it is so vague and uncertain as to be unenforceable, or if it is incomplete in the sense described in *May & Butcher Ltd. v. The King* [*infra*, section 3].

Is the contract in question so incomplete as to be unenforceable within these principles? In my opinion it is not. Unlike in the cases referred to, it does not leave anything unsettled that was necessary to be settled between the parties. It is in itself an entire contract capable of standing on its own feet. The fact that, following on its own performance, there would need to be formed individual service contracts for the carrying out of individual items of aircraft repair and overhaul work did not, to my mind, detract from its central commitment which was to "set-aside" repair and overhaul work and to employ "best efforts" to secure other like work for the respondent within the context of the letter of March 26, 1969.

The more difficult question, it seems to me, is whether the contract is capable of being enforced despite what I think may properly be viewed as a certain looseness of language as, for example, the presence of such terms as "assurances" in the first paragraph, as well as "can guarantee", "set-aside" and "best efforts" appearing in para. (c) of the letter. As to the first of these I have no difficulty in concluding in the circumstances that what were described as "assurances" were, upon acceptance by the respondent, intended to be and did become binding commitments. That this is so is reflected in para. (d) immediately following where the words "In fulfilling the commitment set out in (c) above" appear. Clearly, the Ministers viewed para. (c) as a "commitment" despite the use of the word "assurances" in the first paragraph of the letter. I would view the term "can guarantee" in the same light. It was intended to convey and did convey the limit of "set-aside" repair and overhaul work the respondent could expect to receive if it decided to accept what by that time had become a counter-proposal. Upon acceptance the proposal became a binding commitment guaranteeing provision of "set-aside" work. At the same time that commitment must be construed in a reasonable fashion in the light of the language used, for I would agree that as a guarantee it had to be definite in extent. It is my view that by the language used the parties intended that at least 40,000 direct labour manhours of "set-aside" work would be provided. As both parties conceded before us, any hours in excess of that figure were not within the "set-aside" guarantee.

The term "set-aside" was itself the subject of evidence at trial to the effect that it consisted of work to be directed to the respondent without competition to be performed at full in-plant overhead rates. There was also evidence that it consisted simply of work done without competition and without any contribution to overhead. The trial judge, it appears, accepted that the former was the case and rejected the latter evidence. On the basis of that evidence he concluded . . . that the "set-aside" work was "a guarantee with no strings attached" and that the appellant was bound to carry out this aspect of the agreement even if it was necessary "to take work away from others". I am unable to disagree with his finding in this regard or with the interpretation he placed upon the term based upon his appreciation of the evidence before him. In all of the circumstances surrounding the transaction the explanation of the appellant's witnesses as to the meaning of the term "set-aside" is simply not a reasonable one. That, in effect, was the conclusion which the trial judge drew, perhaps not specifically but as he clearly implies in his reasons.

Finally, I come to the term "best efforts" which the government promised to employ to secure additional work. The appellant attacks it as so lacking in precision as to render it incapable of creating legal rights and obligations enforceable in a court of law. I would agree that it is a rather general term but our task here is to discover, if we can, what the parties intended by it. It was the view of the learned trial judge that it is an equivalent term to "best endeavours" as interpreted in the case of *Sheffield District R. Co. v. Great Central R. Co.* (1911), 27 T.L.R. 451, where A.T. Lawrence J. (sitting as a member of the Railway and Canal Commission) stated . . . that, subject to certain qualifications, the term, broadly speaking, meant "leave no stone unturned". In my view the construction of the term "best efforts" must be approached in the light of the contract itself, the parties to it and its overall purpose as reflected in the language it contains. It created a broad obligation to secure for the respondent aircraft repair and overhaul work up to the limit it lays down.

This did not mean, and the contrary is not suggested, that it required the government to disregard any existing contractual obligations or, certainly, to neglect the public interest. To the extent that that interest required work to be done by persons other than the respondent, there could be no valid complaint that the contract would thereby be breached. Indeed, this limitation seems implicit in the language of the contract itself for the appellant did not bind itself to provide work to the respondent but only to employ its "best efforts" to secure it. I am therefore unable to find anything in the language of the contract which purported to bind the appellant to a course of action that would be contrary to the public interest.

In summary, I would respectfully agree with the conclusion arrived at by the learned trial judge that this feature of the contract obliged the government to employ its "best efforts" to secure additional work from other departments and crown corporations "in respect of any shortfall up to 700,000 hours per year for the years 1971 to 1976". He put it in greater detail (at p. 635) in this way:

> The agreement by the defendant was to provide a guaranteed number of man-hours from DDP and to use its (the Crown's) best efforts to make up any shortfall between what was

realized by the plaintiffs from that and other sources, up to 700,000 hours per annum. I have summarized the agreement in broad terms. From a strict legal view, no further matters had to be agreed upon. Best efforts, from the defendant's side to provide the necessary hours, were required. How those best efforts were to be made, when and if necessary, was up to the defendant. As a matter of commercial and practical necessity, consultation and negotiation as to the work, and cost of it, which would go to any 700,000-hour shortfall, would likely have taken place. In fact, that is what happened. But as a matter of binding legal necessity, no further agreements, to make the March 26 letter valid, were required.

[Pratte J. delivered a dissenting judgment. Urie J. concurred with Stone J. Appeal dismissed, save for one aspect that related to the assessment of the respondent's damages.]

NOTES and QUESTION

1. The symbiotic relationship between the question of intention to contract and that of certainty of terms is illustrated by the decision of the Supreme Court of Canada in *V.K. Mason Construction Ltd. v. Bank of Nova Scotia*, [1985] 1 S.C.R. 271. In that case, a construction company contracted with a property developer to build a retail complex on the strength of what is often called a "comfort letter" provided by the property developer's bank. The letter advised that ". . . we have accorded [the developer] interim financing sufficient to cover the cost of the . . . complex . . .". The construction company completed the project but the bank did not advance sufficient funds to cover the developer's costs, with the result that the construction company was not fully paid. The court acknowledged that, in principle, a "unilateral" contract could have arisen if the letter amounted to a promise on the part of the bank that, if the construction company agreed to build the complex, the bank would ensure that sufficient funding was available to cover the developer's costs. However, it concluded that, given the imprecise wording of the letter, no contract arose. The court's decision on that point was not based on the view that the requirement of certainty as an element of contract formation was not fulfilled. Rather, because the language used did not define the nature and extent of the bank's obligations with sufficient precision, it could not support the conclusion that the bank intended the letter to have contractual effect. Though the bank was therefore not liable for breach of contract, the court did award damages against it in tort on the grounds of negligent misrepresentation. The leading case on so-called "comfort letters" is *Kleinwort, Benson Ltd. v. Malaysia Mining Corp. Bhd.*, [1989] 1 W.L.R. 379 (C.A.), in which the issue of contract formation was also addressed as a matter of intention to contract. See further Clark, " 'Cold Comfort Letter': *Kleinwort, Benson Ltd. v. Malaysia Mining Corp. Bhd*" (1990), 69 C.B.R. 753.

2. The use of ambiguous language in contract drafting often reflects the fact that the subject of the agreement involves performance at a future time in a factual context that is unknowable in points of material detail at the time of the agreement. The best the parties can do is to convey a general idea of the desired outcome of the transaction. In *Leonard H. Cook's Construction Ltd. v. Scott* (1989), 9 R.P.R. (2d) 69 at 71 (N.B. C.A.) the following schedule was attached to an agreement for the sale of the defendant's dairy farm to the plaintiff:

Vendor to keep (1) one lot to be chosen by Leonard Cook and Mary Scott upon approval of Subdivision plan and approved by the proper authorities. Lot to have some view but not of prime location. Lot to be located near center area of property, and not around perimeter of property. The lot size shall be determined by the approved subdivision plan.

The trial judge termed it "hopelessly vague". The Court of Appeal agreed that Schedule A was uncertain and could not be severed.

Did the requirement of certainty make it a practical impossibility for the parties to contract for sale of the dairy farm in a manner that would assure the vendor of a suitable lot? The cases in the next section demonstrate one way in which parties have attempted to deal with a problem of this kind; that is, by agreeing to agree to the precise details of performance when the relevant facts became available (in this case, to identify the lot to be retained by the vendor once the property was subdivided into residential lots from which a choice could be made). As you will see, there is no easy solution to this problem.

3.   Incomplete Terms

The previous section addressed the problem of ascribing meaning to the words of an agreement that is complete on its face, where one or more of the articulated terms are ambiguously expressed. The following trilogy of cases, decided one after the other within a five year span, comprises the foundation of current Canadian law on the issue of whether an agreement that is incomplete on its face may constitute a contract. In these cases, the parties did not stipulate the basis upon which an aspect or aspects of the transaction or relationship under consideration were to proceed. Although delivered more than 70 years ago, these judgments continue to be regularly cited and applied by judges and invoked by legal commentators.

The parties to these cases, like many others, faced a practical problem to which the law has provided no satisfactory solution, notwithstanding the frequency with which it has been presented to the courts. People often wish to establish mutually binding obligations to do something in the future, though they are not able to articulate in advance the precise manner in which those obligations should be performed when the time arrives. The question is how to achieve an enforceable present commitment to a future performance that, at the time of the agreement, cannot be fully defined. The cases comprising the trilogy all involved agreements for the sale of goods. At the time of their agreement, the parties in each case were unable to determine one or more such essential features of the anticipated transaction such as the price to be paid or the quality and exact description of the goods to be provided. Though this sort of problem is endemic to contracts for the supply of goods or services in the future or over a period of time, it can arise in other contexts as well.

The first case, *May & Butcher Ltd. v. R.*, is the likely source of the legal aphorism that; "An agreement to agree is not a contract." Some analysts would place *May & Butcher Ltd.* and *Foley v. Classique Coaches Ltd.* in the category of agreements to agree, differentiating *Hillas & Co. v. Arcos Ltd.* as a case in which the parties' agreement simply lacked essential terms. However, there is no substantive distinction between these cases, notwithstanding that the language employed by the parties in *Hillas & Co. v. Arcos Ltd.* was not expressed in terms of a future agreement on terms. In all three cases, the parties had left an aspect of their agreement unspecified. In such cases, the question is whether it is possible to determine the content of the parties' reciprocal obligations with respect to those elements of their transaction. If it is impossible to ascertain what it is that one or the other of the parties is expected to do or not do to satisfy the agreement, it is impossible either to determine the preliminary question of whether that party is in breach of his or her obligations, or to delineate the basis upon which to fashion a remedy for breach.

MAY & BUTCHER LTD. v. R.

[1934] 2 K.B. 17 (H.L.)

The suppliants entered into an arrangement with the Disposals Board for the purchase of surplus "tentage", which remained in government hands following the end of the first world war. Correspondence from the Controller of the Disposals Board in June 1921 outlined the terms of these arrangements as follows:

> . . . in consideration of your agreeing to deposit with the [Disposals & Liquidation] Commission the sum of 1000*l*. as security for the carrying out of this extended contract, the Commission hereby confirm the sale to you of the whole of the old tentage which may become available . . . up to and including December 31, 1921, upon the following terms:—
>
> (1.) The Commission agrees to sell and [the suppliants] agree to purchase the total stock of old tentage. . . .
>
> (3.) The price or prices to be paid, and the date or dates on which payment is to be made by the purchasers to the Commission for such old tentage shall be agreed upon from time to time between the Commission and the purchasers as the quantities of the said old tentage become available for disposal, and are offered to the purchasers by the Commission.
>
> (4.) Delivery . . . shall be taken by the purchasers in such period or periods as may be agreed upon between the Commission and the purchasers when such quantities of old tentage are offered to the purchasers by the Commission. . . .
>
> (10.) It is understood that all disputes with reference to or arising out of this agreement will be submitted to arbitration in accordance with the provisions of the Arbitration Act, 1889.

By the second letter dated January 7, 1922, the Disposals Controller, referring to verbal negotiations that had taken place for an extension of the agreement between the Commission and the suppliants, confirmed the sale to the latter of the tentage which might become available for disposal up to March 31, 1923.

LORD BUCKMASTER . . . The first arrangement made between the Disposals Board and the appellants was in April, 1920. The transactions between them all appear to have taken a similar form. There was an agreement for the sale of the goods; there was an agreement that the price for the goods should be subsequently fixed between the parties; and there were provisions with regard to arbitration in the event of dispute. A dispute then arose out of the bargain dated January 7, 1922. At or about that time the control of the Disposals Board was changed. . . .

The points that arise for determination are these: Whether or not the terms of the contract were sufficiently defined to constitute a legal binding contract between the parties. The Crown says that the price was never agreed. The suppliants say first, that if it was not agreed, it would be a reasonable price. Secondly, they say that even if the price was not agreed, the arbitration clause in the contract was intended to cover this very question of price, and that consequently the reasonableness of the price was referred to arbitration under the contract. Thirdly, they say that even if they are wrong on their first two contentions the fact that the whole of the bargain was ended in 1922 was doing them a wrong, because in any event they were entitled to have the opportunity of entering into a further agreement for future parcels of the goods which were referred to in the terms of the contract.

My Lords, those being the contentions, it is obvious that the whole matter depends upon the construction of the actual words of the bargain itself. . . .

What resulted was this: it was impossible to agree [to] the prices, and unless the appellants are in a position to establish either that this failure to agree resulted out of a definite agreement to buy at a reasonable price, or that the price had become subject to arbitration, it is plain on the first two points which have been mentioned that this appeal must fail.

In my opinion there never was a concluded contract between the parties. It has long been a well recognized principle of contract law that an agreement between two parties to enter into an agreement in which some critical part of the contract matter is left undetermined is no contract at all. It is of course perfectly possible for two people to contract that they will sign a document which contains all the relevant terms, but it is not open to them to agree that they will in the future agree upon a matter which is vital to the arrangement between them and has not yet been determined. It has been argued that as the fixing of the price has broken down, a reasonable price must be assumed. That depends in part upon the terms of the Sale of Goods Act, which no doubt reproduces, and is known to have reproduced, the old law upon the matter. That provides in s. 8 that "the price in a contract of sale may be fixed by the contract, or may be left to be fixed in manner thereby agreed, or may be determined by the course of dealing between the parties. Where the price is not determined in accordance with the foregoing provisions the buyer must pay a reasonable price"; while, if the agreement is to sell goods on the terms that the price is to be fixed by the valuation of a third party, and such third party cannot or does not make such valuation, s. 9 says that the agreement is avoided. I find myself quite unable to understand the distinction between an agreement to permit the price to be fixed by a third party and an agreement to permit the price to be fixed in the future by the two parties to the contract themselves. In principle it appears to me that they are one and the same thing. . . .

The next question is about the arbitration clause, and there I entirely agree with the majority of the Court of Appeal and also with Rowlatt J. The clause refers "disputes with reference to or arising out of this agreement" to arbitration, but until the price has been fixed, the agreement is not there. The arbitration clause relates to the settlement of whatever may happen when the agreement has been completed and the parties are regularly bound. There is nothing in the arbitration clause to enable a contract to be made which in fact the original bargain has left quite open.

Finally, I cannot take the view that the parties are entitled to an offer for the further parcels, because in my opinion this agreement is not a binding agreement at all, and the suggestion that the payment of the deposit entitled the appellants as of right to these offers, and constituted a valid and binding option, is not to my mind the true construction of what that deposit was for. The deposit was really for the purpose of securing the carrying out of the terms of the bargain when it had been made complete, and for the reasons I have already stated such completion never took place; there never was a complete bargain between the parties, and in my opinion the appellants fail.

[The concurring judgments of Viscount Dunedin and Lord Warrington are omitted.]

NOTE

This case was decided in 1929 but not reported until 1934, and then as a note following the official report of *Foley v. Classique Coaches Ltd.*, *infra*. Nevertheless, it is clear that the judges who sat on both *Hillas & Co. v. Arcos Ltd.*, *infra*, and *Foley v. Classique Coaches Ltd.* were aware of the decision.

HILLAS & CO. v. ARCOS LTD.

(1932), 147 L.T. 503 (H.L.)

Hillas and Co. Ltd., an English timber firm, brought action against Arcos Limited, the business representatives of the Russian government, for breach of a contract to supply 100,000 standards of Russian timber during 1931. Under the agreement on which the action was based, Hillas and Co. had agreed to buy a stipulated amount of timber "of fair specification" on very favourable terms during the 1930 season. The agreement included the following provision in clause 9:

> Buyers shall also have the option of entering into a contract with the sellers for the purchase of 100,000 standards for delivery during 1931. Such contract to stipulate that, whatever the conditions are, buyers shall obtain the goods on conditions and at prices which show to them a reduction of 5 per cent on the f.o.b. value of the official price list at any time ruling during 1931. Such option to be declared before the 1st Jan. 1931. . . .

Shortly after concluding this agreement with Hillas and Co., Arcos entered into a contract with Central Softwood Buying Corporation Limited for sale of its entire timber production for shipment to the British Isles for the 1931 season. Central Softwood Buying Corporation was a collective of two-thirds of the English timber buyers. Though Hillas and Co. had been a member of the collective's predecessor corporation, it was not a member of the new organization, having negotiated the purchase of timber from Russia for the 1931 season on its own account.

The question before the court was whether the option provision reproduced above was a binding agreement. The Court of Appeal's reversal of the trial judge's award of damages in favour of Hillas and Co. was overturned by the House of Lords.

LORD WRIGHT . . . The document of May 21, 1930, cannot be regarded as other than inartistic, and may appear repellant to the trained sense of an equity draftsman. But it is clear that the parties both intended to make a contract and thought they had done so. Business men often record the most important agreements in crude and summary fashion; modes of expression sufficient and clear to them in the course of their business may appear to those unfamiliar with the business far from complete or precise. It is, accordingly, the duty of the court to construe such documents fairly and broadly, without being too astute or subtle in finding defects; but, on the contrary, the court should seek to apply the old maxim of English law, *verba ita sunt intelligenda ut res magis valeat quam pereat*. That maxim, however, does not mean that the court is to make a contract for the parties, or go outside the words they have used, except in so far as there are appropriate implications of law as, for instance, the implication of what is just and reasonable to be ascertained by the court as matter of machinery where the contractual intention is clear but the contract is silent on some detail. Thus in contracts for future performance over a period, the parties may not be able nor may they desire to specify many matters of detail, but leave them to be adjusted in the working out of the contract. Save for the legal implication I have mentioned, such contracts might well be incomplete or uncertain; with that implication in reserve they are neither incomplete nor uncertain. As obvious illustrations I may refer to such matters as prices or times of delivery in contracts for the sale of goods, or times for loading or discharging in a contract of sea carriage. Furthermore, even if the construction of the words used may be difficult, that is not a reason for holding them too ambiguous or uncertain to be enforced if the fair meaning of the parties can be extracted. . . .

The contract [in this case] is clearly an instalment contract "over the season 1930," since the whole quantity could not be delivered in one shipment. It is obvious that the parties either cannot or do not desire to fix precise dates for the plurality of shipments which is contemplated; hence they leave the apportionment of these shipments over the period to be determined as circumstances require, first, by the readiness of the goods, including, no doubt, ports of shipment, which will depend on the position of the respondents, who, accordingly, will have to declare it from time to time and secondly, on the action of the appellants, who on receiving these declarations will be entitled to a reasonable time on each occasion in which to give the necessary shipping instructions in accordance with which the respondents will have to provide tonnage—because it is a c.i.f. [cost, insurance and freight] contract. Such matters may require, as the performance of the contract proceeds, some consultation and even concessions between the sellers and the buyers, but there is no uncertainty involved because, if there eventually emerge differences between the parties, the standard of what is reasonable can, in the last resort, be applied by the law, which thus by ascertaining exact dates makes precise what the parties in the contract have deliberately left undefined. Hence, in view of this legal machinery, *id certum est quod certum reddi potest*. . . .

As to price, that is specifically fixed in this contract by the clauses which have reference to the respondents' new revised schedule supplemented by a further provision in cl. 8 that the appellants were to have the advantage of any beneficial terms granted to any other buyers which directly or in effect reduced the price paid or consideration given for the goods in 1930. . . .

I have, so far, said nothing about the words "of fair specification." The only relevant question is whether these words were too vague or uncertain to give effect to the contractual intention of the parties; and I merely observe here that no one has suggested that any difficulty was experienced in 1930 in applying these words to the actual delivery from time to time of the different instalments that made up the 40,000 standards. I shall discuss these words more fully when I turn, as I now do, to consider cl. 9, which is the crux of this case. That clause must not be construed as if it stood by itself; it is an integral part of the whole agreement; the option under it is given as one of the conditions under which the appellants agree to buy the 22,000 standards, and is part of the consideration for their agreeing to do so. It is, accordingly, a binding offer, which the appellants are entitled, by accepting before Jan. 1, 1931, to turn into a contract if other objections do not prevail. Some confusion has been imported, as I think, into the question by dwelling on the exact words—"the option of entering into a contract," and it is said that this is merely a contract to enter into a contract, whereas in law there cannot be a contract to enter into a contract. The phrase is epigrammatic, but may be either meaningless or misleading. A contract *de praesenti* to enter into what, in law, is an enforceable contract, is simply that enforceable contract, and no more and no less; and if what may, not very accurately, be called the "second contract" is not to take effect till some future date, but is otherwise an enforceable contract, the position is as in the preceding illustration, save that the operation of the contract is postponed. But in each case there is *eo instanti* a complete obligation. If, however, what is meant is that the parties agree to ne-gotiate in the hope of effecting a valid contract, the position is different. There is then no bargain except to negotiate, and negotiations may be fruitless and end without any contract ensuing; yet even then, in strict theory, there is a contract (if there is good consideration) to negotiate, though in the event of repudiation by one party the damages may be nominal, unless a jury think that the opportunity to negotiate was of some appreciable value to the injured party.

However, I think the words of cl. 9 in this case simply mean that the appellants had the option of accepting an offer in the terms of cl. 9 so that when it was exercised a contract at once came into existence, unless, indeed, the terms of the option embodied in the clause were not sufficiently certain and complete; before considering this matter I ought to deal with a further contention based on a construction of the second paragraph of cl. 9, which is in these terms:

> Such contract to stipulate that, whatever the conditions are, buyers shall obtain the goods on conditions and at prices which show to them a reduction of 5 per cent on the f.o.b. value of the official price list at any time ruling during 1931.

It is argued that these words, read with the preceding paragraph, confirm the view that the option was merely for the preparation and agreeing of a formal contract, because the words "whatever the conditions are" mean "whatever the conditions of the contract are." Such an argument involves adding the words "of the contract," which are not expressed, and on other grounds I do not think that it is correct. I think the words "conditions" refers to conditions affecting other people in the trade, primarily as regards price, and such analogous advantages as are dealt with in cl. 8 in connection with the 1930 season. What the appellants are stipulating is that they are to have, throughout the year 1931, such conditions of this character and such prices as will secure to them in any event a clear 5 per cent advantage over other buyers who might compete. On a fair reading of the words, I think the contract is clear and complete in its stipulations as to price. It was contended that no official price list might be issued in 1931, so that the contract price was in that way uncertain and contingent. But in past years in the conduct of this business it had been an invariable practice of the respondents to issue such a list; the evidence and finding in the present case are that an official price list was issued in 1931;

indeed, it is difficult to see how the respondents could carry on the business unless it was issued. I think that as regards the definition of the machinery for fixing the price there is sufficient certainty here for a business transaction; the issue in 1931 of the official price list is not a mere contingency but a practical certainty; it is unnecessary to consider what would have been the legal position if the respondents had ceased to carry on business or had been dispossessed by war or revolution. Such considerations are not relevant to determining whether there is a good contract or not, but relate to such questions as frustration or breach of the contract.

The description of the goods offered to be sold in 1931, in cl. 9, is also, in my judgment, sufficient in law. I so hold simply as a matter of construction, having regard to the context [which related to the sale of timber in 1930 as well as the 1931 option]. "100,000 standards," divorced from the rest of the agreement, no doubt would be too uncertain; abstractly they might be incapable of any definite meaning. But the definition comes from the context. The agreement is headed as being for the purchase of Russian goods which to this extent must define the 100,000 standards; the words "50,000 standards" in cl. 7 have clearly to be read as embodying the same description as in the first paragraph of the agreement, that is, standards of softwood goods of fair specification; and, in my judgment, the same description must apply to the 100,000 standards in cl. 9, not as a matter of implication, but as one of construction. Hence the 100,000 standards are to be of Russian softwood goods of fair specification. In practice, under such a description, the parties will work out the necessary adjustments by a process of give and take in order to arrive at an equitable or reasonable apportionment on the basis of the respondents' actual available output, according to kinds, qualities, sizes and scantlings; but, if they fail to do so, the law can be invoked to determine what is reasonable in the way of specification, and thus the machinery is always available to give the necessary certainty. As a matter of strict procedure, the sellers would make a tender as being of fair specification, the buyers would reject it, and the court or an arbitrator decide whether it was or was not a good tender. It is, however, said that in the present case the contract quantity is too large, and the range of variety in descriptions, qualities, and sizes is too complicated to admit of this being done. But I see no reason in principle to think that such an operation is beyond the power of an expert tribunal, or of a judge of fact assisted by expert witnesses. I cannot find in the record any evidence to justify this contention of the respondents, even if such evidence be at all competent. On the contrary, it seems that a prospective specification for the 500,000 or 600,000 standards which formed the subject of the contract of Nov. 20, 1930, between the respondents and the Central Softwood Corpn., Ltd., was agreed between these parties at Moscow in a few days, which appears to confirm that the ascertainment of a fair specification of Russian softwood goods, even for a very large quantity and over a whole season, is not of insuperable difficulty to experts. Accordingly I see no reason to think that, as regards the quality and description of the goods, the contract is either uncertain or incomplete. Nor can it justly be objected that, though a fair and reasonable specification may not be impossible of ascertainment, the reasonable specification is impossible. The law, in determining what is reasonable, is not concerned with ideal truth, but with something much less ambitious, though more practical.

There still remains the question of shipping dates or times or ports of delivery. I think here again, as matter of construction, cl. 9 is to be read as embodying cl. 6, which, therefore, I think, applies equally to the 100,000 standards as to the 40,000 standards. I have explained my view of the operation and effect of that clause. If I were wrong in that, I should still regard the matter as sufficiently dealt with by the term which the law would imply in such a case, namely, that the deliveries are to be at reasonable times: s. 29(2) of the Sale of Goods Act, 1893, applies, I think, to a contract such as this, where delivery is to be by instalments, equally with a contract under which there is only to be a single delivery, and imports the standard of reasonable time, which, by s. 56 of the same Act, is a question of fact, no doubt to be determined in view of all the relevant circumstances, however complicated. In my judgment, the contract is neither uncertain nor incomplete as regards times of delivery or shipment. . . . In my judgment, the parties here did intend to enter into, and did enter into, a complete and binding agreement, not dependent on any future agreement for its validity. But in any event the cases cited by the Court of Appeal do not, in my judgment, apply here, because this contract contains no such terms as were considered in those cases; it is not stipulated in the contract now in question that such matters as prices or times or quantities were to be agreed. I should certainly share the regret of the lords justices if I were compelled to think such important forward contracts as the present could have no legal effect and were mere "gentlemen's agreements" or honourable obligations. But, for the reasons given, I feel constrained to dissent from their conclusions—I have only with great diffidence arrived at this conclusion—but I am supported by reflecting that I am in agreement with a learned judge very experienced in these questions. . . .

The appeal should, in my judgment, be allowed, with costs in this House and in the courts below, and the judgment of MacKinnon J. restored and the case remitted to the King's Bench Division.

[The concurring opinions of Lord Tomlin and Lord Thankerton are omitted. Lord Warrington and Lord Macmillan concurred in the judgment delivered by Lord Tomlin.]

FOLEY v. CLASSIQUE COACHES LTD.

[1934] 2 K.B. 1 (C.A.)

The defendants, operators of a fleet of motor coaches, agreed to purchase a piece of land from the plaintiffs, who operated a service station on adjacent premises. The sale was made subject to the defendants entering into a supplemental agreement to purchase all the petrol required for their business from the plaintiffs "at a price to be agreed by the parties in writing and from time to time". The supplemental agreement contained an arbitration clause, clause 8, to this effect:

> If any dispute or difference shall arise on the subject matter or construction of this agreement the same shall be submitted to arbitration in the usual way in accordance with the provisions of the Arbitration Act, 1889.

Following the execution of the supplemental agreement on the same day as the agreement for the sale of the land, the land was conveyed to the defendants. For three years, the defendants obtained all their petrol from the plaintiffs until they thought they could purchase their supplies on better terms elsewhere. The defendants then attempted through their solicitor to repudiate the supplemental agreement and the plaintiffs sought a declaration that the agreement was binding and an injunction to prevent the defendants from purchasing their petrol elsewhere.

At trial, the Lord Chief Justice decided in favour of the plaintiffs. The defendants appealed.

SCRUTTON L.J. In this appeal I think that the Lord Chief Justice's decision was right, and I am glad to come to that conclusion, because I do not regard the appellants' contention as an honest one. . . .

I observe that the appellants' solicitor in his letter made no suggestion that the land would be returned, and I suppose the appellants would have been extremely annoyed if they had been asked to return it when they repudiated the condition.

A good deal of the case turns upon the effect of two decisions of the House of Lords which are not easy to fit in with each other. . . . In *Hillas and Co. Ltd. v. Arcos Ltd.*, [*supra*], the House of Lords said that they had not laid down universal principles of construction in *May and Butcher Ltd. v. R.*, [*supra*], and that each case must be decided on the construction of the particular document, while in *Hillas and Co. Ltd. v. Arcos Ltd.* they found that the parties believed they had a contract. In the present case the parties obviously believed they had a contract and they acted for three years as if they had; they had an arbitration clause which relates to the subject-matter of the agreement as to the supply of petrol, and it seems to me that this arbitration clause applies to any failure to agree as to the price. By analogy to the case of a tied house there is to be implied in this contract a term that the petrol shall be supplied at a reasonable price and shall be of reasonable quality. For these reasons I think the Lord Chief Justice was right in holding that there was an effective and enforceable contract, although as to the future no definite price had been agreed with regard to the petrol. . . .

The appeal therefore fails, and no alteration is required in the form of the injunction that has been granted.

[The concurring judgments of Greer and Maugham L.JJ. are omitted.]

NOTES and QUESTIONS

1. Lord Scrutton, who wrote as a member of the Court of Appeal in all three of the foregoing cases, found himself on shifting legal sands. In *May & Butcher Ltd.*, the House of Lords affirmed the majority decision of the Court of Appeal, from which he had dissented, evidently indicating their disapproval of his analysis. Writing for an undivided court in *Hillas & Co. v. Arcos Ltd.*, he accordingly expressed himself bound by the House of Lords decision in *May & Butcher Ltd.* to conclude that the parties' agreement fell short of a contract. Paradoxically, the House of Lords

reversed him, in apparent contradiction of the position they had taken in *May & Butcher Ltd..* In light of that ambivalence, Lord Scrutton can hardly be criticized for having come full circle in *Foley v. Classique Coaches Ltd.*

2. Canadian, British and other Commonwealth courts have repeatedly held that agreements expressly or implicitly leaving out what is regarded as an essential term to be agreed upon in the future are not contracts. Their approach has been criticized by commentators on the grounds that the refusal to enforce what parties evidently viewed as a binding agreement defeats the parties' reasonable expectations and impedes commercial exchange. See *e.g.*, McLauchlan, *Rethinking Agreements to Agree* (1998), 18 N.Z.U.L.R. 77. See also note 5 following *Wellington City Council v. Body Corporate 51702 (Wellington), infra* section 4.

3. The judicial analysis addressed to the question of whether an agreement is too uncertain to be enforced typically focuses on the specificity of the words used by the parties. The agreement is a contract if the court concludes that the words used are clear, or that they accommodate resort to an external standard or frame of reference by which to fill out their content or establish the terms of the contemplated future performance. This approach might be characterized as formalistic rather than substantive; that is, it centres on the form of the parties' agreement rather than the result the agreement was intended to accomplish. In this connection, McEachern C.J., writing for the British Columbia Court of Appeal in *Langley Lo-Cost Builders Ltd. v. 474835 B.C. Ltd.*, [2000] 7 W.W.R. 46 (B.C. C.A.), expressed the view, at 56, that "the courts of this province have been more likely than courts in other provinces to give legal effect to agreements reached through negotiation and discussion." In support of that proposition, he cited *Marquest Industries Ltd. v. Willows Poultry Farms Ltd.* (1968), 1 D.L.R. (3d) 513 (B.C. C.A.) as the leading case in British Columbia, and quoted Bull J.A. at 517-18 as follows, at 57:

> The primary rule of construction has been expressed by the maxim, ut res magis valeat quam pereat or as paraphrased in English, "a deed shall never be void where the words may be applied to any extent to make it good". The maxim has been basic to such authoritative decisions as *Scammell v. Ouston*,. . . as well as many others, which establish that every effort should be made by a Court to find a meaning, looking at substance and not mere form, and that difficulties in interpretation do not make a clause bad as not being capable of interpretation, so long as a definite meaning can properly be extracted. . .

In another recent case, the British Columbia Supreme Court concluded that the following provision as to price did not prevent a contract from arising:

> This Contract will be on the basis of the prices Tendered by the Contractor based on the General Conditions in the Specifications and Drawings (not Lease Documents) unless modifications are made during the short list process . . .

After noting that the parties anticipated ongoing changes in the design of the building to be constructed that would require adjustments in the construction price, Owen-Flood J. said, "it would be entirely unrealistic for the court to expect parties in such circumstances to provide any greater certainty as to price. I find that the Agreement was sufficiently certain in that regard." *Knappett Construction Ltd. v. Axor Engineering Construction Group Inc.* (2003), 25 C.L.R. (3d) 120 (B.C. S.C.) at 145.

4. A thoughtful examination of the cases often suggests unarticulated concerns underlying what appears to be an entirely formalist analysis. Consider whether, in each of the three cases in the trilogy, the party seeking enforcement had materially changed position in the expectation that the agreement would come to fruition. In what position was Hillas and Co. left as a result of Arcos' refusal to supply timber pursuant to their agreement? In what position did the refusal of Classique Coaches to honour its agreement to purchase fuel leave Mr. Foley? Is the extent to which a party has been prejudiced by reliance on the other party's performance of an agreement relevant in determining whether its words are sufficiently certain that the agreement should be enforced?

5. In practice, people often wish to create binding agreements without fixing in advance all of the details of performance, including such material aspects as the price to be paid. As legal advisor to such clients and the drafter of such agreements, you may be obliged to find devices by which that

objective may be fulfiled to the satisfaction of the parties. The cases you have read demonstrate two such devices. One is the incorporation of reference to an objective standard, such as "a reasonable price" or "market price". Another is the use of external valuers or arbitrators, who are empowered to determine price or other matters upon which the parties are unable to reach agreement at the time contemplated.

In the leading case of *Calvan Consolidated Oil & Gas Co. v. Manning*, [1959] S.C.R. 253, the Supreme Court of Canada considered an agreement for the exchange of a percentage of the parties' respective interests in certain petroleum and natural gas permits and the potential development of the properties. The agreement was embodied in a letter written by one of the parties, to which the other had signed his acceptance. Appended to the agreement was the following provision;

> IT IS AGREED THAT the terms of the formal agreement are to be subject to our mutual agreement, and if we are unable to agree, the terms of such agreement are to be settled for us by arbitration by a single arbitrator, pursuant to The Arbitration Act of the Province of Alberta.

In his analysis of whether the agreement was sufficiently certain to be enforced, Judson J. said this regarding the operation of the arbitration provision, at 259-60:

> In an agreement of this kind, where the lands may be first of all sold or made subject to a farmout agreement, it seems to me virtually impossible for the parties at that stage of the proceedings to set out in full what the terms of operation would be if Calvan were to develop the land itself. Here are two co-owners who do not know at the point of time when co-ownership is established what they will do with the land. They realize that they may eventually have to develop it themselves. It is a situation that all co-owners may have to face and if nothing more is said between them, they must agree on the terms of the development. If they cannot agree they are at a standstill and must put up with this situation or wind up their association in some way. There is every reason, therefore, why the parties here introduced an arbitration clause into their agreement to deal with this particular point.
>
> The learned trial judge was of the opinion that the provision for arbitration in relation to a possible operating agreement was meaningless and unenforceable. If this were so, the consequence would be that contracting parties in the position of Calvan and Manning who do not know what their ultimate intentions may be if they retain the property must provide in detail for a contingency that may never arise unless they wish to run the risk of having the rest of their contractual efforts invalidated and declared unenforceable. I agree with the opinion of the Court of Appeal that such a situation may be dealt with by an agreement to arbitrate and I can see no legal or practical difficulty in the way. No more could the learned author of Russell on Arbitration, 17th ed., p. 10, when he said:
>
> > Since an arbitrator can be given such powers as the parties wish, he can be authorised to make a new contract between the parties. The parties to a commercial contract often provide that in certain events their contract shall be added to or modified to fit the circumstances then existing, intending thereby to create a binding obligation although they are unwilling or unable to determine just what the terms of the new or modified agreement shall be. To a court such a provision is ineffective as being at most a mere "agreement to agree"; but a provision that the new or modified terms shall be settled by an arbitrator can without difficulty be made enforceable.
>
> .....
>
> My conclusion therefore is that this contract is not void for uncertainty. There is no need here to invoke the principle of a "fair" and "broad" construction of this contract as mentioned by Lord Wright in *Hillas and Co., Limited v. Arcos Limited* . . .. The parties knew what they were doing and they expressed their intentions with certainty and a complete lack of ambiguity.

6. *Calvan Consolidated Oil & Gas Co.* (*supra*, note 5) has been repeatedly cited and followed. In *Sheer v. Lee* (2000), 263 A.R. 305 (Q.B.), the case was cited as authority for the principle that, if the provision is properly drafted, an arbitrator can be appointed to conclude an agreement for the parties. However, the court expressed this qualification, at para. 28:

However, it is, in my view, a necessary prerequisite to such an arbitration clause that there be a basic agreement in place as to the essential terms to form a binding contract. In this regard, I note that Viscount Simon made this clear in *Heyman* [*v. Darwins Ltd.*, [1942] A.C. 356, at 366], quoted in *Cascade* [*Builders Ltd. v. Alberta Government Telephones Ltd.* (1976), 1 A.R. 257, at 260]:

> If the dispute is whether the contract which contains the clause has ever been entered into at all, that issue cannot go to arbitration under the clause, for the party who denies that he has ever entered into the contract is thereby denying that he has ever joined in the submission. . . . But, in a situation where the parties are at one in asserting that they entered into a binding contract, but a difference has arisen between them . . . such differences should be regarded as differences which have arisen [relative to] the contract, and an arbitration clause . . . should be construed accordingly.

The existence of an arbitration provision in the agreement considered in *May & Butcher Ltd. v. R.* was not regarded as adequate to resolve the uncertainty created by the parties' agreement to agree in the future on the price to be paid for available tentage. However, such a provision supported the conclusion that the agreement in *Foley v. Classique Coaches Ltd.* was enforceable. Does this passage provide a convincing explanation for the difference in result?

7. While incorporation of a mechanism such as arbitration or valuation to establish the specifics of an agreement may provide a basis for the conclusion that the agreement is a contract, drafters should be cognizant of the potential failure of that mechanism. That eventuality materialized in the leading case of *Sudbrook Trading Estate Ltd. v. Eggleton* (1982), [1983] 1 A.C. 444, [1982] 3 All E.R. 1 (H.L.).

In *Sudbrook*, the price for exercise of an option to purchase an interest in land was to be determined by valuers appointed by the parties or, in the event of their inability to reach agreement, by an umpire appointed by the valuers. This mechanism failed when one of the parties refused to appoint a valuer. In support of the majority's decision that the option was enforceable, Scarman L.J. said, at 13:

> Unembarrassed by authority, I would unhesitatingly conclude that the parties intended that the lessee should pay a fair and reasonable price to be determined as at the date when he exercised the option. The valuation formula was introduced into the contract merely as a convenient way of ascertaining the price at that future time. Should we be deterred from so construing the provision by the existence of a line of authority stretching back over 150 years in which provisions remitting to a valuer or arbitrator the ascertainment of a price have been construed as making the machinery of ascertainment an essential term of the contract? . . .
>
> In my view, no "judicial valour" . . . is needed to overrule a line of authority which never reached this House and which, properly considered, is concerned not so much with principle as with construction. . . .

Lord Russell of Killowen dissented, adopting the traditional view, at 12-13, that ". . . if A agrees to sell Blackacre to B the contract must provide for the price to be paid either in express terms or by the establishment of agreed machinery *which is bound to work* by which the price can be ascertained."

8. In *Mitsui & Co. (Canada) v. Royal Bank*, [1995] 2 S.C.R. 187, Pegasus leased two helicopters from Mitsui. Under these leases Pegasus had the option to purchase the helicopters for "reasonable fair market value . . . as established by Lessor." The Supreme Court of Canada held, following *Sudbrook*, that the price was not uncertain and that the lessor had an implied duty to act in good faith to take all reasonable steps to complete the valuation and determine the reasonable fair market value of the helicopters.

9. In some cases, the matter left unspecified by the parties to an agreement is its intended duration. However, failure to stipulate the term of an agreement is not ordinarily regarded as an omission warranting the conclusion that the parties have not reached agreement on essential terms, constituting a failure to contract. The issue has been addressed by the courts as one of contract interpretation rather than formation. The relevant authorities were canvassed in *Rapatax (1987) Inc.*

v. Cantax Corp. (1997), 49 Alta. L.R. (3d) 375 (C.A.), leave to appeal refused, [1997] S.C.C.A. No. 307. After quoting from an early English case illustrating the traditional common law position, Picard J.A. summarized the law as follows, at 381 and 383:

> Several points can be drawn from that passage. First, contracts of indeterminate duration are presumed to be perpetual. Second, that presumption is rebuttable, and in fact, depending upon the circumstances, may be displaced easily. Indeed, in recent times, it has been suggested that parties to a business relationship seldom would wish to be bound in perpetuity and that a contrary presumption would be more consonant with commercial reality. . . .

> It may matter little in practical terms which presumption is applied. In either event, the presumption merely places the onus of proof and is determinative only in the rare (perhaps fanciful) instance in which the scales of proof are equally balanced at the end of a trial. Consequently, there seems no need to depart from the dicta of the Supreme Court of Canada in *Gill Brothers* [*v. Mission Saw Mills Ltd.*, [1945] S.C.R. 766] that contracts of indefinite duration are rebuttably presumed to be perpetual. However, it is necessary for a court to look at the relationship between the parties and the nature and terms of the contract to determine whether there is a basis upon which to conclude that the contract is terminable upon reasonable notice.

4.   Agreements to Negotiate

There are legitimate conceptual and policy reasons for concluding that parties to an agreement who have done no more than agree to agree in the future on essential aspects of a transaction have not accepted reciprocal obligations to perform on ascertainable terms and thus have failed to make a contract. If, for example, there is truly no basis upon which to determine the price to be paid for goods to be delivered at a future date, the judicial determination of a price at which the intended buyer is obliged to purchase may well impose on that party a risk that he or she did not and would not have voluntarily assumed. To illustrate: a person may execute an agreement in the hope of securing a firm source for the supply of goods in the future, though he or she is not prepared to actually purchase at whatever price the market may dictate, regardless of how high. In such a case, a term under which the parties agree to agree on price may reflect the fact that the potential buyer is simply not willing to make a commitment that involves acceptance of the risk of significant market fluctuations. As long as the market price is within the buyer's range, the parties will likely have no difficulty establishing a price when the time comes. However, if the market price has become too high for the buyer's budget, any attempt to fix a price is likely to fail. Since market price is ordinarily the determinant of what amounts to a reasonable price, a judge who decides in such circumstances that the agreement is a contract to purchase at a reasonable price is imposing on the buyer a risk that he or she did not accept.

Though the potential buyer in the scenario postulated may not intend to be bound to purchase at any price, the fact that the parties made an agreement presumably reflects their desire to achieve some substantive result. Each of the parties would no doubt expect that, even if neither would be bound to purchase or sell at absolutely any price, the agreement would at least commit the other to seriously attempt to negotiate terms at the appropriate time with the objective of establishing a mutually satisfactory price. A binding promise to negotiate is often of real practical value, since its fulfilment may offer a much greater likelihood that the parties will complete a transaction than would be the case were they not obliged to make a serious effort to reach agreement. This is particularly true where parties have already agreed on all or most of the primary terms of their transaction and only one or two remain to be determined.

On this view, a distinction may be drawn between an agreement to complete a transaction on unspecified terms or on terms to be agreed, and an agreement to *negotiate* in an endeavour to arrive at terms pursuant to which a transaction will be completed. In the first kind of case, the subject of the agreement is the transaction itself. In the second, the subject of the agreement is the process by which it is hoped a transaction will be concluded. In fact, parties often agree in express language to negotiate a price or other identified terms. The conceptual and practical legitimacy of such an agreement was recognized by Lord Wright in *Hillas & Co. v. Arcos Ltd.*, *supra*, in these words, at 515:

> If, however, what is meant is that the parties agree to negotiate in the hope of effecting a valid contract, the position is different. There is then no bargain except to negotiate, and negotiations may be fruitless and end without any contract ensuing; yet even then, in strict theory, there is a contract (if there is good consideration) to negotiate, though in the event of repudiation by one party the damages may be nominal, unless a jury think that the opportunity to negotiate was of some appreciable value to the injured party.

However, the view that an express or implicit agreement to negotiate may in itself constitute a contract has found few adherents among the judiciary. The primary objections leveled against that analysis are twofold. First, it is impossible to determine the content of a duty to negotiate; the notion is inherently too uncertain to support a contract. What is it that a person subject to such a duty is obliged to do or not do? Secondly, there is no basis upon which to determine damages for breach of such a duty. It cannot be presumed that the negotiations would have succeeded if undertaken. Further, were a presumption of success warranted, there is no way to determine what the terms of the agreement reached would have been. There is therefore no basis upon which to assess in monetary terms what position the party alleging breach would have been in had the other fulfiled the obligation to negotiate. Both points are reflected in Lord Denning's direct rejection of Lord Wright's view in *Courtney & Fairbairn Ltd. v. Tolaini Brothers (Hotels) Ltd.* (1974), [1975] 1 W.L.R. 297 (Eng. C.A.) at 301, expressed as follows:

> That tentative opinion by Lord Wright does not seem to me to be well founded. If the law does not recognise a contract to enter into a contract (when there is a fundamental term yet to be agreed) it seems to me it cannot recognise a contract to negotiate. The reason is because it is too uncertain to have any binding force. No court could estimate the damages because no one can tell whether the negotiations would be successful or would fall through: or if successful, what the result would be. It seems to me that a contract to negotiate, like a contract to enter into a contract, is not a contract known to the law.

The following cases address the enforceability of an agreement to negotiate, as distinguished from an agreement to contract on unspecified terms or on terms to be agreed in the future.

EMPRESS TOWERS LTD. v. BANK OF NOVA SCOTIA

[1991] 1 W.W.R. 537, 50 B.C.L.R. (2d) 126, 48 B.L.R. 212, 14 R.P.R. (2d) 115, 73 D.L.R. (4th) 400 (C.A.), leave to appeal to S.C.C. refused 79 D.L.R. (4th) vii

LAMBERT J.A. The landlord, Empress Towers Ltd., brought a petition under s. 18 of the *Commercial Tenancy Act*, R.S.B.C. 1979, c. 54, against the tenant, the Bank of Nova Scotia, seeking to obtain a writ of possession under s. 21 of the Act.

The first lease between the parties was made in 1972. It expired in 1984. A new lease was made. It contained this clause:

23. RENEWAL:

The Landlord hereby grants to the Tenant rights of renewal of this Lease for two successive periods of five (5) years each, such rights to be exercisable by three (3) months' written notice from the Tenant, subject to all the terms and conditions herein contained excepting any right of renewal beyond the second five (5) year period *and excepting the rental for any renewal period, which shall be the market rental prevailing at the commencement of that renewal term as mutually agreed between the Landlord and the Tenant.* If the Landlord and the Tenant do not agree upon the renewal rental within two (2) months following the exercise of a renewal option, then this agreement may be terminated at the option of either party.

(My emphasis.)

The 1984 lease was due to expire on August 31, 1989. On May 25, 1989, the bank exercised its option to renew the lease for a further term of five years from September 1, 1989. On June 23, 1989, the bank proposed a rental rate of $5,400 a month, up from $3,097.92 under the lease that was about to expire. No written reply was received from Empress Towers. There may have been a telephone response. On July 26, 1989, the bank wrote again to Empress Towers. It said that its proposal of $5,400 a month was a rate which independent appraisers had advised the bank was appropriate. It said it was willing to negotiate. Also on July 26th, the solicitor for Empress Towers wrote to the bank saying that his client was still reviewing the offer. On August 23rd, the bank asked whether Empress Towers was making progress in its deliberations and it said that it remained ready to discuss the matter at Empress Towers' convenience. On August 31st, on the day when the first five-year term was due to expire, Empress Towers made its response. It said it would allow the bank to remain on a month-to-month basis if $15,000 was paid before September 15, 1989, and a rent of $5,400 a month was paid thereafter. The tenancy that Empress Towers wished to create in that way was to be terminable on 90 days' written notice. (There was evidence that an employee of Empress Towers had been robbed of $30,000 in a branch of the bank and that Empress Towers' insurance had paid only $15,000, leaving a loss to Empress Towers of $15,000.)

.....

The principal question in the appeal is whether the renewal clause was void either for uncertainty or, what is fundamentally the same, as an agreement to agree. The obverse of that question is: If the renewal clause is not void, what does it mean?

What was said by this court about interim agreements in *Griffin v. Martens* (1988), 27 B.C.L.R. (2d) 152 at p. 153, . . . is equally true about leases:

> It is not the function of the courts to set interim agreements aside for uncertainty because they contain a clause that is not precisely expressed. If such a clause has an ascertainable meaning, then the courts should strive to find it. See *Hillas & Co. v. Arcos Ltd.* [*supra*] . . . and *Wiebe v. Bobsien* [*infra*, Chapter 6, section 2]. As long as an agreement is not being constructed by the court, to the surprise of the parties, or at least one of them, the courts should try to retain and give effect to the agreement that the parties have created for themselves.

On the other hand, it is well established that if all that the parties say is that they will enter into a lease at a rental to be agreed, no enforceable lease obligation is created: . . . There may, however, be an obligation to negotiate.

The law is generally to the same effect in England. It is discussed by Mr. Justice Megarry in *Brown v. Gould*, [1972] Ch. 53, where three categories of options are analyzed. The first category is where the rent is simply "to be agreed". Usually such a clause cannot be enforced. The second category is where the rent is to be established by a stated formula but no machinery is provided for applying the formula to produce the rental rate. Often the courts will supply the machinery. The third category is where the formula is set out but is defective and the machinery is provided for applying the formula to produce the rental rate. In those cases the machinery may be used to cure the defect in the formula. What is evident from a consideration of all three categories is that the courts will try, wherever possible, to give the proper legal effect to any clause that the parties understood and intended was to have legal effect.

[In *Brown v. Gould*, [1972] Ch. 53 at 56, the following term with respect to an option of renewal of a lease was enforced. The rent was "to be fixed having regard to the market value of the premises . . . taking into account to the advantage of the tenant any increased value . . . attributable to structural improvements made by the tenant during the currency of this present lease".]

In this case, if the parties had intended simply to say that if the tenant wished to renew it could only do so at a rent set by or acceptable to the landlord, then they could have said so. Instead, they said that if the tenant wished to renew it could do so at the market rental prevailing at the commencement of the renewal term. If nothing more had been said then the market rental could have been determined on the basis of valuations and, if necessary, a court could have made the determination. It would have been an objective matter. But the clause goes on to say that not only must the renewal rental be the prevailing market rental but also it must be the prevailing market rental as mutually agreed between the landlord and the tenant. It could be argued that the additional provision for mutual agreement meant only that the first step was to try to agree, but if that step failed then other steps should be adopted to set the market rental. However, the final sentence of cl. 23, which contemplates a failure to agree giving rise to a right of termination, precludes the acceptance of that argument. In my opinion, the effect of the requirement for mutual agreement must be that the landlord cannot be compelled to enter into a renewal tenancy at a rent which it has not accepted as the market rental. But, in my opinion, that is not the only effect of the requirement of mutual agreement. It also carries with it, first, an implied term that the landlord will negotiate in good faith with the tenant with the objective of reaching an agreement on the market rental rate and, secondly, that agreement on a market rental will not be unreasonably withheld: . . . Those terms are to be implied under the officious bystander and business efficacy principles in order to permit the renewal clause, which was clearly intended to have legal effect, from being struck down as uncertain. The key to implying the terms that I have set out is that the parties agreed that there should be a right of renewal at the prevailing market rental. (I do not have to decide in this case whether a bare right of renewal at a rental to be agreed carries with it an obligation to negotiate in good faith or not to withhold agreement unreasonably.)

The conclusion that I have reached is, in my opinion, entirely consistent with the unanimous decision of this court in *Griffin v. Martens* where a "subject" clause in an interim agreement, to the effect that the agreement was subject to the purchaser being able to arrange satisfactory financing, was considered to carry with it an implied obligation on the prospective purchaser to use his best efforts to obtain satisfactory financing. In this case I have said that the requirements are to negotiate in good faith and not to withhold agreement unreasonably. Those requirements carry the same degree of diligence as "best efforts". One would suppose, certainly, that the landlord could not rent to anyone else at a rental rate that the Bank of Nova Scotia would be willing to pay.

The chambers judge decided, on the basis of the affidavit evidence, that the landlord had not negotiated in good faith. It was suggested in argument on the appeal that the chambers judge's finding in that respect was wrong. But there is no basis for interfering with that finding. . . .

Section 21 of the *Commercial Tenancy Act* requires that if a writ of possession is not granted then the petition must be dismissed. . . .

[Taggart J.A. concurred. Wallace J.A. dissented. Appeal dismissed.]

NOTE

Though the agreement under consideration in this case did not expressly contemplate that the parties would negotiate a renewal of the lease, the language used indicated their intention to do so. Does an express or implied contractual term obliging the parties to negotiate *in good faith* overcome the argument, expressed in the introduction to this section, that the content of a duty to negotiate *per se* is inherently too uncertain to support a contract? Does the concept of good faith provide a standard against which the parties' conduct can be measured in order to determine whether an agreement to negotiate has been breached? See Chapter 11, section 3.

MANNPAR ENTERPRISES LTD. v. CANADA

(1999), 173 D.L.R. (4th) 243 (B.C. C.A.)

Mannpar held a permit under contract with the Crown, acting through the Department of Indian and Northern Affairs, to remove and sell sand and gravel located on an Indian reserve. The permit, which had an initial term of five years, included as Clause 7 the following provision:

The Permittee shall have the right to renew this Permit for a further five (5) year period subject to satisfactory performance and renegotiation of the royalty rate and annual surface rental.

> Under no circumstances shall the royalty rate or surface rental be less than the rates received in the preceding term.

The evidence at trial indicated that both Mannpar and the Department expected the operation to extend over a 10-year term, since Mannpar would require a substantial period of time within which to do the reclamation work it was contractually obliged to perform on the area from which sand and gravel was extracted. The trial judge, at 33 B.C.L.R. (3d) 203 at 210, made the following findings, before holding that there was no obligation to negotiate in good faith:

> In early 1993, Mannpar gave written notice of its intention to renew the permit for an additional term of 5 years commencing September 1993. In spite of Mannpar's repeated attempts to renegotiate the royalty rate for the purpose of the renewal, neither the Department nor the [Skyway] Band were prepared to do so prior to the expiration of the original permit on August 31, 1993. Ultimately, Mannpar took the position that the Department was repudiating its obligations to renew and elected to accept the repudiation and sue for damages.

In dismissing the Crown's counterclaim, based on Mannpar's alleged failure to perform the necessary clean up and restoration work, the trial judge said, at 223:

> It is clear that the reclamation was intended to occur over 10 years, yet the plaintiff, through no fault of its own, did not have an opportunity to work over 10 years. In my view, the plaintiff is relieved of the reclamation responsibilities that would have been incurred in the second term.

On appeal, Hall J.A., speaking for the court, also identified as worthy of note two additional provisions of the contract: firstly, one of the recitals to the agreement indicated that the Council of the Skyway Band had authorized the Crown to enter into the permit and secondly, the stipulation that the permit would commence on 1 January 1988 and be fully completed in five years without any further notice as to its termination.

HALL J.A. . . . . On the appeal, two substantial issues were argued:

1) Having regard to the language used in the permit agreement, was clause 7 uncertain as found by the learned trial judge?

2) Ought there to have been implied a term requiring the defendant respondent, Her Majesty the Queen in Right of Canada, to negotiate for a renewal or negotiate in good faith for a renewal?

. . . . .

In arguing that there was a duty cast upon the respondent to negotiate in good faith, the appellant relied upon the earlier judgment of this court in *Empress Towers Ltd. v. Bank of Nova Scotia* (1990), 50 B.C.L.R. (2d) 126. [After quoting from this decision, Hall J.A. continued:]

It is to be noted that in the case of *Empress Towers* [*supra*] there was contained in the relevant document a benchmark that could have been capable of objective assessment, namely "market rental". Such is not the case here. As was pointed out by Greer L.J. in the *Foley* [*supra*] case at p. 12:

> It is a common observation that a decision upon the construction of one contract is not an authority upon the construction of another contract in different words and entered into in different circumstances.

It seems to me that [other cases] are distinguishable from the case at bar because in those cases the courts were implying terms into leases that were continuing leases. That is rather different from the case at bar where the parties only *anticipated* that the business arrangement between them might last for 10 years.

Mannpar submitted that there was a duty cast upon the Crown in this case to exercise good faith by negotiating to see if an agreement could be reached between them. Mannpar asserts that the Crown failed to do this and that the failure should sound in damages with the damages to be assessed by the trial court.

I have earlier referred to the Alberta case of *Mesa Operating Ltd. v. Amoco Canada Resources Ltd.* In that case, Kerans J.A. . . . made this comment concerning the duty to negotiate at [(1994)] 19 Alta. L.R. (3d) [38 at] 44:

> In any event, it is not necessary for this case that I go further into this difficult area. This is because this case turns on a rule founded in the agreement of the parties, not in the law. In my view, as a matter of fact, this contract created certain expectations between the parties about its meaning, and about performance standards. If those expectations are reasonable, they should be enforced because that is what the parties had in mind. They are reasonable if they were shared. Of course, those expectations must also, to be reasonable, be consistent with the express terms agreed upon. This contract should be performed in accordance with the reasonable expectations created by it.

What was at issue in *Mesa* was action taken by one party under a pooling arrangement. It was held that the party who had the capacity under the agreement to make decisions could not act in such a fashion that would effectively nullify the benefits reasonably expected to be obtained from the contract by the other party. As Kerans J.A. pointed out [at 45] of the judgment, the duty to act in accord with the expectations of both parties was not unlike the duty cast upon an individual to use reasonable efforts to satisfy a condition precedent, the situation found to exist in the *Dynamic Transport Ltd.* case [*infra*, Chapter 6, section 4 and see Chapter 6 generally on Contingent Agreements].

. . . I have observed that in *Empress Towers* there was a benchmark, namely, "market value". It seems to me that unless there is a benchmark or a standard by which to measure such a duty, the negotiation concept is unworkable. I refer to the comments of Lord Ackner in *Walford v. Miles*, [1992] 2 A.C. 128.

. . . . .

In *Empress Towers* there was a requirement in the lease for the parties to endeavour to agree on market rental as Lambert J.A. observed at p. 130 of the judgment. He observed that the clause provided:

> . . . that not only must the renewal rental be the prevailing market rental but also it must be the prevailing market rental as *mutually agreed* between the landlord and the tenant. [Emphasis added.]

It was in that context that the majority found there ought to be implied a term that the landlord would negotiate in good faith with the tenant with the objection of reaching an agreement on the market rental rate and that the landlord would have a duty to not unreasonably withhold agreement on a market rental rate. The type of clause considered in that case does not bear any close resemblance to the clause under consideration in the case at bar. Lambert J.A. was careful to note that he did not have to decide whether a bare right of renewal at a rental to be agreed would carry with it an obligation to negotiate in good faith or not to withhold agreement unreasonably.

Mannpar emphasized . . . that central to its argument was the finding of the trial judge that the parties had a general expectation that the permit arrangement would extend over 10 years. That was certainly the basis on which Mannpar predicated its business plan and the amendment to provide an increased working area in 1991 appears consistent with this belief.

However, it must not be forgotten what was the subject matter of the agreement. It was an agreement for the extraction of sand and gravel and the operation of a landfill on the reserve lands of the Skyway Indian Band. The respondent undoubtedly had fiduciary obligations to the Band: *Delgamuukw v. British Columbia*, [1997] 3 S.C.R. 1010. . . . I have noted earlier that each contract must be looked in the context of its own facts and the language used by the parties. The implication of a term can only be made if it is the case that both parties would be likely to agree that such a term should be implied. That would be required to satisfy the so-called officious bystander test. I believe the result of the authorities is that a term can be implied in a contract if this is found to be necessary by a court in order to give business efficacy to the contract. A court will not, however, imply a term into a contract merely because the court may think that such term would be reasonable or would likely be more satisfactory.

Having examined the terms of the permit, I am of the view that the Crown was not insensible to its duties to the Band and wished to ensure that if in future a proposed renewal came to be unacceptable to the Band, the Crown would have the ability to refuse to renew the permit.

There is, as I have noted, a reference in the recitals to the Band "authorizing the grantor to enter into this permit". It was provided in Clause 1 of the agreement that the permit shall "be fully completed and ended on (date) without any further notice as to its termination". There is reference in the permit to the right of renewal being "subject to satisfactory performance and *renegotiation*" (emphasis added). "Renegotiation" is a word of broad import and in the context of this agreement, it appears to me it was employed to convey the meaning or intent that the Crown was reserving unto itself a broad ambit or scope to enter or to refuse to enter into any new arrangements that might be discussed or proposed concerning the possible renewal of the permit. The Crown could not fail to be keenly aware of the likelihood that if the Band was opposed to a renewal, the Crown could very well face legal action from the Band. It should also not be overlooked that there was no arbitration clause inserted into this agreement. Such a clause is frequently found in agreements where some matter is left open to be negotiated in future. I doubt that the absence of such a term was accidental and I should have thought that the Crown might well have been most reluctant to have such a term inserted, bearing in mind previous jurisprudence.

In my opinion, the language chosen in the agreement generally and in the renewal clause in particular reflects a stated desire on the part of the Crown affording it considerable latitude in deciding whether or not to agree to any extension of the five-year permit originally granted and in deciding on what terms might be acceptable if it were to agree to any such renewal.

It must be remembered apropos of the comment above noted in *Foley* about each agreement being construed on it own facts, that this was not just an ordinary commercial arrangement between the parties. Always in the background (and no doubt in the forefront of the mind of the Crown) was the Band and its interests, interests the Crown was bound under existing jurisprudence to keep clearly in mind. The Crown had a trust-like or fiduciary duty to the Band. Given that factual matrix, a great many of the cases involving other very disparate fact situations are of only limited application to the instant case.

In my judgment, the terminology of the permit should not lead to the conclusion that a term or terms ought to be implied as argued for by Mannpar. It appears to me that the matter of future renewal, if any, was left intentionally at large to be "renegotiated". I do not doubt that the Crown wished to ensure that it had the capacity to consult with and take account of Band concerns in the process of discussing any continuation of arrangements with Mannpar. It seems to me that the language used in the agreement was apt to achieve those ends and I concur in the assessment of the learned trial judge that no enforceable agreement arose out of the language of the renewal clause. I do not believe it could be said that there was in this case any duty to negotiate in good faith as alleged since I see no language that could provide an objective benchmark to measure this such as "fair value" or "market value". As I have observed, the clause under consideration here is discernibly different from that considered in the case of *Empress Towers, supra.*

. . . [I]n my opinion the Crown could properly have regard to its fiduciary duties to the Band. This could have significance on the issue of "good faith" or "bad faith", a factor clearly present in cases like *Wiebe v. Bobsien [infra* Chapter 6, section 2] and *Dynamic Transport* referred to *supra.* I believe that the Crown is entitled to invoke its fiduciary duty to the Skyway Band in this case to meet any suggestion that it was in 1993 acting in "bad faith" towards Mannpar.

[Appeal dismissed.]

NOTE and QUESTIONS

Mannpar Enterprises has been cited as authority for the general principle that there is no contract duty to negotiate in good faith. See *e.g., Mellco Developments Ltd. v. Portage la Prairie (City)* (2002), 222 D.L.R. (4th) 67 (Man. C.A.) at 90. Drawing on a passage from the judgment of Hall J.A., Lane J.A. for the Ontario Court of Appeal suggested, in *EdperBrascan Corp. v. 177373 Canada Ltd.* (2000), 50 O.R. (3d) 425 (S.C.J.), affirmed (2002), 22 B.L.R. (3d) 42 (Ont. C.A.), at 444 [O.R.] that *Mannpar Enterprises* established that the concept of a duty to negotiate is unworkable in the absence of an objective benchmark or standard against which to measure the duty. Do these statements accurately represent the decision? Did the court's recognition of the Crown's duty to the Band in connection with the renewal of the permit substantively qualify its conclusion that the Crown did not have a contractual duty to negotiate with Mannpar Enterprises in good faith?

WELLINGTON CITY COUNCIL v. BODY CORPORATE 51702 (WELLINGTON)

[2002] 3 N.Z.L.R. 486 (C.A.)

TIPPING J.

[1] The Wellington City Council (the Council) appeals from a judgment of Wild J holding it liable to pay to the second respondent, Alirae Enterprises Ltd (Alirae) damages of $580,209 for breach of contract. The contract which the Judge found the Council to have breached was what he called a "process" contract. It obliged the Council's officers to "negotiate in good faith" with Alirae the sale of the Council's interest as lessor in premises at 20 Brandon Street, Wellington. Alirae was the lessee. The Judge found that the Council, through its officers, was in breach of that contract by failing to conduct the negotiations in good faith. He assessed damages on the basis that if the Council had not been in breach, a substantive contract for sale and purchase would probably have resulted. On that premise Alirae had lost the profit it would have achieved from developing the premises in the manner it had in mind, if able to acquire the freehold.

[2] The Council's first challenge to Wild J's judgment rests on the proposition that the process contract, upon which the Judge relied for his breach and damages findings, was not a contract enforceable at law. Hence its breach, which the Council in any event denies, did not give rise to any cause of action. The Council's argument, shortly stated, is that the so-called process contract amounted to no more than an agreement to try to agree which the law does not recognise as an enforceable contract. This argument was supported by the contention that an agreement of the present kind is not sufficiently certain to be enforceable in law.

.....

[6] On 2 March 1999 the Council wrote to Alirae the letter which formed the basis of Alirae's later claim. . . . [T]he Council wrote:

"Council officers will negotiate, in good faith, sales of Council's leasehold interests to existing lessees at not less than the current market value of those interests."

[7] Alirae argues, and Wild J found, that the Council thereby offered to negotiate in good faith, which offer Alirae accepted by its conduct in entering into negotiations on that basis. Each party provided consideration to the other by their mutual exchange of promises. The crucial question is whether a legally enforceable contract came about.

[Tipping J. reviewed the decision of Kirby P. in *Coal Cliff Collieries Pty. Ltd. v. Sijehama & Anor* (1991), 24 N.S.W.L.R. 1, in which the New South Wales Court of Appeal concluded that a provision that the parties would "proceed in good faith to consult together upon the formulation of a more comprehensive and detailed Joint Venture Agreement" was not binding as a contractual promise. Tipping J. then continued:]

[14] We are bound, respectfully, to point out that both Kirby P's analysis and his application of it to the facts merged questions of process contract and substantive bargain. A contract purporting to bind the parties to negotiate, whether

expressed in terms of good faith, best endeavours or otherwise, is in substance a contract to try to agree. Breach lies in failure to try, either at all or according to whatever may be required. Breach does not lie in failing to agree. No question of what the terms of the substantive agreement should or might have been directly arises at this stage of the inquiry. Kirby P's references to external standards and an external arbitrator would be relevant to fixing the terms of the substantive contract. It is difficult, however, to see them as relevant to fixing the terms of an agreement to try to agree, when the parties have not themselves provided for any external standard in aid of that exercise.

[15] It is, in this kind of case, important to keep the process aspect conceptually separate from the substantive agreement which the process contract purportedly obliges the parties to endeavour to reach. As will emerge later, we agree with Kirby P that contracts to negotiate should not be held in all circumstances to be unenforceable. Their enforceability will depend on their terms and particularly on the specificity of those terms. It is, in our view, vital to emphasise from the outset that whether the terms of a process contract are sufficiently specific to be enforceable is an issue separate and apart from whether the substantive agreement, if reached, is sufficiently certain to be enforceable. If it is, the process contract will have borne fruit and no question of a breach of that contract can arise. If the substantive agreement is not sufficiently certain to be enforceable, the negotiations will have failed to bring about an enforceable contract. An issue may remain as to whether the process contract itself was enforceable and, if so, whether there was a breach of it. For these reasons we do not regard Kirby P's judgment in *Coal Cliff* as providing much assistance on the present issue, namely whether the process contract in the present case was enforceable.

[16] We turn now to the judgment of Handley JA in *Coal Cliff*. He noted, at 40C, that it was established law both in England and Australia that agreements to agree, or contracts to make contracts containing as yet unascertained terms were not legally enforceable. He cited a number of cases clearly demonstrating that elementary proposition. He then turned to examine whether the introduction into the equation of the concept of good faith, in the form of an obligation to negotiate in good faith, made any difference. For the reasons he gave, at 41F and G, Handley JA held that a promise to negotiate in good faith is illusory and therefore cannot be binding. His primary reasons were that parties negotiating for a contract are free to pursue their own interests. Generally speaking neither party is under any legal duty to consider the interests of the other. Whether and how long and in what manner the parties should negotiate, are matters within their own discretion.

[17] We add, at this point, that an obligation to negotiate in good faith is not the same as an obligation to negotiate reasonably. . .. An obligation to negotiate in good faith essentially means that the parties must honestly try to reach agreement. They remain able to pursue their own interests within what is subjectively honest, rather than what is objectively reasonable. In this respect the absence of an objective external criterion, as mentioned by Kirby P, is clearly relevant. What stance a negotiating party may take within the bounds of subjective honesty is very much more difficult to determine than if the bounds were those of objective

reasonableness. This unexpressed reasoning is what we think underpinned Handley JA's conclusion that a promise to negotiate in good faith is illusory and therefore not binding. The third Judge in *Coal Cliff*, Waddell A-JA, agreed "generally" with Kirby P's reasoning but did not deliver a substantive judgment of his own.

[18] The next case to be considered is *Walford v Miles* [1992] 2 AC 128. The House of Lords held that an agreement to negotiate in good faith was unenforceable for lack of certainty, and amounted to no more than a bare agreement to negotiate. [T]his conclusion is fundamentally inconsistent with Wild J's judgment in the present case. Counsel argued we should prefer the approach of Kirby P in *Coal Cliff*, albeit, as we have said, it is not easy to discern the material ingredients of that approach.

[19] In *Walford*, Lord Ackner delivered the leading speech. . . . At p 136, para G, Lord Ackner noted that an agreement to negotiate did not in English law amount to an enforceable contract. That was first decided by the Court of Appeal in *Courtney and Fairbairn Ltd v Tolaini Brothers (Hotels) Ltd* [*supra*]. . . .

[20] Counsel for the appellant in *Walford* argued that *Courtney* had been wrongly decided. The House of Lords did not accept that proposition. At p 138, para B, Lord Ackner referred to the decision of the United States Court of Appeal, Third Circuit, in *Channel Home Centres, Division of Grace Retail Corporation v Grossman* 795 F 2d 291 (1986), and said of it:

> That case raised the issue whether an agreement to negotiate in good faith, if supported by consideration, is an enforceable contract. I do not find the decision of any assistance. While accepting that an agreement to agree is not an enforceable contract, the Court of Appeal appears to have proceeded on the basis that an agreement to negotiate in good faith is synonymous with an agreement to use best endeavours and as the latter is enforceable, so is the former. This appears to me, with respect, to be an unsustainable proposition.

[21] His Lordship continued at p 138, para D:

> The reason why an agreement to negotiate, like an agreement to agree, is unenforceable, is simply because it lacks the necessary certainty. The same does not apply to an agreement to use best endeavours. This uncertainty is demonstrated in the instant case by the provision which it is said has to be implied in the agreement for the determination of the negotiations. How can a court be expected to decide whether, *subjectively* [Lord Ackner's emphasis], a proper reason existed for the termination of negotiations? The answer suggested depends upon whether the negotiations have been determined "in good faith." However the concept of a duty to carry on negotiations in good faith is inherently repugnant to the adversarial position of the parties when involved in negotiations. Each party to the negotiations is entitled to pursue his (or her) own interest, so long as he avoids making misrepresentations. To advance that interest he must be entitled, if he thinks it appropriate, to threaten to withdraw from further negotiations or to withdraw in fact, in the hope that the opposite party may seek to reopen the negotiations by offering him improved terms. [Counsel] of course, accepts that the agreement upon which he relies does not contain a duty to complete the negotiations. But that still leaves the vital question - how is a vendor ever to know that he is entitled to withdraw from further negotiations? How is the court to police such an "agreement?" A duty to negotiate in good faith is as unworkable in practice as it is inherently inconsistent with the position of a negotiating party. It is here that the uncertainty lies. In my judgment, while negotiations are in existence either party is entitled to withdraw from those negotiations, at any time and for any reason. There can be thus no obligation to continue to negotiate until there is a "proper reason" to withdraw. Accordingly a bare agreement to negotiate has no legal content.

[22] Clearly, if this Court considers it appropriate to follow the approach taken by the House of Lords in *Walford,* the Council's appeal must succeed.

.....

[30] The position can be summed up in the following way. The essence of the common law theory of contract is consensus. It follows that for there to be an enforceable contract, the parties must have reached consensus on all essential terms; or at least upon objective means of sufficient certainty by which those terms may be determined. Those objective means may be expressly agreed or they may be implicit in what has been expressly agreed. Taking price as an example, for a contract to be enforceable the parties must have agreed upon the price, or at least they must have agreed upon objective means of sufficient certainty whereby the price can be determined by someone else, or by the Court. If the price is left for later subjective agreement between the parties, the contract is not enforceable.

[31] As we indicated a little earlier, the same theory of consensus applies by analogy to a process contract which obliges the parties to negotiate in good faith for the purpose of trying to reach agreement on all essential terms. Good faith in this context is essentially a subjective concept, as the House of Lords pointed out in *Walford*. There is thus no sufficiently certain objective criterion by means of which the Court can decide whether either party is in breach of the good faith obligation. The Court is unable in such cases to resolve the question whether a particular negotiating stance was adopted in good faith. The law regards the task of reconciling self interest with the subjective connotation of having to act in good faith as an exercise of such inherent difficulty and uncertainty as not to be justiciable. The ostensible consensus is therefore illusory.

[32] It is implicit in what we have just said that there will be some circumstances in which a process contract is enforceable. The tender cases, although sui generis, provide some analogy:. . . In such cases a specific procedure is in issue, and the Court can reasonably determine what the parties are required to do and whether they have done it. If a contract specifies the way in which the negotiations are to be conducted with enough precision for the Court to be able to determine what the parties are obliged to do, it will be enforceable.

[33] In this case we do not have to address what the position would be if money has changed hands in return for a contractually unenforceable promise to negotiate in good faith. If the recipient refuses to negotiate at all, the Court could well be able to order repayment on restitutionary principles. There would be some parallel with a total failure of consideration. A promise to negotiate in good faith, given in return for a money sum, if wholly unperformed, could well give rise to an equitable obligation to repay; but issues such as this can be left for another day.

[34] The law being as discussed, we are led inexorably to the view that the process contract between the Council and Alirae was unenforceable. It was a contract to negotiate in good faith with no more definition than that of what the obligations of the parties were.

[Appeal dismissed.]

NOTES and QUESTIONS

1. Tipping J. relied upon the decision of the House of Lords in *Walford v. Miles*, [1992] 2 A.C. 128 (U.K. H.L.), in support of the conclusion that the parties' agreement to negotiate in good faith was not enforceable. *Walford v. Miles* has been cited with approval by Canadian courts in a number of recent cases, including *Mannpar Enterprises Ltd. v. Canada (supra)*. See also *Westcom TV Group Ltd. v. CanWest Global Broadcasting Inc.* (1996), [1997] 1 W.W.R. 761 (B.C. S.C. [In Chambers]); Scott C.J.M. in a strong *obiter* passage in *Mellco Developments Ltd. v. Portage la Prairie (City)* (2002), 222 D.L.R. (4th) 67 (Man. C.A.), leave to appeal on a separate point of law refused (2003), [2002] S.C.C.A. No. 502; *P.P. (Portage) Holdings Inc. v. 346 Portage Avenue Inc.* (1999), 177 D.L.R. (4th) 358 (Man. C.A.); *Taylor v. Netron Inc.* (2002), [2002] O.J. No. 3121, 2002 CarswellOnt 2619 (S.C.J.); *EdperBrascan Corp. v. 177373 Canada Ltd., supra*, in the note following *Mannpar Enterprises*.

2. A comprehensive criticism of *Wellington City Council* and of the courts' general refusal to enforce an agreement to negotiate in good faith is advanced in McLauchlan, "The Justiciability of an Agreement to Negotiate in Good Faith" (2003), 20 N.Z.U.L.R. 265. In particular, the author challenges the court's assertion that the question of whether parties have negotiated in good faith is a subjective one and hence impossible to determine. The concept of good faith is compared to that of honesty, with respect to which the author cites authority for the view that the question of whether a person has acted honestly is to be determined on an objective basis. He argues that, by analogy, good faith conduct is what a reasonable person in the position of the party in question would regard as honest and fair dealing, having regard to his or her legitimate self interest.

3. The Supreme Court of Canada has yet to address the question of whether there is, or in some circumstances may be, an enforceable contractual obligation to negotiate in good faith. In *Martel Building Ltd. v. Canada (supra* Chapter 2, section 2, note 2 after *M.J.B. Enterprises Ltd.)*, the court held that there is no duty of care in tort supporting liability for negligence in the conduct of commercial negotiations. In their conclusion on that point, Iacobucci and Major JJ. said, at 887:

> . . . For these reasons we are of the opinion that, in the circumstances of this case, any *prima facie* duty is significantly outweighed by the deleterious effects that would be occasioned through an extension of a duty of care into the conduct of negotiations. We conclude then that, as a general proposition, no duty of care arises in conducting negotiations. While there may well be a set of circumstances in which a duty of care may be found, it has not yet arisen.

> As a final note, we recognize that Martel's claim resembles the assertion of a duty to bargain in good faith. The breach of such a duty was alleged in the Federal Court, but not before this Court. As noted by the courts below, a duty to bargain in good faith has not been recognized to date in Canadian law. These reasons are restricted to whether or not the tort of negligence should be extended to include negotiation. Whether or not negotiations are to be governed by a duty of good faith is a question for another time.

The Supreme Court has, however, acknowledged the existence of a duty of good faith in defined aspects of contract performance, as distinguished from contract negotiation. In *Wallace v. United Grain Growers (supra*, Chapter 14, section 3(iv)), the court held that there is an implied contractual duty of good faith in the manner in which an employee is dismissed. In *Whiten v. Pilot Insurance Co. (supra*, Chapter 14, section 3(iv)), the court established that an insurer is subject to a contractual duty to act in good faith in the assessment and payment of policyholder claims. These decisions support the view that it is possible to determine the meaning of the standard of good faith conduct in a commercial context and to decide whether it has been violated. See also Steyn L.J., "Contract Law: Fulfilling the Reasonable Expectations of Honest Men" (1997), 113 L.Q.R. 433 at 438-39.

4. In the course of his review of the law in this case, Tipping J. referred to two leading text authors, Fridman and Waddams, for the conclusion that in Canada, an agreement to bargain in good faith does not give rise to an enforceable contract. He cited *Empress Towers*, at 495, as authority for the "only exception" to this principle; namely, "where an already concluded contract requires the parties to negotiate a specific contract outside that contract".

This observation raises an important point of distinction. In some of the cases we have considered, parties agreed as a term of an existing contract to negotiate in good faith to arrive at a secondary contract, such as a renewal (*Empress Towers, Mannpar Enterprises*). In others, parties who initially had no existing contractual relationship agreed to negotiate in good faith to conclude a contract (*Wellington City Council, Walford*). Should a court be more willing to enforce an agreement to negotiate in good faith in the first sort of case than in the second?

At least one Canadian court has suggested that there is no distinction between the two types of agreement. In *EdperBrascan Corp. v. 177373 Canada Ltd.* (*supra*, in the note following *Mannpar Enterprises* and discussed in note 5 below), Lane J. concluded his review of the cases relevant to the question of whether an agreement to negotiate is enforceable with this *obiter* observation, at 443-44:

> In the light of these cases, perhaps *Empress Towers* should be regarded as confined to its very narrow set of facts, and not as authority for a general proposition that the duty to bargain in good faith exists whenever a negotiation takes place within an existing contract. To some extent this seems to have happened.

Though *Empress Towers* has been mentioned in a significant number of cases, only a few have acted on the view that an agreement to negotiate, or to negotiate in good faith, is enforceable. For a recent case supporting the enforceability of a duty to negotiate in good faith in the context of renewal of an existing contract, see *Northland Fleet Services Ltd. v. Quintette Operating Corp.* (2001), 16 B.L.R. (3d) 58 (B.C. S.C.). See also *Hargreaves v. Fleming* (1995), 129 Sask. R. 136 (Q.B.).

5. In *EdperBrascan*, the agreement to negotiate under consideration by the court was independent of any other contract between the parties, though they were closely related corporate entities. EdperBrascan, who at the time of the agreement operated under the name Brascan Ltd., owned a controlling interest in Labatt. After Brascan agreed to sell its stake in Labatt to the public, it was agreed that Labatt should dispose of its shareholdings in other companies controlled by Brascan. The parties signed a letter agreement under which Brascan agreed to assist Labatt in liquidating its investments in the Brascan companies. The agreement provided that if any such investments remained unsold at a specified future date, Brascan would purchase them for shares of equivalent value in other named companies. If Labatt determined that the shares offered by Brascan did not represent equivalent value, then Brascan would pay "a price mutually agreed".

EdperBrascan took the position that Labatt's rejection of the shares tendered in satisfaction of the first branch of the agreement amounted to a repudiation, bringing the agreement to an end, and sought a judicial declaration to that effect. Labatt counterclaimed for a declaration that the agreement was in full force and effect, and for an order that EdperBrascan carry it out by delivering either cash or securities of the type contemplated by the agreement.

The court found that the parties' intention was that Brascan would purchase Labatt's investments in the Brascan companies by offering Labatt shares that could be liquidated within a reasonable time for a sum amounting to the book value of the investments. On that view, the shares tendered by EdperBrascan to Labatt did not fulfil Brascan's obligation under the first branch of the agreement. The court concluded that the second branch of the agreement, under which Brascan would pay "a price mutually agreed" in the event that Brascan failed to offer shares of the kind contemplated by the first branch, was unenforceable. In the absence of a formula to determine the price to be agreed or an arbitration clause to resolve any dispute, it constituted an agreement to agree. The court rejected the argument that the provision gave rise to a duty to negotiate in good faith to reach agreement as to price. Hence there was no foundation for EdperBrascan's contention that Labatt had failed to fulfil such a duty.

In its reasons, the court resoundingly affirmed the traditional jurisprudence on agreements to agree and the non-existence of a duty to negotiate in good faith. Notably, however, its analysis did not lead to the conclusion that there was no enforceable contract for sale of Labatt's investments in the Brascan companies to Brascan. On the contrary, EdperBrascan was ordered to pay Labatt in cash the sum of $135.5 million for the remaining investments plus accrued dividends thereon and pre-judgment interest for breach of the first branch of the agreement. In effect, the court severed that portion of the agreement that it regarded as uncertain, leaving the remaining provisions intact. What would the result have been if the provision for purchase of the investments "at a price mutually agreed" were not severable? Had that been the case, do you think the court would have reached the same conclusion regarding the enforceability of that branch of the agreement?

The Ontario Court of Appeal affirmed the decision of the Supreme Court of Justice without addressing the issue of uncertainty.

6. Commentators have suggested that, while the legitimacy of a judicially imposed (*i.e.*, implied) duty to negotiate in good faith to reach agreement on contractual terms may be debatable, there is no good reason for the refusal to enforce an agreement in which the parties voluntarily undertake to do so. On the contrary, such a refusal is widely regarded as defeating the parties' expectations and frustrating their right to determine the terms according to which they wish to conduct their relationship. See the analysis of McLauchlan (cited in note 2); Steyn L.J. (cited in note 3); Berg, "Promises to Negotiate in Good Faith" (2003), 119 L.Q.R. 357; Stewart, "Good Faith in Contractual Performance and in Negotiation" (1998), 72 Aust. L.J. 370; Mason, "Contract, Good Faith and Equitable Standards in Fair Dealing" (2000), 116 L.Q.R. 66 at 80-81; Beatson, *Anson's Law of Contract*, 28th ed. (2002) at 65; Goode, "Commercial Law in the Next Millennium" (The Hamlyn Lectures) (1998) at 33; Paterson, "The Contract to Negotiate in Good Faith: Recognition and Enforcement" (1996), 10 J.C.L. 120; Carter and Furmston, "Good Faith and Fairness in the Negotiation of Contracts" (1994-95) 8 J.C.L. 1, 93; Beale, *Commentary on 'Good Faith and Fairness in Failed Contract Negotiations'* (1995), 8 J.C.L. 120, 123; Beatson, "Commentary on 'Good Faith and Fairness in Negotiated Contract' "(1995), 8 J.C.L. 138.

7. One of the objections raised by Lord Denning to the enforcement of an agreement to negotiate is the difficulty of assessing damages for breach of that duty (see the quotation from *Courtney & Fairbairn Ltd. v. Tolaini Brothers (Hotels) Ltd.* appearing in the introduction to this section). Damages cannot be based on loss of the benefits associated with performance of the contract to be negotiated, since it cannot be presumed that, even if properly pursued, negotiations would have resulted in agreement. Further, there is no way of knowing what the terms of the agreement would have been, had agreement been reached. Lord Denning draws no distinction between the potential benefits associated with negotiation and those associated with the ultimate conclusion of an agreement. Note that in *Wellington City Council*, the court acknowledges the distinction between the parties' agreement as to the negotiation process and the substantive contract towards which negotiations are directed.

Commentators argue that a court can quantify the losses caused by breach of an agreement to negotiate in good faith as well as they can quantify the loss of other benefits that entail a contingency. See Berg, Stewart (*supra*, note 6), and McLauchlan (*supra*, note 2). McLauchlan suggests, at 296-97, that the award that would put the plaintiff in the position he or she would have been in if the contract to negotiate in good faith had been performed may range from purely nominal damages to "substantial damages for loss of the chance to secure the benefits that would have resulted from conclusion of the agreement being negotiated". He quotes noted United States Judge Richard Posner, as follows:

> Damages for breach of an agreement to negotiate may be, although they are unlikely to be, the same as the damages for breach of the final contract that the parties would have signed had it not been for the defendant's bad faith. If, quite apart from any bad faith, the negotiations would have broken down, the party led on by the other party's bad faith to persist in futile negotiations can recover only his reliance damages – the expenses he incurred by being misled, in violation of the parties' agreement to negotiate in good faith, into continuing to negotiate futilely. But if the plaintiff can prove that had it not been for the defendant's bad faith the parties would have made a final contract, then the loss of the benefit of the contract is a consequence of the defendant's bad faith, and, provided that it is a foreseeable consequence, the defendant is liable for the loss – liable, that is, for the plaintiff's consequential damages. . . .

> (*Venture Associates Corp. v. Zenith Data Systems Corp.*,
> 96 F.3d 275 (U.S. 7th Cir., 1996) at 278-79.)

This line of reasoning was applied in *Northland Fleet Services Ltd. v. Quintette Operating Corp.* (2001), 16 B.L.R. (3d) 58 (B.C. S.C.). The court said, at 71:

> It is my view that there is, as yet, no absolute rule or principle of law that automatically precludes the enforceability of an agreement to negotiate with a view to reaching an agreement. Many such agreements may well be too uncertain to enforce, but the court should strive to interpret such agreements in a manner that gives them the legal effect intended by the parties. Given the history of the dealings of these parties, it appears that a compelling reason for including this agreement to negotiate a renewal, vague as it is, might have been to avoid or postpone a tendering process similar to that which Quintette resorted to in 1995, somewhat to the chagrin of Mr. LaPrairie. In that context, even a bare obligation to negotiate would theoretically have some commercial value since it would provide the present contractor with some chance of an advantage over potential competitors. Adding the requirement to negotiate in good faith would add more value if that requirement is equated with "best efforts" diligence, as held by the majority in the *Empress Towers Ltd.* case (*supra*). With the greatest of respect to Lord Denning's comments in *Courtney and Fairburn* (*supra*) the difficulty in estimating damages is a separate question from the vagueness of the contractual obligation, and an obligation to negotiate with a view to entering a contract is very different from an agreement to enter into a contract.

And later, at 72:

> In summary, I find that the agreement to negotiate contained in clause 6.04 is an enforceable provision, and the defendant was in breach by declining to negotiate. The plaintiff did suffer a loss of a chance to obtaining [*sic*] contract and make a profit, but in the circumstances I assess the prospect of the plaintiff obtaining a profitable contract as negligible, and I cannot assign any positive value to the lost chance.

For cases in which damages have been awarded for the loss of a chance to enjoy the benefits of a contract notwithstanding that the prospect of the contract maturing is both uncertain and dependent upon the application of reasonable efforts by one of the contracting parties, see Chapter 6, section 4 (Reciprocal Subsidiary Obligations).

8. Though the case law in the United States is mixed, commentators suggest that the trend is clearly in favour of the enforceability of agreements to negotiate in good faith. See Farnsworth, "Ten Questions about Good Faith and Fair Dealing in United States Contract Law" [2002] 1 A.M.P.L.A. Yearbook 2. This trend may well be a product of the approach explicitly adopted by Article 2 of the Uniform Commercial Code, which governs contracts for the sale of goods in all states except Louisiana. The relevant general provision is as follows:

> §2-204(3) Even though one or more terms are left open a contract for sale does not fail for indefiniteness if the parties have intended to make a contract and there is a reasonably certain basis for giving an appropriate remedy.

Additional provisions of Article 2 address, *inter alia*, agreements that fail to specify terms relating to price (§2-305), place of delivery (§2-308) and time of delivery (§2-309). These provisions have been applied both to the enforcement of agreements in which a term is missing and those that specifically provide for a term to be negotiated. See Choi, "Contracts with Open or Missing Terms under the Uniform Commercial Code and the Common Law: A Proposal for Unification" (2003), 103 Col. L. Rev. 50. Choi prefaces her conclusion that the U.C.C. approach should be extended to contracts for the provision of services with an outline of the policy bases supporting the arguments respectively for and against the enforcement of agreements containing an indefinite term or terms.

5. Anticipation of Formalization

The issue of uncertainty as an impediment to contract formation is often presented in circumstances in which one party seeks to enforce an agreement, either oral or in writing, that is allegedly binding notwithstanding that the parties contemplated that full details of their agreement would be embodied in a further written document. The agreement relied upon in such cases typically addresses in uncomplicated terms the essential points of the contemplated transaction. In some cases, the agreement outlines matters that have been settled and identifies others upon which agreement is to be reached. When in written form, an agreement of either kind may be referred to variously as a letter of intent, memorandum of agreement, memorandum of understanding or heads of agreement.

From the perspective of contract formation, the issues typically arising from such an agreement are whether the parties intended to be bound by its terms and, if they did, whether those terms are sufficiently certain to give rise to a contract. The contract in question may be either an agreement governing the substantive transaction contemplated by the parties, or it may be an agreement to negotiate to finalize the terms of the substantive transaction within the parameters established. The party challenging the enforceability of an agreement of either sort generally does so on the ground that it is simply an agreement to agree or an unenforceable agreement to negotiate, even if, in the latter case, the agreement expressly contemplates negotiation in good faith.

In practical terms, preliminary agreements may play an important role in the negotiation and conclusion of a transaction. They serve the purpose of motivating parties to invest the time and resources required to finalize the details of what may be a complex agreement by providing some assurance that those investments are likely to yield results. In addition, they allow the parties to move forward towards the conclusion of their agreement by stages, addressing a limited number of issues at a time. However, the parties' practical objectives and expectations are not always consistent with the legal outcomes flowing from such agreements. One author, Schueller, "Letters of Intent – A Trap for the Unwary" (2002), 37 R. P.P. and T. J. 509 at 510, has described the situation in these terms:

> A letter of intent is often a trap for the unwary: binding when one of the parties believes it not binding, or not binding when one of the parties hopes to rely on the letter of intent as a binding contract. In other instances, a letter of intent, while not constituting a binding agreement to consummate the transaction described therein, can nevertheless restrict the breadth of a party's ability to negotiate. Considering the widespread use of letters of intent by the business community, understanding how these documents can affect the rights and obligations of the parties is important, particularly if the transaction falls through.

BAWITKO INVESTMENTS LTD. v. KERNELS POPCORN LTD.
(1991), 79 D.L.R. (4th) 97 (Ont. C.A.)

ROBINS J.A. This is an appeal from [a] judgment. . . declaring the appellant in breach of an oral contract to grant the respondent a franchise to operate a retail store at a shopping centre in Hamilton, Ontario, known as "Jackson Square".

The appellant is an Ontario company carrying on business as a retailer of specialty popcorn products under the trade mark "Kernels Gourmet Popcorn". At the time of trial, the appellant sold such products through some 35 "Kernels" stores in Canada and the United States. Approximately one-half of the stores were owned and operated by the appellant. The remaining stores were owned and operated by franchisees pursuant to franchise agreements with the appellant.

In early 1984, the appellant planned to open two stores. One was to be in a shopping centre in London, Ontario, called "White Oaks", and the other in Jackson Square in Hamilton. On March 23, 1984, Anthony Passander approached the appellant with a view to acquiring franchise rights for the Kernels store in Jackson Square. Passander is a real estate broker with wide business experience. For the purposes of this action, he is the sole representative of the respondent, Bawitko Investments Limited, an Ontario company owned by his wife.

On April 3, 1984, the appellant, which was represented throughout this matter by either Richard Sadowski or Scott Staiman, provided Passander with a Kernels "information package". This package contained a variety of promotional items, such as: statements projecting profit and loss for typical locations; statements regarding basic start-up costs; a discussion of questions commonly asked by prospective franchisees about the appellant's franchise; and an application for franchise. Most importantly, the material included a copy of Kernels "draft" or "standard" form of franchise agreement.

The draft agreement is approximately 50 pages in length. It sets out in minute detail the terms and conditions under which the appellant, as franchisor, agrees to grant a franchisee the right to use "the system, methods and procedures" developed by the appellant "for the operation of a retail sales outlet specializing in the sale of popcorn, popcorn related paraphernalia, and beverages under the trademark 'Kernels Gourmet Popcorn'". The extent of the detail governing the franchisor-franchisee relationship can be seen from the headings given to the various sections of the agreement, which include: Grant; Franchisee Fee and Royalty Fee; Term and Renewal; Accounting, Record, Reports, Audits; Duties and Obligations of the Franchisor; Duties and Obligations of the Franchisee; Premises; Construction and Outfitting of Premises; Trademark; Engagement in Similar Business: Non Disclosure of Information; Termination; Effect of Termination; Sale or Encumbrance; Death or Incapacitation; and Guarantor's Covenants. Where the franchisee is a corporation, the agreement provides that the franchisor may, with respect to certain provisions, require the directors, officers or shareholders of the corporation to personally guarantee, acknowledge or agree to be bound by those provisions "in such form of document as may be required by the Franchisor from time to time". Time is made of the essence of the agreement.

This is manifestly a complex document intended to govern a long-term business relationship. Prospective franchisees are advised in the informational material "to make certain to retain professional advisors (e.g. lawyers, accountants, business advisors) to advise you so that you will understand all the terms of the agreement and your obligations thereunder".

Shortly after receiving these documents, Passander met with Sadowski at the appellant's offices. . .on April 18, 1984. . .. Reducing the facts to their essentials, the trial judge, rejecting Sadowski's evidence, found on the basis of Passander's evidence that the appellant had orally contracted on that date to grant the respondent a franchise agreement for the Jackson Square store. The terms of the franchise agreement are not specified in the trial judge's reasons or in the formal judgment which simply adjudges that "the defendant is in breach of an enforceable contract" and directs the master "to assess the damages flowing from the breach of the said contract". Clearly, however, the discussions at this meeting were directed to particular items in the draft franchise agreement and culminated, as the trial judge found, in the parties agreeing:

> (a) that the $5,000 renewal fee provided for in the draft agreement was to be eliminated;
>
> (b) that the term of the draft agreement was to be extended from five to 10 years;
>
> (c) that the fee payable on the resale of the franchise as provided for in the draft agreement would be payable only if the franchise were sold by the respondent within one year; and
>
> (d) that the personal guarantees contemplated by the draft agreement would be eliminated.

The meeting ended with Sadowski shaking hands with Passander and saying, "You've got a deal." The trial judge held that at that point "there was a contract—the defendant granted the franchise". Although the trial judge did not specify all of the terms upon which the franchise was granted or find that the respondent had agreed to the appellant's draft form, he inferentially concluded that the franchise agreement was to be in accordance with the appellant's draft except to the extent that document was amended at the April 18th meeting.

The respondent acknowledged, however, that the parties agreed at the April 18th meeting, and at all pertinent times thereafter, to embody their mutual obligations in a formal written document. Indeed, one would not expect otherwise. In the light of that fact, it is necessary to consider the legal effect to be given the informal oral contract found by the trial judge. The question is whether, on one hand, the oral contract can in itself constitute, as the trial judge held, a complete and legally enforceable contract or, whether, on the other hand, as the appellant contends, the oral contract was not in itself a complete and legally enforceable contract but was subject to and dependent upon a formal written franchise document being settled, approved and executed by the parties. Alternatively, the appellant contends that the respondent was in breach of the oral contract at the relevant time and, in any event, that the oral contract was unenforceable by reason of s. 4 of the *Statute of Frauds*, R.S.O. 1980, c. 481.

Before turning to these issues, it is important to examine briefly the conduct of the parties after April 18th. I should perhaps first note, although, as the appeal was presented, it did not become significant, that as of that date neither party was in a position to enter into or finalize a franchise agreement. The appellant did not yet hold a lease to any premises in Jackson Square, and the respondent had not yet been incorporated. Nevertheless, it was undoubtedly anticipated that the respondent would become the franchisee in premises to be rented by the appellant, and the parties conducted themselves accordingly. Passander made payments by way of deposit towards the initial franchise fee and construction costs pursuant to an extended payment schedule agreed to after April 18th; he took steps to arrange the respondent's financing for the project; and he had discussions with the appellant about the proposed layout of the store. These and similar acts go both to the evidentiary issues that fell to be determined as to whether a contract had been agreed to, and, more particularly, to the question of whether, assuming an otherwise binding oral contract, there had been sufficient part performance to avoid the application of s. 4 of the *Statute of Frauds*.

[Robins J.A. outlined the difficulties that arose between the parties in connection with execution of a written franchise agreement and related documents. The respondent refused to execute the agreement presented by the appellant, which was in the standard form provided to the respondent prior to the meeting of April 18 without the modifications discussed at that meeting. Following an exchange of correspondence, the parties' relationship disintegrated. In August 1984, the respondent commenced an action claiming ". . . specific performance of the franchise agreement between the parties, in accordance with the terms of the draft form of agreement annexed hereto as Schedule "A" [*i.e.*, the appellant's draft franchise agreement], as modified by further agreement of the parties as pleaded in paragraph 5, above; [*i.e.*, the specific items found by the trial judge to have been agreed to on 18th April]." The claim for specific performance was subsequently dropped and the action proceeded to trial as a claim for damages for breach of contract.]

. . . [T]he principal issue in this appeal . . . is essentially this: Was the oral contract found by the trial judge a complete and binding contract or was its enforceability subject to the parties' subsequent agreement on all of the terms and conditions to be contained in the contemplated written franchise agreement? Put another way, did the learned judge err, as the appellant contends, in concluding that Passander was granted the franchise on April 18th and the franchise agreement to which he was "to put his signature" was no more than "a contract already agreed upon"?

As a matter of normal business practice, parties planning to make a formal written document the expression of their agreement, necessarily discuss and negotiate the proposed terms of the agreement before they enter into it. They frequently agree upon all of the terms to be incorporated into the intended written document before it is prepared. Their agreement may be expressed orally or by way of memorandum, by exchange of correspondence, or other informal writings. The parties may "contract to make a contract", that is to say, they may bind themselves to execute at a future date a formal written agreement containing specific terms and conditions. When they agree on all of the essential provisions to be incorporated in a formal document with the intention that their agreement shall thereupon become binding, they will have fulfilled all the requisites for the formation of a contract. The fact that a formal written document to the same effect is to be thereafter prepared and signed does not alter the binding validity of the original contract.

However, when the original contract is incomplete because essential provisions intended to govern the contractual relationship have not been settled or agreed upon; or the contract is too general or uncertain to be valid in itself and is dependent on the making of a formal contract; or the understanding or intention of the parties, even if there is no uncertainty as to the terms of their agreement, is that their legal obligations are to be deferred until a formal contract has been approved and executed, the original or preliminary agreement cannot constitute an enforceable contract. In other words, in such circumstances the "contract to make a contract" is not a contract at all. The execution of the contemplated formal document is not intended only as a solemn record or memorial of an already complete and binding contract but is essential to the formation of the contract itself: see, generally, *Von Hatzfeldt-Wildenburg v. Alexander*, [1912] 1 Ch. 284; *Canada Square Corp. v. Versafood Services Ltd.* (1979), 101 D.L.R. (3d) 742, 8 B.L.R. 21, 25 O.R. (2d) 591 (H.C.J.); affirmed 130 D.L.R. (3d) 205, 15 B.L.R. 89, 34 O.R. (2d) 250 (C.A.); *Bahamaconsult Ltd. v. Kellogg Salada Canada Ltd.* (1975), 61 D.L.R. (3d) 398, 9 O.R. (2d) 630 (H.C.J.); reversed 75 D.L.R. (3d) 522, 15 O.R. (2d) 276 (C.A.); *Chitty on Contracts*, 26th ed. (1990), at pp. 79-91. . . .

In this case, the parties clearly contemplated the signing of a formal written contract. Given this fact, can the oral contract they were found to have reached constitute in law a completed contract which took effect immediately after it was agreed to on April 18th? In determining this question, it is plainly necessary to examine what transpired at that time. In doing so, it must be borne in mind that the franchise agreement which formed the subject-matter of the negotiations was intended to govern a lengthy franchisor-franchisee relationship. The precise terms under which a business relationship of this nature is to be governed are manifestly essential to the formation of a binding contract. If no agreement in respect to essential terms has been reached or the terms have not been agreed to with reasonable certainty, it can only be concluded that such terms were to be agreed upon at a later date and until that time there would be no completed agreement.

It is to be borne in mind that to succeed in this action the respondent was required to prove that a complete agreement was entered into on April 18th. The plaintiff's claim proceeded entirely on the legal basis that the parties had agreed on that date that the final written document granting the franchise was to be in accordance with the terms and conditions set out in the appellant's draft agreement as then amended. If that were established, and the parties manifested an intention to be bound thereby, it could readily be concluded that they had entered into an identifiable and legally enforceable oral contract. In so far as it is contended that the oral contract would be unenforceable by virtue of the *Statute of Frauds*, I may say that I agree with the trial judge that the respondent's acts following April 18th, without detailing them, constituted part performance sufficient to take the oral contract out of *Statute of Frauds*.

However, as I stated earlier, the trial judge did not specify all the essential terms which were to be incorporated into the intended written franchise document other than the specific items to which the parties agreed on April 18th. More particularly, he did not find that it had been agreed at that meeting, or, indeed, at any later time, that the written franchise agreement was to be in the form of the appellant's draft or that this draft had been accepted by the respondent as the document to govern the Jackson Square franchise. In my opinion, such a finding could not be made on the record in this case. Accepting the respondent's testimony in its entirety, the evidence does not establish agreement on the terms to be embodied in the formal written document. Rather, it establishes that the terms, other than those specifically agreed to, were to be settled and agreed to later.

Passander made clear in his testimony that his focus at the April 18th meeting was on what he regarded as the business aspects of the deal, namely, the provisions relating to the personal guarantees, to the renewal and resale fees and to the length of the franchise. The parties were found to have reached agreement on these items. However, the remaining provisions of the draft agreement were not the subject of negotiation or discussion. It would appear that they were not even considered by Passander. . . .

In my view, the terms of the franchise beyond those agreed to cannot be regarded as mere formalities or routine language. This is not a conventional document that requires only the filling in of blank spaces or the completion of minor details which the parties can impliedly be taken to have agreed upon. The terms of the draft clearly include material conditions essential to this kind of specialized contract. The very nature of the franchisor-franchisee relationship mandates that there be express agreement on the detailed provisions set up to regulate the business relationship of the parties. Here, taking the respondent's evidence at its highest, there was no meeting of the minds necessary for a completed contract. Certain terms, as the trial judge found, were agreed to on April 18th, but others essential to the proposed contractual arrangement, with respect to which he made no findings, remained open for negotiation. . . .

The parties' conduct after the April 18th meeting supports the conclusion that no final agreement had been reached. At all relevant times the appellant plainly considered that the terms of the intended formal agreement were not yet settled. Consistent with its position that there was no binding agreement, it invited the respondent, on more than one occasion, to comment on the draft form of agreement, so that, if necessary, terms could be negotiated, presumably, an agreement reached, and the formal written documents thereafter engrossed and executed. . . .

For these reasons, I am of the opinion that the respondent has not established the contract upon which its claim is founded or, in any event, that it was ready and willing at any pertinent time to sign or have signed the various documents contemplated by that contract. The agreement reached on April 18th did not encompass essential aspects of the intended formal agreement. Accordingly, it did not satisfy the standards of certainty which the law requires as a prerequisite to incurring binding and enforceable contractual relations.

[Appeal allowed.]

NOTES

1. Robins J.A. cited, as authority for the principles relevant to the determination of cases involving contemplation of a formal written agreement, the frequently cited decision of the Ontario Court of Appeal in *Canada Square Corp. v. Versafood Services Ltd.* (1979), 101 D.L.R. (3d) 742 (Ont. H.C.), affirmed (1981), 130 D.L.R. (3d) 205 (Ont. C.A.). In that case, the court considered a letter of intention outlining what were described in the letter as "the general principles of our agreement" for the lease of restaurant premises in a building to be constructed by the plaintiff. The court concluded that, particularly in light of their subsequent conduct, the parties intended in exe-

cuting the letter to make a contract. The defendant argued that, notwithstanding an intention to be bound, there was uncertainty with respect to identified terms of the lease precluding the formation of a contract. After quoting from the judgments of Lord Wright in *Hillas & Co. v. Arcos Ltd.*, *supra*, and *G. Scammell & Nephew Ltd. v. Ouston* (1940), [1941] A.C. 251 (U.K. H.L.), Morden J.A. concluded, at 218:

> In this case there is no doubt that the document of October 14, 1969, as an agreement to lease, is crudely expressed and contains some very loose language. Further, a more sophisticated document would probably have covered several other matters in addition to those dealt with in it. Nonetheless, accepting that the parties intended to create a binding relationship and were represented by experienced businessmen who had full authority to represent their respective companies, a Court should not be too astute to hold that there is not that degree of certainty in any of its essential terms which is the requirement of a binding contract.

After reviewing the terms of the letter in the context of the facts of the case, Morden J.A. concluded that it established all essential terms of the contract of lease with sufficient certainty.

2. In *Bawitko Investments Ltd.*, the court accepted that the parties had in fact agreed orally on the terms alleged by the respondent, but concluded that those terms did not give rise to a contract. The Statute of Frauds ordinarily requires that, to be enforceable, a contract for the sale of an interest in land (including a leasehold interest) must be evidenced by a written memorandum. However, the court indicated that, were the oral agreement a contract, the absence of such a memorandum would not have warranted a conclusion that it was unenforceable in this case, in view of the parties' subsequent conduct. The scope and application of the Statute of Frauds and the doctrine of part performance are addressed in Chapter 4, section 8. Assuming that the Statute is not in issue, is there a difference in principle between a preliminary agreement that is oral and one in which the same words are incorporated in a written document?

3. *Bawitko Investments Ltd.* has been cited in many cases, including some in which the courts concluded that the parties did reach an enforceable agreement, notwithstanding that a more formal and detailed written document was to be subsequently executed. See *e.g.*, *Gendis Inc. v. Richardson Oil & Gas Ltd.*, [2000] 9 W.W.R. 1 (Man. C.A.); *1200347 Ontario Ltd. v. Barathon Development Corp.* (2000), [2000] O.J. No. 3002 (S.C.J.); *Mason Homes Ltd. v. Oshawa Group Ltd.* (2003), 12 R.P.R. (4th) 201 (Ont. S.C.J.).

The letter of intent under consideration in *Mason Homes Ltd. v. Oshawa Group Ltd.* stipulated the essential terms of a lease of retail space in a shopping centre upon which the parties had reached agreement. The letter included this provision;

> The lease form to be executed by Landlord [the plaintiff] and Tenant [the defendant] shall be based upon the Tenant's standard lease form (which shall include a construction agreement as a schedule attached to the lease), subject to such changes therein as may be required by this agreement and as may be reasonably requested by the Landlord or its solicitors, *the lease to be settled to the mutual satisfaction of the parties within 45 days after execution hereof, failing which this agreement shall be null and void. Thereafter the said lease shall be executed and delivered as expeditiously as possible* [emphasis added by the court].

The defendant relied on *EdperBrascan Corp. v. 177373 Canada Ltd.*, (see notes 4 and 5 following *Wellington City Council v. Body Corporate 51702 (Wellington)* in section 4 of this chapter) in support of its argument that the letter constituted an unenforceable agreement to agree. The court concluded that, although the parties anticipated that a more elaborate document would be executed, they had reached agreement on the material terms of the lease as stipulated in the Letter of Intent. The Letter of Intent was therefore a binding and enforceable agreement to lease.

4. Parties who anticipate the completion of a further written document embodying their contract may stipulate that the agreement outlined in an informal document is "subject to contract", or use wording to similar effect. Language of that kind is often viewed as an indication that the parties did not intend to be bound until a formal document is executed. In *Calvan Consolidated Oil & Gas Co. v. Manning*, [1959] S.C.R. 253 at 260-61, Judson J. distinguished the agreement before the court, which stipulated that "a formal agreement will be drawn up as soon as possible", from an agreement

"subject to contract". Referring to the latter and to the phrases "subject to the preparation and approval of a formal contract" and "subject to the preparation of a formal contract, its execution by the parties and approval by their solicitors", he suggested that such language represents a qualified acceptance of the terms of the informal agreement. Nevertheless, he appears to leave open the possibility that, even in such cases, a contract may arise before formalization of the written agreement, given the concluding statement that: "Whether the parties intend to hold themselves bound until the execution of a formal agreement is a question of construction. . . ." (*Calvan Consolidated* is also discussed in note 5 following *Foley v. Classique Coaches Ltd.* in section 3). In many other cases, phrases such as "subject to the execution of a formal contract" have been found fatal to the argument that a binding contract exists prior to the execution of the formal document. See the discussion of the case law in *Knowlton Realty Ltd. v. Wyder* (1971), 23 D.L.R. (3d) 69 (B.C. S.C.).

5. If a letter of intent specifies all of the essential terms of a transaction except one or two, with respect to which it is explicitly provided that the parties shall negotiate in good faith to reach agreement, should the court conclude that the letter embodies an enforceable contract to negotiate in good faith? Commentators have suggested that, provided the parties intend to be bound, the enforcement of such agreements is essential to the utilization of letters of intent as effective devices in the negotiation of complex transactions. See Schueller, "Letters of Intent – A Trap for the Unwary" (2002), 37 R. P.P. and T. J. 509; and Gosfield, "The Structure and Use of Letters of Intent as Prenegotiation Contracts for Prospective Real Estate Transactions" (2003), 38 R.P.P. and T.J. 99. The arguments raised in favour of enforcement are largely the same as those raised by the critics of the courts' general refusal to enforce agreements to negotiate (see the Notes and Questions following *Wellington City Council v. Body Corporate 51702 (Wellington)* in section 4 of this chapter).

Chapter 4

THE ENFORCEMENT OF PROMISES

1. Introduction and Study Guide

> So far as human history has gone, the fact is that we do not wish to enforce all promises and the courts have not enforced all promises.
>
> (Corbin, *Contracts* (1963), at 495)

Every society must decide which agreements it will enforce through the legal system and which agreements result in commitments that are binding only as a matter of honour or morality. This issue can be illustrated by taking a number of examples and asking whether they are, or should be, legally enforceable. Consider the following situations:

(i)   A promises to meet B for dinner at 8 p.m. at a favourite restaurant;

(ii) A promises to donate $100 per month to the local United Way campaign;

(iii) A orally agrees to purchase B's business for $100,000;

(iv) B, a contractor, has promised to renovate A's home for the price of $50,000 and to complete the renovations before July 1st. In June, A notices that B is behind schedule and promises the contractor an extra $5,000 if B succeeds in completing the renovations before July 1st.

The previous chapters dealt with whether the parties had reached an agreement and whether the agreement was complete. This chapter is concerned with the criteria which courts employ to determine which of these agreements amount to enforceable contracts. Different legal systems apply different criteria to this basic question, even in the face of similar economic systems. For example, formal contract doctrine in Québec and the United States suggests that the courts in those jurisdictions would reach results in some of the situations set out above that differ from the results that would be achieved under the traditional approach to the common law.

In reading the first case in this chapter, *Dalhousie College v. Boutilier Estate*, it is instructive to ask what theories of liability the Supreme Court of Canada *could* have applied to decide whether Arthur Boutilier's promise to give money to Dalhousie was legally binding. Would any of those theories have achieved a result that differed from the one finally reached by the court? What was the significance to the court of the following factors in determining the possible liability of the estate?

(a) FORMALITY

The donor's promise was in writing, signed and dated. Because these basic formalities were observed, we can be reasonably certain that the donor made the promise and knew what he was doing.

It is often the hallmark of less developed legal systems that promises are legally enforceable only if they satisfy certain basic formalities. For example, at one stage in Roman Law, the donor would have been legally bound by even a verbal pledge if precise language had been used. If, in a case like *Dalhousie College*, a Roman university president had said "Do you solemnly promise (spondesne) to pay $5,000 to the university" and if the donor had replied "I solemnly promise (spondeo)," the donor's promise would have been legally binding. The use of these words may indicate that this form of contracting was based on the idea of a solemn oath.

This early example illustrates a problem with any requirement which states that a contract will be formed if and when the parties observe certain formalities. At least in early Roman law, there was no contractual obligation unless the parties used the precise words required. Because any slip of the tongue could dash the parties' plans, Roman law shows a history of development which first allowed a list of different (but still restricted) verbs to be used, until in the last years of the Empire, a statutory change allowed any expression of the appropriate intention to create this type of contract.

Even in modern times, popular reaction to the question of which agreements should be legally enforced often reflects a variation of the formality test. A person on the street may suggest that the donor's promise should be enforceable "because it is in writing". It would certainly be possible to require that only written promises should be enforceable, but what would be the effect of such a requirement?

There are more general reasons for requirements of formality, such as writing. They were examined by Fuller in "Consideration and Form" (1941), 41 Col. L.R. 799 and synthesized as follows by the Ontario Law Reform Commission in its Report on the Amendment of the Law of Contract (1987) at 95:

> (1) *Evidentiary function.* This function is self-evident and, judging by the preamble to the *Statute of Frauds*, obviously weighed most heavily with the framers of the Statute in 1677. Writing not only avoids the risks of perjury but, more importantly, by providing an objective and permanent record of the parties' agreement, avoids reliance on fallible human memories and eliminates the need to weigh possibly conflicting evidence as to what was said and with what intention.
>
> (2) *Cautionary function.* The danger of parol agreements that are fully enforceable without being reduced to writing, it is said, is that they may result in imposing very significant obligations without the parties fully appreciating the consequences of their actions. A writing requirement introduces a note of deliberation and provides the parties with a period of reflection, thereby, it is argued, preventing unconsidered action. Equally important, a writing requirement provides the parties with a shield behind which they may safely negotiate without the threat of being deemed to have concluded a binding contract.
>
> (3) *Channelling function. . . .* [A] legal formality such as writing not only serves an evidentiary and cautionary function, but "serves also to mark or signalize the enforceable promise; it furnishes a simple and external test of enforceability." However, Professor Fuller also recognized that the requirements of the *Statute of Frauds* serve only a negative effect—they indicate which promises are not enforceable without written evidence, but they do not

> impress the writing with the cachet of conclusive validity and effectiveness. This is because the written promise may be void or unenforceable for lack of consideration, lack of capacity, or because of duress, fraud, or other vitiating factors.

[Footnotes omitted.]

A brief consideration of all the unwritten but enforceable contracts that we make (including those illustrated in Chapter 2, such as *Pharmaceutical Society v. Boots*), demonstrates that the common law does not insist on formalities as a prerequisite to legal liability. Section 7 of this chapter shows that historically some types of promises were always binding if they were made in a particularly formal manner. Section 8 also demonstrates that the test of formality has had a lingering appeal, because in most Canadian jurisdictions certain promises which were once considered socially important still must be in writing in order to be fully enforceable.

(b)   SERIOUSLY INTENDED PROMISES

Some of the central ideas of contract are derived from the institution of promise. As a matter of basic morality, we expect that promises should be kept and it would not be outrageous to say that promises create legal, as well as moral obligations.

A different but related theory would emphasize that perhaps not all promises should be legally binding, but that promises should create legal obligations if they are seriously intended and made for a good reason.

It is probably fair to characterize the donor's promise in *Dalhousie College* as seriously intended and inspired by a good reason. If so, why did this not matter to the Supreme Court of Canada? The result of the case clearly allows the promisor to revoke a freely made and serious promise. Yet, even within Canada, one judge noted in another case before the Supreme Court of Canada that the civil law system of Québec allows promises similar to that of the donor in *Dalhousie College* to be enforced (see *Ross, Re* (1931), [1932] S.C.R. 57, *per* Newcombe J. at p. 68-70).

The Civil Code of Québec, Book 5, Title 1, Chapter 1, provides:

> **Art. 1371.** It is of the essence of an obligation that there be persons between whom it exists, a prestation which forms its object, and, in the case of an obligation arising out of a juridical act, a cause which justifies its existence.

> **Art. 1410.** The cause of a contract is the reason that determines each of the parties to enter into the contract.
> The cause need not be expressed.

The basic concept of *cause* is well discussed in Castel, *The Civil Law System of the Province of Quebec* (1962), at 298-328. Castel's account is an excellent introduction to *cause*. Common law readers may be amused by his comment (at 303) that *cause*, as construed in French doctrine, has 2 defects: "(1) it is false, at least in 2 cases out of 3; (2) it is useless." These views also reflect the tone of critics of the common law doctrine of consideration.

Although it is dangerous to attempt a nutshell definition of a complex concept, for introductory purposes, the concept of "cause" has been described as requiring that "there must be a valid purpose, a reason for, an end to be pursued in the contract". Pollard, *Sourcebook on French Law* (1996) at 193. In the *Ross, Re* decision, Newcombe J., at 68, noted that charitable intention can constitute "cause" when he quoted from an edition of the French jurist Pothier:

> Dans les contrats de bienfaisance, la liberalité que l'une des parties veut exercer envers l'autre, est une cause suffisante de l'engagement qu'elle contracte envers elle.

As you read the materials in this chapter, especially cases such as *Eastwood v. Kenyon, Foakes v. Beer* and *Gilbert Steel v. University Construction*, ask yourself how judges in the 19th and the first portion of the 20th century might have reacted to the argument that a promise that was freely made and intended to be binding should be legally enforceable. You may wish to continue with this inquiry in Chapter 5, when you read *Tweddle v. Atkinson, Dunlop v. Selfridge* and *Beswick v. Beswick*.

After you have read the entire chapter, ask yourself whether the judges who decided cases such as *Ron Engineering* (in Chapter 2, section 2), *Pao On v. Lau Yiu Long, Williams v. Roffey Bros.* and *Robichaud c. Caisse Populaire* would respond to the same question. How does the attitude of the judges in these cases compare with those of their predecessors? Even if the notion of serious intention has not received much formal recognition in the common law approach to enforcing promises, what role has it played in the development of promissory estoppel?

For further reading, some of the lessons to be drawn from the civilian experience are analyzed by Chloros, "The Doctrine of Consideration and the Reform of the Law of Contract" (1968), 17 Int. & Comp. L.Q. 137.

(c) RELIANCE

In the *Dalhousie College* case, the university argued that it made increased expenditures on the strength of the fund-raising campaign in which the donor had made his pledge. In other cases, the reliance of the promisee may be far more explicit and direct. For example, in situation (iv) set out at the beginning of this section, the contractor may have hired more workers and worked longer hours in order to achieve the July 1st completion date for the renovations.

The legal system might well choose to enforce certain promises because of reliance on the part of the promisee. Indeed, in an article entitled "The Reliance Interest in Contract Damages", which is extracted in Chapter 14, section 2, Professors Fuller and Perdue point out that a person who has actually relied on a promise has a particularly pressing claim for relief. Perhaps as a result, the American Restatement of Contracts (2d) 1979, states in para. 90:

> (1) A promise which the promisor should reasonably expect to induce action or forbearance on the part of the promisee or a third person and which does induce such action or forbearance is binding if injustice can be avoided only by enforcement of the promise. The remedy granted for breach may be limited as justice requires.

In contrast to a theory which is based upon the serious nature of the promise, the legal obligation in the reliance theory results not from the fact of the promise or from its serious intention, but from its effect on the promisee.

How far was traditional common law doctrine concerned with reliance in cases such as *Gilbert Steel* and *Foakes v. Beer*? What was the courts' explanation in those cases for finding that the mere reliance of the promisee was an insufficient reason to enforce the promise?

Finally, when you have completed the entire chapter, you may wish to ask how far a theory based on reliance is reflected in the doctrine of promissory estoppel. To what extent does the Canadian version of the doctrine suggest conclusions that differ from those that would be reached under para. 90 of the American Restatement?

(d) EXCHANGE AND BARGAINS

The *Dalhousie College* case shows how the common law did not explicitly adopt the first three theories outlined in this section. What test did the Supreme Court articulate in their place for determining which promises should be enforced?

In insisting upon the existence of consideration, the common law emphasized that contracts were primarily about exchanges or bargains, in which an act or promise was given by the promisee in consideration of the original promise.

There have been many attempts to define "consideration" of which the following are, perhaps, the most often quoted. *Currie v. Misa* (1875), L.R. 10 Exch. 153 (Eng. Exch.) at 162:

> A valuable consideration, in the sense of the law, may consist either in some right, interest, profit, or benefit accruing to the one party, or some forbearance, detriment, loss, or responsibility, given, suffered, or undertaken by the other.

This statement was adopted in *Spruce Grove (Town) v. Yellowhead Regional Library Board* (1982), 143 D.L.R. (3d) 188 (Alta. C.A.).

Pollock, *Principles of Contract*, 13th ed. (1950), at 133:

> An act of forbearance of the one party, or the promise thereof, is the price for which the promise of the other is bought, and the promise thus given for value is enforceable.

American Restatement of Contracts (2d), 1979:

> 71.(1) To constitute consideration, a performance or a return promise must be bargained for.
>
> (2) A performance or return promise is bargained for if it is sought by the promisor in exchange for his promise and is given by the promisee in exchange for that promise.
>
> (3) The performance may consist of
>
>   (a) an act other than a promise, or
>   (b) a forbearance, or
>   (c) the creation, modification or destruction of a legal relation.

The origins of the doctrine of consideration are controversial. Some describe consideration as an historical accident, a legacy of the old forms of action, while others see it as reflecting a free market economy and a commercial society. See, *e.g.*, Fuller, "Consideration and Form" (1941), 41 Colum. L. Rev. 799 at 814-15 for a functional defence of the doctrine of consideration, and Posner, "Gratuitous Promises in Economics and Law" (1977), 6 J. of Legal Stud. 411 for an economic analysis.

With the development of extensive markets and, especially, speculative contracts, the idea of fairness of exchange gave way to the will theory of contract where the agreement of the parties is paramount and the just price or objective value is irrelevant. This was paralleled by a movement in contract damages from reimbursing the plaintiff for what had been given in exchange for the promise to protecting the plaintiff's expectation interest by putting the plaintiff in the same position as if the contract had been performed. See, *e.g.*, Horwitz, "The Historical Foundations of Modern Contract Law" (1974), 87 Harv. L. Rev. 917. The concept of consideration developed to stress a promise, rather than an act, requested and given in exchange for a promise and the executory, bilateral contract became the paradigm of classical contract law. For a defence of the classical theory of contract, see Fried, *Contract as Promise* (1981), reviewed by Atiyah, "The Liberal Theory of Contract" in *Essays on Contract* (1990). It became apparent that the consideration given by each party need not be adequate or equivalent and it was sufficient that there was an exchange between the parties, even if it was not a "fair" exchange. This of course gives rise to the policy question of whether the courts should monitor the fairness of contracts and, if so, by what means.

In considering the materials in this chapter, you may wish to contrast the attitudes of courts in those cases which take a traditional approach to consideration. How do they differ from the attitudes expressed by courts in cases decided since about 1980, including (from Chapter 2, section 2) the *Ron Engineering* decision? What role do the devices of formality, intention and reliance play in determining whether consideration is present? At the present time, what kinds of promises does the doctrine of consideration probably exclude from the arena of legal enforceability?

At the end of the chapter, suppose that you have a roommate with an inquiring mind who is not a lawyer and who asks you to explain the criteria which Canadian courts will apply today to determine which promises and agreements will be legally enforced and which will not. What answer will you provide? Finally, bearing in mind that the materials in this chapter focus on problem areas created by the doctrine of consideration, what impact does consideration have on routine transactions? How would you respond to a roommate who asks you whether consideration really matters at the beginning of the 21st century?

THE GOVERNORS OF DALHOUSIE COLLEGE AT HALIFAX v. THE ESTATE OF ARTHUR BOUTILIER, DECEASED

[1934] S.C.R. 642

CROCKET J. [delivering the judgment of the court]

This appeal concerns a claim which was filed in the Probate Court for the County of Halifax, Nova Scotia, in the year 1931, by the appellant College against the respondent Estate for $5,000, stated as having been "subscribed to Dalhousie Campaign Fund (1920)", and attested by an affidavit of the College Bursar, in which it was alleged that the stated amount was justly and truly owing to the College Corporation.

The subscription, upon which the claim was founded, was obtained from the deceased on June 4, 1920, in the course of a canvass which was being conducted by a committee, known as the Dalhousie College Campaign Committee, for the raising of a fund to increase the general resources and usefulness of the institution and was in the following terms:

> For the purpose of enabling Dalhousie College to maintain and improve the efficiency of its teaching, to construct new buildings and otherwise to keep pace with the growing need of its constituency and in consideration of the subscription of others, I promise to pay to the Treasurer of Dalhousie College the sum of Five Thousand Dollars, payment as follows:

> Terms of payment as per letter from Mr. Boutilier.

> A. 399.

> Name: Arthur Boutilier

> Date June 4th, 1920.

> Make all cheques payable to the Treasurer of Dalhousie College.

So far as the record discloses, the subscription was not accompanied or followed by any letter from the deceased as to the terms of payment. He died on October 29, 1928, without making any payment on account. It appears that some time after he signed the subscription form he met with severe financial reverses which prevented him from honouring his pledge. That he desired and hoped to be able to do so is evidenced by a brief letter addressed by him to the President of the University on April 12, 1926, in reply to a communication from the latter, calling his attention to the subscription and the fact that no payments had been made upon it. The deceased's letter, acknowledging receipt of the President's communication, states:

> In reply I desire to advise you that I have kept my promise to you in mind. As you are probably aware, since making my promise I suffered some rather severe reverses, but I expect before too long to be able to redeem my pledge.

. . . Dr. A. Stanley MacKenzie, who had retired from the Presidency of the University after 20 years' service shortly before the trial, and others gave evidence before the Registrar of Probate. Basing himself apparently upon Dr. MacKenzie's statement that in consideration of the moneys subscribed in the campaign referred to, large sums of money were expended by the College on the objects mentioned in the subscription card, between the years 1920 and 1931, the Registrar decided that there was a good consideration for the deceased's subscription . . . .

An appeal to the Judge of the County Court sitting as Judge of the Probate Court was dismissed, but on a further appeal to the Supreme Court of Nova Scotia *en banc*, this decision was reversed by [a] unanimous judgment . . . on the ground that the subscription was a mere *nudum pactum*, and that nothing was shewn either by the document itself or by the evidence which imposed any binding contractual obligation upon the deceased in connection therewith.

There is, of course, no doubt that the deceased's subscription can be sustained as a binding promise only upon one basis, *viz.*: as a contract, supported by a good and sufficient consideration. The whole controversy between the parties is as to whether such a consideration is to be found, either in the subscription paper itself or in the circumstances as disclosed by the evidence.

So far as the signed subscription itself is concerned, it is contended in behalf of the appellant that it shews upon its face a good and sufficient consideration for the deceased's promise in its statement that it was given in consideration of the subscription of others. As to this, it is first to be observed that the statement of such a consideration in the subscription paper is insufficient to support the promise if, in point of law, the subscriptions of others could not provide a valid consideration therefor. I concur in the opinion of Chisholm, C.J., that the fact that others had signed separate subscription papers for the same common object or were expected so to do does not of itself constitute a legal consideration. Although there have been some cases in the United States in which a contrary opinion has been expressed, these decisions have been rejected as unsound in principle both by the Supreme Court of Massachusetts and the Court of Appeals of the State of New York. See *Cottage Street M.E. Church v. Kendall* [121 Mass. 528 (1877)]; *Hamilton College v. Stewart* [(1848) 1 N.Y. Rep. 517]; and *Albany Presbyterian Church v. Cooper* [(1889), 112 N.Y. Rep. 517]. In the last mentioned case the defendant's intestate subscribed a paper with a number of others, by the terms of which they "in consideration of one dollar " to each of them paid " and of the agreements of each other " severally promised and agreed to and with the plaintiff's trustees to pay to said trustees the sums severally subscribed for the purpose of paying off a mortgage debt on the church edifice on the condition that the sum of $45,000 in the aggregate should be subscribed and paid in for such purpose within one year. The Court of Appeals held that it must reject the consideration recited in the subscription paper, the money consideration, because it had no basis in fact, and the mutual promise between the subscribers, because there was no privity of contract between the plaintiff church and the various subscribers.

A perusal of the reasons for judgment of the Appeal Court of Manitoba, as delivered by Cameron, J.A., in *Sargent v. Nicholson* [(1915), 25 D.L.R. 638 (Man. C.A.)] . . . shews that that court also rejected the contention that it was a sufficient consideration that others were led to subscribe by the subscription of the defendant. . . .

The doctrine of mutual promises was also put forward on the argument as a ground upon which the deceased's promise might be held to be binding. It was suggested that the statement in the subscription of the purpose for which it was made, viz.:" of enabling Dalhousie College to maintain and improve the efficiency of its teaching, to construct new buildings and otherwise to keep pace with the growing need of its constituency," constituted an implied request on the part of the deceased to apply the promised subscription to this object and that the acceptance by the College of his promise created a contract between them, the consideration for the promise of the deceased to pay the money being the promise of the College to apply it to the purpose stated.

I cannot think that any such construction can fairly be placed upon the subscription paper and its acceptance by the College. It certainly contains no express request to the College either "to maintain and improve the efficiency of its teaching" or "to construct new buildings and otherwise to keep pace with the growing need of its constituency," but simply states that the promise to pay the $5,000 is made for the purpose of enabling the College to do so, leaving it perfectly free to pursue what had always been its aims in whatever manner its Governors should choose. No statement is made as to the amount intended to be raised for all or any of the purposes stated. No buildings of any kind are described. The construction of new buildings is merely indicated as a means of the College keeping pace with the growing need of its constituency and apparently to be undertaken as and when the Governors should in their unfettered discretion decide the erection of any one or more buildings for any purpose was necessary or desirable.

It seems to me difficult to conceive that, had the deceased actually paid the promised money, he could have safely relied upon the mere acceptance of his own promise, couched in such vague and uncertain terms regarding its purpose, as the foundation of any action against the College Corporation.

So far as I can discover, there is no English or Canadian case in which it has been authoritatively decided that a reciprocal promise on the part of the promisee may be implied from the mere fact of the acceptance by the promisee of such a subscription paper from the hands of the promisor to do the thing for which the subscription is promised. There is no doubt, of course, that an express agreement by the promisee to do certain acts in return for a subscription is a sufficient consideration for the promise of the subscriber. There may, too, be circumstances proved by evidence, outside the subscription paper itself, from which such a reciprocal promise on the part of the promisee may well be implied, but I have not been able to find any English or Canadian case where it has actually been so decided in the absence of proof that the subscriber has himself either expressly requested the promisee to undertake some definite project or personally taken such a part in connection with the projected enterprise that such a request might be inferred therefrom.

It is true that there are expressions in the judgments of the Manitoba Court of Appeal in *Sargent v. Nicholson* [*supra*] and of Wright, J., of the Supreme Court of Ontario, in *Re Loblaw* [[1933] 4 D.L.R. 2764 (Ont. S.C.)], which seem to support the proposition that a request from the promisor to the promisee may be implied from the mere statement in the subscription paper of the object for which the subscription is promised and a reciprocal promise from the promisee to the promisor to carry out that purpose from the mere fact of the acceptance of the subscription, but an examination of both these judgments makes it clear that these expressions of opinion do not touch the real ground upon which either of the decisions proceeds.

There is no doubt either that some American courts have held that by acceptance of the subscription paper itself the promisee impliedly undertakes to carry out the purpose for which the subscription is made and treated this implied promise of the promisee as the consideration for the promise to pay. This view, however, has been rejected . . . on the ground that the promise implied in the acceptance involves no act advantageous to the subscriber or detrimental to the beneficiary, and hence does not involve a case of mutual promises and that the duty of the payee would arise from trusteeship rather than a contractual promise, citing *Albany Presbyterian Church v. Cooper*, above referred to. No suggestion of mutual promises was made in the last named case, notwithstanding that the subscription there involved was expressly stated to be for the single purpose of erecting a designated church building . . .

As to finding the consideration for the subscription outside the subscription itself, the only evidence relied upon is that of Dr. MacKenzie that increased expenditures were made by the College for the purposes stated between the years 1920 and 1931 on the strength of the subscriptions obtained in the canvass of 1920. It is contended that this fact alone constituted a consideration for the subscription and made it binding. The decisions in *Sargent v. Nicholson* . . . [and] in *Re Loblaw* . . ., are relied upon to sustain this proposition as well as some earlier Ontario cases . . . and several American decisions.

There seems to be no doubt that the first . . . cases above mentioned unqualifiedly support the proposition relied upon, as regards at least a subscription for a single distinct and definite object, such as the erection of a designated building, whether or not the expenditure would not have been made nor any liability incurred by the promisee *but for the promise* or not. The earlier Ontario cases relied upon, however, do not appear to me to go that far. They all show that there was either a direct personal interest on the part of the subscriber in the particular project undertaken or some personal participation in the action of the promisee as a result of which the expenditure or liability was incurred.

Regarding the American decisions, upon which *Sargent v. Nicholson* appears to have entirely proceeded—more particularly perhaps on the dictum of Gray, C.J., in *Cottage Street M.E. Church v. Kendall* [*supra*] than any other—it may be pointed out that there are other American cases which shew that there must be something more than the mere expenditure of money or the incurring of liability by the promisee on the faith of the promise. *Hull v. Pearson* 56 N.Y. Supp. 518 (N.Y.A.D. 1899) . . . in which many of the American cases are reviewed, should perhaps be mentioned in this regard. One W. subscribed a certain sum for the work of the German department of a theological seminary. There was no consideration expressed in the memorandum, and there was no evidence of a request on the part of W. that the work should be continued, or of any expenditures on the part of the theological seminary in reliance on such request. . . . It was held that the subscription was without consideration and could not be enforced. Woodward, J., in the course of his reasons, in which the full court concurred, said:

> It is true that there is evidence that the German department has been continued, but this does not meet the requirement. There is no evidence that it would not have been continued as it had been for a series of years if the subscription of Mr. Wild had not been made.

And further:

> He undoubtedly made the subscription for the purpose of aiding in promoting the work of the German department; but, in the absence of some act or word which clearly indicated that he accompanied his subscription by a request to do something which the corporation would not have done except for his subscription, there is no such request as would justify a constructive consideration in support of this promise.

These latter dicta seem to accord more with the English decisions, which give no countenance to the principle applied in *Sargent v. Nicholson* . . . and in the earlier American cases, as is so pointedly illustrated by the judgments of

Pearson, J., in In *Re Hudson* [(1885), 33 W.R. 819 (Ch.D.)], and Eve, J., in *In Re Cory* [(1912), 29 T.L.R. 18 (Ch.D.)]. The head note in *In Re Hudson* states:

> A. verbally promised to give £20,000 to the Jubilee Fund of the Congregational Union, and also filled up and signed a blank form of promise not addressed to anyone, but headed "Congregational Union of England and Wales Jubilee Fund," whereby he promised to give £20,000, in five equal annual instalments of £4,000 each, for the liquidation of chapel debts. A. paid three instalments of £4,000 to the fund within three years from the date of his promise, and then died, leaving the remaining two instalments unpaid and unprovided for.
>
> The Congregational Union claimed £8,000 from A.'s executors, on the ground that they had been led by A.'s promise to contribute larger sums to churches than they would otherwise have done; that money had been given and promised by other persons in consequence of A.'s promise; that grants from the Jubilee Fund had been promised to cases recommended by A.; and that churches to which promises had been made by the committee, and the committee themselves, had incurred liabilities in consequence of A.'s promise.

His Lordship held there was no consideration for the promise. "There really was," he said, "in this matter, nothing whatever in the shape of a consideration which could form a contract between the parties."

And he added:

> I am bound to say that this is an attempt to turn a charity into something very different from a charity. I think it ought to fail, and I think it does fail. I do not know to what extent a contrary decision might open a new form of posthumous charity. Posthumous charity is already bad enough, and it is quite sufficiently protected by law without establishing a new principle which would extend the doctrine in its favour far more than it has been extended or ought to be extended.

In the *Cory* case a gift of 1,000 guineas was promised to a Y.M.C. Association for the purpose of building a memorial hall. The sum required was £150,000, of which £85,000 had been promised or was available. The committee in charge decided not to commit themselves until they saw that their efforts to raise the whole fund were likely to prove successful. The testator, whose estate it was sought to charge, promised the 1,000 guineas and subsequently the committee felt justified in entering into a building contract, which they alleged they were largely induced to enter into by the testator's promise. Eve, J., held there was no contractual obligation between the parties and therefore no legal debt due from the estate.

Chisholm, C.J., in the case at bar, said that without any want of deference to eminent judges who have held otherwise he felt impelled to follow the decisions in the English cases. I am of opinion that he was fully justified in so doing, rather than apply the principle contended for by the appellant in reliance upon the decision in *Sargent v. Nicholson*, based, as the latter case is, upon the decisions of United States courts, which are not only in conflict with the English cases, but with decisions of the Court of Appeals of the State of New York, as I have, I think, shewn, and which have been subjected to very strong criticism by American legal authors, notably by Prof. Williston, as the learned Chief Justice of Nova Scotia has shewn in his exhaustive and, to my mind, very convincing judgment.

To hold otherwise would be to hold that a naked, voluntary promise may be converted into a binding legal contract by the subsequent action of the promisee alone without the consent, express or implied, of the promisor. There is no evidence here which in any way involves the deceased in the carrying out of the work for which the promised subscription was made other than the signing of the subscription paper itself.

[Appeal dismissed.]

WOOD v. LUCY, LADY DUFF-GORDON

118 N.E. 214 (U.S. N.Y., 1917)

CARDOZO J. [delivering the judgment of the court]

The defendant styles herself "a creator of fashions." Her favor helps a sale. Manufacturers of dresses, millinery and like articles are glad to pay for a certificate of her approval. The things which she designs, fabrics, parasols and what not, have a new value in the public mind when issued in her name. She employed the plaintiff to help her to turn this vogue into money. He was to have the exclusive right, subject always to her approval, to place her indorsements on the designs of others. He was also to have the exclusive right to place her own designs on sale, or to license others to market them. In return, she was to have one-half of 'all profits and revenues' derived from any contracts he might make. The exclusive right was to last at least one year from April 1, 1915, and thereafter from year to year unless terminated by notice of ninety days. The plaintiff says that he kept the contract on his part, and that the defendant broke it. She placed her indorsement on fabrics, dresses and millinery without his knowledge, and withheld the profits. He sues her for the damages, and the case comes here on demurrer.

The agreement of employment is signed by both parties. It has a wealth of recitals. The defendant insists, however, that it lacks the elements of a contract. She says that the plaintiff does not bind himself to anything. It is true that he does not promise in so many words that he will use reasonable efforts to place the defendant's indorsements and market her designs. We think, however, that such a promise is fairly to be implied. The law has outgrown its primitive stage of formalism when the precise word was the sovereign talisman, and every slip was fatal. It takes a broader view to-day. A promise may be lacking, and yet the whole writing may be 'instinct with an obligation,' imperfectly expressed. . . . If that is so, there is a contract.

The implication of a promise here finds support in many circumstances. The defendant gave an exclusive privilege. She was to have no right for at least a year to place her own indorsements or market her own designs except through the agency of the plaintiff. The acceptance of the exclusive agency was an assumption of its duties. . . . We are not to suppose that one party was to be placed at the mercy of the other. . . . Many other terms of the agreement point the same way. We are told at the outset by way of recital that "the said Otis F. Wood possesses a business organization adapted to the placing of such indorsements as the said Lucy, Lady Duff-Gordon has approved." The implication is that the plaintiff's business organization will be used for the purpose for which it is adapted. But the terms of the defendant's compensation are even more significant. Her sole compensation for the grant of an exclusive agency is to be one-half of all the profits resulting from the plaintiff's efforts. Unless he gave his efforts, she could never get anything. Without an implied promise, the transaction cannot have such business "efficacy as both parties must have intended that at all events it should have" (Bowen, L.J., in *The Moorcock*, 14 P. D. 64, 68). But the contract does not stop there. The plaintiff goes on to promise that he will account monthly for all moneys received by him, and that he will take out all such patents and copyrights and trademarks as may in his judgment be necessary to protect the rights and articles affected by the agreement. It is true, of course, as the Appellate Division has said, that if he was under no duty to try to market designs or to place certificates of indorsement, his promise to account for profits or take out copyrights would be valueless. But in determining the intention of the parties, the promise has a value. It helps to enforce the conclusion that the plaintiff had some duties. His promise to pay the defendant one-half of the profits and revenues resulting from the exclusive agency and to render accounts monthly, was a promise to use reasonable efforts to bring profits and revenues into existence. For this conclusion, the authorities are ample. . . .

The judgment of the Appellate Division should be reversed. . . .

QUESTION

1. In *Dalhousie College*, the charitable subscription was not enforced partly because there was "no suggestion of mutual promises". Why was the court willing to enforce the contract in the *Lady Duff-Gordon* case in the absence of an express promise by Mr. Wood?

2.   Past Consideration

EASTWOOD v. KENYON

(1840), 11 Ad. & E. 438, 113 E.R. 482 (Q.B.)

On the death of John Sutcliffe, his infant daughter, Sarah, was left as his sole heiress. The plaintiff, acting as Sarah's guardian, spent money on her education and for the benefit of her estate and for this purpose borrowed money from one Blackburn, to whom in return he gave a promissory note. When Sarah came of age, she promised the plaintiff that she would pay the amount of the note and she did in fact pay Blackburn one year's interest on the note. Subsequently, Sarah married the defendant, who also promised the plaintiff that he would pay the amount of the note. The defendant failed to make any payments and the plaintiff sued him on his promise.

LORD DENMAN C.J. Upon motion in arrest of judgment [for the plaintiff] this promise must be taken to have been proved, and to have been an express promise, as indeed it must of necessity have been, for no such implied promise in law was ever heard of. It was then argued for the plaintiff that the declaration disclosed a sufficient moral consideration to support the promise.

Most of the older cases on this subject are collected in a learned note to the case of *Wennall v. Adney* [(1802), 127 E.R. 137], and the conclusion there arrived at seems to be correct in general, "that an express promise can only revive a precedent good consideration, which might have been enforced at law through the medium of an implied promise, had it not been suspended by some positive rule of law; but can give no original cause of action, if the obligation, on which it is founded, never could have been enforced at law, though not barred by any legal maxim or statute provision." Instances are given of voidable contracts, as those of infants ratified by an express promise after age, and distinguished from void contracts; . . . debts of bankrupts revived by subsequent promise after certificate; and similar cases. Since that time some cases have occurred upon this subject . . . [I]n *Cooper v. Martin* [(1803), 102 E.R. 759] . . . a stepfather was permitted to recover from the son of his wife, after he had attained his full age, upon a declaration for necessaries furnished to him while an infant, for which, after his full age, he promised to pay. . . .

Lord Ellenborough in giving his judgment says, "The plaintiff having done an act beneficial to the defendant in his infancy, it is a good consideration for the defendant's promise after he came of age. In such a case the law will imply a request; and the fact of the promise had been found by the jury;" and undoubtedly the action would have lain against the defendant whilst an infant, inasmuch as it was for necessaries furnished at his request in regard to which the law raises an implied promise. . . .

Lord Mansfield [is alleged to have] considered the rule of nudum pactum as too narrow, and [to have] maintained that all promises deliberately made ought to be held binding. [Such a] doctrine would annihilate the necessity for any consideration at all, inasmuch as the mere fact of giving a promise creates a moral obligation to perform it.

The enforcement of such promises by law, however, plausibly reconciled by the desire to effect all conscientious engagements, might be attended with mischievous consequences to society; one of which would be the frequent preference of voluntary undertakings to claims for just debts. Suits would thereby be multiplied, and voluntary undertakings would also be multiplied, to the prejudice of real creditors. The temptations of executors would be much increased by the prevalence of such a doctrine, and the faithful discharge of their duty be rendered more difficult.

Taking then the promise of the defendant, as stated on this record, to have been an express promise, we find that the consideration for it was past and executed long before, and yet it is not laid to have been at the request of the defendant, nor even of his wife while sole (though if it had, the case of *Mitchinson v. Hewson* [(1797), 101 E.R. 1013], shews that it would not have been sufficient), and the declaration really discloses nothing but a benefit voluntarily conferred by the plaintiff and received by the defendant, with an express promise by the defendant to pay money.

If the subsequent assent of the defendant could have amounted to a ratihabitio, the declaration should have stated the money to have been expended at his request, and the ratification should have been relied on as matter of evidence; but this was obviously impossible, because the defendant was in no way connected with the property or with the plaintiff, when the money was expended. If the ratification of the wife while sole were relied on, then a debt from her would have been shewn, and the defendant could not have been charged in his own right without some further consideration, as of forbearance after marriage, or something of that sort . . . .

In holding this declaration bad because it states no consideration but a past benefit not conferred at the request of the defendant, we conceive that we are justified by the old common law of England. . . .

NOTE and QUESTION

1. Would the plaintiff have succeeded if Sarah had been the defendant?

2. For an argument that courts should once again enforce contracts in moral consideration contexts, see Moller, "Sympathy, Community and Promising: Adam Smith's Case for Reviving Moral Consideration" (1999), 66 U. Chic. L. Rev. 213.

LAMPLEIGH v. BRATHWAIT

(1615), Hobart 105, 80 E.R. 255 (K.B.)

Anthony Lampleigh brought an assumpsit against Thomas Brathwait and declared, that whereas the defendant had feloniously slain one Patrick Mahume, the defendant after the said felony done, instantly required the plaintiff to labour, and do his endeavour to obtain his pardon from the King: whereupon the plaintiff upon the same request did, by all the means he could and many days labour, do his endeavour to obtain the King's pardon for the said felony, viz. in riding and journeying at his own charges from London to Roiston, when the King was there, and to London back, and so to and from New-market, to obtain pardon for the defendant for the said felony. Afterwards, ... in consideration of the premisses, the said defendant did promise the said plaintiff to give him 100 pounds, and that he had not. . . .

To this the defendant pleaded non assumpsit, and found for the plaintiff damage one hundred pounds. It was said in arrest of judgment, that the consideration was passed.

But the chief objection was, that it doth not appear, that he did anything towards the obtaining of the pardon, but riding up and down, and nothing done when he came there. And of this opinion was my brother [Warburton] but my self and the other two Judges were of opinion for the plaintiff, and so he had judgment.

First, it was agreed, that a meer voluntary curtesie will not have a consideration to uphold an assumpsit. But if that curtesie were moved by a suit or request of the party that gives the assumpsit, it will bind, for the promise, though it follows, yet it is not naked, but couples it self with the suit before, and the merits of the party procured by that suit, which is the difference.

[A second point upon which Warburton J. delivered a dissenting judgment is omitted.]

NOTES and QUESTIONS

1. Why did the plaintiff succeed in *Lampleigh v. Brathwait*? Would he have recovered anything if there had been no later promise to pay? What if the later promise had been to pay an exorbitant amount?

2. Harvey Foster served the Canadian Autos Co. Ltd. faithfully for 25 years. Upon his retirement at age 60 the company in gratitude promised to give him a lump sum payment of $10,000 as well as the customary gold watch. These benefits were over and above Harvey's contractual retirement benefits. Canadian Autos, however, found their business profits declining and later told Harvey that unfortunately they were unable to pay the $10,000.

  (a) Can Harvey recover the $10,000?

  (b) Would it make any difference if it were customary for Canadian Autos Ltd. to make a lump sum payment upon retirement?

  (c) Would it make any difference if the promise had been made before the due date of Harvey's retirement?

  (d) Would it make any difference if Canadian Autos had asked Harvey to retire early because of their declining business profits?

  (e) Would it make any difference if Harvey had purchased a new car in the expectation of receiving the $10,000? Should this make any difference? See *Blair v. West. Mut. Benefit Assn.*, [1972] 4 W.W.R. 284 (B.C. C.A.), *supra*, Chapter 2, section 3, and *Moir v. J.P. Porter Co.* (1979), 103 D.L.R. (3d) 22 (N.S. C.A.), *infra*, , section 6(3)(c) of this chapter, note 2 after *Rose and Frank Co. v. J.R. Crompton and Bros.*

3. The O.L.R.C. in its *Report on Amendment of the Law of Contract*, at 33, recommended that:

> A promise made in recognition of a benefit previously received by the promisor or by any third party from the promisee, should be enforceable to the extent necessary to prevent unjust enrichment.
>
> A promise made in recognition of a benefit previously received by the promisor or by any third party from the promisee, should not be enforceable where the promisee conferred the benefit as a gift or where for other reasons the promisor has not been unjustly enriched.
>
> Promises supported by past consideration, where enforceable, should be enforceable only to the extent that the value of the promise is not disproportionate to the benefit.

4. Thel and Yorio, "The Promissory Basis of Past Consideration" (1992), 78 Va. L. Rev. 1045 argue for the full enforcement of promises based on "felt moral obligation", regardless of whether or not a benefit has been received or the extent of that benefit.

THOMAS v. THOMAS

(1842), 2 Q.B. 851, 114 E.R. 330

John Thomas, the deceased husband of the plaintiff, at the time of his death, in 1837, was possessed of a row of seven dwelling houses in Merthyr Tidvil, in one of which, being the dwelling house in question, he was himself residing; and by his will he appointed his brother Samuel Thomas (since deceased) and the defendant executors thereof, to take possession of all his houses, etc., subject to certain payments in the will mentioned, among which were certain charges in money for the benefit of the plaintiff. In the evening before the day of his death, he expressed orally a wish to make some further provision for his wife; and on the following morning he declared orally, in the presence of two witnesses, that it was his wish that his wife should have either the house in which he lived and all that it contained, or an additional sum of 100*l* instead thereof.

This declaration being shortly afterwards brought to the knowledge of Samuel Thomas and the defendant, the executors and residuary legatees, they consented to carry the intentions of the testator so expressed into effect; and, after the lapse of a few days, they and the plaintiff executed the agreement declared upon; which, after stating the parties, and briefly reciting the will, proceeded as follows.

> And, whereas the said testator, shortly before his death, declared, in the presence of several witnesses, that he was desirous his said wife should have and enjoy during her life, or so long as she should continue his widow, all and singular the dwelling house," etc., "or 100*l* out of his personal estate," in addition to the respective legacies and bequests given her in and by his said will; "but such declaration and desire was not reduced to writing in the lifetime of the said John Thomas and read over to him; but the said Samuel Thomas and Benjamin Thomas are fully convinced and satisfied that such was the desire of the said testator, and are willing and desirous that such intention should be carried into full effect: now these presents witness, and it is hereby agreed and declared by and between the parties, that, in consideration of such desire and of the premises," the executors would convey the dwelling house, etc. to the plaintiff and her assigns during her life, or for so long a time as she should continue a widow and unmarried: "provided nevertheless, and it is hereby further agreed and declared, that the said Eleanor Thomas, or her assigns, shall and will, at all times during which she shall have possession of the said dwelling house, etc., pay to the said Samuel Thomas and Benjamin Thomas, their executors, etc., the sum of one pound yearly towards the ground rent payable in respect of the said dwelling house and other premises thereto adjoining, and shall and will keep the said dwelling house and premises in good and tenable repair. . . .

The agreement went on to provide that in case of Eleanor Thomas' "death or second marriage during the term upon which the said premises are held, then and in either such case, the dwelling house and premises shall fall in and form part of the residuary estate of the said testator."

The plaintiff was left in possession of the dwelling house and premises for some time: but the defendant, after the death of his co-executor, refused to execute a conveyance tendered to him for execution pursuant to the agreement, and, shortly before the trial, brought an ejectment, under which he turned the plaintiff out of possession.

PATTESON J. . . . Motive is not the same thing with consideration. Consideration means something which is of some value in the eye of the law, moving from the plaintiff. . . . Now that which is suggested as the consideration here, a pious respect for the wishes of the testator, does not in any way move from the plaintiff; it moves from the testator; therefore, legally speaking, it forms no part of the consideration. Then it is said that, if that be so, there is no consideration at all, it is a mere voluntary gift: but when we look at the agreement we find that this is not a mere proviso that the donee shall take the gift with the burthens; but it is an express agreement to pay what seems to be a fresh apportionment of a ground rent, and which is made payable not to a superior landlord but to the executors. So that this rent is clearly not something incident to the assignment of the house; for in that case, instead of being payable to the executors, it would have been payable to the landlord. Then as to the repairs: these houses may very possibly be held under a lease containing covenants to repair; but we know nothing about it: for any thing that appears, the liability to repair is first created by this instrument. . . .

[Denman C.J. and Coleridge J. delivered concurring judgments for the plaintiff.]

NOTES and QUESTIONS

1. What was the consideration in the opinion of the court for the promise of the deceased? Was this the real reason for the promise?

Rather than analyzing consideration in the technical sense adopted by Patteson J., it was suggested in the Introduction to this chapter that it is useful to think in terms of reasons for enforcing promises. How would this approach apply to cases such as *Thomas v. Thomas*? For an elaboration of this approach, see Atiyah, "Consideration: a Restatement", in *Essays on Contract* (1990) at 187.

2. You will recall that a promise to hold an offer open for a certain period is traditionally not binding in the absence of consideration or a seal, *supra* Chapter 2, section 6(a). What should be the legal position of a person who makes such a promise?

3. According to traditional doctrine, the courts did not enquire into the adequacy of consideration (*e.g.*, *Chappell & Co. v. Nestlé Co.*, [1960] A.C. 87) and it has been argued that this was the case even before the nineteenth century. See Barton, "The Enforcement of Hard Bargains" (1987), 103 L.Q.R. 118. Strictly the inadequacy of consideration was relevant only if it indicated that the contract had been obtained through fraud, misrepresentation, duress, undue influence, mistake or unconscionability. However, Atiyah has raised the question whether the courts should monitor the fairness of the exchange between the parties more directly. See "Contract and Fair Exchange" in *Essays on Contract* (1990), at 329 and also Smith, "In Defence of Substantive Fairness," (1996), 112 L.Q.R. 138.

4. On occasion contracts, *e.g.*, for the sale of land, are made for nominal consideration of $1 and perhaps in consideration of natural love and affection. What is their likely effect? Compare *Harding v. Harding* (1972), 28 D.L.R. (3d) 358 (B.C. S.C.), and *Gilchrist Vending Ltd. v. Sedley Hotel Ltd.* (1967), 66 D.L.R. (2d) 24 (Sask. Q.B.), with *Mountford v. Scott*, [1975] 1 All E.R. 198 (C.A.).

Should a contract be binding where the nominal consideration is a mere formality, pretence or sham? See the comments in the American Restatement of Contracts (2d), 1979, paras. 71 and 79. Compare *Re Hogg Estate* (1987), 83 A.R. 165 (Q.B.).

5. Issues sometimes arise in the context of domestic agreements, where one partner has made a promise with respect to financial or property matters and it is arguable whether consideration was provided. The distinction between motive (such as avoidance of guilt, peace of mind) and consideration can be important here. See, *e.g.*, *Irving v. Irving* (1988), 17 R.F.L. (3d) 318 (B.C. S.C.), where a wife wished to leave a marriage which had broken down but was concerned about the husband's health. She signed an agreement promising him three years' possession of the matrimonial home. The court held there was no consideration to support this promise.

6. Gloria Greer purchases a C.G.E. hairdryer from a local department store and upon opening the box finds a card headed Manufacturers' "Guarantee" and instructing the purchaser to fill in, sign and return the card in order to be covered by the 12-month guarantee. Ten months later the hairdryer short circuits due to a manufacturing defect. Can Gloria sue on the guarantee? See *Trueman v. Maritime Auto & Trailer Sales Ltd.* (1977), 19 N.B.R. (2d) 8 (C.A.); *Kelly v. Mack Canada Inc.* (1988), 53 D.L.R. (4th) 476 (Ont. C.A.); and *Chappell & Co. v. Nestlé Co.*, [1960] A.C. 87. See also the comments of the American court in *Pro CD v. Matthew Zeidenberg and Silken Mountain Web Services Inc.* in Chapter 2, section 4.

7. Harvey Foster Sr. promises to pay Harvey Foster Jr. $500 if he does not smoke cigarettes for a year. If Harvey Foster Jr. does so refrain, can he claim his $500? Would it make any difference if Harvey Foster Sr. had promised to pay the $500 if Harvey Foster Jr. stopped smoking marijuana? See *Hamer v. Sidway*, 27 N.E. 256 (N.Y., 1891); *White v. Bluett* (1853), 23 L.J. Ex. 36; and *Dunton v. Dunton* (1892), 18 V.L.R. 114.

3.   Forbearance

B. (D.C.) v. ARKIN

[1996] 8 W.W.R. 100 (Man. Q.B.); affirmed [1996] 10 W.W.R. 689 (Man. C.A.),
leave to appeal to S.C.C. refused

JEWERS J.: In this small claim appeal, the plaintiff sues the defendants for money she paid to them as compensation for damages the defendant Zellers (Zellers) sustained resulting from thefts committed by her young son. The issue is whether in the particular circumstances of this case having paid over the money, the plaintiff can recover it on the ground that Zellers never had a valid claim against her personally. The proceedings against the defendant Arkin have been discontinued.

A hearing officer dismissed the claim and the plaintiff appeals.

The parties filed the following agreed statement of facts.

1.   On May 26, 1995, [J.B.], along with [R.M.], were apprehended upon leaving the Zellers Store at 969 Henderson Highway, in the City of Winnipeg, by Cathy Clark, a Loss Prevention Officer employed by Zeller's Inc., of four years experience. [J.B.] and [R.M.] had been under surveillance by Ms. Clark in the said store and had placed items from the men's wear department, the toy department, and the book department into the knapsacks that each of them was carrying. No attempt was made to pay for the concealed items at the time that [J.B.] and [R.M.] left the store.

2.   [J.B.] . . . was 14 years of age on May 26, 1995, while [R.M.] . . . was 15 years of age on May 26, 1995. . . .

5.   On July 31, 1995, a letter was sent by . . . legal counsel for Zellers Inc., to [D.B.]. (reproduced hereunder)

6.   Mrs. [B.] did not call or write [counsel's] office after receiving the said letter, other than to remit the sum of $225.00 which was paid by way of a cheque, dated, August 16, 1995.

7.   Prior to May 26, 1995, [J.B.] had no convictions and had not been arrested by the police.

8.   No damage was done to the items recovered from [J.B.] and [R.M.], which items were returned to the said store for purposes of sale.

. . . . .

[The letter from Zellers' counsel read:]

"I act for Zellers to recover their damages in civil court. The civil recovery process is *SEPARATE AND DISTINCT* from any criminal action and the two must not be confused.

It is alleged that on May 26, 1956, [J.B.], a young person for whose supervision my client holds you legally responsible, took unlawful possession of merchandise from Zellers, located at 969 Henderson Highway, Winnipeg, Manitoba, to the value of $59.95.

In accordance with the *Court of Queen's Bench Act* of Manitoba and/or *The Court of Queen's Bench Small Claims Practices Act* of Manitoba, Zellers has a legal right to claim Civil Restitution from you.

> In order to eliminate additional expense to you, Zellers is willing to settle *THE CIVIL CASE ONLY* out of court, providing you pay the following amount by August 25, 1995:
>
> Restitution for cost of incident including damages and costs: $225.00
>
> Should you elect to ignore this demand, refuse or fail to pay the amount of the proposed out of Court settlement, Zellers will take the case before a Civil Court and claim damages, including legal costs and interest pursuant to the *The Court of Queen's Bench Act* of Manitoba and/or *The Court of Queen's Bench Small Claims Practices Act* of Manitoba. Administration charges will continue to increase until the matter is concluded. Payment of the total amount demanded will be deemed full restitution and will halt the *civil court action only.* Any criminal court action which is, or has been undertaken, remains under the jurisdiction of the criminal prosecutor and is separate from this particular court action. Payment should be by cheque or money order made payable to *CIVIL RECOVERY* and sent via the enclosed postage paid envelope. Include your NAME and the CASE NUMBER, shown above. . . .

This claim is part of a loss recovery programme or policy which Zellers initiated several years ago and which commenced in their Manitoba Division in or about February 1995. Zellers wanted to recover what they called their "incremental" costs of shoplifting. These would be the costs of employing loss prevention officers and purchasing their equipment for the purpose of detecting losses (presumably mostly from theft) attributable to their customers and their employees. They concluded that the cost per incident would be approximately $310.00. They conceived the idea of claiming against the parents of children involved in thefts—obviously because it would be futile to pursue the children.

Zellers decided not to use, or hire, their own employees to process these claims but, instead, gave the job to an independent organization called Aclaim Civil Loss Recovery System. That organization reviewed the incident reports regarding the various claims and then engaged lawyers to prosecute them. If there was recovery, Aclaim would get a portion of the recovery and the balance would go to Zellers. Typically, a recovery of $325.00 would result in a fee of $125.00 to Aclaim and $200.00 to Zellers.

If necessary, the lawyers would write two demand letters and the amount claimed in the second letter would be increased somewhat over the amount claimed in the first.

In this case, because two boys were involved, the amount claimed was reduced to $225.00.

There is no general rule that parents are liable for the torts of their children by virtue of their status as parents per se. . . . The parents would only be liable if they, themselves, were in some way negligent or had engaged in tortious conduct in relation to the activities of their children. There is no suggestion in this case that the plaintiff was negligent or had committed any tort in her personal capacity.

Nevertheless, counsel for Zellers submits that, whatever the validity of the underlying claim, the plaintiff voluntarily paid the compensation sought and, in effect, entered into a valid and enforceable contract with Zellers: there was consideration moving both ways; in exchange for Zellers forbearance to bring suit against her, the plaintiff voluntarily paid to them the sum of $225.00.

Counsel for the plaintiff submits that, in the circumstances, the law will not countenance such a contract; that Zellers were never entitled to claim or get any money from the plaintiff; and that the sum in question should be returned to her on equitable principles.

It is well settled that a forbearance to sue is good consideration and that monies paid in exchange for a promise not to sue is a valid and enforceable legal contract. There are qualifications to this general rule and they are well summed in *Chitty on Contracts* 27th Ed. Vol 1, General Principles, Articles 3-041 to 3-045 which are as follows:

> 3-041 *Claims known to be invalid.* A promise is not binding if the sole consideration for it is a forbearance to enforce (or a promise to forbear from enforcing) a claim which is invalid and which is either known by the party forbearing to be invalid or not believed by him to be valid.
> . . .
>
> 3-042 *Claims which are doubtful or not known to be invalid.* If, however, the validity of the claim is doubtful, forbearance to enforce it can be good consideration: . . .
>
> It has, further, been held that the same rule applies even if the claim is clearly invalid in law, so long as it was a "reasonable claim" (i.e. one made on reasonable grounds) which was in good faith believed by the party forbearing to have at any rate a fair chance of success. . . .
>
> 3-043 Two further conditions must be satisfied by a party who relies on his forbearance to enforce an invalid claim as the consideration for a promise made to him. He must not deliberately conceal from the other party (i.e. the promisor) facts which, if known to the latter would enable him to defeat the claim. *And he must show that he seriously intended to pursue the claim.* (Emphasis mine)

In my opinion, the defendant's claim was not merely a doubtful claim—it was an invalid claim. . . .

The plaintiff honestly believed that the claim was a serious one and that if she did not pay it the defendant would sue her. . . . After all, the plaintiff had received a letter from a lawyer who should know something about the law and who was making an apparently serious threat of legal action if the claim was not paid. And she paid. She would not have done so if she had not believed that there was something to it.

In this belief, the plaintiff was mistaken. Whatever legal opinion or opinions Zellers might have had regarding their claims generally, I cannot believe that they seriously thought that this claim could succeed or that they seriously intended to pursue it to court if it was not paid. Mr. Arkin was not called as a witness at the trial and so we do not have the benefit of what his opinion of the claim was. But I assume that as a competent and responsible lawyer, he knew or ought to have known that the claim had no prospect whatsoever of succeeding in court and that it would be futile to pursue it.

The plaintiff subsequently took legal advice, learned of her mistake and now wants her money back. . . . The plaintiff was certainly mislead by the tone and content of the lawyer's letter. In my opinion, in the particular circumstances of this case, the plaintiff is entitled to a refund on the ground of monies paid under a mistake.

The appeal is allowed and the plaintiff's claim is allowed with interest and costs.

NOTES and QUESTION

1. This case led to the enactment of the Parental Responsibility Act C.C.S.M. c. P8. This Act provides:

> 3. The parent of a child who deliberately takes, damages or destroys the property of another person is liable for the loss suffered by the owner . . .

up to $5,000.00, unless the parent proves:

> 7(1) . . . that he or she (a) was exercising reasonable supervision over the child at the time the child engaged in the activity that caused the property loss; and (b) made reasonable efforts in good faith to prevent or discourage the child from engaging in the kind of activity that resulted in the property loss.

Would these provisions change the result in a case such as *B (D.C.) v. Arkin*?

2. Compare *B. (D.C.) v. Arkin* with *Stott v. Merit Investment Co.* (1988), 48 D.L.R. (4th) 288 (Ont. C.A.), leave to appeal refused (1988), 63 O.R. (2d) x (S.C.C.), where the majority found a forbearance to sue on a *bona fide*, though uncertain, claim. In *Stott*, all the judges agreed that there was economic duress, but the majority held that the contract had been affirmed by Stott's subsequent conduct. In *Blackmore v. Cablenet Ltd.*, [1995] 3 W.W.R. 305 (Alta. Q.B.), a settlement by a dismissed employee was set aside for unconscionability.

3. In *Royal Bank v. Kiska*, an extract from which is found in section 7 of this chapter, the defendant, in March 1963, signed a guarantee of his brother's indebtedness to the bank. The bank did not promise to forbear but did not in fact realize upon the brother's securities until June 1963. This was held by the majority (Laskin J.A. dissenting) to be sufficient forbearance.

4. Pre-Existing Legal Duty

(a) PUBLIC DUTY

The traditional view is that if, in exchange for a promise, the promisee agrees to perform, or actually performs, a public duty, there is no consideration. However, the courts were able to find consideration if it could be shown that the promisee provided something extra, beyond the requirements of the public duty, as in *Glasbrook Bros. Ltd. v. Glamorgan C.C.*, [1925] A.C. 270 (H.L.). The traditional view was questioned in *Ward v. Byham*, [1956] 2 All E.R. 318 (C.A.), which was decided at a time when by statute in England, the obligation of maintaining an "illegitimate" child rested entirely on the mother. In that case, the father of a child wrote to the mother, from whom he was separated, as follows:

> Mildred, I am prepared to let you have [the child] and pay you up to £1 per week allowance for her providing you can prove that she will be well looked after and happy and also that she is allowed to decide for herself whether or not she wishes to come and live with you . . . .

Seven months later, when the mother married, the father stopped the payments. In an action brought by the mother for the sum of £1 per week, Morris L.J. found that there was consideration because, irrespective of the statutory obligation, the mother was required to prove that the child was well looked after and happy and also given the choice of whether she lived with the mother. Denning L.J., on the other hand, approached the case, at 319,

> on the footing that, in looking after the child, the mother is only doing what she is legally bound to do. Even so, I think that there was sufficient consideration to support the promise. I have always thought that a promise to perform an existing duty, or the performance of it,

should be regarded as good consideration, because it is a benefit to the person to whom it is given.

QUESTION

The following advertisement appeared in the *Winnipeg Free Tribune*:

"REWARD $500 for information leading to the arrest of Harvey Foster, aged 60, height 5'4", weight 200 lbs., red goatee beard, bald, blue eyes. Offer open for two weeks."

(a) Gloria Greer, a local police sergeant, while on duty sees the person described and immediately rushes to report this to her senior officer.

(b) Gloria while on duty sees the person described and when she goes off duty reports this to her senior officer.

(c) Gloria while at a party notices the person described in the advertisement and immediately phones her superior officer with this information.

In all these situations the information does indeed lead to the apprehension of Harvey. Can Gloria claim the reward in any or all of these cases? Are there any policy reasons why her right to do so might be restricted?

Should cases such as this and *Ward v. Byham* be analyzed in terms of consideration or of public policy?

(b)   DUTY OWED TO A THIRD PARTY

In contrast to the cases involving public duties, the performance of a duty owed to a third party has traditionally been viewed as good consideration, particularly in the family context. In the famous case of *Shadwell v. Shadwell* (1860), 9 C.B. (N.S.) 159, 142 E.R. 62 (C.P.), for example, a nephew became engaged and thus, at that time, incurred a legal obligation to marry his fiancée. When he heard of the engagement, an uncle promised to pay the nephew £150 per year upon his marriage. The majority of the court found that the uncle's promise was legally binding despite the fact that the nephew already (through the engagement) owed a legal obligation to his fiancée. (*N.B.*, in many jurisdictions, engagements no longer create legally binding obligations; see, *e.g.*, the Equality of Status Act, C.C.S.M., c. E130, s. 4(1).)

Should cases in which the pre-existing legal duty is owed to a third party be treated differently than a public duty or a duty to the promisor, discussed in section 4(c), *infra*? See also *Chichester v. Cobb* (1866), 14 L.T. 433, and *Nat. Trust Co. v. Heichman* (1920), 55 D.L.R. 574 (S.C.C.).

This view has been applied in a commercial context in *Scotson v. Pegg* (1861), 158 E.R. 121, and *Prenor Trust Co. of Canada v. Kerkhoff Properties Inc.*, [1994] 9 W.W.R. 170 (Alta. Q.B.), and in modern cases on privity of contract such as *New Zealand Shipping Co. Ltd. v. A.M. Satterthwaite & Co., infra*, Chapter 5, section 3(d), and *ITO-International Terminal Operators Ltd. v. Miida Electronics Inc.*, which is cited in note 2 following the *New Zealand Shipping* case.

PAO ON v. LAU YIU LONG

[1980] A.C. 614 (P.C.)

The plaintiffs owned all the shares in a private company, Shing On, which owned a building as its principal asset. The defendants were majority shareholders in a public company, Fu Chip, which wished to acquire the building. In February 1973 two written agreements were made to give effect to this transaction without cash payments. Under the main agreements the plaintiffs agreed to sell to Fu Chip on 30th April 1973 all their shares in Shing On in exchange for the allotment to the plaintiffs of 4.2 million shares in Fu Chip. In order not to depress the market for Fu Chip by a huge sale, the plaintiffs promised to retain 2.5 million of these shares until April 30, 1974. However, the plaintiffs wanted some protection in case the value of the retained shares fell during that period. As a result, the subsidiary agreement provided that the defendants would buy back from the plaintiffs 2.5 million shares on or before 30th April 1974 at $2.50 per share.

The commercial effect of the agreements was remarkable. The plaintiffs were protected by the subsidiary agreement if the price of Fu Chip shares fell below $2.50 per share on 30th April 1974, but they were also bound to sell back their shares to the defendant if their market value exceeded $2.50 on that date. The plaintiffs had chosen to accept shares in Fu Chip in the transaction because they were expected to rise in value, yet the form of guarantee against a fall in the value of the shares which they accepted deprived them, so far as 60 per cent of their holding was concerned, of the very advantage which by taking their price in shares they hoped to gain—and without receiving any other benefit for having to wait a year before they could realize cash on 60 per cent of their price.

One of the plaintiffs became indignant when she appreciated the effect of the subsidiary agreement and on 25th April 1973, the plaintiffs refused to complete the main agreement unless the subsidiary agreement was cancelled and replaced by a simple guarantee that Fu Chip shares would retain their value. The defendants, fearing a loss of confidence in Fu Chip, signed a written guarantee that, in consideration of the plaintiffs' having agreed to sell their shares in Shing On, the defendants would indemnify the plaintiffs for any loss in respect of the 2.5 million shares retained by the plaintiffs if the closing price of Fu Chip shares on 30th April 1974 fell below $2.50. The main agreement was then completed and the plaintiffs retained 2.5 million shares as agreed. The price of Fu Chip shares slumped to $0.36 per share by 30th April 1974 and the defendants refused to fulfil their guarantee when called upon to do so.

Before the Privy Council, the defendants argued that the consideration for their guarantee was past and that it consisted solely of a promise by the plaintiffs to the defendants to perform their existing contract with Fu Chip.

LORD SCARMAN. . . . An act done before the giving of a promise to make a payment or to confer some other benefit can sometimes be consideration for the promise. The act must have been done at the promisors' request: the parties must have understood that the act was to be remunerated either by a payment or the conferment of some other benefit: and payment, or the conferment of a benefit, must have been legally enforceable had it been promised in advance. All three features are present in this case. The promise given to Fu Chip under the main agreement not to sell the shares for a year was at the first defendant's request. The parties understood at the time of the main agreement that the restriction on selling must be compensated for by the benefit of a guarantee against a drop in price: and such a guarantee would be legally enforceable. The agreed cancellation of the subsidiary agreement left, as the parties knew, the plaintiffs unprotected in a respect in which at the time of the main agreement all were agreed they should be protected. . . .

[Lord Scarman then cited *Lampleigh v. Brathwait, supra,* section 2, and *In re Casey's Patents,* [1892] 1 Ch. 104 (C.A.).]

Their Lordships agree that the mere existence or recital of a prior request is not sufficient in itself to convert what is prima facie past consideration into sufficient consideration in law to support a promise: as they have indicated, it is only the first of three necessary preconditions. As for the second of those preconditions, whether the act done at the request of the promisor raises an implication of promised remuneration or other return is simply one of the construction of the words of the contract in the circumstances of its making. Once it is recognised, as the Board considers it inevitably must be, that the expressed consideration includes a reference to the plaintiff's promise not to sell the shares before April 30, 1974—a promise to be performed in the future, though given in the past—it is not possible to treat the defendants' promise of indemnity as independent of the plaintiffs' antecedent promise, given at the first defendant's request, not to sell. The promise of indemnity was given because at the time of the main agreement the parties intended that the first defendant should confer upon the plaintiffs the benefit of his protection against a fall in price. When the subsidiary agreement was cancelled, all were well aware that the plaintiffs were still to have the benefit of his protection as consideration for the restriction on selling. It matters not whether the indemnity thus given be regarded as the best evidence of the benefit intended to be conferred in return for the promise not to sell, or as the positive bargain which fixes the benefit on the faith of which the promise was given—though where, as here, the subject is a written contract, the better analysis is probably that of the "positive bargain." Their Lordships, therefore, accept the submission that the contract itself states a valid consideration for the promise of indemnity. . . .

[Lord Scarman then considered the argument that any consideration provided by the plaintiffs for the indemnity agreement entered into after April 25, 1973 consisted only of the plaintiffs' promise to perform something they were already bound to do.]

The extrinsic evidence in this case shows that the consideration for the promise of indemnity, while it included the cancellation of the subsidiary agreement, was primarily the promise given by the plaintiffs to the defendants, to perform their contract with Fu Chip, which included the undertaking not to sell 60 per cent of the shares allotted to them before April 30, 1974. Thus the real consideration for the indemnity was the promise to perform, or the performance of, the plaintiffs' pre-existing contractual obligations to Fu Chip. This promise was perfectly consistent with the consideration stated in the guarantee. Indeed, it reinforces it by imposing upon the plaintiffs an obligation now owed to the defendants to do what, at the first defendant's request, they had agreed with Fu Chip to do.

Their Lordships do not doubt that a promise to perform, or the performance of, a pre-existing contractual obligation to a third party can be valid consideration.

In *New Zealand Shipping Co. Ltd. v. A. M. Satterthwaite & Co. Ltd. (The Eurymedon)* [1975] A.C. 154, 168 [*infra*, Chapter 5, section 3(d)] the rule and the reason for the rule were stated:

> An agreement to do an act which the promisor is under an existing obligation to a third party to do, may quite well amount to valid consideration . . . the promisee obtains the benefit of a direct obligation. . . .

Unless, therefore, the guarantee was void as having been made for an illegal consideration or voidable on the ground of economic duress, the extrinsic evidence establishes that it was supported by valid consideration.

Mr. Leggatt for the defendants submits that the consideration is illegal as being against public policy. He submits that to secure a party's promise by a threat of repudiation of a pre-existing contractual obligation owed to another can be, and in the circumstances of this case was, an abuse of a dominant bargaining position and so contrary to public policy. This, he submits, is so even though economic duress cannot be proved. . . .

[The question] is whether, in a case where duress is not established, public policy may nevertheless invalidate the consideration if there has been a threat to repudiate a pre-existing contractual obligation or an unfair use of a dominating bargaining position. Their Lordships' conclusion is that where businessmen are negotiating at arm's length it is unnecessary for the achievement of justice, and unhelpful in the development of the law, to invoke such a rule of public policy.

[The Privy Council went on to find that there was no economic duress in the circumstances of the case.]

NOTES and QUESTION

1. In a case comment the authors praise this decision for the flexible application of consideration rules in order to uphold the reasonable expectations of the parties and for the recognition of the potential availability of relief for duress, but criticize it for "failing to take the opportunity to escape from the straitjacket of consideration in regulating contractual variations." England and Rafferty, "Contractual Variations: Consideration and Duress" (1980), 18 Osgoode Hall L.J. 627.

2. Anson describes a banker's irrevocable credit as follows: There are three stages in the transaction. First, a term is inserted in the contract of sale made between the buyer and the seller whereby the buyer undertakes to furnish an irrevocable letter of credit in favour of the seller. Secondly, the buyer approaches its own banker (usually described as the issuing banker) and instructs it to issue an irrevocable letter of credit, giving the banker details of the transaction. This constitutes a contract between the buyer and the banker. Thirdly, the banker advises the seller that an irrevocable letter of credit has been opened in its favour, that is to say, the banker gives an irrevocable undertaking to pay the seller . . . provided the seller tenders the required shipping documents in compliance with the terms of the credit. The seller can then ship the goods in the secure knowledge that it will be paid for them.

Is there a contract between the banker and the seller, and if so, when does this contract come into existence? See *Anson's Law of Contract*, 28th ed. (2002), at 445-446; Davis, "Relationship Between Banker and Seller Under a Confirmed Credit" (1936), 52 L.Q.R. 225. See also *Aspen Planners Ltd. v. Commerce Masonry & Forming Ltd.* (1979), 100 D.L.R. (3d) 546 (Ont. H.C.).

(c)   DUTY OWED TO THE PROMISOR

GILBERT STEEL LTD. v. UNIVERSITY CONST. LTD.

(1976), 12 O.R. (2d) 19, 67 D.L.R. (3d) 606 (C.A.)

WILSON J.A. [delivering the judgment of the court] This is an appeal from the order of Mr. Justice Pennell dismissing the plaintiff's action for damages for breach of an oral agreement for the supply of fabricated steel bars to be incorporated into apartment buildings being constructed by the defendant. The case raises some fundamental principles of contract law.

The circumstances giving rise to the action are as follows. On September 4, 1968, the plaintiff entered into a written contract to deliver to the defendant fabricated steel for apartment buildings to be erected at three separate sites referred to in the contract as the "Flavin, Tectate and University projects". The price fixed by the contract was $153 per ton for "Hard grade" and $159 per ton for "Grade 60,000". Deliveries for the Flavin and Tectate projects were completed in August, 1969, and October, 1969, respectively, and paid for at the agreed-upon price.

Two apartment buildings calling for the supply of 3,000 tons of fabricated steel were to be erected at the University site. However, prior to the defendant's notifying the plaintiff of its intention to commence construction on the first of these two buildings, the owners of the steel mill announced an increase in the price of unfabricated steel. They also gave warning of a further increase to come. The plaintiff approached the defendant about a new contract for the University project and a written contract dated October 22, 1969, was entered into for the supply of fabricated steel for the first building. The new price was $156 per ton for "Hard grade" and $165 per ton for "Grade 60,000". In fact this increase in price did not reflect the full amount of the initial increase announced by the mill owners.

On March 1, 1970, while the building under construction was still far from completion, the mill owners announced the second increase in price and a further discussion took place between John Gilbert and his brother Harry representing the plaintiff and Mendel Tenenbaum and Hersz Tenenbaum representing the defendant with respect to the price to be paid for the steel required to complete the first building. It is this discussion which the plaintiff alleges resulted in a binding oral agreement that the defendant would pay $166 per ton for "Hard grade" and $178 per ton for "Grade 60,000". Although the plaintiff submitted to the defendant a written contract embodying these revised prices following their meeting, the contract was not executed. It contained, in addition to the increased prices, two new clauses which the trial Judge found had not been the subject of any discussion with the defendant but were unilaterally imported into the document by the plaintiff. The trial Judge also found, however, that the defendant agreed at the meeting to pay the increased price.

From March 12, 1970, until the completion of the first building the defendant accepted deliveries of the steel against invoices which reflected the revised prices but, in making payments on account, it remitted cheques in rounded amounts which at the date of the issuance of the writ resulted in a balance owing to the plaintiff in accordance with the invoices.

Having found on the evidence that the defendant had orally agreed to pay the increased prices, the legal issue confronting Mr. Justice Pennell was whether that agreement was legally binding upon the defendant or whether it failed for want of consideration. Counsel for the defendant submitted at the trial that past consideration is no consideration and that the plaintiff was already obliged before the alleged oral agreement was entered into to deliver the steel at the original prices agreed to in the written contract of October 22, 1969. Where then was the *quid pro quo* for the defendant's promise to pay more?

Counsel for the plaintiff sought to supply this omission from the evidence of Hersz Tenenbaum who, during the course of discussions which took place in September, 1970, with a view to a contract for the supply of steel for the second building at the University site, asked whether the plaintiff would give him "a good price" on steel for this building. Plaintiff's counsel argued that the promise of a good price on the second building was the consideration the defendant received for agreeing to pay the increased price on the first. The trial Judge rejected this submission and found the oral agreement unenforceable for want of consideration. In the course of his reasons for judgment the trial Judge adverted briefly to an alternate submission made by the plaintiff's counsel. He said:

> I should, in conclusion, mention a further point which was argued with ingenuity by Mr. Morphy. His contention was that the consideration for the oral agreement was the mutual abandonment of right under the prior agreement in writing. I must say, with respect, that this argument is not without its attraction for me.

On the appeal Mr. Morphy picked up and elaborated upon this submission which had intrigued the trial Judge. In launching his main attack on the trial Judge's finding that the oral agreement was unenforceable for want of consideration, he submitted that the facts of this case evidenced not a purported oral variation of a written contract which failed for want of consideration but an implied rescission of the written contract and the creation of a whole new contract, albeit oral, which was subsequently reneged on by the defendant. The consideration for this new oral agreement, submitted Mr. Morphy, was the mutual agreement to abandon the previous written contract and to assume the obligations under the new oral one. Mr. Morphy submitted to the Court for its consideration two lines of authority, the first line illustrated by the leading case of *Stilk v. Myrick* (1809), 170 E.R. 1168, in which the subsequent agreement was held to be merely a variation of the earlier agreement and accordingly failed for want of consideration, and the other line illustrated by *Morris v. Baron & Co.*, [1918] A.C. 1 (H.L.), in which the subsequent agreement was held to have rescinded the former one and was therefore supported by the mutual agreement to abandon the old obligations and substitute the new. Mr. Morphy invited us to find that the oral agreement to pay the increased price for steel fell into the second category. There was, he acknowledged, no express rescission of the written contract but price is such a fundamental term of a contract for the supply of goods that the substitution of a new price must connote a new contract and impliedly rescind the old.

It is impossible to accept Mr. Morphy's submission in face of the evidence adduced at the trial. It is clear that the sole reason for the discussions between the parties in March, 1970, concerning the supply of steel to complete the first building at the University site was the increase in the price of steel by the mill owners. No changes other than the change in price were discussed. The trial Judge found that the other two changes sought to be introduced into the written document submitted by the plaintiff to the defendant for signature following the discussions had not even been mentioned at the meeting. Moreover, although repeated references were made at trial by the Gilbert brothers to the fact that the parties had made a "new contract" in March, 1970, it seems fairly clear from the evidence when read as a whole that the "new contract" referred to was the agreement to pay the increased price for the steel, *i.e.*, the agreement which effected the variation of the written contract and not a new contract in the sense of a contract replacing *in toto* the original contract of October 22, 1969.

I am not persuaded that either of the parties intended by their discussions in March, 1970, to rescind their original contract and replace it with a new one. Indeed, it is significant that no such plea was made in the statement of claim which confined itself to an allegation that "it was orally agreed in March 1970 that the prices as set forth in the said contract [*i.e.*, of October 22, 1969] would be varied.. . ." Accordingly, consideration for the oral agreement is not to be found in a mutual agreement to abandon the earlier written contract and assume the obligations under the new oral one.

Nor can I find consideration in the vague references in the evidence to the possibility that the plaintiff would give the defendant "a good price" on the steel for the second building if it went along with the increased prices on the first. The plaintiff, in my opinion, fell far short of making any commitment in this regard.

Counsel for the appellant put before us as an alternate source of consideration for the agreement to pay the increased price, the increased credit afforded by the plaintiff to the defendant as a result of the increased price. The argument went something like this. Whereas previously the defendant had credit outstanding for 60 days in the amount owed on the original prices, after the oral agreement was made he had credit outstanding for 60 days in the amount owed on the higher prices. Therefore, there was consideration flowing from the promise and the law does not inquire into its sufficiency. Reliance was placed by counsel on the decision of Chief Justice Meredith in *Kilbuck Coal Co. v. Turner & Robinson* (1915), 7 O.W.N. 673 (C.A.). This case, however, is clearly distinguishable from the case at bar, as Mr. Justice Pennell pointed out in his reasons, on the basis of the *force majeure* clause which had relieved the plaintiff of its obligations under the original contract. In undertaking to supply coal despite the strike the plaintiff was unquestionably providing consideration of real substance in that case. I cannot accept counsel's contention, ingenious as it is, that the increased credit inherent in the increased price constituted consideration flowing from the promisee for the promisor's agreement to pay the increased price.

The final submission put forward by counsel for the appellant was that the defendant, by his conduct in not repudiating the invoices reflecting the increase in price when and as they were received, had in effect acquiesced in such increase in price and should not subsequently be permitted to repudiate it. There would appear to be two answers to this submission. The first is summed up in the maxim that estoppel can never be used as a sword but only as a shield. A plaintiff cannot found his claim in estoppel. Secondarily, however, it should perhaps be pointed out that in order to found an estoppel the plaintiff must show, not only that the conduct of the defendant was clearly referable to the defendant's having given up its right to insist on the original prices, but also that the plaintiff relied on the defendant's conduct to its detriment. I do not think the plaintiff can discharge either of these burdens on the facts of this case.

In summary, I concur in the findings of the trial Judge that the oral agreement made by the parties in March, 1970, was an agreement to vary the written contract of October 22, 1969, and that it must fail for want of consideration. . . .

[Appeal and cross-appeal dismissed.]

NOTES and QUESTIONS

1. The traditional view is that a promise to perform or performance of a pre-existing contractual duty to the promisor does not constitute consideration, nor does forbearance from breaking the contract. See *Smith v. Dawson* (1923), 53 O.L.R. 615 (C.A.). The plaintiff must do something more or other than he or she is legally bound to do. See *Hartley v. Ponsonby* (1857), 119 E.R. 1471 and *Metric Excavating Ltd. v. 619908 Ontario Ltd.* (1991), 45 C.L.R. 314 (Ont. Gen. Div.), additional reasons at (1991), 45 C.L.R. 314 at 320 (Ont. Gen. Div.).

2. In *Modular Windows of Can. v. Command Const.* (1984), 11 C.L.R. 131 (Ont. H.C.), the plaintiff and defendant had entered into a subcontract whereby the plaintiff agreed to supply windows to the defendant by approximately 15th May 1981. The plaintiff failed to supply the windows as agreed and on 2nd July 1981, the plaintiff presented a letter agreement to the defendant, which provided that the defendant pay the plaintiff an additional $6,000. The defendant signed this agreement because he was "over a barrel", but under its terms, the plaintiff had agreed only to perform its existing contractual obligation to the defendant. The court found that the plaintiff could not recover the additional $6,000, both because there was no consideration for the letter agreement and because that agreement had been procured by economic duress.

3. *Gilbert Steel* leaves open the possibility that if the existing contract can be found to have been terminated, then a valid new contract may be created. In the following case the court found that the parties had agreed to abandon their old contract and substitute a new one.

In *DeLuxe French Fries Ltd. v. McCardle* (1976), 10 Nfld. & P.E.I.R. 414 (P.E.I. C.A.), the plaintiff contracted to purchase from the defendant 20,000 bags of potatoes over a period at a certain price per bag. After 1,975 bags were delivered, the defendant refused to deliver any more at the agreed price, so the plaintiff promised to pay an additional dollar per bag. Some 3,430 further bags were delivered and paid for at the new rate but then the defendant again refused to deliver leaving the plaintiff "holding an empty bag". The plaintiff claimed damages for breach of contract. The court held that a new contract had been created "in the same terms as the original, except as to price", and the plaintiff obtained damages based on the increased price.

4. Alterations to contracts of the type found in *Gilbert Steel* are particularly common in long-term relational contracts in times of inflation or fluctuating markets. They may involve changes to terms dealing with items such as price, quantity, specifications, delivery dates or performance obligations. The modifications may be reasonable business arrangements, but they sometimes raise questions of unfair pressure. Should the validity of modifications depend on a finding of consideration, or should the courts focus on the issue of whether economic duress was present? See Swan, "Consideration and the Reasons for Enforcing Contracts", in Reiter and Swan (eds.), *Studies in Contract Law* (1980), at 23; Reiter, "Contracts, Torts, Relations and Reliance", *ibid.*, at 235, Reiter, "Courts, Consideration and Common Sense" (1977), 27 U.T.L.J. 439 and Cumberbatch, "Of Bar-

gains, Gifts and Extortion: An Essay on the Function of Consideration in the Law of Contract" (1990), 19 Anglo-American L.R. 239.

The courts have developed various techniques to avoid the pre-existing duty rule such as: finding consideration, albeit nominal; finding that circumstances have so changed that the plaintiff's later promise to do exactly what was agreed before is consideration for a promise of more from the defendant; enforcing a modification under seal; enforcing the modification if the parties have rescinded the original agreement and substituted a new one, rather than merely varying the original agreement; or finding a compromise. The use of such devices, however, may lead to arbitrary and unjust results.

The O.L.R.C., in its *Report on Sale of Goods*, suggested that even if consideration is required to create a contract it should never be needed to alter a contract. The same conclusion was reached by the Uniform Law Conference in its proposed Uniform Sale of Goods Act, with the amendment in s. 27 that

> . . . a party may withdraw from an executory portion of the agreement made without consideration and revert to the original contract by giving reasonable notice to the other party, unless the withdrawal would be unjust in view of a material change of position in reliance on the agreement.

The O.L.R.C. in its *Report on Amendment of the Law of Contract* has reiterated its recommendation that:

> (1) an agreement in good faith modifying a contract should not require consideration in order to be binding.

The O.L.R.C. would not require a modification agreement to be in writing except where the original agreement itself so provides.

See also the United Nations Convention on Contracts for the International Sale of Goods, Art. 29, although a party may be precluded by conduct from requiring writing to the extent that the other party has relied on that conduct.

Under the O.L.R.C. proposals, modifications may also be enforceable as a result of the recommendation that reliance should be a basis for the enforcement of promises (see section 1 of this Chapter). However, the enforcement of modifications could also be limited by the O.L.R.C.'s proposal to adopt a general doctrine of unconscionability.

In an important article, the authors suggest "that the abolition of the consideration requirement . . . simply moves the inquiry to another difficult threshold. What is meant by 'good faith', 'extortion' or 'coercion' in this context? What is a 'legitimate commercial reason' for modifying a contract? . . . In an attempt to break out of this vicious circle of inventing new language to restate old problems," they develop an economic analysis to minimize transaction costs. This would render "purely strategic modifications" (no change in the underlying economic conditions) and even modifications in changed circumstances unenforceable, unless the superior risk bearer is indeterminate or the risk is highly remote. They point out that if contractual remedies for breach were fully effective in placing the innocent party in the same position as if the contract had been performed, the enforceability of contractual modifications would arise less frequently. See Aivazian, Trebilcock and Penny, "The Law of Contract Modifications: The Uncertain Quest for a Bench Mark of Enforceability" (1984), 22 Osgoode Hall L.J. 173.

Halson argues that while non-enforcement may discourage "opportunism", it does not always do so. He suggests that all contract modifications should be enforced if there is no economic duress, in particular, if there are adequate alternative remedies available to the promisor: Halson, "Opportunism, Economic Duress and Contractual Modifications" (1991), 107 L.Q.R. 649; Halson, "The Modification of Contractual Obligations" (1991), 44 Current Legal Problems 111.

WILLIAMS v. ROFFEY BROS. & NICHOLLS (CONTRACTORS) LTD.
[1990] 1 All E.R. 512 (C.A.)

The defendant building contractors entered into a contract with the owners, Shepherd's Bush Housing Association, to renovate 27 flats in a block that contained 28 flats in total. The contractors hired the plaintiff as a subcontractor to carry out the carpentry work on the project for a total price of £20,000.

In the course of performing the subcontract, the plaintiff encountered financial difficulties, partly because the agreed price for the work was too low and partly because of problems in the supervision of the plaintiff's work force.

The contractors became concerned that the plaintiff might not complete the subcontract on time, for they were potentially liable to the owners under an agreed damages clause if the entire renovation was not completed by the due date. At this stage, they had made interim payments to the plaintiff of £16,000. As a result of their concerns, the contractors agreed to pay the plaintiff a further £10,300, in addition to the contract price of £20,000, at the rate of £575 for each flat in which the carpentry work was completed.

The contractors made one payment of £1,500 under this arrangement and the plaintiff completed eight further flats. When the contractors failed to make any further payment, the plaintiff stopped work and claimed more than £10,000 damages from the contractors.

GLIDEWELL L.J. . . .

The judge's conclusions

The judge found that the defendants' promise to pay an additional £10,300, at the rate of £575 per completed flat, was part of an oral agreement made between the plaintiff and the defendants on 9 April 1986, by way of variation to the original contract.

The judge also found that before the plaintiff ceased work at the end of May 1986 the carpentry in 17 flats had been substantially (but not totally) completed. This means that between the making of the agreement on 9 April 1986 and the date when the plaintiff ceased work, eight further flats were substantially completed.

The judge calculated that this entitled the plaintiff to receive £4,600 (8 x £575) 'less some small deduction for defective and incomplete items'. He held that the plaintiff was also entitled to a reasonable proportion of the £2,200 which was outstanding from the original contract sum . . . Adding these two amounts, he decided that the plaintiff was entitled to further payments totalling £5,000 against which he had only received £1,500, and that the defendants were therefore in breach of contract, entitling the plaintiff to cease work.

. . . . .

Was there consideration for the defendants' promise made on 9 April 1986 to pay an additional price at the rate of £575 per completed flat?

[The trial judge accepted evidence of the defendants' surveyor] . . . to the effect that a main contractor who agrees too low a price with a sub-contractor is acting contrary to his own interests. He will never get the job finished without paying more money.

The judge therefore concluded:

> In my view where the original sub-contract price is too low, and the parties subsequently agree that the additional moneys shall be paid to the sub-contractor, this agreement is in the interests of both parties. This is what happened in the present case, and in my opinion the agreement of 9 April 1986 does not fail for lack of consideration.'

[C]ounsel for the defendants outlined the benefits to the defendants which arose from their agreement to pay the additional £10,300 as (i) seeking to ensure that the plaintiff continued work and did not stop in breach of the sub-contract, (ii) avoiding the penalty for delay and (iii) avoiding the trouble and expense of engaging other people to complete the carpentry work.

However, counsel submits that, though the defendants may have derived, or hoped to derive, practical benefits from their agreement to pay the 'bonus', they derived no benefit in law, since the plaintiff was promising to do no more than he was already bound to do by his sub-contract, *i.e.*, continue with the carpentry work and complete it on time. Thus there was no consideration for the agreement.

There is, however, another legal concept of relatively recent development which is relevant, namely that of economic duress. Clearly, if a sub-contractor has agreed to undertake work at a fixed price, and before he has completed the work declines to continue with it unless the contractor agrees to pay an increased price, the sub-contractor may be held guilty of securing the contractor's promise by taking unfair advantage of the difficulties he will cause if he does not complete the work. In such a case an agreement to pay an increased price may well be voidable because it was entered into under duress. Thus this concept may provide another answer in law to the question of policy which has troubled the courts since before *Stilk v. Myrick* (1809) 2 Camp 317, 170 ER 1168, and no doubt led at the date of that decision to a rigid adherence to the doctrine of consideration.

This possible application of the concept of economic duress was referred to by Lord Scarman, delivering the judgment of the Judicial Committee of the Privy Council in *Pao On v. Lau Yiu* [*supra* at section 4(b)] . . .

It is true that *Pao On v. Lau Yiu* is a case of a tripartite relationship, *ie* a promise by A to perform a pre-existing contractual obligation owed to B, in return for a promise of payment by C. But Lord Scarman's words seem to me to be of general application, equally applicable to a promise made by one of the original two parties to a contract. . . .

[T]he present state of the law on this subject can be expressed in the following proposition: (i) if A has entered into a contract with B to do work for, or to supply goods or services to B, in return for payment by B and (ii) at some stage before A has completely performed his obligations under the contract B has reason to doubt whether A will, or will be able to, complete his side of the bargain and (iii) B thereupon promises A an additional payment in return for A's promise to perform his contractual obligations on time and (iv) as a result of giving his promise B obtains in practice a benefit, or obviates a disbenefit, and (v) B's promise is not given as a result of economic duress or fraud on the part of A, then

(vi) the benefit to B is capable of being consideration for B's promise, so that the promise will be legally binding.

As I have said, counsel for the defendants accepts that in the present case by promising to pay the extra £10,300 the defendants secured benefits. There is no finding, and no suggestion, that in this case the promise was given as a result of fraud or duress.

If it be objected that the propositions above contravene the principle in *Stilk v. Myrick*, I answer that in my view they do not: they refine and limit the application of that principle, but they leave the principle unscathed, *e.g.*, where B secures no benefit by his promise. It is not in my view surprising that a principle enunciated in relation to the rigours of seafaring life during the Napoleonic wars should be subjected during the succeeding 180 years to a process of refinement and limitation in its application in the present day.

It is therefore my opinion that on his findings of fact in the present case, the judge was entitled to hold, as he did, that the defendants' promise to pay the extra £10,300 was supported by valuable consideration, and thus constituted an enforceable agreement. . . .

RUSSELL L.J. . . . [W]hile consideration remains a fundamental requirement before a contract not under seal can be enforced, the policy of the law in its search to do justice between the parties has developed considerably since the early nineteenth century when *Stilk v. Myrick* was decided by Lord Ellenborough CJ. In the late twentieth century I do not believe that the rigid approach to the concept of consideration to be found in *Stilk v. Myrick* is either necessary or desirable. Consideration there must still be but in my judgment the courts nowadays should be more ready to find its existence so as to reflect the intention of the parties to the contract where the bargaining powers are not unequal and where the finding of consideration reflects the true intention of the parties.

What was the true intention of the parties when they arrived at the agreement. . .? The plaintiff had got into financial difficulties. The defendants, through their employee Mr. Cottrell, recognised that the price that had been agreed originally with the plaintiff was less than what Mr. Cottrell himself regarded as a reasonable price. There was a desire on Mr. Cottrell's part to retain the services of the plaintiff so that the work could be completed without the need to employ another sub-contractor. There was further a need to replace what had hitherto been a haphazard method of payment by a more formalised scheme involving the payment of a specified sum on the completion of each flat. These were all advantages accruing to the defendants which can fairly be said to have been in consideration of their undertaking to pay the additional £10,300. True it was that the plaintiff did not undertake to do any work additional to that which he had originally undertaken to do but the terms on which he was to carry out the work were varied and, in my judgment, that variation was supported by consideration which a pragmatic approach to the true relationship between the parties readily demonstrates.

For my part I wish to make it plain that I do not base my judgment on any reservation as to the correctness of the law long ago enunciated in *Stilk v. Myrick*.

A gratuitous promise, pure and simple, remains unenforceable unless given under seal. But where, as in this case, a party undertakes to make a payment because by so doing it will gain an advantage arising out of the continuing relationship with the promisee the new bargain will not fail for want of consideration . . .

PURCHAS L.J. . . . . This arrangement was beneficial to both sides. By completing one flat at a time rather than half completing all the flats the plaintiff was able to receive moneys on account and the defendants were able to direct their other trades to do work in the completed flats which otherwise would have been held up until the plaintiff had completed his work.

The point of some difficulty which arises on this appeal is whether . . . the agreement reached on 9 April failed for lack of consideration. . . .

In my judgment . . . the rule in *Stilk v. Myrick* remains valid as a matter of principle, namely that a contract not under seal must be supported by consideration. Thus, where the agreement on which reliance is placed provides that an extra payment is to be made for work to be done by the payee which he is already obliged to perform, then unless some other consideration is detected to support the agreement to pay the extra sum that agreement will not be enforceable. . . . *Stilk v. Myrick* involved circumstances of a very special nature, namely the extraordinary conditions existing at the turn of the eighteenth century under which seamen had to serve their contracts of employment on the high seas. There were strong public policy grounds at that time to protect the master and owners of a ship from being held to ransom by disaffected crews. Thus, the decision that the promise to pay extra wages even in the circumstances established in those cases was not supported by consideration is readily understandable. Of course, conditions today on the high seas have changed dramatically and it is at least questionable, counsel for the plaintiff submitted, whether these cases might not well have been decided differently if they were tried today. The modern cases tend to depend more on the defence of duress in a commercial context rather than lack of consideration for the second agreement. In the present case, the question of duress does not arise. The initiative in coming to the agreement of 9 April came from Mr. Cottrell and not from the plaintiff. It would not, therefore, lie in the defendants' mouth to assert a defence of duress. Nevertheless, the court is more ready in the presence of this defence being available in the commercial context to look for mutual advantages which would amount to sufficient consideration to support the second agreement under which the extra money is paid. . . .

The question must be posed: what consideration has moved from the plaintiff to support the promise to pay the extra £10,300 added to the lump sum provision? In the particular circumstances which I have outlined above, there was clearly a commercial advantage to both sides from a pragmatic point of view in reaching the agreement of 9 April. The defendants were on risk that as a result of the bargain they had struck the plaintiff would not or indeed possibly could not comply with his existing obligations without further finance. As a result of the agreement the defendants secured their position commercially. There was, however, no obligation added to the contractual duties imposed on the plaintiff under the original contact. Prima facie this would appear to be a classic *Stilk v. Myrick* case. It was, however, open to the plaintiff to be in deliberate breach of the contract in order to 'cut his losses' commercially. In normal circumstances the suggestion that a contracting party can rely on his own breach to establish consideration is distinctly unattractive. In many cases it obviously would be and if there was any element of duress brought on the other contracting party under the modern development of this branch of the law the proposed breaker of the contract would not benefit. With some hesitation . . . I consider that the modern approach to the question of consideration would be that where there were benefits derived by each party to a contract of variation even though one party did not suffer a detriment this would not be fatal to the establishing of sufficient consideration to support the agreement. If both parties benefit from an agreement it is not necessary that each also suffers a detriment. In my judgment, on the facts as found by the judge, he was entitled to reach the conclusion that consideration existed and in those circumstances I would not disturb that finding. . . .

[Appeal dismissed.]

NOTES and QUESTIONS

1. Much has been written about *Williams v. Roffey*. Halyk, "Consideration, Practical Benefits and Promissory Estoppel: Enforcement of Contract Modification Promises in Light of *Williams v. Roffey Brothers*" (1991), 55 Sask. L. Rev. 393 does not dispute the desirability of the outcome in the case, but suggests that such promises should be enforced by extending the doctrine of promissory estoppel. Chen-Wishart, "The Enforceability of Additional Contractual Promises: A Question of Consideration?" (1990-91), 14 N.Z.U.L.R. 270, suggests that the more appropriate tool is "an expanded concept of economic duress". See also Meyer-Rochow, "The Requirement of Consideration" (1997), 71 Aust. L.J. 532.

2. In October 1981, Canada West Tree Fruits Ltd., apple growers, entered into a "continuing evergreen" contract (terminable with five years' notice on the anniversary date) with the predecessor of the defendant, a wine merchant, for the sale of apple pulp. The defendant agreed to purchase 1,600,000 pounds of product annually from 1982 to 1986; the defendant had the right to request additional quantities of product at any time and after 1986 the parties by mutual agreement could adjust the quantity of product. In June 1984, the defendant agreed to purchase 3,000,000 pounds of product until 1988, with an option for an additional 1,000,000 pounds in each of 1985 and 1986; the parties could by mutual agreement increase the quantities of product. In 1987 the defendant did not want to take any fruit because the cider market was flat and indicated "that if the plaintiff gave concessions for 1987 and 1988 it could lead to a long-term relationship". In September 1987, the plaintiff did agree to reduce the quantity of product to 600,000 pounds for 1987 and 1988, but the defendant gave notice of the termination of the agreement in October 1987. The plaintiff sued for breach of the 1984 agreement. The court held that there was no consideration beyond a "fanciful perception" for the 1987 variation. See *Canada West Tree Fruits Ltd. v. T.G. Bright & Co.* (1990), 48 B.C.L.R. (2d) 91 (C.A.), leave to appeal to S.C.C. refused (1991), 52 B.C.L.R. (2d) xxxviii (note) (S.C.C.).

After you have read the materials in section 5 of this chapter, consider whether the plaintiff should have been estopped from returning to its rights under the 1984 agreement.

3. A specific problem created by the pre-existing duty rule concerns the enforceability of an agreement to extinguish an existing obligation in return for part performance or to forgive the obligation. This problem raises many of the same questions as modification of contracts in general. As a matter of commercial reality, such agreements usually benefit the creditor but may raise questions of exploitation. Again, should these cases depend on a finding of consideration?

Sometimes, arrangements of this nature are enforced on the theory that the parties intended to rescind the original contract and to substitute a new one. Traditionally, the rescission argument is available only where the obligations of both parties are at least partially unperformed (executory), as the consideration is the mutual release of the old obligations. If one party has fully performed (executed) the agreement, an "accord and satisfaction" is normally required at common law to release the other party wholly or partially from the obligations. In *British Russian Gazette and Trade Outlook Ltd. v. Associated Newspapers Ltd.; Talbot v. Associated Newspapers Ltd.*, [1933] 2 K.B. 616 at 643-44 (C.A.), the Court of Appeal adopted the following definition:

> Accord and satisfaction is the purchase of a release from an obligation whether arising under contract or tort by means of any valuable consideration, not being the actual performance of the obligation itself. The accord is the agreement by which the obligation is discharged. The satisfaction is the consideration which makes the agreement operative.

This rule has been somewhat mitigated by statute (*infra*, section 4(c)(ii)), and by the doctrines of waiver and promissory estoppel, which are discussed in detail, in section 5 of this chapter.

(i)   Accord and Satisfaction

FOAKES v. BEER

(1884), 9 App. Cas. 605 (H.L.)

Foakes was the judgment debtor of Mrs. Beer in the amount of £2,090, 19s. On December 21, 1876, the parties entered into the following agreement:

> Whereas the said John Weston Foakes is indebted to the said Julia Beer, and she has obtained a judgment in Her Majesty's High Court of Justice, Exchequer Division, for the sum of £2090 19s. And whereas the said John Weston Foakes has requested the said Julia Beer to give him time in which to pay such judgment, which she has agreed to do on the following conditions. Now this agreement witnesseth that in consideration of the said John Weston Foakes paying to the said Julia Beer on the signing of this agreement the sum of £500, the receipt whereof she doth hereby acknowledge in part satisfaction of the said judgment debt of £2090 19s., and on condition of his paying to her or her executors, administrators, assigns or nominee the sum of £150 on the 1st day of July and the 1st day of January or within one calendar month after each of the said days respectively in every year until the whole of the said sum of £2090 19s. shall have been fully paid and satisfied, the first of such payments to be made on the 1st day of July next, then she the said Julia Beer hereby undertakes and agrees that she, her executors, administrators or assigns, will not take any proceedings whatever on the said judgment.

In June 1882, the respondent, Julian Beer, sought leave to proceed on the judgment. An issue was directed to be tried whether any and what amount was, on the 1st of July 1882, due upon the judgment.

It was found at trial that the whole sum of £2,090 19s. had been paid, but the respondent claimed interest. The Court of Appeal entered judgment for the interest due.

EARL OF SELBORNE L.C. . . . [I] very much doubt whether the effect of the agreement, as a conditional waiver of the interest to which she was by law entitled under the judgment, was really present to the mind of the judgment creditor, still I cannot deny that it might ave that effect, if capable of being legally enforced.

But the question remains, whether the agreement is capable of being legally enforced. Not being under seal, it cannot be legally enforced against the respondent, unless she received consideration for it from the appellant, or unless, though without consideration, it operates by way of accord and satisfaction, so as to extinguish the claim for interest. What is the consideration? On the face of the agreement none is expressed, except a present payment of £500, on account and in part of the larger debt then due and payable by law under the judgment. The appellant did not contract to pay the future instalments of £150 each, at the times therein mentioned; much less did he give any new security, in the shape of negotiable paper, or in any other form. The promise de futuro was only that of the respondent, that if the half-yearly payments of £150 each were regularly paid, she would "take no proceedings whatever on the judgment." No doubt if the appellant had been under no antecedent obligation to pay the whole debt, his fulfilment of the condition might have imported some consideration on his part for that promise. But he was under that antecedent obligation; and payment at those deferred dates, by the forbearance and indulgence of the creditor, of the residue of the principal debt and costs, could not (in my opinion) be a consideration for the relinquishment of interest and discharge of the judgment, unless the payment of the £500, at the time of signing the agreement, was such a consideration. As to accord and satisfaction, in point of fact there could be no complete satisfaction, so long as any future instalment remained payable; and I do not see how any mere payments on account could operate in law as a satisfaction ad interim, conditionally upon other payments being afterwards duly made, unless there was a consideration sufficient to support the agreement while still unexecuted. Nor was anything, in fact, done by the respondent in this case, on the receipt of the last payment, which could be tantamount to an acquittance, if the agreement did not previously bind her.

The question, therefore, is nakedly raised by this appeal, whether your Lordships are now prepared, not only to overrule, as contrary to law, the doctrine stated by Sir Edward Coke to have been laid down by all the judges of the Common Pleas in *Pinnel's Case* [(1602), 77 E.R. 237] in 1602, and repeated in his note to Littleton, sect. 344 [Co. Litt. 212b], but to treat a prospective agreement, not under seal, for satisfaction of a debt, by a series of payments on account to a total amount less than the whole debt, as binding in law, provided those payments are regularly made; the case not being one of a composition with a common debtor, agreed to, inter se, by several creditors. . . . The doctrine itself, as laid down by Sir Edward Coke, may have been criticised, as questionable in principle, by some persons whose opinions are entitled to respect, but it has never been judicially overruled; on the contrary I think it has always, since the sixteenth century, been accepted as law. If so, I cannot think that your Lordships would do right, if you were now to reverse, as erroneous, a judgment of the Court of Appeal, proceeding upon a doctrine which has been accepted as part of the law of England for 280 years.

The doctrine, as stated in *Pinnel's Case*, is "that payment of a lesser sum on the day" (it would of course be the same after the day), "in satisfaction of a greater, cannot be any satisfaction for the whole, because it appears to the Judges, that by no possibility a lesser sum can be a satisfaction to the plaintiff for a greater sum." As stated in Coke Littleton, 212(b), it is "where the condition is for payment of £20, the obligor or feoffor cannot at the time appointed pay a lesser sum in satisfaction of the whole, because it is apparent that a lesser sum of money cannot be a satisfaction of a greater;" adding (what is beyond controversy), that an acquittance under seal, in full satisfaction of the whole, would (under like circumstances) be valid and binding.

The distinction between the effect of a deed under seal, and that of an agreement by parol, or by writing not under seal, may seem arbitrary, but it is established in our law; nor is it really unreasonable or practically inconvenient that the law should require particular solemnities to give to a gratuitous contract the force of a binding obligation. If the question be (as, in the actual state of the law, I think it is), whether consideration is, or is not, given in a case of this kind, by the debtor who pays down part of the debt presently due from him, for a promise by the creditor to relinquish, after certain further payments on account, the residue of the debt, I cannot say that I think consideration is given, in the sense in which I have always understood that word as used in our law. It might be (and indeed I think it would be) an improvement in our law, if a release or acquittance of the whole debt, on payment of any sum which the creditor might be content to receive by way of accord and satisfaction (though less than the whole), were held to be, generally, binding, though not under seal; nor should I be unwilling to see equal force given to a prospective agreement, like the present, in writing though not under seal; but I think it impossible, without refinements which practically alter the sense of the word, to treat such a release or acquittance as supported by any new consideration proceeding from the debtor. All the authorities subsequent to *Cumber v. Wane* [(1721), 93 E.R. 613], which were relied upon by the appellant at your Lordships' Bar have proceeded upon the distinction, that, by giving negotiable paper or otherwise, there had been some new consideration for a new agreement, distinct from mere money payments in or towards discharge of the original liability. I think it unnecessary to go through those cases, or to examine the particular grounds on which each of them was decided. There are no such facts in the case now before your Lordships. What is called "any benefit, or even any legal possibility of benefit," in Mr. Smith's notes to *Cumber v. Wane* is not (as I conceive) that sort of benefit which a creditor may derive from getting payment of part of the money due to him from a debtor who might otherwise keep him at arm's length, or possibly become insolvent, but is some independent benefit, actual or contingent, of a kind which might in law be a good and valuable consideration for any other sort of agreement not under seal.

My conclusion is, that the order appealed from should be affirmed, and the appeal dismissed, with costs, and I so move your Lordships.

[The concurring opinions of Lords Blackburn, Watson and Fitzgerald are omitted.]

NOTE

1. Adams and Brownsword, "Contract, Consideration and the Critical Path" (1990), 53 Mod. L. Rev. 536, suggest that the logic of *Williams v. Roffey* should apply to decisions such as *Pinnel's Case,* and *Foakes v. Beer* as "the economic imperatives may dictate that financial adjustments should be made". This argument was considered in the following decision.

RE SELECTMOVE LTD.

[1995] 2 All E.R. 531 (C.A.)

Selectmove Ltd. ("the company") was required to deduct from payments to its employees certain amounts of money for the purposes of income tax and national insurance contributions and to forward the deductions to the Crown. Over an extended period of time the company had failed to pay the deductions and on July 15, 1991, a collector of taxes met the managing director of the company to discuss the situation. The company was having cash flow problems and the tax collector asked for a proposal to deal with the amounts in arrears. The company proposed that it would begin to make all current payments as they fell due and to pay the arrears at the rate of £1,000 per month from February 1, 1992. The tax collector allegedly said that he would have to seek approval of the proposal from his superiors and that he would get back to the company if it was unacceptable. On October 9, 1991, the Crown demanded payment from the company of all the arrears, in the amount of £24,650.

The company made payment of its current obligations between August and November 1991, though not in strict accordance with the alleged agreement. In 1992, it made seven payments of £1,000 pursuant to the provisions of the alleged agreement for dealing with amounts in arrears. In October, 1991, the company gave notice of dismissal to all of its employees and sold its work in progress to another company. In September, 1992, the Crown brought a winding-up petition, in which it sought the compulsory liquidation of the company and the payment of arrears in the amount of £17,466.60.

It was accepted that the court would dismiss the winding-up petition if the company disputed its debt "in good faith and on substantial grounds." The company claimed that it had an arguable case that the Crown had accepted its proposal of July 15, 1991.

The Court of Appeal found that the Crown had not accepted the proposal but considered, in the alternative, if there had been an acceptance, whether the agreement of July 15, 1991 was supported by consideration. The Crown argued that any such agreement fell within the principle of *Foakes v. Beer*.

PETER GIBSON L.J. . . . . [Counsel] submitted that an additional benefit to the Crown was conferred by the agreement in that the Crown stood to derive practical benefits therefrom: it was likely to recover more from not enforcing its debt against the company, which was known to be in financial difficulties, than from putting the company into liquidation. He pointed to the fact that the company did in fact pay its further . . . [tax and national insurance] liabilities and £7,000 of its arrears. He relied on the decision of this court in *Williams v. Roffey Bros & Nicholls (Contractors) Ltd* [*supra*] for the proposition that a promise to perform an existing obligation can amount to good consideration provided that there are practical benefits to the promisee. . . .

[Counsel] submitted that although Glidewell LJ [in the *Williams* case] in terms confined his remarks to a case where B is to do the work for or supply goods or services to A, the same principle must apply where B's obligation is to pay A, and he referred to an article by Adams and Brownsword 'Contract, Consideration and the Critical Path' (1990) 53 MLR 536 at 539-540 which suggests that *Foakes v. Beer* might need reconsideration. I see the force of the argument, but the difficulty that I feel with it is that if the principle of *Williams'* case is to be extended to an obligation to make payment, it would in effect leave the principle in *Foakes v. Beer* without any application. When a creditor and a debtor who are at arm's length reach agreement on the payment of the debt by instalments to accommodate the debtor, the creditor will no doubt always see a practical benefit to himself in so doing. In the absence of authority there would be much to be said for the enforceability of such a contract. But that was a matter expressly considered in *Foakes v. Beer* yet held not to constitute good consideration in law. *Foakes v. Beer* was not even referred to in *Williams'* case, and it is in my judgment impossible, consistently with the doctrine of precedent, for this court to extend the principle of *Williams'* case to any circumstances governed by the principle of *Foakes v. Beer*. If that extension is to be made, it must be by the House of Lords or, perhaps even more appropriately, by Parliament after consideration by the Law Commission.

In my judgment, the judge was right to hold that if there was an agreement between the company and the Crown it was unenforceable for want of consideration.

[Stuart-Smith and Balcombe L.JJ. concurred in dismissing the appeal.]

NOTES and QUESTIONS

1. In *Robichaud c. Caisse Populaire de Pokemouche Ltée* (1990), 69 D.L.R. (4th) 589 (N.B. C.A.), the Caisse obtained a judgment against the plaintiff for $3,787.80. The Royal Bank had also obtained a judgment in the amount of approximately $10,000 against the plaintiff.

As part of a debt consolidation negotiated by a representative of Avco Financial Services, both the Royal Bank and the Caisse agreed to remove from the registry their judgments against the plaintiff in exchange for the payment of $1,000 to each creditor. A cheque in the amount of $1,000 was duly sent to the Caisse.

Subsequently, the board of directors of the Caisse refused to ratify the agreement, which had been reached through its local manager, and the cheque was not cashed. The plaintiff sued to compel the Caisse to accept the $1,000 as agreed and to remove the judgment.

After reviewing the history of accord and satisfaction and its application in New Brunswick, Angers J.A. concluded at 595-96: (translation)

> It would be easy for the courts to decide that there is or is not consideration or to invent grounds, as several courts have done, to give effect to an agreement such as the one at issue here. However, it cannot be denied that a financial institution, of its own accord and knowing all the consequences of its action, entered into an agreement by which it agreed to waive the priority of a judgment in its favour in return for part payment of the debt due to it. This agreement constituted full satisfaction. The consideration for the Caisse Populaire was the immediate receipt of payment and the saving of time, effort and expense. In my opinion, it is not up to the court to judge the reasons for entering into such an agreement but rather to determine that the agreement was reached with full knowledge and consent. The court must therefore recognize the validity of the agreement. It would be foolish to suppose that financial institutions disdain the old adage, "A bird in the hand is worth two in the bush." Finally, I would go so far as to find that implicit in the agreement to settle for $1,000 is the proviso that if the lesser amount is not paid, the original debt again comes into force.

See a further extract from this case, *infra*, section 5(e).

2. Several articles have discussed the interrelationship of *Foakes v. Beer, Williams v. Roffey* and *Re Selectmove Ltd.* See *e.g.*, Peel, "Part Payment of a Debt Is No Consideration" (1994), 110 LQR 353; O'Sullivan, "In Defence of *Foakes v. Beer*" [1996] Cambridge L.J. 219 and Cumberbatch, "Melting Down to Common Sense" (1997), 48 Northern Ireland L.Q. 48.

3. Harvey Foster borrows $2,000 from his friend Herman, to be repaid on 2nd September.

(a) During the summer, however, Harvey is laid off work and asks Herman if he would take less. Herman agrees to take $1,000. Harvey does pay the $1,000 on 1st July. Can Herman recover the balance?

(b) Would it make any difference if Herman needed $1,000 on 1st July for his summer vacation?

(c) Suppose that on 2nd September Harvey finds that he is unable to pay the full amount. He phones his friend, Herman, who is on holiday in Kenora, and Herman says that he will take $1,000. Harvey takes the $1,000 with him to Kenora on 2nd September, when he goes to visit Herman.

4. Harvey Foster Jr. owes a creditor $1,000, which he cannot pay. Afraid for his son's reputation Harvey Foster Sr. promises to pay the lender $500, if he takes no action against his son. The lender agrees. Can he recover the full amount? See *Hirachand Punamchand v. Temple*, [1911] 2 K.B. 330 (C.A.), and *Budget Rent-A-Car Ltd. v. Goodman*, [1991] 2 N.Z.L.R. 715 (H.C.).

5. For an example of "a composition with a common debtor agreed to by several creditors" referred to in *Foakes v. Beer*, see *Gencon Construction Ltd. (Trustee of) v. M & Y Construction Ltd.* (1988), 48 R.P.R. 148 (Ont. Master).

6. Harvey Foster's business has been severely affected by a recession. When the employees were warned of the possibility of lay-offs, they all met and agreed to accept a 20 per cent salary reduction in return for management's promise to maintain full employment for the duration of the recession. One employee now wishes to claim his full salary, although the recession continues. See *Raggow v. Scougall & Co.* (1915), 31 T.L.R. 564 (Div. Ct.).

FOOT v. RAWLINGS

[1963] S.C.R. 197, 41 W.W.R. 650, 37 D.L.R. (2d) 695

The appellant owed the respondent a large sum under a series of promissory notes, dating from February, 1952 to May, 1958. The parties made an agreement for the payment of the debt on the basis of this letter sent by the respondent to the appellant in July, 1958:

> I have been thinking matters over regarding your indebtedness to me and after a good deal of thought I think that you may be interested in the following proposal:
>
> (1) That I accept the sum of $300.00 per month provided that it is paid on the sixteenth of each and every month without fail, and I agree to lower the interest from eight per cent to five per cent.
>
> (2) The above offer only to take place provided you do not miss any of the Three hundred dollar payments, which are to be paid monthly, starting on 16th August 1958 and to be paid to me on or before the sixteenth of each and every month following until the full account is paid.
>
> (3) These cheques to be for $300.00 each and the first to be payable on the 16th day of August 1958, and every month following, these cheques to be given to cover the following six months starting on the 16th of August 1958 and to the 16th of February 1959, after which you are to give me six more such cheques to carry on the next six months, that would take it to August 1959 after which you are to give me six more such cheques to cover another six months and so on until the account is fully paid.

(4) Should any of these cheques be turned down by the C.B. of C. the whole of the unpaid indebtedness will go back to the present state namely, the interest will revert to the present eight per cent, and the monthly payments revert to $400.00 per month.

(5) My reason for making this offer is not only to help you in your finances but to help me carry on. I realize that I am not going to have many more years to live and would like to be able to do several things before that time comes. This is clearly an advantage to you, as first of all you save three per cent in interest which at the present rate you are paying saves you Fifty dollars per month.

(6) You of course to have the privilege of paying off the whole debt to me at any time you may wish to do so, this offer must be accepted in writing on or before August next.

(7) I, E.H.M. Foot, agree to the above terms of payment.

This was signed by both parties on July 17, 1958.

The appellant substantially complied with the terms of the agreement, but after cashing his November, 1960 cheque, the respondent sued the appellant for the balance of his debt. The respondent succeeded at trial and before the British Columbia Court of Appeal [32 D.L.R. (2d) 320, Davey J.A. dissenting], and the question arose whether he had received consideration in the agreement of July 1958.

CARTWRIGHT J. [delivering the judgment of the court]. . . . I take it then that the factual situation at the date of the issue of the writ was that the agreement between the parties was in existence and the appellant was not in default under its terms. The question calling for decision is whether this rendered the action premature . . .

I have reached the conclusion that the giving of the several series of post-dated cheques constituted good consideration for the agreement by the respondent to forbear from taking action on the promissory notes so long as the appellant continued to deliver the cheques and the same were paid by the bank on presentation. This view of the law has prevailed ever since the Court of Exchequer in *Sibree v. Tripp* (1846), 153 E.R. 745, expressed disapproval of the decision in *Cumber v. Wane* (1721), 93 E.R. 613. In *Sibree v. Tripp* the defendant pleaded in answer to a claim for £500 that the plaintiff had agreed to accept as full payment three promissory notes made by the defendant payable to the plaintiff for £125, £125 and £50 and that the defendant had given these notes to the plaintiff in pursuance of the agreement. It was held that this plea was a good answer to the action in point of law as the acceptance of a negotiable instrument may be in law a satisfaction of a debt of a greater amount. At pp. 751-52 Baron Alderson said:

> . . . [I]f you substitute for a sum of money a piece of paper, or a stick of sealing-wax . . . and the bargain may be carried out in its full integrity. A man may give in satisfaction of a debt of £100, a horse of the value of five pounds, but not five pounds. Again, if the time or place of payment be different, the one sum may be a satisfaction of the other. Let us, then, apply these principles to the present case. If for money you give a negotiable security, you pay it in a different way. The security may be worth more or less, it is of uncertain value. That is a case falling within the rule of law I have referred to. . . .

Sheppard J.A., with whom Tysoe J.A. agreed, was of opinion that there was no consideration for the agreement; he expressed doubts as to whether on the true construction of the agreement the appellant had promised to deliver the cheques and cause them to be paid . . .

On the question of construction I agree with Davey J.A. when he says [p. 324]:

> As a matter of construction the agreement clearly implies that so long as there is no default in its terms the respondent will not sue on the notes, but will forbear from bringing action. A promise to forbear is readily implied from an arrangement such as this.

In my view, when paras. 3 and 7 of the agreement are read together they disclose an undertaking by the appellant to give the cheques from time to time in accordance with para. 3; this undertaking is the consideration for the respondent's agreement to withhold action and so long as the appellant continued to carry it out the respondent's right to sue was suspended.

. . . I agree with the view of Sheppard J.A. that the respondent's right of action on the six promissory notes has not been extinguished. It follows that should the appellant have made default under the agreement of July 17, 1958, it would thereupon have been open to the respondent to bring action for the amount remaining unpaid on the notes; but an agreement for good consideration suspending a right of action so long as the debtor continues to perform the obligations which he has undertaken thereunder is binding. To hold that the claimant in such a case may, in breach of the agreement, pursue his right of action leaving the defendant to a crossaction or counterclaim would be to countenance the circuity of action and multiplicity of proceedings which it was one of the chief objects of the Judicature Acts to abolish and would be contrary to the terms of s-s. (7) of s. 2 of the *Laws Declaratory Act*, R.S.B.C. 1960, c. 213.

. . . So long as the appellant continued to perform his obligations under the agreement of July 17, 1958, the respondent's right to sue on the notes was suspended, consequently his action brought on December 7, 1960, was premature and should have been dismissed on that ground.

The reasons which have brought me to the conclusion that the action was premature make it unnecessary to consider either the ground of estoppel on which Davey J.A., proceeded or the arguments addressed to us as to the effect of s-s. (33) of s. 2 of the *Laws Declaratory Act*. . . .

[Appeal allowed, with costs.]

NOTES and QUESTIONS

1. Consider what should happen if the post-dated cheques were dishonoured. Do you think the creditor should be limited to an action on those cheques or should he be able to enforce the original debt? See *Gyro Capital Inc. v. Franzke*, [1997] O.J. No. 3991 (Gen. Div.).

2. In treating a payment by cheque differently from payment in cash, Cartwright J. adopts Baron Alderson's justification that a negotiable instrument "may be worth more or less: it is of uncertain value". How can a cheque be worth more than a cash payment of the same amount? In the English Court of Appeal case of *D. & C. Bldr. v. Rees, infra*, section 5(b), Lord Denning M.R. commented, at 840 (All E.R.):

> Now, suppose that the debtor, instead of paying the lesser sum in cash, pays it by cheque. He makes out a cheque for the amount. The creditor accepts the cheque and cashes it. Is the position any different? I think not. No sensible distinction can be taken between payment of a lesser sum by cash and payment of it by cheque. The cheque, when given, is conditional

payment. When honoured, it is actual payment. It is then just the same as cash. If a creditor is not bound when he receives payment by cash, he should not be bound when he receives payment by cheque. This view is supported by the leading case of *Cumber v. Wane* [(1721), 1 Stra. 426], which has suffered vicissitudes but was, I think, rightly decided in point of law.

. . .

. . . In point of law payment of a lesser sum, whether by cash or by cheque, is no discharge of a greater sum.

Which of the differing views of the Supreme Court of Canada and the English Court of Appeal is better founded in policy?

3. Harvey Foster owes the Happy Homes Co. Ltd. $1,000 for a sofa. Harvey decides that the sofa is not worth $1,000 and sends a cheque for $500 marked "Payment in Full" on the back to Happy Homes Co. Ltd. Happy Homes Co. Ltd. immediately cashes this cheque. A month later, however, Harvey receives a statement from the company showing a balance owing of $500. See *Day v. McLea* (1889), 22 Q.B.D. 610 (C.A.) and *Ferguson v. Davies*, [1997] 1 All E.R. 315 (C.A.). Compare, *e.g.*, *Phillip v. Massey-Ferguson Fin. Co.*, [1973] 1 W.W.R. 443 (Sask. Dist. Ct.) and *Triple "C" Flooring Ltd. v. Wright Carpets Ltd.*, [1980] 4 W.W.R. 440 (Man. Co. Ct.), with *Woodlot Services Ltd. v. Flemming* (1977), 83 D.L.R. (3d) 201 (N.B. C.A.), and *Fehr v. Robinson Diesel Injection Ltd.* (1985), 47 Sask. R. 12 (Q.B.). Would it make any difference if upon cashing the cheque Happy Homes Co. Ltd. wrote to Harvey acknowledging receipt of the cheque as part payment? Compare *Masur v. McKeran* (1990), 115 A.R. 235 (Master), *Budget Rent-A-Car Ltd. v. Goodman*, [1991] 2 N.Z.L.R. 715 (H.C.) and *Magnum Photo Supplies Ltd. v. Viko New Zealand Ltd.* (N.Z. C.A.), discussed by Keene, "Cheques in Full Satisfaction", [1998] N.Z.L.J. 393, with *Haines House Haulage Co. v. Gamble*, [1989] 3 N.Z.L.R. 221 (H.C.).

This problem appears to have given rise to considerable litigation and controversy in New Zealand. See McLauchlan, "Cheques in Full Satisfaction: Accord Despite Discord?" (1987), 12 N.Z.U.L. Rev. 259 and Keene, "Cheques in Full Satisfaction" [1998] N.Z.L.J. 393.

(ii) *Statute*

JUDICATURE ACT

R.S.A. 2000, c. J-2, s. 13(1)

(1) Part performance of an obligation either before or after a breach thereof shall be held to extinguish the obligation

(*a*) when expressly accepted by a creditor in satisfaction, or

(*b*) when rendered pursuant to an agreement for that purpose though without any new consideration.

NOTES and QUESTIONS

1. There is similar legislation in British Columbia (Law and Equity Act, R.S.B.C. 1996, c. 253, s. 43), Ontario (Mercantile Law Amendment Act, R.S.O. 1990, c. M.10, s. 16), Saskatchewan (Queen's Bench Act, R.S.S. 1998, c. Q-1.01, s. 64), the Northwest Territories (Judicature Act, R.S.N.W.T. 1988, c. J-1, s. 40) and the Yukon (Judicature Act, R.S.Y. 2002, c. 128, s. 25).

Such provisions were originally passed in response to the decision in *Foakes v. Beer* and this helps to explain both their wording and their scope. Would this section have changed the result in *Foakes v. Beer*?

2. The Manitoba equivalent of s. 13(1) is s. 6 of the Mercantile Law Amendment Act, C.C.S.M., c. M120. In The Law Reform (Miscellaneous Amendments) Act, S.M. 1992, c. 32, s. 10, Manitoba added, *inter alia*, the following subsections:

Unconscionability

6(2) Notwithstanding subsection (1), an obligation is not extinguished by part performance where a court of competent jurisdiction finds that it is unconscionable to so allow.

.....

Right of revocation

6(4) A creditor may revoke an agreement under clause 6(1)(b) where

(a) the debtor has not commenced performance of the agreement; or

(b) the debtor has commenced performance of the agreement, but fails to continue performance on a date or within a time provided for in the agreement, and it would be unreasonable in the circumstances for the creditor to give the debtor more time to remedy the default.

3. What is the difference between the two methods of settlement under sections such as s. 13(1) above? See *Triple "C" Flooring Ltd. v. Wright Carpets Ltd.*, [1980] 4 W.W.R. 440 (Man. Co. Ct.). Should a distinction be maintained?

4. In *Graham v. Voth Bros. Const. (1974) Ltd.*, [1982] 6 W.W.R. 365 (B.C. Co. Ct.), the plaintiff sued for the balance due under a trucking contract with the defendant. The defendant, aware that its action threatened to leave the plaintiff virtually bankrupt and unable to pay the truck drivers whom he employed, refused to pay any part of the amount owing to the plaintiff until the plaintiff agreed to reduce his charges. In an action for the difference between the reduced amount accepted by the plaintiff and the original contract price, the defendant relied on the equivalent section of the Law and Equity Act, R.S.B.C. 1996, c. 253, s. 43. Wetmore Co. Ct. J. commented at 369-71:

> The plaintiff says the satisfaction and accord is therefore so tainted with undue influence that the agreement is void. . . .
> The rationale of *Cumber v. Wane, Pinnel's Case* and the many cases dealing with this problem turns on the absence of new consideration for the subsequent contract. In my view, s. 40 [of the *Law and Equity Act*] does no more than remove this question of consideration and does not purport to change the rules of law and equity beyond that point. Hence on this new contract, I am entitled to consider all of the items of undue influence which would be proper considerations in any contract. . . .
> In the case at bar, the funds were payable in 30 days. The defendant then having received the benefit of the services wrongfully refused to pay even the part not in dispute. It was aware of the plaintiff's desperate financial condition. The defendant then deliberately and wrongfully, even in the bare contractual sense, set about to create this inequality of bargaining power. That in my view brings the conscience of equity into play for the benefit of the plaintiff.

The plaintiff was accordingly granted judgment and costs.

5. It is doubtful whether such sections presently apply to partially executed or executory agreements, or outright forgiveness of an obligation. See, *e.g., Bank of Commerce v. Jenkins* (1888), 16 O.R. 215 (C.A.); *Hoolahan v. Hivon*, [1944] 4 D.L.R. 405 (Alta. S.C.), and *Rommerill v. Gardener* (1962), 35 D.L.R. (2d) 717 (B.C. C.A.).

Consider the effect on this problem of the Manitoba legislation, set out in note 2, *supra*.

5. Waiver and Promissory Estoppel

CENTRAL LONDON PROPERTY TRUST LTD. v. HIGH TREES HOUSE LTD.

[1947] 1 K.B. 130, [1956] 1 All E.R. 256

By a lease under seal made on September 24, 1937, the plaintiffs, Central London Property Trust Ltd., granted to the defendants, High Trees House Ltd., a subsidiary of the plaintiff company, a tenancy of a block of flats for the term of ninety-nine years from September 29, 1937, at a ground rent of £2,500 a year. The block of flats was a new one and had not been fully occupied at the beginning of the war owing to the absence of people from London. With war conditions prevailing, it was apparent to those responsible that the rent reserved under the lease could not be paid out of the profits of the flats and, accordingly, discussions took place between the directors of the two companies concerned, which were closely associated, and an arrangement was made between them which was put into writing. On January 3, 1940, the plaintiffs wrote to the defendants in these terms, "we confirm the arrangement made between us by which the ground rent should be reduced as from the commencement of the lease to £1,250 per annum," and on April 2, 1940, a confirmatory resolution to the same effect was passed by the plaintiff company. On March 20, 1941, a receiver was appointed by the debenture holders of the plaintiffs. The defendants paid the reduced rent from 1941 down to the beginning of 1945 by which time all the flats in the block were fully let, and continued to pay it thereafter. In September, 1945, the then receiver of the plaintiff company looked into the matter of the lease and ascertained that the rent actually reserved by it was £2,500. On September 21, 1945, he wrote to the defendants saying that rent must be paid at the full rate and claiming that arrears amounting to £7,916 were due. Subsequently, he instituted the present friendly proceedings to test the legal position in regard to the rate at which rent was payable. In the action the plaintiffs sought to recover £625, being the amount represented by the difference between rent at the rate of £2,500 and £1,250 per annum for the quarters ending September 29, and December 25, 1945. By their defence the defendants pleaded (1.) that the letter of January 3, 1940, constituted an agreement that the rent reserved should be £1,250 only, and that such agreement related to the whole term of the lease, (2.) they pleaded in the alternative that the plaintiff company were estopped from alleging that the rent exceeded £1,250 per annum and (3.) as a further alternative, that by failing to demand rent in excess of £1,250 before their letter of September 21, 1945 (received by the defendants on September 24), they had waived their rights in respect of any rent, in excess of that at the rate of £1,250, which had accrued up to September 24, 1945.

DENNING J. . . . If I were to consider this matter without regard to recent developments in the law, there is no doubt that had the plaintiffs claimed it, they would have been entitled to recover ground rent at the rate of £2,500 a year from the beginning of the term, since the lease under which it was payable was a lease under seal which, according to the old common law, could not be varied by an agreement by parol (whether in writing or not), but only by deed. Equity, however stepped in, and said that if there has been a variation of a deed by a simple contract (which in the case of a lease required to be in writing would have to be evidenced by writing), the courts may give effect to it. . . . That equitable doctrine, however, could hardly apply in the present case because the variation here might be said to have been made without consideration. With regard to estoppel, the representation made in relation to reducing the rent, was not a representation of an existing fact. It was a representation, in effect, as to the future, namely, that payment of the rent would not be enforced at the full rate but only at the reduced rate. Such a representation would not give rise to an estoppel, because, as was said in *Jorden v. Money* [(1854), 10 E.R. 868], a representation as to the future must be embodied as a contract or be nothing.

But what is the position in view of developments in the law in recent years? The law has not been standing still since *Jorden v. Money*. There has been a series of decisions over the last fifty years which, although they are said to be cases of estoppel are not really such. They are cases in which a promise was made which was intended to create legal relations, and which, to the knowledge of the person making the promise, was going to be acted on by the person to whom it was made, and which was in fact so acted on. In such cases the courts have said that the promise must be honoured. The cases to which I particularly desire to refer are: *Fenner v. Blake* [[1900] 1 Q.B. 426 (D.C.)]; *Re Wickham* [(1917), 34 T.L.R. 158]; *Re Porter (William) & Co. Ltd.* [[1937] 2 All E.R. 361] and *Buttery v. Pickard* [(1946), 174 L.T. 144]. As I have said they are not cases of estoppel in the strict sense. They are really promises—promises intended to be binding, intended to be acted on, and in fact acted on. *Jorden v. Money* can be distinguished, because there the promisor made it clear that she did not intend to be legally bound, whereas in the cases to which I refer the proper inference was that the promisor did intend to be bound. In each case the court held the promise to be binding on the party making it, even though under the old common law it might be difficult to find any consideration for it. The courts have not gone so far as to give a cause of action in damages for the breach of such a promise, but they have refused to allow the party making it to act inconsistently with it. It is in that sense, and that sense only, that such a promise gives rise to an estoppel. The decisions are a natural result of the fusion of law and equity: for the cases of *Hughes v. Metropolitan Ry. Co.* [(1877), 2 App. Cas. 439 (H.L.)]; *Birmingham & District Land Co. v. London & North Western Ry. Co.* [(1888), 40 Ch. D. 268 (C.A.)] and *Salisbury v. Gilmore* [[1942] 2 K.B. 38 (C.A.)] afford a sufficient basis for saying that a party would not be allowed in equity to go back on such a promise. In my opinion, the time has now come for the validity of such a promise to be recognized. The logical consequence, no doubt is that a promise to accept a smaller sum in discharge of a larger sum, if acted upon, is binding notwithstanding the absence of consideration: and if the fusion of law and equity leads to this result, so much the better. That aspect was not considered in *Foakes v. Beer* [*supra*]. At this time of day however, when law and equity have been joined together for over seventy years, principles must be reconsidered in the light of their combined effect. It is to be noticed that in the Sixth Interim Report of the Law Revision Committee, pars, 35, 40, [1937], it is recommended that such a promise as that to which I have referred, should be enforceable in law even though no consideration for it has been given by the promisee. It seems to me that, to the extent I have mentioned, that result has now been achieved by the decisions of the courts.

I am satisfied that a promise such as that to which I have referred is binding and the only question remaining for my consideration is the scope of the promise in the present case. I am satisfied on all the evidence that the promise here was that the ground rent should be reduced to £1,250 a year as a temporary expedient while the block of flats was not fully, or substantially fully let, owing to the conditions prevailing. That means that the reduction in the rent applied throughout the years down to the end of 1944, but early in 1945 it is plain that the flats were fully let, and, indeed the rents received from them . . . were increased beyond the figure at which it was originally contemplated that they would be let. At all events the rent from them must have been very considerable. I find that the conditions prevailing at the time when the reduction in rent was made, had completely passed away by the early months of 1945. I am satisfied that the promise was understood by all parties only to apply under the conditions prevailing at the time when it was made, namely, when the flats were only partially let, and that it did not extend any further than that. When the flats became fully let, early in 1945, the reduction ceased to apply.

In those circumstances, under the law as I hold it, it seems to me that rent is payable at the full rate for the quarters ending September 29 and December 25, 1945.

If the case had been one of estoppel, it might be said that in any event the estoppel would cease when the conditions to which the representation applied came to an end, or it also might be said that it would only come to an end on notice. In either case it is only a way of ascertaining what is the scope of the representation. I prefer to apply the principle that a promise intended to be binding, intended to be acted on and in fact acted on, is binding so far as its terms properly apply. Here it was binding as covering the period down to the early part of 1945, and as from that time full rent is payable.

I therefore give judgment for the plaintiff company for the amount claimed.

NOTE and QUESTIONS

1. Would the plaintiffs have recovered the full rent had they sued in March 1943?

2. Had the plaintiffs given notice in March 1943, that they intended to claim the full amount, could they then have done so? From when?

3. Would it make any difference if the apartments had all been let during the war?

4. How did the defendants "act on" the promise in *High Trees*?

5. Would the application of the *High Trees* principle lead to a different result in *Foakes v. Beer*?

6. Throughout this section of the chapter, the reader will find conflicting descriptions of the relationship between waiver and estoppel. A good starting point is found in *Panchaud Frères S.A. v. Etablissement Gen. Grain Co.*, [1970] 1 Lloyd's Rep. 53 (C.A.) where Lord Denning commented at 57, on a distinction between waiver and estoppel by conduct as follows:

> When "waiver" is used in its legal sense, it only takes place when a man, with knowledge of a breach, does an unequivocal act which shows that he has elected to affirm the contract as still existing instead of disaffirming it as, for instance, in waiver of forfeiture. . . .

The basis of [estoppel by conduct] is that a man has so conducted himself that it would be unfair or unjust to allow him to depart from a particular state of affairs which another has taken to be settled or correct. . . .

In the same case, Winn L.J. emphasized, at 59, that the doctrine of waiver is derived either from agreement or quasi-estoppel. However, he saw signs of the emergence in the law of:

a criterion of what is fair conduct between the parties. There may be an inchoate doctrine stemming from the manifest convenience of consistency in pragmatic affairs, negativing any liberty to blow hot and cold in commercial conduct. . . .

(a)   THE NATURE OF THE REPRESENTATION

JOHN BURROWS LTD. v. SUBSURFACE SURVEYS LTD.

[1968] S.C.R. 607, 68 D.L.R. (2d) 354

The defendant, Subsurface Surveys Ltd., purchased a business belonging to the plaintiff for a price in excess of $127,000. Part of the purchase price was secured by a promissory note in the amount of $42,000, which the defendant gave to the plaintiff in March 1963. The note provided for payments in monthly instalments and contained an acceleration clause permitting the creditor to claim the entire amount due if there was a default of more than 10 days on any monthly payment. Over a period of 18 months, the defendant was consistently more than 10 days in default with its monthly payments, although no default had extended beyond 35 days. On each occasion, the creditor accepted the late payments without protest and without invoking the acceleration clause. Finally, following a disagreement between the president of the defendants and the plaintiff, the plaintiff sued for the whole amount owing when the defendant was late with the payment due in November 1964. The defendant then tendered that instalment, but the plaintiff rejected it.

RITCHIE J. [delivering the judgment of the court] . . . It remains to be considered whether the circumstances disclosed by the evidence were such as to justify the majority of the Court of Appeal in concluding that this was a case to which the defence of equitable estoppel or estoppel by representation applied.

Since the decision of the present Lord Denning in the case of *Central London Property Trust Ltd. v. High Trees House Ltd.* [*supra*] there has been a great deal of discussion, both academic and judicial, on the question of whether that decision extended the doctrine of estoppel beyond the limits which had been theretofore fixed, but in this Court in the case of *Conwest Exploration Co. v. Letain*, [1964] S.C.R. 20 at 28, Judson J., speaking for the majority of the Court, expressed the view that Lord Denning's statement had not done anything more than restate the principle expressed by Lord Cairns in *Hughes v. Metropolitan Ry. Co.* (1877), 2 App. Cas. 439 (H.L.) at p. 448, in the following terms:

> . . . it is the first principle upon which all Courts of Equity proceed, that if parties who have entered into definite and distinct terms involving certain legal results—certain penalties or legal forfeiture—afterwards by their own act or with their own consent, enter upon a course of negotiation which has the effect of leading one of the parties to suppose that the strict rights arising under the contract will not be enforced, or will be kept in suspense, or held in abeyance, the person who otherwise might have enforced those rights will not be allowed to enforce them where it would be inequitable having regard to the dealings which have thus taken place between the parties. . . .

It seems clear to me that this type of equitable defence cannot be invoked unless there is some evidence that one of the parties entered into a course of negotiation which had the effect of leading the other to suppose that the strict rights under the contract would not be enforced, and I think that this implies that there must be evidence from which it can be inferred that the first party intended that the legal relations created by the contract would be altered as a result of the negotiations.

It is not enough to show that one party has taken advantage of indulgences granted to him by the other for if this were so in relation to commercial transactions, such as promissory notes, it would mean that the holders of such notes would be required to insist on the very letter being enforced in all cases for fear that any indulgences granted and acted upon could be translated into a waiver of their rights to enforce the contract according to its terms. . . .

I do not think that the evidence warrants the inference that the appellant entered into any negotiations with the respondents which had the effect of leading them to suppose that the appellant had agreed to disregard or hold in suspense or abeyance that part of the contract which provided that:

> . . . on default being made . . . in paying any principal or interest due at any time according to the terms of the said note the Company may forthwith cause the pledged shares to be transferred to the name of the Company on the share register of Subsurface Surveys Ltd. and the pledged shares shall thereupon become the absolute property of the Company.

I am on the other hand of opinion that the behaviour of Mr. Burrows is much more consistent with his having granted friendly indulgences to an old associate while retaining his right to insist on the letter of the obligation, which he did when he and Whitcomb became estranged and when the respondents were in default in payment of an interest payment for a period of 36 days.

For all these reasons I would allow the appeal. . . .

NOTES and QUESTION

1. In Manwaring, "Promissory Estoppel in the Supreme Court of Canada" (1987), 10(3) Dal. L.J. 43, the author reviews a series of decisions which were all decided in part on the absence of an unequivocal representation. As you read the cases in this section, consider the extent to which courts have now departed from the strict requirements set out by Ritchie J.

If the court had found that the creditor was bound by its "indulgences", would it mean that creditors in general would be forced to insist on strict performance? See also, on the effect of "indulgences", *Morrison Lamothe Inc. v. Bedok* (1986), 29 D.L.R. (4th) 255 (Ont. H.C.).

2. In *Owen Sound Pub. Library Bd. v. Mial Developments Ltd.* (1979), 102 D.L.R. (3d) 685 (Ont. C.A.), the contractor contracted with the owner to build an addition to a public library building. The contract provided that payments should be made within a certain number of days from the architect's certificate, otherwise the contractor might terminate the contract upon five days' written notice. The architect issued a certificate for a payment to a subcontractor due on 12th December 1972, but the owner wished to have the subcontractor's seal affixed to its statutory declaration of entitlement, although in fact this was meaningless and unnecessary. Before the due date the contractor agreed to provide the owner with this document, but it was never delivered, nor was there any discussion of the effect of this undertaking on payment. The owner, therefore, put the matter aside. On 20th December 1972, the contractor, anxious to terminate the contract for other reasons, gave notice of termination on the ground that it had not been paid within the specified time. The Court of Appeal held that the contractor's promise to have the corporate seal affixed to the statutory declaration, "could logically or reasonably be interpreted by the Library Board as an agreement by Mial that it would postpone the Board's strict obligation to pay the certificate." While intention to alter legal relations and knowledge that the promisee is likely to so regard the promise are requirements

of promissory estoppel, these can be inferred from reasonable reliance by the promisee. Thus the contractor was estopped from cancelling the contract for late payment, and the owner recovered damages. How would you distinguish this case from the *John Burrows* decision?

In a note on this case in (1979), 8 R.P.R. 113, Swan suggests that it is similar to *Gilbert Steel, supra*: "Both plaintiffs were promised more by the other. One was allowed to keep it: the other was denied it. Both plaintiffs were using the promise to support a claim to remedy against the other." Do you agree?

The *Owen Sound* case was applied in *Re 6781427 Hldg. Ltd. and Alma Mater Soc. of the Univ. of B.C.* (1987), 36 D.L.R. (4th) 753, affirmed 44 D.L.R. (4th) 257 (B.C. C.A.), in the context of an implied extension of time for the exercise of an option to renew a lease.

3. In *Drexel Burnham Lambert Inv. NV v. El Nasr*, [1986] 1 Lloyd's Rep. 356 (Q.B.), the plaintiffs were commodity brokers and the first defendant was one of their clients. The Commodity Customers' Agreement provided for the payment by the client of margins as required by Drexels; if such margins were not provided, Drexels were free to close the client's positions. Among several telex and telephone communications, Drexels sent a telex to the defendant on 24th February indicating that they needed "today at 3 p.m., Ldn. time a confirmation . . . of transfer of 1 1/2 mln. US dollars . . . in order to pursue holding the position." No money was paid by the defendant but the plaintiffs did not close the positions until 28th February and 4th March. The plaintiffs sued for their losses on the defendant's account; the defendant contended that Drexels had promised to close the positions at 3 p.m. on 24th February if they had not received $1.5 million by then, and that they should be placed in the same position as if they had been closed then.

The court held that there was no express or implied promise to close on 24th February. The court thought that "it would be, at the least, unusual that words which were insufficient to constitute a promise should nevertheless be a sufficient representation to give rise to a promissory estoppel . . . There was not a representation or a promise, but a threat." If the promise supporting a promissory estoppel is similar to a contractual promise, what is the purpose of promissory estoppel? At most, the telex was a representation "that Drexels would not close before 3 p.m. on 24th February nor at that time if $1.5 million had been received."

The court doubted whether there could be a promissory estoppel in this situation: "here there was a legal relationship giving rise to certain rights and duties between the parties. But the alleged promise or representation by Drexels was not that they would not enforce their strict legal rights arising out of that relationship—it was that they would enforce them." If promissory estoppel were allowed here, "then any promise or representation whatever by one party to a legal relationship, which is intended to be relied on, will give rise to a promissory estoppel. It seems to me open to question whether the law has yet gone as far as that in emasculating the doctrine of consideration."

On the first point see also *Woodhouse AC Israel Cocoa SA v. Nigerian Produce Marketing Co.*, [1972] A.C. 741 (H.L.).

(b)   THE EQUITIES

D. & C. BUILDERS LTD. v. REES

[1966] 2 Q.B. 617, [1965] 3 All E.R. 837 (C.A.)

LORD DENNING M.R. D. & C. Builders, Ltd. ("the plaintiffs") are a little company. "D" stands for Mr. Donaldson, a decorator, "C" for Mr. Casey, a plumber. They are jobbing builders. The defendant, Mr. Rees, has a shop where he sells builders' materials.

In the spring of 1964 the defendant employed the plaintiffs to do work at his premises, 218, Brick Lane. The plaintiffs did the work and rendered accounts in May and June, which came to £746 13s 1d. altogether. The defendant paid £250 on account. In addition the plaintiffs made an allowance of £14 off the bill. So in

July, 1964, there was owing to the plaintiffs the sum of £482. 13s. 1d. At this stage there was no dispute as to the work done. But the defendant did not pay.

On Aug. 31, 1964, the plaintiffs wrote asking the defendant to pay the remainder of the bill. He did not reply. On Oct. 19, 1964, they wrote again, pointing out that the "outstanding account of £480 is well overdue". Still the defendant did not reply. He did not write or telephone for more than three weeks. Then on Friday, Nov. 13, 1964, the defendant was ill with influenza. His wife telephoned the plaintiffs. She spoke to Mr. Casey. She began to make complaints about the work: and then said: "My husband will offer you £300 in settlement. That is all you'll get. It is to be in satisfaction." Mr. Casey said he would have to discuss it with Mr. Donaldson. The two of them talked it over. Their company was in desperate financial straits. If they did not have the £300, they would be in a state of bankruptcy. So they decided to accept the £300 and see what they could do about the rest afterwards. Thereupon Mr. Donaldson telephoned to the defendant's wife. He said to her: "£300 will not even clear our commitments on the job. We will accept £300 and give you a year to find the balance." She said: "No, we will never have enough money to pay the balance. £300 is better than nothing." He said: "We have no choice but to accept." She said: "Would you like the money by cash or by cheque. If it is cash, you can have it on Monday. If by cheque, you can have it tomorrow (Saturday)." On Saturday, Nov. 14, 1964, Mr. Casey went to collect the money. He took with him a receipt prepared on the company's paper with the simple words: "Received the sum of £300 from Mr. Rees." She gave him a cheque for £300 and asked for a receipt. She insisted that the words "in completion of the account" be added. Mr. Casey did as she asked. He added the words to the receipt. So she had the clean receipt: "Received the sum of £300 from Mr. Rees in completion of the account. Paid. M. Casey." Mr. Casey gave in evidence his reason for giving it: "If I did not have the £300 the company would have gone bankrupt. The only reason we took it was to save the company. She knew the position we were in."

The plaintiffs were so worried about their position that they went to their solicitors. Within a few days, on Nov. 23, 1964, the solicitors wrote complaining that the defendant had "extricated a receipt of some sort or other" from them. They said that they were treating the £300 as a payment on account. On Nov. 28, 1964, the defendant replied alleging bad workmanship. He also set up the receipt which Mr. Casey gave to his wife, adding: "I assure you she had no gun on her." The plaintiffs brought this action for the balance. The defendant set up a defence of bad workmanship and also that there was a binding settlement. The question of settlement was tried as a preliminary issue. The judge made these findings:

> I concluded that by the middle of August the sum due to the plaintiffs was ascertained and not then in dispute. I also concluded that there was no consideration to support the agreement of Nov. 13 and 14. It was a case of agreeing to take a lesser sum, when a larger sum was already due to the plaintiffs. It was not a case of agreeing to take a cheque for a smaller amount instead of receiving cash for a larger account. The payment by cheque was an incidental arrangement.

The judge decided, therefore, the preliminary issue in favour of the plaintiffs. The defendant appeals to this court. He says that there was here an accord and satisfaction, an *accord* when the plaintiffs agreed, however reluctantly, to accept £300 in settlement of the account and *satisfaction* when they accepted the cheque for £300 and it was duly honoured. . . .

This case is of some consequence: for it is a daily occurrence that a merchant or tradesman, who is owed a sum of money, is asked to take less. The debtor says he is in difficulties. He offers a lesser sum in settlement, cash down. He says he cannot pay more. The creditor is considerate. He accepts the proffered sum and forgives him the rest of the debt. The question arises: is the settlement binding on the creditor? The answer is that, in point of law, the creditor is not bound by the settlement. He can the next day sue the debtor for the balance, and get judgment. The law was so stated in 1602 by Lord Coke in *Pinnel's Case* [(1602), 77 E.R. 237]—and accepted in 1884 by the House of Lords in *Foakes v. Beer.* [For the reasons set out *supra*, at section 4(c)(i) of this chapter, Lord Denning M.R. held that the defendants had not provided consideration in paying by cheque.]

This doctrine of the common law has come under heavy fire. It was ridiculed by Sir George Jessel, M.R., in *Couldery v. Bartrum* [(1881), 19 Ch.D. 394, 399]. It was held to be mistaken by Lord Blackburn in *Foakes v. Beer*. It was condemned by the Law Revision Committee in their Sixth Interim Report (Cmnd. 5449), para. 20 and para. 22. But a remedy has been found. The harshness of the common law has been relieved. Equity has stretched out a merciful hand to help the debtor. The courts have invoked the broad principle stated by Lord Cairns, L.C., in *Hughes v. Metropolitan Ry. Co.* [(1877), 2 App. Cas. 439, 448 (H.L.)]:

> . . . it is the first principle upon which all courts of equity proceed if parties, who have entered into definite and distinct terms involving certain legal results . . . afterwards by their own act, or with their own consent, enter upon a course of negotiation which has the effect of leading one of the parties to suppose that *the strict rights arising under the contract will not be enforced*, or will be kept in suspense, or held in abeyance, that the person who otherwise might have enforced those rights *will not be allowed to enforce them where it would be inequitable, having regard to the dealings which have taken place between the parties.*

It is worth noticing that the principle may be applied, not only so as to suspend strict legal rights, but also so as to preclude the enforcement of them.

This principle has been applied to cases where a creditor agrees to accept a lesser sum in discharge of a greater. So much so that we can now say that, when a creditor and a debtor enter on a course of negotiation, which leads the debtor to suppose that, on payment of the lesser sum, the creditor will not enforce payment of the balance, and on the faith thereof the debtor pays the lesser sum and the creditor accepts it as satisfaction: then the creditor will not be allowed to enforce payment of the balance when it would be inequitable to do so. This was well illustrated during the last war. . . see *Central London Property Trust Ltd. v. High Trees House Ltd.* [*supra*]. This caused at the time some eyebrows to be raised in high places. But they have been lowered since. The solution was so obviously just that no one could well gainsay it.

In applying this principle, however, we must note the qualification. The creditor is barred from his legal rights only when it would be inequitable for him to insist on them. Where there has been a *true accord*, under which the creditor voluntarily agrees to accept a lesser sum in satisfaction, and the debtor acts on that accord by paying the lesser sum and the creditor accepts it, then it is inequitable for the creditor afterwards to insist on the balance. But he is not bound unless there has been truly an accord between them.

In the present case, on the facts as found by the judge, it seems to me that there was no true accord. The debtor's wife held the creditor to ransom. The creditor was in need of money to meet his own commitments, and she knew it. When the creditor asked for payment of the £480 due to him, she said to him in effect: "We cannot pay you the £480. But we will pay you £300 if you will accept it in settlement. If you do not accept it on those terms, you will get nothing. £300 is better than nothing." She had no right to say any such thing. She could properly have said: "We cannot pay you more than £300. Please accept it on account." But she had no right to insist on his taking it in settlement. When she said: "We will pay you nothing unless you accept £300 in settlement", she was putting undue pressure on the creditor. She was making a threat to break the contract (by paying nothing) and she was doing it so as to compel the creditor to do what he was unwilling to do (to accept £300 in settlement): and she succeeded. He complied with her demand. That was on recent authority a case of intimidation [see *Rookes v. Barnard*, [1964] A.C. 1129 (H.L.) and *J.T. Stratford & Son Ltd. v. Lindley*, [1965] A.C. 307 (H.L.)]. In these circumstances there was no true accord so as to found a defence of accord and satisfaction [see *Day v. McLea* (1889), 22 Q.B.D. 610 (C.A.)]. There is also no equity in the defendant to warrant any departure from the due course of law. No person can insist on a settlement procured by intimidation.

In my opinion there is no reason in law or equity why the creditor should not enforce the full amount of the debt due to him. I would, therefore, dismiss this appeal.

[The concurring judgments of Danckwerts and Winn L.JJ. are omitted.]

(c)   THE NOTICE

SASKATCHEWAN RIVER BUNGALOWS LTD. v. MARITIME LIFE ASSURANCE CO.
[1994] 2 S.C.R. 490

MAJOR J. [delivering the judgment of the court]

On July 26, 1978, the appellant Maritime Life Assurance Company ("Maritime") issued an insurance policy on the life of Michael Fikowski Sr. to the respondent Saskatchewan River Bungalows Ltd. ("SRB"). In 1984, ownership of the policy was transferred to the respondent Connie Fikowski, at which time she became the beneficiary. SRB retained the responsibility of paying the annual premiums under the policy. . . . The policy contained the following conditions relating to premium payment:

2. PREMIUM PAYMENT PROVISIONS

(1) General

The agreements made by the Company and contained in this contract are conditional upon payment of the premiums as they become due.

Each premium is payable on or before its due date at the Head Office of the Company.

(2) Grace Period

After the first premium has been paid, a grace period of thirty-one days following its due date is allowed for the payment of each subsequent premium. During the grace period, this policy continues in effect.

(3) Non-payment of Premiums

If any premium remains unpaid at the end of the grace period, this policy automatically lapses (terminates because of non-payment of premiums).

Under certain conditions, this policy may be reinstated, as described below.

(4) Reinstatement

This policy may be reinstated within 3 years of the date of the lapse upon written application to the Company subject to the following conditions:

a) evidence that satisfies the Company of the life insured's good health and insurability must be submitted; and

b) all unpaid premiums plus interest, at a rate to be determined by the Company, must be paid to the Company.

Over the years, SRB paid the annual policy premium irregularly. In 1979, the policy lapsed after SRB failed to pay the annual premium within the 31-day grace period. The policy was subsequently reinstated in accordance with the reinstatement provision (cl. 2(4)) of the policy. In 1981, SRB again failed to make payment within the grace period. On this occasion, Maritime accepted late payment and did not require evidence of insurability or an application for reinstatement.

On July 24, 1984, SRB mailed a cheque for $1,316 to pay the annual premium due on July 26, 1984. On August 13, 1984, SRB received a premium due notice from Maritime, requesting payment of $1,361. It sent Maritime a cheque for $45—the difference between the July 24th cheque and the amount demanded in the payment due notice. This second cheque was received by Maritime on August 22, 1984. The first cheque, in the amount of $1,316, was never received by Maritime, nor was it deducted from SRB's bank account.

Subsequent to the expiry of the grace period on August 26, 1984, Maritime sent a late payment offer to SRB. In this offer, Maritime agreed to accept late payment of the July premium if it was "postmarked or, if not mailed, received at the Head Office at Halifax, N.S." on or before September 8, 1984. The offer also contained an explicit reserve of Maritime's right to require evidence of insurability. SRB did not respond to the late payment offer.

On November 28, 1984, Maritime wrote a letter ("the November letter") advising the respondent Connie Fikowski that the premium due on July 26, 1984, remained unpaid. This letter contained the following statement: "Unfortunately this policy is now technically out of force, and we will require immediate payment of $1,361.00 to pay the July 1984-85 premium."

Finally, on February 2, 1985, Maritime sent a notice of policy lapse to the respondents. This notice was originally sent to an incorrect address in Vancouver, but was eventually forwarded to SRB. It read, in part:

> According to our records this policy has lapsed for non-payment of the premium due on the date shown. The policy is no longer in force and no benefits are payable. Because your insurance affords valuable protection and represents a worthwhile investment we invite you to apply for reinstatement of the policy.

The application for reinstatement appended to the lapse notice required evidence of insurability.

SRB closed its hotel business at Lake Louise, Alberta for the winter season around the middle of November, 1984. SRB picked up the corporate mail on an infrequent basis throughout the winter. As a result, SRB did not become aware of the late payment offer, the November letter or the lapse notice until April, 1985. They then began to search for the lost premium cheque. It was not until July, 1985, that SRB sent a replacement cheque to Maritime, and a cheque for the 1985 premium. Both cheques were refused.

On July 9, 1985, SRB's insurance agent informed Maritime that Michael Fikowski Sr. was terminally ill and uninsurable. On August 10, 1985, Michael Fikowski Sr. died. On October 11, 1985, Maritime rejected SRB's claim for benefits under the policy on the ground that it was no longer in force.

. . . . .

Maritime's position is that the policy issued to the respondents lapsed after the expiry of the grace period for payment of the 1984 premium. Fikowski Sr.'s death occurred when the policy was not in force and the respondents had no right to benefits under it.

The respondents' position is that Maritime, through its conduct, waived its right to compel timely payment under the policy. The respondents further submit that none of Maritime's acts were sufficient to retract its waiver of time and that the policy was still in force at the time of death.

Although the parties argued in terms of waiver, Harradence J.A. [in the decision of the Alberta Court of Appeal] considered the doctrine of promissory or equitable estoppel. Recent cases have indicated that waiver and promissory estoppel are closely related: see, *e.g.*, *W. J. Alan & Co. v. El Nasr Export and Import Co.* [*infra*] and *Tudale Explorations Ltd. v. Bruce* (1978), 88 D.L.R. (3d) 584 at p. 587. The noted author Waddams suggests that the principle underlying both doctrines is that a party should not be allowed to go back on a choice when it would be unfair to the other party to do so: S. M. Waddams, *The Law of Contracts*, 3rd ed. (Toronto: Canada Law Book, 1993), at para. 606. It is not necessary for the purpose of this appeal to determine how or whether promissory estoppel and waiver should be distinguished. As the parties have chosen to frame their submissions in waiver, only that doctrine need be dealt with.

Waiver occurs where one party to a contract or to proceedings takes steps which amount to foregoing reliance on some known right or defect in the performance of the other party: *Mitchell and Jewell Ltd. v. Canadian Pacific Express Co.* (1974), 44 D.L.R. (3d) 603 (Alta. C.A.); *Marchischuk v. Dominion Industrial*

Supplies Ltd., [1991] 2 S.C.R. 61 (waiver of a limitation period). The elements of waiver were described in *Federal Business Development Bank v. Steinbock Development Corp.* (1983), 42 A.R. 231 (C.A.), cited by both parties to the present appeal (Laycraft J.A. for the court, at p. 236):

> The essentials of waiver are thus full knowledge of the deficiency which might be relied upon and the unequivocal intention to relinquish the right to rely on it. That intention may be expressed in a formal legal document, it may be expressed in some informal fashion or it may be inferred from conduct. In whatever fashion the intention to relinquish the right is communicated, however, the conscious intention to do so is what must be ascertained.

Waiver will be found only where the evidence demonstrates that the party waiving had (1) a full knowledge of rights; and (2) an unequivocal and conscious intention to abandon them. The creation of such a stringent test is justified since no consideration moves from the party in whose favour a waiver operates. An overly broad interpretation of waiver would undermine the requirement of contractual consideration.

As there is little doubt that Maritime had full knowledge of its rights under the respondents' policy, the waiver issue turns entirely on Maritime's intentions. The respondents have identified several factors which, in their view, support a finding that Maritime "clearly and unequivocally" intended to waive its right to timely payment. In particular, the respondents submit that by encouraging policyholders to pay by mail, by requesting payment of the 1984 premium after the expiry of the policy grace period, by delaying issuance of the February lapse notice, by failing to return the $45 partial payment, and in accepting late payment in 1981, Maritime waived its right to require payment in accordance with the terms of the policy.

It is not necessary to address each of the factors identified by the respondents, for it seems clear that the November letter, taken alone, constituted a waiver of Maritime's right to receive timely payment under the policy. The November letter contained the following statement: "Unfortunately this policy is now technically out of force, and we will require immediate payment of $1,361.00 to pay the July 1984-85 premium."

As late as November 28, 1984, Maritime was willing to continue coverage under the policy upon payment of the July, 1984 premium. The November letter makes no mention of evidence of insurability, nor does it speak of reinstatement. As such, it constitutes clear evidence of Maritime's intention to waive its right to compel timely payment. In this regard, little weight should be given to the assertion that the policy was "technically out of force", for the qualifier "technical" removes all meaning from the expression "out of force". In any event, this assertion does not detract from the clarity of Maritime's demand for payment.

The appellant submits that, whereas the right to compel timely payment is clearly waived where premium payments are received and deposited by an insurance company after the expiry of the policy grace period . . ., a mere demand for payment beyond the grace period is insufficient. Support for that proposition is found in *McGeachie v. North American Life Assurance Co.* (1893), 20 O.A.R. 187 (C.A.); affirmed 23 S.C.R. 148, and in *Northern Life Assurance Co. of Canada v. Reierson*, [1977] 1 S.C.R. 390. In both cases, this court concluded that a demand for payment was equivocal or insufficient to give rise to a waiver. However, in some circumstances a demand for payment may constitute waiver. The nature of waiver is such that hard and fast rules for what can and cannot constitute waiver should not be proposed. The overriding consideration in each case is whether one party communicated a clear intention to waive a right to the other party.

The demand for payment in the present appeal provides stronger evidence of waiver than did the demands in either *McGeachie* or *Reierson.* The demand for payment by the appellant in its November letter was made well beyond the expiry of the grace period. As well, payment in the present case was tendered prior to the occurrence of the event insured against. Any doubt about whether Maritime intended to waive the time requirements of the policy was resolved by the testimony of its legal advisor, who indicated that, having received the $45 partial payment, Maritime was still awaiting payment of the July, 1984 premium in January, 1985. It was for this reason that the lapse notice was not sent until February 2, 1985. In these circumstances, the demand for payment in the November letter was a clear and unequivocal expression of Maritime's intention to continue coverage upon payment of the July premium and, as such, constituted waiver of the time requirements for payment under the policy.

As the November letter constituted waiver, the question is then whether the waiver was still in effect when SRB tendered payment of the missing premium in July, 1985.

Waiver can be retracted if reasonable notice is given to the party in whose favour it operates: *Hartley v. Hymans*, [1920] 3 K.B. 475; *Charles Rickards Ltd. v. Oppenheim*, [1950] 1 K.B. 616; *Guillaume v. Stirton* (1978), 88 D.L.R. (3d) 191 (Sask. C.A.); leave to appeal to S.C.C. refused [1978] 2 S.C.R. vii. As Waddams notes, the "reasonable notice" requirement has the effect of protecting reliance by the person in whose favour waiver operates: The *Law of Contracts, supra*, at paras. 604 and 606. It follows that a notice requirement should not be imposed where reliance is not an issue: *ibid.* at para. 606. In the present appeal, the respondents were not aware of Maritime's waiver until they received the November letter, along with the lapse notice and late payment offer, in April, 1985. It follows that they did not rely on Maritime's waiver. In such circumstances, Maritime was not required to give any notice of its intention to lapse the policy. The statement that "this policy has lapsed", contained in the February lapse notice, took effect on its terms.

In any event, once the respondents opened their mail in April, 1985, they clearly became aware of Maritime's intention to retract its waiver. An informal communication of a party's intention to insist on strict compliance with the terms of a contract is sufficient notice: see, *e.g., Guillaume v. Stirton, supra.* The respondents did not tender a replacement cheque until July, 1985, three months after they became aware of Maritime's intentions. As such, even if a reasonable notice requirement were imposed, it would be adequately met by the respondents' failure to act between April and July.

Maritime's waiver, as contained in the November letter, was no longer in effect when the respondents sought to make payment in July, 1985. Maritime had no obligation to accept the replacement cheque, and the policy lapsed. Maritime was required to reinstate coverage only if the respondents provided evidence of insurability, which was not possible in this case. Therefore, the respondents are not entitled to any of the benefits under the policy.

[The court declined to exercise its equitable power, as enshrined in the Judicature Act, R.S.A. 1980, c. J-1, s. 10, to relieve against the forfeiture of the life insurance policy. Appeal allowed.]

NOTE

In *Kubanowski v Primerica Life Insurance Co. of Canada*, [1997] 9 W.W.R. 101 (Sask. Q.B.), the court held that acceptance and deposit of a premium payment after expiry of the time to pay in a "special offer" after the policy had lapsed, was not in the circumstances sufficient evidence of waiver of the term of timely payment. As in *Saskatchewan River Bungalows*, the "special offer waiver" of the grace period provision was no longer in effect when payment was attempted.

INTERNATIONAL KNITWEAR ARCHITECTS INC. v. KABOB INVESTMENTS LTD.

(1995), 17 B.C.L.R. (3d) 125 (C.A.)

The plaintiff tenant leased commercial premises from the defendant landlord for a five-year term from 1 May, 1987, to 30 April, 1992, for a basic rent of $2,290.93 monthly, increasing yearly to $3,150.03 from 1 May, 1991, plus additional rent (taxes, rates and assessments). On 1 May, 1989, the tenant was experiencing difficulties, and the landlord agreed to reduce the rent to $1,000.00 per month. On 13 December, 1991, no payment having been made on 1 December, 1991, the landlord distrained for arrears of basic rent throughout the term of the lease and on 24 December, 1991, demanded arrears, interest and payment in full from 1 January, 1992. The tenant sued for damages for illegal distress, and the landlord counterclaimed for rent and other moneys owing under the lease for the whole of the term.

SOUTHIN J.A. [delivering the judgment of the court] . . .

Insofar as the counterclaim extends over the whole of the term, it must fail, at least until December 1991 because of the learned judge's findings on the issue of promissory estoppel. The tenant's position is that if the promissory estoppel contained within it a term that the appellant could revive the obligation to pay full rent upon giving reasonable notice, the demand of 24th December, 1991, was ineffective to revive the obligation before the term ended on 30th April, 1992. Failing acceptance of that position, the tenant says the notice could not take effect until at least the 1st February, 1992.

Where notice must be given to effect a purpose, at least two questions arise:

1. Must the notice be for a reasonable period?

2. If so, must the notice specify the period correctly—a so-called "dated notice": see *Australian Blue Metal Ltd. v. Hughes*, [1962] 3 All E.R. 335 (P.C.), especially at 341-343?

Each of these questions must be determined in the absence of express contractual provisions on the facts of the case. In light of the course of conduct between the tenant and the appellant over more than two years, I am of the opinion that the landlord was entitled to give, and the tenant was obliged to accept, notice reasonable in length to revive the obligations of the lease, but the notice need not be a dated notice, and that, in this case, a reasonable time, from the 24th December, 1992 [*sic*], to revive the obligation for both the basic rent and the additional rent, was to the 1st February, 1992.

The tenant is therefore liable for the amounts payable under the lease for the final three months of the term.

.....

[The landlord's appeal was allowed in part.]

NOTES and QUESTIONS

1. Many contracts stipulate that "time is of the essence", which means that the innocent party may terminate the agreement for any delay. Where one party extends the time for performance to a specified date, does this constitute waiver of the condition as to time, requiring reasonable notice to terminate, or merely a substitution of the later date for the one originally stipulated? Compare *Landbank Minerals Ltd. v. Wesgeo Ent. Ltd.*, [1981] 5 W.W.R. 524 (Alta. Q.B.) with *Kapchinsky v. Begam Hldg. Ltd.* (1982), 20 Alta. L.R. (2d) 294 (Q.B.). The *Landbank* approach was approved in British Columbia in *Salama Enterprises (1988) Inc. v. Grewal* (1992), 66 B.C.L.R. (2d) 39 (C.A.), additional reasons at (August 24, 1992), Doc. CA012231 (B.C. C.A.), leave to appeal to S.C.C. refused (1992), 70 B.C.L.R. (2d) xxxiii (note) (S.C.C.).

2. In *Brikom Invts. Ltd. v. Carr*, [1979] Q.B. 467 (C.A.), 99-year apartment leases contained an express covenant by the landlords to repair but also a provision that the tenant would pay a maintenance charge and an annual apportioned contribution in respect of excess expenses incurred by the landlords. Before and after the leases were executed, the landlords promised that they would repair the roofs at their own cost. Some of the tenants later assigned their leases, repeating these assurances to the assignees. The landlords later claimed contributions for the repair of the roofs under the original leases.

Lord Denning M.R. applied the doctrine of promissory estoppel both to the original tenants and to the assignees, saying that the burden and the benefit of an estoppel "run down the line of assignor and assignee on each side."

Roskill and Cumming-Bruce L.JJ. preferred not to rely on the doctrine of promissory estoppel. They held that, in regard to tenants signing the lease on the faith of the representation, there was a binding collateral contract. In regard to the assignees, they held that the assurances constituted a "plain waiver", which ended the obligation to pay contributions for those repairs "once and for all."

Does it make any difference what the assurances are called or whether they are made before or after the contract is executed?

3. The authorities are divided as to whether the parol evidence rule, which is discussed in Chapter 7, section 6, or a contractual clause that requires waivers to be in writing preclude the operation of promissory estoppel. See, *e.g.*, *Sledz v. Edmonton Home Fair Ltd.*, [1997] A.J. No. 1240, , 28 R.P.R. (3d) 132 (Q.B.) (no) and *Manitoba Pool Elevators v. Gorrell*, [1998] M.J. No. 92, , [1998] 6 W.W.R. 596, 127 Man. R. (2d) 4 (Q.B.) (yes, in absence of unconscionable conduct).

4. In *Ajayi v. Briscoe (R.T.) (Nigeria) Ltd.*, [1964] 3 All E.R. 556 (P.C.), Lord Hodson described the principle of promissory estoppel as follows, at 559:

> [W]hen one party to a contract in the absence of fresh consideration agrees not to enforce his rights an equity will be raised in favour of the other party. This equity is, however, subject to the qualification (a) that the other party has altered his position, (b) that the promisor can resile from his promise on giving reasonable notice, which need not be a formal notice, giving the promisee reasonable opportunity of resuming his position, (c) the promise only becomes final and irrevocable if the promisee cannot resume his position.

(d) THE RELIANCE

W.J. ALAN & CO. v. EL NASR EXPORT & IMPORT CO.

[1972] 2 Q.B. 189, [1972] 2 All E.R. 127 (C.A.)

The buyers, an Egyptian company trading in Tanzania purchased 500 tons of coffee from the sellers, Kenyan coffee producers, under two separate contracts of 250 tons each at a price of "Shs. 262/-. . . per c/wt. nett f.o.b. Mombasa." Payment, as is customary, was to be by confirmed, irrevocable letter of credit and the contract was specifically to be governed by English law.

The price in the contracts of sale clearly referred to Kenyan shillings, though at the time the contract was made this was of little importance as there was parity between sterling and Kenyan currency. On September 20th, 1967, the buyers opened a confirmed letter of credit in sterling through a bank in Dar es Salaam.

The sellers raised no complaint when the letter of credit was confirmed in sterling. In September, 1967, the shipped 250 tons of coffee under the first contract and 29 tons in partial fulfilment of the second contract. They immediately operated the letter of credit by invoicing the bank in sterling and by accepting payment in sterling.

On November 16th, 1967, the sellers shipped the remaining 221 tons and on November 18th they prepared an invoice for this shipment in sterling. Before the documents were presented for payment, it was announced that sterling would be devalued, but it was not known whether there would be an equivalent devaluation of Kenyan currency. The sellers nevertheless sent their invoice to the buyers' bank and were duly paid in sterling.

On November 21st, it became known that Kenyan currency would not be devalued and the sellers prepared an invoice for an extra 165,530 Kenyan shillings to offset devaluation and to ensure that they would be paid the full contract price in Kenyan shillings. However, the buyers contended that nothing more was owed to the sellers. The sellers brought an action for the invoice amount.

MEGAW L.J. . . . As I see it, the necessary consequence of that offer and acceptance of a sterling credit is that the original term of the contract of sale as to the money of account was varied from Kenyan currency to sterling. The payment, and the sole payment, stipulated by the contract of sale was by the letter of credit. The buyers, through the confirming bank, had opened a letter of credit which did not conform, because it provided sterling as the money of account. The sellers accepted that offer by making use of the credit to receive payment for a part of the contractual goods. By that acceptance, as the sellers must be deemed to have known, not only did the confirming bank become irrevocably bound by the terms of the offer (and by no other terms), but so also did the buyers become bound. Not only did they incur legal obligations as a result of the sellers' acceptance—for example, an obligation to indemnify the bank—but also the buyers could not thereafter have turned round and said to the sellers (for example, if Kenyan currency had devalued against sterling) that the bank would thereafter pay less for the contractual goods than the promised sterling payment of £262 per ton. If the buyers could not revert unilaterally to the original currency of account, once they had offered a variation which had been accepted by conduct, neither could the sellers so revert. The contract had been varied in that respect.

The sellers, however, contend that they were, indeed, entitled to make use of the non-conforming letter of credit offered to them, without impairing their rights for the future under the original terms of the contract, if and when they chose to revert. They seek to rely on the analogy of a sale of goods contract where the goods are deliverable by instalments, and one instalment falls short of the prescribed quality. The buyer is not obliged, even if in law he could do so, to treat the contract as repudiated. He is not, it is said, even obliged to complain. But he is in no way precluded from insisting that for future instalments of the goods the seller shall conform with the precise terms of the contract as to quality. That is not, in my opinion, a true analogy. The relevant transaction here is not one of instalments. It is a once-for-all transaction. It is the establishment of a credit which is to cover the whole of the payment for the whole of the contract. Once it has been accepted by the sellers, the bank is committed, and is committed in accordance with its accepted terms, and no other terms. Once the credit is established and accepted it is unalterable, except with the consent of all the parties concerned, all of whose legal rights and liabilities have necessarily been affected by the establishment of the credit. Hence the sellers cannot escape from the consequences of the acceptance of the offered credit by any argument that their apparent acceptance involved merely a temporary acquiescence which they could revoke or abandon at will, or on giving notice. It was an acceptance which, once made, related to the totality of the letter of credit transaction; and the letter of credit transaction was, by the contract of sale, the one and only contractual provision for payment. When the letter of credit was accepted as a transaction in sterling as the currency of account, the price under the sale contract could not remain as Kenyan currency.

For the buyers it was submitted further that, if there were not here a variation of the contract, there was at least a waiver, which the sellers could not, or did not properly revoke. I do not propose to go into that submission at any length. On analysis, it covers much the same field as the question of variation. In my view, if there were no variation, the buyers would still be entitled to succeed on the ground of waiver. The relevant principle is, in my opinion, that which was stated by Lord Cairns L.C. in *Hughes v. Metropolitan Ry. Co.* [(1877), 2 App. Cas. 439 (H.L.)]. The acceptance by the sellers of the sterling credit was, as I have said, a once-for-all acceptance. It was not a concession for a specified period of time or one which the sellers could operate as long as they chose and thereafter unilaterally abrogate; any more than the buyers would have been entitled to alter the terms of the credit or to have demanded a refund from the sellers if, after this credit had been partly used, the relative values of the currencies had changed in the opposite way. . . .

LORD DENNING M.R. [Following a clear discussion of the nature of payments under a confirmed, irrevocable letter of credit, Lord Denning continued:] All that I have said so far relates to a 'conforming' letter of credit; that is, one which is in accordance with the stipulations in the contract of sale. But in may cases—and our present case is one—the letter of credit does not conform. Then negotiations may take place as a result of which the letter of credit is modified so as to be satisfactory to the seller. Alternatively, the seller may be content to accept the letter of credit as satisfactory, as it is, without modification. Once this happens, then the letter of credit is to be regarded as if it were a conforming letter of credit. It will rank accordingly as conditional payment.

There are two cases on this subject. One is *Panoutsos v. Raymond Hadley Corpn. of New York* [[1917] 2 K.B. 473 (C.A.)], but the facts are only to be found fully set out in 22 Com. Cas. 308. The other is *Furst (Enrico) & Co. v. Fischer (W.E.)* [[1960] 2 Lloyd's Rep. 340]. In each of those cases the letter of credit did not conform to the contract of sale. In each case the non-conformity was that it was not a confirmed credit. But the sellers took no objection to the letter of credit on that score. On the contrary, they asked for the letter of credit to be extended; and it was extended. In each case the sellers sought afterwards to cancel the contract on the ground that the letter of credit was not in conformity with the contract. In each case the court held that they could not do so.

What is the true basis of those decisions? Is it a variation of the original contract or a waiver of the strict rights thereunder or a promissory estoppel precluding the seller from insisting on his strict rights or what else? In *Enrico Furst* Diplock J. said it was a classic case of waiver. I agree with him. It is an instance of the general principle which was first enunciated by Lord Cairns L.C. in *Hughes v. Metropolitan Ry. Co.* and rescued from oblivion by *Central London Property Trust Ltd. v. High Trees House Ltd.* [*supra*]. The principle is much wider than waiver itself; but waiver is a good instance of its application. The principle of waiver is simply this: if one party by his conduct, leads another to believe that the strict rights arising under the contract will not be insisted on, intending that the other should act on that belief and he does act on it, then the first party will not afterwards be allowed to insist on the strict legal rights when it would be inequitable for him to do so: see *Plasticmoda Societa Per Azioni v. Davidsons (Manchester) Ltd.* [[1952] 1 Lloyd's Rep. 527 (C.A.)]. There may be no consideration moving from him who benefits by the waiver. There may be no detriment to him by acting on it. There may be nothing in writing. Nevertheless, the one who waives his strict rights cannot afterwards insist on them. His strict rights are at any rate suspended so long as the waiver lasts. He may on occasion be able to revert to his strict legal rights for the future by giving reasonable notice in that behalf, or otherwise making it plain by his conduct that he will therafter insist on them. . . . But there are cases where no withdrawal is possible. It may be too late to withdraw; or it cannot be done without injustice to the other party. In that event he is bound by his waiver. He will not be allowed to revert to his strict legal rights. He can only enforce them subject to the waiver he has made.

Instances of these principles are ready to hand in contracts for the sale of goods. A seller may, by his conduct, lead the buyer to believe that he is not insisting on the stipulated time for exercising an option: see *Bruner v. Moore* [[1904] 1 Ch. 305]. A buyer may, by requesting delivery, lead the seller to believe that he is not insisting on the contractual time for delivery: see *Rickards (Charles)*

Ltd. v. Oppenheim [[1950] 1 K.B. 616]. A seller may, by his conduct, lead the buyer to believe that he will not insist on a confirmed letter of credit: see *Plastic-moda*, but will accept an unconfirmed one instead: see *Panoutsos v. Raymond Hadley Corpn. of New York* and *Enrico Furst v. Fischer*. A seller may accept a less sum for his goods than the contracted price, thus inducing him to believe that he will not enforce payment of the balance: see *Central London Property Trust Ltd. v. High Trees House Ltd.* and *D. & C. Builders Ltd. v. Rees* [*supra*]. In none of these cases does the party who acts on the belief suffer any detriment. It is not a detriment, but a benefit to him, to have an extension of time or to pay less, or as the case may be. Nevertheless, he has conducted his affairs on the basis that he has that benefit and it would not be equitable now to deprive him of it.

The judge rejected this doctrine because, he said, "there is no evidence of the [buyers] having acted to their detriment". I know that it has been suggested in some quarters that there must be detriment. But I can find no support for it in the authorities cited by the judge. The nearest approach to it is the statement of Viscount Simonds in the *Tool Metal* case [*Tool Metal Mfg. Co. Ltd. v. Tungsten Electric Co. Ltd.*, [1955] 2 All E.R. 657 (H.L.)] that the other must have been led "to alter his position", which was adopted by Lord Hodson in *Ajayi v. Briscoe (R.T.) (Nigeria) Ltd.* [[1964] 3 All E.R. 556 (P.C.)]. But that only means that he must have been led to act differently from what he otherwise would have done. And, if you study the cases in which the doctrine has been applied, you will see that all that is required is that the one should have "*acted* on the belief induced by the other party". . . .

STEPHENSON L.J. [agreed with Megaw L.J. that the contract had been varied. On the subject of waiver, he said:] . . . I would leave open the question whether the action of the other party induced by the party who "waives" his contractual rights can be any alteration of his position, as Lord Denning M.R. has said, or must, as the judge thought, be an alteration to his detriment, or for the worse, in some sense. In this case the buyers did, I think, contrary to the judge's view, act to their detriment on the sellers' waiver, if that is what it was, and the contract was varied for good consideration, which may be another way of saying the same thing; so that I need not, and do not, express a concluded opinion on that controversial question.

[Appeal allowed.]

QUESTIONS

1. What was the consideration for the variation?

2. If the bank had not honoured the sterling letter of credit, what would have been the sellers' remedy?

3. Is this case distinguishable from *John Burrows Ltd. v. Subsurface Surveys Ltd., supra*?

SOCIÉTÉ ITALO-BELGE POUR LE COMMERCE ET L'INDUSTRIE S.A. v. PALM AND VEGETABLE OILS (MALAYSIA) SDN BHD; THE POST CHASER

[1982] 1 All E.R. 19 (Q.B.)

The plaintiffs agreed to sell palm oil, purchased from Kievit, to the defendants, who in turn contracted to sell the consignment to sub-buyers, Conti, and "in a string" to further sub-buyers, Lewis & Peat, I.C.C., and NOGA. The terms of the contract required "Declaration of ship to be made to buyers in writing as soon as possible after vessel's sailing." The sellers did not give this declaration until more than a month after the ship sailed, but on receipt of the declaration the buyers and Conti made no protest about its lateness, although the other sub-buyers did. Furthermore, on 20th January the buyers sent a message requesting the sellers to hand over the documents covering the consignment to Conti. When the sub-buyers rejected the documents two days later the buyers also rejected them and the sellers were forced to sell the oil elsewhere at a loss. The sellers claimed damages.

The court found that the delay in making the declaration of ship gave the buyers the right to reject the sellers' tender of documents.

ROBERT GOFF J. . . . I turn then to the second question in this case, viz whether the buyers waived their right to reject the sellers' tender of documents. Both counsel . . . were in agreement that the applicable principles were those of equitable estoppel. . . .

[Goff J. discussed whether the buyers' message to the sellers on 20th January constituted an unequivocal representation that they did not intend to enforce their strict legal rights to reject the sellers' tender of documents. He considered that the message] was in terms an unqualified request to Kievit to present the documents to the buyers' own sub-buyers, Conti. Furthermore, it was accompanied by the buyers' request to debit them in respect of the difference between their purchase price ($792.50) and their sale price to Conti ($605) which reinforced the impression that this was not intended to be a provisional presentation in the hope that Conti could persuade Lewis & Peat to accept the documents but was a representation by the buyers that they were prepared to accept the documents, thus waiving any defect in the prior declaration of shipment. In my judgment, this was a sufficiently unequivocal representation for the purposes of waiver.

However, there next arises the question whether there was any sufficient reliance by the sellers on this representation to give rise to an equitable estoppel. Here there arose a difference . . . as to the degree of reliance which is required. It is plain . . . from the speech of Lord Cairns LC in *Hughes v. Metro. Ry. Co.* (1877), 2 App. Cas. 439 at 448, that the representor will not be allowed to enforce his rights 'where it would be inequitable having regard to the dealings which have taken place between the parties'. Accordingly there must be such action, or inaction, by the representee on the faith of the representation as will render it inequitable to permit the representor to enforce his strict legal rights.

On the findings of fact in the award before the court, there is no finding of any reliance by the sellers on the buyers' representation, save the fact that the documents covering the parcel on the Post Chaser were accordingly presented by Kievit (who in this context must be taken to have acted on behalf of the sellers) to Conti. That was done on 20 January; and by 22 January the sellers were informed by the buyers that NOGA had rejected the documents, following which the documents were passed back up the string to the sellers. The question therefore arises whether such action constituted sufficient reliance by the sellers on the buyers' representation to render it inequitable for the buyers thereafter to enforce their right to reject the documents.

The case therefore raises in an acute form the question . . . whether it is sufficient for this purpose that the representee should simply have conducted his affairs on the basis of the representation, or whether by so doing he must have suffered some form of prejudice which renders it inequitable for the representor to go back on his representation. A simple example of the latter could occur where a seller, relying on a representation by his buyer, arranged his affairs and tendered documents to the buyer and by so doing missed an opportunity to dispose of the documents elsewhere for a price greater than that available when the buyer later rejected the documents. Such a conclusion could only be based on findings of fact as to the movement of the market over the relevant period. . . .

[I]n *W.J. Alan & Co. v. El Nasr Export and Import Co.* [*supra*] Lord Denning MR, while stating the principle of equitable estoppel in terms that it must be inequitable for the representor to be allowed to go back on his representation, nevertheless considered that it might be sufficient for that purpose that the representee had conducted his affairs on the basis of the representation, and that it was immaterial whether he has suffered any detriment by doing so.

In the present case . . . the buyers' representation was made on 20 January; it was acted on the same day, by Kievit presenting the documents to Conti; and on 22 January the buyers intimated to the sellers the rejection of the documents. In these circumstances, it is impossible to say that the sellers expended any money at all in consequence of the representation (the presentation of the documents having been made by Kievit); and the time involved was so short that it is difficult to attribute any importance to it. It is impossible therefore, in my judgment, to decide the present case by saying that the sellers acted to their detriment in spending time and money on appropriations. On the other hand, the sellers did (through Kievit) present the documents; and it can therefore be said that they did conduct their affairs on the basis of the buyers' representation.

I approach the matter as follows. The fundamental principle is . . . that the representor will not be allowed to enforce his rights 'where it would be inequitable having regard to the dealings which have thus taken place between the parties'. To establish such inequity, it is not necessary to show detriment; indeed, the representee may have benefited from the representation, and yet it may be inequitable, at least without reasonable notice, for the representor to enforce his legal rights. Take the facts of *Central Property Trust Ltd. v. High Trees House Ltd.* [*supra*] the case in which Denning J breathed new life into the doctrine of equitable estoppel. The representation was by a lessor to the effect that he would be content to accept a reduced rent. In such a case, although the lessee has benefited from the reduction in rent, it may well be inequitable for the lessor to insist on his legal right to the unpaid rent, because the lessee has conducted his affairs on the basis that he would only have to pay rent at the lower rate; and a court might well think it right to conclude that only after reasonable notice could the lessor return to charging rent at the higher rate specified in the lease. Furthermore it would be open to the court, in any particular case, to infer from the circumstances of the case that the representee must have conducted his affairs in such a way that it would be inequitable for the representor to enforce his rights, or to do so without reasonable notice. But it does not follow that in every case in which the representee has acted, or failed to act, in reliance on the representation, it will be inequitable for the representor to enforce his rights for the nature of the action, or inaction, may be insufficient to give rise to the equity, in which event a necessary requirement stated by Lord Cairns LC for the application of the doctrine would not have been fulfilled.

This, in my judgment, is the principle which I have to apply in the present case. Here, all that happened was that the sellers, through Kievit, presented the documents on the same day as the buyers made their representation; and within two days the documents were rejected. Now on these simple facts, although it is plain that the sellers did actively rely on the buyers' representation, and did conduct their affairs in reliance on it, by presenting the documents, I cannot see anything which would render it inequitable for the buyers thereafter to enforce their legal right to reject the documents. In particular, having regard to the very short time which elapsed between the date of the representation and the date of presentation of the documents on the one hand and the date of rejection on the other hand, I cannot see that, in the absence of any evidence that the sellers' position had been prejudiced by reason of their action in reliance on the representation, it is possible to infer that they suffered any such prejudice. In these circumstances, a necessary element for the application of the doctrine of equitable estoppel is lacking; and I decide this point in favour of the buyers. . . .

NOTE and QUESTION

1. From time to time Canadian courts have reiterated the requirement that a party must alter its position to its detriment before promissory estoppel can apply. See, *e.g.*, *Edwards v. Harris-Intertype (Can.) Ltd.* (1983), 40 O.R. (2d) 558, affirmed 9 D.L.R. (4th) 319 (C.A.).

2. Harvey Foster Jr., who has just married, bought a home. He financed his purchase with a bank loan of $60,000 and a loan from his father of $10,000. When Harvey Jr. encountered difficulty in paying off these loans, his father said that he would forgive his debt. With the money which was thus released, Harvey Jr. invested in a new company to develop oil deposits in the Canadian North. The value of Harvey Jr.'s shares in this oil company rose steadily and Harvey Jr. sold when his capital gain was equal to the amount outstanding on the bank loan, which Harvey Jr. paid. Harvey Foster Sr., however, on hearing of his son's success, now claims the $10,000. Discuss. Would it make any difference if Harvey Jr. had not sold when he did but had retained the shares, which have continued to rise steadily in value?

(e) SWORD OR SHIELD?

PETRIDIS v. SHABINSKY

(1982), 132 D.L.R. (3d) 430 (Ont. H.C.)

The plaintiff carried on a restaurant business in a shopping centre owned and managed by the defendant. The lease, expiring on 30th June 1981, gave the plaintiff tenant an option to renew, to be exercised by 31st December 1980. In order to renew, the tenant was required to give to the landlord notice in writing 6 months prior to the expiry of the lease. Any renewal was to be on the same terms as the original lease, except that the renewal lease was not to contain any right of further renewal and the rent, if not agreed, was to be fixed by arbitration.

Towards the end of 1980 the plaintiff allegedly "mentioned to [the defendant] the need to get together on the renewal of the lease to which [the defendant] had replied that he would see the plaintiff after the holidays". From 28th January 1981 to 25th May 1981, negotiations took place both in writing and in person between the plaintiff and the defendant's employees but they were unable to agree on the rent and did not, apparently, consider arbitration. On 2nd June 1981 the defendant gave notice to the plaintiff that they would require vacant possession as of 1st July 1981. "This letter . . . galvanized the plaintiff" into seeing his lawyer who took the position that the option had been exercised. On 4th June 1981 the defendant accepted an offer to lease from HiFi Express (Realty) Inc. The plaintiff had spent some $180,000 on the business and could not relocate on such short notice. He sued for an injunction and a declaration that the lease had been validly renewed.

GRANGE J. . . . Turning now to the plaintiff's position, this is not, in my view, a case of promissory estoppel certainly as that doctrine is generally understood, *i.e.,* an assurance by one party that it will not enforce its legal rights with the intention that the assurance be acted upon by the other party. Even if the doctrine can apply when there is no actual detriment to the other party, and even if the doctrine can be used as a sword to establish a claim rather than as a shield in defence of a claim, the representation must certainly, at least in Canada, be at a time when a legal relationship exists: see *Can. Superior Oil Ltd. v. Paddon-Hughes Dev. Co.,* [1970] S.C.R. 932. Here, while the lease itself continued after December 31, 1980, the option did not, and it is the existence of the option that is the legal relationship upon which promissory estoppel must be founded.

However, promissory estoppel is not the only way of characterizing this transaction. People with rights are entitled to waive or suspend those rights and there may come a time in the course of that waiver or suspension when the rights are either lost or are not permitted to be enforced strictly without some notice to the other side. Ordinarily cases of this nature arise in contracts containing stipulations as to time. Examples are to be seen in *Bonner-Worth Co. v. Geddes Bros.* (1921), 50 O.L.R. 196 (C.A.), (contract for the sale of goods held to subsist after default in delivery); *Norman v. McMurray* (1913), 24 O.W.R. 532 (contract for sale of land with time of essence held to subsist after time for closing because of subsequent negotiations). . . . What happens is this: a party has a right to rescind or repudiate upon the other party's failure and if he exercises that right that is the end of the matter; but he may by word or deed waive or suspend that right and if he does equity will sometimes not permit him or will control him in the strict enforcement of those suspended or waived rights. It was expressed thus by Lord Denning M.R. in *W.J. Alan & Co. v. El Nasr Export & Import Co.* [*supra*].

There is, of course, a difference between contracts for the sale of goods or land, and options to renew leases, but the principles governing terms as to time of performance are not or should not be dissimilar. In sales where time is of the essence, a default by one party will relieve the other who is not in default. In options to renew the landlord may have no obligation other than to grant the renewal on a timely application. If the application is out of time he may refuse it or he may waive the requirement. Perhaps he may enter into negotiations without prejudice to his rights arising from the tenant's default. But here the landlord did not assert any such rights. On the contrary it recognized the continuance of the right of the tenant to renew. As in all questions of waiver, consideration is not a necessary element because the landlord can always reassert its strict right provided it is not inequitable for it to do so.

One can find in the cases many examples of the need for strict compliance with option terms. But one can also find examples of waiver of those strict terms. One such example is *Crosby v. Temple*, [1940] 2 D.L.R. 554 [N.S.C.A.] where an option to purchase contained in a lease was found to continue to exist after the expiry of the time for its exercise simply because the parties continued to negotiate. The case is also authority that the *Statute of Frauds*, R.S.O. 1980, c. 481, is no bar to the action based on waiver. So too is *Iwanczuk v. Center Square Developments Ltd.*, [1967] 1 O.R. 447. There an oral extension of the time for closing a contract for the sale of land was held valid. It is very difficult to distinguish that case from *Brooks v. Stainer*, [1963] 2 O.R. 481, a decision of the same Court to the opposite effect and I will not attempt the distinction. I am content to say that I prefer the reasoning in *Iwanczuk*. I do not regard the extension of time here as a variation of a written contract but as a waiver of a right under that contract.

This is not a case simply of offer and non-acceptance. It is a case of the recognition of the continued existence of rights which would otherwise come to an end. As I have said, there is no doubt that the landlord could have insisted upon the expiry of the option after January 1, 1981, but that is not what it wanted. It wanted the lease to continue and it hoped to persuade the tenant to accept the proposed rent. That being so, it would, in my view, be inequitable to permit the landlord to terminate the negotiations without some reasonable notice to the tenant. What should have happened is not the peremptory immediate termination by the letter of June 2nd, but a reversion to the strict rights not of treating the option as expired but of enforcing it in accordance with an extended time-limit, perhaps in the circumstances one of only a few days. The tenant believing he had the option but without agreement as to rent could not be expected to vacate on such short notice; indeed the tenant should not be expected to vacate at all if he is willing as he obviously is to accept the renewed lease and pay rent in accordance with the contractual terms. . . .

An order will go declaring that the lease is renewed for the first term of five years. The plaintiff may give notice within 30 days of this judgment of his resort to arbitration in accordance with cl. 35.01 to determine the rent. Failing such notice the rent will be as set forth in the landlord's letter of February 24th, and in any event, shall be at that rate pending arbitration.

NOTE and QUESTIONS

1. Had the plaintiff suffered a detriment?

2. How does Grange J. distinguish between promissory estoppel and waiver? Are there grounds for his distinction?

3. In the light of *Petridis v. Shabinsky*, review *Saskatchewan River Bungalows Ltd. v. Maritime Life Assurance Co.*, *supra*, section 5(c).

4. In *Conwest Exploration Co. v. Letain*, [1964] S.C.R. 20, the respondent, L., (the original plaintiff) transferred certain claims to the appellants (defendants), with an option to purchase exercisable by Conwest's incorporating a company on or before 1st October 1958 to hold the claims and allotting to L. not less than 50,000 shares in this company. L. later borrowed money from Conwest and in exchange agreed to transfer 13,000 of these shares and option the rest to Conwest. A company was incorporated, the letters patent bearing the date 25th September 1958, but not signed and sealed until 20th October 1958. L. demanded a reconveyance of the claims and resisted an attempt to enforce the share option.

The majority of the court held that Conwest had caused the company to be incorporated by 1st October 1958, if this was required; in any event L. was estopped by his participation in the incorporation process (in signing a consent to the use of his name on 26th September 1958, and a declaration of substantial interest on 7th October 1958) from insisting on strict performance of the condition. The minority held that the company had not been incorporated by 2nd October 1958; this requirement had not been waived by the share option, or by L.'s conduct, as the option terminated automatically upon the expiration of the option period and could not be extended without consideration.

Martland J. (dissenting) stated, at 31, that the application of the doctrine of equitable estoppel "is not dependent upon which party sues the other. The basic question is as to whether, in the circumstances of the particular case, it is being used as a defence to the strict enforcement of contractual rights, or as a means of proving the existence of a contract made without consideration." Was Conwest asserting a right based on the promissory estoppel?

The facts of *Re Tudale Explorations Ltd. and Bruce* (1978), 88 D.L.R. (3d) 584 (Ont. Div. Ct.), were similar to *Conwest*. Tudale granted to the appellant, Teck, a three-year option to acquire claims, held by an agent. The agreement stated that it could be modified only by writing. The option was extended twice in writing to 30th June 1975. In late June Tudale orally agreed to a further extension, to enable Teck to submit an alternative organizational proposal. In early July, however, Tudale took the position that the agreement was terminated, and applied to recover the claims. On 8th July, Teck purported to exercise the option.

The court said that it made no difference whether one regarded Tudale's assurance as a "waiver or promissory estoppel or variation of the contract or simply [a] binding promise" or "that the promise was oral, that it lacked consideration or that it related to a future event"; as Teck had acted upon the assurance to its detriment, Tudale could not deny the extension, at least without giving Teck a reasonable time to regain its position. The court therefore, dismissed Tudale's application and ordered the claims vested in Teck's company. The court also doubted the view that promissory estoppel can only be raised as a defence and not as a cause of action. Was this necessary to the decision?

ROBICHAUD c. CAISSE POPULAIRE DE POKEMOUCHE LTÉE

(1990), 69 D.L.R. (4th) 589 (N.B. C.A.)

The facts of this case are set out in section 4(c)(i) of this chapter, in note 1 following the extract from *Re: Selectmove Ltd.*

RICE J.A. [translation, delivering a concurring judgment on the basis of promissory estoppel:] . . . In the case at bar, the appellant bases his argument on the principle of promissory estoppel in asking that the judgment in favour of the Caisse Populaire against him be removed. According to the case-law, estoppel is invoked as a grounds of defence and not as grounds for an action. A right of action cannot be founded on the principle of estoppel: *Canadian Superior Oil Ltd. v. Paddon-Hughes Development Co.* (1970), 12 D.L.R. (3d) 247. . .. This principle is invoked as a rule of evidence only against an applicant because, as in the case at bar, it would be unjust to allow him to retract a promise as a result of which the defendant had made commitments to his detriment.

This issue has been the subject of comment in several Canadian decisions. Apparently, the distinction between grounds for action and grounds for defence has been severely criticized: see Osborn J. in *Edwards v. Harris-Intertype (Canada) Ltd.* (1983), 40 O.R. (2d) 558 (H.C.J.).

In Waddams, *The Law of Contracts* (Toronto, Canada Law Book Limited, 1977), the following comments appear at p. 131:

> Some have said that the doctrine can be a shield but not a "sword", implying that it is available only to a defendant. However, it seems irrational to make enforceability depend on the chance of whether the promisee is plaintiff or defendant, and in *Combe v. Combe* itself Denning, L.J., cited cases where estoppel was used as part of the plaintiff's cause of action. If the reason for enforcement is the promisee's reliance, such reliance may be just as strong whether the promisee appears as plaintiff or defendant.

Martland J., in *Conwest Exploration Co. v. Letain* (1964), 41 D.L.R. (2d) 198 at p. 202, [1964] S.C.R. 20, said:

> While it is true that in that case [*Combe v. Combe*] the party seeking to apply the principle was the plaintiff in the action, in my opinion its application is not dependent upon which party sues the other.

In the case at bar, the Caisse Populaire can exercise its rights pre-dating the promise by relying on the judgment in its favour against the appellant without taking action against him and without the appellant being able to exercise the rights he derives from the agreement. If the principle of promissory estoppel could be invoked successfully as grounds of defence in an action by the Caisse Populaire against the appellant, then, considering the relations between them, to refuse its application on the pretext that it is not invoked as grounds of defence is, in my opinion, untenable and contrary to the principles of equity on which the doctrine is based. In the case at bar, the appellant is merely asking that the Caisse Populaire respect the promise that it made to him and on which he relied to his detriment.

. . . . .

[Ayles and Angers JJ.A. concurred that the appeal should be allowed. Appeal allowed.]

QUESTION

Coffee Imports Ltd. in Toronto entered into a contract with Safelaws Ltd. in Winnipeg for the supply of a specified quantity of Brazilian coffee at a fixed price to be delivered on 1st July, time to be of the essence of the contract. In June, Safelaws still had a large quantity of unsold coffee in stock and asked Coffee Imports Ltd. to delay delivery until 1st September. Coffee Imports agreed to this. By 1st September, however, the price of coffee had skyrocketed and Coffee Imports Ltd. refused to deliver at that price on the basis that Safelaws was in breach of contract for non-acceptance of the coffee at the due date. Has Safelaws Ltd. a claim against Coffee Imports Ltd.? How could the damages be measured? See *Charles Rickards Ltd. v. Oppenheim*, [1950] 1 K.B. 616 (C.A.) and *Owen Sound Public Library Bd. v. Mial Developments Ltd.* in section 5(a), note 2 following the extract from the *John Burrows Ltd.* case.

COMBE v. COMBE

[1951] 2 K.B. 215, [1951] 1 All E.R. 767 (C.A.)

The parties were married in 1915, but separated in 1939. On February 1, 1943, on the wife's petition, a decree nisi of divorce was pronounced. On February 9, 1943, the wife's solicitor wrote to the husband's solicitor: "With regard to permanent maintenance, we understand that your client is prepared to make her an allowance of 100*l.* per year, free of income tax". On February 19, 1943, the husband's solicitor replied that the husband had "agreed to allow your client 100*l.* per annum, free of tax". On August 11, 1943, the decree was made absolute. The wife's solicitor wrote for the first instalment of 25*l.* on August 26, and asking that future instalments should be paid on November 11, February 11, May 11, and August 11. The husband, himself, replied that he could not be expected to pay in advance. In fact, he never made any payment. The wife pressed for payment but made no application to the Divorce Court for maintenance. She had an income of between 700*l.* and 800*l.* a year. Her husband had only 650*l.* a year.

On July 28, 1950, the wife brought an action claiming from her husband 675*l.*, being in arrears of payment at the rate of 100*l.* per year for six and three-quarter years. Byrne J. held that the first three quarterly instalments of 25*l.* were barred by the Limitation Act, 1939, but gave judgment for the wife for 600*l.* He held that there was no consideration for the husband's promise to pay his wife 100*l.*, but nevertheless he held that the promise was enforceable on the principle stated in *High Trees* [*supra*] and *Robertson v. Min. of Pensions*, [1949] 1 K.B. 227, because it was an unequivocal acceptance of liability, intended to be binding, intended to be acted on and, in fact, acted on. The husband appealed.

DENNING L.J. . . . . Much as I am inclined to favour the principle stated in the *High Trees* case, it is important that it should not be stretched too far, lest it should be endangered. That principle does not create new causes of action where none existed before. It only prevents a party from insisting upon his strict legal rights, when it would be unjust to allow him to enforce them, having regard to the dealings which have taken place between the parties. That is the way it was put in *Hughes v. Metro. Ry. Co.* [(1877), 2 App. Cas. 439 (H.L.)], the case in the House of Lords in which the principle was first stated, and in *Birmingham & Dist. Land Co. v. London and North Western Ry. Co.* [(1888), 40 Ch.D. 268 (C.A.)], the case in the Court of Appeal where the principle was enlarged. It is also implicit in all the modern cases in which the principle has been developed. Sometimes it is a plaintiff who is not allowed to insist on his strict legal rights. Thus, a creditor is not allowed to enforce a debt which he has deliberately agreed to waive, if the debtor has carried on business or in some other way changed his position in reliance on the waiver. . . . A landlord, who has told his tenant that he can live in his cottage rent-free for the rest of his life, is not allowed to go back on it, if the tenant stays in the house on that footing: *Foster v. Robinson* [[1951] 1 K.B. 149 (C.A.)]. On other occasions it is a defendant who is not allowed to insist on his strict legal rights. His conduct may be such as to debar him from relying on some condition, denying some allegation, or taking some other point in answer to the claim. Thus a government department, which had accepted a disease as due to war service, were not allowed afterwards to say it was not, seeing that the soldier, in reliance of the assurance, had abstained from getting further evidence about it: *Robertson v. Min. of Pensions* [[1949] 1 K.B. 227]. A buyer who had waived the contract date for delivery was not allowed afterwards to set up the stipulated time as an answer to the seller: *Rickards (Charles) Ltd. v. Oppenheim* [[1950] 1 K.B. 616 (C.A.)]. A tenant who had encroached on an adjoining building, asserting that it was comprised in the lease, was not allowed afterwards to say that it was not included in the lease: *Perrott (J.F.) & Co. v. Cohen* [[1951] 1 K.B. 705 (C.A.)]. A tenant who had lived in a house rent-free by permission of his landlord, thereby asserting that his original tenancy had ended, was not afterwards allowed to say that his original tenancy continued. In none of these cases was the defendant sued on the promise, assurance, or assertion as a cause of action in itself: he was sued for some other cause, for example, a pension or a breach of contract, and the promise, assurance or assertion only played a supplementary role—an important role, no doubt, but still a supplementary role. That is, I think, its true function. It may be part of a cause of action, but not a cause of action in itself.

The principle, as I understand it, is that, where one party has, by his words or conduct, made to the other a promise or assurance which was intended to affect the legal relations between them and to be acted on accordingly, then, once the other party has taken him at his word and acted on it, the one who gave the promise or assurance cannot afterwards be allowed to revert to the previous legal relations as if no such promise or assurance had been made by him, but he must accept their legal relations subject to the qualification which he himself has so introduced, even though it is not supported in point of law by any consideration but only by his word.

Seeing that the principle never stands alone as giving a cause of action in itself, it can never do away with the necessity of consideration when that is an essential part of the cause of action. The doctrine of consideration is too firmly fixed to be overthrown by a side-wind. Its ill-effects have been largely mitigated of late, but it still remains a cardinal necessity of the formation of a contract, though not of its modification or discharge. I fear that it was my failure to make this clear which misled Byrne J. in the present case. He held that the wife could sue on the husband's promise as a separate and independent cause of action by itself, although, as he held, there was no consideration for it. That is not correct. The wife can only enforce the promise if there was consideration for it. That is, therefore, the real question in the case: Was there sufficient consideration to support the promise?

[Lord Denning found no consideration on the facts, concluding that:]

It may be that the wife has suffered some detriment because, after forbearing to apply to the court for seven years, she might not now be given leave to apply. . . .

Assuming, however, that she has suffered some detriment by her forbearance, nevertheless, as the forbearance was not at the husband's request, it is no consideration. . . .

The doctrine of consideration is sometimes said to work injustice, but I see none in this case. . . . I do not think it would be right for his wife, who is better off than her husband, to take no action for six or seven years and then come down on him for the whole 600*l*. . . .

[The concurring judgments of Asquith and Birkett L.JJ. are omitted.]

NOTES and QUESTIONS

1. Would it have made any difference if the wife had bought a more expensive car than she could otherwise have afforded on the strength of the husband's promise? Should it make any difference?

2. Is a finding that a promise was intended to be binding, intended to be acted upon, and was, in fact, acted upon equivalent to a finding of consideration?

See *Sloan v. Union Oil Co. of Can.*, [1955] 4 D.L.R. 664 (B.C. S.C.); *Blair v. Western Mutual Benefits Assn., supra,* Chapter 2, section 3; *Wheeldon v. Simon Fraser University* (1970), 15 D.L.R. (3d) 641 (B.C. S.C.).

3. Several cases have questioned the sword/shield dichotomy. See, *e.g., Deer Valley Shopping Centre Ltd. v. Sniderman Radio Sales & Services Ltd.* (1989), 96 A.R. 321 (Q.B.) where the plaintiff landlord was suing the defendant tenant for damages for breach of a lease. On the issue of estoppel the court stated, at 333:

> It has been suggested that estoppel can only be used as a shield, not as a sword. Thus estoppel cannot be used to enforce the promises made, but only as a defence where the promisor attempts to go back in his promise and enforce his rights as they stood before the representation. However, in my view, this is not the present state of law.. . .
>
> The Landlord is therefore entitled to rely on estoppel to prevent the Tenant from denying that there is a lease for the term of years, notwithstanding that he is using it to found his cause of action.

4. Although the doctrine of promissory estoppel may apply in other than contractual contexts, it does not, generally, lie against the Crown to prevent repeal or passage of legislation. Compare *Robertson v. Min. of Pensions*, [1949] 1 K.B. 227, with *Re Apple Meadows Ltd. and Man.* (1985), 18 D.L.R. (4th) 58 (Man. C.A.) and *Reclamation Systems Inc. v. Rae* (1996), 27 O.R. (3d) 419 (Gen. Div.).

WALTONS STORES (INTERSTATE) PTY. LTD. v. MAHER

(1988), 62 A.L.J.R. 110 (H.C.)

Waltons Stores (the appellant) negotiated with the Mahers (the respondents) for a lease of land owned by the Mahers. Waltons proposed the demolition, and replacement in accordance with their specifications, of an existing building on the land. The target date for occupation created a need for a sense of urgency.

The Mahers' solicitor told Waltons' solicitor that the Mahers could not complete construction before the target date, unless demolition began immediately. Some proposed amendments to the lease remained to be agreed. Waltons' solicitor said he had verbal instructions to accept the amendments, but that he would get formal instructions. He then sent fresh documents to the Mahers' solicitor incorporating the amendments, stating in a covering letter:

> You should note that we have not yet obtained our client's specific instructions to each amendment requested, but we believe that approval will be forthcoming. We shall let you know tomorrow if any amendments are not agreed to.

The Mahers were not notified of any objections. Their solicitor then sent to Waltons' solicitor the amended lease proposal, executed "by way of exchange". Some weeks later Waltons' solicitor returned the unsigned lease and stated their intention not to proceed. During these weeks of silence, Waltons knew that the Mahers had demolished the old building and partly erected the new building.

The Mahers sued for a declaration that a binding contract existed, specific performance, or damages in the alternative.

MASON C.J. and WILSON J. The issue in this appeal is whether, in the light of the facts, the appellant is estopped from denying the existence of a binding contract that it would take a lease of the respondents' premises at Nowra and, if so, whether the respondents can support the order made by the primary judge (Kearney J.), affirmed by the New South Wales Court of Appeal, that the appellant pay to the respondent damages in lieu of specific performance of an agreement for a lease.

.....

The estoppel set up by the respondents and found by the primary judge was a common law estoppel in the form of a representation by the appellant constituted by its silence in circumstances where it should have spoken. Likewise, the Court of Appeal based the estoppel on common law principles. . . .

Our conclusion that the respondents assumed that exchange of contracts would take place as a matter of course, not that exchange had in fact taken place, undermines the factual foundation for the common law estoppel by representation found by Kearney J. and the common law estoppel based on omission to correct a mistake favoured by the Court of Appeal. There is, as Mason and Deane JJ. pointed out in *Legione v. Hateley* (1983), 152 C.L.R. 406 at 432, a long line of authority to support the proposition that, to make out a case of common law estoppel by representation, the representation must be as to an existing fact, a promise or representation as to future conduct being insufficient: *Jorden v. Money* (1854) 5 H.L.C. 185; 10 E.R. 868; *Maddison v. Alderson* (1883) 8 App. Cas. 467 at 473. It was pointed out in *Legione*, at 432, that, although in *Thompson* [*v. Palmer* (1933), 49 C.L.R. 507] Dixon J. did not distinguish between an assumption founded upon a representation of existing fact and an assumption founded upon a representation as to future conduct, at the time the doctrine of consideration was thought to be a significant obstacle to the acceptance of an assumption founded upon a representation (or promise) as to future conduct as a basis for common law estoppel by representation. That this was so appears most clearly from the judgment of Isaacs J. in *Ferrier* [*v. Stewart* (1912), 15 C.L.R. 32] at 44. There, his Honour observed that estoppel refers "to an existing fact, and not to a promise de futuro, which must rest, if at all, on contract". However, he went on to say "But a person's conduct has reference to an existing fact, if a given state of things is taken as the assumed basis on which another is induced to act".

Because estoppel by representation is often treated as a separate category, it might be possible to confine the distinction between a representation as to existing fact and one as to future conduct to that category. The adoption of such a course would leave an estoppel based on an omission to correct a mistaken assumption free from that troublesome distinction. However, the result would be to fragment the unity of the common law conception of estoppel and to confine the troublesome distinction at the price of introducing another which is equally artificial. And the result would be even more difficult to justify in a case where, as here, the mistaken assumption as to future conduct arises as a direct consequence of a representation.

If there is any basis at all for holding that common law estoppel arises where there is a mistaken assumption as to future events, that basis must lie in reversing *Jorden v. Money* and in accepting the powerful dissent of Lord St Leonards in that case. The repeated acceptance of *Jorden v. Money* over the years by courts of the highest authority makes this a formidable exercise. We put it to one side as the respondents did not present any argument to us along these lines.

This brings us to the doctrine of promissory estoppel on which the respondents relied in this Court to sustain the judgment in their favour. Promissory estoppel certainly extends to representations (or promises) as to future conduct: *Legione*, at p. 432. So far the doctrine has been mainly confined to precluding departure from a representation by a person in a pre-existing contractual relationship that he will not enforce his contractual rights, whether they be pre-existing or rights to be acquired as a result of the representation. But Denning J. in *Central London Property Trust Ltd. v. High Trees House Ltd.* [*supra*] treated it as a wide-ranging doctrine operating outside the pre-existing contractual relationship . . . In principle there is certainly no reason why the doctrine should not apply so as to preclude departure by a person from a representation that he will not enforce a non-contractual right. . . .

There has been for many years a reluctance to allow promissory estoppel to become the vehicle for the positive enforcement of a representation by a party that he would do something in the future. Promissory estoppel, it has been said, is a defensive equity . . . and the traditional notion has been that estoppel could only be relied upon defensively as a shield and not as a sword . . .

High Trees itself was an instance of the defensive use of promissory estoppel. But this does not mean that a plaintiff cannot rely on an estoppel. Even according to traditional orthodoxy, a plaintiff may rely on an estoppel if he has an independent cause of action, where in the words of Denning LJ in *Combe v. Combe* [*supra*] the estoppel "may be part of a cause of action, but not a cause of action in itself".

But the respondents ask us to drive promissory estoppel one step further by enforcing directly in the absence of a pre-existing relationship of any kind a non-contractual promise on which the representee has relied to his detriment. For the purposes of discussion, we shall assume that there was such a promise in the present case. The principal objection to the enforcement of such a promise is that it would outflank the principles of the law of contract. Holmes J expressed his objection to the operation of promissory estoppel in this situation when he said "It would cut up the doctrine of consideration by the roots, if a promisee could make a gratuitous promise binding by subsequently acting in reliance on it": *Commonwealth v. Scituate Savings Bank*, 137 Mass 301 at 302 (Mass., 1884). . . .

There is force in these objections and it may not be a sufficient answer to repeat the words of Lord Denning MR in *Crabb v. Arun District Council* [1976] Ch. 179 at 187, "Equity comes in, true to form, to mitigate the rigours of strict law". True it is that in the orthodox case of promissory estoppel, where the promisor promises that he will not exercise or enforce an existing right, the elements of reliance and detriment attract equitable intervention on the basis that it is unconscionable for the promisor to depart from his promise, if to do so will result in detriment to the promisee. And it can be argued (see, for example, Greig and Davis, *The Law of Contract*, p. 184) that there is no justification for applying the doctrine of promissory estoppel in this situation, yet denying it in the case of a non-contractual promise in the absence of a pre-existing relationship. The promise, if enforced, works a change in the relationship of the parties, by altering an existing legal relationship in the first situation and by creating a new legal relationship in the second. The point has been made that it would be more logical to say that when the parties have agreed to pursue a course of action, an alteration of the relationship by non-contractual promise will not be countenanced, whereas the creation of a new relationship by a simple promise will be recognised: see D Jackson, "Estoppel as a Sword" (1965) 81 *Law Quarterly Review* 223 at 242.

The direct enforcement of promises made without consideration by means of promissory estoppel has proceeded apace in the United States. The *Restatement on Contracts* 2d §90 states:

> (1) A promise which the promisor should reasonably expect to induce action or forbearance on the part of the promisee or a third person and which does induce such action or forbearance is binding if injustice can be avoided only by enforcement of the promise. The remedy granted for breach may be limited as justice requires.

This general proposition developed from the treatment in particular situations of promissory estoppel as the equivalent of consideration. Thus in *Allegheny College v. National Chautauqua County Bank of Jamestown*, 246 NY 369 (N.Y., 1927), Cardozo CJ said (at 374):

> Certain . . . it is that we have adopted the doctrine of promissory estoppel as the equivalent of consideration in connection with our law of charitable subscriptions.

See Farnsworth, *Contracts* (1982) §2.19; Gilmore, *The Death of Contract* (1974), p. 129.

However, we need to view the development of the doctrine in the United States with some caution. There promissory estoppel developed partly in response to the limiting effects of the adoption of the bargain theory of consideration which has not been expressly adopted in Australia or England. It may be doubted whether our conception of consideration is substantially broader than the bargain theory ... though we may be willing to imply consideration in situations where the bargain theory as implemented in the United States would deny the existence of consideration: see Atiyah, *Consideration in Contracts: A Fundamental Restatement* (1971), pp 6-7, 27, fn 35; Treitel, "Consideration: A Critical Analysis of Professor Atiyah's Fundamental Restatement" (1976) 50 *Australian Law Journal* 439 at 440 et seq. It is perhaps sufficient to say that in the United States, as in Australia, there is an obvious inter-relationship between the doctrines of consideration and promissory estoppel, promissory estoppel tending to occupy ground left vacant due to the constraints affecting consideration.

The proposition stated in §90(1) of the *Restatement* seems on its face to reflect a closer connection with the general law of contract than our doctrine of promissory estoppel, with its origins in the equitable concept of unconscionable conduct, might be thought to allow. This is because in the United States promissory estoppel has become an equivalent or substitute for consideration in contract formation, detriment being an element common to both doctrines. Nonetheless the proposition, by making the enforcement of the promise conditional on (a) a reasonable expectation on the part of the promisor that his promise will induce action or forbearance by the promisee and (b) the impossibility of avoiding injustice by other means, makes it clear that the promise is enforced in circumstances where departure from it is unconscionable. Note that the emphasis is on the promisor's reasonable expectation that his promise will induce action or forbearance, not on the fact that he created or encouraged an expectation in the promisee of performance of the promise.

Some recent English decisions are relevant to this general discussion. *Amalgamated Property Co. v. Texas Bank* [1982] Q.B. 84 in the Court of Appeal and *Pacol Ltd. v. Trade Lines Ltd.* [1982] 1 Lloyd's Rep. 456, are instances of common law or conventional estoppel. However, the comment of Goff J. in *Texas Bank* at first instance (at 107) is significant. His Honour observed:

> Such cases are very different from, for example, a mere promise by a party to make a gift or to increase his obligations under an existing contract; such promise will not generally give rise to an estoppel, even if acted on by the promisee, for the promisee may reasonably be expected to appreciate that, to render it binding, it must be incorporated in a binding contract or contractual variation, and that he cannot therefore safely rely upon it as a legally binding promise without first taking the necessary contractual steps.

The point is that, generally speaking, a plaintiff cannot enforce a voluntary promise because the promisee may reasonably be expected to appreciate that, to render it binding, it must form part of a binding contract.

Crabb was an instance of promissory estoppel. It lends assistance to the view that promissory estoppel may in some circumstances extend to the enforcement of a right not previously in existence where the defendant has encouraged in the plaintiff the belief that it will be granted and has acquiesced in action taken by the plaintiff in that belief. There the defendants, knowing of the plaintiff's intention to sell his land in separate portions, encouraged the plaintiff to believe that he would be granted a right of access over their land and, by erecting gates and failing to disabuse him of his belief, encouraged the plaintiff to act to his detriment in selling part of the land without reservation of a right of way. This raised an equity in favour of the plaintiff which was satisfied by granting him a right of access and a right of way over the defendants' land. The Court of Appeal deduced from the circumstances an equity in the plaintiff to have these rights without having to pay for them. As Oliver J. pointed out in *Taylors Fashions Ltd. v. Liverpool Victoria Trustees Co. Ltd.* [1982] Q.B. 133 at 153, the Court of Appeal treated promissory estoppel and proprietary estoppel or estoppel by acquiescence as mere facets of the same general principle, a point also made by Lord Denning M.R. in *Texas Bank*, at 122, and seemingly accepted by the Privy Council in *Attorney-General of Hong Kong v. Humphreys Estate Ltd.* [1987] 1 A.C. 114 at 123-124. In *Taylors Fashions* Oliver J. also remarked (at 153) that what gave rise to the need for the court to intervene was the defendants' unconscionable attempt to go back on the assumptions which were the foundation of their dealings. Indeed, Scarman LJ in *Crabb* saw the question in terms of whether an equity had arisen from the conduct and relationship of the parties (at 193-194), concluding that the court should determine what was "the minimum equity to do justice to the plaintiff" (at 198). . . .

The decision in *Crabb* is consistent with the principle of proprietary estoppel applied in *Ramsden v. Dyson* (1866) L.R. 1 H.L. 129. Under that principle a person whose conduct creates or lends force to an assumption by another that he will obtain an interest in the first person's land and on the basis of that expectation the other person alters his position or acts to his detriment, may also bring into existence an equity in favour of that other person, the nature and extent of the equity depending on the circumstances. And it should be noted that in *Crabb*, as in *Ramsden v. Dyson*, although equity acted by way of recognising a proprietary interest in the plaintiff, that proprietary interest came into existence as the only appropriate means by which the defendants could be effectively estopped from exercising their existing legal rights.

One may therefore discern in the cases a common thread which links them together, namely, the principle that equity will come to the relief of a plaintiff who has acted to his detriment on the basis of a basic assumption in relation to which the other party to the transaction has "played such a part in the adoption of the assumption that it would be unfair or unjust if he were left free to ignore it": per Dixon J. in *Grundt*, at 675; see also *Thompson*, at 547. Equity comes to the relief of such a plaintiff on the footing that it would be unconscionable conduct on the part of the other party to ignore the assumption.

Before we turn to the very recent decision of the Privy Council in [*Attorney-General (Hong Kong) v.*] *Humphreys Estate* [(1987), 1 A.C. 114], which was not a case of proprietary estoppel, but one, like the present, arising in the course of negotiations antecedent to the making of a contract, we should say something of equity's attitude to the enforcement of voluntary promises. So far equity has set its face against the enforcement of such promises and future representations as such. The support for the exercise of a general equitable jurisdiction to make good expectations created or encouraged by a defendant given by Lord Cottenham L.C. in *Hammersley v. De Biel* (1845) 12 Cl & Fin 45; 8 E.R. 1312, affirmed by the House of Lords in that case, was undermined by the insistence in *Jorden v. Money*

on a representation of existing fact and destroyed by *Maddison v. Alderson* [*supra*]
. . .

Because equitable estoppel has its basis in unconscionable conduct, rather than the making good of representations, the objection, grounded in *Maddison v. Alderson*, that promissory estoppel outflanks the doctrine of part performance [discussed in section 8(c)(ii)(E) of this chapter] loses much of its sting. Equitable estoppel is not a doctrine associated with part performance whose principal purpose is to overcome non-compliance with the formal requirements for the making of contracts. Equitable estoppel, though it may lead to the plaintiff acquiring an estate or interest in land, depends on considerations of a different kind from those on which part performance depends. Holding the representor to his representation is merely one way of doing justice between the parties.

In *Humphreys Estate* the defendants representing the Hong Kong government negotiated with a group of companies (HKL), which included the respondent Humphreys Estate, for an exchange whereby the government would acquire 83 flats, being part of property belonging to HKL, and in exchange HKL would take from the government a Crown lease of property known as Queen's Gardens and be granted the right to develop that property and certain adjoining property held by HKL. The negotiations did not result in a contract, though the exchange of properties was agreed in principle but subject to contract. The government took possession of HKL's property and expended a substantial sum on it. HKL took possession of Queen's Gardens and demolished existing buildings and paid to the government $103,865,608, the agreed difference between the value of the two properties. HKL withdrew from the negotiations and sued to recover the amount paid and possession of the first property. The defendants claimed that HKL was estopped from withdrawing from the agreement in principle. The Privy Council rejected this claim on the ground that the government failed to show (a) that HKL created or encouraged a belief or expectation on the part of the government that HKL would not withdraw from the agreement in principle and (b) that the government relied on that belief or expectation (at 124). Their Lordships observed (at 127-128):

> It is possible but unlikely that in circumstances at present unforeseeable a party to negotiations set out in a document expressed to be 'subject to contract' would be able to satisfy the court that the parties had subsequently agreed to convert the document into a contract or that some form of estoppel had arisen to prevent both parties from refusing to proceed with the transactions envisaged by the document.

The foregoing review of the doctrine of promissory estoppel indicates that the doctrine extends to the enforcement of voluntary promises on the footing that a departure from the basic assumptions underlying the transaction between the parties must be unconscionable. As failure to fulfil a promise does not of itself amount to unconscionable conduct, mere reliance on an executory promise to do something, resulting in the promisee changing his position or suffering detriment, does not bring promissory estoppel into play. Something more would be required. *Humphreys Estate* suggests that this may be found, if at all, in the creation or encouragement by the party estopped in the other party of an assumption that a contract will come into existence or a promise will be performed and that the other party relied on that assumption to his detriment to the knowledge of the first party. *Humphreys Estate* referred in terms to an assumption that the plaintiff would not exercise an existing legal right or liberty, the right or liberty to withdraw from the negotiations, but as a matter of substance such an assumption is indistinguishable from an assumption that a binding contract would eventuate. On the other hand the United States experience, distilled in the *Restatement* (2d §90), suggests that the principle is to be expressed in terms of a reasonable expectation on the part of the promisor that his promise will induce action or forbearance by the promisee, the promise inducing such action or forbearance in circumstances where injustice arising from unconscionable conduct can only be avoided by holding the promisor to his promise.

The application of these principles to the facts of the present case is not without difficulty. The parties were negotiating through their solicitors for an agreement for lease to be concluded by way of customary exchange. *Humphreys Estate* illustrates the difficulty of establishing an estoppel preventing parties from refusing to proceed with a transaction expressed to be "subject to contract". And there is the problem identified in *Texas Bank* (at 107) that a voluntary promise will not generally give rise to an estoppel because the promisee may reasonably be expected to appreciate that he cannot safely rely upon it. This problem is magnified in the present case where the parties were represented by their solicitors.

All this may be conceded. But the crucial question remains: was the appellant entitled to stand by in silence when it must have known that the respondents were proceeding on the assumption that they had an agreement and that completion of the exchange was a formality? The mere exercise of its legal right not to exchange contracts could not be said to amount to unconscionable conduct on the part of the appellant. But there were two other factors present in the situation which require to be taken into consideration. The first was the element of urgency that pervaded the negotiation of the terms of the proposed lease. . . .

The second factor of importance is that the respondents executed the counterpart deed and it was forwarded to the appellant's solicitor on 11 November. The assumption on which the respondents acted thereafter was that completion of the necessary exchange was a formality. The next their solicitor heard from the appellant was a letter from its solicitors dated 19 January, informing him that the appellant did not intend to proceed with the matter. It had known, at least since 10 December, that costly work was proceeding on the site.

It seems to us, in the light of these considerations, that the appellant was under an obligation to communicate with the respondents within a reasonable time after receiving the executed counterpart deed and certainly when it learnt on 10 December that demolition was proceeding. It had to choose whether to complete the contract or to warn the respondents that it had not yet decided upon the course it would take. It was not entitled simply to retain the counterpart deed executed by the respondents and do nothing . . . The appellant's inaction, in all the circumstances, constituted clear encouragement or inducement to the respondents to continue to act on the basis of the assumption which they had made. It was unconscionable for it, knowing that the respondents were exposing themselves to detriment by acting on the basis of a false assumption, to adopt a course of inaction which encouraged them in the course they had adopted. To express the point in the language of promissory estoppel the appellant is estopped in all the circumstances from retreating from its implied promise to complete the contract. . . .

BRENNAN J. [reviewed the nature of estoppel in *pais* and equitable estoppel. He considered the elements of the "unconscionable conduct" required to give rise to an equitable estoppel and concluded:]

In my opinion, to establish an equitable estoppel, it is necessary for a plaintiff to prove that (1) the plaintiff assumed or expected that a particular legal relationship exists between the plaintiff and the defendant or that a particular legal relationship will exist between them and, in the latter case, that the defendant is not free to withdraw from the expected legal relationship; (2) the defendant has induced the plaintiff to adopt that assumption or expectation; (3) the plaintiff acts or abstains from acting in reliance on the assumption or expectation; (4) the defendant knew or intended him to do so; (5) the plaintiff's action or inaction will occasion detriment if the assumption or expectation is not fulfilled; and (6) the defendant has failed to act to avoid that detriment whether by fulfilling the assumption or expectation or otherwise. For the purposes of the second element, a defendant who has not actively induced the plaintiff to adopt an assumption or expectation will nevertheless be held to have done so if the assumption or expectation can be fulfilled only by a transfer of the defendant's property, a diminution of his rights or an increase in his obligations and he, knowing that the plaintiff's reliance on the assumption or expectation may cause detriment to the plaintiff if it is not fulfilled, fails to deny to the plaintiff the correctness of the assumption or expectation on which the plaintiff is conducting his affairs.

[Deane J. found an estoppel by conduct precluding Waltons from denying the existence of a binding contract. In regard to promissory estoppel, he concluded that "once it is recognized that the doctrine of estoppel is one of substantive law and equity, there is no reason why that doctrine cannot be applied as effectively in relation to a representation or assumption of a future state of affairs as to one of an existing state of affairs".

Gaudron J. found that the appellants were estopped from denying that an exchange had occurred. Appeal dismissed.]

NOTES and QUESTION

1. Several writers have discussed *Waltons*. See, *e.g.*, Leopold, "Estoppel: A Practical Appraisal of Recent Developments (1991), 7 Aust. Bar Rev. 47; Dorney, "The New Estoppel" (1991), 7 Aust. Bar Rev. 19); Prindable, "Is Offer and Acceptance No Longer a Consideration? An Examination of the Implications of the *Waltons v. Maher* Concept of Promissory Estoppel" (1996), 16 The Queensland Lawyer 169 and Robertson, "Knowledge and Unconscionability in a Unified Estoppel" (1998), 24 Monash U.L.R. 115. Some emerging themes seem to be the degree to which the different categories of estoppel have been fused, the extent of the remedy (see, *e.g.*, *Giumelli v. Giumelli* (1999), 73 A.L.J.R. 547 (H.C.)) and the limitations on "the new estoppel". You may wish to review the discussions of negotiation in good faith throughout Chapter 3, in light of *Waltons*.

2. The principle of proprietary estoppel (or estoppel by acquiescence or encouragement), as described in *Waltons*, was applied in *Zelmer v. Victor Projects Ltd.*, [1997] 7 W.W.R. 170 (B.C.

C.A.), where the words or conduct of the defendant taken as a whole led the plaintiffs to believe that they had the approval of the defendant to construct a reservoir on his land and would be granted a gratuitous easement. The court concluded that a cause of action can be based on the doctrine of proprietary estoppel, but made no attempt to generalize this principle.

English cases have stressed the element of unconscionable conduct in proprietary estoppel. See, e.g., *Lloyds Bank plc v. Carrick*, [1996] 4 All E.R. 630 (C.A.).

M. (N.) v. A. (A.T.)

(2003), 13 B.C.L.R. (4th) 73 (B.C. C.A.)

[1] HUDDART J.A. [delivering the judgment of the court] This appeal arises out of a failed relationship. It is from an order dismissing Ms. A.'s claim to enforce a promise by Mr. M. to pay the balance outstanding on the mortgage on her home in England (GBP 73,048.53) if she would come to live with him in Canada with a view to marriage.

[2] In reliance on that promise, Ms. A. resigned her permanent job with the Bank of America and moved to Vancouver in July 1993. The relationship was stormy, in part, because Mr. M. did not pay off her mortgage. He did, however, loan her $100,000 on a promissory note dated 6 April 1994. Ms. A. applied those funds to her mortgage. About a week later, Mr. M. evicted Ms. A. from his home. She has not been able to find permanent employment since, in England or Vancouver.

[3] The only issue on this appeal is whether the trial judge erred in refusing to enforce the promise on which Ms. A. relied to her detriment. About that claim, the trial judge wrote, [2001] B.C.J. No. 1986, 2001 BCSC 1358:

> [37] In my opinion, the defendant has not established the primary requirement for the application of the doctrine of promissory estoppel. While I am satisfied that the plaintiff did promise to pay off the mortgage on the defendant's house, and that the defendant relied on his promise to her detriment, the defendant has failed to establish the existence of a legal relationship between the parties at the time the promise was made.

.....

[4] Ms. A.'s counsel frankly acknowledged he was asking this Court, as he had Cohen J., to extend the application of promissory estoppel to right a wrong that is otherwise being done to Ms. A., she having suffered from her reliance on Mr. M.'s promise, albeit in a romantic relationship. He asks us to follow the path already well trod by the courts of New Zealand, Australia, and the United States, and being opened in England to an equitable remedy for injurious reliance on a promise intended to bind its maker and to be acted upon by the promisee, and acted upon by the promisee to the knowledge of the promisor.

[5] This is the approach to promissory estoppel about which Professor Waddams wrote in *The Law of Contracts* (4th ed.) Canada Law Book, 1999, at p. 141.

> ... It may therefore be suggested that Commonwealth law is moving, though rather slowly, in the direction of the Second Restatement, section 90, that is, towards the protection of promises by reason of and to the extent of subsequent reliance.

[6] The relevant part of Restatement of the Law Second, Contracts 2d, The American Law Institute, American Law Institute Publishers (1981) states:

90. Promise Reasonably Inducing Action or Forbearance

(1) A promise which the promisor should reasonably expect to induce action or forbearance on the part of the promisee or a third person and which does induce such action or forbearance is binding if injustice can be avoided only by enforcement of the promise. The remedy granted for breach may be limited as justice requires.

[7] The appellant finds further support for this extension of promissory estoppel beyond its reach as accepted currently in Canadian authorities in *Waltons Stores (Interstate) Limited v. Maher and Another* [*supra*]. At para. 26, Brennan J. summarized the Australian position:

A non-contractual promise can give rise to an equitable estoppel only when the promisor induces the promisee to assume or expect that the promise is intended to affect their legal relations and he knows or intends that the promisee will act or abstain from acting in reliance on the promise, and when the promisee does so act or abstain . . . and the promisee would suffer detriment by his action or inaction if the promisor were not to fulfill the promise.

He went on to state "equitable estoppel almost wears the appearance of contract" because the promisee's action or inaction "looks like consideration . . ."

[8] On the various analyses of the justices in that case the doctrine of promissory estoppel might be seen as the equivalent of consideration, as reason for not requiring proof of consideration for the enforcement of a promise made in the expectation of an action the promisor seeks to induce, or as a remedy comparable to the American remedy for injurious reliance. However, Justices Mason and Wilson noted at para. 25 of their reasons that the development of the doctrine in the United States must be viewed with some caution.

[9] Nevertheless, on the basis of this view of promissory estoppel, Ms. A. considers the minimum equity to do her justice is that she not be required to pay back the loan of $100,000.00 . . .

[10] The respondent says this Court should not make such a revolutionary change to the law in circumstances where the unfulfilled promise was made at the outset of a romantic relationship that by its nature involves risk-taking, and, he might have said, many promises. This is particularly so, he submits, because Parliament and the Legislature have provided statutory remedies for losses suffered on the breakdown of romantic or marriage-like relationships, among which they have not chosen to include the enforcement of an unfulfilled promise. Finally, he asks, what better test is there for the enforcement of a promise than that the common law (as understood in British Columbia) provides: did the parties intend to affect their legal relations? Here, he points out, there is no evidence either party thought a legal relationship had been created by the promise, that their legal relations had been affected, or that the promise was legally binding.

[11] The appellant replies that, if this is the correct test for the enforcement of a promise, Mr. Justice Cohen's order dismissing her claim must be set aside and the matter remitted to the trial court for consideration as to whether the parties thought the promise of Mr. M. to be legally binding.

[12] I find merit in the respondent's submission given the current status of the law of promissory estoppel in Canada, but need consider only the appellant's submission to resolve this appeal. If equitable estoppel is seen as a flexible doctrine

requiring a broad approach to preclude unconscionable conduct or injustice, I am not persuaded by the findings of the trial judge or the evidence in this case that Mr. M.'s failure to keep his promise to Ms. A. is unconscionable as the law understands that concept, and, thus, unjust. This is because, even on the analyses in *Waltons, supra*, a necessary element of promissory estoppel is the promisee's assumption or expectation of a legal relationship.

[13] In *Waltons, supra*, at 406, Mason C.J. and Wilson J. observed that the failure to fulfil a voluntary promise does not amount to unconscionable conduct. "Something more is required." At 407, they noted the crucial question: "was the [promisor] entitled to stand by in silence when it must have known that the [promisees] were proceeding on the assumption that they had an agreement and that completion of the exchange was a formality?" That assumption was the "something extra." was in the promisee's reasonable assumption that an agreement had been reached.

[14] Brennan J. saw the minimum elements required to give rise to an estoppel and, thus, of unconscionable conduct, as including an assumption or expectation as to a legal relationship between the promisor and promisee, induced by the former. This necessary element he drew from Lord Denning's opinion in *Combe v. Combe [supra]*, and maintained despite his preference for an analysis based on remedying detriment rather enforcing a promise. At 428, he identified the first two requirements of equitable estoppel, of whatever variety, in these words:

(1) the plaintiff assumed that a particular legal relationship then existed between the plaintiff and the defendant or expected that a particular legal relationship would exist between them and, in the latter case, that the defendant would not be free to withdraw from the expected legal relationship;

(2) the defendant has induced the plaintiff to adopt that assumption or expectation;

[15] Mr. Justice Deane considered an estoppel in pais had been established by proof that the promisor stood by knowingly and silently while the promisee acted to its detriment on an assumption of existing fact (the existence of a binding agreement between them) induced by the promisor. He saw promissory estoppel as an extension of the doctrine of estoppel by conduct to representations or assumptions of future fact in certain categories of case. He noted various considerations that should be taken into account in extending the doctrine to new categories of cases. Included among them were good conscience and fair dealing, the notion of mutuality, strengthening the doctrine of consideration by preventing its unjust operation in special circumstances, and the effect on the application of other laws.

[16] For Gaudron J., equitable estoppel operated "so as to compel adherence to an assumption as to rights." He was satisfied the promisee had reasonably assumed a binding agreement was in place, and that the promisor had so contributed to the assumption that it would be unfair or unjust to permit the promisor to ignore the assumption.

[17] None of the Australian High Court justices would have extended the reach of the doctrine of promissory estoppel to provide the equivalent of the

American injurious reliance remedy. By no reading of any of their opinions, would the doctrine reach to the facts of this case. 18 While it may be, as Professor Waddams suggests, that the law is moving slowly toward a more generous approach to promissory estoppel than that said by Sopinka J., at para. 13 in *Maracle, v. Travellers Indemnity Co.*, [1991] 2 S.C.R. 50, to be well settled, I can see little evidence of that movement in Canadian authorities, or for that matter, in English authorities. . . .

[19] Counsel could not point to any evidence supporting a finding that Mr. M. intended his voluntary promise to pay the balance outstanding on Ms. A.'s mortgage to have binding effect. Nor did they suggest Ms. A. was of the view his promise was binding. She believed he would follow through on his promise, and took the risk of his not doing so.

[20] The absence of any evidence as to what interest, if any, Mr. M. might acquire in her home, significant references in their correspondence to a future equal partnership and to joint plans for the English house to produce income for them jointly, and the lack of any reference to when the promise was to or could be fulfilled, suggest the promise was made in the context of a relationship both of them thought would be permanent, and result in marriage, at which point they would be life partners, not that it would be fulfilled to compensate Ms. A. for the detriment she would suffer from leaving her job and home. There was also a lack of mutuality, in that Ms. A. could be under no enforceable obligation to stay with Mr. M. if he fulfilled the promise.

[21] In these circumstances, I can see no reason to remit the matter to the trial court for further consideration, even if the trial judge can be said to have erred in requiring proof of an existing legal relationship as a necessary element of promissory estoppel. Whether he did err in that regard I prefer to leave for another case where the question requires to be answered.

[22] It follows I would dismiss the appeal.

[Prowse and Ryan JJ.A. concurred in the judgment of Huddart J.A.]

6.   Intention to Create Legal Relations

(a)   INTRODUCTION

As indicated in the first section of this chapter, civil law systems have traditionally taken intention as the touchstone of the legal enforcement of promises. The central question is whether the promisor had a deliberate and serious intention to make a binding contract. Elements such as consideration, moral obligation or writing are relevant as evidence of that intention.

Because common law rejected intention as the criterion for the enforceability of promises in favour of consideration, the question arose of whether intention had any role to play. Some writers have asserted that the ascendancy of consideration meant that the intention of the parties is irrelevant: see, *e.g.*, Tuck, "Intent to Contract and Mutuality of Assent" (1943), 21 Can. Bar Rev. 123. However, the more traditional Anglo-Canadian view is that the presence of consideration gives rise to a presumption that the parties intended to be legally bound, but this presumption is rebuttable. In a certain group of cases, commonly dealing with social and domestic arrangements, the opposite presumption arises, that the parties are presumed not to intend legal relations in the absence of clear evidence to the contrary.

The following materials deal with these cases in which the parties' intention has traditionally been considered crucial to the creation of contractual obligation. Ironically, they have little to do with the parties' actual intentions. They are more concerned with deciding which disputes are public in nature, and decided by the principles of contract law, and which are private, and not resolved by the courts. They thus deal with judges' views of the proper scope of contract law. The cases raise the question whether this category of agreement should in fact be treated differently from all other types of agreement and, in addition, focus attention on the difficult issue of how courts should ascertain the intentions of the parties. On the latter point, eminent judges have expressed apparently differing opinions. In the Year Books, Brian C.J. is quoted as stating:

> It is common knowledge that the thought of man shall not be tried, for the Devil himself knoweth not the thought of man.

In the 19th century, Bowen L.J. took the more pragmatic position that:

> The state of a man's mind is as much a fact as the state of his digestion.

These quotations are taken from *Winfield and Jolowicz on Tort*, 13th ed. (1989), at 44.

(b)   FAMILY ARRANGEMENTS

BALFOUR v. BALFOUR
[1919] 2 K.B. 571 (Eng. C.A.)

The plaintiff sued her husband for money which she claimed to be due in respect of an agreed allowance of 30*l* a month. The parties were married in August 1900. The husband, a civil engineer, had a job in Ceylon, and after the marriage he and his wife lived there together until the year 1915. In November, 1915, she came to this country with her husband, who was on leave. They remained in England until August, 1916, when the husband had to return. The wife however on the doctor's advice remained in England. On August 8, 1916, the husband being about to sail, the alleged parol agreement sued upon was made. The plaintiff testified: "In August, 1916, defendant's leave was up. I was suffering from rheumatic arthritis. The doctor advised my staying in England for some months, not to go out till November 4. On August 8 my husband sailed. He gave me a cheque from 8th to 31st for 24*l*, and promised to give me 30*l* per month till I returned". . . . In cross-examination she said that they had not agreed to live apart until subsequent differences arose between them, and that the agreement of August, 1916, was one which might be made by a couple in amity. Her husband in consultation with her assessed her needs, and said he would send 30*l* per month for her maintenance. She further said that she then understood that the defendant would be returning to England in a few months, but that he afterwards wrote to her suggesting that they had better remain apart. In March, 1918, she commenced proceedings for restitution of conjugal rights, and on July 30 she obtained a decree nisi. On December 16, 1918, she obtained an order for alimony.

Sargant J. held that the husband was under an obligation to support his wife, and the parties had contracted that the extent of that obligation should be defined in terms of so much a month. The consent of the wife to that arrangement was a usufficient consideration to constitute a contract which could be sued upon.

He accordingly gave judgment for the plaintiff. The husband appealed.

ATKIN L.J. The defence to this action on the alleged contract is that the defendant, the husband, entered into no contract with his wife, and for the determination of that it is necessary to remember that there are agreements between parties which do not result in contracts within the meaning of that term in our law. The ordinary example is where two parties agree to take a walk together, or where there is an offer and an acceptance of hospitality. Nobody would suggest in ordinary circumstances that those agreements result in what we know as a contract, and one of the most usual forms of agreement which does not constitute a contract appears to me to be the arrangements which are made between husband and wife. It is quite common, and it is the natural and inevitable result of the relationship of husband and wife, that the two spouses should make arrangements between themselves—agreements such as are in dispute in this action—agreements for allowances, by which the husband agrees that he will pay to his wife a certain sum of money, per week, or per month, or per year, to cover either her own expenses or the necessary expenses of the household and of the children of the marriage, and in which the wife promises either expressly or impliedly to apply the allowance for the purpose for which it is given. To my mind those agreements, or many of them, do not result in contracts at all, and they do not result in contracts even though there may be what as between other parties would constitute consideration for the agreement. The consideration, as we know, may consist either in some right, interest, profit or benefit accruing to one party, or some forbearance, detriment, loss or responsibility given, suffered or undertaken by the other. That is a well-known definition, and it constantly happens. I think, that such arrangements made between husband and wife are arrangements in which there are mutual promises, or in which there is consideration in form within the definition that I have mentioned. Nevertheless they are not contracts, and they are not contracts because the parties did not intend that they should be attended by legal consequences. To my mind it would be of the worst possible example to hold that agreements such as this resulted in legal obligations which could be enforced in the Courts. It would mean this, that when the husband makes his wife a promise to give her an allowance of 30s. or 2l a week, whatever he can afford to give her, for the maintenance of the household and children, and she promises so to apply it, not only could she sue him for his failure in any week to supply the allowance, but he could sue her for non-performance of the obligation, express or implied, which she had undertaken upon her part. All I can say is that the small Courts of this country would have to be multiplied one hundredfold if these arrangements were held to result in legal obligations. They are not sued upon, not because the parties are reluctant to enforce their legal rights when the agreement is broken, but because the parties, in the inception of the arrangement, never intended that they should be sued upon. Agreements such as these are outside the realm of contracts altogether. The common law does not regulate the form of agreements between spouses. Their promises are not sealed with seals and sealing wax. The consideration that really obtains for them is that natural love and affection which counts for so little in these cold Courts. The terms may be repudiated, varied or renewed as performance proceeds or as disagreements develop, and the principles of the common law as to exoneration and discharge and accord and satisfaction are such as find no place in the domestic code. The parties themselves are advocates, judges, Courts, sheriff's officer and reporter. In respect of these promises each house is a domain into which the King's writ does not seek to run, and to which his officers do not seek to be admitted. The only question in this case is whether or not this promise was of such a class or not. For the reasons given by my brethren it appears to me to be plainly established that the promise here was not intended by either party to be attended by legal consequences. I think the onus was upon the plaintiff, and the plaintiff has not established any contract. The parties were living together, the wife intending to return. The suggestion is that the husband bound himself to pay 30*l* a month under all circumstances, and she bound herself to be satisfied with that sum under all circumstances, and, although she was in ill-health and alone in this country, that out of that sum she undertook to defray the whole of the medical expenses that might fall upon her, whatever might be the development of her illness, and in whatever expenses it might involve her. To my mind neither party contemplated such a result. I think that the parol evidence upon which the case turns does not establish a contract. I think that the letters do not evidence such a contract, or amplify the oral evidence which was given by the wife, which is not in dispute. For these reasons I think the judgment of the Court below was wrong and that this appeal should be allowed.

[The concurring judgments of Warrington L.J. and Duke L.J. are omitted.]

NOTES and QUESTIONS

1. Did the wife give consideration for the husband's promise?

2. Should such an agreement be binding? See generally Hedley, "Keeping Contract in its Place—*Balfour v. Balfour* and the Enforcement of Informal Agreements" (1985), 5 Oxford Jl. of Leg. Stud. 391.

3. The concept of family underlying *Balfour* is of course fluid. For example, the Family Maintenance Act, C.C.S.M., c. F20, s. 4(1) as amended, provides for the mutual support obligation of spouses and common law partners and s. 5 states as follows:

> The right of a spouse or common-law partner to support and maintenance within the meaning of section 4 includes the right, while living with the other spouse or common-law partner, to periodic reasonable amounts for clothing and other personal expenses and the right to sole discretion free of all interference from the other spouse or common-law partner in the use of those amounts.

A common law partner is defined in the Act as "a person who, not being married to the other person, cohabited with him or her in a conjugal relationship (a) for a period of at least three years, or (b) for a period of at least one year and they are together the parents of a child". A mutual support obligation also exists in other provinces, although the provinces vary in their definition of "spouse". In *M. v. H.*, [1999] 2 S.C.R. 3, the Supreme Court of Canada declared the definition of "spouse" in s. 29 of the Family Law Act, R.S.O. 1990, c. F-3 to be unconstitutional in excluding same sex couples. British Columbia had previously amended (Family Relations Amendment Act, S.B.C. 1997, c. 20, s. 1(c)) the definition of "spouse" in this connection in the Family Relations Act R.S.B.C. 1996, c. 128 to include "persons of the same gender".

4. The difficulty of creating enforceable agreements between spouses does not appear to have extended to separation agreements. In *Merritt v. Merritt*, [1970] 2 All E.R. 760 (C.A.), Lord Denning M.R. stated at 762 that " . . . it is altogether different when the parties are not living in amity but are separated, or about to separate. They then bargain keenly. They do not rely on honourable understandings. They want everything cut and dried. It may safely be presumed that they intend to create legal relations." Widgery L.J. said at 763: " . . . I find it unnecessary to go so far as to say that there is a presumption in favour of the creation of legal relationships when the marriage is breaking up, but certainly there is no presumption against the creation of such legal relations as there is when the parties are living happily together."

Separation agreements may be recognized by statute. For example, the Family Maintenance Act, C.C.S.M., c. F20, as amended, states the effect of a separation agreement:

> 9(2) Where two spouses or common-law partners have separated by mutual agreement, and one of them has agreed in writing to release the other from liability for support and maintenance or to accept from the other specified periodic amounts for support and maintenance, no order shall be made under this Act for the support and maintenance of the spouse or common-law partner who has so agreed.

Subsection (2) does not apply where the payer is in default, "where the support and maintenance . . . was inadequate having regard to the circumstances of both spouses or common-law partners at the date of the agreement", or where the payee "has become a public charge or a person in need of public assistance" (s. 9(3)). Section 53 of the Act provides for the filing of separation agreements for the purpose of enforcement.

The Divorce Act, R.S.C. 1985, c. 3 (2nd Supp.) as amended, s. 15.2(4)(*c*), requires the court, in making an order for support, to take into consideration "any . . . agreement or arrangement relating to support of either spouse". The validity of separation agreements has also been recognized by the Marital Property Act, C.C.S.M., c. M45, and similar legislation in other provinces. For commentary on separation agreements, see Shaffer and Melamed, "Separation Agreements Post-*Moge*, *Willick* and *L.G. v. G.B.*: A New Trilogy?" (1999), 16 Can. J. of Fam.L. 51.

5. Traditionally, marriage contracts, made between spouses either before or during the marriage, were largely the preserve of the rich. Jackie and Aristotle Onassis reportedly had a 170-clause marriage contract. Gradually such contracts became more popular among educated middle-class couples. Typical issues were money and property, often including provision for equal sharing; careers; domicile; names; children; sex, including, *e.g.*, extra-marital affairs; freedom and privacy; responsibilities for household chores and other more personal questions: "Ralph agrees not to pick, nag or comment about Wanda's skin blemishes" and both parties agree to avoid using the words "married to, married, husband, wife . . . and other derogatory terms". Many were re-negotiable after a certain period and endeavoured to set out their own grounds for divorce. Do you think such agreements would be enforceable? What would be the remedies for breach?

During the 1970s provinces passed matrimonial property legislation, addressing the equitable division of property, typically on marriage breakdown. Such legislation recognizes the validity of marriage contracts. Contracts, which may be subject to various formal requirements, *e.g.*, that they be in writing or filed in some fashion, may depart from the statutory division of property regime. Such contracts, while enforceable, are nevertheless subject to challenge on the ground of unfairness. See *Hartshorne v. Hartshorne*, 236 D.L.R. (4th) 193, in which a husband and wife made a contract that their property was separate, but with a provision that the wife would be entitled to 3% interest in the matrimonial home for each year the parties were married up to a maximum of 49%. In upholding the agreement, the majority stated at para 46:

> Where, as in the present case, the parties have anticipated with accuracy their personal and financial circumstances at the time of distribution, and where they have truly considered the impact of their choices, then, without more, a finding that their Agreement operates unfairly should not be made lightly. This does not mean that no attention should be given to the possible deficit in the assets and future income of the spouse who chose to stay at home and facilitate the professional development of the other spouse, compared to what they would realistically have been otherwise . . . A fair distribution of assets must of course take into account sacrifices made and their impact, the situation of the parties at the time of distribution, their age, education and true capacity to reintegrate into the work force and achieve economic independence in particular. But this must be done in light of the personal choices made and of the overall situation considering all property rights under the marriage agreement and other entitlements. In the present case, the main feature of the Agreement was the desire that each spouse retain the assets earned before the marriage, sharing equitably assets acquired afterwards being the rule. This will be fair on dissolution of the marriage if Mrs. Hartshorne is not left without means and facing true hardship in reclaiming her professional status and income, in light also of her parental obligations. Consideration must be given to the actual situation as it unfolded.

Thus, aside from the issue of intention to create legal relations, the courts must be attentive to the appropriate balance between freedom of contract and protection of vulnerable family members. For further discussion, see Chapter 12, section 3.

It may be anticipated that marriage contracts will become much more common as they have long been in civil law jurisdictions, such as Québec, which have, traditionally, had community of property systems or, at least, provisions for equal division on termination of the marriage.

6. Some couples enter into cohabitation agreements instead of getting married. Aside from any question of intention to create legal relations, there may be issues of public policy here. See Chapter 13, section 2(b).

7. In *Beaudoin v. Waters* (1997), 31 R.F.L. (4th) 79 (Alta. Q.B.), at 92, the court did not find a binding contract to renovate a home jointly by the defendants, who were separated at the time, despite a written "Construction Agreement" between the female defendant and her then lover, the plaintiff. "Suggesting that there is a presumption against finding an enforceable contract in such situations is perhaps an overstatement of the principle. Nevertheless, a court must exercise great care in finding a contractual relationship when the interpretation of the parties' actions is equally consistent with their having provided the services voluntarily, by reason of friendship or other affinity".

8. Harvey Foster Sr. promises to pay $10,000 per annum to Harvey Jr. as long as Harvey Jr. is attending law school. In Harvey Jr.'s second year, however, Harvey Sr. decides to reduce his son's allowance to $2,000 per annum. Discuss. Would it make any difference if Harvey Sr. had promised to buy Harvey Jr. a house if Harvey Jr., now aged 40, gave up his lucrative position as a realtor in Toronto and moved back to Winnipeg in order to attend the University of Manitoboggan Law School? Could Harvey Sr. sue if Harvey Jr. failed first-year law? See *Jones v. Padavatton*, [1969] 2 All E.R. 616 (C.A.), and *Riches v. Hogben*, [1986] Qd.R. 315 (Full Ct.).

9. Many people provide considerable assistance to elderly relatives and friends from a sense of familial duty or moral obligation. Should such altruistic persons be able to recover on the basis of a promise or expectation of compensation perhaps under the will of the recipient? Compare, *e.g.*, *Hammond v. Hammond*, [1995] 7 W.W.R. 345 (B.C. S.C.) with *Clarkson v. McCrossen Estate* (1995), 122 D.L.R. (4th) 239 (B.C. C.A.) and *Single v. Macharski Estate*, [1996] 3 W.W.R. 23 (Man. C.A.). In *Single*, Helper J.A. stated, at 28: ". . . Mrs. Single's initial and continuing motivation for providing her services, that is, her love for and devotion to Mrs. Macharski, could co-exist with a legitimate expectation for compensation. In my view, the evidence demonstrates clearly that the deceased was aware of Mrs. Single's expectation of compensation as she herself created those expectations with repeated assurances to her."

10. It is common for office staff to contribute a small sum each to purchase a lottery ticket on the understanding that, should they win, the prize money will be divided proportionately. Ought such agreements to be treated as binding? See *Osorio v. Cardona* (1984), 59 B.C.L.R. 29 (S.C.).

11. Might government programmes, expressed in regulations or legislation constitute offers? Compare, *e.g.*, *Esquimalt & Nanaimo Ry v. A.G.B.C.*, [1950] A.C. 87 (P.C.), *Joy Oil Co. v. R.*, [1951] S.C.R. 624, and *Corktown Films Inc. v. Ontario* (1996), 34 B.L.R. (2d) 168, 18 O.T.C. 308 (Gen. Div.) with *Grant v. New Brunswick* (1973), 35 D.L.R. (3d) 141 (N.B. C.A.) and *Dale v. Manitoba*, [1995] 10 W.W.R. 703 (Man. Q.B.), affirmed [1997] 8 W.W.R. 447 (Man. C.A.). In *Puddister Trading Co. v. R.* (1997), 132 F.T.R. 120 (T.D.) a letter from the Department of Fisheries and Oceans confirming the closure of the offshore seal hunt was a contractually binding commitment, not to pay compensation but to complete a broad, independent study of the compensation issue, on which the plaintiff relied. What would be a claimant's consideration in this case or in regard to compensation programmes generally? Should it matter? See section 3 of this chapter.

(c)   COMMERCIAL ARRANGEMENTS

ROSE AND FRANK CO. v. J.R. CROMPTON AND BROS. LTD.

[1923] 2 K.B. 261 (C.A.)

Rose and Frank Co. were the sole agents in the United States for the distribution of the defendant English company's paper products. Down to 1913 there were agreements between the parties which, although vague, were legally binding. In 1913, the parties signed a new document containing the following clause:

> This arrangement is not entered into, nor is this memorandum written, as a formal or legal agreement, and shall not be subject to legal jurisdiction in the Law Courts either of the United States or England, but it is only a definite expression and record of the purpose and intention of the . . . parties concerned to which they each honourably pledge themselves with the fullest confidence, based upon past business with each other, that it will be carried through by each of the . . . parties with mutual loyalty and friendly co-operation.

The defendants refused to fulfil some of the plaintiffs' orders for their products and terminated the agency agreement. At trial, Bailhache J. rejected the honourable pledge clause as repugnant to the rest of the agreement and against public policy, and held the agreement as a whole binding. This judgment was reversed by the Court of Appeal.

SCRUTTON L.J. . . . Now it is quite possible for parties to come to an agreement by accepting a proposal with the result that the agreement concluded does not give rise to legal relations. The reason of this is that the parties do not intend that their agreement shall give rise to legal relations. This intention may be implied from the subject matter of the agreement, but it may also be expressed by the parties. In social and family relations such an intention is readily implied, while in business matters the opposite result would ordinarily follow. But I can see no reason why, even in business matters, the parties should not intend to rely on each other's good faith and honour, and to exclude all idea of settling disputes by any outside intervention, with the accompanying necessity of expressing themselves so precisely that outsiders may have no difficulty in understanding what they mean. If they clearly express such an intention I can see no reason in public policy why effect should not be given to their intention. . . .

Judged by this test, I come to the same conclusion as the learned judge, that the particular clause in question shows a clear intention by the parties that the rest of their arrangement or agreement shall not affect their legal relations, or be enforceable in a Court of law, but in the words of the clause, shall be "only a definite expression and record of the purpose and intention of the . . . parties concerned to which they each honourably pledge themselves, . . . and shall not be subject to legal jurisdiction." If the clause stood first in the document, the intention of the parties would be exceedingly plain. . . .

[Scrutton L.J. went on to hold that the defendants were not bound to fulfil those orders which they had received at the time of termination, as the orders and the defendants' responses to them were made under the arrangements binding in honour only and thus gave rise to no legal obligations. There was, therefore, no legal remedy for non-delivery. However, so far as the defendants had made deliveries which had been accepted in response to earlier orders, "legal consequences as to payments of price would follow."

The opinion of Bankes L.J. also allowing the appeal is omitted. Atkin L.J. agreed that the arrangement of 1913 was not a legally binding contract but decided that the orders and responses constituted enforceable contracts of sale. The House of Lords ([1925] A.C. 445) took the same position as Atkin L.J. and reversed the judgment of the Court of Appeal.]

NOTES and QUESTIONS

1. Would it have made any difference if, instead of the Honourable Pledge clause, the agreement had contained an undertaking by all the parties to submit any dispute to the International Commercial Arbitration Commission [a private body], the decision of the commission to be final and binding on all parties? Compare *Baker v. Jones*, [1954] 2 All E.R. 553 with *Re Portnoy*, [1949] 3 D.L.R. 449 (Man. C.A.).

2. In *Moir v. J.P. Porter Co. Ltd.* (1979), 103 D.L.R. (3d) 22 (N.S. C.A.), the appellant had been employed by the respondent for over 32 years. He wished to retire and after discussions the respondent's president wrote to him as follows:

Dear Mr. Moir:— . . .

Although there may be features you may wish explained in detail, I set forth hereunder the arrangements for your retirement as approved by the Board of Directors of The J.P. Porter Company Limited:—

(a) You will retire on February 28th, 1975 and until that time you will be paid your present salary and automobile expenses.

(b) At your retirement you will acquire, at no cost to you, ownership of the Chrysler automobile which the Company presently rents for your account (obviously, the Company will not defray the operating expenses after February 28th, 1975).

(c) In the sole discretion of the Board of Directors of The J.P. Porter Company Limited and at its pleasure, the Company will, for the period March 1st, 1975 until December 31st, 1979

(i) Pay you a honorarium at the rate of $8,000.00 per annum ($666.66 per month).

(ii) Pay you annually, the premium cost of an annuity which, beginning January 1st, 1980 will pay you during your lifetime an amount of $5,000.00 per annum. The annual premium for this annuity is estimated at $5,300.00 and will be paid to you in a lump-sum in the form of salary in January of each year.

(d) The Company will insist that you accept no employment directly or indirectly in any business or industry that would conflict with the Company's interests. Furthermore, it would be expected that you will be available to act as a consultant when, as and if requested.

This arrangement has been designed to provide you with an income in retirement of approximately $8,000.00 per annum ($5,000.00 from the life annuity mentioned above, plus $3,162.00 from The J.P. Porter Company Limited Pension Plan).

For the period March 1st, 1975-December 31st, 1979, your income would be $13,300.00 from The J.P. Porter Company Limited plus $3,162.00 from the Porter Pension Plan less $5,300.00 premium of the annuity.

As mentioned earlier in this letter there will be no doubt many features of this arrangement which will require explanation and we have here in the office all the details, including the estimated cost of the proposed lifetime annuity. I must, however, repeat and emphasize that this whole arrangement is at the pleasure of the Board of Directors of The J.P. Porter Company Limited and subject to its sole discretion. You will, then, understand that although the Company will make every effort to complete its part of this arrangement there is no commitment to do so.

In discussions of this proposal, the respondent's officer repeated that it was subject to the continuing approval of the Board and the parties agreed that the annuity payments would be paid into an R.R.S.P.

Moir received the honorarium payments up to 1st February 1976 and the payments to the R.R.S.P. for 1975 and 1976. In November 1975, however, the respondent's president wrote to him as follows:

Dear Mr. Moir:—

In the light of conditions current in the dredging industry in Canada, this Company has no alternative but to adopt a policy of severe austerity and to cut costs to the strict minimum.

It is with regret that I must advise you that the retirement allowance of $8,000.00 per annum granted to you by the Board of Directors will terminate on February 29th, 1976. The Company will, however, pay the 1976 deposit of $5,427.00 to your Registered Retirement Savings Plan with the Atlantic Trust Company, but this will be the last such payment.

May I repeat my regret at having to advise you of this decision and the circumstances that have made it necessary.

Moir sued for breach of contract. Do you think that he should succeed? Compare *Parke v. Daily News*, [1962] Ch. 927, with *Edwards v. Skyways*, [1964] 1 All E.R. 494 on the meaning of the phrase "ex gratia" payment.

4. Letters of Comfort also raise issues of intention. One commentator has described the function of a letter of comfort as follows: "If a parent company does not wish to guarantee formally the debts of a subsidiary, it will often furnish the lender with a letter of comfort. Such letters commonly state that the parent is aware of the loan facilities provided and, with varying degrees of formality, there will be an assurance of the parent company's financial involvement with its subsidiary and its overall policy that the subsidiary should be in a position to meet its liabilities to the lender.": Brown, "The Letter of Comfort: Placebo or Promise?", [1990] J.B.L. 281 at 281. The following extract contains the first consideration of letters of comfort by a senior appellate court in Canada.

TORONTO DOMINION BANK v. LEIGH INSTRUMENTS LTD.
(TRUSTEE OF)

(1999), 178 D.L.R. (4th) 634 (Ont. CA), leave to appeal
refused [2000] 1 S.C.R. xxi

BY THE COURT (DOHERTY, AUSTIN and SHARPE JJ.A.)

This is an appeal from the judgment of Winkler J. dismissing all of the appellant's claims. Those claims were based on five letters of comfort provided to the appellant (the Bank) by the Plessey Company plc (Plessey) in connection with a series of loans made at the time of and following Plessey's take-over of Leigh Instruments Limited (Leigh). The respondent, General Electric Company plc (GEC) was in effective control of Plessey when the fifth letter of comfort was provided (December 19, 1989) and the claims against it arise out of that letter. . . .

[Counsel] advanced five grounds of appeal on behalf of the Bank. Four require him to convince us that the trial judge erred in his interpretation of the meaning of para. 3 of the letters of comfort provided by Plessey. Paragraph 3 reads:

> It is our policy that our wholly owned subsidiaries, including Leigh Instruments Limited, be managed in such a way as to be always in a position to meet their financial obligations including repayment of all amounts due under the above facility.

"The above facility" refers to the line of credit made available by the Bank to Leigh. That amount varied and reached $45 million when the fifth comfort letter was provided by Plessey in December 1989.

Throughout his submissions, [counsel] stressed the differences between the contract claim advanced by the Bank and the tort claim in so far as they related to para. 3 of the comfort letters. He did not take issue with the trial judge's analysis of the contract claim, but submitted that the trial judge erroneously applied the same analysis when interpreting para. 3 for the purposes of the negligent misrepresentation claim.

No doubt there are important differences between the two claims; however, the task of determining the meaning to be given to the words in para. 3 was common to both. Before considering the legal effect of those words, the trial judge had to determine what they meant. The same words in the same document cannot have one meaning in the context of a contract claim and a different meaning in the context of a tort claim. Once the meaning of the words is fixed, the legal effect of those words must be considered. It is at this stage of the interpretative process that distinctions between contract and tort claims can become important.

The process of determining the meaning to be given to words in a document is governed by the same principles regardless of whether the process is engaged in the context of a contract claim or a tort claim. Those principles are identified by the trial judge . . . and recently reviewed by the Supreme Court of Canada in *Eli Lily and Co. v. Novopharm Ltd.*, [1998] 2 S.C.R. 129 at pp. 166-67. . . . Essentially, the process is captured in the following question:

> Bearing in mind the relevant background, the purpose of the document, and considering the entirety of the document, what would the parties to the document reasonably have understood the contested words to mean?

The Bank contends, and the respondents agree, that para. 3 contained a representation by Plessey to the Bank as to its policy with respect to the business affairs of Leigh. It is also common ground that the representation was a continuing one. The dispute centres on what the policy was represented to be. The Bank reads para. 3 as a representation by Plessey that it would manage Leigh's affairs in such a way that Leigh would always be in a position to meet its obligations to the Bank. The Bank contends that it was entitled to rely on this representation as to Plessey's policy unless and until given notice of a change in that policy.

The respondents, emphasizing the words "be managed" in para. 3, submit that the paragraph was not a representation that Plessey would manage the affairs of Leigh, but rather a representation that it was Plessey's policy that its subsidiaries, including Leigh, should manage their own affairs in such a way as to be able to meet their financial obligations. The respondents rely not only on the language of para. 3, but on basic corporate law principles which they submit fixed the responsibility of management with the properly appointed officers of Leigh even though ultimate control of the company rested with the sole shareholder, Plessey.

Winkler J. accepted the respondents' interpretation of para. 3. In reaching that conclusion, he emphasized the language of para. 3 considered in the context of the entire letter. . . . He further held that his conclusion as to the meaning of the words in para. 3 was fortified by a consideration of the relevant background facts. . . .

Winkler J. construed para. 3 in the course of his consideration of the contract claim and applied that construction to both the contract claim and the tort claim. For the reasons set out above, we think this was a proper approach. . . .

After giving careful consideration to [counsel's] submissions, we come to the same conclusion as the trial judge. We agree with the trial judge's observation . . . that the appellant's interpretation is inconsistent with the words "be managed" and would require that additional words be inserted in para. 3. The parties chose not to insert any such language. The phrase "be managed" does not suggest that Plessey itself would manage the affairs of Leigh.

Whatever doubt might exist if only the words of para. 3 are considered is dispelled by a consideration of the relevant factual background. The Bank and Plessey were sophisticated commercial entities. Both were familiar with letters of comfort. The Bank knew full well that the letter of comfort was not security in the traditional sense and that its commercial value depended very much on the relationship which existed between the lender and the provider of the letter of comfort. The Bank was very anxious to establish an ongoing relationship with Plessey, a very large multinational corporation. It was well known that Plessey would not provide any guarantee on loans made to Leigh by the Bank. The letter was crafted to avoid any suggestion that Plessey had any legal responsibility for the loans. The interpretation of para. 3 now advanced by the Bank would effectively put Plessey in the position of a guarantor subject to Plessey's ability, on notice to the Bank, to change its "policy". The interpretation urged by the Bank would give it almost exactly the security which it knew full well was not available to it when it chose to proceed with the loan in the hopes of doing more business with Plessey and its many subsidiaries.

It was argued before Winkler J. and here that the respondents' interpretation of para. 3 meant that it amounted to no more than a "motherhood" statement having no real commercial purpose or value to the Bank. The trial judge . . . considered and rejected this argument. He observed that other paragraphs in the letters contained valuable representations and undertakings by Plessey and that the third paragraph gave the Bank a basis, albeit not a legal one, upon which to request that Plessey stand behind the commercial activities of Leigh and honour Leigh's debts. That request, while not based on any legal obligation, had substance and value in the commercial world revealed by the extensive evidence heard by the trial judge.

The trial judge, drawing on the language used by the English Court of Appeal in *Kleinwort Benson v. Malaysia Mining*, [1989] 1 All E.R. 785, referred to para. 3 of the letter as imposing a "moral obligation" on Plessey or as constituting a "gentleman's agreement" between the Bank and Plessey. We prefer the description of the commercial value of comfort letters in general and this one in particular provided in the factum of the respondent GEC. Counsel wrote:

> In this marketplace, both parties have experience in situations where a parent, for reasons it deems appropriate, refuses to give a legally binding assurance and a bank, for reasons it similarly considers appropriate agrees to accept something less, perhaps believing that when, and if, "push comes to shove", the parent would pay for any or all of the "non-legal" commercial considerations of reputation, fear of adverse publicity, higher future borrowing costs and a myriad other reasons and possibilities depending on the circumstances.

The interpretation given to para. 3 by the trial judge did not render the letters of comfort valueless and it cannot be said that his interpretation yields a commercial absurdity. The Bank's primary submission must be rejected. The trial judge correctly construed para. 3 of the letters of comfort. . . .

The Bank's third submission relates only to the fifth letter of comfort. The trial judge found that the fifth letter, like the first four, did not contain a material misrepresentation. He further held . . . that in the circumstances existing when the fifth letter was provided, the Bank could not reasonably have relied on any representation in the letter. In coming to that conclusion, the trial judge placed considerable emphasis on the concluding language of the fifth letter. In that letter Plessey indicated that the letter "does not constitute a legally binding commitment". That language did not appear in the earlier letters.

As we are satisfied that the fifth letter contained no misrepresentation, it is not necessary to address the reliance argument. . . . This ground of appeal must fail as we are satisfied that the fifth letter did not contain any misrepresentation, and in any event any representation in that letter could not reasonably be relied on by the Bank.

The Bank's fifth submission is somewhat different. For the purpose of this submission, the Bank accepts the interpretation of para. 3 given by the trial judge and adopted by this court. Counsel submits that even on that interpretation, the representation became untrue or at least misleading by January or February 1990 when Plessey realized that Leigh's continued fiscal viability was uncertain. Counsel submits that the continuing nature of the representation in para. 3 of the letters required Plessey to put the Bank on notice when it became clear to Plessey that Leigh might not be able to manage itself so as to meet its obligations to the Bank. If this submission is accepted, the Bank is entitled to recover the advances made to Leigh after Plessey knew that Leigh's prospects were not good.

We cannot accept this submission. There is nothing inconsistent with the continued existence of a policy that Leigh should manage its affairs so as to be able to meet its financial obligations and the existence of circumstances which imperiled Leigh's ability to conduct its affairs in accordance with that policy. The policy may remain extant even if circumstances make compliance difficult or doubtful.

The trial judge conducted an extensive review of the evidence surrounding Leigh's slide into insolvency in late 1989 and early 1990. He reviewed the extensive efforts made by Plessey and its owners to salvage Leigh's business. He concluded . . . that the policy referred to in para. 3 of the letters remained in place throughout the material period of time right up until immediately before the bankruptcy of Leigh. We see no basis for interfering with that finding.

There is a second reason why this submission must fail. It is premised on the representations made in the fifth letter of comfort. As indicated above, we agree with the trial judge's conclusion that the Bank could not reasonably rely on any representation in that letter. Consequently, even if we accepted the Bank's argument that the representations in para. 3 became misleading some time in January or February 1990, the Bank could still not establish the requisite reliance on the representations.

We affirm the order of Winkler J. dismissing the Bank's action.

[Appeal dismissed.]

7.   Formality: Promises Under Seal

In section 1 of this chapter, it was emphasized that less developed legal systems often required a degree of formality in order to determine which promises were legally binding. This was certainly true of the common law, because contracts under seal, or deeds, provided a means of enforcing promises from at least the early thirteenth century, long before the doctrine of consideration made its appearance. As in many primitive systems of law, promises were enforced simply because they satisfied certain formalities, regardless of whether the promisor had obtained any consideration.

The original formalities required a party to seal the document by making an impression in sealing wax with a signet ring. This requirement has been considerably relaxed over the centuries, although the distinct history of contracts under seal still means that they are enforced even if they are not supported by consideration.

At the present time, it is a question of fact whether a document is effectively sealed. Some of the issues raised by that question are discussed in the following extract.

ROYAL BANK v. KISKA

[1967] 2 O.R. 379, 63 D.L.R. (2d) 582 (C.A.)

The plaintiff bank brought an action on a guarantee which had been signed by the defendant. At the time of signature, no wafer seal was attached to the guarantee, but the word "seal" was printed on the document, next to the space in which the defendant wrote his signature. The majority of the court found that the guarantee was binding because it was supported by consideration. However, Laskin J.A. thought that there was no consideration and thus in his view the guarantee could be enforced only if it constituted a sealed instrument.

LASKIN J.A. (dissenting). . . . We are in the field of formality; and so long as the doctrine of consideration subsists with its present constituents, it is commercially useful to have an alternative method of concluding a binding transaction. The formal contract under seal is not as formal today as it was in the time of Coke; apart from statute (and there is none on the subject in Ontario relevant to the present case), there has been a recognized relaxation of the ancient common law requirement of a waxed impression. (An account of the origin and development of seals will be found in *Wigmore on Evidence*, vol. VII, 3rd ed., s. 2161.) Neither wax nor an impression is any longer obligatory. A gummed wafer is enough when affixed by or acknowledged by the party executing the document on which it is placed. I would hold also that any representation of a seal made by a signatory will do. The present case is an invitation to be satisfied with less than the foregoing. We confront the question of how far we should, as a common law development, relax formality and still affirm that we are not enforcing a gratuitous promise merely because it is in writing.

The document put forward by the bank has the familiar words "Given under seal at . . ." and "Signed, Sealed and Delivered in the presence of." At the end of the dotted line for the signature of the executing party is the bracketed word "seal". Neither the words "Given under seal" nor the formula of "Signed, Sealed and Delivered" suffice, even when taken collectively, [to] make a signatory chargeable under a sealed instrument when it has not in fact been executed under seal. The respective words are merely anticipatory of a formality which must be observed and are not a substitute for it. I am not tempted by any suggestion that it would be a modern and liberal view to hold that a person who signs a document that states it is under seal should be bound accordingly although there is no seal on it. I have no regret in declining to follow this path in a case where a bank thrusts a printed form under the nose of a young man for his signature. Formality serves a purpose here and some semblance of it should be preserved, especially when it is recalled that the common law did not require either a *testimonium* or an attestation clause to make a sealed instrument enforceable; the operative act was the affixing or adoption of a seal. . . .

I do not think it follows that because want of intention of the executing party to adopt a seal as his own may free him from liability on a sealed instrument that an intention to execute a sealed document will bind him accordingly although no seal is affixed. Here, in any event, there is no evidence of intention save as it may be deduced from the written form which is in question.

This brings me to the final point, namely, whether sufficient formality is preserved by the inclusion in the printed form of the bracketed word "seal". I think not, because this is merely an invitation to place a seal at that spot. It affirms the need of formality rather than dispensing with it. . . . A more difficult situation would exist if, instead of the bracketed word "seal", there was an imprint of a wafer seal reproduced on the document. . . . It is not necessary, for the purpose of the present case, to come to a decision on this question. . . .

I would dismiss the appeal with costs.

[Kelly J.A., with whom McLennan J.A. concurred, delivered a judgment allowing the appeal on the basis that there was consideration.]

NOTES and QUESTIONS

1. Other courts have applied a different test from that envisaged by Laskin J.A., with possibly different results. In *Linton v. Royal Bank of Can.*, [1967] 1 O.R. 315 (H.C.), Hartt J. applied the test from English cases that if a document contains some indication of a seal, the fact that a person intended to execute the document as a deed is sufficient adoption or recognition of the seal. See also *Procopia v. D'Abbondanzo*, [1973] 3 O.R. 8 (H.C.).

2. *Canadian Imperial Bank of Commerce v. Dene Mat Construction Ltd.*, [1988] 4 W.W.R. 344 at 352 (N.W.T.S.C.) is an example of the "more difficult situation" referred to by Laskin J.A. "The formalities of sealing and delivery, in relation to legal deeds, have been eroded as a result of widespread literacy and the demands of a fast-paced commercial world, . . . the evident trend of the authorities is away from mere formalism and towards legal recognition of what the parties intended."

In *872899 Ontario Inc. v. Iacovoni* (1998), 163 D.L.R. (4th) 263 (Ont. C.A.), leave to appeal refused (1999), [1998] S.C.C.A. No. 476, 236 N.R. 199 (note), the purchasers entered into a written agreement to buy a new home to be built by the vendor. Just above the purchasers' signatures, the agreement stated that it was "SIGNED, SEALED AND DELIVERED" by the purchasers, but there was no indication of a seal on the document. The question arose whether, for the purpose of determining the applicable limitation period, the contract was under seal. The Ontario Court of Appeal found, at 271, that the recitals above the parties' signatures did not create a contract under seal and that it could not treat as a contract under seal "a document which bears no trace of a seal".

3. In its *Report on Amendment of the Law of Contract* (1987), at 35-47, the O.L.R.C., influenced by the decline of the seal as a cautionary device, found that the seal no longer plays a useful role in the law of contracts, and should be abolished. It recommended instead that the seal should be replaced by a "witnessed signed writing", which is a document executed by the promisor in the presence of a witness and signed by the witness in the presence of the promisor.

The Law Reform Commission of British Columbia in its *Report on Deeds and Seals* (1988), felt that the deed should be retained to enforce gratuitous promises. They made no recommendation in regard to "the execution requirements necessary to create a deed" as "these are issues already resolved by the current law relying upon the concept of estoppel". They did, however, recommend that a document under seal "shall take effect as if it were created by a simple contract . . . ."

Which of these proposals better fulfils the evidentiary, cautionary and channelling functions of formal instruments outlined in section 1(a) of this chapter? See Romero (1989), 15 Can. Bus. L.J. 368.

8.   Formality: The Requirement of Writing

(a)   INTRODUCTION

The development of the doctrine of consideration emphasized that the common law did not require any particular formality in order to create an enforceable contract. The previous section shows that if a person satisfied the formalities required to create a promise under seal, that promise would be binding even in the absence of consideration.

The formalities discussed in this section fulfil a different role. In 1677, the English Parliament imposed a requirement of writing for specified contracts which meant, in effect, that certain promises might not be enforceable even if they were supported beyond all question by consideration. The Statute of Frauds (29 Car. 2, c. 3) imposed a writing requirement for specified contracts. Section 4 provided:

> And be it further enacted by the authority aforesaid that from and after the said 4 and 20th day of June no action shall be brought whereby to charge any executor or administrator upon any special promise to answer damages out of his own estate or whereby to charge the defendant upon any special promise to answer for the debt, default or miscarriage of another person or to charge any person upon any agreement made upon consideration of marriage or upon any contract or sale of lands, tenements or hereditaments or any interest in or concerning them or upon any agreement that is not to be performed within the space of one year from the making thereof unless the agreement upon which such action shall be brought or some memorandum or note thereof shall be in writing and signed by the party to be charged therewith or some other person thereunto by him lawfully authorized.

Section 17 dealt with contracts for the sale of goods, wares and merchandise for a price of £10 or more but, as reflected in its present-day Canadian equivalents, it also provided for specific evidentiary substitutes for writing not to be found in s. 4:

> Sale of Goods Act, R.S.A. 2000, c. S-2, s. 6.
>
> 6. (1) A contract for the sale of any goods of the value of $50 or upwards is not enforceable by action
>
>> (a) unless the buyer accepts part of the goods so sold and actually receives that part, or gives something in earnest to bind the contract or in part payment, or
>>
>> (b) unless some note or memorandum in writing of the contract is made and signed by the party to be charged or his agent in that behalf.
>
> (2) This section applies to every contract referred to in subsection (1) notwithstanding that the goods may be intended to be delivered at some future time, or may not, at the time of the contract, be actually made, procured or provided or fit or ready for delivery or that some act may be requisite for the making or completing thereof or rendering the goods fit for delivery.
>
> (3) There is an acceptance of goods within the meaning of this section when the buyer does any act, in relation to the goods, that recognizes a pre-existing contract of sale whether there is an acceptance in performance of the contract or not.

The Statute of Frauds became part of the law in some of the provinces of common law Canada by reception, e.g., Alberta, Newfoundland (see the Newfoundland Law Reform Commission, *Discussion Paper on the Statute of Frauds, 1677* (1991)) while in the others, it was re-enacted in substantially the same form (see R.S.O. 1990, c. S.19 am. S.O. 1994, c. 27, s. 55; R.S.N.S. 1989, c. 442 am. 2001, c. 6, s. 126; R.S.N.B. 1973, c. S-14; R.S.P.E.I. 1974, c. S-6). Also, when the English Parliament repealed s. 17 and relocated it in virtually the same form in the 1893 Sale of Goods Act, the common law provinces followed suit as part of the adoption of their own sales statutes. (See the various Sale of Goods Acts referred to in Chapter 2, section 2, in note 4, following *Goldthorpe v. Logan*.)

Over the years, however, as a result of growing discontent on the part of some provinces with all or part of these statutory requirements, changes were made. The following extract summarizes the reforms that have taken place in Canada and elsewhere.

ONTARIO LAW REFORM COMMISSION, REPORT ON AMENDMENT OF THE LAW OF CONTRACT

(1987), at 98-102

The most significant change to the *Statute of Frauds* has occurred recently in Manitoba. In its 1980 *Report on The Statute of Frauds*, the Manitoba Law Reform Commission proposed a radical overhaul of the legislation applicable in that Province, but recommended retention in an amended form of a writing requirement for leases, promises of guarantee and indemnity, and contracts relating to land. The Manitoba Legislative Assembly took a less cautious approach and repealed the Act *in toto*.

The provision in section 4 relating to contracts by executors or administrators to answer damages out of their own estates has been repealed in England, British Columbia, New Zealand, and Western Australia. Its repeal has been recommended in Queensland, South Australia, and Alberta [and now Ontario].

Similarly, the provision relating to agreements not to be performed within a year has been repealed in England, British Columbia, and New Zealand. Its repeal has been recommended in Queensland, South Australia, and Alberta [and now Ontario].

The provisions in section 4 dealing with contracts of guarantee and contracts relating to land have had a more varied history. The repeal of the provision relating to guarantees was recommended in England in 1937 by a majority of the Law Revision Committee. Its retention was recommended by a minority of the Committee and by the later Law Reform Committee in 1953. It was not repealed when the law was amended in 1954. Retention of the original provision was recommended by the Queensland Law Reform Committee. Its repeal was recommended by the South Australia Law Reform Committee.

In British Columbia, the provision dealing with contracts of guarantee was extended in 1958 to cover indemnities as well as guarantees. It now appears as section 59(6) of the *Law and Equity Act*, which reads as follows:

59.(6) A guarantee or indemnity is not enforceable unless

(a) it is evidenced by writing signed by, or by the agent of, the guarantor or indemnitor, or

(b) the alleged guarantor or indemnitor has done an act indicating that a guarantee or indemnity consistent with that alleged has been made.

In Alberta, the writing requirement for a contract of guarantee applies to persons and corporations and is supplemented by the *Guarantees Acknowledgment Act* which requires additional formalities for the giving of guarantees by persons who are not corporations. The Alberta Institute of Law Research and Reform has recently recommended that a guarantee, whether by a person or a corporation, should not be enforceable unless there is some evidence in writing signed by the party to be charged, or by his or her agent, which indicates that the party to be charged has given a guarantee to the party alleging the guarantee and which reasonably identifies the third person whose debt is the subject of the guarantee. The Institute further recommended that the government and the legislature consider whether or not the law should continue to provide for special formalities such as those in the *Guarantees Acknowledgment Act* for the effectiveness of guarantees by persons who are not corporations.

With respect to indemnities, the Alberta Institute recommended that the writing requirement should apply to an agreement under which one person enters into an obligation to another person to pay an existing or future debt of a third person, whether or not the obligation is conditional upon the default of the third person. The Institute recommended several exemptions from the requirement of writing for both guarantees and indemnities. The Institute also recommended the reversal of the common law position that a requirement of writing did not apply to a guarantee given to preserve the guarantor's property.

Turning to the provision relating to contracts for the sale of land, the writing requirement has been retained in England and New Zealand. The British Columbia Law Reform Commission recommended the repeal of the provision and its replacement by a substantially revised version, and this was accomplished by the *Law Reform Amendment Act, 1985*, which amended the *Law and Equity Act*. Its retention has been recommended in Queensland and, with some minor changes, in South Australia. In Alberta, retention of the writing requirement was recommended, but certain substitutes for writing were also suggested.

In the United States, significant changes in the formal requirements relating to land contracts appear in section 2-201 of the Uniform Land Transactions Act. This section requires a writing signed by the party against whom enforcement of the contract is sought. The writing must contain a description of the property sufficiently definite to make identification of the property possible with reasonable certainty; it must state the price or a method of fixing the price; and it must be sufficiently definite to indicate with reasonable certainty that a contract to convey has been made by the parties. There are several exceptions to the writing requirement. These are where the buyer has taken possession and has paid all or part of the contract price; where the buyer has accepted a deed from the seller; where a party has changed its position to its detriment in reasonable reliance on the contract; and where the party against whom enforcement is being sought admits in the pleadings or in evidence that such a contract was made. It will be seen, therefore, that under the Uniform Land Transactions Act, while the requirement of a writing is retained, as is the doctrine of part performance, both features differ substantially in concept and in detail from their Anglo-Canadian counterparts.

.....

The foregoing brief survey indicates that a great majority of the law reform bodies that have reviewed the requirements concerning contracts in the *Statute of Frauds* have favoured retaining writing requirements relating to land contracts and contracts of guarantee, although, in several cases, in a form substantially different from the existing requirements, and also, in the case of land contracts, with extensive provisions relating to the acceptability of acts of part performance. A number of reports have also favoured deleting the other contractual requirements of section 4 on the ground that they no longer serve a useful function.

[Footnotes omitted.]

As well, in Manitoba and British Columbia, the relevant provision in the Sale of Goods Act has been repealed and a similar step has been recommended in other provinces (see, *e.g.*, Ontario Law Reform Commission, *Report on Sale of Goods* (1979), vol. I, at 131).

What this history suggests, of course, is at least some movement away from a policy of requiring contracts to be in writing. As a result, the structure of this section will involve, first, a brief consideration of specific reasons for the enactment of the Statute of Frauds in 1677 as well as more general policy arguments for writing requirements; secondly, an examination of the impact of s. 4 of the Statute of Frauds and its equivalents as interpreted by the courts (including the ways in which it came to be circumvented); and thirdly, a brief reference to the various criticisms of such writing requirements and possible methods of legislative change.

(b)   PURPOSES OF WRITING REQUIREMENTS

Among the factors that led to the enactment of the original statute in 1677 were four that are commonly listed:

(a) Parties to an action, their spouses, and persons with an interest in the action were not competent to testify.

(b) Trial by jury was in a state of transition and it was still possible for jurors to decide cases on the basis of personal knowledge.

(c) Perjury and subornation were rife.

(d) Citizens were extremely litigious.

The first two are not part of present day law and it is thought by most people that the third and fourth considerations are far less common today. In other words, it is assumed that we have moved away from what Simpson described, in *A History of the Common Law of Contract* (1975), as an era where litigation was a form of "sanctioned aggression". (See generally on the history of the Statute of Frauds, pages 599-620 of that work.)

There are other more general reasons why writing requirements might be thought desirable today, which were discussed in section 1(a) of this chapter. With these considerations in mind, consider whether a Statute of Frauds is necessary, and, if so, which types of contract it should cover.

(c)   OPERATION OF THE STATUTE

(i)   *Effects of Non-Compliance*

Requiring that a contract be in writing might suggest that failure to comply with that requirement nullifies or invalidates the parties' attempt to enter into contractual relations. However, while there is no doubt that appropriately-worded legislation could achieve that effect, the phrase in s. 4, "no action shall be brought", has been interpreted as relating to procedure and not validity. What this means is that non-compliance with the Statute only renders a contract unenforceable, *i.e.*, it prevents a plaintiff from bringing a legal action, without affecting the essential validity of the contract.

While an unenforceable valid contract may seem, at first glance, to be somewhat of a contradiction, this is not really the case. An unenforceable but valid contract may have legal significance in the following ways:

(1)   It may be used by way of defence (which does not constitute bringing an action). Thus if A pays money to B by way of deposit on an unenforceable contract for the sale of land, B can raise the validity of the contract by way of *defence* to an action by A to recover the money paid. This would not be the case if the contract were void. However, should the vendor repudiate the contract, the money would be recoverable on the ground of total failure of consideration. See, *e.g.*, *Barber v. Glen*, [1987] 6 W.W.R. 689 at 693 (Sask. C.A.) where an oral amendment to a land contract was allowed to be advanced as a defence.

(2)   The essential validity of an unenforceable contract means that evidence sufficient for a court of common law or equity to permit enforcement may arise *subsequent* to the formation of a contract. At common law this evidence need only be a sufficient note or memorandum (discussed *infra*); in equity this evidence must satisfy the doctrine of part performance (discussed in section 8(c)(iii)). If failure to comply with the Statute had been interpreted as rendering the contract *void* subsequent evidence would be relevant only to the extent that it proved the elements of a *new* valid agreement, including a new offer and acceptance, intent to create legal relations, etc. Many subsequent memoranda and acts of part performance which have been found to be sufficient proof of elements of the originally formed contract would not be sufficient evidence of a newly formed contract. Indeed, it is difficult to see how the doctrine of part performance could ever have been developed by the courts of equity if non-compliance with the Statute rendered the contract void.

(3)   It can be consideration for a new contract or for a negotiable instrument. See *Jones v. Jones* (1840), 151 E.R. 331; *Low v. Fry* (1935), 152 L.T. 585.

(ii) *The Requirement of a Sufficient Note or Memorandum*

(A)   Form of the Note or Memorandum

The Statute requires either that the agreement itself be in writing or that there be a note or a memorandum evidencing the agreement. No particular form of memorandum or writing is required and the note or memorandum need not have been written with the intent of satisfying the Statute. As long as it sufficiently evidences the existence of the contract the note or memorandum will suffice, even if the writing should constitute a repudiation of the contract. However, the writing cannot deny the very existence of the contract.

(B)   Contents of the Note or Memorandum

The note or memorandum must contain all the essential terms. In *McKenzie v. Walsh* (1921), 61 S.C.R. 312 at 313, Sir Louis Davies C.J.C. stated:

> I have reached the conclusion that the memorandum or receipt is sufficient. That it must contain all the essential terms of the contract and thus show that the parties have agreed to those terms is conceded by both sides. That it does so, I conclude. The essential terms are the parties, the property and the price.

Besides the parties, property and the price, other terms, may, depending on the circumstances, be regarded as material. Thus in *Tweddell v. Henderson*, [1975] 2 All E.R. 1096 (Ch. Div.), the payment of the purchase price in stages was regarded as material and in *Huttges v. Verner* (1975), 10 N.B.R. (2d) 533, affirmed 64 D.L.R. (3d) 374 (C.A.), the reservation of a life interest by a vendor was held to be material. As a result, the omission of these orally-settled terms from the writing relied upon was held to have prevented compliance with the Statute.

Whether a given document contains all the material terms is complicated by the principle that it is sufficient if the term is disclosed by reasonable inference and that parol evidence is admissible for the purposes of explanation, though not of adding or varying terms. Precisely what constitutes reasonable inference and the point at which explanation ceases and addition or variation begins are difficult issues. In the following extract, the Supreme Court of Canada provided some illustrations of where the courts have drawn the line.

DYNAMIC TRANSPORT LTD. v. O.K. DETAILING LTD.

[1978] 2 S.C.R. 1072, 6 Alta. L.R. (2d) 156, 4 R.P.R. 208,
85 D.L.R. (3d) 19, 9 A.R. 308, 20 N.R. 500

DICKSON J. [delivering the judgment of the court] . . . On the issue of certainty of description of the land, Courts have gone a long way in finding a memorandum in writing sufficient to satisfy the *Statute of Frauds*. The Judges have consistently attempted to ascertain and effectuate the wishes of the parties, undeterred by lacunas in the language in which those wishes have been expressed. Thus, in *Plant v. Bourne*, [1897] 2 Ch. 281, the defendant agreed to buy a property described in a memorandum signed by him as "twenty-four acres of land, freehold, at T., in the Parish of D". It was held by the Court of Appeal . . . that parol evidence

was admissible to show the subject-matter of the contract. Lindley, L.J., said, at
p. 288:

> That there was an agreement is plain enough. What is it that the agreement refers to? The
> answer to that is, it was the twenty-four acres of freehold land which they were talking about.
> Evidence to shew that is admissible; and if that is once admitted, there is an end of the case.

In *McMurray v. Spicer* (1868), L.R. 5 Eq. 527, the defendant agreed to purchase
from the plaintiff "the mill property, including the cottages, in Esher Village—all
the property to be freehold". In an action for specific performance, it was held
that parol evidence was admissible to identify the property. And in *Bleakley v.
Smith* (1840), 59 E.R. 831, the vendor, who had five houses and no other property
in Cable St., drew up a memorandum in his own handwriting, reading: "John
Bleakley agrees with J.R. Bridges to take the property in Cable Street for the net
sum of £248.10s." It was held that the memorandum was sufficient under the
Statute of Frauds. Parol evidence, of course, was necessary to show that the
vendor had no property in Cable St. other than the property in question. . . .

[The court then contrasted its earlier decision in *Turney v. Zhilka*, [1959] S.C.R.
578.]

In *Turney v. Zhilka* the description of the property contained in the offer to
purchase made by Zhilka was in these terms:

> All and singular the land and not buildings situate on the East side of 5th Line west in
> the township of Toronto and known as 60 acres or more having frontage of about 2046 feet
> on 5th line more or less, by a depth of about . . . feet, more or less (lot boundaries about as
> fenced), being part of west 1/2 of lot 5 Con. 5 west.

It was common ground that this description did not mean the buildings were to
be removed but that certain land around them was to be retained by the vendor.
The exact size of the land to be retained was not specified. The vendor assumed
at the time the contract was made that he had about 65 acres and that he could
retain five acres around his buildings. Actually the vendor only owned 62.37
acres, as he discovered when he had a survey made. When the purchaser sued for
specific performance, he defined his claim in such a way that he left the vendor
with only one and a half acres and a barn, half on the land claimed by the purchaser
and half on the land which the purchaser said the vendor might retain. The
purchaser claimed 60.87 acres out of the total of 62.37 acres. After the Local
Master had been unable to determine what was to be retained as a reasonable
amount of land enclosing the buildings, the trial Judge on appeal from the Master's
report decided that the retained parcel should be 10 acres. There was no basis for
this in the agreement between the parties and thus Judson, J., speaking for this
Court, found that there was not "sufficient certainty of description to enable the
property to be identified once the surrounding facts are pointed to".

QUESTIONS

1. Andrews orally agreed to lease Blackacre to Williams for a period of four years for the sum
of $2,000. On receiving $2,000 in cash, Andrews gave Williams the following signed memorandum:

Dear Sir:

In consideration of you having this day paid me the sum of $2,000 . . . I agree to grant you a lease of four years of Blackacre . . .

"Andrews"

The name of Williams was nowhere stated in this memorandum. Should the memorandum be sufficient? See *Carr v. Lynch*, [1900] 1 Ch. 613.

2. By an agreement in writing signed by both parties Andrews agreed to sell to Barton ". . . 40 acres of land at Williamsburg in the County of Strathcona . . ." for a price of $20,000. Should the writing be sufficient? See *Plant v. Bourne*, discussed *supra* in *Dynamic Transport*.

3. If a material term is omitted and if that term is for the sole benefit of the plaintiff then the omission will not preclude the plaintiff from enforcing the contract, as long as he or she is willing to waive the omitted term. See, *e.g.*, *North v. Loomes*, [1919] 1 Ch. 378.

(C)   The Requisite Signature

The requirement of a signature has been interpreted liberally. Mere initialing has been held to be sufficient (*Chichester v. Cobb* (1866), 14 L.T. 433), the signature may be printed (*Schneider v. Norris* (1814), 105 E.R. 388), and it is not necessary that the signature be at the end of the document (*Durrell v. Evans* (1862), 158 E.R. 848). The alleged "signature" must, however, have been placed with the intention of authenticating the document.

The Statute also provides that the signature may be that of a lawfully authorized agent. Such authorization need not be in writing and it has been held that the agent may sign the agent's own name or that of his or her principal.

It should be noted that the Statute does not require the signatures of both parties, only "the party to be charged", *i.e.*, the defendant. It is thus possible for a plaintiff who has not signed, to enforce a contract against a defendant who has.

A modern exemplification of all these dimensions is afforded by *Moojelsky v. Rexnord Canada Ltd.* (1989), 96 A.R. 91 at 100-02 (Q.B.). Here the court was prepared to accept as a sufficient note or memorandum an apparently internal record of the contract in question set out on company letterhead with the name of an officer in the company's tendering department printed by that officer at the top of the document. The court held that, even though the officer in question might not have been an agent of the company for the purposes of settling the terms of the contract, he was an agent for the purposes of signing a document intended to authenticate the bargain. Moreover, once this was established, the purpose for which the memorandum was prepared did not matter. Implicit here is a holding that a document authenticating the contract for purely internal purposes will be sufficient to satisfy the Statute.

(D)   Joinder of Documents

In certain circumstances where all the material terms do not appear in one document it may be possible to "join" two documents together, even where one of the documents is not signed, for the purposes of producing a sufficient memorandum. There must however be some connection between the two documents for such joinder to be permissible. Either the connection must be obvious when placing the two documents side by side or else there must be a reference, express or implied, in the signed document to the unsigned document. If the only connection that can be made between the two documents is by virtue of parol evidence the joinder will not be permitted. See *Harvie v. Gibbons* (1980), 12 Alta. L.R. (2d) 72 (C.A.), for a review of the authorities on joinder of documents, as well as for an illustration of the application of the above principles.

(iii)   *Categories of Contracts Under the Statute*

Section 4 of the Statute of Frauds covers five categories of contract. However, most of the attention and the litigation involves contracts for the sale or other disposition of land. This is exemplified by the following footnote from the Ontario Law Reform Commission's *Report on Amendment of the Law of Contract* (1987), at 77:

> A non-exhaustive tabulation of Canadian cases involving the *Statute of Frauds* in all provinces and reported between 1970-1979, which was carried out during the course of the Commission's research, reveals the following figures:
>
> | | |
> |---|---:|
> | Contracts involving land | 26 |
> | Contracts of guarantee | 4 |
> | Contracts not to be performed within one year | 2 |
> | Others | 0 |
> | Total | 32 |

The above list does not include contracts for the sale of goods.

Indeed, the only surviving categories in England are contracts of guarantee and land contracts. The same is true in British Columbia, while Manitoba has dispensed with the Statute entirely. As a result, this section deals only briefly with the four categories other than land contracts. We also leave to courses on Commercial Law or Sales the special problems created by what was s. 17, now relocated in the Sale of Goods legislation in all of the common law provinces except British Columbia and Manitoba (where it has been repealed).

(A)   Contracts to Charge an Executor or Administrator on a Special Promise to Answer Damages out of his own Estate

The reason for the inclusion of this particular category is somewhat unclear. While such contracts are rare today, apparently at the time of enactment they were more common. Simpson has speculated, in *A History of the Common Law of Contract* (1975), at 611, that "representatives must often have been harassed by creditors and legatees and tempted to make some incautious promise to buy peace". This provision has been repealed in England, British Columbia and Manitoba.

(B)   Contracts Made upon Consideration of Marriage

This category does not include exchanges of promises to marry; rather it covers contracts wherein a party promises to settle property upon another in consideration of marriage.

(C)   Contracts to Answer for the Debt, Default or Miscarriage of Another Person

The wording " . . . to answer for the debt, default or miscarriage of another" is somewhat archaic. Basically, it has been interpreted as referring to guarantees and not indemnities. The distinction between a guarantee and indemnity is set out in *Lakeman v. Mountstephen* (1874), L.R. 7 H.L. 17; *Birkmyr v. Darnell* (1704), 91 E.R. 27 (K.B.). An indemnity is an undertaking to be liable regardless of whether another person be in default; a guarantee is an undertaking which is conditional on the default or non-performance of someone else. In other words, liability under an indemnity is primary or original whereas liability under a guarantee is secondary. Judicial attempts to distinguish between the two were characterized by Harman L.J. in *Yeoman Credit Ltd. v. Latter*, [1961] 2 All E.R. 294 (C.A.) as being, "hair splitting distinctions of exactly that kind which brings the law into hatred, ridicule and contempt by the public." Note, however, that s. 59(6) of the British Columbia Law and Equity Act, R.S.B.C. 1996, c. 253, covers both indemnities and guarantees.

By the Mercantile Law Amendment Act, 1856 (19 & 20 Vict., c. 97), s. 3, the consideration for the guarantee need not appear in the writing. (Where this provision does not apply by reception, it has been included in the provincial Statutes cited in the Introduction to this section, except in British Columbia.)

A good argument can be made that there indeed should be some special formalities in the case of guarantees. Often, and especially in the case of consumer guarantees, no *direct* benefit flows to the guarantor; rather, the consideration for the promise of guarantee is either the granting of a loan to, or the forbearing to sue a third party (see *Royal Bank v. Kiska* in section 7 of this chapter). Because of this, and because guarantees are often given by private individuals without the benefit of legal advice it is thought that a special cautionary device is useful. The requirement of writing does serve that purpose.

(D)   Contracts not to be Performed within a Year

This particular category has been the subject of extensive criticism. The traditional view was that it was included because witnesses' memories were not thought trustworthy after more than a year. However, if this was the object, the Statute does not accomplish it. For one thing it is possible for an action to be brought on a contract to be performed in less than a year, several years after the cause of action arose (assuming that the limitation of actions statutes have been complied with). Conversely in the instance of a contract to be performed in more than a year, which is repudiated immediately, thus giving rise to an immediate cause of action, the Statute can apply as a defence even though judicial proceedings could be concluded within a year of the making of the contract.

As a result there has been a noticeable judicial reluctance to enforce the Statute in respect of this provision. Most of the litigation over this provision has arisen on the definitional question of what in law constitutes a contract not to be performed within a year and, as the following extract from the O.L.R.C.'s *Report on Amendment of the Law of Contract*, at 82, indicates, the outcome of that litigation depends upon technical considerations which have little or no justifiable policy foundation:

> To illustrate, if a contract is for an indefinite period, but could be performed within a year, it has been held to fall outside the Statute. However, if the contract provides for a specific period for performance of more than a year but also confers a power of determination that may be exercised within the year, it requires a written memorandum. Again, if a contract is to be performed over a period of one year, commencing the day after the formation of the contract, it falls outside the Statute on the principle that the law takes no account of the parts of a day; if, on the other hand, a contract of the same duration commences *two* days after the conclusion of the contract, the Statute will be deemed to apply even though the day immediately following the conclusion is a Sunday. In addition to these constructional vagaries, it has been noted that the statutory provision leads to the curious result that it is in the interest of the defendant to argue that the contract was to run for more than a year, whereas the plaintiff has an incentive to argue equally strenuously that the contract was for less than a year.

[Footnotes omitted.]

(E)   Contracts for the Sale of an Interest in Land

As with the provision relating to contracts not to be performed within a year, the precise reach of this aspect of s. 4 has occasioned considerable difficulties for the courts. Once again, the law is summarized well in the O.L.R.C. *Report*, at 79-82, and we will not dwell upon it here. Rather, in this section we look at an important device which the courts have used to circumvent the strict or literal application of the Statute of Frauds.

Not long after the enactment of the Statute, courts of equity decided to enforce some contracts for the sale of an interest in land, notwithstanding the absence of a sufficient note or memorandum, as long as certain circumstances could be proved. This intervention by equity and the circumstances which must be proved to allow equity to dispense with the writing requirement has become known as the doctrine of part performance. While the first case applying the doctrine, *Butcher v. Stapely* (1685), 23 E.R. 524 (L.C.), occurred as early as 1685, the doctrine was established in its modern sense in the case of *Maddison v. Alderson* (1883), 8 App. Cas. 467 (H.L.).

DEGLMAN v. GUARANTY TRUST CO.

[1954] S.C.R. 725, [1954] 3 D.L.R. 785

RAND J. In this appeal the narrow question is raised as to the nature of part performance which will enable the court to order specific performance of a contract relating to lands unenforceable at law by reason of s. 4 of the Statute of Frauds. The respondent Constantineau claims the benefit of such a contract and the appellant represents the next of kin other than the respondent of the deceased, Laura Brunet, who resist it.

The respondent was the nephew of the deceased. Both lived in Ottawa. When he was about 20 years of age, and while attending a technical school, for six months of the school year 1934-35 he lived with his aunt at No. 550 Besserer Street. Both that and the house on the adjoining lot, No. 548, were owned by the aunt and it was during this time that she is claimed to have agreed that if the nephew would be good to her and do such services for her as she might from time to time request during her lifetime she would make adequate provision for him in her will, and in particular that she would leave to him the premises at No. 548. While staying with her the nephew did the chores around both houses which, except for an apartment used by his aunt, were occupied by tenants. When the term ended he returned to the home of his mother on another street. In the autumn of the year he worked on the national highway in the northern part of Ontario. In the spring of 1936 he took a job on a railway at a point outside of Ottawa and at the end of that year, returning to Ottawa, he obtained a position with the city police force. In 1941 he married. At no time did he live at the house No. 548 or, apart from the six months, at the house No. 550.

The performance consisted of taking his aunt about in her own or his automobile on trips to Montreal and elsewhere, and on pleasure drives, of doing odd jobs about the two houses, and of various accommodations such as errands and minor services for her personal needs. These circumstances, Spence J. at trial and the Court of Appeal, finding a contract, have held to be sufficient grounds for disregarding the prohibition of the statute. . . .

The leading case on this question is *Maddison v. Alderson* [(1883), 8 App. Cas. 467]. The facts there were much stronger than those before us. The plaintiff, giving up all prospects of any other course of life, had spent over twenty years as housekeeper of the intestate until his death without wages on the strength of his promise to leave her the manor on which they lived. A defectively executed will made her a beneficiary to the extent of a life interest in all his property, real and personal. The House of Lords held that, assuming a contract, there had been no such part performance as would answer s. 4.

The Lord Chancellor, Earl Selborne, states the principle in these words:—

> All the acts done must be referred to the actual contract, which is the measure and test of their legal and equitable character and consequence.

At p. 479, referring to the rule that payment of the purchase price is not sufficient, he says:—

> The best explanation of it seems to be, that the payment of money is an equivocal act, not (in itself) until the connection is established by parol testimony, indicative of a contract concerning land . . . All the authorities show that the acts relied upon as part performance must be unequivocally, and in their own nature referable to some such agreement as that alleged.

Lord O'Hagan, at p. 485, uses this language:—

> It must be unequivocal. It must have relation to the one agreement relied upon, and to no other when it must be such, in Lord Hardwick's words, "as could be done with no other view or design than to perform that agreement".

.....

I am quite unable to distinguish that authority from the matter before us. Here, as there, the acts of performance by themselves are wholly neutral and have no more relation to a contract connected with premises No. 548 than with those of No. 550 or than to mere expectation that his aunt would requite his solicitude in her will, or that they were given gratuitously or on terms that the time and outlays would be compensated in money. In relation to specific performance, strict plead-ing would seem to require a demonstrated connection between the acts of perfor-mance and a dealing with the land before evidence of the terms of any agreement is admissible. This exception of part performance is an anomaly; it is based on equities resulting from the acts done; but unless we are to say that, after perfor-mance by one party, any refusal to perform by the other gives rise to them, which would in large measure write off the section, we must draw the line where those acts are referable and referable only to the contract alleged. The facts here are almost the classical case against which the statute is aimed: they have been found to be truly stated and I accept that; but it was the nature of the proof that is condemned, not the facts, and their truth at law is irrelevant. Against this, equity intervenes only in circumstances that are not present here.

There remains the question of recovery for the services rendered on the basis of a *quantum meruit*. On the findings of both courts below the services were not given gratuitously but on the footing of a contractual relation: they were to be paid for. The statute in such a case does not touch the principle of restitution against what would otherwise be an unjust enrichment of the defendant at the expense of the plaintiff. This is exemplified in the simple case of part or full payment in money as the price under an oral contract; it would be inequitable to allow the promissor to keep both the land and the money and the other party to the bargain is entitled to recover what he has paid. Similarly is it in the case of services given.

This matter is elaborated exhaustively in the Restatement of the Law of Contract issued by the American Law Institute and Professor Williston's monu-mental work on Contracts in vol. 2, s. 536 deals with the same topic. On the principles there laid down the respondent is entitled to recover for his services and outlays what the deceased would have had to pay for them on a purely business basis to any other person in the position of the respondent. The evidence covers generally and perhaps in the only way possible the particulars, but enough is shown to enable the court to make a fair determination of the amount called for; and since it would be to the benefit of the other beneficiaries to bring an end to this litigation, I think we should not hesitate to do that by fixing the amount to be allowed. This I place at the sum of $3,000.

The appeal will therefore be allowed and the judgment modified by declaring the respondent entitled to recover against the respondent administrator the sum of $3,000, all costs will be paid out of the estate, those of the administrator as between solicitor and client.

CARTWRIGHT J. [after holding that there were not sufficient acts of part performance the learned judge continued:]. . . . It remains to consider the respon-dent's alternative claim to recover for the value of the services which he performed for the deceased. . . .

I agree with the conclusion of my brother Rand that the respondent is entitled to recover the value of these services from the respondent administrator. This right appears to me to be based, not on the contract, but on an obligation imposed by law. . . .

In my view it was correctly decided in *Britain v. Rossiter* [(1879), 11 Q.B.D. 123 (C.A.)] that where there is an express contract between the parties which turns out to be unenforceable by reason of the Statute of Frauds no other contract between the parties can be implied from the doing of acts in performance of the express but unenforceable contract. At page 127 Brett L.J., after stating that the express contract although unenforceable was not void but continued to exist, said:—

> It seems to me impossible that a new contract can be implied from the doing of acts which were clearly done in performance of the first contract only, and to infer from them a fresh contract would be to draw an inference contrary to the fact. It is a proposition which cannot be disputed that no new contract can be implied from acts done under an express contract, which is still subsisting; all that can be said is that no one can be charged upon the original contract because it is not in writing.

In the case at bar all the acts for which the respondent asks to be paid under his alternative claim were clearly done in performance of the existing but unenforceable contract with the deceased that she would devise 548 Besserer Street to him and to infer from them a fresh contract to pay the value of the services in money would be, in the words of Brett L.J. quoted above, to draw an inference contrary to the fact.

In my opinion when the Statute of Frauds was pleaded the express contract was thereby rendered unenforceable, but, the deceased having received the benefits of the full performance of the contract by the respondent, the law imposed upon her, and so on her estate, the obligation to pay the fair value of the services rendered to her. . . .

For the above reasons I would dispose of the appeal as proposed by my brother Rand.

[Rinfret C.J.C. and Taschereau J. concurred with Rand J.; Estey, Locke and Fauteux JJ. with Cartwright J.]

NOTE

The sum recovered was presumably considerably less than the value of the land claimed. The award therefore ought not to be viewed as an indirect means of enforcing the alleged contract. See, however, Cooper, "The Statute of Frauds and Actions in Restitution and Debt: *Pavey and Matthews Pty. Ltd. v. Paul*" (1989), 19 U.W.A.L. Rev. 56.

THOMPSON v. GUARANTY TRUST CO.

[1974] S.C.R. 1023, [1973] 6 W.W.R. 746, 39 D.L.R. (3d) 408

SPENCE J. [delivering the judgment of the court] This is an appeal from the judgment of the Court of Appeal for Saskatchewan.. . .

The appellant, as plaintiff, had sued for specific performance of an agreement alleged to have been entered into between him and the deceased Richard John Copithorne whereby the said deceased agreed that in consideration of the respondent remaining with the deceased and working and operating the farm lands of the said deceased until the death of the deceased the deceased would devise and bequeath to the respondent the whole of his estate, both land and personalty.

In order to come to a decision in this matter, I find it necessary to outline the facts adduced in the evidence in some considerable detail. I am of the opinion that this would be most efficiently done by quoting extensively from the judgment of MacPherson J. at trial [[1971] 5 W.W.R. 142, at 143]:

At Indian Head in 1921, Gus met Dick and in the spring of 1922 he went to work for him as a farm labourer. He stayed there until Dick died in 1970, 48 years later.

For some of that time, there was a female housekeeper on the farm but during most of those years the two lived alone. Neither ever married.

In 1922, Dick owned two quarter sections of land against which there was debt. He was then 33. When he died at the age of 81, he owned considerably more land and other assets. His estate exceeded $200,000 in value. No will has been found.

For the first two years, Gus was paid by Dick $50 and his keep. In about 1924, Dick became ill and remained unable to work for two years and Gus then did all the farming and kept the home and nursed Dick. Many witnesses describe their relationship through the years as like that of brothers or father and son. Very possibly their intimacy and mutual confidence commenced during this illness. It was then that Dick made his first promise to make Gus his heir. He said that he could then not afford to pay Gus's wages, but, if Gus agreed to stay and work that all this property would be Gus's "if I don't recover".

Again in 1928 Dick was in bed for a good part of the farm season. This time he was injured when he was run over by a one-way plough. Again, he made the same promise and again Gus agreed to stay.

On 28th April 1942 Dick was thrown from a horse and suffered an injury to a leg which left him a cripple for the rest of his life. There were then two papers signed by Dick in the hospital. The smaller one was entirely in his own hand and signed also by Gus. The second was a long document which Gus believed was a will but, as he testified, may not have been. Both were stolen along with all of Dick's duplicate certificates of title and other papers, in 1969, and are beyond my interpretation. I shall refer to these as "the 1942 papers".

As he handed Gus the papers, he said that all the property was Gus's and nobody could bother him. Then he told Gus to look after Christina, who was the housekeeper I have mentioned. He referred to the larger paper as a will.

As a result of Dick's injury, Gus's induction into the Army was deferred and he remained on the farm throughout the war.

Later, in the 1940s, Gus decided to leave Dick and go elsewhere. He decided not to leave, however, because, once again, Dick agreed that upon his death his whole estate would go to Gus, if Gus stayed and worked the farm.

On 4th January 1969 it was necessary to take Dick to hospital. At his request, Mr. and Mrs. Schoenau came to drive him there. Gus went along. Before leaving their home, Dick produced from his strong-box the larger of the 1942 papers, the one which Gus thought was a will, and said to Gus, "Here's everything if I don't come back." Dick wept. Mrs. Schoenau remembers him then saying to Gus, "I am giving everything to you." That night, while Gus was away and the house was empty, the box and its contents, including the presumed will, were stolen.

The duplicate certificates of title were replaced by the procedure under The Land Titles Act, R.S.S. 1965, c. 115.

On 22nd May 1970, Gus, with the assistance of a neighbour, took Dick to the hospital for the last time. Many incidents occurred in the hospital which would indicate to me that Dick, until the end, intended to give his property to Gus.

Gus had in his possession cheques payable to Dick totalling about $4,500. These included two cheques from the Government of Saskatchewan in compensation for land taken for a roadway, and one from the Lutheran Synod, as payment on an agreement for sale of land. Gus gave all the cheques to Dick, who endorsed one and gave them all back to Gus, saying it was all Gus's now, the money and the land, and that he, Dick, did not want to spend any of Gus's money.

Then occurred, the oddest and the most confusing incident in the whole story. Perhaps it was also tragic. Dick told Gus to get Ed Poells to draw a paper turning everything over to Gus. Gus passed the instructions to Poells who drew, in duplicate, a power of attorney. This was signed by Dick, who then told Gus to get himself a lawyer because Dick's property was all now his, and added the precatory injunction that he, Gus, was not to forget Olive, George and Buster, the children of Christina, the deceased housekeeper.

Mr. Poells is of the genus small town factotum—insurance agent, notary public—without whom this province could not carry on, but whose errors sometimes give rise to litigation. Mr. Poells is a very self-assured individual, a bit of an exhibitionist and a most unsatisfactory witness. When Gus told him what Dick wanted, Poells assumed it was a power of attorney. In direct testimony, Poells told us that, although Dick did not read the document, he, Poells, had fully explained it to him. Under cross-examination it appeared that Poells was far from sure what he then said about it. I am satisfied that Poells told Dick that the document turned everything over to Gus but I seriously doubt that he made him or the others present to understand that this was a temporary thing. Mrs. Schoenau who signed as witness said Dick was relieved after signing and he remarked that everything was now Gus's and he could do with it as he pleased.

The document itself is the ordinary printed form of power of attorney, double foolscap size, folded and possessing 2-1/2 pages of small print. The only words added to the printed form were the names of Richard John Copithorne and Angus Reed Thompson. Although Dick's eyes were sharp, he did not read the document. He was told that it turned everything over to Gus, as it did. He saw the names typewritten. He did not understand its temporary quality. I am satisfied on the balance of probabilities that he thought he was signing a will, and that he intended it as such.

The learned trial Judge further stated [at 146]:

Up to about 1924, when Dick's first lengthy illness occurred, Gus was paid normally for work done. Then for two years he did almost everything around the farm and the home, including the care of Dick. Thereafter, except for Dick's season of incapacity when run over by the one-way, apparently the two shared the work until 1942, when Dick was crippled. From 1942 until 1970, the evidence is abundant that Gus was a constant and tireless worker on the farm. He was, in my view, more than a worker, he became a skilled farmer and manager in the sense of making decisions concerning crops, equipment, purchases and sales, or, at least, sharing in the decisions with Dick after consultation.

After 1942, the two were constantly together except when Gus was in the fields. Dick could drive a tractor or truck only for short periods. Mrs. Schoenau, who knew them for the last ten years, never saw Dick drive. He was never anywhere without Gus, she said. She described their visits to the farm where Gus did the cooking and the housework. The house was only fairly clean, said this housewife, but the food was very good.

Gus, some time during the years, with some assistance, rebuilt the house, putting in new floors and constructing a new roof. He built all the granaries.

The learned trial Judge made further extensive references to the evidence and then gave his assessment of the two chief actors in the drama, Richard John Copithorne and the appellant Angus Reed Thompson, in these words, "They were kind, simple, honest people", and again, "The simplicity, humility and honesty of Gus were plain, and I believed him throughout."

Maguire J.A., in giving the judgement of the Court of Appeal for Saskatchewan, said:

The learned trial judge, MacPherson J., in a written judgment, found and held that the respondent [here appellant] had established an oral contract as alleged. There is evidence fully supporting this finding, and it cannot be disturbed.

With this finding I am in complete agreement and, indeed, I am of the view that the appeal was argued in this Court on the basis of the existence of an oral contract whereby the deceased promised to give to the appellant his whole estate if the appellant should remain and work with him on the farm until his, Copithorne's death has been established. . . .

The action has been argued in all Courts upon the basis that there was no sufficient memorandum within s. 4 of the Statute of Frauds and the vital issue in this appeal is whether or not lacking such a memorandum in writing there have been sufficient acts of part performance on the part of the appellant to take the case out of the said s. 4 of the Statute of Frauds.

The learned trial Judge, after his very complete review of the evidence, expressed his conclusion in these words [at 149]:

> Thus, I have no hesitation in holding that Gus's work was directed to the contract and that constituted not only part performance as equity requires, but complete performance. The contract was that Gus was to inherit all of Dick's estate and that, consequently, is enforceable.

On the other hand, Maguire J.A., giving judgment for the Court of Appeal for Saskatchewan, came to another conclusion, stating:

> I cannot, however, construe any act or acts of the respondent as meeting the stated test as expounded in *Deglman v. Guaranty Trust Co.* [*supra*]; *Brownscombe v. Public Trustee*, [1969] S.C.R. 658.

and concluded:

> I must, therefore, with all respect, hold that the learned trial Judge erred in holding that the respondent was entitled to the whole estate of the deceased, pursuant to the terms of the oral agreement.

The test was enunciated by Lord Selborne in the House of Lords in *Maddison v. Alderson* (1883), 8 App. Cas. 467, when he said at p. 479:

> . . . All the authorities shew that the acts relied upon as part performance must be unequivocally, and in their own nature, referable to some such agreement as that alleged. . . .

It is the interpretation of those latter words which has been the subject of a series of cases in this Court. Those cases are *McNeil v. Corbett* (1907), 39 S.C.R. 608; *Deglman v. Guar. Trust Co. of Can.*, *supra*; and *Brownscombe v. Pub. Trustee of Alta.*, *supra*.

In *McNeil v. Corbett*, *supra*, Duff J. (as he then was) considered whether the transfer of a $500 debenture from one party to another was evidence of part performance. The learned Justice quoted from *Maddison v. Alderson* . . . and held that in that particular case there was nothing in the nature of the acts proved which bears any necessary relation to the interest in land said to have been the subject of the agreement in question. A sale and purchase of the stock and bonds actually transferred would suffice to explain them. The acts were held not to be part performance so as to take the case out of the Statute of Frauds. . . .

In the *Deglman* case . . . Cartwright J., as he then was, then said at p. 729:

> It is clear that none of the numerous acts done by the respondent in performance of the contract were in their own nature unequivocally referable to No. 548 Besserer Street, or to any dealing with that land.

This Court, therefore, came to the conclusion that such acts were not acts as to which evidence could be received to establish part performance of the contract and granted to the nephew only a quantum meruit sum, as the Court of Appeal did in the present case.

It should be noted that the very vague and general character of the services performed in *Deglman* bear little resemblance to the services performed in the present case. In the first place, the nephew never lived at 548 Besserer Street, the premises which he alleged his aunt had contracted to leave to him in her will, and had performed services at either 548 or at 550 Besserer Street and had performed various other desultory acts of assistance much more referable to the natural desire of a dutiful nephew to assist an aged aunt than any contract for leaving specific property to him in a will. Moreover, I am of the opinion that the relationship between the claimant and the deceased, that of nephew and aunt, is of some importance in considering the acts of part performance which were alleged. It is also, of course, notable that the nephew had his own life away from the aunt and with his own wife and family.

In *Brownscombe v. Pub. Trustee of Alta., supra*, the Court considered very different circumstances and those which resemble markedly the circumstances in the present case. Brownscombe, when only 16 years of age, had applied to Vercamert at the latter's home for work. Vercamert, as was the deceased in the present case, was a bachelor somewhat severely crippled by heart trouble and able to do but little work on the farm where he lived. The learned trial Judge made a finding which was quoted by Hall J. in giving reasons for judgment in this Court as follows:

> I find that plaintiff worked faithfully for his employer with but little financial reward for a considerable number of years. I find that on a number of occasions when plaintiff thought of leaving Vercamert's employ he was dissuaded by the latter's promised assurance that on his demise the farm would go to plaintiff by Will. In January 1961, Vercamert died intestate and this action is the result.

At p. 664, Hall J. said:

> It is clear that not all the acts relied on as testified to by the appellant and his wife can be regarded as "unequivocally referable in their own nature to some dealing with the land", but in my view the building of the house on the lands in question in the years 1946 and 1947 at the suggestion of Vercamert almost, if not wholly, at the appellant's expense was, as the learned trial judge found "unequivocally referable" to the agreement which the appellant alleged had been made and inconsistent with the ordinary relationship of employee or tenant.

Therefore, this Court held that the plaintiff had proved acts of part performance to take the case out of the Statute of Frauds and directed specific performance.

Counsel made the submission in the present appeal that the acts of part performance which were alleged by the appellant were not so decisive and were not so unequivocally referable to the very lands as were those in *Brownscombe*. I am personally of the opinion that practically every act of part performance as to which evidence was given, and I have read the record carefully, were acts which were unequivocally referable to a contract in reference to the very lands in question, that is, the farm consisting of five one-quarter sections which had been the property of the deceased. The appellant was no mere farm hired man and had not been since about 1924, but from 1924 until the death of Richard John Copithorne on 2nd June 1970 the appellant had been the operator and manager of the whole farm industry owned by the deceased. There was not one part of the work in reference to that farm in which the appellant had not taken, not only a prominent part but the leading part, and both physically and because of age the deceased had relied solely on the intelligent and arduous labour of the appellant. It is quite clear that the deceased, more than anyone else, realized and appreciated the nature and the quality of the appellant's work. We have independent evidence that the deceased told his cousin in 1969, the year before his death, that but for Gus he, Dick, would be in the poorhouse.

In *Brownscombe v. Pub. Trustee of Alta.*, Hall J. found the building of the house to be a factor plainly referable to an agreement as to the very land. Counsel for the respondent here objected that the house was not built by the appellant but the appellant simply renovated and made more comfortable the residence which both he and the deceased had for some time before occupied. I am of the opinion that the distinction is quite unimportant. The evidence is that the house was a wreck, that it was totally rebuilt by the appellant and, in my view, it is exactly the same kind of a circumstance that had occurred in the *Brownscombe* case. Moreover, the appellant changed the farm from a rather run-down marginal proposition to one where the total estate of the deceased at his death amounted to about $200,000. Broken old barns were torn down, granaries were built, a garage building was purchased in the town and hauled on the property, a thoroughbred Hereford cattle business was commenced, and the evidence that the deceased and the appellant had agreed to share the proceeds of this business two-thirds and one-third, in my opinion, rather than being evidence mitigating against the alleged contract, is evidence which will confirm and corroborate it. That was a distribution of proceeds during the lifetime of the deceased and it is quite separable from any contract to give to the appellant what remained at the death of the promisor, the deceased.

I therefore cannot distinguish the circumstances in the present case from those which the Court considered in the *Brownscombe* case except to say that probably the circumstances are stronger in favour of this appellant than they were for Brownscombe in that case. I would, therefore, hold without hesitation that the appellant has proved acts which are unequivocally referable to the very lands and that therefore he has adduced the evidence of part performance which takes the case out of the provisions of s. 4 of the Statute of Frauds.

I would allow the appeal and restore the judgment of the learned trial Judge. . . .

NOTES and QUESTIONS

1. To what extent are the respective courts in *Deglman* and *Thompson* applying the same test for the application of the part performance doctrine? More specifically, do they interpret *Maddison v. Alderson* and the test of "unequivocally referable" in the same way?

2. Virtually all of the part performance litigation involves contracts for the sale of an interest in land. However, consider whether the doctrine can be defended as applicable to the other categories

of contract covered by s. 4. For a discussion, see Barber, "The Operation of the Doctrine of Part Performance, In Particular to Actions for Damages" (1973), 8 U.Q.L.J. 77 at 88 *et seq.*

3. Most commonly, the remedy sought in the part performance cases is specific performance. However, if specific performance is no longer possible because, *e.g.*, the property has been sold to another, an issue arises as to whether the court may award damages instead. While traditionally the courts would not award damages (a common law remedy) to vindicate a claim that was founded in equity, the Chancery Amendment Act, 1858 (21 & 22 Vict., c. 27), or Lord Cairns' Act, as it is more commonly called, and its Canadian equivalents opened up this possibility. However, the availability of equitable damages where the plaintiff is relying upon acts of performance to support the claim remains unclear with some courts holding that, in terms of the language of Lord Cairns' Act, this is not a situation where the courts have "jurisdiction to entertain an application for specific performance". See, *e.g.*, Barber, *supra*, and O.L.R.C.: *Report on Amendment of the Law of Contract* (1987), at 92-93.

However, the better view would now seem to be that, at least where the contract is of a type that is generally susceptible to specific performance and there was some warrant for seeking that form of relief, the disappearance of an entitlement to specific performance between the time the action was commenced and the date of trial will not deprive the plaintiff of the right to rely on the doctrine of part performance as the basis for a claim in damages. See *Dobson v. Winton & Robbins Ltd.*, [1959] S.C.R. 775 and *Price v. Strange*, [1978] Ch. 337 (C.A.). Indeed, with the continued movement in the direction of total fusion of the principles of common law and equity, it may be possible to assert a right to common law damages in aid of equitable interests such as those protected by the doctrine of part performance: *Le Mesurier v. Andrus* (1986), 54 O.R. (2d) 1 (C.A.), leave to appeal to S.C.C. refused (1986), 63 O.R. (2d) x (note) (S.C.C.), and *Canson Enterprises Ltd. v. Boughton & Co.*, [1991] 3 S.C.R. 534. See also *Nicol v. Weigel* (1991), 17 R.P.R. (2d) 213 (B.C. C.A.) holding that the British Columbia statutory form of the doctrine of part performance was not restricted to situations where the plaintiff was entitled to specific performance. There, the defendant had sold the relevant property to a *bona fide* purchaser for value without notice whose interest was registered before the action for specific performance with damages in the alternative was even commenced by the purchaser under the prior oral contract.

4. The mere payment of money was traditionally held not to be a sufficient or even relevant act of part performance (*Johnson v. Can. Co.* (1856), 5 Gr. 558 (C.A.)). However, recent developments in the jurisprudence seen to liberalize the requirements for the application of the doctrine. The House of Lords decision in *Steadman v. Steadman*, [1976] A.C. 536, has been particularly influential in this apparent trend. *Steadman* was approved by the Supreme Court of Canada in a case that did not involve the Statute of Frauds, *Hill v. Nova Scotia (Attorney General)* (1997), 142 D.L.R. (4th) 230 (S.C.C.). The following extract traces some of these judicial developments.

LENSEN v. LENSEN

[1984] 6 W.W.R. 673, 14 D.L.R. (4th) 611, 35 Sask. R. 48 (C.A.)

TALLIS J.A. [delivering the judgment of the court] . . .

There are two theoretical bases for the doctrine of part performance. The more orthodox approach to the doctrine is that of regarding it as a theory that some writers call "alternative evidence". Under this approach acts of part performance are viewed as being evidence sufficiently cogent to allow a court of equity to enforce the contract even though it could not be enforced at common law because of non-compliance with the statute. Under this approach it is necessary that the "acts" of part performance be adduced as a pre-condition to the introduction of parol evidence to prove the contract. However, this raises the question as to what are sufficient acts of part performance to enable the court to consider parol evidence of the contract. Must the acts prove the precise terms of the alleged contract or only that there is a contract?

The second theoretical basis of the doctrine emphasizes the acts of part performance not so much for their evidentiary value but as raising equities in the plaintiff's favour which render it unjust not to enforce the contract. This approach to the doctrine has recently received judicial approval in England: see *Steadman v. Steadman*, [*supra*]. . . .

For many years, the courts in England applied the doctrine of part performance [as stated in *Maddison v. Alderson, supra*] in a stringent fashion. Not only did the acts have to refer to the land in question but, as stated by Fry L.J. in *Fry on Specific Performance*, 6th ed. (1921), p. 276:

> . . . the acts of part performance must be such as not only to be referable to a contract such as alleged, but . . . referable to no other title.

By 1962 this rather stringent test had become liberalized. In *Kingswood Estate Co. v. Anderson*, [1963] 2 Q.B. 169, [1962] 3 W.L.R. 1102, [1962] 3 All E.R. 593 (C.A.), the defendant alleged an oral agreement for a tenancy for life. She contended that her act in quitting her rent-controlled premises and moving into the flat offered her by the plaintiffs was sufficient part performance to render the oral agreement for a life tenancy enforceable. The point was taken that the act of part performance was as referable to a weekly tenancy as to a tenancy for life. Upjohn L.J. categorically rejected the contention that the acts of part performance had to be referable to no other title than alleged, saying, at p. 604 [All E.R.], that "this [was] a long exploded idea" and:

> The true rule is, in my view, stated in FRY ON SPECIFIC PERFORMANCE (6th Edn.), p. 278, s. 582:
>
>> The true principle, however, of the operation of acts of part performance seems only to require that the acts in question be such as must be referred to some contract, and may be referred to the alleged one; that they prove the existence of some contract, and are consistent with the contract alleged.

This test was adopted in *Wakeham v. Mackenzie*, [1968] 1 W.L.R. 1175 at 1181, [1968] 2 All E.R. 783 (Ch.D.). I conclude that these English authorities take the view that the acts need not unequivocally refer to the contract in question but must prove the existence of *some* contract and be *consistent* with the one alleged.

In *Steadman v. Steadman, supra*, Lord Reid emphasized the acts of part performance in the context of raising equities in the plaintiff which render it unjust not to enforce the contract. I refer in particular to the following passages at pp. 981-82:

> The argument for the wife, for which there is a good deal of authority, is that no act can be relied on as an act of part performance unless it relates to the land to be acquired and can only be explained by the existence of a contract relating to the land. . . .
>
> I think that there has been some confusion between this supposed rule and another perfectly good rule. You must not first look at the oral contract and then see whether the alleged acts of part performance are consistent with it. You must first look at the alleged acts of part performance and see whether they prove that there must have been a contract and it is only if they do so prove that you can bring in the oral contract.
>
> A thing is proved in civil litigation by shewing that it is more probably true than not; and I see no reason why there should be any different standard of proof here. If there were what

would the standard be? The only other recognised standard of proof is beyond reasonable doubt but why should that apply here?

I am aware that it has often been said that the acts relied on must necessarily or unequivocally indicate the existence of a contract. It may well be that we should consider whether any prudent reasonable man would have done those acts if there had not been a contract but many people are neither prudent nor reasonable and they might often spend money or prejudice their position not in reliance on a contract but in the optimistic expectation that a contract would follow. So if there were a rule that acts relied on as part performance must of their own nature unequivocally shew that there was a contract, it would be only in the rarest case that all other possible explanations could be excluded.

In my view, unless the law is to be divorced from reason and principle, the rule must be that you take the whole circumstances, leaving aside evidence about the oral contract, and see whether it is proved that the acts relied on were done in reliance on a contract: that will be proved if it is shewn to be more probable than not.

Authorities which seem to require more than that appear to be based on an idea never clearly defined, to the effect that the law of part performance is a rule of evidence rather than an application of an equitable principle. I do not know on what ground any court could say that, although you cannot produce the evidence required by the Statute of Frauds, some other kind of evidence will do instead. But I can see that if part performance is simply regarded as evidence then it would be reasonable to hold not only that the acts of part performance must relate to the land but that they must indicate the nature of the oral contract with regard to the land. But that appears to me to be a fundamental departure from the true doctrine of part performance, and it is not supported by recent authorities such as *Kingswood Estate Co. Ltd. v. Anderson.*

The Canadian approach of the legal interpretation of the phrase "acts unequivocally in their own nature referable" must also be considered because the Supreme Court of Canada has not expressly re-examined the rule in *Maddison v. Alderson* in light of English authorities such as *Steadman v. Steadman* or *Wakeham v. Mackenzie.* For the purposes of this appeal, the appellant accepts that the Supreme Court of Canada has indicated that the acts of alleged part performance must be referable to and must be indicative of some contract dealing with the land: see *Thompson v. Guar. Trust Co., Brownscombe v. Pub. Trustee,* and *Deglman v. Guar. Trust Co.*

Learned counsel submits that the authorities do not go further and dictate that the acts must of necessity be referable to *the* interest in the land or *the* contract which is propounded. I do not read the recent Supreme Court of Canada authorities as applying such a stringent test that the acts must of necessity be referable to either *the* interest in the land or *the* contract which is being propounded. If the acts relied upon are "unequivocally referable in their own nature to *some* dealing with the land" the requisite test is met. . . .

NOTES

1. The decision of the Saskatchewan Court of Appeal in *Lensen* was reversed on other grounds by the Supreme Court of Canada, [1987] 2 S.C.R. 672. The court quoted without comment the views of the Court of Appeal on part performance.

2. Some courts have enthusiastically adopted the reformulation of the doctrine of part performance in *Steadman v. Steadman.* In *Currie v. Thomas* (1985), 19 D.L.R. (4th) 594 (B.C. C.A.), the court described *Steadman v. Steadman,* at 601, as "the leading authority" on the question of part performance and decided the case without referring to the earlier Supreme Court of Canada authorities.

3. After the decision in *Currie v. Thomas*, acting on a recommendation of its Law Reform Commission (*Report on Statute of Frauds* (1977), L.C.R. 33 at 73), the British Columbia legislature enacted the following provision, now the Law and Equity Act, R.S.B.C. 1996, c. 253, s. 59(3) [en. 1985, c. 10, s. 7]:

> (3) A contract respecting land or a disposition of land is not enforceable unless . . .
>
> > (*b*) the party to be charged has done an act, or acquiesced in an act of the party alleging the contract or disposition, that indicates that a contract or disposition not inconsistent with that alleged has been made, or
> >
> > (*c*) the person alleging the contract or disposition has, in reasonable reliance on it, so changed the person's position that an inequitable result, having regard to both parties' interests, can be avoided only by enforcing the contract or disposition.
>
> (4) For the purposes of subsection (3)(*b*), an act of a party alleging a contract or disposition includes a payment or acceptance by that party or on that party's behalf of a deposit or part payment of a purchase price.

To what extent is this a codification of *Steadman*? See the discussion in Bridge, "The Statute of Frauds and Sale of Land Contracts" (1986), 64 Can. Bar Rev. 58 at 103-05.

Under the equitable version of part performance, there still continue to be debates about whether it is only the acts of the plaintiff that should count and about the extent to which the defendant must have known about and/or acquiesced in those actions: see *Taylor v. Rawana* (1990), 74 O.R. (2d) 357 (H.C.), affirmed (1992), 10 O.R. (3d) 736 (C.A.).

(d)   SHOULD WRITING REQUIREMENTS BE RETAINED OR ABOLISHED?

Clearly the Statute of Frauds is the product of conditions which no longer exist. Its retention has also been criticized on a number of other grounds. The Ontario Law Reform Commission for example, pointed out, at 95-97, that the Statute is arbitrary, in that there is no justification for the particular list of contracts which it governs, it does not accord with social practices, because people frequently enter into parol agreements of the type covered by the Statute, and most importantly it can cause unexpected and unjustifiable hardship to a litigant who loses an otherwise good claim on a purely technical defence. In addition, because of the evolution of numerous exceptions, the present requirement of writing does not serve well any cautionary or channelling functions, discussed in section 1(a) of this chapter.

Most jurisdictions, other than Manitoba, have enacted piecemeal reforms. The O.L.R.C., whose *Report* is frequently discussed in this section, recommended more comprehensive change involving, for example, the repeal of the requirement of writing for contracts relating to land, provided that such contracts are not enforceable on the uncorroborated evidence of the party alleging the contract. However, the O.L.R.C. recommended that a writing requirement be retained for guarantees (or indemnities) other than those that are given by a person in the course of business to another person acting in the course of business. For other views on the necessity of writing requirements, see Fridman, "The Necessity for Writing in Contracts Within the Statute of Frauds" (1985), 35 U.T.L.J. 43 and Bridge, "The Statute of Frauds and Sale of Land Contracts", *supra*.

These views and suggestions raise for discussion the entire role of requirements of formality, both in the present law and in any future reforms. What is your view on the wisdom of writing requirements? With respect to land contracts specifically what is your preference: retention of the *status quo*, legislative codification of the part performance doctrine (as in British Columbia), adoption of the O.L.R.C. position, or complete legislative abolition (as in Manitoba)?

In this regard, note the following statement by Huband J.A. of the Manitoba Court of Appeal in *Megill-Stephenson Co. v. Woo* (1989), 59 D.L.R. (4th) 146 at 151, in support of a holding that an apparent oral contract for the sale of land was, having regard to the nature of the negotiations, subject to approval by the vendor's solicitor:

> While the *Statute of Frauds* has been repealed in this jurisdiction, the idea lying behind it remains valid. The courts should be reluctant to impose binding contracts on parties based upon conversations, particularly where the usual practice has been to reduce such contracts into writing. In spite of the repeal of the *Statute of Frauds*, the practice in dealing with the purchase and sale of land is to have the contracts in written form, and that was the obvious expectation between the parties in this dispute. Indeed, the expectation of Woo was that the contract would be reduced into writing and would have no binding legal impact until signed by him. And the signing, of course, would take place only after the contract was reviewed and approved by his solicitor.

Chapter 5

PRIVITY OF CONTRACT

1.   Introduction

The doctrine of privity applies in Canada to prevent two types of persons from enforcing a contract. First, a person who is a complete stranger to the contract has no legal right to enforce the promise of any party to that contract. This aspect of the privity doctrine is uncontroversial. The second type of person affected is the third party beneficiary, the person identified and intended by the promisor and promisee to receive all or part of the benefit of the agreed upon performance. This aspect of the privity doctrine is highly controversial. Gradually, over the course of the past century, the third party bar has been eliminated in almost all common law jurisdictions. The Canadian provinces are now essentially alone in their retention of the formal general prohibition on enforcement of a contract by a third party beneficiary.

2.   The History of the Doctrine of Privity and Third Party Beneficiaries

At least one commentator has asserted that the bar on third party beneficiary actions has been the law of England since before 1700: Bennett, "Considerations Moving From Third Persons" (1895), 9 Harv. L.R. 233 at 234. Such a proposition is quite clearly incorrect. Authorities which unequivocally declare the right of a third party beneficiary to sue on the contract are found well into the nineteenth century. Contrary authorities, of which there were few, appear to proceed on the basis that the third party was a "stranger to the consideration". An independent privity rule clearly appears only at the beginning of the 20th century, albeit without reference to supporting authorities. Additional confusion and uncertainty is caused by the role of the doctrine of consideration in this context. As noted above, the earlier cases barring the third party were all concerned with an absence of consideration on the part of the third party. There is a debate over whether or not the privity rule is just another way of saying that "consideration must move from the promisee". Consider, initially, whether the rule that consideration must move from the promisee is conceptually congruent with the supposed rule that a "stranger to the consideration" cannot enforce the contract. Then decide which of the next three cases, if any, are resolved on the basis of an independent privity rule.

PROVENDER v. WOOD

(1630), Het. 30, 124 E.R. 318

Provender brought an action upon the case against Wood, for that the defendant assumed to the father of the plaintiff upon a marriage to be solemnised between the plaintiff and the daughter of the defendant, to pay him £20. And it was agreed by Richardson and Yelverton nullo contradicent. That the action well lies for the same. And the party to whom the benefit of a promise accrews may bring his action.

TWEDDLE v. ATKINSON

(1861), 1 B. & S. 393, 121 E.R. 762 (Q.B.)

The declaration stated that the plaintiff was the son of John Tweddle, deceased, and before the making of the agreement hereafter mentioned, married the daughter of William Guy, deceased, and before the marriage the parents of both parties to the marriage orally promised to give the plaintiff a marriage portion, and after the marriage the parents entered into the following written agreement:

> High Coniscliffe, July 11th, 1855.

> Memorandum of an agreement made this day between William Guy, of &c., of the one part, and John Tweddle, of &c., of the other part. Whereas it is mutually agreed that the said William Guy shall and will pay the sum of £200. to William Tweddle, his son-in-law; and the said John Tweddle, father to the aforesaid William Tweddle, shall and will pay the sum of £100. to the said William Tweddle, each and severally the said sums on or before the 21st day of August, 1855. And it is hereby further agreed by the aforesaid William Guy and the said John Tweddle that the said William Tweddle has full power to sue the said parties in any Court of law or equity for the aforesaid sums hereby promised and specified.

It was further alleged that afterwards and before this action the plaintiff and his wife, who is still living, ratified and assented to the said agreement, but yet neither William Guy nor his executor has paid the promised sum of £200.

WIGHTMAN J. Some of the old decisions appear to support the proposition that a stranger to the consideration of a contract may maintain an action upon it, if he stands in such a near relationship to the party from whom the consideration proceeds, that he may be considered a party to the consideration. The strongest of those cases is that cited in *Bourne v. Mason* [(1669), 86 E.R. 5] in which it was held that the daughter of a physician might maintain *assumpsit* upon a promise to her father to give her a sum of money if he performed a certain cure. But there is no modern case in which the proposition has been supported. On the contrary, it is now established that no stranger to the consideration can take advantage of a contract, although made for his benefit.

CROMPTON J. It is admitted that the plaintiff cannot succeed unless this case is an exception to the modern and well established doctrine of the action of *assumpsit*. At the time when the cases which have been cited were decided the action of *assumpsit* was treated as an action of trespass upon the case, and therefore in the nature of a tort; and the law was not settled, as it now is, that natural love and affection is not a sufficient consideration for a promise upon which an action may be maintained; nor was it settled that the promisee cannot bring an action unless the consideration for the promise moved from him. The modern cases have, in effect, overruled the old decisions; they shew that the consideration must move from the party entitled to sue upon the contract. It would be a monstrous proposition to say that a person was a party to the contract for the purpose of suing upon it for his own advantage, and not a party to it for the purpose of being sued. It is said that the father in the present case was agent for the son in making the contract, but that argument ought also to make the son liable upon it. I am prepared to overrule the old decisions, and to hold that, by reason of the principles which now govern the action of *assumpsit*, the present action is not maintainable.

BLACKBURN J. . . . [T]he only point is whether, that contract being for the benefit of the children, they can sue upon it. [Counsel] admits that in general no action can be maintained upon a promise, unless the consideration moves from the party to whom it is made. But he says that there is an exception; namely, that when the consideration moves from a father, and the contract is for the benefit of his son, the natural love and affection between the father and son gives the son the right to sue as if the consideration had proceeded from himself. And *Dutton and Wife v. Poole* [(1678), 83 E.R. 523] was cited for this. We cannot overrule a decision of the Exchequer Chamber; but there is a distinct ground on which that case cannot be supported. The cases . . . shew that natural love and affection are not a sufficient consideration whereon an action of *assumpsit* may be founded.

[Judgment for the defendant.]

DUNLOP PNEUMATIC TYRE CO. LTD. v. SELFRIDGE & CO. LTD.
[1915] A.C. 847 (H.L.)

The appellants, tyre manufacturers, sold their tyres to Dew and Company, who were wholesale merchants, on the terms that Dew would not sell the tyres at below Dunlop's list prices, except to customers "legitimately engaged in the motor trade." To such customers, Dew were entitled to sell at 10% below list price if they obtained an undertaking that the customers, in turn, would observe the appellants' list prices.

The respondents, a large department store, agreed to sell Dunlop tyres to two customers at prices below those specified by the appellants. On January 2nd, they obtained the tyres from Dew and signed an agreement under which they promised not to sell or offer them below list price and agreed to pay £5 to the appellants by way of liquidated damages for every tyre sold or offered in breach of the agreement. The respondents then delivered one tyre to a customer and charged him less than the list price. They later informed the second customer that he would be required to pay the full list price.

The appellants commenced an action against the respondents for an injunction and damages in respect of the breach of the agreement of January 2nd. Phillimore J. granted the injunction and gave judgment for the appellants in the amount of £10. This judgment was reversed by the Court of Appeal.

VISCOUNT HALDANE L.C. My Lords, in my opinion this appeal ought to fail. . . . in the law of England certain principles are fundamental. One is that only a person who is a party to a contract can sue on it. Our law knows nothing of a jus quaesitum tertio [the right of a third party to recover] arising by way of contract. Such a right may be conferred by way of property, as, for example, under a trust, but it cannot be conferred on a stranger to a contract as a right to enforce the contract in personam. A second principle is that if a person with whom a contract not under seal has been made is to be able to enforce it consideration must have been given by him to the promisor or to some other person at the promisor's request. These two principles are not recognized in the same fashion by the jurisprudence of certain Continental countries or of Scotland, but here they are well established. A third proposition is that a principal not named in the contract may sue upon it if the promisee really contracted as his agent. But again, in order to entitle him so to sue, he must have given consideration either personally or through the promisee, acting as his agent in giving it.

My Lords, in the case before us, I am of opinion that the consideration, the allowance of what was in reality part of the discount to which Messrs. Dew, the promisees, were entitled as between themselves and the appellants, was to be given by Messrs. Dew on their own account, and was not in substance, any more than in form, an allowance made by the appellants. The case for the appellants is that they permitted and enabled Messrs. Dew, with the knowledge and by the desire of the respondents, to sell to the latter on the terms of the contract of January 2, 1912. But it appears to me that even if this is so the answer is conclusive. Messrs. Dew sold to the respondents goods which they had a title to obtain from the appellants independently of this contract. The consideration by way of discount under the contract of January 2 was to come wholly out of Messrs. Dew's pocket, and neither directly nor indirectly out of that of the appellants. If the appellants enabled them to sell to the respondents on the terms they did, this was not done as any part of the terms of the contract sued on.

No doubt it was provided as part of these terms that the appellants should acquire certain rights, but these rights appear on the face of the contract as jura quaesita tertio, which the appellants could not enforce. Moreover, even if this difficulty can be got over by regarding the appellants as the principals of Messrs. Dew in stipulating for the rights in question, the only consideration disclosed by the contract is one given by Messrs. Dew, not as their agents, but as principals acting on their own account.

The conclusion to which I have come on the point as to consideration renders it unnecessary to decide the further question as to whether the appellants can claim that a bargain was made in this contract by Messrs. Dew as their agents, a bargain which, apart from the point as to consideration, they could therefore enforce. If it were necessary to express an opinion on this further question, a difficulty as to the position of Messrs. Dew would have to be considered. Two contracts—one by a man on his own account as principal, and another by the same man as agent—may be validly comprised in the same piece of paper. But they must be two contracts, and not one as here. I do not think that a man can treat one and the same contract as made by him in two capacities. He cannot be regarded as contracting for himself and for another uno flatu.

My Lords, the form of the contract which we have to interpret leaves the appellants in this dilemma, that, if they say that Messrs. Dew contracted on their behalf, they gave no consideration, and if they say they gave consideration in the shape of a permission to the respondents to buy, they must set up further stipulations, which are neither to be found in the contract sued upon nor are germane to it, but are really inconsistent with its structure. That contract has been reduced to writing, and it is in the writing that we must look for the whole of the terms made between the parties. These terms cannot, in my opinion consistently with the settled principles of English law, be construed as giving to the appellants any enforceable rights as against the respondents.

I think that the judgment of the Court of Appeal was right, and I move that the appeal be dismissed with costs.

LORD DUNEDIN My Lords, I confess that this case is to my mind apt to nip any budding affection which one might have had for the doctrine of consideration. For the effect of that doctrine in the present case is to make it possible for a person to snap his fingers at a bargain deliberately made, a bargain not in itself unfair, and which the person seeking to enforce it has a legitimate interest to enforce. Notwithstanding these considerations I cannot say that I have ever had any doubt that the judgment of the Court of Appeal was right.

My Lords, I am content to adopt from a work of Sir Frederick Pollock, to which I have often been under obligation, the following words as to consideration: "An act or forbearance of one party, or the promise thereof, is the price for which the promise of the other is bought, and the promise thus given for value is enforceable." (Pollock on Contracts, 8th ed., p. 175.)

Now the agreement sued on is an agreement which on the face of it is an agreement between Dew and Selfridge. But speaking for myself, I should have no difficulty in the circumstances of this case in holding it proved that the agreement was truly made by Dew as agent for Dunlop, or in other words that Dunlop was the undisclosed principal, and as such can sue on the agreement. Nonetheless, in order to enforce it he must show consideration, as above defined, moving from Dunlop to Selfridge.

In the circumstances, how can he do so? The agreement in question is not an agreement for sale. It is only collateral to an agreement for sale; but that agreement for sale is an agreement entirely between Dew and Selfridge. The tyres, the property in which upon the bargain is transferred to Selfridge, were the property of Dew, not of Dunlop, for Dew under his agreement with Dunlop held these tyres as proprietor, and not as agent. What then did Dunlop do, or forbear to do, in a question with Selfridge? The answer must be, nothing. He did not do anything, for Dew, having the right of property in the tyres, could give a good title to any one he liked, subject, it might be, to an action of damages at the instance of Dunlop for breach of contract, which action, however, could never create a vitium reale in the property of the tyres. He did not forbear in anything, for he had no action against Dew which he gave up, because Dew had fulfilled his contract with Dunlop in obtaining, on the occasion of the sale, a contract from Selfridge in the terms prescribed.

To my mind, this ends the case. That there are methods of framing a contract which will cause persons in the position of Selfridge to become bound, I do not doubt. But that has not been done in this instance; and as Dunlop's advisers must have known of the law of consideration, it is their affair that they have not so drawn the contract.

I think the appeal should be dismissed.

[Opinions to similar effect were delivered by Lords Atkinson, Parker of Waddington, Sumner, and Parmoor.]

NOTES and QUESTIONS

1. Viscount Haldane merely asserted that the privity and consideration rules were "fundamental" in the law of England. Can you think of reasons why the privity rule is fundamental?

2. Lord Denning attempted on a number of occasions to overcome the bar to third party beneficiary actions. In *Smith v. River Douglas Catchment Bd.*, [1949] 2 K.B. 500 (C.A.), he said at 514:

> [Counsel] says that the plaintiffs cannot sue. He says that there is no privity of contract between them and the Board, and that it is a fundamental principle that no one can sue upon a contract to which he is not a party. That argument can be met either by admitting the principle and saying that it does not apply to this case, or by disputing the principle itself. I make so bold as to dispute it. The principle is not nearly so fundamental as it is sometimes supposed to be. It did not become rooted in our law until the year 1861 (*Tweddle v. Atkinson*), and reached its full growth in 1915 (*Dunlop v. Selfridge*). It has never been able entirely to supplant another principle whose roots go much deeper. I mean the principle that a man who makes a deliberate promise which is intended to be binding, that is to say, under seal or for good consideration, must keep his promise; and the court will hold him to it, not only at the suit of the party who gave the consideration, but also at the suit of one who was not a party to the contract, provided that it was made for his benefit and that he has a sufficient interest to entitle him to enforce it, subject always, of course, to any defences that may be open on the merits.

3. The wholesale rejection of the privity bar in the United States is described by A.J. Waters in "The Property in the Promise: A Study of the Third Party Beneficiary Rule" (1985), 98 Harv. L.R. 1109.

4. What is the relationship between the doctrine of privity and the doctrine of consideration? Is one a consequence of the other, are they two ways of saying the same thing or are they completely distinct from each other? See Furmston, "Return to Dunlop v. Selfridge?" (1960), 23 Mod. L.R. 372 at 382-84.

5. The materials in this chapter focus on enforcement by third party beneficiaries. Consider whether the original parties to a contract can enforce it *against* a third party beneficiary. Has the third party beneficiary promised anything?

3. Ways in Which a Third Party May Acquire the Benefit

In a number of instances the privity rule will not operate to prevent a third party receiving the benefit. There are different reasons why, in each instance, this happens. Thus, for some specific matters, legislatures have decided that a privity bar would be inappropriate or unfair. The effect of the rule may also be avoided if the promisee is able and willing to bring an action for specific performance of the promise. In other cases the privity rule will simply be inapplicable because there is some sort of relationship amongst the parties. Either a trust or agency relationship might exist. There is now also a common law exception for employees claiming the benefit of a limitation of liability clause and another for waivers of subrogation rights. We shall examine all of these possibilities in the next pages. Other potential ways of circumventing the effect of the third party bar would include an earlier assignment or indemnification agreement between the promisee and third party or the possibility of an action founded on a tortious breach of duty.

(a) STATUTE

Specific exceptions to the doctrine of privity were included in the insurance legislation of most common law jurisdictions at an early date. Two sections of the Insurance Act, R.S.O. 1990, c. I.8, are set out below. Section 195 applies to life insurance and s. 258 deals with automobile insurance.

> 195. A beneficiary may enforce for the beneficiary's own benefit, and a trustee appointed pursuant to section 193 may enforce as trustee, the payment of insurance money made payable to him, her or it in the contract or by a declaration and in accordance with the provisions thereof, but the insurer may set up any defence that it could have set up against the insured or the insured's personal representative.

> .....

> 258. (1) Any person who has a claim against an insured for which indemnity is provided by a contract evidenced by a motor vehicle liability policy, even if such person is not a party to the contract, may, upon recovering a judgment therefor in any province or territory of Canada against the insured, have the insurance money payable under the contract applied in or towards satisfaction of the person's judgment and of any other judgments or claims against the insured covered by the contract and may, on the person's own behalf and on behalf of all persons having such judgments or claims, maintain an action against the insurer to have the insurance money so applied.

It has also been thought necessary to exclude the operation of the doctrine of privity in order to make comprehensive consumer protection legislation effective. An example of this is found in the Consumer Protection Act of Saskatchewan, S.S. 1996, c-30. A number of other specific exceptions to the doctrine may be found in various provincial and federal statutes.

Some legislatures have dealt with the doctrine on a general basis. In Australia and New Zealand, for example, legislation now provides that a third party intended to benefit from the agreement may enforce that agreement directly. See the Property Law Act, 1969 (W.A.), s. 11; Property Law Act, 1974 (Qld.); Contracts (Privity) Act, 1982 (N.Z.). In Canada, see the Law Reform Act, S.N.B. 1993, c. L-1.2:

> 4.(1) A person who is not a party to a contract but who is identified by or under the contract as being intended to receive some performance or forbearance under it may, unless the contract provides otherwise, enforce that performance or forbearance by a claim for damages or otherwise.
>
> (2) In proceedings under subsection (1) against a party to a contract, any defence may be raised that could have been raised in proceedings between the parties.
>
> (3) The parties to a contract to which subsection (1) applies may amend or terminate the contract at any time, but where, by doing so, they cause loss to a person described in subsection (1) who has incurred expense or undertaken an obligation in the expectation that the contract

would be performed, that person may recover the loss from any party to the contract who knew or ought to have known that the expenses would be or had been incurred or that the obligation would be or had been undertaken.

(4) This section applies to contracts entered into before or after the commencement of this section, except that subsection (3) does not permit the recovery of loss arising in relation to an expense incurred or an obligation undertaken before the commencement of this section.

In England, in 1999, Parliament passed the Contracts (Rights of Third Parties) Act 1999. The first two sections of the statute read, in part, as follows:

1.(1) Subject to the provisions of this Act, a person who is not a party to a contract (a "third" party) may in his own right enforce a term of the contract if
   (a) the contract expressly provides that he may, or
   (b) subject to subsection (2), the term purports to confer a benefit on him.

(2) Subsection (1)(b) above does not apply if on a proper construction of the contract it appears that the parties did not intend the contract to be enforceable by the third party.

(3) The third party must be expressly identified in the contract by name, as a member of a class or as answering a particular description but need not be in existence when the contract is entered into.

.....

2.(1) Subject to the provisions of this section, where a third party has a right under section 1 to enforce a term of the contract, the parties to the contract may not, by agreement, rescind the contract, or vary it in such a way as to extinguish or alter his entitlement under that right, without his consent if

   (a) the third party has communicated his assent to the term to the promisor;
   (b) the promisor is aware that the third party has relied on the term, or
   (c) the promisor can reasonably be expected to have foreseen that the third party would rely on the term and the third party has in fact relied on it.

(2) The assent referred to in subsection (l)(a)

   (a) may be by words or conduct; and
   (b) if sent to the promisor by post or other means, shall not be regarded as communicated to the promisor until received by him.

(3) Subsection (1) is subject to any express term of the contract under which

   (a) the parties to the contract may by agreement rescind or vary the contract without the consent of the third party, or
   (b) the consent of the third party is required in circumstances specified in the contract instead of those set out in subsection (1)(a) to (c).

NOTES and QUESTIONS

1. What differences are there between the New Brunswick legislation and the English statute?

2. What happens if a New Brunswick resident and an Ontario resident make a contract while in England that gives a benefit to a resident of New Brunswick?

3. Law reform agencies in other Canadian provinces have proposed reform. In its 1987 *Report on Amendment of the Law of Contract*, the O.L.R.C. recommended at 71, that in Ontario "contracts for the benefit of third parties should not be unenforceable for lack of consideration or want of privity". In 1993, the Manitoba Law Reform Commission report on *Privity of Contract* proposed the enactment of the Privity Act to allow for enforcement of the promise by a third party beneficiary unless the promise was "not intended to create, in respect of the benefit, an obligation enforceable at the suit of that person."

(b)   SPECIFIC PERFORMANCE

BESWICK v. BESWICK

[1966] 1 Ch. 538, [1966] 3 All E.R. 1 (C.A.)

LORD DENNING M.R. Old Peter Beswick was a coal merchant in Eccles, Lancashire. He had no business premises. All he had was a lorry, scales and weights. He used to take the lorry to the yard of the National Coal Board, where he bagged coal and took it round to his customers in the neighbourhood. His nephew, John Joseph Beswick, helped him in the business.

In March 1962, old Peter Beswick and his wife were both over 70. He had had his leg amputated and was not in good health. The nephew was anxious to get hold of the business before the old man died. So they went to a solicitor, Mr. Ashcroft, who drew up an agreement for them. The business was to be transferred to the nephew: old Peter Beswick was to be employed as a consultant for the rest of his life at £6 10s. a week. After his death the nephew was to pay to his widow an annuity of £5 per week, which was to come out of the business. . . .

After the agreement was signed, the nephew took over the business and ran it. The old man seems to have found it difficult at first to adjust to the new situation, but he settled down. The nephew paid him £6 10s. a week. But, as expected, he did not live long. He died on November 3, 1963, leaving his widow, who was 74 years of age and in failing health. The nephew paid her the first £5. But he then stopped paying her and has refused to pay her any more.

On June 30, 1964, the widow took out letters of administration to her husband's estate. On July 15, 1964, she brought an action against the nephew for the promised £5 a week. She sued in the capacity of administratrix of the estate of Peter Beswick, deceased, and in her personal capacity she claimed £175 arrears and a declaration. By amendment she claimed specific performance and the appointment of a receiver. The action came for a hearing before the Vice-Chancellor of the County Palatine of Lancaster, who held that she had no right to enforce the agreement. He dismissed the action.

If the decision of the Vice-Chancellor truly represents the law of England, it would be deplorable. It would mean that the nephew could keep the business to himself, and at the same time repudiate his promise to pay the widow. Nothing could be more unjust. . . .

The general rule undoubtedly is that "no third person can sue, or be sued, on a contract to which he is not a party": but at bottom that is only a rule of procedure. It goes to the form of remedy, not to the underlying right. Where a contract is made for the benefit of a third person who has a legitimate interest to enforce it, it can be enforced by the third person in the name of the contracting party or jointly with him or, if he refuses to join, by adding him as a defendant. In that sense, and it is a very real sense, the third person has a right arising by way of contract. He has an interest which will be protected by law. . . .

It is different when a third person has no legitimate interest, as when he is seeking to enforce the maintenance of prices to the public disadvantage, as in

Dunlop Pneumatic Tyre Co. Ltd. v. Selfridge & Co. Ltd. [supra] or when he is seeking to rely, not on any right given to him by the contract, but on an exemption clause seeking to exempt himself from his just liability. He cannot set up an exemption clause in a contract to which he was not a party: see *Scruttons v. Midland Silicones* [[1962] A.C. 446].

The widow here sues in her capacity as executrix of her husband's estate (and therefore as contracting party), and also in her personal capacity (and there-fore as a third person). This joint claim is clearly good. She is entitled to an order for specific performance of the agreement, by ordering the defendant to pay the arrears of £175, and the instalments of £5 a week as they fall due. . . . When the money is recovered, it will go to the widow for her own benefit, and not to her husband's estate. I would allow the appeal accordingly.

[Danckwerts and Salmon L.JJ. were not prepared to go so far as Lord Denning but gave judgments supporting the result arrived at by Lord Denning on the ground that as administratrix of Peter Beswick's estate Mrs. Beswick could sue as a party to the contract between Peter Beswick and the nephew and obtain the remedy of specific performance.

The House of Lords, in the following excerpt, took a similar view to that of Danckwerts and Salmon L.JJ.]

BESWICK v. BESWICK

[1968] A.C. 58, [1967] 2 All E.R. 1197 (H.L.)

LORD REID It so happens that the respondent is administratrix of the estate of her deceased husband and she sues both in that capacity and in her personal capacity. So it is necessary to consider her rights in each capacity.

. . . It is true that a strong Law Revision Committee recommended so long ago as 1937 (Cmd. 5449):

> That where a contract by its express terms purports to confer a benefit directly on a third party it shall be enforceable by the third party in his own name . . . (p. 31).

And, if one had to contemplate a further long period of Parliamentary procrasti-nation, this House might find it necessary to deal with this matter. But if legislation is probable at any early date I would not deal with it in a case where that is not essential. So for the purposes of this case I shall proceed on the footing that the commonly accepted view [view that the third party cannot enforce the contract] is right. [Lord Reid discussed a hypothetical case and continued:]

Applying what I have said to the circumstances of the present case, the respondent in her personal capacity has no right to sue, but she has a right as administratrix of her husband's estate to require the appellant to perform his obligation under the agreement. He has refused to do so and he maintains that the respondent's only right is to sue him for damages for breach of his contract. If that were so, I shall assume that he is right in maintaining that the administratrix could then only recover nominal damages because his breach of contract has caused no loss to the estate of her deceased husband.

If that were the only remedy available the result would be grossly unjust. It would mean that the appellant keeps the business which he bought and for which he has only paid a small part of the price which he agreed to pay. He would avoid paying the rest of the price, the annuity to the respondent, by paying a mere 40s. damages. . . .

The respondent's . . . argument is that she is entitled in her capacity of administratrix of her deceased husband's estate to enforce the provision of the agreement for the benefit of herself in her personal capacity, and that a proper way of enforcing that provision is to order specific performance. That would produce a just result, and, unless there is some technical objection, I am of opinion that specific performance ought to be ordered. For the reasons given by your Lordships I would reject the arguments submitted for the appellant that specific performance is not a possible remedy in this case. I am therefore of opinion that the Court of Appeal reached a correct decision and that this appeal should be dismissed.

LORD PEARCE It is argued that the estate can only recover nominal damages and that no other remedy is open, either to the estate or to the personal plaintiff. Such a result would be wholly repugnant to justice and commonsense. And if the argument were right it would show a very serious defect in the law.

In the first place, I do not accept the view that damages must be nominal. Lush L.J. in *Lloyd's v. Harper* [(1881), 16 Ch. D. 290, 50 L.J. Ch. 140] said:

> Then the next question which, no doubt, is a very important and substantial one, is, that Lloyd's, having sustained no damage themselves, could not recover for the losses sustained by third parties by reason of the default of Robert Henry Harper as an underwriter. That, to my mind, is a startling and alarming doctrine, and a novelty, because I consider it to be an established rule of law that where a contract is made with A for the benefit of B, A can sue on the contract for the benefit of B, and recover all that B could have recovered if the contract had been made with B himself.

I agree with the comment of Windeyer J. in the case of *Coulls v. Bagot's Executor and Trustee Co. Ltd.* [(1967), 119 C.L.R. 460] in the High Court of Australia that the words of Lush L.J. cannot be accepted without qualification and regardless of context and also with his statement:

> I can see no reason why in such cases the damages which A would suffer upon B's breach of his contract to pay C $500 would be merely nominal: I think that in accordance with the ordinary rules for the assessment of damages for breach of contract they could be substantial. They would not necessarily be $500; they could I think be less or more.

In the present case I think that the damages, if assessed, must be substantial. It is not necessary, however, to consider the amount of damages more closely since this is a case in which, as the Court of Appeal rightly decided, the more appropriate remedy is that of specific performance.

The administratrix is entitled, if she so prefers, to enforce the agreement rather than accept its repudiation, and specific performance is more convenient than an action for arrears of payment followed by separate actions as each sum falls due. Moreover, damages for breach would be a less appropriate remedy since the parties to the agreement were intending an annuity for a widow; and a lump sum of damages does not accord with this. And if (contrary to my view) the argument that a derisory sum of damages is all that can be obtained be right, the remedy of damages in this case is manifestly useless.

The present case presents all the features which led the equity courts to apply their remedy of specific performance. The contract was for the sale of a business. The defendant could on his part clearly have obtained specific performance of it if Beswick senior or his administratrix had defaulted. Mutuality is a ground in favour of specific performance.

Moreover, the defendant on his side has received the whole benefit of the contract and it is a matter of conscience for the court to see that he now performs his part of it. Kay J. said in *Hart v. Hart* [(1881), 18 Ch.D. 670]:

> ... when an agreement for valuable consideration ... has been partially performed, the court ought to do its utmost to carry out that agreement by a decree for specific performance.

What then, is the obstacle to granting specific performance?

It is argued that since the widow personally had no rights which she personally could enforce the court will not make an order which will have the effect of enforcing those rights. I can find no principle to this effect. The condition as to payment of an annuity to the widow personally was valid. The estate (though not the widow personally) can enforce it. Why should the estate be barred from exercising its full contractual rights merely because in doing so it secures justice for the widow who, by a mechanical defect of our law, is unable to assert her own rights? Such a principle would be repugnant to justice and fulfil no other object than that of aiding the wrongdoer. I can find no ground on which such a principle should exist. ....

In my opinion, the plaintiff as administratrix is entitled to a decree of specific performance.

[Lords Hodson, Guest, and Upjohn delivered speeches to the same effect.]

QUESTIONS

1. What might have been the result if the administratrix had sued for damages?

2. What are the limitations of the specific performance approach? What if the promisee was unable or unwilling to bear the costs of enforcement? What if, in this case, the will had appointed the nephew as administrator?

(c) TRUST

The doctrine of privity amounts to a conclusion that there is no legal relationship between the promisor and the third party beneficiary. That conclusion cannot be reached, however, where the third party can prove the existence of a relationship of some kind. One such relationship is the trust. (Agency is another.) A trust may be created in different ways. A person (called the settlor) may, gratuitously or for consideration, transfer property or rights to a trustee to be held or managed for the benefit of a third party (called the *cestui que trust* or beneficiary). Alternatively, again gratuitously or for consideration, a person may declare himself or herself to hold property or rights as trustee for the benefit of a specified beneficiary. Once a trust is created, the beneficiary is entitled to enforce the trust obligation directly.

Express words of "trust" are not required in order to create a trust obligation. Generally speaking, it is enough if there is some kind of evidence to establish an "intention" to create a trust. A promise to benefit a third person is evidence of this kind, and in a number of cases a trust has been implied to give effect to such a promise: *Kendrick v. Barkey* (1907), 9 O.W.R. 356 (H.C.); *Dawson v. Dawson* (1911), 23 O.L.R. 1 (C.A.). After the decision of the Privy Council in the next case, however, the use of the trust concept to displace the privity doctrine seemingly became less acceptable.

VANDEPITTE v. PREFERRED ACCIDENT INSURANCE CO.

[1933] A.C. 70, [1932] 3 W.W.R. 573, [1933] 1 D.L.R. 289 (P.C.)

LORD WRIGHT The appellant, Alice Marie Vandepitte, sustained injuries on March 5, 1928, owing to the motor car, in which she was a passenger and which her husband was driving, being involved in a collision with a motor car driven by Jean Berry. Jean Berry was the daughter of R.E. Berry and was driving the car, which was her father's property, with his permission. As she was a minor living with her father, he was civilly liable, under sec. 12 of the *Motor-vehicle Act Amendment Act, 1927*, of British Columbia, ch. 44, for injuries sustained by the appellant due to his daughter's negligence, but in the case the appellant brought her action in the Supreme Court of British Columbia against Jean Berry, claiming that she was injured by Jean Berry's negligent driving. In the proceedings, the appellant's husband, E.J. Vandepitte, was brought in as a third party. On June 13, 1928, judgment was given for the appellant for $4,600 and costs against Jean Berry, and for Jean Berry against E.J. Vandepitte for $2,300 and costs on the basis that both drivers were negligent in the same degree. The appellant issued an execution against Jean Berry, but it was returned unsatisfied. Thereupon, on May 20, 1929, the appellant brought the present action in the Supreme Court of British Columbia, against the respondents, claiming to recover $5,648.71, the amount of the judgment and costs, in virtue of sec. 24 of the *Insurance Act* of British Columbia, 1925, ch. 20. The appellant succeeded in the Supreme Court . . . and on appeal in the Court of Appeal of British Columbia . . .; but in the Supreme Court of Canada the respondents' appeal was allowed, and the appellant's action was dismissed with costs throughout. . . . From that judgment the matter comes on appeal by special leave before their Lordships.

Sec. 24 of the *Insurance Act* is in the following terms:

> Where a person incurs liability for injury or damage to the person or property of another, and is insured against such liability, and fails to satisfy a judgment awarding damages against him in respect of such liability, and an execution against him in respect thereof is returned unsatisfied, the person entitled to the damages may recover by action against the insurer the amount of the judgment up to the face value of the policy, but subject to the same equities as the insurer would have if the judgment had been satisfied.

> .....

The policy here in question was for a period from noon on April 14, 1927,

to noon on April 14, 1928. It was issued on a form of application as required by
the statute, signed by R.E. Berry as the insured. The policy was headed "Combination Automobile Policy No. A. 12498," and embodied contracts between the
insured R.E. Berry and two separate insurance companies, the New Jersey Insurance Company and the Preferred Accident Insurance Company, the respondents.
It embodied the terms of the application by R.E. Berry and the statutory conditions.
Secs. A, B and C defined the obligations of the former company in respect of
damage to or loss of the insured automobile, and sec. D defined the same company's obligation in respect of "legal liability for damage to property of others,"
which was expressed to be to indemnify the insured against loss by reason of the
legal liability imposed by law upon the insured "in respect of damage done to
property." Sec. E embodied the obligations of the respondents and was in the
following terms:

> *Section E.—Legal Liability for Bodily Injuries or Death.*—(1) To indemnify the Insured
> against loss from the liability imposed by law upon the Insured for damages on account of
> bodily injuries (including death, at any time resulting therefrom) accidently suffered or alleged
> to have been suffered by any person or persons . . . as a result of the ownership, maintenance
> or use of the automobile; provided that on account of bodily injuries to or the death of one
> person the Insurer's liability under this section shall not exceed the sum of Five Thousand
> Dollars ($5,000.00), and subject to the same limit for each person the Insurer's liability on
> account of bodily injuries to or the death of more than one person as the result of one accident
> shall not exceed the sum of Ten Thousand dollars ($10,000.00).
> (2) To serve the Insured in the investigation of every accident covered by this Policy and
> in the adjustment, or negotiations therefor, of any claim resulting therefrom.
> (3) To defend in the name and on behalf of the Insured any civil actions which may at
> any time be brought against the Insured on account of such injuries, including actions alleging
> such injuries and demanding damages therefore, although such actions are wholly groundless,
> false or fraudulent, unless the Insurer shall elect to settle such actions.
> (4) To pay all costs taxed against the Insured in any legal proceeding defended by the
> Insurer; and all interest accruing after entry of judgment upon such part of same as is not in
> excess of the Insurer's limit of liability, as hereinbefore expressed.
> (5) To reimburse the Insured for the expense incurred in providing such immediate
> surgical relief as is imperative at the time such injuries are sustained.

The final clause of the policy was as follows:

> The foregoing indemnity provided by Sections D and/or E shall be available in the same
> manner and under the same conditions as it is available to the Insured to any person or persons
> while riding in or legally operating the automobile for private or pleasure purposes, with the
> permission of the Insured, or of an adult member of the Insured's household other than a
> chauffeur or domestic servant; provided that the indemnity payable hereunder shall be applied,
> first, to the protection of the named Insured, and the remainder, if any, to the protection of the
> other persons entitled to indemnity under the terms of this section as the named Insured shall
> in writing direct.

It was contended on behalf of the appellant that under the policy, and in the
events which happened, Jean Berry was the insured within sec. 24 of the Act, and
hence that the respondents were liable to pay the appellant the amount of the loss.
The contention was put in the alternative, either that Jean Berry was directly and
in law a party to the contract being within the description of the persons other
than R.E. Berry to whom the indemnity was available or that if not in law a party
to the contract, she was a *cestui que trust* of the promise contained in the contract

to extend the indemnity to such a person as herself, R.E. Berry having so stipulated as trustee. . . .

The first mode of stating the appellant's case involves that R.E. Berry as his daughter's agent made a contract of insurance between her and the respondents. But a contract can only arise if there is the *animus contrahendi* between the parties. There is here no evidence that Jean Berry ever had any conceptions that she had entered into any contract of insurance. She certainly took no direct part in the conclusion of whatever contract there was; the policy was entirely arranged between R.E. Berry and the respondents and he alone filled in and signed in his own name and behalf the application required by sec. 152 of the statute. . . .

It is, however, argued on behalf of the appellant that even if their Lordships should hold, as they do, that Jean Berry was not a party in law to the insurance contract, she was a party in equity, and in that way was "insured" by the respondents within the meaning of sec. 24. These two steps of the argument require separate consideration.

The contention, firstly, is that R.E. Berry, as part of the bargain and for the consideration proceeding from him, stipulated that the respondents should indemnify his daughter, Jean Berry, as coming under the general words of description, in the same manner and under the same conditions as himself, that is, that he created a trust of that chose in action for her as beneficiary. It cannot be questioned that abstractly such a trusteeship is competent. No doubt at common law no one can sue on a contract except those who are contracting parties and (if the contract is not under seal) from and between whom consideration proceeds. The rule is stated by Lord Haldane in *Dunlop Pneumatic Tyre Co. Ltd. v. Selfridge & Co. Ltd. [supra]*.

In that case, as in *Tweddle v. Atkinson [supra]*, only questions of direct contractual rights in law were in issue, but Lord Haldane states the equitable principle which qualifies the legal rule, and which has received effect in many cases, as for instance, *Robertson v. Wait* (1853) 8 Ex. 299, 22 L.J. Ex. 209; *Affreteurs Reunis Société Anonyme v. Leopold Walford Ltd.* [1919] A.C. 801, 88 L.J.K.B. 861; *Lloyd's v. Harper [supra]*, viz., that a party to a contract can constitute himself a trustee for a third party of a right under the contract and thus confer such rights enforceable in equity on the third party. The trustee then can take steps to enforce performance to the beneficiary by the other contracting party as in the case of other equitable rights. The action should be in the name of the trustee; if, however, he refuses to sue, the beneficiary can sue, joining the trustee as a defendant. But, though the general rule is clear, the present question is whether R.E. Berry can be held in this case to have constituted such a trust. But here again the intention to constitute the trust must be affirmatively proved; the intention cannot necessarily be inferred from the mere general words of the policy. Thus in *Irving v. Richardson* (1831), 109 E.R. 1115, a mortgagee effected in the usual form an insurance on the full value of the ship. He claimed to recover the full amount, which was in excess of the mortgage debt, on the general principle now embodied in sec. 14(2) of the *Marine Insurance Act, 1906*, ch. 41, that a mortgagee may insure on behalf and for the benefit of other persons interested as well as for his own benefit, "and recovering the whole, will hold the surplus beyond his own debt in trust for the mortgagor or other persons interested." It was held that the plaintiff was not entitled beyond the extent of his interest, that is, the mortgage debt, because he did not satisfy the jury of his actual intention in effecting the insurance to cover more than that. In the present case, there was not only the difficulties arising from the statutory provisions quoted above, but there is no evidence that R.E. Berry had any intention to create a beneficial interest for Jean Berry, either specifically or as member of a described class. Indeed, at no time either when the policy was effected or before or after the accident is there any suggestion that R.E. Berry had any such idea. It is true that she was in the habit of driving the insured automobile, but if R.E. Berry read the clause or thought of the matter at all, he would naturally expect that if she did damage the claim would, under the Act quoted, be against him, as she was a minor living in his family.

.....

Their Lordships are of opinion that no trusteeship is here made out but, in any case, they could not hold that the provisions of sec. 24 were satisfied by any but a contract at law, enforceable directly against the insurers by the insured in her own name. That section must be read with the relevant sections of the Act, which have been quoted above, and also with the terms of the policy. In their Lordships' opinion, an equitable right in Jean Berry (even if it were constituted) enforceable only in the name of the statutory insured, R.E. Berry, would not satisfy sec. 24, which involves an added burden on the insurance company, and must be strictly construed.

.....

The decision their Lordships have arrived at involves the conclusion that the final paragraph of the policy gives no enforceable right to anyone. The clause constitutes, in their opinion, merely a promissory representation or statement of an intention on the part of the insurers not binding in law or equity. On the other hand "honour policies" are common insurance business, and any insurance company which failed to fulfil its "honourable obligations" would be liable to pay in loss of business reputation. The defence in the present case is however taken under somewhat unusual circumstances in a claim by strangers on a special statutory enactment; neither Jean Berry nor R.E. Berry is asserting any right.

.....

In their Lordships' opinion the appeal should be dismissed with costs, and they will humbly so advise His Majesty.

(d)   AGENCY

If the "promisee" is actually contracting as agent on behalf of the third party, the doctrine of privity simply has no application. The promisor and third party are the contracting parties. They are in a direct contractual relationship. We will examine a multi-party situation and then the case where agency is used to make an exculpatory clause effective.

McCANNELL v. MABEE McLAREN MOTORS LTD.

36 B.C.R. 369, [1926] 1 W.W.R. 353, [1926] 1 D.L.R. 282 (C.A.)

MACDONALD C.J.B.C. Several grounds of appeal were taken in the notice of appeal, but the only one seriously pressed in argument was that there was not privity of contract between the parties to the action.

The question is an important one. A large volume of business has sprung up of the character of the transactions in question here. The Studebaker Company carries on an extensive business as manufacturers of automobiles which they dispose of in an extensive territory. They make their distribution through dealers or retailers, who are granted the right to purchase the automobiles on terms set out in a written contract, apparently of a standard form and to sell them within a specific territory. These agreements contain a clause reading as follows:

> 20. Infringement of Territory. Dealer agrees to solicit no trade nor sell Studebaker Automobiles to persons residing outside Dealer's territory, except that should such persons come unsolicited to dealer's place of business to buy automobiles off the floor for immediate delivery. Dealer may sell [to] such persons, but in every such case Dealer must pay the Studebaker Dealer in whose territory the customer resides one-half of Dealer's discount profit on such sale. It is mutually agreed that if a Dealer sells a Studebaker Automobile outside of his territory, or if a Studebaker Automobile sold by Dealer, shall be taken from Dealer's territory by purchaser within ninety days from the date of delivery, and remains in the other Dealer's territory for a period of four months or more, Dealer in either event shall pay one-half of Dealer's discount profit to the Studebaker Dealer into whose territory the automobile is taken. It is understood and agreed that this paragraph shall be construed as an agreement between dealer and all other Studebaker Dealers who have signed a similar agreement and that nothing herein contained shall be construed as a liability on the part of the Company to dealer for territorial infringement by any other dealer.

Regarding then this clause as the whole agreement to which the company is one party and the dealer the other, what is the true interpretation of it as affecting other dealers who have entered into precisely similar contracts with the company?

It will be seen that in the earlier part of the main contract it is expressly declared that the dealer is not the agent of the company, and that by clause 20 itself, the company is absolved from liability in respect of the consequences of breach of that clause.

In my opinion, the company must be regarded as the agent of the several dealers to bring about privity of contract between them. Dealer A agrees with dealer B through and in the agent's name, to carry out the reciprocal terms of the clause, which is manifestly for their mutual benefit. Unlike the case of *Dunlop Pneumatic Tyre Co. v. Selfridge & Co.* [*supra*], the consideration is not one moving from the company to the dealer, but from one dealer to the other.

There is nothing novel in regarding the company as the agent for both parties. The bargain between the plaintiff and defendants is, in the words of Lord Dunedin, in the above case:

> A bargain deliberately made, a bargain not in itself unfair and which the person seeking to enforce it has a legitimate interest to enforce.

It is a bargain which can best be brought into existence through the instrumentality of the company, and there is, I think, nothing inconsistent with the character of sellers in their acting in a collateral matter, as agents for the respective dealers in bringing their minds together. Each of the parties to this action have agreed to precisely the same thing; they have each agreed that the clause shall be construed as an agreement between them and not as an agreement as between each and the company as principals. It is not necessary (that), to constitute an agency, the agent shall be designated as such. The function which he fills in bringing the parties together and their recognition of the relationship which his efforts have created is the test of agency. In this case each of the dealers have signed counterparts of clause 20, and while the other contracting party is not named he is specifically designated in the document, and treating as I do the company as the agent for both, each has contracted in each document as a principal in the name of the agent.

I have not failed to notice the words in the clause making it applicable between those dealers "who have signed a similar agreement," nor the argument that the past tense does not include dealers who have signed subsequently to the defendants, but I think the context and object of the clause requires that it be interpreted liberally and in accordance with what all parties must have understood the clause to mean.

I would therefore dismiss the appeal.

MACDONALD J.A. In my opinion the principles laid down in *The "Satanita"* [1895] P. 248, are applicable in this case. From the usual course followed in the sale of cars and from the terms of his own agreement clearly suggesting the course followed, it ought to be presumed that the appellant knew that the respondent—or, at all events, other parties in adjacent territory—would have agreements with the Studebaker Corporation of Canada, Limited, similar to his own. The agreement carries this implication. The appellant and respondent each entered into an agreement with the Studebaker Corporation containing in effect rules and conditions governing their common relations to that company as salesmen in adjoining districts. In the *Satanita Case* the owners of two yachts entered a race under an agreement with the Yacht Racing Association containing rules and regulations governing the contest. One of the association's regulations provided that if certain rules were not observed and as a result damage to another competitor resulted, the delinquent would pay all damages. There was no formal contract between the owners of the competing yachts but each entered into an obligation to the other when they by agreement with the association undertook to observe the rules or pay damages for their breach. A relationship was created between the competitors containing an obligation. To quote Lopes, L.J., at p. 260:

> I have no doubt that there was a contract. Probably a contract with the committee in certain cases, *but also a contract between the owners of the competing yachts amongst themselves*, and that contract was an undertaking that the owner of one competing yacht would pay the owner of any other competing yacht injured by his yacht all the damages arising from any infringement or disobedience of the rules.
>
> In my opinion, directly any owner entered his yacht to sail, this contract arose; and it is clear that the owners of the "Valkyrie" and the "Satanita" did enter their respective yachts and did sail.

So in the case at bar the appellant and respondent did enter into an agreement (not it is true with each other) but with the Studebaker Corporation containing conditions which *ex necessitate* brought them into contractual relations with each other. They entered into agreements with the company to sell only in the territory assigned and upon breach of this condition to account to the other for one half the commission thus earned. The relationship thus created involved an obligation for breach of which an action will lie.

Privity being thus established the question of consideration presents no difficulty.

I may add that this is not the case of a third party suing on a contract made by others for his benefit as in *Tweddle v. Atkinson.*

I would dismiss the appeal.

[Martin, Galliher and McPhillips JJ.A. agreed in dismissing the appeal.]

NEW ZEALAND SHIPPING CO. LTD. v. A.M. SATTERTHWAITE & CO. LTD.

[1975] A.C. 154, [1974] 1 All E.R. 1015 (P.C.)

LORD WILBERFORCE [delivering the majority judgment] The facts of this case are not in dispute. An expensive drilling machine was received on board the ship *Eurymedon* at Liverpool for transhipment to Wellington pursuant to the terms of a bill of lading no. 1262 dated June 5, 1964. The shipper was the maker of the drill, Ajax Machine Tool Co. Ltd. ("the consignor"). The bill of lading was issued by agents for the Federal Steam Navigation Co. Ltd. ("the carrier"). The consignee was A.M. Satterthwaite & Co. Ltd. of Christchurch, New Zealand ("the consignee"). For several years before 1964 the New Zealand Shipping Co. Ltd. ("the stevedore") had carried out all stevedoring work in Wellington in respect of the ships owned by the carrier, which was a wholly owned subsidiary of the stevedore. In addition to this stevedoring work the stevedore generally acted as agent for the carrier in New Zealand; and in such capacity as general agent (not in the course of their stevedoring functions) the stevedore received the bill of lading at Wellington on July 31, 1964. Clause 1 of the bill of lading, on the construction of which this case turns, was in the same terms as bills of lading usually issued by the stevedore and its associated companies in respect of ordinary cargo carried by their ships from the United Kingdom to New Zealand. The consignee became the holder of the bill of lading and owner of the drill prior to August 14, 1964. On that date the drill was damaged as a result of the stevedore's negligence during unloading.

At the foot of the first page of the bill of lading the following words were printed in small capitals:

> In accepting this bill of lading the shipper, consignee and owners of the goods, and the holders of this bill of lading agree to be bound by all of its conditions, exceptions and provisions whether written, printed or stamped on the front or back hereof.

On the back of the bill of lading a number of clauses were printed in small type. It is only necessary to set out the following. . . .

It is hereby expressly agreed that no servant or agent of the carrier (including every independent contractor from time to time employed by the carrier) shall in any circumstances whatsoever be under any liability whatsoever to the shipper, consignee or owner of the goods or to any holder of this bill of lading for any loss or damage or delay of whatsoever kind arising or resulting directly or indirectly from any act neglect or default on his part while acting in the course of or in connection with his employment and, without prejudice to the generality of the foregoing provisions in this clause, every exemption, limitation, condition and liberty herein contained and every right, exemption from liability, defence and immunity of whatsoever nature applicable to the carrier or to which the carrier is entitled hereunder shall also be available and shall extend to protect every such servant or agent of the carrier acting as aforesaid and for the purpose of all the foregoing provisions of this clause the carrier is or shall be deemed to be acting as agent or trustee on behalf of and for the benefit of all persons who are or might be his servants or agents from time to time (including independent contractors as aforesaid) and all such persons shall to this extent be or be deemed to be parties to the contract in or evidenced by this bill of lading.

Clause 11 provided:

The carrier will not be accountable for goods of any description beyond £100 in respect of any one package or unit unless the value thereof shall have been stated in writing both on the broker's order which must be obtained before shipment and on the shipping note presented on shipment and extra freight agreed upon and paid and bills of lading signed with a declaration of the nature and value of the goods appearing thereon. When the value is declared and extra freight agreed as aforesaid the carrier's liability shall not exceed such value or pro rata on that basis in the event of partial loss or damage.

No declaration as to the nature and value of the goods having appeared in the bill of lading, and no extra freight having been agreed upon or paid, it was acknowledged by the consignee that the liability of the carrier was accordingly limited to £100 by the application of clause 11 of the bill of lading. Moreover, the incorporation in the bill of lading of the rules scheduled to the Carriage of Goods by Sea Act 1924 meant that the carrier and the ship were discharged from all liability in respect of damage to the drill unless suit was brought against them within one year after delivery. No action was commenced until April 1967, when the consignee sued the stevedore in negligence, claiming £880 the cost of repairing the damaged drill.

The question in the appeal is whether the stevedore can take the benefit of the time limitation provision. The starting point, in discussion of this question, is provided by the House of Lords decision in *Scruttons v. Midland Silicones* [[1962] A.C. 446]. There is no need to question or even to qualify that case in so far as it affirms the general proposition that a contract between two parties cannot be sued on by a third person even though the contract is expressed to be for his benefit. Nor is it necessary to disagree with anything which was said to the same effect in the Australian case of *Wilson v. Darling Island Stevedoring and Lighterage Co. Ltd.* [(1956), 95 C.L.R. 43 (H.C.)]. Each of these cases was dealing with a simple case of a contract the benefit of which was sought to be taken by a third person not a party to it, and the emphatic pronouncements in the speeches and judgments were directed to this situation. But *Scruttons* left open the case where one of the parties contracts as agent for the third person: in particular Lord Reid's speech spelt out, in four propositions, the prerequisites for the validity of such an agency contract. There is of course nothing unique to this case in the conception of agency contracts: well known and common instances exist in the field of hire purchase, of bankers' commercial credits and other transactions. Lord Reid said, at p. 474:

> I can see a possibility of success of the agency argument if (first) the bill of lading makes it clear that the stevedore is intended to be protected by the provisions in it which limit liability, (secondly) the bill of lading makes it clear that the carrier, in addition to contracting for these provisions on his own behalf, is also contracting as agent for the stevedore that these provisions should apply to the stevedore, (thirdly) the carrier has authority from the stevedore to do that, or perhaps later ratification by the stevedore would suffice, and (fourthly) that any difficulties about consideration moving from the stevedore were overcome. And then to affect the consignee it would be necessary to show that the provisions of the Bills of Lading Act 1855 apply.

The question in this appeal is whether the contract satisfies these propositions.

Clause 1 of the bill of lading, whatever the defects in its drafting, is clear in its relevant terms. The carrier, on his own account, stipulates for certain exemptions and immunities: among these is that conferred by article III, rule 6, of the Hague Rules which discharges the carrier from all liability for loss or damage unless suit is brought within one year after delivery. In addition to these stipulations on his own account, the carrier as agent for, inter alios, independent contractors stipulates for the same exemptions.

Much was made of the fact that the carrier also contracts as agent for numerous other persons; the relevance of this argument is not apparent. It cannot be disputed that among such independent contractors, for whom, as agent, the carrier contracted, is the appellant company which habitually acts as stevedore in New Zealand by arrangement with the carrier and which is, moreover, the parent company of the carrier. The carrier was, indisputably, authorised by the appellant to contract as its agent for the purposes of clause 1. All of this is quite straightforward and was accepted by all the judges in New Zealand. The only question was, and is, the fourth question presented by Lord Reid, namely that of consideration.

It was on this point that the Court of Appeal differed from Beattie J., holding that it had not been shown that any consideration for the shipper's promise as to exemption moved from the promisee, i.e., the appellant company.

If the choice, and the antithesis, is between a gratuitous promise, and a promise for consideration, as it must be in the absence of a tertium quid, there can be little doubt which, in commercial reality, this is. The whole contract is of a commercial character, involving service on one side, rates of payment on the other, and qualifying stipulations as to both. The relations of all parties to each other are commercial relations entered into for business reasons of ultimate profit. To describe one set of promises, in this context, as gratuitous, or nudum pactum, seems paradoxical and is prima facie implausible. It is only the precise analysis of this complex of relations into the classical offer and acceptance, with identifiable consideration, that seems to present difficulty. . . .

In their Lordships' opinion the present contract presents much less difficulty than many of those above referred to. It is one of carriage from Liverpool to Wellington. The carrier assumes an obligation to transport the goods and to discharge at the port of arrival. The goods are to be carried and discharged, so the transaction is inherently contractual. It is contemplated that a part of this contract, viz. discharge, may be performed by independent contractors—viz. the appellant. By clause 1 of the bill of lading the shipper agrees to exempt from liability the carrier, his servants and independent contractors in respect of the performance of this contract of carriage. Thus, if the carriage, including the discharge, is wholly carried out by the carrier, he is exempt. If part is carried out by him, and part by his servants, he and they are exempt. If part is carried out by him and part by an independent contractor, he and the independent contractor are exempt. The exemption is designed to cover the whole carriage from loading to discharge, by whomsoever it is performed: the performance attracts the exemption or immunity in favour of whoever the performer turns out to be. There is possibly more than one way of analyzing this business transaction into the necessary components; that which their Lordships would accept is to say that the bill of lading brought into existence a bargain initially unilateral but capable of becoming mutual, between the shipper and the appellant, made through the carrier as agent. This became a full contract when the appellant performed services by discharging the goods. The performance of these services for the benefit of the shipper was the consideration for the agreement by the shipper that the appellant should have the benefit of the exemptions and limitations contained in the bill of lading. The conception of a "unilateral" contract of this kind was recognised in *Great Northern Ry. Co. v. Witham* [(1873), L.R. 9 C.P. 16] and is well established. This way of regarding the matter is very close to if not identical to that accepted by Beattie J. in the Supreme Court: he analysed the transaction as one of an offer open to acceptance by action such as was found in *Carlill v. Carbolic Smoke Ball Co.* [*supra*, Chapter 1, section 2]. But whether one describes the shipper's promise to exempt as an offer to be accepted by performance or as a promise in exchange for an act seems in the present context to be a matter of semantics. The words of Bowen L.J. in *Carlill v. Carbolic Smoke Ball Co.* "why should not an offer be made to all the world which is to ripen into a contract with anybody who comes forward and performs the condition?" seem to bridge both conceptions: he certainly seems to draw no distinction between an offer which matures into a contract when accepted and a promise which matures into a contract after performance, and, though in some special contexts (such as in connection with the right to withdraw) some further refinement may be needed, either analysis may be equally valid. On the main point in the appeal, their Lordships are in substantial agreement with Beattie J.

.....

In the opinion of their Lordships, to give the appellant the benefit of the exemptions and limitations contained in the bill of lading is to give effect to the clear intentions of a commercial document, and can be given within existing principles. They see no reason to strain the law or the facts in order to defeat these intentions. It should not be overlooked that the effect of denying validity to the clause would be to encourage actions against servants, agents and independent contractors in order to get round exemptions (which are almost invariable and often compulsory) accepted by shippers against carriers, the existence, and presumed efficacy, of which is reflected in the rates of freight. They see no attraction in this consequence.

Their Lordships will humbly advise Her Majesty that the appeal be allowed and the judgment of Beattie J. restored. The respondent must pay the costs of the appeal and in the Court of Appeal.

[Lords Dilhorne and Simon of Glaisdale delivered separate dissenting judgments.]

NOTES and QUESTION

1. Do you see any difficulties with the "unilateral" contract analysis used by Lord Wilberforce?

2. The Supreme Court of Canada allowed an action against negligent employees in *Greenwood Shopping Plaza v. Beattie*, [1980] 2 S.C.R. 228. The employees were not entitled to take the benefit of a clause in the lease agreement between their employer and the lessor that would have prevented the action. The evidence before the court was insufficient to establish a contractual link, of the type found in the *New Zealand Shipping Co.* case, between the employer and employees. The Supreme Court, however, did subsequently apply the agency analysis in *ITO-International Terminal Operators Ltd. v. Miida Electronics Inc.*, [1986] 1 S.C.R. 752 to exclude the liability of a stevedore – terminal operator company that negligently stored goods.

3. The line of stevedore cases involved economic loss. However, the issue of exemption of liability for third parties can arise in the context of personal injuries. The Supreme Court of Canada has shown a willingness to side-step the doctrine of privity in these cases as well. In *Dyck v. Man. Snowmobile Assn. Inc.*, [1985] 1 S.C.R. 589, the court denied recovery for injuries negligently caused to Dyck by an official of the Snowmobile Association. Dyck had signed the following release.

Indemnifying Release

I have read the supplementary regulations issued for this event and agree to be bound by them. In consideration of acceptance of this entry or my being permitted to take part in this event, I AGREE TO SAVE HARMLESS AND KEEP INDEMNIFIED the M.S.A. and/or the M.S.A., its organizers, and their respective agents, officials, servants and representatives from and against all claims, actions, costs and expenses and demands in respect to death, injury, loss or damage to my person or property, howsoever caused, arising out of or in connection with my taking part in this event and not withstanding [sic] that the same may have been contributed to or occasioned by the negligence of the said bodies, or any of them, their agents, officials, servants or representatives. It is understood and agreed that this Agreement is to be binding on myself, my heirs, executors and assigns.

IN WITNESS WHEREOF I/we have hereunder set my/our hand and seal this day of 'February 23, 1975'

'[*illegible*]' X 'Ron Dyck'

(witness)

The court was of the view that this clause satisfied the four requirements for agency. What is your view? Do you think that an approach developed in economic loss cases should be applied in personal injury cases?

(e) EMPLOYMENT

LONDON DRUGS LTD. v. KUEHNE & NAGEL INTERNATIONAL LTD.

[1992] 3 S.C.R. 299, 97 D.L.R. (4th) 261

IACOBUCCI J. This appeal and cross-appeal raise two principal issues: (1) the duty of care owed by employees to their employer's customers, and (2) the extent to which employees can claim the benefit of their employer's contractual limitation of liability clause.

.....

The facts are not complicated. On August 31, 1981, London Drugs Limited (hereinafter "appellant"), delivered a transformer weighing some 7,500 lbs. to Kuehne and Nagel International Ltd. (hereinafter "Kuehne & Nagel") for storage pursuant to the terms and conditions of a standard form contract of storage. The transformer had been purchased from its manufacturer, Federal Pioneer Limited, and was to be installed in the new warehouse facility being built by the appellant. The contract of storage included the following limitation of liability clause:

> LIABILITY – Sec. 11(*a*) The responsibility of a warehouseman in the absence of written provisions is the reasonable care and diligence required by the law.
>
> (*b*) The warehouseman's liability on any one package is limited to $40 unless the holder has declared in writing a valuation in excess of $40 and paid the additional charge specified to cover warehouse liability.

With full knowledge and understanding of this clause, the appellant chose not to obtain additional insurance from Kuehne & Nagel and instead arranged for its own all-risk coverage. At the time of entering into the contract, the appellant knew, or can be assumed to have known, that Kuehne & Nagel's employees would be responsible for moving and upkeeping the transformer.

On September 22, 1981, Dennis Gerrard Brassart and Hank Vanwinkel (hereinafter "respondents"), both employees of Kuehne & Nagel, received orders to load the transformer onto a truck which would deliver it to the appellant's new warehouse. The respondents attempted to move the transformer by lifting it with two forklift vehicles when safe practice required it to be lifted from above using brackets which were attached to the transformer and which were clearly marked for that purpose. While being lifted, the transformer toppled over and fell causing damages in the amount of $33,955.41.

Alleging breach of contract and negligence, the appellant brought an action for damages against Kuehne & Nagel, Federal Pioneer Limited, and the respondents. In a judgment rendered on April 14, 1986, Trainor J. of the Supreme Court of British Columbia held that the respondents were personally liable for the full amount of damages, limiting Kuehne & Nagel's liability to $40 and dismissing the claim against Federal Pioneer Limited. On March 30, 1990, the majority of the Court of Appeal allowed the respondents' appeal and reduced their liability to $40. The appellant was granted leave to appeal to this court on December 7, 1990. The respondents have cross-appealed in order to argue that they should be completely free of liability.

III ISSUES

The cross-appeal raises the following question:

(1) Did the respondents, acting in the course of their employment and performing the very essence of their employer's contractual obligations with the appellant, owe a duty of care to the appellant?

If so, it is not disputed before this court that the respondents were negligent in their handling of the appellant's transformer. In other words, the finding of the trial judge that the respondents breached their duty of care is not contested. Moreover, it is not disputed that it is the respondents' negligence which was the cause of the damages to the transformer and that these damages amount to $33,955.41. The next question which is raised by the appeal would thus become one of the appropriate liability for this breach, namely:

(2) Can the respondents obtain the benefit of the limitation of liability clause contained in the contract of storage between their employer and the appellant so as to limit their liability to $40?

For reasons that follow, I am of the opinion that both questions should be answered in the affirmative. By so concluding, both the cross-appeal and the appeal should therefore be dismissed.

IV ANALYSIS

A. *Duty of care*

.....

In my opinion, the respondents unquestionably owed a duty of care to the appellant when handling the transformer.

.....

B. *Limitation of liability clause*

Accepting the finding of the trial judge that the respondents breached their duty of care thereby causing damages fixed at $33,955.41 to the appellant, I must now consider whether they are allowed to benefit from the limitation of liability clause found in the contract of storage between their employer, Kuehne & Nagel, and the appellant.

.....

The appellant argues that the respondents should not benefit, in any way, from a limitation of liability clause contained in a contract to which they are not parties. In its submissions, the appellant strongly, if not exclusively, relies upon the doctrine of privity of contract and upon its application by this court in *Canadian General Electric*, [[1971] S.C.R. 41], *Greenwood Shopping Plaza, supra*, and *ITO-International Terminal Operators, supra*. It is submitted that these decisions have unequivocally established the legal principles to be applied in determining whether a tortfeasor may rely upon a limitation of liability clause in a contract to which the tortfeasor is not a party. The appellant submits that, in so doing, this court has repeatedly rejected attempts to abrogate or weaken the doctrine of privity of contract. In particular, it is argued that contractual protection can be extended to non-contracting parties only in limited circumstances where the facts support a finding of agency or trust. In the present case, the appellant states that there exists no evidence which would allow this court to make such a finding. Accordingly, it is submitted that the majority of the Court of Appeal has abandoned "longstanding, established and fundamental principles of law" in affording contractual protection to the respondents.

.....

For their part, the respondents submit that they are entitled to benefit from the limitation of liability clause and suggest three alternative ways to arrive at such a result. First, they argue for a judicial reconsideration, or a relaxation of, the doctrine of privity of contract as it applies to the case at bar. It is submitted that this doctrine, in the facts of the present case, is radically out of step with commercial reality, with the expectations of the parties and with the way in which the parties allocated the risk of loss or damage. The respondents argue that employees can, without consideration and without invoking traditional exceptions such as trust or agency, claim the benefit of their employer's contractual limitation of liability when: (1) there is a contractual limitation of liability between their employer and another party; (2) a loss occurs during the employer's performance of its contractual obligations to that third party; and (3) the employees are acting in the course of their employment when the loss occurs. [Discussion of the second (implied term) and the third (duty of care in tort) alternatives are omitted.]

.....

For my part, I prefer to deal head-on with the doctrine of privity and to relax its ambit in the circumstances of this case. . . .

I accept the respondents' submission that this is both the time and the case for a judicial reconsideration of the rule regarding privity of contract as applied to employers' contractual limitation of liability clauses.

.....

In my view, the respondents were third party beneficiaries to the limitation of liability clause found in the contract of storage between their employer and the appellant and, in view of the circumstances involved, may benefit directly from this clause notwithstanding that they are not a signing party to the contract. I recognize that such a conclusion collides with privity of contract in its strictest sense; however, for reasons that follow, I believe that this court is presented with an appropriate factual opportunity in which to reconsider the scope of this doctrine and decide whether its application in cases such as the one at bar should be limited or modified. It is my opinion that commercial reality and common sense require that it should.

.....

Many have noted that an application of the doctrine so as to prevent a third party from relying on a limitation of liability clause which was intended to benefit him

or her frustrates sound commercial practice and justice. It does not respect allocations and assumptions of risk made by the parties to the contract and it ignores
the practical realities of insurance coverage. In essence, it permits one party to
make a unilateral modification to the contract by circumventing its provisions
and the express or implied intention of the parties. In addition, it is inconsistent
with the reasonable expectations of all the parties to the transaction, including the
third party beneficiary who is made to support the entire burden of liability. The
doctrine has also been criticized for creating uncertainty in the law. While most
commentators welcome, at least in principle, the various judicial exceptions to
privity of contract, concerns about the predictability of their use have been raised.
Moreover, it is said, in cases where the recognized exceptions do not appear to
apply, the underlying concerns of commercial reality and justice still militate for
the recognition of a third party beneficiary right.

.....

Without doubt, major reforms to the rule denying third parties the right to
enforce contractual provisions made for their benefit must come from the legislature. Although I have strong reservations about the rigid retention of a doctrine
that has undergone systematic and substantial attack, privity of contract is an
established principle in the law of contracts and should not be discarded lightly.
Simply to abolish the doctrine of privity or to ignore it, without more, would
represent a major change to the common law involving complex and uncertain
ramifications. This court has in the past indicated an unwillingness to sanction
judge-made changes of this magnitude. . . .

.....

This court has also recognized, however, that in appropriate circumstances
courts have not only the power but the duty to make incremental changes to the
common law to see that it reflects the emerging needs and values of our society:
. . . It is my view that the present appeal is an appropriate situation for making
such an incremental change to the doctrine of privity of contract in order to allow
the respondents to benefit from the limitation of liability clause.

As we have seen earlier, the doctrine of privity has come under serious attack
for its refusal to recognize the right of a third party beneficiary to enforce contractual provisions made for his or her benefit. Law reformers, commentators and
judges have pointed out the gaps that sometimes exist between contract theory
on the one hand, and commercial reality and justice on the other. We have also
seen that many jurisdictions around the world, including Quebec and the United
States, have chosen from an early point (as early as the doctrine became "settled"
in the English common law) to recognize third party beneficiary rights in certain
circumstances. As noted by the appellant, the common law recognizes certain
exceptions to the doctrine, such as agency and trust, which enable courts, in
appropriate circumstances, to arrive at results which conform with the true intentions of the contracting parties and commercial reality. However, as many have
observed, the availability of these exceptions does not always correspond with
their need. Accordingly, this court should not be precluded from developing the

common law so as to recognize a further exception to privity of contract merely on the ground that some exceptions already exist. . . .

There are few principled reasons for upholding the doctrine of privity in the circumstances of this case. Maintaining the alleged *status quo* by itself is an unhelpful consideration since I am considering whether or not a relaxation, or change, to the law should be made. Similarly, most of the traditional reasons or justifications behind the doctrine are of little application in cases such as this one, when a third party beneficiary is relying on a contractual provision as a defence in an action brought by one of the contracting parties. There are no concerns about double recovery or floodgates of litigation brought by third party beneficiaries. The fact that a contract is a very personal affair, affecting only the parties to it, is simply a restatement of the doctrine of privity rather than a reason for its maintenance. Nor is there any concern about "reciprocity", that is, there is no concern that it would be unjust to allow a party to sue on a contract when he or she cannot be sued on it.

Moreover, recognizing a right for a third party beneficiary to rely on a limitation of liability clause should have relatively little impact on the rights of contracting parties to rescind or vary their contracts, in comparison with the recognition of a third party right to sue on a contract. In the end, the most that can be said against the extension of exceptions to the doctrine of privity in this case is that the respondent employees are mere donees and have provided no consideration for the contractual limitation of liability.

The doctrine of privity fails to appreciate the special considerations which arise from the relationships of employer-employee and employer-customer. There is clearly an identity of interest between the employer and his or her employees as far as the performance of the employer's contractual obligations is concerned. When a person contracts with an employer for certain services, there can be little doubt in most cases that employees will have the prime responsibilities related to the performance of the obligations which arise under the contract. This was the case in the present appeal, clearly to the knowledge of the appellant. While such a similarity or closeness might not be present when an employer performs his or her obligations *through* someone who is not an employee, it is virtually always present when employees are involved. Of course, I am in no way suggesting that employees are a party to their employer's contracts in the traditional sense so that they can bring an action on the contract or be sued for breach of contract. However, when an employer and a customer enter into a contract for service and include a clause limiting the liability of the employer for damages arising from what will normally be conduct contemplated by the contracting parties to be performed by the employer's employees, and in fact so performed, there is simply no valid reason for denying the benefit of the clause to employees who perform the contractual obligations. The nature and scope of the limitation of liability clause in such a case coincides essentially with the nature and scope of the contractual obligations performed by the third party beneficiaries (employees).

Upholding a strict application of the doctrine of privity in the circumstances of this case would also have the effect of allowing the appellant to circumvent or escape the limitation of liability clause to which it had expressly consented.. . .

[I]t would be absurd in the circumstances of this case to let the appellant go around the limitation of liability clause by suing the respondent employees in tort. The appellant consented to limit the "warehouseman"'s liability to $40 for anything that would happen during the performance of the contract. When the loss occurred, the respondents were acting in the course of their employment and performing the very services, albeit negligently, for which the appellant had contracted with Kuehne & Nagel. The appellant cannot obtain more than $40 from Kuehne & Nagel, whether the action is based in contract or in tort, because of the limitation of liability clause. However, resorting to exactly the same actions, it is trying to obtain the full amount from the individuals ("warehousemen") who were directly responsible for the storing of its goods in accordance with the contract. As stated earlier, there is an identity of interest between the respondents and Kuehne & Nagel as far as performance of the latter's contractual obligations is concerned. When these facts are taken into account, and it is recalled that the appellant knew the role to be played by employees pursuant to the contract, it is clear to me that this court is witnessing an attempt in effect to "circumvent or escape a contractual exclusion or limitation of liability or the act or omission that would constitute the tort". In my view, we should not sanction such an endeavour in the name of privity of contract.

Finally, there are sound policy reasons why the doctrine of privity should be relaxed in the circumstances of this case. A clause such as one in a contract of storage limiting the liability of a "warehouseman" to $40 in the absence of a declaration by the owner of the goods of their value and the payment of an additional insurance fee makes perfect commercial sense. It enables the contracting parties to allocate the risk of damage to the goods and to procure insurance accordingly. If the owner declares the value of the goods, which he or she alone knows, and pays the additional premium, the bargain will have placed the entire risk on the shoulders of the "warehouseman". On the other hand, if the owner refuses the offer of additional coverage, the bargain will have placed only a limited risk on the "warehouseman" and the owner will be left with the burden of procuring private insurance if he or she decides to diminish its own risk. In either scenario, the parties to the contract agree to a certain allocation and then proceed, based on this agreement, to make additional insurance arrangements if required. It stretches commercial credulity to suggest that a customer, acting prudently, will not obtain insurance because he or she is looking to the employees for recovery when generally little or nothing is known about the financial capacity and professional skills of the employees involved. That does not make sense in the modern world.

In addition, employees such as the respondents do not reasonably expect to be subject to unlimited liability for damages that occur in the performance of the contract when said contract specifically limits the liability of the "warehouseman" to a fixed amount. According to modern commercial practice, an employer such as Kuehne & Nagel performs its contractual obligations with a party such as the appellant *through* its employees. As far as the contractual obligations are concerned, there is an identity of interest between the employer and the employees. It simply does not make commercial sense to hold that the term "warehouseman" was not intended to cover the respondent employees and as a result to deny them the benefit of the limitation of liability clause for a loss which occurred during the performance of the very services contracted for. Holding the employees liable in these circumstances could lead to serious injustice especially when one considers that the financial position of the affected employees could vary considerably such that, for example, more well-off employees would be sued and left to look for contribution from the less well-off employees. Such a result creates also uncertainty and requires excessive expenditures on insurance in that it defeats the allocations of risk specifically made by the contracting parties and the reasonable expectations of everyone involved, including the employees. When parties enter into commercial agreements and decide that one of them *and* its employees will benefit from limited liability, or when these parties choose language such as "warehouseman" which implies that employees will also benefit from a protection, the doctrine of privity should not stand in the way of commercial reality and justice.

For all the above reasons, I conclude that it is entirely appropriate in the circumstances of this case to call for a relaxation of the doctrine of privity.

.....

In the end, the narrow question before this court is: in what circumstances should employees be entitled to benefit from a limitation of liability clause found in a contract between their employer and the plaintiff (customer)? Keeping in mind the comments made earlier and the circumstances of this appeal, I am of the view that employees may obtain such a benefit if the following requirements are satisfied:

(1) the limitation of liability clause must, either expressly or impliedly, extend its benefit to the employees (or employee) seeking to rely on it; and

(2) the employees (or employee) seeking the benefit of the limitation of liability clause must have been acting in the course of their employment *and* must have been performing the very services provided for in the contract between their employer and the plaintiff (customer) when the loss occurred.

Although these requirements, if satisfied, permit a departure from the strict application of the doctrine of privity of contract, they represent an incremental change to the common law. I say "incremental change" for a number of reasons.

First and foremost, this new exception to privity is dependent on the intention of the contracting parties. An employer and his or her customer may choose the appropriate language when drafting their contacts [*sic*] so as to extend, expressly or impliedly, the benefit of any limitation of liability to employees. It is their intention as stipulated in the contract which will determine whether the first requirement is met. In this connection, I agree with the view that the intention to extend the benefit of a limitation of liability clause to employees may be express or *implied* in all the circumstances: . . .

Second, taken as a whole, this new exception involves very similar bench-
marks to the recognized agency exception, applied in *The Eurymedon* and by this
court in *ITO-International Terminal Operators, supra*. As discussed in the latter
decision, the four requirements for the agency exception were inspired from the
following passage of Lord Reid's judgment in *Midland Silicones*, [Iacobucci J.
here set out the four requirements for establishing an agency relationship that are
reproduced in the *New Zealand Shipping Co.* case, *supra*.]

. . . . .

The first requirement of both exceptions is virtually identical. The second and
third requirements of the agency exception are supplied by the identity of interest
between an employer and his or her employees as far as the performance of
contractual obligations are concerned; this is implicit in the recognition of this
new exception. As for the fourth requirement of agency, while this new exception
makes no specific mention of consideration moving from the employees to the
customer, the second requirement of the new exception embraces the same elements which were adopted by courts to recognize consideration moving from
stevedores in cases involving "Himalaya clauses". [The term "Himalaya clause"
owes its origin to the case of *Adler v. Dickson*, [1955] 1 Q.B. 158 (C.A.). In that
case a passenger on the ship "Himalaya" successfully sued the captain and boat-
swain for personal injuries caused by their negligence despite a clause in her
ticket which absolved the company that owned the ship from liability for any
injury suffered by passengers.]

Third, it must be remembered that I am proposing a very specific and limited
exception to privity in the case at bar; *viz.*, permitting employees who qualify as
third party beneficiaries to use their employer's limitation of liability clauses as
"shields" in actions brought against them, when the damage they have caused
was done in the course of their employment and while they were carrying out the
very services for which the plaintiff (customer) had contracted with their employer. In sum, I am recognizing a limited *jus tertii*.

In closing on this point, I wish to add the obvious comment that nothing in
the above reasons should be taken as affecting in any way recognized exceptions
to privity of contract such as trust and agency. In other words, even if the above
requirements are not satisfied, an employee may still establish the existence of a
trust or agency so as to obtain a benefit which the contracting parties intended
him or her to have, notwithstanding lack of privity.

The only question in the case at bar is whether the respondents are third
party beneficiaries with respect to the limitation of liability clause so as to come
within the first requirement of the test I set forth above. Based on uncontested
findings of fact, the respondents were acting in the course of their employment
when they caused the transformer to topple over. Moreover, at that time they were
performing the very services provided for in the contract between Kuehne &
Nagel and the appellant, namely, the storage and upkeep of the transformer.

For convenience, I reproduce again the limitation of liability clause:

LIABILITY – Sec. 11(*a*) The responsibility of a warehouseman in the absence of written
provisions is the reasonable care and diligence required by the law.

(b) The warehouseman's liability on any one package is limited to $40 unless the holder has declared in writing a valuation in excess of $40 and paid the additional charge specified to cover warehouse liability.

Does the language chosen indicate that the benefit of the clause is specifically restricted to Kuehne & Nagel? I think not. On the contrary, when all of the relevant circumstances are considered, it is my view that the parties must be taken as having intended that the benefit of this clause would also extend to Kuehne & Nagel's employees.

It is clear that the parties did not choose express language in order to extend the benefit of the clause to employees. For example, there is no mention of words such as "servants" or "employees" in s. 11(b) of the contract. As such, it cannot be said that the respondents are express third party beneficiaries with respect to the limitation of liability clause. However, this does not preclude a finding that they are *implied* third party beneficiaries. In view of the identity of interest between an employer and his or her employees with respect to the performance of the former's contractual obligations and the policy considerations discussed above, it is surely open to a court, in appropriate circumstances, to conclude that a limitation of liability clause in a commercial contract between an employer and his or her customer impliedly extends its benefit to employees.

In the case at bar, the parties have not chosen language which inevitably leads to the conclusion that the respondents were not to benefit from s. 11(b) of the contract of storage. The term "warehouseman" as used in s. 11(b) is not defined in the contract and the definition provided in the *Warehouse Receipt Act*, s. 1, is of no use in determining whether it includes employees for the purpose of the contractual limitation of liability. While it is true that s. 10(e) of the contract uses the term "warehouse employee", this by itself does not preclude an interpretation of "warehouseman" in s. 11 (b) of the same contract as implicitly including employees for the purposes of the limitation of liability clause. Such a conclusion does not offend the words chosen by the parties.

When all the circumstances of this case are taken into account, including the nature of the relationship between employees and their employer, the identity of interest with respect to contractual obligations, the fact that the appellant knew that employees would be involved in performing the contractual obligations, and the absence of a clear indication in the contract to the contrary, the term "warehouseman" in s. 11(b) of the contract must be interpreted as meaning "warehousemen". As such, the respondents are not complete strangers to the limitation of liability clause. Rather, they are unexpressed or implicit third party beneficiaries with respect to this clause. Accordingly, the first requirement of this new exception to the doctrine of privity is also met.

The respondents owed a duty of care to the appellant in their handling of its transformer. According to the uncontested findings of the trial judge, they breached this duty causing damages in the amount of $33,955.41. While neither trust nor agency is applicable, the respondents are entitled to benefit directly from the limitation of liability clause in the contract between their employer and the appellant. This is so because they are third party beneficiaries with respect to that clause and because they were acting in the course of their employment and performing the very services contracted for by the appellant when the damages occurred. I acknowledge that this, in effect, relaxes the doctrine of privity and creates a limited *jus tertii*. However, when viewed in its proper context, it merely represents an incremental change to the law, necessary to see that the common law develops in a manner that is consistent with modern notions of commercial reality and justice.

[McLachlin J. agreed that the appeal should be dismissed, but based her conclusion on a voluntary assumption of risk. La Forest J. dissented in part, concluding that the employees did not owe a duty of care to the appellant. L'Heureux-Dubé, Sopinka and Cory JJ. concurred with Iacobucci J. Appeal and cross-appeal dismissed.]

NOTES and QUESTIONS

1. Four years earlier, in *Trident General Insurance Co. v. NcNiece Bros. Pty. Ltd.* (1988), 165 C.L.R. 107, the Australian High Court had rejected a blanket application of the third party beneficiary bar.

2. Consider the reasons Iacobucci J. offered for his conclusion. Do these reasons have general application beyond the circumstances of the exception created by his judgment?

3. In *London Drugs*, the Supreme Court created a true common law exception to the third party beneficiary bar. It is distinguishable, in this respect, from trust or agency, which are not exceptions, but rather, relationships that preclude the "third party" beneficiary characterization. The employment exception applies to a third party beneficiary who has no direct relationship with the promisor but, who, for the reasons given in *London Drugs*, is now able to insist on the benefit. The result, effectively, is to create a contractual relationship between the employee and the person contracting with the employer.

4. In what way does this employment exception differ from the notion of vicarious immunity? Is the difference found in the expressed intention of the parties to benefit the third party? Is there really any difference at all if the court will easily imply that intention?

5. Are there reasons why an employer would choose not to extend the benefit of a limitation or exculpatory clause to employees? Might an employer believe that employees would exercise less care if they were relieved of liability *ex ante*? Do you think all workers appreciate their potential liability in tort to other parties? Would it be prudent for many types of workers to carry liability insurance covering their work activities? Would variable premiums and deductibles based on such factors as training or claims experience provide similar incentives to exercise due care? How costly would this insurance be if purchased to the same extent, and at the same time (to avoid additional transaction costs), as vehicle insurance? What is the significance of the workers' compensation regime in this context? Are other workers the main victims of employee negligence? If workers did begin generally to insure, would their premium payments be matched by a corresponding reduction in premiums paid by employers? Would any benefit realized by the employer be transferred back to the workers (through bargaining) in the form of wages to reflect the increased cost of being an employee? Is it right, in the absence of an exculpatory clause, to hold both employers (vicariously) and employees liable for negligence in the performance of the work undertaken? Do both groups affect the level of risk associated with the enterprise? See Flannigan, "Enterprise Control: The Servant-Independent Contractor Distinction" (1987), 37 U.T.L.J. 25.

6. Iacobucci J. insists that his decision represents an "incremental change" and not a major reform. Do you agree? What remains subject to the third party beneficiary bar?

7. In *Froese v. Montreal Trust Co. of Canada* (1996), 137 D.L.R. (4th) 725, the British Columbia Court of Appeal refused to use *London Drugs* to justify the imposition of a "burden" on a beneficiary of a pension trust. Arguably, however, there was no privity issue in the case. If the employees/beneficiaries made contributions to the pension fund, they accepted a "unilateral" offer

made by the company and the trustee. Accordingly, the beneficiaries had either trust and/or contract rights, subject to whatever exclusion clauses applied.

EDGEWORTH CONSTRUCTION LTD. v. N.D. LEA & ASSOCIATES LTD.

(1993), 107 D.L.R. (4th) 169 (S.C.C.)

McLACHLIN J. The appellant, Edgeworth Construction Ltd. (hereinafter Edgeworth), is engaged in the business of building roads in the Province of British Columbia. In 1977, it bid on a contract to build a section of highway in the Revelstoke area. Its bid was successful, and Edgeworth entered into a contract with the province for the work. Edgeworth alleges that it lost money on the project due to errors in the specifications and construction drawings. It commenced proceedings for negligent misrepresentation against the engineering firm which prepared those drawings, N.D. Lea & Associates Ltd. (hereinafter N.D. Lea) as well as the individual engineers who affixed their seals to the drawings.

.....

Liability for negligent misrepresentation arises where a person makes a representation knowing that another may rely on it, and the plaintiff in fact relies on the representation to its detriment: *Hedley Byrne & Co. Ltd. v. Heller & Partners Ltd.*, [1964] A.C. 465 (H.L.); *Haig v. Bamford* (1976), 72 D.L.R. (3d) 68. . . .

The facts alleged in this case meet this test, leaving the contract between the contractor and the province to one side. The engineers undertook to provide information (the tender package) for use by a definable group of persons with whom it did not have any contractual relationship. The purpose of supplying the information was to allow tenderers to prepare a price to be submitted. The engineers knew this. The plaintiff contractor was one of the tenderers. It relied on the information prepared by the engineers in preparing its bid. Its reliance upon the engineers' work was reasonable. It alleges it suffered loss as a consequence. These facts establish a *prima facie* cause of action against the engineering firm.

The only question which remains is whether the contract between the contractor and the province negated the duty of care which would otherwise have arisen on the facts pleaded.

The argument that the contract between Edgeworth and the province negated or subsumed the duty of care owed by the engineers to Edgeworth is put in a number of ways. It is said that the contract converted the representation from one made by the engineering firm to one made by the province. It is argued that the contract destroyed the proximity which would otherwise have lain between the contractor and the engineers. And it is said that the proper course of the law and policy precludes reliance on tort principles when a contract such as this has been made.

The essence of the position adopted below is that the Ministry assumed all risks previously held by the engineers. The material provided to prospective bidders, which incorporated the impugned work of the engineers, was "adopted and promulgated by [the Ministry] as [the Ministry's] representations". Thus, it is argued, the Ministry assumed all risks, and the duty between the engineers and contractor is negated.

I cannot accede to this argument. It is true that the engineers' work was incorporated in the tender package and thereafter in the contract. This establishes that the representations in the design became the representations of the province. But it does not, without more, and with great respect to the differing views below, establish the further proposition that when the representations became the representations of the province they ceased to be the representations of the engineers. The contractor was relying on the accuracy of the engineers' design just as much after it entered into the contract as before. Neither the Ministry nor the contractor ever assumed the risk of errors in the engineers' work. Throughout, Edgeworth, if its contentions are borne out at trial, was relying on the expertise of the engineers and not of the province with respect to the accuracy of the design.

The contract, by cl. 42, stipulated that any representation in the tender documents were "furnished merely for the general information of bidders and [were] not in anywise warranted or guaranteed by or on behalf of the Minister . . .". This arguably absolved the province from any liability for the plans. The exemption extends, on its express words, only to warranties "by or on behalf of the Minister". It does not purport to protect the engineers against liability for their representations.

There is a further problem of whether the engineers, not parties to the contract, could claim the benefit of its exclusion of liability for the representations in the tender documents. This court in *London Drugs Ltd. v. Kuehne & Nagel International Ltd.*, *supra*, held that the doctrine of privity of contract did not preclude contractual exclusions for negligence being extended to provide protection for the employees actually charged with doing the work. But before such an argument can succeed, it must be established that the contract clause provides protection, or should by implication be held to provide protection, for the persons who, although not parties to the contract, are claiming the benefit of the exclusion. In the case at bar this has not been done. In *London Drugs* the fact that the work for which the exemption was given could only be done by the employees, taken together with other circumstances including the powerlessness of the employees to protect themselves otherwise, suggested that a term should be implied that the clause was intended to benefit them, or alternatively, that the intention of the parties manifested in the contract must be taken to limit the duty of care owed in tort. The facts in this case do not give rise to such an inference: rather, cl. 42 is entirely consistent with the conclusion that the protection was intended for the benefit of the province alone. Moreover, the engineering firm, unlike the employees in *London Drugs*, could have taken measures to protect itself from the liability in question, It could have placed a disclaimer of responsibility on the design documents, Alternatively, it could have refused to agree to provide the design without ongoing supervision duties which would have permitted it to make alterations as the contract was being performed; I raise this point in the context of the engineers' argument that much of the loss might have been avoided had it had ongoing supervisory duties. Finally, the engineering firm might have decided to accept the risk that tenderers would rely on its design to their detriment, and have insured itself accordingly. In short, the circumstances of the case, combined with the wording of the exclusion clause, negate any inference that the contractor should be taken as having excluded its right to sue the engineers for design deficiencies by its contract with the province. For these reasons, I conclude that cl. 42 of the contract between the contractor and the province does not assist the engineering firm.

[La Forest J. delivered a concurring judgment. Sopinka, Gonthier, Cory, Iacobucci and Major JJ. concurred. Appeal allowed.]

NOTES and QUESTIONS

1. Do you agree with McLachlin J. that the employees in the *London Drugs* case were unable to take measures to protect themselves?

2. Before the employment exception will apply, a court must be satisfied that the parties expressly or impliedly intended for the benefit of the exculpatory clause to extend to the employees. This was the first requirement of Iacobucci J. in *London Drugs*, and was reiterated by McLachlin J. in the *Edgeworth* case. Although Iacobucci J.'s "identity of interest" rationale may as a practical matter create a status immunity, the availability of the exception is supposedly dependent on the actual intention of the parties, and not on the "employee" status of the worker. Accordingly, it is not enough for a court merely to assess whether or not a worker is an employee. In *M.A.N. - B & W Diesel v. Kingsway Transports Ltd.* (1997), 33 O.R. (3d) 355 (C.A.), however, the Ontario Court of Appeal apparently proceeded on that basis. Finlayson J.A., at 358 and 362, stated:

> The argument on appeal centred on whether Tremblay was an employee of Kingsway or an independent contractor. If he was an employee, then on the authority of *London Drugs Ltd. v. Kuehne & Nagel International Ltd.*, *supra*, he was entitled to the benefit of the limitation of liability clause contained in the bill of lading.
>
> .....
>
> The respondents were entitled to rely on the limitation of liability clause to limit their damages payable as a result of the accident. At the time of the accident, Tremblay was an employee of Kingsway and Servall. On the principles enunciated in *London Drugs Ltd. v. Kuehne & Nagel International Ltd.*, *supra*, this is a suitable case to relax the doctrine of privity to allow Tremblay to rely on the clause. This holding would be consistent with the commercial reality that employers such as the respondents perform their contractual obligations through their employees. It would also more closely reflect the reasonable expectations of the parties with respect to the allocation of risks.

Consider whether the commercial reality, reasonable expectation or risk allocation factors mentioned by the court support an intention test or a status test. Contrast the analysis in this case with that of a different panel of the Ontario Court of Appeal in *Madison Developments Ltd. v. Plan Electric Co.* (1997), 152 D.L.R. (4th) 653 (Ont. C.A.).

(f)   SUBROGATION

FRASER RIVER PILE & DREDGE LTD. v. CAN-DIVE SERVICES LTD.
[1999] 3 S.C.R. 108, 176 D.L.R. (4th) 257,

A barge, the "Sceptre Squamish" belonging to the appellant, Fraser River, sank. At the time, it was under charter to Can-Dive. Insurance companies generally have the right to step into the shoes of the insured and sue the wrongdoer. The contract of insurance between Fraser River and the insurer contained a clause under which the insurer waived its right of subrogation against "any charterer", and extended coverage to affiliated companies and charterers. The insurer paid Fraser River the amount stipulated in the policy for the loss of the barge. Fraser River made a further agreement with the insurer to pursue a negligence action against Can-Dive and to waive any right to the waiver of subrogation clause. The insurer then sued Can-Dive, who relied in the waiver of subrogation. At trial, Can-Dive was held liable for $949,503, the court taking the view that Can-Dive, as a third party, could not enforce the waiver in the contract of insurance. Its appeal on the ground that it could not be held liable in a subrogated action was allowed.

IACOBUCCI J. [delivering the judgment of the court]. . . .

B. Is Can-Dive, as a third-party beneficiary under the insurance policy pursuant to the waiver of subrogation clause, entitled to rely on that clause to defend against the insurer's subrogated action on the basis of the principled exception to the privity of contract doctrine established by the Court's decision in *London Drugs*?

. . . . .

As a preliminary matter, I note that it was not our intention in *London Drugs*, [*supra*, at section 3(e)], to limit application of the principled approach to situations involving only an employer-employee relationship. That the discussion focussed on the nature of this relationship simply reflects the prudent jurisprudential principle that a case should not be decided beyond the scope of its immediate facts.

In terms of extending the principled approach to establishing a new exception to the doctrine of privity of contract relevant to the circumstances of the appeal, regard must be had to the emphasis in *London Drugs* that a new exception first and foremost must be dependent upon the intention of the contracting parties. Accordingly, extrapolating from the specific requirements as set out in *London Drugs* the determination in general terms is made on the basis of two critical and cumulative factors: (a) Did the parties to the contract intend to extend the benefit in question to the third party seeking to rely on the contractual provision? and (b) Are the activities performed by the third party seeking to rely on the contractual provision the very activities contemplated as coming within the scope of the contract in general, or the provision in particular, again as determined by reference to the intentions of the parties?

(a) Intentions of the Parties

As to the first inquiry, Can-Dive has a very compelling case in favour of relaxing the doctrine of privity in these circumstances, given the express reference in the waiver of subrogation clause to "charterer(s)", a class of intended third-party beneficiaries that, on a plain reading of the contract, includes Can-Dive within the scope of the term. Indeed, there is no dispute between the parties as to the meaning of the term within the waiver of subrogation clause; disagreement exists only as to whether the clause has legal effect. Accordingly, there can be no question that the parties intended to extend the benefit in question to a class of third-party beneficiaries whose membership includes Can-Dive. . . .

In essence, Fraser River's argument in terms of the intention of the parties is not that the scope of the waiver of subrogation clause does not extend to third parties such as Can-Dive, but that the provision can only be enforced by Fraser River on Can-Dive's behalf, and not by Can-Dive acting independently. A plain reading of the provision, however, does not support this conclusion. There is no language in the clause indicating that the waiver of subrogation is intended to be conditional upon Fraser River's initiative in favour of any particular third-party beneficiary. It appears to me that Fraser River has conflated arguments concerning the intentions of the parties in drafting the provision and the legal effect to be given to the provision. In no uncertain terms, the waiver of subrogation clause indicates that the insurers are precluded from proceeding with an action against third-party beneficiaries coming within the class of "charterer(s)", and the relevant inquiry is whether to give effect to these intentions by enforcing the contractual term, notwithstanding the doctrine of privity of contract.

In my opinion, the case in favour of relaxing the doctrine of privity is even stronger in the circumstances of this appeal than was the case in *London Drugs* wherein the parties did not expressly extend the benefit of a limitation of liability clause covering a "warehouseman" to employees. Instead, it was necessary to support an implicit extension of the benefit on the basis of the relationship between the employers and its employees, that is to say, the identity of interest between the employer and its employees in terms of performing the contractual obligations. In contrast, given the express reference to "charterer(s)" in the waiver of subrogation clause in the policy, there is no need to look for any additional factors to justify characterizing Can-Dive as a third-party beneficiary rather than a mere stranger to the contract.

Having concluded that the parties intended to extend the benefit of the waiver of subrogation clause to third parties such as Can-Dive, it is necessary to address Fraser River's argument that its agreement with the insurers to pursue legal action against Can-Dive nonetheless effectively deleted the third-party benefit from the contract. A significant concern with relaxing the doctrine of privity is the potential restrictions on freedom of contract which could result if the interests of a third-party beneficiary must be taken into account by the parties to the initial agreement before any adjustment to the contract could occur. It is important to note, however, that the agreement in question was concluded subsequent to the point at which what might be termed Can-Dive's inchoate right under the contract crystallized into an actual benefit in the form of a defence against an action in negligence by Fraser River's insurers. Having contracted in favour of Can-Dive as within the class of potential third-party beneficiaries, Fraser River and the insurers cannot revoke unilaterally Can-Dive's rights once they have developed into an actual benefit. At the point at which Can-Dive's rights crystallized, it became for all intents and purposes a party to the initial contract for the limited purposes of relying on the waiver of subrogation clause. Any subsequent alteration of the waiver provision is subject to further negotiation and agreement among all of the parties involved, including Can-Dive.

I am mindful, however, that the principle of freedom of contract must not be dismissed lightly. Accordingly, nothing in these reasons concerning the ability of the initial parties to amend contractual provisions subsequently should be taken as applying other than to the limited situation of a third-party's seeking to rely on a benefit conferred by the contract to defend against an action initiated by one of the parties, and only then in circumstances where the inchoate contractual right has crystallized prior to any purported amendment. Within this narrow exception, however, the doctrine of privity presents no obstacle to contractual rights conferred on third-party beneficiaries.

(b) Third-Party Beneficiary is Performing the Activities Contemplated in the Contract

As to the second requirement that the intended third-party beneficiary must rely on a contractual provision in connection with the very activities contemplated by the contract in general, or by the relevant clause in particular, Fraser River has argued that a significant distinction exists between the situation in *London Drugs* and the circumstances of the present appeal. In *London Drugs* the relationship between the contracting parties and the third-party beneficiary involved a single contract for the provision of services, whereas in the present circumstances, such a "contractual nexus", to use Fraser River's phrase, does not exist. In other words, the waiver of subrogation clause upon which Can-Dive seeks to rely is contained in an unrelated contract that does not pertain to the charter contract in effect between Fraser River and Can-Dive.

With respect, I do not find this argument compelling, given that a similar contractual relationship could be said to exist in *London Drugs* in terms of the service contract between the parties and a contract of employment which presumably existed between the employer and employees. At issue is whether the purported third-party beneficiary is involved in the very activity contemplated by the contract containing the provision upon which he or she seeks to rely. In this case, the relevant activities arose in the context of the relationship of Can-Dive to Fraser River as a charterer, the very activity anticipated in the policy pursuant to the waiver of subrogation clause. Accordingly, I conclude that the second requirement for relaxing the doctrine of privity has been met.

(c) Policy Reasons in Favour of an Exception in These Circumstances

Having found that Can-Dive has satisfied both of the cumulative threshold requirements for the purposes of introducing a new, principled exception to the doctrine of privity of contract as it applies to third-party beneficiaries, I nonetheless wish to add that there are also sound policy reasons for relaxing the doctrine in these circumstances. In this respect, it is time to put to rest the unreasonable application of the doctrine of privity to contracts of insurance established by the Privy Council in *Vandepitte* [v. *Preferred Accident Insurance Corpn. of New York*, *supra*], a decision characterized since its inception by both legislatures and the judiciary as out of touch with commercial reality. As Esson J.A. noted [in the

Court of Appeal], the decision in *Vandepitte* received little attention outside the field of automobile insurance, where it had been promptly overruled by legislative amendment in British Columbia and other provinces. In addition, Esson J.A. was correct in holding that *Vandepitte* has been impliedly overruled in the course of decisions by the Court, given that in cases where the rule of privity might have been applied, the decision was ignored: . . . Of particular interest is the Court's decision in *Commonwealth Construction Co.* [*v. Imperial Oil Ltd.*, [1978] 1 S.C.R. 317]. The case concerned a general contractor's "builder's risk" policy that purported to extend coverage to subcontractors who were not parties to the original contract. In holding that subrogation was not available against the subcontractors, de Grandpré J., writing for the Court, made the following comments regarding the "Additional Insureds" and "Trustee" clauses, at p. 324:

> While these conditions may have been inserted to avoid the pitfalls that were the lot of the unnamed insured in *Vandepitte* . . . a precaution that in my view was not needed, they without doubt cover additional ground.

When considered in light of the Court's discussion of the necessary interdependence of various contractors involved in a common construction enterprise, the comment reflects the Court's acknowledgment that the rule of privity set out in *Vandepitte* was inconsistent with commercial reality. In a similar fashion, Fraser River in the course of this appeal has been unable to provide any commercial reason for failing to enforce a bargain entered into by sophisticated commercial actors. In the absence of any indication to the contrary, I must conclude that relaxing the doctrine of privity in these circumstances establishes a default rule that most closely corresponds to commercial reality as is evidenced by the inclusion of the waiver of subrogation clause within the contract itself.

A plain reading of the waiver of subrogation clause indicates that the benefit accruing in favour of third parties is not subject to any qualifying language or limiting conditions. When sophisticated commercial parties enter into a contract of insurance which expressly extends the benefit of a waiver of subrogation clause to an ascertainable class of third-party beneficiary, any conditions purporting to limit the extent of the benefit or the terms under which the benefit is to be available must be clearly expressed. The rationale for this requirement is that the obligation to contract for exceptional terms most logically rests with those parties whose intentions do not accord with what I assume to be standard commercial practice. Otherwise, notwithstanding the doctrine of privity of contract, courts will enforce the bargain agreed to by the parties and will not undertake to rewrite the terms of the agreement.

Fraser River has also argued that to relax the doctrine of privity of contract in the circumstances of this appeal would be to introduce a significant change to the law that is better left to the legislature. As was noted in *London Drugs* privity of contract is an established doctrine of contract law, and should not be lightly discarded through the process of judicial decree. Wholesale abolition of the doctrine would result in complex repercussions that exceed the ability of the courts to anticipate and address. It is by now a well-established principle that courts will not undertake judicial reform of this magnitude, recognizing instead that the legislature is better placed to appreciate and accommodate the economic and policy issues involved in introducing sweeping legal reforms.

That being said, the corollary principle is equally compelling, which is that in appropriate circumstances, courts must not abdicate their judicial duty to decide on incremental changes to the common law necessary to address emerging needs and values in society: *Watkins v. Olafson*, [1989] 2 S.C.R. 750, at pp. 760-61, and *R. v. Salituro*, [1991] 3 S.C.R. 654, at pp. 665-70. In this case, I do not accept Fraser River's submission that permitting third-party beneficiaries to rely on a waiver of subrogation clause represents other than an incremental development. To the contrary, the factors present in *London Drugs*, in support of the incremental nature of the exception, are present as well in the circumstances of this appeal. As in *London Drugs*, a third-party beneficiary is seeking to rely on a contractual provision in order to defend against an action initiated by one of the contracting parties. Fraser River's concerns regarding the potential for double recovery are unfounded, as relaxing the doctrine to the extent contemplated by these reasons does not permit Can-Dive to rely on any provision in the policy to establish a separate claim. In addition, the exception is dependent upon the express intentions of the parties, evident in the language of the waiver of subrogation clause, to extend the benefit of the provision to certain named classes of third-party beneficiaries.

V. Conclusion and Disposition

I conclude that the circumstances of this appeal nonetheless meet the requirements established in *London Drugs* for a third-party beneficiary to rely on the terms of a contract to defend against a claim initiated by one of the parties to the contract. As a third-party beneficiary to the policy, Can-Dive is entitled to rely on the waiver of subrogation clause whereby the insurers expressly waived any right of subrogation against Can-Dive as a "charterer" of a vessel included within the policy's coverage.

Accordingly, I would dismiss the appeal with costs.

NOTES and QUESTIONS

1. Did the Supreme Court create a narrow exception for subrogation matters or a general test of enforceability for third parties? Would you agree, as some have suggested, that the decision essentially abolishes the third party beneficiary bar?

2. Subsequent cases have focused on whether the parties to the contract intended to benefit the third party. That will be the primary issue even in jurisdictions where the third party bar has been jettisoned. See *Manitoba Hydro Electric Board v. John Inglis Co.* (1999), 181 D.L.R. (4th) 470 (Man. C.A.); *Dryburgh v. Oak Bay Marina (1992) Ltd.* (2001), 206 F.T.R. 255 (Fed. T.D.); *Attis v. Canada (Minister of Health)* (2003), 29 C.P.C. (5th) 242 (Ont. S.C.J.); *Marble (Litigation Guardian of) v. Saskatchewan*, [2003] S.J. No. 479, 2003 CarswellSask 496 (Q.B.); and *Daishowa-Marubeni International Ltd. v. Toshiba International Corp.*, [2003] A.J. No. 1189, 2003 CarswellAlta 1373 (C.A.).

3. Is it correct to say that the *Fraser* exception can be used as a "shield" but not as a "sword"? See *Parwinn Developments Ltd. v. 375069 Alberta Ltd.* (2000), 30 R.P.R. (3d) 74 (Alta. Q.B.).

4.   Privity and Contract Theory

It is commonly assumed that the doctrine of privity is a necessary or fundamental feature of contract theory. That assumption seems to be the major reason why some still hesitate to discard the doctrine.

It would appear however that the third party bar is not theoretically sound. Consider the remarks of Dowrick in "A Jus Quaesitum Tertio By Way of Contract in English Law" (1956), 19 Mod. L.R. 374, at 390-91:

> Using the term principle in its widest sense, is a *jus quaesitum tertio* in accordance with the fundamental theory of contract law? The sceptical common lawyer will immediately ask—which theory? It is only proposed to consider two theories which are at least congenial to the modern English common law. Pound's theory is that the common law of contract is based upon the postulate that men must be able to assume that those with whom they deal will act in good faith, and hence, that the latter will make good reasonable expectations created by their promises or other conduct. Pollock's first principle of contract is substantially similar. If A promises under a contract with B to benefit T, would it be in accord with or opposed to this theory to grant T a right to the performance of the promise by A? Clearly, if T knows of the promise and as a reasonable man would expect performance, the law should grant him a legal right to that end. An alternative theory which has wide currency amongst English lawyers, is that the law of contracts has as its objective the enforcement of promises provided they are parts of bargains: all agreements are not to be enforced, only agreements consisting essentially of a promise on one side in return for consideration on the other. Should T be granted legal remedies to enforce a promise made by A to B in which B has provided the consideration? The bargain exists. The only question is should T be given a right to enforce it as well as B? If the object of the law is to *enforce* bargains the additional means of enforcement are justified, especially in cases where B's undoubted right of action would only entitle him to nominal damages, or where B refused to sue. While either theoretical approach to the problem yields a result favouring a doctrine of *jus quaesitum tertio* it must readily be admitted that such a deductive approach rarely convinces English lawyers.

Elsewhere it has been argued that the third party bar is inconsistent with *every* theory or approach that has been offered to justify either the existing or the ideal state of contract law. See Flannigan, "Privity—The End of an Era (Error)" (1987), 103 L.Q.R. 564.

If the doctrine is a theoretical error, and if there are no *reasons* for its retention, can we not profitably abolish it? A great number of judges, commentators and law reform commissions have advocated that the doctrine be put to rest. Does the legislative and judicial activity in other jurisdictions over the past several years suggest that the third party beneficiary bar will eventually be wholly discarded in Canada? Why do you think most provincial legislatures in Canada have to date failed to reform this area of contract? Is the need for reform less compelling relative to the other matters the legislatures have addressed? Should the Supreme Court now generally reverse this judicial error, or is it preferable for the court to chip away at the doctrine?

Chapter 6

CONTINGENT AGREEMENTS

1.   Introduction

The characterization of an agreement as a contract entails a defined set of legal outcomes. The parties are, from the point of contract formation, bound to perform the obligations imposed by its terms. Neither party is thereafter free to refuse to proceed in the manner agreed, or at all. So doing will constitute a breach of the contract supporting an award of damages or specific performance. This reality may put a person who wishes to "nail down" a deal in a difficult position if his or her own willingness to perform depends upon information that is not immediately available, or upon a state of affairs that has not yet materialized.

Perhaps the most common instance of such a situation is the case of the home buyer who has found the house he or she wants to purchase, but cannot commit to paying for it until financing has been arranged. If the prospective buyer defers entering into a contract until financing is confirmed, the seller might sell to someone else before that can be accomplished and the house will have been lost. On the other hand, if the prospective buyer agrees to buy the house but is then unable to arrange the financing required to pay the price, the prospective buyer will find him- or herself in breach of contract and liable to pay damages if the seller ultimately sells at a lower price. As the material in Chapter 14 demonstrates, the seller would be entitled to recover as damages the sum that would put him or her in the position of having had the contract of sale performed; that is, of having actually received the agreed purchase price from the defaulting buyer. The quantum of the award would be roughly the difference between what the original buyer agreed to pay, and the price the seller was able to obtain on the subsequent sale. The defaulting buyer would not only be left without the house, but with a potential liability to pay thousands of dollars by way of damages.

One can think of countless examples of situations of this kind. An art lover wishes to purchase what she believes to be a rare painting and is willing to pay a substantial price for it, but only if she can confirm its authenticity through a qualified appraisal. A businessperson wishes to buy a parcel of land for purposes of development, but only if the municipal authority is prepared to change the property zoning to authorize the contemplated structure or use. A car dealer wishes to conclude the sale of a vehicle to an interested buyer on deferred payment terms, but only if a credit check confirms that the buyer enjoys a satisfactory credit rating. In all these instances, one prospective contracting party wants to prevent the other prospective party from dealing with someone else, without making a present contractual commitment to proceed with the transaction until certain information can be obtained or a particular state of affairs has come to pass. The parties may be in a position to agree on the terms of a transaction that both wish to conclude, but one or the other is willing to perform on those terms only if some contingency is satisfied.

The need to create a presently binding contract on established terms subject to a proviso that will release one or both of the parties from the obligation to actually perform under those terms if a contingency does not materialize may be met by making the contract conditional. The prospective home buyer may make her offer to purchase the house subject to the "condition" of financing being arranged by a specified date. The art buyer will agree to purchase the painting subject to the "condition" of obtaining an appraiser's confirmation of authenticity. A condition of this kind is generally, though perhaps not helpfully, referred to as a *condition precedent*.

The terminology of condition precedent can be misleading. First, it may lead to confusion about whether a stipulated condition is a condition precedent to the *formation* of a contract, or only to the *performance* of obligations imposed by a contract. This distinction will be explored shortly. Further, the word "condition" is inherently confusing, since it is used to convey a number of different doctrinal ideas (sometimes improperly). Used without qualification, "condition" is properly understood to refer to a contractual term of such importance that its breach by one party entitles the other, not only to claim damages, but also to terminate the contract, thereby relieving both from any further obligation to perform. Used in this sense (and further discussed in Chapter 7, section 7), it is the failure of a promised performance or state of affairs to materialize that constitutes a discharging breach by the promisor; hence the condition is *promissory*. In contrast, a *contingent* condition describes an event or state of affairs that neither party to a contract has promised will come about, but the occurrence of which is a prerequisite of their obligation to perform their contractual obligations. Since a contingent condition does not embody an obligation undertaken by either party, it cannot be breached. Unless the parties have stipulated otherwise, the failure of the condition simply brings the contract to an end. While the conceptual distinction between promissory and contingent conditions seems clear enough, the concepts are not infrequently confused and the terminology is all too often misplaced. As a result, it is necessary in each case to ascertain what the parties actually intended in terms of their reciprocal obligations.

A so-called *condition precedent* is a contingent condition. It is (i) a term of an existing contract, as opposed to a term of an offer to contract, (ii) which describes an event or state of affairs the occurrence of which has not been promised by either party, and (iii) whose fulfilment is a prerequisite of the obligation of both to complete the contract.

There is a second category of contingent conditions, called *conditions subsequent*. The distinction between a condition precedent and a condition subsequent was addressed in *Dawson v. Helicopter Exploration Co.*, [1955] S.C.R. 868, an extract of which is included in Chapter 2. Estey J relied upon the following passage from Anson's *Law of Contract*, 20th ed. at 310-11 in his characterization of the obligation of the respondent company as a condition subsequent:

> A contract may contain within itself the elements of its own discharge, in the form of provisions, express or implied, for its determination in certain circumstances. These circumstances may be the non-fulfilment of a condition precedent [or] the occurrence of a condition subsequent. . . .
>
> In the second case the parties introduce a provision that the fulfilment of a condition or the occurrence of an event shall discharge either one of them or both from further liabilities under the contract.

On close analysis, there is little substantive difference between contingent conditions precedent and subsequent, given that both are terms of an existing contract and both operate to prevent contractual obligations from arising or falling due after the date of their non-fulfilment. In the sixth edition of this book, Professor Donald Clark argued that "condition subsequent as a distinct concept has meaning only when restricted to a contingency the occurrence (or non-occurrence) of which brings to an end not merely an existing contract, but a contractual obligation that has already become enforceable or would otherwise by the mere passage of time have become enforceable."

In any event, the decision to limit further discussion in this chapter to conditions precedent is prompted by the fact that conditions subsequent are not only far less common than conditions precedent, but also less likely to raise difficult conceptual issues of the kind hereafter addressed.

2. Offer, Option or Contract?

If one of the parties involved in a transaction does not intend to enter into a contract at all unless and until a contingency is satisfied, written or oral communications embodying the terms of a proposed agreement can be no more than an offer to contract on those terms, which offer can be accepted upon satisfaction of the contingency. An offer expressed as being conditional in this sense cannot support the immediate creation of a contract through acceptance, since the offer is not immediately capable of acceptance. To use the example of the home purchase, the prospective buyer's offer may simply amount to a statement of willingness to contract on the agreed terms at such time as he or she procures the necessary financing. Though the seller may purport to accept that offer, the acceptance cannot take effect until financing is in place, since the offer is open for acceptance only if and when that has occurred. In this instance, no contract arises until financing is confirmed. Pending confirmation, there is nothing to prevent the prospective buyer from withdrawing the offer, or the prospective seller from recanting his or her stated willingness to accept. Regrettably, the parties' intention may be obscured rather than clarified by the statement that the offer is subject to a condition precedent.

Language that expresses an agreement as "subject to" a predetermined event or state of affairs is often ambiguous. If the intention of the parties is to conclude an immediately binding contract, a stipulated condition does not qualify the creation of the contract, but only the parties' obligation to perform the obligations arising under it. If the condition is not satisfied, the contract is terminated and neither party is obliged to proceed. However, before failure of the condition precedent, withdrawal from the agreement by either party will constitute a breach of contract. In this scenario, there is truly a "conditional contract", since there *is* a contract, the full performance of which is conditional on fulfilment of the stipulated condition.

The case of *Weibe v. Bobsein* exemplifies the distinction between a conditional offer and a contract incorporating a condition precedent. It also suggests, though in rather oblique terms, an alternative approach that enables one party to hold the other to performance of a contractual obligation without making an immediate present commitment to contract; namely through the use of an option.

An option entails a contract preliminary to the primary contract contemplated by the parties. Under an option contract, one party provides consideration, usually by way of a deposit or payment of money, for the other's agreement to enter into the primary contract at a future specified time, at the "option" of the first. To illustrate: Ann pays Bob $1,000 for an option to purchase property owned by Bob on specified terms, exercisable on or before the expiry of 30 days. Exercise of the option gives rise to a contract of sale on the terms agreed. Ordinarily, the money paid by Ann for the option will be applied to the purchase price payable under the primary contract. If Ann does not exercise the option, the deposit will be forfeit to Bob. In effect, Ann is paying for time in which to decide whether or not she wishes or is able to buy the property, without risking its loss to another potential buyer in the interim. The option ensures that Bob will not sell before Ann is ready to make a final decision. If Bob sells to another buyer during the term of the option, he will be in breach of contract and liable to pay damages to Ann for her loss of the opportunity to purchase the property through exercise of the option. The distinction between an option and a conditional offer to contract lies in the presence or absence of consideration. An option entails a present contractual obligation on the part of Bob to refrain from taking action that will preclude the eventual formation of the contemplated primary contract.

WIEBE v. BOBSIEN

[1985] 1 W.W.R. 644, 59 B.C.L.R. 183, 36 R.P.R. 277, 14 D.L.R. (4th) 754 (S.C.)

BOUCK J.

.....

Adolf Bobsien is a contractor. He owns the subject property at 14241 Crescent Beach Road, Surrey, British Columbia. On 14th May 1984 he listed it for sale with a realtor.

John Allen Wiebe is a dentist. In the early summer of 1984 he had title to a house at 537 Yale Road, Port Moody, British Columbia. He made the offer to purchase the Crescent Beach Property owned by the defendant. Eventually, they both signed an interim agreement dated 22nd June 1984. Its essential terms are as follows:

1) A deposit on account of the proposed purchase price—$1,000.
2) Purchase price—$360,000.
3) Completion date—29th August 1984.
4) The sale was subject to the plaintiff selling his Port Moody residence on or before 18th August 1984.
5) Pending the sale of the Port Moody home, the seller retained the right to sell his Crescent Beach property to another purchaser if one could be found. In the event the defendant received a bona fide offer from a third party, the plaintiff then had 72 hours to remove the "condition precedent" from the interim agreement dated 22nd June 1984 "so that it was no longer subject to the sale" of the plaintiff's Port Moody home.
6) On its face the interim agreement is not under seal.

During argument counsel for the plaintiff conceded that if the plaintiff did not sell his Port Moody residence by 18th August 1984 he was entitled to terminate the agreement and receive back the deposit of $1,000.

On 22nd July 1984 the defendant decided he did not wish to go through with the sale. He informed the plaintiff of this fact by telegram on that date. In summary it states the interim agreement dated 22nd June 1984 "is cancelled".

Dr. Wiebe did not accept his cancellation but continued in his efforts to sell the Port Moody property. On 18th August 1984 he was successful in obtaining a buyer for the sum of $165,000. On that day he notified the defendant that the "subject clause" was removed. In accordance with another term of the contract he increased the deposit to $10,000.

When the completion date of 29th August 1984 arrived, the defendant refused to close. At that time the plaintiff was ready, willing and able to complete.

.....

ISSUE

Is the interim agreement a form of option that could be cancelled by the defendant prior to 18th August 1984 or is it a binding agreement for sale and purchase of the Crescent Beach property?

LAW

It is the position of the plaintiff that the interim agreement of 22nd June 1984 was a binding contract of purchase and sale. Apart from any deposit of $1,000, consideration passed between the parties by way of corresponding commitments to buy and sell. A condition precedent to completion of the agreement was the sale of the Port Moody property owned by the plaintiff on or before 18th August 1984. The contractual obligation imposed upon the defendant to deliver up possession and complete the conveyance in accordance with the contract was merely in suspense pending the sale of the plaintiff's home.

On the other hand, the defendant says the contract of 22nd June 1984 was no contract at all. At most it was a form of option agreement and since the deposit of $1,000 could be claimed by the purchaser if the transaction collapsed, the option lacked consideration. Therefore the defendant was entitled to withdraw from its terms any time prior to 18th August 1984. He did so by his telegram of 22nd July 1984.

Authorities on this area of the law are not easy to reconcile. First, I will discuss the leading cases from both camps. Then I will say why I think the plaintiff should succeed.

One should keep in mind there is written support for the position of the plaintiff that the parties treated the sale of the Port Moody home as a "condition precedent" because those are the exact two words they used in the contract documents.

How a condition precedent operates is the subject of much judicial analysis. Generally speaking, its effect is characterized in one of two ways. It either:

1) prevents the creation of a contract, or it

2) merely suspends performance of some or all of the obligation [*sic*] set out in the contract until the condition is met.

I will try to analyze the case law following this order.

1. *Circumstances where a condition precedent prevents the formation of a contract*

Aberfoyle Plantations Ltd. v. Cheng, [1960] A.C. 115, is an example of the application of the first rule. A summary of the facts is as follows:

In 1955 the parties agreed to sell and to buy a plantation, part of which consisted of 182 acres comprised in seven leases that had expired in 1950. In the intervening years the vendor had tried but failed to obtain a renewal of the leases. Clause 4 of the agreement therefore provided that "the purchase is conditional on the vendor obtaining a renewal" of the leases. If he proved "unable to fulfil this condition this agreement shall become null and void".

The vendor failed to obtain renewal and the judicial committee held that the purchaser could recover the deposit he had paid. Lord Jenkins said [p. 128]:

> . . . at the very outset of the agreement the vendor's obligation to sell, and the purchaser's obligation to buy, were by clause 1 expressed to be subject to the condition contained in clause 4. It was thus made plain beyond argument that the condition was a condition precedent on the fulfilment of which the formation of a binding contract of sale was made to depend."

In other words, no binding contract was made because the purchase was subject to a condition precedent which the seller could elect not to perform.

A similar result was reached by Taylor J. of this court in two recent cases he decided. The first is *Black Gavin & Co. v. Cheung* (1980), 20 B.C.L.R. 21 (S.C.). Here, the interim agreement for the purchase of a hotel was [p. 23]:

> . . . subject to Liquor Administration Branch approval, subject to my inspection of and approval of premises and chattels, subject to my approval of the financial statements, and subject to me increasing present 2nd mortgage by $140,000.

His Lordship decided the parties did not enter into any contract at all. At p. 25 he said this:

> But in no sense does it become a binding agreement of sale and purchase. That can happen only if the purchaser approves the property, chattels and financial statements and obtains

governmental approval for transfer of the liquor licence. . ... A document signed by both parties, in which one says to the other "you may buy on these terms if you like the property" and the other says he will if he does, is not, I think, an agreement subject to a condition precedent, or an agreement at all. It remains an offer by the proposed vendor to the proposed purchaser, and nothing more, until the proposed purchaser says that he does indeed approve of the property.

I would add that, while the transaction may have the appearance of an option, it cannot be a true option if given neither under seal nor for consideration. There was no seal in the present instance, and the "deposit" money could not be consideration. The intended vendor was entitled to the deposit either as part payment, in the event of sale, or by forfeiture, in the event of default in completion; but there could be neither sale nor obligation to complete unless and until the intended purchaser said "I approve". The only effect in law which could be given to the so called "interim agreement" is as a bare offer by Mr. Cheung to the intended purchaser, Mr. Bewza, to sell to him on the terms mentioned if Mr. Bewza should indicate later that he wished to buy.

It follows that the offer bound Mr. Cheung and the other defendants no more than it bound the proposed purchaser; it could be withdrawn by the defendants at any time before receipt of an unequivocal acceptance.

Taylor J. found the contract was not one which was subject to a condition precedent but was merely in the form of an offer which either side could choose to withdraw prior to the time the purchaser said he approved of the property. He decided no binding agreement was ever reached in the first instance.

The second case is along the same lines. It is *Murray McDermid Hldg. Ltd. v. Thater* (1983), 42 B.C.L.R. 119 (S.C.). A summary of the relevant facts is contained in the headnote:

The interim agreement between the parties stated that the plaintiff company's offer to purchase was "subject to" the approval of the company president on or before a certain date. A deposit of $100 was paid. Prior to the date specified the defendant revoked her acceptance of the offer whereupon the plaintiff's agent purported to remove the "subject to" clause. The defendant refused to complete the transaction and the plaintiff commenced an action for specific performance.

At p. 125 Taylor J. said this:

I find the "subject clause" not to be a condition precedent . . .

I conclude that the "interim agreement" was one which imposed no obligation on the plaintiff purchaser unless and until its president, within the time stipulated, gave his approval to the proposed price and terms, and that it stood as a bare offer on the part of the defendant vendor, unsupported by consideration, and accordingly such as she might revoke at any time before that approval was given.

He went on to hold that the vendor was entitled to revoke the offer to sell before the time came for completion of the "subject to" clause. When the vendor did this, the agreement was terminated.

American experience in this area of the law is similar to that of Canada and the United Kingdom. Here is what Corpus Juris Secundum says about the effect of a condition precedent on a contract: vol. 17A, p. 318, para. 338:

A condition precedent may relate to the binding effect of an agreement or to the duty to perform an existing contract. The existence of such a condition depends upon the intent of the parties as gathered from the words they have employed, and it will be interpreted according to general rules of construction.

And at p. 319, there is the following editorial comment as a footnote to the text:

> Generally in contracts, when reference is made to conditions, what is meant are conditions which become operative after formation of the contract and qualify the duty of immediate performance of a promise or promises thereunder, not conditions which qualify the existence of a contract or promise.

These statements are in line with most Canadian authorities. A condition precedent may be of a nature that creates no binding agreement or it may just act as an ingredient which suspends performance of an otherwise complete contract. It all depends upon the intention of the parties as expressed in the contract itself and as shown by surrounding events.

United States texts and case law say that when a condition precedent is "illusory", it may prevent the formation of a binding contract: Corbin on Contracts, vol. 3A, p. 78, para. 644. A condition is illusory when it involves "fancy [or] taste": *Mattei v. Hopper*, 330 P. 2d 625 at 627 (California S.C.), 1958. An example of such a clause might be the following:

> I promise to buy your house subject to me deciding whether I like it or not.

That kind of condition precedent is contained in the two cases decided by Taylor J. of this court. In *Black Gavin & Co. v. Cheung*, supra, the purchaser made the agreement subject to five conditions [set out above] . . .

[The conditions relating to the approval of the premises and of the chattels] imply a condition of whim, fancy, like or dislike. If the purchaser fancies it or approves the premises or the chattels, then it would buy the hotel. These two conditions plus the combined effect of all taken together constituted an illusory contract that was no agreement at all.

A similar situation occurred in *Murray McDermid Holdg. Ltd. v. Thater, supra*. In that case the condition precedent to the purchaser completing the sale depended upon the approval of the purchaser's president. In other words, whether the purchaser really fancied the property. An obvious inference arose that the parties did not actually intend to execute a binding agreement because they left an escape hatch for the purchaser should its president decide he did not "approve" the agreement.

While a purchaser must use his best efforts in doing such things as obtaining financing, getting subdivision approval or selling his own home, there is no way the law can test whether he used his best efforts in deciding if he really likes a particular piece of property or not. Therefore there can be no contract in the first instance.

2. *Circumstances where a condition precedent suspends the performance of the contract*

While each contract must be interpreted according to its own terms and surrounding circumstances, nonetheless, the law seems to lean in favour of the concept that where there is a condition precedent such as a "subject to" clause, a contract is formed on signing by the parties. It is merely in suspense pending the completion of the condition. *Aberfoyle Plantations Ltd. v. Cheng, supra*, is not necessarily in line with this statement but it is generally restricted to its own peculiar facts.

In *Property & Bloodstock Ltd. v. Emerton; Bush v. Property & Bloodstock Ltd.*, [1967] 3 All E.R. 321 (C.A.), the court approved this second rule as the one which is most consistent with proper contractual interpretation.

That was a case where a sale was "subject to" the vendor obtaining the consent of his landlord to an assignment of the lease to the purchaser. It was held that the landlord's consent was not a condition precedent to the formation of the contract of sale or the creation of the relationship of vendor and purchaser.

In passing Danckwerts L.J. had this to say about the decision of Lord Jenkins in the *Aberfoyle* case at p. 328:

> Lord Jenkins thought that the contract was so conditional that even the relationship of vendor and purchaser was never created by it. This is a proposition which, with all respect, I find it very difficult to accept.

Following upon the lead of Danckwerts L.J., Lord Denning M.R. articulated the second principle more fully in *Smallman v. Smallman*, [1971] 3 W.L.R. 588, [1971] 3 All E.R. 717 (C.A.). This was an instance where a husband and wife reached an agreement "subject to the approval in due course of the court". The husband tried to escape the consequences of the contract by arguing the condition precedent really meant there was no agreement at all. At p. 720 His Lordship said:

> In my opinion, if the parties have reached an agreement on all essential matters, then the clause 'subject to the approval of the court' does not mean there is no agreement at all. There is an agreement, but the operation of it is suspended until the court approves it. It is the duty of one party or the other to bring the agreement before the court for approval. If the court approves, it is binding on the parties. If the court does not approve, it is not binding. But, pending the application to the court, it remains a binding agreement which neither party can disavow. Orr LJ has drawn my attention to a useful analogy. Many contracts for the sale of goods are made subject to an export or import licence being obtained. Such a condition does not mean there is no contract at all. It is the duty of the seller, or the buyer, as the case may be, to take reasonable steps to obtain a licence. If he applies for a licence and gets it, the contract operates. If he takes all reasonable steps to obtain it, and it is refused, he is released from his obligation. If he fails to apply for it or to do what is reasonable to obtain it, he is in breach and liable to damages; see *Brauer & Co. (Great Britain) Ltd. v. James Clark (Brush Materials) Ltd.* [1952] 2 All ER 497 and *AV Pound & Co. Ltd. v. MW Hardy & Co. Inc.* [1956] 1 All ER 639, [1956] AC 588. Similarly when a man agrees to buy property 'subject to the title being approved by our solicitor', there is a binding contract. There is an implied promise by the buyer that he will appoint a solicitor and shall consult him in good faith, and that the solicitor shall give his honest opinion. If the solicitor honestly disapproves, the contract does not bind. But until he does disapprove, the contract binds.

Our Supreme Court of Canada followed this line of reasoning in *Dynamic Tpt. Ltd. v. O.K. Detailing Ltd.*, [1978] 2 S.C.R. 1072, [*infra*].

From these English, Canadian and American authorities a general rule is laid down that in a real estate transaction a condition precedent which must be performed by the purchaser will not usually prevent the formation of a contract but will simply suspend the covenant of the vendor to complete until the condition precedent is met by the purchaser.

SUMMARY

From this review of the law, the following summary falls into place:

1) A real estate contract containing a condition precedent will usually result in a binding agreement of sale and purchase. The obligation to complete the contract is merely in suspense pending the occurrence of the event constituting the condition precedent.

2) However, in some instances, such a condition may prevent the formation of a contract if the agreement itself and the surrounding events indicate it was never the intention of the parties to bind themselves to a contract of sale and purchase.

3) In this case, the contract and the surrounding events indicate the parties intended to reach a consensus when they executed the interim agreement on 22nd June 1984.

4) Completion of the sale was suspended pending disposition of the plaintiff's Port Moody home on or before 18th August 1984. He had a duty to take all reasonable steps to sell this house. If he failed to do so, he would be in breach of his agreement and liable in damages to the plaintiff.

5) When the Port Moody residence was sold on 18th August 1984, the defendant was then contractually bound to sell the Crescent Beach property to the purchaser because the agreement was no longer in suspense. Hence, the defendant had no legal right to cancel the contract by his telegram of 22nd July 1984.

. . . . .

[Judgment for plaintiff. This decision was affirmed on appeal. Lambert J.A., in dissent, accepted the governing principle set out by Bouck J., but took a different view of its application to the instant facts. His judgment illustrates how difficult it can be to determine whether the satisfaction of a condition precedent is so dependent on one party's subjective evaluation as to render agreement illusory.]

WIEBE v. BOBSIEN

[1986] 4 W.W.R. 270, 64 B.C.L.R. 295, 39 R.P.R. 228, 20 D.L.R. (4th) 475
(C.A.)

LAMBERT J.A. [dissenting] . . . Each "condition precedent" case must be considered on its own facts. As Bouck J. indicated, some conditions precedent are so imprecise, or depend so entirely on the subjective state of mind of the purchaser, that the contract process must still be regarded as at the offer stage. An example would be "subject to the approval of the president of the corporate purchaser". In other cases, the condition precedent is clear, precise and objective. In those cases, a contract is completed; neither party can withdraw, but performance is held in suspense until the parties know whether the objective condition precedent is fulfilled. An example would be "subject to John Smith being elected as Mayor in the municipal election on 15 October of this year".

But there is a third class of condition precedent. Into that class fall the types of conditions which are partly subjective and partly objective. An example would be "subject to planning department approval of the attached plan of subdivision". This looks objective, but it differs from a truly objective condition in that someone has to solicit the approval of the planning department. Perhaps some persuasion of the planning department will be required. Can the purchaser prevent the condition from being fulfilled by refusing to present the plan of subdivision to the planning department? This type of case has been dealt with by implying a term that the purchaser will take all reasonable steps to cause the plan to be presented to the planning department, and will, at the proper time and in the proper way, take all reasonable steps to have the plan approved by the planning department.

The law in relation to implying terms in an agreement is no different in relation to conditions precedent than it is for other terms of an agreement. Business contracts should not be permitted to fail over an omission that the parties would immediately have corrected if the parties had noticed the omission at the time the contract was made. And we have the "business efficacy" test and the "officious bystander" test to guide us. In the example I have given, it is clear that business efficacy requires that someone must present the plan of subdivision to the planning department, and the officious bystander test would be met by both parties answering the hypothetical question of the hypothetical onlooker, as to who will present the plan, by saying: "Of course the purchaser will do it".

But there are cases that fall in this third class of condition precedent where it will not be possible to imply the missing term, and the agreement will fail for uncertainty. In those cases the court cannot write a contract for the parties.

I think this case falls in that category of incurable uncertainty. What term should be implied? A term requiring the purchaser to make all reasonable efforts to sell his house sounds all right. But what does it mean? Does it meet the officious bystander test? I do not think so because it leaves unresolved the question of whether he must sell at the price he can get, on the market, in the time allotted, or whether he is entitled to insist that the sale can only take place at a price he considers reasonable and is willing to accept.

I think that what the parties usually intend by this type of clause is the second alternative. That is, that the purchaser is only committed to sell his own house if he gets the price he has in mind. The reason is that in the residential housing market the purchaser is likely to be unfamiliar with the market, but he is almost sure to know how much cash he has and what size of mortgage he can count on being able to service.

Let us say he owns his own house in which he thinks he has a $100,000 equity. He knows he can service a mortgage of $50,000, and he has just received a legacy of $100,000. He has no access to any other resources. As long as he can recover his equity of $100,000 on the sale of his own house, on which there is now a mortgage of $50,000, he has the resources to pay $250,000 for a better house. So he makes an offer to purchase the better house of $250,000, subject to the sale of his existing house. He proposes to realize his equity of $100,000 by selling his own house for $150,000. But the market has sagged. All the offers he receives turn out to be less than $100,000. If he sells at that price he will not be able to complete the purchase of the new house. He will be $50,000 short.

As I say, I think that is the most usual type of situation where this kind of "subject to" clause is used in the residential housing market. I think that a purchaser who accepts the recommendation of a real estate agent to put this type of subject clause in his offer would be astounded to find that he has committed himself to sell his own house at the best offer he receives in the time allotted, no matter whether it meets his expectations or approval, or not.

In my opinion, the condition precedent in this case is uncertain. The uncertainty could have been turned to sufficient certainty by the purchaser removing the condition, or by the purchaser, in fact, selling his house. At that time a contract would have been formed. Until then, the interim agreement remained a standing offer by the vendor to sell at $360,000, revocable at the will of the vendor, on reasonable notice to the purchaser. The standing offer was withdrawn in ample time before the purchaser sold his own house. So no contract of purchase and sale ever arose.

The way to deal with this problem in the real estate market is for the form of subject clause to state the price and the essential terms upon which the purchaser must sell his own house. Then a court would have no trouble in implying a term that the purchaser must make all reasonable efforts to sell at that price and on those terms. And the court could assess whether the purchaser had made reasonable efforts to do so.

[The majority of the court, Seaton and Carrothers JJ.A., dismissed the appeal.]

NOTES and QUESTIONS

1. The threefold categorization established by Lambert J.A. in his dissenting opinion has been applied in several subsequent cases. See *e.g.*, *Mark 7 Development Ltd. v. Peace Holdings Ltd.* (1991), 53 B.C.L.R. (2d) 217, 15 R.P.R. (2d) 101 (B.C. C.A.), *Swan Creek Developments Ltd. v. G.A. Brown Associates Ltd.* (1999), [1999] B.C.J. No. 1056, 1999 CarswellBC 991 (S.C.), and *Harvey v. Black* (1992), 7 Alta. L.R. (3d) 103, 137 A.R. 111, [1993] 3 W.W.R. 527 (Q.B.).

2. Both Bouck J. and Lambert J.A. suggest that there cannot be an immediately binding contract where an agreement is made conditional upon the subjective state of mind of one of the parties, such as "approval" or "best efforts". Does the framing of a condition precedent in those terms inevitably lead to the conclusion that the agreement is not a contract? How might that conclusion be avoided? See section 3 below.

3. The question of whether a contract is or is not created by an agreement that contemplates satisfaction of a condition depends, as does any question of contract formation, on the intention of the parties. The language used is not necessarily determinative, particularly when it is susceptible to competing interpretations. Note that while Bouck J. suggested that the parties' use of the term "condition precedent" supported the plaintiff's argument that the agreement was a contract, he proceeded in the immediately following paragraph to say that a condition precedent may either prevent the creation of a contract or suspend the performance of an extant contract.

Clear language will ordinarily compel the Court to arrive at the conclusion it plainly dictates. In *Taberner v. Ernest & Twin Development Inc.* (2001), 89 B.C.L.R. (3d) 104, 38 E.T.R. (2d) 120, 39 R.P.R. (3d) 140 (S.C.), a property owner argued that an offer to purchase conditional upon the purchaser's approval of a property inspection and specified documentation was no more than a standing offer, since by effectively reserving the right to change her mind by the expedient of refusing her approval, the prospective purchaser had not committed herself to a contract. Lowry J. concluded that the British Columbia Court of Appeal's decision in *Mark 7 Development Ltd. v. Peace Holdings*

Ltd., supra, note 1, would support the vendor's argument that its acceptance of the offer could not create a contract, were it not for the inclusion in the written agreement of the following clause:

> This offer, or counter-offer, will be open for acceptance until 9 o'clock pm on July 21, 2000 and *upon acceptance of the offer*, or counter-offer, by accepting in writing and notifying the other party of such acceptance *there shall be a binding Contract of Purchase and Sale* on the terms and conditions set forth [emphasis added].

The vendor was accordingly not entitled to refuse to complete the sale when the purchaser advised that she was ready and willing to do so. However, the parties' written assertion that their agreement is a contract will not make it so if the court concludes that its terms do not in fact create reciprocal binding obligations. In *Saveheli v. Philp*, 2000 BCSC 815, 33 R.P.R. (3d) 149 (S.C. [In Chambers]), Owen-Flood J. concluded, in the face of the same wording deemed decisive by Lowry J. in *Taberner*, that an accepted offer did not give rise to a contract, because the stated condition that the buyer receive and approve certain information regarding the tax implications of the transaction was so broad that it was impossible to determine what would constitute a reasonable approval or unreasonable rejection of such information. In the result, there was no contract of sale that could be enforced by the prospective purchaser. See also *Black Gavin & Co. v. Cheung* (1980), 20 B.C.L.R. 21 (S.C.) at 24.

   4. Consider the following scenario: Black listed his house for sale with Greenacre Realty. The exclusive listing agreement contained the following provision:

> I agree to pay a commission of 5 per cent of the sale price on any sale or exchange howsoever effected during the currency of this authority . . . or if the property is sold by me within 90 days after the expiration of this authority to anyone who has been made aware of the property through the marketing activities of you or your sub-agents during the term of this authority.

On the final day of the 60-day exclusive listing period Greenacre mailed information about Black's house to White. On 12th June, 80 days later, Black personally concluded an agreement for sale with White that was expressly "conditional on my arranging a suitable mortgage within 15 business days". Thirteen days thereafter White notified Black that financing was arranged, and completion took place a few days later. Is Black liable to Greenacre Realty for commission? On what date did Black sell to White? See *H.W. Liebig & Co. v. Leading Investments Ltd.*, [1986] 1 S.C.R. 70.

   5. The agreement under review in *Weibe v. Bobsein* was typical in that it provided for a deposit on account of the purchase price to be made by the purchaser at the time the agreement was made. The question of whether a deposit supports characterization of the agreement as an option to purchase on the terms stipulated was addressed by the British Columbia Court of Appeal in *Mark 7 Development Ltd. v. Peace Holdings Ltd.*, *supra*, note 1. Hinds J.A. first concluded that conditions imposed for the benefit of the putative purchaser in a multimillion dollar real estate transaction meant that there was no binding contract of sale, but only a standing offer to sell that could be and was revoked by the vendor. Hinds J.A. then considered the purchaser's argument that, having paid a deposit on account of the purchase price, he had acquired an option to purchase that precluded the vendor's retraction of its offer to sell. On that view, the vendor's refusal to proceed allegedly amounted to breach of its obligations under the option contract. The following is an extract from the discussion of the issue, at 226-27:

> The case of *Murray McDermid Holdings Ltd. v. Thater* [(1982), 42 B.C.L.R. 119, (S.C.)], involved a "subject to" clause. The plaintiff's offer to purchase the defendant's property was subject to the approval of the president of the plaintiff company. Taylor J. (as he then was) held that the interim agreement was simply an offer to sell which was revocable by the defendant prior to the assent of the president of the plaintiff being given or the expiry of the time specified for that purpose.

> In dealing with the issue of consideration Taylor J. had this to say at pp. 122 - 23:

>> A somewhat similar transaction was involved in *Black Gavin & Co. Ltd. v. Cheung* (1980), 20 B.C.L.R. 21 (S.C.).

There the interim agreement said that the purchaser's offer was subject to his inspection and approval of the premises, chattels and accounts. I held that such an interim agreement, under which one party in effect says to the other "you may buy on these terms if you like the property", and the other says he will if he does, is not an agreement to buy subject to a condition precedent or agreement at all. I held it to be an offer by the vendor to sell on those terms if the purchaser should later indicate that he wishes to buy, and went on to say (at p. 25):

I would add that, while the transaction may have the appearance of an option, it cannot be a true option if given neither under seal nor for consideration. There was no seal in the present instance, and the 'deposit' money could not be consideration. The intended vendor was entitled to the deposit either as part payment, in the event of sale, or by forfeiture, in the event of default in completion; but there could be neither sale nor obligation to complete unless and until the intended purchaser said "I approve. . . .

The amount paid as consideration for an option may, of course, form part of the purchase price if the option is exercised, but an option can be enforceable only if there is some consideration which must be given by the optionee in any event. In order for there to be an enforceable option in the present case the terms of the agreement must be such that the vendor would have received the deposit even if the plaintiff did not approve the deal.

After considering the wording of the "time is of the essence" clause and the effect thereof, Taylor J. concluded that the interim agreement could not operate as an option because it lacked consideration.

In *Kitsilano Ent. Ltd. v. G. & A. Developments Ltd.* [(1990), 48 B.C.L.R. (2d) 70 (S.C.)] Macdonell J. quoted with approval long segments of the judgment of Taylor J. in *Murray McDermid*. He concluded that the agreement was not an option because there was no consideration. In *Kitsilano Ent.*, as in this case, the deposit was completely refundable in the event of non-completion of the proposed sale. I therefore conclude that the interim agreement in this case cannot be construed as an option due to lack of consideration flowing from the plaintiff to the defendant.

6. You have been retained to advise Andy, who is considering purchasing an expensive used sports car from Barb. Andy wants the car, but needs to arrange a loan to finance its purchase. In addition, he wishes to have the car inspected and its condition approved by a qualified mechanic before he pays Barb the purchase money. The only mechanic whose opinion he trusts is presently away on vacation. What language would you use to draft the agreement so as to create (i) a conditional offer that will, if it is accepted by Barb, mature into a contract only when the loan and the inspection are in place, (ii) a conditional contract under which Andy will not be obliged to pay for the car until the loan and the inspection are in place, and (iii) an option to purchase the car, exercisable by Andy at such time as the loan and inspection are in place. What are the advantages and disadvantages of each approach?

7. What is the status of a contingent agreement when the event on which it is conditioned has in fact occurred, but the party with knowledge of this fails to communicate notice of the fulfilment of the condition before the expiration of the period contractually specified for its satisfaction? *Halsbury's Laws* (4th ed.), vol. 9, para. 514, sets out the following general principle:

Where a promise is conditional upon the happening of a particular event, and there is no express stipulation that notice is to be given of the happening of the event, a condition to that effect will not, as a rule, be implied, except where the nature of the contract requires it; for instance, where the event is a matter which lies within the peculiar knowledge of the other party to the contract or depends upon an option to be exercised by him.

The familiar "subject to financing" clause would appear to be a clear example of a condition falling within the latter category. Even here, however, the cautious contractual drafter may be tempted to include an express provision to place the matter beyond doubt.

3. Absence of Consideration and Uncertain Terms

You saw in Chapter 4 that the concept of consideration, in the context of a bilateral contract, requires the exchange of promises that entail an obligation on the part of each party either to do something or to refrain from doing something. Though the language of an agreement may appear to suggest reciprocal commitments, a purported contract will fail for lack of consideration if one of the parties has in fact not assumed a definite obligation (recall the analysis in *Dalhousie College v. Boutilier Estate, supra,* Chapter 4, section 1(d)). This issue has frequently arisen in connection with agreements expressed to be conditional upon one of the parties' approval of information to be procured or provided in connection with the subject matter of the contract. The attempt to draft wording that gives rise to an immediate contract while preserving the right of one of the parties to refuse to complete the transaction contemplated if he or she is not satisfied with certain information or documentation has met with mixed success (see *e.g., Savelhi v. Philp,* note 3 above). If the condition permits the person for whose benefit it is included to refuse to grant approval for any reason whatsoever or for no reason at all, that person has in effect not promised that he or she will do or not do anything. Even if he or she genuinely wishes to proceed with the transaction, the other party may refuse to do so if the terms of the condition are such that there is no consideration to support a contract. In *Wiebe v. Bobsein,* the trial judge referred to United States authority describing such a condition precedent as "illusory". It would be more accurate to say that the *consideration* that may superficially appear to flow from the party relying upon the condition is illusory.

In *Mark 7 Development Ltd. v. Peace Holdings Ltd., supra,* Hinds J.A., speaking for the British Columbia Court of Appeal, said of the conditions imposed by a purchaser of real estate, at p. 225:

> I have earlier quoted para. 2 (2.4) of the conditions. It provides for the purchaser to indicate by February 17, 1989, whether the leases, financial statements and list of fixtures are acceptable to the purchaser. It further provides "the purchaser may be arbitrary in his acceptance of these". Those conditions precedent are manifestly dependent upon the subjective state of mind of the purchaser and, as such, they fall into the first category referred by Lambert J.A. [in *Wiebe v. Bobsein*]. They precluded the interim agreement from coming into existence as a binding agreement. It remained a standing offer by the defendant to sell the property to the plaintiff revocable at the will of the defendant prior to acceptance by the plaintiff.

In many cases, the courts have injected consideration into a condition that appears on its face to depend entirely on the subjective state of mind of a party by fettering that party's caprice through recognition of an implied obligation of reasonableness. In *Tau Holdings Ltd. v. Alderbridge Development Corp.* (1991), 7 B.C.A.C. 151, 60 B.C.L.R. (2d) 161 (C.A.), the defendant argued that there was no contract for the purchase of land where the offer to sell included a term providing that the purchaser's obligation to complete the transaction was subject to, *inter alia,* the purchaser's approval of engineering, soils, and traffic reports in respect of the property and his having obtained financing. The court rejected the contention that, notwithstanding the purchaser's purported acceptance, the offer remained an outstanding offer to sell that had never matured into a contract. Lambert J.A. distinguished *Mark 7 Development Ltd.* as follows, at 166:

> The first distinction between the two cases is that in the *Mark 7* case the condition precedent was entirely subjective and it was particularly specified that the Purchaser could be arbitrary in deciding whether to accept the leases. On the authority of *Wiebe v. Bobsein* [*supra*, section 2 of this chapter], *Griffin v. Martens* (1988), 27 B.C.L.R. (2d) 152 at p. 154, and *Empress Towers v. Bank of Nova Scotia* [Chapter 3, section 4] at p. 130, all decisions of this Court, I conclude that in this case the conditions precedent cannot be considered to be entirely subjective nor can they be considered to impose no obligations on the Purchaser. On the contrary, I consider that the conditions precedent oblige the Purchaser to consider the engineering, soils, and traffic reports and *not to reject them arbitrarily but only on reasonable specified grounds.* In addition, the condition precedent in relation to financing imposed an obligation on the Purchaser to *pursue financing actively and not to reject financing unreasonably.* Under the authorities to which I have referred those terms should be implied, in accordance with the structure of the agreement, which was not framed as if it were, after acceptance, to be only an offer or an option, and to give it business efficacy [emphasis added].

For a more recent example of this approach, see *Drabinsky v. Heffel Gallery Ltd.* (2000), 13 B.L.R. (3d) 190 (B.C. S.C. [In Chambers]).

In other instances, courts have scrutinized conditions requiring that a purchaser obtain "satisfactory" or "suitable" financing through the lens, not of consideration, but of another requirement of contract formation, namely, certainty of terms. Some courts have concluded that the condition is so ambiguous as to render the agreement void for uncertainty (*Pietrobon v. McIntyre* (1987), 15 B.C.L.R. (2d) 350 (S.C.)). Others have avoided that conclusion by implying an objective qualification that the condition is fulfilled by financing satisfactory to a reasonable person in the purchaser's position (*Griffin v. Martens* (1988), 27 B.C.L.R. (2d) 152 (C.A.)), or that the purchaser will use reasonable efforts to obtain financing (*Gennis v. Madore* (1988), 72 Nfld. & P.E.I.R. 104 (P.E.I. T.D.)). Recall that in *Wiebe v. Bobsein*, Lambert J.A. dissented from the majority's view that the agreement constituted an enforceable contract of sale on the ground that it was not possible to imply an intelligible term requiring the purchaser to take reasonable steps to sell his house, with the result that the agreement failed for uncertainty. The difficulty, in his view, was that it was impossible to ascertain what price the purchaser was bound to find acceptable.

4. Reciprocal Subsidiary Obligations

The fact that a condition precedent is contingent, rather than promissory, means that a court cannot satisfy a moral intuition that one of the contracting parties is blameworthy through the imposition of liability for breach of contract. If a condition precedent is not satisfied, the "deal" will be off regardless of whether any effort was or was not made by anyone to bring about the event or state of affairs contemplated. Thus the prospective home vendor who contracts to sell subject to the unqualified condition that the buyer procure financing by a specified date will be in breach of contract if he or she accepts another offer before that date has arrived, even if it becomes clear that the original buyer has had a change of heart and is making no effort to actually put financing in place. The perceived unfairness of this result has motivated the courts to imply in such contracts a term subsidiary to the condition precedent, obliging the appropriate party to make reasonable and genuine efforts to procure satisfaction of the condition. The prospective buyer subject to such an obligation will be in breach by failing to make such efforts.

Contractual obligations that fall to be performed only upon satisfaction of a condition precedent may be described as the parties' *primary* obligations. They are the obligations that relate to the ultimate objective of the contract. In the context of the posited real estate transaction, the primary obligations of the parties are those that give effect to the sale; essentially, payment of the purchase price on the one hand, and delivery of title and possession on the other. However, the conclusion that a contract exists before the primary obligations become operative suggests that parties are subject to other obligations in the meantime. For purposes of differentiation, those interstitial obligations may be described as *subsidiary*.

Where a condition precedent is unaccompanied by a requirement that either of the parties take steps to procure its fulfilment, their reciprocal subsidiary obligation may be defined as the simple obligation to refrain from withdrawing from the contract. A refusal to proceed manifested before the time stipulated for satisfaction of the condition precedent has arrived will accordingly constitute a breach of contract, supporting the opposite party's claim for a contract remedy. However, contracts that include a condition precedent usually require more than mere restraint from withdrawal on the part of one or both of the parties. In the vast majority of cases, the condition precedent contemplates an event or a state of affairs that will not occur unless action is taken. In *Wiebe v. Bobsein*, for example, the purchaser had an implied subsidiary obligation to make reasonable efforts to bring about the sale of his Port Moody residence by the specified date.

Among the most common conditions precedent are those relating to the procurement of such third party action as zoning or subdivision approval. A well drafted contract will designate which of the parties, if either, is expected to undertake efforts to obtain the required approval or other event, and may even indicate the nature of the action to be taken. However, many agreements are silent on the point. The next case addresses the question of whether subsidiary obligations relating to the satisfaction of a condition precedent exist in the absence of express contractual provision.

DYNAMIC TRANSPORT LTD. v. O.K. DETAILING LTD.

[1978] 2 S.C.R. 1072, 6 Alta. L.R. (2d) 156, 4 R.P.R. 208, 85 D.L.R. (3d) 19,9 A.R. 308, 20 N.R. 500

DICKSON J. [delivering the judgment of the court] This is an action for specific performance brought by the appellant, Dynamic Transport Ltd., to enforce a contract in writing between the respondent, O.K. Detailing Ltd. as vendor, and the appellant as purchaser, for the sale of land in the City of Edmonton. The price was $53,000. The land is now said to be worth $200,000. The respondent refuses to complete, maintaining that the contract is unenforceable on two grounds: (i) the description of the land is so vague and uncertain as to make identification impossible; and (ii) the contract is silent as to which party will obtain the subdivision approval required under the terms of the *Planning Act*, R.S.A. 1970, c. 276.

[Some comments from the judgment of the court on the sufficiency of the description of the land are set out in Chapter 4, section 8(c)(ii). The court found that the contract provided a description of the land which satisfied the Statute of Frauds and went on to consider the effect of the necessity of obtaining subdivision approval under the Planning Act.]

. . . Both parties were aware that subdivision approval, pursuant to the *Planning Act*, was required, but the agreement is silent as to whether vendor or purchaser would obtain this approval. The statutory prerequisite became an implied term of the agreement. The obtaining of subdivision approval was, in effect, a condition precedent to the performance of the obligations to sell and to buy. . . . The parties created a binding agreement. It is true that the performance of some of the provisions of that agreement was not due unless and until the condition was fulfilled, but that in no way negates or dilutes the force of the obligations imposed by those provisions, in particular, the obligation of the vendor to sell and the obligation of the purchaser to buy. These obligations were merely in suspense pending the occurrence of the event constituting the condition precedent.

The existence of a condition precedent does not preclude the possibility of some provisions of a contract being operative before the condition is fulfilled, as for example, a provision obligating one party to take steps to bring about the event constituting the condition precedent. . . .

In appropriate circumstances the Courts will find an implied promise by one party to take steps to bring about the event constituting the condition precedent: see Cheshire and Fifoot's *Law of Contract*, 9th ed. (1976), at pp. 137-8:

> Where there is a contract but the obligations of one or both parties are subject to conditions a number of subsidiary problems arise. So there may be a question of whether one of the parties has undertaken to bring the condition about . . . There is a clear distinction between a promise, for breach of which an action lies and a condition, upon which an obligation is dependent. But the same event may be both promised and conditional, when it may be called a promissory condition. A common form of contract is one where land is sold "subject to planning permission." In such a contract one could hardly imply a promise to obtain planning permission, since this would be without the control of the parties but the courts have frequently implied a promise by the purchaser to use his best endeavours to obtain planning permission.

There are many cases in which provisions of a contract were subject to the condition precedent of an approval or a licence being obtained, and one party was, by inference in the circumstances, held to have undertaken to apply for the approval or licence: see *Hargreaves Tpt. Ltd. v. Lynch*, [1969] 1 W.L.R. 215; *Brauer & Co. (Great Britain) Ltd. v. James Clark (Brush Materials) Ltd.*, [1952] 2 All E.R. 497; *Société d'Avances Commerciales (London) Ltd. v. A. Besse & Co. (London) Ltd.*, [1952] 1 T.L.R. 644, and *Smallman v. Smallman*, [1971] 3 All E.R. 717. This type of case is merely a specific instance of the general principle that "the court will readily imply a promise on the part of each party to do all that is necessary to secure performance of the contract": 9 Hals., 4th ed., p. 234, para. 350. . . .

Section 19(1) of the *Planning Act* of Alberta provides:

> 19(1) A person who proposes to carry out a division of land shall apply for approval of the proposed subdivision in the manner prescribed by The Subdivision and Transfer Regulations.

"Subdivision" is defined in s. 2(*s*) as follows:

> (*s*) "subdivision" means a division of a parcel by means of a plan of subdivision, plan of survey, agreement or any instrument, including a caveat, transferring or creating an estate or interest in part of the parcel.

In a purchase and sale situation, the "person who proposes to carry out a subdivision of land" is the intending vendor. It is he who must divide his parcel of land, which has hitherto been one unit, for the purpose of sale. If a purchaser carried out the actual work in connection with the application, he could only do so in the vendor's name and as his agent. The vendor is under a duty to act in good faith and to take all reasonable steps to complete the sale. I cannot accept the proposition that failure to fix responsibility for obtaining planning approval renders a contract unenforceable. The common intention to transfer a parcel of land in the knowledge that a subdivision is required in order to effect such transfer must be taken to include agreement that the vendor will make a proper application for subdivision and use his best efforts to obtain such subdivision. This is the only way in which business efficacy can be given to their agreement. In the circumstances of this case, the only reasonable inference to be drawn is that an implied obligation rested on the vendor to apply for subdivision. In making a similar finding on the facts in *Hogg v. Wilken* (1974), 51 D.L.R. (3d) 511 at p. 513, Lerner, J., said:

> In this contract the only inference to be drawn is that it was the vendors' obligation to make the application. An application for such consent would have to be carried out in good faith to its logical conclusion by presentation of same to the committee, the necessary appearance before the committee and furnishing any answers or material that would be reasonably within the power of the vendors to supply if requested by that committee.

In *Hogg v. Wilken* a mandatory order was made in these terms.

The procedure for application is set forth in detail in the *Planning Act* and the Regulations promulgated thereunder. There is no problem in determining the mechanics of what is to be done. . . . In my opinion, the appellant is entitled to a declaration that the contract between the parties mentioned above is a binding contract in accordance with its terms, including the implied term that the respondent will seek subdivision approval.

[Appeal allowed.]

NOTES and QUESTIONS

1. What outcome did Dynamic Transport Ltd. seek to achieve through this litigation? What would the result have been if the court had not found that O.K. Detailing Ltd. was, under an implied term of the contract, obliged to seek subdivision approval? To what extent do you think a court's reasoning is, or should be, influenced by the outcomes flowing from the alternative analyses available to it?

2. In *Marleau v. Savage* (2000), [2000] O.J. No. 2399, 34 R.P.R. (3d) 277 (S.C.J.) at 290 [R.P.R.], Lalonde J. cited *Dynamic Transport* in support of the general proposition that, "The common

intention of entering into a contract which is made subject to a condition precedent requiring the approval of a third party must be taken to include an agreement that one of the parties to the contract will be under an obligation to act in good faith and to use best efforts to seek satisfaction of the condition precedent." Does *Dynamic Transport* support that statement? Should a subsidiary obligation of that kind be implied in all cases?

3. Where a statute obliges one party to a contract to obtain certain approvals or take other specified action in order to create the circumstances required for completion of the contemplated transaction, should a contractual term automatically be implied to the effect that that party is to make reasonable efforts to satisfy the statutory requirement? In *Dynamic Transport*, the parties knew that completion of the sale depended on subdivision approval under the *Planning Act*. In *Russell v. Pfeiffer*, [1999] B.C.J. No. 2253, 1999 CarswellBC 2276 (S.C.), the parties to an agreement for the sale of a parcel of land did not know that subdivision approval was required by the British Columbia *Property Law Act*, as they were under the misimpression that the subject property was already subdivided. The Provincial Court judge's award of damages to the purchaser at trial was affirmed on appeal to the British Columbia Supreme Court. Both courts concluded that, in imposing an express obligation on a vendor of land to deliver a registerable transfer of title, the *Act* obliged the vendor to make efforts to obtain the subdivision approval that was a prerequisite of registration of a transfer. *International Paper Industries Ltd. v. Top Line Industries Inc.* (1996), 135 D.L.R. (4th) 423 (B.C. C.A.) was distinguished. In that case, the court denied a putative tenant's action to enforce an agreement for lease of part of an unsubdivided parcel of land, where the parties were unaware of the subdivision requirements of the *Property Law Act*. In support of the court's decision, Newbury J.A. said, at 438:

> . . . we ought not to imply into the terms of the Lease before us, a covenant or obligation on the part of one party or the other to seek and obtain subdivision approval, notwithstanding that such a result would on one view merely give business efficacy to the Lease. No Canadian case cited to us has gone this far where the parties were unaware of the statutory requirement and there seems much wisdom in the comment that courts should be cautious in implying or imposing terms into contracts. This is especially true where, as here, such terms may involve major expense and the Court cannot be confident that had the parties thought of the subdivision issue, they would have provided for it in a particular way. In my view, then, it would not be appropriate for us to regard the Lease as being subject to a condition precedent, namely compliance with s. 73, or for us to impose a duty on either party now to make the effort and expenditures necessary to obtain subdivision, assuming it could be obtained.

In *BC Rail Ltd. v. Domtar Inc.* (2001), 86 B.C.L.R. (3d) 48 (B.C. C.A.), counsel for the appellant asked the Court of Appeal to hear an appeal that had become moot, in part on the basis that observations made in the decisions in *Russell v. Pfeiffer* supported a reconsideration of the Court's judgment in *International Paper*. The court declined to hear the appeal, without commenting on the merits of that argument.

4. It is not always easy to identify the doctrinal basis upon which the question of enforceability of a contract involving a condition precedent should be addressed. This is exemplified by the divergent approaches taken by the trial and appeal courts respectively in *Century Services Inc. v. Multi-Corp. Inc.* (1998), 228 A.R. 41, 188 W.A.C. 41, 67 Alta. L.R. (3d) 287 (C.A.), leave to appeal refused (1999), 237 N.R. 390 (note) (S.C.C.). Century Services Inc. sued Multi-Corp. for its alleged breach of a contract under which the plaintiff was to sell by auction the assets of a corporate subsidiary of the defendant. Negotiations were conducted by employees of the corporate parties to the dispute. The plaintiff alleged that a contract had been concluded, subject to the approval of the defendant's Board of Directors by a stipulated date. However, the defendant's representative, Mr. Lobsinger, never presented the plaintiff's offer to the Board. Instead, he recommended the offer of a third party, which offer was approved. The reasoning of the trial judge in support of his award of damages for breach of contract was summarized by the Court of Appeal as follows, at 291:

> He also relied on *Dynamic Transport v. O.K. Detailing* [*supra*] which "went further and required that a party to a contract who has said that subdivision approval was required has a

duty to use his best efforts to obtain such approval." He decided that these principles would require Mr. Lobsinger "not only to place the plaintiff's agreement before the Board for its approval but to, at the very least, not speak negatively about it".

The Court of Appeal reversed the trial decision, but its own decision did not turn on the question of whether the defendant was in breach of an implied subsidiary obligation to take action to put the Board's approval in place. Rather, the court concluded that a contract could not arise without the approval of the Board, since only the Board could act for the defendant company. The possibility that Mr. Lobsinger had ostensible authority to bind the company was not in issue, since the plaintiff's representative knew that Board approval was required to finalize the transaction. The court's analysis pre-empted the question of whether the defendant was in breach of a subsidiary obligation under the contract, since it meant that no contract arose in the first place. Though the judgment does not explicitly identify the deciding issue as failure of consideration, the case clearly falls within that category. In substance, it was one in which a party agreed to contract, conditional on its own approval of terms (see section 3 above). To borrow the words of Taylor J. in *Black Gavin & Co. v. Cheung* (1980), 20 B.C.L.R. 21 (S.C.) at 25, an agreement under which one party says to the other "you may buy on these terms if you like the property" and the other says he will, if he does, is not an agreement subject to a condition precedent, or an agreement at all. It remains an offer until that party says that he does indeed approve.

(a)   Remedies for Breach of Subsidiary Obligation

In the introduction to this chapter, reference was made to the general principle governing the award of damages for a breach of contract; that is, that the victim of breach should, so far as can be done through an award of money, be put in the position he or she would have been in had the contract been performed. Application of that principle presumes that it is possible to prove, on the civil standard of balance of probabilities, what that position would have been. In many cases, that onus is readily satisfied. In an unconditional contract for the sale of land, for example, a purchaser can prove that had the vendor performed the obligation to transfer title, the purchaser would have had the ownership and possession of land of a quantifiable value. In contrast, where a contracting party fails to perform a contractual obligation to make reasonable efforts to bring about the satisfaction of a condition precedent involving the action of a third party, it is difficult to know what the result would have been if reasonable efforts had been exerted. There is no guarantee that the third party would have taken the requisite action. The problem of framing an appropriate remedy for breach of a subsidiary obligation of this kind is addressed in the next case.

EASTWALSH HOMES LTD. v. ANATAL DEVELOPMENTS LTD.

(1993), 12 O.R. (3d) 675, 100 D.L.R. (4th) 469, 30 R.P.R. (2d) 276 (C.A.)

GRIFFITHS J.A. The appellant, Anatal Developments Limited ("Anatal"), a land developer, entered into an agreement to sell to the respondent, Eastwalsh Homes Ltd. ("Eastwalsh"), a builder of homes, 147 building lots outlined in a proposed plan of subdivision in Mississauga, Ontario. It was an express condition of the agreement that Anatal would use its best efforts to have the plan of subdivision registered prior to the date fixed for closing of the sale. The agreement further provided that, failing such registration, the agreement would be terminated.

The plan was not registered within the requisite time period and the sale fell through. Eastwalsh brought this action against Anatal, claiming specific performance of the agreement or, alternatively, damages for breach of the agreement.

The trial judge, Mr. Justice Ewaschuk, found that Anatal, in breach of its contractual obligations, did not use its best efforts to have the plan of subdivision registered by the date specified in the contract. The trial judge found that had Anatal used its best efforts, there would have been a 50% chance that the plan of subdivision could have been registered within the contractual time-period and the transaction could have closed. Accordingly, the trial judge awarded Eastwalsh 50% of the increased market value of the lots over the sale price, amounting to damages of $2,020,780. Anatal appeals the finding of liability. Eastwalsh cross-appeals against the quantum of damages awarded.

.....

The trial judge declined to award Eastwalsh specific performance of the agreement and held that Eastwalsh was entitled to damages only for the breach. The trial judge rejected Eastwalsh's claim for loss of profits, holding that Eastwalsh could reasonably have mitigated its losses by buying similar lots available in Mississauga but that Eastwalsh took no steps to mitigate.

The trial judge held that the measure of damages was the loss to Eastwalsh in being deprived of the opportunity to purchase the 147 lots. He said in his reasons [at pp. 264-5]:

> I find that Anatal probably caused Eastwalsh to be deprived of the 147 building lots in the sense that Eastwalsh was deprived of the chance that the plan of subdivision would have been registered on time because Anatal did not discharge its best efforts in pursuing that goal. I also find that the chance consisted of a substantial possibility that the plan would have been registered on time, again had Anatal discharged its best efforts on behalf of Eastwalsh, as the contract required it to do.

And later he said [at p. 267]:

> I conclude that the defendant, Anatal, had a 50% chance of having the plan of subdivision registered by December 31, 1987, had it discharged its best efforts. This is with respect to the plan which Anatal had pursued during the summer of 1986, and which it finally submitted to Peel Region on March 17, 1987. Anatal never pursued or submitted the plan attached to the agreement, at least not after August 29, 1986.

The trial judge found that the 147 lots had increased in value from $6,809,150 at the contract date to $10,850,710 at the time of the repudiation. He then stated [at p. 268]:

> Thus, the difference in value between mitigation date and repudiation date is $4,041,560. On the basis that it had only a 50% chance of having the plan registered on time and thereby getting the lots, Eastwalsh is only entitled to $2,020,780 in damages.

.....

[The court concurred with the trial judge's conclusion that Anatal had committed a breach by failing to discharge its best efforts to achieve registration of the plan of subdivision by the date stipulated in the contract. It then turned to the issues of causation and loss.]

The general rule is that the burden is on the plaintiff to establish on the balance of probabilities that, as a reasonable and probable consequence of the breach of contract, the plaintiff suffered the damages claimed. If the plaintiff is not able to establish a loss, or where the loss proven is trivial, the plaintiff may recover only nominal damages.

A second fundamental principle is that where it is clear that the breach of contract caused loss to the plaintiff, but it is very difficult to quantify that loss, the difficulty in assessing damages is not a basis for refusal to make an award in the plaintiff's favour. One of the frequent difficulties in assessing damages is that the plaintiff is unable to prove loss of a definite benefit but only the "chance" of receiving a benefit had the contract been performed. In those circumstances, rather than refusing to award damages, the courts have attempted to estimate the value of the lost chance and awarded damages on a proportionate basis.

This was the approach that the trial judge took here. He found that had Anatal not breached the contract, there was a 50% chance that the plan of subdivision would have been registered by December 31, 1987, and the transaction of sale could have closed. In this respect, he was not referring to the agreed plan, the plan attached to the agreement of purchase and sale, but to the plan which had been extensively negotiated in 1985 and 1986 by Anatal and not submitted to Peel Region for circulation until March 17, 1987.

In taking the approach that a chance of 50% had compensable value to Eastwalsh, the trial judge followed the principle laid down in the leading English Court of Appeal decision of *Chaplin v. Hicks*, [*infra*, Chapter 14, section 3(a)(i)], which has been followed in the Supreme Court of Canada and more recently in this court in the decision of *Multi-Malls Inc. v. Tex-Mall Properties Ltd.* (1980), 108 D.L.R. (3d) 399; affirmed 128 D.L.R. (3d) 192n; leave to appeal to Supreme Court of Canada refused [1982] 1 S.C.R. xiii, 41 N.R. 360n.

.....

In short, in assessing damages, the court must discount the value of the chance by the improbability of its occurrence.

.....

[After referring to the Supreme Court of Canada decisions in *Webb & Knapp (Canada) Ltd. v. City of Edmonton*, [1970] S.C.R. 588 and *Kinkel v. Hyman*, [1939] S.C.R. 364, Griffiths J.A. continued as follows:]

On my analysis these two Supreme Court of Canada decisions stand for the following propositions. The burden rests on the plaintiff alleging breach of contract to prove on the balance of probabilities that the breach and not some intervening factor or factors has caused loss to the plaintiff. In this respect the courts have not relaxed the basic standard of proof. Where it is clear that the defendant's breach has caused loss to the plaintiff, it is no answer to the claim that the loss is difficult to assess or calculate. The concept of the loss of a chance then begins to operate and the court will estimate the plaintiff's chance of obtaining a benefit had the contract been performed. But even in this situation, the Supreme Court of Canada has said in *Kinkel v. Hyman, supra,* that proof of the loss of a mere chance is not enough; the plaintiff must prove that the chance constitutes "some reasonable probability" of realizing "an advantage of some real substantial monetary value".

In the present case, the trial judge applied the correct approach in separating the question of causation from the question of loss. One cannot quarrel with his conclusion on causation that the breach of contract by Anatal denied Eastwalsh the chance of closing the transaction. Where I respectfully disagree with the trial judge is that, even accepting a causal connection between the breach and the loss of a chance, in my opinion the evidence does not support a finding that Eastwalsh lost a 50% chance of closing the sale. The evidence in fact compels the conclusion that, notwithstanding the breach, the transaction would not have been completed within the contract period.

·····

In this case, the burden rested on Eastwalsh to prove not only a breach of contract by Anatal but also that if Anatal had discharged its best efforts to secure registration of the agreed plan or an alternative conforming plan of subdivision, there was a reasonable probability of registration of the plan being achieved within the time-frame of the contract. In my view, Eastwalsh failed to satisfy that burden in this case. The irresistible conclusion on the evidence is that Anatal, devoting the most reasonable efforts, could not have succeeded in registering a plan of subdivision, whether conforming or not, within the time-frame of the contract. The chance Eastwalsh lost is too insubstantial to justify anything more than nominal damages.

NOTES and QUESTIONS

1. An application for leave to appeal to the Supreme Court of Canada was refused, (1993), 15 O.R. (3d) xvi, 104 D.L.R. (4th) vii, 34 R.P.R. (2d) 90 (note).

2. In *John E. Dodge Holdings Ltd. v. 805062 Ontario Ltd.* (2001), 56 O.R. (3d) 341, 46 R.P.R. (3d) 239 (S.C.J.), affirmed (2003), 223 D.L.R. (4th) 541, 63 O.R. (3d) 304, 10 R.P.R. (4th) 98 (C.A.), leave to appeal refused, [2003] S.C.C.A. No. 145, 2003 CarswellOnt 4375, 2003 CarswellOnt 4376, the courts considered a provision in an agreement for the sale of land that required the vendor to "proceed diligently at his expense to obtain any necessary consent [under the subdivision control provisions of the *Planning Act*] by completion." The vendor purported to terminate the agreement on the grounds that the required approvals had not been obtained by the closing date. The trial judge held that the vendor was in breach of the obligation to take reasonable action to obtain consent, and granted the purchaser the remedy of specific performance. The order did not oblige the vendor to transfer title to the land to the purchaser, but rather to perform its obligations with respect to procurement of the required subdivision approvals. The award of specific performance thus required the vendor (i) to reapply to the City of Vaughan for severance approval with respect to the property subject to the contract of sale, (ii) in the event that unacceptable conditions were imposed by the Committee of Adjustment, to exercise its statutory right of appeal to the Ontario Municipal Board and (iii) subject to the Ontario Municipal Board's decision, comply with all severance conditions. The Court of Appeal upheld the award.

3. By the time the appeal of the lower court's ruling in *John E. Dodge Holdings Ltd.* was heard, the vendor had complied to the point of procuring severance approval, subject to a requirement to grant a utility corridor easement imposed by the Ontario Municipal Board on the vendor's appeal from the decision of the Committee of Adjustment. The effect of the Court of Appeal's confirmation

of the trial decision was to require the vendor not only to perform the subsidiary obligations associated with procurement of severance approval, but to complete the contract of sale, since the condition precedent to completion was by then satisfied. In the event, the purchaser's decision to pursue an award of specific performance rather than damages proved to be a well calculated one. Would the purchaser have been equally well served had the vendor made the required effort to obtain severance approval, but failed? Could an award of damages have been granted at that juncture? In *Dynamic Transport*, the court directed the vendor to "make and pursue a *bona fide* application as may be necessary to obtain registration of an approved plan of subdivision", in default of which the purchaser was declared to be entitled to damages for loss of its bargain. The court further stipulated that "In the event that the respondent makes and pursues a *bona fide* application as aforesaid, and such application is rejected, then the appellant's claim for specific performance of the provisions concerning sale and purchase stands dismissed, as does the claim for damages in the alternative. . ." (1978), 85 D.L.R. (3d) 19 at 30. For an argument that the court's reasoning on this point was flawed, see Clark, "Rethinking the Role of Specific Relief in the Contractual Setting", in Berryman (ed.), *Remedies: Issues and Perspectives* (1991), 139 at 161.

4. Assuming it is established that a vendor of land is in breach of a subsidiary obligation to make reasonable efforts to satisfy a condition precedent, would it ever be appropriate for a court to award specific performance of the vendor's *primary* obligation to convey the subject property? Consider in this regard the relevance of whether the condition precedent can be waived and, if so, by which party, a matter discussed under the next heading.

5.   Unilateral Waiver

There is no doubt that parties to a contract that includes a condition precedent as one of its terms can agree to vary or waive satisfaction of the condition. However, in many cases one of the parties wishes to waive the condition in order to proceed with the contract, while the other does not. For example, the home buyer hypothesized at the beginning of this chapter may wish to proceed with purchase of the house, even though he or she is not able to obtain financing by the date specified in the condition precedent. If he or she purports to waive fulfilment of the condition, is the seller obliged to proceed with the transaction? Common sense would suggest that, since the condition was included to ensure that the purchaser would have funds available to complete the purchase and was thus intended for the purchaser's benefit, he or she should be permitted to waive it if she so chooses. Waiver would, of course, put the purchaser in the position of being subject to an unconditional contractual obligation to pay the purchase price on the agreed date, regardless of whether he or she has succeeded in arranging the necessary funds.

A contracting party who has received good legal advice can and should address this issue by making explicit provision in the contract permitting or precluding waiver of any conditions precedent. However, in many instances the contract is silent on the point. The dissenting judgment of Laskin J. in *Barnett v. Harrison* articulates in compelling terms the rationale supporting the proposition that satisfaction of a condition precedent can be waived by the party for whose benefit it is primarily intended. However, the majority of the court rejected his analysis, reaffirming the test articulated by the so-called "rule in *Turney v. Zilka*."

TURNEY v. ZHILKA

[1959] S.C.R. 578, 18 D.L.R. (2d) 447

JUDSON J. [delivering the judgment of the court] . . . The other defence pleaded was that the purchaser failed to comply with the following condition of the contract:

> Providing the property can be annexed to the Village of Streetsville and a plan is approved by the Village Council for subdivision.

The date for the completion of the sale is fixed with reference to the performance of this condition—"60 days after plans are approved". Neither party to the contract undertakes to fulfil this condition, and neither party reserves a power of waiver. The purchaser made some enquiries of the Village council but the evidence indicates that he made little or no progress and received little encouragement, and that the prospects of annexation were very remote. After the trouble arose over the quantity and description of the land, the purchaser purported to waive this condition on the ground that it was solely for his benefit and was severable, and sued immediately for specific performance without reference to the condition and the time for performance fixed by the condition. The learned trial judge found that the condition was one introduced for the sole benefit of the purchaser and that he could waive it.

I have doubts whether this inference may be drawn from the evidence adduced in this case, but, in any event, the defence falls to be decided on broader grounds. The cases on which the judgment is founded are *Hawksley v. Outram*, [1892] 3 Ch. 359 and *Morrell v. Studd*, [1913] 2 Ch. 648. In the first case a purchaser of a business stipulated in the contract of sale that he should have the right to carry on under the old name and that the vendors would not compete within a certain area. A dispute arose whether one of the vendors, who had signed the contract of sale under a power of attorney from another, had acted within his power. The purchaser then said that he would waive these rights and successfully sued for specific performance. In the second case, the contract provided that the purchaser should pay a certain sum on completion and the balance within two years. He also promised to secure the balance to the vendor's satisfaction. The purchaser raised difficulties about the performance of this promise, and the vendor said that he would waive it and take the purchaser's unsecured promise. It was held that he was entitled to do so. All that waiver means in these circumstances is that one party to a contract may forgo a promised advantage or may dispense with part of the promised performance of the other party which is simply and solely for the benefit of the first party and is severable from the rest of the contract.

But here there is no right to be waived. The obligations under the contract, on both sides, depend upon a future uncertain event, the happening of which depends entirely on the will of a third party—the Village Council. This is a true condition precedent—an external condition upon which the existence of the obligation depends. Until the event occurs there is no right to performance on either side. The parties have not promised that it will occur. The purchaser now seeks to make the vendor liable on his promise to convey in spite of the non-performance of the condition and this to suit his own convenience only. This is not a case of renunciation or relinquishment of a right but rather an attempt by one party, without the consent of the other, to write a new contract. Waiver has often been referred to as a troublesome and uncertain term in the law but it does at least presuppose the existence of a right to be relinquished.

BEAUCHAMP v. BEAUCHAMP

[1973] 2 O.R. 43, 32 D.L.R. (3d) 693 (C.A.)

GALE C.J.O. [delivering the judgment of the court] On April 13, 1971, the appellants signed an offer to purchase certain lands in the township of Gloucester for the sum of $15,500 in cash. I emphasize that the purchasers were to pay cash and nothing else, in the form of a deposit of $500, and the balance on closing. The closing was to take place on July 1st. The agreement also had the following condition included in it:

> This sale is conditional for a period of 15 days from date of acceptance of same upon the Purchaser or his Agent being able to obtain a first mortgage in the amount of Ten Thousand Dollars ($10,000.00) bearing interest at the current rate otherwise, this offer shall be null and void and all deposit monies shall be returned to the Purchaser without interest or any other charge. This offer is also conditional for a period of 15 days from date of acceptance of same upon the Purchaser or his Agent being able to secure a second mortgage in the amount of $2,500.00 for a period of five (5) years, bearing interest at the current rate, otherwise, this offer shall be null and void and all deposit monies returned to the Purchaser without interest or any other charge.

The appellants were able to arrange for a first mortgage of $12,000 and, on April 28, 1971, as found by the trial Judge, they caused a notice in the following form to be delivered to the respondents:

> This is to notify you that the condition specified on the agreement of purchase and sale between Mr. Vianney Beauchamp (*sic*) and Carmen Beauchamp herein called the Vendors and Mr. Ronald Beauchamp and Pauline Beauchamp herein called the Purchasers has been met. The transaction will therefore close as per the agreement.

The Judge also found that there was an anticipatory breach by the respondents which excused the appellants from the need to make formal tender. However, he dismissed the appellants' action for specific performance, holding that the respondents were excused from completing the sale on the ground that the condition which I have quoted was a condition precedent which had not been strictly complied with by the appellants' arranging a first mortgage of $10,000 and a second mortgage of $2,500.

We point out, as did the trial Judge, that the condition was solely for the protection of the appellants, and all the respondents were interested in was receiving the sum of $15,500 in cash. The notice to which I referred brought home to the respondents the fact that payment of the $15,500 in cash would be made and that the appellants had met the condition referred to in the offer, or, alternatively, were waiving it.

In those circumstances, we are of the view that the learned trial Judge erred in declining to order specific performance. Counsel for the respondents relied upon . . . the *Turney v. Zhilka* [line of cases] for the proposition that a true condition precedent cannot be waived, even though it is in favour of one party only and the fulfilment of the condition is completely within the control of that one party. We do not think that those cases are appropriate to the circumstances here; they are distinguishable, as the condition herein is not such as is dealt with in those cases.

The appeal will therefore be allowed and judgment given for specific performance, with costs to the appellants throughout.

[An appeal to the Supreme Court of Canada was dismissed without counsel for the respondents being called upon: (1974), 40 D.L.R. (3d) 160.]

BARNETT v. HARRISON

[1976] 2 S.C.R. 531, 57 D.L.R. (3d) 225, 5 N.R. 131

LASKIN C.J.C. [dissenting] This case raises the correctness and, if correct, the applicability of the judgments of this Court in *Turney v. Zhilka [supra]*, *F.T. Dev. Ltd. v. Sherman*, [1969] S.C.R. 203 and *O'Reilly v. Marketers Diversified Inc.*, [1969] S.C.R. 741. It was twice argued, first before a Bench of five (as was each of the three cases just mentioned) and then before the Full Court.

On the first argument, counsel for the respondent vendors admitted that the unperformed condition in the contract of sale, upon which they rested their resistance to specific performance sought by the appellant purchaser, was one solely for the benefit of the purchaser who had effected a timely waiver before bringing his suit. On the argument before the Full Court, a different position was taken by way of a submission that the unperformed condition was a "true condition precedent", was for the benefit of both parties and hence could not be waived by the purchaser alone. The concession on the first argument that the vendors had no interest in the performance of the particular condition, as being one exacted by the purchaser solely for his benefit, was in effect withdrawn.

·····

Two provisions of this contract of sale are relevant to the determination of the question at issue. The first is a lengthy clause which is alleged by the purchaser to embody a condition which was solely for his benefit. The second is another clause expressing certain conditions which, on the respondents' submission, highlights, by comparison with the language of the first clause, why the latter is a "true condition precedent". For proper context I set out hereafter not only the two clauses but as well two other provisions of the agreement, numbering them for convenience from one to four. They are as follows:

> 1. The purchaser shall prepare and have ready for presentation to the said Town of Stoney Creek (and obtain an appointment from the said Municipality) his site plan within four months of acceptance of this offer.

> If this offer is accepted by the vendors, the contract of purchase and sale will be subject to the condition that the necessary approvals of the Ontario Municipal Board and the Town of Stoney Creek to the site plan and proposed changes in zoning, and any approval of the Committee of Adjustment or Planning Board required are given. The applications for and all matters and appearances relating to such approvals shall be prepared by and at the expense of the purchaser but may be brought in the names of the vendors. The vendors agree and undertake to give all help and co-operation required by the purchaser and to execute all necessary documents and make all attendances necessary (without costs to the purchaser) to

assist in and facilitate the obtaining of the approvals and registrations required by the purchaser. It is agreed between the parties that the Application and hearing before the Ontario Municipal Board shall be completed on or before the 30th day of September, 1968 (without the decision necessarily having been made). Provided however, if any adjournment results from opposition beyond the control of the purchaser, then the said date for completion of the application and hearing shall be extended to the 31st day of January, 1969 at the latest. Provided further, that the purchaser shall within two months after all Municipal approvals have been granted, cause an appointment to be obtained for a hearing before the Ontario Municipal Board. In the event that these conditions are not complied with then notwithstanding anything herein contained, the agreement of purchase and sale shall be null and void and the deposit monies returned to the purchaser.

2. If this Offer is accepted by the vendors, the contract of Purchase and Sale will be conditional upon:

(a) The said lands being serviced with adequate water and adequate sanitary sewer facilities to accommodate the purchaser's site plan of commercial and residential requirements within the terms of the zoning by-law.

(b) There being no charges for services against the lands other than those charges in existence at the date of acceptance of this agreement.

(c) There being no capital contribution required by the Town of Stoney Creek other than the usual five per cent (5%) for land dedication.

In the event that any of the above conditions are not complied with, the purchaser shall have the option to declare this agreement null and void and to have the deposit returned or to accept the changes and complete the agreement.

3. It is understood and agreed that the purchaser shall not be required to make any amendments to his proposed site plan in the event that approval by all necessary persons, departments or agencies is not obtained. In the event that the proposed site plan submitted by the purchaser is not approved by all persons, departments and agencies, then the said agreement shall be null and void and the deposit returned to the purchaser forthwith. Provided, however, the purchaser may at his option, make any necessary amendments to meet the requirements of the persons, departments or agencies. Notice of the exercise of such Option by the purchaser shall be given to the vendors within forty-five days of the said refusal of approval having been communicated to the purchaser.

4. This offer shall be accepted on or before the 11th day of February, 1967, otherwise void. The sale shall be completed sixty days after the date the Ontario Municipal Board approves the proposed site plan prepared by the purchaser on which date possession of the lands is to be given to the purchaser.

The offer to purchase, under the above and other terms of the offer made by the purchaser, was duly accepted. Time was of the essence under the contract. The purchaser had sought the property for an apartment project and he proceeded to submit site plans for approval by the municipal authorities. After he had submitted some 15 plans to no avail (although he was prepared to accept all amendments proposed by the municipality), it became quite obvious that he was not going to succeed in obtaining the necessary approval for his apartment project. Thereupon, he advised that he was prepared to take and use the land under the existing zoning.

The vendors took no part in and were not consulted on the preparation of any of the site plans. The record of the evidence adduced at the trial shows that the vendors regarded the condition numbered 1 above as of no interest or consequence to them. I draw attention to this because, in my opinion, the construction mutually placed upon a contract by the parties thereto is not to be ignored when the benefit and obligations of the contract come to be considered. What happened in this case, as counsel for the vendors was candid to admit on the first argument, was that the vendors got a better offer for their land and looked for a way to recede from their contract with the appellant.

The purchaser made a formal waiver in writing of all conditions save as to title, and avowed his readiness and willingness to complete in accordance with the prescriptions of the agreement otherwise governing completion. The vendors then took the position that approvals of the site plan and consequent changes in zoning constituted a condition precedent which they would not waive, and since the date by which to secure such approvals had not been met they regarded the agreement as null and void. In the ensuing action brought by the purchaser for specific performance, the trial Judge held that the case was governed by *Turney v. Zhilka* in that there was here, as there, a "true condition precedent" whose performance depended on the will of third parties, that is the municipal authorities, and that unless there was performance in accordance with its terms specific performance could not be had by the purchaser.

A majority of the Ontario Court of Appeal took the same position in affirming dismissal of the purchaser's action. Jessup J.A., dissented, holding that *Turney v. Zhilka* was distinguishable because in the present case, unlike that one, the purchaser was given an unlimited right of amendment to meet the requirements of the proper authorities and hence it was open to him to accept the present zoning, as he in fact did. This conclusion by Jessup J.A., goes to support the purchaser's view of the contract as involving a condition solely for his benefit.

I pass now to a consideration of *Turney v. Zhilka* and to the principle on which it was based. The condition in that case, upon which the suit for specific performance foundered, was one fixed by the contract without reference to any obligation of performance being placed on either the vendor or the purchaser. Judson, J., speaking for this Court read this [condition] as depending (to use his words) "entirely on the will of a third party". That is not the present case, it being quite clear under the contract (even apart from the evidence of the vendors) that it was the purchaser who was to prepare and seek approval of a site plan, and of necessary rezoning, in order to carry out his apartment project which was the known and particularized use to which the land was to be put. Since the obligation to proceed with a site plan and to seek rezoning was expressly put on the purchaser, and since, on the evidence, the condition was one extracted by him solely for his benefit, there is a marked difference between the present case and *Turney v. Zhilka*.

The issue raised by *Turney v. Zhilka* and by the cases that have followed it, such as the *F.T. Dev.* case and the *O'Reilly* case, appears to me to require a proper understanding of the phrase "true condition precedent" which was used by Judson J. in *Turney v. Zhilka.* . . . ...

. . . . .

A condition which is characterized as a condition precedent may be one in which both parties have an interest and yet it may be subject to waiver at the suit of one only of the parties. That is because their interest in it may not be the same. The condition may be for the protection of one party only in the sense that it is solely for his benefit, but it may be important to the other party in the sense that he is entitled to know the consequence of its performance or waiver by the date fixed for its performance so that he may, if he is the vendor, either collect his money or be free to look for another purchaser. It would, in my view, be a mistake to move from the fact that both parties have an interest in the performance or non-performance of a condition of the contract to the conclusion that the condition cannot therefore be waived at the suit of the one party for whose sole benefit the condition was introduced into the contract. Some of the submissions made here, especially on the re-argument of the appeal, failed to draw this distinction which, to me, is a vital one.

Another distinction that appears to me to be vital is one that is clear upon a comparison of the relevant conditions in *Turney v. Zhilka* and in the present case. The fact that the conduct or action of a third party is involved in the proper performance of a condition does not on that ground alone make it a "true condition precedent" which cannot be waived. Thus, to take a homely example, the fact that a purchaser may make it a condition of completion that he be able to obtain mortgage financing within a fixed period does not, in my opinion, preclude him from waiving the condition and paying in cash, provided, of course, he makes his election to waive the condition within the period fixed by the contract: see *Scott v. Rania*, [1966] N.Z.L.R. 527 (C.A.). In principle, there is no difference between the foregoing situation and one where the duty of one of the parties to the contract arises only upon the act of a third party, as for example, the obligation to pay money upon the certificate of an architect or engineer. Of course, the obligor is not likely to make the payment unless the certificate is provided, but the fact that he could insist on its production does not mean that he could not waive this condition of his duty to pay.

There is a parallel situation where title defects are involved. It is unquestionable that a purchaser may choose to accept the subject property notwithstanding an impediment to perfect title upon whose removal he could insist: see *Bennett v. Fowler* (1840), 48 E.R. 1197. As Cardozo J. put it in *Catholic Foreign Mission Society of America v. Oussani* (1915), 215 N.Y. 1 at 8:

> . . . a buyer in such circumstances is not bound to rescind. He may waive the condition, and accept the title though defective. If he does, the seller may not refuse to convey because the buyer could not have been compelled to waive.

. . . . .

The principle operates in favour of a vendor as well as in favour of a purchaser. *Morrell v. Studd & Millington*, [1913] 2 Ch. 648, is illustrative. There it was held that a vendor could waive a provision that the balance of the purchase price be secured to his satisfaction and could sue the purchaser for specific performance after forgoing that provision which was solely for his benefit.

In this class of case, whether it be action or conduct by one of the parties that is involved or action or conduct of a third party, what is important is whether that action or conduct is a condition of an obligation of one of the parties only or of both. If of one only, there is no reason why he should not be able to offer performance of his own obligation or duty without insisting on the condition and then call on the other to perform his side of the bargain.

What has sometimes complicated the application of this principle are cases which involved not the performance of a concluded contract but rather the question whether there was a concluded contract. *Lloyd v. Nowell*, [1895] 2 Ch. 744, is referred to by *Fry on Specific Performance*, 6th ed. (1921), at pp. 175 and 461 to point up the distinction. Thus, where a transaction was subject to "the preparation by my solicitor and completion of a formal contract", it would not be said that the vendor could waive this provision and create a contract by his unilateral act. Nor could a purchaser do so under a similar provision respecting the preparation of a formal contract by his solicitor: see *Von Hatzfeldt-Wildenburg v. Alexander*, [1912] 1 Ch. 284.

I take *Turney v. Zhilka* to have involved, as a matter of construction, a condition which was applicable to the duty of both parties. As Judson J. put it, at p. 450 D.L.R., "the obligations under contract, *on both sides*, depend upon a future uncertain event, the happening of which depends entirely on the will of a third party—the village council". (The emphasis is mine.) It is on this basis only that it can be said, as Judson J., did, that there was here a "true condition precedent", that is one external to the obligations of both parties and one where the contract did not give the carriage of the matter to either one of the parties so as to provide a basis for contending that it was for his benefit alone and could be waived by him. This construction of a condition involving some action of a third party is not a necessary one: see, for example, *Funke v. Paist* (1947), 52 A. (2d) 655 (Pa.), and *Richardson v. Snipes* (1959), 330 S.W. (2d) 381 (Tenn.), holding required zoning approvals to be conditions of the duty of the purchaser only and hence open to waiver by him. Nevertheless, there can be no doubt that, in particular situations of which *Turney v. Zhilka* is illustrative, a provision for rezoning or redevelopment consent may be construed as one for the mutual advantage or benefit of both of the parties to a contract of sale of land and hence not open to unilateral waiver. This was the result reached in the recent English case of *Heron Garage Properties Ltd. v. Moss*, [1974] 1 All E.R. 421. There is one point in that case which also calls for consideration here and that is the fact that the date of completion is geared to the obtaining of planning consent or zoning approval, thus raising the question of the severability of the provision which the purchaser purported to waive. I will return to this point later in these reasons.

.....

I cannot but think that if the condition in the present case and the condition in the *O'Reilly* case are not instances of conditions which can be waived by the one party to whose duty of performance they go, there can hardly be any case in which waiver can be lawfully effected short of an express provision therefor in the contract of sale. No doubt this is a salutary procedure, but the law of contract has long ago ceased to depend on exact expression of every consequence of a contractual provision.

An examination of the case law in England, in Australia, in New Zealand and in the United States discloses no differentiation in applicable principle between those provisions where action of a third party is involved and those where only the action of the opposite party is involved so far as concerns the right of waiver of a provision which is found to be for the benefit of one party only. Of course, a party cannot base a claim for performance by the opposite party of a conditional obligation on his own failure to perform, unless it can be said that the failure relates to a mere promise rather than to the condition; but, even as to a condition to which a party is obliged in favour of the opposite party, the latter may elect to enforce the contract rather than rescind upon breach of the condition.

The present case, in a sense, shows the opposite side of the coin because if the provision in question is solely for the benefit of a party who decides to renounce that benefit, there is then no impediment to calling for the opposite party's performance provided the provision waived is not tied in with other terms from which it cannot be extricated by way of unilateral relinquishment. What the earlier observation shows, however, is that failure to perform a condition does not necessarily mean that there is no contract to enforce since the innocent party may elect to keep it alive. This also goes to a point raised in the present case and I shall deal with it now.

Counsel for the respondent vendors urged that the provisions of the contract of sale themselves set up a distinction between provisions open to waiver by the purchaser and those that were not. The submission related to the provision numbered 2 in these reasons which stated that if the conditions therein were not complied with "the purchaser shall have the option to declare this agreement null and void". The contrast alleged was with the site plan condition, the one central to this appeal, numbered 1 in these reasons, which concluded that "in the event that these conditions are not complied with . . . the agreement of purchase and sale shall be null and void". Here there was no express "option" to that end given to the purchaser.

There are two comments that I would make on the foregoing submissions. First, the provision numbered 2, respecting water and sewer facilities and protection of the purchaser against service charges and capital contributions, did not call for any action or initiative by the purchaser and he would have been entitled to resist enforcement of the contract by the vendors if the conditions stated to be such, were not fulfilled, even if the contract had not expressly so stated. Further, the presence of a waiver clause did not make the conditions any more directly conditions of the buyer's duty of performance than they would have been without it. In short, the situation here was simply one where the waiver clause emphasized that the provisions in question were for the purchaser's benefit; and, to recall an earlier observation here, the purchaser could insist on them if he so desired, and it would be no defence to the vendors to say that because the purchaser could not be compelled to waive they would not perform.

The second comment relates to the site plan provision and to the concluding stipulation that the agreement should be null and void (without giving either party a power so to elect) "in the event that these conditions are not complied with". I accept the proposition stated in *Corbin on Contracts*, vol. 3A, at p. 517, that a provision that the contract shall be null and void "seldom means what it appears to say" and that "generally what is meant is that the duty of one of the parties shall be conditional on [performance] by the other party exactly as agreed"; otherwise the contract would in effect be giving an option to the party who is to render the performance on the failure of which the contract is to be null and void. This proposition does not, however, preclude a party entitled to call for such performance from waiving it where it is solely for his benefit. In relation to the present case, it invites consideration of the conditions to which the "null and void" provision relates. In my view, those conditions are the provisions as to the time fixed for completion of the hearings before the municipal board and related time provisions, all annexed to the site plan provisions. If the latter can be waived, the time provisions go with them, and there is consequently no bar in them to the purchaser's right to call for performance by the vendors.

In the *Heron Garage* case, one where the vendor retained adjoining land on which he proposed to carry on a business (sale of motor vehicles) to a degree related to the business proposed to be carried on by the purchaser (a gasoline station), the provision for completion was one calendar month after receipt by the purchaser of unconditional consent to its planning application or one calendar month after the purchaser approved any conditional planning consent (which he had to do within 28 days thereof), but in either case not before January 1, 1973. The Judge in the *Heron Garage* case, after holding the planning condition to be for the benefit of both parties and hence not to be waived by the purchaser alone, also felt that the nexus between that condition and the completion date precluded waiver because it would leave the completion date in the air.

I find no such difficulty in the present case once it is decided, as in my opinion it should be, that on the very face of the site plan condition, it was for the sole benefit of the purchaser. Since it was open to the purchaser to pay cash and he offered to do so, it would follow that a reasonable period following the refusal of site plan approval, a period measured by the 60 days mentioned in the completion condition, would govern completion following waiver of the condition. In fact, nothing turned on the completion date in the present case since the purchaser was ready and willing to complete, with waiver of all conditions save as to title, within 60 days after September 30, 1968, being the date fixed by the contract for the conclusion of the hearings by the Ontario Municipal Board.

Having had the benefit of seeing the reasons prepared by my brother Dickson before completing my own, I would underline two of the points of difference between us. I do not view waiver as involving a rewriting of an agreement any more than I regard estoppel of a party from insisting upon a term of an agreement as a rewriting thereof. A party that is entitled to a range of benefits under an agreement does not rewrite it against the opposite party by forgoing some of those benefits. Second, I find nothing offensive or prejudicial in the fact that a vendor may not know until completion date whether the contract will be performed according to its very terms or whether there will be a waiver so as to give the purchaser a choice to opt out or to insist on performance by the vendor. This is not an uncommon situation in contracts and depends simply on their terms.

In the result, while recognizing the basis upon which *Turney v. Zhilka* proceeded, I do not find that it precludes a contrary conclusion in the present case, and I would, accordingly, allow the appeal, set aside the judgments below and enter a decree of specific performance in favour of the purchaser with costs throughout.

DICKSON J. [After reviewing the facts of the case, Dickson J continued as follows:]

The trial Judge, Thompson J., made these findings [22 D.L.R. (3d) 29 at 37]:

> It becomes very obvious that the conditions of the contract relative to zone changing, including the approvals necessary therefor by law, were made conditions precedent by the very terms of the instrument and from the language of the parties there used, were intended so to be.

The obligations under this contract on both sides depend upon a future uncertain event, the amendment of the zoning by-law, the happening of which depends entirely upon the will of third parties—the Town Council, the Planning Board, the Minister and the Municipal Board. This is a true condition precedent—an external condition or conditions upon which the very existence of such obligations depend.

The Judge considered *Turney v. Zhilka* and concluded [at 38]:

> I can see no real distinction between the condition in that case and those in the instant case and must therefore hold that the plaintiff is not entitled to waive the conditions in question without the consent of the defendants, nor to enforce the contract less the conditions.

The action was dismissed with costs and the purchaser appealed.

It would appear from the judgments rendered in the Court of Appeal that the principal issue canvassed in that Court was the force of the proviso reading: "Provided, however, the purchaser may at his option, make any necessary amendments to meet the requirements of the persons, departments or agencies." On this point Schroeder J.A., said [33 D.L.R. (3d) 272 at 275]:

> It is contended on behalf of the appellant that the provision above set forth giving him the right to revise his application from time to time must be interpreted as conferring upon him the right to withdraw his application in its entirety and that, carrying the interpretation thereof to its extreme length, it bestowed upon him a right to waive performance of the said conditions at his option.
>
> My brother Brooke and I do not agree with this submission. In the view which we take, the vendors and the purchaser contemplated an alteration in the zoning provisions affecting the area in question and on a proper construction of the terms of the agreement the conditions above-quoted were true conditions precedent, the nonfulfilment of which rendered this agreement null and void. In our opinion, the case in hand is indistinguishable from *Turney v. Zhilka*, *supra*.

Jessup J.A., dissenting, said [at 275-76]:

> In my view, this unlimited right of amendment necessarily includes the right to dispense with any rezoning of the property, in other words, a complete capitulation to the requirements of the persons, departments or agencies involved. For that reason, I would allow the appeal as I have stated.

I agree with the conclusion of the majority in the Court of Appeal. First, the right to amend is limited to "necessary amendments to meet the requirements" of the planning authorities; it is in my view merely a right to alter or correct or improve the plan in response to the demands of the authorities. Second, the right to amend, it will be observed, relates only to the site plan and there is no mention of amending the proposal for a change in zoning.

It was urged that the provisions in the agreement respecting the proposed site plan and zoning changes were so vague as to afford the purchaser the opportunity of complying by filing any kind of plan and by accepting the existing zoning, and in any event the vendors had no real interest in the site plan or the zoning to be adopted. This is true to a point but it ignores realities, it speaks of what might have happened, not of what did happen. As the trial Judge observed, there had been long and protracted negotiations and discussions between the parties as to the purpose to which the lands were to be put by the purchaser. The plans of the purchaser initially contemplated six apartment buildings of nine storeys each or five apartment buildings of 12 storeys each, housing some 3,000 persons. The plans were later modified to four apartment buildings containing 780 apartment units. This proposal was under study by the Town Council and various highway, engineering and other authorities when time ran out on September 30, 1968. The proposal continued under such study until withdrawn by the appellant in a letter dated November 8, 1968. There can be no doubt on the evidence that the purchaser seriously planned and assiduously sought approval of a major housing development. The approval, a future uncertain event, was entirely dependent upon the will of third parties, the Town of Stoney Creek, the Planning Board, the Minister and the Ontario Municipal Board. The factual infrastructure of this case may differ in detail from *Turney v. Zhilka* and is perhaps more analogous to that of the two later cases which came before the Court; in *F.T. Dev. Ltd. v. Sherman, supra*, the offer was conditional upon the purchaser obtaining rezoning on a specified (M-5) zoning basis. I do not think, however, it can be very seriously questioned that the general principle laid down in *Turney v. Zhilka* applies.

The Court was invited by counsel for the appellant to reappraise the rule in *Turney v. Zhilka* if that case was found to be controlling. Counsel cited a number of American and English authorities which support the broad proposition that a party to a contract can waive a condition that is for his benefit. Despite the support elsewhere for such a general proposition, I am of the view the rule expressed in *Turney v. Zhilka* should not be disturbed for several reasons. First, the distinction made in *Turney v. Zhilka* between (i) the manifest right of A to waive default by B in the performance of a severable condition intended for the benefit of A, and (ii) the attempt by A to waive his own default or the default of C, upon whom depends the performance which gives rise to the obligation, *i.e.*, the true condition precedent, seems to me, with respect, to be valid. Second, when parties, as here, aided by legal advisors, make a contract subject to explicit conditions precedent and provide therein specifically that in the event of non-compliance with one or more of the conditions, the contract shall be void, the Court runs roughshod over the agreement by introducing an implied provision conceding to the purchaser the right to waive compliance. In the instant case the conditions for water and sewer requirements were expressed to be subject to waiver at the option of the purchaser but the conditions respecting site plan and zoning were not; if all of these various conditions were to be placed on the same footing, the Court would be simply rewriting the agreement. Third, if the purchaser is to be put in the position of being able to rely on the conditions precedent or to waive them, depending on which course is to his greater benefit, the result may be that the purchaser has been given an option to purchase, for which he has paid nothing; if the property increases in value, the purchaser waives compliance and demands specific performance but if property declines in value, the purchaser does not waive compliance and the agreement becomes null and void in accordance with its terms. It is right to say that this opportunity to select against the vendors will not arise in every case. The zoning changes or other contingency, the subject-matter of the conditions precedent, may be approved by the third party or other-wise satisfied within the purchase. He will not be permitted purposely to fail to perform his obligations in order to avoid the contract. But even when, as here, no question of bad faith arises, approvals may not be forthcoming within the pre-scribed time, and the vendors, whose lands have been tied up for 20 months, can be in the position where they do not know until the final day whether or not the purchaser will waive compliance and whether or not the sale will be completed. If what has been termed an agreement of purchase and sale is to be in reality an option, the purchaser will take the benefit of the appreciation in land value during the intervening months but if the agreement takes effect in accordance with its terms the vendors will have that benefit. I can see no injustice to the purchaser if the contract terms prevail and possible injustice to vendors if they do not. Fourth, application of the rule in *Turney v. Zhilka* may avoid determination of two questions which can give rise to difficulty (i) whether the condition precedent is for the benefit of the purchaser alone or for the joint benefit and (ii) whether the conditions precedent are severable from the balance of the agreement. I am inclined to the view in the present case that they are not. Finally, the rule in *Turney v. Zhilka* has been in effect since 1959, and has been applied many times. In the interests of certainty and predictability in the law, the rule should endure unless compelling reason for change be shown. If in any case the parties agree that the rule shall not apply, that can be readily written into the agreement. *Genern Invts. Ltd. v. Back* (1969), 3 D.L.R. (3d) 611 (Ont. H.C.), and *Dennis v. Evans* (1972), 23 D.L.R. (3d) 625, affirmed 27 D.L.R. (3d) 680*n* (Ont. C.A.), are ex-amples of cases in which the contract expressly provided that a condition could be waived by the party for whose benefit it had been inserted.

The case of *Beauchamp v. Beauchamp* was cited by counsel for the appellant. . . . The patent purpose of the condition [in that case] was to afford the purchasers an opportunity of raising the moneys with which to complete the purchase; in this they were successful and so advised the vendors timeously. It was of no impor-tance whatever that the funds required by the purchasers came from a first mort-gage for $12,000 rather than a first mortgage for $10,000 and a second mortgage for $2,500. That case should, I think, be regarded as one in which the condition precedent was satisfied and not as one in which it was waived.

I would dismiss the appeal with costs.

[Beetz, de Grandpré, Pigeon, Martland, Judson and Ritchie JJ. concurred with Dickson J.; Spence J. concurred with Laskin C.J.C. Appeal dismissed.]

NOTES and QUESTIONS

1. It is important to remember that the converse of the rule in *Turney v. Zilka* is that a *promissory* condition can be waived by the party in whose favour it operates. For example, the obligation of a vendor of land to deliver title clear of encumbrances amounts to a promise to do so. If the vendor is unable to obtain discharge of a caveat or other claim registered against the title, the purchaser may waive performance of that condition and accept title subject to the caveat. However, the distinction between a promissory condition and a true condition precedent has not always been observed. In *Bayerische Landesbank Girozentrale v. R.S.W.H. Vegetable Farmers Inc.* (2001), 53 O.R. (3d) 374 (S.C.J.) at 380 Molloy J. said;

> It is well settled that if a condition in an agreement is inserted solely for the benefit of one of the parties, it may be waived by that party. As was stated by the Supreme Court of Canada in *Zhilka v. Turney*, [*supra*], at p. 583 S.C.R.:
>
>> . . . one party to a contract may forego a promised advantage or may dispense with part of the promised performance of the other party which is simply and solely for the benefit of the first party and is severable from the rest of the contract.

The condition to which this statement of the law was applied was clearly not promissory in nature.

2. With the hindsight provided by the decision in *Barnett v. Harrison*, how might a condition be drawn to protect the interests of someone in the same position as the purchaser in that case? For a helpful discussion, see Davies, "Some Thoughts on the Drafting of Conditions in Contracts for the Sale of Land" (1977), 15 Alta. L. Rev. 422.

3. Consider the effect of s. 54 of the Law and Equity Act, R.S.B.C. 1996, c. 253:

Conditions precedent

> 54. If the performance of a contract is suspended until the fulfillment of a condition precedent, a party to the contract may waive the fulfillment of the condition precedent, even if the fulfillment of the condition precedent is dependent on the will or actions of a person who is not a party to the contract if
>
> (a) the condition precedent benefits only that party to the contract;
>
> (b) the contract is capable of being performed without fulfillment of the condition precedent; and
>
> (c) where a time is stipulated for fulfillment of the condition precedent, the waiver is made before the time stipulated, and where a time is not stipulated for fulfillment of the condition precedent, the waiver is made within a reasonable time.

4. If satisfaction of a condition precedent is validly waived, *primary obligations become unconditionally enforceable by both parties*. In the absence of any contractual provision to the contrary, the non-fulfilment of a condition precedent terminates the contract. That consequence was articulated by the Manitoba Court of Appeal in this passage from *Kiernicki v. Jaworski* (1956), 18 W.W.R. 289 (Man. C.A.) at 293;

> In a contract, "subject to" a stipulated condition, such as the conditions here, means that the dominant but conditional obligation of the contract, namely to purchase, is to become operative and effective only on fulfilment of the condition or occurrence of the event stipulated in the condition; unless there is such fulfilment or occurrence the conditional contract never becomes unconditional, operative or binding, and the parties are in the same position as if no contract has been entered into.

Does the line of authority following from *Dynamic Transport* call for qualification of this statement?

Chapter 7

REPRESENTATIONS AND TERMS; CLASSIFICATIONS AND CONSEQUENCES

1.   Introduction

Statements made during the course of negotiations leading up to a contract may or may not become terms of the contract. Indeed, they fall into three broad categories. Firstly, there are statements made without contractual intent, picturesquely described by Bowen L.J. in *Carlill v. Carbolic Smoke Ball Company*, *supra* in Chapter 2, section 2, as "mere puffs". More modern commentators have characterized such expressions as "sales talk" and no liability attaches to them. Secondly, pre-contractual statements may be categorized as mere representations, which are not terms of the contract, but which can lead to the limited legal consequences indicated in section 2 of this chapter. Thirdly, a statement may be construed as a term of the contract, leading to more serious legal liabilities in the event that it is broken.

Because of the different remedies available, the distinction between mere representations and terms is vital. It is discussed in section 3 of this chapter. Recent statutory reforms, which appear to break down this distinction to some extent, are set forth in section 4, and the possibility of liability in tort for negligent misstatements that induce contracts is considered in section 5.

Returning to the scope of the contract, section 6 contains materials on the "parol evidence" rule, a doctrine which affects analysis of the scope of contracts in writing. The rule is that no extrinsic evidence is admissible for the purposes of adding to, varying, contradicting or subtracting from a contract which has been reduced to writing. Here you should consider the strength of the tendency to assume that a written contract contains all the terms.

Once one has determined the boundaries of a particular contract, in the sense of deciding what statements can be classified as contractual terms, a further classification is made with respect to such terms. A distinction is drawn between the more important terms of the contract, called conditions, and the less important terms, which are known as warranties. A third, hybrid type of term has also become well recognized and is called, in Lord Denning's terminology, an intermediate term. These classifications are discussed in section 7 and again they dictate the remedies available to an aggrieved party. The remedies in turn are analyzed in the *Hong Kong Fir Shipping* case and succeeding cases, *infra*, in section 7 of the chapter, and in the final segment of this chapter entitled Discharge by Performance or Breach.

2.   Misrepresentation and Rescission

In this part, three basic issues relating to the availability of the remedy of rescission for misrepresentation will be addressed:

1.   What kinds of pre-contractual statements will, if false, be characterized as misrepresentations giving rise to rescission?

2.   What is the nature of the remedy of rescission?

3.   What limitations are imposed on one's ability to rescind for misrepresentation?

As a preliminary point, it is important to draw a clear distinction between the remedy of rescission and the remedies available where one party has failed to do all that he or she promised by breaking a term of the contract.

"Rescission" is an expression which is used in a variety of ways, at least three of which can be clearly identified:

(a)   It is commonly used to denote the setting aside of a contract because of some defect affecting its formation, such as misrepresentation, duress or undue influence.

(b)   It is also used to describe the discharge of an existing contract by subsequent agreement of the parties.

(c)   It is incorrectly, but commonly, used to refer to the situation in which an innocent party is discharged from having to carry out his or her obligations under the contract because of the other party's serious breach of contract or failure to perform. Here, the contract is not "wiped out" but, on the contrary, the innocent party is entitled to be compensated by virtue of its previous existence to the extent necessary to put him or her in the position he or she would have been in had the contract been performed.

The difference between a claim for damages and a suit to rescind an agreement has been explained in the following terms. The action for damages is an action to enforce the agreement and thus has as its object the substitution of money damages for the performance which should have been rendered under the binding agreement between the parties. (The innocent party may also wish to be freed from the obligation to perform.) The effect of a suit for rescission, on the other hand, is to determine that the contract is one that ought not to be enforced. Hence any monetary award (or other order) made upon rescission should have as its object the restoration of the parties to their pre-contract positions. The Supreme Court of Canada in *Guarantee Co. of North America v. Gordon Capital Corp.* (1999), 178 D.L.R. (4th) 1 (S.C.C.) has, at paras. 39-45, discussed the confusion over the meaning of the term rescission, showing a preference for it to be used to mean the contract is voided *ab initio*. In this case, sophisticated business parties were assumed to have used the term in that sense.

REDGRAVE v. HURD

(1881), 20 Ch. D. 1 (C.A.)

The plaintiff, an elderly solicitor engaged in practice in Birmingham, advertised that he would "take as a partner an efficient lawyer and advocate about forty, who would not object to purchase advertiser's suburban residence". The defendant, a solicitor practising in Stroud, entered into negotiations with the plaintiff with a view to purchasing the home and a share in the practice. The defendant asked for some idea of the income yielded annually by the practice and was advised by the plaintiff that it amounted to £300 to £400 a year. This matter was explored further in an interview at which time the plaintiff produced summaries of business done in 1877, 1878 and 1879 which indicated receipts of approximately £200 per year. When asked how the difference was made up, the plaintiff showed the defendant a quantity of papers and letters which he said related to additional business. The defendant did not examine the papers and ultimately agreed to purchase the house and a share in the business for £1600. The parties entered into a written agreement which referred only to the sale of the house. The defendant paid a deposit of £100 and in due course, moved his family to Birmingham and took possession of the house. On learning, however, that the practice was "utterly worthless", he refused to complete the transaction. The plaintiff brought suit for specific performance. The defendant, alleging that he had been induced to enter the agreement by a misrepresentation, counterclaimed for rescission, return of the deposit, and damages in deceit for the loss and trouble of the move and for having given up his practice in Stroud.

At trial, Fry J. held for the plaintiff and dismissed the counterclaim. Although it was his view that the letters and papers shown to the defendant by the plaintiff would have indicated additional business of only £5 or £6 per year, Fry J. concluded that the defendant, by failing to examine the documents, must be taken not to have relied on the representations as to the value of the practice.

JESSEL M.R. . . . As regards the Defendant's counter-claim, we consider that it fails so far as damages are concerned, because he has not pleaded knowledge on the part of the Plaintiff that the allegations made by the Plaintiff were untrue, nor has he pleaded the allegations themselves in sufficient detail to found an action for deceit. It only remains to consider the claim of the Plaintiff for specific performance, and so much of the counter-claim of the Defendant as asks to have the contract rescinded. . . .

As regards the rescission of a contract, there was no doubt a difference between the rules of Courts of Equity and the rules of Courts of Common Law—a difference which of course has now disappeared by the operation of the Judicature Act, which makes the rules of equity prevail. According to the decisions of the Courts of Equity it was not necessary, in order to set aside a contract obtained by material false representation, to prove that the party who obtained it knew at the time when the representation was made that it was false. It was put in two ways, either of which was sufficient. One way of putting the case was, "A man is not to be allowed to get a benefit from a statement which he now admits to be false. He is not to be allowed to say, for the purpose of civil jurisdiction, that when he made it he did not know it to be false; he ought to have found that out before he made it." The other way of putting it was this: "Even assuming that moral fraud must be shown in order to set aside a contract, you have it where a man, having obtained a beneficial contract by a statement which he now knows to be false, insists upon keeping the contract. To do so is a moral delinquency: no man ought to seek to take advantage of his own false statements." The rule in equity was settled, and it does not matter on which of the two grounds it was rested. As regards the rule of Common Law there is no doubt it was not quite so wide. There were, indeed, cases in which, even at Common Law, a contract could be rescinded for misrepresentation, although it could not be shewn that the person making it knew the representation to be false. They are variously stated, but I think, according to the later decisions, the statements must have been made recklessly and without care, whether it was true or false, and not with the belief that it was true. But, as I have said, the doctrine in equity was settled beyond controversy, and it is enough to refer to the judgment of Lord Cairns in the *Reese River Silver Mining Company v. Smith* [(1869), L.R. 4 H.L. 64], in which he lays it down in the way which I have stated.

There is another proposition of law of very great importance which I think it is necessary for me to state, because, with great deference to the very learned Judge from whom this appeal comes, I think it is not quite accurately stated in his judgment. If a man is induced to enter into a contract by a false representation it is not a sufficient answer to him to say, "If you had used due diligence you would have found out that the statement was untrue. You had the means afforded you of discovering its falsity, and did not choose to avail yourself of them." I take it to be a settled doctrine of equity, not only as regards specific performance but also as regards rescission, that this is not an answer unless there is such delay as constitutes a defence under the Statute of Limitations. That, of course, is quite a different thing. Under the statute delay deprives a man of his right to rescind on the ground of fraud, and the only question to be considered is from what time the delay is to be reckoned. It had been decided, and the rule was adopted by the statute, that the delay counts from the time when by due diligence the fraud might have been discovered. Nothing can be plainer, I take it, on the authorities in equity than that the effect of false representation is not got rid of on the ground that the person to whom it was made has been guilty of negligence. One of the most familiar instances in modern times is where men issue a prospectus in which they make false statements of the contracts made before the formation of a company, and then say that the contracts themselves may be inspected at the offices of the solicitors. It has always been held that those who accepted those false statements as true were not deprived of their remedy merely because they neglected to go and look at the contracts. Another instance with which we are familiar is where a vendor makes a false statement as to the contents of a lease, as, for instance, that it contains no covenant preventing the carrying on of the trade which the purchaser is known by the vendor to be desirous of carrying on upon the property. Although the lease itself might be produced at the sale, or might have been open to the inspection of the purchaser long previously to the sale, it has been repeatedly held that the vendor cannot be allowed to say, "You were not entitled to give credit to my statement." It is not sufficient, therefore, to say that the purchaser had the opportunity of investigating the real state of the case, but did not avail himself of that opportunity. . . .

As regards the facts of this case, I agree with the conclusions of Mr. Justice Fry on every point but one, and my failure to agree with him in that one is the cause of my concurring in reversing his decision. What he finds in effect is that the Defendant Hurd was induced to enter into the contract by a material misrepresentation made to him by the Plaintiff Redgrave, but he comes to the conclusion that either he did not finally rely upon that representation, or that if he did rely upon it he made an inquiry which, although ineffectual and made, as he says, carelessly and inefficiently, bound him in a Court of Equity, and prevented him from saying that he relied on the representation. I have already dealt with that as a matter of law, and I will deal with it presently as a matter of fact, because I think there was an omission to notice a most material fact, or rather, I should say, an omission to give sufficient weight to it, for it is noticed in the judgment which is now appealed from. . . .

[Jessel M.R. then reviewed the evidence relating to the negotiations between the parties and the findings of the trial judge.]

Then the learned Judge goes on to say: "According to the conclusion which I come to upon the evidence, the books were there before the Defendant, and although he did not trouble to look into them he had the opportunity of doing so. In my judgment if he had intended to rely upon that parol representation of business beyond that which appeared in the papers, having the materials before him, he would have made some inquiry into it. But he did nothing of the sort." Now in that respect I am sorry to say that the learned Judge was not correct. There were no books which shewed the business done. The Plaintiff did not keep any such books, and had nothing but his diaries, and some letter books; and therefore, it is a mistake to suppose that there were any books before the Defendant which he could look into to ascertain the correctness of the statements made by the Plaintiff; and the whole foundation of the judgment on this part of the case, even if it had been well founded in law, fails in fact, because the Defendant was not guilty of negligence in not doing that which it was impossible to do, no books being in existence which would shew the amount of business done. Then the learned Judge continues: "He did nothing of the sort: I think the true result of the evidence is this, that the Defendant thought that if he could have even such a nucleus of business as these papers disclosed, he could by the energy and skill which he possessed make himself a good business in Birmingham." Then that being so the learned Judge came to the conclusion either that the Defendant did not rely on the statement, or that if he did rely upon it he had shewn such negligence as to deprive him of his title to relief from this Court. As I have already said, the latter proposition is in my opinion not founded in law, and the former part is not founded in fact; I think also it is not founded in law, for when a person makes a material representation to another to induce him to enter into a contract, and the other enters into that contract, it is not sufficient to say that the party to whom the representation is made does not prove that he entered into the contract, relying upon the representation. If it is a material representation calculated to induce him to enter into the contract, it is an inference of law that he was induced by the representation to enter into it, and in order to take away his title to be relieved from the contract on the ground that the representation was untrue, it must be shewn either that he had knowledge of the facts contrary to the representation, or that he stated in terms, or shewed clearly by his conduct, that he did not rely on the representation. If you tell a man, "You may enter into partnership with me, my business is bringing in between £300 and £400 a year," the man who makes that representation must know that it is a material inducement to the other to enter into the partnership, and you cannot investigate as to whether it was more or less probable that the inducement would operate on the mind of the party to whom the representation was made. Where you have neither evidence that he knew facts to shew that the statement was untrue, or that he said or did anything to shew that he did not actually rely upon the statement, the inference remains that he did so rely, and the statement being a material statement, its being untrue is a sufficient ground for rescinding the contract. For these reasons I am of opinion that the judgment of the learned Judge must be reversed and the appeal allowed.

As regards the form of the judgment, as the appellant succeeds on the counter-claim, I think it would be safer to make an order both in the action and the counter-claim, rescinding the contract and ordering the deposit to be returned.

[Concurring judgments were delivered by Baggallay and Lush L.JJ.]

QUESTIONS

1. Was the defendant fully restored to the position he was in before he entered the contract?

2. Why was the counterclaim for damages dismissed?

3. Jessel M.R. states that "it is an inference of law" that a material representation calculated to induce did induce in the absence of evidence to the contrary. Others have suggested that such inferences are inferences of fact. Indeed, in *Smith v. Chadwick* (1884), 9 App. Cas. 187 at 196, Lord Blackburn opined that it is "not possible to maintain that it is an inference of law." Similarly, in the decision of the Alberta Court of Appeal in *L.K. Oil & Gas Ltd. v. Canalands Energy Corp.* (1989) 60 D.L.R. (4th) 490 [leave to appeal to S.C.C. refused [1990] 1 W.W.R. lxxi (note) (S.C.C.)]. Harradence J.A. stated, at 498:

> In my view, the approach taken by Canadian courts is to consider all of the relevant facts of a case in order to decide whether a statement was relied upon. Where nothing else but the representation could have induced the contract, then a logical inference is that the represen-tation did, in fact, induce the contract. Where other factors could be operative, the evidence must be considered to determine which factors were relied upon.

Which approach do you favour? In what circumstances would it make a difference whether the inference was factual or legal? What if the defendant did not wish to testify?

SMITH v. LAND AND HOUSE PROPERTY CORP.

(1884), 28 Ch. D. 7 (C.A.)

The plaintiffs offered for sale a hotel, stating that it was currently leased to Frederick Fleck, "a most desirable tenant". The defendants agreed to buy the hotel. Shortly thereafter Fleck went into bankruptcy. The defendants refused to complete the transaction and defended the plaintiffs' suit for specific performance on the basis that the misdescription of Fleck's virtues amounted to a misrepresentation. The plaintiffs argued that the reference to Fleck was a mere expression of opinion and not a statement of fact.

BOWEN L.J. . . . It is material to observe that it is often fallaciously assumed that a statement of opinion cannot involve the statement of a fact. In a case where the facts are equally well known to both parties, what one of them says to the other is frequently nothing but an expression of opinion. The statement of such opinion is in a sense a statement of a fact, about the condition of the man's own mind, but only of an irrelevant fact, for it is of no consequence what the opinion is. But if the facts are not equally known to both sides, then a statement of opinion by the one who knows the facts best involves very often a statement of a material fact, for he impliedly states that he knows facts which justify his opinion. Now a landlord knows the relations between himself and his tenant, other persons either do not know them at all or do not know them equally well, and if the landlord says that he considers that the relations between himself and his tenant are satisfactory, he really avers that the facts peculiarly within his knowledge are such as to render that opinion reasonable. Now are the statements here statements which involved such a representation of material facts? They are statements on a subject as to which *prima facie* the vendors know everything and the purchasers nothing. The vendors state that the property is let to a most desirable tenant, what does that mean? I agree that it is not a guarantee that the tenant will go on paying his rent, but it is to my mind a guarantee of a different sort, and amounts at least to an assertion that nothing has occurred in the relations between the landlords and the tenant which can be considered to make the tenant an unsatisfactory one. That is an assertion of a specific fact. Was it a true assertion? Having regard to what took place between Lady Day and Midsummer, I think that it was not. On the 25th of March, a quarter's rent became due. On the 1st of May, it was wholly unpaid and a distress was threatened. The tenant wrote to ask for time. The Plaintiffs replied that the rent could not be allowed to remain over Whitsuntide. The tenant paid on the 6th of May £30, on the 13th of June £40, and the remaining £30 shortly before the auction. Now could it at the time of the auction, be said that nothing had occurred to make Fleck an undesirable tenant? In my opinion a tenant who had paid his last quarter's rent by driblets under pressure must be regarded as an undesirable tenant. . . .

[Concurring judgments of Baggallay and Fry L.JJ. are omitted.]

NOTES and QUESTIONS

1. What rationale could be offered for the proposition that statements of opinion should not serve as a basis for rescission?

2. If, in the course of the negotiations that occurred in *Redgrave v. Hurd*, the plaintiff had stated that he and his wife were of the view that Birmingham is a lovely place to live, would this provide an additional ground of relief if Birmingham did not, in fact, offer a particularly attractive urban environment?

3. For a further illustration of the fact/opinion dichotomy, see *Esso Petroleum Co. v. Mardon*, [1976] 2 All E.R. 5 (C.A.), in which Esso's estimate of annual consumption of petrol at a service station was held to be a representation that the forecast was sound and reliable.

4. Should both parties be taken to know (or have equal access to opinions about) their legal position under a proposed transaction? Although it is sometimes said that misrepresentations of law (at least those that are innocently erroneous) do not give rise to rescission, the courts have been willing to construe statements as to another's legal position as representations of fact. See *Wauton v. Coppard*, [1899] 1 Ch. D. 92. If the misstatement were made by a solicitor, what tacit representation of fact might you argue to be inherent in the statement of opinion? See *Brown v. Raphael*, [1958] 1 Ch. D. 636 (C.A.).

BANK OF BRITISH COLUMBIA v. WREN DEVELOPMENTS LTD.

(1973), 38 D.L.R. (3d) 759 (B.C. S.C.)

MUNROE J. In this action the plaintiff claims the sum of $25,301.63 against the defendant Allan upon certain written guarantees executed and delivered by said defendant to the plaintiff as security for a loan of $30,000 made by the plaintiff to the defendant Wren Developments Ltd. on October 24, 1969, which loan was renewed on January 20, 1970. . . . The plaintiff has already recovered default judgment against the corporate defendant and summary judgment against the defendant Gordon Smith, the other person who executed and delivered the said guarantees. At all material times, the defendant Smith was the president and managing director of the corporate defendant and the defendant Allan was a director, secretary and minority shareholder thereof. Two other persons were also shareholders. . . .

As collateral security for the loan aforesaid the corporate defendant deposited with the plaintiff on October 24, 1969, 1,050 shares of Dynasty Explorations Limited (N.P.L.) and 33,400 shares of Spartan Exploration Ltd. (N.P.L.) owned by it. On December 10, 1969, the plaintiff released 17,000 shares of Spartan and received in exchange 17,500 shares of Fairborn Mines Ltd. On February 25, 1970, the plaintiff released 15,000 shares of Spartan and received in exchange 16,000 shares of Fairborn. On June 11, 1970, the plaintiff released 25,000 shares of Fairborn and received a part only of the proceeds of the sale thereof to apply upon and in reduction of the loan. On November 13, 1970, the plaintiff released 50 shares of Dynasty and 8,500 shares of Fairborn. It is not clear upon the evidence what consideration, if any, the plaintiff received therefor. All such releases were made by the plaintiff at the request of the defendant Smith and without the knowledge or consent of the defendant Allan or of the corporate defendant. Under the terms of the general hypothecation agreement the plaintiff was authorized to "sell the security or any part thereof and to apply the proceeds in reduction of the liabilities as the bank may see fit without prejudice to its claim for any deficiency". The plaintiff has not proved that it did sell the securities and apply the proceeds in reduction of the loan. . . .

Is the defendant Allan liable for the balance of the amount claimed under and by virtue of his written guarantees? He signed the first guarantee on October 28, 1969, when the original loan was made. That guarantee was replaced by a later guarantee signed on June 21, 1971, whereunder for the first time his personal guarantee for the debt of the company was limited to the sum of $28,258.90, the amount then owing upon the loan. On June 2, 1971, the defendant Allan received ex. 15 advising him that the plaintiff was not prepared to carry the loan in its present unsatisfactory condition and that unless satisfactory arrangements for payment were made by June 15th, legal steps would be instituted against the company and the guarantors. The fact that the loan payments were in arrears came as a complete surprise to Allan. On June 21, 1971, he went to see plaintiff's credit supervisor who told him that Smith had recently made satisfactory arrangements for payment of the company loan and had signed a new guarantee and asked Allan to do likewise, saying it was a routine procedure. Allan inquired of the credit supervisor as to the collateral security (shares) held by the bank and was told by the latter that he did not know particulars thereof but would make an investigation and report later to Allan. Thereupon Allan signed the new form of guarantee. When he did so, he did not know that any of the shares had been released or exchanged by the bank as aforesaid. On the contrary, since he had not been informed of any sale or exchange of shares and because his signature was required on banking transactions entered into by the company, and because neither he nor the company had ever authorized Smith to act as their agent, he felt reasonably certain that the collateral security pledged by the company was still held by the bank. In that mistaken belief he executed and delivered the new guarantee to the plaintiff. The financial position of Allan had been materially prejudiced by the dealings with the shares of the company pledged as collateral security for its loan. . . .

I reject the submission of counsel for the plaintiff [—] the shares were not released or dealt with by the plaintiff in pursuance of [the term giving the plaintiff authority to sell the security, quoted above] but, rather, were released to Smith and sold or exchanged by him with the consent of the plaintiff in the mistaken belief on the part of the plaintiff that Smith was the owner thereof, which he was not—nor did Smith have the authority of the owner (the company) to deal with the shares as he did.

Upon the evidence I find that the defendant Allan, when he signed the second guarantee, was misled by the words, acts and conduct of the plaintiff into believing that there had been no change in the collateral securities held by the plaintiff, and otherwise he would not have signed it. In short, there was a unilateral mistake on the part of the defendant Allan which was induced by the misrepresentation of the plaintiff in failing to disclose material facts to him. In those circumstances, the defendant Allan is not liable to the plaintiff upon the second personal guarantee: *Royal Bank v. Hale* (1961), 30 D.L.R. (2d) 138 (B.C. S.C.). The first guarantee was discharged by novation when the second guarantee was delivered and accepted.

Because of its negligence, the plaintiff is not now in a position to return the collateral security pledged with it. In *Ellis & Co.'s Trustee v. Dixon-Johnson*, [1925] A.C. 489 at 491 (H.L.), Viscount Cave, L.C., said:

> I have always understood the rule in equity to be that, if a creditor holding security sues for his debt, he is under an obligation on payment of the debt to hand over the security; and

if, having improperly made away with the security, he is unable to return it to his debtor, he cannot have judgment for the debt.

In the absence of evidence that the missing securities can now be replaced, the claim of the plaintiff must fail also upon this ground. . . .

The action is dismissed with costs.

NOTE and QUESTIONS

1. Did Allan indicate that he would execute the guarantee only if there had been no change in the collateral security?

2. The general position taken by the common law is that silence does not constitute a misrepresentation. On the other hand, it is well established that if a true representation is followed by a change of circumstances prior to agreement which renders the statement false, the representer has a duty to draw the change to the representee's attention. In *With v. O'Flanagan*, [1936] Ch. 575, for example, the seller of a medical practice accurately represented the current income from the practice, but committed a misrepresentation by failing to disclose subsequently changed conditions rendering the practice worthless.

Further, a number of cases hold so-called "half-truths" to constitute misrepresentation. For example, in *Notts Patent Brick v. Butler* (1886), 16 Q.B.D. 778, a purchaser of land, intending to use the property as a brickyard, asked the vendor's solicitor whether the land was subject to any restrictive covenants. The solicitor responded that he was not aware of any. In fact, there was a covenant prohibiting its use as a brickyard. The solicitor's response was literally true but only a half-truth because he failed to disclose that he had not made an appropriate investigation to determine whether there were such covenants.

Conduct amounting to a deliberate concealment of the truth may also be characterized as a misrepresentation. In *Gronau v. Schlamp Investments Ltd.* (1974), 52 D.L.R. (3d) 631 (Man. Q.B.), the defendant vendor of an apartment building discovered, prior to sale, a serious crack in one of the walls of the building. When advised by an engineer that repairing the crack would be quite expensive, the vendor decided to conceal the crack by covering it over with matching bricks. The plaintiff purchaser was held entitled to rescind. Would this principle apply to a vendor of residential premises who wallpapers the dining room to hide the cracks in the plaster on its walls?

Do any of the above exceptions to the general principle that silence is not a misrepresentation apply to the facts of *Bank of British Columbia v. Wren Developments*?

3. In earlier chapters, we explored the possibility that parties negotiating an agreement might be subjected to a duty to bargain in good faith. See Chapters 3 and 5. Under American law, a duty to disclose information in the course of bargaining has been recognized in circumstances where non-disclosure "amounts to a failure to act in good faith". See American Law Institute, Restatement of the Law Second, Contracts, sec. 161 (b). Recently, the Court of Appeal for Ontario, *obiter*, suggested that a similar duty to disclose ought to be recognized in Canadian common law. In *978011 Ontario Ltd. v. Cornell Engineering Co.* (2001), 198 D.L.R. (4th) 615 (Ont. C.A.), Weiler J.A. suggested that the following five factors are indicative of when such a duty should be imposed:

(1) A past course of dealing between the parties in which reliance for advice, etc., has been an accepted feature;

(2) The explicit assumption by one party of advisory responsibilities;

(3) The relevant positions of the parties particularly in their access to information and in their understanding of possible demands of the deal;

(4) The manner in which the parties were brought together, and the expectations that could create in the relying parties; and

(5) [W]hether "trust and confidence knowingly [has] been reposed by one party or the other."

These factors were drawn from Finn, "The Fiduciary Principle", in Youdan (ed.), Equity, Fiduciaries and Trusts (1989) at p. 20. They were inapplicable to the facts of the *Cornell Engineering* case. Is such a principle workable? How would it apply to the facts of *Wren*?

KUPCHAK v. DAYSON HOLDINGS LTD.

(1965), 53 W.W.R. 65, 53 D.L.R. (2d) 482 (B.C. C.A.)

The appellants (the Kupchaks) had purchased the shares of a motel company, Palms Motel Ltd., from the respondents (Dayson Holdings) in return for two properties conveyed to the respondents and mortgages given to the respondents by the appellants on the land and chattels owned by the motel company. The transaction was completed on 30th March 1960 and the appellants thereupon took possession of the hotel premises and began to operate the business. Two months later, learning that representations made by the respondents' agent as to the past earnings of the hotel were false, the appellants stopped making payments on the mortgages and consulted their solicitors. Subsequently, an exchange of communications between the solicitors for both parties occurred. The respondents obtained (but did not execute) a warrant to seize the furniture of the hotel pursuant to the terms of the chattel mortgage. One week later the appellants' solicitors notified the respondents of an intention to continue withholding payments until a proposed lawsuit had been determined.

Subsequently, respondents sold an undivided half interest in one of the properties conveyed to them by the appellants, tore down the existing building and erected an apartment building. The amount of an existing mortgage on the other property was increased and the interest rate was raised. Over a year after the sale of the half interest, the respondents launched an unsuccessful foreclosure action against the appellants and the appellants commenced an action for rescission. The appellants continued to live in and operate the hotel. The trial judge denied rescission but awarded the appellants damages.

DAVEY J.A. The learned trial Judge found the Kupchaks had been induced by fraud of the respondents to exchange their Haro Street and North Vancouver properties for shares of the Palms Motel Ltd., and to give mortgages over land and chattels of the motel in the sum of $64,500 to Dayson Holdings Ltd. to secure the difference in the value of two sets of property. However, he held that the appellants were not entitled to rescission, because, while they were able to restore to the respondents the shares in the motel, the respondents could not restore the Haro St. property, as they had conveyed an undivided one-half interest in it to Marks Estates Ltd. on October 19, 1960, and as the buildings had been torn down, and a modern apartment house had been erected. . . .

Certificates of encumbrance show that on April 26, 1962, the Haro St. property was registered in the names of Dayson Holdings Ltd. and Marks Estates Ltd., subject to two mortgages for $400,000 and $175,000. The evidence at the trial was taken on May 2, 3, 4, 24 and 25, 1962. Judgment was delivered on September 4, 1962, finding fraud, but refusing rescission, and giving leave to speak to damages. After having received various submissions on damages over a period of two years, concluding with an oral argument on May 14, 1964, the learned trial Judge on the afternoon of that day awarded the appellants damages in the sum of $28,012.67. . . .

The appellants appeal against the learned trial Judge's refusal to grant rescission, and the respondents cross-appeal against the finding of fraud and the amount of damages.

Having read all the evidence of the principal actors in this litigation, I think there is ample evidence to support the finding of fraud inducing the contract, and there remains for consideration only the question of the relief to be granted appellants.

The appellants are able to restore the shares in the Palms Motel Ltd. to the respondents, and since as directors they have continued to operate the business and maintain it as a going concern there has been no change in the character of the company, or its shares. The respondents, the wrongdoers, can return the North Vancouver property, but because of their own dealing with the Haro St. property they can only return the remaining undivided one-half interest in it, and that in a form so completely changed that its identity may be said to have been destroyed. In *Spence v. Crawford*, [1939] 3 All E.R. 271 at 281 (H.L.), Lord Thankerton stated that broadly speaking a defender, who, as purchaser, has been guilty of fraud, is not entitled to raise in bar of restitution his own dealing with the property that he has acquired by fraud. At p. 279 he repeated Lord Cranworth's observations in *Western Bank of Scotland v. Addie* (1867), L.R. 1. Sc. & Div. 145 (H.L.), and noted that the condition of rescission is the restoration of the defendant to his precontract position, and that no stress is placed on whether the pursuer is so restored. The respondents are purchasers *qua* the Haro St. property, and so fall within the scope of the first principle enunciated by Lord Thankerton.

In *Spence v. Crawford*, Lord Wright said at p. 288:

> On the basis that the fraud is established, I think that this is a case where the remedy of rescission, accompanied by *restitutio in integrum*, is proper to be given. The principles governing that form of relief are the same in Scotland as in England. The remedy is equitable. Its application is discretionary, and, where the remedy is applied, it must be moulded in accordance with the exigencies of the particular case. The general principle is authoritatively stated in a few words by Lord Blackburn in *Erlanger v. New Sombrero Phosphate Co.* (1878), 3 App. Cas. 1218 (C.A.), where, after referring to the common law remedy of damages, he went on to say, at p. 1278:

> But a court of equity could not give damages, and, unless it can rescind the contract, can give no relief. And on the other hand, it can take accounts of profits, and make allowance for deterioration. And I think the practice has always been for a court of equity to give this relief whenever, by the exercise of its powers, it can do what is practically just, though it cannot restore the parties precisely to the state they were in before the contract.

> In that case, Lord Blackburn is careful not to seek to tie the hands of the court by attempting to form any rigid rules. The court must fix its eyes on the goal of doing "what is practically just." How that goal may be reached must depend on the circumstances of the case, but the court will be more drastic in exercising its discretionary powers in a case of fraud than in a case of innocent misrepresentation. . . . There is no doubt good reason for the distinction. A case of innocent misrepresentation may be regarded rather as one of misfortune than as one of moral obliquity. There is no deceit or intention to defraud. The court will be less ready to pull a transaction to pieces where the defendant is innocent, whereas in the case of fraud the court will exercise its jurisdiction to the full in order, if possible, to prevent the defendant from enjoying the benefit of his fraud at the expense of the innocent plaintiff. . . .

In the result, under the authorities the respondents' dealing with the Haro St. property, which they acquired by fraud, ought not to bar rescission of the transaction unless it be impractical, or so unjust to the respondents that it ought not to be imposed upon a guilty party.

In determining whether rescission is practical, equity's power to remove inequities resulting from rescission and deficiencies in restitution by compensation, account, or indemnity must be kept in mind. It is, of course, impossible for the respondents to return the Haro St. property because they have sold an undivided one-half interest to Marks Estates Ltd., but even if they still owned the entire interest, the character of the property has been so greatly changed and improved physically by industry, planning, and the expenditure of a large sum of money that it would be unjust to deprive respondents of the property and give it to the appellants. Nor do the appellants ask for that. Instead, they ask for its value on March 31, 1960, and they say that value is the sum of $80,000 put upon the property in the exchange.

My brother Sheppard has suggested that the jurisdiction to order the payment of a sum of money incidental to a decree for rescission in order to effect substantial restitution is limited to those cases in which account or indemnity may be ordered under equitable principles to work out the rights of the parties consequent upon rescission, and, that this appears from Lord Blackburn's judgment in *Erlanger v. New Sombrero Phosphate Co.* (1878), 3 App. Cas. 1218 (C.A.). I agree that the compensation sought by the appellants for the Haro St. property does not flow from account or indemnity, and is more like damages, which equity cannot award as such. However, with respect, I am unable to interpret Lord Blackburn's judgment in *Erlanger v. New Sombrero Phosphate Co.* so narrowly. Rescission is an equitable remedy, and in my opinion equity has the same power, operating on the conscience of the parties, to order one to pay compensation to the other in order to effect substantial restitution under a decree for rescission, as it has to order one party to pay money on account, or by way of indemnity. The jurisdiction to order compensation is, I think, inherent in the decree for rescission and incidental to it, and flows from what Lord Blackburn described in the *Erlanger* case as equity's power to do what is practically just, though it cannot restore the parties precisely to the state they were in before the contract. . . . I think the allowance of compensation as incident of rescission and restitution is one of the things Lord Wright had in mind in *Spence v. Crawford, supra,* at p. 288, where he said the application of that remedy is discretionary, and when it is applied it must be moulded in accordance with the exigencies of the particular case. He observed that Lord Blackburn in *Erlanger v. New Sombrero Phosphate Co., supra,* was careful not to tie the hands of the Court in attempting to do what is practically just by any rigid rules; that in the case of fraud the Court will exercise the jurisdiction to the full in order, if possible, to prevent the defendant from enjoying the benefit of his fraud at the expense of the innocent plaintiff. At p. 289 Lord Wright stated that in a case of fraud the Court will do its best to unravel the complexities of any particular case, which may involve adjustments on both sides. The easiest way to effect adjustments is by the allowance of money. In *Spence v. Crawford, supra,* the compensation was directed to be paid by the plaintiff, in accordance with his offer, to the defendant as a condition of the restoration of the plaintiff's shares. Here it is proposed that the respondents be compelled to pay compensation to the appellants for that part of appellants' property that respondents cannot, or ought not to be required to restore on rescission, because of their own dealings with that property. That distinction, in my opinion, has no bearing on the present question, which is whether there is power to award the payment of money under equitable principles to adjust the rights consequent upon rescission, otherwise than in the course of equity's auxiliary jurisdiction to order accounts and indemnity. Rescission is just as much an equitable remedy as account and indemnity, and in applying that remedy, equity may order the payment of compensation to adjust the rights of the parties consequent upon rescission, just as it may order the payment of money upon account or by way of indemnity.

But even on the narrowest aspect of that suggestion, compensation is a form of equitable relief just as much as account, indemnity, or declaration of trust, and payment of it may be ordered under equitable principles for breach of a fiduciary obligation. *Nocton v. Lord Ashburton*, [1914] A.C. 932 (H.L.), was such a case. Lord Haldane, at p. 946, referred to the old bill in Chancery to enforce compensation for breach of such an obligation. Also at p. 952 he said that equity operating *in personam* as a Court of conscience could order the defendant, not to pay damages as such, but to make restitution, or to compensate the plaintiff by putting him in as good a position pecuniarily as that in which he was before the injury.

That being so, in my opinion, equity as an incident of its peculiar remedy of rescission, or under its power to award compensation, may adjust the rights of the parties by ordering either one to pay compensation to the other to make good some deficiency in perfect restitution.

It being impractical and unjust to require the respondents upon rescission to restore the Haro St. property they had acquired from the appellants by fraud, the respondents ought to compensate the appellants for the property respondents are allowed to keep, the more so as their dealing with the property was after September 16, 1960, when they had notice of appellants' claim of fraud. If the entire interest in Haro St. had been sold at a fair price in an arm's length deal, the amount of compensation would be the purchase price. But in the present circumstances it should be the value of the property on March 31, 1960. However, I do not think the value placed upon a piece of real estate in an exchange, while some evidence of value, by itself constitutes a safe guide, for there is sometimes a tendency on each side to exaggerate the value of their respective parcels, and this mutual exaggeration is immaterial so long as the amount of the difference between those values is acceptable. Accordingly, I would order rescission, unless barred by defences I consider next, and order the respondents to compensate the appellants for their equity in the Haro St. property based upon its value on March 31, 1960, to be ascertained by an inquiry, with interest at 5% per annum from that date. . . .

That leads to the question whether the appellants by conduct, word, or silence have elected to affirm the exchange, and whether their right to rescission is barred by laches. If a guilty party intends to allege that this victim has affirmed the contract or has been guilty of laches, he must plead and prove those defences to rescission. But in neither action did the respondents plead these bars to rescission.

Nevertheless these defences were argued before us without objection by the appellants, who did object, however, that the respondents had not pleaded in bar of rescission that they could not restore the Haro St. property. Any objection that these defences to rescission had not been pleaded would fail if the evidence thereon had been fully canvassed at the trial. But the difficulty is that neither appellants nor respondents directed their attention at the trial to evidence of election or laches.

As to the definition and elements of election, it will be sufficient to quote the language of Mellor, J., in *Clough v. London & North Western Ry. Co.* (1871), L.R. 7 Ex. 26 (Ex. Ch.), which has been approved many times by the highest authority. . . .

At pp. 35-6 [he said]:

> In such cases the question is, has the person on whom the fraud was practised, having notice of the fraud, elected not to avoid the contract? or has he elected to avoid it? or has he made no election?
>
> We think that so long as he has made no election he retains the right to determine it either way, subject to this, that if in the interval whilst he is deliberating, an innocent third party has acquired an interest in the property, or if in consequence of his delay the position even of the wrong-doer is affected, it will preclude him from exercising his right to rescind.
>
> And lapse of time without rescinding will furnish evidence that he has determined to affirm the contract; and when the lapse of time is great, it probably would in practice be treated as conclusive evidence to shew that he has so determined. . . .
>
> Neither can we see the principle or discover the authority for saying that it is necessary that there should be a declaration of his intention to rescind prior to the plea.

In 26 Hals., 3rd ed., pp. 884-85, para. 1643, the learned author states:

> 1643. Affirmation of contract. A fourth defence is that the representee has elected to affirm the contract. It follows, from what has already been stated, that if, after discovery of the whole of the material facts giving him a right to avoid the contract, the representee has, by word or act, definitely elected to adhere to it, the representor has a complete defence to any proceedings for rescission. The acts and conduct relied upon as evincing the representee's affirmance must be such as are more consistent, on a reasonable view of them, with that than with any other theory. It is not sufficient to point to acts of a neutral character, or acts which are equally consistent with a possible ultimate intention to disaffirm, or with a mere suspension of judgment. . . .

Before turning to the facts, I quote Sir Barnes Peacock's explanation of laches in *Lindsay Petroleum Oil Co. v. Hurd* (1874), L.R. 5 P.C. 221 at pp. 239-40, which has been approved by the Privy Council, the House of Lords, and the Supreme Court of Canada, the latest occasion being in *Nwakobi (Osha of Obosi) v. Nzekwu*, [1964] 1 W.L.R. 1019 (P.C.):

> Now the doctrine of laches in Courts of Equity is not an arbitrary or a technical doctrine. Where it would be practically unjust to give a remedy, either because the party has, by his conduct, done that which might fairly be regarded as equivalent to a waiver of it, or where by his conduct and neglect he has, though perhaps not waiving that remedy, yet put the other party in a situation in which it would not be reasonable to place him if the remedy were afterwards to be asserted, in either of these cases, lapse of time and delay are most material. But in every case, if an argument against relief, which otherwise would be just, is founded upon mere delay, that delay of course not amounting to a bar by any statute of limitations, the validity of that defence must be tried upon principles substantially equitable. Two circumstances, always important in such cases, are, the length of the delay and the nature of the acts

done during the interval, which might affect either party and cause a balance of justice or injustice in taking the one course or the other, so far as relates to the remedy.

The facts on which the respondents rely to constitute election and laches were all elicited by the appellants as part of the narrative of their case, and the respondents directed no cross-examination to those defences to rescission.

The first fact to be ascertained is the date appellants learned of the misrepresentation. The only evidence of that is the testimony of Dan Kupchak that he refused to pay the third and subsequent monthly instalments accruing due on the third mortgage to the Daysons, because he had learned the property had been misrepresented, and because he could not make the payments. He paid the payments due on May 1st, and June 1st, 1960, but made default on the payments due on July 1st and August 1st. Kupchak must have learned during June, 1960, that the property had been misrepresented in some respect, but in what respect it is not known.

It is said that the appellants affirmed the transaction by retaining the shares and remaining as directors of the company, by continuing to manage the motel, and by keeping up the payments on the first and second mortgages against the company's property. On the evidence the significance of those circumstances is obscure since they were not explored by either party, and at the best they remain equivocal. The appellants could not divest themselves of the shares by transferring them to the respondents without the respondents' signatures as transferees; under the usual form of articles the appellants would continue as directors until their successors had been appointed, and the only persons they dare appoint, without prejudicing their right to rescind, would be nominees of the respondents. There is not the slightest suggestion that the respondents would accept rescission or responsibility for the management of the company or its business by accepting a retransfer of the shares, and again becoming directors. As the shareholders and directors of record, the appellants were responsible for operating the business of Palms Motel Ltd., and could not abandon the operation without ensuring its proper management, and that they could only do through the co-operation of the Daysons.

. . .

Furthermore, as to laches and delay, the letter of appellants' solicitors of September 16, 1960, referring to the "proposed action against your client", and the discussions of which it speaks, clearly implied repudiation, for it was only repudiation that would justify the non-payment of the monthly instalments of the mortgage. Therefore the sale of a half-interest in the Haro St. property to Marks Estates Ltd. on October 19, 1960, was made, and the apartment block was built after notice of the repudiation. The respondents proceeded immediately to deal with the Haro St. property in spite of knowledge of the claim of fraud and of the impending action for rescission. They were not misled by any delay. It is true that the appellants' action against respondents was not commenced until November 21, 1961, but the appellants' solicitors had written the letter of September 16, 1960, and the respondents had issued their writ for foreclosure on February 28, 1961, to which the appellants by their statement of defence and counterclaim had pleaded fraud and prayed for rescission. I am unable, with respect, to see in the circumstances how such delay as there was requires an inference of affirmation, or supports laches or waiver, even if those pleas are open to the respondents, which in my opinion they are not.

Apart from the letter, the defence and counterclaim in the foreclosure action was a sufficient repudiation. . . . Some two years elapsed between trial and judgment, but for what reason I am unable to say. There is nothing to show that respondents were responsible. I am at a loss to see on what principle the appellants' right to a rescission in this case was prejudiced or lost by their dilatoriness after trial, if the delay was their fault. I do not say that delay in prosecuting an action for rescission could never have that result, but in the present case the respondents were sufficiently protected by remedies available under the rules, if they objected to the delay. . . .

SHEPPARD J.A. [dissenting] . . . In the case at bar the Kupchaks have retained the shares and have remained on the register which in itself is evidence of affirmation, and the positive acts of continuing in management of the motel can only be evidence of asserting rights in respect to the shares and therefore of affirming the transaction. In *Barron v. Kelly* (1918), 56 S.C.R. 455, the Court held that there had been an election to affirm by reason of the purchaser, after learning of the fraudulent misrepresentations, having made subsequent payments and having made an offer to exchange whereby he had thereby elected not to rescind. That must be said of the Kupchaks. . . .

[Norris J.A. concurred with Davey J.A. in setting aside the judgment for damages and ordering rescission and compensation.]

NOTES and QUESTIONS

1. If the Kupchaks had induced the agreement by misrepresentations of the value of the properties transferred to Dayson Holdings, would the latter be entitled to rescind if the facts were otherwise as presented in this case?

2. Would rescission have been ordered if the misrepresentation had been innocent?

3. In *Whittington v. Seale Hayne* (1900), 82 L.T. 49, the plaintiff sued for rescission of a lease of a farm. The plaintiff had entered the lease on the faith of the lessor's statement that the premises were in a good sanitary condition. The plaintiff took possession and incurred various expenses. The plaintiff invested in poultry stock, made improvements to the premises and paid certain taxes. As well, of course, he paid rent to the lessor. The premises were quite insanitary and the plaintiff's poultry perished as a result. Which, if any, of these expenses should be reimbursed in a rescission claim? In a claim for damages for breach of contract?

4. For affirmation of the flexible nature of the equitable remedy of rescission described in *Erlanger*, see *Wandinger v. Lake* (1977), 78 D.L.R. (3d) 305 at 315 (Ont. H.C.), *per* Lerner J. (". . . the Court does have full power to do what is practically just to restore the parties to their former position").

5. In *Bank of Montreal v. Murphy*, [1986] 6 W.W.R. 610, the British Columbia Court of Appeal suggested in *obiter dicta*, at 615-16, "if the circumstances are appropriate, the courts of British Columbia should not regard themselves as confined to the remedy of rescission where a contract is induced by a misrepresentation and the awarding of the remedy of rescission would not do justice between the parties." For discussion of *Murphy* in the context of the parol evidence rule, see *infra*, section 6(a), note 3 after *J. Evans & Son (Portsmouth) Ltd. v. Merzario (Andrea) Ltd.* in this chapter.

6. For an award of damages in lieu of rescission in a case of unconscionability, see *Dusik v. Newton* (1985), 62 B.C.L.R. 1 (C.A.). The court noted the trend toward increasing remedial flexibility and the need to avoid unjust enrichment.

REDICAN v. NESBITT

[1924] S.C.R. 135, [1924] 1 W.W.R. 305, [1924] 1 D.L.R. 536

ANGLIN J. The defendants entered into a contract to purchase a leasehold property from the plaintiff represented by one Wing, her agent. In due course an assignment of lease executed by the plaintiff and assented to by the landlord (the city of Toronto) was delivered to the defendants' solicitor with the keys of the property, the cheque of one of the defendants for the purchase money being simultaneously handed to the plaintiff's solicitor. The defendants also took an assignment of insurance and paid some arrears of taxes. On inspecting the property two days later—which is said to have been their first opportunity of doing so—they discovered, as they allege, that it had been misrepresented to them by Wing in several particulars, which they claim are of such importance that, had they known the truth in regard to them, they would not have purchased. On learning of these matters they stopped payment of the cheque given for the purchase money having first notified the vendor's husband that that would be done. An action by the vendor was at once begun [for the sum of $2,969.84, being the amount owing by the defendants to the plaintiff under the contract of sale].
. . .

Innocent misrepresentation, such as will support a demand for rescission in equity, though unavailing at common law, will serve as a good equitable defence to a claim for payment under the contract as well as afford ground for a counter-claim for rescission. Rescission is, of course, destructive of the basis of the plaintiff's claim; the right to rescission when established is an effective defence. But whether misrepresentation is set up by way of equitable defence or as the basis of a counter-claim for rescission, the burden on the defendant is the same. If the case made by him would not warrant a decree for rescission it will not avail as a defence to the claim for payment. In preferring this defence a defendant assumes the role of actor and a plea which, if established, would defeat a counter-claim for rescission is equally effective by way of reply to the defence of misrepresentation if set up by the plaintiff. . . .

In the present case the defendants plead misrepresentation as a ground both of defence and of counter-claim. They assert that it was fraudulent and, alternatively, that if innocent it was so material as to afford ground for rescission.

The jury negatived fraud and on this branch of the case, if they are not entitled to have the action dismissed on the other, the defendants ask for a new trial on the ground of misdirection and refusal by the learned trial judge to submit an essential element of it to the jury. I defer dealing with that aspect of the appeal.

The jury found that innocent misrepresentations inducing the contract had been made by the plaintiff's agent, and upon them the defendants maintain they are entitled to rescission. The trial judge rejected this claim on the ground that the contract for sale had been fully executed by the delivery of the deed and the acceptance of the cheque in payment, and that rescission of a contract after execution cannot be had for mere innocent misrepresentation unless it be such as renders the subject of sale different in substance from what was contracted for (*Kennedy v. Panama etc. Mail Co.* (1867), L.R. 2 Q.B. 580). The suggestion that the property differed so completely in substance from what the defendants intended to acquire that there was a failure of consideration is not borne out by the facts. Neither is there any foundation for a suggestion of mutual mistake as a basis for rescission. . . . The trial judge regarded the handing over of the cheque as absolute payment and as a completion of the contract by the defendants just as the delivery of the conveyance and possession constituted completion on the part of the plaintiff.

In the Appellate Divisional Court this judgment was sustained, the late Sir W.R. Meredith C.J.O. giving the judgment of the majority of the court, on the ground that the contract became "executed" upon delivery and acceptance of the conveyance, whether the giving and taking of the cheque should or should not be regarded as payment of the purchase money. . . .

But on the question when a contract will, for the purposes of this rule, be deemed to have ceased to be "executory" and to have become "executed" the authorities are not so clear. I have not found any reported case in which it has been determined whether or not after delivery and acceptance of the conveyance and taking of possession a contract of sale remains "executory" until actual payment of the purchase money then due; nor indeed have I found any authority in which the contrary has been categorically determined. . . .

The foundation of the rule that an executed contract will not be rescinded for innocent misrepresentation appears to be somewhat obscure. In *Angel v. Jay*, [1911] 1 K.B. 666 (D.C.), Darling J. states, apparently without disapproval, the contention of counsel that "the foundation of the doctrine" is that

> when property has passed the persons concerned cannot be placed in the same position as they were in before the estate became vested.

In numerous cases the vesting of the property has been referred to as a serious obstacle to rescission. In other cases the supersession of the contract for sale by the executed conveyance accepted by the purchaser and the resultant restriction of his rights to those assured by the latter instrument appears to be the ground upon which rescission of the contract after acceptance of conveyance is refused. So far does the court go in maintaining this doctrine that, where under a court sale the purchase money was still in court, the purchaser who had accepted the title and taken his conveyance was refused relief in respect of subsequently discovered incumbrances. . . .

In the case now before us it is probably unnecessary to determine the effect on the right of a purchaser to rescission of his acceptance of a conveyance and taking of possession without making payment. What might have been a formidable obstacle to the granting of rescission to the defendants was suggested by the trial judge, namely, the inability of the court to compel the landlord's assent to a re-assignment of the leasehold to the plaintiff. The effect of the acceptance of the conveyance assented to by the lessor and of the taking of possession of the property by the defendants may have been to give to the lessor rights against them as tenants the relinquishment of which the court could not exact.

Although the execution of the contract does not afford an answer to a claim for rescission in cases of fraudulent misrepresentation, inability to effect *restitutio in integrum*, unless that has become impossible owing to action of the wrong-doer, will ordinarily preclude rescission. Kerr on Fraud (5th ed.) 387-90. *A fortiori* is this the case where innocent misrepresentation only is relied upon. . . .

Here, however, neither the impossibility of *restitutio in integrum* nor the intervention of a *jus tertii* has been pleaded by the plaintiff, as it should have been if she meant to rely upon it either by way of reply to the defence or of defence to the counter-claim. Had that issue been raised on the pleadings the defendants might have produced at the trial and tendered for the plaintiff's acceptance a re-assignment of the lease duly assented to by the landlord or other satisfactory assurance that such assent would be forthcoming; or, if not, a judgment might have been pronounced in terms similar to those of the decree made in *Lindsay Petroleum Oil Co. v. Hurd* (1874), L.R. 5 P.C. 221.

But I strongly incline to the view that, while the acceptance of the cheque as payment was in this sense conditional that, if it should be dishonoured, the right to sue for the money due under the contract would revive, the transaction was, nevertheless, intended to be closed and the contract completely executed so far as the purchasers were concerned by their taking of the deed and the keys and handing over the cheque. They had obtained the full consideration for which they contracted and, if the vendor saw fit to accept the cheque they tendered in payment in lieu of cash, they should not be heard to say that the contract had not been fully executed. I cannot think that the vendor's right to have the contract treated as executed and completed can be defeated by the fact that she took a cheque as the equivalent of a cash payment, and still less by the accident that the cheque was not presented for payment during the two days which intervened between the closing of the sale and the stopping of payment. Bearing in mind the well estab-lished custom of solicitors with regard to the closing of sales of real estate, when delivery of conveyance and possession was given and accepted and a cheque (then good) for the purchase money was tendered and taken, what was performed was what the parties intended should be done when they contracted.

Without, therefore, necessarily affirming the position taken in the judgment of the majority of the learned judges of the Appellate Divisional Court, I am of the opinion that, under all the circumstances of this case, the contract for sale was executed and that, according to a well settled rule in equity, rescission for innocent misrepresentation is not an available remedy for the defendants.

I am clearly of the opinion, however, that a new trial must be directed because the issue of fraud was not properly presented to the jury. In substance the learned trial judge charged that, in order to establish fraud, the defendants must show that Wing actually knew his representations were false. He did not tell the jury that the representations would be fraudulent if they were false and were made without belief in their truth, or recklessly, careless of whether they were true or false. *Derry v. Peek* (1889), 14 App. Cas. 337 (H.L.). Wing denied having made the statement that the house was lighted by electricity and added that he "did not know how it was lighted." The jury found that he had made the statement. If adequately instructed, or if a properly framed question had been submitted to them, they might have found that it had been fraudulently made. . . .

[Separate concurring judgments of Idington, Duff and Mignault JJ. are omitted. Davies C.J. concurred with Anglin J.]

NOTES and QUESTIONS

1. The notion that execution of an agreement may preclude rescission for misrepresentation has surfaced in other contexts. See, for example, *Seddon v. North Eastern Salt Co. Ltd.*, [1905] 1 Ch. 326, applying the rule to a sale of securities. What justification, if any, could be offered for extending the rule into this context?

2. Application of this approach in the context of contracts for the sale of goods where the goods have been delivered has also been considered. In *Ennis v. Klassen* (1990), 70 D.L.R. (4th) 321, the Manitoba Court of Appeal held that the rule relating to real estate transactions should not apply to sales of goods cases. Huband J.A. commented, at 331:

> Where a misrepresentation induces a person to purchase a chattel, an equitable remedy should be available in spite of execution of the contract where the purchaser's conduct has been reasonable, and where the absence of an equitable remedy will produce an unfair result. Rescission ceases to be available where the contract has been accepted, which in most instances will mean after the passage of a reasonable period of time for the purchaser to determine whether representations are true.

Do you think this approach is likely to lead to a reconsideration and revision of the analysis of real estate transactions? For an example of an agreement being accepted by the passage of time, see *Leaf v. International Galleries*, [1950] 2 K.B. 86 (C.A.), *infra*, section 3 of this chapter.

3.   Representations and Terms

The problem addressed in this section is easily illustrated in the context of contracts for the sale of goods. If, in the course of negotiating the sale of a car, the seller should say to the prospective buyer, "It's a good little bus . . . you will have no trouble with it", the buyer may well come to consider whether these utterances form part of the contractual obligation of the seller. Is the seller liable in damages for breach of contract, if, in fact, the car could not be fairly described as a "good little bus"?

Before turning to consider the variety of solutions proposed by the courts and by the legislatures for such questions, it may be useful to speculate for a moment about the range of factors which might be considered material in fashioning a rule which would isolate the cases in which liability seems appropriate or just. Would it be sufficient to simply ask whether the parties *intended* the utterance to be part of their contract? Would it be relevant that the seller did not say that he "promised" that the car was a good little bus? Is it relevant that the seller is or is not a mechanic? A car dealer? Or that the buyer is a mechanic or car dealer? Is it relevant that the seller knew or should have known that the car was in poor mechanical condition? Should it matter when the utterance occurred—whether before or after the buyer agreed to purchase the car? How important is it that the seller's comments were not made in writing?

The modern treatment of these problems at common law may be dated from 1913, the year of the important decision of the House of Lords in *Heilbut, Symons & Co. v. Buckleton*, reproduced in part below. As will be seen, the debate as to what their proper resolution should be continues unabated, both in the courts and in the legislatures, to the present day.

For a decision dealing with the "good little bus" problem, see *Andrews v. Hopkinson*, [1957] 1 Q.B. 229.

HEILBUT, SYMONS & CO. v. BUCKLETON

[1913] A.C. 30 (H.L.)

VISCOUNT HALDANE L.C. My Lords, the appellants, who were rubber merchants in London, in the spring of 1910 underwrote a large number of shares in a company called the Filisola Rubber and Produce Estates, Limited, a company which was promoted and registered by other persons about that time. They instructed a Mr. Johnston, who was the manager of their Liverpool business, to obtain applications for shares in Liverpool. Johnston, who had seen a draft prospectus in London but had at the time no copy of the prospectus, mentioned the company to several people in Liverpool, including a Mr. Wright, who sometimes acted as broker for the respondent. On April 14 the respondent telephoned to Johnston from Wright's office. As to what passed there is no dispute. The respondent said "I understand you are bringing out a rubber company." The reply was "We are." The respondent then asked whether Johnston had any prospectuses, and his reply was in the negative. The respondent then asked "if it was all right," and Johnston replied "We are bringing it out," to which the respondent rejoined "That is good enough for me." He went on to ask how many shares he could have, and to say that he would take almost any number. He explained in his evidence in chief that his reason for being willing to do this was that the position the appellants occupied in the rubber trade was of such high standing that "any company they should see fit to bring out was a sufficient warranty" to him "that it was all right in every respect." Afterwards, as a result of the conversation, a large number of shares were allotted to the respondent.

About this time the rubber boom of 1910 was at its height and the shares of the Filisola Company were, and for a short time remained, at a premium. Later on it was discovered that there was a large deficiency in the rubber trees which were said in the prospectus to exist on the Filisola Estate, and the shares fell in value. The respondent brought an action against the appellants for fraudulent misrepresentation, and alternatively for damages for breach of warranty that the company was a rubber company whose main object was to produce rubber.

The action was tried at Liverpool Assizes before Lush J. and a special jury. The jury found that there was no fraudulent representation by the appellants or Johnston, but they found that the company could not be properly described as a rubber company, and that the appellants or Johnston, or both, had warranted that the company was a rubber company. . . .

LORD MOULTON . . . It is not contested that . . . the reply of Mr. Johnston to the plaintiff's question over the telephone was a representation by the defendants that the company was a "rubber company," whatever may be the meaning of that phrase; nor is there any controversy as to the legal nature of that which the plaintiff must establish. He must shew a warranty, i.e., a contract collateral to the main contract to take shares, whereby the defendants in consideration of the plaintiff taking the shares promised that the company itself was a rubber company. The question in issue is whether there was any evidence that such a contract was made between the parties.

It is evident, both on principle and on authority, that there may be a contract the consideration for which is the making of some other contract. "If you will make such and such a contract I will give you one hundred pounds," is in every sense of the word a complete legal contract. It is collateral to the main contract, but each has an independent existence, and they do not differ in respect of their possessing to the full the character and status of a contract. But such collateral contracts must from their very nature be rare. The effect of a collateral contract such as that which I have instanced would be to increase the consideration of the main contract by 100l., and the more natural and usual way of carrying this out would be by so modifying the main contract and not by executing a concurrent and collateral contract. Such collateral contracts, the sole effect of which is to vary or add to the terms of the principal contract, are therefore viewed with suspicion by the law. They must be proved strictly. Not only the terms of such contracts but the existence of an animus contrahendi on the part of all the parties to them must be clearly shown. Any laxity on these points would enable parties to escape from the full performance of the obligations of contracts unquestionably entered into by them and more especially would have the effect of lessening the authority of written contracts by making it possible to vary them by suggesting the existence of verbal collateral agreements relating to the same subject-matter.

There is in the present case an entire absence of any evidence to support the existence of such a collateral contract. The statement of Mr. Johnston in answer to plaintiff's question was beyond controversy a mere statement of fact, for it was in reply to a question for information and nothing more. No doubt it was a representation as to fact, and indeed it was the actual representation upon which the main case of the plaintiff rested. It was this representation which he alleged to have been false and fraudulent and which he alleged induced him to enter into the contracts and take the shares. There is no suggestion throughout the whole of his evidence that he regarded it as anything but a representation. Neither the plaintiff nor the defendants were asked any question or gave any evidence tending to shew the existence of any animus contrahendi other than as regards the main contracts. The whole case for the existence of a collateral contract therefore rests on the mere fact that the statement was made as to the character of the company, and if this is to be treated as evidence sufficient to establish the existence of a collateral contract of the kind alleged the same result must follow with regard to any other statement relating to the subject-matter of a contract made by a contracting party prior to its execution. This would negative entirely the firmly established rule that an innocent representation gives no right to damages. It would amount to saying that the making of any representation prior to a contract relating to its subject-matter is sufficient to establish the existence of a collateral contract that the statement is true and therefore to give a right to damages if such should not be the case.

In the history of English law we find many attempts to make persons responsible in damages by reason of innocent misrepresentations, and at times it has seemed as though the attempts would succeed. On the Chancery side of the Court the decisions favouring this view usually took the form of extending the scope of the action for deceit. There was a tendency to recognize the existence of what was sometimes called "legal fraud," i.e., that the making of an incorrect statement of fact without reasonable grounds, or of one which was inconsistent with information which the person had received or had the means of obtaining, entailed the same legal consequences as making it fraudulently. Such a doctrine would make a man liable for forgetfulness or mistake or even for honestly interpreting the facts known to him or drawing conclusions from them in a way which the Court did not think to be legally warranted. The high-water mark of these decisions is to be found in the judgment pronounced by the Court of Appeal in the case of *Peek v. Derry* (1887), 37 Ch. D. 541 (C.A.), where they laid down that where a defendant has made a misstatement of fact and the Court is of opinion that he had no reasonable grounds for believing that it was true he may be made liable in an action of deceit if it has materially tended to induce the plaintiff to do an act by which he has incurred damage. But on appeal to your Lordships' House this decision was unanimously reversed, and it was definitely laid down that, in order to establish a cause of action sounding in damages for misrepresentation, the statement must be fraudulent or, what is equivalent thereto, must be made recklessly, not caring whether it be true or not. The opinions pronounced in your Lordships' House in that case shew that both in substance and in form the decision was, and was intended to be, a reaffirmation of the old common law doctrine that actual fraud was essential to an action for deceit, and it finally settled the law that an innocent misrepresentation gives no right of action sounding in damages.

On the Common Law side of the Court the attempts to make a person liable for an innocent misrepresentation have usually taken the form of attempts to extend the doctrine of warranty beyond its just limits and to find that a warranty existed in cases where there was nothing more than an innocent misrepresentation. The present case is, in my opinion, an instance of this. But in respect of the question of the existence of a warranty the Courts have had the advantage of an admirable enunciation of the true principle of law which was made in very early days by Holt C.J. with respect to the contract of sale. He says: "An affirmation at the time of the sale is a warranty, provided it appear on evidence to be so intended." So far as decisions are concerned, this has, on the whole, been consistently followed in the Courts of Common Law. But from time to time there have been dicta inconsistent with it which have, unfortunately, found their way into textbooks and have given rise to confusion and uncertainty in this branch of the law. For example, one often sees quoted the dictum of Bayley J. in *Cave v. Coleman*, (1828), 3 Man. & Ry. K.B. 2, where, in respect of a representation made verbally during the sale of a horse, he says that "being made in the course of dealing, and before the bargain was complete, it amounted to a warranty"—a proposition that is far too sweeping and cannot be supported. A still more serious deviation from the correct principle is to be found in a passage in the judgment of the Court of Appeal in *De Lassalle v. Guildford*, [1901] 2 K.B. 215 at 221 (C.A.), which was cited to us in the argument in the present case. In discussing the question whether a representation amounts to a warranty or not the judgment says:

> In determining whether it was so intended, a decisive test is whether the vendor assumes to assert a fact of which the buyer is ignorant, or merely states an opinion or judgment upon a matter of which the vendor has no special knowledge, and on which the buyer may be expected also to have an opinion and to exercise his judgment.

With all deference to the authority of the Court that decided that case, the proposition which it thus formulates cannot be supported. It is clear that the Court did not intend to depart from the law laid down by Holt C.J. and cited above, for in the same judgment that dictum is referred to and accepted as a correct statement of the law. It is, therefore, evident that the use of the phrase "decisive test" cannot be defended. Otherwise it would be the duty of a judge to direct a jury that if a vendor states a fact of which the buyer is ignorant, they must, as a matter of law, find the existence of a warranty, whether or not the totality of the evidence shews that the parties intended the affirmation to form part of the contract; and this would be inconsistent with the law as laid down by Holt C.J. It may well be that the features thus referred to in the judgment of the Court of Appeal in that case may be criteria of value in guiding a jury in coming to a decision whether or not a warranty was intended; but they cannot be said to furnish decisive tests, because it cannot be said as a matter of law that the presence or absence of those features is conclusive of the intention of the parties. The intention of the parties can only be deduced from the totality of the evidence, and no secondary principles of such a kind can be universally true.

It is, my Lords, of the greatest importance, in my opinion, that this House should maintain in its full integrity the principle that a person is not liable in damages for an innocent misrepresentation, no matter in what way or under what form the attack is made. In the present case the statement was made in answer to an inquiry for information. There is nothing which can by any possibility be taken as evidence of an intention on the party of either or both of the parties that there should be a contractual liability in respect of the accuracy of the statement. It is a representation as to a specific thing and nothing more. The judge, therefore, ought not to have left the question of warranty to the jury, and if, as a matter of prudence, he did so in order to obtain their opinion in case of appeal, he ought then to have entered judgment for the defendants notwithstanding the verdict.

It will, of course, be evident that I have been dealing only with warranty or representation relating to a specific thing. This is wholly distinct from the question which arises when goods are sold by description and their answering to that description becomes a condition of the contract. It is, in my opinion, a failure to recognize that in the present case the parties were referring (as is evident by the written contracts) to one specific thing only that led Farwell L.J. to come to a different conclusion from that to which your Lordships ought, in my opinion, to come in this appeal.

[Concurring judgments were delivered by Viscount Haldane L.C. and Lord Atkinson.]

NOTE and QUESTIONS

1. How would you articulate the policy rationale underlying the decision in this case?

2. The disclosure of material information concerning the distribution to the public of new issues of shares is now extensively regulated by provincial securities regulation legislation. Typically, new issues must be accompanied by a prospectus which provides full disclosure of material information to prospective purchasers. The issuing company and its promoters and underwriters are liable for misrepresentations in the prospectus. Statutory rights of rescission are conferred on purchasers in such circumstances.

What would the policy rationale for a legislative scheme of this kind be? Does the fact that such legislation has been enacted suggest that the common law doctrine applied in *Heilbut* was misconceived?

DICK BENTLEY PRODUCTIONS LTD. v. HAROLD SMITH (MOTORS) LTD.

[1965] 1 W.L.R. 623, [1965] 2 All E.R. 65 (C.A.)

LORD DENNING M.R. The second plaintiff, Mr. Charles Walter Bentley, sometimes known as Dick Bentley, brings an action against Harold Smith (Motors), Ltd., for damages for breach of warranty on the sale of a car. Mr. Bentley had been dealing with Mr. Smith (to whom I shall refer in the stead of the defendant company) for a couple of years and told Mr. Smith he was on the look-out for a well vetted Bentley car. In January, 1960, Mr. Smith found one and bought it for £1,500 from a firm in Leicester. He wrote to Mr. Bentley and said: "I have just purchased a Park Ward power operated hood convertible. It is one of the nicest cars we have had in for quite a long time." Mr. Smith had told Mr. Bentley earlier that he was in a position to find out the history of cars. It appears that with a car of this quality the makers do keep a complete biography of it.

Mr. Bentley went to see the car. Mr. Smith told him that a German baron had had this car. He said that it had been fitted at one time with a replacement engine and gearbox, and had done twenty thousand miles only since it had been so fitted. The speedometer on the car showed only twenty thousand miles. Mr. Smith said the price was £1,850, and he would guarantee the car for twelve months, including parts and labour. That was on the morning of Jan. 23, 1960. In the afternoon Mr. Bentley took his wife over to see the car. Mr. Bentley repeated to his wife in Mr. Smith's presence what Mr. Smith had told him in the morning. In particular that Mr. Smith said it had done only twenty thousand miles since it had been refitted with a replacement engine and gearbox. Mr. Bentley took it for a short run. He bought the car for £1,850, gave his cheque and the sale was concluded. The car was a considerable disappointment to him. He took it back to Mr. Smith from time to time. [His Lordship referred briefly to some work done on the car and continued:] Eventually he brought this action for breach of warranty. The county court judge found that there was a warranty, that it was broken, and that the damages were more then £400, but as the claim was limited to £400, he gave judgment for the plaintiffs for that amount.

The first point is whether this representation, namely that the car had done twenty thousand miles only since it had been fitted with a replacement engine and gearbox, was an innocent misrepresentation (which does not give rise to damages), or whether it was a warranty. It was said . . . in *Heilbut, Symons & Co. v. Buckleton* [*supra*]:

> An affirmation at the time of sale is a warranty, provided it appear on evidence to be so intended.

But that word "intended" has given rise to difficulties. I endeavoured to explain in *Oscar Chess Ltd. v. Williams* [[1957] 1 All E.R. 325 (C.A.)], that the question whether a warranty was intended depends on the conduct of the parties, on their words and behaviour, rather than on their thoughts. If an intelligent bystander would reasonably infer that a warranty was intended, that will suffice. What conduct, then? What words and behaviour, lead to the inference of a warranty?

Looking at the cases once more, as we have done so often, it seems to me that if a representation is made in the course of dealings for a contract for the very purpose of inducing the other party to act on it, and it actually induces him to act on it by entering into the contract, that is prima facie ground for inferring that the representation was intended as a warranty. It is not necessary to speak of it as being collateral. Suffice it that the representation was intended to be acted on and was in fact acted on. But the maker of the representation can rebut this inference if he can show that it really was an innocent misrepresentation, in that he was in fact innocent of fault in making it, and that it would not be reasonable in the circumstances for him to be bound by it. In the *Oscar Chess* case the inference was rebutted. There a man had bought a second-hand car and received with it a log-book, which stated the year of the car, 1948. He afterwards resold the car. When he resold it he simply repeated what was in the log-book and passed it on to the buyer. He honestly believed on reasonable grounds that it was true. He was completely innocent of any fault. There was no warranty by him and only an innocent misrepresentation. Whereas in the present case it is very different. The inference is not rebutted. Here we have a dealer, Mr. Smith, who was in a position to know, or at least to find out, the history of the car. He could get it by writing to the makers. He did not do so. Indeed it was done later. When the history of this car was examined, his statement turned out to be quite wrong. He ought to have known better. There was no reasonable foundation for it.

[His Lordship summarised the history of the car, and continued:] The county court judge found that the representations were not dishonest. Mr. Smith was not guilty of fraud. But he made the statement as to twenty thousand miles without any foundation. And the judge was well justified in finding that there was a warranty. He said:

> I have no hesitation that as a matter of law the statement was a warranty. Mr. Smith stated a fact that should be within his own knowledge. He had jumped to a conclusion and stated it as a fact. A fact that a buyer would act on.

This is ample foundation for the inference of a warranty.

SALMON L.J. I agree. I have no doubt at all that the learned county court judge reached a correct conclusion when he decided that Mr. Smith gave a warranty to the second plaintiff, Mr. Bentley, and that that warranty was broken. Was what Mr. Smith said intended and understood as a legally binding promise? If so, it was a warranty and as such may be part of the contract of sale or collateral to it. In effect, Mr. Smith said:

> If you will enter into a contract to buy this motor car from me for £1,850, I undertake that you will be getting a motor car which has done no more than twenty thousand miles since it was fitted with a new engine and a new gearbox.

I have no doubt at all that what was said by Mr. Smith was so understood and was intended to be so understood by Mr. Bentley.

[Danckwerts L.J. concurred with Lord Denning M.R. Appeal dismissed.]

QUESTIONS

1. Is it possible to reconcile this decision with *Heilbut Symons v. Buckleton*? What is the policy rationale underlying Lord Denning's reasons and how does it differ from that underlying *Heilbut Symons*?

2. How does the *Redgrave v. Hurd* test for misrepresentation differ from Lord Denning's test for contractual term?

3. Would the *Dick Bentley* decision be of assistance to a buyer who purchased a car from a dealer having been induced to purchase by false statements contained in an advertisement published by the manufacturer of the car in the local newspaper? Could you construct some theory for imposing contractual duties on the manufacturer?

LEAF v. INTERNATIONAL GALLERIES

[1950] 2 K.B. 86, [1950] 1 All E.R. 693 (C.A.)

DENNING L.J. In March, 1944, the buyer bought from the sellers an oil painting of Salisbury Cathedral. On the back of the picture was a label indicating that it had been exhibited as a Constable, and during the negotiations for the purchase the sellers represented that it was a painting by Constable. That representation, the judge has found, was incorporated as one of the terms of the contract. The receipt for the price, £85, was given in these terms: "Mar. 6, 1944. One original oil painting Salisbury Cathedral by J. Constable, £85." Nearly five years later the buyer was minded to sell the picture. He took it to Christie's to be put into an auction, and he was then advised that it was not a Constable. So he took it back to the sellers and told them he wanted to return it and get his money back. They did take the picture back temporarily for investigation, and they still adhered to the view that it was a Constable. Eventually the buyer brought a claim in the county court claiming rescission of the contract. In his particulars of claim he pleaded that the picture had been represented to be a Constable, and that he had paid £85 in reliance on that representation. The sellers resisted the claim. After hearing expert evidence the judge found as a fact, and this must be accepted, that the painting was not by Constable and was worth little.

The question is whether the buyer is entitled to rescind the contract on that account. I emphasize that this is a claim to rescind only. There is no claim in this action for damages for breach of condition or breach of warranty. The claim is simply one for rescission. At a very late stage before the county court judge counsel for the buyer did ask for leave to amend by claiming damages for breach of warranty, but it was not allowed. So no claim for damages is before us. The only question is whether the buyer is entitled to rescind. The way in which the case is put by counsel for the buyer is this. He says this was an innocent misrepresentation and that in equity he is entitled to claim rescission even of an executed contract of sale on that account. He points out that the judge has found that it is quite possible to restore the parties to the same position that they were in originally, by the buyer simply handing back the picture to the sellers in return for the repayment of the purchase price.

In my opinion, this case is to be decided according to the well known principles applicable to the sale of goods. This was a contract for the sale of goods. There was a mistake about the quality of the subject-matter, because both parties believed the picture to be a Constable, and that mistake was in one sense essential or fundamental. Such a mistake, however, does not avoid the contract. There was no mistake about the subject-matter of the sale. It was a specific picture of "Salisbury Cathedral." The parties were agreed on the terms on the same subject-matter, and that is sufficient to make a contract. . . . There was a term in the contract as to the quality of the subject-matter, namely, as to the person by whom the picture was painted—that it was by Constable. That term of the contract was either a condition or a warranty. If it was a condition, the buyer could reject the picture for breach of the condition at any time before he accepted it or was deemed to have accepted it, whereas, if it was only a warranty, he could not reject it but was confined to a claim for damages.

I think it right to assume in the buyer's favour that this term was a condition, and that, if he had come in proper time, he could have rejected the picture, but the right to reject for breach of condition has always been limited by the rule that once the buyer has accepted, or is deemed to have accepted, the goods in performance of the contract, he cannot thereafter reject, but is relegated to his claim for damages: see s. 11(1)(c) of the Sale of Goods Act, 1893. . . . The circumstances in which a buyer is deemed to have accepted goods in performance of the contract are set out in s. 35 of the Act which provides that the buyer is deemed to have accepted the goods, among other things,

> . . . when after a lapse of a reasonable time, he retains the goods without intimating to the seller that he has rejected them.

In this case this buyer took the picture into his house, and five years passed before he intimated any rejection. That, I need hardly say, is much more than a reasonable time. It is far too late for him at the end of five years to reject this picture for breach of any condition. His remedy after that length of time is for damages only, a claim which he has not brought before the court.

Is it to be said that the buyer is in any better position by relying on the representation, not as a condition, but as an innocent misrepresentation? I agree that on a contract for the sale of goods an innocent material misrepresentation may in a proper case be a ground for rescission even after the contract has been executed. The observations of Joyce J., in *Seddon v. North Eastern Salt Co. Ltd.*, [[1905] 1 Ch. 326] are, in my opinion, too widely stated. Many judges have treated it as plain that an executed contract of sale may, in a proper case, be rescinded for innocent misrepresentation. ... It is unnecessary, however, to pronounce finally on these matters because, although rescission may in some cases be a proper remedy, nevertheless it is to be remembered that an innocent misrepresentation is much less potent than a breach of condition. A condition is a term of the contract of a most material character, and, if a claim to reject for breach of condition is barred, it seems to me *a fortiori* that a claim to rescission on the ground of innocent misrepresentation is also barred. So, assuming that a contract for the sale of goods may be rescinded in a proper case for innocent misrepresentation, nevertheless, once the buyer has accepted, or is deemed to have accepted, the goods, the claim is barred. In this case the buyer must clearly be deemed to have accepted the picture. He had ample opportunity to examine it in the first few days after he bought it. Then was the time to see if the condition or representation was fulfilled, yet he has kept it all this time and five years have elapsed without any notice of rejection. In my judgment, he cannot now claim to rescind, and the appeal should be dismissed.

SIR RAYMOND EVERSHED M.R. I also agree that this appeal should be dismissed, for the reasons which have already been given. On the facts of this case it seems to me that the buyer ought not now to be allowed to rescind this contract. In the circumstances it is unnecessary, as my brethren have already observed, to express any conclusion on the more general matter whether the so-called doctrine which finds expression in the headnote to *Seddon v. North Eastern Salt Co.* [*supra*] ought now to be treated as of full effect and validity. The doubt on that matter is the greater since the observations of the majority of this court in *Solle v. Butcher* [1949] 2 All E.R. 1107 but out of respect to the argument of counsel for the buyer and because the matter is one of interest to lawyers (see, for example, the article in the Law Quarterly Review of January, 1939, p. 90), I venture to add some observations which may be relevant when the general application of the doctrine has to be further considered.

The buyer's case rested fundamentally on this statement which he made: "I contracted to buy a Constable. I have not had, and never had, a Constable." Though that is, as a matter of language, perfectly intelligible, it, nevertheless, needs a little expansion if it is to be accurate. What he contracted to buy and what he bought was a specific chattel, namely, an oil painting of Salisbury Cathedral, but he bought it on the faith of a representation, innocently made, that the painting had been painted by Constable. It turns out that it was not so painted. Nevertheless, it remains true to say that the buyer still has the article he contracted to buy. The difference in value is, no doubt, considerable, but it is, as Denning L.J. has observed, a difference in quality rather than in the substance of the thing itself.

That leads me to suggest this matter for consideration. The attribution of works of art to particular artists is often a matter of great controversy and increasing difficulty as time goes on. If the buyer is right in saying that he is entitled, perhaps years after the purchase, to raise the question whether in truth a particular painting was rightly attributed to a particular artist, it may result in most costly and difficult litigation in which there will be found divergent views of artists and critics of great eminence, and the prevailing view at one date may be quite different from that which prevails at a later date. There is, moreover, a further point. The judge has found here that *restitutio in integrum* is possible, meaning thereby, as I understand it, that the picture itself retains the condition which it possessed at the time of the sale in 1944 and can, therefore, be returned to the sellers, and the sellers can return to the buyer the £85 which he paid. It can be well understood that, if the view for which counsel for the buyer contended is of general application, many cases will arise in which other controversies of equal difficulty and complexity may have to be determined—namely, whether in the interval there has been a change through wear and tear or otherwise in the article which has been sold. A set of chairs attributed to Chippendale after being used for six years might well be said to have suffered damage which appreciably diminishes their value. Again, the fashion in these things, and consequently their value, varies from time to time.

It seems to me, therefore, that, if the view of counsel for the buyer is to be accepted, there may arise matters for determination of great difficulty and complexity leading to uncertainty and considerable litigation. And as between one case and another the rule of equity may work somewhat capriciously. Those results, it seems to me, are undesirable. If a man elects to buy a work of art or any other chattel on the faith of some representation, innocently made, and delivery of the article is accepted, then it seems to me that there is much to be said for the view that on acceptance there is an end of that particular transaction, and that, if it were otherwise, business dealings in these things would become hazardous, difficult, and uncertain. A representation of this kind may either be a warranty or not, or equivalent to a warranty or not. If not, then the matters to which I have already referred seem to me to gain in importance. I need not elaborate the point by example, but, if the representation does amount to a warranty, then, as Jenkins L.J. has pointed out, there is available to the buyer a remedy at law for the breach which is reasonably certain and capable of giving perfectly adequate compensation to the injured party. If such a remedy at law is available, there is less ground for invoking a rule of equity to supplement the law. Finally, I add this. True it is that since the observations of Scrutton L.J. in *Bell v. Lever Bros., Ltd.* [*infra*, Chapter 9, section 3(a)] and those of this court in *Solle v. Butcher* much greater doubt may be entertained about the validity of the decision of Joyce J., in *Seddon v. North Eastern Salt Co.* in 1905—forty-five years ago. The article in the Law Quarterly Review read to us by counsel for the buyer was written eleven years ago. There has been opportunity for Parliament to alter the law if it was thought to be inadequate. I am not saying that that is a ground on which we should conclude the so-called doctrine of *Seddon v. North Eastern Salt Co.* is well stated or is in all respects correct, but the fact that it has stood for such a length of time, even though qualified, is, I think, another consideration deserving of some weight when this matter has further to be debated and to be adjudicated on. I have added those remarks out of respect to the argument and because of the importance of the case, but I base my conclusion on those grounds which have already been stated by my brethren and which it would be mere repetition on my part to state again.

[Jenkins L.J. delivered a concurring judgment. Appeal dismissed.]

QUESTIONS

1. In *Dick Bentley*, the plaintiff sought damages for breach of contract. In *Leaf*, the plaintiff sought rescission only. What are the differences between these two remedies? Would Mr. Leaf be awarded any money if his suit for rescission had succeeded? Would he be obliged to return the picture? Was Mr. Bentley obliged to restore the car to the seller? If Mr. Leaf had brought a successful claim for damages for breach of contract on the assumption that the seller's representation was a contractual undertaking, what would his damages be?

2. The extent to which "execution" of the agreement should preclude the right to rescind has been considered above. See *Redican v. Nesbitt*, *supra*, and the notes which follow it. What different limitation on the right to rescind is proposed in *Leaf*? If the limitation is imposed, should *Leaf* be entitled to bring a claim for damages of some kind? On what theory of liability?

3. Could the statement that the painting is a Constable be *both* a representation and a term of the contract? Could the plaintiff sue both for rescission and for damages for breach of contract?

4. Statutory Reform

The rules concerning the availability of remedies of various kinds in the context of agreements induced by misrepresentation have attracted the interest of law reform bodies and legislatures. Fuelled in the main by a desire to increase the remedies available to consumers who have been subjected to misleading sales practices, these reform efforts have been required to address a number of difficult issues. Should representations be made part of the agreement between the parties so that their falsity will engage the remedies for breach of contract? Or is the more satisfactory path for reform an enlargement of rescissionary relief? Or should both devices be adopted, leaving the misrepresentee the option to choose the most attractive solution? Or, should the choice be left to the courts and, if so, can some guidelines for the exercise of such a discretion be developed? Should reforms of this kind apply only to consumer transactions or only to transactions for the purchase and sale of property? Should all misrepresentations give rise to the new remedies or, say, only those relating to the nature and quality of the subject-matter of the contract?

The following extract offers a set of proposals dealing with these issues.

ONTARIO LAW REFORM COMMISSION, REPORT ON AMENDMENT OF THE LAW OF CONTRACT

(1987), at 238-42

2. PRECEDENTS FOR REFORM

(a)   SOLUTIONS THAT TREAT REPRESENTATIONS AS CONTRACTUAL TERMS

A number of jurisdictions have enacted legislation that departs from the common law test for determining when a statement is a term of the contract. To varying degrees, these jurisdictions, in effect, have treated as terms of the contract, or warranties, representations that at common law would not satisfy the test of contractual intention.

(i) The United States

The American Uniform Sales Act, adopted in 1906, defined as an express warranty "any affirmation of fact or any promise by the seller relating to the goods if the natural tendency of such affirmation or promise is to induce the buyer to purchase the goods, and if the buyer purchases the goods relying thereon". The Uniform Commercial Code has now superseded the Uniform Sales Act, and adds the rather ambiguous requirement that the statement must become "part of the basis of the bargain".

(ii) Ontario

In our *Report on Consumer Warranties and Guarantees in the Sale of Goods* published in 1972, we recommended that all statements by business sellers inducing consumer sales should be treated as warranties. This proposal, although not implemented in Ontario, has been adopted in Saskatchewan, [Consumer Protection Act, S.S. 1996, c. C-30.1, s. 45] and New Brunswick [Consumer Product Warranty and Liability Act, S.N.B. 1978, c. C-18.1, s. 4(1)] in consumer product warranty statutes.

In our 1979 *Report on Sale of Goods*, we recommended that all representations relating to goods, by both business and non-business sellers, should be treated as warranties. While we were concerned about the possibility of imposing heavy damages on non-business sellers, we decided, in the end, to make no special provision on the point.

When the Commission's Report came to be considered by the Uniform Law Conference of Canada, the Conference felt it necessary to maintain the distinction between representations and terms. . . .

(iii) New Zealand

The New Zealand *Contractual Remedies Act 1979* also contains a provision that treats a representation as a contractual term. Section 6(1) provides as follows:

> 6.–(1) If a party to a contract has been induced to enter into it by a misrepresentation, whether innocent or fraudulent, made to him by or on behalf of another party to that contract—

> (a) He shall be entitled to damages from that other party in the same manner and to the same extent as if the representation were a term of the contract that has been broken; and

> (b) He shall not, in the case of fraudulent misrepresentation, or of an innocent misrepresentation made negligently, be entitled to damages from that other party for deceit or negligence in respect of that misrepresentation.

This provision is criticized by Dawson and McLauchlan in their book on the New Zealand Act [*The Contractual Remedies Act 1979* (1981)] on the ground that the imposition of damages measured by the contractual expectation would place "an unfair burden" on an innocent misrepresentor.

(b)   OTHER SOLUTIONS

(i)   *United Kingdom*

The *Misrepresentation Act, 1967*, [c. 7] is a complex piece of legislation that modifies the law relating to representations in several respects. Section 1 enlarges the common law power of rescission, making it available even where the representation has become a term of the contract or where the contract has been performed. Section 2(1) entitles a representee to claim damages unless the representor proves that the representation was not negligently made. Section 2(2) reduces the right to rescission by giving the court power to refuse rescission and to award damages in lieu thereof, but only in cases where the representee "would be entitled, by reason of the misrepresentation, to rescind the contract". Thus, in a case where rescission is barred, for example because of the inability of the plaintiff to restore benefits received under the contract, the Act still makes no provision for a money award in substitution for rescission.

(ii)   *Ontario Business Practices Act*

The Ontario *Business Practices Act* [now R.S.O. 1990, c. B 18, repealed 2002, c. 30, Sch. E, s. 1, to come into force on proclamation] gives a right of rescission in respect of misrepresentations inducing contracts for the sale of goods and certain services supplied to consumers. The Act also provides, in section 4(1)(b), that:

> ... where rescission is not possible because restitution is no longer possible, or because rescission would deprive a third party of a right in the subject matter of the agreement that he has acquired in good faith and for value, the consumer is entitled to recover the amount by which the amount paid under the agreement exceeds the fair value of the goods or services received under the agreement or damages, or both.

This provision empowers the court to make a money award in lieu of rescission, for which the primary measure envisaged rests on restitutionary principles.

3. PROPOSALS FOR REFORM

The defects in the present law may be summarized as follows. A misrepresentation that is neither fraudulent nor negligent and that does not constitute a term of a contract is actionable neither in tort nor in contract. While a plaintiff who has been induced to enter into a transaction by a defendant's false statement may seek rescission of the transaction, in some cases the right of rescission may be too narrow and, in others, too broad. For example, if the law is that rescission is barred merely by execution of a contract, the right of rescission may be too narrow. Moreover, cases can be envisaged in which a *prima facie* right of rescission should be restricted because of the difficulty of unwinding a contractual transaction or the intervention of third party rights. Finally, the court has no power to make a money award in substitution for, or in addition to, rescission.

A simple amalgamation of representations with contractual terms would, in our opinion, impose too great a liability on the innocent non-business representor.

Rather, we would propose the following modifications to the existing law. First, we believe that the right to rescind on the basis of misrepresentation should be enlarged by removing execution as an automatic bar, even in land sale cases. Accordingly, we recommend that, subject to the following recommendation, a representee should be able to rescind a contract that has been induced by misrepresentation even though the contract has been wholly or partly performed and even though, in the case of a contract for the sale of an interest in land, the interest has been conveyed to the representee.

Secondly, and balancing this enlarged right of rescission, we recommend that, where a party to a contract would otherwise have a *prima facie* right to rescission, the court should have power to deny rescission, or to declare it ineffective, awarding damages in lieu thereof. We further recommend that, in exercising this power, the court should take into consideration, *inter alia*, the following factors: undue hardship to the representor or to third parties; difficulty in reversing performance or long lapse of time after performance; whether a money award would give adequate compensation to the representee; the nature and scope of the representation; and the conduct of the representor and whether or not he or she was negligent in making the representation.

We recognize that in some cases there will be a period of uncertainty during which it will not be clear whether or not a purported rescission is valid, but this is bound to occur under any system. The Rules of Civil Procedure make provision for interim preservation orders of property, which can be used in appropriate cases.

Thirdly, we recommend that, whether or not a contract is rescinded, the court should have the power to allow just compensation by way of restitution, or for losses incurred in reliance on the representation. In exercising this power the court should take into account such factors as whether the misrepresentation was made in the course of a business, whether the representor had personal knowledge of the facts, and whether he or she used reasonable care.

There has been some uncertainty about whether the law relating to misrepresentation applies to misrepresentations of law. Since misrepresentations of law can be just as misleading as misrepresentations of fact, we recommend that legislation should make it clear that misrepresentation includes a misrepresentation of law.

We have directed our attention to innocent, that is, non-fraudulent misrepresentations, intending to leave in place the existing law relating to fraudulent misrepresentations. However, it would seem that there is no need to exclude fraudulent misrepresentations from the scope of our first recommendation, removing certain bars to rescission. We would not want to open the door to an argument that the rights of a misrepresentee were less in the case of fraud than in the case of innocent misrepresentation. In respect of the other recommendations, it should be made clear that they apply to innocent misrepresentations, including negligent misrepresentations.

On one matter that was dealt with in the U.K. *Misrepresentation Act 1967* we make no recommendation. This is the question of control of contractual clauses excluding liability for misrepresentation. In our opinion, such clauses can be satisfactorily dealt with under our general recommendations on unconscionability.

[Footnotes partially omitted.]

NOTE and QUESTIONS

1. As the report notes, the O.L.R.C. had, in previous reports, recommended that certain kinds of representations be treated as warranties. Is this approach adopted here? Why or why not?

2. Assume that legislation has been enacted implementing these recommendations. Further assume that you are a judge who must apply the new legislation to the facts of the *Dick Bentley* and *Leaf* cases. What results?

3. Under the new statute, could a court refuse both rescission and damages?

4. In what way would the new legislation be more generous to the "innocent non-business" representor than "a simple amalgam of representations with contractual terms"?

FAIR TRADING ACT

R.S.A. 2000, C.F.-2

Unfair practices

6.(1) In this section, "material fact" means any information that would reasonably be expected to affect the decision of a consumer to enter into a consumer transaction.

(2) It is an unfair practice for a supplier, in a consumer transaction or a proposed consumer transaction,

   (a) to exert undue pressure or influence on the consumer to enter into the consumer transaction;

   (b) to take advantage of the consumer as a result of the consumer's inability to understand the character, nature, language or effect of the consumer transaction or any matter related to the transaction;

   (c) to use exaggeration, innuendo or ambiguity as to a material fact with respect to the consumer transaction;

   (d) to charge a price for goods or services that grossly exceeds the price at which similar goods or services are readily available without informing the consumer of the difference in price and the reason for the difference;

   (e) to charge a price for goods or services that is materially higher than the estimate given for those goods or services unless the consumer has expressly consented to the higher price before the goods or services are supplied.

(3) It is an unfair practice for a supplier

   (a) to enter into a consumer transaction if the supplier knows or ought to know that the consumer is unable to receive any reasonable benefit from the goods or services;

   (b) to enter into a consumer transaction if the supplier knows or ought to know that there is no reasonable probability that the consumer is able to pay the full price for the goods or services;

    (c) to include in a consumer transaction terms or conditions that are harsh, oppressive or excessively one-sided;

    (d) to make a representation that a consumer transaction involves or does not involve rights, remedies or obligations that is different from the fact.

(4) Without limiting subsections (2) and (3), the following are unfair practices if they are directed at one or more potential consumers:

    (a) a supplier's doing or saying anything that might reasonably deceive or mislead a consumer;

    (b) a supplier's misleading statement of opinion if the consumer is likely to rely on that opinion to the consumer's disadvantage;

    (c) a supplier's representation that goods or services have sponsorship, approval, performance, characteristics, accessories, ingredients, quantities, components, uses, benefits or other attributes that they do not have;

    (d) a supplier's representation that the supplier has a sponsorship, approval, status, qualification, affiliation or connection that the supplier does not have;

    (e) a supplier's representation that goods or services are of a particular standard, quality, grade, style or model, if they are not;

    (f) a supplier's representation that goods have or have not been used to an extent that is different from the fact;

    (g) a supplier's representation that goods are new if they are used, deteriorated, altered or reconditioned;

    (h) a supplier's representation that goods have or do not have a particular prior history or usage if that is different from the fact;

    (i) a supplier's representation that goods or services are available for a reason that is different from the fact;

    (j) a supplier's representation that goods or services have been made available in accordance with a previous representation, if they have not;

    (k) a supplier's representation that the supplier can supply goods or services if the supplier cannot;

    (l) a supplier's representation involving a voucher that another supplier will provide goods or a service at a discounted or reduced price if the first-mentioned supplier knows or ought to know that the second-mentioned supplier will not;

    (m) a supplier's representation that goods are available in a particular quantity if they are not;

    (n) a supplier's representation that goods or services will be supplied within a stated period if the supplier knows or ought to know that they will not;

    (o) a supplier's representation that a specific price benefit or advantage exists if it does not;

    (p) a supplier's representation that a part, replacement, repair or adjustment is needed, or desirable if it is not;

(q) a supplier's representation that the supplier is requesting information, conducting a survey or making a solicitation for a particular purpose if that is not the case;

(r) a supplier's representation that a person does or does not have the authority to negotiate the terms of consumer transaction, if the representation is different from the fact;

(s) when the price of any part of goods or services is given in any representation by a supplier,

   (i) failure to give the total price of the goods or services, or

   (ii) giving less prominence to the total price of the goods or services than to the price of the part;

(t) when the amount of any instalment to be paid in respect of goods or services is given in any representation by a supplier,

   (i) failure to give the total price of the goods or services, or

   (ii) giving less prominence to the total price of the goods and services than to the amount of the instalment;

(u) a supplier's giving an estimate of the price of goods or services if the goods or services cannot be provided for that price;

(v) a supplier's representation of the price of goods or services in such a way that a consumer might reasonably believe that the price refers to a larger package of goods or services than is the case;

(w) a supplier's representation that a consumer will obtain a benefit for helping the supplier to find other potential customers if it is unlikely that the consumer will obtain such a benefit;

(x) a supplier's representation about the performance, capability or length of life of goods or services unless

   (i) the representation is based on adequate and proper independent testing that was done before the representation is made,

   (ii) the testing substantiates the claim, and

   (iii) the representation accurately and fairly reflects the results of the testing;

(y) a supplier's representation that goods or services are available at an advantageous price if reasonable quantities of them are not available at such price, unless it is made clear that quantities are limited;

(z) a supplier's representation that appears in an objective form such as an editorial, documentary or scientific report when the representation is primarily made to sell goods or services, unless the representation states that it is an advertisement or promotion;

(aa) anything specified in the regulations.

Unfair practices prohibited

7. No supplier may commit an unfair practice.

Court action by consumer

13.(1) When a consumer

(a) has entered into a consumer transaction, and

(b) in respect of that consumer transaction, has suffered damage or loss due
to an unfair practice,

that consumer may commence an action in the Court of Queen's Bench for relief
from that damage or loss against any supplier who engaged in or acquiesced in
the unfair practice that caused that damage or loss.

(2) In an action under this section, the Court of Queen's Bench may

(a) declare that the practice is an unfair practice;

(b) award damages for damage or loss suffered;

(c) award punitive or exemplary damages;

(d) make an order for

(i)   specific performance of the consumer transaction,

(ii) restitution of property or funds, or

(iii) rescission of the consumer transaction;

(e) grant an order in the nature of an injunction restraining the supplier from
engaging in the unfair practice;

(f) make any directions and grant any other relief the Court considers
proper.

(3) In determining whether to grant any relief under this section and the
nature and extent of the relief, the Court of Queen's Bench must consider whether
the consumer made a reasonable effort to minimize any damage resulting from
the unfair practice and to resolve the dispute with the supplier before commencing
the action in the Court.

NOTES and QUESTIONS

1. Similar legislation has been enacted in British Columbia (Trade Practice Act, R.S.B.C. 1996,
c. 457), Manitoba (Business Practices Act, S.M. 1990-91, c. 6), Newfoundland (Trade Practices Act,
R.S.N.L. 1990, c. T-7), Ontario (Business Practices Act, R.S.O. 1990, c. B.18 (repealed 2002, c. 30,
Sch. E. s. 1, to come into force on proclamation)) and Prince Edward Island (Business Practices Act,
R.S.P.E.I., 1988, c. B-7).

2. Which of the "unfair practices" set out in s. 6(2) of the Alberta Act would fall outside the
common law definition of misrepresentation? Section 13 appears to limit relief only by requiring the
court to consider whether the consumer has made reasonable efforts to minimize loss and resolve
the dispute. How does this approach differ from the common law? Is the remedial scheme desirably
flexible or undesirably discretionary?

3. The new Ontario legislation (Consumer Protection Act, S.O. 2002, c. 30) stipulates the
following with respect to civil redress:

18. (1) Any agreement, whether written, oral or implied, entered into by a consumer after
or while a person has engaged in an unfair practice may be rescinded by the consumer and the
consumer is entitled to any remedy that is available in law, including damages.

(2) A consumer is entitled to recover the amount by which the consumer's payment under the agreement exceeds the value that the goods or services have to the consumer or to damages, or both, if rescission of the agreement under subsection (1) is not possible,

    (a) because the return or restitution of the goods or services is no longer possible; or

    (b) because rescission would deprive a third party of a right in the subject-matter of the agreement that the third party has acquired in good faith and for value.

(3) A consumer must give notice within one year after entering into the agreement if,

    (a) the consumer seeks to rescind an agreement under subsection (1); or

    (b) the consumer seeks recovery under subsection (2), if rescission is not possible.

How does this provision reform the common law. Which of the "bars" to rescission have been retained?

4. Saskatchewan enacted legislation which covers much of the same ground as the business practices legislation in a more comprehensive Act dealing with consumer purchases. See Consumer Products Warranties Act, now the Consumer Protection Act, S.S. 1996, c. C-30.1, and its analysis by Romero in (1979), 43 Sask. L. Rev. 81.

5. The plaintiff purchased a used car after material misrepresentations were made by the seller. Four months later the plaintiff purported to rescind by giving notice of an election to do so to the seller. The seller refused to agree to this. By the time of trial, the plaintiff had owned the car for 22 months and driven it 40,000 kilometres. Can the court order rescission? See *Lasby v. Royal City Chrysler Plymouth* (1987), 59 O.R. (2d) 323 at 330, leave to appeal to Ont. C.A. refused 59 O.R. (2d) 323n.

5. Concurrent Liability in Contract and Tort

There has been a considerable amount of litigation in Canada dealing with the relationship between tort and contract remedies for misrepresentation. To a great extent, the controversy was triggered by the famous House of Lords decision in *Hedley Byrne & Co. v. Heller & Partners*, [1964] A.C. 465, in which it was assumed that there could be liability in tort for a negligent misrepresentation causing pecuniary loss where a "special relationship" existed between the parties.

Once this proposition was accepted, it became at least theoretically possible that a particular misrepresentation could give rise to liability both in tort and contract. Thus, where a careless misrepresentation induces an agreement, it might be argued that the making of such a misrepresentation is, in accordance with the analysis set forth in section 3 of this chapter, a breach of a term of the agreement itself. Could it not at the same time, or at least alternatively, be a tortious wrong? Similarly, the possibility of concurrent liability arises where an agreement to provide a service requires the making of statements. Such agreements are normally interpreted to include an implied undertaking to exercise reasonable skill and care. Thus a careless misstatement would constitute a breach of the implied covenant. Could it not also constitute a tort?

For a time, the answer to both of these questions seemed to be in the negative as a result of the decision of the Supreme Court of Canada in *J. Nunes Diamonds Ltd. v. Dom. Elec. Protection Co.*, [1972] S.C.R. 769. This case appeared to reject the possibility of tortious liability for a misrepresentation made in the course of performing an agreement. Pigeon J., writing for the majority, at 777-78, stated that "the basis of tort liability considered in *Hedley Byrne* is inapplicable to any case where the relationship between the parties is governed by a contract, unless the negligence relied on can properly be considered as 'an independent tort' unconnected with the performance of that contract. . . ." Some lower courts attempted to narrow the holding in *Nunes* either by treating it as a decision which was dependent on the fact that the agreement had contained a clause which appeared to exclude liability for "representations . . . other than those endorsed herein in writing" or by assuming that the holding in *Nunes* was inapplicable to pre-contractual statements. See, *e.g.*, *Surrey (Dist.) v. Carroll-Hatch & Assoc. Ltd.* (1979), 101 D.L.R. (3d) 218 (B.C. C.A.), and *Sodd Corp. v. N. Tessis, infra.* Nonetheless, the broad language of Pigeon J.'s opinion in *Nunes* presented an obstacle to the development of tortious liability for misrepresentations related to the creation or performance of contractual obligations until the decision of the Supreme Court of Canada in *Central Trust Co. v. Rafuse*, [1986] 2 S.C.R. 147. In that case, the court adopted a general principle favouring the possibility of concurrent liability in tort and contract in contractual contexts. Le Dain J., writing for a unanimous court, carefully examined the mass of conflicting Canadian and English authority on this issue and held that such liability could arise where a relationship of sufficient proximity to create a duty of care in tort is established by the contract and where the resulting tort duty is co-extensive with an obligation also imposed by the contract itself. Le Dain J. went on to note, at 206, that:

> A concurrent or alternative liability in tort will not be admitted if its effect would be to permit the plaintiff to circumvent or escape a contractual exclusion or limitation of liability for the act or omission that would constitute the tort. Subject to this qualification, where concurrent liability in tort and contract exists the plaintiff has the right to assert the cause of action that appears to be most advantageous to him in respect of any particular legal consequence.

Our particular concern in this chapter is the possibility of tortious liability for pre-contractual misrepresentations. In what circumstances would the misrepresentee wish to be able to make a claim in tort? Would every contractual relationship be a relationship of sufficient "proximity" to give rise to a duty of care? Consider the following authorities.

SODD CORP. v. N. TESSIS

(1977), 17 O.R. (2d) 158, 25 C.B.R. (N.S.) 16, 2 C.C.L.T. 245,
79 D.L.R. (3d) 632 (C.A.)

LACOURCIÈRE J.A. This is an appeal by the defendant from the judgment of Her Honour Judge Sydney Dymond granting the plaintiff judgment against the defendant in the amount of $4,500 on the basis of negligent misrepresentation on the sale by tender of certain stock-in-trade contained in a warehouse.

The defendant, a chartered accountant and licensed trustee in bankruptcy, advertised for sale by tender the stock of a furniture business carried on by the bankrupt under the name and style of Riteway Furniture. The plaintiff submitted a tender after its principal officer made a cursory examination of the stock in the warehouse. This officer testified that the defendant represented to him that the method of calculating the retail value of the goods in the warehouse ($33,500) was by doubling the wholesale cost, and that he relied upon that representation in deciding to submit the plaintiff's tender.

The learned trial Judge found as a fact that the goods in the warehouse were overvalued by approximately 100% in comparison with the invoices and price catalogues found in the store. She found that the defendant was negligent in misrepresenting the quantity and value of the items included in the assets of the bankrupt advertised for sale, and that the defendant was not entitled to rely on an exemption clause in the advertisement which reads as follows:

> Tenders will be accepted on the basis that the Purchaser has inspected the assets and title thereto, and no warranty or condition is expressed or can be implied as to designation, classification, quality or condition or in any manner whatsoever.

After the learned trial Judge reviewed the evidence, made her findings of fact and discussed the submissions of counsel, she concluded, orally, as follows:

> I consider that the trustee in bankruptcy had a duty to act responsibly, both in his advertisement for tenders and in his advice given at the time of the inspection and that if he did not expect prospective purchasers to rely on his representations, he should not have made the representations. On the *Hedley Byrne* principle, the defendant failed in his duty to the plaintiff. He made negligent representations which he should have known would and did induce the plaintiff to prepare his tender in a certain manner and, as a result of that tender being accepted, the plaintiff has suffered damage. I believe that the general principle enunciated in the *Hedley Byrne* case and applied in our Courts, has overruled [the former principle] that only fraudulent misrepresentation gives rise to an action for damages in cases of this nature. I, therefore, find that the defendant is liable to the plaintiff.

In a careful argument, Mr. Blair submitted that the principle in *Hedley Byrne & Co. v. Heller & Partners*, could not be applied in the circumstances of this case because there was no special relationship between the parties giving rise to a duty of care. He relied on the words of Lord Reid in *Hedley Byrne & Co. v. Heller & Partners*, who, after quoting from *Derry v. Peek* (1889), 14 App. Cas. 337 (H.L.), said at p. 583:

> This passage makes it clear that Lord Haldane did not think that a duty to take care must be limited to cases of fiduciary relationship in the narrow sense of relationships which had been recognised by the Court of Chancery as being of a fiduciary character. He speaks of other special relationships, and I can see no logical stopping place short of all those relationships where it is plain that the party seeking information or advice when he knew or ought to have known that the inquirer was relying on him. I say "ought to have known" because in questions of negligence we now apply the objective standard of what the reasonable man would have done.
>
> A reasonable man, knowing that he was being trusted or that his skill and judgment were being relied on, would, I think, have three courses open to him. He could keep silent or decline to give the information or advice sought: or he could give an answer with a clear qualification that he accepted no responsibility for it or that it was given without that reflection or inquiry which a careful answer would require: or he could simply answer without any such qualification. If he chooses to adopt the last course he must, I think, be held to have accepted some responsibility for his answer being given carefully, or to have accepted a relationship with the inquirer which requires him to exercise such care as the circumstances require.

He argued further that the defendant did not hold himself out as possessing any "special skill and competence", in the words of Lord Diplock in *Mutual Life & Citizens' Assurance Co. v. Evatt*, [1971] A.C. 793 (P.C.).

In our view, the defendant as a professional accountant and trustee in bankruptcy was in a special relationship creating a duty of care to the plaintiff and was negligent in his representation concerning the retail value of the stock-in-trade.

We are also unable to accept the appellant's argument that since the relationship between the parties was contractual, the *Hedley Byrne* principle does not apply on the basis of *Nunes (J.) Diamonds Ltd. v. Dominion Electric Protection Co. [supra]* . . . [T]he present case did, in fact, involve a pre-contractual negligent misrepresentation which induced the plaintiff to submit its tender, and the defendant's liability follows on the authority of *Esso Petroleum Co. v. Mardon*, [1976] Q.B. 801; see also *Walter Cabott Const. Ltd. v. R.* (1974), 44 D.L.R. (3d) 82, varied 69 D.L.R. (3d) 542 (Fed. C.A.).

In our view, the trial Judge was correct in finding that the plaintiff was not negligent in relying on a licensed trustee who had caused an inventory of the stock to be taken, when the plaintiff's opportunity for inspection was, at best, limited.

There is one further aspect to consider with respect to liability. While the plaintiff's claim was pleaded on the basis of contract, it was clearly presented at trial as being founded upon the tort of negligent misrepresentation, without any amendments being sought or granted. In our view, while an amendment at this stage would not be unfair, it is unnecessary inasmuch as the defendant's negligent misstatement also constituted a collateral warranty inducing the plaintiff to submit its tender. The defendant's stipulation amounted, in our view, to a binding promise, depriving him of the terms of the exemption. On that basis, the conclusion can be supported in contract: *Couchman v. Hill*, [1947] K.B. 554 (C.A.); *Esso Petroleum Co. v. Mardon [supra]*. It is clear from the cases that the defendant's representation, whether characterized as a negligent misstatement or as a collateral warranty, falls outside the exemption clause. . . .

In the result, we are unanimously agreed that the appeal should be dismissed with costs.

NOTES and QUESTIONS

1. The Ontario Court of Appeal appears to place some emphasis on the fact that the defendant in this case is a professional accountant and thus possesses "special skill and competence". What is the rationale underlying this requirement? Do you believe that it should be an invariable requirement? For cases which seem to ignore or place less emphasis on this requirement see *R.H. Peden Const. Ltd. v. Resolute Const. (1977) Ltd.* (1980), 31 A.R. 453 (Q.B.); *Nelson Lumber Co. v. Koch* (1980), 111 D.L.R. (3d) 140 (Sask. C.A.). But see *Kingu v. Walmar Ventures Ltd.* (1986), 38 C.C.L.T. 51 (B.C. C.A.). While the occupation of the defendant is no doubt of some relevance, the critical question to which it is relevant seems to be whether the plaintiff's reliance on the defendant's statement is reasonable and, on the defendant's part, foreseeable. See *Hercules Management Ltd. v. Ernst & Young* (1997), 146 D.L.R. (4th) 577 (S.C.C.) at para 24.

2. According to the Ontario Court of Appeal, this misrepresentation could also be characterized as a collateral warranty. How would you formulate that warranty? Was it a promise that the value of the goods was as represented by the defendant? In *Esso Petroleum Co. v. Mardon, supra*, Esso communicated a misleading estimate of the annual consumption of petrol at a service station in the course of negotiating a lease of the station to Mardon. The Court of Appeal held that Esso had, in effect, misrepresented (or promised) that the forecast was sound and reliable (which it was not) but had not guaranteed its accuracy.

3. There is a vast literature concerning the availability of concurrent liability. For discussions of this issue, see Fridman, "The Interaction of Tort and Contract" (1977), 93 L.Q.R. 422; O'Connell, "The Interlocking Death and Rebirth of Contract and Tort" (1977), 75 Mich. L.R. 659; Symmons, "The Problem of the Applicability of Tort Liability in Contractual Situations" (1975), 21 McGill L.J. 79; Schwartz, "Hedley Byrne and Precontractual Misrepresentations: Tort Law to the Aid of Contract?" (1978), 10 Ottawa L.R. 581; Morgan, "The Negligent Contract Breaker" (1980), 58 Can. Bar Rev. 299; Bridge, "The Overlap of Tort and Contract" (1982), 27 McGill L.J. 872; Blom, "Tort Recovery for Economic Loss and the Intersection between Contract and Tort" (1996), 54(3) The Advocate 367; Ogilvie, "Concurrent Liability in Contract and Tort: Cautionary Tales from the Supreme Court of Canada" [1997] Journal of Business Law 372.

4. A problem which has surfaced with some frequency relates to the effect of exemption clauses on tortious liability for pre-contractual statements. How is this matter resolved in *Sodd*? Where the exception clause appears in the very document in which the pre-contractual misstatement is expressed, would you be more or less inclined to give it the effect of precluding liability? Where the exemption clause appears in a written contract which contains the terms of the agreement ultimately entered into by the parties, and stipulates, for example, that "no representation, statement, understanding or agreement has been made or exists, either oral or in writing", should it have the effect of precluding tortious liability for careless misstatements which induced the representee to enter the agreement? See *Ronald Elwyn Lister Ltd. v. Dunlop Can. Ltd.* (1978), 85 D.L.R. (3d) 321 (Ont. H.C.), in which the trial court permitted the provision to have this effect, though emphasizing that the plaintiffs had, prior to signing the document, received advice from a lawyer who had advised them that they were "taking an awful chance" in signing an agreement containing a provision of this kind. This decision was reversed on other grounds by the Ontario Court of Appeal, 105 D.L.R. (3d) 684, but ultimately restored on further appeal by the Supreme Court of Canada. See (1982), 135 D.L.R. (3d).

5. In *Beer v. Townsgate I Ltd.* (1997), 152 D.L.R. (4th) 671 (Ont. C.A.) [facts briefly set out in Chapter 2, section 6(b), note 1 after *Barrick v. Clark*], the Ontario Court of Appeal suggested that such a provision in a contract to purchase a condominium would not preclude liability where the agreement was signed in a frenzied atmosphere and the clause "was not drawn to the attention of [the purchasers], the contract was signed in haste with no opportunity for them to read it . . . [and there was] no reasonable expectation they were assenting to the clause". See *ibid.*, at 682.

Are lay persons likely to understand the significance of contractual provisions of this kind? If not, would you favour the courts adopting the view that such provisions should be construed so as to preclude liability for careless precontractual statements only if the language clearly so indicates? See, in support of this view, McCamus and Maddaugh, "Some Problems in the Borderland of Tort, Contract and Restitution", [1983] Special Lectures of The Law Society of Upper Canada 273 at 284-87. In *Hayward v. Mellick* (1984), 5 D.L.R. (4th) 740 (Ont. C.A.), Houlden J.A. took this view in a dissenting judgment. The majority opinion of Weatherston J.A. appeared to suggest, at 748, that strict construction of this kind would be appropriate only where the precontractual statement related to "some overriding or collateral matter" but not where the representation is as to the "quality or fitness of the subject-matter of the contract". What argument, if any, could be made in support of a distinction of this kind?

Would the analysis of these problems be any different if the exemption clause appearing in the written contract stipulates that the representee "does not rely upon any information given or statement made to him" prior to entering the agreement? In *Carman Const. Ltd. v. C.P.R.*, [1982] 1 S.C.R. 958, Martland J., on behalf of the Supreme Court of Canada, expressed the view that a "non-reliance" provision of this kind would not properly be characterized as an exemption clause and therefore would not be subject to strict construction of the kind suggested above. His Lordship also noted, however, that it was his view that the plaintiff was aware of the existence of this contractual provision and understood that he could not rely on any information communicated to him by the defendant. For discussion, see McCamus and Maddaugh, *supra*; Hayek, "Collateral Contracts and The Supreme Court of Canada" (1983), 7 Can. Bus. L.J. 328. For a discussion of the decisions, see Swan and Reiter, "The Effectiveness of Contractual Allocations of Risk: *Carman Const. Ltd. v. Canadian*

Pacific Railway; Ronald Elwyn Lister Ltd. v. Dunlop Can. Ltd." (1982), 6 Can. Bus. L.J. 219. This issue is discussed in more detail later in this chapter.

These issues surfaced for reconsideration in the following case.

BG CHECO INTERNATIONAL LTD. v. BRITISH COLUMBIA HYDRO & POWER AUTHORITY

[1993] 1 S.C.R. 12, 99 D.L.R. (4th) 577, 75 B.C.L.R. (2d) 145, 14 C.C.L.T. (2d) 233, 5 C.L.R. (2d) 173, [1993] 2 W.W.R. 321, 20 B.C.A.C. 241, 147 N.R. 81, 35 W.A.C. 241

[The following statement of facts is taken from the judgment of Iacobucci J., who dissented in part from the decision of the majority.]

. . . The appellant and respondent on the cross-appeal, B.C. Hydro and Power Authority [Hydro], is a British Columbia Crown corporation. The respondent and appellant on the cross-appeal, BG Checo International Ltd. [Checo], is a large corporation in the business of constructing electrical transmission lines and distribution systems . . .

In November of 1982, Hydro called for tenders to erect transmission towers and to string transmission lines. In December, 1982, prior to submitting its tender for the contract, Checo's representative inspected the area by helicopter. He noted that the right of way had been partially cleared, and also noted evidence of ongoing clearing activity. The representative assumed that the right of way would be further cleared prior to the commencement of Checo's work. On January 2, 1983, Checo submitted its tender, and on February 15, 1983, Hydro accepted Checo's tender and the parties entered into a written contract. Checo contracted to construct 130 towers and install insulators, hardware and conductors over 42 kilometres of right of way near Sechelt, British Columbia.

In fact, no further clearing of the right of way ever took place. The "dirty" condition of the right of way caused Checo a number of difficulties in completing its work. Checo sued Hydro seeking damages for negligent misrepresentation, or, in the alternative, for breach of contract.

The evidence at trial indicated that Hydro had contracted the clearing-out to another company, and that, to Hydro's knowledge, the work was not done adequately. There was no direct discussion between the representatives of Checo and Hydro concerning this issue. There was evidence led at trial that the contract between the parties did not specify clearing standards with the same degree of detail as was present in similar contracts entered into by Hydro.

During the trial, Hydro tendered documents in evidence which Checo had unsuccessfully attempted to discover. These documents indicated that Hydro was aware of the problem with the clearing and of the impact that these problems would have on the successful tenderer. As a result, Checo amended its statement of claim to include a claim in fraud.

The trial judge . . . found that Hydro had acted fraudulently in its dealings with Checo and awarded Checo $2,591,580.56, being "the total loss suffered by [Checo] as a result of being fraudulently induced to enter into this contract". Hydro appealed to the Court of Appeal for British Columbia, which rejected the finding of fraud, but found that there had been a negligent misrepresentation which induced Checo to enter into the contract. The Court of Appeal awarded the sum of $1,087,729.81, for the misrepresentation, and referred the question of breach of contract and damages flowing therefrom to the British Columbia Supreme Court. Checo's cross-appeal for punitive damages and for a higher scale of costs was dismissed. . . .

It will be helpful to set out the relevant provisions of the contract. The terms of the contract, No. HA-8071, are identical to the tender documents. The critical clauses are 2.03, 4.04 and 6.01.03. I have highlighted that portion of cl. 6.01.03 which Checo alleges founds the misrepresentation by Hydro.

2.03 TENDERER'S RESPONSIBILITY

It shall be the Tenderer's responsibility to inform himself of all aspects of the Work and no claim will be considered at any time for reimbursement for any expenses incurred as a result of any misunderstanding in regard to the conditions of the Work. Should any details necessary for a clear and comprehensive understanding be omitted or any error appear in the Tender Documents or should the Tenderer note facts or conditions which in any way conflict with the letter or spirit of the Tender Documents, it shall be the responsibility of the Tenderer to obtain clarifications before submitting his Tender. [There follow some technical details.]

Neither B.C. Hydro nor the Engineer shall be responsible for any instructions or information given to any Tenderer other than by the Purchasing Agent, in accordance with this Clause.

4.04 INSPECTION OF SITE AND SUFFICIENCY OF TENDER

The Contractor shall inspect and examine the Site and its surroundings and shall satisfy himself before submitting his Tender as to the nature of the ground and sub-soil, the form and nature of the Site, the quantities and nature of work and materials necessary for completion of the Work, the means of access to the Site, the accommodation and facilities he may require, and in general shall himself obtain all necessary information as to risks, contingencies, and other circumstances which may influence or affect his Tender. Without limiting the generality of the foregoing, the Contractor shall satisfy himself of any special risks, contingencies, regulations, safety requirements, and other circumstances which may be encountered.

The Contractor shall be deemed to have satisfied himself before tendering as to the correctness and sufficiency of his Tender for the Work and of the prices stated in the Schedule of Prices which prices shall (except insofar as it is otherwise provided in the Contract) cover all his obligations under the Contract and all matters and things necessary for the proper execution of the Work.

6.01.03 WORK DONE BY OTHERS

Clearing of the right-of-way and foundation installation has been carried out by others and will not form part of this Contract.

Standing trees and brush have not been removed from the right-of-way in certain valley and gully crossings. The Contractor shall be responsible for such further site preparation as required by Section 7.01. [Emphasis added.]

7.01.02 PREPARATION OF THE SITE

The Contractor shall carry out any preparation of the Site, including removal of logs, stumps and boulders, as is necessary to perform his operations.

The Contractor shall ensure that the transmission line is protected from possible slides, washouts or other hazards resulting from his road construction, grading, benching, and other site preparation work and operations. Surface drainage shall be directed away from any structure foundations and guy anchors.

> Any condition resulting from the Contractor's work and which, in the opinion of the Engineer constitutes a hazard to the transmission line shall be corrected to the satisfaction of the Engineer.

.....

LA FOREST and McLACHLIN JJ. We have had the advantage of reading the reasons of our colleague Justice Iacobucci. We agree with his conclusion that Hydro is liable to Checo for breach of contract. We disagree, however, with his conclusion that the contract precludes Checo from suing in tort. In our view, our colleague's approach would have the effect of eliminating much of the rationalizing thrust behind the movement towards concurrency in tort and contract. Rather than attempting to establish new barriers to tort liability in contractual contexts, the law should move towards the elimination of unjustified differences between the remedial rules applicable to the two actions, thereby reducing the significance of the existence of the two different forms of action and allowing a person who has suffered a wrong full access to all relevant legal remedies.

The facts have been fully set out by our colleague and need not be repeated. The tender documents (subsequently incorporated in the contract) stated that clearing of the right of way would be done by others and formed no part of the work to be performed by Checo. The tender documents and contract documents also stated that it was Checo's responsibility to inform itself of all aspects of the work and that should any errors appear in the tender documents, or should Checo note any conditions conflicting with the letter or spirit of the tender documents, it was the responsibility of Checo to obtain clarification before submitting its tender. The tender documents also provided that Checo would satisfy itself of all site conditions and the correctness and sufficiency of the tender for the work and the stipulated prices.

Checo argues that the right of way was not properly cleared and that the statement in the tender documents and the contract that it had been cleared constituted a breach of contract and negligent misrepresentation.

Hydro argues first that it carried out the clearing required by cl. 6.01.03 of the contract and, second, that in any event it was up to Checo to satisfy itself that the site was adequately cleared before tendering. In other words, if there was ambiguity as to what was meant by "cleared" Checo had assumed the risk of clearing which might not meet its expectations.

The trial judge found Hydro liable for the tort of deceit. The Court of Appeal found that the evidence fell short of supporting that finding, there being no evidence of intention to deceive. That conclusion cannot seriously be contested and Checo's cross-appeal on the issue of fraudulent misrepresentation must accordingly be dismissed. The only issues therefore are whether claims lie in contract and tort and, if so, what is the measure of damages.

The claim in contract

The parties chose to set out their respective rights and obligations in the contract they signed. They chose to incorporate the tender documents into the contract. Thus, all rights and obligations flowing from the tender documents onward are set by the parties' own agreement.

It follows that a court, in assessing the rights and obligations of the parties, must commence with the contract. It must look to what the parties themselves had to say about those rights and obligations.

This brings us to construction of the contract. The problem is that of reconciling provisions in the contract which are said to be inconsistent. One, the provision that placed on Hydro the obligation of clearing the right of way, was specific. Clause 6.01.03 stated that "[c]learing of the right-of-way and foundation installation has been carried out by others and will not form part of this Contract". It went on to state a limited exception for two areas, again drafted in specific terms: "Standing trees and brush have not been removed from the right-of-way in certain valley and gully crossings." The other relevant provisions are the general provisions placing on Checo the responsibility for any misunderstandings as to the conditions of the work or errors in the tender documents (cl. 2.03), and for satisfying itself before bidding as to site conditions, quantities of work, etc., and requiring it to "obtain all necessary information as to risks, contingencies, and other circumstances which may influence or affect [its] Tender" (cl. 4.04).

It is a cardinal rule of the construction of contracts that the various parts of the contract are to be interpreted in the context of the intentions of the parties as evident from the contract as a whole. . . . Where there are apparent inconsistencies between different terms of a contract, the court should attempt to find an interpretation which can reasonably give meaning to each of the terms in question. Only if an interpretation giving reasonable consistency to the terms in question cannot be found will the court rule one clause or the other ineffective. . . . In this process, the terms will, if reasonably possible, be reconciled by construing one term as a qualification of the other term: . . . A frequent result of this kind of analysis will be that general terms of a contract will be seen to be qualified by specific terms—or, to put it another way, where there is apparent conflict between a general term and a specific term, the terms may be reconciled by taking the parties to have intended the scope of the general term to not extend to the subject-matter of the specific term.

Approaching the matter in this way, the provisions referred to above are capable of reconciliation. The parties agreed that Hydro should bear the responsibility of clearing the right of way. The only exception was as to the removal of trees and debris in certain valley and gully crossings. The general obligation of Checo for misunderstandings and errors in the tender documents and for satisfying itself as to the site, the work and all contingencies must not have been intended to negate the specific obligation for clearing which the contract placed squarely on the shoulders of Hydro. The failure to discharge that responsibility was not a "misunderstanding" or "error" in the tender documents within cl. 2.03. Nor was it relevant to the tenderer's inspection of the site or responsibility for risks and contingencies that might affect the bid within cl. 4.04. Given the specific nature of Hydro's obligation to clear the right of way, the site inspection and contingencies referred to can reasonably be read as relating to matters other than clearing, which was a clearly assigned obligation and thus not a contingency. The same applies to the provision for preparation of the site (cl. 7.01.02). In this way, the clause placing on Hydro the obligation to clear the right of way can be reconciled with the clauses placing on Checo the consequences of errors and misunderstandings in the tender documents and the obligation to satisfy itself as to the site, the work and contingencies.

We thus conclude that the contract required Hydro to clear the right of way as specified in cl. 6.01.03 of the contract and that duty was not negated by the more general clauses relating to errors and misunderstandings in tendering, site conditions and contingencies. This was the view of the trial judge . . . and the majority in the Court of Appeal. . . . The trial judge, based on the evidence he heard, went on to define what "clearing" meant in the contract; it meant that "the right-of-way would be free of logs and debris". The majority of the Court of Appeal accepted this conclusion. So must we. Since it is not seriously contended that Hydro cleared the right of way to this standard, Hydro's breach of contract is established.

. . . The measure of damages is what is required to put Checo in the position it would have been in had the contract been performed as agreed. If the contract had been performed as agreed, Hydro would have removed the logs and debris from the right of way. Checo would not have been required to do the additional work that was necessitated by reason of the worksite being improperly cleared. It might also have avoided certain overhead. The contract stipulated 15% for overhead and profit on extra work. Checo may be entitled to a portion of this sum for overhead. It would not be entitled to profit on the cost of clearing the right of way, since that would put Checo in a better position than it would have been had Hydro performed its contract; Checo never bargained for profit on this work, which was totally outside the parties' expectations. [W]e share Iacobucci J.'s view that if damages are to be assessed for breach of contract regarding the improper clearing of the worksite, the case should be returned to trial for that to be done.

The claim in tort

The theory of concurrency

The first question is whether the contract precludes Checo from suing in tort.

Iacobucci J. concludes that a contract between the parties may preclude the possibility of suing in tort for a given wrong where there is an express term in the contract dealing with the matter. We would phrase the applicable principle somewhat more narrowly. As we see it, the right to sue in tort is not taken away by the contract in such a case, although the contract, by limiting the scope of the tort duty or waiving the right to sue in tort, may limit or negate tort liability.

In our view, the general rule emerging from this court's decision in *Central Trust Co. v. Rafuse* [*supra*] is that where a given wrong *prima facie* supports an action in contract and in tort, the party may sue in either or both, except where the contract indicates that the parties intended to limit or negative the right to sue in tort. This limitation on the general rule of concurrency arises because it is always open to parties to limit or waive the duties which the common law would impose on them for negligence. This principle is of great importance in preserving a sphere of individual liberty and commercial flexibility. Thus, if a person wishes to engage in a dangerous sport, the person may stipulate in advance that he or she waives any right of action against the person who operates the sport facility: *Dyck v. Manitoba Snowmobile Ass'n Inc.*, [1985] 1 S.C.R. 589. Similarly, if two business firms agree that a particular risk should lie on a party who would not ordinarily bear that risk at common law, they may do so. So a plaintiff may sue either in contract or tort, subject to any limit the parties themselves have placed on that right by their contract. The mere fact that the parties have dealt with a matter expressly in their contract does not mean that they intended to exclude the right to sue in tort. It all depends on *how* they have dealt with it.

Viewed thus, the only limit on the right to choose one's action is the principle of primacy of private ordering—the right of individuals to arrange their affairs and assume risks in a different way than would be done by the law of tort. It is only to the extent that this private ordering contradicts the tort duty that the tort duty is diminished. The rule is not that one cannot sue concurrently in contract and tort where the contract limits or contradicts the tort duty. It is rather that the tort duty, a general duty imputed by the law in all the relevant circumstances, must yield to the parties' superior right to arrange their rights and duties in a different way. In so far as the tort duty is not contradicted by the contract, it remains intact and may be sued upon. For example, where the contractual limitation on the tort duty is partial, a tort action founded on the modified duty might lie. The tort duty as modified by the contractual agreement between the parties might be raised in a case where the limitation period for an action for breach of contract has expired but the limitation period for a tort action has not. If one says categorically, as we understand Iacobucci J. to say, that where the contract deals with a matter expressly, the right to sue in tort vanishes altogether, then the latter two possibilities vanish.

This is illustrated by consideration of the three situations that may arise when contract and tort are applied to the same wrong. The first class of case arises where the contract stipulates a more stringent obligation than the general law of tort would impose. In that case, the parties are hardly likely to sue in tort, since they could not recover in tort for the higher contractual duty. The vast majority of commercial transactions fall into this class. The right to sue in tort is not extinguished, however, and may remain important, as where suit in contract is barred by expiry of a limitation period.

The second class of case arises where the contract stipulates a lower duty than that which would be presumed by the law of tort in similar circumstances. This occurs when the parties by their contract indicate their intention that the usual liability imposed by the law of tort is not to bind them. The most common means by which such an intention is indicated is the inclusion of a clause of exemption or exclusion of liability in the contract. Generally, the duty imposed by the law of tort can be nullified only by clear terms. We do not rule out, however, the possibility that cases may arise in which merely inconsistent contract terms could negative or limit a duty in tort, an issue that may be left to a case in which it arises. The issue raises difficult policy considerations, *viz.*, an assessment of the circumstances in which contracting parties should be permitted to agree to contractual duties that would subtract from their general obligations under the law of tort. These important questions are best left to a case in which the proper factual foundation is available, so as to provide an appropriate context for the decision. In the second class of case, as in the first, there is usually little point in suing in tort since the duty in tort and consequently any tort liability is limited by the specific limitation to which the parties have agreed. An exception might arise where the contract does not entirely negate tort liability (*e.g.*, the exemption clause applies only above a certain amount) and the plaintiff wishes to sue in tort to avail itself of a more generous limitation period or some other procedural advantage offered by tort.

The third class of case arises where the duty in contract and the common law duty in tort are co-extensive. In this class of case, like the others, the plaintiff may seek to sue concurrently or alternatively in tort to secure some advantage peculiar to the law of tort, such as a more generous limitation period. The contract may expressly provide for a duty that is the same as that imposed by the common law; or the contractual duty may be implied. The common calling cases, which have long permitted concurrent actions in contract and tort, generally fall into this class. There is a contract. But the obligation under that contract is typically defined by implied terms, *i.e.*, by the courts. Thus, there is no issue of private ordering as opposed to publicly imposed liability. Whether the action is styled in contract or tort, its source is an objective expectation, defined by the courts, of the appropriate obligation and the correlative right.

The case at bar, as we see it, falls into this third category of case. The contract, read as we have proposed, did not negate Hydro's common law duty not to negligently misrepresent that it would have the right of way cleared by others. Had Checo known the truth, it would have bid for a higher amount. That duty is not excluded by the contract, which confirmed Hydro's obligation to clear the right of way. Accordingly, Checo may sue in tort.

We conclude that actions in contract and tort may be concurrently pursued unless the parties by a valid contractual provision indicate that they intended otherwise. This excludes, of course, cases where the contractual limitation is invalid, as by fraud, mistake or unconscionability. Similarly, a contractual limitation may not apply where the tort is independent of the contract in the sense of falling outside the scope of the contract, as the example given in *Elder, Dempster & Co., Ltd. v. Paterson, Zochonis & Co., Ltd.*, [1924] A.C. 522 (H.L.), of the captain of a vessel falling asleep and starting a fire in relation to a claim for cargo damage.

The express-implied distinction

Our colleague asserts that where the parties deal with a matter expressly in their contract, all right to sue in tort is lost. We have suggested, with great respect, that this proposition in unnecessarily Draconian. The converse of this proposition is that implied terms of contracts do not oust tort liability.

Although Iacobucci J. states . . . that he is leaving open the question of "Whether or not an implied term of a contract can define a duty of care in such a way that a plaintiff is confined to a remedy in contract", the distinction between implied and express terms figures in his discussion of the effect of contract terms on tort liability. For example, . . . our colleague states:

> The compromise position adopted by Le Dain J. was that any duty arising in tort will be concurrent with duties arising under the contract, *unless the duty which the plaintiff seeks to rely on in tort is also a duty defined by an express term of the contract.*

(The emphasis is Iacobucci J.'s.) It would seem to follow from this statement that concurrent duties in contract and tort would lie where the contract duty is defined by an *implied* term of the contract, but not where the term is express. In these circumstances, it is not amiss to consider the utility of the distinction between express and implied terms of the contract as a basis for determining when a contract term may affect tort liability.

In our view, using the express-implied distinction as a basis for determining whether there is a right to sue in tort poses a number of problems. The law has always treated express and implied contract terms as being equivalent in effect. Breach of an implied term is just as serious as breach of an express term. Moreover, it is difficult to distinguish between them in some cases. Implied terms may arise from custom, for example, or from the conduct of the parties. In some cases words and conduct intermingle. Why should parties who were so certain in their obligations that they did not take the trouble to spell them out find themselves able to sue in tort, while parties who put the same matters in writing cannot?

Nor is it evident to us that if parties to a contract choose to include an express term in the contract dealing with a particular duty relevant to the contract, they intended to oust the availability of tort remedies in respect of that duty. In such cases, the intention may more likely be:

(a) to make it clear that the parties understand particular contractual duties to exist as between them, rather than having the more uncertain situation of not knowing whether a court will imply a particular duty under the contract; and/or

(b) to prevent litigation (for breach of contract) in the event of disputes arising—the more certain the parties' respective rights and obligations (as is usually the case when those rights and obligations are set out in express contractual terms), the more likely it will be that disputes between the parties can be settled.

While the tort duty may be limited by the contractual terms so as to be no broader than the contract duty, there is no reason to suppose that merely by stipulating a duty in the contract, the parties intended to negate all possibility of suing in tort.

Indeed, a little further on in his reasons, our colleague appears to concede that the ouster of recourse to tort law must depend on more than the fact the contract has expressly dealt with the matter. He indicates . . . that whether the parties will be held to have intended to oust tort remedies in favour of contracts will depend on the context, including:

(a) whether the contract is commercial or non-commercial:

(b) whether the parties were of equal bargaining power;

(c) whether the court is of the view that to find such an intention will lead to an unjust result in the court action.

Thus, the question of whether a concurrent action in tort lies would depend not only on whether the contract expressly deals with the matter, but also on the elastic distinctions between commercial and non-commercial contracts, the court's perception of relative bargaining power and, finally, whether the court sees the result as just or unjust. We do not agree that parties contracting in a commercial context should be presumed to be more desirous of ousting the availability of tort remedies than parties contracting in a non-commercial context. If there are particular commercial relationships in which the parties wish remedies for disputes between them to be in contract only, then they may be expected to indicate this intention by including an express clause in the contract waiving the right to sue in tort. As for equality of bargaining power and the court's view of whether the result would be just or unjust, we fear they would introduce too great a measure of uncertainty. Parties should be able to predict in advance whether their remedies are confined to contract or whether they can sue concurrently in tort and contract. Finally, it seems to us that Iacobucci J.'s test for determining when concurrent liability is precluded will be difficult to apply in situations where the express contractual term does not exactly overlap a tort duty. In the present case, the contractual term was identical to the negligent misrepresentation, but that is not often to be expected.

[La Forest and McLachlin JJ. then reviewed the authorities and concluded that they do not support the view "that the express mention of a matter in the contract, and only its express mention in the contract, ousts any possibility of suing in tort". They then concluded that it was open to the plaintiff, on the present facts, to claim for negligent misrepresentation in tort as well as breach of contract. Sopinka J. concurred with Iacobucci J. L'Heureux-Dubé and Gonthier JJ. concurred with La Forest and McLachlin JJ. The appeal was dismissed and the cross-appeal was allowed in part.]

NOTE and QUESTION

1. Why would a plaintiff prefer to sue in tort or in contract in a case where both causes of action are available?

2. On the same day the court handed down its decision in *BG Checo, supra*, the court released its decision in *Queen v. Cognos Inc.*, [1993] 1 S.C.R. 87. In that case, the defendant employer, while negotiating a contract of employment with the plaintiff, failed to reveal that the project for which the plaintiff was to be hired had not received final approval. The employment agreement which the parties entered provided for termination on one month's notice. The project was not approved. Upon termination, the plaintiff brought a claim for damages for negligent misrepresentation. The Supreme Court allowed recovery on this basis.

La Forest J., with L'Heureux-Dubé and Gonthier JJ. concurring, concluded that the tort was independent of the contract and, accordingly, that no issue of concurrency arose. Iacobucci J., with Sopinka J. concurring, stated that neither the termination clause nor any other provision of the agreement precluded the defendant's liability in tort. McLachlin J. came to the same conclusion on the basis that the pre-contractual representation was different in scope and effect from the contractual obligation.

6.   The Parol Evidence Rule

(a)   THE SCOPE AND RATIONALE OF THE RULE

Section 3 of this chapter addressed the distinction between terms of the contract and mere representations outside the contract. What if there is a document that appears to contain all the terms of the contract, indeed it may even say so, but one party argues that there was a further oral term? Consider, for example, a variation of the "good little bus" issue introducing section 3. Smith sells Jones a two-year old, one owner car for $5,000. At the time the contract is being negotiated, Smith tells Jones that the car has only done 40,000 kilometres. On hearing this Jones says, "In that case, I'll take it." He then signs a document presented to him by Smith which, among other clauses, states the following:

(34) This car has clocked between 60,000 and 70,000 kilometres.

(35) This written contract contains all the agreement between the parties and none of the parties shall be bound by any representation not contained herein.

Jones then drives off and, before he is half-way home, the car breaks down. A mechanic pronounces it beyond repair and indicates that it has been driven for 65,000 kilometres. The parol evidence rule relates to the question of whether Jones can rely on Smith's fraudulent misrepresentation in endeavouring to obtain relief.

If the rule is applied, it has the effect of excluding from the court's consideration evidence as to oral (and indeed written) statements preceding or contemporaneous with completion of "the" written contract. Prior statements, whether promises or affirmations, are thus confined to the status of mere representations. In other words, the rule presents a possible barrier to the analysis examined in section 3.

The rule should be distinguished from the body of law relating to extrinsic evidence in aid of the interpretation rather than the modification of written contracts. The distinction is pointed out by the English Law Commission in its 1986 Report, *The Parol Evidence Rule*, Law Comm. No. 154, at 1-2. However, it added that this distinction is "not always easy to see in practice; for example, where parol evidence is admitted to the effect that the expression '1000 rabbits' in a contract means '1200 rabbits', it is not clear", at least without further information, whether that evidence is being admitted for the purposes of interpretation (*i.e.*, for the parties "1000" means "1200") or for the purposes of modifying "the" written contract in some way. In most cases, particularly given the restrictions placed by Canadian courts on the admissibility of extrinsic evidence to interpret a document, it will in fact be the latter, most commonly in the context of an action for the equitable remedy of rectification.

Both the rule limiting the use of extrinsic evidence as a guide to interpretation and the parol evidence rule which is the subject of this section were used by the Supreme Court of Canada in *R. v. Horse*, [1988] 1 S.C.R. 187. In this case Treaty Indians in Saskatchewan tried to use the transcript of negotiations surrounding Treaty No. 6 between the Indians and the Queen's representatives to show that they had a right to hunt on private land. The passage relied upon was as follows:

[Chief Tee-Tee-Quay-Say said at p. 215:] '. . . We want to be at liberty to hunt on any place as usual . . .'

"[Lieutenant Governor Morris replied at p. 218:] 'You want to be at liberty to hunt as before. I told you we do not want to take that means of living from you, you have it the same as before, only this, if a man, whether Indian or half-breed, had a good field of grain, you would not destroy it with your hunt . . .'" Morris, *The Treaties of Canada with the Indians of Manitoba and the North-West Territories* (1880).

The Treaty, however, excepted "such tracts as may from time to time be required or taken up for settlement" from the right to hunt. Estey J., delivering the judgment of the court, stated at 222:

I have some reservations about the use of this material as an aid to interpreting the terms of Treaty No. 6. In my view the terms are not ambiguous. The normal rule with respect to interpretation of contractual documents is that extrinsic evidence is not to be used in the absence of ambiguity; nor can it be invoked where the result would be to alter the terms of a document by adding to or subtracting from the written agreement.

The result was that the Treaty Indians were convicted of hunting contrary to the Wildlife Act, S.S. 1979, c. W-13.1. (Though see now *Marshall v. Canada* (1999), 177 D.L.R. (4th) 513 (S.C.C.) in which the court held that even in the context of a treaty document that purports to contain all the terms, extrinsic evidence of the historical and cultural context is admissible even without any ambiguity on the face of the treaty.)

There are "exceptions". Rectification, which is considered in Chapter 9, section 5, involves one of the most readily court accepted "exceptions" to the parol evidence rule in its traditional form. Rectification allows proof by extrinsic evidence that the parties made an agreement, but then recorded it incorrectly, so that the court may correct the inaccurate written document.

However, even beyond the ready acceptance by the courts of parol evidence extrinsic to the contract when rectification is being sought, there are also numerous other situations, where in interpreting an agreement such evidence will be admitted for the purposes of modifying the written contract in some way. Canadian courts continue, nevertheless, to mouth the parol evidence rule as if it still represents a severe limitation on the use of extrinsic evidence. For example, in *Leitch Tpt. Ltd. v. Neonex Int. Ltd.* (1979), 106 D.L.R. (3d) 315, the Ontario Court of Appeal stated, in a case which was really about the use of extrinsic evidence as a guide to interpretation, that it was "a cardinal rule" of the common law.

The question that you should be asking yourselves, however, as you work your way through this section, is whether it is a "cardinal rule" without any substance or it in fact involves a tautology. At the outset, consider the following problem and the extent to which the parol evidence rule might or should affect the resolution of it. Then, at the end of the section, return to it and consider it in the light of the readings.

ZELL v. AMERICAN SEATING CO.

183 F. 2d 642 (C.C.A., 2nd Circ., 1943)

Appeal from a summary judgment dismissing the plaintiff's action.

FRANK C.J. Plaintiff, by a letter addressed to defendant company dated October 17, 1941, offered to make efforts to procure for defendant contracts for manufacturing products for national defence or war purposes, in consideration of defendant's agreement to pay him $1,000 per month for a three months' period if he were unsuccessful in his efforts, but, if he were successful, to pay him a further sum in an amount not to be less than 3% nor more than 8% of the "purchase price of said contracts." On October 31, 1941, at a meeting in Grand Rapids, Michigan, between plaintiff and defendant's President, the latter, on behalf of his company, orally made an agreement with plaintiff substantially on the terms set forth in plaintiff's letter, one of the terms being that mentioned in plaintiff's letter as to commissions; it was orally agreed that the exact amount within the two percentages was to be later determined by the parties. After this agreement was made, the parties executed, in Grand Rapids, a written instrument dated October 31, 1941, appearing on its face to embody a complete agreement between them; but that writing omitted the provision of their agreement that plaintiff, if successful, was to receive a bonus varying from three to eight per cent; instead, there was inserted in the writing a clause that the $1,000 per month "will be full compensation, but the company may, if it desires, pay you something in the nature of a bonus." However, at the time when they executed this writing, the parties orally agreed that the previous oral agreement was still their actual contract, that the writing was deliberately erroneous with respect to plaintiff's commissions, and that the misstatement in that writing was made solely in order to "avoid any possible stigma which might result: from putting such a provision "in writing," the defendant's President stating that "his fears were based upon the criticism of contingent fee contracts." Nothing in the record discloses whose criticism the defendant feared, but plaintiff, in his brief, says that defendant was apprehensive because adverse comments had been made in Congress of such contingent fee arrangements in connection with war contracts. The parties subsequently executed further writings extending, for two three-month periods, their "agreement under date of October 31, 1941." Through plaintiff's efforts and expenditures of large sums for travelling expenses, defendant, within this extended period, procured contracts between it and companies supplying aircraft to the government for war purposes, the aggregate purchase price named in said contracts being $5,950,000. The defendant has refused to pay the plaintiff commissions thereon in the agreed amount (i.e., not less than three percent) but has paid him merely $8,950 (at the rate of $1,000 a month) and has offered him, by way of settlement, an additional sum of $9,000 which he has refused to accept as full payment.

Defendant argues that the summary judgment was proper on the ground that, under the parol evidence rule, the court could not properly consider as relevant anything except the writing of October 31, 1941, which appears on its face to set forth a complete and unambiguous agreement between the parties. If defendant on this point is in error, then, if the plaintiff at a trial proves the facts as alleged by him, and no other defenses are successfully interposed, he will be entitled to a sum equal to 3% of $5,950,000. . . .

It is not surprising that confusion results from a rule called "the parol evidence rule" which is not a rule of evidence, which relates to extrinsic proof whether written or parol, and which has been said to be virtually no rule at all. As Thayer said of it, "Few things are darker than this, or fuller of subtle difficulties." The rule is often loosely and confusingly stated as if, once the evidence establishes that the parties executed a writing containing what appears to be a complete and unambiguous agreement, then no evidence may be received of previous or contemporaneous oral understandings which contradict or vary its terms. But, under the parol evidence rule correctly stated, such a writing does not acquire that dominating position if it has been proved by extrinsic evidence that the parties did not intend it to be an exclusive authoritative memorial of their agreement. If they did intend it to occupy that position, their secret mutual intentions as to the terms of the contract or its meaning are usually irrelevant, so that parties who exchange promises may be bound, at least "at law" as distinguished from "equity," in a way which neither intended, since their so called "objective" intent governs. When, however, they have previously agreed that their written promises are not to bind them, that agreement controls and no legal obligations flow from the writing. It has been held virtually everywhere, when the question has arisen that (certainly in the absence of any fraudulent or illegal purpose) a purported written agreement, which the parties designed as a mere sham, lacks legal efficacy, and that extrinsic parol or other extrinsic evidence will always be received on that issue. So the highest court of Michigan has several times held. It has gone further. In *Woodward v. Walker*, 158 N.W. 846, that court specifically enforced against the seller an oral agreement for the sale of land which had been followed by a sham written agreement, for sale of the same land at a higher price, intended to deceive the seller's children who were jealous of the buyer. . . .

Candor compels the admission that, were we enthusiastic devotees of that rule, we might so construe the record as to bring this case within the rule's scope; we could dwell on the fact that plaintiff, in his complaint, states that the acceptance of his offer "was partly oral and partly contained" in the October 31 writing, and could then hold that, as that writing unambiguously covers the item of commissions, the plaintiff is trying to use extrinsic evidence to "contradict" the writing. But the plaintiff's affidavit, if accepted as true and liberally construed, makes it plain that the parties deliberately intended the October 31 writing to be a misleading, untrue statement of their real agreement.

We thus construe the record because we do not share defendant's belief that the rule is so beneficent, so promotive of the administration of justice, and so necessary to business stability, that it should be given the widest possible application. The truth is that the rule does but little to achieve the ends it supposedly serves. Although seldom mentioned in modern decisions, the most important motive for perpetuation of the rule is distrust of juries, fear that they cannot adequately cope with, or will be unfairly prejudiced by, conflicting "parol" testimony. If the rule were frankly recognized as primarily a device to control juries, its shortcomings would become obvious, since it is not true that the execution by the parties of an unambiguous writing, "facially complete," bars extrinsic proof. The courts admit such "parol" testimony (other than the parties' statements of what they meant by the writing) for a variety of purposes: to show "all the operative usages" and "all the surrounding circumstances prior to and contemporaneous with the making" of a writing; to show an agreed oral condition, nowhere referred to in the writing, that the writing was not to be binding until some third person approved; to show that a deed, absolute on its face, is but a mortgage. These and numerous other exceptions have removed most of that insulation of the jury from "oral" testimony which the rule is said to provide.

The rule, then, does relatively little to deserve its much advertised virtue of reducing the dangers of successful fraudulent recoveries and defenses brought about through perjury. The rule is too small a hook to catch such a leviathan. Moreover, if at times it does prevent a person from winning, by lying witnesses, a lawsuit which he should lose, it also, at times, by shutting out the true facts, unjustly aids other persons to win lawsuits they should and would lose, were the suppressed evidence known to the courts. Exclusionary rules, which frequently result in injustice, have always been defended—as was the rule, now fortunately extinct, excluding testimony of the parties to an action—with the danger-of-perjury argument. Perjury, of course, is pernicious and doubtless much of it is used in our courts daily with unfortunate success. The problem of avoiding its efficacious use should be met head on. Were it consistently met in an indirect manner—in accordance with the viewpoint of the adulators of the parol evidence rule—by wiping out substantive rights provable only through oral testimony, we would have wholesale destruction of familiar causes of action such as, for instance, suits for personal injury and for enforcement of wholly oral agreements.

The parol evidence rule is lauded as an important aid in the judicial quest for "objectivity," a quest which aims to avoid that problem the solution of which was judicially said in the latter part of the fifteenth century to be beyond even the powers of Satan—the discovery of the inner thoughts of man. The policy of stern refusal to consider subjective intention, prevalent in the centralized common law courts of that period, later gave way; in the latter part of the 18th and the early part of the 19th century, the recession from that policy went far, and there was much talk of the "meeting of the minds" in the formation of contracts, of giving effect to the actual "will" of the contracting parties. The obstacles to learning that actual intention have, more recently, induced a partial reversion to the older view. Today a court generally restricts its attention to the outward behaviour of the parties: the meaning of their acts is not what either party or both parties intended but the meaning which a "reasonable man" puts on those acts; the expression of mutual assent, not the assent itself, is usually the essential element. We now speak of "externality," insisting on judicial consideration of only those manifestations of intention which are public ("open to the scrutiny and knowledge of the community") and not private ("secreted in the heart" of a person). This objective approach is of great value, for a legal system can be more effectively administered if legal rights and obligations ordinarily attach only to overt conduct. Moreover, to call the standard "objective" and candidly to confess that the actual intention is not the guiding factor serves desirably to high-light the fact that much of the "law of contracts" has nothing whatever to do with what the parties contemplated but consists of rules—founded on considerations of public policy—by which the courts impose on the contracting parties obligations of which the parties were often unaware; this "objective" perspective discloses that the voluntary act of entering into a contract creates a jural "relation" or "status" much in the same way as does being married or holding a public office.

But we should not demand too much of this concept of "objectivity"; like all useful concepts it becomes a thought-muddler if its limitations are disregarded. We can largely rid ourselves of concern with the subjective reasons of the parties; when, however, we test their public behavior by inquiring how it appears to the "reasonable man," we must recognize, unless we wish to fool ourselves, that although one area of subjectivity has been conquered, another remains unsubdued. For instance, under the parol evidence rule, the standard of interpretation of a written contract is usually "the meaning that would be attached to" it "by a *reasonably intelligent person* acquainted with all operative usages and knowing all the circumstances prior to, and contemporaneous with, the making" of the contract, "other than oral statements by the parties of what they intended it to mean." We say that "the objective viewpoint of a third person is used." But where do we find that "objective" third person? We ask judges or juries to discover that "objective viewpoint"—through their own subjective processes. Being but human, their beliefs cannot be objectified, in the sense of being standardized. Doubtless, there is some moderate approximation to objectivity, that is, to uniformity of beliefs, among judges—men with substantially similar training—although less than is sometimes supposed. But no one can seriously maintain that such uniformity exists among the multitude of jurymen, men with the greatest conceivable variety of training and background. When juries try cases, objectivity is largely a mirage; most of the objectivity inheres in the words of the "reasonable man" standard which the judges, often futilely, admonish juries to apply to the evidence. Certain aspects of subjectivity common to all men seem to have been successfully eliminated in the field of science through the "relativity theory"—which might better be called the "anti-relativity" or "absolute" theory. But equal success has not attended the anti-relativity or objective theory in the legal field. Perhaps nine-tenths of legal uncertainty is caused by uncertainty as to what courts will find, on conflicting evidence, to be the facts of cases. Early in the history of our legal institutions, litigants strongly objected to a determination of the facts by mere fallible human beings. A man, they felt, ought to be allowed to demonstrate the facts "by supernatural means, by some such process as the ordeal or the judicial combat; God may be for him, though his neighbors be against him." We have accepted the "rational" method of trial based on evidence but the longing persists for some means of counter-acting the fallibility of the triers of the facts. Mechanical devices, like the parol evidence rule, are symptoms of that longing, a longing particularly strong when juries participate in trials. But a mechanical device like the parol evidence rule cannot satisfy that longing, especially because the injustice of applying the rule rigidly has led to its being riddled with exceptions.

Those exceptions have, too, played havoc with the contention that business stability depends upon that rule, that, as one court put it "the tremendous but closely adjusted machinery of modern business cannot function at all without" the assurance afforded by the rule and that, "if such assurance were removed today from our law, general disaster would result. . . ." We are asked to believe that the rule enables businessmen, advised by their lawyers, to rely with indispensable confidence on written contracts unimpeachable by oral testimony. In fact, seldom can a conscientious lawyer advise his client, about to sign an agreement, that, should the client become involved in litigation relating to that agreement, one of the many exceptions to the rule will not permit the introduction of uncertainty-producing oral testimony. As Corbin says, "That rule has so many exceptions that only with difficulty can it be correctly stated in the form of a rule." One need but thumb the pages of Wigmore, Williston, or the Restatement of Contracts to see how illusory is the certainty that the rule supplies. "Collateral parol agreements contradicting a writing are inadmissible," runs the rule as ordinarily stated; but in the application of that standard there exists, as Williston notes, "no final test which can be applied with unvarying regularity." Wigmore more bluntly says that only vague generalizations are possible, since the application of the rule, "resting as it does on the parties' intent, can properly be made only after a comparison of the kind of transaction, the terms of the document, and the circumstances of the parties . . ." Such is the complexity of circumstances and the variety of documentary phraseology, and so minute the indicia of intent, that one ruling can seldom be controlling authority or even of utility for a subsequent one. The recognized exceptions to the rule demonstrate strikingly that business can endure even when oral testimony competes with written instruments. If business stability has not been ruined by the deed-mortgage exception, or because juries may hear witnesses narrate oral understandings that written contracts were not to be operative except on the performance of extrinsic conditions, it is unlikely that commercial disaster would follow even if legislatures abolished the rule in its entirety.

In sum, a rule so leaky cannot fairly be described as a stout container of legal certainty. John Chipman Gray, a seasoned practical lawyer, expressed grave doubts concerning the reliance of businessmen on legal precedents generally. If they rely on the parol evidence rule in particular, they will often be duped. It has been seriously questioned whether in fact they do so to any considerable extent. We see no good reason why we should strain to interpret the record facts here to bring them within such a rule.

Reversed and remanded.

[Footnotes omitted.]

NOTES and QUESTIONS

1. On further appeal *Zell* was reversed by the Supreme Court of the United States, 322 U.S. 709 (1943), with a 7 to 2 majority. Four members of the majority considered that the parol evidence rule precluded use of the affidavit evidence and three considered the contract void as being contrary to public policy.

2. Frank C.J. asserts that there is a "loosely and confusingly stated" version of the rule which he then sets out to correct. What are the two versions of the rule and what is the difference between them? What are the policy arguments for and against each version?

3. Why is Frank C.J. out of sympathy with the parol evidence rule and its perceived objectives? Should his arguments prevail in Canada?

4. Consider the gloss that he places upon the so-called "objective" theory of contract. In the light of your previous readings, do you find this acceptable?

5. Why precisely did Frank C.J. consider the parol evidence as to the commission in this case? Does this not add to, vary, or contradict the written instrument? It has been asserted that to accept the proposition put forward in *Zell* results in the whole parol evidence rule becoming a tautology. Consider the following comments by Wedderburn, "Collateral Contracts", [1959] Camb. L.J. 58 at 60:

> [There is] . . . another limitation upon the parol evidence rule, one which causes the rule to be no more than a self-evident tautology. The rule applies only if the document is intended to be the whole contract. If, therefore, the parties intended to make a contract partly oral and partly written, there is no objection to parol evidence being introduced to prove the oral terms. Thus, the "rule" comes to this: when the writing is the whole contract, the parties are bound by it and parol evidence is excluded; when it is not, evidence of the other terms must be admitted! To say this is to say little more than that the parties are bound, as usual, by the terms which, from an objective point of view, were "intended" by them to be contractually binding; and the peculiar difficulties introduced by the writing have been conjured away.

Later, at 62, Wedderburn summarizes the effect of the jurisprudence on the parol evidence rule in these terms:

> What the parol evidence rule has bequeathed to the modern law is a presumption—namely that a document which *looks* like a contract is to be treated as a *whole* contract. This presumption is "very strong" but it is a presumption only, and it is open to either of the parties to allege that there was, in addition to what appears in the written agreement, an antecedent express stipulation not intended by the parties to be excluded, but intended to continue in force with the express written agreement. [Quoting Lord Russell of Killowen C.J. in *Gillespie Bros v. Cheney, Eggar & Co.*, [1896] 2 Q.B. 59 at 62.]

6. If it is correct, as Wedderburn suggests, to treat the rule as no more than a presumption, what factors would be relevant in considering whether effect should be given to the presumption? Mc-Lauchlan in his book, *The Parol Evidence Rule* (1976) at 144 provides this analysis:

> The following are the most important factors which will affect the strength of the presumption of completeness or the weight to be attached to the parol testimony:
>
> (a) the nature of the writing, its form and contents.
>
> (b) whether the writing has been signed.
>
> (c) the status of the parties.
>
> (d) the circumstances surrounding the preparation of the document.
>
> (e) the subsequent conduct of the parties.
>
> (f) whether the contract is in a standard form.
>
> (g) the nature and effect of the parol testimony.
>
> (h) the presence of a merger clause in the writing.

Although some of these factors will be stronger indications of the parties' supposed intention than others, none will necessarily be decisive. They only affect the quality of the evidence required to rebut the presumption. The whole question is one of *weight*, not *admissibility*. For instance, the fact that the alleged oral term is *inconsistent* with, and not merely *additional* to, the written terms, is not decisive. Although it is more likely that evidence of an additional oral term will be believed, the mere fact that the evidence contradicts the written terms does not necessarily prove that it is untrue. Other evidence may convince the court that the oral agreement was in fact made. In this event, there is a contract partly in writing and partly oral, an unwritten contract which is partly evidenced in writing. It is for the court to reconcile inconsistencies and to determine as best it can from all the evidence what was the parties' true agreement in accordance with the same principles of interpretation as apply when a contract is contained in two or more documents.

7. Frank C.J. notes a few of the so-called "exceptions" to the rule, including the well established exception that evidence is admissible to show that the parties' intention was that the enforceability of the agreement was to be dependent on the approval of a third party. (*Pym v. Campbell* (1856), 119 E.R. 903.) Similarly, it has been held that evidence that the agreement is dependent on the happening of a certain event is admissible. (*Western Log Exchange Ltd. v. Soucie Const. Ltd.* (1979), 14 B.C.L.R. 293, affirmed on other grounds, 21 B.C.L.R. 57 (C.A.).) Evidence is also admissible to show that a consideration stated to have passed in a deed has not, in fact, been paid. (*Re Lang Estate*, [1919] 1 W.W.R. 651.) Conversely, where a deed does not show a consideration, evidence that it has passed is also admissible. (*Cleveland v. Boak* (1906), 39 N.S.R. 39 (C.A.).) The rule does not preclude evidence of collateral agreements (*Long v. Smith* (1911), 23 O.L.R. 121 (C.A.); *Ferland v. Keith* (1958), 15 D.L.R. (2d) 472 (Ont. C.A.).) Nor does it preclude evidence of subsequent agreements to vary or rescind an existing agreement. (*Barber v. Glen*, [1987] 6 W.W.R. 689 (Sask C.A.).) Nor would the rule preclude evidence relating to the validity of an agreement on grounds such as fraud, undue influence, mistake and the like. It is also sometimes stated, as in *Zell*, that the rule does not apply where it is demonstrated that the agreement is intended to be partly oral and partly in writing. (*Wake v. Harrop* (1861), 158 E.R. 317 at 320. See also, *J. Evans & Son (Portsmouth) Ltd. v. Merzario (Andrea) Ltd., infra*). The status of this exception in Canadian law must be considered carefully in the light of the two following decisions of the Supreme Court of Canada.

HAWRISH v. BANK OF MONTREAL

[1969] S.C.R. 515, 66 W.W.R. 673, 2 D.L.R. (3d) 600

JUDSON J. [delivering the judgment of the court] This action was brought by the Bank of Montreal against Andrew Hawrish, a solicitor in Saskatoon, on a guarantee which the solicitor had signed for the indebtedness and liability of a newly formed company, Crescent Dairies Limited. This company had been formed for the purpose of buying the assets of Waldheim Dairies Limited, a cheese factory in which Hawrish had an interest.

By January, 1959, the line of credit granted by the bank to the new company was almost exhausted. The bank then asked Hawrish for a guarantee, which he signed on January 30, 1959. The guarantee was on the bank's usual form and stated that it was to be a continuing guarantee and to cover existing as well as future indebtedness of the company up to the amount of $6,000.

The defence was that when he signed the guarantee, Hawrish had an oral assurance from the assistant manager of the branch that the guarantee was to cover only existing indebtedness and that he would be released from his guarantee when the bank obtained a joint guarantee from the directors of the company. The bank did obtain a joint guarantee from the directors on July 22, 1959, for the sum of $10,000. Another joint guarantee for the same amount was signed by the directors on March 22, 1960. Between the dates of these two last-mentioned guarantees there had been some changes in the directorate.

Hawrish was never a director or officer of the new company but at the time when the action was commenced, he was a shareholder and he was interested in the vendor company. At all times the new company was indebted to the vendor company in an amount between $10,000 and $15,000. Hawrish says that he did not read the guarantee before signing. On February 20, 1961, Crescent Dairies Ltd., whose overdraft was at that time $8,000, became insolvent. The bank then brought its action against Hawrish for the full amount of his guarantee—$6,000.

The trial Judge dismissed the bank's action. He accepted the guarantor's evidence of what was said before the guarantee was signed and held that parol evidence was admissible on the ground that it was a condition of signing the guarantee that the appellant would be released as soon as a joint guarantee was obtained from the directors. . . .

The relevant provisions of this guarantee may be summarized as follows:

(a) It guarantees the present and future debts and liabilities of the customer (Crescent Dairies Ltd.) up to the sum of $6,000.

(b) It is a continuing guarantee and secures the ultimate balance owing by the customer.

(c) The guarantor may determine at any time his further liability under the guarantee by notice in writing to the bank. The liability of the guarantor continues until determined by such notice.

(d) The guarantor acknowledges that no representations have been made to him on behalf of the bank; that the liability of the guarantor is embraced in the guarantee; that the guarantee has nothing to do with any other guarantee; and that the guarantor intends the guarantee to be binding whether any other guarantee or security is given to the bank or not.

The argument before us was confined to two submissions of error contained in the reasons of the Court of Appeal:

(a) that the contemporaneous oral agreement found by the trial Judge neither varied nor contradicted the terms of the written guarantee but simply provided by an independent agreement a manner in which the liability of the appellant would be terminated; and

(b) that oral evidence proving the making of such agreement, the consideration for which was the signing of the guarantee, was admissible.

I cannot accept these submissions. In my opinion, there was no error in the reasons of the Court of Appeal. This guarantee was to be immediately effective. According to the oral evidence it was to terminate as to all liability, present or future, when the new guarantees were obtained from the directors. But the document itself states that it was to be a continuing guarantee for all present and future liabilities and could only be terminated by notice in writing, and then only as to future liabilities incurred by the customer after the giving of the notice. The oral evidence is also in plain contradiction of the terms of para. (d) of my summary above made. There is nothing in this case to permit the introduction of the principle in *Pym v. Campbell* (1856), 119 E.R. 903, which holds that the parol evidence rule does not prevent a defendant from showing that a document formally complete and signed as a contract, was in fact only an escrow.

The appellant further submitted that the parol evidence was admissible on the ground that it established an oral agreement which was independent of and collateral to the main contract.

In the last half of the 19th century a group of English decisions, of which *Lindley v. Lacey* (1864), 144 E.R. 232; *Morgan v. Griffith* (1871), L.R. 6 Exch. 70, and *Erskine v. Adeane* (1873), 8 Ch. App. 756, are representative, established that where there was parol evidence of a distinct collateral agreement which did not contradict nor was inconsistent with the written instrument, it was admissible. These were cases between landlord and tenant in which parol evidence of stipulations as to repairs and other incidental matters and as to keeping down game and dealing with game was held to be admissible although the written leases were silent on these points. These were held to be independent agreements which were not required to be in writing and which were not in any way inconsistent with or contradictory of the written agreement.

The principle formulated in these cases was applied in *Byers v. McMillan* (1887), 15 S.C.R. 194. In this case Byers, a woodcutter, agreed in writing with one Andrew to cut and deliver 500 cords of wood from certain lands. The agreement contained no provision for security in the event that Byers was not paid upon making delivery. However, before he signed it, it was orally agreed that Byers was to have a lien on the wood for the amount to which he would be entitled for his work and labour. Byers was not paid and eventually sold the wood. The respondents, the McMillans, in whom the contract was vested as a result of various assignments, brought an action of replevin. It was held by a majority of this Court that they could not succeed on the ground that the parol evidence of the oral agreement in respect of the lien was admissible. Strong J., with whom the other members of the majority agreed, said at pp. 202-3:

> *Erskine v. Adeane; Morgan v. Griffith; Lindley v. Lacey,* afford illustrations of the rule in question by the terms of which any agreement collateral or supplementary to the written agreement may be established by parol evidence, provided it is one which as an independent agreement could be made without writing, and that it is not in any way inconsistent with or contradictory of the written agreement.

> .....

> These cases (particularly *Erskine v. Adeane* which was a judgment of the Court of Appeal) appear to be all stronger decisions than that which the appellant calls upon us to make in the present case, for it is difficult to see how an agreement, that one who in writing had undertaken by his labor to produce a chattel which is to become the property of another shall have a lien on such product for the money to be paid as the reward of his labor, in any way derogates from the contemporaneous or prior writing. By such a stipulation no term or provision of the writing is varied or in the slightest degree infringed upon; both agreements can well stand together; the writing provides for the performance of the contract, and the consideration to be paid for it, and the parol agreement merely adds something respecting security for the payment of the price to these terms.

[Judson J. here quoted from *Heilbut, Symons & Co. v. Buckleton, supra,* to the effect that the courts should be slow to find a collateral contract.]

Bearing in mind these remarks to the effect that there must be a clear intention to create a binding agreement, I am not convinced that the evidence in this case indicates clearly the existence of such intention. Indeed, I am disposed to agree with what the Court of Appeal said on this point. However, this is not an issue in this appeal. My opinion is that the appellant's argument fails on the ground that the collateral agreement allowing for the discharge of the appellant cannot stand as it clearly contradicts the terms of the guarantee bond which state that it is a continuing guarantee.

The appellant has relied upon *Byers v. McMillan*. But upon my interpretation that the terms of the two contracts conflict, this case is really against him as it is there stated by Strong J., that a collateral agreement cannot be established where it is inconsistent with or contradicts the written agreement. To the same effect is the unanimous judgment of the High Court of Australia in *Hoyt's Proprietary Ltd. v. Spencer* (1919), 27 C.L.R. 133, which rejected the argument that a collateral contract which contradicted the written agreement could stand with it. Knox C.J. said at p. 139:

> A distinct collateral agreement, whether oral or in writing, and whether prior to or contemporaneous with the main agreement, is valid and enforceable even though the main agreement be in writing, provided the two may consistently stand together so that the provisions of the main agreement remain in full force and effect notwithstanding the collateral agreement. This proposition is illustrated by the decisions in *Lindley v. Lacey* (1864), 144 E.R. 232; *Erskine v. Adeane* (1873), L.R. 8 Ch. App. 756; *De Lassalle v. Guildford*, [1901] 2 K.B. 215 (C.A.), and other cases.

I would dismiss the appeal with costs.

NOTE and QUESTIONS

1. Can the reasoning in this case be reconciled with that in *Zell*? On what basis did the defendant try to argue for the enforcement of the oral undertaking limiting his liability? Did these grounds have any merit?

2. Do you think the result in this case would have been different were it not for the integration or merger clause in the guarantee by which the guarantor acknowledged the completeness of the written document? Would or should the presence of such a clause have influenced the judgment of Frank C.J. in *Zell*?

3. The collateral contract argument raised in this case has been a device for courts and advocates wishing to circumvent the parol evidence rule. A collateral contract is a contract the consideration for which is the making of another contract. See Fridman, *The Law of Contract,* 3rd ed. (1994), Chapter 13. You should consider under what circumstances the Statute of Frauds will prevent the use of this device. Does the Statute of Frauds have any impact on the Zell/McLauchlan theories? See *supra*, Chapter 4, 8(c)(ii) "The Requirement of a Sufficient Note or Memorandum". Also, generally, see McLauchlan, "The Inconsistent Collateral Contract" (1976), 3 Dal. L.J. 136, Dawson, "Parol Evidence, Misrepresentation and Collateral Contracts" (1982), 27 McGill L.J. 403, and Stewart, "Oral Promises, Ad Hoc Implication and the Sanctity of Written Agreements" (1987), 61 Aust. L.J. 119.

BAUER v. BANK OF MONTREAL

[1980] 2 S.C.R. 102, 33 C.B.R. (N.S.) 291, 110 D.L.R. (3d) 424

B was guarantor of a loan made by the bank to a company of which at the time he was the principal officer and major shareholder. As part of the loan arrangement, there was an assignment of the book debts of the company to the bank. However, the bank did not register the assignment properly with the result that, on the subsequent bankruptcy of the company, it was not a preferred creditor. The book debts therefore became part of the assets available to all general creditors and did little or nothing to reduce B's obligation under the guarantee to the bank. Normally, at law, the failure of the bank to perfect its security (the book debts) by proper registration would have provided B with a defence to the bank's action on the guarantee. However, the relevant contract contained the following clause:

> It is further agreed that said bank, without exonerating in whole or in part the undersigned, or any of them (if more than one), may grant time, renewals, extensions, indulgences, releases and discharges to, may take securities from and give the same and any or all existing securities up to, may abstain from taking securities from, or from perfecting securities of . . . the customer.

Notwithstanding this clause, B resisted judgment on a number of grounds, one of which was the following.

McINTYRE J. [delivering the judgment of the court] . . . Finally, it was the contention of the guarantor that the bank could not rely on the above-quoted provision in the facts of this case because it was an express condition of the giving of the guarantee that the accounts be preserved for the benefit of the guarantor and reassigned to him on payment of the company's indebtedness. The bank was, therefore, in breach of its undertaking in this regard and was not entitled to take advantage of the provision. The argument had not been raised at trial presumably because no reliance had been placed upon the relieving provision above-quoted.

I have examined the evidence with care and find it difficult to discover any very clear support for the existence of any such collateral or qualifying agreement. However, Galligan, J., considered there was such an agreement for he said:

> Not only is it the law that a surety upon payment of the debt is entitled to the benefit of the security held by the creditor (see *Household Fin. Corp. Ltd. v. Foster*, [1949] O.R. 123 (C.A.)), in this case I am satisfied that it was understood between the plaintiff's branch manager and the defendant that if the defendant paid the indebtedness of Grey Electronics to the plaintiff, the plaintiff would deliver to him the book debts of Grey Electronic, the assignment of which was held by it.

To make such a finding, he would necessarily have had to rely on evidence. The only evidence I can find in the record of such an arrangement is a statement by the bank manager that the bank would have reassigned the accounts on payment by the guarantor as normal practice, and the assertion by the guarantor that he had been told by the bank manager that if he made good on his guarantee the accounts would be reassigned to him. He said as well that he would not have given his guarantee otherwise. There was then some evidence for the finding of the trial Judge and its sufficiency is not for this Court to judge. However, it seems clear to me that this evidence would go towards imposing a limit on the bank's rights with respect to the security given by the debtor. This would clearly contradict the terms of the guarantee which, as has been pointed out, gave the bank the right to abstain from registration and perfection of security. On this basis, it would be inadmissible under the parol evidence rule and any collateral agreement founded upon it could not stand. I can see no distinction between the case at bar and that of *Hawrish v. Bank of Montreal*. . . .

Any such collateral oral agreement as contended for by the appellant therefore may not stand in the face of the written guarantee. It follows that an additional argument raised by the guarantor relating to a claim that the collateral contract had been fundamentally breached will not require to be dealt with. I would dismiss the appeal. In all circumstances of this case, I would not award costs to the respondent in any of the Courts.

[Appeal dismissed.]

NOTES and QUESTIONS

1. For a critical discussion of the Supreme Court of Canada's judgment in this case, see Swan and Reiter, "Developments in Contract Law: The 1979-80 Term" (1981), 2 Supreme Court L.R. 125 at 153-58. In this article, the authors speculate that the use of the parol evidence rule in both *Hawrish* and *Bauer* was a surrogate for the Supreme Court's view that there was simply insufficient proof of the alleged separate, collateral agreement. If true, can such a judicial approach be justified?

2. Subsequently, Swan and Reiter return to their criticisms of the Supreme Court and its use of the parol evidence rule, this time in the context of their discussion of *Barton v. Agincourt Football Ent. Ltd.*, [1982] 1 S.C.R. 666, a case where they see the court in effect applying the rule where there was clear proof of a particular prior understanding as to the effect of an agreement. See "Developments in Contract Law: The 1981-82 Term" (1983), 5 Supreme Court L.R. 139 at 152-54.

3. In the light of the traditional statement of the rule that the collateral contract device may only be used where such a contract is consistent with the terms of the written contract, can the following decision be explained?

J. EVANS & SON (PORTSMOUTH) LTD. v. MERZARIO (ANDREA) LTD.

[1976] 1 W.L.R. 1078, [1976] 2 All E.R. 930 (C.A.)

The plaintiffs were importers of machinery and had a shipping agreement with the defendant forwarding agents for the transportation of machinery from Italy to England. The plaintiffs and defendants had done business previously but this was the first occasion on which the possibility of the goods being carried in containers rather than crates had been raised. There was some discussion prior to the written contract about this and, because of the plaintiff's concern that the machinery would rust if carried on deck, the defendants promised orally that they would arrange for the container to be transported below deck. Unfortunately, in arranging with another company for the sea part of the transportation, the defendants neglected this aspect. A machine (worth £3,000) was shipped in a container and travelled on the deck. During the voyage, the container fell off the deck into the sea and the machinery was lost. The plaintiffs sued the defendants for damages and the defendants relied, *inter alia*, upon the following contractual provisions:

4. Subject to express instructions in writing given by the customer, the Company reserves to itself complete freedom in respect of means route and procedure to be followed in the handling and transportation of the goods.

11. The Company shall not be liable for loss or damage to goods unless such loss or damage occurs whilst the goods are in actual custody of the Company and under its actual control and unless such loss or damage is due to the wilful neglect or default of the Company or its own servants.

13. In no case shall the liability of the Company exceed . . . £50 per ton.

At trial, Kerr J. held . . . that the defendants were entitled to rely on clause 11 and avoid all liability. The plaintiffs appealed.

LORD DENNING M.R. . . . The judge quoted largely from the well known case of *Heilbut, Symons & Co. v. Buckleton*, [*supra*], in which it was held that a person is not liable in damages for an innocent misrepresentation; and that the courts should be slow to hold that there was a collateral contract. I must say that much of what was said in that case is entirely out of date . . . even in respect of promises as to the future, we have a different approach nowadays to collateral contracts. When a person gives a promise or an assurance to another, intending that he should act on it by entering into a contract, and he does act on it by entering into the contract, we hold that it is binding: see *Bentley (Dick) Productions Ltd. v. Smith (Harold) (Motors) Ltd.* [*supra*]. That case was concerned with a representation of fact, but it applies also to promises as to the future. Following this approach, it seems to me plain that Mr. Spano gave an oral promise or assurance that the goods in this new container traffic would be carried under deck. He made the promise in order to induce Mr. Leonard to agree to the goods being carried in containers. On the faith of it, Mr. Leonard accepted the quotations and gave orders for transport. In those circumstances the promise was binding. There was a breach of that promise and the forwarding agents are liable—unless they can rely on the printed conditions.

It is common ground that the course of dealing was on the standard conditions of the forwarding trade. Those conditions were relied upon: condition 4 which gives the company complete freedom in respect of means, route and procedure in the transportation of goods; condition 11 which says that the company will not be liable for loss or damage unless it occurs while in their actual custody and then only if they are guilty of wilful neglect or default; condition 13 which says that their liability shall not exceed the value of the goods or a sum at the rate of £50 per ton of 20 cwt.

The question is whether the company can rely on those exemptions. I do not think so. The cases are numerous in which oral promises have been held binding in spite of written exempting conditions: such as *Couchman v. Hill*, [1947] K.B. 554 (C.A.); *Harling v. Eddy*, [1951] 2 K.B. 739 (C.A.); *City and Westminster Properties (1934) Ltd. v. Mudd*, [1959] Ch. 129. The most recent is *Mendelssohn v. Normand*, [1970] 1 Q.B. 177 at 184, where I said: "The printed condition is rejected because it is repugnant to the express oral promise or representation." During the argument Roskill L.J. put the case of the Hague Rules. If a carrier made a promise that goods would be shipped under deck, and, contrary to that promise, they were carried on deck and there was a loss, the carrier could not rely on the limitation clause. Following the authorities, it seems to me that the forwarding agents cannot rely on the condition. There was a plain breach of the oral promise by the forwarding agents. I would allow the appeal.

ROSKILL L.J. . . . The matter was apparently argued before the judge on behalf of the plaintiffs on the basis that the defendants' promise (if any) was what the lawyers sometimes call a collateral oral warranty. That phrase is normally only applicable where the original promise was external to the main contract, that main contract being a contract in writing, so that usually parol evidence cannot be given to contradict the terms of the written contract. The basic rule is clearly stated in paragraph 742 of *Benjamin's Sale of Goods*, 9th ed. (1974) to which I refer but which I will not repeat. But that doctrine, as it seems to me, has little or no application where one is not concerned with a contract in writing (with respect, I cannot accept [counsel's] argument that there was here a contract in writing) but with a contract which, as I think, was partly oral, partly in writing, and partly by conduct. In such a case the court does not require to have recourse to lawyers' devices such as collateral oral warranty in order to seek to adduce evidence which would not otherwise be admissible. The court is entitled to look at and should look at all the evidence from start to finish in order to see what the bargain was that was struck between the parties. That is what we have done in this case and what, with great respect, I think the judge did not do in the course of his judgment. I unreservedly accept [counsel's] submission that one must not look at one or two isolated answers given in evidence; one should look at the totality of the evidence. When one does that, one finds, first, as I have already mentioned, that these parties had been doing business in transporting goods from Milan to England for some time before; secondly, that transportation of goods from Milan to England was always done on trailers which were always under deck; thirdly, that the defendants wanted a change in the practice—they wanted containers used instead of trailers; fourthly, that the plaintiffs were only willing to agree to that change if they were promised by the defendants that those containers would be shipped under deck, and would not have agreed to the change but for that promise. The defendants gave such a promise, which to my mind against this background plainly amounted to an enforceable contractual promise. In those circumstances it seems to me that the contract was this: "If we continue to give you our business, you will ensure that those goods in containers are shipped under deck"; and the defendants agreed that this would be so. Thus there was a breach of that contract by the defendants when this container was shipped on deck; and it seems to me to be plain that the damage which the plaintiff suffered resulted from that breach. That being the position, I think that [counsel's] first argument fails.

I will deal very briefly with the second point, with which Lord Denning M.R. has already dealt fully. It is suggested that even so these exemption clauses apply. I [asked] what the position would have been if when the defendants' first quotation had come along there had been stamped on the face of that quotation: "No containers to be shipped on deck": and this container had then been shipped on deck. [Counsel] bravely said that the exemption clauses would still have applied. With great respect, I think that is an impossible argument. In the words which Devlin J. used in *Firestone Tyre and Rubber Co. Ltd. v. Vokins & Co. Ltd.*, [1951] 1 Lloyd's Rep. 32 at 39, and approved by Lord Denning M.R. in *Mendelssohn v. Normand Ltd.*, [1970] 1 Q.B. 177 at 184, the defendants' promise that the container would be shipped under deck would be wholly illusory. This is not a case of fundamental breach. It is a question of construction. Interpreting the contract as I find it to have been, I feel driven to the conclusion that none of these exemption clauses can be applied, because one has to treat the promise that no container would be shipped on deck as overriding any question of exempting conditions. Otherwise, as I have already said, the promise would be illusory. . . .

[Geoffrey Lane L.J. delivered a judgment to the same effect as Roskill L.J. Appeal allowed.]

NOTES and QUESTIONS

1. To what extent does the judgment of Lord Denning M.R. differ from that of Roskill L.J.? Which approach better enables a circumvention of the Supreme Court of Canada decisions in *Hawrish* and *Bauer*?

2. In *Lister (Ronald Elwyn) Ltd. v. Dunlop Can. Ltd.* (1978), 85 D.L.R. (3d) 321 (Ont. H.C.), Rutherford J. approved the *Evans* line of authority in the following terms at 331-32:

> Certainly, I have no doubt that in certain cases, evidence of oral collateral contracts existing apart from a subsequent written agreement may be given effect to even where they are repugnant to the terms of the subsequent agreement.

Nevertheless, he then refused to give effect to prior oral assurances in the face of the following clause in the relevant agreement at 330:

> Dunlop and the Dealer agree that, except as herein expressly stated, no representation, statement, understanding or agreement has been made or exists, either oral or in writing, and that in entering into this Agreement the Dealer has not relied upon any presumption of fact or of law which in any way affects this Agreement, or any provision of the consideration for, or the validity of, this Agreement, or which relates to the subject matter hereof or which imposes any liability upon Dunlop in connection with this Agreement.

His reasons for this, at 332, were as follows:

> I have come to the conclusion, however, that the present case is not one where relief should be granted on the basis of alleged oral agreements. In reaching this decision, I was influenced by the circumstances in which the franchise agreement was entered into. The Listers, and particularly Mr. Lister, who negotiated the franchise agreement on behalf of the yet-to-be incorporated corporate plaintiff, were experienced in business and cognizant of the legal consequences of entering into a commercial contract. Although there was a marked economic disparity between the parties to the franchise agreement, the situation in this regard appeared to be similar to that in *Jirna* [*Jirna Ltd. v. Mr. Donut of Can. Ltd.* (1971), 22 D.L.R. (3d) 639 (Ont. C.A.), affirmed [1975] 1 S.C.R. 2] case where the Court of Appeal concluded that there was no inequality of bargaining power of the nature which would allow the plaintiff to avoid the clear terms of the written agreement. In the present case, the Listers gave the following explanation as to why they would sign a document with provisions clearly repugnant to previous oral assurances: Dunlop's representatives had told them that the franchise agreement was a matter of standard form and could not be altered, but that all previous representations and assurances would be honoured. However, according to the undisputed evidence of Mr. Gifford, their solicitor, the Listers were advised that they were "taking an awful chance" in signing the agreement in the form which Dunlop proposed. Notwithstanding Mr. Gifford's warnings, the plaintiffs chose to sign the agreement in that form, doing so without any coercion or duress from any quarter. Clause 11 (set out above) of that document, by its terms, was clearly intended to exclude contractual liability upon Dunlop arising apart from the express terms of the franchise agreement. In the circumstances of the present case, I would find that this intention should be given effect to.

Should the solicitor's advice have been crucial? If you had been the plaintiff's solicitor, what would you have said?

When *Lister* went on appeal this aspect of the judgment was not challenged although the appeal was allowed on other grounds: 105 D.L.R. (3d) 684 (Ont. C.A.), only to be reversed again on further appeal: 135 D.L.R. (3d) 1 (S.C.C.).

3. In *Curtis v. Chemical Cleaning and Dyeing Co.*, [1951] 1 K.B. 805 (C.A.), it was held that where there is a misrepresentation (fraudulent or innocent) as to the effect or meaning of a contractual document, whether signed or unsigned, the misrepresenting party cannot rely upon the written contract in contradiction of the misrepresentation. This possibility was acknowledged in *Bauer v. Bank of Montreal, supra*, but held not to be established on the facts. Subsequently, in another bank guarantee case, the Ontario Court of Appeal allowed such a defence to proceed: *Bank of N.S. v. Zackheim* (1983), 3 D.L.R. (4th) 760. See also Dawson, "Parol Evidence, Misrepresentation and Collateral Contracts" (1983), 27 McGill L.J. 403. This, of course, is different from the plaintiff's argument in *Hawrish* and *Lister*, where the misrepresentations were not as to the effect or meaning of the written documents but as to whether the written document would be relied upon. Consider, however, the extent to which an equitable estoppel argument might be made in cases such as *Hawrish, Lister* and *Bauer*. The traditional argument would, of course, be that equitable estoppel cannot be used because there was no pre-existing contractual or legal relationship between the parties: the representations were pre-contractual rather than post-contractual. Now see, however, *Bojtar v. Parker* (1979), 99 D.L.R. (3d) 147, affirmed 103 D.L.R. (3d) 577 (Ont. C.A.); *Re Tudale Explorations Ltd. and Bruce* (1978), 88 D.L.R. (3d) 584 (Ont. D.C.); *Crabb v. Arun District Council*, [1976] Ch. 179 (C.A.); *Evenden v. Guildford City Assn. Football Club*, [1975] Q.B. 917 (C.A.); *Enquist v. Hass* (1979), 15 B.C.L.R. 139 (S.C.).

This evolution in the doctrine of estoppel to cover pre-contractual negotiations has in fact been applied by the British Columbia Court of Appeal in *Bank of Montreal v. Murphy*, [1986] 6 W.W.R. 610, in the context of a misrepresentation as to the effect of a guarantee or the extent to which it would be enforced. The bank's representation that the guarantors were responsible for only half of the relevant debt was held to have induced the giving of the guarantee, and the Court of Appeal then applied the doctrine of estoppel to prevent the bank from asserting a claim for the full amount. Lambert J.A. (delivering the judgment of the court) held at 38-39:

> In my opinion, the findings of fact of the trial Judge, founded as they are on the pleadings, encompass all the elements of an estoppel against the bank. There was a representation that was intended to be relied on, and that was in fact relied on, to the detriment of the Murphys. The representation was intended to modify the legal relationships of the parties. In those circumstances, the bank is estopped from denying that the legal relationships between the parties are otherwise than in accordance with the representation. If the representation is viewed as a statement about the effect of the guarantee in law, then the defence would be one of estoppel. If the represention is viewed as a statement about the effect to be given to the guarantee by the bank, the defence would be one of promissory estoppel.

He then held that the same result could be reached by a collateral contract analysis. The case also has another interesting aspect to it. At trial, the court had denied enforcement to any part of the guarantee on the traditional theory that it had been induced by a material misrepresentation. This had the effect of absolving the guarantors completely. Not so, said the Court of Appeal. The bank was held to be entitled to that half of the debt for which the guarantors assumed they would be held accountable. Do you agree?

In contrast to *Murphy*, in *Chant v. Infinitum Growth Fund Inc.* (1986), 28 D.L.R. (4th) 577, the Ontario Court of Appeal, reversing the trial judge, refused to rectify a document to give effect to assurance as to when a guarantee would be enforced. Parol evidence of such assurances was also held to be inadmissible on the basis of *Hawrish* and *Bauer*. (This judgment has been criticized strongly by Waddams, "Two Contrasting Approaches to the Parol Evidence Rule" (1986-87), 12 Can. Bus. L.J. 207.)

4. Consider also *Roberts v. Montex Dev. Corp.* (1979), 100 D.L.R. (3d) 660 (B.C. S.C.). Here the court was concerned with whether representations in a brochure could constitute an actionable warranty notwithstanding an integration clause in a contract for the sale of a suite in a condominium. McKenzie J. held that as the purchaser had had no independent legal advice and as the escape clause had not been drawn to her attention, *Lister* was distinguishable. At 667 he stated:

> The expression "inequality of bargaining power" has to be translated in the present case to "inequality of capacity to obtain truthful information" and on that basis the scales were unequally tipped against the purchaser.

This suggests a significant expansion of *Curtis*. Silence as to the existence of a contractual provision may in some instances be treated the same as misrepresentation as to the effect or meaning of a contract. In what situations should this be accepted? Compare this decision with *L'Estrange v. Graucob*, [1934] 2 K.B. 394, discussed in *McCutcheon v. David MacBrayne Ltd.*, *infra*, Chapter 8, section 3(d)(i).

5. Surfacing very obviously in *Lister*, *Curtis*, *Roberts* and other cases is the existence of a judicial policy that the parol evidence rule is less likely to be invoked where there is unconscionable dealing or use of superior bargaining power. At its most extreme, the doctrine of unconscionability will deny any recognition at all to an apparent written contract (see Chapter 12). However, as *Lister*, *Curtis* and *Roberts* suggest, it also provides a basis on which particular oral assurances may overcome exemption and other specific clauses in contracts. The unwary consumer may achieve protection if the effect of a standard form document is misrepresented, if a statement is made that particular clauses will not have effect or be relied on, as in *Roberts*, and where the promotional literature gives assurances not replicated, indeed apparently excluded by "the" contract.

In fact, even outside unconscionable transaction and unfair bargaining situations, and notwithstanding *Hawrish* and *Bauer*, some Canadian courts are indicating considerable sympathy for the philosophy of *Evans*, as well as *Murphy*. Consider the following British Columbia Court of Appeal decision, which was relied upon in *Murphy*.

GALLEN v. BUTTERLEY

(1984), 53 B.C.L.R. 38, 25 B.L.R. 314, 9 D.L.R. (4th) 496 (C.A.)

As a result of oral assurances as to the nature of buckwheat as a crop, specifically that buckwheat would act as a blanket and smother weeds, some experienced farmers entered into a contract for the purchase of buckwheat seed.

Contrary to the assurances, weeds smothered and destroyed the crop. The farmers then sued and were successful at trial on the basis of breach of warranty.

An appeal was argued in part on the basis that the trial judge should not have admitted the evidence as to the oral assurances, particularly as they conflicted with a clause in the written, standard form of agreement signed by the plaintiffs. That clause provided that the defendant gave

> no warranty as to the productiveness or any other matter pertaining to the seed sold to the producer and will not in any way be responsible for the crop.

It was also contended that, irrespective of the clause, the evidence, even if admitted, did not establish a contractual warranty by the defendants.

LAMBERT J.A. . . . In Pt. III of these reasons, I concluded that evidence of the oral representation was admissible in this case either on the basis that the document did not contain the whole agreement (the "one contract" theory), or on the basis that the document contained one complete agreement but that the oral representation formed the basic term of another complete agreement (the "two contract" theory).

But I wish to emphasize that these theories are legal analysis only. They are not real life. So the substantive law ought to be the same, whichever theory is adopted. It makes no sense to say that if the warranty is cast as part of a single contract ("I am selling you a rust-proof car"), the consequence in law is different from if the warranty is cast as part of a separate collateral contract ("If you buy this car for me, I will guarantee that it is rust-proof").

The crucial parol evidence principle of substantive law, for the purposes of this case, is the principle that forms one of the reasons for decision in *Hawrish v. Bank of Montreal*, [*supra*]; *Bauer v. Bank of Montreal*, [*supra*]; and *Carman Const. Ltd. v. C.P.R.*, [1982] 1 S.C.R. 958, all decisions of the Supreme Court of Canada, and also in *First Nat. Mtge. Co. v. Grouse Nest Resorts* (1977), 2 B.C.L.R. 300, a decision of this court. That principle was stated in this way by Martland J., for the Supreme Court of Canada, in the *Carman Const.* case, at p. 969:

> ". . . a collateral agreement cannot be established where it is inconsistent with or contradicts the written agreement".

I propose to make eight comments about that principle.

The first is that the principle has its root in the parol evidence rule as a rule of evidence, and in the "two contract" or "collateral contract" exception to that rule of evidence. There is no objection to the introduction of evidence to establish an oral agreement separate from the written agreement and made at the same time: see *Heilbut, Symons & Co. v. Buckleton*, [*supra*]. But it is unreasonable to contemplate that, at the same time, and between the same parties, two contracts will be made dealing with the same subject matter, one of which contradicts the other. So, since the written one was clearly and demonstrably made, reason requires one to conclude that the oral one, contradicting it, was never made. This point was set out clearly by Isaacs J. in the High Court of Australia, in *Hoyt's Proprietary Ltd. v. Spencer* (1919), 27 C.L.R. 133 at 145-46, and it is consistent with the reasons of Strong J. in the Supreme Court of Canada, in *Byers v. McMillan* (1887), 15 S.C.R. 194. Those are the two roots which Judson J. relied on in *Hawrish v. Bank of Montreal* when he framed the modern restatement of the principle.

The second is that the principle cannot be an absolute one. Let us suppose that a bank manager, acting within his authority, agrees that if his customer will agree to sign and be bound by the bank's standard form of guarantee, then the guarantee will only be in effect for one year. The customer agrees on the basis of that assurance and he signs the standard form of guarantee which contains no mention of the one-year period. Two years pass by. The bank manager is replaced. The principal debtor goes bankrupt and the bank sues the guarantor, who pleads the collateral agreement as a defence. At trial, evidence is given by the former bank manager. He says that he agreed on behalf of the bank that the guarantee would only be in effect for a year. The second bank manager says that he knows about the agreement made by the first bank manager, but he also knows about the *Hawrish* case, which he thinks says that the agreement made by the first bank manager on behalf of the bank does not bind the bank, and that, if that is so, then he thinks that his duty to the bank's shareholders is to sue on the written guarantee. I do not consider that the bank would succeed in that case. The principle in *Hawrish* is not a tool for the unscrupulous to dupe the unwary.

The third comment is that *Hawrish, Bauer* and *Carman Const.* illustrate, by the attention given to the evidence, that the principle is not an absolute one. In *Hawrish*, at p. 520, Judson J. said:

> Bearing in mind these remarks to the effect that there must be a clear intention to create a binding agreement, I am not convinced that the evidence in this case indicates clearly the existence of such intention. Indeed, I am disposed to agree with what the Court of Appeal said on this point.

In *Bauer*, at p. 111, McIntyre J. said:

> For reasons which will appear later in that part of this judgment dealing with the collateral contract argument, I am of the view that there is no evidence which would support any such finding against the bank.

In *Carman Const.* at p. 967, Martland J. said:

> In my opinion, there is no evidence in the present case to establish an intention to warrant the accuracy of the statement made by the C.P.R. employee to Fielding, *i.e.* no promise to make it good.

If the principle were an absolute one, there would have been no need in those cases to mention the evidence because the statement alleged in each case, if established by the evidence, clearly contradicted the document. So the cases could have been disposed of by the application of the absolute principle, no matter how convincing the evidence, even if both parties agreed that the oral warranty was given, and was intended to be binding, and was intended to override or modify the document.

The fourth point is that *Bauer v. Bank of Montreal* explicitly recognizes a particular exception to the principle, where, at p. 111, McIntyre J., for the Supreme Court of Canada, said:

> Various authorities were cited for the proposition that a contract induced by misrepresentation or by an oral representation, inconsistent with the form of the written contract, would not stand and could not bind the party to whom the representation had been made. These authorities included *Can. Indemnity Co. v. Okanagan Mainline Real Estate Bd.*, [[1971] S.C.R. 493], per Judson J. at p. 500, *Jaques v. Lloyd D. George & Partners* [[1968] 1 W.L.R. 625], per Lord Denning at pp. 630-631, *Firestone Tyre & Rubber Co. v. Vokins & Co.*, [[1951] 1 Lloyds Rep. 32 (K.B.D.)], see Devlin J. at p. 39, and *Mendelssohn v. Normand Ltd.* [[1970] 1 Q.B. 177].
>
> No quarrel can be made with the general proposition advanced on this point by the appellant. To succeed, however, this argument must rest upon a finding of some misrepresentation by the bank, innocent or not, or on some oral representation inconsistent with the written document which caused a misimpression in the guarantor's mind, or upon some omission on the part of the bank manager to explain the contents of the document which induced the guarantor to enter into the guarantee upon a misunderstanding as to its nature.

So, if the contract is induced by an oral misrepresentation that is inconsistent with the written contract, the written contract cannot stand.

The fifth point is that the rationale of the principle, as discussed in the first point, above, does not apply with equal force where the oral representation adds to, subtracts from or varies the agreement recorded in the document, as it does where the oral representation contradicts the document. As far as "adding to" is concerned, there is nothing inherently unreasonable about two agreements which add to each other. "Subtracting from" and "varying" represent a halfway stage between "adding to", on the one hand, which is wholly reasonable, and "contra-dicting", on the other hand, which is wholly unreasonable.

The sixth point is that, if *Hawrish, Bauer* and *Carman Const.* are properly considered on their facts, the law in Canada is no different from that stated by K. W. Wedderburn in his article "Collateral Contracts", [1959] Cambridge L.J. 58 at 62, where he says:

> What the parol evidence rule has bequeathed to the modern law is a presumption—namely that a document which *looks* like a contract is to be treated as the *whole* contract. This presumption is "very strong", but "it is a presumption only, and it is open to either of the parties to allege that there was, in addition to what appears in the written agreement, an antecedent express stipulation not intended by the parties to be excluded, but intended to continue in force with the express written agreement".

The presumption is always strong. But it is strongest when the oral representation is alleged to be contrary to the document, and somewhat less strong when the oral representation only adds to the document.

The seventh point is that, if it is correct to view the principle only as a strong presumption, which I think is the correct view of *Hawrish, Bauer* and *Carman*, then that presumption would be more rigorous in a case where the parties had produced an individually negotiated document than it would be where a printed form was used, though it would be a strong presumption in both cases.

The eighth and final point is that, if it is correct to consider the principle only as a strong presumption, then the presumption would be less strong where the contradiction was between a specific oral representation, on the one hand, and a general exemption or exclusion clauses that excludes liability for any oral representation, whatsoever, on the other hand, than it would be in a case where the specific oral representation was contradictory to an equally specific clause in the document. This point is made by Anderson J.A., whose reasons I have read in draft, and I agree with him that the point is established by the cases to which he refers.

I will return to this principle, on the facts of this case, in Pt. VII of the reasons.

VI

Is there a contradiction between the oral representation and the signed document?

I propose to set out the oral representation and cl. 23. If the oral representation is to have effect at all, it can be stated in this way:

> Allstate warrants that weeds will not be a cause of loss; the buckwheat will grow up and smother the weeds.

Clause 23 reads:

> 23. Allstate gives no warranty as to the productiveness or any other matter pertaining to the seed sold to the producer and will not in any way be responsible for the crop.

In my opinion, the oral warranty and the printed document do not contradict each other. Taking cl. 23 without regard to the oral warranty, and having regard to the fact that the clause does not exclude all warranties, I think that the proper inter-pretation of cl. 23, in its context, is that all warranties pertaining to the seed are excluded, and that Allstate is not responsible for the yield. In the context, I think that the word "crop" means "yield".

But even if I am wrong and cl. 23, if it stood alone, would bear the meaning that Allstate was not to be liable for anything that prevented the production and harvesting of a buckwheat crop grown from the seed, I think it is proper to interpret cl. 23 in its relationship with the oral representation that was made in this case, because it is in the light of that representation that the parties would have interpreted cl. 23 when they read it over before signing the document. If that approach to interpretation is the correct one, then the oral representation and cl. 23 must be interpreted harmoniously, if that can be done without depriving cl. 23 of a natural and sensible meaning. Under that interpretation, Allstate would not be responsible for matters relating to the seed, for the yield, or for matters that might affect the production of the buckwheat arising from soil conditions or from farming methods or practices, but Allstate would assume any risk that the crop would be destroyed by weeds. There is no reason why the usual rule that a harmonious construction should be preferred to a contradictory construction should not apply.

But, of course, the rationale of the harmonious construction rule is that the parties cannot have intended to agree to inconsistent obligations. So the rule only applies where both obligations have contractual force. And that depends on whether the oral representation was a warranty. But the question of whether it was a warranty or a bare representation is a question of fact, determined by the objective evidence of whether it was intended to have contractual force. So the interpretation of the representation and the document, on the one hand, and the question of whether the representation is a warranty, on the other hand, are bound together and should be answered together.

VII

Conclusion

The trial judge said:

> It is clear on the law that the exclusionary clause in the contract will not avail the defendant Allstate if such a warranty is made out on the evidence. Is it so made out?

For the reasons I have set out in Pts. V and VI, I think that it is a considerable oversimplification of the law to say that an exclusionary clause will not avail the defendant if a collateral warranty is made out on the evidence. Sometimes it will, sometimes it will not; the court must strive to reach the true contractual intention of the parties, guided, in the case of contradiction, by the strong presumption in favour of the document.

But even if the trial judge oversimplified the law, he considered the right question on the evidence, namely: Is a warranty made out as a matter of fact? I do not think that he misdirected himself on the principles to be applied in answering that question of fact. It involved a nice question of judgment and an assessment of the testimony and demeanour of the witnesses. Paris J. concluded that Mr. Nunweiler's statement regarding weed control constituted a warranty. There is ample evidence to support that conclusion, much of it referred to by Paris J. in his reasons. I do not think that it is open to me to consider that matter afresh or, if I were to reach a different conclusion on the facts from Paris J., to substitute my view of the facts for his.

Once it has been decided that the oral representation was a warranty, then, in my opinion,

(*a*) evidence accepted on the basis that there would be a subsequent ruling on admissibility becomes admissible;

(*b*) the oral warranty and the document must be interpreted together and, if possible, harmoniously, to attach the correct contractual effect to each;

(*c*) if no contradiction becomes apparent in following that process, then the principle in *Hawrish, Bauer* and *Carman* has no application; and

(*d*) if there is a contradiction, then the principle in *Hawrish, Bauer* and *Carman* is that there is a strong presumption in favour of the written document, but the rule is not absolute, and if on the evidence it is clear that the oral warranty was intended to prevail, it will prevail.

Since, in my opinion, there is no contradiction in this case between the specific oral warranty and the signed standard form, buckwheat marketing agreement, 1980, I have concluded that the warranty has contractual effect and that the defendant Allstate Grain Co. Ltd. is liable to the plaintiffs for breach of that warranty.

But if it were correct, in this case, to conclude that the oral representation and the buckwheat marketing agreement, 1980 contradicted each other, then, on the basis of the facts found by the trial judge and his conclusion that the oral representation was intended to affect the contractual relationship of the parties, as a warranty, I would have concluded that, in spite of the strong presumption in favour of the document, the oral warranty should prevail.

I would dismiss the appeal.

ANDERSON J.A. . . . In my opinion, while the words "not responsible for the crop" would be in the abstract, without reference to the negotiations and assurances leading up to the execution of the written contract lead to the conclusion that all matters relating to the crop, including the question of weed control, were solely for the plaintiffs, as the clause in question is an exemption or exclusionary clause, the words "not responsible for the crop" must be construed in the light of the express promise made by the defendants. The words "not responsible for the crop" are not, in my opinion, so clear and unequivocal as to exclude the assurances given in respect of weed control. In the light of all the circumstances, as a matter of construction, I have reached the conclusion that the defendants must have meant by the words "not responsible for the crop" that the plaintiffs were to be "responsible for the crop" in all aspects, except that the plaintiffs could rely on the express promise made by the defendants with respect to weed control.

The defendants rely in the main on two judgments of the Supreme Court of Canada, namely, *Bauer v. Bank of Montreal* and *Carman Const. Ltd. v. C.P.R.* These cases are, in my opinion, of no assistance because, in the first place, they do not purport to deal with exemption or exclusionary clauses and, in the second place, in those cases the alleged oral representations were contrary to the clear and plain terms contained in the written contracts.

With respect to *Bauer*, McIntyre J. specifically held that the clause in question was not an exemption clause and was, therefore, not subject to any special rules of construction. He went on to conclude that the submission that the contract of guarantee was executed after a misrepresentation by the bank as to its effect was well founded in law but lacked any evidentiary foundation on which such an argument could succeed. He set out the law at p. 110 as follows:

> The third argument involves the assertion that the execution of the guarantee was procured by misrepresentation of its full nature and effect by the bank or, alternatively, that there was a failure to explain its nature and effect. The misrepresentation alleged is that the bank manager told the guarantor that upon his paying the amount secured under the guarantee, the book debts would be reassigned to him. The representation was false for the reason that it contradicted the bank's own document. It was contended that the guarantee would not have been executed in its absence. Various authorities were cited for the proposition that a contract induced by misrepresentation or by an oral representation, inconsistent with the form of the written contract, would not stand and could not bind the party to whom the representation had been made. [See the authorities listed in Lambert J.A.'s judgment, quoting McIntyre J., at 457.]
>
> No quarrel can be made with the general proposition advanced on this point by the appellant. To succeed, however, this argument must rest upon a finding of some misrepresentation by the bank, innocent or not, or on some oral representation inconsistent with the written document which caused a misimpression in the guarantor's mind, or upon some omission on the part of the bank manager to explain the contents of the document which induced the guarantor to enter into the guarantee upon a misunderstanding as to its nature. For reasons which will appear later in that part of this judgment dealing with the collateral contract argument, I am of the view that there is no evidence which would support any such finding against the bank. The cases referred to above support the general proposition advanced but rest upon a factual basis providing support for the argument. In each case there is a clear finding of a specific misrepresentation which led to the formation of the contract in question, a circumstance not to be found here. This argument must fail as well.

The cases cited with approval by McIntyre J. deal specifically with exemption or exclusionary clauses and make it clear that the words contained in such clauses will be narrowly construed, so that the written words purporting to exclude warranties will not, except in very clear cases, be utilized to defeat an express promise or warranty.

I quote from several of the judgments approved by McIntyre J. in *Bauer*. In giving the judgment of the Supreme Court of Canada in *Can. Indemnity Co. v. Okanagan Mainline Real Estate Bd.*, *supra*, Judson J. at p. 500 said in part:

> Whillis-Harding, in getting the indemnity agreement from the Board was acting as agent for Canadian Indemnity. After the policy had been issued and delivered it misrepresented the reason for the request for the execution of the application and it was this misrepresentation as to the contents of the document that induced the Board to sign. A party who misrepresents, albeit innocently, the contents or effect of a clause inserted by him into a contract cannot rely on the clause in the face of his misrepresentation: *Mendelssohn v. Normand Ltd.* [*supra*]; *Curtis v. Chemical Cleaning & Dyeing Co.* [*supra*]; *Jaques v. Lloyd D. George & Partners Ltd.* [*supra*].

See also judgment of Devlin J. in *Firestone Tyre & Rubber Co. v. Vokins & Co.*, *supra*, at p. 39 as follows:

> One may test the point by considering the construction of the contract if the phrase about pilferage of goods were not there. The position then would be that the lightermen have said: "We will deliver your goods; we promise to deliver your goods at such and such a place, and in the condition in which we receive them; but we are not liable if they are lost or damaged from any cause whatsoever." That is not in law a contract at all. It is illusory to say: "We promise to do a thing, but we are not liable if we do not do it." If the matter rested there, there would be nothing in the contract. The words that are introduced about theft and pilferage must do one of two things. Either they must impose a liability to do something in respect of theft or pilferage, or they must modify the construction of the clause.

See also judgment of Lord Denning M.R. in *Mendelssohn v. Normand Ltd.*, at pp. 183-84, as follows:

> There are many cases in the books when a man has made, by word of mouth, a promise or a representation of fact, on which the other party acts by entering into the contract. In all such cases the man is not allowed to repudiate his representation by reference to a printed condition, see *Couchman v. Hill* [[1947] K.B. 554 (C.A.)]; *Curtis v. Chemical Cleaning & Dyeing Co.*; and *Harling v. Eddy* [[1951] 2 K.B. 739 (C.A.)]; nor is he allowed to go back on his promise by reliance on a written clause, see *City and Westminster Properties (1934) Ltd. v. Mudd* [[1959] Ch. 129, 145], by Harman J. The reason is because the oral promise or representation has a decisive influence on the transaction—it is the very thing which induces the other to contract—and it would be most unjust to allow the maker to go back on it. The printed condition is rejected because it is repugnant to the express oral promise or representation. As Devlin J. said in *Firestone Tyre & Rubber Co. v. Vokins & Co.* [*supra* at] 39: "It is illusory to say: 'We promise to do a thing, but we are not liable if we do not do it'." To avoid this illusion, the laws gives the oral promise priority over the printed clause.

It follows from the above that McIntyre J. would not have applied the parol evidence rule, as enunciated in *Bauer*, to exemption clauses.

In my opinion, the proper course to be followed in determining whether an exemption clause excludes an express warranty is to determine as a matter of construction, having regard to all circumstances including the warranty, whether the exemption clause was, in fact, intended by the parties to exclude the express warranty.

SEATON J.A. [dissenting] . . . The evidence makes clear that this is not the case of a salesman making reckless statements to outwit a dull customer. The defendant Nunweiler passed on the best information that was available to him. The plaintiffs described themselves in their statement of claim as businessmen and they appear to be accurate in so doing.

This is not the case of a contract being shoved across a counter with a curt "sign here". Mr. Jack Guichon examined the contract at home and filled out part of it. That appears not to have happened until May. The cases of want of knowledge by the signer of a printed form are inapplicable.

The provision in the written contract that Allstate "will not in any way be responsible for the crop" is neither unreasonable nor unconscionable. It cannot be construed to permit a warranty that the crop would not be lost to weeds. I agree with the trial judge that the oral and the written cannot stand together; the words used simply will not permit it. There is no basis for saying that weed growth is an exception that the contract will permit and there is no reason to put the weed statement on a different level from the other statements made at the March meeting.

The oral term cannot be found to be a condition precedent. Nor can it be said to be a misrepresentation of the nature or effect of the contract.

It is difficult to know what bargain would have been arrived at had the plaintiffs been unwilling to accept the risk of crop failure, that is, if they had said to Allstate that the statements made at the March meeting about the planting procedures, yield, return, details of growth and weed control were part of the contract. It may be that there would have been agreement to share the risk, to share both the losses and the profits. That question was not discussed and the bargain that was entered into assigned the risk in clear language to the plaintiffs. Nothing could be clearer than: "Allstate . . . will not in any way be responsible for the crop". . . .

[He then went on to hold that the assurances were not intended as a contractual warranty before continuing:]

If I were free to do as I choose I would not give any encouragement to the parol evidence rule as an admissibility rule. I am not attracted to deciding a point by refusing to hear evidence on an aspect of it. I am not free to choose and the rule does not seem to need my support. I would favour retention of a respect for the written contract that makes it difficult to persuade the court that a term not recorded was intended to be part of the bargain.

I do not see how people can safely act through an agent or take an assignment of a contract if written documents are not treated with some respect. Lawyers cannot give useful advice to people considering whether to contract if the written part is of little importance. Certainty, though no longer the only aim, remains an important aim in contract law.

Take this case. These plaintiffs did not make the claim that the defendants were responsible for weeds until Allstate had claimed in small debts court for the cost of the seed. The parties did not know the extent of their bargain until the trial judge ruled on it. They still do not. In the March discussions the defendant Nunweiler talked about yield, return, details of growth and other things. There is nothing to distinguish what he said about weed control from his other statements. Was Allstate responsible for all those things? The parties do not know what their bargain is. If the trial judge is right nothing is to be gained by looking at what they wrote down, what they called their contract. . . .

[Appeal dismissed.]

NOTE and QUESTIONS

1. As in *Evans*, the judgments of the majority judges differ quite dramatically in the approach they take in giving effect to the oral assurances. Which approach is more desirable?

2. Does Anderson J.A.'s discussion of *Bauer* and citation of an extract from McIntyre J.'s judgment not reproduced earlier suggest that *Bauer* might not be such a restrictive authority after all?

3. Seaton J.A. in dissent was concerned because the facts here did not exhibit any inequality of bargaining power. To what extent does this weaken the majority position?

4. For recent decisions that appear to assume that *Gallen* provides an escape route from the rigidity of *Bauer* and *Hawrish*, see *Corey Developments Inc. v. Eastbridge Developments (Waterloo)*

Ltd. (1997), 34 O.R. (3d) 73 (Gen. Div.), affirmed on other grounds (1999), 44 O.R. (3d) 95 (C.A.); *Douglas Lake Cattle Co. v. Smith* (1991), 78 D.L.R. (4th) 319 (B.C. C.A.). See also *Ahone v. Holloway* (1988), 30 B.C.L.R. (2d) 368 (C.A.) at 372-73 *per* McLachlin J.A., relying on *Gallen* to this effect and on Corbin's articulation of the parol evidence rule that is consistent with the formulation in *Gallen*.

(b)   STATUTORY MODIFICATION OF THE PAROL EVIDENCE RULE

In many provinces, consumer protection legislation has dealt with the parol evidence rule. See, *e.g.*, the following British Columbia section.

TRADE PRACTICE ACT

R.S.B.C. 1996, c. 457

29. In a proceeding in respect of a consumer transaction, a rule of law respecting parole or extrinsic evidence, or a term or provision in a consumer transaction, does not operate to exclude or limit the admissibility of evidence relating to the understanding of the parties as to the consumer transaction or a particular term or provision of it.

NOTES and QUESTIONS

1. The scope of this legislation was examined by Fridman, *The Law of Contract in Canada*, 4th ed. (1999) at 358-360. He noted that the statute made it impossible to exclude or limit its operation. See generally McCloy, "Report on the Panel on Consumer Affairs and Trade Practices Act" (1975), 33 Advocate 119, and Zysblat, "Amendments to the British Columbia Trade Practices Act: The Refinement of Omnibus Legislation" (1975), 1 Can. Bus. L.J. 99.

2. To what extent, if at all, does the provision modify the common law parol evidence rule?

3. In England, in 1976, the Law Commission reached a provisional conclusion that the parol evidence rule should be abolished (Working Paper No. 70). This was then echoed in 1979 in both the British Columbia Law Reform Commission's *Report on Parol Evidence*, and the O.L.R.C.'s *Report on Sale of Goods* (1979), vol. 1, at 110-17. The Ontario Law Reform Commission listed six major defects in the parol evidence rule:

   (i)   The rule is seriously ambiguous.

   (ii)   The rule is more honoured in its breach than in its observance.

   (iii)   The rule does not recognize the realities of modern standard form agreements.

   (iv)   The rule draws an artificial distinction between contractual and non-contractual representations.

   (v)   The rule runs against the modern trend in the law of evidence.

   (vi)   The rule does not, in fact, lead to more efficient or speedier trials.

The Commission continued:

> Considerations such as the above led the English Law Commission to conclude that the "parol evidence rule no longer serves any useful purpose. It is a technical rule of uncertain ambit which, at best, adds to the complications of litigation without affecting the outcome and, at worst, prevents the courts from getting at the truth." We agree with this verdict, and now proceed to consider a number of possible solutions to the present impasse.

> ALTERNATIVE SOLUTIONS

> We have already indicated the English Law Commission's proposal to abolish the parol evidence rule. The New South Wales Law Reform Commission in its *Working Paper on the*

Sale of Goods has made a recommendation which, although it appears to be similar in effect, is expressed differently. The Commission proposed that the rule be modified "so that if a contract for the sale of goods is in writing the presumption is that it is not intended to be the conclusive and exclusive record of the transaction and that the onus of proof that it is so intended should be on the party alleging such to be the case". The Commission also felt that the use of standard clauses to establish such an intention should be frowned upon, and that they should be given little or no weight. We construe these recommendations as involving the abolition of the existing rule, coupled with a shifting of the burden of proof to the party alleging the integrated nature of the writing. It is not, however, clear from the Working Paper how the burden is to be discharged in practice, or what would be sufficient to discharge the burden.

Another alternative would be to confer upon the court the power not to apply the rule in a given case where, in the court's opinion, it would be unreasonable to do so. Although initially attracted to this solution as a compromise between total abolition and maintenance of the status quo, we are of the view that it suffers from two important weaknesses. The first is that it does not address itself directly to the artificial nature of the rule: it seeks to mitigate, rather than eliminate, the rule. The second is that it would add one more element of uncertainty in an area already abounding in uncertainty. The Commission therefore rejects this approach.

[The Report here sets out UCC s. 2-202.]

This section goes a substantial distance towards removing the objections to the parol evidence rule; but, in our opinion, it does not go far enough. The strengths of the section are as follows: (a) it rejects any assumption that, because some of the terms of an agreement have been reduced to writing, the parties intended it to be the final expression of all the terms; and, (b) its inferential rejection of the "four corners" or "appearance" test in determining the finality and exclusiveness of a writing. The weaknesses of the section are two-fold. First, it disallows the admissibility of extrinsic evidence that contradicts an express written term, whether or not the writing was intended to be an integrated document. Secondly, it fails to indicate how much weight is to be given to an integration or merger clause. As might be expected, the first weakness has proved to be particularly troublesome in practice, and some courts have been forced to resort to some rather artificial reasoning to justify the admissibility of extrinsic evidence that conflicts with the parties' writing.

CONCLUSION

Having reviewed the various alternatives, a majority of the Commission is impressed by the simplicity and flexibility of the English Law Commission's proposal, and adopts it as its own. Accordingly, we recommend that the parol evidence rule should not apply to a contract for the sale of goods. In the view of the majority of the Commissioners, the principal weakness of the parol evidence rule, as traditionally applied in England and Canada, has been the near-conclusive presumption of exclusiveness attached to formal instruments. If this hurdle is removed (and this, in our opinion, is all that the abolition of the parol evidence rule implies) it merely clouds the issue to encumber the reform with the type of qualifying language used in the Code. The majority finds support for this conclusion in the apparent success with which the provisions abolishing the rule have been applied in *The Business Practices Act* and in comparable statutes elsewhere.

It needs to be emphasized, however, as the English Law Commission also emphasized, that the abolition of the parol evidence rule is not likely to effect a radical change. The courts will continue to attach very great weight, and rightly so, to written terms freely consented to by the parties; they will continue to express scepticism with respect to the consensual nature of unbargained terms contained in printed forms of agreement. The main difference is likely to be that there will be less frequent recourse to circumstances that now constitute exceptions to the rule, especially the exception based on collateral agreements. This result would follow because, in the light of the evidence, the court would find it easier than under existing law to hold that the writing could not have been intended as the final and exclusive expression of the parties' agreement.

CONSEQUENTIAL ISSUES

We deal with two such issues. The first involves the conclusive character of merger or integration clauses. In our opinion, it would be futile to abolish the parol evidence rule without also indicating the status of such clauses. Canadian courts have generally tended to take them at face value. American courts have been divided in their approach, but those courts that have rejected the "four corners" rule have also rejected the conclusive character of merger clauses. This seems to us to be correct in principle. We therefore recommend that a provision in writing, purporting to state that the writing represents the exclusive expression of the parties' agreement, should have no conclusive effect. Our Draft Bill contains a provision to this effect. An alternative approach would have been to let the general unconscionability provision in the revised Act police the reasonableness of such clauses. In view of the importance and ubiquitousness of merger clauses, however, we think it better to provide some specific guidance than to leave the question completely at large.

The second issue is whether the abolition of the rules should be accompanied by special provisions with respect to the position of third parties claiming rights under the writing. We have decided that this is not necessary for a number of reasons. First, the rule in equity is that the assignee of a chose in action (which includes, of course, an assignee of contract rights) takes subject to equities; hence, an assignee is already very vulnerable under existing law, and the abolition of the parol evidence rule will not change his position materially. For example, in an action by an assignee of the seller's right to payment, the buyer is free to allege that the goods were never delivered, were not satisfactory, or that the agreement was induced by misrepresentation. Another reason is that, in the comparable provision in section 4(7) of *The Business Practices Act* abolishing the parol evidence rule in consumer transactions, no exception is made in favour of third parties. Further, the proposed provision only addresses itself to contracts of sale and does not purport to affect other transactions such as negotiable instruments, documents of title, or real estate conveyances where the rights of third parties do not depend upon equitable rules of assignment. A fourth reason is that, in sales situations, the problem is most likely to arise when an executed agreement has been discounted with a financial intermediary as, for example, in the case of consumer credit agreements and "factored" accounts. In such cases it is customary, or open, to the assignee to protect himself by various devices such as obtaining an acknowledgement of the account from the buyer, insertion of a "cut-off" clause in favour of the assignee, and the execution of a promissory note. The abolition of the parol evidence rule should not interfere with these practices. Finally, in our view, if it is desired to attach negotiable incidents to particular types of writing, it should be done by other means.

Accordingly, the Commission does not recommend that the abolition of the parol evidence rule should be accompanied by special provisions with respect to the position of third parties claiming rights under the writing.

Subsequently, the O.L.R.C.'s position was adopted by the Uniform Law Conference of Canada in 1981 and encapsulated by the following provision in its draft Uniform Sale of Goods Act.

17. No rule of law or equity respecting parol or extrinsic evidence and no provision in a writing prevents or limits the admissibility of evidence to prove the true terms of the agreement, including evidence of any collateral agreement or representation or evidence as to the true identity of the parties.

The O.L.R.C. then returned to the issue as part of its consideration of the general law of Contract and made the following recommendations: *Report on Amendment of the Law of Contract* (1987), at 163:

1. (a) Evidence or oral agreement to terms not included in, or inconsistent with, a written document should be admissible to prove the real bargain between the parties.

 (b) Conclusive effect should not be attached to merger and integration clauses.

2. In order to give effect to the above-mentioned recommendations, a provision similar to section 17 of the Uniform Sale of Goods Act, but applicable to all types of contracts, should be enacted.

Interestingly, in the interim, the English Law Commission produced its final *Report on the Parol Evidence Rule* (Law Comm. Report No. 154) and concluded that in the light of judicial developments, legislative abolition of the Rule was no longer needed. See Marston, "The Parol Evidence Rule: The Law Commission Speaks" (1986), 45 Cambridge L.J. 192. To this, the O.L.R.C. responded, at 162, that the judicial development of the Rule in Ontario could not allow the same conclusion to be drawn.

4. In "Do We Need a Parol Evidence Rule?" (1991), 19 Can. Bus. L.J. 385 at 394-96, Waddams responds to the proposals for "abolition" of the parol evidence rule as follows:

Let us suppose an express oral agreement, amply proved by convincing evidence, after lengthy negotiations between equal parties as follows: "In the course of the negotiations over the past week, we have both offered concessions on various points at various times. We recognize the difficulties of reconstructing an agreement from diffuse negotiations and we both affirm that all statements, concessions, offers, promises and negotiations are superseded by this document [pointing to it] which we both agree is the exclusive record of our agreement." That is a very reasonable agreement, potentially to the advantage of both parties. It can be said to be efficient, for it saves the need to identify and deny expressly every concession made during negotiations. If such an agreement is made orally, or is included in the writing, or is inferred from the parties' conduct, and genuinely represents their intentions, and is not obtained by a misuse of superior bargaining power, there is, I would suggest, every reason to enforce it.

For this reason some of the proposals for "abolition" of the parol evidence rule seem to me to go too far, at least where they are not limited to cases of standard forms or of consumer transactions where possibly a case might be made that mistake and unconscionability are common. In my view some of the proposals deprive parties of power to make what is a sensible, efficient and commercially useful agreement, and I see no justification for such a limitation on freedom of contract subject, I would repeat, to considerations of mistake and unconscionability.

It is difficult to oppose a proposal so attractive sounding as that the "true terms" of an agreement should prevail. But the proposal appears to rest on false assumption. It is unrealistic to suppose that parties to a complex agreement have all the terms in mind at the moment of signature, as though there were a "true" subjective agreement on every point. The only true agreement often is that the document will prevail. Where a signer does direct his mind to a point on which he has earlier received oral assurances that are not reflected in the document, his attitude will often be that he does not expect the problem to arise; that if it does, he will hope to renegotiate; and that insisting on a clear revision of the document in his favour may well alarm the other party or her advisers, and jeopardize the whole agreement. Documents can never deal with every conceivable situation, and it is probably undesirable that they should. At the point of agreement the parties say to each other, in effect: the drafting process must stop somewhere if we are ever to implement this agreement. Despite the imperfections of this document, we agree to be bound, for better or worse, by what it says. Even an actual mistake about the effect of the document is insufficient ground for relief unless the other party had reason to know of it. There are, therefore, a large number of cases in which enforcement of the terms of a written document against a promisor is fully in accordance with justice and with general principles of contract formation, even though the content of those terms was not in the conscious mind of the promisor at the moment of contract formation. This point may appear to be obvious, but reference to the "true" terms of the agreement tends to obscure it.

The approach suggested by these considerations is that, while a rule that treats documents as always conclusive is unacceptable, so also is a rule that lays down that a document can never be conclusive. Signature to a document should create a strong presumption, but a presumption only, that the writing is to prevail. Whether it does prevail must depend on the determination of the parties' contractual intention in the particular case.

This approach, in my view, gives power to the court to do justice in every case where there has been reliance on extrinsic statements, while not depriving the parties of the power, if such is indeed their true intention, of agreeing that a document shall be conclusive. All relevant evidence is admissible to establish whether or not it has been agreed that a document is to be conclusive. If and when (but only when) such an agreement has been established, it should be enforced.

A rule to the effect proposed in the preceding paragraph is not a rule of evidence, though it has evidentiary consequences because it makes the detailed content of any antecedent agreements or negotiations that have been superseded by the document irrelevant. It is doubtful whether such a principle requires any special name. Preferably it should not be called the parol evidence rule. But it represents, in my opinion, a sound application of general principles of contract law. It would remove the excessive sanctity that some cases have attributed to contractual documents, while at the same time preserving general contractual principles and useful commercial practice.

[Footnotes omitted.]

5. Does the following Article in a proposed plain English Australian Contract Code reflect adequately Waddams' position?

Article 25

A court may exclude evidence which is inconsistent with an obviously genuine, complete and unequivocal document recording a contract.

See *An Australian Contract Code* (Discussion Paper No. 27, Law Reform Commission of Victoria, 1992) at 15. How might a court determine what is "obviously" such a document?

7. Classification of Terms

In previous sections, problems associated with defining the outer limits of one's contractual obligation were considered. In this section, we assume that the affirmation or promise in question is a term of the agreement and consider a further range of problems which arise when one asks whether the party who has given a contractual undertaking is invariably bound to perform it, whether or not the other party has given or is prepared to give the performance which he or she has promised to render in return.

A brief illustration indicates the issues which must be considered. A promises to employ B for 12 months at a salary of $4,000 per month. Must A continue to pay B even though B refuses to work after the first month? Must B continue to work if A refuses to pay? Must B complete one month's work before A can be obliged to pay? In short, what is the order of performance in this agreement? Further, what are the consequences of one party's failure to perform? May the other party refuse to perform or must he or she continue to perform and be content with a lawsuit for damages for breach of contract?

It is evident that a rule which bound the promisor to perform in any event would be capable of working great hardship on the non-defaulting party. The solution which the courts developed for this problem was to infer that in appropriate cases the performance of one party's obligation was conditioned or contingent upon the completion of performance by the other party. Thus if, in our example, it was determined that continued performance by B was required only if A had performed the obligation to pay, it might be said that it is a condition of B's obligation to serve that A performs his or her duty to pay. An elliptical (and rather confusing) way of expressing the same notion is to say that the term of the agreement in which A promises to pay is a "condition" of the agreement.

If it were concluded that B is obliged to perform in any event, A's obligation to pay would be described as a mere "warranty". Breach of that obligation by A would not relieve B from continuing to perform. B's sole remedy, in effect, would be to sue for damages for breach of contract.

The historical development of the rules by which the courts attempted to distinguish mere warranties from terms which are of such a nature that their performance is a condition of the other party's obligation to perform is described in the reasons for judgment rendered by Diplock L.J. in the *Hong Kong Fir Shipping* case, reproduced *infra*.

Compare the more traditional approach which concentrates on the interpretation of the contract, with the more modern approach suggested in *Hong Kong Fir*, which goes hand-in-hand with the recognition of innominate terms or intermediate stipulations.

HONG KONG FIR SHIPPING CO. LTD. v. KAWASAKI KISEN KAISHA LTD.

[1962] 2 Q.B. 26, [1962] 1 All E.R. 474 (C.A.)

By a time charter, it was mutually agreed between the owners of the vessel Hong Kong Fir and the charterers that (cl. 1) the owners would let and that the charterers hire the vessel for twenty-four months from the date of her delivery to the charterers at Liverpool "she being in every way fitted for ordinary cargo service", and that (cl. 3) the owners would "maintain her in a thoroughly efficient state in hull and machinery during service". Hire was payable at the rate of 47s. per ton, but it was provided that no hire should be paid for time lost exceeding twenty-four hours in carrying out repairs to the vessel and that such off-hire periods might at the charterers' option be added to the charter time. The vessel was delivered to the charterers at Liverpool on Feb. 13, 1957, and on the same day she sailed for Newport News, U.S.A., to load a cargo of coal which she was to carry to Osaka. When she was delivered to the charterers at Liverpool, her engine-room was undermanned and her engine-room staff incompetent, although the owners knew that the vessel's machinery was very old and, therefore, required an ample and efficient engine-room staff to maintain it. During the voyage to Osaka, the vessel was off hire for repairs to her engines for a total period of about five weeks, and when she arrived at Osaka, on May 25, 1957, it was found that the engines were in a very bad state and that it would take a further fifteen weeks to make the vessel seaworthy. The condition of the engines at Osaka was due mainly to the inefficiency of the engine-room staff on the voyage from Liverpool. By Sept. 15, 1957, the vessel had been made seaworthy in every respect and then had an efficient and adequate engine-room staff; at that date she was still available to the charterers for seventeen months. In mid-June, there had been a steep fall in freight rates from 47s. to 24s. per ton, and by mid-August the rates had dropped again to 13s. 6d. per ton. On June 6 and on Sept. 11, 1957, the charterers had written to the owners repudiating the charter. In an action by the owners for wrongful repudiation, the trial judge found that the owners were in breach of cl. 1 of the charter in delivering a vessel that was unseaworthy with regard to her engine-room staff, and were also in breach of cl. 3 in negligently failing to maintain the vessel in an efficient state, but that in June there were no reasonable grounds for thinking that the owners were unable to make the vessel seaworthy by mid-September at the latest. The charterers contended that the owners' breaches of charter entitled them to repudiate the charter, alternatively that the charter had been frustrated. At trial, Salmon J. found that the vessel was unseaworthy, but rejected the alternative contentions of the charterer that the contract was frustrated or that it was entitled to repudiate for breach of contract.

DIPLOCK L.J. . . . . Every synallagmatic contract contains in it the seeds of the problem: in what event will a party be relieved of his undertaking to do that which he has agreed to do but has not yet done? The contract may itself expressly define some of these events, as in the cancellation clause in a charterparty, but, human prescience being limited, it seldom does so exhaustively and often fails to do so at all. In some classes of contracts, such as sale of goods, marine insurance, contracts of affreightment evidenced by bills of lading and those between parties to bills of exchange, Parliament has defined by statute some of the events not provided for expressly in individual contracts of that class; but, where an event occurs the occurrence of which neither the parties nor Parliament have expressly stated will discharge one of the parties from further performance of his undertakings, it is for the court to determine whether the event has this effect or not. The test whether an event has this effect or not has been stated in a number of metaphors all of which I think amount to the same thing: does the occurrence of the event deprive the party who has further undertakings still to perform of substantially the whole benefit which it was the intention of the parties as expressed in the contract that he should obtain as the consideration for performing those undertakings? This test is applicable whether or not the event occurs as a result of the default of one of the parties to the contract, but the consequences of the event are different in the two cases. Where the event occurs as a result of the default of one party, the party in default cannot rely on it as relieving himself of the performance of any further undertakings on his part and the innocent party, although entitled to, need not treat the event as relieving him of the performance of his own undertakings. This is only a specific application of the fundamental legal and moral rule that a man should not be allowed to take advantage of his own wrong. Where the event occurs as a result of the default of neither party, each is relieved of the further performance of his own undertakings, and their rights in respect of undertakings previously performed are now regulated by the Law Reform (Frustrated Contracts) Act, 1943. . . .

In the earlier cases before the Common Law Procedure Act, 1852, the problem tends to be obscured to modern readers by the rules of pleading peculiar to the relevant forms of action—covenant, debt and assumpsit, and the nomenclature adopted in the judgments, which were mainly on demurrer, reflects this. It was early recognized that contractual undertakings were of two different kinds: those collateral to the main purpose of the parties as expressed in the contract, and those which were mutually dependent so that the non-performance of an undertaking of this class was an event which excused the other party from the performance of his corresponding undertakings. In nomenclature of the eighteenth and early nineteenth centuries, undertakings of the latter class were called "conditions precedent", and a plaintiff under the rules of pleading had to aver specially in his declaration his performance or readiness and willingness to perform all those contractual undertakings on his part which constituted conditions precedent to the defendant's undertaking for non-performance of which the action was brought. . . .

The fact that the emphasis in the earlier cases was on the breach by one party to the contract of his contractual undertakings, for this was the commonest circumstance in which the question arose, tended to obscure the fact that it was really the event resulting from the breach which relieved the other party of further performance of his obligations; but the principle was applied early in the nineteenth century and without analysis to cases where the event relied on was one brought about by a party to a contract before the time performance of his undertakings arose, but which would make it impossible to perform those obligations when the time to do so did arrive. . . . It was not, however, until *Jackson v. Union Marine Ins. Co.* (1874), L.R. 10 C.P. 125 (Ex. Ch.), that it was recognized that it was the happening of the event and not the fact that the event was the result of a breach by one party of his contractual obligations that relieved the other party from further performance of his obligations. Bramwell B. . . . said:

> . . . there are cases which hold that, where the shipowner has not merely broken his contract, but so broken it that the condition precedent is not performed, the charterer is discharged . . . Why? Not merely because the contract is broken. If it is not a condition precedent, what matters is whether it is unperformed with or without excuse? Not arriving with due diligence, or at a day named, is the subject of a cross-action only. But, not arriving in time for the voyage contemplated, but at such a time that it is frustrated, is not only a breach of contract, but discharges the charterer. And so it should, though he has such an excuse that no action lies.

Once it is appreciated that it is the event and not the fact that the event is a result of a breach of contract which relieves the party not in default of further performance of his obligations, two consequences follow: (i) The test whether the event relied on has this consequence is the same whether the event is the result of the other party's breach of contract or not. . . . (ii) The question whether an event which is the result of the other party's breach of contract has this consequence cannot be answered by treating all contractual undertakings as falling into one of two separate categories: "conditions", the breach of which gives rise to an event which relieves the party not in default of further performance of his obligations, and "warranties", the breach of which does not give rise to such an event. Lawyers tend to speak of this classification as if it were comprehensive, partly for the historical reasons which I have already mentioned, and partly because Parliament itself adopted it in the Sale of Goods Act, 1893, as respects a number of implied terms in contracts for the sale of goods and has in that Act used the expressions "condition" and "warranty" in that meaning. But it is by no means true of contractual undertakings in general at common law.

No doubt there are many simple contractual undertakings, sometimes express, but more often because of their very simplicity ("It goes without saying") to be implied, of which it can be predicated that every breach of such an undertaking must give rise to an event which will deprive the party not in default of substantially the whole benefit which it was intended that he should obtain from the contract. And such a stipulation, unless the parties have agreed that breach of it shall not entitle the non-defaulting party to treat the contract as repudiated, is a "condition". So, too, there may be other simple contractual undertakings of which it can be predicated that *no* breach can give rise to an event which will deprive the party not in default of substantially the whole benefit which it was intended that he should obtain from the contract; and such a stipulation, unless the parties have agreed that breach of it shall entitle the non-defaulting party to treat the contract as repudiated, is a "warranty". There are, however, many contractual undertakings of a more complex character which cannot be categorized as being "conditions" or "warranties". . . . Of such undertakings, all that can be predicated is that some breaches will, and others will not, give rise to an event which will deprive the party not in default of substantially the whole benefit which it was intended that he should obtain from the contract; and the legal consequences of a breach of such an undertaking, unless provided for expressly in the contract, depend on the nature of the event to which the breach gives rise and do not follow automatically from a prior classification of the undertaking as a "condition" or a "warranty". For instance, to take the example of Bramwell B. in *Jackson v. Union Marine Ins. Co.*, by itself breach of an undertaking by a shipowner to sail with all possible dispatch to a named port does not necessarily relieve the charterer of further performance of his obligation under the charter-party, but, if the breach is so prolonged that the contemplated voyage is frustrated, it does have this effect.

In 1874, when the doctrine of frustration was being foaled by "impossibility of performance" out of "condition precedent", it is not surprising that the explanation given by Bramwell B., should give full credit to the dam by suggesting that in addition to the express *warranty* to sail with all possible dispatch there was an implied *condition precedent* that the ship should arrive at the named port in time for the voyage contemplated. In *Jackson v. Union Marine Ins. Co.*, there was no breach of the express warranty; but, if there had been, to engraft the implied condition on the express warranty would have been merely a more complicated way of saying that a breach of a shipowner's undertaking to sail with all possible dispatch may, but will not necessarily, give rise to an event which will deprive the charterer of substantially the whole benefit which it was intended that he should obtain from the charter. Now that the doctrine of frustration has matured and flourished for nearly a century and the old technicalities of pleading "conditions precedent" are more than a century out of date, it does not clarify, but on the contrary obscures, the modern principle of law where such an event *has* occurred as a result of a breach of an express stipulation in a contract, to continue to add the now unnecessary colophon

> therefore it was an implied *condition* of the contract that a particular kind of breach of an express *warranty* should not occur.

The common law evolves not merely by breeding new principles but also, when they are fully grown, by burying their ancestors.

As my brethren have already pointed out, the shipowner's undertaking to tender a seaworthy ship has, as a result of numerous decisions as to what can amount to "unseaworthiness", become one of the most complex of contractual undertakings. It embraces obligations with respect to every part of the hull and machinery, stores and equipment and the crew itself. It can be broken by the presence of trivial defects easily and rapidly remediable as well as by defects which must inevitably result in a total loss of the vessel. Consequently, the problem in this case is, in my view, neither solved nor soluble by debating whether the owners' express or implied undertaking to tender a seaworthy ship is a "condition" or a "warranty". It is, like so many other contractual terms, an undertaking one breach of which may give rise to an event which relieves the charterer of further performance of his undertakings if he so elects, and another breach of which may not give rise to such an event but entitle him only to monetary compensation in the form of damages. It is, with all deference to counsel for the charterers' skilful argument, by no means surprising that, among the many hundreds of previous cases about the shipowner's undertaking to deliver a seaworthy ship, there is none where it was found profitable to discuss in the judgments the question whether that undertaking is a "condition" or a "warranty"; for the true answer, as I have already indicated, is that it is neither, but one of that large class of contractual undertakings, one breach of which may have the same effect as that ascribed to a breach of "condition" under the Sale of Goods Act, 1893, and a different breach of which may have only the same effect as that ascribed to a breach of "warranty" under that Act. . . .

What the learned judge had to do in the present case, as in any other case where one party to a contract relies on a breach by the other party as giving him a right to elect to rescind the contract, was to look at the events which had occurred as a result of the breach at the time at which the charterers purported to rescind the charterparty, and to decide whether the occurrence of those events deprived the charterers of substantially the whole benefit which it was the intention of the parties as expressed in the charterparty that the charterers should obtain from the further performance of their own contractual undertakings. One turns, therefore, to the contract, the Baltime 1939 Charter. Clause 13, the "due diligence" clause, which exempts the shipowners from responsibility for delay or loss or damage to goods on board due to unseaworthiness unless such delay or loss or damage has been caused by want of due diligence of the owners in making the vessel seaworthy and fitted for the voyage, is in itself sufficient to show that the mere occurrence of the events that the vessel was in some respect unseaworthy when tendered or that such unseaworthiness had caused some delay in performance of the charterparty would not deprive the charterer of the whole benefit which it was the intention of the parties he should obtain from the performance of his obligations under the contract—for he undertakes to continue to perform his obligations notwithstanding the occurrence of such events if they fall short of frustration of the contract and even deprives himself of any remedy in damages unless such events are the consequence of want of due diligence on the part of the shipowner.

The question which the learned judge had to ask himself was, as he rightly decided, whether or not, at the date when the charterers purported to rescind the contract, namely June 6, 1957, or when the owners purported to accept such rescission, namely Aug. 8, 1957, the delay which had already occurred as a result of the incompetence of the engine-room staff, and the delay which was likely to occur in repairing the engines of the vessel and the conduct of the owners by that date in taking steps to remedy these two matters, were, when taken together, such as to deprive the charterers of substantially the whole benefit which it was the intention of the parties they should obtain from further use of the vessel under the charterparty. In my view, in his judgment—on which I would not seek to improve—the learned judge took into account and gave due weight to all the relevant considerations and arrived at the right answer for the right reasons.

[Sellers and Upjohn L.JJ. delivered concurring judgments.]

NOTES and QUESTIONS

1. What does the term "condition" mean? Are all "conditions" promises? Are any "conditions" promises? Is a "condition" a "state of affairs"?

2. What does the term "warranty" mean? How can one distinguish terms of agreements which are "mere" warranties from terms which are such that their performance is a condition of the other party's duty to perform?

3. What is the third category of terms identified in *Hong Kong Fir*? Does the introduction of this concept into the law of contractual performance render the law more uncertain or unpredictable in its application?

4. Would it be preferable to have a simple rule that breach of "condition" would entitle the innocent party to repudiate but that all other breaches would sound in damages only? What are the disadvantages of such a rule? Consider the following provisions of the Ontario Sale of Goods Act, R.S.O. 1990, c. S.1, s. 12, which are common to the sales legislation in Commonwealth jurisdictions:

> 12.(1) Where a contract of sale is subject to a condition to be fulfilled by the seller, the buyer may waive the condition or may elect to treat the breach of the condition as a breach of warranty and not as a ground for treating the contract as repudiated.
>
> (2) Whether a stipulation in a contract of sale is a condition the breach of which may give rise to a right to treat the contract as repudiated or a warranty the breach of which may give rise to a claim for damages but not to a right to reject the goods and treat the contract as repudiated depends in each case on the construction of the contract, and a stipulation may be a condition, though called a warranty in the contract.
>
> (3) Where a contract of sale is not severable and the buyer has accepted the goods or part thereof, or where the contract is for specific goods the property in which has passed to the buyer, the breach of any condition to be fulfilled by the seller can only be treated as a breach of warranty and not as a ground for rejecting the goods and treating the contract as repudiated, unless there is a term of the contract, express or implied, to that effect.
>
> (4) Nothing in this section affects the case of a condition or warranty, fulfilment of which is excused by law by reason of impossibility or otherwise.

The Sale of Goods Acts also contain a provision preserving the rules of common law except insofar as they are inconsistent with the provisions of the Acts. Would *Hong Kong Fir* be applicable to a sale of goods transaction? See *Cehave N.V. v. Bremer Handelsgesellschaft m.b.h.; Hansa Nord, The*, [1976] Q.B. 44 (C.A.), in which Lord Denning M.R. used the expression "intermediate stipulation". See also, *Reardon Smith Line v. Yngvar Hansen-Tangen*, [1976] 3 All E.R. 570 (H.L.).

5. A offers to sell B a car for $500, delivery to take place at the end of the week. B accepts A's offer. Are there any "conditions" in their agreement? Consider the application of s. 27 of the Ontario

Sale of Goods Act, R.S.O. 1990, c. S.1 (a provision found in the sales legislation of other common law provinces):

> 27. Unless otherwise agreed, delivery of the goods and payment of the price are concurrent conditions, that is to say, the seller shall be ready and willing to give possession of the goods to the buyer in exchange for the price and the buyer shall be ready and willing to pay the price in exchange for possession of the goods.

Would you have been able to persuade a court to adopt this approach without the assistance of s. 27?

6. Your client wishes to purchase a business. You have been retained to draft the agreement in terms favourable to the purchaser. How would you secure to your client the right to withdraw from the agreement in the event that the seller's business does not comply with representations made during negotiations? How would you secure the purchaser's right to withdraw in the event that the seller fails to perform his contractual promises?

7. Since the suggestion in *Hong Kong Fir* that the proper way to categorize a breach is to concentrate on its practical effect, there have been a number of important English decisions relating to the question of the proper test to be used. In *The Mihalis Angelos*, [1971] 1 Q.B. 164, the Court of Appeal used the more traditional test for determining whether the innocent party was released from further performance of the contract by construing the terms of the contract themselves rather than examining the seriousness of the breach. In that case, on the basis of accepted usage, it was held that a promise that a ship would be ready to load by a certain date was a condition of a charterparty.

8. In *Bunge Corp. v. Tradax S.A.*, [1981] 2 All E.R. 513 (H.L.) the validity of the *Hong Kong Fir* approach was reaffirmed but the House of Lords held that the provision which required purchasers of a large tonnage of a commodity to give fifteen consecutive days' notice of the probable readiness of vessels hired to ship the commodity was a "condition" of the agreement in the traditional sense, notwithstanding the fact that the agreement did not clearly stipulate the consequences of breach. This decision was applied by the Alberta Court of Appeal in *Bank of B.C. v. Turbo Resources Ltd.* (1983), 148 D.L.R. (3d) 598. For a discussion of the decision in *Bunge*, see Hutchinson and Wakefield, "Contracts—Innominate Terms: Contractual Encounters of the Third Kind" (1982), 60 Can. Bar Rev. 335. The authors argue that the *Hong Kong Fir* test could usefully be restated in the following terms, at 343-44:

> A contractual term would be a condition if every breach of it *might* deprive the innocent party of substantially the whole benefit of the contract; a right to repudiate the contract would be available whatever the actual effects of the breach. A contractual term would be an innominate clause if some, but not necessarily every breach *might* deprive the innocent party of substantially the whole benefit of the contract; a right to repudiate the contract would only be available if the breach did in fact result in the innocent party being deprived of substantially the whole benefit of the contract. A contractual term would be a warranty if its breach would *never* deprive the innocent party of substantially the whole benefit of the contract; a right to repudiate the contract would never arise [emphasis added].

Do you agree that this represents an improvement of the *Hong Kong Fir* test and, if so, why?

KRAWCHUK v. ULRYCHOVA

(1996), 40 Alta. L.R. (3d) 196 (Prov. Ct.)

The plaintiff, Krawchuk, purchased an eight year old Arabian horse from the defendant as a riding horse for her eleven year old daughter. The plaintiff insisted on a guarantee of good health and soundness supported by a veterinarian's certificate. The defendant supplied a letter from a Dr. Rach stating that the horse was sound which was accepted in lieu of a formal certificate. The plaintiff took possession of and boarded the horse. Shortly thereafter, the horse was observed to be "cribbing" on a wooden fence, "that is, seizing a rail in its teeth and sucking air". According to Dr. Rach this habit releases stimuli into the horse's system giving it a "high." Some horses with a cribbing habit retain normal health. Others go off their food—preferring "cribbing" to oats—thereby suffering weight loss, and some develop colic. These conditions affect the horse's performance. The defendant denied any knowledge of the cribbing problem.

Dr. Rach, at trial, confirmed that when he examined the horse he noticed that the front teeth of the horse were worn - a sign of cribbing - but that the horse did not have the negative physical conditions which sometimes accompany cribbing. He further conceded that a cribbing habit meant that the horse was unsound and that he should have noted this problem in his letter. He failed to do so, he said, as he thought the transaction was between friends and that he need not mention bad habits. When the cribbing was discovered, the plaintiff was advised to provide a "cribbing" collar. This was done and the horse had not cribbed since.

The plaintiff sought to set aside the transaction and claimed for damages for breach of the guarantee of soundness. The trial judge found a breach in that the horse was "unsound" at the time of sale, and then turned to consider whether the breach gave rise to the right to repudiate. As the transaction was one for the sale of goods, it was necessary for the judge to consider the effect of various provisions of the Sale of Goods Act on this question.

SCOTT PROV J. . . . I must determine the second issue [the ability of the purchaser to repudiate the agreement] with which I have more difficulty. No one disputes that at the time of the purchase the horse was in good health and has generally remained so. The matter of soundness, however, relates to a vice or habit developed by this horse of "cribbing". The evidence indicates this "cribbing" is treatable and has in fact been treated by the use of a "cribbing" collar which prevents a horse from so doing.

The Sale of Goods Act, R.S.A. 1980, c. S-2, provides, in s. 14 thereof under the heading "Conditions and Warranties", as follows:

> 14(1) When a contract of sale is subject to any condition to be fulfilled by the seller, the buyer may waive the condition or may elect to treat the breach of the condition as a breach of warranty and not as a ground for treating the contract as repudiated.
> (2) Whether a stipulation in a contract of sale is a condition the breach of which may give rise to a right to treat the contract as repudiated or a warranty the breach of which may give rise to a claim for damages but not to a right to reject the goods and treat the contract as repudiated depends in each case on the construction of the contract.
> (3) A stipulation may be a condition though called a warranty in the contract.
> (4) When a contract of a sale is not severable and the buyer has accepted the goods or part of them, or a contract of sale is for specific goods the property in which has passed to the buyer, the breach of any condition to be fulfilled by the seller shall only be treated as a breach of warranty and not as a ground for rejecting the goods and treating the contract as repudiate unless there is a term of the contract expressed or implied to that effect.

This in my view merely codifies, in general terms, the common law in this regard. In this particular case there is certainly no express term in the contract that the buyer may repudiate same in the event of breach. Whether a term can be implied to be a fundamental condition, the breach of which allows the party to repudiate the contract, has in recent years given the Court some difficulty because of, as stated by Mr. Justice Stratton on behalf of the Alberta Court of Appeal in the case of *First City Trust Co. v. Triple Five Corp.* (1989), 57 D.L.R. (4th) 554 at 562: "the wide variety of expressions which have been used to define the nature of a term which, if breached by one party, entitles the party not in default to repudiate."

[T]he review of the applicable case law in this area of conditions and warranties by Mr. Justice Stratton including the case of *Hong Kong Fir Shipping Co. v. Kawasaki Kisen Kaisha Ltd.*, [*supra*], which introduced the proposition that the gravity of the consequences of the breach should be looked at to determine if the innocent party may repudiate the contract, is worthy of note, Mr. Justice Stratton stating at pages 564 through 566:

> In my view the House of Lords in *Bunge Corp. v. Tradax S.A.*, [1981] 2 All E.R. 513, places the correct interpretation on the effect of *Hongkong Fir* and clarifies the present law on the point.
>
> .....
>
> Lord Scarman, at p. 543 of the report of the *Bunge* case, succinctly summarized the law on the point as he felt it should be in the light of the *Hongkong Fir* decision:
>
>> "The first question is always, therefore, whether, on the true construction of a stipulation and the contract of which it is part, it is a condition, an innominate term, or only a warranty. If the stipulation is one which on the true construction of the contract the parties have not made a condition, and breach of which may be attended by trivial, minor or very grave consequences, it is innominate, and the court (or an arbitrator) will, in the event of dispute, have the task of deciding whether the breach that has arisen is such as the parties would have said, had they been asked at the time they made their contract, 'It goes without saying that, if that happens, the contract is at an end.'"
>
> He then draws the following conclusion:
>
>> "Unless the contract makes it clear, either by express provision or by necessary implication arising from its nature, purpose and circumstances ("the factual matrix" as spelt out, for example, by Lord Wilberforce in his speech in *Reardon Smith Line Ltd v. Hansen-Tangen*, [1976] 3 All E.R. 570 at 573-575, (1976) 1 WLR 989 at 995-997), that a particular stipulation is a condition or only a warranty, it is an innominate term the remedy for breach of which depends on the nature, consequences and effect of the breach."
>
> .....
>
> Although the decision in *Bunge* is not binding on this court, its persuasive effect is substantial. I am satisfied that the test set out in *Hongkong Fir*, as explained by *Bunge* does not replace the earlier and traditional rules as to when an innocent party is excused from a breach by the other party. It did, however, introduce a new test, namely, one based on a consideration of the gravity of the consequences of a breach, which under certain circumstances should be applied.
>
> The traditional test that has consistently been cited with approval and applied by the courts is that stated by Bowen L. J. in *Bentsen v. Taylor, Sons & Co. (2)*, (1893) 2 Q.B. 274 (C.A.) at p. 281:
>
>> "There is no way of deciding that question except by looking at the contract in the light of the surrounding circumstances, and then making up one's mind whether the intention of the parties, as gathered from the instrument itself, will best be carried out by treating the promise as a warranty sounding only in damages, or as a condition precedent by the failure to perform which the other party is relieved of his liability."

.....

It will be noted that the test to determine intent as enunciated by Bowen L. J. requires one to look not only at the words of the contract but at surrounding circumstances.

In *Reardon Smith Line Ltd. v. Hansen-Tangen*, [1976] 3 All E.R. 570 (H.L.), Lord Wilberforce, in noting that the term "surrounding circumstances" was imprecise said, at p. 574:

> "In a commercial contract it is certainly right that the court should know the commercial purpose of the contract and this in turn presupposes knowledge of the genesis of the transaction, the background, the context, the market which the parties are operating."

Then later in his judgment at p. 575 he observed: ". . . what the court must do must be to place itself in thought in the same factual matrix as that in which the parties were".

In *Bank of British Columbia v. Turbo Resources Ltd.* (1983), 148 D.L.R. (3d) 598, 46 A.R. 22, 27 Alta. L.R. (2d) 17, this court after citing *Bunge*, *supra*, held that all the circumstances of the commercial setting of the contract must be considered in determining whether a breach went to the root of the contract.

The traditional test, in my view, can be readily reconciled with the so-called "third category" approach put forward in *Hongkong Fir*. The approach which I believe to have been accepted by the authorities can briefly be summarized as follows: (1) the test enunciated by Bowen L. J. remains the starting point; (2) the surrounding circumstances referred to in that test must include the commercial setting, and (3) if it cannot be determined by those considerations whether the parties intended the obligation in question to be a warranty sounding only in damages or a condition, the breach of which would release the innocent party, then the basis for seeking out that intent should be, as put forward by *Hongkong Fir*, namely, an assessment of the gravity of the event to which the breach gave rise.

As to the applicability of the *Hong Kong Fir* case to the provisions of the Sale of Goods Act, referred to earlier Section 59 thereof provides:

> 59(1) The rules of the common law including the law merchant except insofar as they are inconsistent with the express provisions of this Act, and in particular the rules relating to the law of principal and agent and the effect of fraud, misrepresentation, duress or coercion mistake or other invalidating cause, continue to apply to contracts for the sale of goods.

I agree with the comments . . . of the English Court of Appeal in the English case of *Cehave N.V. v. Bremer Handelgesellschaft mbH*, [1976] Q.B. 44 (C.A.), and in particular those of Lord Denning at p.60, in reference to the similar section of the *Sale of Goods Act*, 1893 (U.K.), 56 & 57 Vict., c. 71, referring to the division between conditions and warranties as set out in that act as being non exhaustive stated:

> It left out of account the vast majority of stipulations which were neither "conditions" nor "warranties" strictly so called: but were intermediate stipulations, the effect of which depended on the breach. The cases about these stipulations were legion. They stretched continuously from . . . 1777 to . . . 1884 . . . Those cases expressed the rules of the common law. They were preserved by . . . the 1893 Act, which said:
>
> > "The rules of the common law including the law merchant, save in so far as they are inconsistent with the express provisions of this Act . . . shall continue to apply to contract for the sale of goods."
>
> There was nothing in the Act inconsistent with those cases. So they continue to apply.
>
> In 1962 in . . . *Hongkong Fir* . . ., the Court of Appeal drew attention to this vast body of case law. They showed that, besides conditions and warranties, strictly so called, there are many stipulations of which the effect depends on this: if the breach goes to the root of the contract,

the other party is entitled to treat himself as discharged: but if it does not go to the root, he is not. In my opinion, the principle embodied in these cases applies to contracts for the sale of goods just as to all other contracts.

In view of Mr. Justice Stratton's conclusions in the *First City Trust* case that *Hong Kong Fir* does not alter the traditional rules and those rules are not inconsistent with the provisions of the Alberta *Sale of Goods Act*, the test set out by Mr. Justice Stratton should apply in this case. Applying those tests to the circumstances of this case, the horse was being purchased by the Plaintiff as a riding horse for her daughter and not as competition or show horse. The evidence of Dr. Rach is that the fact that a horse is a "cribber" and therefore unsound does not prevent its use for a particular purpose such as riding but that one has to take care to prevent the horse from "cribbing" which can be accomplished by the use of a collar. As stated, the evidence indicated that in November 1995 after a crib collar was applied to the horse the horse ceased "cribbing".

It is interesting to note that during the course of the trial some evidence was given that on two occasions since purchase, the horse had bucked and the Plaintiff was concerned about her daughter's safety. There was no suggestion nor can any inference be drawn from the evidence that the bucking of the horse was in any way attributable to its "cribbing". The Plaintiff, her daughter, and her cousin had each ridden the horse either on or both of the Saturday and Sunday April 14 and 15, 1995 with no evidence that the horse had a propensity to buck. Such a propensity goes neither to the question of the good health nor soundness of the horse which the Defendant "guaranteed". Nor is there any evidence to show that the Defendant knew or ought to have known that the horse had such a propensity. In that respect at least, I am of the view, that the principle of buyer beware must be applied. It would appear that the bucking gave more concern to the Plaintiff than the question of "cribbing" in that when the horse was first noticed to "crib" the Plaintiff contacted the Defendant and requested that the latter supply her with a cribbing collar. At that point there was no suggestion that she considered the "cribbing" was of grave concern and wished to repudiate the contract.

I am satisfied therefore both in terms of the construction of the contract, the surrounding circumstances and, if necessary to considering, "the gravity of the event to which the breach gave rise" the breach must be considered a breach of warranty and not breach of fundamental condition giving rise to repudiation of the contract.

As a result of that breach of warranty what damages flow? No hard evidence was presented as to what value one might place on a horse which "cribbs". Certainly I am satisfied that one would not pay "top dollar" for such a horse but there is no reason why with the use of a crib collar when it is not being ridden, it would prevent the horse from having a useful career as a riding horse. . . .

[Damages were assessed at $1500.]

NOTES and QUESTIONS

1. The damages awarded in *Krawchuk* represent approximately half the purchase price of the horse. Do you agree with the result?

2. The *Hong Kong Fir* analysis has been adopted in other Canadian decisions. See *First City Capital Ltd. v. Petrosar Ltd.* (1987), 61 O.R. (2d) 193 (H.C.); *Lehndorff Canadian Pension Properties Ltd. v. Davis Management Ltd.* (1989), 59 D.L.R. (4th) 1 (B.C. C.A.); *First City Trust Co. v. Triple Five Trust Corp. Ltd.* (1989), 57 D.L.R. (4th) 554 (Alta. C.A.); *Ramrod Investments Ltd. v. Matsumoto Shipyards Ltd.* (1990), 47 B.C.L.R. (2d) 86 (C.A.).

3. A rents an airplane from B for two years, starting January 1st, 2002. The lease provides for renewal for a further two years if A so notifies B in writing prior to midnight September 30th, 2003. A attempts to exercise this option on October 3rd, 2003. B refuses. B has suffered no prejudice as a result of the delay. Can A rely on the *Hong Kong Fir* analysis to establish that B's exclusive remedy for the late renewal is a claim in damages? See *United Dominions Trust (Commercial) Ltd. v. Eagle Aircraft Services Ltd.*, [1968] 1 W.L.R. 74, [1968] 1 All E.R. 104 (C.A.); *Dow Chemical of Canada Ltd. v. R V Industries Ltd.* (1979), 9 Alta. L.R. (2d) 129 (Q.B.).

4. In *Field v. Zien*, [1963] S.C.R. 632, the Supreme Court of Canada adopted an analytical method similar to that employed by Diplock L.J. in *Hong Kong Fir*. The contractual term in issue provided that on the closing of a transaction for the sale of a business, the total of the cash on hand, accounts receivable and inventory would exceed the accounts payable by $109,865. The contract did not stipulate that the term was either a "condition" or a "warranty". Judson J., at 635, writing for the court, stated:

> In deciding whether the remedy is rescission, with all its consequences or damages, the emphasis should be on the seriousness of the defective performance in the particular contract. Nothing in the way of clarity is gained by attaching a label to the clause.

Having regard to the relative significance of the shortage which had, in fact, occurred ($14,000) as against the contract price ($175,000), the ascertainable probability of its occurrence at the time of formation of the agreement, and the fact that the contract provided that final payment of $50,000 of the contract price was to be held back until four months after closing, Judson J. held that this was a proper case for damages.

5. In *968703 Ontario Ltd. v. Vernon* (2002), 58 O.R. (3d) 215 (C.A.), a more refined version of the Hong Kong Fir test for substantial or repudiatory breach was articulated. Vernon, through a group of companies, operated a gravel pit and processing plant. Having decided to sell off the assets of the business, he retained Headline, an auctioneering firm, to conduct an auction of the assets. The auction agreement stipulated that Headline would place all proceeds from sales arranged by Headline in a joint bank account with Vernon. It was envisaged that the auction would be followed by subsequent private sales. After the auction occurred, Headline breached the agreement by failing to deposit more than $100,000 of the proceeds into a joint bank account. Vernon then refused to allow Headline to sell the remaining assets. The Ontario Court of Appeal held that Vernon would be entitled to terminate the contract only if the breach by Headline was "substantial" not "minor". In applying this standard, the following factors were to be considered:

    (a) the ratio of the party's obligation not performed to the obligation as a whole;

    (b) the seriousness of the breach to the innocent party;

    (c) the likelihood of repetition of the breach;

    (d) the seriousness of the consequences of the breach; and

    (e) the relationship of the part of the obligation performed to the whole obligation.

See *ibid.*, at 222 *per* Weiler J.A. The court held that, in the circumstances, the breach was substantial and justified Vernon's refusal to allow Headline access to further assets. Is it important in such a case that the nature of the breach is suggestive of a lack of either integrity or a willingness to perform satisfactorily in the future?

WICKMAN MACHINE TOOL SALES LTD. v. L. SCHULER A.G.

[1974] A.C. 235, [1973] 2 All E.R. 39 (H.L.)

Schuler, a German manufacturing firm, entered into a written agreement with Wickman, an English company, which granted to Wickman the sole right to sell Schuler products, including panel presses, in a territory which included the United Kingdom. In order to ensure that aggressive sales efforts were undertaken by Wickman, the agreement contained the following provisions:

> 7. Promotion by [Wickman].
>
> > (a) Subject to Clause 17 [Wickman] will use its best endeavours to promote and extend the sale of Schuler products in the Territory.
> >
> > (b) It shall be condition of this Agreement that:—
> >
> > > (i) [Wickman] shall send its representatives to visit six [largest U.K. car manufacturers] at least once in every week for the purpose of soliciting orders for panel presses;
> > >
> > > (ii) that the same representative shall visit each firm on each occasion unless there are unavoidable reasons preventing the visit being made by that representative in which case the visit shall be made by an alternative representative and [Wickman] will ensure that such a visit is always made by the same alternate representative.
>
> [Wickman] agrees to inform Schuler of the names of the representatives and alternative representatives instructed to make the visits required by this clause.

Clause 11 provided for a power to determine the agreement in the following terms:

> 11. Duration of Agreement.
>
> > (a) This Agreement and the rights granted hereunder to [Wickman] shall commence on the First day of May 1963 and shall continue in force (unless previously determined as hereinafter provided) until the 31st day of December 1967 and thereafter unless and until determined by either party upon giving to the other not less than 12 months' notice in writing to that effect expiring on the said 31st day of December 1967 or any subsequent anniversary thereof PROVIDED that Schuler or [Wickman] may by notice in writing to the other determine this Agreement forthwith if:—
> >
> > > (i) the other shall have committed a material breach of its obligations hereunder and shall have failed to remedy the same within 60 days of being required in writing so to do or
> > >
> > > (ii) the other shall cease to carry on business or shall enter into liquidation (other than a members' voluntary liquidation for the purposes of reconstruction or amalgamation) or shall suffer the appointment of a Receiver of the whole or a material part of its undertaking;
> >
> > and PROVIDED FURTHER that Schuler may by notice determine this Agreement forthwith if [Wickman] shall cease to be a wholly-owned subsidiary of Wickman Limited. . . .

Wickman failed to comply strictly with its obligations under 7(b). Although Wickman representatives visited the named firms in most weeks, on a few occasions they failed to do so. Schuler repudiated the agreement, claiming that these defaults amounted to a breach of 'condition' and therefore conferred an absolute right to terminate the agreement.

At trial, Mocatta J. acceded to Schuler's argument and held that the agreement had been lawfully terminated. An appeal taken to the Court of Appeal was successful. Lord Denning M.R. suggested that the use of the term 'condition' in the agreement might draw upon any one of three possible meanings of that term ([1972] 2 All E.R. 1173 at 1180):

(a) *The proper meaning*

There are three meanings of 'condition' open to us. The first is the proper meaning, which is given pride of place in the Oxford English Dictionary: 'Something demanded or required as a prerequisite to the granting or performance of something else'; and which is carried over into the law in this way: 'In a legal instrument, e.g. a . . . contract, a provision on which its legal force or effect is made to depend.'

Applying this proper meaning, I ask myself: was this requirement (sending of a representative every week) 'a condition of the agreement' in this sense, that it was a prerequisite to the *very existence* of the agreement? . . . I do not think the word 'condition' was used in that sense in this clause. Even if Wickman Sales did not send the representative every week, the contract would not be void. That is obvious.

Alternatively, I next ask myself, was this requirement (sending of a representative every week) a 'condition of the agreement' in this sense, that it was a prerequisite to the *right to recover* on the agreement? So that, if Wickman Sales did not fulfil the requirement, they could not sue Schuler for a breach of the agreement? . . . I do not think the word 'condition' was used in that sense in this clause. For instance, if Wickman Sales introduced a purchaser and became entitled to commission, Schuler could not resist payment on the ground that Wickman Sales had failed to make one weekly visit. . . . This clause was an independent covenant, the breach of which could be paid for in damages, and was not a ground for refusing to pay commission.

So I would hold that the word 'condition'; is not used in this clause in its proper meaning.

(b) *The common meaning*

The second meaning of 'condition' is the common meaning which receives little attention in the Oxford English Dictionary: 'a provision, a stipulation'.

The word is frequently used by laymen and lawyers in this sense. When an agreement is made for the sale of land, it is always subject to 'conditions of sale'. The Law Society's 'Conditions of Sale' are in everyday use. . . . Whenever a quotation is given or invoice sent, the printed form invariably says it is subject to the 'conditions' on the back. In all these cases the word 'conditions' simply means *terms* of the contract. Sometimes these 'conditions' may contain a provision which is so expressed as to be a 'condition' proper, e.g. when something or other is a prerequisite of an obligation to pay. At other times it is simply a term of the contract which gives rise to damages if it is broken. Its effect depends solely on the true interpretation of the clause itself and not in the least on the fact that it is labelled a 'condition'.

(c) *The term of art*

I must turn to the third meaning of 'condition'. It is the meaning given to it by lawyers as a term of art. A 'condition' in this sense is a stipulation in a contract which carries with it this consequence: if the promisor breaks a 'condition' in any respect, however slight, it gives the other party a right to be quit of his future obligations and to sue for damages unless he, by his conduct, waives the condition, in which case he is bound to perform his future obligations, but can sue for the damages he has suffered. A 'condition' in this sense is used in contrast to a 'warranty'. If a promisor breaks a warranty in any respect, however serious, the other party is not quit of his future obligations. He has to perform them. His only remedy is to sue for damages. . . .

Lord Denning concluded that the word 'condition' in 7(b) should be interpreted as meaning an ordinary term of the contract and accordingly, that only material breaches would confer a right to determine in accordance with clause

11. Edmund Davies L.J. delivered concurring reasons; Stephenson L.J. dissented. The decision of the Court of Appeal was upheld by the House of Lords (Lord Wilberforce dissenting).

LORD REID Wickman's main contention is that Schuler were only entitled to determine the agreement for the reasons and in the manner proved in cl 11. Schuler, on the other hand, contend that the terms of cl 7 are decisive in their favour: they say that 'It shall be condition of this Agreement' in cl 7(b) means that any breach of cl 7(b)(i) or 7(b)(ii) entitles them forthwith to terminate the agreement. So as there were admittedly breaches of cl 7(b)(i) which were not waived they were entitled to terminate the contract.

I think it right first to consider the meaning of cl 11 because, if Wickman's contention with regard to this is right, then cl 7 must be construed in light of the provisions of cl 11. Clause 11 expressly provides that the agreement 'shall continue in force (unless previously determined as hereinafter provided) until' 31st December 1967. That appears to imply the corollary that the agreement shall not be determined before that date in any other way than as provided in cl 11. It is argued for Schuler that those words cannot have been intended to have that implication. In the first place Schuler say that anticipatory breach cannot be brought within the scope of cl 11 and the parties cannot have intended to exclude any remedy for an anticipatory breach. And, secondly, they say that cl 11 fails to provide any remedy for an irremediable breach however fundamental such breach might be.

There is much force in this criticism. But on any view the interrelation and consequences of the various provisions of this agreement are so ill-thought out that I am not disposed to discard the natural meaning of the words which I have quoted merely because giving to them their natural meaning implies that the draftsman has forgotten something which a better draftsman would have remembered. If the terms of cl 11 are wide enough to apply to breaches of cl 7 then I am inclined to hold that cl 7 must be read subject to the provisions of cl 11.

It appears to me that cl 11(a)(i) is intended to apply to all material breaches of the agreement which are capable of being remedied. The question then is what is meant in this context by the word 'remedy'. It could mean obviate or nullify the effect of a breach so that any damage already done is in some way made good. Or it could mean cure so that matters are put right for the future. I think that the latter is the more natural meaning. The word is commonly used in connection with diseases or ailments and they would normally be said to be remedied if they were cured although no cure can remove the past effect or result of the disease before the cure took place. And in general it can only be in a rare case that any remedy of something that has gone wrong in the performance of a continuing positive obligation will, in addition to putting it right for the future, remove or nullify damage already incurred before the remedy was applied. To restrict the meaning of remedy to cases where all damage past and future can be put right would leave hardly any scope at all for this clause. On the other hand, there are cases where it would seem a misuse of language to say that a breach can be remedied. For example, a breach of cl 14 by disclosure of confidential information could not be said to be remedied by a promise not to do it again.

So the question is whether a breach of Wickman's obligation under cl 7(b)(i) is capable of being remedied within the meaning of this agreement. On the one hand, failure to make one particular visit might have irremediable consequences, e.g. a valuable order might have been lost when making that visit would have obtained it. By looking at the position broadly I incline to the view that breaches of this obligation should be held to be capable of remedy within the meaning of cl 11. Each firm had to be visited more than 200 times. If one visit is missed I think that one would normally say that making arrangements to prevent a recurrence of that breach would remedy the breach. If that is right and if cl 11 is intended to have general application then cl 7 must be read so that a breach of cl 7(b)(i) does not give to Schuler a right to rescind but only to require the breach to be remedied within 60 days under cl 11 (a)(i). I do not feel at all confident that this is the true view but I would adopt it unless the provisions of cl 7 point strongly in the opposite direction; so I turn to cl 7.

Clause 7 begins with the general requirement that Wickman shall 'use its best endeavours' to promote sales of Schuler products. Then there is in cl 7(b)(i) specification of those best endeavours with regard to panel presses, and in cl 12(b) a much more general statement of what Wickman must do with regard to other Schuler products. This intention to impose a stricter obligation with regard to panel presses is borne out by the use of the word 'condition' in cl 7(b). I cannot accept Wickman's argument that condition here merely means term. It must be intended to emphasize the importance of the obligations in sub-cl (b)(i) and (b)(ii). But what is the extent of that emphasis?

Schuler maintain that the word 'condition' has now acquired a precise legal meaning; that, particularly since the enactment of the Sale of Goods Act 1893, its recognised meaning in English law is a term of contract any breach of which by one party gives to the other party an immediate right to rescind the whole contract. Undoubtedly the word is frequently used in that sense. There may, indeed, be some presumption that in a formal legal document it has that meaning. But it is frequently used with a less stringent meaning. One is familiar with printed 'conditions of sale' incorporated into a contract, and with the words 'for conditions see back' printed on a ticket. There it simply means that the 'conditions' are terms of the contract.

In the ordinary use of the English language 'conditions' has many meanings, some of which have nothing to do with agreements. In connection with an agreement it may mean a pre-condition: something which must happen or be done before the agreement can take effect. Or it may mean some state of affairs which must continue to exist if the agreement is to remain in force. The legal meaning on which Schuler rely is, I think, one which would not occur to a layman; a condition in that sense is not something which has an automatic effect. It is a term the breach of which by one party gives to the other an option either to terminate the contract or to let the contract proceed and, if he so desires, sue for damages for the breach.

Sometimes a breach of a term gives that option to the aggrieved party because it is of a fundamental character going to the root of the contract, sometimes it gives that option because the parties have chosen to stipulate that it shall have that effect. Blackburn J. said in *Bettini v. Gye*, 1 Q.B.D. 183 at 187: 'Parties may think some matter, apparently of very little importance, essential; and if they sufficiently express an intention to make the literal fulfilment of such a thing a condition precedent, it will be one.'

In the present case it is not contended that Wickman's failures to make visits amounted in themselves to fundamental breaches. What is contended is that the terms of cl 7 'sufficiently express an intention' to make any breach, however small, of the obligation to make visits a condition so that any such breach shall entitle Schuler to rescind the whole contract if they so desire.

Schuler maintain that the use of the word 'condition' is in itself enough to establish this intention. No doubt some words used by lawyers do have a rigid inflexible meaning. But we must remember that we are seeking to discover intention as disclosed by the contract as a whole. Use of the word 'condition' is an indication—even a strong indication—of such an intention but it is by no means conclusive. The fact that a particular construction leads to a very unreasonable result must be a relevant consideration. The more unreasonable the result the more unlikely it is that the parties can have intended it, and if they do intend it the more necessary it is that they shall make that intention abundantly clear.

Clause 7(b) requires that over a long period each of the six firms shall be visited every week by one or other of two named representatives. It makes no provision for Wickman being entitled to substitute others even on the death or retirement of one of the named representatives. Even if one could imply some right to do this, it makes no provision for both representatives being ill during a particular week. And it makes no provision for the possibility that one or other of the firms may tell Wickman that they cannot receive Wickman's representative during a particular week. So if the parties gave any thought to the matter at all they must have realised the probability that in a few cases out of the 1,400 required visits a visit as stipulated would be impossible. But if Schuler's contention is right failure to make even one visit entitles them to terminate the contract however blameless Wickman might be. This is so unreasonable that it must make me search for some other possible meaning of the contract. If none can be found then Wickman must suffer the consequences. But only if that is the only possible interpretation.

If I have to construe cl 7 standing by itself then I do find difficulty in reaching any other interpretation. But if cl 7 must be read with cl 11 the difficulty disappears. The word 'condition' would make any breach of cl 7(b), however excusable, a material breach. That would then entitle Schuler to give notice under cl 11(a)(i) requiring the breach to be remedied. There would be no point in giving such a notice if Wickman were clearly not in fault but if it were given Wickman would have no difficulty in shewing that the breach had been remedied. If Wickman were at fault then on receiving such a notice they would have to amend their system so that they could shew that the breach had been remedied. If they did not do that within the period of the notice then Schuler would be entitled to rescind.

In my view, that is a possible and reasonable construction of the contract and I would therefore adopt it. The contract is so obscure that I can have no confidence that this is its true meaning but for the reasons which I have given I think that it is the preferable construction. It follows that Schuler were not entitled to rescind the contract as they purported to do. So I would dismiss this appeal.

I must add some observations about a matter which was fully argued before your Lordships. The majority of the Court of Appeal were influenced by a consideration of actings subsequent to the making of the contract. In my view, this was inconsistent with the decision of this House in *James Miller and Partners Ltd. v. Whitworth Street Estates (Manchester) Ltd.*, [1970] A.C. 583 (H.L.). We were asked by Wickman to reconsider that decision on this point and I have done so. As a result I see no reason to change the view which I expressed in that case. . . .

LORD WILBERFORCE [agreeing that the subsequent actions should have been left out of account, but dissenting on the meaning of condition. In his opinion, the use of the word indicated that the term was one the breach of which entitled the aggrieved party to treat the contract as at an end]. . . . I would only add that, for my part, to call the clause arbitrary, capricious or fantastic, or to introduce as a test of its validity the ubiquitous reasonable man (I do not know whether he is English or German) is to assume, contrary to the evidence, that both parties to this contract adopted a standard of easygoing tolerance rather than one of aggressive, insistent punctuality and efficiency. This is not an assumption I am prepared to make, nor do I think myself entitled to impose the former standard on the parties if their words indicate, as they plainly do, the latter. . . .

[Lords Morris of Borth-Y-Gest, Simon of Glaisdale and Kilbrandon delivered judgments concurring in dismissing the appeal.]

QUESTIONS

1. How would you improve the drafting of the agreements in *Hong Kong Fir* and *Schuler*? More generally, how would you avoid the risk of a court determining that the consequences intended by the parties are "unreasonable" and hence, not a permissible construction of the agreement?

2. Do you think it makes any difference which test is used? If it does, which do you consider to be the better approach? Is it really a conflict between the values of certainty and flexibility?

3. See the section on fundamental breach, *infra*, Chapter 8, section 3(d)(v). Although conditions are often referred to as fundamental terms, the doctrine of fundamental breach was developed for a particular purpose, that of dealing with extremely wide disclaimer clauses. Once you have reviewed this material, consider whether every breach of a "condition" would constitute a fundamental breach for the purposes envisaged by the fundamental breach doctrine.

8.   Discharge by Performance or Breach

In previous sections of this chapter, the effect of a significant breach of contract in releasing an innocent party from the obligation to render further performance has been examined. In a later chapter, we will consider the various remedies available to the innocent party which may have the effect either of requiring the defaulting party to perform the agreement or to pay money damages which will be, in effect, a substitution for performance of the agreement. In this part, we consider the problems of the party in default. Two related questions are considered.

First, we consider the question of the extent to which the party in default may be able to enforce the agreement itself. Again, as it is not every breach of contract that releases the innocent party from the obligation to perform, it is obvious that in the case of breaches which do not release the innocent party, the contract remains in force and can be enforced by the defaulting party if the innocent party subsequently refuses one of its obligations under the agreement.

This may be an unattractive state of affairs for the innocent party and it is not surprising, therefore, that agreements are often drafted in such a way as to attempt to preclude a situation of this kind from arising. The problem can be conveniently illustrated in the context of building contracts. The owner of land who hires a contractor to erect a building might well wish to stipulate that it is a "condition" of the obligation to pay the contract price that the construction work be fully completed and, indeed, perhaps completed to the satisfaction of the owner's architect. If such an arrangement survives the analysis indicated by previous sections of this chapter, the consequence would be that the contractor would be unable to enforce the agreement until the work was fully and satisfactorily completed.

Even in the absence of an explicit arrangement of this kind, the common law has taken the position that in the case of so-called "entire contracts", that is to say, agreements to do specified work for a lump sum, it will be presumed that the performance must be "complete" before the hirer becomes liable to pay the lump sum. While this approach affords generous protection of the owner or hirer's interest in satisfactory performance, it is obviously capable of working great hardship on the supplier of work. For example, in *Cutter v. Powell* (1795), 101 E.R. 573, a seaman contracted to serve on a ship bound from Jamaica for Liverpool. He died before the voyage was completed and his estate was unable to recover for that part of the work which he did perform. Until the seaman's *entire* promise was performed, there was no obligation to pay. The rigorous approach taken in the earlier cases has been ameliorated to some extent by the development of a doctrine of "substantial performance" which is the subject of the first two cases reproduced below.

The second and related issue considered in this part concerns the extent to which a defaulting party who cannot enforce the agreement may have some other remedy which will enable him or her to recover the value of benefits conferred on the other party through partial performance of the agreement. If, for example, a building contractor completes four-fifths of a building project before becoming insolvent and therefore unable to complete the project, the contractor would normally not be able to enforce the agreement for reasons suggested above. But should the owner or hirer, on the other hand, be able to retain all or some of the benefits conferred without paying anything for them? Similarly, where a purchaser of goods pays a deposit or makes a partial payment of the purchase price before becoming insolvent and unable to complete the agreement, should the seller be able to retain the monies advanced even if the goods are easily resold at a profit to another purchaser? If the party in default can successfully sue to recover the value of benefits conferred in such circumstances, it is evident that these would not be claims for breach of contract. It is also obvious that they are not claims arising in tort. Are you familiar with any other theory of liability that might provide a basis for actions of this kind?

The two problems considered in this part are interrelated inasmuch as they together make up the armoury of remedial weapons available to the party in default. More than this, however, it may well be that the extent to which remedies of the latter kind are unavailable to the party in default may influence courts in developing an approach to the doctrine of substantial performance which is more generous to the party in default. Conversely, to the extent that remedies of the second type become more widely available, the need for a doctrine of substantial performance may be thought to diminish.

FAIRBANKS SOAP CO. v. SHEPPARD

[1953] 1 S.C.R. 314, [1953] 2 D.L.R. 193

S contracted to build a machine for F for a price of $9,800. F paid $1,000 on account. When the machine was nearly completed S refused to do more unless he was paid a further $3,000. F sued to recover the $1,000 and for other consequential losses. S counterclaimed for the contract price.

CARTWRIGHT J. [delivering the judgment of the court] ... I did not understand counsel to differ as to the present state of the law in Ontario but rather as to its application to the facts of the case at bar. In *Appleby v. Myers* (1867), L.R. 2 C.P. 651 (Ex. Ch.), a decision of the Exchequer Chamber in which the unanimous judgment of the Court ... was delivered by Blackburn J., that learned judge stated the general rule at page 661, as follows:

> ... the plaintiffs, having contracted to do an entire work for a specific sum, can recover nothing unless the work be done, or it can be shown that it was the defendant's fault that the work was incomplete, or that there is something to justify the conclusion that the parties have entered into a fresh contract.

The judgment in *Appleby v. Myers* was approved and acted upon by the Judicial Committee in *Forman & Co. Proprietary Ltd. v. The Liddesdale*, [1900] A.C. 190 (P.C.), particularly at page 202. In *Sumpter v. Hedges*, [*infra*] A.L. Smith L.J. said [at 674]:

> The law is that, where there is a contract to do work for a lump sum, until the work is completed the price of it cannot be recovered.

This rule was recognized by the Court of Appeal in *H. Dakin and Co. Ltd. v. Lee*, [1916] 1 K.B. 566 (C.A.), but it was pointed out that the word "completed" as used in the rule is, in certain circumstances, equivalent to "substantially completed". The judgments in *Dakin v. Lee* have been repeatedly approved and followed in Ontario, *vide, e.g., Taylor Hardware Co. v. Hunt* (1917), 35 D.L.R. 504 at 507, and in my respectful opinion they correctly state the law.

The real question on this appeal is whether the respondent substantially completed his contract to construct the machine. With the greatest respect for the contrary view held by the learned trial judge and the Court of Appeal, I have reached the conclusion that he did not. From a perusal of the written record I would have inclined to the view that the evidence of the appellant's expert witness Mitchell, who was of opinion that the machine when completed would not be capable of producing soap chips of commercial quality should be preferred to that of the experts called by the respondent not only because of his admitted high qualifications but because he appeared to have based his opinion on a much more thorough examination of the machine than was made by the other witnesses; but I do not rest my judgment on this view. In my opinion on the evidence of the respondent himself and of the witnesses called on his behalf there was no sub-stantial completion of the contract. At the time when the respondent definitely refused to proceed further with the construction of the machine it was incomplete in the following respects: the "knife" and "flange" were missing, baffles were required for the canvas apron screening on the dryer, further work was required on the fans and the speed of the machine had to be changed, being about six times as fast as was proper. It is urged on behalf of the respondent that these are comparatively unimportant details and that the allowance of $600 for the com-pletion of the machine made by the learned trial judge is a generous one. But it appears from the evidence of the respondent and his witnesses that what remained to be done required engineering skill and knowledge. The record is silent as to whether the services of an engineer other than the respondent possessing the necessary skills were available to the appellant. The situation was, I think, accu-rately summed up in the following answer made in re-examination by the expert witness Stokes called for the respondent:

> I think I know what both you gentlemen are trying to get at, and let me put it this way, it may not be legal or it may not be orthodox, but I am going to say this, if Fairbanks and Sheppard do not get together that machine will never run, it has to depend on the co-operation of two individuals just the same as ours at Guelph. If we had sat on the sidelines looking at it, it would never run. We had to co-operate with Sheppard and he had to co-operate with us. Everyone has to co-operate to operate the machine.

The respondent in his own evidence made it clear that he decided to desist from further construction at a time when the machine was not capable of producing soap chips and to refuse to bring it to the state where it would produce them unless and until he was paid moneys to which under the contract he was not then entitled. He says in effect that he had intentionally put in sprockets of the wrong size so that the appellant could not use the machine to produce soap chips. After stating that one reason for putting in a small sprocket was to "run the machine in" he added that he had another reason. He was questioned as to this by the learned trial judge as follows:

> His Lordship: You asked him what reason and he is not finished his answer. A. Will I give the other reason? Q. Yes. A. Because of the fact if I had gone and put the proper speeds on that dryer and I had put the knife on the dryer and operated that dryer producing chips, from my previous experience about the loan on the machine, with my dealings with Mr. Fairbanks with the machine, I had come to the firm conclusion I would have been locked out of the plant the same as Arneil, I would have been locked out and I would have had to sue him for my money. He could have fooled around for years and been making soap chips at my

expense. I have $6,000 tied up in the machine and I think I have a right to get something out of it before I operate it and he could go on and operate it for years.

I can find nothing in *Dakin v. Lee* (*supra*) or in the numerous other authorities referred to by counsel to indicate that under all these circumstances it could be said that the respondent had substantially completed his contract. The contract was to construct a machine to produce soap chips of a certain standard. The respondent refused to do anything further at a time when on his own evidence the partially constructed machine would not produce soap chips at all. In my opinion on the view of the evidence most favourable to the respondent he abandoned the work and left it unfinished. The difference between the facts of the case at bar and those in *Dakin v. Lee* (*supra*) are apparent on reading all the judgments in the last mentioned case, and it will be sufficient to refer to the following passage from the judgment of Lord Cozens-Hardy M.R. at pages 578 and 579:

> In these circumstances it has been argued before us that, in a contract of this kind to do work for a lump sum, the defect in some of the items in the specification, or the failure to do every item contained in the specification, puts an end to the whole contract, and prevents the builders from making any claim upon it; and therefore, where there is no ground for presuming any fresh contract, he cannot obtain any payment. The matter has been treated in the argument as though the omission to do every item perfectly was an abandonment of the contract. That seems to me, with great respect, to be absolutely and entirely wrong. An illustration of the abandonment of a contract which was given from one of the authorities was that of a builder who, when he had half finished his work, said to the employer "I cannot finish it, because I have no money," and left the job undone at that stage. That is an abandonment of the contract, and prevents the builder, therefore, from making any claim, unless there be some other circumstances leading to a different conclusion. But to say that a builder cannot recover from a building owner merely because some item of the work has been done negligently or inefficiently or improperly is a proposition which I should not listen to unless compelled by a decision of the House of Lords. Take a contract for a lump sum to decorate a house; the contract provides that there shall be three coats of oil paint, but in one of the rooms only two coats of paint are put on. Can anybody seriously say that under these circumstances the building owner could go and occupy the house and take the benefit of all the decorations which had been done in the other rooms without paying a penny for all the work done by the builder, just because only two coats of paint had been put on in one room where there ought to have been three?
>
> I regard the present case as one of negligence and bad workmanship, and not as a case where there has been an omission of any one of the items in the specification. The builders thought apparently, or so they have sworn, that they had done all that was intended to be done in reference to the contract; and I suppose the defects are due to carelessness on the part of some of the workmen or of the foreman: but the existence of these defects does not amount to a refusal by them to perform part of the contract; it simply shows negligence in the way in which they have done the work.

In the case at bar when the respondent knew the machine was not capable of producing soap chips he said to the appellant: "I will not finish it unless you pay me $3,000." In my opinion the conduct of the respondent falls within the illustration of abandonment of a contract given by the Master of Rolls in the above quoted passage.

Counsel for the respondent did not seek to base any claim in regard to this contract on a quantum meruit and I think it clear that, if, as I have held to be the case, there was no substantial completion of the contract, there was no evidence from which any new contract to accept and pay for the work done could be inferred. From the evidence it seems probable that the machine in its present state has become part of the realty which belongs to the appellant. Assuming this is to be so it is clear from the reasons in *Sumpter v. Hedges* [*infra*], that the mere fact of the appellant remaining in possession of his land is no evidence upon which an inference of a new contract can be founded. At page 676 Collins L.J. puts the matter as follows:

> There are cases in which, though the plaintiff has abandoned the performance of a contract, it is possible for him to raise the inference of a new contract to pay for the work done on a quantum meruit from the defendant's having taken the benefit of that work, but, in order that that may be done, the circumstances must be such as to give an option to the defendant to take or not to take the benefit of the work done. It is only where the circumstances are such as to give that option that there is any evidence on which to ground the inference of a new contract.

In the case at bar the appellant has never elected to take any benefit available to him from the unfinished work and Mr. Williston stated that he was willing that, in the event of his appeal succeeding, a term should be inserted in the judgment permitting the respondent to remove the machine within a reasonable time.

For the above reasons I am of opinion that the respondent's claim based on the contract to construct the machine fails and that the appellant is entitled to a declaration that the contract was cancelled and to the return of the $1,000 paid to the respondent in November 1946.

In the result the appeal should be allowed and judgment should be entered (a) declaring that the contract between the parties dated the 21st of September 1945 has been cancelled, (b) providing that the appellant recover from the respondent the sum of $2,684.68, (c) providing that the respondent shall have the right to remove the incomplete machine from the premises of the appellant within sixty days from the date of the delivery of this judgment. . . .

MARKLAND ASSOCIATES LTD. v. LOHNES

(1973), 33 D.L.R. (3d) 493 (N.S. S.C.)

L contracted with M for the supply and installation of building materials and for the renovation of her property. L made certain payments but refused to pay the balance of the contract price because of defects in the workmanship. M brought an action for the balance of the price due under the contract.

GILLIS J. . . . I find that the contract, between the parties, was a lump sum or entire contract. On consideration of the express provision for performance and payment, and all of the evidence, I find it is not possible to sever or apportion the price and performance. The fact that two interim payments, total $4,000, were made does not change that finding. I find that the undertaking of the plaintiff was to complete the work for the definite price of $8,300 which was payable on completion.

The plaintiff not having performed fully, and in some parts of performance having done badly, is all or part of the price to be paid? There arises the questions: Is entire performance a condition precedent to payment? Having found defects and omissions was there, in fact, substantial performance? If substantial performance is found can the owner set off against the price the cost of correcting defects and omissions. The leading cases are *H. Dakin & Co., Ltd. v. Lee*, [1916] 1 K.B. 566 (C.A.), and *Hoenig v. Isaacs*, [1952] 2 All E.R. 176 (C.A.), the first having been applied in the second. In *Hoenig v. Isaacs* at p. 180-1, Denning L.J. said:

> In determining this issue the first question is whether, on the true construction of the contract, entire performance was a condition precedent to payment. It was a lump sum contract, but that does not mean that entire performance was a condition precedent to payment. When a contract provides for a specific sum to be paid on completion of specified work, the courts lean against a construction of the contract which would deprive the contractor of any payment at all simply because there are some defects or omissions. The promise to complete the work is, therefore, construed as a term of the contract, but not as a condition. It is not every breach of that term which absolves the employer from his promise to pay the price, but only a breach which goes to the root of the contract, such as an abandonment of the work when it is only half done. Unless the breach does go to the root of the matter, the employer cannot resist payment of the price. He must pay it and bring a cross-claim for the defects and omissions, or, alternatively, set them up in diminution of the price.

In the case under consideration the finding of defects and omissions had been made. In that respect there has been, by the plaintiff, breach of some terms implicit in the contract. That finding, however, is based more on the fact of work badly done than on work not entirely done. In effect there was, in my judgment, substantial performance of the work but workmanship content mainly and some material was not of a proper standard and quality. My assessment of the many authorities leads me to the opinion that where the work was done, but badly, and the defects have been or can be remedied, the tendency of the Courts is to find there has been substantial performance and the builder should have the price less the cost of adjusting the defects and omissions. For a very complete review of cases and essays, up to the date of opinion, see *Fred Pierce Ltd. v. Troke* (1957), 8 D.L.R. (2d) 5 (N.S. C.A.). Among the many cases cited, Ilsley C.J., set out *H. Dakin & Co. Ltd. v. Lee, supra*, in a complete way but began with the headnote (p. 14) as follows: . . .

> Where a builder has supplied work and labour for the erection or repair of a house under a lump sum contract, but has departed from the terms of the contract, he is entitled to recover for his services, unless (1) the work that has been done has been of no benefit to the owner; and (2) the work he has done is entirely different from the work which he has contracted to do; or (3) he has abandoned the work and left it unfinished. . . .

Many writers and opinions come to a statement such as found in Goldsmith, *Canadian Building Contracts* (1968), at p. 74:

> It is virtually impossible to lay down any general principles for determining whether or not a particular contract has been substantially completed, and each case must be determined on its own facts.

I find substantial performance by the plaintiff in the case at bar. Nevertheless, the defendant is entitled to damages for breach of terms of the contract, not a condition precedent to payment of the price. [The court went on to find that the measure of damage was the cost of making good the defects and omissions.]

NOTES and QUESTIONS

1. See Stoljar, "The Great Case of *Cutter v. Powell*" (1956), 34 Can. Bar Rev. 288, and Glanville Williams, "Partial Performance of Entire Contracts" (1941), 57 L.Q.R. 373 and 490.

2. How should the courts view a plaintiff who is not ready and willing to perform? See Lloyd, "Ready and Willing to Perform: The Problem of Prospective Inability in the Law of Contract" (1974), 37 Mod. L.R. 121.

3. Late performance is not conceptually different from any other type of defective performance, but merits some separate consideration for historical reasons. The general rule is that delay in performance is not a sufficiently serious breach to discharge the other party unless time "is of the essence". Time is not usually of the essence in equity unless the parties have agreed that it should be so or because of the nature of the subject-matter of the contract.

4. For an illustration of the application of the test of abandonment, see *Nu-West Homes Ltd. v. Thunderbird Petroleums Ltd.*, *infra*, Chapter 14, section 3(a)(ii).

SUMPTER v. HEDGES

[1898] 1 Q.B. 673 (C.A.)

CHITTY L.J. . . . The plaintiff had contracted to erect certain buildings for a lump sum. When the work was only partly done, the plaintiff said that he could not go on with it, and the judge has found that he abandoned the contract. The position therefore was that the defendant found his land with unfinished buildings upon it, and he thereupon completed the work. That is no evidence from which the inference can be drawn that he entered into a fresh contract to pay for the work done by the plaintiff. If we held that the plaintiff could recover, we should in my opinion be overruling *Cutter v. Powell* [(1795), 101 E.R. 573], and a long series of cases in which it has been decided that there must in such a case be some evidence of a new contract to enable the plaintiff to recover on a quantum meruit. There was nothing new in the decision in *Pattinson v. Luckley* [(1875), L.R. 10 Ex. Ch. 330], but Bramwell B. there pointed out with his usual clearness that in the case of a building erected upon land the mere fact that the defendant remains in possession of his land is no evidence upon which an inference of a new contract can be founded. He says: "In the case of goods sold and delivered, it is easy to shew a contract from the retention of the goods; but that is not so where work is done on real property." I think the learned judge was quite right in holding that in this case there was no evidence from which a fresh contract to pay for the work done could be inferred.

COLLINS L.J. I agree. I think the case is really concluded by the finding of the learned judge to the effect that the plaintiff had abandoned the contract. If the plaintiff had merely broken his contract in some way so as not to give the defendant the right to treat him as having abandoned the contract, and the defendant had then proceeded to finish the work himself, the plaintiff might perhaps have been entitled to sue on a quantum meruit on the ground that the defendant had taken the benefit of the work done. But that is not the present case. There are cases in which, though the plaintiff has abandoned the performance of a contract, it is possible for him to raise the inference of a new contract to pay for the work done on a quantum meruit from the defendant's having taken the benefit of that work, but, in order that that may be done, the circumstances must be such as to give an option to the defendant to take or not to take the benefit of the work done. It is only where the circumstances are such as to give that option that there is any evidence on which to ground the inference of a new contract. Where, as in the case of work done on land, the circumstances are such as to give the defendant no option whether he will take the benefit of the work or not, then one must look to other facts than the mere taking the benefit of the work in order to ground the inference of a new contract. In this case, I see no other facts on which such an inference can be founded. the mere fact that a defendant is in possession of what he cannot help keeping, or even has done work upon it, affords no grounds for such an inference. He is not bound to keep unfinished a building which in an incomplete state would be a nuisance on his land. I am therefore of opinion the plaintiff was not entitled to recover for the work which he had done. . . .

[The concurring reasons of A.L. Smith L.J. are omitted.]

QUESTIONS

1. Is the plaintiff suing for breach of contract or for restitutionary or "quasi-contractual" relief?

2. Has the defendant been unjustly enriched? Reconsider *Deglman v. Guaranty Trust, supra,* Chapter 4, section 8(c)(iii)(E). See also the Summary of Recommendations of the Law Commission (for England and Wales), Report No. 121, *Pecuniary Restitution on Breach of Contract* (1983), at 34-36. The Report recommends that a party in breach, having conferred a benefit on the other party, should have a right of recovery with respect to the partial performance.

3. Since the work performed was required by the agreement between the parties (and therefore something which the defendant wanted to have done), why is it necessary to demonstrate a further decision by the defendant to derive advantage from the plaintiff's work? Is this merely a manifestation of the "implied contract" theory of restitutionary liability which met its demise, in Canada at least, in *Deglman v. Guaranty Trust,* [1954] S.C.R. 725? If so, would (or should) a contemporary Canadian court follow *Sumpter v. Hedges*?

HOWE v. SMITH

(1884), 27 Ch. D. 89 (C.A.)

FRY L.J. On the 24th of March, 1881, the defendant and plaintiff entered into an agreement in writing, by which the defendant agreed to sell and the purchaser agreed to buy certain real estate for £12,500, of which £500 was in the contract stated to have been paid on the signing of the agreement as a deposit and in part payment of the purchase-money. The contract provided for the payment of the balance on the 24th of April, 1881, and it further provided by the 8th condition that if the purchaser should fail to comply with the agreement the vendor should be at liberty to resell the premises, and the deficiency of such second sale thereof, with all expenses attending the same, should be made good by the defaulter and be recoverable as liquidated damages.

The plaintiff, the purchaser, did not pay the balance of his purchase-money on the day stipulated, and he has been guilty of such delay and neglect in completing that, according to our judgment already expressed, he has lost all right to the specific performance of the contract in equity.

The question then arises which has been argued before us, although not before Mr. Justice Kay, whether or not the plaintiff is entitled to recover the £500 paid on the signing of the contract.

The £500 was paid, in the words of the contract, as "a deposit and in part payment of the purchase-money." What is the meaning of this expression? The authorities seem to leave the matter in some doubt. [Fry L.J.'s discussion of the case law is omitted.]

These authorities appear to afford no certain light to answer the inquiry whether, in the absence of express stipulation, money paid as a deposit on the signing of a contract can be recovered by the payer if he has made such default in performance of his part as to have lost all right to performance by the other party to the contract or damages for his own non-performance.

Money paid as a deposit must, I conceive, be paid on some terms implied or expressed. In this case no terms are expressed, and we must therefore inquire what terms are to be implied. The terms most naturally to be implied appear to me in the case of money paid on the signing of a contract to be that in the event of the contract being performed it shall be brought into account, but if the contract is not performed by the payer it shall remain the property of the payee. It is not merely a part payment, but is then also an earnest to bind the bargain so entered into, and creates by the fear of its forfeiture a motive in the payer to perform the rest of the contract.

The practice of giving something to signify the conclusion of the contract, sometimes a sum of money, sometimes a ring or other object, to be repaid or redelivered on the completion of the contract, appears to be one of great antiquity and very general prevalence. It may not be unimportant to observe as evidence of this antiquity that our own word "earnest" has been supposed to flow from a Phoenician source through the . . . Greeks, the *arra* or *arrha* of the Latins, and the *arrhes* of the French. It was familiar to the law of Rome. . . .

Taking these early authorities into consideration, I think we may conclude that the deposit in the present case is the earnest or *arrha* of our earlier writers; that the expression used in the present contract that the money is paid "as a deposit and in part payment of the purchase-money," relates to the two alternatives, and declares that in the event of the purchaser making default the money is to be forfeited, and that in the event of the purchase being completed the sum is to be taken in part payment.

Such being my view of the nature of the deposit, it appears to me to be clear that the purchaser has lost all right to recover it if he has lost both his right to specific performance in equity and his right to sue for damages for its non-performance at law. That the purchaser has by his delay lost all right to specific performance we have already decided. It remains to inquire whether he has also lost all right to sue for damages for its non-performance. [Fry L.J. went on to hold that the plaintiff had lost this right and would, therefore, be denied recovery of the deposit. The concurring reasons of Cotton and Bowen L.JJ. are omitted.]

NOTE and QUESTIONS

1. Is the argument for dismissing the plaintiff's restitutionary claim stronger in *Howe v. Smith* than it was in *Sumpter v. Hedges*?

2. Are there circumstances in which a deposit should be recoverable by a party who is unable or unwilling to perform?

3. In certain circumstances, it can be argued that a deposit can be recovered because it constitutes a penalty out of all proportion to the loss suffered by the recipient. See *Stockloser v. Johnson, infra,* Chapter 14, section 3(e).

STEVENSON v. COLONIAL HOMES LTD.

[1961] O.R. 407 (C.A.)

KELLY J.A. The appellant sued in the County Court of the County of York for the return of $1,000, a down payment made by him on the execution on April 24, 1958, of a written contract for the purchase of a prefabricated cottage, delivery of which the appellant subsequently refused; the defendant by its defence alleged that it was entitled to retain the $1,000 as having been forfeited by the appellant and in the alternative counterclaimed for damages for breach of contract.

Judgment was rendered on February 1, 1960, dismissing the plaintiff's action and the defendant's counterclaim, both without costs. From that judgment the appellant appeals to this Court. . . .

As to the return of the sum of $1,000, it was contended by the appellant that this sum was a partial payment of the purchase-price and as such the appellant, upon the rescission of the contract was entitled to its return subject, of course, to any rights of the respondent to claim damages for the breach of contract. For the respondent it was argued first that the $1,000 payment was a deposit and as such was forfeited to the respondent when the appellant failed to complete the contract, and second, that even if the $1,000 payment were a part payment of the purchase-price the appellant having failed to complete the contract, the respondent was entitled to declare the contract rescinded and to retain as its own property all payments which had been up to that time made on account of the purchase-price.

The only authority in support of the latter proposition is to be found in the judgment of Bankes L.J., in *Harrison v. Holland,* [1922] 1 K.B. 211 at 212-3 (C.A.);

> This 100,000*l* which the plaintiff seeks to recover was stated in the contract to be payable in advance on account of the purchase price. If nothing more had been said about it, as the contract came to an end in consequence of the purchasers' own default, neither they nor their assignee would have been able to get the money back.

This cannot be now taken as a correct statement of the law. It was pointed out in *Mayson v. Clouet,* [1924] A.C. 980 at 986-87 (P.C.), that this remark was *obiter* and that the members of the Judicial Committee of the Privy Council, before whom the case was argued, thought the *dictum* of Bankes L.J., to be unsound.

A proper statement of the law on this subject appears in *Benjamin on Sale,* (8th ed.), p. 946: "And in ordinary circumstances, unless the contract otherwise provides, the seller, on rescission following the buyer's default, becomes liable to repay the part of the price paid." . . .

I do not consider that this case can be decided solely upon the fact that the contract was rescinded by the respondent upon the default of the appellant. Whether or not the appellant is entitled to the return of the $1,000, in the view I take of the case, depends upon whether the $1,000 was paid as a deposit or whether it was part payment of the purchase-price.

A useful summary of the law upon this point is to be found in the judgment of Finnemore J., in *Gallagher v. Shilcock*, [1949] 2 K.B. 765 at 768-69:

> The first question is whether the 200*l* which the plaintiff buyer paid on May 17 was a deposit or merely a pre-payment of part of the purchase price. When money is paid in advance, it may be a deposit strictly so called, that is something which binds the contract and guarantees its performance; or it may be a part payment—merely money pre-paid on account of the purchase price; or, again it may be both: in the latter case, as was said by Lord Macnaghten in *Soper v. Arnold* (1889), 14 App. Cas. 429 at 435 (H.L.): "The deposit serves two purposes—if the purchase is carried out it goes against the purchase-money—but its primary purpose is this, it is a guarantee that the purchaser means business." If it is a deposit, or both a deposit and pre-payment, and the contract is rescinded, it is not returnable to the person who pre-paid it if the rescission was due to his default. If, on the other hand, it is part-payment only, and not a deposit in the strict sense at all, then it is recoverable even if the person who paid it is himself in default. That, I think, follows from *Howe v. Smith* (1884), 27 Ch. D. 89 (C.A.), and from *Mayson v. Clouet*, [1924] A.C. 980 (P.C.), a case in the Privy Council. As I understand the position, in each case the question is whether the payment was in fact intended by the parties to be a deposit in the strict sense or no more than a part payment: and, in deciding this question, regard may be had to the circumstances of the case, to the actual words of the contract, and to the evidence of what was said.

As was stated by Lord Dunedin in *Mayson v. Clouet*, at p. 985: "Their Lordships think that the solution of a question of this sort must always depend on the terms of the particular contract." The contract between the appellant and the respondent should be critically examined to see if from it can be drawn the intention of the parties as to whether the $1,000 was to be a deposit or a part payment of purchase-price only. . . .

The evidence indicates that on April 24, 1958, one O'Gorman, a salesman, brought to the office of the appellant printed forms which had been prepared by the respondent, apparently in quantities. It is to be assumed from the evidence that these forms were in blank when O'Gorman came to the appellant's office and that they were filled in during the course of his interview with the appellant. The pertinent part of the contract is contained in the lower left-hand portion of the printed form. As filled out by O'Gorman and signed by the appellant, this portion of the contract reads as follows:

> Please enter my/our order for the above cottage and additions for delivery as indicated. I/we agree to pay Colonial Homes Ltd. the sum of *$2,206.00, Twenty Two Hundred and Six $*, Payment to be made as follows *$1,000.00* as down payment with this order and the balance of funds *$1,206.00* as follows: *C.O.D.*

The words and figures italicized were written in in handwriting the balance were printed. Below this appears the signature of the appellant, witnessed by O'Gorman. Immediately to the right of the foregoing on the printed form in a box headed "For Head Office Use Only", are the printed words "Order Approved".

"Price Approved", "Deposit Rec'd", "Credit Approved". Although the blanks after these phrases have been filled in on ex. 6, the absence of anything following these words on ex. 2 indicates that this portion was entirely blank at the time it was signed by the appellant. It is to be noted that on the portion of the contract which was signed by the appellant, the $1,000 is described as down payment, while the word "deposit" is contained in the box which I have referred to as being to the right of the portion of the contract which was signed.

The fact that the word "deposit" was contained in the box headed "For Office Use Only" and that the blanks after the phrases in this box were not filled in at the time of the execution of the contract would, in my opinion, make it unlikely that the appellant's attention was ever directed to this portion of the contract in the box. Nor do I believe that what impression he gathered as to his obligations, when he signed agreeing to pay and paying a "down payment", can be determined from the presence of the printed word "deposit" in the box.

While, as I have said, if the $1,000 were paid as a deposit, it would not be recoverable by the appellant, no authority was quoted nor am I able to find any which hold that the use of the words "down payment" is sufficient to impose on the payment the characteristics of a deposit. Where, as in this case, the contract is in writing and has been made on a printed form, drawn for its own use and supplied by the respondent, there seems to be no room to imply any terms in it which are to give rights to the respondent which are not clearly intelligible to the ordinary laymen to whom the contract will be submitted for signature. It is one thing for a Court to be asked to place an interpretation on words which the parties have used either verbally or in correspondence in good faith and which, while understood in one sense by the seller, are to the buyer of average intelligence capable of another meaning. It is an entirely different matter when a skilled and experienced seller prepares for the use of the purchaser of his product, a document which could have been written in unambiguous language and could have contained an express statement calling to the attention of the prospective purchaser the right of forfeiture reserved by the seller with respect to any payment made on account of the purchase-price. If the seller chooses to use words of uncertain meaning when he could have removed all room for doubt by the use of more specific language, a Court should not be asked to imply terms for the benefit of the seller. If the respondent had intended to induce the appellant to enter into a contract and pay money under conditions whereby the money would have been forfeited in the event of default, it should have included the word "deposit" in its contract in place of the word "down payment" or it should have spelled out with some particularity the obligation which the appellant was undertaking by signing the contract. Having failed to do so, the Court should not be asked to interpret the contract in its favour unless the document is capable of no other meaning when read by a reasonably intelligent man.

Two passages in the judgment of Stable J., in *Dies v. British Internat. Mining & Finance Corp.*, [1939] 1 K.B. 724, seem to be applicable to the facts of the present case. The first of these, appearing at p. 742, is as follows:

> In the present case, neither by the use of the word "deposit" or otherwise, is there anything to indicate that the payment of 100,000*l* was intended or was believed by either party to be in

the nature of a guarantee or earnest for the due performance of the contract. It was a part payment of the price of the goods sold and was so described.

And again at p. 743, after quoting with approval the statement from *Benjamin on Sale*, which has already been set out, the learned Judge goes on to say:

> If this passage accurately states the law as, in my judgment, it does where the language used in a contract is neutral, the general rule is that the law confers on the purchaser the right to recover his money, and that to enable the seller to keep it he must be able to point to some language in the contract from which the inference to be drawn is that the parties intended and agreed that he should.

I have no difficulty in coming to the conclusion that the $1,000 paid by the appellant on the execution of the contract was a part payment of purchase-price and that, even granting that the rescission of the contract has been brought about by the default of the appellant, the appellant is entitled to the return of his part payment, subject, of course, to the respondent's claim for damages for breach of contract.

In view of the right of the appellant to receive back the part payment, the respondent is entitled to recover on his counterclaim for damages for breach of contract. While some doubt may be raised by ex. 7 as to whether the sales commission payable by the respondent is to be calculated on the quantum of the contract price or the cash receipt, the only evidence before the Court is that tendered on behalf of the respondent in which it claims that it is liable to pay the full commission of the 13%; based on the purchase-price of $2,298, being the amount as revised by the amending contract of May 6th, the total commission would be $310.23. In addition to this the respondent is entitled to the other items of damages for office expense, cost of reconverting material and loss of profit set out in his counterclaim, amounting in the aggregate, along with commission, to $645.20.

I would allow the appeal and direct that the judgment below be varied by allowing the plaintiff's claim for $1,000 with costs and directing that judgment be entered for the defendant on its counterclaim in the sum of $645.20 with costs.

The success on the appeal being divided, there should be no costs of the appeal.

QUESTIONS

1. Why should moneys paid over by the defaulting party be accorded different treatment than services rendered or goods supplied?

2. Does the ability of defaulting parties to recover part payments offer an additional reason for suggesting that *Sumpter v. Hedges* ought not to be followed by a Canadian court?

Chapter 8

STANDARD FORM CONTRACTS AND EXCLUSION CLAUSES

1. Introduction

This chapter is unusual, for it addresses primarily the judicial treatment of certain types of contractual terms, whose function is to limit or exclude the ordinary liability of one of the parties to the contract. These provisions occur commonly, though by no means exclusively, in standard form agreements which are prepared by one party for use in a large number of transactions.

Because the chapter deals with certain types of contractual terms, which are not theoretically distinct from other terms, it raises few unique legal concepts. Instead, in a manner that will already be familiar to the reader, it relates closely to many of the topics that both precede and follow this chapter. The reader will note, for example, how in dealing with the so-called ticket cases, the courts must return to a basic review of the principles of offer and acceptance. In examining other aspects of exclusion clauses, the courts use the concepts of unconscionability and inequality of bargaining power, which are considered more fully in Chapter 12.

Much of the topic deals with the judicial interpretation of exclusion clauses as part of the entire agreement to which they belong. Courts face in this context some of the classic problems of interpretation. Therefore, at an early stage in this chapter, general issues of interpretation are discussed.

Much of the process of interpretation, broadly understood, involves the implication by the courts of terms into the contract. This technique has already been illustrated many times throughout the book, such as in the areas of offer and acceptance discussed in Chapter 2, certainty of terms discussed in Chapter 3 and contingent agreements discussed in Chapter 6. Some terms are implied into contracts as a result of statutory mandate. Familiar examples are provided by provincial sale of goods and consumer protection legislation. Indeed, often in the consumer context terms are imposed rather than implied since the parties are not free to exclude or diminish their effect. In the absence of statutory directive, however, the courts have broad powers to imply terms into contracts.

Of particular importance in recent years has been the readiness of the courts to imply or impose obligations of good faith in the performance of even commercial contracts: see generally O'Byrne, "Good Faith in Contractual Performance: Recent Developments" (1995), 74 Can. Bar Rev. 70. Sometimes such an obligation is characterized as an implied term of the contractual relationship. In

Wallace v. United Grain Growers Ltd. (1997), 152 D.L.R. (4th) 1 (S.C.C.), *infra*, Chapter 14, section 3(a)(iv), for example, a wrongful dismissal case, McLachlin J., in dissent on this question but with the concurrence of La Forest and L'Heureux-Dubé JJ., determined that it was an implied term of a contract of employment that an employer act in good faith in dismissing an employee. She saw the implication of such a term as being "necessary" within the meaning of the authorities cited in *Machtinger v. HOJ Industries Ltd.*, below. Even the majority in *Wallace* recognized on the part of the employer the existence of an obligation of good faith and fair dealing in the manner of dismissing an employee, the breach of which resulted in an increase in the length of the required notice period and, hence, in the damages awarded to the plaintiff.

Concern with the need for good faith dealings undoubtedly operates behind the scenes in the courts' treatment of exclusion clauses and standard form contracts. Sometimes it is brought into the open, as with Bingham L.J.'s judgment in *Interfoto Picture Library Ltd. v. Stiletto Visual Programmes Ltd.*, *infra*, section 3(d)(i). For further discussion of the duty of good faith and other limitations upon a contracting party's pursuit of self interest, see Chapter 11, section 3(b).

The various powers to imply terms are well described in the following case dealing with the basis for implying a provision into a contract of employment that the employee be given reasonable notice of the termination of employment.

MACHTINGER v. HOJ INDUSTRIES LTD.

[1992] 1 S.C.R. 986, 91 D.L.R. (4th) 491, 40 C.C.E.L. 1, 92 C.L.L.C. 14,022, 136 N.R. 40, 53 O.A.C. 200

McLACHLIN J. . . . So the real issue is this: in the absence in a contract of employment of a legally enforceable term providing for notice on termination, on what basis is a court to imply a notice period and, in particular, to what extent is intention to be taken into account in fixing an implied term of reasonable notice in an employment contract?

This question cannot be answered without examining the legal principles governing the implication of terms. The intention of the contracting parties is relevant to the determination of some implied terms, but not all. Intention is relevant to terms implied as a matter of *fact*, where the question is what the parties would have stipulated had their attention been drawn at the time of contracting to the matter at issue. Intention is not, however, relevant to terms implied as a matter of *law*. As to the distinction between types of implied terms see G.H. Treitel, *The Law of Contract*, 7th ed. (London: Stevens: Sweet & Maxwell, 1987), at pp. 158-65 (dividing them into three groups: terms implied in fact; terms implied in law, and terms implied as a matter of custom or usage), and *Canadian Pacific Hotels Ltd. v. Bank of Montreal* (1987), 40 D.L.R. (4th) 385, [1987] 1 S.C.R. 711, 41 C.C.L.T. 1.

Requirements for reasonable notice in employment contracts fall into the category of terms implied by law: *Allison v. Amoco Production Co.* (1975), 58 D.L.R. (3d) 233 at p. 240, [1975] 5 W.W.R. 501 (Alta. S.C.), *per* MacDonald J. They do not depend upon custom or usage, although custom and usage can be an element in determining the nature and scope of the legal duty imposed. Nor do they fall into the category of terms implied as a matter of fact, where the law supplies a term which the parties overlooked but obviously assumed.

Terms implied in contracts of employment imposing reasonable notice requirements depend rather on a number of factors, which

> ... must be decided with reference to each particular case, having regard to the character of the employment, the length of service of the servant, the age of the servant and the availability of similar employment, having regard to the experience, training and qualifications of the servant.

(*Bardal v. Globe & Mail Ltd.* (1960), 24 D.L.R. (2d) 140 at p. 145, [1960] O.W.N. 253 (H.C.J.), *per* McRuer C.J.H.C.)

These considerations determine the appropriate notice period on termination. They do not depend upon contractual intention. Indeed, some of them—such as the length of service and prospects of employment—are usually not known at the time the contract is made. Thus, the term of notice fixed by the court is, to borrow the language of Treitel, *op. cit.*, at p. 162, a "legal incident" of a particular kind of contractual relationship

In my opinion, this analysis is fully in accordance with the decision of this court in *Canadian Pacific Hotels, supra*. In that case Le Dain J. analyzed the bases upon which a term may be implied in a contract. The first category includes terms implied as a matter of custom or usage. In order for a term to be implied on this basis there must be evidence to support an inference that the parties to the contract would have understood such a custom or usage to be applicable; terms are implied in this manner on the basis of a presumed intention. The second category encompasses terms implied as necessary to give business efficacy to a contract. These are terms which the parties to a given contract would obviously have assumed. They are thus also implied on the basis of presumed intention, and correspond to Treitel's category of terms implied in fact.

The final category of implied terms considered in *Canadian Pacific Hotels, supra*, is the one applicable in the present case. These are terms implied not on the basis of presumed intention, but "as legal incidents of a particular class or kind of contract, the nature and content of which have to be largely determined by implication" (p. 431). These correspond to Treitel's category of terms implied in law.

Relying on the decision of the House of Lords in *Liverpool City Council v. Irwin*, [1977] A.C. 239, Le Dain J. suggested that the test for implication of a term as a matter of law is necessity. An examination of that case reveals what is meant by "necessity" in this context. In that case the House of Lords was concerned to reject the test for implication of such terms proposed by Lord Denning M.R. in dissent in the Court of Appeal, [1976] 1 Q.B. 319, under which a court could imply in law whatever term it thought "reasonable", including anticipating the recommendations for statutory reform of Law Reform Commissions. This, the House of Lords thought, seemed "to extend a long, and undesirable, way beyond sound authority" (p. 254, *per* Lord Wilberforce). In its place Lord Wilberforce said that the applicable test was that "such obligation should be read into the contract as the nature of the contract implicitly requires, no more, no less: a test, in other words, of necessity" (p. 254).

The test for "necessity" adopted by the House of Lords in *Liverpool City Council* is not whether the term is "necessary" for the very existence of the contract. All members of the House approved the implication of a term that a landlord in a tenancy agreement had an obligation to keep common parts of the building in repair. While the tenancy agreement could have continued without this term, it was necessary in a practical sense to the fair functioning of the agreement, given the relationship between the parties. As Cons J.A. described it in *Tai Hing Cotton Mill Ltd. v. Liu Chong Hing Bank Ltd.*, [1984] 1 Lloyd's Rep. 555 (Hong Kong C.A.), the House of Lords took a "practical view of necessity" (p. 560). I note that although the Privy Council reversed Cons J.A. in the result, it specifically approved as correct the analytical approach adopted by him: [1968] A.C. 80 at pp. 104-5.

Lord Wilberforce relied on the earlier decision of the House in *Lister v. Romford Ice & Cold Storage Co. Ltd.*, [1957] A.C. 555, in stating that in determining what is necessary regard must be had to both "the inherent nature of a contract and of the relationship thereby established" (pp. 254-5). As Viscount Simonds said in that case, the question is whether the term sought to be implied is a "necessary condition" of the contractual relationship. Thus (at p. 576, citations omitted):

> ... the real question becomes, not what terms can be implied in a contract between two individuals who are assumed to be making a bargain in regard to a particular transaction or course of business; we have to take a wider view, for we are concerned with a general question, which, if not correctly described as a question of status, yet can only be answered by considering the relation in which the drivers of motor-vehicles and their employers generally stand to each other. Just as the duty of care, rightly regarded as a contractual obligation, is imposed on the servant, or the duty not to disclose confidential information, or the duty not to betray secret processes, just as the duty is imposed on the master not to require his servant to do any illegal act, just so the question must be asked and answered whether in the world in which we live today it is a necessary condition of the relation of master and man that the master should, to use a broad colloquialism, look after the whole matter of insurance.

In the same way, the question which courts have been asking themselves is whether in the world in which we live today it is a necessary condition of the relation (to use more modern language) of employer and employee that there should be a contractual duty imposed on the employer to provide the employee with reasonable notice of termination. The answer provided has been a resounding "Yes". I agree with the following comment of Treitel on the *Liverpool City Council* necessity test: "it is, with respect, hard to see any difference between attaching a legal incident to a contract on the ground of necessity and imposing a duty" (p. 162). To my mind, where the law has for many years imposed a legal duty on contracting parties, as it has in implying the term that employers must give employees reasonable notice of termination, that duty has clearly been found to be "necessary" in the sense required by both the House of Lords in *Liverpool City Council* and this court in *Canadian Pacific Hotels*.

Viewed thus, the error of the Court of Appeal was to characterize a term properly implied in law as a term to be implied in fact. This led the court to look to the intention of the parties, as revealed in their course of dealing and the notice terms (now null and void) of their employment contracts, in determining what notice period ought to be implied. As the parties had contracted for less than reasonable notice of termination, the court held that it would be improper to imply a reasonable notice term into the contracts, and held the plaintiffs to be entitled only to the minimum notice periods required by the Act.

But what is at issue is not the intention of the parties, but the legal obligations of the employer, implied in law as a necessary incident of this class of contract. That duty can be displaced only by an express contrary agreement: see *Sterling Engineering Co. Ltd. v. Patchett*, [1955] A.C. 534 (H.L.) at pp. 543-4 *per* Viscount Simonds and at p. 547 *per* Lord Reid; Treitel, *op. cit.*, at pp. 161-2. Since there is no contrary agreement here, the Act having rendered what contrary agreement there was null and void, the reasonable term of notice implied by the law is not displaced and will be imposed by the court. . . .

[McLachlin J. concurred in the decision reached by Iacobucci J. (La Forest, L'Heureux-Dubé, Sopinka, Gonthier and Cory JJ. concurring). However, the majority resolved the case on the narrower ground that the common law principle of termination only on reasonable notice was a presumption, rebuttable if the contract of employment clearly specified, whether expressly or impliedly, some other period of notice.]

2.   Some General Principles of Contractual Interpretation

A basic starting point to the interpretation of a contract is that the courts are attempting to give expression to the intention of the parties; however, that intention must be found in the words the parties have used. In construing those words, the court should prefer the "natural" or "ordinary" meaning they would have for a layperson, but there may be circumstances to justify construction of the words according to some special meaning developed by trade usage or other custom.

As a general proposition, it is important to bear in mind the working principle that extrinsic evidence cannot be used to explain the plain meaning of words, but can be employed, as intimated in the previous paragraph, to show that words have acquired a special meaning as a result of some custom (*Campbell-Bennett Ltd. v. G.L. McNicol Co.*, [1952] 3 D.L.R. 247 (B.C. S.C.)) or to resolve an ambiguity (*Alampi v. Swartz* (1964), 43 D.L.R. (2d) 11 (Ont. C.A.); *St. Lawrence Petroleum Ltd. v. Bailey Selburn Oil & Gas Ltd.* (1961), 36 W.W.R. 167 (Alta. S.C.), affirmed (1962), 41 W.W.R. 210 (Alta. C.A.), affirmed [1963] S.C.R. 482). Thus, in *Eli Lilly & Co. v. Novopharm Ltd.*, [1998] 2 S.C.R. 129 at 166, Iacobucci J. said: "[I]t is unnecessary to consider any extrinsic evidence at all when the document is clear and unambiguous on its face."

Other evidentiary matters arise in the interpretation of contracts in general and of exclusion clauses in particular. It is said that evidence of the prior negotiations of the parties is generally inadmissible as an aid to interpretation, at least in the absence of ambiguity, because "such evidence is unhelpful. By the nature of things, where negotiations are difficult, the parties' positions, with each passing letter, are changing and until the final agreement, although converging, still divergent. It is only the final document which records a consensus": *Prenn v. Simmonds,* [1971] 1 W.L.R. 1381 at 1384 (H.L.), *per* Lord Wilberforce. Equally, the English courts have held that evidence of the subsequent conduct of the parties is not admissible as an aid to the interpretation of a contract: *Wickman Machine Tool Sales Ltd. v. L. Schuler A.G.,* [*supra,* Chapter 7, section 7]. As Waddams, *The Law of Contracts,* 4th ed. (1999) at 230, has pointed out, however, citing Lambert J.A. in *Re Canadian National Railways and Canadian Pacific Ltd.* (1978), 95 D.L.R. (3d) 242 (B.C. C.A.), the modern Canadian position is more flexible and is in favour of admitting such evidence, though weighing it carefully, where there are at least two reasonable interpretations of the contract in question.

There is also authority for the proposition that direct evidence of the parties' subjective intentions or purposes is inadmissible. Lord Wilberforce made the point in *Reardon Smith Line Ltd. v. Hansen-Tangen,* [1976] 1 W.L.R. 989 at 996 in the following way:

> When one speaks of the intention of the parties to the contract, one is speaking objectively—and what must be ascertained is what is to be taken as the intention which reasonable people would have had if placed in the situation of the parties. Similarly, when one is speaking of aim, or object, or commercial purpose, one is speaking objectively of what reasonable persons would have in mind in the situation of the parties.

Equally, in *Eli Lilly, supra,* Iacobucci J. said at 166:

> The trial judge [held that] it is open to the trier of fact to admit extrinsic evidence as to the subjective intentions of the parties at [the] time [of entering into the contract]. In my view, this approach is not quite accurate. The contractual intent of the parties is to be determined by reference to the words they used in drafting the document, possibly read in light of the surrounding circumstances which were prevalent at the time. Evidence of one party's subjective intention has no independent place in this determination.

The courts, however, do recognize that contracts are not made in a vacuum and they are willing to consider evidence as to the background circumstances surrounding the making of the contract. Lord Wilberforce explained the scope of this power, again in the *Reardon Smith* case, *supra,* at 995-96:

> The nature of what is legitimate to have regard to is usually described as "the surrounding circumstances" but this phrase is imprecise: it can be illustrated but hardly defined. In a commercial contract it is certainly right that the court should know the commercial purpose of the contract and this in turn presupposes knowledge of the genesis of the transaction, the background, the context, the market in which the parties are operating.

In *Investors Compensation Scheme Ltd. v. West Bromwich Building Society,* [1998] 1 All E.R. 98 (H.L.) at 114, Lord Hoffmann gave a broader scope to what constituted the background by saying that "it includes absolutely anything which would have affected the way in which the language of the document would have been understood by a reasonable man."

There are various specific principles of interpretation to which the courts will resort in the process of construction. Thus, if a contract is in printed form, to which typed or handwritten provisions have been added, or if a typewritten contract contains clauses added by hand, any conflict between the language of the basic document and these additional provisions will be resolved in favour of the latter on the assumption that they more reliably express the intention of the parties.

As with statutory interpretation, the courts will use the *ejusdem generis* principle to assist in construing contracts: see, *e.g., Atlantic Paper Stock Ltd. v. St. Anne-Nackawic Pulp & Paper Co., infra*, Chapter 10, section 5.

If the contract document has been drafted by one of the parties, any ambiguities are likely to be construed against that party and in favour of the other. This, the *contra proferentem* principle, will be developed further in the next section. It is clearly of particular significance in the realm of standard form contracts and exclusion clauses.

Of the many principles of construction applied by the courts, it may be that the one most frequently and most significantly helpful is the principle which emphasizes interpretation in context. A word or a phrase of debatable import may achieve a clear meaning when the entire document is read, giving effect to all its language where that is possible, or when the "surrounding circumstances" are examined.

The following case deals with the classic standard form contract, the insurance policy, and the interpretation of exclusions contained therein. It illustrates many of the principles of construction already discussed, such as the need to interpret in context and the application of the *contra proferentem* rule. It exemplifies the difficulty in a given case of identifying contractual language as either clear on the one hand or as ambiguous on the other. It also introduces some items to be addressed later in the chapter, such as the requirement that the effect of particularly onerous provisions be clearly brought to the attention of the party affected thereby.

SCOTT v. WAWANESA MUTUAL INSURANCE CO.

[1989] 1 S.C.R. 1445, 59 D.L.R. (4th) 660, [1989] 4 W.W.R. 728, 37 B.C.L.R. (2d) 273, 9 C.C.L.I. (2d) 268, [1989] I.L.R. 1-2462, 94 N.R. 261

LA FOREST J. [dissenting] . . . The appellants, Mr. and Mrs. Scott, took out a fire insurance policy on their dwelling with the respondent insurer. As is usual with these "homeowner's" policies, the protection of the policy extended to the relatives and to any other residents of the household under 21. This was done by defining "Insured" to include these persons. The definition section provided as follows:

DEFINITIONS

    (a) INSURED: The unqualified word "Insured" includes (1) the Named Insured, and (2) if residents of his household, his spouse, the relatives of either, and any other person under the age of 21 in the care of an Insured.

The Scotts' 15-year-old son Charles was thus an insured and his personal property was covered by the policy by virtue of the following clause:

COVERAGE C—PERSONAL PROPERTY:

    (1) On Premises—This Policy insures personal property, whether required to be specifically mentioned by any applicable Statutory Conditions of the Policy or not,

> usual or incidental to the occupancy of the premises as a dwelling, owned, worn or
> used by an Insured, while on the Principal Residence Premises, or at the option of
> the Named Insured, personal property owned by others, while on the portion of the
> premises occupied by the Insured.

On March 29, 1983, the dwelling was damaged by a fire which was deliberately set by the son, Charles Scott, acting alone. The appellants filed a proof of loss, but the respondent insurer denied coverage relying on the following clause:

LOSSES EXCLUDED

This Policy does not insure:

> .....

> (d) loss or damage caused by a criminal or wilful act or omission of the Insured or of
> any person whose property is insured hereunder

Charles Scott, the insurer stated, was an insured under this provision by virtue of the definition earlier quoted; thus, it maintained, it was absolved from liability . . .

The issue

There can be no gainsaying the insurer's proposition that the Scotts' son was an insured. His property was covered by the policy. That, however, is not the issue. The issue is whether the exclusion from coverage caused by the wrongful act or omission of an insured applies only to the insured responsible for the act or omission or whether it applies not only to that insured but also to an innocent insured . . .

[W]hile it is true that the exemption clause as worded can be made to bear the interpretation urged by the respondent, the language is far from clear; in a word, it is ambiguous. In the face of this ambiguity, the Ontario Court of Appeal in *Rankin* [*v. North Waterloo Farmers Mutual Ins. Co.* (1979), 100 D.L.R. (3d) 564] applied the *contra proferentem* doctrine and construed the language in a manner favourable to the insured. In my opinion, they were correct to do so. Policies of insurance are prepared by the insurers and in doing so they not unnaturally are minded to protect their own interests. To avoid the consequent injustices that may ensue to an insured, courts have long insisted that any ambiguity be resolved in favour of the insured. And where, as is the case here, the ambiguity bears on a clause that stands significantly to defeat the objective of the purchaser in buying insurance, the case for application of the doctrine is compelling. A clause intended to achieve the purpose argued for by the insurer would, in my view, have to be drawn so as to bring it clearly to the attention of the insured.

It may not be necessary to go the length of having the clause "printed in red ink with a red hand pointing to it" to use the expression of Lord Denning M.R., in *Thornton v. Shoe Lane Parking Ltd.*, [*infra*, section 3(d)(i)], but its alleged purpose should be clearly brought home to the ordinary insured. That the insurer knows just how to do this is evident from one of the clauses used by the insurer to define the different perils for which it provides coverage under the policy. The heading entitled "VANDALISM OR MALICIOUS ACTS" reads in relevant part:

13. VANDALISM OR MALICIOUS ACTS: There is no liability for loss or damage

.....

(c) caused by the Insured's spouse or any member of the same household.

By virtue of having itself defined "FIRE OR LIGHTNING" as a separate and distinct peril, the insurer must have concluded that the incident in question in the present case was not covered by clause 13 for it did not rely upon or even mention it in its argument. Nevertheless, I note that the very clear words of exception used in cl. 13 serve only to underscore the ambiguity that permeates the "losses excluded" clause on which the insurer does rely, and thereby to strengthen the case for construing that clause in a manner favourable to the insured . . .

L'HEUREUX-DUBÉ J. The issue in this case is whether Charles Scott, the son of appellant Cecil Scott, is included within this definition of the "Insured", such that the loss incurred is excluded from compensation by the above cited exception clause.

At first instance, the chambers judge held that the definition of "Insured" did not include Charles Scott: 13 D.L.R. (4th) 752, Wood J. found that the loss suffered by the appellants affected their joint interest in the home and its contents. This loss, according to Wood J. [at p. 756] was "clearly distinct and separate from any loss which their son may have suffered in the same fire". Because of these separate interests, the loss suffered by the appellants was not affected by the exception clause in the policy . . .

The Court of Appeal of British Columbia, 30 D.L.R. (4th) 414 . . . reversed the decision of Wood J. It is the appeal from this reversal which is before us.

In my view, the terms of the insurance policy are perfectly clear and unambiguous. The policy does not cover the type of risk which occasioned this loss. Such risk was specifically excluded. The wording of the exclusion clause for the purposes of the present case is unambiguous, as is the definition of "Insured". I am in complete agreement with the statement of Macdonald J.A., writing for the Court of Appeal, at p. 420, that:

> In the case at bar the policy does not insure "loss or damage caused by a criminal or wilful act or omission of the Insured or of any person whose property is insured hereunder". Clearly Charles Scott falls within the definition of "Insured" which I quoted earlier. He was a resident of the household and a relative of a named insured. And he was an "other person under the age of 21 in the care of an Insured".
>
> It is unnecessary to decide whether the indemnification obligation is joint or several. The exclusionary clause is unambiguous. Assuming the position more favourable to the respondents [here appellants], that it is several, the exclusionary clause bars recovery where the loss is caused by a wilful act of the insured. This clause is, therefore, fatal to the respondent's [here appellant] claim. *Rankin, supra,* is right in point. The exclusion clause in that case was in the same language as provision (d). It follows that, in my opinion, *Rankin* should not be followed.

In this particular case, the plain meaning of the clause at issue is given additional support by another term of the policy itself:

PERILS INSURED AGAINST

The Insurance provided by Section I of this Policy is against direct loss or damage caused by the following perils, as defined and limited:

.....

13. VANDALISM OR MALICIOUS ACTS: There is no liability for loss or damage

.....

(c) caused by the Insured's spouse or any member of the same household.

It is clear that the policy does not cover damage caused to the insured premises by either the insured or by members of his household . . .

Were I convinced that a different interpretation would advance the true intent of the parties, I would gladly subscribe to it. However, when the wording of a contract is unambiguous, as in my view it is in this case, courts should not give it a meaning different from that which is expressed by its clear terms, unless the contract is unreasonable or has an effect contrary to the intention of the parties. In the present case, the policy of insurance excludes liability of the insurer for damage caused by the criminal or wilful acts of the insured. The definition of "insured" clearly includes the minor children living in the home. It may well be that insurance companies do not wish to pay for the delinquency of teenagers within the home. I do not see how they could word their policy to exclude such a risk other than by the precise terms used in this policy.

Given the facts of the case, the exclusion clause, and the definition of insured contained in the policy, the damages suffered by the appellants in this case are clearly excluded. I cannot think of any words which could more clearly exclude coverage in these circumstances than those used in the policy.

In the result, I would dismiss the appeal with costs.

[Dickson C.J.C. and Sopinka J. concurred with La Forest J. McIntyre, Lamer and Wilson JJ. concurred with L'Heureux-Dubé J. Appeal dismissed.]

NOTE

For commentary on this decision, see Rafferty, "Developments in Contract and Tort Law: The 1988-89 Term" (1990), 1 S.C.L.R. (2d) 269 at 311-19. For a thoughtful discussion of contractual interpretation in general, see Sullivan, "Contract Interpretation in Practice and Theory" (2000), 13 S.C.L.R. (2d) 369.

3.   Control of Standard Form Contracts and Exclusion Clauses

(a)   INTRODUCTION

As you read the cases in this section, you will observe that many of the disputes involving standard form agreements arose from an exclusion clause of one sort or another and *vice versa*. The standard form contract and the exclusion clause do tend to go hand in hand (or "hand in glove"). And it is perfectly true that many cases deal with problems arising in part from the use of a standard form and in part from the attempt to disclaim liability. However, you should recognize that these are really two different problems arising from different sources.

The standard form contract may give rise to difficulties of interpretation, incorporation and general effectiveness of terms which have nothing to do with limiting liability, and the use of a standard form contract may be offensive or disquieting quite apart from any question of exclusion clauses. Conversely, exclusion clauses may appear in contracts which are not in standard form and their use, in any contract, may occasion problems of interpretation and may demand careful consideration of the extent to which a party should be entitled to rely on them.

Although this chapter will follow the traditional practice of dealing with the issues of standard form agreements and exclusion clauses together, you should be careful to separate, where appropriate, the problems that result from the standard form contract and those that arise from the exclusion clause.

(b)   DEVELOPMENT AND USE OF THE STANDARD FORM

In this chapter you will encounter cases which illustrate three different types of contracts and contexts in which standard forms are used.

The so-called "ticket cases" illustrate one of the earliest uses of a standardized written form. Entrepreneurs, engaged in hundreds or thousands of daily transactions, usually involving a contract of bailment or of carriage or both, had neither the time nor the desire to negotiate the terms of each contract. They had certain fixed terms upon which they would do business. Their customers frequently gave no thought to the terms they desired. To the extent that they gave the matter any thought, they were perhaps also too rushed to negotiate terms, or they were not seriously enough concerned to object to the terms insisted upon by entrepreneurs, or a sense of passiveness was induced by recognition of the fact that entrepreneurs would not vary the terms upon which they would do business and their competitors, if there were any, probably did business on very much the same terms.

In these cases, the contract is frequently formed quickly, casually, and with no discussion of terms, and a ticket is handed over which purports to set out the terms in very brief compass, or in some cases, to incorporate terms which are not printed on the ticket, but which the ticket attempts to incorporate by reference. These additional terms may be discoverable by the customer, but perhaps only at great inconvenience.

A second group of cases involve contractual dealings by businesses which lead almost inevitably to the use of standard forms. The transactions are so numerous that the entrepreneur could not afford to negotiate terms with each customer, but this does not distinguish the bailment and carriage businesses we have referred to above. What is distinctive about this second group of businesses is that the contract is necessarily so complex that the customer could not sensibly expect to negotiate terms without the assistance of a lawyer or other expert adviser, and the entrepreneur could not leave negotiation of terms to the inexpert agents through whom he or she must deal with customers. Thus, financial institutions adopt standard forms of financing and lending agreements; real property or auto rental businesses use standard form lease agreements. Typical of this group is the insurance business.

The third group of cases involves transactions, often of sale, in which a vendor, for example, may use a standard form for some of the reasons already mentioned, but is also largely concerned to introduce into the contract a disclaimer clause which is intended to limit or eliminate liability to the purchaser to which the vendor might otherwise be exposed.

The standard form contract is a convenient and valuable tool for parties who are in a position to bargain for terms reasonably fair to both. Its most objectionable characteristic is said to lie in its propensity for oppressiveness when used by a party in a dominant position who is able to dictate terms to the other contracting party.

In *Federal Commerce & Navigation Co. v. Tradax Export S.A.*, [1978] A.C. 1 at 8 (H.L.), Lord Diplock, when dealing with a contract of charterparty, pointed out the crucial importance of standard form agreements in the commercial arena:

> No market such as a freight, insurance or commodity market, in which dealings involve the parties entering into legal relations of some complexity with one another, can operate efficiently without the use of standard forms of contract and standard clauses to be used in them. Apart from enabling negotiations to be conducted quickly, standard clauses serve two purposes. First, they enable those making use of the market to compare one offer with another to see which is the better; and this, as I have pointed out, involves considering not only the figures for freight, demurrage and desparch money, but those clauses of the charterparty that deal with the allocation of misfortune risks between charterer and shipowner, particularly those risks which may result in delay. The second purpose served by standard clauses is that they become the subject of exegesis by the courts so that the way in which they will apply to the adventure contemplated by the charterparty will be understood in the same sense by both the parties when they are negotiating its terms and carrying them out.

In the earlier decision of *A. Schroeder Music Publishing Co. v. Macaulay*, [1974] 3 All E.R. 616 (H.L.), which involved a contract between a songwriter and a music publisher, the same judge stressed the need to distinguish standard form agreements made by commercial equals from those, such as the one before him, characterized by a marked disparity in the respective bargaining power of the parties (at 624):

> Standard forms of contracts are of two kinds. The first, of very ancient origin, are those which set out the terms on which mercantile transactions of common occurrence are to be carried out. Examples are bills of lading, charterparties, policies of insurance, contracts of sale in the commodity markets. The standard clauses in these contracts have been settled over the years by negotiation by representatives of the commercial interests involved and have been widely adopted because experience has shown that they facilitate the conduct of trade. Contracts of these kinds affect not only the actual parties to them but also others who may have a commercial interest in the transactions to which they relate, as buyers or sellers, charterers or shipowners, insurers or bankers. If fairness or reasonableness were relevant to their enforceability the fact that they are widely used by parties whose bargaining power is fairly matched would raise a strong presumption that their terms are fair and reasonable.
>
> The same presumption, however, does not apply to the other kind of standard form of contract. This is of comparatively modern origin. It is the result of the concentration of particular kinds of business in relatively few hands. The ticket cases in the 19th century provide what are probably the first examples. The terms of this kind of standard form of contract have not been the subject of negotiation between the parties to it, or approved by any organisation representing the interests of the weaker party. They have been dictated by that party whose bargaining power, either exercised alone or in conjunction with others providing similar goods or services, enables him to say: 'If you want these goods or services at all, these are the only terms on which they are obtainable. Take it or leave it.

The following extract, using the *Schroeder* case as an illustration, provides important economic insights on the general notion of inequality of bargaining power and on the use of the standard form contract

TREBILCOCK, THE COMMON LAW OF RESTRAINT OF TRADE

(1986), at 165-71

[In discussing the *Schroeder* case, Trebilcock noted that Lord Diplock had characterized the contract as of the second variety of standard form agreement and pointed out that the House of Lords struck down the contract because it felt that the publisher had abused its bargaining power in exacting the terms of the contract from the plaintiff. He continued:]

While recognizing that the assumptions underlying this analysis of the use of standard-form contracts have enjoyed considerable academic currency, it is submitted that they are largely fallacious. First, the proposition that the use of consumer standard-form contracts is the result of the concentration of market power is often entirely without factual foundation. The reason why such contracts are used is mostly exactly the same as for their use in the commercial context, that is, to "facilitate the conduct of trade", or in economic terms, to reduce transaction costs. If an agreement had to be negotiated and drafted from scratch every time a relatively standard transaction was entered into, the costs of trans-acting for all parties involved would escalate dramatically. Moreover, it is a matter of common observation that standard forms are used (for this reason) in countless contexts where no significant degree of market concentration exists. Dry-cleaners have standard dry-cleaning agreements, hotels standard registration forms, credit-grantors standard financing agreements, insurance companies standard life, fire, and automobile insurance policies, real estate agents standard sale and purchase agreements, landlords standard leases, restaurants set menu and price lists, and, for that matter, department and grocery stores set product ranges and price terms. The fact that in these cases a supplier's products are offered on a take-it-or-leave-it basis is evidence not of market power but of a recognition that neither producer nor consumer interests in aggregate are served by incurring the costs involved in negotiating separately every transaction. The use of standard forms is a totally spurious proxy for the existence of market power. The real measure of market power is not whether a supplier presents his terms on a take-it-or-leave-it basis but whether the consumer, if he decides to "leave it", has available to him a workably competitive range of alternative sources of supply. Whether this is or is not so cannot be simply inferred from the fact that a particular supplier is offering non-negotiable standard-form terms. It is a matter for independent in-quiry. If the market is workably competitive, any supplier offering uncompetitive standard-form terms will have to reformulate his total package of price and non-price terms to prevent consumers (at least consumers at the margin, who are the decisive consideration in such a market) from switching their business to other competitors.

It is, of course, true that general use of common standard-form contracts throughout an industry may, on occasion, be evidence of cartelization. But here one must be discriminating. If a reasonable choice of different packages of price and non-price terms is available in the market, albeit all through the medium of different standard-form contracts, then obviously the allegation of a "fix" will not stand up. Even where all contracts are the same, in perfectly competitive markets where the product is homogeneous, one would expect to find commonality of terms (for example, the wheat market). Every supplier simply "takes" his price and probably other terms from the market and is powerless to vary them. In a perfectly competitive market, with many sellers and many buyers, each supplying or demanding too insignificant a share of total market output to influence terms, all participants, sellers and buyers, are necessarily confronted with a take-it-or-leave-it proposition. Thus uniformity of terms, standing alone, is ambiguous as between the presence or absence of competition.

It is clear that the music publishing industry does not conform to all the criteria of a perfectly competitive market, given that the products (that is, the service packages) offered by different suppliers to composers are presumably somewhat differentiated. Because each package may possess a degree of uniqueness, each supplier may have a small measure of ability to adjust price and output combinations in relation to his differentiated product. But, provided that a substantial measure of substitutability is possible between one supplier's product and those of others, the market is as workably competitive as most real-world markets are likely to be. Moreover, as experience in the antitrust context has demonstrated, an industry whose products are widely differentiated will almost never be able to sustain a stable cartel, as the possibilities for cheating on agreed price and output restrictions are extensive and largely unpoliceable. This difficulty in the way of effective cartelization is, of course, compounded if the industry comprises many firms and entry barriers are low, both features of the music-publishing industry, as we shall see.

The suggestion by Lord Diplock that consumer standard-form contracts are explicable only on the basis that they are dictated by a party whose bargaining power, either exercised alone (monopolization) or in conjunction with others (cartelization), enables him to adopt the position that these are the only terms on which the product is obtainable, simply does not stand up as a matter of *a priori* analysis. This is not to suggest that monopolization or cartelization may not in fact have been present in *Macaulay* [*Shroeder*]. But not a shred of relevant evidence was adduced on this issue. Indeed, had the court chosen to examine data on the structure and performance of the music industry (which it did not), it is unlikely that it could have defended contractual invalidation on a monopolization or cartelization rationale. Before looking at these data, several preliminary observations are in order.

First, even if one assumes abuse of market power through monopolization or cartelization . . . a monopolist will typically monopolize the price (here the royalty) terms of trade, not the non-price terms (here, in particular, the unconditional assignments of copyrights)—he will give his customer what the latter wants but at a higher price or, in the case of a monopsonist, at a lower wage (or royalty rate).

Second, even if market concentration exists, there will still be the intractable problem, highlighted in many antitrust cases, of determining whether, and to what extent, it has produced anti-competitive effects. Relative long-term industry profit rates are sometimes considered an alternative, or additional, indicator of non-competitive behaviour, and may be equally relevant in a case such as *Macaulay*. However, for a variety of reasons, neither the market concentration test, the profit rate test nor related tests, can be readily applied in practice to yield reliable predictions of non-competitive behaviour. Whether in ordinary civil litigation between private parties there will normally be sufficient economic incentive for parties to invest in the complex task of producing reliable economic evidence on the issue of abuse of market power raises further problems.

Third, the corporate structure of the defendants in *Macaulay* made it presumptively implausible that they had monopoly power or were playing a dominant firm role in the industry. The defendants were a wholly owned subsidiary of a United States parent company, whose sole shareholders and directors were a husband and wife. They were also the sole directors of the defendant subsidiary.

[From a brief study of readily available economic data, Trebilcock concluded that the British and United States music publishing industries were highly competitive and composed of many competing firms. He then analyzed Lord Reid's discussion of unconscionability in the contract formation process (as opposed to its outcome).] [Lord Reid] found no evidence, "nor does it seem probable, that this form of contract made between a publisher and an unknown composer has been moulded by any pressure of negotiation. Indeed, it appears that established composers who can bargain on equal terms can and do make their own contracts." Lord Diplock himself also adverted to this latter issue in passing [in] his judgment: "It is not without significance that on the evidence in the present case, music publishers in negotiating with song-writers whose success has been already established do not insist on adhering to a contract in the standard form they offered to the [plaintiff]."

Despite Lord Diplock's statement that this fact was not without significance, it is not clear what its significance is. Both he and Lord Reid appear to be saying no more than that established song-writers were able to obtain better contracts than unknown ones, which, one would have thought, was unremarkable. Indeed, if this were not the case, good song-writers could then claim that they were being oppressed, which would mean that music-publishing firms could do nothing right.

Further, as has already been argued, the fact that there was no negotiation with this particular publisher over his terms (that is, they were offered on a take-it-or-leave-it basis) is quite beside the point, if choice from across the market of different packages of terms was possible. This possibility itself constitutes the "pressure of negotiation" vis-à-vis particular suppliers. Moreover, even the presence of dickering between parties, standing alone, is ambiguous as between the presence or absence of competition. Dickering may, for example, be merely a reflection of attempts by a monopolist to price-discriminate among customers by ascertaining and exploiting different demand elasticities.

Finally, there appears in fact to have been some *inter-* and *intra-*supplier negotiations in this case. Russell L.J. in the Court of Appeal stated that prior to the contract with the defendants, the plaintiff had composed some popular songs and "entered into individual agreements with music publishers by which he assigned the copyright . . . for a share in royalties." Apparently, none of these had been published. He and a collaborator had then chosen to approach the defendants, partly in the hope that a relationship with them would eventually lead them into the production side of record-making, partly because the defendants, with wholly owned affiliates world-wide, offered better royalty arrangements on sales in foreign markets, and presumably partly because the defendants offered the plaintiff greater prospects of access to foreign markets than purely domestic competitors.

Thus, the plaintiff having some knowledge of terms available from other publishers because of prior dealings with them, he and his collaborator initiated the contact with the defendants, and in dealing with them, they apparently began with clear views on the terms desired.

[Footnotes omitted.]

(c)   THE USE OF EXCLUSION CLAUSES

There is nothing inherently offensive about a contract which limits or denies liability. In many cases it may be the only satisfactory technique for carefully defining the bargain between the parties. For example, a life insurer, perhaps reasonably enough, is unwilling to contract to pay insurance benefits in all cases where death has occurred. Two common exclusions are death resulting from suicide within two years of issue of the policy and death resulting from war risks.

Similarly, it may be reasonable enough for a carrier or bailee to state a limit on the value for which it will be liable for lost or damaged goods. Indeed, if the charge for carriage or safe-keeping is modest, it might be unreasonable to permit a shipper or bailor to claim a large sum for, say, a small package of precious jewels which were not identified as having an unusually high value.

The shipper or bailor may be able to insure its goods and perhaps should do so. The carrier or bailee may be insured against liability but, to obtain a favourable premium, the policy may limit the amount of insurance on any one package or article. Thus, it may be a perfectly reasonable term of a contract of shipment that the carrier will not be liable for more than $50 for loss of or damage to any one package unless a higher value is declared. Declaration of a higher value may result in a small additional charge to cover the cost of additional insurance.

Where the limiting or exempting clauses are a reasonable device for defining the bargain reached by freely consenting parties in a situation of reasonably equivalent bargaining power, no real problem exists.

However, a problem does arise when an exemption is inserted in a standard form contract insisted upon by a dominant party, or when an exclusion clause appears to relieve a contracting party of the very responsibility which the contract seemed intended to impose.

Thus, when a carrier relies upon a clause which denies any liability for loss or damage however caused and whether or not by the negligence, or even the intentional wrongdoing, of the carrier's servants, we may all react with the same sense of pique as the judge who commented: "They could throw my car in the sea for all they cared". Similarly, the law may be expected to look with disfavour upon an insurance contract in which the exclusions erode the cover provided so seriously as to make the policy deceptive, or a contract of sale which includes a provision purporting to exculpate the vendor even if the purchaser discovers that she has bought a piece of junk.

You will observe in the materials that follow that there are three distinct questions that may be raised in the process of deciding how to deal with a particular limiting clause that is relied on by one contracting party and is challenged by the other. First, has the clause been effectively included as a term of the contact? This may involve, among other things, an enquiry into the notice of the clause given to the party who challenges it. Second, what does the clause mean? This may involve a very strict reading of the clause to narrow its effect; a narrow application of a limiting clause may be justified on the ground that the tendency of such a clause is to subtract from the benefit the contract would otherwise extend to the party who now challenges the clause. Third, independently of the resolution of the first two questions, and of particular importance if the clause survives those tests, is there some reason why we will simply refuse to apply the clause to a particular set of facts? In a particular case we may conclude that application of the clause would produce a result that is just too unfair, too unjust, too oppressive, too unconscionable. Clearly, it is especially difficult to give any meaningful form to this third question.

(d)   JUDICIAL TREATMENT OF STANDARD FORM CONTRACTS AND EXCLUSION CLAUSES

(i)   *Incorporation—Unsigned Documents*

PARKER v. SOUTH EASTERN RY. CO.; GABELL v. SOUTH EASTERN RY. CO.

(1877), 2 C.P.D. 416 (C.A.)

Actions against the South Eastern Railway Company for the value of bags and their contents lost to the plaintiffs respectively by the negligence of the company's servants.

The plaintiff in each case had deposited a bag in a cloak-room at the defendants' railway station, had paid the clerk 2*d*., and had received a paper ticket, on one side of which were written a number and a date, and were printed notices as to when the office would be opened and closed, and the words "See back." On the other side were printed several clauses relating to articles left by passengers, the last of which was, "The company will not be responsible for any package exceeding the value of £10." In each case the plaintiff on the same day presented his ticket and demanded his bag, and in each case the bag could not be found, and had not been since found. Parker claimed £24 10*s*. as the value of his bag, and Gabell claimed £50 16*s*. The company in each case pleaded that they had accepted the goods on the condition that they would not be responsible for the value if it exceeded £10; and on the trial they relied on the words printed on the back of the ticket, and also on the fact that a notice to the same effect was printed and hung up in the cloak-room. Each plaintiff gave evidence and denied that he had seen the notice, or read what was printed on the ticket. Each plaintiff admitted that he had often received such tickets, and knew there was printed matter on them, but said that he did not know what it was. Parker said that he imagined the ticket to be a receipt for the money paid by him; and Gabell said he supposed it was evidence of the company having received the bag, and that he knew that the number on it corresponded with a number on his goods.

The questions left in each case by the judge to the jury were: 1. Did the plaintiff read or was he aware of the special condition upon which the articles were deposited? 2. Was the plaintiff, under the circumstances, under any obligation, in the exercise of reasonable and proper caution, to read or make himself aware of the condition?

The jury in each case answered both questions in the negative, and the judge thereupon directed judgment to be entered for the plaintiff for the amount claimed.

MELLISH L.J. In this case we have to consider whether a person who deposits in the cloak-room of a railway company, articles which are lost through the carelessness of the company's servants, is prevented from recovering, by a condition on the back of the ticket, that the company would not be liable for the loss of goods exceeding the value of £10. . . .

The directors may have thought, and no doubt did think, that the delivering the ticket to the person depositing the article would be sufficient to make him bound by the conditions contained in the ticket, and if they were mistaken in that, the company must bear the consequences.

The question then is, whether the plaintiff was bound by the conditions contained in the ticket. In an ordinary case, where an action is brought on a written agreement which is signed by the defendant, the agreement is proved by proving his signature, and, in the absence of fraud, it is wholly immaterial that he has not read the agreement and does not know its contents. The parties may, however, reduce their agreement into writing, so that the writing constitutes the sole evidence of the agreement, without signing it; but in that case there must be evidence independently of the agreement itself to prove that the defendant has assented to it. In that case, also, if it is proved that the defendant has assented to the writing constituting the agreement between the parties, it is, in the absence of fraud, immaterial that the defendant had not read the agreement and did not know its contents. Now if in the course of making a contract one party delivers to another a paper containing writing, and the party receiving the paper knows that the paper contains conditions which the party delivering it intends to constitute the contract, I have no doubt that the party receiving the paper does, by receiving and keeping it, assent to the conditions contained in it, although he does not read them, and does not know what they are. I hold therefore that the case of *Harris v. Great Western Ry. Co.* [(1876), 1 Q.B.D. 515] was rightly decided, because in that case the plaintiff admitted, on cross-examination, that he believed there were some conditions on the ticket. On the other hand, the case of *Henderson v. Stevenson* [(1875), L.R. 2 Sc. & Div. 470 (H.L.)] is a conclusive authority that if the person receiving the ticket does not know that there is any writing upon the back of the ticket, he is not bound by a condition printed on the back. The facts in the cases before us differ from those in both *Henderson v. Stevenson* and *Harris v. Great Western Ry. Co.*, because in both the cases which have been argued before us, though the plaintiffs admitted that they knew there was writing on the back of the ticket, they swore not only that they did not read it, but that they did not know or believe that the writing contained conditions, and we are to consider whether, under those circumstances, we can lay down as a matter of law either that the plaintiff is bound or that he is not bound by the conditions contained in the ticket, or whether his being bound depends on some question of fact to be determined by the jury, and if so, whether, in the present case, the right question was left to the jury.

Now, I am of opinion that we cannot lay down, as a matter of law, either that the plaintiff was bound or that he was not bound by the conditions printed on the ticket, from the mere fact that he knew there was writing on the ticket, but did not know that the writing contained conditions. I think there may be cases in which a paper containing writing is delivered by one party to another in the course of a business transaction, where it would be quite reasonable that the party receiving it should assume that the writing contained in it no condition, and should put it in his pocket unread. For instance, if a person driving through a turnpike-gate received a ticket upon paying the toll, he might reasonably assume that the object of the ticket was that by producing it he might be free from paying toll at some other turnpike-gate, and might put it in his pocket unread. On the other hand, if a person who ships goods to be carried on a voyage by sea receives a bill of lading signed by the master, he would plainly be bound by it, although afterwards in an action against the shipowner for the loss of the goods, he might swear that he had never read the bill of lading, and that he did not know that it contained the terms of the contract of carriage, and that the shipowner was protected by the exceptions contained in it. Now the reason why the person receiving the bill of lading would be bound seems to me to be that in the great majority of cases persons shipping goods do know that the bill of lading contains the terms of the contract of carriage; and the shipowner, or the master delivering the bill of lading, is entitled to assume that the person shipping goods has that knowledge. It is, however, quite possible to suppose that a person who is neither a man of business nor a lawyer might on some particular occasion ship goods without the least knowledge of what a bill of lading was, but in my opinion such a person must bear the consequences of his own exceptional ignorance, it being plainly impossible that business could be carried on if every person who delivers a bill of lading had to stop to explain what a bill of lading was.

Now the question we have to consider is whether the railway company were entitled to assume that a person depositing luggage, and receiving a ticket in such a way that he could see that some writing was printed on it, would understand that the writing contained the conditions of contract, and this seems to me to depend upon whether people in general would in fact, and naturally, draw that inference. The railway company, as it seems to me, must be entitled to make some assumptions respecting the person who deposits luggage with them: I think they are entitled to assume that he can read, and that he understands the English language, and that he pays such attention to what he is about as may be reasonably expected from a person in such a transaction as that of depositing luggage in a cloak-room. The railway company must, however, take mankind as they find them, and if what they do is sufficient to inform people in general that the ticket contains conditions, I think that a particular plaintiff ought not to be in a better position than other persons on account of his exceptional ignorance or stupidity or carelessness. But if what the railway company do is not sufficient to convey to the minds of people in general that the ticket contains conditions, then they have received goods on deposit without obtaining the consent of the persons depositing them to the conditions limiting their liability. I am of opinion, therefore, that the proper direction to leave to the jury in these cases is, that if the person receiving the ticket did not see or know that there was any writing on the ticket, he is not bound by the conditions; that if he knew there was writing, and knew or believed that the writing contained conditions, then he is bound by the conditions; that if he knew there was writing on the ticket, but did not know or believe that the writing contained conditions, nevertheless he would be bound, if the delivering of the ticket to him in such a manner that he could see there was writing upon it, was, in the opinion of the jury, reasonable notice that the writing contained conditions.

I have lastly to consider whether the direction of the learned judge was correct, namely, "Was the plaintiff, under the circumstances, under any obligation, in the exercise of reasonable and proper caution, to read or to make himself aware of the condition?" I think that this direction was not strictly accurate, and was calculated to mislead the jury. The plaintiff was certainly under no obligation to read the ticket, but was entitled to leave it unread if he pleased, and the question does not appear to me to direct the attention of the jury to the real question, namely, whether the railway company did what was reasonably sufficient to give the plaintiff notice of the condition.

On the whole, I am of opinion that there ought to be a new trial.

[Baggallay L.J. delivered a concurring judgment, while Bramwell L.J. felt that, as a matter of law, judgment ought to be entered for the defendants. Orders absolute for new trials.]

NOTES and QUESTIONS

1. In the *Parker* case Baggallay L.J. said at 424 that "[i]f the practice of issuing cloak-room tickets, containing statements of conditions intended to be binding on depositors, had become general, it might well be that a person depositing his property and accepting a ticket, even though himself ignorant of the practice, must be treated as aware of it, and as bound to ascertain whether any such conditions were stated on the ticket delivered to him; but no such practice has been shewn or even suggested in either of the present cases, nor does it, so far as I am aware, exist."

Could a judge today make the same observation concerning the tickets given by cloak-room attendants, dry cleaners, car parks, carriers and others from whom a customer receives a "ticket" or "claim check"? As you read the more recent cases which follow, reflect upon changing business practices and how they affect the legal rights of the parties.

2. In *Parker*, Mellish L.J. indicated that the degree of notice required would depend in part upon the type of document involved. He gave as an example a bill of lading and concluded that a shipper of goods, receiving such a document, would be bound by the terms contained therein despite never having read it and being unaware that it embodied the terms of the contract of carriage. Such a document was involved in *Promech Sorting Systems B.V. v. Bronco Rentals and Leasing Ltd.* (1995), 123 D.L.R. (4th) 111 (Man. C.A.), where the court also stressed that the reasonableness of any notice given may well depend upon the particular recipient involved. In that case, the question arose as to whether the plaintiff, the owner of goods, acting through the agency of a shipping company, was bound by the terms of a bill of lading issued by the defendant railway company. The bill of lading acknowledged receipt of the goods "subject to the classifications and tariffs in effect". The reverse side of the bill provided in part:

> The amount of any loss or damage for which any carrier is liable shall be computed on the basis of the value of the goods . . . unless a lower value . . . is determined by the classification or tariff upon which the rate is based in any of which events such lower value shall be the amount to govern such computation whether or not such loss or damage occurs from negligence.

The tariffs effectively limited the carrier's liability to $500. The court held that the defendant had done what was reasonably sufficient to give the agent, and therefore the plaintiff, notice of the limitation of liability clause. In reaching that conclusion, Tweddle J.A. said at 117, 118-19:

> That which is reasonable notice for one class of customers may not be reasonable for another class . . .
>
> .....
>
> If the contract had been made with a man or woman off the street, with little or no experience in shipping goods, the words would probably have been insufficient. The defendant railway company was dealing, however, with a shipping company which regularly did business with it. Indeed, the trial judge found that the shipping company "may have been aware that C.P. Rail often made use of such clauses". As the authorities show, that which is insufficient notice to one class of customers may be sufficient notice to another. The shipping company was of a class which regularly dealt with the defendant railway company and for whom the use of bills of lading was routine. It was undoubtedly familiar with the language used in the land bill.
>
> It may well be that customers without experience in the shipment of goods would regard the word "tariff", as the trial judge did, as meaning no more than a schedule of rates. But a shipping company would be well aware that the rate charged for the carriage of freight varies according to the responsibility undertaken by the carrier. The shipping company itself had limited its responsibility by a condition in the ocean bill. For such a customer, a reference to the tariffs would surely mean that an examination of them was required to ascertain the conditions on which the carriage was being undertaken at the rate being charged.
>
> Quite apart from the words on the face of the land bill, which make the shipment subject to the tariffs, the terms and conditions on the reverse side of the bill refer to limitations on liability. The particular limitation now relied on is not set out, but the fact that a limitation might be determined by the tariff upon which the rate is based is stipulated expressly. The land bill is a standard form with which the shipping company, regularly doing business with the defendant railway company, must have been familiar.
>
> In my view, the words "subject to the tariffs" on the land bill were reasonably sufficient to effect notice to the class of customers to which the shipping company belonged, that the carriage of the plaintiff's sorting system was subject to conditions. That being so, the limitation of liability contained in the tariffs applied.

3. Consider the effectiveness of the following clause appearing in small print on the back of a ferry ticket, the front of which provided in red ink: "SEE REVERSE SIDE OF TICKET":

> This ticket is issued subject to certain terms and conditions which are hereby incorporated into and form part of this ticket and of contract of carriage hereby evidenced, some of which terms

and conditions limit or exclude the liability of the carrier, its masters, agents, servants or employees, which conditions of carriage may be seen upon request at any terminal office, aboard ship or at the head office of the carrier. This is not a negotiable instrument.

THORNTON v. SHOE LANE PARKING LTD.

[1971] 2 Q.B. 163, [1971] 1 All E.R. 686 (C.A.)

At trial, the defendants, Shoe Lane Parking, were held liable for the personal injuries suffered by the plaintiff as the result of an accident which occurred in a multi-storey car park of which the defendants were the occupiers. The defendants appealed.

LORD DENNING M.R. In 1964 Mr. Thornton, the plaintiff, who was a freelance trumpeter of the highest quality, had an engagement with the BBC at Farringdon Hall. He drove to the City in his motor car and went to park it at a multi-storey automatic car park. It had only been open a few months. He had never gone there before. There was a notice on the outside headed 'Shoe Lane Parking'. It gave the parking charges, 5s for two hours, 7s 6d for three hours, and so forth; and at the bottom: 'ALL CARS PARKED AT OWNERS RISK'. The plaintiff drove up to the entrance. There was not a man in attendance. There was a traffic light which showed red. As he drove in and got to the appropriate place, the traffic light turned green and a ticket was pushed out from the machine. The plaintiff took it. He drove on into the garage. The motor car was taken up by mechanical means to a floor above. The plaintiff left it there and went off to keep his appointment with the BBC. Three hours later he came back. He went to the office and paid the charge for the time that the car was there. His car was brought down from the upper floor. He went to put his belongings into the boot of the car, but unfortunately there was an accident. The plaintiff was severely injured. The judge has found it was half his own fault, but half the fault of Shoe Lane Parking Ltd., the defendants. The judge awarded him £3,637 6s. 11d.

On this appeal the defendants do not contest the judge's findings about the accident. They acknowledge that they were at fault, but they claim that they are protected by some exempting conditions. They rely on the ticket which was issued to the plaintiff by the machine. They say that it was a contractual document and that it incorporated a condition which exempts them from liability to him. The ticket was headed 'Shoe Lane Parking'. Just below there was a 'box' in which was automatically recorded the time when the car went into the garage. There was a notice alongside: 'Please present this ticket to cashier to claim your car.' Just below the time, there was some small print in the left hand corner which said: 'This ticket is issued subject to the conditions of issue as displayed on the premises.' That is all.

The plaintiff says that he looked at the ticket to see the time on it, and put it in his pocket. He could see that there was printing on the ticket, but he did not read it. He only read the time. He did not read the words which said that the ticket was issued subject to the conditions as displayed on the premises. If the plaintiff had read those words on the ticket and had looked around the premises to see where the conditions were displayed, he would have had to have driven his car into the garage and walked round. Then he would have found, on a pillar opposite the ticket machine, a set of printed conditions in a panel. He would also have found, in the paying office (to be visited when coming back for the car) two more panels containing the printed conditions. If he had the time to read the conditions—it would have taken him a very considerable time—he would have read this:

CONDITIONS

The following are the conditions upon which alone motor vehicles are accepted for parking;—

1. The Customer agrees to pay the charges of [the defendants] . . .

2. The Customer is deemed to be fully insured at all times against all risks (including, without prejudice to the generality of the foregoing, fire, damage and theft, whether due to the negligence of others or not) and the [defendants] shall not be responsible or liable for any loss or misdelivery of or damage of whatever kind to the Customer's motor vehicle, or any articles carried therein or thereon or of or to any accessories carried thereon or therein or *injury to the Customer* or any other person *occurring when the Customer's motor vehicle is in the Parking Building howsoever that loss, misdelivery, damage or injury shall be caused*; and it is agreed and understood that the Customer's motor vehicle is parked and permitted by the [defendants] to be parked in the Parking Building in accordance with this Licence entirely at the Customer's risk . . .

There is a lot more. I have only read about one-tenth of the conditions. The important thing to notice is that the defendants seek by this condition to exempt themselves from liability, not only for damage to the car, but also for injury to the customer howsoever caused. The condition talks about insurance. It is well known that the customer is usually insured against damage to the car; but he is not insured against damage to himself. If the condition is incorporated into the contract of parking, it means that the plaintiff will be unable to recover any damages for his personal injuries which were caused by the negligence of the company.

We have been referred to the ticket cases of former times? They were concerned with railways, steamships and cloakrooms where booking clerks issued tickets to customers who took them away without reading them. In those cases the issue of the ticket was regarded as an *offer* by the company. If the customer took it and retained it without objection, his act was regarded as an *acceptance* of the offer. . . . These cases were based on the theory that the customer, on being handed the ticket, could refuse it and decline to enter into a contract on those terms. He could ask for his money back. That theory was, of course, a fiction. No customer in a thousand ever read the conditions. If he had stopped to do so, he would have missed the train or the boat.

None of those cases has any application to a ticket which is issued by an automatic machine. The customer pays his money and gets a ticket. He cannot refuse it. He cannot get his money back. He may protest to the machine, even swear at it; but it will remain unmoved. He is committed beyond recall. He was committed at the very moment when he put his money into the machine. The contract was concluded at that time. It can be translated into offer and acceptance in this way. The offer is made when the proprietor of the machine holds it out as being ready to receive the money. The acceptance takes place when the customer puts his money into the slot. The terms of the offer are contained in the notice placed on or near the machine stating what is offered for the money. The customer is bound by those terms as long as they are sufficiently brought to his notice beforehand, but not otherwise. He is not bound by the terms printed on the ticket if they differ from the notice, because the ticket comes too late. The contract has already been made. . . . The ticket is no more than a voucher or receipt for the money that has been paid . . . on terms which have been offered and accepted before the ticket is issued. In the present case the offer was contained in the notice at the entrance giving the charges for garaging and saying 'at owners risk', i.e. at the risk of the owner so far as damage to the car was concerned. The offer was accepted when the plaintiff drove up to the entrance and, by the movement of his car, turned the light from red to green, and the ticket was thrust at him. The contract was then concluded, and it could not be altered by any words printed on the ticket itself. In particular, it could not be altered so as to exempt the company from liability for personal injury due to their negligence.

Assuming, however, that an automatic machine is a booking clerk in disguise, so that the old fashioned ticket cases still apply to it, we then have to go back to the three questions put by Mellish LJ in *Parker v. South Eastern Ry. Co.* [*supra*], subject to this qualification: Mellish LJ used the word 'conditions' in the plural, whereas it would be more apt to use the word 'condition' in the singular, as indeed Mellish LJ himself did at the end of his judgment. After all, the only condition that matters for this purpose is the exempting condition. It is no use telling the customer that the ticket is issued subject to some 'conditions' or other, without more; for he may reasonably regard 'conditions' in general as merely regulatory, and not as taking away his rights, unless the exempting condition is drawn specifically to his attention. (Alternatively, if the plural 'conditions' is used, it would be better prefaced with the word 'exempting', because the exempting conditions are the only conditions that matter for this purpose.) Telescoping the three questions, they come to this: the customer is bound by the exempting condition if he knows that the ticket is issued subject to it; or, if the company did what was reasonably sufficient to give him notice of it. Counsel for the defendants admitted here that the defendants did not do what was reasonably sufficient to give the plaintiff notice of the exempting condition. That admission was properly made. I do not pause to enquire whether the exempting condition is void for unreasonableness. All I say is that it is so wide and so destructive of rights that the court should not hold any man bound by it unless it is drawn to his attention in the most explicit way. . . . In order to give sufficient notice, it would need to be printed in red ink with a red hand pointing to it – or something equally startling.

However, although reasonable notice of it was not given, counsel for the defendants said that this case came within the second question propounded by Mellish LJ, namely that the plaintiff 'knew or believed that the writing contained conditions'. There was no finding to that effect. The burden was on the defendants to prove it, and they did not do so. Certainly there was no evidence that the plaintiff knew of this exempting condition. He is not, therefore, bound by it. . . .

[In the present case] the whole question is whether the exempting condition formed part of the contract. I do not think it did. The plaintiff did not know of the condition, and the defendants did not do what was reasonably sufficient to give him notice of it.

I do not think the defendants can escape liability by reason of the exempting condition. I would, therefore, dismiss the appeal. . . .

MEGAW L.J. . . . I think it is a highly relevant factor in considering whether proper steps were taken fairly to bring that matter to the notice of the plaintiff that the first attempt to bring to his notice the intended inclusion of those conditions was at a time when as a matter of hard reality it would have been practically impossible for him to withdraw from his intended entry on the premises for the purpose of leaving his car there. It does not take much imagination to picture the indignation of the defendants if their potential customers, having taken their tickets and observed the reference therein to contractual conditions which, they said, could be seen in notices on the premises, were one after the other to get out of their cars, leaving the cars blocking the entrances to the garage, in order to search for it, find and peruse the notices. Yet, unless the defendants genuinely intended the potential customers should do just that, it would be fiction, if not farce, to treat those customers as persons who have been given a fair opportunity, before the contracts are made, of discovering the conditions by which they are to be bound.

[Sir Gordon Willmer delivered a concurring judgment. Appeal dismissed.]

NOTE

The leading case on the requirement that notice of the terms of the contract must be given prior to the conclusion of the contract is *Olley v. Marlborough Ct. Ltd.*, [1949] 1 K.B. 532 (C.A.), discussed by Nemetz C.J. in *Delaney v. Cascade River Holidays, infra*, section 3(d)(ii) of this chapter.

INTERFOTO PICTURE LIBRARY LTD. v. STILETTO VISUAL PROGRAMMES LTD.

[1989] Q.B. 433, [1988] 1 All E.R. 348 (C.A.)

DILLON LJ. . . . The plaintiffs run a library of photographic transparencies. The defendants are engaged in advertising. On 5 March 1984 Mr Beeching, a director of the defendants, wanting photographs for a presentation for a client, telephoned the plaintiffs, whom the defendants had never dealt with before. He spoke to a Miss Fraser of the plaintiffs and asked her whether the plaintiffs had any photographs of the 1950s which might be suitable for the defendants' presentation. Miss Fraser said that she would research his request, and a little later on the same day she sent round by hand to the defendants 47 transparencies packed in a Jiffy bag. Also packed in the bag, among the transparencies, was a delivery note which she had typed out, and to which I shall have to refer later.

Having received the transparencies, Mr Beeching telephoned the plaintiffs at about 3:10 on the afternoon of 5 March, and told Miss Fraser, according to a contemporary note which the judge accepted, that he was very impressed with the plaintiffs' fast service, that one or two of the transparencies could be of interest, and that he would get back to the plaintiffs.

Unfortunately he did not get back to the plaintiffs and the transparencies seem to have been put on one side and overlooked by the defendants. The plaintiffs tried to telephone Mr Beeching on 20 March and again on 23 March, but only spoke to his secretary. In the upshot the transparencies, which the defendants did not use for their presentation, were not returned to the plaintiffs until 2 April.

The plaintiffs thereupon sent an invoice to the defendants for £3,783.50 as a holding charge for the transparencies. The invoice was rejected by the defendants, and accordingly in May 1984, the plaintiffs started this action claiming the £3,783.50, the amount of the invoice. That is the sum for which the judge awarded the plaintiffs judgment by this order now under appeal.

The plaintiffs' claim is based on conditions printed on their delivery note, which I have briefly mentioned, and must now describe in greater detail.

It is addressed to Mr Beeching of the defendants at the defendants' address and in the body of it the 47 transparencies are listed by number. In the top right-hand corner the date of dispatch is given as 5 March 1984 and the date for return is clearly specified as 19 March. Across the bottom, under the heading 'Conditions' fairly prominently printed in capitals, there are set out nine conditions, printed in four columns. Of these the important one is no 2 in the first column, which reads as follows:

> All transparencies must be returned to us within 14 days from the date of posting/delivery/collection. A holding fee of £5.00 plus VAT per day will be charged for each transparency which is retained by you longer than the said period of 14 days save where a copyright licence is granted or we agree a longer period in writing with you.

Condition 8 provides:

> When sent by post/delivered/collected the above conditions are understood to have been accepted unless the package is returned to us immediately by registered mail or by hand containing all the transparencies whole and undefaced and these conditions shall apply to all transparencies submitted to you whether or not you have completed a request form.

The conditions purport to be merely the conditions of the bailment of transparencies to a customer. If the customer wishes to make use of transparencies so submitted to him, a fresh contract has to be agreed with the plaintiffs, but, as that did not happen so far as the defendants are concerned, it is unnecessary to consider that aspect further.

The sum of £3,783.50 is calculated by the plaintiffs in strict accordance with condition 2 as the fee for the retention of 47 transparencies from 19 March to 2 April 1984. It is of course important to the plaintiffs to get their transparencies back reasonably quickly, if they are not wanted, since if a transparency is out with one customer it cannot be offered to another customer, should occasion arise. It has to be said, however, that the holding fee charged by the plaintiffs by condition 2 is extremely high, and in my view exorbitant. The judge held that on a quantum meruit a reasonable charge would have been £3.50 per transparency per week, and not £5 per day, and he had evidence before him of the terms charged by some ten other photographic libraries, most of which charged less than £3.50 per week and only one of which charged more (£4 per transparency per week). It would seem therefore that the defendants would have had a strong case for saying that condition was void and unenforceable as a penalty clause; but that point was not taken in the court below or in the notice of appeal.

The primary point taken in the court below was that condition 2 was not part of the contract between the parties because the delivery note was never supplied to the defendants at all. That the judge rejected on the facts; he found that the delivery note was supplied in the same Jiffy bag with the transparencies, and that finding is not challenged in this court. He made no finding however that Mr Beeching or any other representative of the defendants read condition 2 or any of the other printed conditions, and it is overwhelmingly probable that they did not.

An alternative argument for the defendants, in this court as below, was to the effect that any contract between the parties was made before the defendants knew of the existence of the delivery note, viz either in the course of the preliminary telephone conversation between Mr Beeching and Miss Fraser or when the Jiffy bag containing the transparencies was received in the defendants' premises but before the bag was opened. I regard these submissions as unrealistic and unarguable. The original telephone call was merely a preliminary inquiry and did not give rise to any contract. But the contract came into existence when the plaintiffs sent the transparencies to the defendants and the defendants, after opening the bag, accepted them by Mr Beeching's phone call to the plaintiffs at 3.10 on 5 March. The question is whether condition 2 was a term of that contract.

There was never any oral discussion of terms between the parties before the contract was made. In particular there was no discussion whatever of terms in the original telephone conversation when Mr Beeching made his preliminary inquiry. The question is therefore whether condition 2 was sufficiently brought to the defendants' attention to make it a term of the contract which was only concluded after the defendants had received, and must have known that they had received the transparencies *and* the delivery note.

This sort of question was posed, in relation to printed conditions, in the ticket cases, such [as] *Parker v. South Eastern Rly Co* [*supra*], in the last century. At that stage the printed conditions were looked at as a whole and the question considered by the courts was whether the printed conditions as a whole had been sufficiently drawn to a customer's attention to make the whole set of conditions part of the contract; if so the customer was bound by the printed conditions even though he never read them.

More recently the question has been discussed whether it is enough to look at a set of printed conditions as a whole. When for instance one condition in a set is particularly onerous does something need to be done to draw customers' attention to that particular condition?

. . . [I]n *Thornton v. Shoe Lane Parking Ltd* [*supra*] both Lord Denning MR and Megaw LJ held as one of their grounds of decision, as I read their judgments, that where a condition is particularly onerous or unusual the party seeking to enforce it must show that that condition, or an unusual condition of that particular nature, was fairly brought to the notice of the other party. . . .

Counsel for the plaintiffs submits that *Thornton v. Shoe Lane Parking Ltd* was a case of an exemption clause and that what their Lordships said must be read as limited to exemption clauses and in particular exemption clauses which would deprive the party on whom they are imposed of statutory rights. But what their Lordships said was said by way of interpretation and application of the general statement of the law by Mellish LJ in *Parker v. South Eastern Rly Co* and the logic of it is applicable to any particularly onerous clause in a printed set of conditions of the one contracting party which would not be generally known to the other party.

Condition 2 of these plaintiffs' conditions is in my judgment a very onerous clause. The defendants could not conceivably have known, if their attention were not drawn to the clause, that the plaintiffs were proposing to charge a 'holding fee' for the retention of the transparencies at such a very high and exorbitant rate.

At the time of the ticket cases in the last century it was notorious that people hardly ever troubled to read printed conditions on a ticket or delivery note or similar document. That remains the case now. In the intervening years the printed conditions have tended to become more and more complicated and more and more one-sided in favour of the party who is imposing them, but the other parties, if they notice that there are printed conditions at all, generally still tend to assume that such conditions are only concerned with ancillary matters of form and are not of importance. In the ticket cases the courts held that the common law required that reasonable steps be taken to draw the other parties' attention to the printed conditions or they would not be part of the contract. It is in my judgment a logical development of the common law into modern conditions that it should be held, as it was in *Thornton v. Shoe Lane Parking Ltd*, that, if one condition in a set of printed conditions is particularly onerous or unusual, the party seeking to enforce it must show that that particular condition was fairly brought to the attention of the other party.

In the present case, nothing was done by the plaintiffs to draw the defendants' attention particularly to condition 2; it was merely one of four columns' width of conditions printed across the foot of the delivery note. Consequently condition 2 never, in my judgment, became part of the contract between the parties.

I would therefore allow this appeal and reduce the amount of the judgment which the judge awarded against the defendants to the amount which he would have awarded on a quantum meruit on his alternative findings, i e the reasonable charge of £3.50 per transparency per week for the retention of the transparencies beyond a reasonable period, which he fixed at 14 days from the date of their receipt by the defendants.

BINGHAM LJ. In many civil law systems, and perhaps in most legal systems outside the common law world, the law of obligations recognises and enforces an overriding principle that in making and carrying out contracts parties should act in good faith. This does not simply mean that they should not deceive each other, a principle which any legal system must recognise; its effect is perhaps most aptly conveyed by such metaphorical colloquialisms as 'playing fair', 'coming clean' or 'putting one's cards face upwards on the table'. It is in essence a principle of fair and open dealing. In such a forum it might, I think, be held on the facts of this case that the plaintiffs were under a duty in all fairness to draw the defendants' attention specifically to the high price payable if the transparencies were not returned in time and, when the 14 days had expired, to point out to the defendants the high cost of continued failure to return them.

English law has, characteristically, committed itself to no such overriding principle but has developed piecemeal solutions in response to demonstrated problems of unfairness. Many examples could be given. Thus equity has intervened to strike down unconscionable bargains. Parliament has stepped in to regulate the imposition of exemption clauses and the form of certain hire-purchase agreements. The common law also has made its contribution, by holding that certain classes of contract require the utmost good faith, by treating as irrecoverable what purport to be agreed estimates of damage but are in truth a disguised penalty for breach, and in many other ways.

The well-known cases on sufficiency of notice are in my view properly to be read in this context. At one level they are concerned with a question of pure contractual analysis, whether one party has done enough to give the other notice of the incorporation of a term in the contract. At another level they are concerned with a somewhat different question, whether it would in all the circumstances be fair (or reasonable) to hold a party bound by any conditions or by a particular condition of an unusual and stringent nature. . . .

[Bingham L.J. then discussed *Parker v. South Eastern Railway Co.*, supra, *Hood v. Anchor Line (Henderson Brothers) Ltd.*, [1918] A.C. 837 (H.L.), *J. Spurling Ltd. v. Bradshaw*, [1956] 2 All E.R. 121 (C.A.), *McCutcheon v. David MacBrayne Ltd.*, infra, and *Thornton v. Shoe Lane Parking Ltd.*, supra. He reached the conclusion from these authorities that the fundamental question to be addressed was whether it would be fair to hold one party bound to the other's terms. He continued:]

The tendency of the English authorities has, I think, been to look at the nature of the transaction in question and the character of the parties to it; to consider what notice the party alleged to be bound was given of the particular condition said to bind him; and to resolve whether in all the circumstances it is fair to hold him bound by the condition in question. This may yield a result not very different from the civil law principle of good faith, at any rate so far as the formation of the contract is concerned.

Turning to the present case, I am satisfied for reasons which Dillon LJ has given that no contract was made on the telephone when the defendants made their initial request. I am equally satisfied that no contract was made on delivery of the transparencies to the defendants before the opening of the Jiffy bag in which they were contained. Once the Jiffy bag was opened and the transparencies taken out with the delivery note, it is in my judgment an inescapable inference that the defendants would have recognised the delivery note as a document of a kind likely to contain contractual terms and would have seen that there were conditions printed in small but visible lettering on the face of the document. To the extent that the conditions so displayed were common form or usual terms regularly encountered in this business, I do not think the defendants could successfully contend that they were not incorporated into the contract.

The crucial question in the case is whether the plaintiffs can be said fairly and reasonably to have brought condition 2 to the notice of the defendants. The judge made no finding on the point, but I think that it is open to this court to draw an inference from the primary findings which he did make. In my opinion the plaintiffs did not do so. They delivered 47 transparencies, which was a number the defendants had not specifically asked for. Condition 2 contained a daily rate per transparency after the initial period of 14 days many times greater than was usual or (so far as the evidence shows) heard of. For these 47 transparencies there was to be a charge for each day of delay of £235 plus value added tax. The result would be that a venial period of delay, as here, would lead to an inordinate liability. The defendants are not to be relieved of that liability because they did not read the condition, although doubtless they did not; but in my judgment they are to be relieved because the plaintiffs did not do what was necessary to draw this unreasonable and extortionate clause fairly to their attention. I would accordingly allow the defendants' appeal and substitute for the judge's award the sum which he assessed on the alternative basis of quantum meruit. . . .

[Appeal allowed.]

McCUTCHEON v. DAVID MacBRAYNE LTD.

[1964] 1 W.L.R. 125, [1964] 1 All E.R. 430 (H.L.)

LORD REID My Lords, the appellant is a farm grieve in Islay. While on the mainland in October, 1960, he asked his brother-in-law, Mr. McSporran, a farmer in Islay, to have his car sent by the respondents to West Loch Tarbert. Mr. McSporran took the car to Port Askaig. He found in the respondents' office there the purser of their vessel "Lochiel", who quoted the freight for a return journey for the car. He paid the money, obtained a receipt and delivered the car to the respondents. It was shipped on the "Lochiel" but the vessel never reached West Loch Tarbert. She sank owing to negligent navigation by the respondents' servants, and the car was a total loss. The appellant sues for its value, agreed at £480.

The question is, what was the contract between the parties? The contract was an oral one. No document was signed or changed hands until the contract was completed. I agree with the unanimous view of the learned judges of the Court of Session that the terms of the receipt which was made out by the purser and handed to Mr. McSporran after he paid the freight cannot be regarded as terms of the contract. So the case is not one of the familiar ticket cases where the question is whether conditions endorsed on or referred to in a ticket or other document handed to the consignor in making the contract are binding on the consignor. If conditions, not mentioned when this contract was made, are to be added to or regarded as part of this contract it must be for some reason different from those principles which are now well settled in ticket cases. If this oral contract stands unqualified there can be no doubt that the respondents are liable for the damage caused by the negligence of their servants.

. . . . .

LORD DEVLIN My Lords, when a person in the Isle of Islay wishes to send goods to the mainland he goes into the office of MacBrayne (the respondents) in Port Askaig which is conveniently combined with the local Post Office. There he is presented with a document headed "Conditions" containing three or four thousand words of small print divided into twenty-seven paragraphs. Beneath them there is a space for the sender's signature which he puts below his statement in quite legible print that he thereby agrees to ship on the conditions stated above. The appellant, Mr. McCutcheon, described the negotiations which preceded the making of this formidable contract in the following terms:

> Q. Tell us about that document; how did you come to sign it?
> A. You just walk in the office and the document is filled up ready and all you have to do is sign your name and go out.
> Q. Did you ever read the conditions?
> A. No.
> Q. Did you know what was in them?
> A. No.

There are many other passages in which the appellant and his brother-in-law, Mr. McSporran, endeavour more or less successfully to appease the forensic astonishment aroused by this statement. People shipping calves, the appellant said, (he was dealing with an occasion when he had shipped thirty-six calves) had not much time to give to the reading. Asked to deal with another occasion when he was unhampered by livestock, he said that people generally just tried to be in time for the boat's sailing; it would, he thought, take half a day to read and understand the conditions and then he would miss the boat. In another part of his evidence he went so far as to say that if everybody took time to read the document, "MacBrayne's office would be packed out the door". Mr. McSporran evidently thought the whole matter rather academic because, as he pointed out, there was no other way to send a car.

There came a day, Oct. 8, 1960, when one of the respondents' vessels was negligently sailed into a rock and sank. She had on board a car belonging to the appellant, which he had got Mr. McSporran to ship for him, and the car was a total loss. It would be a strangely generous set of conditions in which the persistent reader, after wading through the verbiage, could not find something to protect the carrier against "any loss . . . wheresoever or whensoever occurring"; and condition 19 by itself is enough to absolve the respondents several times over for all their negligence. It is conceded that if the form had been signed as usual, the appellant would have had no case. But by a stroke of ill luck for the respondents it was on this day of all days that they omitted to get Mr. McSporran to sign the conditions. What difference does that make? If it were possible for your lordships to escape from the world of make-believe, which the law has created, into the real world in which transactions of this sort are actually done, the answer would be short and simple. It should make no difference whatever. This sort of document is not meant to be read, still less to be understood. Its signature is in truth about as significant as a handshake that marks the formal conclusion of a bargain.

Your lordships were referred to the dictum of Blackburn J., in *Harris v. Great Western Ry. Co.* [(1876), 1 Q.B.D. 515, at p. 530]. The passage is as follows:

> And it is clear law that where there is a writing, into which the terms of any agreement are reduced, the terms are to be regulated by that writing. And though one of the parties may not have read the writing, yet, in general, he is bound to the other by those terms; and that, I apprehend, is on the ground that, by assenting to the contract thus reduced to writing, he represents to the other side that he has made himself acquainted with the contents of that writing and assents to them, and so induces the other side to act upon that representation by entering into the contract with him, and is consequently precluded from denying that he did make himself acquainted with those terms. But then the preclusion only exists when the case is brought within the rule so carefully and accurately laid down by Parke, B., in delivering the judgment of the Exchequer in *Freeman v. Cooke* [(1848), 2 Exch. 654] that is, if he 'means his representation to be acted upon, and it is acted upon accordingly: or if, whatever a man's real intentions may be, he so conduct himself that a reasonable man would take the representation to be true, and believe that it was meant that he should act upon it, and did act upon it as true'.

If the ordinary law of estoppel was applicable to this case, it might well be argued that the circumstances leave no room for any representation by the sender on which the carrier acted. I believe that any other member of the public in the appellant's place,—and this goes for lawyers as well as for laymen,—would have found himself compelled to give the same sort of answers as the appellant gave; and I doubt if any carrier who serves out documents of this type could honestly say that he acted in the belief that the recipient had "made himself acquainted with the contents". But Blackburn J. was dealing with an unsigned document, a cloakroom ticket. Unless your Lordships are to disapprove the decision in *L'Estrange v. F. Graucob Ltd.* [[1934] 2 K.B. 394]—and there has been no suggestion in this case that you should,—the law is clear, without any recourse to the doctrine of estoppel, that a signature to a contract is conclusive.

This is a matter that is relevant to the way in which the respondents put their case. They say that the previous dealings between themselves and the appellant, being always on the terms of their "risk note", as they call their written conditions, the contract between themselves and the appellant must be deemed to import the same conditions. In my opinion, the bare fact that there have been previous dealings between the parties does not assist the respondents at all. The fact that a man has made a contract in the same form ninety-nine times (let alone three or four times which are here alleged) will not of itself affect the hundredth contract, in which the form is not used. Previous dealings are relevant only if they prove knowledge of the terms, actual and not constructive, and assent to them. If a term is not expressed in a contract, there is only one other way in which it can come into it and that is by implication. No implication can be made against a party of a term which was unknown to him. If previous dealings show that a man knew of and agreed to a term on ninety-nine occasions, there is a basis for saying that it can be imported into the hundredth contract without an express statement. It may or may not be sufficient to justify the importation,—that depends on the circumstances; but at least by proving knowledge the essential beginning is made. Without knowledge there is nothing.

It is for the purpose of proving knowledge that the respondents rely on the dictum of Blackburn J. which I have cited. My lords, in spite of the great authority of Blackburn J., I think that this is a dictum which some day your lordships may have to examine more closely. It seems to me that when a party assents to a document forming the whole or a part of his contract, he is bound by the terms of the document, read or unread, signed or unsigned, simply because they are in the contract; and it is unnecessary, and possibly misleading, to say that he is bound by them because he represents to the other party that he has made himself acquainted with them. But if there be an estoppel of this sort, its effect is in my opinion limited to the contract in relation to which the representation is made; and it cannot (unless of course there be something else on which the estoppel is founded besides the mere receipt of the document) assist the other party in relation to other transactions. The respondents in the present case have quite failed to prove that the appellant made himself acquainted with the conditions that they had introduced into previous dealings. He is not estopped from saying that for good reasons or bad he signed the previous contracts without the slightest idea of what was in them. If that is so, previous dealings are no evidence of knowledge, and so are of little or no use to the respondents in this case. I say "of little or no use" because the appellant did admit that he knew that there were some conditions, though he did not know what they were. . . .

If a man is given a blank ticket without conditions or any reference to them, even if he knows in detail what the conditions usually exacted are, he is not, in the absence of any allegation of fraud or of that sort of mistake for which the law gives relief, bound by such conditions. It may seem a narrow and artificial line that divides a ticket that is blank on the back from one that says "For conditions see time-tables", or something of that sort, that has been held to be enough notice. I agree that it is an artificial line and one that has little relevance to every day conditions. It may be beyond your lordships' power to make the artificial line more natural: but at least you can see that it is drawn fairly for both sides, and that there is not one law for individuals and another for organizations that can issue printed documents. If the respondents had remembered to issue a risk note in this case, they would have invited your lordships to give a curt answer to any complaint by the appellant. He might say that the terms were unfair and unreasonable, that he had never voluntarily agreed to them, that it was impossible to read or understand them and that anyway, if he had tried to negotiate any change, the respondents would not have listened to him. The respondents would expect him to be told that he had made his contract and must abide by it. Now the boot is on the other foot. It is just as legitimate, but also just as vain, for the respondents to say that it was only a slip on their part, that it is unfair and unreasonable of the appellant to take advantage of it and that he knew perfectly well that they never carried goods except on conditions. The law must give the same answer: they must abide by the contract which they made. What is sauce for the goose is sauce for the gander. It will remain unpalatable sauce for both animals until the legislature, if the courts cannot do it, intervenes to secure that when contracts are made in circumstances in which there is no scope for free negotiation of the terms, they are made on terms that are clear, fair and reasonable and settled independently as such. That is what Parliament has done in the case of carriage of goods by rail and on the high seas.

[Concurring judgments were delivered by Lords Reid, Hodson, Guest and Pearce.]

NOTES and QUESTION

1. This case illustrates the problem of implying a term, such as an exclusion clause, from past dealings. Lord Devlin's judgment has been criticized as requiring a subjective assessment of the plaintiff's knowledge of the term in question and is inconsistent with the earlier decision of *J. Spurling Ltd. v. Bradshaw*, [1956] 2 All E.R. 121 (C.A.). In reaching the same conclusion, the other judges relied more on the fact that there was no evidence of a consistent course of dealing between the parties either in the sense that sometimes the plaintiff, or his agent, was required to sign a "risk note" and sometimes not (Lord Reid) or in the sense that the oral contract reached in *McCutcheon* was inconsistent with the defendant's previous practice of requiring a written contract (Lords Hodson, Guest and Pearce). In *Hardwick Game Farm v. Suffolk Agricultural Poultry Producers Assn.*, [1969] 2 A.C. 31, the House of Lords emphasized that the test of knowledge should be objective. See also *Hollier v. Rambler Motors (A.M.C.) Ltd.*, [1972] 2 Q.B. 71 (C.A.). For comment, see Clarke, "Incorporating Terms into a Contract by a Course of Dealing", [1979] J.B.L. 23.

2. In *British Crane Hire Corp. v. Ipswich Plant Hire Ltd.*, [1974] 1 All E.R. 1059 (C.A.), the defendant agreed over the telephone to hire one of the plaintiff's cranes. Nothing was said about the conditions of hire. Soon after the crane was delivered, the plaintiff, in accordance with its normal business practice, sent the defendant a printed form to be signed setting out the conditions of hire. Before the defendant signed the form, the crane sank in marshy ground. By the printed conditions, the defendant was required *inter alia* to indemnify the plaintiff against the expenses incurred in connection with the use of the crane. The question arose as to whether the plaintiff's conditions had been incorporated into the oral contract of hire. The court rejected incorporation based on a course of dealing between the parties because there were insufficient prior transactions to constitute a course of dealing. It pointed out, however, that the parties were of equal bargaining power and were both in the trade of plant hire. It also stressed the fact that the defendant knew that conditions along these lines were habitually imposed by the supplier of such machines and that the defendant itself used similar conditions to the plaintiff, both versions being variations of the standard form in the industry. On this basis, the court held that the plaintiff's conditions had been incorporated into the contract as a result of the common understanding that the hiring was to be on the basis of the plaintiff's usual terms.

3. Consider whether a case like *McCutcheon* can, or should, be resolved exclusively as a problem of communication of terms of the contract and mutual assent. What importance should be given to problems of exploitation of a monopoly market or of unequal bargaining positions? Is the concept of unconscionability applicable?

4. Like many of the cases in the context of standard form agreements and exclusion clauses, *McCutcheon* involved a bailment relationship between the parties. In such a situation, though not in *McCutcheon* itself, the outcome might well depend in part upon the application of the principle, unique to bailment, that once the bailor shows that the goods have been lost or damaged during the term of the bailment, the onus shifts to the bailee to establish that it was not in breach of any relevant duty or that any breach of duty was protected by a suitably worded exemption clause: see, for example, *J. Spurling Ltd. v. Bradshaw*, [1956] 2 All E.R. 121 (C.A.); *Levison v. Patent Steam Carpet Cleaning Co.*, [1977] 3 All E.R. 498 (C.A.); and *Punch v. Savoy's Jewellers Ltd.* (1986), 26 D.L.R. (4th) 546 (Ont. C.A.).

(ii) *Incorporation—Signed Documents*

The traditional view, as expressed in *L'Estrange v. F. Graucob Ltd.*, [1934] 2 K.B. 394, discussed in the following case, and as assumed in *McCutcheon*, was that one party's signature to a document containing terms established that party's assent to those terms, in the absence of fraud or misrepresentation. The following decision, however, has significantly altered that position.

TILDEN RENT-A-CAR CO. v. CLENDENNING

(1978), 18 O.R. (2d) 601, 4 B.L.R. 50, 83 D.L.R. (3d) 400 (C.A.)

DUBIN J.A. Upon his arrival at Vancouver Airport, Mr. Clendenning, a resident of Woodstock, Ontario, attended upon the office of Tilden Rent-A-Car Company for the purpose of renting a car while he was in Vancouver. He was an experienced traveller and had used Tilden Rent-A-Car Company on many prior occasions. He provided the clerk employed at the airport office of Tilden Rent-A-Car Company with the minimum information which was asked of him, and produced his American Express credit card. He was asked by the clerk whether he desired additional coverage, and, as was his practice, he said "yes". A contract was submitted to him for his signature, which he signed in the presence of the clerk, and he returned the contract to her. She placed his copy of it in an envelope and gave him the keys to the car. He then placed the contract in the glove compartment of the vehicle. He did not read the terms of the contract before signing it, as was readily apparent to the clerk, and in fact he did not read the contract until this litigation was commenced, nor had he read a copy of a similar contract on any prior occasion.

The issue on the appeal is whether the defendant is liable for the damage caused to the automobile while being driven by him by reason of the exclusionary provisions which appear in the contract.

On the front of the contract are two relevant clauses set forth in box form. They are as follows:

15. COLLISION DAMAGE WAIVER BY CUSTOMERS INITIALS "J.C."

   In consideration of the payment of 2.00 per day customers liability for damage to rental vehicle including windshield is limited to NIL. But notwithstanding payment of said fee, customer shall be fully liable for all collision damage if vehicle is used, operated or driven in violation of any of the provisions of this rental agreement or off highways serviced by federal, provincial, or municipal governments, and for all damages to vehicle by striking overhead objects.

16. I, the undersigned have read and received a copy of above and reverse side of this contract

   Signature of customer or employee of customer "John T. Clendenning"

   (Emphasis added.)

On the back of the contract in particularly small type and so faint in the customer's copy as to be hardly legible, there are a series of conditions, the relevant ones being as follows:

6. The customer agrees not to use the vehicle in violation of any law, ordinance, rule or regulation of any public authority.

7. The customer agrees that the vehicle will not be operated:

   (a) By any person who has drunk or consumed any intoxicating liquor, whatever be the quantity, or who is under the influence of drugs or narcotics;

The rented vehicle was damaged while being driven by Mr. Clendenning in Vancouver. His evidence at trial, which was accepted by the trial Judge, was to the effect that in endeavouring to avoid a collision with another vehicle and acting out of a sudden emergency he drove the car into a pole. He stated that although he had pleaded guilty to a charge of driving while impaired in Vancouver, he did so on the advice of counsel, and at the time of the impact he was capable of the proper control of a motor vehicle. This evidence was also accepted by the trial Judge.

Mr. Clendenning testified that on earlier occasions when he had inquired as to what added coverage he would receive for the payment of $2 per day, he had been advised that "such payment provided full non-deductible coverage". It is to be observed that the portion of the contract reproduced above does provide that "In consideration of the payment of $2.00 per day customers liability for damage to rented vehicle including windshield is limited to NIL".

A witness called on behalf of the plaintiff gave evidence as to the instructions given to its employees as to what was to be said by them to their customers about the conditions in the contract. He stated that unless inquiries were made, nothing was to be said by its clerks to the customer with respect to the exclusionary conditions. He went on to state that if inquiries were made, the clerks were instructed to advise the customer that by the payment of the $2 additional fee the customer had complete coverage "unless he were intoxicated, or unless he committed an offence under the *Criminal Code* such as intoxication".

Mr. Clendenning acknowledged that he had assumed, either by what had been told to him in the past or otherwise, that he would not be responsible for any damage to the vehicle on payment of the extra premium unless such damage was caused by reason of his being so intoxicated as to be incapable of the proper control of the vehicle, a provision with which he was familiar as being a statutory provision in his own insurance contract.

The provisions fastening liability for damage to the vehicle on the hirer, as contained in the clauses hereinbefore referred to, are completely inconsistent with the express terms which purport to provide complete coverage for damage to the vehicle in exchange for the additional premium. It is to be noted, for example, that if the driver of the vehicle exceeded the speed-limit even by one mile per hour, or parked the vehicle in a no-parking area, or even had one glass of wine or one bottle of beer, the contract purports to make the hirer completely responsible for all damage to the vehicle. Indeed, if the vehicle at the time of any damage to it was being driven off a federal, provincial or municipal highway, such as a shopping plaza for instance, the hirer purportedly would be responsible for all damage to the vehicle.

Mr. Clendenning stated that if he had known of the full terms of the written instrument, he would not have entered into such a contract. Having regard to the findings made by the trial Judge, it is apparent that Mr. Clendenning had not in fact acquiesced to such terms.

It was urged that the rights of the parties were governed by what has come to be known as "the rule in *L'Estrange v. F. Graucob Ltd.*", [1934] 2 K.B. 394, and in particular the following portion from the judgment of Scrutton, L.J., at p. 403:

> In cases in which the contract is contained in a railway ticket or other unsigned document, it is necessary to prove that an alleged party was aware, or ought to have been aware, of its terms and conditions. These cases have no application when the document has been signed. *When a document containing contractual terms is signed, then, in the absence of fraud, or I will add, misrepresentation, the party signing it is bound, and it is wholly immaterial whether he has read the document or not.*

(Emphasis added.) . . .

Consensus ad idem is as much a part of the law of written contracts as it is of oral contracts. The signature to a contract is only one way of manifesting assent to contractual terms . . .

Even accepting the objective theory to determine whether Mr. Clendenning had entered into a contract which included all the terms of the written instrument, it is to be observed that an essential part of that test is whether the other party entered into the contract in the belief that Mr. Clendenning was assenting to all such terms. In the instant case, it was apparent to the employee of Tilden-Rent-A-Car that Mr. Clendenning had not in fact read the document in its entirety before he signed it. It follows under such circumstances that Tilden-Rent-A-Car cannot rely on provisions of the contract which it had no reason to believe were being assented to by the other contracting party.

As stated in Waddams, *The Law of Contracts*, p. 191:

> One who signs a written document cannot complain if the other party reasonably relies on the signature as a manifestation of assent to the contents, or ascribes to words he uses their reasonable meaning. But the other side of the same coin is that only a reasonable expectation will be protected. If the party seeking to enforce the document knew or had reason to know of the other's mistake the document should not be enforced.

In ordinary commercial practice where there is frequently a sense of formality in the transaction, and where there is a full opportunity for the parties to consider the terms of the proposed contract submitted for signature, it might well be safe to assume that the party who attaches his signature to the contract intends by so doing to acknowledge his acquiescence to its terms, and that the other party entered into the contract upon that belief. This can hardly be said, however, where the contract is entered into in circumstances such as were present in this case.

A transaction, such as this one, is invariably carried out in a hurried, informal manner. The speed with which the transaction is completed is said to be one of the attractive features of the services provided.

The clauses relied on in this case, as I have already stated, are inconsistent with the over-all purpose for which the contract is entered into by the hirer. Under such circumstances, something more should be done by the party submitting the contract for signature than merely handing it over to be signed. . . .

I see no real distinction in contracts such as these, where the signature by itself does not truly represent an acquiescence of [*sic*] unusual and onerous terms which are inconsistent with the true object of the contract, and the ticket cases. . . .

In modern commercial practice, many standard form printed documents are signed without being read or understood. In many cases the parties seeking to rely on the terms of the contract know or ought to know that the signature of a party to the contract does not represent the true intention of the signer, and that the party signing is unaware of the stringent and onerous provisions which the standard form contains. Under such circumstances, I am of the opinion that the party seeking to rely on such terms should not be able to do so in the absence of first having taken reasonable measures to draw such terms to the attention of the other party, and, in the absence of such reasonable measures, it is not necessary for the party denying knowledge of such terms to prove either fraud, misrepresentation or *non est factum*.

In the case at bar, Tilden Rent-A-Car took no steps to alert Mr. Clendenning to the onerous provisions in the standard form of contract presented by it. The clerk could not help but have known that Mr. Clendenning had not in fact read the contract before signing it. Indeed the form of the contract itself with the important provisions on the reverse side and in very small type would discourage even the most cautious customer from endeavouring to read and understand it. Mr. Clendenning was in fact unaware of the exempting provisions. Under such circumstances, it was not open to Tilden Rent-A-Car to rely on those clauses, and it was not incumbent on Mr. Clendenning to establish fraud, misrepresentation or *non est factum*. Having paid the premium, he was not liable for any damage to the vehicle while being driven by him . . .

In the result, therefore, I would dismiss the appeal with costs.

LACOURCIÈRE J.A. [dissenting] . . . In my view the printing is not difficult to read, and the presence of conditions on the reverse side of the signed contract is brought to the signatory's attention in a very clear way.

It is not in dispute that the respondent violated two conditions of the contract: he drove the company's vehicle into a post, after drinking an unrecalled quantity of alcohol between 11:30 p.m. and 2 a.m. He was given a breathalyzer test, indicating a police officer's belief, on reasonable and probable grounds, that he had committed an offence of driving a motor vehicle while his ability to drive was impaired by alcohol or after having consumed alcohol in such quantity that the proportion of alcohol in his blood exceeded the penal limit. On the advice of counsel he pleaded guilty to a charge of impaired driving. I have set this out only to show that the respondent's violation of the contractual conditions was not a mere technical breach of an admittedly strict clause.

The clause is undoubtedly a strict one. It is not for a Court to nullify its effect by branding it unfair, unreasonable and oppressive. It may be perfectly sound and reasonable from an insurance risk viewpoint, and may indeed be necessary in the competitive business of car rental, where rates are calculated on the basis of the whole contract. On this point, see the majority judgment delivered by Lord Wilberforce in *New Zealand Shipping Co. Ltd. v. A.M. Satterthwaite & Co. Ltd.* [*supra*, Chapter 5, section 3(d)], where it was held that the Court must give effect to the clear intent of a commercial document.

I am of the view that, even if the respondent's signature is not conclusive, the terms of the contract are not unusual, oppressive or unreasonable and are binding on the respondent. I would, therefore, allow the appeal with costs, set aside the judgment below and in lieu thereof substitute a judgment for the amount of the agreed damages and costs.

[Zuber J.A. concurred with Dubin J.A. Appeal dismissed.]

DELANEY v. CASCADE RIVER HOLIDAYS LTD.

(1983), 44 B.C.L.R. 24, 24 C.C.L.T. 6 (C.A.)

NEMETZ C.J.B.C. [dissenting] Dr. Fergus Delaney, an Ontario veterinarian, visited British Columbia on business on the weekend of May 5, 1979. While in Vancouver he met a school friend, Dr. Stein Hoff. Dr. Hoff told Dr. Delaney that he (Hoff) was taking part in a "white water adventure" down the Fraser River and invited Delaney to join him. Delaney was enthusiastic about the idea. Inquiries were made and, because the raft was not full for that trip, Delaney's name was added to the passenger list. The trip ended in tragedy with the drowning of Dr. Delaney and two other passengers. The plaintiff (widow), executrix of the estate of Fergus Michael Delaney, brought this action under the provisions of the Family Compensation Act, R.S.B.C. 1979, c. 120, for the benefit of herself and for three infant children of Dr. Delaney. Her action was dismissed [reported (1981), 34 B.C.L.R. 62, 19 C.C.L.T. 78, 16 B.L.R. 114]. She now appeals to this Court.

The history of the disastrous trip is as follows: The passenger group travelled to Yale on Friday night. On Saturday morning, May 5, 1979, they assembled in a parking lot and met with representatives of Cascade River Holidays Ltd. (Cascade) including the reservations manager, Louella Morrison, and the defendant, Philip Reambeault, the raftsman. Sometime prior to this meeting Delaney paid $100 to Mr. Sims, president of Cascade, for the trip. The other passengers had made earlier bookings and paid in advance.

It was an overcast, rainy day. As Cascade's van was being loaded with gear and passengers, and T-shirts were being distributed, Louella Morrison obtained the signature of the eight paying passengers on a form entitled "Standard Liability Release". I will discuss the effect of Delaney's signing of this release later. All passengers, save Delaney, had received brochures from Cascade which contained the following statement:

LIABILITY

Cascade River Holidays Ltd. does not guarantee safe passage and assumes no responsibility for patrons' safety or property. Patrons must sign our liability release before departure. Cascade River Holidays has operated since 1973 without major loss and uses all the standard safety devices. We recommend the patron purchase personal insurance to protect himself.

Dr. Hoff had received one of these brochures, but there is no evidence that Dr. Delaney saw it. Hoff, who had been on such an expedition before, described the trip to Delaney as being "not necessarily a terribly adventuresome trip" and said that some elderly people had been on it the previous occasion. Hoff gave Delaney the impression that it was a safe thing to do. . . .

[At the time of embarkation, life jackets with 21 pound buoyancy were provided to each passenger. The operator of the defendant was aware that jackets of this nature were inadequate for the Fraser River and had corresponded with the federal Department of Transport about the possibility of using life jackets of 32 pound buoyancy, which were of the type employed on the Colorado River. Although he received no satisfactory response from the Department, which provided an answer that "reached a new level in bureaucratic non sequiturs", the trial judge found that the defendant was negligent in not providing more buoyant life jackets.

The raft overturned in the narrows at Scuzzy Rock; Dr. Delaney's life jacket proved inadequate for turbulent conditions and he drowned. The majority of the court found that the plaintiff had failed to show that the defendant's negligence caused Dr. Delaney's death, because it could not be shown that he would have survived if he had worn a jacket of more buoyant specifications. Nemetz C.J.B.C., however, found that the plaintiff had sufficiently proved causation of loss and continued to consider the finding of the trial judge that the liability release was an effective bar to the action. He found that it was not, for two reasons.]

(1) Past Consideration

It is contended for the plaintiff that notice of the terms of the liability release were not contemporaneous with the entry into the contract; in other words, the terms of the liability release are not a part of the contract, and since there was no "new" consideration for them, the release is unenforceable. This raises the question whether the maxim "past consideration is no consideration" is applicable to the facts of this case. The trial Judge found that Dr. Delaney paid his $100 at or about the time the release was signed. Since the issue of past consideration was not canvassed by the trial Judge, it was not essential for him to analyze the timing of the payment. There is evidence before the Court from Mr. Sims that Dr. Delaney paid his fare to take the trip on the morning of May 5, 1979 before the release was presented for signature. Mr. Sims testified that he received the payment personally and that he was not present later when the release was signed. Therefore, we know that some time elapsed between the two events.

The crucial factor is that notice of the terms, or indeed of the existence of a liability release was not contemporaneous with the entry into the contract evidenced by the payment of the fare to Sims earlier that morning. At the moment of payment, Cascade was obliged to take Dr. Delaney on the expedition on the terms existing at that moment. The subsequent requirement of signing the release was an attempt by Cascade to impose additional and onerous terms to a contract which had already been finalized. Although the company policy was that no one could go on the trip without signing the release, they had no more right to require him to agree to the additional contractual terms of the release than they would have had to try to exact a higher fare from him to secure their performance of the contract (*Gilbert Steel Ltd. v. University Const. Ltd.* [*supra*, Chapter 4, section 4(c)]). Simply stated, there was no consideration for Dr. Delaney's signature on the release form because Cascade was bound to take him whether or not he signed.

The leading case on the question of timing of consideration is *Olley v. Marlborough Ct. Ltd.*, [1949] 1 K.B. 532, [1949] 1 All E.R. 127 (C.A.). There, a husband and wife, on arrival at the defendant hotel registered and paid for a week's lodging in advance. They then went upstairs to the bedroom allotted to them where a notice was posted which purported to release the proprietors of the hotel from liability for articles lost or stolen unless they were left with the manageress for safe custody. The couple had not been notified of this release at the time they registered. Some of the wife's belongings were stolen from the room. The Court held that the terms of the notice in the bedroom formed no part of the contract made between the guests and the proprietor of the hotel. The contract had been made before the guests could see the notice. The couple in question had resided in the hotel for several months at the time of the theft. There was evidence to the effect that during the prolonged period they had occupied the room it is likely they would have read the notice posted on the door. The plaintiffs paid for the room on a weekly basis and it was contended for the defendants that each payment constituted a new contract and that at the time of the theft the plaintiffs had been reasonably notified of the release, having had it posted in their room for a period of months. The Court found that this was a continuing contract and since notice had not been given at the very beginning, the release was unenforceable. Singleton L.J. put it this way at p. 547 [K.B.]:

> If the defendants who would prima facie be liable for their own negligence, seek to exempt themselves by words of some kind, they must show, first, that those words form part of the contract between the parties and, secondly, that those words are so clear that they must be understood by the parties in the circumstances as absolving the defendants from the results of their own negligence . . . It is clear that when the plaintiff and her husband went to the hotel they had not seen the notice. Apparently by the custom of the hotel, they were asked to pay a week in advance, and when they went to the bedroom for the first time they had not seen the notice, and the words at the head of the notice could not be part of the contract between the parties.

The case at Bar is even stronger. There can be no presumption of advance knowledge of disclaimer of responsibility.

Lord Denning, in *Olley*, summarized the law as follows, at p. 549:

> The only other point in the case is whether the hotel company are protected by the notice which they put in the bedrooms, "The proprietors will not hold themselves responsible for articles lost or stolen, unless handed to the manageress for safe custody." The first question is whether that notice formed part of the contract. Now people who rely on a contract to exempt themselves from their common law liability must prove that contract strictly. Not only must the terms of the contract be clearly proved, but also the intention to create legal relations—the intention to be legally bound—must also be clearly proved. The best way of proving it is by a written document signed by the party to be bound. Another way is by handing him before or at the time of the contract a written notice specifying its terms and making it clear to him that the contract is on those terms. A prominent public notice which is plain for him to see when he makes the contract or an express oral stipulation would, no doubt, have the same effect. But nothing short of one of these three ways will suffice. . . . The hotel company no doubt hope that the guest will be held bound by them, but the hope is vain unless they clearly show that he agreed to be bound by them, which is rarely the case.

(2) The Insufficiency of the Notice

I reproduce the principal portion of the liability release:

CASCADE RIVER HOLIDAYS

P.O. Box 65, Yale,
B.C., Canada V0K 2S0
Phone (604) 863-2332

Standard Liability Release

TRIP NAME 2 day Fraser
TRIP NO. C10
TRIP DATE May 5-6 1979

DISCLAIMER CLAUSE: Cascade River Holidays Ltd. is not responsible for any loss or damage suffered by any person either in travelling to the location of the trip, before, during or after the trip, for any reasons whatsoever including negligence on the part of the company, its agents or servants.

AGREEMENT: I agree to assume all risks involved in taking the trip including travelling before and after, and agree to pay the cost of any emergency evacuation of my person and belongings that may become necessary. I agree to Cascade River Holidays Ltd. its agents and servants relieving themselves of all liability for losses and damages of all and every descriptions. I acknowledge having read this Liability release and that I am of full age and my acceptance of the above disclaimer clause by my signature and seal. (Parents or Guardians please sign for minors.)

(Signatures follow)

This document must be read together with the relevant portions of the brochure. . . . [which is set out above. Nemetz C.J.B.C. found that there was no evidence that Dr. Delaney had seen or read the brochure and recognised that his position may have been different from that of other passengers. Nemetz C.J.B.C. then considered whether the action was barred by *L'Estrange v. Graucob, supra*, and discussed the circumstances in which the release was signed.]

On the morning of May 5, Miss Morrison met with the members of the group in the hotel parking lot at Yale and either singly or in groups presented them with the release. She asked each to read it and sign it and said that those who would not sign would not be allowed to embark on the journey on the river. All passengers signed. It is evident that the releases were signed in a hurried manner. Miss Morrison's evidence is clear and frank. She pointed out that "it always seemed we were always in a hurry trying to get everybody out." She approached the passengers for signature when they were busy with other matters, i.e., "getting things out of their car and they are getting fishing things and things like that. . . ." This testimony is amply supported by a number of the passengers. Dr. Hoff, when asked in cross-examination, "If you wished to read the release it would not have taken you very long, at all, would it?" He replied, "It would under the circumstances have taken an inappropriate time." The reason was, of course, that he was anxious to get onto the van for the embarkation place. Mr. Lundie, a chartered accountant, was also a passenger. He described the signing operation:

As I understood it one of the procedures that we had to do was sign that standard form of liability and it was done in a rather perfunctory manner by somebody just standing by the van or sitting at the opening of the side door of the van and thus they could ask people to come

> over and they did. I think as we stowed our gear in the van, we signed the liability document
> and got a T-shirt.

He did not read the document. He was told it was a standard liability form but there was no discussion as to implications. Mr. Steeves, another passenger, confirms that the signing was done "very quickly". He said, "I think I can compare it to signing a rent-a-car form." Miss Morrison was not sure whether Delaney read the release.

L'Estrange was decided in England almost 50 years ago. It was the decision of two judges sitting in the Divisional Court. It was a case where there was no consensus. Miss L'Estrange owned a restaurant. The company's salesmen sold her a cigarette machine. They presented her with an order form which she signed without reading. A clause in the form stated: "any express or implied condition, statement or warrant[y], statutory or otherwise not stated herein is hereby excluded." The machine was defective so she sued. The Court held that the exemption clause was a bar because, as Scrutton L.J. said, "When a document containing contractual terms is signed, then, in the absence of fraud, or I will add, misrepresentation, the party signing it is bound, and it is wholly immaterial whether he has read the document or not." It must not be forgotten that Maugham L.J. cautioned that there were two possibilities to be kept in mind. One was where, though signed by the person, it was signed in circumstances which did not make it that person's act. And the other situation would, he said, be where the person was induced to sign by misrepresentation. . . .

[Nemetz C.J.B.C. then quoted from the *Tilden Rent-A-Car* case, *supra*, found that the signing of the release could be compared to the signing of a car rental form and found that the language of the release was misleading in the following respects:]

(1) The use of the adjective "standard" would tend to induce a sense of security in the passenger asked to sign the release. This is borne out in the testimony of Lundie, who, having read the word "standard", refrained from reading further.

(2) The clause speaks generally of "loss or damage" but does not mention the risk of personal injury or death. Cascade's president, Sims, conceded that if he mentioned the possibility of a fatal accident, his business would suffer.

(3) The release provides that the passenger assumes "all risks involved in taking the trip. . . ." It does not refer to all risks arising from the supply of inadequate equipment, i.e., inadequate life jackets.

This may have been innocent misrepresentation but it will not avail Cascade the use of such an all-embracing exclusionary clause because, as was said by Lord Denning in *Photo Production Ltd. v. Securicor Tpt. Ltd.* [*infra*, section 3(v) of this chapter]:

> Thus we reach, after long years, the principle which lies behind all our striving: the court will
> not allow a party to rely on an exemption or limitation clause in circumstances in which it
> would not be fair or reasonable to allow reliance on it; and, in considering whether it is fair
> and reasonable, the court will consider whether it was in standard form, whether there was
> equality of bargaining power, the nature of the breach, and so forth.

The release contained provisions so onerous and unusual that it was the duty of Cascade to see that the provisions were "effectively called to the attention of the other party under the penalty of their being held non-binding on the latter party". . . . It was not sufficient that a clerk, minutes before passengers were to depart on this unusual voyage, when the passengers' minds were directed to the voyage and packing their gear, should place before them this document containing the onerous terms it did. A reasonably intelligent person was entitled to assume that a form titled "standard" did not contain the unusual provisions contained in this one. This was indeed what Professor Waddams has termed "misrepresentation by omission" (see *Tilden, supra*). In the case of Delaney, Cascade had not sent him a brochure. They could not assume that he had a clear idea of the risk of which they had forewarned the others in the brochure under the heading "Liability" which speaks of Cascade not guaranteeing safe passage and not assuming responsibility for the patron's safety. And, *a fortiori*, the brochure recommended that "the patron purchase personal insurance to protect himself". Had Delaney been so warned, would he have assumed the risk to absolve Cascade from negligence of not providing him with the best life-saving jackets available? I do not think so. . . .

[Accordingly Nemetz C.J.B.C. would have allowed the appeal.]

McFARLANE J.A. [TAGGART J.A. concurring] [having resolved the issue of causation against the plaintiff continued to consider the effect of the release.] . . . I think the argument of "past consideration" must fail. It seems clear that the deceased was informed that unless he signed the release form he would not be taken on the trip. The immediate consideration which he received was, therefore, that he was permitted to enter the van and carry on with the venture.

While it is possible to criticize the language of the "Standard Liability Release", I think it must be interpreted and understood, having regard to the whole purpose of the relationship between the deceased and the corporate respondent. That purpose, so far as the deceased was concerned, was to engage in what must have been intended to be an exciting and thrilling challenge of the power of the Fraser River in the Canyon. Construed in that way, there is, in my opinion, no doubt of the intent involved in the language of the release. I think also the trial Judge was correct in applying the principles stated in *L'Estrange v. F. Graucob Ltd.* [*supra*]. Having regard to the nature of the venture involved I think that there is no sufficient ground for making an exception to the general principles enunciated in that case.

[The appeal was dismissed. Leave to appeal to the Supreme Court of Canada was granted, but the appeal was discontinued on 24th September 1984.]

NOTES

1. In *Trigg v. MI Movers International Transport Services Ltd.* (1991), 4 O.R. (3d) 562, leave to appeal to S.C.C. refused (1992), 7 O.R. (3d) xii (note) (S.C.C.), the Ontario Court of Appeal extended the *Clendenning* principle by applying it to a situation where there was no evidence that the contract had been executed in hurried circumstances and to a less unusual and onerous exclusion clause. The court simply held that a limitation or exclusion clause could not be imported into a contract merely by the signature of the party sought to be bound. The onus was on the party attempting

to rely upon the clause to establish that the clause had properly been brought to the other party's attention so that it was reasonable for the first party to believe that the other had assented to the terms of the contract. The court also endorsed Nemetz C.J.B.C.'s judgment in *Delaney* that, to be effective, the notice must be given before or at the time that the contract was made.

2. The *Clendenning* principle was implicitly accepted by the Supreme Court in *Crocker v. Sundance Northwest Resorts Ltd.*, [1988] 1 S.C.R. 1186, where the document signed was not lengthy, but really contained just one clause.

3. It must not be forgotten that, as a general proposition, parties who have executed contracts cannot escape from the effect of particular contractual provisions by failing to read the contracts in question. They have an obligation to familiarize themselves with the contents of their contracts. A failure to do so can be justified only by special circumstances. The nature of those circumstances was discussed in *978011 Ontario Ltd. v. Cornell Engineering Co.* (2001), 53 O.R. (3d) 783 (C.A.), leave to appeal refused (2001), 158 O.A.C. 195 (note) (S.C.C.). The defendant company ("Cornell") carried on the business of stamping metal to be used in the manufacturing of household appliances. The company was owned by Stevens (51%) and Bimboga (49%). Bimboga decided to sell his shares in Cornell. Stevens discussed the purchase by Macdonald of Bimboga's interest with Macdonald. Stevens and Macdonald orally agreed that Macdonald was to go to work for the defendant, Cornell, at an annual salary of $55,000 and, during a two-year period, Macdonald had to satisfy Bimboga that he had the ability and the experience to take over Bimboga's role as president of the defendant. As a result of that agreement, Macdonald turned down another post at a salary of $135,000 and started working for the defendant in January 1993.

In February 1993, the defendant's accountant advised Macdonald that it would be beneficial for both sides for his services to be provided to the defendant through a corporation and pursuant to a written services agreement. Stevens asked Macdonald to prepare a written document. Macdonald obtained a standard form contract from his professional association and made a number of revisions. In particular, he struck out the termination provisions in the printed contract and inserted, in slightly larger print, a provision that, if either the personal services contract or the agreement to purchase Bimboga's shares at the completion of the contract were terminated or changed, the defendant would pay compensation to Macdonald equal to twice the total remuneration paid to Macdonald up to that date. Macdonald presented the contract to Stevens and asked him to read it. Before signing, Stevens read only the first page of the 11-page contract, and not the termination clause. Later, the defendant unilaterally terminated the services agreement and the question was whether Macdonald could enforce the termination clause. Weiler J.A., for the court, said at 793–800:

> [W]e have a judicial system that emphasizes individual responsibility and self-reliance. Generally, parties negotiating a contract expect that each will act entirely in the party's own interests. Absent a special relationship, the common law in Canada has yet to recognize that in the negotiation of a contract, there is a duty to have regard to the other person's interests, namely, to act in good faith. . . . In keeping with the principle of self-reliance imposed by law on each party to a contract, the failure to read a contract before signing it is not a legally acceptable basis for refusing to abide by it. Nor is the fact that the clause was not subject to negotiations sufficient in itself. . . .
>
> The law does, however, regulate contractual conduct between individuals through the imposition of three types of standards: unconscionability, good faith and the fiduciary standard. All three standards are points on a continuum in which the law acknowledges a limitation on the principle of self-reliance and imposes an obligation to respect the interests of the other. [The court then quoted from P. Finn, "the Fiduciary Princple", in T. Youdan, ed., *Equity, Fidicuaries and Trusts* (Scarborough, Ont: Carswell, 1989) at 1. The relevant section is summarized, *infra*, Chapter 11, section 3.]
>
> The circumstances where the law requires more than self-interested dealing on the part of a party share certain characteristics. First, one party relies on the other for information necessary to make an informed choice and, second, the party in possession of the information has an opportunity, by withholding (or concealing) information, to bring about the choice made by the other party. . . . If one party to a contract relies on the other for information, that

reliance must be justified in the circumstances. Finn, *supra*, suggests . . . that the following five factors are indicative of situations where reliance is justified . . . [See the five factors as applied by the court below.]

The presence of one of these elements alone will not necessarily suffice to justify the imposition of a duty in law on the other. Dependence, influence, vulnerability, trust and confidence are of importance only to the extent that they evidence a relationship suggesting an entitlement not to be self-reliant: . . . While the relationship may be the foundation for the entitlement, in and of itself, the relationship does not create the entitlement. The entitlement arises either because one party has no ability to readily inform himself or herself by accessing important information or because one party has an inability to appreciate the significance of the information. That inability may be due to a cognitive disability or it may arise out of the circumstances created by the other party. To determine whether the entitlement is created, regard must be had to all the circumstances . . .

.....

[B]ased upon Stevens' complete trust in Macdonald, the trial judge found that Macdonald had an obligation to act in good faith towards Stevens. He went on to hold that this obligation to act in good faith required Macdonald to disclose the existence of the termination clause to Stevens, and that Stevens should not be held responsible for his own negligence in failing to read the agreement because he had trusted Macdonald and relied on him to prepare the Services Agreement.

I respectfully disagree [applying the five factors].

(1) Past course of dealing

When Stevens signed the Services Agreement, he did so on behalf of Cornell. Although Stevens and Macdonald were friends and Stevens acted as a mentor in advising Macdonald on his career, Macdonald had no prior dealing and no relationship with Bimboga, the other person affected by the Agreement. The undisputed purpose of the Services Agreement was to facilitate the transfer of Bimboga's shares in Cornell to Macdonald. Macdonald was at the mercy of Bimboga's discretion in the sense that even if he raised the money for the first payment towards the purchase of Bimboga's shares, Bimboga still had to be satisfied of Macdonald's ability to run the company before transferring his shares. Without the termination clause, Macdonald had no protection from Bimboga.

It is also important to recall that Macdonald turned down a salary of $135,000 . . . for an indefinite period in return for a two-year employee position for $55,000. In this context, the termination clause in the Services Agreement, although one-sided, was not unreasonable. Furthermore, by entering into the Services Agreement, Macdonald was potentially relinquishing his common law protection from wrongful dismissal. In these circumstances, the inclusion of a termination clause in the agreement was not unusual . . .

It appears that the trial judge was of the opinion that since Macdonald had already started work for Cornell, all of the terms of his employment had been agreed upon and therefore the termination clause was a unilateral change to the oral agreement. Technically, the parties to the oral contract were not the same as the parties to the written contract. The oral contract was entered into by Macdonald personally, the written contract was entered into by the appellant corporation. More importantly, there was no discussion, and no prior agreement between any of the parties regarding termination.

Upon seeing the 11-page agreement, Stevens must have known from the length of the document that it contained terms other than the few that had been agreed upon orally. The terms that had been agreed upon orally, namely, compensation of $55,000 per annum, at the rate of 1/12 per month, and the duration of the agreement, two years, were all on the first page which Stevens read.

(2) Explicit assumption by one party of advisory responsibilities

It was Stevens who explicitly assumed advisory responsibilities and it was Stevens who was in a position to influence Macdonald.

(3) Relative positions of the parties, particularly in their access to information and in their understanding of the possible demands of the dealing

Macdonald intended to leave the agreement with Stevens to read and in fact advised him to read it. Stevens and Bimboga would have had ready access to the necessary information had it not been for Stevens' precipitous act in deciding to sign the agreement after reading only the first page. Macdonald did nothing to pressure Stevens to sign the agreement without reading it.

The Agreement was easy to read with clear headings including the heading "Termination" in bold. The changes to the standard form were easy to detect . . .

[This is not] a case where a party has accepted a standard form contract containing onerous and verbose provisions in small type and in circumstances where it could not reasonably be expected for the signing party to read the contract: see *Tilden Rent-A-Car Co. v. Clendenning* [*supra*]. In this case, Stevens, an experienced person in signing contracts, had the opportunity to examine the documents, and was encouraged to do so. The clause is plainly visible, clearly worded and capable of being detected . . .

(4) The manner in which the parties were brought together and the expectation that could be created in the relying party

.....

. . . The actions of Stevens do not suggest that he on behalf of Cornell was a "relying party" on Macdonald

(5) Whether trust or confidence has knowingly been reposed by one party in the other

. . . Stevens was in an advisory position to Macdonald, it was not the other way around. Quite apart from advancing Macdonald's interests, when their interests did not coincide, Stevens appears to have had no regard for Macdonald's interests in his dealings with him. As a sophisticated and experienced businessperson, Stevens had the cognitive ability to appreciate the significance of the document he was signing. That ability was not impaired as a result of any act by Macdonald.

Having regard to all of the circumstances, Stevens was not justified in law in expecting that he would not be bound by the termination clause in the Services Agreement when he signed the agreement without reading it . . .

(iii) *Statutory Notice Provisions*

In deciding whether a particular clause on which one contracting party relies should be given effect, a natural first question to consider is whether the clause should be treated as part of the contract at all. To treat a clause as part of the contract we must satisfy ourselves that both parties have agreed to the clause or, at least, that the party who now objects to the clause should reasonably be taken as having agreed to it. Thus, you have observed the courts, in the cases you have just read, considering, among other things, whether the clause was sufficiently brought to the notice of the party who now objects to it.

The following provision, drawn from the Ontario Insurance Act, is an example of an attempt to prescribe by statute for adequate notice of a limiting clause which may bear onerously on the purchaser of an insurance policy:

INSURANCE ACT

R.S.O. 1990, c. I.8, s. 149

149. A contract containing,

(a) a deductible clause;

(b) a co-insurance, average or similar clause; or

> (c) a clause limiting recovery by the insured to a specified percentage of the value of any property insured at the time of loss, whether or not that clause is conditional or unconditional,
>
> shall have printed or stamped upon its face in red ink or bold type the words "The policy contains a clause that may limit the amount payable", or the French equivalent failing which the clause is not binding upon the insured.

The efficacy of such a statutory notice requirement may well be questioned. Professor Leff has observed that "Many people don't read contracts at all; even a clear one won't help them. And some people would sign a contract even if 'THIS IS A SWINDLE' were embossed across its top in electric pink" ("Contract as a Thing" (1970), 19 Am. U.L. Rev. 131 at 157). While that may be true, it does not diminish the case for stipulating for fair notice for those who do read their contracts. Statutory prescription of notice in red ink on the face of the document, however, is of little value if the rest of the document is printed in red ink. It is notorious that some insurance companies complied with the requirement imposed by the Insurance Act by printing the prescribed warning in large red letters that were visible but were superimposed across other print in the document in a manner which did not tend to draw obvious attention to the warning. The face of the policy also carried the insurer's name and its insignia in bold red characters.

(iv) Strict Construction

As has already been seen in the discussion of *Scott v. Wawanesa Mutual Insurance Co., supra*, section 2, it is well established that, where a contract has been drafted by one of the parties, any ambiguities in it are likely to be construed against that party *(contra proferentem)* and in favour of the other: *Mobil Oil Canada Ltd. v. Beta Well Service Ltd.*, [1974] 3 W.W.R. 273 (Alta. C.A.), affirmed (1974), 2 A.R. 183 (S.C.C.).

Indeed, there are numerous cases in which a standard form contract has been interpreted in a way which can only be described as a benevolent reading in favour of the party who did not draft or proffer the standard form. In *Staples v. Great American Ins. Co.*, [1941] S.C.R. 213, for example, a motor yacht was insured subject to the following condition:

> Warranted by the insured that the yacht shall be used solely for private pleasure purposes and not to be hired or chartered unless approved and permission endorsed hereon.

There was some evidence that the insured had used the yacht, or allowed others to use it, for various business purposes on a few occasions. The yacht was destroyed by fire while being used by the insured's friend, Racicot, to take his uncle across the lake to inspect a mine property.

The Supreme Court of Canada noted that the yacht had not been hired or chartered by Racicot and concluded that there had been no breach of the warranty.

The trial judge had found that Racicot's use of the boat was a breach of the warranty in that it was not "for pleasure purposes" but for a purpose connected with his uncle's business. On this point, Kerwin J. in the Supreme Court of Canada said at 222-23:

> In the first place, there is nothing in the statement attached to the policy to prohibit the use of the yacht by someone other than the insured. The word "private" must be read in

conjunction with the words "and not to be hired or chartered unless approved and permission endorsed hereon." So read, the "pleasure purposes" may be private even when the yacht was used by Racicot with the appellant's implied permission. On the day of the fire, it was certainly not hired or chartered, and the question is whether Racicot, who "took his uncle up to another part of the lake, without remuneration, to a dam where the uncle was to inspect a mine for his own benefit," was using the yacht solely for private pleasure purposes. That question, in my view, must be answered in the affirmative. The yacht was not hired or chartered either by Racicot or by his uncle. The word "pleasure" has various meanings, depending upon the context in which it is used, and I think that on the occasion in question, it must be held that Racicot experienced "enjoyment, delight, gratification" (Oxford Dictionary), in transporting his uncle from one part of the lake to another, equally as well as if he had taken his uncle as a matter of friendship to a part of the lake in order to board a train or bus. . . .

Similar principles of strict construction and *contra proferentem* apply to the interpretation of exclusion clauses generally: see most recently *Bow Valley Husky (Bermuda) Ltd. v. Saint John Shipbuilding Ltd.* (1997), 153 D.L.R. (4th) 385 (S.C.C.). In the famous case of *Wallis, Son & Wells v. Pratt & Haynes*, [1911] A.C. 394 (H.L.), for example, a provision that the seller gave "no warranty expressed or implied . . . as to description" of goods being sold did not protect it from liability for breach of an implied *condition* as to the description of the goods even though the buyer, having accepted the goods, was required to treat the breach of condition as a breach of warranty.

One important line of cases deals with the exclusion of liability for negligence. As a general proposition, very clear words must be employed in order for one party to protect itself from liability for negligence: *Canada Steamship Lines Ltd. v. R.*, [1952] 2 D.L.R. 786 (P.C.). Thus, where a defendant is potentially subject to two liabilities, one strict and the other for negligence, general words of exclusion will not be construed as protecting the defendant from its liability for negligence: *White v. John Warrick & Co.*, [1953] 1 W.L.R. 1285 (C.A.); *Canadian Pacific Forest Products Ltd. v. Belships (Far East) Shipping (PTE.) Ltd.* (1999), 175 D.L.R. (4th) 449 (Fed. C.A.). Where a defendant's potential liability rests only in negligence, then general words of exclusion are capable of covering negligence since otherwise the clause would lack subject-matter: *Alderslade v. Hendon Laundry Ltd.*, [1945] K.B. 189 (C.A.); but the courts are not averse to construing the clause merely as a warning by the defendant that it is not liable in the absence of negligence: *Olley v. Marlborough Ct. Ltd.*, [1949] 1 K.B. 532 (C.A.); *Hollier v. Rambler Motors (A.M.C.) Ltd.*, [1972] 2 Q.B. 71 (C.A.).

A less restrictive approach, however, was taken by the Supreme Court of Canada in ITO—*International Terminal Operators Ltd. v. Miida Electronics Inc.* (1986), 28 D.L.R. (4th) 641 in the commercial context. A carrier (Mitsui) had undertaken the storage of goods pending delivery. Once the goods had been unloaded from the ship, Mitsui was relieved of the liability as a carrier. Its liability became that of a bailee. The contract contained general words releasing the carrier from liability "in any capacity whatsoever for any . . . loss of . . . the goods occurring before loading and/or after discharge". Did they exclude liability for negligence? McIntyre J. pointed out that the courts have generally accepted *Canada Steamship Lines* as authoritative, but he relaxed the principle that negligence had to be addressed specifically by the exclusion clause. With the support of the court on this issue, he stated at 675-76:

> The exempting provision relieves of liability in any capacity which would include that of bailee after discharge and during storage. There is no express mention of negligence, so the question is: Do the words extend to include it? This is a question of construction and the answer must be found in the context of the whole contract. The contract of carriage contemplated the exclusion of all liability upon the carrier for preloading, and after-discharge, loss. The liability of the carrier *qua* carrier is not touched in this exemption clause and the focus in our case is on liability regarding the storage of the goods after discharge. It has been said that a general exemption from all liability will not of itself exclude negligence. In this case, however, where the exemption clause relates only to a small part of the full, agreed performance, such a general rule is not necessarily applicable. Here the carrier is protected in specific terms from liability for the loss of the goods. The only duty of the bailee is to exercise reasonable care in the safeguarding of the goods and it is difficult to see how a loss, in this case by theft, could occur but for the negligence of the bailee. I would therefore conclude that the words employed here are wide enough to include negligence as being within the reasonable contemplation of the parties in formulating their agreement.
>
> I think it is important, in determining what was within reasonable contemplation, to recognize that this is a commercial contract between two parties who, in essence, are determining which of them is to bear the responsibility for insurance at the various stages of the contract.
>
> The remaining question, whether there is any other possible head of liability upon which the exemption clause could operate, must be answered in the negative. The goods were in short-term storage awaiting delivery. The only liability which could be imposed on the bailee would be based on negligence. I am therefore of the opinion that Mitsui, as the carrier, has the benefit of the exemption clause.

This approach was followed by the Federal Court of Appeal in *MacKay v. Scott Packing and Warehousing Co. (Canada) Ltd.*, [1996] 2 F.C. 36 and by Iacobucci J. for the majority of the Supreme Court in the *Bow Valley Husky* case, *supra*. In the latter case, his Lordship also suggested (at 430) that a different approach should be adopted for the construction of clauses that expressly provided for "the *assumption* of liability limited to a specific circumstance" as opposed to those that provided for "general *exclusion* from liability". In that case, the majority held that a shipbuilder was not liable for breach of a duty to warn the owner of the dangerously inflammable property of a certain product, whose use had been mandated by the owner, because that duty had been precluded by the terms of the contract between the parties. The contract stated in part: "Builder's liability with respect to the Owner Directed Supply shall extend only to installation thereof . . ." By expressly extending liability only to (negligence) in the installation of such materials, the parties had by necessary implication excluded all other grounds for the liability of the builder, including the duty to warn.

In contrast, McLachlin J. for the minority concluded that the contractual exclusion clause did not protect the builder from breach of a duty to warn. The relevant clause fell under an article in the contract headed "Warranties". She determined that warranties ordinarily related to the quality of goods and workmanship and not to warnings about the risks associated with the use of particular products. The purpose of the clause, when strictly construed as it had to be, was to narrow the scope of any warranty for owner-directed materials. The builder was not to be responsible for defects in the items chosen by the owner but only for the defective installation of those items. The clause simply did not address the separate and independent question of whether the builder was under a tortious duty to warn the owner.

In *Ailsa Craig Fishing Co. v. Malvern Fishing Co.,* [1983] 1 All E.R. 101, the House of Lords suggested that clauses limiting liability should not be regarded with the same hostility as those excluding liability and hence should be construed more liberally. In *Hunter Engineering Co. v. Syncrude Canada Ltd., infra,* section 3(v), however, Wilson J. rightly rejected any categorical distinction between the two types of clauses because, in a given case, an exclusion clause could be fair and a limitation of liability clause unfair.

(v) *Fundamental Breach*

In the 1950s and 1960s, drawing upon the concept of deviation in bailment cases, the courts developed a doctrine of fundamental breach of contract to the effect that a party could not rely upon an exclusion clause, however widely expressed, where it had committed a fundamental breach of contract. The primary proponent of this doctrine was Lord Denning in the English Court of Appeal and his judgment in the following case is typical.

KARSALES (HARROW) LTD. v. WALLIS

[1956] 1 W.L.R. 936, [1956] 2 All E.R. 866 (C.A.)

Wallis inspected a second-hand Buick motor car which Stinton was offering to sell for £600. He found the car in excellent condition and agreed to buy it if Stinton could arrange financing through a hire-purchase company. Karsales (Harrow) Ltd. bought the car from Stinton and sold it to Mutual Finance Ltd. which let the car out to Wallis on hire-purchase terms. When this agreement was concluded the car was still in Stinton's possession and Wallis had not seen it since the initial inspection.

DENNING L.J. About a week later the vehicle was left, late at night, outside the defendant's garage. It was examined by the defendant the next morning and was found to be the same Buick car as he had previously inspected in this sense, that it had the same body and engine registration number, but it had been badly damaged. It had evidently been towed in. There was a rope attached to the front bumper. It was, as the judge found, "in a deplorable state". The new tyres had been taken off and old ones put on; the wireless set had been removed from it; the chrome strips round the body were missing; and when the defendant's fitter looked at the engine, the cylinder head was off, all the valves were burnt, and there were two broken pistons. The car would not go. The defendant said to Mr. Stinton "I will not accept the car in this condition"; the car was towed away to Mr. Stinton's place and was never repaired. It would have cost £150 to put it into the condition in which the defendant had first seen it.

Mutual Finance, Ltd., after several months, assigned all their rights under the hire-purchase agreement to Karsales (Harrow) Ltd., the intermediary to which

I have referred, and Karsales (Harrow) Ltd. now sue the defendant for ten months' instalments of payments under the hire-purchase agreement. The judge has found that they are entitled to those payments as having become due under the agreement, and the question is whether that decision is right in point of law or not.

On this matter, counsel on behalf of the defendant says that he agreed to take on hire-purchase terms a Buick motor car which he had seen a week or two before he had signed these documents. He says that it was the duty of Mutual Finance Ltd. to see that there was delivered to the defendant a motor car which corresponded to the car which he had seen; further that, owing to the condition of the car on delivery, there was a fundamental breach by Mutual Finance Ltd. and that Karsales (Harrow) Ltd. (to whom I will hereafter refer as the plaintiffs) cannot recover the instalments. In answer, counsel on behalf of the plaintiffs says that there was delivered to the defendant a Buick motor car of the registration number specified in the agreement and they are in no way responsible for its condition on delivery. They rely on cl. 3(g) of the hire-purchase agreement:

> No condition or warranty that the vehicle is roadworthy or as to its age, condition or fitness for any purpose is given by the owner or implied herein.

The judge held that the clause meant that the hire-purchase company were not responsible in any way for the condition of this car when it was delivered, and that although it was in this deplorable condition they could still recover the instalments due under the agreement; and that, even though the car was rejected by the defendant, they could still recover them

In my opinion, under a hire-purchase agreement of this kind, when the hirer has himself previously seen and examined the motor car and made application for hire-purchase on the basis of his inspection of it, there is an obligation on the lender to deliver the car in substantially the same condition as when it was seen. It makes no difference that the lender is a finance company which has bought the car in the interval without seeing it. The lender must know, from the ordinary course of business, that the hirer applies on the faith of his inspection and on the understanding that the car will be delivered in substantially the same condition: and it is an implied term of the agreement that pending delivery the car will be kept in suitable order and repair for the purposes of the bailment. This is supported by *Story on Bailment*, arts. 383 to 385, and *Robertson v. Amazon Tug & Lighterage Co.* [(1881), 7 Q.B.D. 598 (C.A.)]. The plaintiffs say that there can be no such implication in this case in view of the express terms of cl. 3(g). The law about exempting clauses, however, has been much developed in recent years, at any rate about printed exempting clauses, which so often pass unread. Notwithstanding earlier cases which might suggest the contrary, it is now settled that exempting clauses of this kind, no matter how widely they are expressed, only avail the party when he is carrying out his contract in its essential respects. He is not allowed to use them as a cover for misconduct or indifference or to enable him to turn a blind eye to his obligations. They do not avail him when he is guilty of a breach which goes to the root of the contract. It is necessary to look at the contract apart from the exempting clauses and see what are the terms, express or implied, which impose an obligation on the party. If he has been guilty of a breach of those obligations in a respect which goes to the very root of the contract, he cannot rely on the exempting clauses.

The principle is sometimes said to be that the party cannot rely on an exempting clause when he delivers something "different in kind" from that contracted for, or has broken a "fundamental term" or a "fundamental contractual obligation". However, I think that these are all comprehended by the general principle that a breach which goes to the root of the contract disentitles the party from relying on the exempting clause. In the present case the lender was in breach of the implied obligation that I have mentioned. When the defendant inspected the car prior to signing the application form, the car was in excellent condition and would go: whereas the car which was subsequently delivered to him was no doubt the same car but it was in a deplorable state and would not go. That breach went to the root of the contract and disentitled the lender from relying on the exempting clause. . . .

[Concurring judgments were delivered by Birkett and Parker L.JJ. The appeal was allowed.]

NOTE

In *Suisse Atlantique Société D'Armement Maritime S.A. v. N.V. Rotterdamsche Kolen Centrale,* [1967] 1 A.C. 361, the House of Lords attempted to put an end to the doctrine of fundamental breach by determining that it was simply a question of construction of the contract as to whether a particular breach fell within the protection of a particular clause or, indeed, whether a particular clause prevented a breach from having occurred at all. In so doing, their Lordships recognized that the process of construction was flexible. There was the overarching principle to be borne in mind that the more serious the breach the clearer the language required to protect the defendant. There were also a number of subsidiary principles of construction, such as the maxims that an exclusion clause would not be interpreted so as to lead to an absurdity or so as to defeat the main object of the contract.

In a series of decisions the English Court of Appeal led by Lord Denning attempted to resurrect the doctrine of fundamental breach as a rule of law. One of the earliest and most notorious of these was *Harbutt's "Plasticine" Ltd. v. Wayne Tank & Pump Co.,* [1970] 1 Q.B. 447 (C.A.). There, the court held that, where a contract has come to an end because of a fundamental breach, either through the election of the innocent party or (more controversially) automatically because the serious consequences of the breach have rendered any election otiose, then the exclusion clause also falls to the ground. In the following case, the House of Lords again, and more vigorously, endorsed a construction approach.

PHOTO PRODUCTION LTD. v. SECURICOR TRANSPORT LTD.

[1980] A.C. 827, [1980] 2 W.L.R. 283, [1980] 1 All E.R. 556 (H.L.)

LORD WILBERFORCE My Lords, this appeal arises from the destruction by fire of the respondents' factory involving loss and damage agreed to amount to £615,000. The question is whether the appellant is liable to the respondents for this sum.

The appellant is a company which provides security services. In 1968 it entered into a contract with the respondents by which for a charge of £8 15s. 0d. (old currency) per week it agreed to "provide their night patrol service whereby four visits per night shall be made seven nights per week and two visits shall be made during the afternoon of Saturday and four visits shall be made during the day of Sunday." The contract incorporated printed standard conditions which, in some circumstances, might exclude or limit the appellant's liability. The questions in this appeal are (i) whether these conditions can be invoked at all in the events which happened and (ii) if so, whether either the exclusion provision, or a provision limiting liability, can be applied on the facts. The trial judge . . . decided these issues in favour of the appellant. The Court of Appeal decided issue (i) in the respondents' favour invoking the doctrine of fundamental breach. Waller L.J. in addition would have decided for the respondents on issue (ii).

What happened was that on a Sunday night the duty employee of the appellant was one Musgrove. It was not suggested that he was unsuitable for the job or that the appellant was negligent in employing him. He visited the factory at the correct time, but when inside he deliberately started a fire by throwing a match on to some cartons. The fire got out of control and a large part of the premises was burnt down. Though what he did was deliberate, it was not established that he intended to destroy the factory. The judge's finding was in these words:

> Whether Musgrove intended to light only a small fire (which was the very least he meant to do) or whether he intended to cause much more serious damage, and, in either case, what was the reason for his act, are mysteries I am unable to solve.

This, and it is important to bear it in mind when considering the judgments in the Court of Appeal, falls short of a finding that Musgrove deliberately burnt or intended to burn the respondents' factory.

The condition upon which the appellant relies reads, relevantly, as follows:

> Under no circumstances shall the company [Securicor] be responsible for any injurious act or default by any employee of the company unless such act or default could have been foreseen and avoided by the exercise of due diligence on the part of the company as his employer; nor, in any event, shall the company be held responsible for (1) any loss suffered by the customer through burglary, theft, fire or any other cause, except insofar as such loss is solely attributable to the negligence of the company's employees acting within the course of their employment. . . .

There are further provisions limiting to stated amounts the liability of the appellant upon which it relies in the alternative if held not to be totally exempt.

It is first necessary to decide upon the correct approach to a case such as this where it is sought to invoke an exception or limitation clause in the contract. The approach of Lord Denning M.R. in the Court of Appeal was to consider first whether the breach was "fundamental." If so, he said, the court itself deprives the party of the benefit of an exemption or limitation clause ([1978] 1 W.L.R. 856 at 863). Shaw and Waller L.JJ. substantially followed him in this argument.

·····

Much has been written about the *Suisse Atlantique* case [[1967] 1 A.C. 361]. Each speech has been subject to various degrees of analysis and criticism, much of it constructive. Speaking for myself I am conscious of imperfections of terminology, though sometimes in good company. But I do not think that I should be conducing to the clarity of the law by adding to what was already too ample a discussion a further analysis which in turn would have to be interpreted. I have no second thoughts as to the main proposition that the question whether, and to what extent, an exclusion clause is to be applied to a fundamental breach, or a breach of a fundamental term, or indeed to any breach of contract, is a matter of construction of the contract. Many difficult questions arise and will continue to arise in the infinitely varied situations in which contracts come to be breached—by repudiatory breaches, accepted or not, by anticipatory breaches, by breaches of conditions or of various terms and whether by negligent, or deliberate action or otherwise. But there are ample resources in the normal rules of contract law for dealing with these without the superimposition of a judicially invented rule of law. I am content to leave the matter there with some supplementary observations.

1. The doctrine of "fundamental breach" in spite of its imperfections and doubtful parentage has served a useful purpose. There was a large number of problems, productive of injustice, in which it was worse than unsatisfactory to leave exception clauses to operate. Lord Reid referred to these in the *Suisse Atlantique* case, pointing out at the same time that the doctrine of fundamental breach was a dubious specific. But since then Parliament has taken a hand: it has passed the Unfair Contract Terms Act 1977. This Act applies to consumer contracts and those based on standard terms and enables exception clauses to be applied with regard to what is just and reasonable. It is significant that Parliament refrained from legislating over the whole field of contract. After this Act, in commercial matters generally, when the parties are not of unequal bargaining power, and when risks are normally borne by insurance, not only is the case for judicial intervention undemonstrated, but there is everything to be said, and this seems to have been Parliament's intention, for leaving the parties free to apportion the risks as they think fit and for respecting their decisions. . . .

2. The case of *Harbutt* [[1970] 1 Q.B. 447 (C.A.)] must clearly be overruled. It would be enough to put that upon its radical inconsistency with the *Suisse Atlantique* case. But even if the matter were res integra I would find the decision to be based upon unsatisfactory reasoning as to the "termination" of the contract and the effect of "termination" on the plaintiffs' claim for damage. I have, indeed, been unable to understand how the doctrine can be reconciled with the well accepted principle of law, stated by the highest modern authority, that when in the context of a breach of contract one speaks of "termination," what is meant is no more than that the innocent party or, in some cases, both parties, are excused from further performance. Damages, in such cases, are then claimed under the contract, so what reason in principle can there be for disregarding what the contract itself says about damages—whether it "liquidates" them, or limits them, or excludes them? These difficulties arise in part from uncertain or inconsistent terminology. A vast number of expressions are used to describe situations where a breach has been committed by one party of such a character as to entitle the other party to refuse further performance: discharge, rescission, termination, the contract is at an end, or dead, or displaced; clauses cannot survive, or simply go. I have come to think that some of these difficulties can be avoided; in particular the use of "rescission," even if distinguished from rescission ab initio, as an equivalent for discharge, though justifiable in some contexts . . . may lead to

confusion in others. To plead for complete uniformity may be to cry for the moon. But what can and ought to be avoided is to make use of these confusions in order to produce a concealed and unreasoned legal innovation: to pass, for example, from saying that a party, victim of a breach of contract, is entitled to refuse further performance, to saying that he may treat the contract as at an end, or as rescinded, and to draw from this the proposition, which is not analytical but one of policy, that all or (arbitrarily) some of the clauses of the contract lose, automatically, their force, regardless of intention.

.....

[Point 3 has been omitted.]

4. It is not necessary to review fully the numerous cases in which the doctrine of fundamental breach has been applied or discussed. Many of these have now been superseded by the Unfair Contract Terms Act 1977. Others, as decisions, may be justified as depending upon the construction of the contract . . .

In this situation the present case has to be decided. As a preliminary, the nature of the contract has to be understood. Securicor undertook to provide a service of periodical visits for a very modest charge which works out at 26p. per visit. It did not agree to provide equipment. It would have no knowledge of the value of the plaintiffs' factory: that, and the efficacy of their fire precautions, would be known to the respondents. In these circumstances nobody could consider it unreasonable, that as between these two equal parties the risk assumed by Securicor should be a modest one, and that the respondents should carry the substantial risk of damage or destruction.

The duty of Securicor was, as stated, to provide a service. There must be implied an obligation to use due care in selecting their patrolmen, to take care of the keys and, I would think, to operate the service with due and proper regard to the safety and security of the premises. The breach of duty committed by Securicor lay in a failure to discharge this latter obligation. Alternatively it could be put upon a vicarious responsibility for the wrongful act of Musgrove—viz., starting a fire on the premises: Securicor would be responsible for this upon the principle stated in *Morris v. C.W. Martin & Sons Ltd.*, [1966] 1 Q.B. 716 at 739. This being the breach, does condition 1 apply? It is drafted in strong terms, "Under no circumstances"? "any injurious act or default by any employee." These words have to be approached with the aid of the cardinal rules of construction that they must be read contra proferentem and that in order to escape from the consequences of one's own wrongdoing, or that of one's servant, clear words are necessary. I think that these words are clear. The respondents in fact relied upon them for an argument that since they exempted from negligence they must be taken as not exempting from the consequence of deliberate acts. But this is a perversion of the rule that if a clause can cover something other than negligence, it will not be applied to negligence. Whether, in addition to negligence, it covers, e.g. deliberate, acts, remains a matter of construction requiring, of course, clear words. I am of opinion that it does, and being free to construe and apply the clause, I must hold that liability is excluded. On this part of the case I agree with the judge and adopt his reasons for judgment. I would allow the appeal.

LORD DIPLOCK . . . My Lords, it is characteristic of commercial contracts, nearly all of which today are entered into not by natural legal persons, but by fictitious ones, i.e. companies, that the parties promise to one another that some thing will be done; for instance, that property and possession of goods will be transferred, that goods will be carried by ship from one port to another, that a building will be constructed in accordance with agreed plans, that services of a particular kind will be provided. Such a contract is the source of primary legal obligations upon each party to it to procure that whatever he has promised will be done is done. (I leave aside arbitration clauses which do not come into operation until a party to the contract claims that a primary obligation has not been observed.)
. . .

A basic principle of the common law of contract, to which there are no exceptions that are relevant in the instant case, is that parties to a contract are free to determine for themselves what primary obligations they will accept. They may state these in express words in the contract itself and, where they do, the statement is determinative; but in practice a commercial contract never states all the primary obligations of the parties in full; many are left to be incorporated by implication of law from the legal nature of the contract into which the parties are entering. But if the parties wish to reject or modify primary obligations which would otherwise be so incorporated, they are fully at liberty to do so by express words.

Leaving aside those comparatively rare cases in which the court is able to enforce a primary obligation by decreeing specific performance of it, breaches of primary obligations give rise to substituted or secondary obligations on the part of the party in default, and, in some cases, may entitle the other party to be relieved from further performance of his own primary obligations. These secondary obligations of the contract breaker and any concomitant relief of the other party from his own primary obligations also arise by implication of law—generally common law, but sometimes statute, as in the case of codifying statutes passed as the turn of the century, notably the Sale of Goods Act 1893. The contract, however, is just as much the source of secondary obligations as it is of primary obligations; and like primary obligations that are implied by law, secondary obligations too can be modified by agreement between the parties, although, for reasons to be mentioned later, they cannot, in my view, be totally excluded. In the instant case, the only secondary obligations and concomitant reliefs that are applicable arise by implication of the common law as modified by the express words of the contract.

Every failure to perform a primary obligation is a breach of contract. The secondary obligation on the part of the contract breaker to which it gives rise by implication of the common law is to pay monetary compensation to the other party for the loss sustained by him in consequence of the breach; but, with two exceptions, the primary obligations of both parties so far as they have not yet been fully performed remained unchanged. This secondary obligation to pay compensation (damages) for non-performance of primary obligations I will call the "general secondary obligation." It applies in the cases of the two exceptions as well.

The exceptions are: (1) Where the event resulting from the failure by one party to perform a primary obligation has the effect of depriving the other party of substantially the whole benefit which it was the intention of the parties that he should obtain from the contract, the party not in default may elect to put an end to all primary obligations of both parties remaining unperformed. (If the expression "fundamental breach" is to be retained, it should, in the interests of clarity, be confined to this exception.) (2) Where the contracting parties have agreed, whether by express words or by implication of law, that *any* failure by one party to perform a particular primary obligation ("condition" in the nomenclature of the Sale of Goods Act 1893), irrespective of the gravity of the event that has in fact resulted from the breach, shall entitle the other party to elect to put an end to all primary obligations of both parties remaining unperformed. (In the interest of clarity, the nomenclature of the Sale of Goods Act 1893, "breach of condition" should be reserved for this exception.)

Where such an election is made (a) there is substituted by implication of law for the primary obligations of the party in default which remain unperformed a secondary obligation to pay monetary compensation to the other party for the loss sustained by him in consequence of their non-performance in the future and (b) the unperformed primary obligations of that other party are discharged. This secondary obligation is additional to the general secondary obligation; I will call it "the anticipatory secondary obligation." . . .

My Lords, an exclusion clause is one which excludes or modifies an obligation, whether primary, general secondary or anticipatory secondary, that would otherwise arise under the contract by implication of law. Parties are free to agree to whatever exclusion or modification of all types of obligations as they please within the limits that the agreement must retain the legal characteristics of a contract; and must not offend against the equitable rule against penalties; that is to say, it must not impose upon the breaker of a primary obligation a general secondary obligation to pay to the other party a sum of money that is manifestly intended to be in excess of the amount which would fully compensate the other party for the loss sustained by him in consequence of the breach of the primary obligation. Since the presumption is that the parties by entering into the contract intended to accept the implied obligations exclusion clauses are to be construed strictly and the degree of strictness appropriate to be applied to their construction may properly depend upon the extent to which they involve departure from the implied obligations. Since the obligations implied by law in a commercial contract are those which, by judicial consensus over the years or by Parliament in passing a statute, have been regarded as obligations which a reasonable businessman would realise that he was accepting when he entered into a contract of a particular kind, the court's view of the reasonableness of any departure from the implied obligations which would be involved in construing the express words of an exclusion clause in one sense that they are capable of bearing rather than another, is a relevant consideration in deciding what meaning the words were intended by the parties to bear. But this does not entitle the court to reject the exclusion clause, however unreasonable the court itself may think it is, if the words are clear and fairly susceptible of one meaning only.

My Lords, the reports are full of cases in which what would appear to be very strained constructions have been placed upon exclusion clauses, mainly in what today would be called consumer contracts and contracts of adhesion. As Lord Wilberforce has pointed out, any need for this kind of judicial distortion of the English language has been banished by Parliament's having made these kinds of contracts subject to the Unfair Contract Terms Act 1977. In commercial contracts negotiated between business-men capable of looking after their own interests and of deciding how risks inherent in the performance of various kinds of contract can be most economically borne (generally by insurance), it is, in my view, wrong to place a strained construction upon words in an exclusion clause which are clear and fairly susceptible of one meaning only even after due allowance has been made for the presumption in favour of the implied primary and secondary obligations.

Applying these principles to the instant case; in the absence of the exclusion clause which Lord Wilberforce has cited, a primary obligation of Securicor under the contract, which would be implied by law, would be an absolute obligation to procure that the visits by the night patrol to the factory were conducted by natural persons who would exercise reasonable skill and care for the safety of the factory. That primary obligation is modified by the exclusion clause. Securicor's obligation to do this is not to be absolute, but is limited to exercising due diligence in its capacity as employer of the natural persons by whom the visits are conducted, to procure that those persons shall exercise reasonable skill and care for the safety of the factory.

For the reasons given by Lord Wilberforce it seems to me that this apportionment of the risk of the factory being damaged or destroyed by the injurious act of an employee of Securicor while carrying out a visit to the factory is one which reasonable business-men in the position of Securicor and the factory owners might well think was the most economical. An analogous apportionment of risk is provided for by the Hague Rules in the case of goods carried by sea under bills of lading. The risk that a servant of Securicor would damage or destroy the factory or steal goods from it, despite the exercise of all reasonable diligence by Securicor to prevent it, is what in the context of maritime law would be called a "misfortune risk"—something which reasonable diligence of neither party to the contract can prevent. Either party can insure against it. It is generally more economical for the person by whom the loss will be directly sustained to do so rather than that it should be covered by the other party by liability insurance. This makes it unnecessary to consider whether a later exclusion clause in the contract which modifies the general secondary obligation implied by law by placing limits on the amount of damages recoverable for breaches of primary obligations, would have applied in the instant case.

For the reasons given by Lord Wilberforce and in application of the principles that I have here stated, I would allow this appeal.

[Lords Keith of Kinkel and Scarman adopted the reasons of Lord Wilberforce while Lord Salmon delivered a concurring judgment.]

NOTES and QUESTIONS

1. Following *Photo Production*, the tendency of the Canadian courts was, on the surface at least, to apply a principle of construction. They were still inclined, however, to pose the initial question, arguably irrelevant under a construction approach, of whether the defendant's conduct constituted a fundamental breach of contract: see for example *Gallant v. Hobbs* (1982), 37 O.R. (2d) 1 (Co. Ct.), affirmed (1983), 40 O.R. (2d) 377 (C.A.); *Gafco Enterprises Ltd. v. Schofield*, [1983] 4 W.W.R. 135 (Alta. C.A.); and *Punch v. Savoy's Jewellers Ltd.* (1986), 26 D.L.R. (4th) 546 (Ont. C.A.).

2. In *Beaufort Realties (1964) Inc. v. Chomedey Aluminum Co.* (1980), 116 D.L.R. (3d) 193, the Supreme Court of Canada, in a judgment given by Ritchie J., followed *Photo Production* and supported the construction approach. In so doing, however, Ritchie J. approved of Wilson J.'s judgment in the Ontario Court of Appeal (1979), 97 D.L.R. (3d) 170. In actuality, Wilson J.'s judgment in *Beaufort Realties* provided the basis for her later judgment in *Hunter Engineering, infra*. Do you agree that her approach is in line with *Photo Production*?

3. In *Photo Production*, the House of Lords felt free to apply a principle of construction to a commercial case happy in the knowledge that exclusion clauses in the consumer context had been dealt with by way of statutory reform in the Unfair Contract Terms Act 1977 (U.K.), c. 50. There is no such encompassing legislation in Canada. What attitudes should Canadian courts take in jurisdictions which do not have similar legislation? The issue is also addressed to some extent in the following case.

HUNTER ENGINEERING CO. INC. v. SYNCRUDE CANADA LTD.

[1989] 1 S.C.R. 426, 57 D.L.R. (4th) 321, [1989] 3 W.W.R. 385, 35 B.C.L.R. (2d) 145, 92 N.R. 1

Syncrude contracted with Hunter for the supply of 32 "mining gearboxes" for use in Syncrude's tar sands project. The gearboxes were delivered to Syncrude and were put in service on July 4, 1978. Under a second contract made by Syncrude, Allis-Chalmers supplied extraction conveyor systems, priced at $4.1 million, which included four "extraction gearboxes". These gearboxes were placed in service on November 24, 1977. All of the gearboxes, under both contracts, were designed by Hunter. Each of the contracts contained the following clause:

> 8. WARRANTIES—GUARANTEES: Seller warrants that the goods shall be free from defects in design, material, workmanship, and title, and shall conform in all respects to the terms of this purchase order, and shall be of the best quality, if no quality is specified. If it appears within one year from the date of placing the equipment into service for the purpose for which it was purchased, that the equipment, or any part thereof, does not conform to these warranties and Buyer so notifies Seller within a reasonable time after its discovery, Seller shall thereupon promptly correct such nonconformity at its sole expense. The conditions of any subsequent tests shall be mutually agreed upon and Seller shall be notified of and may be represented at all tests that may be made. Except as otherwise provided in this purchase order, Seller's liability hereunder shall extend to all damages proximately caused by the breach of any of the foregoing warranties or guarantees, but such liability shall in no event include loss of profit or loss of use.

In each contract, the purchase order modified the clause so that the warranty expired within 24 months after delivery or 12 months after the gearboxes entered service, whichever occurred first. In addition, the Allis-Chalmers purchase order contained this variation of the warranty clause:

The final sentence of Paragraph 8 is hereby deleted. In its place shall be, "The Provisions of this paragraph represent the only warranty of the Seller and no other warranty or conditions, statutory or otherwise shall be implied."

Each contract also included a clause stipulating that the contract was governed by Ontario law. The Sale of Goods Act, R.S.O. 1970, c. 421 contained this statutory warranty of fitness in s. 15:

15. Subject to this Act and any statute in that behalf, there is no implied warranty or condition as to the quality of fitness for any particular purpose of goods supplied under a contract of sale, except as follows:

1. Where the buyer, expressly or by implication, makes known to the seller the particular purpose for which the goods are required so as to show that the buyer relies on the seller's skill or judgment, and the goods are of a description that it is in the course of the seller's business to supply (whether he is the manufacturer or not), there is an implied condition that the goods will be reasonably fit for such purpose, but in the case of a contract for the sale of a specified article under its patent or other trade name there is no implied condition as to its fitness for any particular purpose.

.....

4. An express warranty or condition does not negative a warranty or condition implied by this Act unless inconsistent therewith.

In September and October 1979, defects were discovered in the gearboxes which were then taken out of service and repaired at a cost of $750,000 for the mining gearboxes and of $400,000 for the extraction gearboxes. Both Hunter and Allis-Chalmers denied responsibility for the cost of repairs. Both relied on expiry of the contractual warranties.

Syncrude sued Hunter and Allis-Chalmers. At trial Hunter was found to be liable. Gibbs J. concluded that the contractual time limit had expired under the contract, but that clause 8, the warranty clause in the contract, did not serve to exclude the statutory warranty introduced by s. 15 of the Sale of Goods Act. That provision applied in that the gearboxes were supplied in the course of Hunter's business, Hunter knew the purpose for which they were required, and Syncrude relied on Hunter's skill and judgment. Allis-Chalmers, however, was found not to be liable. Although the statutory warranty was not excluded by clause 8 in its standard formulation, Gibbs J. concluded that it was excluded by the variation of clause 8 in Allis-Chalmers' purchase order.

Gibbs J. rejected a further argument by Syncrude that Allis-Chalmers had committed a fundamental breach so that the exclusion clause was negated. He said that Syncrude had freely accepted the time limitations and that the problems with the gearboxes did not amount to a fundamental breach; they were repaired at a cost well below the purchase price; Syncrude got what it bargained for.

Syncrude appealed from the finding that there was no fundamental breach by Allis-Chalmers. Hunter cross-appealed. The Court of Appeal rejected Hunter's appeal and allowed Syncrude's appeal. It concluded that there was a fundamental breach in that the cost of repairs was 86 per cent of the purchase price and the gearboxes failed within two years when they should have lasted for ten years. The court also said that the warranty clause was not intended to exclude liability for fundamental breach, and it derived support from the following clause which made specific reference to fundamental breach in respect of special or consequential damages:

Paragraph 14—Limitation of Liability

Notwithstanding any other provision in this contract or any applicable statutory provisions neither the Seller nor the Buyer shall be liable to the other for special or consequential damages or damages for loss of use arising directly or indirectly from any breach of this contract, *fundamental* or otherwise or from any tortious act or omissions of their respective employees [*sic*] or agents and in no event shall the liability of the Seller exceed the unit price of the defective product or of the product subject to late delivery. [Emphasis added.]

There was a further appeal and cross-appeal (on an issue not relevant to fundamental breach) to the Supreme Court of Canada.

WILSON J. [dissenting in the cross-appeal] . . . The Court of Appeal's judgment thus gave Syncrude the $750,000 it had won at trial plus $400,000 for repairs to the extraction gearboxes. Interest on both these sums brought the total to $1.535M.

3. THE ISSUES BEFORE THIS COURT

Both Hunter U.S. and Allis-Chalmers appealed to this court? Four separate grounds of appeal were argued. I will deal with them in the following order:

  (i) the liability of Hunter U.S. for the design faults which caused the gearboxes to fail;

      [On this issue, Wilson J. agreed with the courts below that Hunter was responsible for the design faults in the gearboxes.]

  (ii) the liability of Hunter U.S. under the statutory warranty in the *Sale of Goods Act*;

  (iii) the liability of Allis-Chalmers under the doctrine of fundamental breach;

      [The fourth ground of appeal is omitted.]

          .....

(ii)   *The statutory warranty*

Although Hunter U.S. was liable for the design fault that caused the gearboxes to fail, the failure was discovered after the contractual warranty period had expired. For Syncrude to succeed, therefore, it must find an alternative route to establishing Hunter U.S.'s liability. Two issues are of concern here. The first is whether either or both of the exclusionary clauses in the Hunter U.S. and Allis-Chalmers contracts are sufficient to preclude the application of the statutory warranty. If not, then a second issue arises as to whether the gearboxes were "reasonably fit" for their purpose.

I would answer these questions in the same way as Gibbs J. and the British Columbia Court of Appeal. Section 15, para. 4 of the *Sale of Goods Act* provides that an express warranty "does not negative a warranty or condition implied by this Act unless inconsistent therewith". Hunter U.S. argues that it may invoke s. 15, para. 4 because the specific limitation period in its express warranty serves to exclude any other warranty which would extend beyond that period. This argument runs counter to two long-established and related principles in the law of contract, (1) that an exclusion clause should be strictly construed against the party seeking to invoke it and (2) that clear and unambiguous language is required to oust an implied statutory warranty?. I would adopt the following statement of the law by Eberle J. of the Ontario Supreme Court in *Chabot v. Ford Motor Co. of Canada Ltd.* (1982), 138 D.L.R. (3d) 417 at p. 430, 39 O.R. (2d) 162, 19 B.L.R. 147:

> ... although a vendor may exclude conditions implied by the *Sale of Goods Act*, he must use explicit language, in the absence of which the court will not be prepared to find that the conditions have been excluded.

In the present case there is clearly no explicit exclusion of the implied warranty contained in the Hunter U.S. contract. I find it equally clear that the revision to the Allis-Chalmers agreement did explicitly and unambiguously oust the statutory warranty by stating: "The Provisions of this paragraph represent the only warranty of the seller and *no other warranty* or conditions, *statutory or otherwise* shall be implied" (my emphasis). The explicit reference to the statutory warranty is crucial here and in my view serves to prevent the application of s. 15, para. 1 of the *Sale of Goods Act* to the Allis-Chalmers contract.

This finding on the Hunter U.S. warranty requires a consideration of whether the gearboxes were, in the words of s. 15, para. 1 of the Act, "reasonably fit" for the purpose for which they were supplied. I think this issue can be disposed of very shortly. It is abundantly clear that Syncrude informed Hunter U.S. of the purpose for which the gearboxes were required, that Syncrude relied on Hunter U.S.'s expertise, and that the gears were "goods . . . which it is in the course of the seller's business to supply". It is equally clear that the gears were not reasonably fit for their purpose. The trial judge found as facts that:

(a) the gears would normally be expected to work for ten years before needing extensive overhauling;

(b) the gears needed to be replaced after only 15 months or so, despite never being put to more than 60% of their intended workload;

(c) the cost of repairing the extraction gearboxes was $400,000 compared to the original price of $464,300.

Gibbs J.'s conclusion was that in such circumstances the gears could not be considered reasonably fit for their purpose. The Court of Appeal endorsed that finding and I would unequivocally affirm it also. The defects in design were crucial. The cracking was not something that would be expected to happen in the normal lifetime of the gearboxes. I would conclude therefore that Hunter U.S. is liable for the cost of repairs to the mining gearboxes.

(iii)   *Fundamental breach*

Fundamental breach has been the subject of many judicial definitions. It has been described as "a breach going to the root of the contract" (*Suisse Atlantique Société d'Armement Maritime S.A. v. N.V. Rotterdamsche Kolen Centrale*, [*supra*], *per* Lord Reid at p. 399) and as one which results "in performance totally different from what the parties had in contemplation" (*R.G. McLean Ltd. v.*

Canadian Vickers Ltd. (1970), 15 D.L.R. (3d) 15 at p. 20, [1971] 1 O.R. 207 (C.A.), *per* Arnup J.A.). In *Canso Chemicals Ltd. v. Canadian Westinghouse Co. Ltd.* (1974), 54 D.L.R. (3d) 517, 10 N.S.R. (2d) 306 (C.A.), MacKeigan C.J.N.S. gave nine different definitions from leading Canadian and United Kingdom cases. The definitional uncertainty that has pervaded this area of the law is further illustrated by Fridman, *Law of Contract in Canada*, 2nd ed. (1986), at p. 531, and the cases cited therein.

The formulation that I prefer is that given by Lord Diplock in *Photo Production Ltd. v. Securicor Transport Ltd.*, [*supra*]. A fundamental breach occurs "Where the event resulting from the failure by one party to perform a primary obligation has the effect of depriving the other party of *substantially the whole benefit* which it was the intention of the parties that he should obtain from the contract" (p. 849). (Emphasis added.) This is a restrictive definition and rightly so, I believe. As Lord Diplock points out, the usual remedy for breach of a "primary" contractual obligation (the thing bargained for) is a concomitant "secondary" obligation to pay damages. The other primary obligations of both parties yet unperformed remain in place. Fundamental breach represents an exception to this rule for it gives to the innocent party an additional remedy, an election to "put an end to all primary obligations of both parties remaining unperformed" (p. 849). It seems to me that this exceptional remedy should be available only in circumstances where the foundation of the contract has been undermined, where the very thing bargained for has not been provided.

I do not think the present case involves a fundamental breach. The trial judge had this to say on the question at pp. 77-8:

> As to the nature of the defect, in my opinion it was not so fundamental that it went to the root of the contract. The contract between the parties was still a contract for gearboxes. Gearboxes were supplied. They were capable of performing their function and did perform it for in excess of a year which, given the agreed time limitations, was the "cost free to Syncrude" period contemplated by the parties. It was conceded that the gearboxes were not fit for the service. However, the unfitness, or defect, was repairable and was repaired at a cost significantly less than the original purchase price. No doubt the bull gear is an important component of the gearbox but no more important than the engine in an automobile and in the *Gafco Ent.* case the failure of the engine was not a sufficiently fundamental breach to lead the Court to set aside the contract of sale. On my appreciation of the evidence Syncrude got what it bargained for from Stephens-Adamson. It has not convinced me that there was fundamental breach.

The Court of Appeal, in overturning this finding, seems to have been influenced by two factors: that the repair cost was 85% of the original contract price and that the gear which should have lasted ten years failed after less than two. I will deal with each of these factors in turn.

There is an obvious conflict between the judgments below over the relationship between the size of the contract and the cost of repairs. The Court of Appeal treated the contract for the gearboxes as a discrete transaction in coming to its conclusion. The trial judge, however, was influenced by the fact that the overall contract with Allis-Chalmers was for 14 conveyor systems, only four of which contained extraction gearboxes. The total cost of these systems was in excess of $4M. It seems to me that the trial judge was right to take this into account. If he was, then Allis-Chalmers breached only one aspect of its contract with Syncrude, one "primary obligation". Although the gears were obviously an important component of the conveyor system, their inferior performance did not have the effect of depriving Syncrude of "substantially the whole benefit of the contract" to use Lord Diplock's phrase. The cost of repair was only a small part of the total cost.

Syncrude bargained for and received bull gears. Clearly, they were not very good gears. They were not reasonably fit for the purposes they were intended to serve. But they did work for a period of time and were repairable. There are numerous cases in which serious but repairable defects in machinery of various kinds have been found not to amount to fundamental breach. In *Gafco Enterprises Ltd. v. Schofield*, [(1983), 43 A.R. 262 (C.A.)], a case relied on by Gibbs J. in this case, the purchaser bought a second-hand car for $12,000 which immediately required some $4,000 worth of engine repairs. Harradence J.A. held that the defects "do not amount to a breach going to the root of the contract. They are repairable, albeit at some expense" (p. 267 A.R.). Similarly, in *Peters v. Parkway Mercury Sales Ltd.* (1975), 58 D.L.R. (3d) 128, 10 N.B.R. (2d) 703 (C.A.), a transmission failure shortly after the expiration of a 30-day warranty on a used car was found not to be a fundamental breach. Hughes C.J.N.B. said at p. 711 N.B.R.:

> In my view the car which the defendant sold to the plaintiff was not essentially different in character from what the parties should have had in contemplation. Although the car was in poorer condition than either party probably knew, I do not think the defects amounted to "such a congeries of defects as to destroy the workable character of the machine" and consequently the plaintiff's claim for a declaration that there has been a fundamental breach entitled him to rescission if [*sic*] the contract fails.

In *Keefe v. Fort* (1978), 89 D.L.R. (3d) 275 (S.C.A.D.), another case involving a faulty but repairable car, Pace J.A. said at p. 279 that "the doctrine of fundamental breach was never intended to be applied to situations where the parties have received substantially what they had bargained for".

In the present case the Court of Appeal relied on its own prior judgment in *Beldessi v. Island Equipment Ltd.* (1973), 41 D.L.R. (3d) 147 (B.C. C.A.), which it said was "very similar" to this one (p. 390). *Beldessi*, however, involved a log skidding machine which, despite numerous repairs, never worked properly. It was therefore similar to *R.G. McLean Ltd. v. Canadian Vickers Ltd.* [[1969] 2 O.R. 219 (H.C.)], in which a printing press could not be made to function adequately. It seems to me that the present case is more akin to those cited above where the purchaser got a poor, but none the less repairable, version of what it contracted for. I do not think that in these circumstances it can be said that the breach undermined the entire contractual setting or that it went to the very root of the contract. It was not, in other words, fundamental. I would therefore allow the appeal by Allis-Chalmers on this issue.

However, if I am wrong in this and the breach by Allis-Chalmers is properly characterized as fundamental, the liability of Allis-Chalmers would, in my view, be excluded by the terms of the contractual warranty.

Prior to 1980, in both the United Kingdom and in Canada, there were two competing views of the consequences of fundamental breach. One held that there was a rule of law that a fundamental breach brought a contract to an end, thereby preventing the contract breaker from relying on any clause exempting liability. This view was most closely identified with Lord Denning in the English Court of Appeal? The other view was that exemption clauses should be construed by the same rules of contract interpretation on whether a fundamental breach had occurred or not. Whether or not liability was excluded was to be decided simply on the construction of the contract: see *Suisse Atlantique, supra*. . . .

In England, the issue was unequivocally resolved by the House of Lords in favour of the construction approach in the *Photo Production* case . . .

The construction approach to exclusionary clauses in the face of a fundamental breach affirmed in *Photo Production* was adopted by this court as the law in Canada in *Beaufort Realties (1964) Inc. v. Chomedey Aluminum Co. Ltd.* (1980), 116 D.L.R. (3d) 193 . . . The court did not, however, reject the concept of fundamental breach. The respondent entered into a construction contract with Beaufort in which it agreed to waive all liens for work and materials provided in the event of a failure to make payments. Such a failure took place and Justice Ritchie had no difficulty in concluding that the failure constituted a fundamental breach. He adopted Lord Wilberforce's construction approach to the exclusion clause and stated at p. 197 D.L.R. . . ., "that the question of whether such a clause was applicable where there was a fundamental breach was to be determined according to the true construction of the contract."

As Professor Waddams noted (see (1981), 15 U.B.C. Law Rev. 189) shortly after this court's decision in *Beaufort Realties*:

> . . . the Supreme Court of Canada followed the House of Lords in holding that there is no rule of law preventing the operation of exclusionary clauses in cases of fundamental breach of contract. The effect of such clauses is now said to depend in each case on the true construction of the contract.

Thus, the law in Canada on this point appears to be settled. Some uncertainty, however, does remain primarily with regard to the application of the construction approach. Some decisions of our courts clearly follow the construction approach in both theory and practice. In *Hayward v. Mellick* (1984), 5 D.L.R. (4th) 740 (C.A.), for example, Weatherston J.A. noted that as "the courts of this province adopted the doctrine from the English courts, I think we should now follow their lead in rejecting it as a rule of law" (p. 749 D.L.R.). Even when the exclusion clause in issue was "strictly construed" Weatherston J.A. recognized that "it would be too strained a construction of the disclaimer clause to say that it applies only to representations that are not negligent. I think that effect must be given to it . . .". He went on to hold that the exclusion clause in that case was sufficient to cover any breach of contract.

Commentators seem to be in agreement, however, that the courts, while paying lip service to the construction approach, have continued to apply a modified "rule of law" doctrine in some cases. Professor Fridman in *Law of Contract in Canada*, 2nd ed. (1986), has suggested at p. 558 that:

> Under the guise of "construction", some courts appear to be utilizing something very much akin to the "rule of law" doctrine. What Canadian courts may be doing is to apply a concept of "fair and reasonable" construction in relation to the survival of the exclusion clause after a fundamental breach, and the application of such a clause where the breach in question

involves not just a negligent performance of the contract, but the complete failure of the party obliged to fulfil the contract in any way whatsoever.

Professor Ogilvie, in a review of Canadian cases decided shortly after *Photo Production*, including *Beaufort Realties* itself, argues that the rule of law approach "has been replaced by a substantive test of reasonableness which bestows on the courts at least as much judicial discretion to intervene in contractual relationships as fundamental breach ever did": see Ogilvie, "The Reception of *Photo Production Ltd. v. Securicor Transport Ltd.* in Canada: *Nec Tamen Consumebatur*" (1982), 27 McGill L.J. 424 at p. 441.

Little is to be gained from a review of the recent cases which have inspired these comments. Suffice it to say that the law in this area seems to be in need of clarification. The uncertainty might be resolved in either of two ways. The first way would be to adopt *Photo Production* in its entirety. This would include discarding the concept of fundamental breach. The courts would give effect to exclusion clauses on their true construction regardless of the nature of the breach. Even the party who had committed a breach such that the foundation of the contract was undermined and the very thing bargained for not provided could rely on provisions in the contract limiting or excluding his or her liability. The only relevant question for the court would be: on a true and natural construction of the provisions of the contract did the parties, *at the time the contract was made*, succeed in excluding liability? This approach would have the merit of importing greater simplicity into the law and consequently greater certainty into commercial dealings, although the results of enforcing such exclusion clauses could be harsh if the parties had not adequately anticipated or considered the possibility of the contract's disintegration through fundamental breach.

The other way would be to import some "reasonableness" requirement into the law so that courts could refuse to enforce exclusion clauses in strict accordance with their terms if to do so would be unfair and unreasonable. One far-reaching "reasonableness" requirement which I would reject (and which I believe was rejected in *Beaufort Realties* both by this court and the Ontario Court of Appeal) would be to require that the exclusion clause be *per se* a fair and reasonable contractual term in the contractual setting or bargain made by the parties. I would reject this approach because the courts, in my view, are quite unsuited to assess the fairness or reasonableness of contractual provisions as the parties negotiated them. Too many elements are involved in such an assessment, some of them quite subjective. It was partly for this reason that this court in *Beaufort Realties* and the House of Lords in *Photo Production* clearly stated that exclusion clauses, like all contractual provisions, should be given their natural and true construction. Great uncertainty and needless complications in the drafting of contracts will obviously result if courts give exclusion clauses strained and artificial interpretations in order, indirectly and obliquely, to avoid the impact of what seems to them *ex post facto* to have been an unfair and unreasonable clause.

I would accordingly reject the concept that an exclusion clause in order to be enforceable must be *per se* a fair and reasonable provision at the time it was negotiated. The exclusion clause cannot be considered in isolation from the other provisions of the contract and the circumstances in which it was entered into. The purchaser may have been prepared to assume some risk if he could get the article at a modest price or if he was very anxious to get it. Conversely, if he was having to pay a high price for the article and had to be talked into the purchase, he may have been concerned to impose the broadest possible liability on his vendor. A contractual provision that seems unfair to a third party may have been the product of hard bargaining between the parties and, in my view, deserves to be enforced by the courts in accordance with its terms.

It is, however, in my view an entirely different matter for the courts to determine *after a particular breach has occurred* whether an exclusion clause should be enforced or not. This, I believe, was the issue addressed by this court in *Beaufort Realties*. In *Beaufort* this court accepted the proposition enunciated in *Photo Production* that no rule of law invalidated or extinguished exclusion clauses in the event of fundamental breach but rather that they should be given their natural and true construction so that the parties' agreement would be given effect. Nevertheless the court, in approving the approach taken by the Ontario Court of Appeal in *Beaufort*, recognized at the same time the need for courts to determine whether *in the context of the particular breach which had occurred* it was fair and reasonable to enforce the clause in favour of the party who had committed that breach even if the exclusion clause was clear and unambiguous. The relevant question for the court in *Beaufort* was: is it fair and reasonable in the context of this fundamental breach that the exclusion clause continue to operate for the benefit of the party responsible for the fundamental breach? In other words, should a party be able to commit a fundamental breach secure in the knowledge that no liability can attend it? Or should there be room for the courts to say: this party is now trying to have his cake and eat it too. He is seeking to escape almost entirely the burdens of the transaction but enlist the support of the courts to enforce its benefits.

It seems to me that the House of Lords was able to come to a decision in *Photo Production* untrammelled by the need to reconcile the competing values sought to be advanced in a system of contract law such as ours. We do not have in this country legislation comparable to the United Kingdom's *Unfair Contract Terms Act 1977*. I believe that in the absence of such legislation Canadian courts must continue to develop through the common law a balance between the obvious desirability of allowing the parties to make their own bargains and have them enforced through the courts and the obvious undesirability of having the courts used to enforce bargains in favour of parties who are totally repudiating such bargains themselves. I fully agree with the commentators that the balance which the courts reach will be made much clearer if we do not clothe our reasoning "in the guise of interpretation". Exclusion clauses do not automatically lose their validity in the event of a fundamental breach by virtue of some hard and fast rule of law. They should be given their natural and true construction so that the meaning and effect of the exclusion clause the parties agreed to at the time the contract was entered into is fully understood and appreciated. But, in my view, the court must still decide, having ascertained the parties' intention at the time the contract was made, whether or not to give effect to it in the context of subsequent events such as a fundamental breach committed by the party seeking its enforcement through the courts. Whether the courts address this narrowly in terms of fairness as between the parties (and I believe this has been a source of confusion, the parties being, in the absence of inequality of bargaining power, the best judges of what is fair as between themselves) or on the broader policy basis of the need for the courts (apart from the interests of the parties) to balance conflicting values inherent in our contract law (the approach which I prefer), I believe the result will be the same since the question essentially is: in the circumstances that have happened should the court lend its aid to A to hold B to this clause?

In affirming the legitimate role of our courts at common law to decide whether or not to enforce an exclusion clause in the event of a fundamental breach, I am not unmindful of the fact that means are available to render exclusion clauses unenforceable even in the absence of a finding of fundamental breach.

[Wilson J. referred to six consumer protection statutes and then turned to the doctrine of unconscionability.]

While this is perhaps not the place for a detailed examination of the doctrine of unconscionability as it relates to exclusion clauses, I believe that the equitable principles on which the doctrine is based are broad enough to cover many of the factual situations which have perhaps deservedly attracted the application of the "fair and reasonable" approach in cases of fundamental breach. In particular, the circumstances surrounding the making of a consumer standard-form contract could permit the purchaser to argue that it would be unconscionable to enforce an exclusion clause.

[Wilson J. discussed, *inter alia*, *Davidson v. Three Spruces Realty Ltd.* [*infra*, section 3(d)(vi).]

. . . I do not necessarily endorse the approaches taken in the cases to which I have just referred. I use them merely to illustrate the broader point that in situations involving contractual terms which result from inequality of bargaining power the judicial armoury has weapons apart from strained and artificial constructions of exclusion clauses. Where, however, there is no such inequality of bargaining power (as in the present case) the courts should, as a general rule, give effect to the bargain freely negotiated by the parties. The question is whether this is an absolute rule or whether *as a policy matter* the courts should have the power to refuse to enforce a clear and unambiguous exclusion clause freely negotiated by parties of equal bargaining power and, if so, in what circumstances? In the present state of the law in Canada the doctrine of fundamental breach provides one answer.

To dispense with the doctrine of fundamental breach and rely solely on the principle of unconscionability, as has been suggested by some commentators, would, in my view, require an extension of the principle of unconscionability beyond its traditional bounds of inequality of bargaining power. The court, in effect, would be in the position of saying that terms freely negotiated by parties of equal bargaining power were unconscionable. Yet it was the inequality of bargaining power which traditionally was the source of the unconscionability.

What was unconscionable was to permit the strong to take advantage of the weak in the making of the contract. Remove the inequality and we must ask, wherein lies the unconscionability? It seems to me that it must have its roots in subsequent events, given that the parties themselves are the best judges of what is fair at the time they make their bargain. The policy of the common law is, I believe, that having regard to the conduct (pursuant to the contract) of the party seeking the indulgence of the court to enforce the clause, the court refuses. This conduct is described for convenience as "fundamental breach". It marks off the boundaries of tolerable conduct. But the boundaries are admittedly uncertain. Will replacing it with a general concept of unconscionability reduce the uncertainty?

When and in what circumstances will an exclusion clause in a contract freely negotiated by parties of equal bargaining power be unconscionable? If both fundamental breach and unconscionability are viewed as legal tools designed to relieve parties in light of subsequent events from the harsh consequences of an automatic enforcement of an exclusion clause in accordance with its terms, is there anything to choose between them as far as certainty of law is concerned? Arguably, unconscionability is even less certain than fundamental breach. Indeed, it may be described as "the length of the Chancellor's foot". Lord Wilberforce may be right that parties of equal bargaining power should be left to live with their bargains regardless of subsequent events. I believe, however, that there is some virtue in a residual power residing in the court to withhold its assistance on policy grounds in appropriate circumstances.

Turning to the case at bar, it seems to me that, even if the breach of contract was a fundamental one, there would be nothing unfair or unreasonable (and even less so unconscionable, if this is a stricter test) in giving effect to the exclusion clause. The contract was made between two companies in the commercial market place who are of roughly equal bargaining power. Both are familiar and experienced with this type of contract. As the trial judge noted (at p. 77):

> Warranty cl. 8 was put forward by Syncrude. Presumably it provided the protection Syncrude wanted. Indeed, the first sentence thereof is sufficiently all-embracing that it is difficult to conceive a defect which would not be caught by it. Syncrude freely accepted the time limitations; there is no evidence that they were under any disadvantage or disability in the negotiating of them. There is no reason why they should not be held to their bargain, including that part which effectively excludes the implied condition of s. 15(1) of the Ontario Sale of Goods Act.

There is no evidence to suggest that Allis-Chalmers who seeks to rely on the exclusion clause was guilty of any sharp or unfair dealing. It supplied what was bargained for (even although it had defects) and its contractual relationship with Syncrude, which included not only the gears but the entire conveyer system, continued on after the supply of the gears. It cannot be said, in Lord Diplock's words, that Syncrude was "deprived of substantially the whole benefit" of the contract. This is not a case in which the vendor or supplier was seeking to repudiate almost entirely the burdens of the transaction and invoking the assistance of the courts to enforce its benefits. There is no abuse of freedom of contract here.

In deciding to enforce the exclusion clause the trial judge relied in part on the fact that the exclusion clause limited but did not completely exclude the liability of Allis-Chalmers. In relying on this fact the trial judge was supported by some dicta of Lord Wilberforce in the House of Lords in *Ailsa Craig Fishing Co. v. Malvern Fishing Co.*, [1983] 1 All E.R. 101 (H.L.) at pp. 102-3. It seems to me, however, that any categorical distinction between clauses limiting and clauses excluding liability is inherently unreliable in that, depending on the circumstances, "exclusions can be perfectly fair and limitations very unfair": Waddams, *The Law of Contracts*, 2nd ed. (1977), at p. 349. It is preferable, I believe, to determine whether or not the impugned clause should be enforced in all the circumstances of the case and avoid reliance on awkward and artificial labels. When this is done, it becomes clear that there is no reason in this case not to enforce the clause excluding the statutory warranty.

.....

DICKSON C.J.C. [Dickson C.J.C. agreed with Wilson J. that Hunter was in breach of the implied term that the gearboxes be reasonably fit for their purpose. He then considered the applicability of the doctrine of fundamental breach with respect to the contract with Allis-Chalmers.]

.....

The House of Lords' cases decided that liability for breach of a fundamental term may be excluded by a suitably worded exclusion clause. However, counsel contended that there is a rule of construction that exemption clauses must be very clearly worded if they are to be sufficient to exclude liability for fundamental breach. It was said that this approach to the construction of a contract was confirmed in this court in *Beaufort Realties (1964) Inc. v. Chomedey Aluminum Co. Ltd.* [*supra*].

On the application of the principles to the present case, Syncrude asked the question whether Allis-Chalmers and Syncrude intended that Allis-Chalmers could supply gearboxes which were so fundamentally defective as to require complete replacement, or in this case, complete reconstruction, after 15 months' service, at Syncrude's sole cost. Syncrude would give a negative response to this question.

I have had the advantage of reading the reasons for judgment prepared by my colleague, Justice Wilson, in this appeal and I agree with her disposition of the liability of Allis-Chalmers. In my view, the warranty clauses in the Allis-Chalmers contract effectively excluded liability for defective gearboxes after the warranty period expired. With respect, I disagree, however, with Wilson J.'s approach to the doctrine of fundamental breach. I am inclined to adopt the course charted by the House of Lords in *Photo Production Ltd. v. Securicor Transport Ltd.*, [*supra*], and to treat fundamental breach as a matter of contract construction. I do not favour, as suggested by Wilson J., requiring the court to assess the reasonableness of enforcing the contract terms after the court has already determined the meaning of the contract based on ordinary principles of contract interpretation. In my view, the courts should not disturb the bargain the parties have struck, and I am inclined to replace the doctrine of fundamental breach with a rule that holds the parties to the terms of their agreement, provided the agreement is not unconscionable.

The doctrine of fundamental breach in the context of clauses excluding a party from contractual liability has been confusing at the best of times. Simply put, the doctrine has served to relieve parties from the effects of contractual terms, excluding liability for deficient performance where the effects of these terms have seemed particularly harsh. Lord Wilberforce acknowledged this in *Photo Production*, at p. 843:

> 1. The doctrine of "fundamental breach" in spite of its imperfections and doubtful parentage has served a useful purpose. There was a large number of problems, productive of injustice, in which it was worse than unsatisfactory to leave exception clauses to operate.

In cases where extreme unfairness would result from the operation of an exclusion clause, a fundamental breach of contract was said to have occurred. The consequence of fundamental breach was that the party in breach was not entitled to rely on the contractual exclusion of liability but was required to pay damages for contract breach. In the doctrine's most common formulation, by Lord Denning in *Karsales (Harrow) Ltd. v. Wallis*, [*supra*], fundamental breach was said to be a rule of law that operated regardless of the intentions of the contracting parties. Thus, even if the parties excluded liability by clear and express language, they could still be liable for fundamental breach of contract. This rule of law was rapidly embraced by both English and Canadian courts.

A decade later in the *Suisse Atlantique* case, the House of Lords rejected the rule of law concept in favour of an approach based on the true construction of the contract. The Law Lords expressed the view that a court considering the concept of fundamental breach must determine whether the contract, properly interpreted, excluded liability for the fundamental breach. If the parties clearly intended an exclusion clause to apply in the event of fundamental breach, the party in breach would be exempted from liability. . . . The renunciation of the rule of law approach by the House of Lords and by this court, however, had little effect on the practice of lower courts in England or in Canada . . .

Finally, in 1980, the House of Lords definitively rejected the rule of law approach to fundamental breach in *Photo Production, supra* . . .

As Wilson J. notes in her reasons, Canadian courts have tended to pay lip service to contract construction but to apply the doctrine of fundamental breach as if it were a rule of law. While the modification underlying the continuing use of fundamental breach as a rule of law may be laudatory, as a tool for relieving parties from the effects of unfair bargains, the doctrine of fundamental breach has spawned a host of difficulties; the most obvious is how to determine whether a particular breach is fundamental. From this very first step the doctrine of fundamental breach invites the parties to engage in games of characterization, each party emphasizing different aspects of the contract to show either that the breach that occurred went to the very root of the contract or that it did not. The difficulty of characterizing a breach as fundamental for the purposes of exclusion clauses is vividly illustrated by the differing views of the trial judge and the Court of Appeal in the present case.

The many shortcomings of the doctrine as a means of circumventing the effects of unfair contracts are succinctly explained by Professor Waddams (*The Law of Contracts*, 2nd ed. (Toronto: C.L.B. Inc., 1984), at pp. 352-53):

> The doctrine of fundamental breach has, however, many serious deficiencies as a technique of controlling unfair agreements. The doctrine requires the court to identify the offending provision as an "exemption clause", then to consider the agreement apart from the exemption clause, to ask itself whether there would have been a breach of that part of the agreement and then to consider whether that breach was "fundamental". These enquiries are artificial and irrelevant to the real questions at issue. An exemption clause is not always unfair and there are many unfair provisions that are not exemption clauses. It is quite unsatisfactory to look at the agreement apart from the exemption clause, because the exemption clause is itself part of the agreement, and if fair and reasonable a perfectly legitimate part. Nor is there any reason to associate unfairness with breach or with fundamental breach. . . .
>
> More serious is the danger that suppression of the true criterion leads, as elsewhere, to the striking down of agreements that are perfectly fair and reasonable.

Professor Waddams makes two crucially important points. One is that not all exclusion clauses are unreasonable. This fact is ignored by the rule of law approach to fundamental breach. In the commercial context, clauses limiting or excluding liability are negotiated as part of the general contract. As they do with all other contractual terms, the parties bargain for the consequences of deficient performance. In the usual situation, exclusion clauses will be reflected in the contract price. Professor Waddams' second point is that exclusion clauses are not the only contractual provisions which may lead to unfairness. There appears to be no sound reason for applying special rules in the case of clauses excluding liability than for other clauses producing harsh results.

In light of the unnecessary complexities the doctrine of fundamental breach has created, the resulting uncertainty in the law, and the unrefined nature of the doctrine as a tool for averting unfairness, I am much inclined to lay the doctrine of fundamental breach to rest, and where necessary and appropriate, to deal explicitly with unconscionability. In my view, there is much to be gained by addressing directly the protection of the weak from over-reaching by the strong, rather than relying on the artificial legal doctrine of "fundamental breach". There is little value in cloaking the inquiry behind a construction that takes on its own idiosyncratic traits, sometimes at odds with concerns of fairness. This is precisely what has happened with the doctrine of fundamental breach. It is preferable to interpret the terms of the contract, in an attempt to determine exactly what the parties agreed. If on its true construction the contract excludes liability for the kind of breach that occurred, the party in breach will generally be saved from liability. Only where the contract is unconscionable, as might arise from situations of unequal bargaining power between the parties, should the courts interfere with agreements the parties have freely concluded. The courts do not blindly enforce harsh or unconscionable bargains and, as Professor Waddams has argued, the doctrine of "fundamental breach" may best be understood as but one manifestation of a general underlying principle which explains judicial intervention in a variety of contractual settings. Explicitly addressing concerns of unconscionability and inequality of bargaining power allows the courts to focus expressly on the real grounds for refusing to give force to a contractual term said to have been agreed to by the parties.

I wish to add that, in my view, directly considering the issues of contract construction and unconscionability will often lead to the same result as would have been reached using the doctrine of fundamental breach, but with the advantage of clearly addressing the real issues at stake.

In rejecting the doctrine of fundamental breach and adopting an approach that binds the parties to the bargains they make, subject to unconscionability, I do not wish to be taken as expressing an opinion on the substantial failure of contract performance, sometimes described as fundamental breach, that will relieve a party from future obligations under the contract. The concept of fundamental breach in the context of refusal to enforce exclusion clauses and of substantial failure of performance have often been confused, even though the two are quite distinct. In *Suisse Atlantique*, Lord Wilberforce noted the importance of distinguishing the two uses of the term fundamental breach, at p. 431:

> Next for consideration is the argument, based on "fundamental breach" or, which is presumably the same thing, a breach going "to the root of the contract." These expressions are used in the cases to denote two quite different things, namely, (i) a performance totally different from that which the contract contemplates, (ii) a breach of contract more serious than one which would entitle the other party merely to damages and which (at least) would entitle him to refuse performance or further performance under the contract.
>
> Both of these situations have long been familiar in the English law of contract . . . What is certain is that to use the expression without distinguishing to which of these, or to what other, situations it refers is to invite confusion.
>
> The importance of the difference between these meanings lies in this, that they relate to two separate questions which may arise in relation to any contract.

I wish to be clear that my comments are restricted to the use of fundamental breach in the context of enforcing contractual exclusion clauses.

Turning to the case at bar, I am of the view that Allis-Chalmers is not liable for the defective gearboxes. The warranty provision of the contract between Allis-Chalmers and Syncrude clearly limited the liability of Allis-Chalmers to defects appearing within one year from the date of placing the equipment into service. The trial judge found that the defects in the gearboxes did not become apparent until after the warranty of Allis-Chalmers had expired. It is clear, therefore, that the warranty clause excluded liability for the defects that materialized, and subject to the existence of any unconscionability between the two parties there can be no liability on the part of Allis-Chalmers. I have no doubt that unconscionability is not an issue in this case. Both Allis-Chalmers and Syncrude are large and commercially sophisticated companies. Both parties knew or should have known what they were doing and what they had bargained for when they entered into the contract. There is no suggestion that Syncrude was pressured in any way to agree to terms to which it did not wish to assent. I am therefore of the view that the parties should be held to the terms of their bargain and that the warranty clause freed Allis-Chalmers from any liability for the defective gearboxes . . .

[L'Heureux-Dubé J. concurred with Wilson J. La Forest J. concurred with Dickson C.J.C. McIntyre J. delivered a short judgment agreeing with Wilson J. that any breach of contract by Allis-Chalmers was not fundamental and, in any event, if the breach was properly characterized as fundamental, the liability of Allis-Chalmers would be excluded by the terms of the contractual warranty. Estey and Le Dain JJ. also heard the appeal but took no part in the judgment. Appeal of Hunter dismissed, and appeal of Allis-Chalmers and cross-appeal of Syncrude allowed.]

NOTES

1. For commentary on this case, see Flannigan, "*Hunter Engineering*: The Judicial Regulation of Exculpatory Clauses" (1990), 69 Can. Bar Rev. 514; Rafferty, "Developments in Contract and Tort Law: The 1988-89 Term" (1990), 1 S.C.L.R. (2d) 269 at 278-99.

2. We noted above s.149 of the Ontario Insurance Act as an example of a statutory attempt at prescription of the notice that must be given by an insurer that desires to include a particular kind of clause limiting cover. It is not surprising that we do not have legislative attempts to define how limiting clauses are to be interpreted; what could a statutory provision stipulate except that such a clause must be read narrowly? Most of the statutory interventions have in fact been directed at the third question in our analytical framework—which clauses will we simply refuse to apply?

As we noted earlier, it is perhaps impossible to provide an answer to that question which would provide a reliable guide in advance that could be used effectively by a court when a particular set of facts is under review. The theory of "fundamental breach" may have enjoyed such popularity because of its deceptive appearance of certainty of form; compared with "fairness" or "unconscionability", a test of "fundamental breach" may seem to be less vague, to involve a desirable degree of certainty. Whatever might be said on that point, the courts have apparently turned away from "fundamental breach" in favour of a more frankly uncertain test—"is this a clause which we will not enforce?" or, as Wilson J. expressed it in *Hunter*, "in the circumstances that have happened should the court lend its aid to A to hold B to this clause?"

In fact, Wilson J. seemed to deny the usefulness of any advance descriptor to identify the clauses that will be struck down. She considered "unconscionability" to be an inappropriate test, and she was dismissive of tests such as "fairness" or "reasonableness":

> [T]he courts, in my view, are quite unsuited to assess the fairness or reasonableness of contractual provisions as the parties negotiated them . . . [T]he parties [are], in the absence of inequality of bargaining power, the best judges of what is fair as between themselves . . .

Perhaps Wilson J.'s remarks help to explain why statutory attempts to control unfair contract terms have not been a spectacular success. One of the earliest legislative interventions was the statutory implied warranty of fitness in the Sale of Goods Act. The implied warranty in s.15 of the Ontario statute was applied to the contract between Syncrude and Hunter Engineering and led to the judgment against Hunter. However, the ease with which the implied warranty could be displaced was illustrated by the Allis-Chalmers contract with Syncrude.

One statutory technique then, is the prescriptive term, such as the implied warranty of fitness. The problem is twofold. First, whether necessarily or not, there has been a lack of willingness to impose it in all cases, that is to prevent the parties from contracting out of the statutory term. Secondly, such a specific prescriptive term deals with only one of a numberless array of possible unfair contract terms. It is one thing to specify a particular term which must be included, but quite a different matter to frame a general prohibition against terms which may not be included in a contract.

Various statutory attempts have been made to control unfair terms more generally. Again, the Insurance Act, R.S.O. 1990, c. I.8 contains an example:

151. Where a contract,

.....

(b) contains any stipulation, condition or warranty that is or may be material to the risk

> including, but not restricted to, a provision in respect to the use, condition, location or maintenance of the insured property,

the exclusion, stipulation, condition or warranty is not binding upon the insured, if it is held to be unjust or unreasonable by the court before which a question relating thereto is tried.

There are some few cases in which this provision has been considered, but hardly any in which it has been applied to strike down a clause in an insurance policy. Should we expect such statutory attempts to be effective? A statute is necessarily prospective in its design. It must prescribe in advance for what is permissible. Is a legislature any more "suited" than a court "to assess [in advance] the fairness or reasonableness of contractual provisions as the parties [may negotiate] them"? Or rather, does a statutory stipulation for fairness and reasonableness assist a court in dealing with a particular challenge to a particular contract term?

You might note that the Unfair Contract Terms Act 1977, (U.K.), c. 50 adopts "reasonableness" as its dominant test for permissible contract terms. S. 3 provides that a party contracting with a consumer, or contracting on the basis of its own standard form, cannot rely on a clause to limit its liability for breach "except in so far as . . . the contract term satisfies the requirement of reasonableness."

(vi)   *Unconscionability and Unreasonableness*

In *Hunter*, Dickson C.J.C. suggested that the problem of exclusion clauses in the context of an inequality of bargaining power should, as a matter of common law, be addressed by the concept of unconscionability rather than by a doctrine of fundamental breach. He provided little guidance, however, as to when an exclusion clause might be struck down on grounds of unconscionability; nor did he refer to any decisions adopting that approach, such as the following case.

DAVIDSON v. THREE SPRUCES REALTY LTD.

[1977] 6 W.W.R. 460, 79 D.L.R. (3d) 481 (B.C. S.C.)

ANDERSON J. The plaintiffs' claims are for damages for breach of contract of bailment or, alternatively, for negligence.

The three actions were consolidated for the purposes of trial, and it was agreed by counsel that the evidence of all witnesses and the discovery read in by counsel for Mr. and Mrs. Farr could be considered by me in reaching my decision in each of the cases.

The defendant "The Three Spruces Realty Ltd." (hereinafter called the "bailee") carried on the business and operation of "safety deposit" vaults at 402 West Pender St., Vancouver, British Columbia. These vaults provided bulk storage space for the safekeeping of the property of customers. The property of the customers was stored in the vaults in containers supplied by the customers. The bailee also rented "safety deposit" boxes to its customers. This aspect of the bailee's business is not in issue here except perhaps to demonstrate the higher risk involved in placing valuables in bulk storage as opposed to placing such valuables in a safety deposit box.

Each of the plaintiffs entered into an agreement with the bailee whereby the bailee agreed to keep their valuables in safekeeping. Each of the plaintiffs paid an annual fee for this service.

In the Farr and Elsdon cases a written agreement was executed by the plaintiffs, which agreement contained a "limitation of liability" clause. In the

Davidson case the agreement was simply an oral contract whereby the bailee, for a fee, agreed to keep the Davidsons' valuables in safekeeping. . . .

The bailee did not take reasonable precautions to safeguard the goods placed in bulk storage by the plaintiffs. In fact, the evidence is clear that the bailee did not take any of the precautions normally taken by prudent persons engaged in this type of business.

The particulars of negligence and breach of contract which have been alleged and proved, are as follows:

(a) The bailee neglected to require persons entering the vaults to identify themselves or to sign admission slips.

(b) Customers and strangers were permitted to enter the bulk storage area, unattended by any of the employees of the bailee.

(c) No evidence was adduced to show that there had been a proper, or any, investigation of potential customers.

(d) Identification tags were placed on the containers placed in the vaults by the plaintiffs, thereby enabling strangers to know the identity of the owners of the containers.

(e) In December of 1975, a theft from one of the containers in the bulk storage vault occurred but none of the plaintiffs were warned that this theft had taken place.

(f) No evidence was called by the bailee to show that any precautions had been taken to protect the plaintiffs' valuables from theft.

In the spring and summer of 1976, each of the plaintiffs attended at the "safety deposit" vaults and ascertained that their containers had been opened and the contents removed. In each case the old locks had been removed and new locks inserted in their stead. In each case concrete bricks, wrapped in plastic bags, were substituted for the plaintiffs' valuables, namely, gold and silver coinage . . .

The bailee relies on cl. 9 appearing on the back page of the contract, which clause reads as follows:

> 9. Neither the lessor nor its officers, agents and servants, shall be in any way liable directly or indirectly for any theft, robbery, embezzlement, loss or destruction of, or any injury or damage whatsoever to any papers or property which may at any time be deposited or stored in the box or held by the lessor under clause 11 below, or for any act, neglect, or omission whatsoever of the lessor or its officers, agents and servants, or of the tenant or any deputy or any stranger.

The following matters may be relevant in determining whether the limitation clause is applicable in the circumstances:

(a) The contract is a standard form prepared by the bailee.

(b) The contract refers to the rental of a safety deposit box and not to bulk storage.

(c) A copy of the contract was not given to any of the plaintiffs.

(d) The contract was executed by each of the plaintiffs after representation of almost absolute safety had been made by the bailee.

(e) The contract was not read by any of the plaintiffs and their attention was not drawn to the limitation clause.

(f) The rules and regulations made it clear that, in so far as safety deposit boxes are concerned, access to the box is limited to the holder of the box or his agent, and that the contents of the box are to be examined outside the vault in rooms specially provided for that purpose (see rules 2 and 4).

(g) The contract contains a release form whereby the customer may waive the liability of the bailee.

(h) Almost immediately after the contract was signed the plaintiffs were assured that it was not necessary to insure their valuables against loss by theft or otherwise.

Counsel for the bailee makes the following submissions:

(1) While the printed portions of the contract refer to a "safety deposit box" the contract should be interpreted in accordance with the written words "floor space".

In summary, counsel submits that the contract should be interpreted as a contract for "floor space" and that the clauses referring to the "box" should be interpreted as referring to "floor space". Where the clauses are clearly inapplicable to "floor space" they should be disregarded.

(2) While the limitation clause appears to be harsh and onerous, the necessity for upholding freedom of contract is so important that the Courts should not seek to escape from the language of the limitation clause.

Counsel for the plaintiffs make the following submissions:

(1) The contract must be strictly construed against the maker thereof, the bailee, and it follows that the contract is not applicable to "floor space" but only to "safety deposit boxes".

(2) The words of limitation should not be interpreted as excluding the duty of reasonable care but should be construed as meaning that the bailee is not an insurer.

(3) The words of limitation are not applicable where there has been a fundamental breach of the contract.

(4) The representation by the bailee that there was no necessity for the plaintiffs to insure their goods amounted to a representation that their goods were insured.

(5) The representations made by the bailee amounted to a promise that proper precautions were being taken to safeguard the property of the plaintiffs and that the contract should be construed so as not to permit the bailee to break its promise.

I am convinced that while the contract can be interpreted as being a contract for "floor space" it cannot be contended that the limitation clause can be read to apply to "floor space". The limitation clause refers to a "box" and not to "floor space". Limitation clauses of the type relied upon here will be strictly construed. The contract was, moreover, drawn up by the bailee and it lies ill in the mouth of the bailee to ask that the word "box" be read as "floor space" so that it can avoid its responsibilities on the basis of a highly technical "fine print" escape clause.

I point out, moreover, that the risks involved in "floor space" storage are much greater than the risks involved in the use of safety deposit boxes. Before anyone can enter the safety deposit box of another person he must first obtain that person's key. He must also gain entry to the "safety deposit box" vault by causing the custodial officers to believe that he is the registered holder of the box. He can only open the box in the presence and with the assistance of the custodial officer. He can only remove the goods contained in the box in a room specially designated for that purpose. While some care is required to prevent the contents of safety deposit boxes from being stolen it is obvious that much greater custodial care is required in the case of bulk storage. The holder of a safety box would have little to lose by agreeing to the terms of cl. 9. The same cannot be said of a customer renting "floor space". It follows, therefore, that as the limitation clause is concerned only with the risks relating to the use of "safety deposit boxes" that it would not be correct to apply the clause in respect of risks relating to the use of "floor space". It cannot be said that the parties must have intended that wherever the contract contained the word "box" the words "floor space" were to be substituted for the word "box".

In any event, it appears to me that the rules and regulations were drawn up solely for fixing the terms and conditions for the lease of a safety deposit box and are not applicable to "floor space".

If I am wrong in concluding that the limitation clause is not applicable to contracts for "floor space", I hold that the limitation clause does not apply where, as here, there has been a fundamental breach of the contract of bailment. While such a clause might (not must) protect against an isolated careless act or a momentary error of judgment, it cannot prevail where the conduct of the bailee has been such as to demonstrate almost complete lack of care. If a defendant relies upon a limitation clause of this kind he must show that he has not been guilty of a fundamental breach. . . .

With respect to the lack of care, while it is apparent that ordinary precautions were not taken, the worst aspect of this case is that with knowledge by the bailee that a theft from the "bulk storage" vault had taken place the plaintiffs were not warned of the theft or that their valuables might be in jeopardy or that they should obtain insurance coverage. Surely, such deliberate disregard for the safety of the plaintiffs' property amounts to gross negligence on the part of the bailee and constitutes conduct not protected by the limitation clause.

Counsel for the bailee submits that the Courts should not interfere with freedom of contract. He submits that if the parties to contracts are not held to the terms of their bargain, however harsh or one-sided, the element of certainty so important in the commercial world will be eliminated. He submits that the plaintiffs agreed in writing, in clear terms, that the bailee would not be responsible for any negligence on its part. He submits that negligence cannot in itself constitute a fundamental breach or, in any event, the limitation clause protected the bailee in respect of all acts of negligence.

I agree that as a general rule, apart from fraud, it would be a dangerous thing to hold that contracts freely entered into should not be enforced. It is not correct, however, to suppose that there are no limitations on freedom of contract. The point has been reached in the development of the common law where, in my opinion, the Courts may say, in certain circumstances, that the terms of a contract, although perfectly clear, will not be enforced because they are entirely unreasonable. I quote from the judgment of Lord Denning, M.R., in *Gillespie Brothers & Co. Ltd. v. Roy Bowles Transport Ltd.*, [1973] Q.B. 400 at pp. 415-6, as follows:

> The time may come when this process of "construing" the contract can be pursued no further. The words are too clear to permit of it. Are the courts then powerless? Are they to permit the party to enforce his unreasonable clause, even when it is so unreasonable, or applied so unreasonably, as to be unconscionable? When it gets to this point, I would say, as I said many years ago: "there is the vigilance of the common law which, while allowing freedom of contract, watches to see that it is not abused": *John Lee & Son (Grantham) Ltd. v. Railway Executive*, [1949] 2 All E.R. 581 at 584 (C.A.). It will not allow a party to exempt himself from his liability at common law when it would be quite unconscionable for him to do so.

I take the view that the Courts are not bound to accept all contracts at face value and enforce those contracts without some regard to the surrounding circumstances. I do not think that standard form contracts should be construed in a vacuum. I do not think that mere formal consensus is enough. I am of the opinion that the terms of a contract may be declared to be void as being unreasonable where it can be said that in all the circumstances it is unreasonable and unconscionable to bind the parties to their formal bargain.

In ascertaining whether "freedom of contract has been abused" so as to make it unconscionable for the bailee to exempt itself from liability, I think regard may be had to the following:

(1) Was the contract a standard form contract drawn up by the bailee?

(2) Were there any negotiations as to the terms of the contract or was it a commercial form which may be described as a "sign here" contract?

(3) Was the attention of the plaintiffs drawn to the limitation clause?

(4) Was the exemption clause unusual in character?

(5) Were representations made which would lead an ordinary person to believe that the limitation clause did not apply?

(6) Was the language of the contract when read in conjunction with the limitation clause such as to render the implied covenant made by the bailee to use reasonable care to protect the plaintiffs' property meaningless?

(7) Having regard to all the facts including the representations made by the bailee and the circumstances leading up to the execution of the contract, would not the enforcement of the limitation clause be a tacit approval by the Courts of unacceptable commercial practices?

In the case at bar, the plaintiffs were not asked to read the contract. They were not advised of the contents of the contract. They were asked to "sign here" and pay the annual rental fee. Prior to signing the contract they were assured that proper precautions would be taken to secure their valuables. When the plaintiffs asked whether they should obtain insurance coverage they were advised that it was not necessary to obtain such coverage. The plaintiffs were not given a copy of the contract. The fact a theft had taken place was not made known to them.

Even if the language of the limitation clause extends to all acts or omissions on the part of the bailee, including such negligence as would amount to a fundamental breach of contract, I hold, in the circumstances here, that the limitation clause is so unreasonable that it cannot be enforced. It amounts to a clear "abuse of freedom of contract".

Apart from the fact that the limitation clause is, in the circumstances of this case, so unreasonable that it cannot be enforced, the bailee cannot rely on the clause because the plaintiffs were induced to believe, by means of innocent misrepresentations, that the clause would not be enforced. . . .

In summary, the limitation clause will not assist the bailee because:

(a) It does not apply to "floor space".

(b) The conduct of the bailee was such as to amount to a fundamental breach of the contract.

(c) Even if the limitation clause was such as to protect the bailee against conduct amounting to a fundamental breach, the clause is, in all the circumstances, so offensive to all right-thinking persons that the Courts will hold that to allow the bailee to rely on the limitation clause would be unconscionable and an abuse of freedom of contract.

(d) The representations made by the bailee were such as would induce an ordinary person to believe that the limitation clause would not be enforced and therefore the bailee cannot rely on it. . . .

[Judgment for plaintiffs.]

NOTES and QUESTION

1. In reaching his judgment, Anderson J. was clearly influenced by the work of Lord Denning. In addition to the *Gillespie Brothers* case cited in the above extract, Anderson J. also relied upon Lord Denning's later judgment in *Levison v. Patent Steam Carpet Cleaning Co.*, [1977] 3 All E.R. 498 (C.A.). There, as in *Gillespie Brothers*, Lord Denning expressed the view that an exclusion clause should not be given effect where it was unreasonable, or where it would be unreasonable to apply it in the circumstances of the case, at least where there was inequality of bargaining power. It is worth noting, however, that he did not confine his principle to that context. Inequality of bargaining power was just one factor to be taken into account. Thus, he applied his principle in the Court of Appeal in the *Photo Production* case, [1978] 3 All E.R. 146 to deny Securicor the right to rely on its exclusion clause. He stated the principle in the following way (at 153):

> [T]he court will not allow a party to rely on an exemption or limitation clause in circumstances in which it would not be fair or reasonable to allow reliance on it; and, in considering whether it is fair and reasonable, the court will consider whether it was in a standard form, whether there was equality of bargaining power, the nature of the breach, and so forth.

2. In 1987, the O.L.R.C. recommended that legislation be enacted giving the courts the power to grant relief from contracts and contractual provisions, like exclusion clauses, that are unconscionable. These recommendations are set out *infra* in Chapter 12, section 4(d), note 3 after the *Unconscionable Transactions Relief Act*. The approach of the O.L.R.C. is similar to that of Anderson J. in

Davidson. It provides a shopping list of factors to which the courts may have regard in determining whether a contract, or part thereof, is unconscionable.

3. The tendency in post-*Hunter Engineering* cases has been for the courts to avoid making a choice between Dickson C.J.C.'s and Wilson J.'s approach: see, for example, *Catre Industries Ltd. v. Alberta* (1989), 63 D.L.R. (4th) 74 (Alta. C.A.), leave to appeal to S.C.C. refused (1990), 108 N.R. 170 (note) (S.C.C.); *Kordas v. Stokes Seeds Ltd.* (1992), 11 O.R. (3d) 129 (C.A.), leave to appeal to S.C.C. refused (1993), 10 B.L.R. (2d) 201 (note) (S.C.C.); *MacKay v. Scott Packaging and Warehousing Co. (Canada) Ltd.*, [1996] 2 F.C. 36 (C.A.).

In *Atlas Supply Co. of Canada Ltd. v. Yarmouth Equipment Ltd.* (1991), 103 N.S.R. (2d) 1 (C.A.), the majority of the Nova Scotia Court of Appeal applied Dickson C.J.C.'s unconscionability approach to strike down an exclusion clause favouring the franchisor in a franchise agreement. At the same time, however, it indicated that there was little, if any, difference between Dickson C.J.C.'s unconscionability principle and Wilson J.s "fair and reasonable" test. Matthews J.A. said at 24:

> Although the principle of unconscionability should be used sparingly to avoid an exclusion clause, this appellant should not be permitted to engage in such conduct secure in the knowledge that no liability could be imposed upon it because of the exclusionary clause or, as Wilson J. said . . . in *Hunter*:
>
>> ". . . this party is now trying to have his cake and eat it too. He is seeking to escape almost entirely the burdens of the transaction but enlist the support of the courts to enforce its benefits."

The impugned conduct in *Atlas Supply* consisted of the franchisor, "a large national company with international connections", inducing "a small businessman . . . with little or no retail experience", to enter into a franchise agreement by presenting favourable financial forecasts while, at the same time, deliberately withholding available information projecting the non-viability of the proposed franchise and then inserting a clause to the effect that the franchisor did not warrant the sales volumes and profit projections.

How different are the approaches of Dickson C.J.C. and Wilson J.? In *MacKay, supra*, the Federal Court of Appeal suggested that the basic distinction lay in the fact that, under Dickson C.J.C.'s approach, the question of unconscionability had to be assessed at the time that the contract was concluded and, therefore, the nature and degree of the particular breach were irrelevant; under Wilson J.'s approach, however, the fairness and reasonableness of enforcing the clause had to be determined at the time of the breach and, therefore, "the nature and degree of the breach may well be of fundamental significance" (at 45-46).

4. The Supreme Court of Canada has considered its decision in *Hunter Engineering, supra* on just a few subsequent occasions. In *Guarantee Co. of North America v. Gordon Capital Corp.* (1999), 178 D.L.R. (4th) 1 (S.C.C.), the court pointed out that the approaches of both Dickson C.J.C. and Wilson J. centred upon the construction of the exclusion clause in question. Iacobucci and Bastarache JJ., for the court, thus concluded at 20:

> If, as a matter of contractual interpretation, the parties clearly intended an exclusion clause to continue to apply in the event of fundamental breach, courts [are] required to enforce the bargain agreed to by the parties, rather than applying a rule of law to rewrite the terms of the contract.

Their Lordships then determined that the same policy rationale, which supported judicial respect for the bargain struck between commercial actors of equal bargaining power, applied to clauses other than just exclusion clauses, such as those designed to limit the time within which an action could be brought.

In describing the situations in which an exclusion, or similar, clause would not be enforced despite its applicability as a matter of construction, Iacobucci and Bastarache JJ. said at 21:

> The only limitation placed upon enforcing the contract as written in the event of a fundamental breach would be to refuse to enforce an exclusion of liability in circumstances where to do so would be unconscionable, according to Dickson C.J.C., or unfair, unreasonable or otherwise contrary to public policy, according to Wilson J.

It is interesting to observe the way in which the approaches of Dickson C.J.C. and Wilson J. were assimilated. The one approach that ultimately emerges bears a greater resemblance to Dickson C.J.C.'s position than Wilson J.'s. There was no real attempt in the case to determine whether it would be unfair or unreasonable to apply the time limitation provision in light of the breach of contract that had occurred. The *Gordon Capital* case was approved by the Supreme Court in *Z.I. Pompey Industrie v. ECU-Line N.V.* (2003), 224 D.L.R. (4th) 577 (S.C.C.) where, at 594, "the policy rationale in support of the construction approach applied to exclusion clauses and time limitation clauses [was determined to be] equally applicable to forum selection clauses in bills of lading."

5. In *Shelanu Inc. v. Print Three Franchising Corp.* (2003), 226 D.L.R. (4th) 577 (Ont. C.A.), the court followed the *Gordon Capital* case, discussed in the introduction to this chapter, the Ontario Court of Appeal followed the *Gordon Capital* case, with its rationalization and conflation of the approaches of Dickson C.J.C. and Wilson J. The case concerned a formal franchise argument which the franchisee argued had been varied by a subsequent oral agreement. In denying the enforceability of the oral agreement, the franchisor relied upon clauses in the franchise agreement to the effect that the written contract constituted the entire agreement between the parties and that any amendment to that agreement had to be effected in writing and signed by the parties. The court held that, as a matter of construction, the clauses did not conflict with the subsequent oral agreement. Weiler J.A. then continued at 595-597:

> In view of my conclusion above it is not strictly necessary for me to address the enforceability of the exclusion clauses. However, given the trial judge's conclusion and the extent of argument on the question of whether he erred in refusing to give effect to the clauses, I will consider this issue.
>
> .....
>
> On appeal, the appellant has conceded the existence of the oral agreement and its terms but asks this court to enforce the written agreement instead. That submission, in effect, asks this court not to give effect to the intention of the parties. Such a submission is contrary to the classical theory of contract interpretation which emphasizes that courts should ascertain and give effect to the intention of the parties: R. Sullivan, "Contract Interpretation in Practice and Theory" (2000), 13 Sup. Ct. L. Rev. (2d) 369.
>
> Sullivan states, at 378, that, "if a conflict arises between the intention of the parties as inferred from the totality of the evidence on the one hand and the meaning of the text on the other, intention should win." Professor Waddams has also argued that if a party knows or has reason to know that a written contract on which that party relies does not represent the intention of the other party, it should not be enforced. See S.M. Waddams, *The Law of Contracts*, 3rd ed. (Toronto: Canada Law Book, 1993) at paras. 328-329.
>
> The rationale of Sullivan and Waddams is similar, namely, that in addition to certainty, legal values such as fairness, equity and justice underlie contractual interpretation and enforcement. Before the court allows the coercive power of the state to be used to serve the private interests of a party to a contract, the court will want to endure the contract does not offend these legal values.
>
> I would also note that the agreement that we are dealing with is a franchise agreement. A franchise agreement is a type of contract of adhesion, that is, a type of contract whose main provisions are presented on a "take it or leave it basis". In such situations, the case for holding that an exclusion clause represents the intention of the signer and that the signer should be bound by it is weaker because there is usually an inherent inequality of bargaining power between the parties. See Waddams, *supra*, at para. 342.
>
> .....
>
> Enforcing an exclusion clause that is contrary to the reasonable expectation and understanding of the parties in these circumstances would not be fair or reasonable and would also come within the exception enunciated in *Gordon Capital, supra*.
>
> I would hold that even if the exclusion clauses applied, the trial judge was entitled to refuse to enforce [them].

6. In the case below, *Fraser Jewellers*, the trial judge had fairly clearly applied Anderson J.'s judgment in *Davidson, supra*. The Ontario Court of Appeal, however, emphasized how difficult it is to establish unconscionability in the commercial context as well as the likelihood that Dickson C.J.C.'s and Wilson J.'s approach from *Hunter Engineering, supra*, would yield the same result on a given set of facts. *Solway*, the case that follows *Fraser Jewellers*, is one of the few where it has been determined that it would be unconscionable to apply an exclusion clause.

FRASER JEWELLERS (1982) LTD. v. DOMINION ELECTRIC PROTECTION CO.

(1997), 148 D.L.R. (4th) 496 (Ont. C.A.)

The plaintiff operated a jewellery store in Cornwall, Ontario. It entered into a contract with the defendant, operating under the name of "ADT", whereby ADT was to furnish a burglar alarm system and, for an annual fee, provide the plaintiff with a monitoring service pursuant to which ADT was to notify the Cornwall police if the alarm system should be activated.

Paragraph E of the agreement provided:

> It is understood that ADT is not an insurer, that insurance, if any, shall be obtained by the customer and that the amounts payable to ADT hereunder are based upon the value of the services and the scope of liability as herein set forth and are unrelated to the value of the customer's property or property of others located in customer's premises. ADT makes no guarantee or warranty, including any implied warranty of merchantability or fitness, that the system or services supplied, will avert or prevent occurrences of the consequences therefrom, which the system or service is designed to detect or avert; that if ADT should be found liable for loss, damage or injury due to a failure of service or equipment in any respect, its liability shall be limited to a sum equal to 100% of the annual service charge or $10,000.00, whichever is less, as the agreed upon damages and not as a penalty, as the exclusive remedy; and that the provisions of this paragraph shall apply if loss, damage or injury irrespective of cause or origin, results, directly or indirectly to person or property from performance or non-performance of obligations imposed by this contract or from negligence, active or otherwise, of ADT, its agents or employees.

The plaintiff's owner (Mr. Gordon) testified that he had not read the agreement, that he was unaware of the exclusionary provision and that it was not pointed out to him by the defendant. He also indicated that he had not insured against losses resulting from robbery.

Two years later, robbers escaped from the plaintiff's premises with $50,000 worth of jewellery. The defendant, however, failed to respond to the plaintiff's alarm signal for about ten minutes and, by the time ADT called the police, the robbers were gone.

The plaintiff sued to recover its loss from ADT. It succeeded at trial. The defendant appealed. The Court of Appeal held, first, that there was sufficient evidence to support the trial judge's finding that the robbers could have been caught or the jewellery recovered had ADT not negligently delayed contacting the police. It then turned its attention to the issue of whether ADT, in accordance with paragraph E, was entitled to limit its liability to the amount of the annual monitoring charge ($890).

ROBINS J.A. [delivering the judgment of the court] . . .

The Limitation of Liability Issue

On this aspect of the case, the trial judge held that ADT was not entitled to rely on para. E of the agreement to limit its liability to the plaintiff. For all practical purposes, he held the clause to be unenforceable. In reaching this conclusion, he had reference to *Hunter Engineering Co. v. Syncrude Canada Ltd.*, [*supra*], the most recent decision of the Supreme Court of Canada on the question of judicial control of exclusionary provisions designed to reduce or eliminate liability in private contracts.

In that case, the Supreme Court of Canada was unanimous in holding that, while such provisions, *prima facie*, were enforceable according to their true meaning, a court was empowered in limited circumstances to grant relief against provisions of this nature. The Supreme Court of Canada, however; was evenly divided on the question of the test to be used to determine when or in what circumstances the power to grant relief should be exercised.

[The court discussed the differing approaches of Dickson C.J.C. and Wilson J. It then turned its attention to the question of whether the defendant had committed a fundamental breach and continued:]

The defendant's negligence in failing to respond appropriately to the alarm cannot be equated to a fundamental breach of the agreement. It is important to recognize that this was not a deliberate or wilful breach or a refusal of ADT to perform its contractual duty. . . .

At most, the untimely response was the consequence of a lapse or error on the part of an ADT employee. The commercial purpose of the transaction was not thereby destroyed. Indeed, as I have noted, the contract has continued intact. In these circumstances, the breach, while entitling the plaintiff to damages, cannot be characterized as fundamental.

However, whether the breach is fundamental or not, an exclusionary clause of this kind, in my opinion, should, *prima facie*, be enforced according to its true meaning. Relief should be granted only if the clause, seen in the light of the entire agreement, can be said, on Dickson's C.J.C.'s test, to be "unconscionable" or, on Wilson J.'s test, to be "unfair or unreasonable". The difference in practice between these alternatives, as Professor Waddams has observed, "is unlikely to be large": S.M. Waddams, *The Law of Contracts*, 3rd ed. (Toronto: Canada Law Book, 1993) at p. 323.

The trial judge concluded that para. E was unfair, unreasonable or unconscionable on the basis of his findings to the effect, in summary, that: the agreement was not read by Mr. Gordon; para. E was not brought to his attention; the agreement was on a standard printed form and was not negotiated; the exemption clause was "unusual in character"; and there was an "inequality of bargaining power" between the parties. In my respectful opinion, these factors are either immaterial to the issue or, on the facts of this case, not such as to render this limitation clause unenforceable.

As a general proposition, in the absence of fraud or misrepresentation, a person is bound by an agreement to which he has put his signature whether he has read its contents or has chosen to leave them unread.? Failure to read a contract before signing it is not a legally acceptable basis for refusing to abide by it. A businessman executing an agreement on behalf of a company must be presumed to be aware of its terms and to have intended that the company would be bound by them. The fact that Mr. Gordon chose not to read the contract can place him in no better position than a person who has. Nor is the fact that the clause is in a standard pre-printed form and was not a subject of negotiations sufficient in itself to vitiate the clause. . . .

This is not a case in which the clause limiting liability was so obscured as to make it probable that it would escape attention. This contract was printed and contained on essentially one sheet of paper. The limitation provision was high-lighted in bold block letters. The language is clear and unambiguous. There was no need to resort to a magnifying glass to see it or a dictionary to understand it. Nothing was done to mislead a reader. Had Mr. Gordon perused the contract, he would have been aware of the limitation. The fact that he did not is irrelevant to the question of the fairness or conscionability of the contract.

The trial judge held that it was the defendant's responsibility to bring the clause to the "specific attention" of the plaintiff and to explain its effect. Not to have done so, he found, constituted an "unacceptable commercial practice". As I view the matter, there was no special relationship existing between these parties that imposed any such obligation on the defendant. This is an ordinary commercial contract between business people. If anything, given that the plaintiff contacted the defendant to upgrade an existing system whose installation was governed by a contract containing a similar limitation provision, it could reasonably be as-sumed that the plaintiff was aware of the limitation imposed on ADT's potential liability. Be that as it may, in this commercial setting, in the absence of fraud or other improper conduct inducing the plaintiff to enter the contract, the onus must rest upon the plaintiff to review the document and satisfy itself of its advantages and disadvantages before signing it. There is no justification for shifting the plaintiff's responsibility to act with elementary prudence onto the defendant.

It is not suggested that the plaintiff was rushed or pressured in any way into signing the contract. Nor is it suggested that the defendant engaged in any dubious conduct to achieve this end. The plaintiff had all the time needed to read the contract and consider its terms and, admittedly, could have questioned ADT's representative on any provision about which it may have had doubt. It accordingly must be treated in the same manner as a subscriber who signed the contract with full knowledge of the exclusion provision. . . .

The trial judge was of the opinion that there was an inequality of bargaining position between the plaintiff, a small retailer, and the defendant, a large security protection firm, and treated this as militating in favour of striking the clause. While I agree that such inequality is a relevant criterion, the fact that the parties may have different bargaining power does not in itself render an agreement unconscionable or unenforceable. Mere inequality of bargaining power does not entitle a party to repudiate an agreement. The question is not whether there was an inequality of bargaining power. Rather; the question is whether there was an abuse of the bargaining power.

On the facts of this case, there is no evidence of any such abuse. Nothing in this record indicates that the defendant obtained the contract by any unfair use of its stronger position or sought to take undue advantage of the plaintiff or, indeed, that the plaintiff was victimized as a consequence of its weaker position. The fact that the plaintiff is a small business is not sufficient to justify the court's interference with the parties' contractual arrangements. Nor, as I indicated earlier, is the fact that the agreement is in the form of a standard printed contract.

The remaining question is whether the terms of the exclusion provision are, as the trial judge viewed them, so "unusual in character" or so unfair or unconscionable that their enforcement would constitute an "unacceptable commercial practice". In deciding this question, the provision, as I have already stated, must be considered in the light of the entire agreement.

Paragraph E makes it clear that ADT is not an insurer; that insurance, if any, should be obtained by the customer; that the amounts payable by the customer are based on the value of the services; and that the scope of liability is unrelated to the value of the customer's property.

Having regard to the potential value of property kept on a customer's premises, and the many ways in which a loss may be incurred, the rationale underlying this type of limitation clause is apparent and makes sound commercial sense. ADT is not an insurer and its monitoring fee bears no relationship to the area of risk and the extent of exposure ordinarily taken into account in the determination of insurance policy premiums. Limiting liability in this situation is manifestly reasonable. The clause, in effect, allocates risk in a certain fashion and alerts the customer to the need to make its own insurance arrangements. ADT has no control over the value of its customer's inventory and can hardly be expected, in exchange for a relatively modest annual fee, to insure a jeweller against negligent acts on the part of its employees up to the value of the entire jewellery stock whatever that value, from time to time, may be.

The alarm services were to be provided on the understanding that the charges were based upon "the value of the services and the scope of liability" set out in the agreement and not upon "the value of the customer's property". To now make the security company liable, effectively as an insurer, for the value of the customer's property and not for the stipulated damages would be to fundamentally change the contract agreed to by the parties. . . .

Furthermore, the exemption clause with which we are concerned here cannot properly be said to be unusual. Indeed, it appears from the decided cases that clauses limiting a security company's liability for acts arising out of its own negligence are a common feature of commercial relations of this type. These clauses have been upheld in this province in a number of cases, none of which was referred to by the trial judge, and generally in the United States where the same issue has arisen in cases involving companies doing business in Ontario pursuant to contracts containing similar exclusion clauses. . . .

In my opinion, the parties should be held to their bargain. . . .

[Appeal allowed.]

SOLWAY v. DAVIS MOVING & STORAGE INC.
(c.o.b. Kennedy Moving Systems)

(2002), 62 O.R. (3d) 522 (C.A.), leave to appeal refused (2003), 2003 CarswellOnt 2018, 2003 CarswellOnt 2019 (S.C.C.)

The plaintiffs, Akler and Solway, contracted with the defendant, Kennedy Moving, to have their household goods, including rare and valuable artifacts and antiques, removed from their house, stored briefly, and delivered to their new home. The trailer containing their goods was left on a public street overnight, to enable snowploughing to be done on the Kennedy parking lot, and stolen.

LABROSSE J.A. (GILLESE J.A. concurring) The plaintiffs claimed for the replacement cost of their possessions. . . . Kennedy Moving, admitted liability for the loss of the goods, but only to the extent of the terms of the bill of lading and Regulation 1088 passed pursuant to the *Truck Transportation Act*, R.S.O. 1990, c. T.22. The bill of lading and the Regulation would limit the claim to $0.60 per pound, for a total of $7,089.60.

The trial judge found that the plaintiffs were aware of the limitation of liability clause when they entered into the transaction and that they had taken steps to obtain additional insurance coverage with their own insurer.

The plaintiffs had initially contacted Kennedy Moving because they had been satisfied with its performance in an earlier move. Although they had obtained a quotation from a competitor, they opted to go with Kennedy Moving because of both their past experience and because it seemed so professional. Akler testified that Kennedy Moving's affiliation with Atlas Van Lines, which was a household name, gave them comfort and assurance.

The plaintiffs testified that Kennedy Moving had represented that their goods would be secure during the move. Kennedy Moving would provide safekeeping of their goods by parking the trailer in the Kennedy Moving yard, removing the loading gear, locking the trailer, and locking the air brakes. Akler testified that she did not tell anyone at Kennedy Moving the value of her goods, but did emphasize the importance of certain items. It was clearly important to the plaintiffs that their goods be secure. The trial judge found that they were given assurances to that effect.

. . . . .

. . . Since Peterson [a member of Kennedy Moving's sales staff] did attend at the plaintiffs' home, he was likely aware that their possessions were not simply ordinary household goods.

. . . . .

The trial judge found that Kennedy Moving had given false assurances that the goods would be secured that had induced the plaintiffs to agree to the limitation clause [and were never advised that their goods would be left unattended].

In considering whether or not Kennedy Moving should be permitted to invoke the limitation of liability clause, the trial judge relied on the decision of the Supreme Court of Canada in *Hunter Engineering Co. v. Syncrude Canada Ltd.* [*supra*].

In *Fraser Jewellers (1982) Ltd. v. Dominion Electric Protection Co.* [*supra*], this court reviewed the decision in *Hunter Engineering* and noted that, in that case, the Supreme Court of Canada was unanimous in holding that, while limitation of liability provisions, *prima facie*, were enforceable according to their true meaning, a court was empowered in limited circumstances to grant relief against provisions of this nature. The Supreme Court of Canada, however, was evenly divided on the question of the test to be used to determine when or in what circumstances the power to grant relief should be exercised. . . .

Robins J.A., speaking for this court, reconciled these two approaches in *Fraser Jewellers*, [(1997), 34 O.R. (3d) 1, at 10] as follows:

> [W]hether the breach is fundamental or not, an exclusionary clause of this kind, in my opinion, should, *prima facie*, be enforced according to its true meaning. Relief should be granted only if the clause, seen in the light of the agreement, can be said, on Dickson C.J.C.'s test, to be "unconscionable" or, on Wilson J.'s test, to be "unfair or unreasonable". The difference in practice between these alternatives, as Professor Waddams has observed, "is unlikely to be large": *Waddams, The Law of Contract*, 3rd ed. (1993), at p. 323.

. . . . .

In this case, the plaintiffs' goods were highly valuable, both in monetary and sentimental terms. As such, they took special care to choose a moving company that would provide the security they felt was essential. Based on their past experience with Kennedy Moving, its apparent professionalism, and its affiliation with Atlas Van Lines, the plaintiffs made what they thought was an informed decision to opt for Kennedy Moving.

. . . . .

In deciding not to enforce the limitation clause, the trial judge appears to have equated the words, "unconscionable" and "unreasonable" as these terms were discussed in *Hunter Engineering*. In our view, on the facts as found by the trial judge, to limit the loss of the plaintiffs to $7,089.60 would, in the words of Dickson C.J.C. be "unconscionable", or in the words of Wilson J. be "unfair or unreasonable". This is one of those cases where relief should be granted.

The conclusion of the trial judge is amply supported by the evidence. It also accords with principles of contract law. We see no basis to interfere. . . .

CARTHY J.A. (dissenting) In my view [the] loss . . . is clearly covered by the statutory limitations of liability embodied in the contract with the appellants and should have limited the liability to $7,089.60. . . .

My major disagreement with the trial judge's reasons is with her application of the reasons in *Hunter*. It is generally considered that there is little room remaining for setting aside an exemption provision on the basis of fundamental breach following *Hunter*. . . . Yet here we find what I would consider a minor transgression in the performance of the contract justifying just that.

[Carthy J.A. then considered the approaches of Dickson C.J.C. and Wilson J. in *Hunter Engineering*.]

It isn't necessary to my reasoning to choose between these two approaches. If it were, I would favour that of Dickson C.J.C. There is no need for an undefined discretion in the enforceability of exclusion clauses. Contracting parties, insurers, business persons and litigants are all better served by the certainty of standards. And it must be kept in mind that this debate is not about fundamental breach as it may excuse continuing performance under a contract. . . .

Turning to the facts of this case, Dickson C.J.C. would not take a moment to conclude that there was no unconscionability in the terms of this contract. The liability clause was imposed by statute, and in this case upon knowledgeable and sophisticated persons. Wilson J. would have looked as well at the outcome, but surely would have concluded that all policy concerns pointed to enforcement of a provision born in legislation which itself was driven by policy.

That legislation is the *Truck Transportation Act*, R.S.O. 1990, c. T.22. Regulation 1088 thereunder sets forth a lengthy schedule of conditions that are deemed to be a part of every contract for the carriage for compensation of household goods. One condition imposes absolute liability on the carrier for loss or damage to goods accepted for carriage, with some noted exceptions that have no present relevance.

Condition 9 reads in part:

> 9. Valuation
>
> Subject to Article 10, the amount of any loss or damage for which the carrier is liable, whether or not the loss or damage results from negligence of the carrier or the carrier's employees or agents, shall be the lesser of, . . . [60 cents a pound]

The policy concerns addressed by this legislation are longstanding and widespread. For at least 200 years, a carrier of goods has been absolutely liable at common law for their safekeeping. The policy for this sweeping liability is summarized by John McNeil, Q.C. in his text *Motor Carrier Cargo Claims*, 3rd ed. (Toronto: Carswell, 1997) at p. 3 in these terms:

> [T]he cargo owner's separation from his cargo involves relinquishment of any opportunity to protect it; the carrier's exclusive possession gives the carrier exclusive access to all evidentiary considerations in the event of a loss; the ability of the owner to prove a cause of action based on fault would be completely illusory; and imposing liability without fault on the carrier would encourage his diligence and care in the safeguard of the cargo.

Eventually it was found that commercial realities required a limit to that liability. The carrier has no means of knowing the value of the goods and, even if it did, the cost of insurance for the most valuable of goods in a cargo would impose prohibitive charges on the consignor of lesser valued goods. Thus statutes or regulations emerged maintaining the concept of absolute liability but limiting that liability to a declared value or, more often, to a value measured by weight. In this fashion the consignor can either insure the goods or bear the risk of their loss or damage, knowing the value of such goods. The carrier also bears some risk, which will act as an incentive to act prudently, while knowing that the extent of liability is tied to the weight of the goods being transported.

Provisions similar to those under our *Truck Transportation Act* are found in each of the provinces and extend internationally in treaties such as the Warsaw Convention, 1929, applying in Canada to international carriage by air, and the Hague-Visby Rules in respect of international carriage by water.

Thus we have a legislative policy that has developed over many years, permeates all facets of the transportation of goods industry and is based upon a sensible business and commercial rationale. I see no policy basis for not applying the limitation provision against the respondents in the present case. To the contrary, allowing the respondents' claim opens the door to every imaginable complaint of misfeasance and would undermine the entire structure built up under this longstanding policy.

The incident that gave rise to the present litigation fits precisely within the policy and the wording of condition 9 of the regulation. The appellants were in the course of performing a common carriage and a misadventure occurred which, at most, could be found to be caused in part by their negligence. It was the manner of performance, not the failure to perform which was the subject of complaint. On their part, the householders recognized the burden of risk and sought out their own insurance, armed with knowledge of the goods' value that was essential to that task and not reasonably available to the moving company. The movers did know how many pounds they were carrying and thus could readily cover themselves with insurance to meet the statutory limit. In my view, this was how the regulation was intended to work in facilitating carriage of goods and it would be totally disruptive of its purpose if carriers are to be exposed to liability for undetermined amounts whenever, in the trial judge's words, "it would be unreasonable to enforce [the exemption]" or some standardless variation on those words.

In direct response to the reasons of Labrosse J.A., I do not agree that the standard of care is affected by the fact that the cargo was not "ordinary household goods". Movers should treat all belongings alike. If the goods were of special value then the consignors should have purchased a corresponding amount of insurance.

The fulcrum of Labrosse J.A.'s argument seems to be that the respondents were induced to accept the limited liability by false assurances that their goods would be secure. ... [A]ssurances that the goods would be kept secure are superfluous in a contract of bailment. That is so because a carrier's obligation to keep their consignment secure is implicit in every contract of carriage of goods. The assurances did not need to be made explicit. Aside from being superfluous, there was nothing false about the assurances. The overnight storage on the street was not anticipated. It was, at the highest, a negligent performance of the duty to keep the goods secure. Finally, there was no inducement because the limitation of liability was mandated by statute. ...

[Appeal allowed in part on a matter not addressed in the above extract, but otherwise dismissed.]

QUESTIONS

1. How was the majority able to ignore entirely the fact that the limitation of liability clause was prescribed by statute? Apart from any issue about the primacy of legislation, how could it be unconscionable to enforce a clause mandated by statute?

2. The defendant had presumably insured on the basis of its potential statutory and contractual liability. The plaintiffs had taken out additional insurance coverage. Why should the loss above the statutory limit be shifted from the plaintiffs' insurer on to the defendant personally? If the plaintiffs had failed to insure or, as was apparently the case, had underinsured, why should the defendant be responsible to the plaintiffs who were aware of the limitation of liability and who presumably knew the value of their own goods?

Chapter 9

MISTAKE

1. Introduction

The law of contract generally adopts an unsympathetic stance reflected, for instance, in the principle of *caveat emptor*, toward parties who have made mistakes which were not caused by misrepresentations. Disappointed house buyers, investors, tenants, car purchasers, etc., are left to bear the costs of their own mistakes. Thus, mistake often seems to operate as an argument of last resort for an aggrieved party who is unable to fit within other categories of relief. Most cases which can be broadly categorized as involving a mistake are routinely dealt with in other areas of contract law. For example, the disappointed purchasers in the cases considered in Chapter 7, section 3 can readily be described as mistaken. In *Dick Bentley Productions Ltd. v. Harold Smith (Motors) Ltd.*, the purchaser was mistaken about the condition of the car, in *Oscar Chess Ltd. v. Williams*, which is considered within the extract from *Dick Bentley Productions Ltd.*, the buyer was mistaken about the model year of the car, and in *Leaf International Galleries* about whether the painting was a genuine Constable. In all of these cases, the courts dealt with the problem as one involving the law relating to misrepresentations and terms. Only in *Leaf* was there even a suggestion that the purchaser's mistake might have any independent significance.

Similarly, many mistake issues can be analysed using doctrines relating to the formation of the contract, such as offer, acceptance and certainty of terms. For instance, the phenomenon of mistakes in the tendering process was touched on in Chapter 2, section 2. This chapter returns to mistake issues in the formation of a contract in more detail.

The reality that a remedy for mistake is rare outside of the analysis of formation and representations and terms suggests a fruitful analytical approach. It is often helpful to consider whether any of the ordinary categories of contract law provide a response to the problem. Thus, for instance, one party may have been mistaken about the other's intentions so that no agreement has been reached. If the contract was formed, relief might be available for a misrepresentation or the breach of a term that covers one party's mistake or, in the absence of a misrepresentation or breach, the buyer may have taken the risk that the subject matter of the contract is different than expected, as in *Oscar Chess Ltd.* If the ordinary categories do not supply a remedy, then as a second step it is necessary to explore whether there is any applicable independent doctrine of mistake which provides relief.

This exploration is complicated by several related factors. First, the doctrine has developed in a somewhat disorderly way. The Ontario Law Reform Commission noted in the *Report on Amendment of the Law of Contract* (1987), at 252:

> There is great uncertainty about what the present Anglo-Canadian law of mistake is. No two authors agree in their analysis of it and the same confusion exists in the case law. Reputable scholars often disagree about the interpretation of the same case. Some scholars deny altogether that English contract law recognizes an independent doctrine of mistake. Others acknowledge its existence but give it a very limited scope while a third group is prepared to concede the doctrine of mistake a substantially larger role. . . . Further difficulties arise because equity has asserted a jurisdiction in this area that is significantly wider and more flexible than the jurisdiction exercised by the common law courts. However, no one is quite sure how the two bodies of rules mesh (if indeed they mesh at all) and what the precise boundary is between them.

Second, there are inconsistencies in the vocabulary used to describe recurring problems. However, a useful distinction, reflected in the organisation of this chapter, is between mistake as to the terms of the contract and mistake as to assumptions, or facts. This distinction may be subtle in its application to the facts of particular cases. For example, did B mistakenly think she was buying a cat that was white (an assumption to which the principle of *caveat emptor* would apply) or did she mistakenly think A was promising to sell her a cat that was white (a mistake as to a term which would require the court to consider whether a contract had been formed).

As well, the following labels, from Cheshire, Fifoot and Furmston, *The Law of Contract* 14th ed., (2001), at 252-253, are sometimes, though far from consistently, used, perhaps because it is a matter of debate whether they contribute a great deal to the functional analysis of mistake problems.

Common Mistake

This term may be used to describe a situation where the parties have the same mistaken perception. They have reached agreement but share a common mistake about an important fact. For example, A agrees to buy B's car, located in the parking lot. Unknown to both of them, the car was destroyed by fire a few minutes before they reached agreement.

Mutual Mistake

This term may be used to indicate that both parties are mistaken but do not share the same mistake. They are at cross-purposes. Here, unlike the analysis of common mistake, the question is whether they reached agreement at all. For example, A owns a black cat and a white cat. A intends to offer the black cat for sale, but B, the would-be buyer, believes that A's offer refers to the white cat.

Unilateral Mistake

This term may be used to describe a situation where one party makes a mistake, while the other knows of it. For example, A is negotiating to sell her car for a price in the region of $5,000. A sends a formal offer of sale to B by e-mail, but accidentally omits a zero, so that the e-mail reads "I hereby offer to sell you my car for $500." This analysis has even been used in cases of mistaken identity induced by fraud, which are discussed in section 4 of this chapter.

In practice, courts tend to deal with cases of mutual and unilateral mistake by asking whether a contract was properly formed. In contrast, in cases of common mistake courts tend to assume that a contract has been properly formed and to view the issues as a matter of contractual interpretation and who should bear the costs of a shared mistaken assumption.

The following materials will consider first cases which involve mistake as to terms. These commonly raise issues of mutual and unilateral mistake. Section 3 deals with mistaken assumptions, mostly relating to common mistake. The final section raises issues of mistake and the interests of third parties.

2. Mistake as to Terms

(a) APPROACHES TO INTERPRETATION

LINDSEY v. HERON & CO.

(1921), 50 O.L.R. 1, 64 D.L.R. 92 (C.A.)

MIDDLETON J. The law applicable to this case is most clearly expressed in Corpus Juris, vol. 13, p. 265:

> The apparent mutual assent of the parties essential to the formation of a contract must be gathered from the language employed by them, and the law imputes to a person an intention corresponding to the reasonable meaning of his words and acts. It judges of his intention by his outward expressions and excludes all questions in regard to his unexpressed intention. If his words or acts, judged by a reasonable standard, manifest an intention to agree in regard to the matter in question, that agreement is established, and it is immaterial what may be the real but unexpressed state of his mind on the subject.
>
> If, whatever a man's real intention may be, he so conducts himself that a reasonable man would believe that he was assenting to the terms proposed by the other party, and that other party upon that belief enters into the contract with him, the man thus conducting himself would be equally bound as if he had intended to agree to the other party's terms. . . .

. . . Here the vital parts of the transaction are the question put by the plaintiff to the defendants, "What will you give me for 75 shares of Eastern Cafeterias of Canada?" To which the defendants' manager in effect answered: "I shall look into it and let you know." The defendants' manager made such inquiry as he saw fit, and then telephoned the plaintiff, "I will give you $10.50 a share for your Eastern Cafeterias," and the plaintiff replied "I accept your offer," He then delivered his Eastern Cafeterias of Canada Limited and received the cheque sued upon. The defendants' manager now says that he meant to buy "Eastern Cafeterias Limited," another stock and so, the parties not being *ad idem*, there was no contract.

Applying the principles quoted above, I cannot agree. I think that, judged by any reasonable standard, the words used by the defendants manifested an intention to offer the named price for the thing which the plaintiff proposed to sell, i.e., stock in the Eastern Cafeterias of Canada Limited. Had the plaintiff spoken of "Eastern Cafeterias," the words used would have been ambiguous, and

I should find no contract, for each might have used the ambiguous term in a different sense; but the defendants, by use of these ambiguous terms in response to the plaintiff's request couched in unambiguous language, must be taken to have used it in the same sense. . . . The appeal should be dismissed.

LENNOX J. [dissenting]. . . . I am not assailing the findings of fact; I am, however, with respect, very decidedly of opinion that, admitting every fact as found and every legitimate inference of fact, the plaintiff was not entitled to recover. Counsel for the plaintiff, "as he lawfully might," both at the trial and on the argument of the appeal, very adroitly kept away from the fundamental issue, "What did the defendants offer to buy?"

Nobody is likely to controvert the soundness of the proposition of law upon which the decision at the trial manifestly turned, and which was so much dwelt upon during the argument of the appeal, namely: "If whatever a man's real intention may be, he so conducts himself that a reasonable man would believe that he was assenting to the terms proposed by the other party, and that other party upon that belief enters into the contract with him, the man thus conducting himself would be equally bound as if he had intended to agree to the other party's terms:" *Freeman v. Cooke* (1848), 154 E.R. 652, as paraphrased in *Smith v. Hughes* [*infra*]. But *Freeman v. Cooke* was a case of estoppel, and the defendants here were entitled to offer to buy what they liked, and to refuse to accept what they did not offer to buy, however similar in name, and even if it were "just as good"—which it was not. Their offer was the beginning of the contract—I do not mean the beginning of communication—it was the first step in the negotiation. The action was decided and the judgment supported on appeal as if the alleged contract were made out in this way: an offer by the plaintiff to sell 75 shares of Eastern Cafeterias of Canada Limited; a telephone reply from the defendants to the plaintiff that they "would be willing to pay $10.50 a share;" and acceptance by the plaintiff by delivery of 75 shares of Eastern Cafeterias of Canada and receipt of cheque. If this had been what occurred, this would, I think, constitute a binding contract, even though the defendants, by mistake, inquired about the wrong stock, to wit "Eastern Cafeterias Limited," and, in consequence, were misled as to the value. The plaintiff upon this assumption had done all he was called upon to do, and the appeal might quite properly be decided against the defendants. . . .

This, however, is not what occurred; there was no offer by the plaintiff to sell anything. I let the plaintiff speak for himself, and to his own counsel upon examination in chief, and for the rest I quote from the reasons for judgment:—

Q. Then what did you do?

A. When I went back from lunch to the office I phoned up Heron & Company.

Q. Do you know to whom you spoke?

A. I found out afterwards it was Mr. Lewis.

Q. What was the conversation?

A. I asked him for a quotation on 75 shares of Eastern Cafeterias of Canada Limited stock.

Q. What was his answer to that?

> A. He told me that he would have to find out and he would let me know in the course of half an hour or so . . .
>
> Q. When next did you have any conversation with Mr. Lewis?
>
> A. About half an hour later . . .
>
> Q. What did he say to you?
>
> A. He told me he would be willing to pay $10.50 a share for the stock.

He did not say "for the stock," he said "for Eastern Cafeterias," as sworn to by two witnesses and found by the Judge.

I quote from the reasons for judgment:—

> Lewis, on the other hand, says the name he gave him was 'Eastern Cafeterias Limited,' and at this time

(that is, when the plaintiff telephoned asking for a quotation)

> neither the plaintiff nor Lewis nor Heron & Company knew anything about the old company being reorganised, or that there was or had been any more than one company, and I think the defendants were not very clear about the exact name of the original company, and assumed that the one respecting which the inquiry of the plaintiff made was 'Eastern Cafeterias Limited.'
>
> Mr. Lewis told the plaintiff to wait a short time. He thereupon wired his Montreal agents and got a quotation on 'Eastern Cafeterias Limited,' and thereupon called up the plaintiff on the phone and made him an offer of $10.50 per share for his 75 shares.

(The learned Judge inadvertently used the word "his," as is shown by what immediately follows).

> Lewis says in making this offer he used the name 'Eastern Cafeterias Limited,' but the plaintiff says that, as brokers always abbreviate the names of companies when referring to them, especially in conversation, he assumed, quite naturally, that, even if Mr. Lewis did abbreviate the name, this was the company he mentioned to him.

The last sentence quoted is surely conclusive. I quite agree that the plaintiff "assumed quite naturally" that the defendants were referring to "his 75 shares." We are all prone to assume that other people are thinking of what for the time being is uppermost in our own thoughts; but the question is not what he assumed, but what the others said, and their offer was to buy "Eastern Cafeterias," leaving out it may be the word "Limited," common to both. The mistake was in beginning at the wrong point, and one result of it is a misapplication of the doctrine of *Freeman v. Cooke*. Quite too much importance was attached to the question as to whether or not the plaintiff used the words "of Canada" when he inquired for prices in the morning. The question is of no consequence whatever except in so far as it might assist in determining the weight of evidence. If the plaintiff did inquire as to Eastern Cafeterias of Canada Limited, there is no finding that he made himself understood: on the contrary, it is specifically found that the defendants understood him to ask about Eastern Cafeterias, wired to their agents in Montreal in consequence, asking a quotation on this stock, and, having received a quotation, and acting upon it, 'phoned the plaintiff offering $10.50 per share for Eastern Cafeterias. There was no duty cast upon the defendants to find out what the plaintiff had to sell—he hardly knew himself for that matter—the defendants' offer to the plaintiff had a definite legal and commercial meaning; and the plaintiff could not alter its meaning by attempting to deliver something else.

There is no getting away from the fact that the alleged contract took this form:—

(a) An offer by the defendants to purchase 75 shares of Eastern Cafeterias Limited.

(b) A nominal or apparent acceptance by the plaintiff by delivery of a certificate for 75 shares of Eastern Cafeterias of Canada Limited, and receipt of a cheque in payment, on the understanding, common to both parties at the time, that the certificate was for the shares the defendant offered to buy.

It is to no purpose to suggest that the defendants would not have appreciated the difference if they had noticed the words "of Canada" on the face of the certificate. It is not to any purpose, either, to argue that they were lacking in vigilance. On discovery they promptly repudiated the transaction, and the plaintiff had not "altered his position" in the meantime. The matter appears to me to be very simple. There was no agreement. The parties were never of one mind, they were not referring to the same thing—there was no *consensus ad idem*. There must be mutual assent, and to the same thing, and in the same sense—without this there can be no contract. . . .

[Appeal dismissed.]

QUESTION

"The courts enforce apparent agreement rather than hidden states of mind." Why? In what other contexts have you noticed that the law of contracts is concerned with interpreting words and actions objectively rather than subjectively?

STAIMAN STEEL LTD. v. COMMERCIAL & HOME BUILDERS LTD.

(1976), 13 O.R. (2d) 315, 71 D.L.R. (3d) 17 (H.C.)

SOUTHEY J. This is an action for damages for breach of an alleged contract for the sale of goods from the defendant Commercial & Home Builders Limited ("Commercial") to the plaintiff. The contract was alleged to have been made by the defendant F. Caldarone Auctions Limited ("Caldarone Auctions") as agent for Commercial at an auction sale conducted by Caldarone Auctions on the premises of Commercial on June 15, 1972. . . .

[In the course of an auction, the plaintiff had made a successful bid for a bulk lot of steel. He gave evidence that he understood the lot to include both building steel and used steel, while the defendants gave evidence that the lot consisted of used steel only. The defendants had refused to deliver any of the steel to the plaintiff because he would not sign a waiver to the effect that the lot did not include the building steel. The judge held that the bulk lot did not include the building steel.]

Counsel for Commercial sought to justify the position . . . taken by Commercial on the ground that if the plaintiff intended to buy a bulk lot containing the building steel, whereas Commercial intended to sell a lot without that steel, then there was no *consensus ad idem* and, therefore, no contract for the sale of any steel.

Counsel for Commercial relied on *Raffles v. Wichelhaus* (1864), 159 E.R. 375, involving two ships named "Peerless" which sailed from Bombay, one in October and one in December, . . . [in which case the court] held that there was no contract, apparently because there was no *consensus ad idem*.

Counsel for the plaintiff, on the other hand, relied on the basic rule of contract law that it is not a party's actual intention that determines contractual relationships, but rather the intention manifested by the words and actions of the parties . . . [based on the first paragraph of the judgment of Middleton J. in *Lindsey v. Heron & Co., supra.*]

[Counsel] submitted that if the Court found that the building steel was not a part of the bulk lot, then the result should not be a finding that there was no contract. He contended that there should then be a finding that there was a contract for the sale of the lot without the building steel, even though it was not the plaintiff's intention to bid for the lot without the building steel.

In my judgment the plaintiff must succeed on this secondary point. The basis of the successful defence by Commercial on the first point is that the circumstances were such that a reasonable man would infer that the auctioneer, despite his words, was manifesting an intention to offer for sale the bulk lot without the building steel. By making the highest bid, Staiman so conducted himself that a reasonable man would believe that he was assenting to the purchase of that lot. A contract for the sale of that lot to the plaintiff thereupon came into existence. That contract was never subsequently repudiated by Staiman. The plaintiff was at all times willing to take delivery of and to pay for the bulk lot without the building steel, which was what Commercial and Caldarone Auctions said was the subject of the contract of sale, although the plaintiff made it quite clear that it might still commence proceedings to establish that the bulk lot should have included the building steel.

Commercial had the right to insist that the plaintiff take delivery and pay for the bulk lot excluding the building steel, but Commercial had no right, in my judgment, to require the plaintiff to give up its claim that the contract included the building steel as well as the remainder of the bulk lot. By insisting on such waiver or acknowledgement, Commercial was attempting to introduce unilaterally a new term into the contract of sale.

If, as appears to have been the case, the plaintiff thought the bulk lot he was purchasing included the building steel and the defendants thought that the bulk lot they were selling did not include the building steel, then the case was one of mutual mistake, as that expression is used in Cheshire and Fifoot's *Law of Contract*, 8th ed. (1972), p. 221. In such a case, the Court must decide what reasonable third parties would infer to be the contract from the words and conduct of the parties who entered into it. It is only a case where the circumstances are so ambiguous that a reasonable bystander could not infer a common intention that the Court will hold that no contract was created. As pointed out in Cheshire and Fifoot at p. 212:

> If the evidence is so conflicting that there is nothing sufficiently solid from which to infer a contract in any final form without indulging in mere speculation, the court must of necessity declare that no contract whatsoever has been created.

In this case, in my judgment, a reasonable man would infer the existence of a contract to buy and sell the bulk lot without the building steel and therefore I have held that there was a contract to that effect binding on both parties, notwithstanding such mutual mistake.

The case is quite unlike *Raffles v. Wichelhaus* . . . because, in [that case], it was impossible for the Court to impute any definite agreements to the parties.

In *Raffles v. Wichelhaus*, the Court had no more reason to find that both parties had manifested an intention to deal in cotton shipped on the "Peerless" sailing in October than to deal with cotton shipped in the "Peerless" sailing in December . . .

By refusing to deliver any steel from the bulk lot to the plaintiff, Commercial has clearly breached its contract for the sale of such bulk lot to the plaintiff. It remains to assess the damages suffered by the plaintiff because of such breach of contract.

[The damages were assessed at $16,436.]

NOTE

Both cases considered so far resolve the issue of mistake by enquiring into the reasonable interpretation of the parties' words, objectively assessed. In principle, when is an objective approach not justified? Consider the following examples.

A offers to sell a black cat to B, a stranger. If A subsequently claims that A meant to sell a white cat, how should the court resolve the question of interpretation?

A offers to sell a black cat to C, a good friend, who knows that A suffers from a rare speech defect, so that every time that A says "black", A really means "white". How should a court determine whether the offer relates to a black cat or a white cat?

GLASNER v. ROYAL LEPAGE REAL ESTATE SERVICES LTD.

(1992), 28 R.P.R. (2d) 72 (B.C. S.C.)

The plaintiff listed his home for sale with a real estate agent. The defendants offered to buy the home when they signed an interim agreement which contained a warranty that the building did not, and had never been insulated with urea formaldehyde foam insulation ("UFFI"). The plaintiff knew that he could not accept such a warranty, as his house had once been insulated with UFFI, although he had had the material removed and there was now no trace of UFFI in the home. Rather than amend the defendants' offer, the plaintiff drew an entirely new interim agreement which warranted only that the home did not presently contain UFFI. The plaintiff instructed his real estate agent not to tell the defendants that there had once been UFFI in the home and the defendants signed the plaintiff's version of the interim agreement. The plaintiff's real estate agent went against her instructions and told the defendants that the house had once contained UFFI. The defendants refused to complete the transaction or to tender the agreed deposit. The plaintiff sued to recover the deposit and, in an application for summary judgment, the court dealt with the question of a unilateral mistake as to a material term.

SPENCER J. [in Chambers] . . . With respect to the duty on one party who knows, or should have known, that the other is concluding a contract under a unilateral mistake about a material term, I respectfully adopt the words of Grange J., as he then was, in *Stepps Investments Ltd. v. Security Capital Corp.* (1976), 73 D.L.R. (3d) 351 (H.C.), at p. 364:

> In the circumstances of this case I believe that the plaintiffs should have known of the mistake made by the defendant and I believe it would be equitable accordingly to grant relief to the defendant. It is not unreasonable, in my view, in modern commercial relations, to require the parties, where an important amendment is being made, to ensure that knowledge of such amendment comes to the other side. I do not mean that a party must overcome obtuseness in his opposite number but he must at least give him a real opportunity to appreciate the change. And if the circumstances are such that the amendment might readily be missed he should be particularly reluctant to assume such knowledge. Here the plaintiffs could have resolved the whole problem by a clear reference to the amendment in the correspondence or in the recitals or the operative parts of the agreement itself. It could even have been resolved in a clear, unambiguous, oral conversation with the defendant's solicitors and I cannot find that such a clear and unambiguous conversation ever took place.

There were other authorities cited to me by counsel for the intending pur-chasers for the same proposition, including *Beverly Motel (1972) Ltd. v. Klyne Properties Ltd.* (1981), 126 D.L.R. (3d) 757 (S.C.); *McMaster University v. Wilchar Construction Ltd.*, [*infra*, section 2(b)]; *First City Capital Ltd. v. British Columbia Building Corp.* (1989), 43 B.L.R. 29 (B.C. S.C.), and *Windjammer Homes Inc. v. Generation Enterprises* (1989), 43 B.L.R. 315 (B.C. S.C.). The thrust of those authorities is to show that equity will relieve against performance of a contract obtained by a party who knew the other side was mistaken about a material fact and who took advantage of that mistake. . . .

Based upon those authorities, where a plaintiff comes to equity seeking specific performance of a contract, the courts may refuse performance because of the defendant's mistake about a material term of which the plaintiff was or should have been aware. That is particularly so where the cause of the defendant's mistake was the plaintiff's calculated decision to say nothing about a change he has made in the terms of the contract under negotiation.

[Action dismissed.]

(b)   "SNAPPING UP" A MISTAKEN OFFER

The idea expressed in the *Glasner* decision, that there should be relief when one party knew that the other had made a mistake is raised also in a group of cases where the question arises whether an offeree who knows that an offer is mistaken in some way should be permitted to "snap it up". In *Hartog v. Colin & Shields*, [1939] 3 All E.R. 566 (K.B.), the parties had been negotiating the sale of Argentinian hare skins and had discussed a possible sale at a price of 10 3/4 pence per piece. By mistake, the defendants offered the goods at 10-1/4 pence per pound, which corresponded to a price of approximately 3 3/4 pence per piece. The court found that the plaintiff must have realized a mistake had occurred before "snapping up" the offer and his claim for breach of contract was therefore denied.

The *Hartog* case, which involved a mistake as to terms, may be contrasted with *Imp. Glass Ltd. v. Consol. Supplies Ltd.* (1960), 22 D.L.R. (2d) 759 (B.C.C.A.). The appellant, Imperial, had been invited to bid on the supply and installation of window glass on a construction project. Prior to submitting a bid, Imperial sought a quotation from the respondent whose employee inadvertently calculated the square footage at one-tenth of what it ought to have been. Based on this calculation, a price of $2,000 was quoted to Imperial, which in turn used this figure in calculating its own bid to the subcontractor. After its tender was accepted, Imperial requested and received written confirmation of the respondent's quotation of $2,000 and placed its order with the respondent. Shortly after receiving the order the respondent discovered its mistake, notified the appellant that its purchase order was not accepted and rebuked the appellant for even sending the order since it must have known of the error.

The court agreed that the appellant knew of the respondent's mistake when it accepted the offer but held, at 763, that:

> The mistake was not in the offer. All that is claimed is that the offer would not have been made had the mistake been detected. The mistake was therefore in the motive or reason for making the offer, not in the offer. There was consequently a consensus and a valid contract.

In other words, there was no mistake as to the terms of the offer since the respondent always intended to offer the glass at the price quoted; instead, the mistake was in the assumption that the square footage was accurate and in the calculations based on that figure.

The decision in *Imperial Glass* has been strongly criticized (*e.g.*, see Carr, "Comment" (1961), 39 Can. Bar Rev. 625) and it has not prevented other courts from protecting a party whose mistaken offer had been "snapped up". In *McMaster Univ. v. Wilchar Const. Ltd.* (1971), 22 D.L.R. (3d) 9, affirmed without reasons 69 D.L.R. (3d) 400n (C.A.), the Ontario High Court gave a more reasoned decision. Thompson J. made some general comments on the law of mistake at 17-19:

> If the mistake is as to a term of the contract and is known to the other party, it will avoid the contract: see *Chitty on Contracts*, 23rd ed. (1968), vol. 1, p. 104, art. 211. Mistake merely as to the quality or the substance of the thing contracted for must be distinguished from mistake as to a term of the contract, for in the former case it will be an error merely as to motive which will not avoid a contract: *Chitty op. cit.*, p. 104, art. 212.
>
> In the application of any particular decided authority relating to the topic of mistake as applied to contracts, one must exercise caution. Not only is it a difficult and elusive topic, but some confusion has arisen in the cases as to the distinction between the legal and equitable principles to be applied. Although the fusion of law and equity has to some extent alleviated this situation, there still is a tendency to apply the more narrow common law principles where justice could more readily be done by the discretionary use of equitable remedy. Thus, it is that the principles upon which the Courts will intervene and the circumstances in which they will do so have not been precisely settled and the decided cases are open to a number of varying interpretations and are difficult to reconcile.
>
> The distinction between cases of common or mutual mistake and, on the other hand, unilateral mistake, must be kept in mind. In mutual or common mistake the error or mistake in order to avoid the contract at law, must have been based either upon a fundamental mistaken assumption as to the subject-matter of the contract or upon a mistake relating to a fundamental

term of the contract. There, the law applies the objective test as to the validity of the contract. Its rigour in this aspect has been designed to protect innocent third parties who have acquired rights under the contract.

Normally a man is bound by an agreement to which he has expressed assent. If he exhibits all the outward signs of agreement, at law it will be held that he has agreed. The exception to this is in the case where there has been fundamental mistake or error in the sense above stated. In such case, the contract is void *ab initio*. At law, in unilateral mistake, that is when a mistake of one party relating to the contract is known to the other party, the Courts will apply the subjective test and permit evidence of the intention of the mistaken party to be adduced. In such case, even if one party knows that the other is contracting under a misapprehension, there is, generally speaking, no duty cast upon him to disclose to the other circumstances which might affect the bargain known to him alone or to disillusion that other, unless the failure to do so under the circumstances would amount to fraud. This situation, of course, must be distinguished from the case in which the mistake is known to or realized by both parties prior to the acceptance of the offer.

The law also draws a distinction between mistake simply nullifying consent and mistake negativing consent. Error or mistake which negatives consent is really not mistake technically speaking in law at all, as it prevents the formation of contract due to the lack of consensus and the parties are never *ad idem*. It is rather an illustration of the fundamental principle that there can be no contract without consensus of all parties as to the terms intended. This is but another way of saying that the offer and the acceptance must be coincident or must exactly correspond before a valid contract results.

A promiser is not bound to fulfil a promise in a sense in which the promisee knew at the time that the promiser did not intend it. In considering this question, it matters not in what way the knowledge of the meaning is brought to the mind of the promisee, whether by express words, by conduct, previous dealings or other circumstances. If by any means he knows that there was no real agreement between him and the promisee, he is not entitled to insist that the promise be fulfilled in a sense to which the mind of the promiser did not assent. . . .

As a general rule, equity follows the law in its attitude towards contracts which are void by reason of mistake. If the contract is void at common law, equity will also treat it as a nullity. Equity, however, will intervene in certain cases to relieve against the rigours of the common law, even though the mistake would not be operative at law. If, for lack of consensus, no contract comes into existence, there, of course, is nothing to which an equity can attach. It is only in cases where the contract is not void at law that equity may afford relief by declaring the contract voidable. It gives relief for certain types of mistakes which the common law disregards and its remedies are more flexible. Thus, equity does not require the certainty which had led to the narrow common law doctrine of fundamental mistake. It seeks rather the more broad and more elastic approach by attempting to do justice and to relieve against hardship. In equity, to admit of correction, mistake need not relate to the essential substance of the contract, and provided that there is mistake as to the promise or as to some material term of the contract, if the Court finds that there has been honest, even though inadvertent, mistake, it will afford relief in any case where it considers that it would be unfair, unjust or unconscionable not to correct it: *Hartog v. Colin & Shields*, *supra*.

A similar approach was taken in *Belle River Community Arena Inc. v. W.J.C. Kaufmann Co.* (1978), 87 D.L.R. (3d) 761 (Ont. C.A.), a case involving a mistake in a tender. Kaufmann had submitted a tender to build the Belle River Community Arena for $641,603. After the tenders had been opened and it transpired that the Kaufmann tender was the lowest, Kaufmann discovered an error amounting to $70,800 in the tender. Kaufmann sent a telegram: "Re new Tri-Community arena building please withdraw our quotation dated January 11, 1973 due to a serious error in our tender." Belle River then tried to accept the tender, but was found to be unable to do so.

The *Belle River* decision was discussed by the Supreme Court of Canada in the following case, which has had an enormous impact on the application of the law of mistake in tenders.

R. v. RON ENGINEERING & CONSTRUCTION (EASTERN) LTD.

[1981] 1 S.C.R. 111, 13 B.L.R. 72, 119 D.L.R. (3d) 267, 35 N.R. 40

[Re-read the extract from this case in Chapter 2, section 2, in which the court found that the contractor's tender was irrevocable.]

ESTEY J. [delivering the judgment of the court] The Ontario Court of Appeal, reversing the trial Judge, directed the return to the respondent-contractor (hereinafter referred to as the "contractor") of $150,000 paid by the contractor to the appellant-owner (hereinafter referred to as the "owner") by way of a tender deposit at the time of filing a bid in response to a call for tenders by the owner. . . .

The core of the submission by the contractor is simply that a mistake by a tenderer, be it patent or latent, renders the tender revocable or the deposit recoverable by the tenderer, . . . so long as notice is given to the owner of the mistake prior to the acceptance by the owner of the contractor's tender. There are subsidiary arguments advanced by the contractor to which I will later make reference.

We are not here concerned with a case where the mistake committed by the tendering contractor is apparent on the face of the tender. Rather the mistake here involved is one which requires an explanation outside of the tender documents themselves. The trial Judge has so found and there is evidence in support of that finding. Nor do we have here a case where a trial Court has found impropriety on the part of the contractor such as the attempted recall of an intended, legitimate bid once the contractor has become aware that it is the lowest bidder by a wide margin. . . .

Relying on its decision in *Belle River Community Arena Inc. v. W.J.C. Kaufmann Co. Ltd. et al* [*supra*], decided by the Court of Appeal after the trial judgment herein had been handed down, the Court of Appeal concluded "that an offeree cannot accept an offer which he knows has been made by mistake and which affects a fundamental term of the contract". The Court, speaking through Arnup J.A., continued [(1979), 98 D.L.R. (3d) 548 at 550]:

> In our view, the principles enunciated in that case ought to be applied in this case. The error in question has been found to be, as it obviously was, material and important. It was drawn to the attention of the Commission almost at once after the opening of tenders. Notwithstanding that, the Commission proceeded as if the error had not been made and on the footing that it was entitled to treat the tender for what it said on its face.

and concluded [pp. 550-1]:

> As I said in the course of the argument, a commission or other owner calling for tenders is entitled to be sceptical when a bidder who is the low tenderer by a very substantial amount attempts to say, after the opening of tenders, that a mistake has been made. However, when that mistake is proven by the production of reasonable evidence, the person to whom the tender is made is not in a position to accept the tender or to seek to forfeit the bid deposit.

In the *Belle River* case the contractor purported to withdraw the tender before any action to accept was taken by the owner. . . . Arnup J.A. in that case found that the owner was unable to accept the offer once he became aware that it contained a mistake which affected a fundamental term of the contract. At p. 766 D.L.R., the learned Justice in Appeal put it this way:

> In substance, the purported offer, because of the mistake, is not the offer the offeror intended to make, and the offeree knows that.
>
> The principle applies even if there is a provision binding the offeror to keep the offer open for acceptance for a given period.

And continuing on p. 767 D.L.R.:

> In view of the conclusion I have reached as to the inability of the plaintiff to accept the tender, it does not matter, in my opinion, whether the purported tender could be withdrawn, or was in fact withdrawn, before the purported acceptance.
>
> .....
>
> If Kaufmann's tender could be withdrawn before acceptance (as occurred in *Hamilton Bd. Ed.* case, *supra* [*Hamilton Bd. Ed. v. U.S.F. & G.*, [1960] O.R. 594]), then Kauffman's [*sic*] tender was so withdrawn, and no contract came into existence. If it could not be withdrawn for 60 days, it nevertheless could not be accepted, for the reason already stated, and hence no contract came into existence.

This judgment is the basis for that given by the Court of Appeal in these proceedings. . . .

[The court then concluded that the tender was irrevocable on the basis of the contract "A" analysis set out in Chapter 2, section 2.]

We are then left with the bare submission on behalf of the contractor that while the offer was not withdrawn it was not capable of acceptance and that by reason thereof the contractor is entitled to a return of the deposit.

I share the view expressed by the Court of Appeal that integrity of the bidding system must be protected where under the law of contracts it is possible so to do. I further share the view expressed by that Court that there may be circumstances where a tender may not be accepted as for example where in law it does not constitute a tender, and hence the bid deposit might not be forfeited. That is so in my view, however, simply because contract A cannot come into being. It puts it another way to say that the purported tender does not in law amount to an acceptance of the call for tenders and hence the unilateral contract does not come into existence. Therefore, with the greatest of respect, I diverge from that Court where it is stated in the judgment below [p. 551]:

> However, when that mistake is proven by the production of reasonable evidence, the person to whom the tender is made is not in a position to accept the tender or to seek to forfeit the deposit.

The test, in my respectful view, must be imposed at the time the tender is submitted and not at some later date after a demonstration by the tenderer of a calculation error. Contract A (being the contract arising forthwith upon the submission of the tender) comes into being forthwith and without further formality upon the submission of the tender. If the tenderer has committed an error in the calculation leading to the tender submitted with the tender deposit, and at least in those circumstances where at that moment the tender is capable of acceptance in law, the rights of the parties under contract A have thereupon crystallized. The tender deposit, designed to ensure the performance of the obligations of the tenderer under contract A, must therefore stand exposed to the risk of forfeiture upon the breach of those obligations by the tenderer. Where the conduct of the tenderer might indeed expose him to other claims in damages by the owner, the tender deposit might well be the lesser pain to be suffered by reason of the error in the preparation of the tender. This I will return to later.

Much argument was undertaken in the Court on the bearing of the law of mistake on the outcome of this appeal. In approaching the application of the principles of mistake it is imperative here to bear in mind that the only contract up to now in existence between the parties to this appeal is the contract arising on the submission of the tender whereunder the tender is irrevocable during the period of time stipulated in the contract. Contract B (the construction contract, the form of which is set out in the documents relating to the call for tenders) has not and did not come into existence. We are concerned therefore with the law of mistake, if at all, only in connection with contract A.

.....

There is no question of a mistake on the part of either party up to the moment in time when contract A came into existence. The employee of the respondent intended to submit the very tender submitted, including the price therein stipulated. Indeed, the president, in instructing the respondent's employee, intended the tender to be as submitted. However, the contractor submits that as the tender was the product of a mistake in calculation, it cannot form the basis of a construction contract since it is not capable of acceptance and hence it cannot be subject to the terms and conditions of contract A so as to cause a forfeiture thereunder of the deposit. The fallacy in this argument is twofold. Firstly, there was no mistake in the sense that the contractor did not intend to submit the tender as in form and substance it was. Secondly, there is no principle in law under which the tender was rendered incapable of acceptance by the appellant. For a mutual contract such as contract B to arise, there must of course be a meeting of minds, a shared *animus contrahendi*, but when the contract in question is the product of other contractual arrangements, different considerations apply. However, as already stated, we never reach that problem here as the rights of the parties fall to be decided according to the tender arrangements, contract A. At the point when the tender was submitted the owner had not been told about the mistake in calculation. Unlike the case of *McMaster University v. Wilchar Const. Ltd.* [discussed earlier in this section] there was nothing on the face of the tender to reveal an error. There was no inference to be drawn by the quantum of the tender . . . that there had indeed been a miscalculation.

In . . . *McMaster University*, . . . the case appears to have turned upon the fact that the mistake was known to the offeree and therefore the offer could not be accepted and hence the formation of the contract could not occur. In that case the offer mistakenly omitted one page of the tender and the learned trial Judge, at p. 12 D.L.R., stated: "It undoubtedly must have been apparent to Mr. Hedden [employee of the owner], if not to the entire tender committee, that this page was missing from the Wilchar [contractor] tender as delivered." And again at p. 16

D.L.R.: "To me this is patently a case where the offeree, for its own advantage, snapped at the offeror's offer well knowing that the offer as made was made by mistake." The Court was therefore, in that case, not so much concerned with mistake as with the inability of the parties to comply on the facts with the fundamental rules pertaining to the formation of contracts. There could be no *consensus ad idem* and hence construction contract B could not come into being. More important to the issue now before us, the document submitted by the contractor was on its face incomplete and could not in law amount to a tender as required by the conditions established in the call for tenders.

It was not seriously advanced that this was a case of patent error in the tender offer and I proceed on the basis that there was not a patent error present.

On the facts as found by the learned trial Judge, no mistake existed which impeded or affected the coming into being of contract A. The "mistake" occurred in the calculations leading to the figures that the contractor admittedly intended to submit in his tender. Therefore, the issue in my view concerns not the law of mistake but the application of the forfeiture provisions contained in the tender documents. The effect a mistake may have on the enforceability or interpretation of a contract subsequently arising is an entirely different question, and one not before us. Neither are we here concerned with a question as to whether a construction contract can arise between parties in the presence of a mutually known error in a tender be it, at least initially, either patent or latent.

It might be argued that by some abstract doctrine of law a tender which could not form the basis of a contract upon acceptance in the sense of contract B, could not operate as a tender to bring into being contract A. It is unnecessary to consider such a theory because it was not and could not be argued that the tender as actually submitted by the contractor herein was not in law capable of acceptance immediately upon its receipt by the owner, the appellant. There may well be, as I have indicated, a situation in the contemplation of the law where a form of tender was so lacking as not to amount in law to a tender in the sense of the terms and conditions established in the call for tenders, and it may well be that such a form of tender could not be "snapped up" by the owner, as some cases have put it, and therefore it would not operate to trigger the birth of contract A. Such a situation might arise in the circumstances described in Fridman, *The Law of Contract in Canada* (1976), at p. 81: "An offer that is made in error, *e.g.*, as where the offeror intended to say $200 a ton but wrote $20 by mistake, may be an offer that cannot be validly accepted by the other party." . . . We do not have to decide that question here.

Nor are we concerned with the position of the parties where an action is brought upon a refusal to form contract B as was the case in *McMaster, supra*. It is true that the appellant-owner here has made a counterclaim for damages resulting from the refusal of the respondent to enter into the construction contract but such counterclaim was dismissed and the appeal herein is concerned only with the claim made by the respondent for the return of the tender deposit.

Left to itself, therefore, the law of contract would result in a confirmation of a dismissal by the learned trial Judge of the claim by the contractor for the return of the tender deposit. The terms of contract A, already set out, clearly indicate a contractual right in the owner to forfeit this money.

As the respondent has not raised the principle of the law of penalty as it applies to the retention of the deposit here by the appellant, it is not necessary to deal with that branch of the law . . .

For these reasons I would allow the appeal, set aside the order of the Court of Appeal, and restore the judgment of J. Holland J. at trial with costs, here and in all Courts below, to the appellant.

[Appeal allowed.]

NOTE and QUESTIONS

1. *Ron Engineering* involved the forfeiture of a deposit under contract A. The court expressly said that it was not dealing with the impact of mistake on contract B and thus the question remained whether mistake had any role to play with respect to contract B. In *Calgary (City) v. Northern Construction Co.* (1985), [1986] 2 W.W.R. 426 (Alta. C.A.), the trial judge had found in favour of a contractor who had submitted a mistaken tender on the ground that in that case the owner had accepted the contractor's tender and had sought damages for the contractor's refusal to perform the construction contract. The trial judge commented, at 433, that this "fact removes the case from a contract A situation and creates the contract B situation not considered by the Supreme Court of Canada in *Ron Engineering*". However, the Court of Appeal exploded any notion that *Ron Engineering* might have left open the possibility that a mistake in a tender, though ineffective in contract A, might still impair the validity of contract B. McDermid J.A. commented, at 600-601:

> By virtue of the terms of contract A, the city had the right to elect as to what contractor it would select to do the construction or in fact it could have refused to select any. Rather than considering the terminology of contract law and considering the tender of Northern as an offer and the city's selection of Northern as the acceptance of an offer, thus forming a new contract B, I think the situation, as I have said, is that the city was exercising a right granted it by contract A. One writer has compared the situation with a lease which grants an option to purchase. I think it may be also compared to where a manufacturer grants to a purchaser the right to purchase a manufactured article with rights of the purchaser to elect to purchase additional units of the article at a set price. If a mistake were made by the lessor or manufacturer in setting the purchase price which was not apparent at the time the contract was made, surely the time to consider whether the contract was enforceable was the time that it was made and not the time of the exercise of the option or right to purchase.
>
> If this is the correct view, the contractor is placed in a dilemma, for if he executes contract B I do not think he could then raise the question of mistake, while if he does not do so, he is in breach of contract A.
>
> In my opinion, therefore, contract B, the construction contract, would not come into being until such time as it was actually executed by both parties. In this case, contract B never came into being, for Northern refused to execute the construction contract sent it by the city.

As a result, the contractor's refusal to sign contract B because of the mistake in its tender constituted a breach of contract A. The City was thus entitled to recover as damages the difference between the contractor's tender and the second lowest tender, which the City accepted upon the contractor's refusal to sign contract B.

Northern Construction appealed to the Supreme Court of Canada, [1987] 2 S.C.R. 757. In judgments extending to two brief paragraphs each, McIntyre J. and Wilson J. dismissed the appeal as being governed by *Ron Engineering*. What role, if any, remains for the doctrine of mistake in the tendering system? Does this case mean that, in effect, contract B can be enforced irrespective of a mistake?

2. Do you think that there is a justifiable legal distinction between a mistake on the face of a tender and a mistake drawn to the attention of the other party five minutes after tenders have been opened? Are the courts not simply allowing owners to "snap up" offers which, at the time of acceptance, they know to be mistaken? How much reliance did the owner place on Ron Engineering's tender before it became aware of the mistake?

3. In *Hartog v. Colin & Shields and Belle River*, both discussed earlier, what considerations led the courts to say that the offeree could not take advantage of the mistakes in the respective offers?

Stripping away the technicalities of the contract A analysis, are there reasons why the same considerations should not apply to mistaken tenders?

On the same day that the Supreme Court of Canada handed down its judgment in *Ron Engineering*, it denied leave to appeal in *Metro Toronto v. Poole Const. Ltd.* (January 27, 1981, S.C.C. File No. 16038). In an unreported judgment (February 21, 1980) in that case, the Ontario Court of Appeal had again applied the reasoning of the *Belle River* case to prevent Metro Toronto from accepting the tender of a contractor which it knew to be mistaken. Initially, Metro Toronto had sought the advice of their consulting engineers on what to do with the contractor's mistaken tender. The engineers reported, in part:

> Based on the proceedings of our meeting of May 31st, we are of the opinion that Poole Construction Ltd. . . . truly made an inadvertent error in their tendered price in the amount of $537,988. Should they be required to execute a contract based on their tendered price, they will probably sustain a loss in excess of $250,000. This sum would represent a substantial fine to a convicted felon let alone an honest businessman who made a mistake at no one's expense but his own.
>
> We hold that everyone is due just recompense for honest labour, and that nothing is served by exacting one's pound of flesh. The second-low bid is still well within the project's budget estimate. We look upon a Bid Bond as a deterrent to frivolous tendering and not as a means of entrapping the unwary, albeit culpably negligent. It is realized that this line of thinking leads to the question: 'Where does one draw the line?'. We do not have the answer and believe, that as a general norm, there is none. We do not think, however, that a peril to maintaining precedent and ease of administration is any justification in this case to exact such an extreme penalty. . . .

> (*Metro Toronto v. Poole Constr. Ltd.* (1979), 10 M.P.L.R. 157, 159-160 (Ont. S.C.))

4. *Northern Construction* supports *Ron Engineering* despite trenchant criticism of the earlier case; see comments by Blom (1981), 6 Can. Bus. L.J. 80; Nozick (1982), 60 Can. Bar Rev. 345; Swan (1981), 15 U.B.C.L. Rev. 447. The whole issue of mistake in this context has attracted a great deal of academic interest. See, *e.g.*, Blom, "Three More Mistaken Bid Cases" (1987), 13 Can. Bus. L.J. 203, for a discussion of the trend of denying relief for mistake in order to preserve the stability of the tendering process. Should stability be the overriding concern? See also Rafferty, "Mistaken Tenders: An Examination of the Recent Case Law" (1985), 23 Alta. L. Rev. 491; Fridman, "Tendering Problems" (1987), 66 Can. Bar Rev. 582, and Percy, "Radical Developments in the Law of Tenders: A Canadian Re-formulation of Common Law Principles" (1988), 4 Const. L.J. 171.

5. The contract A analysis of *Ron Engineering* was soon extended to mistaken tenders made by subcontractors to general contractors. See *e.g.*, *Gloge Heating & Plumbing Ltd. v. Nor. Const. Co.*, [1986] 2 W.W.R. 649 (Alta. C.A.).

6. For many years *Ron Engineering* appeared to have closed the door in practice on successful mistake arguments in tender cases. The extent to which *Ron Engineering* contradicts the principle illustrated, for example, in *Glasner v. Royal Le Page Real Estate Services Ltd.*, *supra*, that an offeree should not benefit from a mistake in the offer which is known, or ought to be known, to the offeree was emphasized in a 1999 trial decision. In *Ottawa (City) Non-Profit Housing Corp v. Canvar Construction (1991) Inc.* (1999), 46 C.L.R. (2d) 116 (Ont. Gen Div.), the contractor, as the result of a clerical error, made a bid of $2,289,000 for a project, instead of the intended amount of $2,989,000. The contractor was required to submit a bid bond in the amount of five percent of its tender price and provided a bid bond in the amount of $149,450. The next lowest tender was $3,130,000. The owner nevertheless accepted the original tender of the contractor for $2,289,000 and the contractor

at trial was found liable for damages of $845,000 when it refused to perform the construction project at the tendered price.

The Ontario Court of Appeal reversed the decision (2000),13 O.A.C. 116, on the basis of the narrow exception that in this case the magnitude of the error and the amount of the bid bond meant that the mistake was apparent on the face of the tender, within the narrow exception left in *Ron Engineering*.

Although the decision of the Court of Appeal prevented the owner from receiving a huge windfall at the expense of the contractor, is there any reason why the contractor should be able to obtain a remedy for a mistake only in the case of an obviously defective tender or an error on the face of the tender, as *Ron Engineering* suggests?

7. In a separate judgment in *Calgary v. Northern Construction Co.*, *supra*, note 1, Kerans J.A. commented that before a contractor's mistake in a tender could affect the validity of the contract, it must be a mistake as to the terms of the contract. Kerans J.A. commented at 439 that the contractor's calculation error was not a mistake as to the terms of its offer and thus did not provide the basis for any relief to the contractor. This portion of the judgment of Kerans J.A. is based on the classic case of *Smith v. Hughes*, which is set out in the following extract.

SMITH v. HUGHES

(1871), L.R. 6 Q.B. 597 (Div. Ct.)

COCKBURN C.J. This was an action brought upon a contract for the sale of a quantity of oats by plaintiff to defendant, which contract the defendant had refused to complete, on the ground that the contract had been for the sale and purchase of *old* oats, whereas the oats tendered by the plaintiff had been oats of the last crop, and therefore not in accordance with the contract.

The plaintiff was a farmer, the defendant a trainer of racehorses. And it appeared that the plaintiff, having some good winter oats to sell, had applied to the defendant's manager to know if he wanted to buy oats, and having received for answer that he (the manager) was always ready to buy good oats, exhibited to him a sample, saying at the same time that he had forty or fifty quarters of the same oats for sale, at the price of 35*s*. per quarter. The manager took the sample, and on the following day wrote to say he would take the whole quantity at the price of 34*s*. a quarter.

Thus far the parties were agreed; but there was a conflict of evidence between them as to whether anything passed at the interview between the plaintiff and defendant's manager on the subject of the oats being *old* oats, the defendant asserting that he had expressly said that he was ready to buy old oats, and that the plaintiff had replied that the oats were old oats, while the plaintiff denied that any reference had been made to the oats being old or new.

The plaintiff having sent in a portion of the oats, the defendant, on meeting him afterwards, said, "Why those were new oats you sent me;" to which the plaintiff having answered, "I knew they were; I had none other." The defendant replied, "I though I was buying old oats: new oats are useless to me; you must take them back." This the plaintiff refused to do, and brought this action.

It was stated by the defendant's manager that trainers as a rule always use old oats, and that his own practice was never to buy new oats if he could get old.

But the plaintiff denied having known that the defendant never bought new oats, or that trainers did not use them; and, on the contrary, asserted that a trainer had recently offered him a price for new oats. Evidence was given for the defendant that 34*s*. a quarter was a very high price for new oats, and such as a prudent man of business would not have given. On the other hand, it appeared that oats were at the time very scarce and dear.

The learned judge of the county court left two questions to the jury: first, whether the word "old" had been used with reference to the oats in the conversation between the plaintiff and the defendant's manager; secondly, whether the plaintiff had believed that the defendant believed, or was under the impression, that he was contracting for old oats; in either of which cases he directed the jury to find for the defendant.

It is to be regretted that the jury were not required to give specific answers to the questions so left to them. For, it is quite possible that their verdict may have been given for the defendant on the first ground; in which case there could, I think, be no doubt as to the propriety of the judge's direction; whereas now, as it is possible that the verdict of the jury—or at all events of some of them—may have proceeded on the second ground, we are called upon to consider and decide whether the ruling of the learned judge with reference to the second question was right.

[Cockburn C.J. went on to discuss the principle of *caveat emptor.*]

It only remains to deal with an argument which was pressed upon us, that the defendant in the present case intended to buy old oats, and the plaintiff to sell new, so that the two minds were not ad idem; and that consequently there was no contract. This argument proceeds on the fallacy of confounding what was merely a motive operating on the buyer to induce him to buy with one of the essential conditions of the contract. Both parties were agreed as to the sale and purchase of this particular parcel of oats. The defendant believed the oats to be old, and was thus induced to agree to buy them, but he omitted to make their age a condition of the contract. All that can be said is, that the two minds were not ad idem as to the age of the oats; they certainly were ad idem as to the sale and purchase of them. Suppose a person to buy a horse without a warranty, believing him to be sound, and the horse turns out unsound, could it be contended that it would be open to him to say that, as he had intended to buy a sound horse, and the seller to sell an unsound one, the contract was void, because the seller must have known from the price the buyer was willing to give, or from his general habits as a buyer of horses, that he thought the horse was sound? The cases are exactly parallel.

The result is that, in my opinion, the learned judge of the county court was wrong in leaving the second question to the jury, and that, consequently, the case must go down to a new trial.

BLACKBURN J. In this case I agree that on the sale of a specific article, unless there be a warranty making it part of the bargain that it possesses some particular quality, the purchaser must take the article he has bought though it does not possess that quality. And I agree that even if the vendor was aware that the purchaser thought that the article possessed that quality, and would not have entered into the contract unless he had so thought, still the purchaser is bound, unless the vendor was guilty of some fraud or deceit upon him, and that a mere abstinence from disabusing the purchaser of that impression is not fraud or deceit; for, whatever may be the case in a court of morals, there is no legal obligation on the vendor to inform the purchaser that he is under a mistake, not induced by the act of the vendor. And I also agree that where a specific lot of goods are sold by a sample, which the purchaser inspects instead of the bulk, the law is exactly the same, if the sample truly represents the bulk; though, as it is more probable that the purchaser in such a case would ask for some further warranty, slighter evidence would suffice to prove that, in fact, it was intended there should be such a warranty. On this part of the case I have nothing to add to what the Lord Chief Justice has stated.

But I have more difficulty about the second point raised in the case. I apprehend that if one of the parties intends to make a contract on one set of terms, and the other intends to make a contract on another set of terms, or, as it is sometimes expressed, if the parties are not ad idem, there is no contract, unless the circumstances are such as to preclude one of the parties from denying that he has agreed to the terms of the other. The rule of law is that stated in *Freeman v. Cooke* [(1848), 154 E.R. 652]. If, whatever a man's real intention may be, he so conducts himself that a reasonable man would believe that he was assenting to the terms proposed by the other party, and that other party upon that belief enters into the contract with him, the man thus conducting himself would be equally bound as if he had intended to agree to the other party's terms.

The jury were directed that, if they believed the word "old" was used, they should find for the defendant—and this was right; for if that was the case, it is obvious that neither did the defendant intend to enter into a contract on the plaintiff's terms, that is, to buy this parcel of oats without any stipulation as to their quality; nor could the plaintiff have been led to believe he was intending to do so.

But the second direction raises the difficulty. I think that, if from that direction the jury would understand that they were first to consider whether they were satisfied that the defendant intended to buy this parcel of oats on the terms that it was part of his contract with the plaintiff that they were old oats, so as to have the warranty of the plaintiff to that effect, they were properly told that, if that was so, the defendant could not be bound to a contract without any such warranty unless the plaintiff was misled. But I doubt whether the direction would bring to the minds of the jury the distinction between agreeing to take the oats under the belief that they were old, and agreeing to take the oats under the belief that the plaintiff contracted that they were old.

The difference is the same as that between buying a horse believed to be sound, and buying one believed to be warranted sound; but I doubt if it was made obvious to the jury, and I doubt this the more because I do not see much evidence to justify a finding for the defendant on this latter ground if the word "old" was not used. There may have been more evidence than is stated in this case; and the demeanour of the witnesses may have strengthened the impression produced by the evidence there was; but it does not seem a very satisfactory verdict if it proceeded on this latter ground. I agree, therefore, in the result that there should be a new trial.

HANNEN J. I think there should be a new trial in this case not because the ruling of the county court judge was incorrect, but because, having regard to the evidence, I think it doubtful whether the jury sufficiently understood the direction they received to enable them to take it as their guide in determining the question submitted to them.

It appears from the evidence on both sides that the plaintiff sold the oats in question by a sample which the defendant's agent took away for examination. The bargain was only completed after this sample had been in the defendant's possession for two days. This, without more, would lead to the conclusion that the defendant bought on his own judgment as to the quality of the oats represented by the sample and with the usual warranty only, that the bulk should correspond with it. There might, however, be super-added to this warranty an express condition that the oats should be old, and the defendant endeavoured by his evidence to establish that there was such an express bargain between him and the plaintiff. This was the first question which the jury had to consider; but as they have not stated whether they answered it in favour of the defendant, it is possible—and, from the judge's report, it is most probable—that they did not so answer it, and the case must be considered on the assumption that there was no express stipulation that the oats were old.

There might have been an implied term in the contract, arising from previous dealings or other circumstances, that the oats should be old; but the learned judge probably thought the evidence did not make it necessary that he should leave this question to the jury. And the second question, which he did leave to them, seems intended to ascertain whether there was any contract at all between the parties.

It is essential to the creation of a contract that both parties should agree to the same thing in the same sense. Thus, if two persons enter into an apparent contract concerning a particular person or ship, and it turns out that each of them, misled by a similarity of name, had a different person or ship in his mind, no contract would exist between them: *Raffles v. Wichelhaus* [(1864), 159 E.R. 375].

But one of the parties to an apparent contract may, by his own fault, be precluded from setting up that he had entered into it in a different sense to that in which it was understood by the other party. Thus in the case of a sale by sample where the vendor, by mistake, exhibited a wrong sample, it was held that the contract was not avoided by this error of the vendor. . . .

But if in the last-mentioned case the purchaser, in the course of negotiations preliminary to the contract, had discovered that the vendor was under a misapprehension as to the sample he was offering the vendor would have been entitled to shew that he had not intended to enter into the contract by which the purchaser sought to bind him. The rule of law applicable to such a case is a corollary from the rule of morality . . . that a promise is to be performed "in that sense in which the promiser apprehended at the time the promisee received it," and may be thus expressed: "The promiser is not bound to fulfil a promise in a sense in which the promisee knew at the time the promiser did not intend it." And in considering the question, in what sense a promisee is entitled to enforce a promise, it matters not in what way the knowledge of the meaning in which the promiser made it is brought to the mind of the promisee, whether by express words, or by conduct, or previous dealings, or other circumstances. If by any means he knows that there was no real agreement between him and the promiser, he is not entitled to insist that the promise shall be fulfilled in a sense to which the mind of the promiser did not assent.

If, therefore, in the present case, the plaintiff knew that the defendant, in dealing with him for oats, did so on the assumption that the plaintiff was contracting to sell him old oats, he was aware that the defendant apprehended the contract in a different sense to that in which he meant it, and he is thereby deprived of the right to insist that the defendant shall be bound by that which was only the apparent, and not the real bargain.

This was the question which the learned judge intended to leave to the jury; and, as I have already said, I do not think it was incorrect in its terms, but I think that it was likely to be misunderstood by the jury. The jury were asked, "whether they were of opinion, on the whole of the evidence, that the plaintiff believed the defendant to believe, or to be under the impression that he was contracting for the purchase of old oats? If so, there would be a verdict for the defendant." The jury may have understood this to mean that, if the plaintiff believed the defendant to believe that he was buying old oats, the defendant would be entitled to the verdict; but a belief on the part of the plaintiff that the defendant was making a contract to buy the oats, of which he offered him a sample, under a mistaken belief that they were old, would not relieve the defendant from liability unless his mistaken belief were induced by some misrepresentation of the plaintiff, or concealment by him of a fact which it became his duty to communicate. In order to relieve the defendant it was necessary that the jury should find not merely that the plaintiff believed the defendant to believe that he was buying old oats, but that he believed the defendant to believe that he, the plaintiff, was contracting to sell old oats.

I am the more disposed to think that the jury did not understand the question in this last sense because I can find very little, if any, evidence to support a finding upon it in favour of the defendant. It may be assumed that the defendant believed the oats were old, and it may be suspected that the plaintiff thought he so believed, but the only evidence from which it can be inferred that the plaintiff believed that the defendant thought that the plaintiff was making it a term of the contract that the oats were old is that the defendant was a trainer, and that trainers, as a rule, use old oats; and that the price given was high for new oats, and more than a prudent man would have given.

Having regard to the admitted fact that the defendant bought the oats after two days' detention of the sample, I think that the evidence was not sufficient to justify the jury in answering the question put to them in the defendant's favour, if they rightly understood it; and I therefore think there should be a new trial.

QUESTIONS

1. Why does a mistake as to a warranty of quality (a mistake as to a term of the contract) negative consent when a mistake as to the existence of the quality (a mistaken assumption) does not? See Waddams, *The Law of Contracts*, 4th ed. (1999) at 223-24.

2. If the plaintiff did not use the word "old", but knew that the defendant believed him to be so warranting, then according to *Smith v. Hughes*, the plaintiff's suit should not succeed. Is the reason that there was never any contract, or that there was a contract which was not performed? For an illustration, see *McMaster University v. Wilchar Construction Ltd.*, discussed in the extract of *Ron Engineering*, where the plaintiff knew of a mistake in the defendant's construction bid and was therefore not allowed to enforce the agreement.

3. Mistaken Assumptions

(a)   COMMON LAW

This section deals with situations where the parties have reached an agreement and it has been correctly recorded but one or more of the parties has made a false assumption concerning a matter material to the decision to enter into the contract. These cases of mistaken assumptions as to existing facts are to be distinguished from those where circumstances unexpectedly change in the future, after formation of the contract; the latter are dealt with under the doctrine of frustration, discussed in Chapter 10. Note also that mistakes in reducing terms to writing, resulting in the written document's failure to reflect the real agreement between the parties, may be relieved by the remedy of rectification, discussed in section 5 of this chapter.

The following case is generally recognized as the leading English decision on mistake and has often been followed and approved by Canadian courts.

BELL v. LEVER BROTHERS LTD.

[1932] A.C. 161 (H.L.)

Lever Brothers, which had a controlling interest in the Niger Company, appointed Bell and Snelling chairman and vice-chairman of the Board of Directors. Unknown to Lever Brothers, Bell and Snelling speculated in the company's business to their private advantage, thereby committing breaches of duty which would have justified Lever Brothers in terminating their appointments. Later, the Niger Company was amalgamated with another company on terms which left no room for the defendants and Lever Brothers negotiated their termination. An agreement was reached and Bell and Snelling were paid £30,000 and £20,000 respectively as compensation.

Lever Brothers claimed, *inter alia*, that the agreement was reached and money paid under a mistake of fact. At trial, the jury found that the defendants had not acted fraudulently but that Lever Brothers would have dismissed them without promising to pay compensation had they known of the defendants' breaches of contract. Wright J. found that Lever Brothers would have been justified in dismissing the defendants.

The trial court and the Court of Appeal held that the compensation agreements were void as having been made under mistake. The House of Lords, consisting of Lords Atkin, Blanesburgh, Thankerton with Lord Warrington and Viscount Hailsham dissenting, disagreed and allowed the appeal.

LORD ATKIN . . . My Lords, the rules of law dealing with the effect of mistake on contract appear to be established with reasonable clearness. If mistake operates at all it operates so as to negative or in some cases to nullify consent. The parties may be mistaken in the identity of the contracting parties, or in the existence of the subject-matter of the contract at the date of the contract, or in the quality of the subject-matter of the contract. These mistakes may be by one party, or by both, and the legal effect may depend upon the class of mistake above mentioned. Thus a mistaken belief by A. that he is contracting with B., whereas in fact he is contracting with C., will negative consent where it is clear that the intention of A. was to contract only with B. So the agreement of A. and B. to purchase a specific article is void if in fact the article had perished before the date of sale. In this case, though the parties in fact were agreed about the subject-matter, yet a consent to transfer or take delivery of something not existent is deemed useless, the consent is nullified. As codified in the Sale of Goods Act the contract is expressed to be void if the seller was in ignorance of the destruction of the specific chattel. I apprehend that if the seller with knowledge that a chattel was destroyed purported to sell it to a purchaser, the latter might sue for damages for non-delivery though the former could not sue for non-acceptance, but I know of no case where a seller has so committed himself. This is a case where mutual mistake certainly and unilateral mistake by the seller of goods will prevent a contract from arising. Corresponding to mistake as to the existence of the subject-matter is mistake as to title in cases where, unknown to the parties, the buyer is already the owner of that which the seller purports to sell to him. The parties intended to effectuate a transfer of ownership: such a transfer is impossible: the stipulation is naturali rationer inutilis. This is the case of *Cooper v. Phibbs* [(1867), L.R. 2 H.L. 149 (H.L.)] where A. agreed to take a lease of a fishery from B., though contrary to the belief of both parties at the time A. was tenant for life of the fishery and B. appears to have had no title at all. To such a case Lord Westbury applied the principle that if parties contract under a mutual mistake and misapprehension as to their relative and respective rights the result is that the agreement is liable to be set aside as having proceeded upon a common mistake. Applied to the context the statement is only subject to the criticism that the agreement would appear to be void rather than voidable. Applied to mistake as to rights generally it would appear to be too wide. Even where the vendor has no title, though both parties think he has, the correct view would appear to be that there is a contract: but that the vendor has either committed a breach of stipulation as to title, or is not able to perform his contract. The contract is unenforceable by him but is not void.

Mistake as to quality of the thing contracted for raises more difficult questions. In such a case a mistake will not affect assent unless it is the mistake of both parties, and is as to the existence of some quality which makes the thing without the quality essentially different from the thing as it was believed to be. Of course it may appear that the parties contracted that the article should possess the quality which one or other or both mistakenly believed it to possess. But in such a case there is a contract and the inquiry is a different one, being whether the contract as to quality amounts to a condition or a warranty, a different branch of the law. The principles to be applied are to be found in two cases which, as far as my knowledge goes, have always been treated as authoritative expositions of the law. The first is *Kennedy v. Panama, etc. Mail Co.* [(1867), L.R. 2 Q.B. 580].

In that case the plaintiff had applied for shares in the defendant company on the faith of a prospectus which stated falsely but innocently that the company had a binding contract with the Government of New Zealand for the carriage of mails. On discovering the true facts the plaintiff brought an action for the recovery of the sums he had paid on calls. The defendants brought a cross action for further calls. Blackburn J., in delivering the judgment of the Court, said:

> The only remaining question is one of much greater difficulty. It was contended by Mr. Mellis, on behalf of Lord Gilbert Kennedy, that the effect of the prospectus was to warrant to the intended shareholders that there really was such a contract as is there represented, and not merely to represent that the company *bona fide* believed it; and that the difference in substance between shares in a company with such a contract and shares in a company whose supposed contract was not binding, was a difference in substance in the nature of the thing; and that the shareholder was entitled to return the shares as soon as he discovered this, quite independently of fraud, on the ground that he had applied for one thing and got another. And, if the invalidity of the contract really made the shares he obtained different things in substance from those which he applied for, this would, we think, be good law. . . . There is, however, a very important difference between cases where a contract may be rescinded on account of fraud, and those in which it may be rescinded on the ground that there is a difference in substance between the thing bargained for and that obtained. It is enough to show that there was a fraudulent representation as to any part of that which induced the party to enter into the contract which he seeks to rescind; but where there has been an innocent misrepresentation or misapprehension, it does not authorize a rescission unless it is such as to show that there is a complete difference in substance between what was supposed to be and what was taken, so as to constitute a failure of consideration. For example, where a horse is bought under a belief that it is sound, if the purchaser was induced to buy by a fraudulent misrepresentation as to the horse's soundness, the contract may be rescinded. If it was induced by an honest misrepresentation as to its soundness, though it may be clear that both vendor and purchaser thought that they were dealing about a sound horse and were in error, yet the purchaser must pay the whole price unless there was a warranty; and even if there was a warranty, he cannot return the horse and claim back the whole price, unless there was a condition to that effect in the contract.

The Court came to the conclusion in that case that, though there was a misapprehension as to that which was a material part of the motive inducing the applicant to ask for the shares, it did not prevent the shares from being in substance those he applied for.

[Here Lord Atkin discussed *Smith v. Hughes, supra.*]

. . . In these cases I am inclined to think that the true analysis is that there is a contract, but that the one party is not able to supply the very thing whether goods or services that the other party contracted to take; and therefore the contract is unenforceable by the one if executory, while if executed the other can recover back money paid on the ground of failure of the consideration.

We are now in a position to apply to the facts of this case the law as to mistake so far as it has been stated. It is essential on this part of the discussion to keep in mind the finding of the jury acquitting the defendants of fraudulent misrepresentation or concealment in procuring the agreements in question. Grave injustice may be done to the defendants and confusion introduced into the legal conclusion, unless it is quite clear that in considering mistake in this case no suggestion of fraud is admissible and cannot strictly be regarded by the judge who has to determine the legal issues raised. The agreement which is said to be void is the agreement contained in the letter of March 19, 1929, that Bell would retire from the Board of the Niger Company and its subsidiaries, and that in consideration of his doing so Levers would pay him as compensation for the termination of his agreements and consequent loss of office the sum of £30,000 in full satisfaction and discharge of all claims and demands of any kind against Lever Brothers, the Niger Company or its subsidiaries. The agreement, which as part of the contract was terminated, had been broken so that it could be repudiated. Is an agreement to terminate a broken contract different in kind from an agreement to terminate an unbroken contract, assuming that the breach has given the one party the right to declare the contract at an end? I feel the weight of the plaintiffs' contention that a contract immediately determinable is a different thing from a contract for an unexpired term, and that the difference in kind can be illustrated by the immense price of release from the longer contract as compared with the shorter. And I agree that an agreement to take an assignment of lease for five years is not the same thing as to take an assignment of a lease for three years, still less a term for a few months. But, on the whole, I have come to the conclusion that it would be wrong to decide that an agreement to terminate a definite specified contract is void if it turns out that the agreement had already been broken and could have been terminated otherwise. The contract released is the identical contract in both cases, and the party paying for release gets exactly what he bargains for. It seems immaterial that he could have got the same result in another way, or that if he had known the true facts he would not have entered into the bargain. A. buys B.'s horse; he thinks the horse is sound and he pays the price of a sound horse; he would certainly not have bought the horse if he had known 'as the fact is' that the horse is unsound. If B. has made no representation as to the soundness and has not contracted that the horse is sound, A. is bound and cannot recover back the price. A. buys a picture from B.; both A. and B. believe it to be the work of an old master, and a high price is paid. It turns out to be a modern copy. A. has no remedy in the absence of representation or warranty. A. agrees to take on lease or to buy from B. an unfurnished dwelling-house. The house is in fact uninhabitable. A. would never have entered into the bargain if he had known the fact. A. has no remedy, and the position is the same whether B. knew the facts or not, so long as he made no representation or gave no warranty. A. buys a roadside garage business from B. abutting on a public thoroughfare: unknown to A., but known to B., it has already been decided to construct a by-pass road which will divert substantially the whole of the traffic from passing A.'s garage. Again A. has no remedy. All these cases involve hardship on A. and benefit B., as most people would say, unjustly. They can be supported on the ground that it is of paramount importance that contracts should be observed, and that if parties honestly comply with the essentials of the formation of con-tracts—i.e., agree in the same terms on the same subject-matter—they are bound, and must rely on the stipulations of the contract for protection from the effect of facts unknown to them.

This brings the discussion to the alternative mode of expressing the result of a mutual mistake. It is said that in such a case as the present there is to be implied a stipulation in the contract that a condition of its efficacy is that the facts should be as understood by both parties—namely, that the contract could not be terminated till the end of the current term. The question of the existence of conditions, express or implied, is obviously one that affects not the formation of contract, but the investigation of the terms of the contract when made. A condition derives its efficacy from the consent of the parties, express or implied. They have agreed, but on what terms. One term may be that unless the facts are or are not of a particular nature, or unless an event has or has not happened, the contract is not to take effect. With regard to future facts such a condition is obviously contractual. Till the event occurs the parties are bound. Thus the condition (the exact terms of which need not here be investigated) that is generally accepted as underlying the principle of the frustration cases is contractual, an implied condition. Sir John Simon formulated for the assistance of your Lordships a proposition which should be recorded:

> Whenever it is to be inferred from the terms of a contract or its surrounding circumstances that the consensus has been reached upon the basis of a particular contractual assumption, and that assumption is not true, the contract is avoided: i.e., it is void ab initio if the assumption is of present fact and it ceases to bind if the assumption is of future fact.

I think few would demur to this statement, but its value depends upon the meaning of "a contractual assumption," and also upon the true meaning to be attached to "basis," a metaphor which may mislead. When used expressly in contracts, for instance, in policies of insurance, which state that the truth of the statements in the proposal is to be the basis of the contract of insurance, the meaning is clear. The truth of the statements is made a condition of the contract, which failing, the contract is void unless the condition is waived. The proposition does not amount to more than this that, if the contract expressly or impliedly contains a term that a particular assumption is a condition of the contract, the contract is avoided if the assumption is not true. But we have not advanced far on the inquiry how to ascertain whether the contract does contain such a condition. Various words are to be found to define the state of things which make a condition. "In the contemplation of both parties fundamental to the continued validity of the contract," "a foundation essential to its existence," "a fundamental reason for making it," are phrases found in the important judgment of Scrutton L.J. in the present case. The first two phrases appear to me to be unexceptionable. They cover the case of a contract to serve in a particular place, the existence of which is fundamental to the service, or to procure the services of a professional vocalist, whose continued health is essential to performance. But "a fundamental reason for making a contract" may, with respect, be misleading. The reason of one party only is presumedly not intended, but in the cases I have suggested above, of the sale of a horse or of a picture, it might be said that the fundamental reason for making the contract was the belief of both parties that the horse was sound or the picture an old master, yet in neither case would the condition as I think exist. Nothing is more dangerous than to allow oneself liberty to construct for the parties contracts which they have not in terms made by importing implications which would appear to make the contract more businesslike or more just. The implications to be made are to be no more than are "necessary" for giving business efficacy to the transaction, and it appears to me that, both as to existing facts and future facts, a condition would not be implied unless the new state of facts makes the contract something different in kind from the contract in the original state of facts. . . .

I have already stated my reasons for deciding that in the present case the identity of the subject-matter was not destroyed by the mutual mistake, if any, and need not repeat them. . . .

NOTE and QUESTIONS

1. What was the mistake in *Bell v. Lever Brothers*? Does the House of Lords recognize a doctrine of mistake under which a contract would be rendered void *ab initio*? What alternative explanations does it offer for the conclusion that a contract might be void?

2. In *Gullison (A.L.) & Sons Ltd. v. Corey* (1979), 24 N.B.R. (2d) 638, affirmed on the mistake issue 29 N.B.R. (2d) 86 (C.A.), the owner of a house under construction and the builder shared a mistaken belief that the plans would produce a house of a certain size. Although the decision was based on another point, the court indicated that a mistake not relating to the existence of the subject matter but only to its "quality" would not render a contract void. Would the House of Lords in *Bell v. Lever Brothers* ever grant relief for a mistake of quality?

McRAE v. COMMONWEALTH DISPOSALS COMMISSION

(1951), 84 C.L.R. 377 (Aust. H.C.)

The Commission entered into a contract to sell to the plaintiff "one oil tanker including contents wrecked on Jourmand Reef approximately 100 miles north of Samarai. Price £285". The plaintiff fitted out a salvage expedition at considerable expense but found no tanker. Indeed, there was no such tanker at the locality specified by the Commission, nor did it appear that there was any such place as the Jourmand Reef. At first instance Webb J. held that as there was no tanker there was no contract, although the plaintiff could recover damages for deceit. On appeal, McRae sought damages in contract.

DIXON and FULLAGAR JJ. . . . In the assumed background of the case lay the facts that during the war a considerable number of ships, including "oil tankers", became wrecked or stranded in the waters adjacent to New Guinea, that after the war the Commission had the function of disposing of these as it thought fit, and that a purchaser from the Commission of any of these wrecked or stranded vessels might, but not necessarily would, make a very large profit by salving and selling the vessel, or the materials of her hull and equipment, or her cargo. The realization of a profit in this way (and the evidence suggests that a purchaser would not contemplate a realization of profit by an immediate resale of what he had bought as such) could, of course, only be achieved after the expenditure of large sums of money. Such a purchaser would naturally regard himself as acquiring, at best, a chance of making a profit. But he would not regard himself as acquiring a certainty of making a loss. . . .

Now, the simple fact is that there was not at any material time any oil tanker lying at or anywhere near the location specified in the letter of 18th April. There was, at a point about eleven miles east of the location specified, a wrecked vessel described as an "oil barge". . . . The existence of the wrecked barge in question here is not, we think, a directly relevant factor in the case, though it may serve to explain to some extent how a rumour that there was a wrecked tanker somewhere began to circulate in the offices of the Commission.

We say advisedly that such a rumour began to circulate, because there was indeed no better foundation for any supposition on the part of the officers of the Commission that they had a tanker to sell. They had no more definite information than was derived from an offer by a man named Jarrett to buy for £50 the contents of a wrecked vessel, which he said was within a radius of 200 miles from Samarai, and from what can be quite fairly described as mere gossip. The reckless and irresponsible attitude of the Commission's officers is clearly indicated by the description in the advertisement of the locality of the tanker. In an even worse light appears an attempt which was made later, without any foundation whatever, to suggest that at the time of the making of the contract there had been a tanker in the place specified but that she had since been washed off the reef in a storm. Unfortunately the plaintiffs, for their part, took the matter seriously. They believed, and there is evidence that they had some reason for believing, that an oil tanker wrecked at the place indicated was likely to prove a profitable proposition, and accordingly they paid on 23rd April the balance of their purchase money, and then proceeded to fit up a small ship, which they owned, with diving and salvage equipment, and they engaged personnel, and proceeded from Melbourne to New Guinea. It is sufficient at this stage to say that they expended a large sum of money in discovering that they had bought a non-existent tanker.

The plaintiffs, as has been said, based their claim for damages on three alternative grounds. They claimed, in the first place, for damages for breach of a contract to sell a tanker lying at a particular place. Alternatively they claimed damages for a fraudulent representation that there was a tanker lying at the place specified. In the further alternative, they claimed damages for a negligent failure to disclose that there was no tanker at the place specified after that fact became known to the Commission. . . .

The first question to be determined is whether a contract was made between the plaintiffs and the Commission. The argument that the contract was void, or, in other words, there was no contract, was based, as has been observed, on *Couturier v. Hastie* [(1856), 10 E.R. 1065 (H.L.)]. It is true that *Couturier v. Hastie* has been commonly treated in the text-books as a case of a contract avoided by mutual mistake. . . .

The case has not, however, been universally regarded as resting on mistake, and Sir Frederick Pollock, in his preface to vol. 101 of the Revised Reports, at p. vi, says:—"*Couturier v. Hastie* shows how a large proportion of the cases which swell the rubric of relief against mistake in the textbooks (with or without protest from the text-writer) are really cases of construction". And in *Solle v. Butcher*, [[1950] 1 K.B. 671 (C.A.)], Denning L.J. observed that the cases which it had been usual to classify under the head of "mistake" needed reconsideration since the decision of the House of Lords in *Bell v. Lever Bros. Ltd. [supra]*. No occasion seems to have arisen for a close examination of *Couturier v. Hastie*, but such an occasion does now arise.

The facts of the case were simple enough. . . . A sold to B "1,180 quarters of Salonica Indian corn of fair average quality when shipped, at 27s. per quarter f.o.b., and including freight and insurance, to a safe port in the United Kingdom, payment at two months from date upon handing over shipping documents." At the date of the contract the vessel containing the corn had sailed from Salonica, but, having encountered very heavy weather, had put in at Tunis. Here the cargo had been found to have become so heated and fermented that it could not be safely carried further. It had accordingly been landed at Tunis and sold there. These facts were unknown to either party at the date of the contract. On discovering them, B repudiated the contract. After the expiration of the two months mentioned in the contract, A, being able and willing to hand over the shipping documents, sued B for the price. The case came on for trial before Martin B. and a jury. Martin B. directed the jury that "the contract imported that, at the time of the sale, the corn was in existence as such, and capable of delivery" [(1852), 155 E.R. 1250 at 1254]. The jury found a verdict for the defendant, and the plaintiff had leave to move. The Court of Exchequer made absolute a rule to enter a verdict for the plaintiff. This decision was reversed in the Court of Exchequer Chamber, and the House of Lords, after consulting the Judges, affirmed the decisions of the Exchequer Chamber, so that the defendant ultimately had judgment.

In considering *Couturier v. Hastie* it is necessary to remember that it was, in substance, a case in which a vendor was suing for the price of goods which he was unable to deliver. If there had been nothing more in the case, it would probably never have been reported: indeed the action would probably never have been brought. But the vendor founded his claim on the provision for "payment upon handing over shipping documents". He was not called upon to prove a tender of the documents, because the defendant had "repudiated" the contract, but he was able and willing to hand them over, and his argument was, in effect, that by handing them over he would be doing all that the contract required of him. The question thus raised would seem to depend entirely on the construction of the contract, and it appears really to have been so treated throughout. In the Court of Exchequer, Pollock C.B., in the course of argument, said [(1852), 155 E.R. 1250 at 1254]:—"This question is purely one of construction. I certainly think that the plain and literal meaning of the language here used imports that the thing sold, namely, the cargo, was in existence and capable of being transferred." This was, in effect, what Martin B. had told the jury, and what it means is that the plaintiff had contracted that there was a cargo in existence and capable of delivery. . . .

The judgment of the Exchequer Chamber was delivered by Coleridge J. The view that the contract was void is probably derived from certain expressions which were used in the course of this judgment. But it does seem clear that again the question of construction was regarded as the fundamental question in the case. . . . [Here their Lordships quoted a number of passages to this effect.] In the light of these passages it seems impossible to regard the expressions [(1853), 156 E.R. 43 at 46] "If the contract for the sale of the cargo was valid" and "the contract failed as to the principal subject-matter of it" as meaning that the contract was treated as being void. All that the passages in which those expressions occur seem in their context to mean is that the principal subject matter of the contract was a cargo of goods, that the purchaser did not buy shipping documents representing non-existent goods, that the consideration to the purchaser had failed, and that he could not therefore be liable to pay the contract price.

In the House of Lords again the Lord Chancellor, in giving judgment [(1856), 10 E.R. 1065 at 1068, 1069], said:—"The whole question turns upon the making and construction of the contract". A little later he said:—"What the parties contemplated . . . was that there was an existing something to be sold and bought, and, if sold and bought, then the benefit of insurance should go with it." In other words, there was not an absolute obligation to pay the price on delivery of the shipping documents (as the plaintiff contended), but an obligation to pay on delivery of those documents only if they represented at the time of the making of the contract goods in existence and capable of delivery. And this is all that the Lord Chancellor really had in mind, we think, when later he says:—"If the contract of the 15th May had been an operating contract, and there had been a valid contract at that time existing. I think the purchaser would have had the benefit of insurance in respect of all damage previously existing."

In *Bell v. Lever Bros. Ltd.* Lord Atkin, though he does not mention *Couturier v. Hastie* itself, discusses . . . other cases which have sometimes been regarded as turning on mistake avoiding a contract *ab initio*, and His Lordship concludes the discussion with a very important observation. He says . . . :—"In these cases I am inclined to think that the true analysis is that there *is* a contract, but that the one party is not able to supply the very thing, whether goods or services, that the other party contracted to take; and therefore the contract is unenforceable by the one if executory, while, if executed, the other can recover back money paid on the ground of failure of the consideration". . . .

The observation of Lord Atkin in *Bell v. Lever Bros. Ltd.* seems entirely appropriate to *Couturier v. Hastie*. In that case there was a failure of consideration, and the purchaser was not bound to pay the price: if he had paid it before the truth was discovered, he could have recovered it back as money had and received. The construction of the contract was the vital thing in the case because, and only because, on the construction of the contract depended the question whether the consideration had really failed, the vendor maintaining that, since he was able to hand over the shipping documents, it had not failed. The truth is that the question whether the contract was void, or the vendor excused from performance by reason of the non-existence of the supposed subject matter, did not arise in *Couturier v. Hastie*. It would have arisen if the purchaser had suffered loss through non-delivery of the corn and had sued the vendor for damages. If it had so arisen, we think that the real question would have been whether the contract was subject to an implied condition precedent that the goods were in existence. Prima facie, one would think, there would be no such implied condition precedent, the position being simply that the vendor *promised* that the goods *were* in existence. . . . It should be noted in this connection that in *Solle v. Butcher* Denning L.J. said that the doctrine of French law, as enunciated by Pothier, is no part of English law.

His Lordship was without doubt thinking of the passage quoted from Pothier in a note of the report of the argument in the House of Lords in *Couturier v. Hastie*. Although we would not be prepared to assent to everything that is said by Denning L.J. in the course of this judgment, we respectfully agree with this observation. When once the common law had made up its mind that a promise supported by consideration ought to be performed, it was inevitable that the theorisings of the civilians about "mistake" should mean little or nothing to it. On the other hand, the question whether a promisor was excused from performance by existing or supervening impossibility without fault on his part was a practical every-day question to which the common law has been vividly conscious, as witness *Taylor v. Caldwell* [(1863), 122 E.R. 309, *infra*, Chapter 10, section 2], with its innumerable (if sometimes dubious) successors. But here too the common law has generally been true to its theory of simple contract, and it has always regarded the fundamental question as being: "What did the promisor really promise?" Did he promise to perform his part at all events, or only subject to the mutually contemplated original or continued existence of a particular subject-matter? So questions of intention or "presumed intention" arise, and these must be determined in the light of the words used by the parties and reasonable inferences from all the surrounding circumstances. . . .

If the view so far indicated be correct, as we believe it to be, it seems clear that the case of *Couturier v. Hastie* does not compel one to say that the contract in the present case was void. But, even if the view that *Couturier v. Hastie* was a case of a void contract be correct, we would still think that it could not govern the present case. Denning L.J. indeed says in *Solle v. Butcher* . . . :—"Neither party can rely on his own mistake to say it was a nullity from the beginning, no matter that it was a mistake which to his mind was fundamental, and no matter that the other party knew he was under a mistake. *A fortiori* if the other party did not know of the mistake, but shared it". But, even if this be not wholly and strictly correct, yet at least it must be true to say that a party cannot rely on mutual mistake where the mistake consists of a belief which is, on the one hand, entertained by him without any reasonable ground, and, on the other hand, deliberately induced by him in the mind of the other party. . . . even if they [officials of the Commission] be credited with a real belief in the existence of a tanker, they were guilty of the grossest negligence. It is impossible to say that they had any reasonable grounds for such a belief. Having no reasonable grounds for such a belief, they asserted by their advertisement to the world at large, and by their later specification of locality to the plaintiffs, that they had a tanker to sell. They must have known that any tenderer would rely implicitly on their assertion of the existence of a tanker, and they must have known that the plaintiffs would rely implicitly on their later assertion of the existence of a tanker in the latitude and longitude given. They took no steps to verify what they were asserting, and any "mistake" that existed was induced by their own culpable conduct. In these circumstances it seems out of the question that they should be able to assert that no contract was concluded. It is not unfair or inaccurate to say that the only "mistake" the plaintiffs made was that they believed what the Commission told them.

The position so far, then, may be summed up as follows. It was not decided in *Couturier v. Hastie* that the contract in that case was void. The question whether it was void or not did not arise. If it had arisen, as in an action by the purchaser for damages, it would have turned on the ulterior question whether the contract was subject to an implied condition precedent. Whatever might then have been held on the facts of *Couturier v. Hastie*, it is impossible in this case to imply any such term. The terms of the contract and the surrounding circumstances clearly exclude any such implication. The buyers relied upon, and acted upon, the assertion of the seller that there was a tanker in existence. It is not a case in which the parties can be seen to have proceeded on the basis of a common assumption of fact so as to justify the conclusion that the correctness of the assumption was intended by both parties to be a condition precedent to the creation of contractual obligations. The officers of the Commission made an assumption, but the plaintiffs did not make an assumption in the same sense. They knew nothing except what the Commission had told them. If they had been asked, they would certainly not have said: "Of course, if there is no tanker, there is no contract". They would have said: "We shall have to go and take possession of the tanker. We simply accept the Commission's assurance that there is a tanker and the Commission's promise to give us that tanker." The only proper construction of the contract is that it included a promise by the Commission that there was a tanker in the position specified. The Commission contracted that there was a tanker there. . . . If, on the other hand, the case of *Couturier v. Hastie* and this case ought to be treated as cases raising a question of "mistake", then the Commission cannot in this case rely on any mistake as avoiding the contract, because any mistake was induced by the serious fault of their own servants, who asserted the existence of a tanker recklessly and without any reasonable ground. There *was* a contract, and the Commission contracted that a tanker existed in the position specified. Since there was no such tanker, there has been a breach of contract, and the plaintiffs are entitled to damages for that breach. . . .

The conclusion that there was an enforceable contract makes it unnecessary to consider the other two causes of action raised by the plaintiffs. . . .

[The question of the quantification of the plaintiffs' damages is discussed, *infra*, Chapter 14, section 2(b). McTurnan J. concurred. Appeal allowed.]

NOTES and QUESTIONS

1. Would this case be dealt with differently in light of the subsequent decision of the House of Lords in *Hedley Byrne & Co. v. Heller & Partners*, [1964] A.C. 465, discussed *supra*, Chapter 7, section 5, in the context of *Sodd Corp. v. Tessis*?

2. The Sale of Goods Acts contain provisions which state that a contract for the sale of specific goods is *void* where they have perished at the time the contract is made. This provision is found in R.S.O. 1990, c. S.1, s. 8. Equivalent provisions are found in the sales legislation of the common law provinces and territories.

3. G entered into a contract to sell a farm to B. Both G and B anticipated that B would use the land to grow tobacco and the following term was included in the contract: "It is expressly understood that this offer to purchase and acceptance thereof includes 14 acres of tobacco growing quota." However, the Tobacco Growers' Marketing Board would only allocate a 10 acre quota. When this

became known to the parties, B asked for a reduction in price, but G refused to proceed with the sale, feeling that an honest mistake had been made and that this should nullify the whole transaction. (a) How do you think the House of Lords in *Bell v. Lever Brothers* might decide this case? (b) How do you think the Australian High Court in *McRae v. Commonwealth Disposals Comm.* might decide this case? In *R. v. Ont. Flue-Cured Tobacco Growers' Marketing Bd.; Ex parte Grigg* (1965), 51 D.L.R. (2d) 7, the Ontario Court of Appeal held that the contract was void.

4. Both the test set out in *Bell v. Lever Brothers* and the illustrations of its application provided in Lord Atkin's judgment suggest that there is little room at common law for any mistaken assumptions to negative or nullify the consent of the parties.

Does the precise formulation of the test for operative mistake by Lord Atkin provide any opportunity for a creative argument that mistaken assumptions might have an effect outside the narrow confines suggested by the judgment?

5. *Bell v. Lever Brothers* was broadly interpreted in *Associated Japanese Bank (International) Ltd. v. Crédit du Nord S.A.*, [1989] 1 W.L.R. 255 (Q.B.). The plaintiffs, relying on representations by one Bennett that he owned four industrial machines, purchased them from Bennett and leased them back to him. The defendants then contracted separately with the plaintiffs to guarantee Bennett's obligations under the purchase and leaseback agreement. Bennett defaulted and went into bankruptcy after making only one payment under the lease. The machines were found never to have existed.

The plaintiffs brought action against the defendants under the guarantee for the entire amount of unpaid rent. The court held, following *Bell v. Lever Brothers*, that the non-existence of the subject-matter of the guarantee made it essentially different from what the parties believed it to be. Accordingly, the contract of guarantee was held to be void *ab initio* for common mistake. The court made the following observations at 267-68:

> No one could fairly suggest that in this difficult area of law there is only one correct approach or solution. But a narrow doctrine of common law mistake (as enunciated in *Bell v. Lever Brothers Ltd.* [*supra*], supplemented by the more flexible doctrine of mistake in equity (as developed in *Solle v. Butcher* [discussed in the next section of this chapter] and later cases), seems to me to be an entirely sensible and satisfactory state of the law: see *Sheikh Bros. Ltd. v. Ochsner* [1957] A.C. 136. And there ought to be no reason to struggle to avoid its application by artificial interpretations of *Bell v. Lever Brothers Ltd.*
>
> It might be useful if I now summarised what appears to me to be a satisfactory way of approaching this subject. Logically, before one can turn to the rules as to mistake, whether at common law or in equity, one must first determine whether the contract itself, by express or implied condition precedent or otherwise, provides who bears the risk of the relevant mistake. It is at this hurdle that many pleas of mistake will either fail or prove to have been unnecessary. Only if the contract is silent on the point, is there scope for invoking mistake. That brings me to the relationship between common law mistake and mistake in equity. Where common law mistake has been pleaded, the court must first consider this plea. If the contract is held to be void, no question of mistake in equity arises. But, if the contract is held to be valid, a plea of mistake in equity may still have to be considered: see *Grist v. Bailey* [1967] Ch. 532 and the analysis in *Anson's Law of Contract*, 26th ed. (1984), p. 290.

6. How might you attack the compensation agreements in *Bell v. Lever Brothers* on behalf of the employer today? See *Sybron Corp. v. Rochem Ltd.*, [1983] 2 All E.R. 707 (C.A.).

TORONTO-DOMINION BANK v. FORTIN (NO. 2)

[1978] 5 W.W.R. 302, 27 C.B.R. (N.S.) 232, 88 D.L.R. (3d) 232 (B.C. S.C.)

Fortin was one of several nominal defendants (most of them corporate) who executed a joint debenture (a document acknowledging indebtedness and undertaking to pay) in favour of the nominal plaintiff, the Toronto-Dominion Bank. However, the real plaintiff was a prospective purchaser of the companies who was suing the real defendant, the receiver/manager of the companies, to recover the $10,000 portion of the deposit retained by the receiver-manager.

ANDREWS J. On June 21, 1976, Mr. Harold Sigurdson was appointed receiver/manager of Chimo Structures Ltd., Chimo Industries Ltd. and Chimo Construction Ltd. (hereinafter referred to as the "Chimo Companies"). During the last week of August and the first week of September, 1976, the receiver/manager placed a newspaper advertisement inviting offers with respect to the sale of the Chimo Companies as a going concern. On October 14, 1976, Mr. M.P. Flynn, through his solicitor, tendered an offer for the purchase of the property and assets of the Chimo Companies pursuant to the terms of the advertisement placed by the receiver/manager. These terms included a provision, *inter alia*, that all offers must be accompanied by a deposit of a certified cheque payable to the receiver/manager in an amount equal to 5% of the amount of the offer and that this deposit would be returned to the offerer if not accepted, but subject to forfeiture if the offerer failed to complete. Mr. Flynn's offer was duly accompanied by a cheque for 5% of the offered purchase price, in the amount of $24,658. After some further negotiations between the parties, Mr. Sigurdson accepted Mr. Flynn's offer on November 3, 1976. He indicated he would apply forthwith to the Court for approval of the sale, as was required by the order appointing him receiver.

On November 4, 1976, Mr. Flynn requested that the receiver delay applying for Court approval of the sale in question. In response to this request the application was postponed to November 16, 1976. On the morning of this latter date the parties met to further discuss the terms of the offer and certain points which Mr. Flynn felt were ambiguous. As a result of this discussion Mr. Flynn instructed his solicitor to withdraw his offer and request the return of the $24,658 deposit.

The solicitors for Mr. Sigurdson advised Mr. Flynn that, acting within the terms of their agreement, the full amount of the deposit moneys would not be returned; however, the receiver/manager would accept $10,000 as a compromise in satisfaction of all claims against Mr. Flynn arising out of the agreement.

Mr. Flynn agreed to the terms of the compromise agreement on November 18, 1976. On November 23, 1976, the receiver/manager received an offer from another potential purchaser.

On November 30, 1976, the Supreme Court of British Columbia ruled, on an application to approve this latter sale, that "the assets" of the Chimo Companies "cannot be offered for sale and sold without an order authorizing the same". The Court stated that the receiver had acted beyond the powers accorded to him by the order of the Court appointing him in offering the assets for sale and in entering into an agreement for sale. The order authorized and required the receiver to preserve the goodwill and assets of the companies, not to dispose of them. He did not become, in effect, a liquidator until authorized by the Court to sell the assets. This ruling was upheld by the British Columbia Court of Appeal on February 11, 1977.

As a result of that decision the applicant now contends that the receiver/manager had no legal right to enter into a contract with the applicant for the sale of the assets of the Chimo Companies. Thus, the applicant feels that the receiver/manager's position as an officer of the Court obliges him to return the $10,000 paid under the compromise agreement, as the said sum was paid under a mistake of law.

The basic rule respecting a compromise agreement is that it cannot be attacked by reason of a common mistake of law provided the claim compromised is a *bona fide* or "honest" claim, however mistaken the parties are as to its validity. Thus forbearance to sue is said to be good consideration regardless of whether the claim compromised is unfounded and could not be sustained.

One rationale for this rule is given in Cheshire & Fifoot's *Law of Contract*, 9th ed. (1976), p. 76, where the learned author states that the consideration for a compromise agreement is not found in the compromise of a legal right but rather in the surrender of the *claim* to such a right. The traditional reason cited in the case law is the policy desire to effect reasonable settlements. Such a desire would be frustrated if the compromise of a doubtful claim could be set aside on demonstration that the claim could not succeed.

As an example of the numerous cases following this rule and concluding that the validity or invalidity of the claim is not a relevant consideration, see *A.G.B.C. v. Deeks Sand & Gravel Co. Ltd.*, [1956] S.C.R. 336 [and the discussion in *B (D.C.) v. Arkin* in Chapter 4, section 3]. There are, however, exceptions to the general rule as stated above. In *A.G.B.C. v. Deeks* the Court recognized that lack of capacity to enter into a compromise may render it invalid, referring to *Dixon v. Evans* (1872), L.R. 5 H.L. 606; *Holsworthy Urban Council v. Holsworthy Rural Council*, [1907] 2 Ch. 62. In *Dixon v. Evans* a compromise was effected between the directors of a company and a shareholder who wished to have his shares cancelled. The compromise was disputed on the grounds that the directors acted beyond the scope of their authority by entering into the compromise agreement. The Court, however, ruled that the directors had the power to make a compromise of a disputed claim with a shareholder and thus the compromise was valid. The House of Lords at pp. 618-9 stated:

> In dealing with a compromise, always supposing it to be a thing that is within the power of each party, if honestly done, all that a Court of justice has to do is to ascertain that the claim or the representation of the one side is *bona fide* and truly made, and that on the other side, the answer, or defence, or counter claim, is also *bona fide* and truly made. . . . That is the characteristic of a compromise, and if it be not manifestly *ultra vires* of the parties, it is one that a Court of justice ought to respect, and ought not to permit to be questioned.

This paragraph was cited with approval by the Supreme Court of Canada in the *Deeks* case at p. 345 S.C.R. In *Holsworthy Urban Council v. Holsworthy Rural Council* the compromise dealt with money the plaintiff claimed was owed to it by the defendant. Subsequent to the compromise a House of Lords decision altered lower Court decisions respecting the validity of the plaintiff's original claim. The Court in *Holsworthy*, in upholding the compromise, noted at p. 393 "that a compromise, if entered into *bona fide* and if it does not involve the doing of an act by one of the parties which is itself *ultra vires* may be . . . binding". In *Holsworthy* the Court held it was not *ultra vires* of the council to pay the money in compromise of a *bona fide* claim. Thus the council in *Holsworthy*, like the directors in the *Dixon* case, had the capacity to enter into a compromise agreement.

The applicant in the case at bar says that the receiver's powers are derived from an order of the Court appointing him, and since that appointment did not contain the power to sell the assets he therefore could not have any power to compromise an agreement for sale. A similar position was advanced in the *Deeks* case where the Province of British Columbia sought to enforce a compromise relating to the renewal of certain leases. The compromise provided that there would be an adjustment both as regard to rental and royalties. It was later determined to be beyond the powers of the Province to impose a royalty on the leases in question; thus it was argued that the compromise must be invalid as the subject-matter of the attempted compromise was *ultra vires* the Province. The Supreme Court of Canada in rejecting that argument found the compromise valid as affecting the settlement of an honest disagreement over the construction of the leases. The *Deeks* case is distinguished from the case at bar in that, in the *Deeks* case, the parties specifically sought legal advice on that part of the compromise settlement later in dispute. In the *Deeks* case at p. 345 S.C.R., the Court says:

> Although the respondent was at the time acting under the advice of solicitors and had been advised that it was entitled to receive renewals free from the claims being put forward by the Province, it saw fit to enter into the compromise which involved concessions on both sides.

Thus the parties had put their minds to the capacity of the Province to impose the royalties. This is different from the case at bar, where neither party had considered the capacity of the receiver to enter the contract of sale or the compromise. Had they sought legal advice on this point and decided, even if erroneously, that the receiver had the capacity to enter into the agreement of sale, they would be bound by the compromise agreement. This is a recurring theme running throughout the case law as to whether the parties at any time considered and received legal advice respecting the validity of the claim to be compromised. . . .

At some point a mistake can be so fundamental that the compromise agreement cannot stand. Such a proposition is set out by S. M. Waddams in the *Law of Contracts* (1977), p. 85. Similarly, G. H. Treitel in the *Law of Contracts*, 4th ed. (1975), p. 60, comments that where the claim is clearly untenable the compromise of it should not be good consideration. This concept of a fundamental mistake was enunciated by the House of Lords in *Bell v. Lever Bros. Ltd.* [*supra*], and cited with approval in the following quotation adopted in the judgment of Fenton Atkinson, L.J., in *Magee v. Pennine Ins. Co.*, [1969] 2 All E.R. 891 at p. 896:

> Whenever it is to be inferred from the terms of a contract or its surrounding circumstances that the *consensus* has been reached upon the basis of a particular contractual assumption, and that assumption is not true, the contract is avoided. [And to that has to be added the additional rider] . . . the assumption must have been fundamental to the continued validity of the contract, or a foundation essential to its existence.

The *Magee* case is analogous to the case at bar. . . . As the plaintiff [in that case] had no valid claim on the insurance policy [Lord Denning M.R. held] that it would be inequitable for him to have the advantage of the mistake.

In the context of the case at bar the contract of sale is void *ab initio* and, it being the basis of the later compromise, following *Magee*, though not a nullity at law is liable to be set aside in equity. The case at bar is stronger for the applicant, as the contract of insurance in *Magee* was merely voidable for misrepresentation as opposed to being void from inception, as here.

The applicant can also rely on the proposition that a higher onus rests on an officer of the Court to return money obtained under a mistake of law than it does on the ordinary individual. . . .

In the circumstances the receiver/manager will return the deposit of $10,000 to the applicant. Costs will follow the event.

[Application allowed.]

NOTES and QUESTIONS

1. In *Magee v. Pennine Ins. Co. Ltd.*, to which Andrews J. referred, the parties were under the mistaken impression that a policy of car insurance was valid and enforceable when it was not. A majority of the court held that the mistake was fundamental and therefore vitiated a compromise agreement reached between the parties in respect of an insurance claim. Lord Denning stated at 893:

> What is the effect of this common mistake? . . . [Counsel for Magee] relied much on *Bell v. Lever Brothers Ltd.* and its similarity to the present case. . . . I do not propose to go through the speeches in that case. They have given enough trouble to commentators already. I would say simply this. A common mistake, even on a most fundamental matter, does not make a contract void at law: but it makes it voidable in equity.

Fenton Atkinson L.J. simply said, at 896:

> I think it is clear that when the agreement relied on by the plaintiff was made it was made on the basis of a particular and essential contractual assumption, namely, that there was in existence a valid and enforceable policy of insurance and that assumption was not true. In my view it is the right and equitable result of this case that the insurance company should be entitled to avoid that agreement on the ground of mutual mistake in a fundamental and vital matter.

Ought a contract to be voidable rather than void for mistake? The effects of mistake in equity are considered in the following section of this chapter.

2. Although a compromise agreement "cannot be attacked by reason of a common mistake of law . . . however mistaken the parties are as to its validity", the court in *T.D. Bank v. Fortin* (No. 2) holds that "[a]t some point a mistake can be so fundamental that the compromise agreement cannot stand". Is the fact that the mistake was fundamental a sufficient justification for relieving the plaintiff? Does it explain why the defendant should bear the risk that the original agreement was void? See Swan, "The Allocation of Risk in the Analysis of Mistake and Frustration", Study No. 7 in *Studies in Contract Law*, Reiter and Swan (eds.) (1980), at 181, especially the discussion of *T.D. Bank v. Fortin (No. 2)* at 204-10.

3. The fundamental question of who should bear the loss caused by a mistake is seldom dealt with directly by the courts. The study by Swan, *supra*, focuses on allocation of risk in presenting a framework for a general approach to mistake; a shorter discussion of the economic implications of the allocation of risk in this context is found in Kronman, "Mistake, Disclosure, Information and the Law of Contracts", in *The Economics of Contract Law*, Kronman and Posner (eds.) (1979), at 114-16.

4. As *T.D. Bank v. Fortin (No. 2)* emphasizes, the notion that there can be no relief in contract for a mistake of law has a long history, although numerous cases exist where relief was granted in apparent cases of mistake of law, or at least of mixed law and fact. See Waddams, *The Law of Contracts*, 4th ed. (1999), at para. 393.

A similar rule existed in the law of restitution where a person sought to recover money paid to another, with whom the payer was not in any contractual relationship. The supposed inability to recover a payment made under mistake of law was subjected to severe criticism and finally removed in *Air Canada v. British Columbia*, [1989] 1 S.C.R. 1161, where La Forest J. commented, at 1201, that "the distinction between mistake of fact and mistake of law should play no part in the law of restitution". See further McCamus, "Restitution and the Supreme Court: The Continuing Progress of the Unjust Enrichment Principle" (1991), 2 S.C.L.R. (2d) 505 at 513-15.

(b) EQUITY

For nearly two decades, it appeared that *Bell v. Lever Brothers* had set out all the basic principles that applied to the controversial area of contracts founded on mistaken assumptions. However, in *Solle v. Butcher* (1949), [1950] 1 K.B. 671 (Eng. C.A.), Denning, L.J. suggested that cases of mistaken assumptions should be subjected to a two-stage analysis. First, it should be asked whether a mistake had occurred which rendered the contract void at common law, following essentially the analysis of Lord Atkin in *Bell v. Lever Brothers*. If the contract was valid at common law, it was then necessary to ask whether it was voidable on grounds of equitable mistake. According to Denning L.J., at 692, equity could provide relief for common mistake "so long as it could do so without injustice to third parties" where it was unconscientious for one party to retain the legal advantage which had been obtained through the mistake of the other. As an example of when it would be unconscientious to retain the legal advantage, Lord Denning commented, at 693, that a contract could be set aside "if the parties were under a common misapprehension either as to facts or as to their relative and respective rights, provided that the misapprehension was fundamental and that the party seeking to set it aside was not himself at fault".

Lord Denning's version of equitable mistake had two attractions. First, it allowed relief on much less restrictive grounds than the common law doctrine set out in *Bell v. Lever Brothers*. Secondly, because equitable mistake rendered the contract voidable, rather than void, it enabled the courts to avoid injustice to third parties who had relied on the existence of a valid contract.

Despite these attractions, there were doubts as to both the authenticity of Lord Denning's version of equitable mistake and its consequences. Perhaps Lord Denning himself indicated the dubious lineage of his own doctrine when he commented in the case, at 695: "if the rules of equity have become so rigid that they cannot remedy . . . an injustice [of the type that arose in *Solle v. Butcher*], it is time we had a new equity, to make good the omissions of the old". In any event the decision in *Solle v. Butcher* aroused some harsh criticism. For example, Davies, "Mistake in Equity: *Solle v. Butcher* Re-examined" (1969), 3 Man. L.J. 79 at 82 commented:

> [I]t is submitted that the cure proposed by Lord Denning is worse than the disease and that Lord Denning's doctrine is objectionable not only because it is flatly contrary to authority, [but also because] [a]ccording to Lord Denning's doctrine a contract will be set aside if it is unjust in all the circumstances to enforce it and the party seeking to set aside has not been at fault. But who is to say what is "unjust in all the circumstances" or what constitutes "fault"? Under Lord Denning's doctrine equity would vary not only with the length of the chancellor's foot, but with the feet of every judge in the land."

The controversial nature of the legal reasoning in *Solle v. Butcher* perhaps explains why the English Court of Appeal appeared to bury the doctrine in the following case.

GREAT PEACE SHIPPING v. TSAVLIRIS SALVAGE
[2002] 4 All E.R. 689 (C.A.)

The facts of *The Great Peace* are stated succinctly by Professor McCamus in "Mistaken Assumptions in Equity: Sound Doctrine or Chimera" (2004), 40 Can. Bus. L.J. 46, at 69-70, as follows:

> En route from Brazil to China, a vessel, The Cape Providence, suffered serious structural damage with consequent risk to both the vessel and its crew. The defendant salvor was retained to provide assistance. The defendant sought assistance from a third party, Marint, in locating a tug. When it appeared that the tug would only be available in five or six days, Marint was asked to try to locate another vessel in the vicinity of The Cape Providence that might be prepared to offer assistance with the evacuation of the crew, should that become necessary. Marint advised that The Great Peace, a vessel owned by the plaintiffs, was the vessel closest to the current location of The Cape Providence and that it should be able to rendezvous with the The Cape Providence in about twelve hours. Acting on the instructions of The Cape Providence, the defendant commenced negotiations with the plaintiff for suitable arrangements by which The Great Peace would alter its course and proceed to the location of The Cape Providence. Within a few hours, such arrangements were reached and The Great Peace altered its course. The arrangements included a term permitting the defendant to cancel the agreement on payment of a minimum five-day fee.

> Within a few hours, it became apparent that The Great Peace was actually 410 miles, rather than the initially estimated 35 miles, away from The Cape Providence. At this point, the defendants advised Marint that they were expecting to cancel The Great Peace but would not do so yet, as they wish to determine whether a closer vessel could be identified. Shortly thereafter, having learned that The Cape Providence had been passed by a vessel called The Nordfarer, the defendants contracted with the owners of The Nordfarer for similar assistance and instructed Marint to cancel the arrangements with the plaintiffs. Marint then confirmed the cancellation and indicated that it would recommend, in the circumstances, the payment of a lesser cancellation fee of two days' hire. The defendants were unwilling, however, to pay any sum at all to the plaintiff with respect to the cancellation of the agreement.

> In response to the plaintiff's claim for the five-day cancellation fee payable under the agreement, the defendants argued, both at trial and at the Court of Appeal, that the agreement had been entered into on the basis of a shared fundamental assumption that The Great Peace was "in close proximity" to the Cape Providence whereas, in fact, she was not. Accordingly, the agreement was either voided common law or, at least, voidable in equity.

LORD PHILLIPS M.R. [delivering the judgment of the court]

[T]he judgment of Lord Alverstone CJ in *Hobson v. Pattenden* [(1903), 19 T.L.R. 186] . . . suggests that the following elements must be present if common mistake is to avoid a contract: (i) there must be a common assumption as to the existence of a state of affairs; (ii) there must be no warranty by either party that that state of affairs exists; (iii) the non-existence of the state of affairs must not be attributable to the fault of either party; (iv) the non-existence of the state of affairs must render performance of the contract impossible; (v) the state of affairs may be the existence, or a vital attribute, of the consideration to be provided or circumstances which must subsist if performance of the contractual adventure is to be possible.

The second and third of these elements are well exemplified by the decision of the High Court of Australia in *McRae v. Commonwealth Disposals Commission* (1951) 84 CLR 377. . . .

[T]he English doctrine of mistake . . . fills a gap in the contract where it transpires that it is impossible of performance without the fault of either party and the parties have not, expressly or by implication, dealt with their rights and obligations in that eventuality. . . .

[W]hile we do not consider that the doctrine of common mistake can be satisfactorily explained by an implied term, an allegation that a contract is void for common mistake will often raise important issues of construction. Where it is possible to perform the letter of the contract, but it is alleged that there was a common mistake in relation to a fundamental assumption which renders performance of the essence of the obligation impossible, it will be necessary, by construing the contract in the light of all the material circumstances, to decide whether this is indeed the case. In performing this exercise, the test advanced by Lord Diplock, applicable alike to both frustration and to fundamental breach, in *Hong Kong Fir Shipping Co. Ltd v. Kawasaki Kisen Kaisha Ltd* [*supra*, Chapter 7, section 7] can be of assistance.

[The Court of Appeal here quoted the test of substantial deprivation of the whole benefit of the contract set out in the *Hong Kong Fir*]. . . .

This test may not, however, be adequate in the context of mistake, for there are cases where contracts have been held void for mistake, notwithstanding that the effect of the mistake was that the consideration proved to have substantially greater value than the parties had contemplated.

Once the court determines that unforeseen circumstances have, indeed, resulted in the contract being impossible of performance, it is next necessary to determine whether, on true construction of the contract, one or other party has undertaken responsibility for the subsistence of the assumed state of affairs. This is another way of asking whether one or other party has undertaken the risk that it may not prove possible to perform the contract, and the answer to this question may well be the same as the answer to the question of whether the impossibility of performance is attributable to the fault of one or other of the parties.

Circumstances where a contract is void as a result of common mistake are likely to be less common than instances of frustration [discussed in Chapter 10]. Supervening events which defeat the contractual adventure will frequently not be the responsibility of either party. Where, however, the parties agree that something shall be done which is impossible at the time of making the agreement, it is much more likely that, on true construction of the agreement, one or other will have undertaken responsibility for the mistaken state of affairs. This may well explain why cases where contracts have been found to be void in consequence of common mistake are few and far between.

Lord Atkin himself gave no examples of cases where a contract was rendered void because of a mistake as to quality which made "the thing without the quality essentially different from the thing as it was believed to be". He gave a number of examples of mistakes which did not satisfy this test, which served to demonstrate just how narrow he considered the test to be. . . .

We agree with [the trial judge] that, on the facts of the present case, the issue in relation to common mistake turns on the question of whether the mistake as to the distance apart of the two vessels had the effect that the services that the "*Great Peace*" was in a position to provide were something essentially different from that to which the parties had agreed. We shall defer answering that question until we have considered whether principles of equity provide a second string to the defendants' bow.

Mistake in equity

In *Solle v. Butcher* Denning LJ held that a court has an equitable power to set aside a contract that is binding in law on the ground of common mistake. . . .

A number of cases, albeit a small number, in the course of the last 50 years have purported to follow *Solle v. Butcher*, yet none of them defines the test of mistake that gives rise to the equitable jurisdiction to rescind in a manner that distinguishes this from the test of a mistake that renders a contract void in law, as identified in *Bell v. Lever Brothers*. This is, perhaps, not surprising, for Lord Denning, the author of the test in *Solle v. Butcher*, set *Bell v. Lever Brothers* at nought. It is possible to reconcile *Solle v. Butcher* and *Magee v. Pennine Insurance* [*supra*] with *Bell v. Lever Brothers* only by postulating that there are two categories of mistake, one that renders a contract void at law and one that renders it voidable in equity. Although later cases have proceeded on this basis, it is not possible to identify that proposition in the judgment of any of the three Lords Justices, Denning, Bucknill or Fenton Atkinson, who participated in the majority decisions in the former two cases. Nor, over 50 years, has it proved possible to define satisfactorily two different qualities of mistake, one operating in law and one in equity.

In *Solle v. Butcher* Denning LJ identified the requirement of a common misapprehension that was "fundamental", and that adjective has been used to describe the mistake in those cases which have followed *Solle v. Butcher*. We do not find it possible to distinguish, by a process of definition, a mistake which is "fundamental" from Lord Atkin's mistake as to quality which "makes the thing contracted for essentially different from the thing that it was believed to be".

A common factor in *Solle v. Butcher* and the cases which have followed it can be identified. The effect of the mistake has been to make the contract a particularly bad bargain for one of the parties. Is there a principle of equity which justifies the court in rescinding a contract where a common mistake has produced this result?

> "Equity is . . . a body of rules or principles which form an appendage to the general rules of law, or a gloss upon them. In origin at least, it represents the attempt of the English legal system to meet a problem which confronts all legal systems reaching a certain stage of development. In order to ensure the smooth running of society it is necessary to formulate general rules which work well enough in the majority of cases. Sooner or later, however, cases arise in which, in some unforeseen set of facts, the general rules produce substantial unfairness . . ." (*Snell's Equity*, 30th edn. Paragraph 1-03)

Thus the premise of equity's intrusion into the effects of the common law is that the common law rule in question is seen in the particular case to work injustice, and for some reason the common law cannot cure itself. But it is difficult to see how that can apply here. Cases of fraud and misrepresentation, and undue influence, are all catered for under other existing and uncontentious equitable rules. We are only concerned with the question whether relief might be given for common mistake in circumstances wider than those stipulated in *Bell v. Lever Brothers*. But that, surely, is a question as to where the common law should draw the line; not whether, given the common law rule, it needs to be mitigated by application of some other doctrine. The common law has drawn the line in *Bell v. Lever Brothers*. The effect of *Solle v. Butcher* is not to supplement or mitigate the common law; it is to say that *Bell v. Lever Brothers* was wrongly decided.

Our conclusion is that it is impossible to reconcile *Solle v. Butcher* with *Bell v. Lever Brothers*. The jurisdiction asserted in the former case has not developed. It has been a fertile source of academic debate, but in practice it has given rise to a handful of cases that have merely emphasised the confusion of this area of our jurisprudence. . . . If coherence is to be restored to this area of our law, it can only be by declaring that there is no jurisdiction to grant rescission of a contract on the ground of common mistake where that contract is valid and enforceable on ordinary principles of contract law.

We are very conscious that we are not only scrutinising the reasoning of Lord Denning in *Solle v. Butcher* and in *Magee v. Pennine Insurance Co [supra]*, but are also faced with a number of later decisions in which Lord Denning's approach has been approved and followed. . . . In this case we have heard full argument, which has provided what we believe has been the first opportunity in this court for a full and mature consideration of the relation between *Bell v. Lever Brothers Ltd* and *Solle v. Butcher*. In the light of that consideration we can see no way that *Solle v. Butcher* can stand with *Bell v. Lever Brothers*. In these circumstances we can see no option but so to hold.

We can understand why the decision in *Bell v. Lever Brothers Ltd* did not find favour with Lord Denning. An equitable jurisdiction to grant rescission on terms where a common fundamental mistake has induced a contract gives greater flexibility than a doctrine of common law which holds the contract void in such circumstances. Just as the Law Reform (Frustrated Contracts) Act 1943 was needed to temper the effect of the common law doctrine of frustration, so there is scope for legislation to give greater flexibility to our law of mistake than the common law allows.

The result in this case

We revert to the question that we [earlier] left unanswered. . . . It was unquestionably a common assumption of both parties when the contract was concluded that the two vessels were in sufficiently close proximity to enable the *"Great Peace"* to carry out the service that she was engaged to perform. Was the distance between the two vessels so great as to confound that assumption and to render the contractual adventure impossible of performance? If so, the appellants would have an arguable case that the contract was void under the principle in *Bell v. Lever Brothers Ltd*.

[The trial judge] addressed this issue in the following paragraph:

Was the *"Great Peace"* so far away from the *"Cape Providence"* at the time of the contract as to defeat the contractual purpose - or in other words to turn it into something essentially different from that for which the parties bargained? This is a question of fact and degree, but in my view the answer is no. If it had been thought really necessary, the *"Cape Providence"* could have altered course so that both vessels were heading toward each other. At a closing speed of 19 knots, it would have taken them about 22 hours to meet. A telling point is the reaction of the defendants on learning the true positions of the vessels. They did not want to cancel the agreement until they knew if they could find a nearer vessel to assist. Evidently the defendants did not regard the contract as devoid of purpose, or they would have cancelled at once.

[Counsel for the appellant] submitted that it was not legitimate for the Judge to have regard to the fact that the appellants did not want to cancel the agreement with the *"Great Peace"* until they knew whether they could get a nearer vessel to assist. We do not agree. This reaction was a telling indication that the fact that the vessels were considerably further apart than the appellants had believed did not mean that the services that the *"Great Peace"* was in a position to provide were essentially different from those which the parties had envisaged when the contract was concluded. The *"Great Peace"* would arrive in time to provide several days of escort service. The appellants would have wished the contract to be performed but for the adventitious arrival on the scene of a vessel prepared to perform the same services. The fact that the vessels were further apart than both parties had appreciated did not mean that it was impossible to perform the contractual adventure.

The parties entered into a binding contract for the hire of the *"Great Peace"*. That contract gave the appellants an express right to cancel the contract subject to the obligation to pay the "cancellation fee" of 5 days hire. When they engaged the *"Nordfairer"* they cancelled the *"Great Peace"*. They became liable in consequence to pay the cancellation fee. There is no injustice in this result.

For the reasons that we have given, we would dismiss this appeal.

NOTE and QUESTIONS

1. *The Great Peace* is an unusual example of the English Court of Appeal finding that one of its own decisions, *Solle v. Butcher*, is no longer good law. It thus undermines the cases which relied on *Solle v. Butcher*.

In his article "Mistaken Assumptions in Equity: Sound Doctrine or Chimera?", *supra*, Professor McCamus concluded, at 68, that the correct view would be that the doctrine of equitable mistake has been accepted as a feature of Canadian law.

What impact might *The Great Peace* have on the future of equitable mistake in Canada? In his article, Professors McCamus, at 75-76, offers three reasons why Canadian courts should be reluctant to follow the path of the English Court of Appeal in *The Great Peace*:

(i) The test for operative mistake defined by the Court of Appeal in the *The Great Peace* appears unduly restrictive and is likely, therefore, to lead to the manipulations characteristic of the earlier narrow versions of the test.

(ii) By failing to address the impact of the common law void for mistake doctrine on the interest of third parties, the Court of Appeal has breathed renewed life into a doctrine that is quite unattractive from a policy perspective.

(iii) The attempted suppression of the equitable doctrine carries with it the suppression of the remedial flexibility afforded by the doctrine. The result is to leave mistaken assumptions doctrine in a very unsatisfactory state.

The objections set out by Professor McCamus are important. Are they sufficient to outweigh the benefits of certainty emphasized by the opponents of equitable mistake?

2. The Court of Appeal emphasizes that in any case of mistaken assumptions, it is vital to assess whether the contract allocates the risk of the mistake that occurred. What does the presence of the cancellation fee in the *The Great Peace* indicate about the way in which the parties allocated the risk in that case?

If the court had concluded that the appellant had taken the risk that it might have to terminate the contract with *The Great Peace* early, would it have been necessary to proceed to the analysis of whether the performance of the contract had become impossible?

4.   Mistake and Third Party Interests

(a)   MISTAKEN IDENTITY

Cases of mistaken identity usually arise because of fraud. A rogue fraudulently represents to the owner of goods that he or she is another identifiable person in order to induce the owner to part with goods to the rogue.

Formerly, these cases appeared to raise obscure issues of contract formation in circumstances that were tragic for the participants but sometimes morbidly amusing to the detached reader. However, the increasing incidence of identity theft has emphasized that the cases involve fundamental principles of policy. The cases concern the rights of mistaken owners, not as against the parties with whom they contract, but as against the interests of the innocent third parties into whose hands the subject of the transaction has passed. The following recent decision illustrates both the traditional analytical approach of the English courts to the problem of mistaken identity and a closely contested debate over an important issue of policy.

SHOGUN FINANCE LTD. v. HUDSON

[2003] UKHL 62

A rogue had dishonestly acquired the driver's licence of Mr. Durlabh Patel of Mayflower Road in Leicester, England. The rogue then went to a car dealership, posing as Mr. Patel, and agreed to buy a Mitsubishi Shogun car for £22,250, subject to obtaining financing.

The dealer produced an English form of financing agreement known as a hire-purchase contract, under which the dealer sells the car to a finance company, in this case, Shogun Finance. The finance company then "hires" the car to the purchaser, who agrees to make monthly payments until the entire amount of financing has been paid off. At that stage, the finance company normally transfers title in the car to the purchaser.

The judgment of Lord Phillips describes the circumstances surrounding the formation of the hire-purchase contract. After the financing was arranged, the dealer allowed the rogue to take possession of the car and he purported to sell it to a private purchaser, the defendant Hudson, for £17,000. The rogue vanished and in this action Shogun claimed the car, or its value, from Hudson.

Under English law, if a hire-purchase agreement was concluded between the dealer and the rogue, then Hudson could take advantage of a statutory exception to the principle that the vendor of a chattel (the rogue) cannot convey to the purchaser a better title than the one held by the vendor. Shogun, however, contended that because they were mistaken about the identity of the person with whom they were dealing, no hire-purchase agreement was ever concluded with the rogue. If there was no agreement, then the normal rule applied and Hudson did not obtain title to the car from the rogue. Under these circumstances, Shogun would have a valid claim against Hudson for the car or its value.

LORD PHILLIPS

This appeal is a variation on a theme that has bemused courts and commentators alike for over 150 years. Two individuals conduct negotiations in which all the terms necessary to constitute a binding contract are agreed. One of those individuals has, however, been masquerading as a third party. Does a binding contract result? . . .

[In the showroom, the dealer produced a copy of Shogun's standard hire-purchase agreement.]

The form had a box for insertion of 'Customer Details'. Into this was entered the name and address of Mr Durlabh Patel together with the number of his driving licence. The rogue signed the form 'D.J. Patel' with a signature which matched that on the stolen driving licence, which he produced.

[The dealer] telephoned Shogun's sales support centre and relayed to one of the clerks there the details which the rogue had provided, and then faxed to them a copy of Mr. Patel's driving licence and the draft agreement. Shogun made a computer search to check Mr. Patel's name and address, . . . then to check whether any . . . judgments or bankruptcy orders were registered against him, then to check his credit rating with one or more credit reference agencies. In the space of about five minutes they learned how long Mr. Patel had lived at his address, where he worked and how long he had worked there, his bank account number and how long he had held the account, his date of birth and his driving licence number. They also learned that he had no adverse credit references.

Shogun compared the signatures on the driving licence and the draft agreement and concluded that they matched. They then phoned the dealer and told him that the proposal was accepted. The form was signed on behalf of Shogun, but it is not clear precisely when this was done. The rogue paid the dealer a deposit of 10% of the purchase price, partly in cash and partly by cheque. [T]he cheque was in due course dishonoured. The dealer handed over the vehicle to the rogue, with complete documentation. . . .

The rogue then sold the vehicle to the defendant, Mr. Hudson, for £17,000. Mr. Hudson bought the vehicle for himself, and not as a dealer. He bought it in good faith. The rogue has vanished without trace. Shogun contend that the vehicle has at all times been their property and claim its return, or its value in lieu. Mr. Hudson claims that the rogue passed a good title to him, by reason of the provisions of the Hire-Purchase Act 1964.

Formation of contract

A contract is normally concluded when an offer made by one party ('the offeror') is accepted by the party to whom the offer has been made ('the offeree'). Normally the contract is only concluded when the acceptance is communicated by the offeree to the offeror. A contract will not be concluded unless the parties are agreed as to its material terms. There must be *'consensus ad idem'*. Whether the parties have reached agreement on the terms is not determined by evidence of the subjective intention of each party. It is, in large measure, determined by making an objective appraisal of the exchanges between the parties. If an offeree understands an offer in accordance with its natural meaning and accepts it, the offeror cannot be heard to say that he intended the words of his offer to have a different meaning. The contract stands according to the natural meaning of the words used. There is one important exception to this principle. If the offeree knows that the offeror does not intend the terms of the offer to be those that the natural meaning of the words would suggest, he cannot, by purporting to accept the offer, bind the offeror to a contract—*Hartog v Colin and Shields* [[1939] 3 All E.R. 566 (K.B.), discussed in section 2(b) of chapter] . . . *Smith v Hughes* (1871) LR 6 QB 597. Thus the task of ascertaining whether the parties have reached agreement as to the terms of a contract can involve quite a complex amalgam of the objective and the subjective and involve the application of a principle that bears close comparison with the doctrine of estoppel. Normally, however, the task involves no more than an objective analysis of the words used by the parties. The object of the exercise is to determine what each party *intended,* or must be deemed to have *intended.*

The task of ascertaining whether the parties have reached agreement as to the terms of a contract largely overlaps with the task of ascertaining what it is that the parties have agreed. The approach is the same. It requires the construction of the words used by the parties in order to deduce the *intention* of the parties—see *Chitty on Contracts, 28th Ed Volume 1, paragraphs 12-042,3* and the cases there cited. This is true, whether the contract is oral or in writing. The words used fall to be construed having regard to the relevant background facts and extrinsic evidence may be admitted to explain or interpret the words used. Equally, extrinsic evidence may be necessary to identify the subject matter of the contract to which the words refer.

Just as the parties must be shown to have agreed on the terms of the contract, so they must also be shown to have agreed the one with the other. If A makes an offer to B, but C purports to accept it, there will be no contract. Equally, if A makes an offer to B and B addresses his acceptance to C there will be no contract. Where there is an issue as to whether two persons have reached an agreement, the one with the other, the courts have tended to adopt the same approach to resolving that issue as they adopt when considering whether there has been agreement as to the terms of the contract. The court asks the question whether each intended, or must be deemed to have intended, to contract with the other. That approach gives rise to a problem where one person is mistaken as to the identity of the person with whom he is dealing, as the cases demonstrate. I propose at this point to consider those cases.

.....

[Lord Phillips, in paras 126-166 of the judgment, considered the many authorities on mistaken identity. This extract contains his comments on three of the key cases.]

In *Cundy v Lindsay* (1878) 3 App Cas 459 a dispute about title to goods reached the House of Lords. A rogue called Blenkarn had a room at 37 Wood Street, Cheapside. A well-known firm called W Blenkiron & Son carried on business at 123 Wood Street. Blenkarn placed written orders for goods from 37 Wood Street with the plaintiffs. He signed the orders in such a way that the signature appeared to be Blenkiron & Co. The plaintiffs, who knew of Blenkiron & Son, though not the number at which they carried on business in Wood Street, accepted the orders and despatched goods addressed to 'Messrs Blenkiron & Co, 37 Wood Street, Cheapside.' Blenkarn sold some of these goods to the defendants, against whom the plaintiffs claimed in conversion.

The House held that no contract had been concluded with Blenkarn and that, accordingly, the property in the goods had remained vested in the plaintiffs. . . .

Here, once again, the focus was on the intention of the offeree. In deciding that his intention was to contract with Blenkiron & Co, the House had regard to the fact that the order was apparently signed 'Blenkiron & Co' and to the fact that the plaintiffs knew of a firm of that name and intended to deal with that firm. Thus extrinsic evidence was admitted in addition to the wording of the order in order to ascertain the intention of the plaintiffs. . . .

Phillips v. Brooks Ltd. [1919] 2 KB 243 is the first case that involved a face-to-face transaction. A rogue called North entered the plaintiff's jewellery shop. He selected some pearls and a ring and wrote out a cheque for the total price of £3,000. He stated that he was Sir George Bullough and gave an address in St James' Square. The plaintiff, who knew of the existence of Sir George Bullough, referred to a directory and found that Sir George did, indeed, live at that address. He then permitted North to take away the ring before the cheque was cleared. Horridge J held that a contract was concluded between the plaintiff and North. . . .

Phillips v. Brooks well illustrates the conundrum that the application of the test of *intention* raises when terms are negotiated between two persons who are face to face. It arises where the two persons, A and B, are not known to each other and where A gives a name which is not his own. If B is unaware of the existence of a third person who bears that name, there will be no problem. B will clearly intend to contract with A, treating the name given by A simply as the label by which A identifies himself. Equally A will know that B intends to contract with him. The problem arises where B is aware of a third person, C, who bears the name falsely adopted by A. In that situation it is B's intention to contract both with A and with C, for he does not distinguish between the two. No sensible answer can be given to the question: does B intend to contract with A or C? Nor can any sensible answer be given to the question: does A believe that B intends to contract with him or with C?

Horridge J. solved the conundrum by drawing an 'inference' that the plaintiff intended to contract with the rogue, who was present, and not with the individual whose identity the rogue had assumed. . . .

In *Lewis v. Averay* [1972] 1 QB 198 the plaintiff advertised his car for sale in a newspaper. A rogue telephoned and asked to see it. He arrived and told the plaintiff and his fiancée that he was Richard Green and led them to believe that he was a well-known film actor of that name, who was playing the role of Robin Hood in a television series. A sale was agreed and the rogue wrote out a cheque for the purchase price. The plaintiff demurred at letting the rogue take the car before his cheque was cleared, whereupon the rogue produced a pass of admission to Pinewood Studios, with an official stamp on it, the name Richard A. Green and the rogue's photograph. On sight of this the plaintiff permitted the rogue to take the car and the documents that related to it. The cheque bounced and the rogue sold the car to the defendant pretending at this point that he had the plaintiff's name. The Court of Appeal held that a valid contract had been concluded between the plaintiff and the rogue and that good title had passed to the defendant.

Giving the leading judgment, Lord Denning MR commented . . . at p. 207:

"When two parties have come to a contract – or rather what appears, on the face of it, to be a contract – the fact that one party is mistaken as to the identity of the other does not mean that there is no contract, or that the contract is a nullity and void from the beginning. It only means that the contract is voidable, that, liable to be set aside at the instance of the mistaken person, so long as he does so before third parties have in good faith acquired rights under it.

In this case Mr. Lewis made a contract of sale with the very man, the rogue, who came to the flat. I say that he 'made a contract' because in this regard we do not look into intentions, or into his mind to know what he was thinking or into the mind of the rogue. We look to the outward appearances. On the face of the dealing, Mr. Lewis made a contract under which he sold the car to the rogue, delivered the car and the logbook to him, and took a cheque in return. The contract is evidenced by the receipts which were signed. It was, of course, induced by fraud. The rogue made false representations as to his identity. But it was still a contract, though voidable for fraud. It was a contract under which this property passed to the rogue, and in due course passed from the rogue to Mr. Averay, before the contract was avoided"

. . . . .

[In this appeal], Lord Hobhouse of Woodborough and Lord Walker of Gestingthorpe have concluded that, as the contract was a written document, the identity of the hirer falls to be ascertained by construing that document. Adopting that approach, the hirer was, or more accurately purported to be, Mr. Patel. As he had not authorised the conclusion of the contract, it was void.

Lord Nicholls of Birkenhead and Lord Millett have adopted a different approach. They point out the illogicality of applying a special approach to face-to-face dealings. What of dealings on the telephone, or by videolink? There also it could be said that each of the parties to the dealings is seeking to make a contract with the other party to the dealings. And this can even be said when the dealings are conducted by correspondence. If A writes to B making an offer and B writes back responding to that offer, B is intending to contract with the person who made that offer. If a contract is concluded in face-to-face dealings, notwithstanding that one party is masquerading as a third party, why should the result be different when the dealings are by letter?

Lord Nicholls of Birkenhead and Lord Millett propose an elegant solution to this illogicality. Where two individuals *deal with each other*, by whatever medium, and agree terms of a contract, then a contract will be concluded between them, notwithstanding that one has deceived the other into thinking that he has the identity of a third party. In such a situation the contract will be voidable but not void. While they accept that this approach cannot be reconciled with *Cundy v. Lindsay*, they conclude that *Cundy v. Lindsay* was wrongly decided and should no longer be followed.

While I was strongly attracted to this solution, I have found myself unable to adopt it. *Cundy v. Lindsay* exemplifies the application by English law of the same approach to identifying the parties as is applied to identifying the terms of the contract. In essence this focuses on deducing the intention of the parties from their words and conduct. Where there is some form of personal contact between individuals who are conducting negotiations, this approach gives rise to problems. In such a situation I would favour the application of a strong presumption that each intends to contract with the other, with whom he is dealing. Where, however, the dealings are exclusively conducted in writing, there is no scope or need for such a presumption. This can be illustrated by a slight adaption of the facts of the present case. Assume that the rogue had himself filled in the application form and sent it and a photocopy of Mr. Patel's driving licence to Shogun. Assume further that he had been authorised to do so by Mr. Patel. There can be no doubt that a contract would have been concluded between Shogun and Mr. Patel. Mr. Patel would have intended to contract with Shogun; Shogun would have intended to contract with Mr. Patel; and this would have been demonstrated by the application form.

Assume now that the rogue had wrongly understood that he had been re-quested by Mr. Patel to fill in and submit the application form on his behalf, but in fact had no authority to do so. In this situation, according to established principles of the law of agency, an apparent contract would have been concluded between Shogun and Mr. Patel but, being concluded without the latter's authority, it would be a nullity. Shogun might have a claim against the rogue for breach of warranty of authority, but could not have demonstrated that a contract had been concluded with the rogue.

Turning to the true position—that the rogue knew he had no authority to conclude a contract in the name of Mr. Patel, but fraudulently wished to induce Shogun to believe that they were entering into such a contract—I do not see by what legal principle this change in the mental attitude of the rogue could result in a binding contract being concluded with him.

The position is not, of course, as simple as that. Negotiations between the rogue and Shogun were not conducted exclusively by written correspondence. They were conducted with the aid of the dealer and the use of faxes and telephone communications. Acceptance of the offer was conveyed by telephone via the dealer—and this might have been capable of concluding a contract, notwithstanding that Clause 1 of the standard terms provided for acceptance by signature. . . .

Shogun's representatives were aware of the presence of the prospective hirer in the dealer's showrooms in Leicester. To an extent the dealings were interpersonal through the medium of the dealer. Should one treat them as comparable to face-to-face dealings and conclude that there was a presumption that Shogun intended to contract with the man with whom they were dealing? Should one treat the written agreement as no more than peripheral to the dealings and conclude that it does not override that presumption? I have concluded that the answer to these questions is 'no'.

Shogun had, on the evidence, set up a formal system under which contracts would be concluded in writing on a standard form . . . which provided essential information, including the identity of the parties to the agreement.

These considerations lead me to conclude that the correct approach in the present case is to treat the agreement as one concluded in writing and to approach the identification of the parties to that agreement as turning upon its construction. The particulars given in the agreement are only capable of applying to Mr. Patel. It was the intention of the rogue that they should identify Mr. Patel as the hirer. The hirer was so identified by Shogun. Before deciding to enter into the agreement they checked that Mr. Patel existed and that he was worthy of credit. On that basis they decided to contract with him and with no-one else. Mr. Patel was the hirer under the agreement. As the agreement was concluded without his authority, it was a nullity. The rogue took no title under it and was in no position to convey any title to Mr. Hudson.

For these reasons I would dismiss this appeal.

[Lords Hobhouse and Walker delivered separate concurring speeches. Lords Nicholls and Millett dissented. The appeal was dismissed.]

QUESTIONS

1. Consider the implications for the innocent third party of a finding that a contract is void rather than voidable as suggested by Lord Denning. As is pointed out by the O.L.R.C., in its *Report on Sale of Goods* 1979, vol 2, at 286, the relevance of the distinction between void and voidable titles in this context has been questioned.

As a matter of policy, rather than detailed analysis, who should bear the risk of dealing with the rogue, Shogun or Mr. Hudson?

2. Lord Phillips disagreed with the "elegant solution" suggested by the dissenting judges, Lords Nicholls and Millett, in which the contract would have been voidable rather than void. Lord Nicholls, at para 35, noted that this result was consistent with the approach adopted elsewhere in the common law world, notably under the Uniform Commercial Code. He continued:

and this course makes practical sense. In a case such as the present the owner of goods has no interest in the identity of the buyer. He is interested only in creditworthiness. It is little short of absurd that a subsequent purchaser's rights depend on the precise manner in which the crook seeks to persuade the owner of his creditworthiness and permit him to take the goods away with him. This ought not to be so. The purchaser's rights should not depend upon the precise form the crook's misrepresentation takes.

Is Lord Phillips' rebuttal of this view convincing?

(b)   DOCUMENTS MISTAKENLY SIGNED: *NON EST FACTUM*

The problem of documents mistakenly signed is described by Fridman, *The Law of Contract*, 4th ed. (1999), at 295-296:

> Another possibly operative kind of mistake occurs when a party has mistaken the kind of contract, that is, transaction, that is involved. For example, a party believes that he is giving a guarantee for another's debt, when he is in fact selling his property. Originally, where a contract was by deed, that is, *under seal*, a party could plead such error in certain limited circumstances, by alleging, *non est factum*, that is, that the deed, though appearing to be his, was in fact not his, as he had assented and affixed his seal to something other than what he had intended. Such a plea was a denial of consent. In more modern times, the plea has been allowed to be raised in the case of *any* written contract, not necessarily one under seal.

Again, we are here faced with the problem of the intervening rights of a third party who has relied on the signature of one party to a contract when that signature was induced by the co-contractant's fraudulent misrepresentation as to the nature of the document.

Prudential Trust Co. v. Cugnet, [1956] S.C.R. 914, was the first major Canadian decision concerning the plea of *non est factum*. In that case, Hunter, acting as agent for Amigo Petroleums Ltd., called upon the respondent Cugnet, a retired farmer, at his home. At the time of the visit the respondent was playing cards. Hunter told him that he wanted to talk about mineral rights so they went into another room. After a short conversation, Cugnet signed what was fraudulently misrepresented as a mere grant of an option of mineral rights, but which was in fact an assignment and transfer of a share in those rights. Amigo Petroleums Ltd. assigned its rights to Canuck Freehold Royalties Ltd. (for which Prudential Trust Co. Ltd. was a bare trustee). An action brought to establish Canuck's rights under the agreement was met by a plea of *non est factum* by Cugnet and his son (who had filed a caveat against the titles of the lands, based on an earlier agreement of sale between his father as vendor and himself as purchaser). The trial court and the Court of Appeal granted relief on the basis of *non est factum*.

A majority of the Supreme Court of Canada agreed that the case was one of *non est factum* and held that the transfer was therefore void and the appellant had acquired no title. Applying the English decision in *Carlisle & Cumberland Banking Co. v. Bragg*, [1911] 1 K.B. 489 (C.A.), the court upheld the "class/contents" distinction, holding that the mistake was as to the class or character of the document and not merely as to its contents. Even more important, given the issue of third party interests, the court held the *Carlisle* case to establish that, except in the case of a negotiable instrument, carelessness on the part of the signatory is immaterial and cannot preclude a plea of *non est factum* even as against innocent third parties.

Cartwright J., in dissent, found no mistake as to the character of the document but only as to its effect: Cugnet knew that it dealt with his mineral interests and was mistaken only in that it effected a transfer and not simply an option of those interests. Furthermore, even if the mistake did go to the class or character of the document, Cartwright J. held that the respondent should not be allowed to plead *non est factum* against an innocent third party when it was only through his own carelessness that he failed to discover the misrepresentation.

More recent decisions have vindicated the views of Cartwright J. In *Saunders v. Anglia Bldg. Soc.*, the House of Lords overruled *Carlisle* and the Supreme Court of Canada followed in *Marvco Color Research Ltd. v. Harris* by overruling *Prudential Trust Co. v. Cugnet*. Extracts from both decisions are set out below.

SAUNDERS v. ANGLIA BUILDING SOCIETY

[1971] A.C. 1004, [1970] 3 All E.R. 961 (H.L.)

On an appeal from a judgment, sub nom. *Gallie v. Lee*, [1969] 2 Ch. 17, the House of Lords had to deal with the issues of negligence and the degree of difference between the document as signed and the document as represented.

LORD PEARSON . . .

Negligence: It is clear that by the law as it was laid down in *Foster v. Mackinnon* [(1869), L.R. 4 C.P. 704] a person who had signed a document differing fundamentally from what he believed it to be would be disentitled from successfully pleading non est factum if his signing of the document was due to his own negligence. The word "negligence" in this connection had no special, technical meaning. It meant carelessness, and in each case it was a question of fact for the jury to decide whether the person relying on the plea had been negligent or not. In *Foster v. Mackinnon* the Lord Chief Justice had told the jury that, if the indorsement was not the defendant's signature, or if, being his signature, it was obtained upon a fraudulent representation that it was a guarantee, and the defendant signed it without knowing that it was a bill, and under the belief that it was a guarantee and if the defendant was not guilty of any negligence in so signing the paper, the defendant was entitled to the verdict. On appeal this decision was held to be correct. In *Vorley v. Cooke* (1857), 65 E.R. 898 at 900, Stuart V.C. said:

> It cannot be said that Cooke's conduct was careless or rash. He was deceived, as anyone with the ordinary amount of intelligence and caution would have been deceived, and he is therefore entitled to be relieved.

Whatever may be thought of the merits of the decision in that case, this passage illustrates the simple approach to the question whether the signer of the deed had been negligent or not. Similarly, in *Lewis v. Clay* (1897), 67 L.J.Q.B. 224 at 225 Lord Russell of Killowen C.J. left to the jury the question:

> Was the defendant, in signing his name as he did recklessly careless, and did he thereby enable Lord William Nevill to perpetrate the fraud?

Unfortunately this simple and satisfactory view as to the meaning and effect of negligence in relation to the plea of non est factum became distorted in the case of *Carlisle & Cumberland Banking Co. v. Bragg* [*supra*]. The defendant was induced to sign the document by fraud, and did not know that it was a guarantee, but thought that it was a mere proposal for insurance. The jury found that he had been negligent. Pickford J. considered that the finding of negligence was immaterial, and on appeal his view was upheld. Vaughan Williams L.J. said at 494:

> I do not know whether the jury understood that there could be no material negligence unless there was a duty on the defendant towards the plaintiffs. Even if they did understand that, in my opinion, in the case of this instrument, the signature to which was obtained by fraud, and which was not a negotiable instrument, Pickford J. was right in saying that the finding of negligence was immaterial. I wish to add for myself that in my judgment there is no evidence whatsoever to show that the proximate cause of the plaintiff's advancing money on this document was the mere signature of it by the defendant. In my opinion, the proximate cause of the plaintiff's making the advance was that Rigg fraudulently took the document to

the bank, having fraudulently altered it by adding the forged signature of an attesting witness, and but for Rigg having done those things the plaintiffs would never have advanced the money at all.

. . . In my opinion *Carlisle & Cumberland Banking Co. v. Bragg* was wrong in the reasoning and the decision.

I think it is not right to say that in relation to the plea of non est factum, negligence operates by way of estoppel. The phrase "estoppel by negligence" tends, in this connection at any rate, to be misleading in several ways:

(1) The phrase is inaccurate in itself, as has been pointed out in *Spencer Bower and Turner on Estoppel by Representation*, 2nd ed. (1966), p. 69 and in the judgments of the Court of Appeal in this case. Estoppel in the normal sense of the word does not arise from negligence: it arises from a representation made by words or conduct.

(2) The phrase tends to bring in the technicalities of estoppel, and the requirement that the representation must be intended to be acted upon may cause difficulties.

(3) The phrase tends to bring in the technicalities of negligence as they have been developed in the tort of negligence. This is what happened in *Carlisle & Cumberland Banking Co. v. Bragg*, as shown by the passage cited above. The innocent third party who has paid or lent money on the faith of a negligently signed document should not have to prove the signer owed a duty to him, nor that the signer's negligence was the proximate cause of the money being paid or lent.

(4) An estoppel must be pleaded and proved by the party relying on it. In relation to the plea of non est factum, this could put the burden of proof on the wrong party. The person who has signed the document knows with what knowledge or lack of knowledge and with what intention he signed the document, and how he was induced or came to sign it. He should have the burden of proving that his signature was not brought about by negligence on his part.

Salmon L.J. has said in his judgment in this case [1969] 2 Ch. 17 at 48:

If . . . a person signs a document because he negligently failed to read it, I think he is precluded from relying on his own negligent act for the purpose of escaping from the ordinary consequences of his signature. In such circumstances he cannot succeed on a plea of non est factum. This is not in my view a true estoppel, but an illustration of the principle that no man may take advantage of his own wrong.

I agree.

The degree of difference required: The judgments in the older cases used a variety of expressions to signify the degree or kind of difference that, for the purposes of the plea of non est factum, must be shown to exist between the document as it was and the document as it was believed to be. More recently there has been a tendency to draw a firm distinction between (a) a difference in character or class, which is sufficient for the purposes of the plea, and (b) a difference only in contents, which is not sufficient. This distinction has been helpful in some cases, but, as the judgments of the Court of Appeal have shown, it would produce wrong results if it were applied as a rigid rule for all cases. In my opinion, one has to use a more general phrase, such as "fundamentally different" or "radically different" or "totally different."

[Lords Reid, Hodson, Wilberforce and Pearson and Viscount Dilhorne all rendered separate concurring judgments. The appeal was dismissed.]

MARVCO COLOR RESEARCH LTD. v. HARRIS

[1982] 2 S.C.R. 774, 20 B.L.R. 143, 26 R.P.R. 48, 141 D.L.R. (3d) 577, 45 N.R. 302

ESTEY J. [delivering the judgment of the court] This is an action for fore-closure on a mortgage (or more accurately, a charge under the *Land Titles Act*, R.S.O. 1970, c. 234) securing the sum of $55,650.43 granted by the respondents to the appellant. The only defence raised in the action was that of *non est factum*. The respondents unquestionably executed the charge in favour of the appellant and it is clear that the appellant has not been guilty of fraud or improper conduct of any kind, and in concurrent findings below has been found to be, but for *non est factum*, fully entitled to the relief requested. The respondents executed the charge at the request of a third party, Johnston, in connection with the acquisition by Johnston of an interest of an associate in a firm owned by Johnston and the associate. In connection with this acquisition the respondents had advanced $15,000 in cash raised by them through an earlier mortgage on the same property, granted by them to the Bank of Montreal. The husband, Dennis Harris, one of the respondents, had also executed a contract of guarantee in favour of the appellant of the same principal sum as secured by the mortgage which is the subject of this action. In this guarantee the appellant in consideration of the covenants by the respondent husband and Johnston, released its claims against Suwald, the person whose interest in the firm was being purchased by Johnston. Prior to the release, Suwald had been liable to the appellant on a covenant in a chattel mortgage which had been given by Johnston and Suwald at the time of the purchase of the firm from the appellant. Apparently on the same day, but after this contract of guarantee was executed, the respondents signed the mortgage or charge in question, the last paragraph of which included the following passage typed in a blank space in the form of charge used by the parties:

> This mortgage is given as collateral security for the liability of Dennis Albert Harris under the terms of a Deed of Covenants bearing even date wherein the said Dennis Albert Harris and the Mortgagee are (inter alia) parties as co-covenantor and covenantee respectively. No finan-cial liability on the part of the Mortgagors shall arise hereunder unless and until there shall be default on the part of the covenantors of the terms of the said Deed of Covenants and no rights shall accrue to the Mortgagee prior to any such default. The Mortgagee agrees with the Mortgagors that it will pursue all other remedies under the Deed of Covenants and Chattel Mortgage referred to therein before enforcing the security hereby constituted. Discharge of the liabilities arising under the Deed of Covenants and the said Chattel Mortgage shall rank pro tanto as a discharge (or partial discharge, as the case may be) of the principal secured hereby. All other terms and conditions of this Mortgage shall be read and construed accord-ingly.

The mortgage was in fact, therefore, a collateral security granted by the respondents in favour of the appellant securing the performance by the covenantors, including the respondent husband, and it was relied upon by the appellant in releasing Suwald from his obligations under the chattel mortgage.

Johnston was at all material times living with the daughter of the respondents. The daughter also executed the aforementioned contract of guarantee as trustee because she had been the trustee under a bill of sale executed by the appellant in favour of a company owned or controlled by Suwald and Johnston at the time the appellant sold its business to those individuals or their corporate nominee. The daughter did not personally guarantee the indebtedness to the appellant. Other than the association of their daughter with Johnston, the purchaser of the Suwald interest in the firm in question, there appears to be no reason for the participation by the respondents in the financing of Johnston's purchase of Suwald's interest in the firm.

The mortgage in question was executed by the respondents individually at different times and places on the same date, apparently January 27, 1976. When the respondent wife signed the document her daughter was present, but the finding is that in executing the mortgage the respondent wife relied upon the representations made by Johnston, who was also present, as to the nature and content of the document, and did not do so in reliance upon anything said by the daughter. The respondent husband executed the mortgage later on the same day in the presence of Johnston upon whose representations he likewise apparently relied. The learned trial judge stated this about the execution of the mortgage by the respondents [107 D.L.R. (3d) 632 at 634 (affirmed 115 D.L.R. (3d) 512*n* (C.A.))]:

> When she [the respondent wife] arrived Johnston said they were to wait for Clay [an employee in the lawyer's office] who was bringing a paper for her to sign. Clay arrived, said there was an error in the document, left and returned and presented the document to the wife. At some point Johnston, perhaps in the presence of Clay, said it was "just to correct the date" in the Bank of Montreal mortgage. In any event the defendant wife signed it without reading it. Later that day Johnston and Clay attended upon her husband at home and got him to sign as well. The husband testified they told him it related to discrepancies in the date of the Bank of Montreal mortgage. He signed without question and without reading.

> .....

> There is also no doubt that the defendants were careless in not reading the document before signing. The wife is well educated, the husband less so, but both are literate and English-speaking and both have a basic understanding of mortgages, having executed at least three others since the purchase of their home. It is undisputed evidence, however, that they were told it was an unimportant amendment to the Bank of Montreal mortgage when in reality it was a second substantial mortgage to the plaintiff.

The mortgage in favour of the Bank of Montreal has been paid off and the only issue arising on this appeal concerns the mortgage which is the subject of the action, and in that connection this issue was put by the appellant:

> Is the defence of *non est factum* available to a party who, knowing that a document has legal effect, carelessly fails to read the document thereby permitting a third party to perpetrate a fraud on another innocent party?

This issue turns on the decision of this Court in *Prudential Trust Co. v. Cugnet* [*supra*], a four-to-one decision. The majority . . . found that where a document was executed as a result of a misrepresentation as to its nature and character and not merely its contents the defendant was entitled to raise the plea of *non est factum* on the basis that his mind at the time of the execution of the document did not follow his hand. In such a circumstance the document was void *ab initio*. So went the judgment of Nolan J. with whom Justices Taschereau and Fauteux, as they then were, concurred. Locke J. reached the same result, but added the following comment on the effect of careless conduct on the ability of the defendant to raise the plea of *non est factum* (at p. 929 S.C.R.):

> It is my opinion that the result of the authorities was correctly stated in the *Bragg's* case. To say that a person may be estopped by careless conduct such as that in the present case, when the instrument is not negotiable, is to assert the existence of some duty on the part of the person owing to the public at large, or to other persons unknown to him who might suffer damage by acting upon the instrument on the footing that it is valid in the hands of the holder. I do not consider that the authorities support the view that there is any such general duty, the breach of which imposes a liability in negligence.

Cartwright J., as he then was, dissented. His Lordship commenced with a recitation of the general proprieties (at p. 932 S.C.R.):

> . . . [G]enerally speaking, a person who executes a document without taking the trouble to read it is liable on it and cannot plead that he mistook its contents, at all events, as against a person who acting in good faith in the ordinary course of business has changed his position in reliance on such document.

and then moved to the exception arising under the principle of *non est factum*. After making reference to *Carlisle v. Bragg, supra*, His Lordship said (at p. 934 S.C.R.):

> An anxious consideration of all the authorities referred to by counsel and in the Courts below has brought me to the conclusion that, insofar as *Carlisle v. Bragg* decides that the rule that negligence excludes a plea of *non est factum* is limited to the case of negotiable instruments and does not extend to a deed such as the one before us, we should refuse to follow it.

He concluded, therefore, that any person who fails to exercise reasonable care in signing a document is precluded from relying on the plea of *non est factum* as against a person who relies upon that document in good faith and for value.

As the basis for the judgments of Justice Nolan, concurred in by two other members of the court, and of Justice Locke was the judgment of the Court of Appeal of England in *Carlisle v. Bragg, supra*, it should be pointed out at once that that case has been overruled by the House of Lords in *Saunders v. Anglia Bldg. Soc.* . . . .

The doctrine of *non est factum* sprang into prominence with the judgment in *Foster v. Mackinnon* (1869), L.R. 4 C.P. 704. At trial in that case the jury was directed that if the defendant's signature on the document in question "was obtained upon a fraudulent representation that it was a guarantee and that the defendant signed it without knowing that it was a bill, and under the belief that it was a guarantee, and if the defendant was not guilty of any negligence in so signing the paper, he was entitled to the verdict". On appeal, the Court of Common Pleas endorsed the direction of the trial judge, and held that (at p. 712):

> . . . [I]n the case now under consideration, the defendant, according to the evidence, if believed, and the finding of the jury, never intended to indorse a bill of exchange at all, but intended to

sign a contract of an entirely different nature. It was not his design, and, if he were guilty of no negligence, it was not even his fault that the instrument he signed turned out to be a bill of exchange.

In *Foster v. Mackinnon* a distinction is drawn between negotiable instruments and other documents. A qualification of the general rule was felt to be necessary when applied to negotiable instruments in order to protect innocent transferees for value. As a result, the court concluded that where "the party signing knows what he is doing: the indorser intended to indorse, and the acceptor intended to accept, a bill of exchange", the party signing the document cannot deny its validity against a holder in due course whether or not he was negligent in affixing his signature. This rule was said to be a limitation on the general principle of *non est factum* established in earlier cases under which the signor, in order to deny successfully his signature, had to show that he had not been careless in executing the document. This general rule was applicable to deeds, and "equally applicable to other written contracts" (at p. 712).

Following the decision in *Foster v. Mackinnon*, and prior to the decision of the Court of Appeal in *Carlisle v. Bragg*, it is clear that the presence or absence of negligence on the part of the defendant was a critical factor in determining his ability to raise successfully the plea of *non est factum*. The rule . . . of the day was as follows:

> So a man may avoid a deed or other instrument, which he was induced to execute by a fraudulent misrepresentation of its contents, as was held in *Foster v. Mackinnon* . . .
>
> And if the party who executes an instrument in such circumstances had not been guilty of negligence in so doing, he may avoid it, not only against him who made the fraudulent misrepresentation, but as against a third party who has acted innocently, on the faith of the instrument being genuine.

> (*Chitty on Contracts*, 15th ed. (1909), at pp. 673-4)

.....

Only one exception to this rule was recognized: if the document signed was a bill of exchange and the signor intended to sign a bill of exchange, he could not successfully plead *non est factum*, even though he had not been negligent.

Almost a half a century after the decision in *Foster v. Mackinnon*, *supra*, the Court of Appeal in *Carlisle v. Bragg*, *supra*, substantially modified the law in the United Kingdom with reference to the plea of *non est factum*. In that case the court allowed the plea to be entered by a defendant who had executed a guarantee believing it to be a document of a different character, and went on to hold that the defendant was not estopped from raising the plea even though it was the negligence of the defendant which lead to the loss in question. The jury indeed had found the defendant to be negligent in signing the document. The Court of Appeal concluded that any doctrine which limited the application of the plea where the defendant was negligent was confined to negotiable instruments.

The decision of the Court of Appeal in *Carlisle v. Bragg* may be summarized as follows:

(1) *Foster v. Mackinnon* applies only to bills of exchange.

(2) Negligence on the part of the signor is therefore relevant only to bills of exchange.

(3) Negligence is used in the tortious sense, and therefore, only when a duty of care exists in the signor and his act is the proximate cause of the loss by the third party, can it be a bar to a successful plea of *non est factum*.

(4) In all other cases negligence is irrelevant, and *non est factum* may be pleaded where the document signed is of a different nature from that which the signor intended to execute: *vide Chitty on Contracts*, 18th ed. (1930), at p. 803, and Anson, *Law of Contracts*, 14th ed. (1917), at p. 164.

Carlisle v. Bragg has attracted unfavourable comment in legal writings and the following is an example of the criticisms of the judgment written shortly after its issuance:

> A man who signs a document which he has not taken the trouble to read, who makes therein a promise on which other persons may act to their detriment, and who is found by a jury to have acted without reasonable care, is not liable for the consequences of his act to the party who has suffered by reliance on his promise, unless the document, the nature and contents of which he has neglected to ascertain, should chance to be a negotiable instrument; or unless the promisee, whose identity he has also neglected to ascertain, should chance to be a person to whom he owes a duty to take care. Such is the decision of the Court of Appeal in *Carlisle and Cumberland Banking Co. v. Bragg*, [1911] 1 K.B. 489, 80 L.J.K.B. 472.
>
> Shortly stated, the Court was asked to say which of the two innocent parties should suffer for the fraud of a third, and the Lords Justices decided in favour of the man whose admitted negligence was the cause of the trouble.

(Anson, *Carlisle and Cumberland Banking Co. v. Bragg*, 28 L.Q.R. 190 (1912) at p. 190.)

Although the decision in *Carlisle v. Bragg* was the subject of much criticism, it was adopted by the majority of this court in *Prudential Trust Co. Ltd. v. Cugnet*, *supra*. As previously mentioned, Cartwright J. in his dissenting judgment recognized the flaws in the Court of Appeal's decision and refused to follow it, adopting instead the rule recognized prior to *Carlisle v. Bragg* that a person who was negligent in executing a written instrument, whether or not it was a bill of exchange, was estopped, as against an innocent transferee, from denying the validity of the document. He also recognized that "negligence" in the sense that the term was used in relation to the plea of *non est factum*, connoted carelessness, rather than the attributes of the term in the law of tort. This aspect of the matter was dealt with in this way (at p. 935 S.C.R.):

> It may be said that the term negligence is inappropriate because it presupposes a duty owed by Cugnet Senior to Canuck, but in the passages quoted the term is, I think, used as meaning that lack of reasonable care in statement which gives rise to an estoppel. As it was put by Sir William Anson in an article on *Carlisle & Cumberland Banking Co. v. Bragg* in 28 L.Q. Rev. 190 at p. 194: "And further, there seems some confusion between the negligence which creates a liability in tort, and the lack of reasonable care in statement which gives rise to an estoppel. Bragg might well have been precluded by carelessness from resisting the effect of his written words, though the Bank might not have been able to sue him for negligence."

The law in Canada prior to the decision of the House of Lords in *Saunders* has been summarized by Professor Fridman as follows:

The Canadian situation, prior to the *Saunders* case, would appear to have been that there was considerable sympathy for the position of some illiterate, ill-educated, or otherwise disadvantaged parties, who signed a document, perhaps not fully realizing what was involved. But for *non est factum* to be pleaded successfully, the party raising the plea would have to show some kind of misconception, not necessarily fraudulently induced, as to the intended legal effect of the document. Negligence does not seem to have played a very large part in the thinking of Canadian judges in this context: although they were concerned with the sort of *intent* shown by the signer of the document.

(Fridman, *The Law of Contract* (1976), at p. 109)

It was not until *Saunders v. Anglia Building Society, supra,* that the law was put back to the position which it was in after *Foster v. Mackinnon.* It is interesting to note that in doing so all the judges dealt with the meaning of the word negligence as employed by the court in *Foster v. Mackinnon* as meaning "carelessness" in the same way that Cartwright J. did in *Prudential, supra.* Thus the rule with reference to *non est factum* in the United Kingdom requires that the defendant be not guilty of carelessness in order to be entitled to raise the defence of *non est factum.*

It is not necessary for us to concern ourselves with the second leg of *Saunders v. Anglia,* namely, those circumstances in which a defendant who has not been guilty of negligence may raise the defence of *non est factum.* Here the respondents, by concurrent findings below, were found to be negligent or careless. I do note in passing, however, that it was the consensus of the several members of the House of Lords participating in the *Saunders* case that for the principle to operate, the document must be fundamentally different, either as to content, character or otherwise from the document that the signor intended to execute. Prior to this decision the plea of *non est factum* was available only if the mistake was as to the very nature or character of the transaction. It was not sufficient that there be a mistake as to the contents of the document: *Howatson v. Webb,* [1907] 1 Ch. 537, affirmed [1908] 1 Ch. 1; *Muskham Fin. Ltd. v. Howard,* [1963] 1 Q.B. 904. This distinction was rejected by the House of Lords in favour of a more flexible test. In the words of Lord Pearson (at p. 1039); "In my opinion, one has to use a more general phrase, such as 'fundamentally different' or 'radically different' or 'totally different.'" Lord Wilberforce at pp. 1026-7 concluded that the principle would come into play on "rare occasions".

In my view, with all due respect to those who have expressed views to the contrary, the dissenting view of Cartwright J. (as he then was) in *Prudential, supra,* correctly enunciated the principles of the law of *non est factum.* In the result the defendants-respondents are barred by reason of their carelessness from pleading that their minds did not follow their hands when executing the mortgage so as to be able to plead that the mortgage is not binding upon them. The rationale of the rule is simple and clear. As between an innocent party (the appellant) and the respondents, the law must take into account the fact that the appellant was completely innocent of any negligence, carelessness or wrongdoing, whereas the respondents by their careless conduct have made it possible for the wrongdoers to inflict a loss. As between the appellant and the respondents, simple justice requires that the party, who by the application of reasonable care was in a position to avoid a loss to any of the parties, should bear any loss that results when the only alternative available to the courts would be to place the loss upon the innocent appellant. In the final analysis, therefore, the question raised cannot be put more aptly than in the words of Cartwright J. in *Prudential, supra,* at p. 929 S.C.R.: ". . . which of two innocent parties is to suffer for the fraud of a third". The two parties are innocent in the sense that they were not guilty of wrongdoing as against any other person, but as between the two innocent parties there remains a distinction significant in the law, namely, that the respondents, by their carelessness, have exposed the innocent appellant to risk of loss, and even though no duty in law was owed by the respondents to the appellant to safeguard the appellant from such loss, nonetheless the law must take this discarded opportunity into account.

In my view, this is so for the compelling reason that in this case, and no doubt generally in similar cases, the respondents' carelessness is but another description of a state of mind into which the respondents have fallen because of their determination to assist themselves and/or a third party for whom the transaction has been entered into in the first place. Here the respondents apparently sought to attain some advantage indirectly for their daughter by assisting Johnston in his commercial venture. In the *Saunders* case, *supra,* the aunt set out to apply her property for the benefit of her nephew. In both cases the carelessness took the form of a failure to determine the nature of the document the respective defendants were executing. Whether the carelessness stemmed from an enthusiasm for their immediate purpose or from a confidence in the intended beneficiary to save them harmless matters not. This may explain the origin of the careless state of mind but is not a factor limiting the operation of the principle of *non est factum* and its application. The defendants, in executing the security without the simple precaution of ascertaining its nature in fact and in law, have nonetheless taken an intended and deliberate step in signing the document and have caused it to be legally binding upon themselves. In the words of *Foster v. Mackinnon* this negligence, even though it may have sprung from good intentions, precludes the defendants in this circumstance from disowning the document, that is to say, from pleading that their minds did not follow their respective hands when signing the document and hence that no document in law was executed by them.

This principle of law is based not only upon the principle of placing the loss on the person guilty of carelessness, but also upon a recognition of the need for certainty and security in commerce. This has been recognized since the earliest days of the plea of *non est factum.* In *Waberley v. Cockerel* (1542), 73 E.R. 112, for example, it was said that:

> . . . although the truth be, that the plaintiff is paid his money, still it is better to suffer a mischief to one man than an inconvenience to many, which would subvert a law; for if matter in writing may be so easily defeated, and avoided by such surmise and naked breath, a matter in writing would be of no greater authority than a matter of fact. . . .

The appellant, as it was entitled to do, accepted the mortgage as valid, and adjusted its affairs accordingly. For example, the appellant released Suwald from the chattel mortgage held by the appellant.

I wish only to add that the application of the principle that carelessness will disentitle a party to the document of the right to disown the document in law must depend upon the circumstances of each case. This has been said throughout the judgments written on the principle of *non est factum* from the earliest times. The magnitude and extent of carelessness, the circumstances which may have contributed to such carelessness, and all other circumstances must be taken into account in each case before a court may determine whether estoppel shall arise in the defendant so as to prevent the raising of this defence. The policy considerations inherent in the plea of *non est factum* were well stated by Lord Wilberforce in his judgment in *Saunders, supra*, at pp. 1023-4:

> . . . the law . . . has two conflicting objectives: relief to a signer whose consent is genuinely lacking . . . protection to innocent third parties who have acted upon an apparently regular and properly executed document. Because each of these factors may involve questions of degree or shading any rule of law must represent a compromise and must allow to the court some flexibility in application.

The result in this case has depended upon the intervention by this court in the development of the principle of *non est factum* and its invocation in a way inconsistent with that applied many years ago in the *Prudential* case, *supra*. The respondents have pleaded their case in the courts below and in this court consistent with the result in the *Prudential* judgment. In these circumstances consideration can and should be given to the application of the general principle that costs follow the event. The appellant, of course, was required to persevere to the level of this court in order to bring about a review of the reasoning which led to the determination in the *Prudential* case. The respondents, on the other hand, acted reasonably in founding their position upon that decision notwithstanding the revision of the law of England consequent upon the judgments in *Saunders*. In all these circumstances, therefore, I would award to the appellant costs only before the court of first instance with no costs being awarded either party in the Court of Appeal or in this court.

[Appeal allowed.]

NOTES and QUESTIONS

1. For a discussion of the situation where one party signs a blank form to be filled in later by another; see *United Dominion Trust Ltd. v. Western*, [1976] Q.B. 513 (C.A.). See also *Royal Bank of Canada v. Gill* (1986), 6 B.C.L.R. (2d) 359 (S.C.), affirmed [1988] 3 W.W.R. 441 (B.C.C.A.), where the defence of *non est factum* was held not to be available to an illiterate person who signed a guarantee on behalf of his son in the son's presence and without asking the son to explain the guarantee document.

2. Consider the relation between *non est factum* and the doctrine of unconscionability when you read Chapter 12. See, *e.g., Taylor v. Armstrong* (1979), 99 D.L.R. (3d) 547 (Ont. H.C.).

3. *Non est factum* was successfully pleaded in *Northside Economic Development Assistance Corp. v. Strickland* (1990), 96 N.S.R. (2d) 4 (T.D.) by a wife who signed two chattel mortgages and promissory notes as security. After deciding that Mrs. Strickland was not guilty of negligence or carelessness, Glube C.J.T.D. stated at 10-11:

> . . . I am perfectly satisfied that . . . Mrs. Strickland was totally under the will of her husband when it came to any financial arrangements, that she had no independent views, and if she had them, she was not permitted to express them.

Under a strict application of *Saunders v. Anglia Building Society* should this plea have succeeded? Was the judge overly sympathetic to Mrs. Strickland's situation and, if so, was there a better way of attacking the transactions?

4. For a judicial history of *non est factum* in Canada see Schwartz, "*Non Est Factum* in Canada After *Marvco Color Research Ltd. v. Harris*" (1985), 34 U.N.B.L.J. 92.

5. Rectification

As noted in Chapter 7, section 6, one of the most common "exceptions" to the parol evidence rule arises out of the use of the equitable remedy of rectification, which enables the courts to correct written documents that do not reflect the real agreement between the parties, where there has been a mistake in the reduction of the terms into writing. In order to decide if the remedy is appropriate, the courts of necessity must admit extrinsic evidence of matters preceding the written contract.

BERCOVICI v. PALMER

(1966), 59 D.L.R. (2d) 513 (Sask. Q.B.)

MACPHERSON J. The plaintiff claims rectification of an agreement in writing. The defendant counterclaims for rectification in another respect.

The plaintiff and her late husband for many years carried on two retail businesses at Regina Beach, a resort where the businesses were open only in the summer. In July, 1958, a few months after her husband's death, the plaintiff realized she could not carry them on and decided to sell.

She agreed to sell to the defendant for $24,000 to be paid on terms which do not concern the issues before me. The [defendant] took over the businesses on July 26, 1958, and on July 28, 1958, the parties and the defendant's husband, who negotiated the deal, went to the office of the plaintiff's solicitor to put it in writing. The solicitor was on holiday but one of his partners took instructions and prepared a brief memorandum which the parties and the defendant's husband then and there signed.

The defendant then instructed her own solicitor and correspondence ensued between him and the plaintiff's solicitor on his return. On August 21, 1958, a formal agreement was signed.

This litigation arises from the fact that there is included in the recitals of the agreement of August 21st a parcel of land which the plaintiff says was there in error and which the defendant says was always part of the deal.

The parcel is not contiguous with any other land concerned and is occupied by a summer cottage known as Rob Roy. It is legally described as "Lot 6 in Block 33, Lakeview, Regina Beach, etc." It was then owned by the plaintiff. The store premises agreed to be sold are described as "Lot 1 in Block 33A, Lakeview, Regina Beach, etc." Blocks 33 and 33A are distinct. The agreement mentions, in addition to the store property, "Lot 6 in Block 33A, Lakeview, Regina Beach, etc." The plaintiff never has owned Lot 6 in Block 33A.

Thus the plaintiff seeks rectification to delete reference to Lot 6 altogether and the defendant seeks rectification to correct the description from Block 33A to Block 33.

[His Lordship considered the applicable law and continued:]

On the evidence I am satisfied beyond any fair and reasonable doubt that the property Rob Roy was not intended by either of the parties to be included in their transaction. If it is Rob Roy which is described in the agreement as Lot 6, etc., it got in it by some inexplicable error on the part of the plaintiff's solicitor and its inclusion went unnoticed until late in 1963 by all parties and their solicitors.

The facts which so satisfy me are best listed:

The defendant and her husband were interested in buying the business interests of the plaintiff in Regina Beach, that is the store and the lease on the pavilion. There was no relationship between these businesses and Rob Roy cottage.

Rob Roy was never mentioned by any of the parties in any of their negotiations or in the memorandum of July 28, 1958, even by inference, and their solicitors were never instructed to include it.

The purchase price was calculated without Rob Roy being in the mind of either party.

I do not accept Mr. Palmer's statement that in a quarrel between him and the plaintiff concerning certain stock invoices within a week of the takeover, that the plaintiff said: "Now I will not include Rob Roy." If this were true he should have instructed his wife's solicitor to ensure it was included, if, in fact, the parties so intended. Furthermore, he did not check the final agreement or attend the signing of it only because he was not, by then, on speaking terms with the plaintiff.

From the date of the takeover, July, 1958, until October, 1963, the defendant did not demand possession of Rob Roy or its keys or its rent although she and her husband, who was the business head of the family, knew of its existence and location and must have known it was occupied. Neither said that they had even gone to look at it after the transaction.

Similarly the defendant never paid taxes or sought to insure Rob Roy. The fire policies assigned by the plaintiff were checked fully after a fire in August, 1961.

The defendant and her husband were not shy of quarreling with the plaintiff. In fact disagreement started within a few days of the first memorandum and continued for over five years. This disagreement was in relation to liability for certain invoices totalling, the defendant said, between $1,000 and $1,500. Why would they overlook an asset worth twice as much? The plaintiff sold Rob Roy in 1960 for $2,700.

The letter from the defendant's solicitor to the plaintiff's solicitor of August 6, 1958, refers to "both properties", *i.e.*, the store and the pavilion. If Rob Roy were intended to be included one would think he would use a term indicating more than two.

The agreement of August 21, 1958, lists contents of all buildings except Rob Roy.

The plaintiff in my view did nothing before or after the agreement in question inconsistent with the position she now takes, that Rob Roy was not included. Her failure to observe that Rob Roy was in the agreement was satisfactorily explained by her lack of knowledge of lot numbers and her reliance on her solicitor who had acted for her and her late husband for many years. I found her quite believable.

There will therefore be an order for rectification of the agreement between the parties dated August 21, 1958, deleting therefrom the second paragraph of the recitals, that is, all reference to Lot 6. The plaintiff shall have her costs.

The counterclaim is dismissed with costs to the plaintiff.

[The defendant appealed.]

BERCOVICI v. PALMER

(1966), 58 W.W.R. 111, 59 D.L.R. (2d) 513 (Sask. C.A.)

CULLITON C.J.S. [delivering the judgment of the court] . . . The principles to be followed by the Court in an action for rectification have been clearly stated in numerous judicial decisions. Duff J. (as he then was), in delivering one of the judgments of the Supreme Court of Canada in *Hart v. Boutilier* (1916), 56 D.L.R. 620 at 630, said:

> The power of rectification must be used with great caution; and only after the Court has been satisfied by evidence which leave no "fair and reasonable doubt" (*Fowler v. Fowler* (1859), 45 E.R. 97), that the deed impeached does not embody the final intention of the parties. This evidence must make it clear that the alleged intention to which the plaintiff asks that the deed be made to conform, continued concurrently in the minds of all the parties down to the time of its execution; and the plaintiff must succeed in shewing also the precise form in which the instrument will express this intention.

The same principles have been followed by the English Court of Appeal. In *Rose (Frederick E.) (London) Ltd. v. Pim (Wm. H.) Jr. & Co.*, [1953] 2 All E.R. 739 at 747 (C.A.), Denning L.J. said:

> Rectification is concerned with contracts and documents, not with intentions. In order to get rectification, it is necessary to show that the parties were in complete agreement on the terms of their contract, but by an error wrote them down wrongly.

It is clear from the judgment of the learned trial Judge that in the disposition of the case he directed himself in accordance with the foregoing principles. It is equally clear that there was evidence upon which he could properly make the findings of fact upon which he founded the order for rectification. Such findings were in part based upon his determination of the credibility of the witnesses and there are no circumstances that would warrant this Court in reversing the same:. . . .

Learned counsel contended that in an action for rectification the only evidence that can be considered is the evidence of what took place prior to the execution of the written document and that in the instant case the learned trial Judge erred in law in considering the conduct of the parties subsequent to that time. In support of this argument learned counsel relied upon the judgments in *Lovell and Christmas Ltd. v. Wall* (1911), 104 L.T. 85 (C.A.); *Earl of Bradford v. Earl of Romney* (1862), 54 E.R. 956, and *Brown v. Hillar*, [1951] 4 D.L.R. 383 (Ont. H.C.). With all deference I must say that I do not think the judgments in these cases advance the appellant's argument. In each case there is reiterated the established principle that subsequent declarations of the parties are not admissible for the purpose of construing a written contract. In this case the learned trial Judge was not faced with the question of construction but with the question of rectification. . . .

In *Hart v. Boutilier, supra*, it is obvious that Duff J. gave effect to considerations arising from the conduct of the parties for at p. 636 he said: "The respondent's subsequent conduct is not less difficult to understand." In the same case Idington J., makes it clear that in an action for rectification reliance may be placed upon considerations arising from the conduct of the parties. At p. 630 he stated:

> The conduct of the parties and the outstanding features and nature of the transaction must in such cases often be relied upon as a better guide than what either may merely swear to.

The case of *Smith v. Hemeon*, [1953] 4 D.L.R. 157 (N.S. S.C.), was an action for rectification. MacDonald J., in the application of the principles propounded in *Hart v. Boutilier, supra*, at p. 161 had this to say:

> Here there is no evidence other than the testimony of the plaintiff; for the defendant neither took the stand nor introduced any evidence. In such a case as this one must make up his mind definitely as to the credibility of the plaintiff as a witness, remembering that the issue is not merely as to the plaintiff's intention, but also as to the defendant's. Whilst a plaintiff cannot testify as to the intention of the defendant as such, his testimony may well make clear what the subject of the transaction was. In this case the plaintiff has satisfied me that the negotiations between the parties and the oral agreement they reached related to the Red Lot and to it alone. *Very germane to such a case is consideration of the subsequent conduct of the parties: cf. Hart v. Boutilier, supra*. . . .

(The italics are mine.) With the views so expressed by MacDonald J., I am in complete agreement.

There was, as would be expected, a denial by the appellant of the evidence given by the respondent, as to what was the real contract between the parties. The learned trial Judge, in satisfying himself beyond any reasonable doubt that the appellant did in truth enter into the agreement as alleged by the respondent, looked to certain documentary evidence and to the consideration arising from the conduct of the parties. This he was entitled to do. In my opinion the learned trial Judge properly stated and applied the law and as his findings of fact cannot be disturbed, the appeal will be dismissed with costs.

NOTE and QUESTION

1. Here the Court of Appeal admitted evidence of conduct subsequent to the execution of the contract for the purposes of deciding whether or not to grant relief. In doing so, the judge contrasted the use of such evidence for this purpose and the use of the same kind of evidence for the construction of a contract. Is there any rationale for treating such evidence differently, depending upon the purpose for which it is being used? See also *Man. Dev. Corp. v. Columbia Forest Products Ltd.* (1974), 43 D.L.R. (3d) 107 (Man. C.A.), where subsequent conduct was admitted for interpretative purposes.

2. Consider whether there has to be evidence of a prior concluded agreement between the parties or whether the court needs only to be "satisfied" of a "common intention."

SYLVAN LAKE GOLF & TENNIS CLUB LTD.
v. PERFORMANCE INDUSTRIES LTD.

[2002] 1 S.C.R. 678

BINNIE J. [delivering the judgment of McLachlin C.J., and L'Heureux-Dubé, Gonthier, Major, and Arbour JJ.]

In this appeal the Court is called on to deal with rectification of a contract for a real estate development dream that turned into a nightmare for the warring partners. Houses were to have been built along the 18th fairway of the Sylvan Lake Golf Course, within commuting distance of Red Deer, Alberta. It did not happen because the parties fell out over the amount of land to be included in the development contract.

There was a written contract but the respondent's President [Bell] did not bother to read it before it was signed. Had he done so, the error in reducing the parties' prior oral agreement to writing would likely have been detected and the development would have gone ahead. The appellants, who rely on the written document, say that a party who fails to exercise due diligence in its business affairs should be refused the equitable remedy of rectification. That is their strongest argument.

The principal witness and "directing mind" of the appellant Performance Industries Ltd. ("Performance"), which stands firm on the written document, is Terrance O'Connor. For him, the joint venture ended with his actions being characterized by the trial judge as "fraudulent, dishonest and deceitful". . . . The trial judgment made him personally liable (jointly and severally with his company Performance Industries Ltd.) for $1,047,810, including a $200,000 award of punitive damages, plus costs on a solicitor-client basis.

. . . . .

[Sylvan Lake Golf & Tennis Club Ltd. ("Sylvan") had operated an 18 hole golf course under a lease which gave it the right of first refusal in the event that the owner decided to sell the land. A third party offered to purchase the land from the owner in November 1989 for $1.3M and Sylvan had until December 31, 1989 to make the purchase on the same terms and conditions as the third party.

Near the end of November, Bell and O'Connor began to discuss purchasing the golf course as a joint venture.]

After a number of preliminary meetings, O'Connor spent about two and a half hours at Bell's home during the December 16-17 weekend. The two men met at length in O'Connor's truck a day or two later. The trial judge found that Bell and O'Connor came to a verbal agreement on the terms of their joint venture. They would pool their resources plus a $700,000 mortgage . . . to purchase the property. Sylvan (Bell) would thereafter operate the facilities for five years for its own account without any day-to-day involvement of O'Connor. In brief, at the conclusion of five years, Sylvan would be bought out by Performance (O'Connor) for an agreed sum less any money then outstanding on the . . . mortgage.

For present purposes, the only contentious issue was the option for a residential development to be undertaken by Bell [as a project to secure his retirement] (or a third party) "along the 18th fairway". O'Connor and Bell did not discuss a metes and bounds description of the optioned land, but Bell testified, and the trial judge accepted, that he showed O'Connor photographs and plans of the sort of development he had in mind, namely a *double* row of houses (i.e., on both sides of a street) clustered around a *cul-de-sac* along the length of the 18th fairway (480 yards). A photograph of a comparable golf course development where Bell had lived in the Bayview area of Toronto formed part of the negotiations. . . . O'Connor agreed to option the land to permit such a development, otherwise (as the trial judge found) Bell would not have agreed to the five-year joint venture. The parties agreed that the purchase price of the optioned land would be $400,000 by a third party (or $200,000 if the existing owner Sylvan (Bell) chose to develop the parcel).

As part of the agreement, O'Connor undertook to have his lawyer reduce the verbal terms to writing. In due course, a document was produced. Clause 18, the option, accurately specified the 480-yard length of the proposed development, but instead of sufficient width to permit a double row of houses (approximately 110 *yards*), clause 18 allowed only enough land for a single row of houses (110 *feet*). This misstatement of the oral agreement was thus pleaded in para. 9 of the Statement of Claim:

> Paragraph 18 of the December 21st, 1989 written Agreement did not accurately reflect the terms of the oral agreement made between Performance and Sylvan in that it misdescribed the width of the lands subject to the Agreement as "One Hundred and Ten (110 ft.) feet in width east to west", when the width of the lands comprising the 18th hole was approximately 110 *yards* in width east to west. [Emphasis in original.]

Bell had in mind a development of about 58 homes on about 11 acres. O'Connor's draft allowed 3.6 acres. Bell testified, and the trial judge accepted, that he had specifically told O'Connor during the negotiations that a single row housing development (which is all that clause 18 would permit) would "be a waste of land and an uneconomic use of the 18th hole" (para. 42).

.....

[The parties also signed a joint venture agreement which expressly mentioned the contemplated sale of land along the eighteenth fairway "110 feet in width".]

Bell subsequently retained Norman Trouth, a development consultant, who produced alternative plans and sketches for developments of 50 and 58 houses along the 18th fairway. Trouth estimated the 58-house project on or about 10.9 acres would net $820,100. In some respects, Bell was looking for more land than O'Connor had verbally agreed to. The proposals would, as contemplated from the outset, involve a measure of realignment of the 18th fairway. Bell therefore left these development proposals with O'Connor, who said he would review them. In the meantime, the lands in the golf course had been annexed to the Town of Sylvan Lake and there was potential for development of the entire 171.5 acres, much to O'Connor's benefit.

Time went by. In May 1993, Bell again contacted O'Connor, who promised to review the proposal, but did not respond either then or even after a later meeting arranged by Bell's wife. The clock was running because the option required the development to be completed by December 31, 1994. Finally, by letter dated June 8, 1993, O'Connor's lawyer advised Bell that "[i]t is very unlikely that Performance Industries Ltd. will approve of any development plan which is not strictly in line with the Agreement".

Bell testified that at that point, for the first time, he read clause 18 and realized that it did not conform to the oral agreement. O'Connor, he concluded, had slipped in a change of dimensions that turned a viable project into "a waste of land". Bell says he was incensed. He attended at O'Connor's office for what he described as a heated meeting.

Attempts were made to resolve the dispute, but O'Connor continued to insist that Bell's right to develop the property was limited under clause 18 of the Agreement to a strip of land 110 feet wide on the easterly boundary of the golf course adjacent to the 18th hole. Bell continued to insist that O'Connor live up to the verbal agreement, which would require 110 feet being read as 110 yards.

In December 1994, the 5-year duration of the joint venture coming up for expiry, O'Connor tendered the funds required to buy out Sylvan's interest. Bell refused to allow Sylvan to relinquish possession of the land, and O'Connor commenced an action for specific performance. The Alberta Court of Queen's Bench granted an order for specific performance and O'Connor assumed possession of the property and built a clubhouse at the 18th hole. Also in late 1994, Sylvan commenced the present action against Performance and O'Connor for rectification of the Agreement or damages in lieu thereof, punitive damages and solicitor-client costs.

.....

Rectification of the Contract

Rectification is an equitable remedy whose purpose is to prevent a written document from being used as an engine of fraud or misconduct "equivalent to fraud". The traditional rule was to permit rectification only for mutual mistake, but rectification is now available for unilateral mistake (as here), provided certain demanding preconditions are met. Insofar as they are relevant to this appeal, these preconditions can be summarized as follows. Rectification is predicated on the existence of a prior oral contract whose terms are definite and ascertainable. The plaintiff must establish that the terms agreed to orally were not written down properly. The error may be fraudulent, or it may be innocent. What is essential is that at the time of execution of the written document the defendant knew or ought to have known of the error and the plaintiff did not. Moreover, the attempt of the defendant to rely on the erroneous written document must amount to "fraud or the equivalent of fraud". The court's task in a rectification case is corrective, not speculative. It is to restore the parties to their original bargain, not to rectify a belatedly recognized error of judgment by one party or the other: *Hart v. Boutilier* (1916), 56 D.L.R. 620 (S.C.C.), at p. 630; *Ship M. F. Whalen v. Pointe Anne*

Quarries Ltd. (1921), 63 S.C.R. 109, at pp. 126-27; *Downtown King West De-velopment Corp. v. Massey Ferguson Industries Ltd.* (1996), 133 D.L.R. (4th) 550 (Ont. C.A.), at p. 558. . . . In *Hart, supra,* at p. 630, Duff J. (as he then was) stressed that "[t]he power of rectification must be used with great caution". Apart from everything else, a relaxed approach to rectification as a substitute for due diligence at the time a document is signed would undermine the confidence of the commercial world in written contracts.

. . . . .

The Conditions Precedent to Rectification

As stated, high hurdles are placed in the way of a businessperson who relies on his or her own unilateral mistake to resile from the written terms of a document which he or she has signed and which, on its face, seems perfectly clear. The law is determined not to open the proverbial floodgates to dissatisfied contract makers who want to extricate themselves from a poor bargain.

I referred earlier to the four conditions precedent, or "hurdles" that a plaintiff must overcome. To these the appellants wish to add a fifth. Rectification, they say, should not be available to a plaintiff who is negligent in reviewing the documentation of a commercial agreement. To the extent the appellants' argument is that in such circumstances the Court *may* exercise its discretion to refuse the equitable remedy to such a plaintiff, I agree with them. To the extent they say the want of due diligence (or negligence) on the plaintiff's part is an absolute bar, I think their proposition is inconsistent with principle and authority and should be rejected.

The first of the traditional hurdles is that Sylvan (Bell) must show the existence and content of the inconsistent prior oral agreement. Rectification is "[t]he most venerable breach in the parol evidence rule" (Waddams, [*The Law of Contracts*] at para. 336). The requirement of a prior oral agreement closes the "floodgate" to unhappy contract makers who simply failed to read the contractual documents, or who now have misgivings about the merits of what they have signed.

The second hurdle is that not only must Sylvan (Bell) show that the written document does not correspond with the prior oral agreement, but that O'Connor either knew or ought to have known of the mistake in reducing the oral terms to writing. It is only where permitting O'Connor to take advantage of the error would amount to "fraud or the equivalent of fraud" that rectification is available. This requirement closes the "floodgate" to unhappy contract makers who simply made a mistake. Equity acts on the conscience of a defendant who seeks to take advan-tage of an error which he or she either knew or ought reasonably to have known about at the time the document was signed. Mere unilateral mistake alone is not sufficient to support rectification but if permitting the non-mistaken party to take advantage of the document would be fraud or equivalent to fraud, rectification may be available: *Hart, supra,* at p. 630; *Ship M. F. Whalen, supra,* at pp. 126-27.

What amounts to "fraud or the equivalent of fraud" is, of course, a crucial question. In *First City Capital Ltd. v. British Columbia Building Corp.* (1989), 43 B.L.R. 29 (B.C.S.C.), McLachlin C.J.S.C. (as she then was) observed that "in this context 'fraud or the equivalent of fraud' refers not to the tort of deceit or strict fraud in the legal sense, but rather to the broader category of equitable fraud or constructive fraud. . . . Fraud in this wider sense refers to transactions falling short of deceit but where the Court is of the opinion that it is unconscientious for a person to avail himself of the advantage obtained" (p. 37). Fraud in the "wider sense" of a ground for equitable relief "is so infinite in its varieties that the Courts have not attempted to define it", but "all kinds of unfair dealing and unconscionable conduct in matters of contract come within its ken": *McMaster University v. Wilchar Construction Ltd.* (1971), 22 D.L.R. (3d) 9 (Ont. H.C.), at p. 19. See also *Montreal Trust Co. v. Maley* (1992), 99 D.L.R. (4th) 257 (Sask. C.A.), *per* Wakeling J.A.; *Alampi v. Swartz* (1964), 43 D.L.R. (2d) 11 (Ont. C.A.); *Stepps Investments Ltd. v. Security Capital Corp.* (1976), 73 D.L.R. (3d) 351 (Ont. H.C.), *per* Grange J. (as he then was), at pp. 362-63; and Waddams, *supra*, at para. 342.

The third hurdle is that Sylvan (Bell) must show "the precise form" in which the written instrument can be made to express the prior intention (*Hart*, *supra*, *per* Duff J., at p. 630). This requirement closes the "floodgates" to those who would invite the court to speculate about the parties' unexpressed intentions, or impose what in hindsight seems to be a sensible arrangement that the parties might have made but did not. The court's equitable jurisdiction is limited to putting into words that—and only that—which the parties had already orally agreed to.

The fourth hurdle is that all of the foregoing must be established by proof which this Court has variously described as "beyond reasonable doubt" (*Ship M. F. Whalen*, *supra*, at p. 127), or "evidence which leaves no 'fair and reasonable doubt'" (*Hart*, *supra*, at p. 630), or "convincing proof" or "more than sufficient evidence" (*Augdome Corp. v. Gray*, [1975] 2 S.C.R. 354, at pp. 371-72). The modern approach, I think, is captured by the expression "convincing proof", i.e., proof that may fall well short of the criminal standard, but which goes beyond the sort of proof that only reluctantly and with hesitation scrapes over the low end of the civil "more probable than not" standard.

Some critics argue that anything more demanding than the ordinary civil standard of proof is unnecessary (e.g., Waddams, *supra*, at para. 343), but, again, the objective is to promote the utility of written agreements by closing the "floodgate" against marginal cases that dilute what are rightly seen to be demanding preconditions to rectification.

It was formerly held that it was not sufficient if the evidence merely comes from the party seeking rectification. In *Ship M. F. Whalen*, *supra*, Duff J. (as he then was) said, at p. 127, "[s]uch parol evidence must be adequately supported by documentary evidence and by considerations arising from the conduct of the parties". Modern practice has moved away from insistence on documentary corroboration (Waddams, *supra*, at para. 337; Fridman, [*The Law of Contract*], at p. 879). In some situations, documentary corroboration is simply not available, but if the parol evidence is corroborated by the conduct of the parties or other proof, rectification may, in the discretion of the court, be available.

                                        .....

The Existence and Content of the Prior Oral Agreement

The Court should attempt to uphold the parties' bargain where the terms can be ascertained with a reasonable level of comfort, i.e., convincing proof. Here the trial judge predicated his award of compensatory damages on the finding that the optioned land could accommodate 58 single family houses located along the 480 yard length of the 18th fairway. There is no argument about the 480 yards. O'Connor himself plucked the 480 figure from the length of play listed on the Sylvan Lake Golf Club score card. O'Connor's number for the width of the development (110) may also be accepted. The issue is whether the number was intended to express yards or feet. The trial judge appears to have concluded that the dispute about the depth of the residential development (which is all that divided the parties) came down to a simple choice between Bell's version (Plan A) and O'Connor's version (Plan B). Both plans were predicated on the length of the 18th fairway, namely 480 yards. Plan B, which O'Connor had described in the document, contemplated a single row of houses on a development plan 110 *feet* deep. Bell's Plan A was based on two rows of housing separated by a road allowance, in a configuration similar to that shown in the aerial photo of the Bayview development discussed by Bell and O'Connor at their December 16-17 meeting. Plan A called for a depth of about 110 *yards*. If Plan B's 110-*foot* depth is tripled to 110 *yards*, the acreage under option would be roughly tripled from about 3.6 acres (Plan B) to about 10.9 acres (Plan A), which accommodates the 58 lots plus the standard municipal road allowance. . . .

The trial judge . . . found that the parties had made a verbal agreement with reference to a residential development along the 18th hole. It was more than an agreement to agree. He concluded that there was a definite project in a definite location to which O'Connor and Bell had given their definite assent.

Although the parties did not discuss a metes and bounds description, they were working on a defined development proposal. O'Connor cannot complain if the numbers he inserted in clause 18 (110 x 480) are accepted and confirmed. The issue, then, is the error created by his apparently duplicitous substitution of feet for yards in one dimension. We know the 480 must be yards because it measures the 18th fairway. If the 110 is converted from feet to yards, symmetry is achieved, certainty is preserved and Bell's position is vindicated.

Fraud or Conduct Equivalent to Fraud

The notion of "*equivalent* to fraud" as distinguished from fraud itself, is often utilized where "the court is unwilling to go so far as to find actual knowledge on the side of the party seeking enforcement" (Waddams, *supra*, at para. 342). The trial judge had no such hesitation in this case. He characterized O'Connor's actions as "fraudulent, dishonest and deceitful" (para. 114).

The trial judge was persuaded not only of the terms of the prior oral agreement and of Bell's mistake but "beyond any reasonable doubt" of O'Connor's knowledge of that mistake. He states (at para. 79):

> This court is satisfied beyond any reasonable doubt that O'Connor knew of Bell's mistake and he chose to permit Bell to sign it in the mistaken belief that it represented the verbal agreement. He did so with the full intention that he would in the future rely on the terms of the Agreement to thwart or reduce any plan by Bell to develop an increased area of the golf course for residential development.

O'Connor thus fraudulently misrepresented the written document as accurately reflecting the terms of the prior oral contract. He knew that Bell would not sign an agreement without the option for sufficient land to create the "Bayview" layout development with two rows of housing as specified in the prior oral contract. O'Connor therefore knew when Bell signed the document that he had not detected the substitution of 110 feet for 110 yards. O'Connor knowingly snapped at Bell's mistake "to thwart or reduce any plan by Bell to develop an increased area of the golf course for residential development". Bell's loss would be O'Connor's gain, as O'Connor (Performance) would come into sole ownership of the optioned land as of December 31, 1994.

Although on occasion the trial judge describes O'Connor's conduct as "equivalent to a fraud", and elsewhere he describes it as actual fraud, his reasons taken as a whole can only be characterized as a finding of actual fraud.

Precise Terms of Rectification

It follows from the foregoing that "the precise form" in which the written document can be made to conform to the oral agreement would be simply to change the word "feet" in the phrase "one hundred ten (110) *feet* in width" to "yards".

Existence of "Convincing Proof"

The trial judge made his key findings in respect of the prior oral agreement, Bell's unilateral mistake and O'Connor's knowledge of that mistake to a standard of "beyond any reasonable doubt".

He also found that Bell's version of the verbal agreement was sufficiently corroborated on significant points by other witnesses (including his wife, his former partner, his lawyer and, subsequently, the development consultants), and documents (including his lawyer's notes and the plan of the Bayview Golf Course development discussed in mid-December 1989).

Bell's Lack of Due Diligence

The appellants seek, in effect, to add a fifth hurdle (or condition precedent) to the availability of rectification. A plaintiff, they say, should be denied such a remedy unless the error in the written document could not have been discovered with due diligence.

O'Connor says that Bell's failure to read clause 18 and note the mixture of yards and feet should be fatal to his claim because the Court ought not to assist businesspersons who are negligent in protecting their own interests. Alternatively, the effective cause of Bell's loss is not the fraudulent document but Bell's failure to detect the fraud when he had an opportunity to do so.

I agree that Bell, an experienced businessman, ought to have examined the text of clause 18 before signing the document. The terms of clause 18 were clear on their face (even though many readers might have misread a description of land that mixed units of measurement as clause 18 did here). He had time to review the document with his lawyer. He did so. Changes were requested. He did not catch the substitution of 110 feet for 110 yards; indeed, he says he did not read clause 18 at all. . . .

It is undoubtedly true that courts ought to hold commercial entities to a reasonable level of due diligence in documenting their transactions. Otherwise, written agreements will lose their utility and commercial life will suffer. Rectification should not become a belated substitute for due diligence.

On the other hand, most cases of unilateral mistake involve a degree of carelessness on the part of the plaintiff. A diligent reading of the written document would generally have disclosed the error that the plaintiff, after the fact, seeks to have corrected. The mistaken party will often have failed to read the document entirely, or may have read it too hastily or without parsing each word. As the American *Restatement of the Law, Second: Contracts (2d)* (1981) points out in its commentary under s. 157 ("Effect of Fault of Party Seeking Relief"), "since a party can often avoid a mistake by the exercise of such care, the availability of relief would be severely circumscribed if he were to be barred by his negligence". Comment B discusses "[f]ailure to read writing". "Generally, one who assents to a writing is presumed to know its contents and cannot escape being bound by its terms merely by contending that he did not read them; his assent is deemed to cover unknown as well as known terms." But this proposition is qualified by that Comment's further statement that the "exceptional rule" in s. 157 (which permits rectification or "reformation" of the contract) applies only where there has been an agreement that preceded the writing. "In such a case, a party's negligence in failing to read the writing does not preclude reformation if the writing does not correctly express the prior agreement".

One reason why the defence of contributory negligence or want of due diligence is not persuasive in a rectification case is because the plaintiff seeks no more than enforcement of the prior oral agreement to which the defendant has already bound itself.

. . . . .

Discretionary Relief

I conclude, therefore that due diligence on the part of the plaintiff is not a condition precedent to rectification. However, it should be added at once that rectification is an equitable remedy and its award is in the discretion of the court. The conduct of the plaintiff is relevant to the exercise of that discretion. In a case where the court concludes that it would be unjust to impose on a defendant a liability that ought more properly to be attributed to the plaintiff's negligence, rectification may be denied. That was not the case here.

Fraud

There is, on the facts of this case, a more fundamental reason why the appellants' complaint about Bell's lack of due diligence provides no defence. O'Connor did more than "snap" at a business partner's mistake. O'Connor undertook as part of the verbal agreement to have a document prepared that set out its terms. According to the trial judge, he not only breached that term, it became part of his fraudulent scheme to have the document wrongly state the terms of the option, to fraudulently misrepresent to Bell that it did accurately set out their verbal agreement, to allow Bell to sign it when O'Connor knew Bell was mistaken in doing so, then to delay any response to Bell's development proposals (and thus bring the error to Bell's attention) until it was almost too late for the development to proceed. O'Connor admitted providing his lawyer with the erroneous metes and bounds description in clause 18. It should not, I think, lie in his mouth to say that he should not be responsible for what followed because his fraud was so obvious that it ought to have been detected.

"[F]raud 'unravels everything'": *Farah v. Barki*, [1955] S.C.R. 107, at p. 115 (Kellock J. quoting Farwell J. in *May v. Platt*, [1900] 1 Ch. 616, at p. 623).

The appellants' concept of a due diligence defence in a fraud case was rejected over 125 years ago by Lord Chelmsford L.C. who said, "when once it is established that there has been any fraudulent misrepresentation or wilful concealment by which a person has been induced to enter into a contract, it is no answer to his claim to be relieved from it to tell him that he might have known the truth by proper inquiry. He has a right to retort upon his objector, 'You, at least, who have stated what is untrue, or have concealed the truth, for the purpose of drawing me into a contract, cannot accuse me of want of caution because I relied implicitly upon your fairness and honesty'": *Central R. Co. of Venezuela v. Kisch* (1867), L.R. 2 H.L. 99, at pp. 120-21. . . .

The appellants having failed to establish that due diligence on the part of the plaintiff is a precondition to rectification, or to shake the trial judge's findings with respect to the traditional preconditions discussed above, their appeal on the rectification issues must be rejected.

[Binnie J. agreed with the Alberta Court of Appeal in refusing to award punitive damages in this case. Although O'Connor's conduct was reprehensible, even fraudulent conduct attracts punitive damages only in exceptional cases. The court pointed out that, in accordance with *Whiten v. Pilot Insurance, infra,* Chapter 14, section 3(iv), the plaintiff had received generous compensatory damages and that punitive damages were rational only if compensatory damages failed to adequately achieve the objectives of retribution, deterrence and denunciation. LeBel J. concurred, subject only to the same reservations on the role of punitive damages that he expressed in *Whiten*.]

NOTES

1. In the *Sylvan Lake* case, as in many other decisions involving rectification of contracts, the court went to some lengths to emphasize the restrictions on the remedy in order to avoid opening the floodgates for litigation. In other contexts, the courts have been liberal in allowing rectification,

particularly in a series of tax cases, the best known of which is *Juliar v. Canada (Attorney General)* (2000), 50 O.R. (3d) 728 (C.A.). In *Juliar*, family members entered into an agreement to restructure a business. It was always intended that the transaction should not attract immediate tax liabilities to the parties. However, the agreement resulted in adverse tax consequences that the parties had not anticipated. The court found that if a mistake is made in a document deliberately designed to avoid the payment of tax, there is no reason why it should not be corrected (at para. 25). The Crown, which contested the application for rectification, was in no privileged position in relation to such a document (at paras. 33 - 34).

2. Sections 4 and 5 of this chapter have raised many issues relating to the impact on third parties when a court invalidates a transaction on the grounds of mistake. For a discussion of the effect of rectification on third parties, see *Augdome Corp. v. Gray* (1974), [1975] 2 S.C.R. 354.

Chapter 10

FRUSTRATION

1. Introduction

As noted elsewhere in this book, "sanctity of contract" has been identified as one of the cornerstones of the classical model of contracts. However, as the previous chapter on mistake indicated, in certain limited situations parties may be excused from their contractual obligations. Frustration provides another example of an excuse from performance obligations. Whereas mistake deals with inaccurate assumptions or lack of knowledge about past or existing circumstances, frustration relates to inaccurate assumptions about future circumstances. Sometimes it is not clear whether a mistake or a frustration analysis is appropriate.

For example, assume that a popular rock band has been scheduled to play in the only outdoor stadium in your hometown. Two days before the concert, the local municipality revokes the licence because it is discovered that the stadium has become very dangerous due to serious architectural flaws. No other venue is available. All the parties involved in the concert—the band, the promoters, the airlines, the trucking companies, the roadies, security companies, franchises and the fans—had assumed that the stadium would be available. Large sums of money have been expended in anticipation and significant profits expected. What is to be done? If the situation (the revocation of the licence) is seen as linked to danger arising after the contract, then the doctrine of frustration would be applicable. If, on the other hand, the revocation is seen as linked to a problem of architectural flaws pre-existing the contract, then the doctrine of mistake could be applicable.

Under the regime of "sanctity of contract" all the parties would be locked in: they would have to perform their respective obligations or pay damages for breach. Contractual liability is absolute. But, as we shall see in this chapter, in the course of the last century the courts have been gradually widening the ambit of the doctrine of frustration, thereby allowing the parties to walk away from their future obligations because of a supervening contingency. Thus the focus of section 2 of this chapter, Development and Application of the Doctrine, is to identify some of the limited circumstances in which a claim of frustration might possibly succeed. Such circumstances might include: death, incapacity or unavailability of a contracting party; destruction or unavailability of the subject matter; illegality; method of performance becoming impossible; and thwarting of a common venture. As will become apparent, certain types of arrangements, such as shipping, building and export sales contracts, are particularly vulnerable to unforeseen upheavals.

Section 3 addresses the issue of self-induced frustration. Section 4 raises the question of whether the doctrine should be expanded further while section 5 deals with the judicial response to efforts by the drafters of contracts to plan for the unforeseen via *force majeure* clauses. Finally, section 6 discusses the effects of frustration.

Frustration also provides a particularly good illustration of the debate on the role of the judiciary in developing contract law. Over the years, a variety of theories have been espoused by judges and academics as to the underlying rationale and justifications for the doctrine. In relation to the question of whether a contract has been frustrated they are usually catalogued as the "implied term", "construction", and "foundation of the contract" theories. With respect to the effect of a frustrated contract, they are commonly described as the "failure of consideration" or "just solution" approaches. One way to conceptualize the debate is between those who espouse judicial restraint and those who favour judicial activism.

Those who favour restraint proclaim that "no court has an absolving power" (*Tamplin (F.A.) S.S. Co. Ltd. v. Anglo-Mexican Petroleum Co. Ltd.*, [1916] 2 A.C. 397 (H.L.) at 404). They explain the rare cases of frustration on the basis that there is an implied term which allows the parties to avoid their contractual obligations.

On the other hand, those who perceive themselves as more realistic claim it is better if we acknowledge that in these situations the courts are actually making aspects of the contract for the parties. An example is Lord Radcliffe's unusually frank (for a judge) acknowledgment that the "reasonable man" is simply the court's "anthropomorphic conception of justice" (*Davis Contractors v. Fareham U.D.C.*, *infra*, section 2 of this chapter at 728). The most explicit version of this view is to be found in Lord Wright's assertion that "[t]he truth is . . . the Court . . . decides the question in accordance with what seems to be just and reasonable in its eyes. The judge finds in himself the criterion of what is reasonable. The Court is in this sense making a contract for the parties—though it is almost blasphemy to say so". (*Legal Essays and Addresses* (1939), at 259.)

Those who advocate an interventionist analysis often appeal to "fairness" or "efficient allocation of risk" as the benchmark for an appropriate resolution of the case. The following four discussions are attempts by academics to identify guiding principles that can help resolve problems of frustration. In reading the cases that follow the extracts, you might consider (a) whether the courts are adopting a literalist or an interventionist approach and (b) whether any of the extracts can provide guidance in explaining the current state of the law.

COLLINS, THE LAW OF CONTRACT

4th ed. (2003), at 300-301

Although the courts prefer to describe their practices that are analogous to judicial revision as either construction of the contract in order to fulfil the intentions of the parties or as independent rules of law concerned with impossibility, neither of these accounts appears strongly persuasive. If the [judicial] intervention is described as merely construction of the contract, given that the parties did not foresee and have any clear intentions towards the events which have occurred, we must suspect that the courts use a further criterion for determining the intent of the parties. This criterion may be one which takes fairness in the sense of the preservation of the balance of advantage of the contract as the unacknowledged but vital guide to interpretation. Alternatively, if the intervention is described as the application of a rule about impossibility, again the decision whether an unexpected event renders an obligation impossible seems likely to depend upon a judgment as to whether to continue to insist upon performance would upset the balance of advantage contained in the contract. . . .

Although many judges deny that fairness is relevant to the question of whether or not a contract is frustrated, they frequently acknowledge that their interventions are required by the need to do justice between the parties. In a representative description of the doctrine of frustration, Bingham LJ states [*J Lauritzen AS v. Wijsmuller BV, The Super Servant Two,* [1990] 1 Lloyd's Rep. 1 CA]:

> The object of the doctrine was to give effect to the demands of justice, to achieve a just and reasonable result, to do what is reasonable and fair, as an expedient to escape from injustice where such would result from enforcement of a contract in its literal terms after a significant change in circumstances . . .

These references to injustice, or as we prefer to say unfairness, require further elucidation.

The process of judicial revision is not so simple as to compare the obligation of one party before and after the unexpected event in order to discover whether the event has substantially increased the cost of performance of his obligation. The criterion of fairness must also be sensitive both to the sophistication of the parties when they established their contract and the precise allocation of risks by the contract. Where the parties enjoyed comparable resources for devising a complex commercial transaction and exercised those resources in order to create a contract which attempted to allocate all the risks between the parties, then it is unlikely except in calamitous circumstances that the courts will be prepared to accept that unexpected events have created any imbalance in the obligations. If, on the other hand, either one or both parties lack these skills, the terms of the contract are less likely to be regarded as a presumptively fair allocation of the burdens of unforeseen eventualities. In these cases, the courts are more likely to use the techniques of judicial revision such as construction or frustration in order to restore the expectations of the parties with respect to the balance of advantage contained in the contract. . . .

[Footnotes omitted.]

ATIYAH, AN INTRODUCTION TO THE LAW OF CONTRACT

5th ed. (1995), at 240-243

But if the contract does not expressly allocate the risks, the question is how the law (or the court, speaking for the law) should allocate them. If it is not reasonable to place the risk of the relevant events on either party the contract is frustrated whereas, if the risk is placed on either party, that party will be bound to perform or to pay damages if he cannot do so. The following factors may be considered as very general guides in deciding whether the court will place a certain risk on one or other of the parties.

First . . . it can be said that a party takes the risk of any changes in circumstances which affect only his own purposes in contracting, and do not affect the common object of both parties. Similarly, a change in circumstances which only affects *the way* in which one of the parties is to carry out his obligations does not normally frustrate a contract. . . .

Secondly, it may happen that a party enters into a contract whereby he receives remuneration so abnormally large that it is clear that in effect he is receiving a sort of insurance premium against special risks. Then it must be reasonable to place on him those risks. . . .

The third rule is perhaps the most important of all: generally speaking, a person who undertakes to do something takes the risk that performance of his undertaking may prove more onerous than expected, or even impossible, as a result of changes in circumstances which are normal, or merely slight deviations from the normal, whereas he does not take the risk of performance proving impossible owing to utterly abnormal or extraordinary occurrences. . . .

Fourthly, even though a person does not normally take the risk of non-performance where performance is rendered impossible as a result of utterly abnormal developments, he does take the risk, or at all events the courts think it reasonable to place on him the risk, of non-performance, if the result of the impossibility is to give him a remedy over against some other person. . . .

Finally, it may be laid down as a very rough general rule that, if parties make a contract which is only to be performed at some distant future date, one or other of them will be held to have assumed the risk of performance whatever the future may bring. The point is that a whole object of such contracts is frequently to eliminate the dangers of later events.

[Footnotes omitted]

POSNER, ECONOMIC ANALYSIS OF LAW

6th ed. (2003), at 105-108

Suppose I agree to supply someone with 1,000 widgets by July 1; my factory burns to the ground; and I cannot procure widgets from anyone else in time to fulfill the contract. Suppose, further, that there was no way in which I could have anticipated or prevented the fire, so that fulfillment of the contract was genuinely impossible. It does not follow that I should escape liability for the buyer's losses that resulted from my failure to perform. My undertaking may have implicitly included a promise to insure him in the event of my inability to deliver the promised goods on time. And if such a contract of insurance was implicit in the transaction, it should be enforced.

The distinction between *prevention* and *insurance* as methods of minimizing loss is fundamental to the analysis of contract law. A loss that can be averted by an expenditure smaller than the expected loss is preventable, but not all losses are preventable in this sense; the fire that destroyed the factory in the preceding example was assumed not to be. Through insurance, however, it may be possible to reduce the costs created by the risk of loss. The insured exchanges the possibility of a loss for a smaller, but certain, cost (the insurance premium). . . .

[I]f an event rendering the contract uneconomical (such as unexpectedly severe weather) is not preventable at a cost less than the expected loss caused by nonperformance, one of the contracting parties may be the cheaper insurer. This is a reason independent of ability to prevent the event from occurring for assuming that the parties, had they made provision for this contingency, would have assigned that party the risk. If the promisee is the intended risk bearer, the promisor is discharged if the risk materializes and prevents him from completing performance.

To determine the cheaper insurer, it is convenient to divide the costs of insurance into two categories: (1) measurement costs and (2) transaction costs. The first consists of the costs of estimating (a) the probability that the risk will materialize and (b) the magnitude of the loss if the risk does materialize. The product of the two is the expected value of the loss and is the basis for computing the appropriate insurance premium that will be built into the contract price. . . . The main transaction cost is that of pooling the risk with other risks to reduce or eliminate it; where self-insurance is feasible, this cost may be lower than if market insurance has to be purchased. . . .

This analysis of the insurance function of contracts is helpful for understanding the doctrine of impossibility and related grounds for discharging a contract. It explains, for example, why physical impossibility as such is not a ground for discharge. If the promisor is the cheaper insurer, the fact that he could not have prevented the occurrence of the event that prevented him from performing should not discharge him. Conversely, the fact that performance remains physically possible, but is uneconomical, should not *ipso facto* defeat discharge. If the promisor could not have prevented at reasonable cost the event that has prevented him from fulfilling his promise and the promisee was the cheaper insurer of the resulting loss, the promisor has a good argument that he did not break the contract. So impossibility is ill-named—but maybe not, because it dramatizes the critical fact that mere difficulty or unforeseen expense of performance is not an excuse for failure to perform. Ordinarily, a fixed-price contract is intended to assign to the performing party the risk of problems encountered in performance, since that party is better able to overcome them.

Discharge is routinely allowed in personal service contracts where the death of the promisor prevents performance, unless the promisor had reason to believe (and failed to warn the promisee) that his life expectancy was less than normal for someone of his age. The event, death, is probably not preventable at reasonable cost by either party, but the promisee is the cheaper insurer; although both parties are in an equally good position to estimate the probability of the promisor's death, the promisee is in a better position to estimate the cost to him if the promisor is unable to provide the agreed-upon services.

Another example is a contract to drill for water. The contractor who, because of unexpectedly difficult soil conditions, is unable to complete performance at the cost he projected is not excused. He probably is the superior insurer, even if he could not have anticipated the soil conditions. He will know better than the promisee both the likelihood, and the consequences for the costs of drilling, of encountering subsoil conditions that make drilling difficult. So he will be better able to estimate the risk. He may also be able to self-insure at low cost because he does a lot of drilling in different areas and the risks of encountering unexpectedly difficult conditions are independent.

Now suppose a grower agrees before the growing season to sell his crop to a grain elevator, and the crop is destroyed by blight. Should the grower be excused from liability? Probably. He has every incentive to avoid a blight, so if it occurs, it probably could not have been prevented; and the grain elevator, which doubtless buys from a variety of growers, not all of whom will be hit by blight in the same growing season, is in a better position to buffer the risk of blight than the grower is—though it must be added that in this age of future contracts both parties may be able to insure against the loss quite inexpensively.

Often parties will include in their contract a *force majeure* ("greater force") clause, specifying the circumstances in which failure to perform will be excused. If they do, should impossibility, impracticability, and related judicial doctrines be applicable to the contract?

Examples of the operation of these doctrines could be multiplied, but instead let us consider the related case where completion of performance by one of the parties is prevented, again by circumstances beyond his control, and that party wants to be excused from further performance or even wants to be paid for what he has done although it is not what the contract called for him to do. I hire a contractor to build a house and midway through construction the building burns down. The contractor demands to be paid for the material and labor that he expended on the construction or, alternatively, refuses to rebuild the house without a new contract. The fact that he was prevented through no fault of his own from performing as contemplated by the contract should not automatically entitle him to cancel it or to be paid as if the burned-down building had been what I contracted for. The issue should be which of us was intended to bear the risk of fire. In the absence of evidence of the parties' actual intentions, we have to compare relative costs of preventing or insuring against fire. Like a manufacturer whose goods are destroyed by fire before delivery, the contractor generally is better placed for fire protection than the owner because he controls the premises and is knowledgeable about the fire hazards of buildings under construction.

[Footnotes omitted.]

TREBILCOCK, THE LIMITS OF FREEDOM OF CONTRACT

(1993), at 135-136

Posner and Rosenfield ["Impossibility and Related Doctrines in Contract Law: An Economic Analysis" (1977), 6 J. of Leg. Stud. 83] acknowledge that

often (I would be inclined to argue, typically) the criteria they propose for identifying the most efficient insurer or risk-bearer will point in opposite directions—one party is better placed to estimate the probability of a given contingency
materializing (typically the party whose performance is in issue); the other party,
who is to receive the performance in issue, can better evaluate the magnitude of
the loss if the contingency does materialize; and either party may be better placed
to diversify away or absorb the risk through self-insurance, market insurance, or,
more debatably, superior wealth. Uncertainties surrounding these issues are likely
to render judicially determined insurance extremely expensive compared with
most forms of explicit first-party insurance. Moreover, in contractual settings
such as entailed in the frustration cases, at least in the absence of major information
asymmetries between the parties, it is not clear that the courts are likely to improve
on the risk allocations of the parties by engaging in highly particularistic *ex post*
assignments of losses. A clear, albeit austere, rule of literal contract enforcement
in most cases provides the clearest signal to parties to future contractual relationships as to when they might find it mutually advantageous to contract away from
the rule.

[Footnotes omitted.]

2. Development and Application of the Doctrine

PARADINE v. JANE
(1647), Aleyn 26, 82 E.R. 897, Sty. 47; 82 E.R. 519 (K.B.)

[Paradine had leased certain lands to Jane and brought this action in debt for
rent which the defendant had failed to pay. The action occurred during the period
of the English Civil War and, in response to it, the defendant pleaded] that Prince
Rupert, an alien, and an enemy of the King invaded the land with an army, and
with divers armed men did enter upon him, and did drive away his cattell, and
expelled him from the lands let unto him by the plaintiff, and kept him out that
he could not enjoy the lands for such a time. [His counsel argued strenuously
that] by the law of reason it seems the defendant in our case ought not to be
charged with the rent, because he could not enjoy that that was let to him, and it
was no fault of his own that he could not.

ROLL J. . . . . When the party by his own contract creates a duty or charge
upon himself, he is bound to make it good, if he may, notwithstanding any accident
by inevitable necessity, because he might have provided against it by his contract.
And therefore if the lessee covenant to repair a house though it be burnt by
lightning or thrown down by enemies, yet he ought to repair it. . . . Another reason
was added, that as the lessee is to have the advantage of casual profits, so he must
run the hazard of casual losses, and not lay the whole burthen of them upon his
lessor; and though the land be surrounded or gained by the sea, or made barren
by wildfire, yet the lessor shall have his whole rent.

[Judgment for plaintiff.]

NOTE and QUESTION

1. The above extract is taken from a combination of two private reports of the case.

For discussions of the curious history of how *Paradine v. Jane* became a leading case see Page, "The Development of the Doctrine of Impossibility of Performance" (1919-1920), 18 Michigan L. Rev. 589 and Swan, "The Allocation of Risk in the Analysis of Mistake and Frustration" in Reiter and Swan, *Studies in Contract Law* (1980) 181 at 185 footnote 13. See also, more generally, Treitel, *Frustration and Force Majeure* (1994) Ch. 2.

2. Is the rule in *Paradine v. Jane* excessively harsh? What would have been the result if the lessee had been willing to take up possession of the premises, but the lessor had been prevented by the Civil War from delivering them up?

TAYLOR v. CALDWELL

(1863), 3 B. & S. 826, 122 E.R. 309 (Q.B.)

BLACKBURN J. [delivering the judgment of the court] In this case the plaintiffs and defendants had, on the 27th May, 1861, entered into a contract by which the defendants agreed to let the plaintiffs have the use of The Surrey Gardens and Music Hall on four days then to come, viz., the 17th June, 15th July, 5th August and 19th August, for the purpose of giving a series of four grand concerts, and day and night fetes at the Gardens and Hall on those days respectively; and the plaintiffs agreed to take the Gardens and Hall on those days, and pay 100*l* for each day.

. . . The agreement then proceeds to set out various stipulations between the parties as to what each was to supply for these concerts and entertainments, and as to the manner in which they should be carried on. The effect of the whole is to shew that the existence of the Music Hall in the Surrey Gardens in a state fit for a concert was essential for the fulfilment of the contract,—such entertainments as the parties contemplated in their agreement could not be given without it.

After the making of the agreement, and before the first day on which a concert was to be given, the Hall was destroyed by fire. This destruction, we must take it on the evidence, was without the fault of either party, and was so complete that in consequence the concerts could not be given as intended. And the question we have to decide is whether, under these circumstances, the loss which the plaintiffs have sustained is to fall upon the defendants. The parties when framing their agreement evidently had not present to their minds the possibility of such a disaster, and have made no express stipulation with reference to it, so that the answer to the question must depend upon the general rules of law applicable to such a contract.

There seems no doubt that where there is a positive contract to do a thing, not in itself unlawful, the contractor must perform it or pay damages for not doing it, although in consequence of unforeseen accidents, the performance of his contract has become unexpectedly burthensome or even impossible. . . . But this rule is only applicable when the contract is positive and absolute, and not subject to any condition either express or implied: and there are authorities which, as we think, establish the principle that where, from the nature of the contract, it appears that the parties must from the beginning have known that it could not be fulfilled unless when the time for fulfilment of the contract arrived some particular specified thing continued to exist, so that, when entering the contract, they must have contemplated such continuing existence as the foundation of what was to be done; there, in the absence of any express or implied warranty that the thing shall exist, the contract is not to be construed as a positive contract, but as subject to an implied condition that the parties shall be excused in case, before breach, performance becomes impossible from the perishing of the thing without default of the contractor.

There seems little doubt that this implication tends to further the great object of making the legal construction such as to fulfil the intention of those who entered into the contract. For in the course of affairs men in making such contracts in general would, if it were brought to their minds, say that there should be such a condition. . . .

There is a class of contracts in which a person binds himself to do something which requires to be performed by him in person; and such promises, e.g. promises to marry, or promises to serve for a certain time, are never in practice qualified by an express exception of the death of the party; and therefore in such cases the contract is in terms broken if the promisor dies before fulfilment. Yet it was very early determined that, if the performance is personal, the executors are not liable. . . . [Thus, a learned author states,]

> if an author undertakes to compose a work, and dies before completing it, his executors are discharged from this contract: for the undertaking is merely personal in its nature, and, by the intervention of the contractor's death, has become impossible to be performed.

. . . In *Hall v. Wright* [(1859), 120 E.R. 688 at 695], Crompton J., in his judgment, puts another case.

> Where a contract depends upon personal skill, and the act of God renders it impossible, as, for instance, in the case of a painter employed to paint a picture who is struck blind, it may be that the performance might be excused.

It seems that in those cases the only ground on which the parties or their executors, can be excused from the consequences of the breach of the contract is, that from the nature of the contract there is an implied condition of the continued existence of the life of the contractor, and, perhaps in the case of the painter of his eyesight. . . .

It may, we think, be safely asserted to be now English law, that in all contracts of loan of chattels or bailments if the performance of the promise of the borrower or bailee to return the things lent or bailed, becomes impossible because it has perished, this impossibility (if not arising from the fault of the borrower or bailee from some risk which he has taken upon himself) excuses the borrower or bailee from the performance of his promise to redeliver the chattel. . . .

In none of these cases is the promise in words other than positive, nor is there any express stipulation that the destruction of the person or thing shall excuse the performance; but that excuse is by law implied, because from the nature of the contract it is apparent that the parties contracted on the basis of the continued existence of the particular person or chattel. In the present case, looking at the whole contract, we find that the parties contracted on the basis of the continued existence of the Music Hall at the time when the concerts were to be given; that being essential to their performance.

We think, therefore, that the Music Hall having ceased to exist, without fault of either party, both parties are excused, the plaintiffs from taking the Gardens and paying the money, the defendants from performing their promise to give the use of the Hall and Gardens and other things.

NOTE

Statute law also has dealt with the issue of destruction of the subject matter. Section 9 of The Sale of Goods Act, R.S.N.S. 1989, c. 408 (as amended) provides the following presumptive rule:

Where there is a contract for the sale of specific goods, and the goods without the knowledge of the seller have perished at the time when the contract is made, the contract is void.

CAN. GOVT. MERCHANT MARINE LTD. v. CAN. TRADING CO.

64 S.C.R. 106, [1922] 3 W.W.R. 197, 68 D.L.R. 544

The appellants contracted with the Canadian Trading Company (the respondent) to transport lumber from Vancouver to Australia in two vessels, the Canadian Prospector and the Canadian Inventor. To the knowledge of both parties, the ships were, at the time of contracting, under construction for the appellants. Apparently, because of a dispute between the appellants and the shipbuilders, the vessels were not ready in time and the contracted voyage could not be made. In an action by the Canadian Trading Company, the appellants claimed, *inter alia*, that their contract had been frustrated because the ships were unfit for sailing at the time set for performance.

DUFF J. . . . The principle of *Taylor v. Caldwell* [*supra*] has unquestionably been extended to cases in which parties having entered into a contract in terms unqualified it is found when the time for performance arrives, that a state of things contemplated by both parties as essential to performance according to the true intent of both of them fails to exist. For the purpose of deciding whether a particular case falls within the principle you must consider the nature of the contract and the circumstances in which it was made in order to see from the nature of the contract whether the parties must have made their bargain on the footing that a particular thing or state of facts should be in existence when the time for performance should occur. And if reasonable persons situated as the parties were must have agreed that the promisor's contractual obligations should come to an end if that state of circumstances should not exist then a term to that effect may be implied. . . . But it is most important to remember that no such term should be implied when it is possible to hold that reasonable men could have contemplated the taking the risk of the circumstances being what they in fact proved to be when the time for performance arrived.

The doctrine of English law is that generally a promisor except to the extent to which his promise is qualified warrants his ability to perform it and this notwithstanding he may thereby make himself answerable for the conduct of other persons. . . .

The contracts were made on the 19th of March and provided for shipment at the end of April or the beginning of May. Is there anything in the circumstances affording a ground for saying that the agents of appellant and of the respondent as reasonable men could not have contracted on the footing that the appellants should assume the risk of what subsequently happened?

It is important to remember that there is no evidence to indicate that the delay was due to any extraordinary occurrence, to anything outside the ordinary course of events. There is a suggestion of a strike and there is a suggestion of a dispute between the Government and the contractors who were building the ships. The respondents were not aware of the precise relations between the appellants and the contractors and were entitled to assume that the contractors in entering into the contract were duly taking into account the possibilities incidental to those relations. There was nothing in the facts known to them making it unreasonable from the respondents' point of view that they should expect an undertaking as touching the date of sailing unqualified, at all events, in respect of any of the matters which have been suggested as accounting for the appellants' default. Real impossibility of performance arising from destruction of the ships by fire, for example, would have presented a different case. There is nothing in the evidence inconsistent with the hypothesis that the impossibility which no doubt did arise at the last moment was due to lack of energy on part of the Government or to supineness or indifference on part of the appellants. Impossibility arising from such causes is not the impossibility contemplated by the case of *Taylor v. Caldwell.*

MIGNAULT J. [concurring] . . . It seems to me . . . that the contingency which relieves a party from performing a contract on the ground of impossibility of performance, is an unforeseen event. . . .
So that if the event which causes the impossibility could have been anticipated and guarded against in the contract, the party in default cannot claim relief because it has happened. . . .

But here the appellant undertook to carry a cargo on a ship nearing completion. It could certainly have been foreseen that something might occur in the ship yard, especially in these days of labour troubles, to delay completion, and by making an absolute contract without providing against the contingency of non-completion in time, the appellant, in my opinion, assumed the risk of this contingency. The respondent prepared all its cargo for the ship in time and would be subject to considerable loss if the appellant were relieved from the consequences of non-performance. Such a condition, if it had been stipulated, might not have been accepted by the respondent, which possibly would have preferred to ship its lumber through another steamship company. And I think that the risk of such a contingency cannot be imposed on the respondent as an implied condition now that the loss has occurred.

[Idington, Anglin and Brodeur JJ. delivered concurring judgments dismissing the appeal.]

NOTES and QUESTION

1. An example of the tendency of courts to place the risk of unforeseen developments on the promisor is provided by *Graham v. Wagman* (1976), 73 D.L.R. (3d) 667, appeal allowed as to measure of damages 89 D.L.R. (3d) 282 (Ont. C.A.). The defendants agreed to lease to the plaintiffs 150 parking spaces in a building which they intended to erect. However, the defendants were unable to proceed with the building, because they failed to obtain the necessary financing. Their argument that this failure excused their breach of contract met with no success. Weatherston J. commented at 352: "I have never heard that impecuniosity is an excuse for non-performance of a promise."

2. In *O'Connell v. Harkema Express Lines Ltd.* (1982), 141 D.L.R. (3d) 291 (Ont. Co. Ct.), a strike which forced a trucking company out of business was found to have frustrated the contract of employment of the company's sales manager. But compare *St. John v. TNT Canada* (1991), 56 B.C.L.R. (2d) 311 (S.C.).

3. In the well-known consideration case of *Smith v. Dawson* (1923), 53 O.L.R. 615 (C.A.), the plaintiff contractors agreed to build a house for the defendant for $6,464. When the house was almost complete, a fire occurred, causing considerable damage. The defendant had insured the house and some furniture which she had moved in, and she received $2,150 from the insurers. The plaintiffs effected no insurance, but the defendant asked them to go ahead and complete the work on the basis that she would pay over the insurance money to them. Upon completion, the defendant refused to pay the insurance money and the plaintiff's claim to it was denied on the ground that the only consideration provided by the contractors for this promise was the performance of that which they were already legally obliged to do. In the case, Middleton J. commented: "In the absence of any provision to the contrary in the contract, the destruction of the building by fire would not afford any excuse for non-performance of the contract." Why is this the case? In practice, how would you expect contractors to react to this definition of their obligations?

CLAUDE NEON GENERAL ADVERTISING LTD. v. SING

[1942] 1 D.L.R. 26 (N.S. S.C.)

The defendant rented a neon sign for the Oriental Café Parlor. Lighting restrictions were introduced when Canada entered the second world war.

DOULL J. . . . [The defendant] says that the carrying out of the contract has become impossible by a change of the law and in effect that he is relieved from further [rental] payment on the principles established by the cases which are referred to as cases of frustration. . . .

Since the beginning of the present century, these rules have been considerably extended and the doctrine which has been applied has been called frustration. There are two classes of these cases: (1) The "Coronation Cases," in which the contract could be carried out but the circumstances which formed its basis had wholly changed; (2) Cases in which a change in the law or the advent of war involved such a fundamental change in the contract that it might be said that any contract that could be carried out would essentially differ from what the parties had in contemplation.

In *Krell v. Henry*, [1903] 2 K.B. 740 (C.A.), the defendant had made an agreement to hire certain rooms of the plaintiff which would provide a view of the Coronation procession of King Edward VII. Owing to the illness of the King, the procession was cancelled and it was held that the contract was thereby frustrated. Vaughan Williams L.J. in the Court of Appeal said (p. 749):

I think that you first have to ascertain, not necessarily from the terms of the contract, but, if required, from necessary inferences, drawn from surrounding circumstances recognized by both contracting parties, what is the substance of the contract, and then to ask the question whether the substantial contract needs for its foundation the assumption of the existence of a particular state of things.

. . . . .

In *Bell v. Lever Bros. Ltd.* [*supra*, Chapter 9, section 3(a)], Lord Atkin says:

The implications to be made are to be no more than are 'necessary' for giving business efficacy to the transaction, and it appears to me that, both as to existing facts and future facts, a condition would not be implied unless the new state of facts make the contract something different in kind from the contract in the original state of facts. Thus, in *Krell v. Henry*, Vaughan Williams L.J. finds that the subject of the contract was 'rooms to view the procession': the postponement, therefore, made the rooms not rooms to view the procession. This also is the test finally chosen by Lord Sumner in *Bank Line v. Capel (A.) & Co.*, [1919] A.C. 435 (H.L.), where dealing with the criterion for determining the effect of interruption in 'frustrating' a contract, he says: 'An interruption may be so long as to destroy the identity of the work or service, when resumed, with the work or service when interrupted.' We therefore get a common standard for mutual mistake, and implied conditions whether as to existing or as to future facts. Does the state of the new facts destroy the identity of the subject matter as it was in the original state of facts?

Later the Judicial Committee in *Maritime Nat. Fish Ltd. v. Ocean Trawlers Ltd.* [*infra*, section 3 of this chapter], said:

This case is more analogous to such a case as *Krell v. Henry*, where the contract was for the hire of a window for a particular day: it was not expressed but it was mutually understood that the hirers wanted the window in order to view the Coronation procession: when the procession was postponed by reason of the unexpected illness of King Edward, it was held that the contract was avoided by that event: the person who was letting the window was ready and willing to place it at the hirer's disposal on the agreed date; the hirer, however, could not use it for the purpose which he desired. It was held that the contract was dissolved because the basis of the contract was that the procession should take place as contemplated.

The correctness of this decision has been questioned, for instance, by Lord Finlay L.C., in *Larrinaga & Co. v. Société Franco-Americaine des Phosphates de Medulla* (1923), 39 T.L.R. 316 at p. 318, Lord Finlay observes:

It may be that the parties contracted in the expectation that a particular event would happen, each taking his chance, but that the actual happening of the event was not made the basis of the contract.

The authority is certainly not one to be extended: it is particularly difficult to apply where . . . the possibility of the event . . . was known to both parties when the contract was made, but the contract entered into was absolute in terms so far as concerned that known possibility. It may be asked whether in such cases there is any reason to throw the loss on those who have undertaken to place the thing or service . . . at the other parties' disposal and are able and willing to do so.

It is worth while noting that in the same volume of reports one of the "Coronation Cases" was decided differently from *Krell v. Henry* by the same Court. *Herne Bay Steam Boat Co. v. Hutton*, [1903] 2 K.B. 683 (C.A.), where the defendant had chartered a ship to take a party of persons to see the Naval Review and for a day's cruise around the fleet following the King's Coronation. The Naval Review did not take place and the defendant repudiated the contract. It was held that the venture was at the defendant's risk and that there was not total failure of consideration or subject matter. The defendant could have had the cruise around the fleet although he would not have seen any Naval Review. The plaintiff therefore recovered. . . .

In the case which we are considering, the neon sign was constructed for the purposes of the defendant, it was erected on the defendant's premises and was operated for some time. The monthly rental was for the purpose of paying the cost of construction and erection as well as maintenance over a period of 60 months. No part of the contract between the parties became impossible. The defendant certainly gets very much less benefit from the sign, but it is not entirely useless as a daylight sign. The lighting of it, even when legal, is a matter for the defendant. It is true that the defendant does not get an illuminated sign and in that respect the case approaches *Krell v. Henry*; but having regard to the remarks concerning *Krell v. Henry* in the *Trawlers* case, I do not think that I should say that the contract is for an illuminated sign. The *Herne Bay* case was not so very different from *Krell v. Henry*, but it was there held that the charterer took the risk.

[Judgment for the plaintiff.]

NOTES and QUESTIONS

1. Sir Frederick Pollock commented on the *Herne Bay* case: "In point of fact the fleet was still there, as Stirling L.J. observed, and as the writer of these lines can bear witness, it was very well worth seeing without the review." See "Note" (1904), 20 L.Q.R. 3 at 4.

2. Seller sold land to Buyer and reserved the right to remove from the property within five years a historic barn. One year later, the provincial government designated the barn a heritage property and refused to allow its removal. Does Seller have any remedy? See *Some Fine Investments Ltd. v. Ertolahti* (1991), 107 N.S.R. (2d) 1 (T.D.).

3. The coronation cases are some of the most controversial in the law of frustration. Do you believe that the allocation of risk approach advocated at the beginning of this chapter can provide determinative results? For further discussions see Posner and Rosenfield, "Impossibility and Related Doctrines in Contract Law: An Economic Analysis" (1977), 6 J. of Legal Studies 83 at 110-111; Reiter, Comment (1978), 56 Can. Bar Rev 98 at 113; Swan, "The Allocation of Risk in the Analysis of Mistake and Frustration" in Reiter & Swan, *Studies in Contract Law* (1980) 181 at 210-212. For a feminist critique of the "cockiness" of Posner's economic analysis see Frug, "Rescuing Impossibility Doctrine: A Postmodern Feminist Analysis of Contract Law" (1991-92), 140 U. Pa. L. Rev. 1029 at 1034-41.

4. Do you think that the difference between *Krell v. Henry* and *Herne Bay v. Hutton* can be explained by the fact that Henry was a consumer while Hutton was a business person who was hiring the boat to take other paying consumers to see the fleet? (See Brownsword, "Towards a Rational Law of Contract" in Wilhelmsson, ed., *Perspectives of Critical Contract Law* (1993) 242 at 246-7). Why do you think this fact is not addressed in traditional accounts of the case?

DAVIS CONTRACTORS LTD. v. FAREHAM U.D.C.

[1956] A.C. 696, [1956] 2 All E.R. 145 (H.L.)

In July, 1946, the plaintiff contractors entered into a building contract to build 78 houses for the defendant municipality within a period of eight months. The contract price was fixed at £92,425. Owing to unexpected circumstances, and without fault of either party, adequate supplies of labour were not available in the post-war market and the work took 22 months to complete. The contractors claimed, in part, that the contract was frustrated and that they were entitled to a sum of money on a *quantum meruit* basis in addition to the contract price.

LORD RADCLIFFE . . . I do not think that there has been a better expression of that general idea [of frustration] than the one offered by Lord Loreburn in *Tamplin (F.A.) SS. Co. Ltd. v. Anglo-Mexican Petroleum Products Co. Ltd.,* [1916] 2 A.C. 397 at 403 (C.A.). It is shorter to quote than to try to paraphrase it:

> . . . a court can and ought to examine the contract and the circumstances in which it was made, not of course to vary, but only to explain it, in order to see whether or not from the nature of it the parties must have made their bargain on the footing that a particular thing or state of things would continue to exist. And if they must have done so, then a term to that effect will be implied, though it be not expressed in the contract. . . . no court has an absolving power, but it can infer from the nature of the contract and the surrounding circumstances that a condition which is not expressed was a foundation on which the parties contracted.

So expressed, the principle of frustration, the origin of which seems to lie in the development of commercial law, is seen to be a branch of a wider principle which forms part of the English law of contract as a whole. But, in my opinion, full weight ought to be given to the requirement that the parties "must have made" their bargain on the particular footing. Frustration is not to be lightly invoked as the dissolvent of a contract.

Lord Loreburn ascribes the dissolution to an implied term of the contract that was actually made. This approach is in line with the tendency of English courts to refer all the consequences of a contract to the will of those who made it. But there is something of a logical difficulty in seeing how the parties could even impliedly have provided for something which ex hypothesi they neither expected nor foresaw; and the ascription of frustration to an implied term of the contract has been criticized as obscuring the true action of the court which consists in applying an objective rule of the law of contract to the contractual obligations that the parties have imposed upon themselves. So long as each theory produces the same result as the other, as normally it does, it matters little which theory is avowed. But it may still be of some importance to recall that, if the matter is to be approached by way of implied term, the solution of any particular case is not to be found by inquiring what the parties themselves would have agreed on had they been, as they were not, forewarned. It is not merely that no one can answer that hypothetical question: it is also that the decision must be given "irrespective of the individuals concerned, their temperaments and failings, their interest and circumstances." The legal effect of frustration "does not depend on their intention or their opinions, or even knowledge, as to the event." On the contrary, it seems that when the event occurs "the meaning of the contract must be taken to be, not what the parties did intend (for they had neither thought nor intention regarding it), but that which the parties, as fair and reasonable men, would presumably have agreed upon if, having such possibility in view, they had made express provisions as to their several rights and liabilities in the event of its occurrence" [*Dahl v. Nelson, Donkin & Co.* (1881), 6 App. Cas. 38 (H.L.) *per* Lord Watson].

By this time it might seem that the parties themselves have become so far disembodied spirits that their actual persons should be allowed to rest in peace.

In their place there rises the figure of the fair and reasonable man. And the spokesman of the fair and reasonable man, who represents after all no more than the anthropomorphic conception of justice, is and must be the court itself. So perhaps it would be simpler to say at the outset that frustration occurs whenever the law recognizes that without default of either party a contractual obligation has become incapable of being performed because the circumstances in which performance is called for would render it a thing radically different from that which was undertaken by the contract. Non haec in foedera veni. It was not this that I promised to do.

There is, however, no uncertainty as to the materials upon which the court must proceed.

> The data for decision are, on the one hand, the terms and construction of the contract, read in the light of the then existing circumstances, and on the other hand the events which have occurred.

(*Denny, Mott & Dickson Ltd. v. Fraser (James B.) & Co. Ltd.*, [1944] A.C. 265 at 274 (H.L.), *per* Lord Wright).

In the nature of things there is often no room for any elaborate inquiry. The court must act upon a general impression of what its rule requires. It is for that reason that special importance is necessarily attached to the occurrence of any unexpected event that, as it were, changes the face of things. But, even so, it is not hardship or inconvenience or material loss itself which calls the principle of frustration into play. There must be as well such a change in the significance of the obligation that the thing undertaken would, if performed, be a different thing from that contracted for.

I am bound to say that, if this is the law, the appellants' case seems to me a long way from a case of frustration. Here is a building contract entered into by a housing authority and a big firm of contractors in all the uncertainties of the post-war world. Work was begun shortly before the formal contract was executed and continued, with impediments and minor stoppages but without actual interruption, until the 78 houses contracted for had all been built. After the work had been in progress for a time the appellants raised the claim, which they repeated more than once, that they ought to be paid a larger sum for their work than the contract allowed; but the respondents refused to admit the claim and, so far as appears, no conclusive action was taken by either side which would make the conduct of one or the other a determining element in the case.

That is not in any obvious sense a frustrated contract. But the appellants' argument, which certainly found favour with the arbitrator, is that at some stage before completion the original contract was dissolved because it became incapable of being performed according to its true significance and its place was taken by a new arrangement under which they were entitled to be paid, not the contract sum, but a fair price on quantum meruit for the work that they carried out during the 22 months that elapsed between commencement and completion. The contract, it is said, was an eight months' contract, as indeed it was. Through no fault of the parties it turned out that it took 22 months to do the work contracted for. The main reason for this was that, whereas both parties had expected that adequate supplies of labour and material would be available for completion in eight months, the supplies that were in fact available were much less than adequate for the purpose. Hence, it is said, the basis or the footing of the contract was removed before the work was completed; or, slightly altering the metaphor, the footing of the contract was so changed by the circumstance that the expected supplies were not available that the contract built upon that footing became void. These are the findings which the arbitrator has recorded in his supplemental award.

In my view, these are in substance conclusions of law, and I do not think that they are good law. All that anyone, arbitrator or court, can do is to study the contract in the light of the circumstances that prevailed at the time when it was made and, having done so, to relate it to the circumstances that are said to have brought about its frustration. It may be a finding of fact that at the time of making the contract both parties anticipated that adequate supplies of labour and material would be available to enable the contract to be completed in the stipulated time. I doubt whether it is, but, even if it is, it is no more than to say that when one party stipulated for completion in eight months, and the other party undertook it, each assumed that what was promised could be satisfactorily performed. That is a statement of the obvious that could be made with regard to most contracts. I think that a good deal more than that is needed to form a "basis" for the principle of frustration.

The justice of the arbitrator's conclusion depends upon the weight to be given to the fact that this was a contract for specified work to be completed in a fixed time at a price determined by those conditions. I think that his view was that, if without default on either side the contract period was substantially extended, that circumstance itself rendered the fixed price so unfair to the contractor that he ought not to be held to his original price. I have much sympathy for the contractor, but, in my opinion, if that sort of consideration were to be sufficient to establish a case of frustration, there would be an untold range of contractual obligations rendered uncertain and, possibly, unenforceable.

Two things seem to me to prevent the application of the principle of frustration to this case. One is that the cause of the delay was not any new state of things which the parties could not reasonably be thought to have foreseen. On the contrary, the possibility of enough labour and materials not being available was before their eyes and could have been the subject of special contractual stipulation. It was not made so. The other thing is that, though timely completion was no doubt important to both sides, it is not right to treat the possibility of delay as having the same significance for each. The owner draws up his conditions in detail, specifies the time within which he requires completion, protects himself both by a penalty clause for time exceeded and by calling for the deposit of a guarantee bond and offers a certain measure of security to a contractor by his escalator clause with regard to wages and prices. In the light of these conditions the contractor makes his tender, and the tender must necessarily take into account the margin of profit that he hopes to obtain upon his adventure and in that any appropriate allowance for the obvious risks of delay. To my mind, it is useless to pretend that the contractor is not at risk if delay does occur, even serious delay.

And I think it a misuse of legal terms to call in frustration to get him out of his unfortunate predicament.

[Viscount Simonds and Lords Morton, Reid and Somervell delivered judgments dismissing the appeal.]

NOTES

1. Lord Radcliffe's test of "radical difference" has been specifically approved in a number of Canadian courts, especially in construction cases. See, *e.g.*, *Peter Kiewit and Sons' Co. v. Eakins Const. Ltd.*, [1960] S.C.R. 361 at 368; *Swanson Const. Co. v. Govt. of Man.* (1963), 40 D.L.R. (2d) 162, affirmed 47 W.W.R. 640 (S.C.C.) at 172 [D.L.R.]; *Elec. Power Equipment Ltd. v. R.C.A. Victor Co.* (1964), 46 D.L.R. (2d) 722 (B.C. C.A.). It does not, however, represent the only modern description of the circumstances in which a court will find a contract frustrated. For example, in the *Hong Kong Fir* case, *supra*, Chapter 7, section 7, Lord Diplock envisaged that an event which deprives a party of "substantially the whole benefit" that it was intended to receive under a contract would relieve that party of its duty of further performance in cases of frustration, as well as where there had been a breach of an innominate term. In *Bell v. Lever Brothers Ltd.*, *supra*, Chapter 9, section 3(a), Lord Atkin contemplated that the "difference in kind" test would apply in the area of frustration as well as mistake.

2. In *Naylor Group Inc. v. Ellis-Don Construction Ltd.*, [2001] 2 S.C.R. 943, the Court explicitly adopted the "radical difference" test at paras. 53-56. In this case, Ellis-Don agreed to subcontract electrical work to Naylor on a hospital renovation project. Naylor told Ellis-Don that it did not have workers affiliated with the International Brotherhood of Electrical Workers (IBEW) to which Ellis-Don did not object. However, an Ontario Labour Relations Board (OLRB) decision had confirmed Ellis-Don's collective bargaining commitment to use only electrical subcontractors whose employees were affiliated with the IBEW; Naylor was not told by Ellis-Don of this ruling. Nevertheless, Ellis-Don included Naylor as the subcontractor in its tender and was awarded the prime hospital contract. Ellis-Don then told Naylor it could not use it as the subcontractor because of the collective agreement with the electrical workers and hired another electrical subcontractor. Naylor sued for breach of contract and unjust enrichment. Naylor won at both the trial and appeal levels and Ellis-Don appealed to the Supreme Court of Canada arguing that the agreement was frustrated due to the OLRB decision. The court found that the doctrine of frustration was inapplicable for two reasons. First, the OLRB decision did not qualify as a "supervening event" as required by the doctrine, because it was a foreseeable outcome; Ellis-Don had a 30-year collective bargaining commitment with the IBEW. Second, the contract between Ellis-Don and Naylor included a provision for Ellis-Don to "reasonably object" to the awarding of the subcontract to Naylor, which it had not done. Consequently, the Supreme Court dismissed the appeal.

CAPITAL QUALITY HOMES LTD. v. COLWYN CONSTRUCTION LTD.

(1975), 9 O.R. (2d) 617, 61 D.L.R. (3d) 385 (C.A.)

EVANS J.A. [delivering the judgment of the court] . . .

Under an agreement dated January 15, 1969, the plaintiff, purchaser, agreed to purchase from the defendant, vendor, 26 building lots each comprising parts of lots within a registered plan of subdivision. The date fixed for closing was July 30, 1970. Both parties were aware that the purchaser was buying building lots for the purpose of erecting a home on each lot with the intention of selling the several homes by way of separate conveyances. Under the terms of the agreement it was entitled to a conveyance of a building lot upon payment of $6,000 and, upon full payment, to 26 separate deeds of conveyance each representing one building lot.

It is agreed that no demand for any conveyance was made prior to the date of closing.

When the sale agreement was executed the designated land was not within an area of subdivision control and not subject to any restriction limiting the right to convey. On June 27, 1970, certain amendments . . . came into effect whereby these lands came under the provisions of what is now s. 29 of the *Planning Act*, R.S.O. 1970, c. 349, which in certain circumstances restricts an owner's right to convey and makes necessary the obtaining of a consent from the relevant committee of adjustment designated in the amending legislation. In the absence of such consent no interest in part of a lot within a registered plan of subdivision can be conveyed.

The vendor was accordingly precluded from conveying the 26 building lots in 26 separate deeds without proper consents and while a conveyance to the purchaser of all lots in one deed may have been permissible, the purchaser in any event would be unable to reconvey individual building lots to prospective home buyers as it had intended without complying with the restrictive provisions of the new legislation.

This substantial change in the law, prohibiting and restricting conveyancing of the lands 33 days prior to the anticipated closing date, resulted in some discussion between the parties relative to possible postponement of the closing date in order to devise some method of circumventing the restrictions to which the lands were now subject. No arrangement was made to extend closing. On the agreed date of closing the purchaser insisted that the vendor deliver conveyances for each individual building lot with the consents necessary to effectually transfer the lots. The vendor insisted that it was the responsibility of the purchaser to obtain the necessary consents. On the closing date the balance of the agreed purchase price was tendered by the solicitors for the purchaser but no conveyances were forthcoming in the mode contemplated by the agreement. It is common ground that the purchaser would not withdraw its demand for 26 individual conveyances with consents attached and that the vendor did not provide such conveyances. Following failure to close on the agreed date, the purchaser contended that the vendor was in default and on August 5, 1970, repudiated the agreement and made demand upon the vendor for the return of the balance of the deposit.

Although the statement of facts agreed to by counsel does not state that the relatively short period of time, 33 days, between the effective date of the amending legislation and the stipulated closing date made impossible the obtaining of the necessary consents, the argument indicated that such was the understanding and I have accordingly assumed that the time factor was so limited that the parties were in agreement that it would have been impossible to process the applications for consents prior to the closing date. . . .

Accordingly, I propose to deal with this appeal on the basis of the argument advanced before us, i.e., on the doctrine of frustration and its applicability to contracts involving the sale and purchase of land. . . .

[T]he appellant, vendor, submitted that the supervening legislation which restricted transfer of the lots was a burden falling upon the purchaser. The argument was that upon execution of an agreement for the sale of land the purchaser became the equitable owner of the lands and any amending legislation which affected either zoning or alienation of land was a burden to be assumed by the purchaser. Accordingly, the purchaser was in error in attempting to repudiate the agreement and could not recover the deposit paid.

The respondent, purchaser, took the position that the effect of the new legislation was to make impossible the fulfillment of the terms of the contract; that there was a failure of consideration and that equity would not force the purchaser to take something fundamentally different from that for which it had bargained.

The vendor also argued that the obligation to obtain the consent of the committee of adjustment rested upon the purchaser. I do not agree. Unless otherwise provided in the agreement of sale the vendor is required to convey a marketable title in fee simple. There was no provision in the instant agreement which would permit the vendor to escape from that normal obligation.

That default alone was sufficient to entitle the purchaser to the return of its deposit.

There can be no frustration if the supervening event results from the voluntary act of one of the parties or if the possibility of such event arising during the term of the agreement was contemplated by the parties and provided for in the agreement. In the instant case the planning legislation which supervened was not contemplated by the parties, not provided for in the agreement and not brought about through a voluntary act of either party. The factor remaining to be considered is whether the effect of the planning legislation is of such a nature that the law would consider the fundamental character of the agreement to have been so altered as to no longer reflect the original basis of the agreement. In my opinion the legislation destroyed the very foundation of the agreement. The purchaser was purchasing 26 separate building lots upon which it proposed to build houses for resale involving a reconveyance in each instance. This purpose was known to the vendor. The lack of ability to do so creates a situation not within the contemplation of the parties when they entered the agreement. I believe that all the factors necessary to constitute impossibility of performance have been established and that the doctrine of frustration can be invoked to terminate the agreement. . . .

If the factual situation is such that there is a clear "frustration of the common venture" then the contract, whether it is a contract for the sale of land or otherwise, is at an end and the parties are discharged from further performance and the adjustment of the rights and liabilities of the parties are left to be determined under the *Frustrated Contracts Act*. In my opinion, on the facts of this case, the contract was frustrated; the doctrine was applicable and should be invoked with the result that both parties are discharged from performance of the contract and the purchaser is entitled to recover the full amount paid as it is not claimed that the vendor incurred any expenses in connection with the performance of the contract, prior to frustration, which would entitle it to retain a portion of the money paid as provided for in s. 3(2) of the *Frustrated Contracts Act*. Accordingly, the vendor must refund to the purchaser the balance of the deposit money, that is, $13,980.

[Appeal dismissed.]

QUESTION and NOTE

1. Is there an alternative analysis by which the return of the purchaser's deposit might be justified?

2. In cases such as *Capital Quality Homes*, the date at which the contract was frustrated is clear. In others, the question is more complex. In *Finelvet A.G. v. Vinava Shipping Co.*, [1983] 2 All E.R. 658 (Q.B.D.), a chartered ship, the Chrysalis, was docked at the port of Basrah when, on 22nd September 1980, war broke out between Iran and Iraq. On 1st October the ship was ready to leave, but it was prevented from doing so by the Iraqi port authorities and by the risk of damage from the hostilities. On 14th November the charterers cancelled the charter party and the question arose as to when the contract had become frustrated.

Mustill J. found that frustration depended, not on the declaration of war, but on the effect of acts done in furtherance of the war. The court refused to disturb the arbitrator's finding that the contract was not frustrated until 24th November when most informed people took the view that ships would be unable to leave Basrah for several months and probably much longer.

VICTORIA WOOD DEVELOPMENT CORP. v. ONDREY

(1977), 14 O.R. (2d) 723, 1 R.P.R. 141, 74 D.L.R. (3d) 528 (H.C.)

The plaintiff, Victoria Wood, entered into a contract on 6th April 1973 to purchase from the defendants 90 acres of land bordering the Queen Elizabeth Way in Oakville, with the sale to be completed on 31st October 1973. To the knowledge of the defendants, the plaintiff intended to subdivide and develop the land, but amendments to Ontario planning legislation, which were passed on 22nd June 1973, and regulations filed under the new legislation on 4th August 1973 effectively brought the property within a restricted development area and precluded its subdivision development. The plaintiff sought a declaration that the contract was frustrated and the return of their deposit. They relied, *inter alia*, on the *Capital Quality Homes Ltd.* case [*supra*].

OSLER J. [distinguishing *Capital Quality Homes*] . . . In my view, in the present instance, "the very foundation of the agreement" has not been destroyed. Though it was as I have found well known to the vendor that the purchaser intended to make commercial use of its property by some form of subdivision, the agreement is in no sense made conditional upon the ability of the purchaser to carry out its intention. The "very foundation of the agreement" was that the vendor would sell and the purchaser would buy the property therein described upon the terms therein set out. The only obligations assumed by the vendor were to provide a deed and to join in or consent to any subsequent applications respecting the zoning and to give partial discharges of the mortgage it was taking back under certain circumstances. The only obligation of the purchaser was to complete the cash balance agreed to, execute and give back a mortgage and to pay such mortgage in accordance with its terms. Nothing in the supervening legislation affects, in the slightest degree, the abilities of the parties to carry out their respective obligations.

As it was put by counsel for the Ondreys, a developer in purchasing land is always conscious of the risk that zoning or similar changes may make the carrying out of his intention impossible, or may delay it. He may attempt to guard against such risk by the insertion of proper conditions in the contract and thereby persuade the vendor to assume some of the risk. In the present case he has not done so and, indeed, there is no evidence that he has attempted to do so. "The very foundation of the agreement" is not affected and there is no room for the application of the doctrine of frustration.

Counsel for the Ondreys advanced as a secondary argument the proposition that there is no absolute prohibition against development as now, some four years after the passage of the legislation, it has been shown to be possible to make application to a hearing board set up by the Minister for a recommendation to the Minister that any land affected by the legislation be exempted from such effect. Had I found that the ability to develop the land had formed part of the agreement between the parties, I would not have given effect to this second argument. Under the legislation, no development is permitted and the fact that it may, at some future time, become possible to persuade the Minister *ex gratia* to exempt the lands, would not, in my view, have affected the matter if I had found that development was at the heart of the agreement. . . .

[The plaintiff's action was dismissed and the vendors' concurrent action for specific performance was successful. Affirmed (1978), 22 O.R. (2d) 1, 7 R.P.R. 60, 92 D.L.R. (3d) 229 (C.A.).]

QUESTION

1. Why was the "fundamental character" of the agreement altered in *Capital Quality Homes*, but the "very foundation of the agreement" not destroyed in *Victoria Wood*? For further examples of decisions in which courts have found that an inability to obtain planning changes can amount to frustration, see *Focal Properties Ltd. v. George Wimpey (Canada) Ltd.* (1975), 73 D.L.R. (3d) 387 (Ont. C.A.), affirmed [1978] 1 S.C.R. 2, and *British Columbia (Minister of Crown Lands) v. Cressey Development Corp.*, [1992] 4 W.W.R. 357 (B.C. S.C.). See also, *Amalg. Invt. & Property Co. v. Walker (John) & Sons Ltd.*, [1976] 3 All E.R. 509 (C.A.), in which the purchaser agreed to buy a warehouse for development purposes for £1,700,000. The next day, the building was designated a historic site, which meant that it could not be redeveloped and reduced its value to £200,000. The purchaser's argument of frustration failed, on the ground that the possibility that a building might be so designated was an inherent risk which it had to bear.

KBK NO. 138 VENTURES LTD. v. CANADA SAFEWAY LTD.

(2000), 185 D.L.R. (4th) 650 (B.C. C.A.)

[1] BRAIDWOOD J.A. The issue in this appeal is whether or not an agreement between the parties for the sale of land has been frustrated . . . so that the appellant must return the $150,000 deposit that it received pursuant to the contract of sale.

Facts

[2] The facts are not in dispute. The appellant Canada Safeway Limited ("Safeway") owned certain property on Victoria Drive in East Vancouver. It decided to sell the property as "prime redevelopment opportunity" and issued an advertisement providing a description of the property and listing the price at $8.5

million. The property was described as being zoned C-2 with a maximum floor space ratio ("FSR") of 3.22 except where the property was used for dwelling purposes for which the maximum FSR was 2.5.

[3] The respondent KBK No. 138 Ventures Ltd. ("KBK") was interested in purchasing the property and developing it as a mixed commercial and residential condominium project . . .

[4] On 28 October 1996, KBK and Safeway entered into a contract for the sale of the property. The contract specified that the purchase price would be the greater of $8.8 million or $38 multiplied by the number of square feet of floor area (as determined by the maximum FSR permitted by the City on the closing date).

[5] Pursuant to the contract, KBK paid Safeway $150,000 as a first instalment on the purchase price. This is the sum of money now in dispute.

[6] On 29 November 1996, the Director of Planning for the City ("the Director") submitted an application on his own motion to the City to rezone the property from C-2 to CD-1 and to decrease the maximum FSR to 0.3.

[7] On 2 December 1996, the parties received letters advising them of the Director's application. Neither party had contemplated such an eventuality . . .

[8] Both KBK and Safeway registered their objections to the Director's application. However, on 25 March 1997, after a public hearing and a second reading by Council, a bylaw was passed that formally rezoned the property from C-2 to CD-1. This zoning change had the result of restricting the FSR of any new buildings to a maximum of 0.3.

[9] On 13 March 1997, KBK advised Safeway that the contract had been frustrated and demanded that Safeway return the first instalment. Safeway refused to do so.

[10] Safeway ultimately entered into another agreement to sell the property to Westbank Holdings Ltd. The purchase price was now set at $5.4 million to reflect the development restrictions associated with the rezoning of the property.

[11] In her reasons for judgment, . . . the trial judge found that the contract between the parties had been frustrated. Pursuant to s. 5(2) of the *Frustrated Contract Act*, R.S.B.C. 1996, c. 166, she ordered that KBK is entitled to restitution of the first instalment that it made to Safeway, which amounted to $150,000 . . .

1. The Test for Frustration

[13] The leading case on the doctrine of frustration is *Davis Contractors Ltd. v. Fareham U.D.C.*, [*supra*] in which the House of Lords articulated the so-called "radical change in the obligation" test . . .

[19] Counsel for Safeway argued that the facts in this case are similar to *Victoria Wood Development Corp. v. Ondrey* [*supra*] . . .

3. The Case at Bar

[22] It was argued before us that the purpose of the agreement in this case was not the development of the Victoria Drive property as prime commercial and residential property; rather, it was simply the sale and purchase of property. This

Court should therefore follow the decision of *Victoria Wood* and find that the contract has not been frustrated. However, I think that the facts of the case at bar clearly distinguish it from the facts in *Victoria Wood*. In particular, the circumstances surrounding the contract demonstrate that Safeway had more than "mere knowledge" that KBK had the intention of redeveloping the property.

[23] I first turn to the advertisement placed by Safeway that introduced the property to KBK. It read in part:

FOR SALE

PRIME RE-DEVELOPMENT OPPORTUNITY

.....

Zoning:

The subject property is zoned C-2, a commercial zoning district intended to provide a wide range of goods and services and commercial activities to serve large neighbourhoods.

Some, but not all, permitted uses include: general office; financial institution; retail store; grocery or drug store; restaurant—Class 1. Conditional approval uses include dwelling units in conjunction with any of the outright approved uses but limited generally to the upper floors of a building; and also liquor stores.

The maximum floor space ratio shall not exceed 3.22, except that the FSR for dwelling uses shall not exceed 2.50 . . . [Emphasis added.]

[24] I next turn to the clauses in the contract itself. Clause 1 specifically referred to KBK's intentions in purchasing the property when it defined the term "development" as follows:

. . . the Buyer's intended development on the Lands, being a condominium development for mixed commercial and/or residential use.

I also point to Clause 6.2 of the contract, which the learned trial judge also noted. It read in part:

The Purchase Price shall also be adjusted on the Closing Date *by increasing the Purchase Price to an amount equal to the product of $38.00 times the number of square feet of floor area for the Lands approved in accordance with the FSR for the Lands* . . . The Purchase Price will not be adjusted if the above calculation gives a result of less than the original Purchase Price, or if the FSR is not determined on the Closing Date due to a final development permit not having been approved and issued by the City of Vancouver. [Emphasis added.]

The deal was therefore structured with an eye on KBK's ultimate goal of redeveloping the property as a condominium development for mixed commercial and/or residential use. It was on the basis of the FSR allowable for such a development that the purchase price of $8.5 million was calculated.

[25] Schedule 3 of the contract included a non-competition clause prohibiting KBK from using the property as a grocery store, drugstore or convenience store. The implication of this provision is that KBK was bound to develop the land into something other than a grocery store like Safeway. Such a non-competition clause was not included in the agreement of purchase and sale concluded between Safeway and Westbank at the reduced price of $5.4 million.

[26] The appellant Safeway argued that other clauses in the contract specifically allocated the risk of such a downzoning to KBK. However, I agree with the trial judge that the contract cannot be interpreted in this manner. She stated at paragraph 30:

Safeway submitted that clauses 4.2, 7.1 and 9.0, all operated to expressly allocate the risk of inability to develop the Property to the Plaintiff. Clause 4.2 stated that:

> "The transaction contemplated by this agreement is not conditional on the Buyer ob-taining a development permit for the Development, and the transaction contemplated hereby shall be completed on the closing date whether or not a development permit is obtained by the Buyer."

Clause 7.2 stated [that] the Buyer acknowledges and agrees that the seller neither makes nor gives any representation, warranty or covenant with respect to:

> (a) zoning, inclusive of permitted uses, of the lands;
>
> (b) the availability of the development permit or building permit in respect of the lands, for any development and construction by the buyer of any building or structure, which the buyer may desire at any time to develop and construct upon the lands . . .

I do not find that the above clauses expressly allocate to [KBK] the risk of the Director's application to re-zone the Property. At best, these clauses are of general wording and serve as a disclaimer, by Safeway, as to anything it may have said during the course of negotiations with respect to the zoning or development of the Property.

[27] Finally, I turn to the question as to whether the change in zoning was foreseeable. The learned trial judge wrote at paragraph 39:

> It is clear from the evidence that the parties did not actually contemplate the event which I have found to have frustrated the Contract. I am satisfied that any reasonable person in the position of the parties likely would not have contemplated such an event. It was most unusual for the Director to take such a step on his own accord. He appeared to have done so as a result of a new concept amongst planning authorities of "visioning" by communities. It was both the Plaintiff's and the Defendant's misfortune that the Property was located in one of the areas chosen to be a pilot project for input from the community as to its vision of the future for that community . . .

Summary and Disposition

[28] In all the circumstances, I agree with the conclusion of the trial judge. This is not a case like *Victoria Wood*, supra, since there is more than "mere knowledge of the vendor that land was being bought for development or even for a particular kind of development". Rather, there is an intervening event and change of circumstances so fundamental as to be regarded as striking at the root of the agreement and as entirely beyond what was contemplated by the parties when they entered into the agreement. The Director's application "radically altered" the contract between the parties within the meaning of the test set out in *Davis Contractors* and the above cases. The change in zoning and the consequent reduction in FSR from 3.22 to 0.3, which meant a change in the allowable buildable square footage from 231,800 square feet to 30,230 square feet, did not amount to a mere inconvenience but, rather, transformed the contract into some-thing totally different from what the parties intended.

[29] Accordingly, I would dismiss this appeal.

QUESTION

Farmer agrees to sell to Developer at a price of $3,000 per acre 160 acres of farmland, situated in a restricted development area adjacent to Metropolis. Between the date of the interim agreement and the scheduled date of closing, the provincial legislature unexpectedly repeals its restricted development area legislation and the value of the land increases to $8,000 per acre. Does Farmer have any remedy?

KESMAT INVT. INC. v. INDUST. MACHINERY CO. & CANADIAN INDEMNITY CO.

(1986), 70 N.S.R. (2d) 341 (N.S. C.A.)

Industrial Machinery Co. (Industrial) obtained an easement from Kesmat to enable it to build a sewer line across Kesmat's property. In exchange, Industrial undertook to obtain a rezoning and subdivision of Kesmat's lands and to pay Kesmat $50,000 if it was unsuccessful in doing so. Canadian Indemnity issued a bond in Kesmat's favour in the amount of $50,000 guaranteeing the performance of Industrial's undertakings.

Industrial met with considerable difficulty in its rezoning application and it became clear that before the application would be granted, Industrial would first have to conduct an environmental study. The cost of the study was estimated at $25,000 to $50,000. Industrial did not carry out the study, and failed to obtain the rezoning. In an action by Kesmat to recover $50,000 from Industrial and Canadian Indemnity, Glube C.J.T.D. at trial found that the contract was frustrated, *inter alia*, by the requirement of an environmental study. Kesmat appealed.

MACDONALD J.A. [delivering the judgment of the court] . . . It is clear from the authorities that hardship, inconvenience or material loss or the fact that the work has become more onerous than originally anticipated are not sufficient to amount to frustration in law so as to terminate a contract and relieve the parties thereto of their obligations to each other: see Goldsmith, Canadian Building Contracts at p. 105. Courts have, however, interpreted impossibility of performance to encompass not only absolute impossibility but also impossibility in the sense of impracticality of performance due to extreme and unreasonable difficulty, expense, injury or loss. . . .

It is common knowledge that the public are becoming increasingly concerned with protecting the environment from pollution, damage and deterioration. Ecologists and environmentalists are constantly drawing attention to the need to conserve our natural resources and to preserve our environment. As Chief Justice Glube found, the requirement of an environmental impact report was not an unknown requirement. It might well be said that even if such requirement had been contemplated by the parties they still would have entered into the contract they did. In any event the requirement of the study was known to Industrial when the last bond extension was obtained.

I have reached the following conclusions based on a consideration of the relevant circumstances against the background of the applicable legal principles.

1. Requirement of an environmental impact report was an intervening event that made more onerous and expensive performance by Industrial of its obligations to Kesmat. The cost of the study, however, based on the evidence, has not been shown to be so onerous or unreasonable so as to render performance of the contract impractical—it simply cannot be said that the cost of the study is so enormous

"that no man of common sense would incur the outlay"—per Maule J. in *Moss v. Smith* (1850), 137 E.R. 827 at 831.

2. The requirement of such study or report was not an unheard of request. It was one that . . . Industrial, prior to the last extension of both the principal agreement and the bond, knew or ought to have known might be made. It follows that the request for such study or report is not so catastrophic an intervening event as to justify the invocation of the doctrine of frustration. . . .

It is clear that the rezoning and resubdivision was not completed in accordance with the terms of the agreement as extended. The appellant contends that there was therefore a default by Industrial which activated the penal provisions of the principal agreement and of the bond.

[Kesmat was found to be entitled to judgment in the amount of $50,000 against Industrial and Canadian Indemnity. Appeal allowed.]

NOTES and QUESTIONS

1. *Kesmat Investment Inc.* was followed in *Yellowknife Condominium Corp. No. 7 v. Creative Spirit Ltd.*, [1999] N.W.T.J. No. 1 (S.C.). In that case, Yellowknife negotiated a contract with Creative for the exterior painting of its four buildings and fencing. Creative incurred unexpected cost overruns and requested an increase in the material budget, but Yellowknife refused. Creative completed one building and decided not to paint the remaining buildings. Creative submitted an invoice to Yellowknife, which it did not pay, so Creative sued. The trial judge found that the contract had become impossible to perform and was frustrated. Yellowknife appealed. After reiterating the "impracticality of performance" test suggested in *Kesmat*, the appeal court found that:

> . . . the trial judge's determination that the contract had become frustrated had its foundation in certain findings made by the trial judge: (a) the owner's budgeted figure of $40,000.00 was totally artificial and not related to the cost of the work, (b) the actual absorption rate/process of the paint by the buildings' exterior, experienced during the painting of the first building, was not anticipated, (c) there was no trial evidence that a journeyman painter can determine in advance by a visual inspection how many coats of paint will be required, and (d) the contract "is just not going to work at $40,000.00". He stated, "You can't get a Cadillac for a hundred dollars." These were findings of fact available to the trial judge on the evidence at trial. On these findings it was open to the trial judge to conclude that the contract had become impossible to perform and was frustrated. No error of law was made in reaching this conclusion and hence this Court on appeal ought not to interfere.

Do you agree with this disposition?

2. Can an employee's disability suffice for an employer to claim that the contract of employment has been frustrated? If so, what sort of criteria should the court consider? See *Marshall v. Harland & Wolff Ltd.*, [1972] 2 All E.R. 715 (N.I.R.C.); *Yeager v. R.J. Hastings Agencies Ltd.*, [1985] 1 W.W.R. 218 (B.C. S.C.); *Parks v. Atlantic Provinces Special Education Authority Resource Centre for the Visually Impaired* (1992), 109 N.S.R. (2d) 113 (C.A.); *Bishop v. Carleton Co-operative Ltd.* (1996), 176 N.B.R. (2d) 206 (C.A.); *White v. F.W. Woolworth Co.* (1996), 22 C.C.E.L. (2d) 110 (Nfld. C.A.); *Miller v. Fetterly & Associates Inc.*, [1999] N.S.J. No. 203 (S.C.); *Demuynck v. Agentis Information Services Inc.*, [2003] B.C.J. No. 113 (S.C.). A number of cases rely on the distinction between a temporary and a permanent disability. How does one know whether a particular disability, mental or physical, is permanent or temporary? At what moment does one determine that a disability is permanent — at the time of the dismissal or with hindsight, at the time of the litigation?

3. There has always been considerable controversy in the common law world as to whether contracts conveying an interest in land, and particularly leases, could be frustrated. The rationale for such a limitation is that "estates in land . . . give rise to proprietary rights in addition to purely

personal rights as found in all commercial contracts" [*Capital Quality Homes Ltd. v. Colwyn Construction Ltd.* (1975), *supra* at 392 (*per* Evans J.A)]. The House of Lords in *National Carriers Ltd. v. Panalpina (Northern) Ltd.*, [1981] A.C. 675 (U.K. H.L.), held that in principle a lease could be frustrated, but only in very rare circumstances. See also *Holbeck Hall Hotel Ltd. v. Scarborough Borough Council*, [1997] E.W.J. No. 4452 at paras. 149-151. The decision in *Panalpina* has been subject to criticism. See, for example, Barr, "Frustration of Leases – The Hazards of Contractualization" (2001), 52 N.I.L.Q. 82.

4. Although the Supreme Court of Canada has not dealt with the question, several courts of appeal have ruled that the doctrine of frustration can apply to land. See, for example, *Capital Quality Homes, supra, Turner v. Clark* (1983), 30 R.P.R. 164 (N.B. C.A) and *KBK No. 38 Venture Properties Ltd. v. Canada Safeway Ltd., supra* at para. 15. As Braidwood J.A. noted in this last case, "[s]uch case law is in harmony with the well established idea in Canada that commercial conveyances of land are also contracts: *Highway Properties Ltd. v. Kelly, Douglas & Co.,* [1971] S.C.R. 562." Do the reasons that favour the application of the doctrine of frustration to a lease necessarily support its application to sales of land?

3.   Self-Induced Frustration

MARITIME NATIONAL FISH LTD. v. OCEAN TRAWLERS LTD.

[1935] A.C. 524, [1935] 2 W.W.R. 606, [1935] 3 D.L.R. 12 (P.C.)

In July 1932, the appellants chartered a trawler, the St. Cuthbert, from the respondents for a period of one year, commencing 25th October 1932 at a rate of $590 per month.

LORD WRIGHT [delivering the judgment of the court] . . . When the parties entered into the new agreement in July, 1932, they were well aware of certain legislation consisting of an amendment of the Fisheries Act . . . which in substance made it a punishable offence to leave or depart from any port in Canada with intent to fish with a vessel that uses an otter or other similar trawl for catching fish, except under licence from the Minister: it was left to the Minister to determine the number of such vessels eligible to be licensed, and Regulations were to be made defining the conditions in respect of licences. . . .

The St. Cuthbert was a vessel which was fitted with, and could only operate as a trawler with, an otter trawl.

The appellants, in addition to the St. Cuthbert, also operated four other trawlers, all fitted with otter trawling gear.

On March 11, 1933, the appellants applied to the Minister of Fisheries for licences for the trawlers they were operating, and in so doing complied with all the requirements of the Regulations, but on April 5, 1933, the Acting Minister replied that it had been decided (as had shortly before been announced in the House of Commons) that licences were only to be granted to three of the five trawlers operated by the appellants: he accordingly requested the appellants to advise the Department for which three of the five trawlers they desired to have licences. The appellants thereupon gave the names of three trawlers other than the St. Cuthbert, and for these three trawlers licences were issued, but no licence was granted for the St. Cuthbert. In consequence, as from April 30, 1933, it was no longer lawful for the appellants to employ the St. Cuthbert as a trawler in their business. On May 1, 1933, the appellants gave notice that the St. Cuthbert was available for redelivery to the respondents; they claimed that they were no longer bound by the charter.

On June 19, 1933, the respondents commenced their action claiming $590.97 as being hire due under the charter for the month ending May 25, 1933: it is agreed that if that claim is justified, hire at the same rate is also recoverable for June, July, August, September and October, 1933.

[Lord Wright indicated that he would be inclined to concur with the judgment of the Supreme Court of Nova Scotia in holding the contract was not frustrated because the appellants, being aware of the legislation, took the risk that the necessary licence would not be granted. However, the Judicial Committee disposed of the case on the shorter ground that:] . . . in their judgment the case could be properly decided on the simple conclusion that it was the act and election of the appellants which prevented the St. Cuthbert from being licensed for fishing with an otter trawl. It is clear that the appellants were free to select any three of the five trawlers they were operating and could, had they willed, have selected the St. Cuthbert as one, in which event a licence would have been granted to her. It is immaterial to speculate why they preferred to put forward for licences the three trawlers which they actually selected. Nor is it material, as between the appellants and the respondents, that the appellants were operating other trawlers to three of which they gave the preference. What matters is that they could have got a licence for the St. Cuthbert if they had so minded. If the case be figured as one in which the St. Cuthbert was removed from the category of privileged trawlers, it was by the appellants' hand that she was so removed, because it was their hand that guided the hand of the Minister in placing the licences where he did and thereby excluding the St. Cuthbert. The essence of "frustration" is that it should not be due to the act or election of the party. . . .

. . . [T]heir Lordships are of opinion that the loss of the St. Cuthbert's licence can correctly be described . . . as "a self induced frustration." . . . Lord Blackburn in *Dahl v. Nelson, Donkin & Co.* (1881), 6 App. Cas. 38 at 53 (H.L.), . . . refers to a "frustration" as being a matter "caused by something for which neither party was responsible" . . . [I]t cannot in their Lordships' judgment be predicated that what is here claimed to be a frustration, that is, by reason of the withholding of the licence, was a matter for which the appellants were not responsible or which happened without any default on their part. In truth, it happened in consequence of their election. If it be assumed that the performance of the contract was dependent on a licence being granted, it was that election which prevented performance, and on that assumption it was the appellants' own default which frustrated the adventure: the appellants cannot rely on their own default to excuse them from liability under the contract.

NOTES and QUESTIONS

1. In *Paal Wilson & Co. v. Partenreederei Hannah Blumenthal*, [1983] 1 A.C. 854 (U.K. H.L.), Lord Brandon of Oakbrook in the House of Lords (with whom Lords Diplock, Keith of Kinken, Roskill and Brightman agreed) said at 909:

> . . . there are two essential factors which must be present in order to frustrate a contract. The first essential factor is that there must be some outside event or extraneous change of situation,

not foreseen or provided for by the parties at the time of contracting, which either makes it impossible for the contract to be performed at all, or at least renders its performance something radically different from what the parties contemplated when they entered into it. The second essential factor is that the outside event or extraneous change of situation concerned, and the consequences of either in relation to the performance of the contract, must have occurred without either the fault or the default of either party to the contract.

2. In *J. Lauritzen A.S. v. Wijsmuller B.V. (The "Super Servant Two")*, [1989] 1 Lloyd's Rep. 148, affirmed [1990] 1 Lloyd's Rep. 1 (C.A.), Lauritzen owned a large and heavy drilling rig, which was under construction in Japan. Wijsmuller agreed to transport the rig to the Rotterdam area of the North Sea on one of its large semi-submersible, self-propelled barges. The rig was to be delivered to Wijsmuller for carriage between June 20 and August 20, 1981 and the transportation unit was described in the contract as "Super Servant One or Super Servant Two in Wijsmuller's option".

Ultimately, Wijsmuller planned to use Super Servant Two to transport the rig and engaged Super Servant One on other contracts for the period between June and August, 1981. On January 29, 1981, Super Servant Two sank and was declared a total loss. On February 16, 1981, Wijsmuller informed Lauritzen that they would not carry out the transportation of the rig and Lauritzen claimed damages for breach of contract. Wijsmuller pleaded that the contract had been frustrated.

    (a) Should Wijsmuller's defence of frustration succeed?
    (b) If Wijsmuller knew on February 16, 1981, that its defence of frustration might not succeed, what might it have chosen to do?
    (c) What if the Super Servant Two had sunk because of Wijsmuller's negligence?

3. A, a peach grower in the Okanagan Valley, has agreed to sell 100 kilograms of peaches from A's orchard to each of five customers. A severe hailstorm damages the orchard with the result that only 100 kilograms of peaches in total are produced. What should A do? See *Hollinger Consol. Gold Mines Ltd. v. Northern Can. Power*, [1923] 4 D.L.R. 1205 (Ont. C.A.); *Samuel v. Black Lake Asbestos & Chrome Co.* (1920), 58 D.L.R. 270, reversed on other grounds 62 S.C.R. 472. What if A's contract with each customer contained a *force majeure* clause, which absolved A of liability for failure to deliver in these circumstances? See *J. Lauritzen A.S. v. Wijsmuller B.V.*, *supra* at 158-59.

4. A agrees to purchase a condominium in a building yet to be constructed by the vendor/ developer. The developer then gets into a "war" with the planning authority which ultimately refuses the building permit and downzones the site. Is the contract frustrated? See *Dinicola v. Huang & Danczkay Properties* (1996), 135 D.L.R. (4th) 525 (Ont. Gen. Div.), affirmed on other grounds (1998), 163 D.L.R. (4th) 286 (Ont. C.A.).

4.   Should the Doctrine of Frustration be Expanded: Commercial Impracticality and Social Force Majeure?

It is apparent that the courts have been reluctant to expand the doctrine of frustration because of the threat that it poses for the shibboleth of sanctity of contract. Anglo-Canadian courts have reiterated on many occasions that even a dramatic increase in expense or the fact that performance has become significantly more onerous will not suffice. Bad bargains are not enough. But there are several hints that the doctrine could be expanded.

First, there are long term supply contracts, a phenomenon that has become increasingly common in the twentieth century. In these situations parties may bind themselves to provide goods and/or services (water, fuel or electricity) for many decades. Obviously, such contracts are vulnerable to the possibility that some unanticipated exogenous events (for example, hyperinflation, transformation in the marketplace by the emergence of a price-inflating cartel, or environmental protection legislation) could thwart (at least one of the parties' expectations). With the exception of Lord Denning (*Staffordshire Area Health Authority v. South Staffordshire Waterworks Co.*, [1978] 3 All E.R. 769 (C.A.)), English and Canadian courts have been unsympathetic to such arguments. (For a critique of this absolute prohibition, on the basis of both policy and principle, see Beatson, "Increased Expense and Frustration" in Rose, ed., *Consensus ad Idem: Essays in the Law of Contract in Honour of Guenter Treitel* (1996) 121.)

However, in several other jurisdictions there has been greater openness to the possibility of excusing performance on the basis of extreme economic hardship. McBryde, in "Frustration of Contract" (1980), 25 Juridical Rev. (N.S.) 1 at 11 draws our attention to an old Scottish case, *Wilkie v. Bethune* (1848), 11 D. 132 where

> [a]n employer was bound to pay his servant in potatoes. There was a dramatic rise in the price of potatoes due to the failure of the crop in 1846. If the servant had been paid in potatoes he would have greatly benefitted. However, the court applied an equitable construction to the contract and held the servant entitled, not to his potatoes, but to a sum which would purchase the equivalent of other food.

In the United States there is the doctrine of "commercial impracticality". U.C.C. Section 2-615 and the American Law Institute, *Restatement of the Law of Contracts*, 2nd ed. (1979) 261 both provide that the obligation to perform is excused if "performance as agreed has been made impractical by the occurrence of a contingency the non-occurrence of which was a basic assumption on which the contract was made." See for example *Mineral Park Land Co. v. Howard*, 172 Cal. 289, 156 P. 458 (1916); *Aluminum Co. of America (Alcoa) v. Essex Group Inc.*, 499 F. Supp. 53 (W.D. Pa., 1980); *Florida Power and Light Co. v. Westinghouse Electric Co.*, 826 F.2d 239 (1987). Another example is to be found in *Codelfa Construction Pty. Ltd. v. State Rail Authority of NSW* (1982), 149 C.L.R. 337, where the Australian High Court found that, despite the long list of precedent to the contrary, extreme financial hardship for a builder could ground frustration.

In the light of these cases reconsider the *Capital Quality Homes*, *KBK* and *Yellowknife Condominium* cases. Are they truly situations of impossibility, or are they examples of commercial impracticality?

Commercial impracticality primarily relates to supervening events that affect the relations between two corporations. In some jurisdictions there is a cognate doctrine for consumers who experience a significant change in their financial circumstances that renders their contractual obligations for leases, credit cards or loans significantly more onerous. This is sometimes called social *force majeure*. Wilhelmsson provides the following introduction to the concept as it has emerged in Scandinavia.

WILHELMSSON, "'SOCIAL FORCE MAJEURE'—A NEW CONCEPT IN NORDIC CONSUMER LAW"

(1990) 13 Journal of Consumer Policy 1 at 7-8

The principle of social force majeure could be applied when the following four conditions are fulfilled:

1.   The consumer is affected by some *special occurrence* such as an unfa-

vourable change in his health (physical or mental illness, personal injury), work (unemployment, reduced work, strike and lockout), housing
(termination of lease) or family (divorce, death or injury of family
member). The list is not exhaustive; other occurrences may be relevant,
too.

2.   There is a *causal connection* between this occurrence and the consumer's
      difficulties in paying. If the occurrence has not led to economic diffi-
      culties for the person concerned—if he is wealthy and has other re-
      sources—he may not invoke the principle of social force majeure.

3.   If the consumer *foresaw* the special occurrence when he concluded the
      contract, he cannot rely on it.

4.   If the occurrence was caused by the *fault* of the consumer, he is also
      prevented from invoking the principle of social force majeure.

There are various legal consequences which may be attached to social force
majeure. . . .

•   Many of the acts, such as the legislation on interest, prescribe that social
     force should lead to a *mitigation of the sanctions* imposed on a consumer
     who has not been able to pay on time. It therefore seems quite natural
     that social force majeure should form a relevant defence against, e.g.,
     the liability to pay damages in case of delay.

•   In some cases, when avoidance of a contract would cause economic
     losses to the consumer, social force majeure should *prevent the other
     party from avoiding* the contract, at least for some time. Such a conse-
     quence would be especially important in the case of permanent contracts
     concerning necessary utilities like electricity, telephone, and heating.

•   In some cases . . . one might recognize the right of the consumer to
     withdraw from a binding contract or to *terminate* a long term contract
     when he is hit by social force majeure.

QUESTION

Is the following provision of the *Residential Tenancies Act*, R.S.N.S. 1989, c. 401 an example
of social *force majeure* in the Canadian context?

Early termination upon income reduction

10B Notwithstanding Section 10, where the income of a tenant, or one of a group of the
tenants in the same residential premises, is so reduced because of a significant deterioration
of a tenant's health that it is not reasonably sufficient to pay the rent in addition to the tenant's
other reasonable expenses, or if there is more than one tenant, the tenant may terminate a year-
to-year tenancy by giving the landlord

(1) one month's notice to quit; and

(2) a certificate of a medical practitioner evidencing the significant deterioration of
health.

In light of the ideas of commercial impracticality and social *force majeure* consider the following
discussion of the context and impact of the recession of 1981-1983.

CONKLIN, A CONTRACT

Devlin, ed., *Canadian Perspectives on Legal Theory* (1991), at 213-215

[The author had discussed language as a system of signs, which in the case of law mediates the lawyer's interpretation of facts with the consequences of separating the law from social practices which the sign system does not incorporate.] The possibility that there might be victims beyond or outside of the legal sign system is difficult for Canadian lawyers to fathom because they have been so successfully assimilated into a language that precludes that possibility. First, the sign system induces the belief that a contract is a private matter in that it regulates the private relationships between two parties in contrast to the public matters that concern the state. So, the lawyer demarcates the contract as falling within private law as opposed to public law. Second, the legal sign system reinforces the belief that financial institutions are independent of the state. . . . This belief is strong notwithstanding the fact that the state formally creates and regulates financial institutions and notwithstanding the fact that the Minister of Finance is theoretically responsible for monetary policy in Canada. Being considered private institutions independent of the government, we tend to contrast the banker to the police officer. We tend to believe that raw physical force is associated with the criminal code and not with the contract. Third, the sign system of which the contract is only a part induces the belief that, in contrast to prisoners, businesspersons retain their liberty to live freely from physical restraint within society. This freedom from physical coercion is called civil liberty. We are also led to believe that, notwithstanding the enforcement of the contract, borrowers retain their liberty to express themselves, to vote, to travel interprovincially, to assemble in a group, and to associate with others without constraint from the state. The sign system calls this political liberty. The sign system of law, then, induces us to believe that the contract is the epitome of freedom in that it is a private matter involving a private dispute independent of the state. With the help of the sign system in the subject area of constitutional law, we are led to believe that freedom is still retained during the enforcement of the contract.

The recession of 1981-83 in Southwestern Ontario suggests that such beliefs are illusory. When one looks beyond the legal system to empirically oriented studies of the financial industry, to the testimony before legislative committees, to the interviews and statistical studies of the financial industry carried out by respected journalists, to studies in banking and business journals, and to other nonlegal resource material, one is struck by the public issues that envelop the contract. Moreover, one is struck by how the sign system of lawyers misdescribes and even conceals the suffering as practised in Canada.

And yet, the lawyer's sign system concentrated upon the contract as the source of a dispute during the recession of 1981-83. That contract involved two "independent" parties, alone isolated from other human beings, scissored from the indigenous community of fellow farmers and businesspersons, and estranged from the indigenous community at large. The sign system constructed the parties as two atomistic individuals at civil war.

The sign system of the lawyer at the time presupposed, for example, that if individuals were granted fair opportunities to fulfill their duties, they should be able to do so. So, if they could not obtain alternate financing within a few hours or days, then they deserved to have their assets seized. The outcome was deemed a just one. But the public record drawn from outside the lawyer's sign system seems to suggest that the factors triggering many loan calls during the 1981-83 recession were external to the debtor's competence, foreseeability, blameworthiness, and control. The most important factor during the period, for example, was the extraordinarily rapid rise in interest rates beginning in late 1979. The interest rate charged to the preferred customers of the chartered banks climbed from 12.75 percent on February 28, 1979, to 23.5 percent in August 1981 where it remained until September 11, 1981. Trust companies and credit unions, to the extent that they financed small businesses and farms at the time, charged still higher rates. By 1984, the financial institutions had lowered their interest rates to their former level. Farmers and small businesspersons could not have foreseen the rapid and radical escalation of the interest rate. Nor could they have controlled it, notwithstanding the fact that most contracts allowed for a floating interest rate, which the debtor theoretically could have renegotiated into a fixed rate (at a possibly still higher level). Further, regionally declining employment and markets also lay outside the borrower's control. Not infrequently, the very circumstances that brought on the enforcement of one person's contract reverberated throughout the regional economy as a whole. In one industry towns, the enforcement of the dominant company's contract undermined the whole community's self-confidence. This, in turn, affected the lender's expectations about the future economy of a region or industry. And this, in turn, affected how lenders would consider the financial position of other farmers and small businesspersons. . . .

Let us take one more example of how the focus upon the contract lopped off a great deal of social practice. A focus upon the contract encouraged the lawyer to consider how the lender could be placed in the *status quo ante* —that is, how could the situation be corrected so as to repair the particular economic loss caused to the lender by the borrower's failure to pay upon demand? This question, in turn, carried with it an isolated time sequence of the two individual parties leading up to the enforcement of the contract. It lopped off the social and economic conditions leading up to the borrower's decision to take out a loan during the 1970s. At that time, financial institutions and government agencies were rapidly expanding credit. As Donald Fullerton, the President of the CIBC, once acknowledged, this expanding credit constituted "the mistakes of the '70s": "What were we thinking of when we made the loans?" The Central Mortgage and Housing Corporation influenced expectations through loans at below-market interest rates; capital contributions to low income housing and rental construction; loans and grants to municipalities for land assembly, sewage, and water projects; and subsidies for home insulation. Similarly, by March 1979, the Farm Credit Corporation had granted 71,722 outstanding loans totalling 2.7 billion dollars for the purchase of farm equipment, livestock, buildings, and land. And the Export Development Corporation had extended commercial credit for exports and for the creation of large capital projects in Canada by foreign companies. By the end of the 1970s, these four government agencies had flushed 8.7 billion dollars into businesses in Canada. And this was all in addition to the great expansion of loans by financial institutions. Unlimited optimism in a crassly materialistic culture permeated the decisions of farmers and small businesspersons to take out loans. But the contract was read into a preexisting sign system that excluded all these factors from its scope.

For lawyers, the sign system induced them to interpret the circumstances as isolated disputes between two socially atomistic and isolated parties. The sign system projected the judge's role as one of adjudicating that dispute. By focusing upon the contract as the source of all relevant rights and duties, the sign system estranged the two atomistic parties from any connection with other human beings. The sign system just could not allow lawyers to ask whether borrowers' defaults were caused by economic factors outside of their control; whether the financing of small business in Canada allowed for a competition among commercial lenders at the time; whether there was even a semblance of bargaining power between the two "self-sufficient" parties when the lender drew up the initial draft of the contract; whether financial institutions did in fact draw up the contract and, if so, how frequently did borrowers attempt or succeed in amending lenders' drafts; whether particular lenders controlled a relatively large proportion of all borrowing funds in the Canadian economy; whether lenders possessed an expansive and diversified asset basis; whether they effectively lobbied for regulatory protection throughout the 1970s; whether they advised the central bankers of monetary and interest rate policy; and whether they had effectively acted as partners with the farmers and small businesspersons generally since the nineteenth century. The sign system in which lawyers found themselves prevented them from considering such issues as legally relevant to the facts and circumstances of cases. The door to the social world could hardly budge. Its hinges were seized. No light could be detected beyond a lawyer's gaze. And this occurred despite the sign system's professed appeal to the facts and circumstances of each case.

[Footnotes omitted.]

5. Anticipating the Unforeseeable: Force Majeure Clauses

While it is true that one may not be able to anticipate the specific impact of unforeseen contingencies, many business people recognize that given the nature of their business there may be some general contingencies beyond their control that might make performance either impossible or more onerous than they expect. To facilitate forward planning and provide for flexibility, many contracts include *force majeure* clauses. Generally speaking, such clauses can provide a variety of options: first, performance can be suspended for a specified period of time; secondly, the contract might be varied; and third, if necessary, there may be an option to terminate the contract without having to pay damages for non-performance. Clearly, *force majeure* clauses are an attempt to allocate risk in the event that an exogenous contingency arises.

Because such clauses are designed to avoid the doctrine of absolute contracts and excuse performance, thereby transferring all risk of loss onto the other party, the courts tend to worry that there might be an inequitable allocation of risk. Consequently, courts are inclined to construe such clauses quite strictly although there is no rule of law to this effect.

ATLANTIC PAPER STOCK LTD. v. ST. ANNE-NACKAWIC PULP & PAPER CO.

[1976] 1 S.C.R. 580, 10 N.B.R. (2d) 513, 56 D.L.R. (3d) 409, 4 N.R. 539

DICKSON J. [delivering the judgment of the court] This litigation arises out of a contract for the sale by Atlantic Paper Stock Limited and Elliot Krever & Associates (Maritimes) Ltd. to St. Anne-Nackawic Pulp and Paper Company, Ltd. of 10,000 tons of waste paper a year for 10 years, to be used as secondary fibre in the manufacture of corrugating medium at St. Anne's mill. After 14 months, St. Anne advised Atlantic and Elliot Krever it would not accept any more secondary fibre and the latter sued for damages. In defence, St. Anne pleaded non-availability of markets for pulp or corrugating medium with the meaning of the concluding words of cl. 2(a) of the contract, reading:

> St. Anne warrants and represents that its requirements under this contract shall be approximately 15,000 tons a year, and further warrants that in any one year its requirements for Secondary Fibre shall not be less than 10,000 tons, unless as a result of an act of God, the Queen's or public enemies, war, the authority of the law, labour unrest, or strikes, the destruction of or damages to production facilities, or the non-availability of markets for pulp or corrugating medium.

. . . Quantum of damages aside, the sole question is whether non-availability of markets for pulp or corrugated medium discharged St. Anne from its obligations under the contract.

St. Anne owns and operates a mill at Nackawic, New Brunswick, which was designed to manufacture pulp and paper. St. Anne is a wholly-owned subsidiary of Parsons & Whittemore, an American company with world-wide interests in the pulp and paper industry. Construction of the mill was started in 1968, and completed in 1970, at a cost of $72,000,000, of which $18,000,000 was invested in the section designed for the manufacture of paper. The mill began to manufacture paper in April of 1970, and bleached hardwood Kraft pulp in June of 1970. The paper manufactured was a semi-chemical medium commonly referred to as corrugating medium, which is used in the packaging and box industry. Corrugating medium is placed between two sheets of what is known as liner board, a product not produced by St. Anne, to form the stuff of which cardboard cartons are made. The raw materials required to produce the type of corrugating medium manufactured by St. Anne included 15% so-called secondary fibre, which is waste paper salvaged from used corrugated cartons and shipping cases.

The contract in issue in these proceedings is dated April 10, 1970, and obligates St. Anne to purchase, on stated terms, exclusively from or through Atlantic and Elliot Krever, all its requirements, maximal 18,000 tons and minimal 10,000 tons, of secondary fibre for its mill. Following upon the execution of this contract, Atlantic and Elliot Krever entered into agreements with the City of St. John and with two New Brunswick breweries for the provision of the secondary fibre needed under the contract with St. Anne. Atlantic and Elliot Krever furnished St. Anne with secondary fibre in accordance with the terms of the contract until they received, without warning, advice by telegram on June 9, 1971, that St. Anne would not accept any more fibre. The paper machine closed down on June 16, 1971, and has since stood idle.

An act of God clause or *force majeure* clause, and it is within such a clause that the words "non-availability of markets" are found, generally operates to discharge a contracting party when a supervening, sometimes supernatural, event, beyond control of either party, makes performance impossible. The common thread is that of the unexpected, something beyond reasonable human foresight and skill. If markets were unavailable to St. Anne, did they become so because of something unexpected happening after April 10, 1970? Was the change so radical as to strike at the root of the contract? Could the company, through the exercise of reasonable skill, have found markets in which to trade? Clause 2(a) contemplates the following frustrating events: an act of God, the Queen's or public enemies, war, the authority of the law, labour unrest or strikes, the destruction of or damage to production facilities. Reading the clause *ejusdem generis*, it seems to me that "non-availability of markets" as a discharging condition must be limited to an event over which the respondent exercises no control. . . .

[Dickson J. then commented that the primary cause of the failure of St. Anne's corrugating medium facility was a lack of an effective marketing plan for the product.] St. Anne's had known prior to the present contract that the U.S. market was foreclosed to it. It then appeared that St. Anne's had greatly overestimated its ability to sell in the Canadian market, which was dominated by integrated companies, with parent companies manufacturing corrugating medium and selling to subsidiaries manufacturing cardboard cartons. In addition in 1970 and 1971, a number of technological and competitive factors caused a decline of perhaps 10% in the export potential to European markets. The trial Judge summed up St. Anne's marketing problems as follows:

> Feasibility studies had been done for the defendant, prior to construction and the reports were optimistic. Needless to say, the predictions on all points have been incorrect so far. The situation at the time of cancellation of the contract herein was substantially the same as at the time of the studies.

The difference between the conclusion of the trial Judge and that of the Appeal Division turned essentially on whether the words "non-availability of markets" meant non-availability of economic markets for St. Anne. Mr. Justice Barry found no such connotation in the language of the clause. The effect of the Appeal Division opinion would be to relieve St. Anne of contractual obligation if St. Anne could not operate at a profit. I doubt that reasonable men would have made such a bargain. It would in my opinion be doing violence to the plain words "non-availability of markets for pulp or corrugating medium" in the context of the entire clause within which the words are found, to permit St. Anne to rely upon its soaring production costs to absolve it of contractual liability. . . .

[On the basis of a market survey it] would appear, therefore, that on an average selling price per ton of $120 St. Anne would lose $30.29 per ton in June, 1970, and $66.94 per ton in June, 1971. In the first year of operation St. Anne's mill operated at a loss of $9,000,000 as against a projected loss of $782,000. As Mr. Justice Barry said, "the defendant simply priced itself out of any available market existing".

The trial Judge made [the following critical finding of fact]:

> . . . the conditions existing in the market on April 10, 1970, when the parties executed P-1 were and are substantially the same as at the time of cancellation in June, 1971, and at present.

Exhibit P-1 is the contract to which I have referred. He also held:

> I find that there is a market for corrugated medium, albeit a declining one, and very competitive market, and certainly, not an economic market at the defendant's cost per ton.

Mr. Wiltshire, senior vice-president of St. Anne, was asked by counsel to state the factors on which the decision to stop production were based. He prefaced his answer by the words: "It was an accumulation of circumstances", and then referred to a change of agents in Germany, failure to get repeat business, competition from bogus medium, unsold inventory of more than half of production, re-evaluation of the Canadian dollar. The factors confirm beyond doubt the presence of many serious marketing difficulties, but, in my opinion, they do not establish, in the face of evidence of a strong demand for corrugated medium throughout the world and of competitors of St. Anne selling to the limit of their respective productive capacities, that markets for corrugating medium were not available to St. Anne.

I do not think St. Anne can rely on a condition which it brought upon itself. A fair reading of the evidence leads one to conclude that the whole St. Anne project for the manufacture of corrugating medium was misconceived. The problems which plagued it proceeded, however, not from non-availability of markets for corrugating medium but from (i) lack of an effective marketing plan, as I have stated; St. Anne spent $16,000,000 to produce a product without any notion of where the product would be sold, and (ii) inordinate operating costs, aggravated by two subsidiary factors: (a) lack of captive outlets, and (b) failure to produce liner board; customers needed both corrugating medium and liner board, and preferred manufacturers who could offer both. The project, conceived in ephemeral hopes and not the harsh realities of the market place, resulted in failure for which St. Anne and not changes in the market for corrugating medium during the period April 10, 1970 to June 9, 1971 must be held accountable.

[Accordingly, the appeal was allowed and St. Anne was held liable for damages in the amount of $108,250.]

NOTES AND QUESTIONS

1. Why do courts tend to construe *force majeure* clauses strictly? The restrictive approach to the interpretation of such clauses seems to be continued in *Atcor Ltd. v. Continental Energy Marketing Ltd.* (1996), 38 Alta. L.R. (3d) 229 (C.A.).

Atcor and Continental entered into a contract whereby Atcor would supply Continental with natural gas by means of a pipeline operated by a third party, Nova Corporation. The contract contained the following *force majeure* clause:

> 9. Subject to the other provisions of this paragraph, if either party to this Agreement fails to observe or perform any of the covenants or obligations herein imposed upon it and such failure shall have been occasioned by, or in consequence of force majeure, as hereinafter defined, such failure shall be deemed not to be a breach of such covenants or obligations.
>
>> (a) For the purposes of this Agreement, the term "force majeure" shall mean any acts of God, including therein, but without restricting the generality thereof, lightning, earthquakes and storms and in addition shall mean any strikes, lockouts or other industrial disturbances, acts of the Queen's enemies, sabotage, wars, blockades, insurrections, riots, epidemics, landslides, floods, fires, washouts, arrests and restraints, civil disturbances, explosions, breakages of or accidents to plant, machinery or lines of pipe, hydrate obstructions of lines of pipe, freezings of wells or delivery facilities, well blowouts, cratering, pipeline tie-ins, pipeline connections, pipeline repairs and reconditioning, the orders of any court or governmental authority, the invoking of force majeure pursuant to any gas purchase contracts, any acts or omissions (including failure to take gas) of a transporter of gas to or for Seller which is excused by any event or occurrence of the character herein defined as constituting force majeure, or any other causes, whether of the kind herein enumerated or otherwise, not within the control of the party claiming suspension and which, by the exercise of due diligence, such party is unable to overcome.

Thus the clause explicitly provided that problems with the pipeline would constitute *force majeure*, and further provided that a party could not have the benefit of the *force majeure* clause if the *force majeure* event were within its power or could be overcome by due diligence.

During the course of the contract numerous pipeline problems forced Nova to decrease the amount of natural gas that Atcor was allowed to transport via the pipeline. Atcor drastically reduced its shipments to Continental, declaring *force majeure*, but continued to supply other customers via the Nova pipeline.

At trial, the court ruled that Nova's reduction of service to Atcor constituted *force majeure* under the agreement between Atcor and Continental and that the reduction was not within Atcor's power and could not be remedied by due diligence. Continental appealed, arguing that the pipeline restrictions did not cause Atcor's drastic reductions in supply; rather, they argued that Atcor's decision to direct what natural gas it could ship to other customers was the reason for the curtailment of service. The Alberta Court of Appeal allowed Continental's appeal, ruling that the trial judge erred in focusing only on the *force majeure* event and not on the effects of that event. Although the pipeline restrictions were not themselves within Atcor's power, the court ruled that Atcor was obliged to demonstrate that it could not mitigate the effects of the reductions by other means, provided those means were concordant with reasonable industry practice. The Court of Appeal remitted the case for a new trial, since the trial judge had not considered the largely factual question of whether Atcor could have mitigated the effects of the pipeline restrictions while remaining within the bounds of reasonable business standards.

2. For comprehensive reviews of the law in relation to *force majeure* see Treitel, *Frustration and Force Majeure* (1994) and McKendrick, ed., *Force Majeure and Frustration of Contract* (1991).

3. Does the judicial approach to *force majeure* clauses shed any light on the more general question as to the role of the judiciary in developing the common law of frustration?

6. Effect of Frustration

The effect of frustration is to automatically terminate the contract as of the moment of frustration, regardless of the wishes of the parties. Two points should be noted. First, unlike mistake, frustration is not retrospective, it does not render the contract void *ab initio*; rather parties are released from further obligations. Second, unlike a serious breach where the innocent party can choose whether to treat the contract as repudiated or not, frustration does not allow for a power of election. Both parties are automatically discharged from future performance of obligations. However, rights and obligations accrued prior to the frustration remain enforceable. This rule leads to some unfortunate financial consequences and has resulted in legislative intervention in every province but Nova Scotia. The following extract outlines a) the common law position; b) two different legislative regimes.

ONTARIO LAW REFORM COMMISSION, REPORT ON AMENDMENT OF THE LAW OF CONTRACT

(1987), at 279-82

(i)   *The Common Law Position*

Three principal issues arise in considering what relief should be made available following the frustration of a contract. The first is whether compensation should be allowed for benefits conferred on a party prior to frustration even though the contract does not provide for it and, where the benefit consists of non-pecuniary performance, performance is only partial. The second issue is whether reliance expenditures incurred by the parties in performance of their obligations should be recoverable and to what extent. The third issue is whether a court should be free to examine the surrounding circumstances to determine whether it is appropriate to allocate the reliance losses on some other basis than would otherwise be appropriate because of the implied agreement of the parties, trade usages, or general economic considerations.

The common law answers to these questions are both rigid and unsatisfactory. Briefly, the general position at common law regarding compensation for benefits conferred may be considered under two heads: recovery of monies paid and recompense for non-pecuniary benefits conferred. Turning first to recovery of monies paid, the 1904 case of *Chandler v. Webster* [[1904] 1 K.B. 493] held that money paid under a frustrated contract could not be recovered on the theory that the action for money had and received would not lie unless the contract was void *ab initio*. A frustrated contract was avoided, it was thought, only from the occurrence of the frustrating event. Moreover, obligations accrued before the frustrating event would remain enforceable on the same theory.

The decision of the House of Lords in *Fibrosa Spolka Akcyjna v. Fairbairn Lawson Combe Barbour, Ltd.* [[1943] A.C. 32] overruled *Chandler* and discredited the theory underlying it. In *Fibrosa*, a buyer who had made partial payment before the frustrating event sought recovery. The House of Lords recognized the buyer's right to recover money paid, provided that the seller's consideration wholly failed.

[Viscount Simon stated, at 46-47:

> To claim the return of money paid on the ground of total failure of consideration is not to vary the terms of the contract in any way. The claim arises not because the right to be repaid is one of the stipulated conditions of the contract, but because, in the circumstances that have

> happened, the law gives the remedy. . . . [I]t does not follow that because the plaintiff cannot sue "on the contract" he cannot sue dehors [ie outside] the contract for the recovery of a payment in respect of which consideration has failed.

However, he continued, at 49:

> While this result [the return of money paid] obviates the harshness with which the previous view in some instances treated the party who had made a prepayment, it cannot be regarded as dealing fairly between the parties in all cases and must sometimes have the result of leaving the recipient who has to return the money at a grave disadvantage. He may have incurred expenses in connexion with the partial carrying out of the contract which are equivalent, or more than equivalent, to the money which he prudently stipulated should be prepaid but which he now has to return for reasons which are no fault of his. He may have to repay the money, though he has executed almost the whole of the contractual work, which will be left on his hands. These results follow from the fact that the English common law does not undertake to apportion a prepaid sum in such circumstances. . . ."]

In the absence of total failure of consideration, however, it would seem that restitutionary relief would be denied.

As to recompense for non-pecuniary benefits conferred, in England, recovery for the value of partial performance is made difficult by the rule in *Appleby v. Myers*, [(1867), L.R. 2 C.P. 651 (Ex.)]. This case held that, in the case of non-pecuniary benefits conferred under a contract that has been frustrated, recovery is not available for partial performance of an entire contract: the performing party must perform fully to earn his or her payment.

In Canada, the position of a party who has partly performed should be more promising in the light of the Supreme Court of Canada's embrace of a general doctrine of unjust enrichment in *Deglman v. Guaranty Trust Co. of Canada*, [*supra*, Chapter 4, section 8(c)(iii)(E)]. However, the *Deglman* doctrine only applies (assuming it is applied to frustration cases) to restitutionary claims for benefits conferred. Neither Canadian nor English law offers indemnification to a party who has incurred reliance expenditures in preparation for, or partial performance of, contractual obligations not resulting in benefits conferred on the other party. The loss lies where it falls. Given this rule, the common law courts obviously do not have to concern themselves with any implied agreement between the parties for the allocation of reliance expenditures. The common law rule on the non-recoverability of reliance expenditures is defensible on policy grounds, but it may lead to anomalies. It means, for example, that a party who has prepaid all or part of the price but received no return benefits is entitled to recover his payments in full, while the other party who may have spent as much or more in part performance of his obligations is entitled to nothing.

(ii) *Legislative Developments*

. . . The principal features of the [Act that applies in Ontario, and the majority of the common law provinces] are these. The Act abolishes the rule in *Chandler v. Webster* by relieving a contracting party from liability to make payments accruing before the date of frustration, but without affecting any claim against him or her for damages, and allows recovery of any payments made before this time. So far as non-pecuniary benefits are concerned, the court may, not must, allow recovery of their value. The recovery of reliance expenditures is still more circumscribed.

. . . [T]he Act provides that the court may permit the party incurring such expenses to retain so much of any payments received from the other party as is necessary to indemnify him or her for such expenses or to recover them from the other party if monies were payable to the other party before the date of frustration. These limited rights of recovery for reliance expenditures appear to have been animated by the theory that prepayment of the price is intended to protect the other party's reliance interests. The theory has little to commend it and has justly been criticized.

Finally, certain exclusions in the Ontario Act that follow those in the British Act should be noted. The Ontario Act does not apply to maritime contracts, insurance contracts, or to a contract for the sale of specific goods. . . .

In 1974 British Columbia enacted a new *Frustrated Contract Act* [R.S.B.C. 1996, c. 166]. The Act was also adopted at the same time by the Uniform Law Conference of Canada as a new *Uniform Frustrated Contracts Act*. The British Columbia Act ("the Act") was based on the recommendations in a Report of the British Columbia Law Reform Commission and was designed to remove the shortcomings in the first Uniform Act. It was largely successful in this objective although, in our view, a number of further improvements are desirable.

The Act introduces three important changes. First, it removes a discretionary element in the first Uniform Act in allowing, as of right, the recovery of compensation for non-pecuniary benefits conferred before discharge of the contract. Second, it provides that reliance losses shall be divided equally between the parties without regard to any prepayments that may have been made under the contract. Third, it recognizes explicitly that the parties may have intended to allocate the risk of loss of reliance expenditures on a basis different from that provided for in the Act, and establishes criteria for determining whether they have done so in fact.

[Footnotes partially omitted.]

NOTES and QUESTIONS

1. The O.L.R.C. recommended adoption of a modified version of the B.C. legislation. See *Report on Amendment of the Law of Contract* (1987), at 285.

2. For a critique of the approach taken under the Frustrated Contracts Acts and the British Columbia legislation and a consideration of alternative models that have been adopted in New South Wales and Victoria, see Stewart and Carter, "Frustrated Contracts and Statutory Adjustment: The Case for Reappraisal" (1992), 51 Camb. L.J. 66.

3. Citations of other versions of the Frustrated Contracts Act are: R.S.A. 2000, c. F-27; C.C.S.M., c. F190; R.S.N.B. 1973, c. F-24; R.S.N.L. 1990, c. F-26; R.S.N.W.T. 1988, c. F-12; R.S.O. 1990, c. F.34 as amended S.O. 1993, c. 27, Schd.; R.S.P.E.I. 1988, c. F-16, S.S. 1994, c. F-22.2, R.S.Y. 2002, c. 96.

Sections II and V of the Civil Code of Québec respectively provide for an "exception from liability" and "impossibility of performance":

1470. A person may free himself from his liability for injury caused to another by proving that the injury results from superior force, unless he has undertaken to make reparation for it.

A superior force is an unforeseeable and irresistible event, including external causes with the same characteristics.

1693. A debtor is released where he cannot perform an obligation by reason of a superior force and before he is in default, or where, although he was in default, the creditor could not, in any case, benefit by the performance of the obligation by reason of that superior force, unless, in either case, the debtor has expressly assumed the risk of superior force.

The burden of proof of superior force is on the debtor.

1694. A debtor released by impossibility of performance may not exact performance of the correlative obligation of the creditor; if the performance has already been rendered, restitution is owed.

Where the debtor has performed part of his obligation, the creditor remains bound to perform his own obligation to the extent of his enrichment.

Would either of these be relevant in a situation where a tenant has been unable to inhabit an apartment for one month due to a catastrophic ice storm?

4. What difference would the different forms of Frustrated Contracts Acts make to the following cases?

(a) *Krell v. Henry*, discussed in *Claude Neon General Advertising Ltd. v. Sing*, *supra*, section 2 of this chapter, in which the would-be renter had made a down payment of £25 for the rooms and promised to pay a further £50, for which the owner sued.

(b) *Taylor v. Caldwell*, *supra*, section 2 of this chapter.

(c) *Capital Quality Homes Ltd. v. Colwyn Const. Ltd.*, *supra*, section 2 of this chapter.

5. Does the fact that some legislative interventions specifically empower a court to exercise its discretion "if it considers it just to do so having regard to all the circumstances" provide any assistance in determining which is the most appropriate theory to explain the doctrine of frustration?

Chapter 11

LIMITS ON THE PURSUIT OF SELF INTEREST: AN EDITOR'S COMMENT

1. The Traditional View

Chapter 1 showed that the law of contracts, as it developed in the 19th century, was based on the general assumption that the parties were free to vigorously pursue their own interests and not obliged to take into account the position of their contracting partner. Each side was (and in most respects still is) expected to look after its own interests and the courts had no recognized right to intervene solely on the ground that one party had taken unfair advantage of another. Although there were always limits on this model of freedom of contract, it reflected the fundamental assumption of welfare economics, that people in general will rationally maximize their own self interest and that this conduct results in a net social benefit.

The principle of freedom of contract, and its underlying assumption, continues to pervade the subject. It explains the cornerstones of the law of contract, such as the notion that the courts will not investigate the adequacy of consideration. As long as there is an exchange, the courts will not examine whether the exchange is fair. It underlies the maxim of *caveat emptor*, which is at the heart of Chapter 7, so that the buyer of goods must look after his or her own interests in the absence of an actionable misrepresentation by the seller or a relevant term in the contract.

The philosophy of this view of contract law has been described by Hugh Collins as follows:

> The latent social ideal of the nineteenth-century law of contract embodies a libertarian state, in which the law maximizes the liberty of individual citizens, encourages self-reliance, and adopts an avowedly neutral stance with regard to permissible patterns of social life. The law of contract secures these goals perhaps more effectively than any other category of the law by facilitating the creation of legal obligations on any terms which individuals freely choose. We should recognize, therefore, that not only was the law of contract a convenient way of understanding the social relations of a market economy, but also it represented a particular theory of the legitimacy of state power, one which limited the exercise of such power in the name of respecting the liberty of citizens under the banner of freedom of contract.
>
> The fundamental analytical framework of the law of contract became one which focused upon the voluntary choices of individuals. The role of the law of contract was conceived principally as a facilitation of voluntary choices by giving them legal effect.

(Collins, *The Law of Contract*, 4th ed. (2003) at 6.)

The courts have provided innumerable practical examples of the ideal that Collins describes, even in recent times. In *Walford v. Miles*, a decision noted in Chapter 3, section 4, discussed in the *Mannpar Enterprises* and *Wellington City Council* decisions, and note 4 following *Wellington*, the House of Lords rejected, at 460 (All E.R.), the notion that there was a duty to carry on negotiations in good faith as repugnant to the inherently "adversarial position of the parties when involved in negotiations. Each party is entitled to pursue his (or her) own interest, so long as he avoids making misrepresentations."

Despite the power of the ideal of freedom of contract, it was never perfectly realized. An obvious manifestation of the manner in which the law of contract reflected a particular theory about how state power should be exercised (and avoided a neutral stance in relation to permissible patterns of social life) is illustrated in Chapter 13, section 2, where the materials consider types of contracts that have been found to be contrary to public policy. More importantly for the purposes of this chapter, the law always placed some express limits on the pursuit of self interest. For example, the law of contracts directly protects those who, because of their youth or mental disability, are presumed to transact at a disadvantage. This long-standing concern for specific categories of vulnerable people is considered in section 5 of Chapter 12. The law of duress and undue influence, which is discussed in sections 2 and 3 of Chapter 12, places broad limits on the ability of parties to relentlessly pursue their self interest.

This type of expressly acknowledged intervention by the judiciary was traditionally limited to specific areas of contract. However, within the traditional categories of contract law, the judges were always prepared, even in the nineteenth century, to mould the rules in an instrumental way in order to limit the advantage that one party can take over another. Lord Denning's interventions, referred to throughout the book, often illustrate the flexibility of contractual principles. Dozens of less spectacular cases also provide examples of this tendency. For example, in Chapter 4, section 5(e), *Robichaud v. Caisse Populaire de Pokemouche Ltée.* arguably provides an instance of the court limiting the power of a creditor over a debtor in a manner that conventional law appeared to prevent. *Bank of British Columbia v. Wren Developments*, in Chapter 7, section 2, may well illustrate the imposition by a court of a duty to disclose, while preserving the facade that there can be no misrepresentation in the absence of a statement of fact. The portion of Chapter 8 dealing with the judicial control of exclusion clauses provides many examples of the manipulation of doctrine within the traditional categories of the law of contracts in favour of a weaker party.

The covert use of traditional contract rules provides a measure of protection to the weaker parties, but in a manner that is often unpredictable and unsatisfactory and that can hide the real reasons for the decision. A failure by judges to openly discuss the real reasons for their decisions may mislead the appeal courts and commentators. New or modified approaches may be given effect without being critically evaluated. Moreover, there is a danger that the rule pressed into service to provide a fair result will itself be distorted. Subsequent applications of the distorted rule in a different fact situation may lead to arbitrary or unfair results. It may be questioned whether these sorts of consequences are worth bearing for the marginal protection thereby provided to either party.

2.   The Relationship Between Contracts and Other Areas of Private Law

The traditional approach of the courts tended to result in Contracts courses that were organized on the basis of the individual categories of doctrine as they are set out in this book. However, it is now clear that some general principles have emerged which are capable of transcending the individual categories of the subject and which in many cases limit the pursuit of self interest. This movement seems to have resulted from a changing conception of the nature of a contract.

In Chapter 7, section 5, the materials considered the development of concurrent liability in contract and tort. The introductory portion of that section referred to the decision of the Supreme Court of Canada in *J. Nunes Diamonds Ltd. v. Dominion Electric Protection Company*, [1972] S.C.R. 769, where the court decided that an action in negligent misrepresentation could not be brought when the relations of the parties were governed by a contract. In that case, Pigeon J. commented, at 777-78, that the tort of negligent misrepresentation was "inapplicable to any case where the relationship between the parties is governed by a contract, unless the negligence relied on can properly be described as an 'independent tort' unconnected with the performance of that contract".

This view was based on the assumption that a contract was a comprehensive code which set out all the rules that governed the parties' relationship in a particular transaction. By the act of contracting, the parties had set out all the applicable rules, which precluded the importation into contracts of legal principles which would otherwise govern the parties' relationship in a particular transaction. The mere existence of a contract impliedly excluded the operation of the principles of negligence in relation to that transaction. Dr. Flannigan has characterised this view as based on the hegemony of contract. In respect of the related issue of whether the presence of a contract precludes the existence of fiduciary duties, he has described it as based on the assumption that "commercial actors set their own bargain and, consequently, if they do not *contract into* fiduciary responsibility, it does not govern their arrangement." (Flannigan, "Commercial Fiduciary Obligation" (1998), 36 Alta. L. Rev. 905, 918.)

The notion that a contract was a comprehensive code was based on an odd view of the legal obligations that result from the existence of a particular relationship. Negligence principles and fiduciary duties apply because of the relationship between the parties, or because the parties have a particular status in relation to each other. In principle, the parties should continue to be bound by those duties unless they agree not to be. In any event, the contract as code view did not prove very workable in practice, because courts tended to be drawn to the idea that both tort and fiduciary duties should apply, unless expressly excluded, regardless of seemingly authoritative statements to the contrary. In relation to negligence, the view was decisively rejected by the Supreme Court of Canada in

Central Trust Co. v. Rafuse, which was cited in the introductory portion of Chapter 7, section 5, and in *BG Checo International Ltd. v. British Columbia Hydro & Power Authority*, which is extracted above in Chapter 7, section 5. Some echoes of the theory remain in the dissenting judgment of Iacobucci J. in the *BG Checo* decision, in which he suggested that a contract may preclude the possibility of a negligence action where there is an express term that deals with the matter, even though it does not expressly exclude tort liability. However the majority view, which reflects the everyday decisions of Canadian courts, was that an action in negligence is always available, when the pre-requisites of negligence are fulfilled, unless the contract excludes or limits the action. A similar approach is reflected in some fiduciary duty cases, such as *Molchan v. Omega Oil & Gas Ltd.* (1988), 47 D.L.R. (4th) 481 (S.C.C.), though for a discussion of the extent to which the parties can exclude liability for breach of fiduciary duty, see Feasby, "Fiduciary Obligations and Exclusion Clauses" (1998), 36 Alta. L.Rev. 923.

Decisions such as *B.G. Checo International* and *Central Trust* suggest a different view of the role of a contract. People in ordinary circumstances owe each other duties imposed by the general law, whether they find their source in torts, property (arising, for example, in the law of bailment), fiduciary law or any other area. These general duties apply unless they are limited or excluded by the terms of the contract.

The collapse of the idea that a contract sets out a comprehensive code of rules had its most obvious impact in the context of negligence actions that arise in contractual settings, as discussed in Chapter 7. It is now clear that the demise of this concept affected many other areas and that it has resulted in the emergence of a different perspective on the function of contracts. A contract no longer ousts the general legal principles that govern the parties' relationship, but it complements them, with the important difference that contract rules can exclude or limit the application of general principles if they do so explicitly. This view has led to an appreciation that various general principles, in addition to those of negligence, can apply across all the categories of contract law.

3.   Overriding General Principles

The emergence of general principles that transcend the individual categories of the law of contract has been illustrated by many decisions in recent years, particularly at the Supreme Court of Canada level. In one case, which involved a contractual relationship between a financial advisor and a client, La Forest J. offered both a partial summary of these "category-busting" principles and a justification for their existence. La Forest J. commented:

> Vulnerability is common to many relationships in which the law will intervene to protect one of the parties. It is, in fact, the "golden thread" that unites such related causes of action as breach of fiduciary duty, undue influence, unconscionability and negligent misrepresentation.

(*Hodgkinson v. Simms* (1995), 117 D.L.R. (4th) 161, 173 (S.C.C.).)

For the purposes of this account, it is possible to add the doctrine of good faith to the catalogue of broad principles set out in *Hodgkinson v. Simms*. Good faith is a relative newcomer to Anglo-Canadian contract law and lacks the definition provided by the longer history that the concepts of undue influence and unconscionability have enjoyed. It differs from fiduciary duty and negligence, because it does not arise out of a particular relationship between the parties. Instead, it seems to occur as a default rule in certain contractual situations, in much the same manner as some of the more frequently implied terms. However, along with unconscionability and the fiduciary principle, good faith is capable of limiting the pursuit of self interest in contractual relationships, with the result that it is important to deal with the inter-relationship of the three doctrines at this stage. The following extract provides an introduction to this topic. Of the remaining causes of action listed by La Forest J., negligent misrepresentation was dealt with in Chapter 7, section 5 and undue influence is considered in section 3 of Chapter 12.

O'BYRNE, GOOD FAITH IN CONTRACTUAL PERFORMANCE: RECENT DEVELOPMENTS

(1995), 74 Can. Bar Rev. 70, at 72-73

I. *Locating the good faith requirement relative to other standards*

Finn, in his article "The Fiduciary Principle" [in T.G. Youdan, ed., *Equity, Fiduciaries and Trusts* (1989) at 1] provides a useful treatment of the good faith standard regulating consensual relationships relative to both unconscionability and the obligations of a fiduciary. What follows are certain highlights from Finn's analysis:

THE FIDUCIARY STANDARD

- requires the fiduciary "to act selflessly and with undivided loyalty" to the other party.

THE GOOD FAITH STANDARD

- requires the parties to have regard for each other's "legitimate interests."
- applies even though the purpose of the contract is for each party to promote its own interests.
- means that the parties have only a qualified entitlement to act self-interestedly.
- arises in arms-length transactions.

THE UNCONSCIONABILITY STANDARD

- prohibits the parties from being "excessively self-interested or exploitative."
- means that the parties have a virtually absolute entitlement to act self-interestedly and with minimum regard for the other party.
- arises, generally, where one party is vulnerable or weaker than the other.

These foregoing standards force each party to acknowledge and respect the interests of the other, thereby putting a relative brake on self-promotion. Parties are not free to do exactly as they please: their conduct must meet the threshold standard governing the relationship in question.

[Footnotes omitted.]

Unconscionability is considered in detail in section 4 of Chapter 12. However, it is useful first to examine briefly the role of the fiduciary principle and the doctrine of good faith.

(a)   The Fiduciary Principle

A detailed account of fiduciary law is far beyond the scope of a course in Contracts. However, because the courts can employ the fiduciary principle in a contractual setting, it is necessary to be aware of its general dimensions.

A fiduciary is a person who in a broad sense occupies a position of trust and confidence. Because fiduciaries have expressly or impliedly undertaken to do so, they are required to relinquish their self interest and to act solely on behalf of another. The relationship between a trustee and a beneficiary is the most familiar example of a fiduciary relationship, in which the trustee assumes a high level of duty to act in the beneficiary's interest at the expense of the trustee's own self interest.

Fiduciary duties also arise in other traditional categories, such as relationships between partners and between solicitor and client. However, in recent years the courts have recognized that fiduciary relationships can arise outside of the traditional categories, if the facts surrounding the relationship show that there is evidence of "a mutual understanding that one party has relinquished its self-interest and agreed to act solely on behalf of the other party" (*Hodgkinson v. Simms, supra*, at 176-177).

The courts have found that a fiduciary duty arises in a number of commercial relationships in particular. For example, fiduciary duties were found to exist in *Hodgkinson v. Simms, supra*, between a financial adviser and the client who hired him, in *Erewhon Exploration v. Northstar Energy Corporation* (1994), 15 Alta. L.R. (3d) 200 (Q.B.) between an operator under a joint operating agreement and its contracting partner and in *Roe, McNeill & Co. v. McNeill* (1998), 45 B.C.L.R. (3d) 35 (C.A.) between the vendor and the purchaser of an accounting practice.

A fiduciary duty places the strictest limitation on the pursuit of self interest by the fiduciary. Although the courts suggest that they will find only rarely that the parties in a commercial relationship have surrendered their self interest in such a way as to invoke the fiduciary principle, it is undeniable that they have imposed fiduciary duties in a number of cases which were previously purely contractual in nature.

(b)   Good Faith

The doctrine of good faith in contracts is illustrated on numerous occasions throughout the book. Particularly vivid examples are found in Chapter 3, section 5 in *Empress Towers, Mannpar Enterprises Ltd. v. Canada, Wellington City Council v. Body Corporate 51702 (Wellington)* and the materials which follow and in *Wallace v. United Grain Growers Ltd.* in Chapter 14, section 3 (a)(iv). Although the notion of good faith has been described as "undeveloped and seriously controversial" (Flannigan, *supra*, at 921), it is clear that it too requires one contracting party to have regard for the legitimate interests of the other and to limit the pursuit of his or her own self interest. The limitation is less than that placed on a fiduciary, but greater than that imposed by the doctrine of unconscionability.

It is difficult to provide a definitive account of the nature of the duty of good faith and the situations in which it might apply. Sometimes such an obligation is characterized as an implied term of the contractual relationship. In the *Wallace v. United Grain Growers Ltd.* case, *supra*, McLachlin J., in dissent on this question but with the concurrence of La Forest and L'Heureux-Dubé JJ., determined that it was an implied term of a contract of employment that an employer act in good faith in dismissing an employee. In *Shelanu Inc. v. Print Three Franchising Corp.* (2003), 226 D.L.R. (4th) 577 (Ont. C.A.), noted in Chapter 8, sections 1 and 3(d)(vi), the court determined that a duty of good faith existed in the context of a franchisor-franchisee relationship because such contracts typically possessed the same characteristics as the employment contract considered in *Wallace.* Weiler J.A. said at 598-599:

> The relative position of the parties as outlined by Iacobucci J. in *Wallace* also exists in the typical franchisor-franchisee relationship. First, it is unusual for a franchisee to be in the position of being equal in bargaining power to the franchisor. . . .. The second characteristic, inability to negotiate more favourable terms, is met by the fact that a franchise agreement is a contract of adhesion. As I have indicated, a contract of adhesion is a contract in which the essential clauses were not freely negotiated but were drawn up by one of the parties on its behalf and imposed on the other. Further, insofar as access to information is concerned, the franchisee is dependent on the franchisor for information about the franchise, its location and projected cash flow, and is typically required to take a training program devised by the franchisor. The third characteristic, namely that the relationship continues to be affected by the power imbalance, is also met by the fact the franchisee is required to submit to inspections of its premises and audits of its books on demand, to comply with operation bulletins, and, often is dependent on, or required to buy, equipment or product from the franchisor.

Of course, an obligation to act in good faith is not restricted to certain classes of contract and it may arise simply out of the circumstances of a particular contractual relationship: see *978011 Ontario Ltd. v. Cornell Engineering Co.*, discussed in section 3(d)(ii) of Chapter 8.

In *Mesa Operating Ltd. Partnership v. Amoco Canada Resources Ltd.* (1994), 19 Alta. L.R. (3d) 38 (C.A.), the majority of the Alberta Court of Appeal described good faith as an interpretive guide, which enabled them to construe the contract in accordance with the parties' settled expectations. The court appeared to treat good faith as a term that was implicit in the parties' own agreement about how Amoco was to exercise a discretionary power under the contract. However, in *Opron Construction Co. v. Alberta* (1994), 151 A.R. 241 (Q.B.), an Alberta trial court seemed to treat the duty of good faith more as a general default rule, when it described it in terms of a rebuttable presumption.

In what circumstances are courts likely to become concerned about the absence of good faith? As the examples of *Empress Towers* and *Wallace v. United*

Grain Growers demonstrate, the courts typically resort to good faith where one party exercises a discretionary contractual power or makes a unilateral contractual decision.

Just as it is difficult to define when the courts will find a duty of good faith, it is impossible to identify with precision the standards of conduct which the duty demands. The concept is most often defined in the negative, as this overview will illustrate through two examples.

In the *Amoco* decision, *supra*, the court emphasized that the contract, properly interpreted, required Amoco not to act in a manner that substantially nullified the contractual objectives of, or caused significant harm to, the other party in a manner that was contrary to the original purposes or expectations of the parties. In that case, Amoco drilled a successful gas well on the south half of a section of land in which Mesa held a royalty interest that entitled it to 12 1/2% of the proceeds of all gas sales. However, in order to produce gas, a company must have the rights to a full drilling spacing unit, which ordinarily requires an entire section of land. If a company does not have rights to an entire section, it must "pool" its land with the other owners of the section in order to obtain an entire drilling spacing unit. When gas is then produced, the proceeds of production can be allocated to all the owners of the lands on an "areal" basis, that is according to the proportion that the surface acreage of each parcel bears to the entire section. However, if the characteristics of the reservoir are well known, production is normally allocated on a "reserves" basis, so that owners receive a share of production determined by the proportion of the gas in the lands that they contributed to the drilling spacing unit. Amoco pooled the south half of the section with the north half (which Amoco happened to own outright) on an areal basis, although it probably knew that all the gas was situated under the south half. Their discretionary decision effectively meant that Mesa received only half the royalty that it would have received if Amoco had pooled on a "reserves" basis. Amoco was thus in breach of a contractual obligation which the court recognized could readily be expressed in terms of good faith.

In *Gateway Realty Ltd. v. Arton Holdings Ltd.* (1991), 106 N.S.R. (2d) 180 (S.C.), affirmed (1992), 112 N.S.R. (2d) 180 (C.A.), the court recognized that the same elements that were identified in the *Amoco* decision could constitute bad faith and added that good faith also required that a party's conduct must not be contrary to community standards of honesty, reasonableness or fairness. Professor O'Byrne has summarised the *Gateway* case as follows, *supra*, at 73-74:

> Gateway Realty Ltd. ("Gateway") owned a shopping mall in which Zellers was the anchor tenant. The lease permitted Zellers to occupy the premises, leave them vacant, or assign to a third party without any obligation to secure the consent of the Landlord. After being approached by the defendant Arton Holdings Ltd. ("Arton")—a competitor of Gateway's—Zellers agreed to locate in Arton's mall. As part of this arrangement, the defendant agreed to take an assignment of the remaining 17 years of Zellers's lease with Gateway. The upshot was that 60,000 square feet of Gateway's mall had been assigned to its largest competitor. Pursuant to a subsequent agreement between Gateway and Arton, the companies agreed to "use their best efforts" to lease the space formerly occupied by Zellers. According to the court, this agreement bound Arton's exercise of its tenancy rights "either as a clarification of its tenancy obligations, as an amendment to the lease clause allowing it to 'go dark', or as a collateral agreement to

the same effect." When Arton continued to reject prospective tenants which it thought would strengthen Gateway's mall at the expense of its own operation, Gateway brought an action claiming, *inter alia*, that Arton had breached an obligation of good faith by not taking reasonable steps to sublet and had failed to discharge its obligation to use "best efforts."

Kelly J. found for Gateway on both grounds and therefore terminated the assignment. Not only was Arton in breach of its obligation to use "best efforts," it had failed to discharge its more generalized duty to perform in good faith. According to the court [at 212]:

> The law requires that parties to a contract exercise their rights under that agreement honestly, fairly and in good faith. This standard is breached when a party acts in a bad faith manner in the performance of its rights and obligations under the contract. "Good faith" conduct is the guide to the manner in which the parties should pursue their mutual contractual objectives. Such conduct is breached when a party acts in "bad faith"—a conduct that is contrary to community standards of honesty, reasonableness or fairness.

> [footnotes omitted.]

Professor O'Byrne's article provides a useful and detailed account of the development of good faith in Canada.

The fiduciary principle and the doctrine of good faith are relatively novel methods of limiting the pursuit of self interest in contractual relationships. Chapter 12 deals with the more long-standing doctrines which the courts have used to prevent the excessive promotion of self-interest at the expense of a weaker party.

THE PROTECTION OF WEAKER PARTIES

1. Introduction

Contract law does not hold weaker parties to all the bargains they make. Infants and persons with mental disabilities, for example, are presumed to transact at a disadvantage and, with some exceptions, their contracts are either void or voidable. Other persons, who are not presumed in advance to be disadvantaged, may be in a special relationship with another or may find themselves actually coerced, dominated or taken advantage of in a given situation. These persons may be able to claim relief under the doctrines of duress, undue influence or unconscionability.

The foregoing are explicit contractual bases upon which a weaker party might seek relief. It may be that weaker parties are also given protection more covertly. It has been suggested that judges will use other contract rules in an instrumental way to achieve what they believe to be a fair result in the circumstances. This can be problematic if it occurs, because the real reasons for the decision are hidden. A failure by judges to openly discuss their views misleads appeal courts and commentators. New or modified approaches are given effect without being critically evaluated. Moreover, there is a danger that the rule pressed into service to provide the fair result will itself be distorted. Subsequent application of the distorted rule in different circumstances may lead to arbitrary or unfair results. It may be questioned whether these sorts of consequences are worth bearing for the marginal protection thereby provided to weaker parties.

The extent to which judges utilize this kind of technique is open to debate. Presumably, however, where it does occur, it would be motivated by a feeling that the traditional bases for relief are too narrow. Keep this in mind as you now investigate the various doctrines and see how, in recent years, their scope of application has expanded in some respects and contracted in others.

We will examine these explicit bases for relief under four headings: (1) duress, (2) undue influence, (3) unconscionability and (4) incapacity. Note that persons may be weaker parties relative to others in a variety of ways. They may be intellectually weaker by reason of a disease of the mind, economically weaker or simply situationally weaker because of temporary circumstances. Alternatively, the "weakness" may arise out of a special relationship in which trust and confidence has been reposed in the other party. The weakness or special relationship is, in every case, a fact to be proven.

2. Duress

Historically the legal doctrine of duress was a narrow one. A contract could be set aside on this basis only if it had been procured as a result of actual or threatened physical violence ("duress to the person"). Thus, a contract brought about through a beating or a threat to commit a crime or a tort was voidable. With one qualification, this was the only kind of duress that was actionable.

Strictly speaking, neither a threatened improper refusal to release goods nor a threat to wrongfully seize goods (*i.e.*, "duress of goods") is an instance of physical violence and therefore would not qualify as legal duress. Nevertheless, there were cases in which it was held that money paid to avoid the threatened action could be recovered. In effect, therefore, some relief was given for duress of goods.

Times have changed. It is now accepted that relief for duress is no longer limited to these narrow circumstances. In particular, commercial pressure may amount to actionable duress.

PAO ON v. LAU YIU LONG
[1980] A.C. 614, [1979] 3 All E.R. 65 (P.C.)

The facts of this case are set out *supra*, in Chapter 4, section 4(b). It involved a defence, which was rejected by the Privy Council, that the consideration for a guarantee executed by the defendants (the Laus) consisted of a promise by the plaintiffs to perform their existing contract with a company in which the defendants were principal shareholders. In addition, the defendants argued that their guarantee was procured by economic duress. On this point, the Privy Council offered the following analysis.

LORD SCARMAN Duress, whatever form it takes, is a coercion of the will so as to vitiate consent. Their Lordships agree with the observation of Kerr J. in *The Siboen and The Sibotre* [[1976] 1 Lloyd's Rep. 293 (Q.B.)] that in a contractual situation commercial pressure is not enough. There must be present some factor 'which could in law be regarded as a coercion of his will so as to vitiate his consent'. This conception is in line with what was said in this Board's decision in *Barton v. Armstrong* [[1976] A.C. 104 (P.C.)] by Lord Wilberforce and Lord Simon of Glaisdale, observations with which the majority judgment appears to be in agreement. In determining whether there was a coercion of will such that there was no true consent, it is material to enquire whether the person alleged to have been coerced did or did not protest; whether, at the time he was allegedly coerced into making the contract, he did or did not have an alternative course open to him such as an adequate legal remedy; whether he was independently advised; and whether after entering the contract he took steps to avoid it. All these matters are, as was recognised in *Maskell v. Horner* [[1915] 3 K.B. 106 (C.A.)], relevant in determining whether he acted voluntarily or not.

In the present case there is unanimity amongst the judges below that there was no coercion of Lau's will. In the Court of Appeal the trial judge's finding . . . that Lau considered the matter thoroughly, chose to avoid litigation, and formed the opinion that the risk in giving the guarantee was more apparent than real was upheld. In short, there was commercial pressure, but no coercion. Even if this Board was disposed, which it is not, to take a different view, it would not substitute its opinion for that of the judges below on this question of fact.

It is, therefore, unnecessary for the Board to embark on an enquiry into the question whether English law recognises a category of duress known as 'economic duress'. But, since the question has been fully argued in this appeal, their Lordships will indicate very briefly the view which they have formed. At common law money paid under economic compulsion could be recovered in an action for money had and received. . . . The compulsion had to be such that the party was deprived of 'his freedom of exercising his will'. It is doubtful, however, whether at common law any duress other than duress to the person sufficed to render a contract voidable. . . . American law now recognises that a contract may be avoided on the ground of economic duress. The commercial pressure alleged to constitute such duress must, however, be such that the victim must have entered the contract against his will, must have had no alternative course open to him, and must have been confronted with coercive acts by the party exerting the pressure: see Williston on Contracts [3rd ed. (1970) ch. 47, s. 1603]. American judges pay great attention to such evidential matters as the effectiveness of the alternative remedy available, the fact or absence of protest, the availability of independent advice, the benefit received, and the speed with which the victim has sought to avoid the contract. Recently two English judges have recognised that commercial pressure may constitute duress the pressure of which can render a contract voidable: see Kerr J. in *The Siboen and The Sibotre* [*supra*] and Mocatta J. in *North Ocean Shipping Co. v. Hyundai Const. Co.* [[1979] Q.B. 705]. Both stressed that the pressure must be such that the victim's consent to the contract was not a voluntary act on his part. In their Lordship's view, there is nothing contrary to principle in recognising economic duress as a factor which may render a contract voidable, provided always that the basis of such recognition is that it must amount to a coercion of will, which vitiates consent. It must be shown that the payment made or the contract entered into was not a voluntary act.

NOTE and QUESTIONS

1. In *The Siboen and The Sibotre* (referred to in *Pao On*), Kerr J., at 336, stated that "the Court must in every case at least be satisfied that the consent of the other party was overborne by compulsion so as to deprive him of any animus contrahendi". Is it preferable to describe duress as a "coercion of will" rather than as a situation where the person's will is "overborne"? See Atiyah, "Economic Duress and the 'Overborne Will'" (1982), 98 L.Q.R. 197.

2. The approach taken by the Privy Council in *Pao On* was to examine the effect of the threat on the will of the other party. Do you think the seriousness of the consequences of the threatened conduct is or should be a factor in the judicial conclusion? See Coote, "Duress by Threatened Breach of Contract" (1980), 39 Camb. L.J. 40.

3. Is it relevant that the pressure exerted would or would not have coerced the will of a reasonable person?

GORDON v. ROEBUCK

(1992), 9 O.R. (3d) 1, 92 D.L.R. (4th) 670 (C.A.)

Gordon and Roebuck were both solicitors (and experienced businessmen), each acting as trustee for different investors in a joint venture development of two apartment buildings. Roebuck, as trustee, held mortgages on the buildings as security for monies advanced to the project by his beneficiary clients. The first building was sold in 1979. On January 10, 1980, the parties to the joint venture contracted to give absolute authority to Gordon to deal with the second building. The document also stated that, in return for Gordon repaying the monies secured by the mortgages, Roebuck would execute any documents required upon a sale of the property. Subsequently, but before repayment of the monies, Gordon agreed to sell the second building to a multiple urban residential building (MURB) tax shelter syndicate. The transaction was to close on December 31, 1980. In order to close, Roebuck would have to provide a discharge of the mortgage and execute a statutory declaration that had been prepared for the purpose of obtaining financing from Canada Mortgage and Housing Corporation. On December 25, 1980, Roebuck advised Gordon that he would not provide the discharge or execute any other document unless Gordon agreed to pay $162,500 out of the proceeds of the sale to Roebuck, primarily as trustee for Hyman Satok, one of the joint venture participants. Roebuck insisted that the Satok money had originally been advanced by way of loan rather than as a contribution of capital to the joint venture. Gordon and Roebuck then negotiated a settlement on December 29, 1980 whereby Roebuck agreed to execute the documents in return for a $50,000 payment and a series of promissory notes totalling $80,000. The sale of the building was then able to close. Gordon subsequently refused to honour the promissory notes and commenced an action, as trustee, to have the December 29, 1980 contract declared voidable by reason of economic duress. The trial judge dismissed the claim concluding that there was no exertion of pressure that was not legitimate. Gordon appealed.

McKINLAY, J.A. [delivering the judgment of the court] . . . On p. 8 of his reasons [p. 205 O.R., pp. 572-73 D.L.R.] the trial judge states:

> To succeed on the ground of economic duress, the plaintiff must prove that his will was coerced and that the pressure exerted to do that was not legitimate. Lord Scarman [in *Pao On v. Lau Yiu, supra*]has set out four factors to consider in determining if a party's will has been coerced. They are:
>
> (1) Did he protest?
> (2) Was there an alternative course open to him?
> (3) Was he independently advised?
> (4) After entering the contract did he take steps to avoid it?
>
> There is no evidence the plaintiff protested at the time of the alleged coercion of his will. He had an alternative course, an adequate legal remedy. He was independently advised. He did not take steps to avoid the contract for over a year after entering it.
>
> The plaintiff did not testify and there is, therefore, no direct evidence, as there might have been, as to the coercion of his will.
>
> I hold that there was not a coercion of the plaintiff's will in the sense that that is required to avoid a contract on the ground of economic duress.

The appellant takes the position that none of the answers which the trial judge gave to the questions posed above is supported by the evidence. I shall address them *seriatim*.

(1) *Did he protest?*

The trial judge found that there was no evidence that the appellant protested at the time of the alleged coercion of his will. He placed some reliance on the fact that the appellant himself did not testify and that, therefore, there was no direct evidence as to the coercion of this will. On Christmas Day 1980, Mr. Roebuck advised the appellant through the appellant's solicitor that he would not attend at the closing of the MURB sales and would not provide the required discharge of mortgage unless an amount of $162,500 was paid to him on closing. That amount was alleged to have included the $100,000 obtained from Mr. Satok and other monies advanced by Manning Roebuck, in trust. The alleged coercion culminated at a meeting on December 29, 1980, attended by Mr. Roebuck, by his solicitor Norman Endicott, by Daniel Gordon, son of the appellant, and by Arthur Gans, a solicitor who acted for the appellant. Daniel Gordon, also a solicitor, acted at all times as agent for his father.

Evidence from Wilferd Gordon would have been of little or no assistance with respect to the fact of coercion, since he was not present at the December 29, 1980 meeting. . . . The position of the appellant was clear: that a mortgage discharge, and a statutory declaration giving names of the persons entitled to the funds on discharge of the mortgage, were required to close the transaction; that Mr. Roebuck was aware of that requirement; that he had undertaken to provide all documents necessary for the closing in an agreement executed by him on January 10, 1980; and that he improperly refused to provide those documents—and, more particularly, the statutory declaration—other than in return for $162,500. It was the appellant's position that he was entitled to both the mortgage discharge and the statutory declaration, the first by virtue of payment of the amount owing on the mortgage plus interest, and the second as a result of an agreement the parties executed on January 10, 1980. It was also the position of the appellant that the respondents were not entitled to any funds advanced by Mr. Roebuck on behalf of Mr. Satok until all mortgage loans and unsecured loans to the joint venture had been repaid in full. Their position was that Mr. Satok was an investor in the project through Mr. Roebuck, and that he would only be entitled to a return of investment *pro rata* with other investors.

There can be no doubt that there was substantial objection by Daniel Gordon on behalf of his father to payment of any amount representing alleged advances by Mr. Satok. The agreement entered into at the meeting on December 29, 1980—just prior to closing—was solely for the purpose of obtaining the statutory declaration required for closing. The appellant's son on his behalf had protested by correspondence and during his attendance at the December 29 meeting. The final outcome of that meeting was a handwritten agreement to pay $50,000 in cash and to deliver a series of promissory notes totalling $80,000 on closing.

(2) *Was there an alternative course open to him?*

With respect to whether or not the appellant had an alternative course open to him, the trial judge found that he did—namely, the obtaining of a court order requiring execution of the required documents. It is true that application to the court was considered, and a notice of motion was actually drafted by the appellant's counsel on December 29, 1980, returnable Tuesday, December 30, 1980. It was not proceeded with because of the agreement finally entered into between the parties on December 29 for the payment of $50,000 plus the delivery of the promissory notes. It is the position of the appellant that he had no realistic alternative, given the complexity and the immediacy of the closing of the transaction, and the difficulty in getting a matter of such complexity before the court and having it decided by the court between December 29 and December 30. Any alternative course, he says, was an unrealistic one. In my view, the "adequate legal remedy" which the trial judge found available to the appellant was non-existent in practical terms.

(3) *Was he independently advised?*

With respect to the issue of independent legal advice, the trial judge found that the appellant was independently advised, and there is no doubt that that is so. However, independent advice in such circumstances would likely have been that there was no other practical course available but to capitulate to the demands of the party exerting the pressure.

(4) *After entering the contract did he take steps to avoid it?*

With respect to the question whether the appellant took steps to avoid the contract within a reasonable time after its execution, the learned trial judge was clearly incorrect in his conclusion that the appellant took no steps to avoid the contract for over a year after entering it. This action was commenced on May 13, 1981—three and a half months after execution of the impugned contract, after payment of $50,000, and one month after the due date of the first promissory note.

I have difficulty in finding evidence on which the trial judge could base the findings referred to above. With respect to the first question, there was substantial evidence of protest by the appellant's agent both prior to and at the meeting of December 29, 1980. With respect to the second, the alternative course open to the appellant was not, under the circumstances, a realistic alternative. With respect to the third, independent advice in this particular situation was not relevant, since appropriate advice could only have been to yield to the pressure because of the exigencies of the situation. With respect to the fourth, the finding of the trial judge was clearly in error. I see no alternative to a finding that economic duress was exerted in this case.

However, that does not end the matter. As stated by the trial judge, one must determine whether the coercion exerted on the appellant was legitimate. This requires an assessment of whether Mr. Roebuck was required by the agreement of January 10, 1980 to execute the statutory declaration required by the appellant, and whether he had a *bona fide* claim to the monies demanded at the time he demanded them.

The trial judge seems to have had some doubt as to the appellant's entitlement to the documents demanded from Mr. Roebuck for the purpose of closing the transaction. On January 10, 1980 the parties entered into a contract in which Mr. Roebuck quit-claimed all his right, title and interest in the property to Wilferd Gordon, and in which he gave Mr. Gordon authority to deal with the property in any manner he saw fit, including the ongoing management, development and sale of the property. For the purpose of carrying out that agreement Mr. Roebuck agreed to execute any and all documentation which Wilferd Gordon, in his sole discretion, considered necessary to give effect to the agreement. Mr. Roebuck conceded that he had entered into that contract voluntarily and was bound by it. It is clear that that agreement required Mr. Roebuck to execute the mortgage and statutory declaration requested of him.

Mr. Roebuck gave evidence that he was of the view that the amount of $162,500 was loaned to the joint venture by him on behalf of clients. Records of the project show the $162,500 to be owed to Palroe, a company controlled by Mr. Roebuck, which was one of the original joint venturers. The appellant takes the position that those monies were investments in the project and not loans made to it. However, accounts entered at trial were confusing and inadequate to say the least. The trial judge correctly considered that the appellant, in claiming unjustifiable economic duress, had the onus of proving that Mr. Roebuck was not entitled to the amounts required under the impugned agreement. The trial judge was entitled to hold, as he did, that the appellant had not satisfied that onus.

In summary, I am of the view that coercion was exerted on the appellant's agent to execute the December 29, 1980 agreement which amounted to economic duress at law. However, I am also of the view that the pressure exerted was justified on the facts of this case on the basis *only* that there was some evidence from which the trial judge could conclude that the appellant had not shown that Mr. Roebuck was not entitled to the funds demanded by him on closing of the transaction. Consequently the agreement was not one which could be set aside as one executed under *unjustifiable* economic duress.

The appellant argued that there was no consideration given by the respondent for the promises made by the appellant in the December 29 agreement. The document was executed under seal, all signatories were lawyers, and there is no indication in any of the facts that the seal was intended for any other purpose than to import consideration. I agree with the trial judge that there was no merit in that argument.

[Appeal dismissed, but judgment against Gordon in his capacity as trustee.]

QUESTIONS

1. Is it conceptually advantageous to distinguish between justified and unjustified economic *duress* rather than between economic *pressure* and economic *duress*? The former analysis involves initially ascertaining whether the pressure exerted amounts to duress at law and then going on to consider whether that duress is justified. What advantage, if any, does this offer over simply determining whether the pressure applied, given all the relevant factors, amounted to duress?

2. Does the *Gordon* case suggest that the four factors assessed by the Ontario Court of Appeal are the exclusive determinants of legal duress? Judges in several subsequent cases have addressed only those four considerations. What, ultimately, is the test for economic duress? Are there potentially many other factors that might be relevant in the application of that test?

3. If the complaining party had independent advice, does it matter that the advice was to "capitulate to the demands"? Whatever the nature of the advice, does it matter whether or not it was followed? Does it matter that the advice was based on wrong or incomplete facts or was given under severe time constraints?

4. In what sense is it relevant that an alternative course of action is "unrealistic"? Does a court undermine its own authority by discounting the alternative of legal enforcement of rights? Do you suppose legal enforcement was the kind of alternative course contemplated by Lord Scarman in *Pao On*?

3.   Undue Influence

Duress was a common law doctrine. The courts of equity exercised a somewhat wider jurisdiction in granting relief where there had been undue influence. The two doctrines were compared by Henry J. in *Brooks v. Alker* (1975), 60 D.L.R. (3d) 577 at 583-84 (Ont. H.C.).

> The concept of duress at common law and of undue influence in equity is well established and needs no elaboration. . . . By duress is meant the compulsion under which a person acts through fear of personal suffering as from injury to the body, or from confinement, actual or threatened. A contract obtained by duress of one party over another is voidable not void. The duress must exist at the time of making the contract and the personal suffering may be that of the spouse or near relative of the contracting party, but that of a stranger is not sufficient.
>
> Undue influence has been defined as the unconscientious use by one person of power possessed by him over another in order to induce the other to enter a contract: *Earl of Aylesford v. Morris* (1873), 8 Ch. App. 484, *per* Lord Selborne at p. 490. It is my understanding that duress falling short of the common law requirements may also constitute undue influence in equity.

Undue influence is found where there is an ability to exercise exceptional power in relation to another person's choices. It is something well beyond the making of suggestions. It is a power of persuasion that is objectionable usually because it arises out of a confidential or other special relationship between the parties.

A claim of undue influence can be established in either of two ways. The first is to prove *actual* undue influence, that is, an actual operating influence on the choice that was made. The second way is to prove a special relationship between the parties. For example, evidence that one party advised the other on matters germane to the wisdom of the transaction entered into may be sufficient to establish a "special relationship" between them. Proof of the required relationship raises the presumption that undue influence was exercised. Once this presumption is raised the claim of undue influence is made out unless the other party is able to rebut the presumption.

The decision of the House of Lords in *Nat. Westminster Bank v. Morgan*, [1985] 1 All E.R. 821, deals with a number of aspects of the doctrine of undue influence. In the following passage Lord Scarman, at 827, described the rationale for the doctrine and asserted that there must be a disadvantageous bargain before a claim for relief can be advanced:

> ... I know of no reported authority where the transaction set aside was not to the manifest disadvantage of the person influenced. It would not always be a gift: it can be a 'hard and inequitable' agreement (see *Ormes v. Beadel* (1860) 2 Giff 166 at 174, 66 ER 70 at 74); or a transaction 'immoderate and irrational' (see *Bank of Montreal v. Stuart* [1911] AC 120 at 137) or 'unconscionable' in that it was a sale at an undervalue (see *Poosathurai v. Kannappa Chettiar* (1919) LR 47 Ind App 1 at 3-4). Whatever the legal character of the transaction, the authorities show that it must constitute a disadvantage sufficiently serious to require evidence to rebut the presumption that in the circumstances of the relationship between the parties it was procured by the exercise of undue influence. In my judgment, therefore, the Court of Appeal erred in law in holding that the presumption of undue influence can arise from the evidence of the relationship of the parties without also evidence that the transaction itself was wrongful in that it constituted an advantage taken of the person subjected to the influence which, failing proof to the contrary, was explicable only on the basis that undue influence had been exercised to procure it.
>
> The principle justifying the court in setting aside a transaction for undue influence can now be seen to have been established by Lindley LJ in *Allcard v. Skinner* [(1887), 36 Ch. D. 145 (C.A.) at 182-83]. It is not a vague 'public policy' but specifically the victimisation of one party by the other . . .:
>
>> The principle must be examined. What then is the principle? Is it that it is right and expedient to save persons from the consequences of their own folly? or is it that it is right and expedient to save them from being victimised by other people? In my opinion the doctrine of undue influence is founded on the second of these two principles. Courts of Equity have never set aside gifts on the ground of the folly, imprudence, or want of foresight on the part of donors. The Courts have always repudiated any such jurisdiction. *Huguenin v. Baseley* ((1807) 14 Ves. 273, [1803-13] All ER Rep 1) is itself a clear authority to this effect. It would obviously be to encourage folly, recklessness, extravagance and vice if persons could get back property which they foolishly made away with, whether by giving it to charitable institutions or by bestowing it on less worthy objects. On the other hand, to protect people from being forced, tricked or misled in any way by others into parting with their property is one of the most legitimate objects of all laws; and the equitable doctrine of undue influence has grown out of and been developed by the necessity of grappling with insidious forms of spiritual tyranny and with infinite varieties of fraud.

In the *Morgan* case Lord Scarman had used terminology which suggested that "domination" was the degree of influence necessary to support the action. That suggestion was addressed by the English Court of Appeal two years later in *Goldsworthy v. Brickell*, [1987] 1 All E.R. 853. Nourse L.J. reviewed the case law on the issue of "domination" and stated, at 868, that.

> It will be observed that none of these eminent judges thought it necessary, in order to make out a case based on the presumption, to show that the relationship was one of domination of one party by the other. Everything which they said is consistent with the notion that it is enough to show that the party in whom the trust and confidence is reposed is in a position to exert influence over him who reposes it. The improbability of there being any other standard is emphasised by a consideration of some of the well-defined relationships, for example doctor and patient or solicitor and client. The reason why the presumption applies to those relationships is that doctors and solicitors are trusted and confided in by their patients and clients to give them conscientious and disinterested advice on matters which profoundly affect, in the one case, their physical and mental and, in the other, their material well-being. It is natural to presume that out of that trust and confidence grows influence. But it would run contrary to human experience to presume that every patient is dominated by his doctor or every client by

his solicitor. Even in jest such cases must be rare. And while that may not be equally true of other relationships, for example, parent and child, it is not the function of a presumption to presume the generally improbable.

The Supreme Court of Canada examined the doctrine of undue influence in the following case. The decision deals with a trust but the court does refer to "commercial transactions" in the course of discussing the issues of "domination" and "manifest disadvantage". Consider whether the subsequent decision of the House of Lords in *Etridge* sufficiently clarified the jurisprudence.

GEFFEN v. GOODMAN ESTATE

[1991] 2 S.C.R. 353, 81 D.L.R. (4th) 211

WILSON J. The respondent, Stacy Randall Goodman, as executor of his mother's estate and on his own behalf, commenced an action claiming that he and his siblings were entitled to certain property left to his mother, Tzina Goodman, by his grandmother, Annie Sanofsky. The appellants, Sam, William and Ted Geffen are the brothers and nephew of Stacy's mother. They are the trustees of a certain trust agreement in which Stacy's mother is named as the settlor and under which the trust property is to be distributed amongst all of Annie Sanofsky's grandchildren. This appeal concerns the validity of the trust agreement.

Annie Sanofsky had four children, Sam, Ted, Jack and Tzina. Sam and Ted Geffen are both successful businessmen currently living in the United States. Their brother Jack is an insurance underwriter who lives in Edmonton. Their sister Tzina (Mrs. Goodman), now deceased, had a less than trouble-free life. She first came under the care of a psychiatrist while a teenager. Psychiatric intervention became a common feature of her existence. She was hospitalized many times over the years and was eventually diagnosed as suffering from bipolar affective disorder, formerly known as manic depressive disorder, and immature personality. Tzina's illness caused strain in her family relationships. Her disorder tended to drive people away from her. Although she married and had children she did not have much contact with her children after her separation from her husband. Her contact with them was purely casual.

In 1968, with the help of her son Jack, Annie Sanofsky executed a will providing for a life estate to her daughter Tzina and directing that on Tzina's death her estate should be distributed to all of her (Annie's) grandchildren. At the time of their mother's death the four children were surprised to learn that a new will had been executed in 1975 which superseded the 1968 will. Under the new will Annie Sanofsky left the property which had been her home outright to her daughter Tzina, provided bequests of $1,000 each to her sons, and directed that the residue of her estate be held in trust for Tzina during her lifetime and pass on Tzina's death to her (Tzina's) children.

The three Geffen brothers, not surprisingly, were unhappy with the way in which their mother had disposed of her estate. They thought it unfair that their children had been cut out of the will. Their sister agreed. They were especially concerned, however, with their mother's decision to bequeath her home in Calgary outright to their sister. Tzina had a history of mental illness and they feared that her disability would interfere with her capacity to act responsibly in relation to the property she had inherited. They were particularly concerned that Tzina might divest herself of the assets she needed for her own support. If this happened they might be called upon to contribute to her support. They, along with their sister, decided to seek legal advice as to whether or not the second will was valid.

They retained the services of Mr. Pearce, a Calgary lawyer, and explained the situation to him. Jack Geffen acted as spokesman for the family. The options open to Tzina were canvassed. It was suggested that the house be transferred by Tzina to her brothers' children. A disagreement ensued between Tzina and her brother Jack. She did not like the idea of transferring title to the house immediately, leaving herself with only a life interest in it. Mr. Pearce suggested that she take some time to think things over. The meeting disbanded, the brothers paid for the consultation and all concerned returned to their respective homes.

Mrs. Goodman thereafter had only casual contact with her brothers but continued to seek the advice of counsel and communicated with Mr. Pearce on several occasions. As a result of these consultations it was suggested to Mrs. Goodman that the Calgary residence be put into a trust for her for life with her brothers as trustees but that she would retain the right to dispose of the property by will. This suggestion was vehemently rejected by Jack but accepted by Ted and Sam Geffen. Jack indicated that he would have nothing further to do with the trust and it was agreed that Ted's son William would replace him as a trustee.

Mr. Pearce then went ahead and prepared the trust deed. The trust property was conveyed to the trustees on terms that Mrs. Goodman retained a life interest in the Calgary residence and that on her request the trustees would consider a sale of the property so long as the sale was in Mrs. Goodman's best interests. The trust deed further provided that upon Mrs. Goodman's death the trust property would be divided equally among her surviving children, nephews and nieces, *i.e.*, all Annie Sanofsky's grandchildren.

After the deed was executed Mrs. Goodman was apparently not too sure of the effect of what she had done. She attempted twice to put the property on the market. Her attempts were thwarted by Mr. Pearce. Mrs. Goodman died in May of 1984, leaving a last will and testament in which she left her entire estate to her children.

.....

The presumption of undue influence

This appeal raises important questions concerning the doctrine of undue influence and, in particular, the application of the presumption of undue influence. It was over this issue that the trial judge and the Court of Appeal parted company. As well, the scope of the doctrine of undue influence and its evidentiary companion, the presumption of undue influence, has recently been addressed by the House of Lords in *Morgan* [*supra*]. Not surprisingly, the parties to this appeal devoted the bulk of their argument both on the leave application and the appeal itself to the question whether or not we should follow the House of Lords in Canada. Indeed, the primary ground of appeal advanced by the appellant was whether there could be a presumption of undue influence where the trust agreement was not found by the trial judge to be "manifestly disadvantageous" to the party seeking to have it set aside. The respondent's response was that the doctrine of "manifest disadvantage" applies only to commercial transactions and does not apply to gifts. The court has thus been called upon not only to resolve the dispute between the parties to this appeal but to clarify the law and provide some guidance to our courts in this area.

In the present case there was no evidence of undue influence as such and it therefore remains to consider whether the relationship between the parties gave rise to a presumption of undue influence.

What are the factors that go to establishing a presumption of undue influence? This question has been the focus of much debate in recent years. Equity has recognized that transactions between persons standing in certain relationships with one another will be presumed to be relationships of influence until the contrary is shown. These include the relationship between trustee and beneficiary (*Ellis v. Barker* (1871), L.R. 7 Ch. App. 104); solicitor and client (*Wright v. Carter*, [1903] 1 Ch. 27 (C.A.)); doctor and patient (*Mitchell v. Homfray* (1881), 8 Q.B.D. 587 (C.A.)); parent and child (*Lancashire Loans Ltd. v. Black*, [1934] 1 K.B. 380 (C.A.)); guardian and ward (*Hylton v. Hylton* (1754), 2 Ves. Sen. 547, 28 E.R. 349); and future husband and fiancee (*Re Lloyds Bank, Ltd.*, [1931] 1 Ch. 289). Beginning, however, with *Zamet v. Hyman*, [1961] 3 All E.R. 933 (C.A.), it came to be accepted that the relationships in which undue influence will be presumed are not confined to fixed categories and that each case must be considered on its own facts. Since then it has been generally agreed that the existence of some "special" relationship must be shown in order to support the presumption although what constitutes such a "special" relationship is a matter of some doubt.
. . .

The growing debate in the academic literature over the kind of relationship to which the presumption of undue influence should apply is echoed in the decision of the English courts following *Morgan*. For instance, in *Midland Bank plc v. Shephard*, [1988] 3 All E.R. 17 (C.A.), and *Simpson v. Simpson*, [1989] Fam. L. 20, a test of "dominating influence" was applied, while in *Goldsworthy v. Brickell*, [*supra*], the Court of Appeal applied the confidentiality test and explicitly rejected the domination approach. . . .

Similar debate and disagreement has arisen over another factor thought to be relevant in establishing a presumption of undue influence. At the Court of Appeal level in *Morgan* [[1983] 3 All E.R. 85] the two-judge panel agreed that it was not necessary for a plaintiff invoking the presumption to show that the transaction entered into worked to his or her disadvantage. Dunn L.J. acknowledged that the decided cases all involved instances of disadvantage to the party influenced but went on to state that considerations of public policy required that transactions brought about through the possible abuse of a confidential relationship should not be permitted by a court of equity to stand. Slade L.J. agreed, adding that this did not mean that proof of a fair transaction was irrelevant. In his opinion, such proof could in fact make it easier for a party to rebut the presumption once applied.

The House of Lords, however, specifically overruled the Court of Appeal on this point. . . .

The requirement that the plaintiff show manifest disadvantage was subsequently applied even to the first class of undue influence cases, *i.e.*, those in which actual undue influence must be affirmatively shown by the person allegedly influenced: see *Bank of Credit & Commerce International S.A. v. Aboody*, [1989] 2 W.L.R. 759 (C.A.). . . .

This court is not, of course, bound to follow decisions of the House of Lords. Nor is it, strictly speaking, necessary for us for the purposes of the present appeal to examine all aspects of the *Morgan* decision and in particular the rule of the House of Lords respecting the requirement of a showing of manifest disadvantage in cases involving commercial transactions. It is my view, however, that the resolution of this appeal should proceed from first principles and this necessarily leads us into a consideration of the law as set out in *Morgan*. . . .

What then is the nature of the relationship that must exist in order to give rise to a presumption of undue influence? Bearing in mind the decision in *Morgan*, its critics and the divergence in the jurisprudence which it spawned, it is my opinion that concepts such as "confidence" and "reliance" do not adequately capture the essence of relationships which may give rise to the presumption. I would respectfully agree with Lord Scarman that there are many confidential relationships that do not give rise to the presumption just as there are many non-confidential relationships that do. It seems to me rather than when one speaks of "influence" one is really referring to the ability of one person to dominate the will of another, whether through manipulation, coercion, or outright but subtle abuse of power. I disagree with the Court of Appeal's decision in *Goldsworthy v. Brickell, supra*, that it runs contrary to human experience to characterize relationships of trust or confidence as relationships of dominance. To dominate the will of another simply means to exercise a persuasive influence over him or her. The ability to exercise such influence may arise from other relationships as well. The point is that there is nothing *per se* reprehensible about persons in a relationship of trust or confidence exerting influence, even undue influence, over their beneficiaries. It depends on their motivation and the objective they seek to achieve thereby.

What of the controversial requirement of "manifest disadvantage" articulated in *Morgan*? In my view, the critics were correct in pointing out that this test, while perhaps appropriate in a purely commercial setting, limits the doctrine of undue influence too much. In the case of gifts or bequests, for example, it makes no sense to insist that the donor or testator prove that their generosity placed them at a disadvantage. While one could say that giving away anything is in a literal sense *ipso facto* disadvantageous, it seems to me that this is a wholly unrealistic test to apply to a gift. A donor who wishes to make a gift is not really disadvantaged by doing so. On the contrary, his or her own purpose is served by doing so. Disadvantage is accordingly, to my mind, not a particularly appropriate concept for general application to the wide variety of situations to which the doctrine of undue influence could conceivably apply.

What then must a plaintiff establish in order to trigger a presumption of undue influence? In my view, the inquiry should begin with an examination of the relationship between the parties. The first question to be addressed in all cases is whether the potential for domination inheres in the nature of the relationship itself. This test embraces those relationships which equity has already recognized as giving rise to the presumption, such as solicitor and client, parent and child, and guardian and ward, as well as other relationships of dependency which defy easy categorization.

Having established the requisite type of relationship to support the presumption, the next phase of the inquiry involves an examination of the nature of the transaction. When dealing with commercial transactions, I believe that the plaintiff should be obliged to show, in addition to the required relationship between the parties, that the contract worked unfairness either in the sense that he or she was unduly disadvantaged by it or that the defendant was unduly benefited by it. From the court's point of view this added requirement is justified when dealing with commercial transactions because, as already mentioned, a court of equity, even while tempering the harshness of the common law, must accord some degree of deference to the principle of freedom of contract and the inviolability of bargains. Moreover, it can be assumed in the vast majority of commercial transactions that parties act in pursuance of their own self-interest. The mere fact, therefore, that the plaintiff seems to be giving more than he is getting is insufficient to trigger the presumption.

By way of contrast, in situations where consideration is not an issue, *e.g.*, gifts and bequests, it seems to me quite inappropriate to put a plaintiff to the proof of undue disadvantage or benefit in the result. In these situations the concern of the court is that such acts of beneficence not be tainted. It is enough, therefore, to establish the presence of a dominant relationship.

Once the plaintiff has established that the circumstances are such as to trigger the application of the presumption, *i.e.*, that apart from the details of the particular impugned transaction the nature of the relationship between the plaintiff and defendant was such that the potential for influence existed, the onus moves to the defendant to rebut it. As Lord Evershed M.R. stated in *Zamet v. Hyman, supra*, at p. 938, the plaintiff must be shown to have entered into the transaction as a result of his own "full, free and informed thought". Substantively, this may entail a showing that no actual influence was deployed in the particular transaction, that the plaintiff had independent advice, and so on. Additionally, I agree with those authors who suggest that the magnitude of the disadvantage or benefit is cogent evidence going to the issue of whether influence was exercised.

In the present case neither the trial judge nor the Court of Appeal went into very much detail as to why the presumption of undue influence was properly applicable given the nature of the relationship between Mrs. Goodman and her older brothers. They focused instead on the details of the execution of the trust agreement itself. A review of the circumstances between the deceased and her brothers *at the relevant time* does, however, disclose that the relationship between them was such that a potential existed for the brothers to exercise a persuasive influence over their sister. . . .

It is true that the trial judge found as a fact that there was very little contact between Mrs. Goodman and her brothers over the years prior to the death of their mother. Uncontradicted evidence disclosed that Mrs. Goodman had a history of mental health problems and that she suffered from both bipolar affective disorder and a personality disorder which at times made her domineering and aggressive but at other times withdrawn and helpless depending on her mood swings. The brothers were aware that their sister's condition made her a difficult person to deal with and affected her ability to act responsibly on her own behalf and to make an adequate living for herself. They knew that their mother had shouldered the bulk of responsibility for their sister and that without her help they would likely have to step in to assist. Even though the brothers were successful businessmen who were significantly better off than their sister, they regarded her as a potential liability and sought to avoid any financial responsibility for her. Indeed, it was the suspicion that they might be placed in a position of responsibility for their sister that prompted Jack to play a role in assisting their mother in the preparation of her first will the terms of which ensured that this would not happen.

It was when the mother died and the brothers discovered that she had executed a second will which removed the protections contained in the first one that the real potential for the brothers to influence their sister arose. The evidence discloses that Mrs. Goodman had sought the assistance of her brothers to see her through the emotional crisis of the death of her mother, her primary care-giver. Communications between Mrs. Goodman and her brothers increased during this period. They knew she needed support and protection. She consulted with them as to what the best arrangement would be. The brothers were well aware that their sister had reposed her trust and confidence in them to help her straighten out her legal and financial affairs. It was a situation where the brothers knew their sister was vulnerable, knew that she was relying upon them to help her and knew that they had interests of their own which did not necessarily coincide with hers. Thus, apart from the particular circumstances surrounding the execution of the trust agreement, the relationship between the deceased and the appellants was such that it could have afforded them the potential to exercise undue influence over her.

Since the trust instrument is unquestionably more akin to a gift or bequest than a commercial transaction, the existence of the required relationship without more is sufficient to trigger the presumption. It remains, therefore, to be determined whether the presumption has been rebutted. . . .

Given that the trial judge found that there was very little contact between the brothers and the deceased at the relevant time, that the deceased was not in fact relying on her brothers to advise her, and that the prime motivation of the brothers was to advance their sister's welfare, it is difficult to conclude that the appellants have not successfully rebutted the presumption of undue influence. In addition to these findings it is also relevant that the evidence establishes that the deceased received some independent advice from Mr. Pearce and that the agreement ultimately concluded was in accord with her wishes. I acknowledge that in other situations the fact that the brothers took a leading role in the initial meeting with Mr. Pearce might militate against a finding of independent advice. However, after the departure of the brothers for their respective homes, Mrs. Goodman continued on her own initiative to seek Mr. Pearce's advice. . . .

LA FOREST J. I have had the advantage of reading the reasons of my colleague, Madame Justice Wilson. While I agree with the result she has reached, I have found it necessary to express my own separate views for reasons that will appear.

As my colleague has noted, the first issue to be considered is whether the circumstances in this case are such as to give rise to a presumption of undue influence. Wilson J. concludes that such a presumption will arise only when the parties are in a relationship of "influence", where one person is in a position to dominate the will of another. I agree with this.

My colleague then proceeds to consider whether the additional requirement of "manifest disadvantage" must be present before a presumption of undue influence will be applied. The "manifest disadvantage" requirement was adopted by the House of Lords in *National Westminster Bank Plc. v. Morgan*, [1985] A.C. 686, a case in which undue influence was alleged in a loan transaction between a bank and one of its customers. At issue there was whether to apply a presumption of undue influence in the context of such a transaction. Lord Scarman found such a presumption will be applied in appropriate circumstances, but only when manifest disadvantage to the party influenced can be shown. He stated, at p. 707:

> A commercial relationship can become a relationship in which one party assumes a role of dominating influence over the other . . . Similarly a relationship of banker and customer may become one in which the banker acquires a dominating influence. If he does and a manifestly disadvantageous transaction is proved, there would then be room for the court to presume that it resulted from the exercise of undue influence.

Wilson J. finds that the requirement of manifest disadvantage simply does not make sense in the context of this case, where the challenged transaction concerns a gift. I would agree. A gift is by its nature inherently disadvantageous, at least in a material sense, so the requirement is superfluous. Having made this finding, it seems to me that it becomes unnecessary to discuss the issue of manifest disadvantage further on the facts of this case. My colleague nonetheless proceeds to elaborate upon this point at some length, and I accordingly feel obliged to say a few words about it.

It may well be appropriate to require a showing of undue disadvantage or benefit before a presumption of undue influence will be applied. Given that the effect of the presumption of undue influence is to shift the burden of proof to the defendant, it may not be unreasonable to require that there be some showing of undue disadvantage or benefit in a commercial transaction before the presumption will arise. It is a substantially different question, however, whether undue influence itself must always involve undue disadvantage or benefit.

As my colleague correctly points out, there is a difference of opinion as to whether manifest disadvantage should be a required element of undue influence in a commercial transaction. This stems from differing views on what the doctrine of undue influence is designed to protect. One view is that it should protect against abuses of trust, confidence or power. From this perspective, the focus is upon the process of the undue influence itself, rather than the result. Manifest disadvantage to the person influenced is not a requirement, but merely evidence that goes to show whether or not an abuse of confidence took place. The opposing view is that the law should not interfere with reasonable bargains, and that the doctrine of undue influence should only address abuses of trust or confidence resulting in a significant and demonstrable disadvantage to the person influenced.

It is unnecessary for us to choose between these two opposing positions in the context of this case, which does not even concern a commercial transaction, and I think it is unwise to do so. I therefore cannot adopt my colleague's comment . . . that there is "nothing *per se* reprehensible about persons in a relationship of trust or confidence exerting influence, *even undue influence*, over their beneficiaries" (emphasis added). Nor would I want to be taken as agreeing with the proposition that the law will never interfere with a contract that does not necessarily lead to a material disadvantage, even where it is clear that the process leading up to the contract has been tainted. . . .

SOPINKA J. I have had the advantage of reading the reasons herein of my colleagues Madame Justice Wilson and Mr. Justice La Forest which differ as to whether a presumption of undue influence arises in this case. In my view, given the positive finding by the trial judge, supported by the evidence, that there was no undue influence, the existence of a presumption is immaterial and any discussion of it by the trial judge and the Court of Appeal was unnecessary and *obiter*. The same applies to the consideration of this matter here.

[Cory J. concurred with Wilson J. McLachlin J. concurred with La Forest J. Appeal allowed.]

NOTES and QUESTIONS

1. The presumption of undue influence arising out of a special relationship is designed to control the same opportunism mischief addressed by the general law of fiduciary obligation. Fiduciary responsibility may exist independently of, or be created by, contractual agreement. The contract and fiduciary liability regimes will often have concurrent application. See Flannigan, "Fiduciary Obligation in the Supreme Court" (1990), 54 Sask. L. Rev. 45 at 49-50, "Commercial Fiduciary Obligation" (1998), 36 Alta. L. R. 905 and, generally, "The Boundaries of Fiduciary Accountability" forthcoming in (2004) 83 Can. Bar Rev.

2. As with other equitable principles, there are a number of bars to relief on the ground of undue influence. These include affirmation of the transaction after the undue influence has ended, the impossibility of restitution and the intervention of third party rights.

3. Donna needed working capital for her struggling business. The bank agreed to provide the loan after Donna indicated that it could be secured by a mortgage on her parents' home which, at the time, was free of encumbrances. Donna said she would get her parents' signatures to the mortgage. Execution of the mortgage was subsequently procured through undue influence exercised by Donna over her parents. Donna loses everything. Does the undue influence exercised by Donna allow her parents to avoid foreclosure of the mortgage on their home? See *Bertolo v. Bank of Montreal* (1986), 57 O.R. (2d) 577 (C.A.); *Barclays Bank plc v. O'Brien*, [1993] 4 All E.R. 417 (H.L.).

4. In your view, should there be a requirement that the transaction be disadvantageous?

5. What would constitute satisfactory independent legal advice to a person asked to give security for an obligation of their spouse?

ROYAL BANK OF SCOTLAND PLC v. ETRIDGE (No. 2)

[2001] 3 W.L.R. 1021, [2001] 4 All E.R. 449

LORD NICHOLLS OF BIRKENHEAD [with whom the other law lords agreed in concurring judgments] My Lords, before your Lordships' House are appeals in eight cases. Each case arises out of a transaction in which a wife charged her interest in her home in favour of a bank as security for her husband's indebtedness or the indebtedness of a company through which he carried on business. The wife later asserted she signed the charge under the undue influence of her husband. In *Barclays Bank Plc v. O'Brien* [1994] 1 AC 180 your Lordships enunciated the principles applicable in this type of case. Since then, many cases have come before the courts, testing the implications of the O'Brien decision in a variety of different factual situations. Seven of the present appeals are of this character. In each case the bank sought to enforce the charge signed by the wife. The bank claimed an order for possession of the matrimonial home. The wife raised a defence that the bank was on notice that her concurrence in the transaction had been procured by her husband's undue influence. The eighth appeal concerns a claim by a wife for damages from a solicitor who advised her before she entered into a guarantee obligation of this character.

Undue influence

The issues raised by these appeals make it necessary to go back to first principles. Undue influence is one of the grounds of relief developed by the courts of equity as a court of conscience. The objective is to ensure that the influence of one person over another is not abused. In everyday life people constantly seek to influence the decisions of others. They seek to persuade those with whom they are dealing to enter into transactions, whether great or small. The law has set limits to the means properly employable for this purpose. To this end the common law developed a principle of duress. Originally this was narrow in its scope, restricted to the more blatant forms of physical coercion, such as personal violence.

Here, as elsewhere in the law, equity supplemented the common law. Equity extended the reach of the law to other unacceptable forms of persuasion. The law will investigate the manner in which the intention to enter into the transaction was secured . . . If the intention was produced by an unacceptable means, the law will not permit the transaction to stand. The means used is regarded as an exercise of improper or 'undue' influence, and hence unacceptable, whenever the consent thus procured ought not fairly to be treated as the expression of a person's free will. It is impossible to be more precise or definitive. The circumstances in which one person acquires influence over another, and the manner in which influence may be exercised, vary too widely to permit of any more specific criterion.

Equity identified broadly two forms of unacceptable conduct. The first comprises overt acts of improper pressure or coercion such as unlawful threats. Today there is much overlap with the principle of duress as this principle has subsequently developed. The second form arises out of a relationship between two persons where one has acquired over another a measure of influence, or ascendancy, of which the ascendant person then takes unfair advantage. An example from the 19th century, when much of this law developed, is a case where an impoverished father prevailed upon his inexperienced children to charge their reversionary interests under their parents' marriage settlement with payment of his mortgage debts. . . .

In cases of this latter nature the influence one person has over another provides scope for misuse without any specific overt acts of persuasion. The relationship between two individuals may be such that, without more, one of them is disposed to agree a course of action proposed by the other. Typically this occurs when one person places trust in another to look after his affairs and interests, and the latter betrays this trust by preferring his own interests. He abuses the influence he has acquired. In *Allcard v. Skinner* (1887) 36 Ch. D. 145, a case well known to every law student, Lindley LJ, at p 181, described this class of cases as those in which it was the duty of one party to advise the other or to manage his property for him. . . .

The law has long recognised the need to prevent abuse of influence in these 'relationship' cases despite the absence of evidence of overt acts of persuasive conduct. The types of relationship, such as parent and child, in which this principle falls to be applied cannot be listed exhaustively. Relationships are infinitely various. . . . For example, the relation of banker and customer will not normally meet this criterion, but exceptionally it may: see *National Westminster Bank Plc v. Morgan* [1985] AC 686, 707-709.

Even this test is not comprehensive. The principle is not confined to cases of abuse of trust and confidence. It also includes, for instance, cases where a vulnerable person has been exploited. Indeed, there is no single touchstone for determining whether the principle is applicable. Several expressions have been used in an endeavour to encapsulate the essence: trust and confidence, reliance, dependence or vulnerability on the one hand and ascendancy, domination or control on the other. None of these descriptions is perfect. None is all embracing. Each has its proper place.

In *CIBC Mortgages Plc v. Pitt* [1994] 1 AC 200 your Lordships' House decided that in cases of undue influence disadvantage is not a necessary ingredient of the cause of action. It is not essential that the transaction should be disadvantageous to the pressurised or influenced person, either in financial terms or in any other way. However, in the nature of things, questions of undue influence will not usually arise, and the exercise of undue influence is unlikely to occur, where the transaction is innocuous. The issue is likely to arise only when, in some respect, the transaction was disadvantageous either from the outset or as matters turned out.

Burden of proof and presumptions

Whether a transaction was brought about by the exercise of undue influence is a question of fact. Here, as elsewhere, the general principle is that he who asserts a wrong has been committed must prove it. The burden of proving an allegation of undue influence rests upon the person who claims to have been wronged. This is the general rule. The evidence required to discharge the burden of proof depends on the nature of the alleged undue influence, the personality of the parties, their relationship, the extent to which the transaction cannot readily be accounted for by the ordinary motives of ordinary persons in that relationship, and all the circumstances of the case.

Proof that the complainant placed trust and confidence in the other party in relation to the management of the complainant's financial affairs, coupled with a transaction which calls for explanation, will normally be sufficient, failing satisfactory evidence to the contrary, to discharge the burden of proof. On proof of these two matters the stage is set for the court to infer that, in the absence of a satisfactory explanation, the transaction can only have been procured by undue influence. In other words, proof of these two facts is prima facie evidence that the defendant abused the influence he acquired in the parties' relationship. He preferred his own interests. He did not behave fairly to the other. So the evidential burden then shifts to him. It is for him to produce evidence to counter the inference which otherwise should be drawn.

The case of *Bainbrigge v. Browne*, 18 Ch. D. 188 . . . provides a good illustration of this commonplace type of forensic exercise. Fry J. held, at p 196, that there was no direct evidence upon which he could rely as proving undue pressure by the father. But there existed circumstances 'from which the court will infer pressure and undue influence.' None of the children were entirely emancipated from their father's control. None seemed conversant with business. These circumstances were such as to cast the burden of proof upon the father. He had made no attempt to discharge that burden. He did not appear in court at all. So the children's claim succeeded. Again, more recently, in *National Westminster Bank Plc v. Morgan* [*supra* at] 707, Lord Scarman noted that a relationship of banker and customer may become one in which a banker acquires a dominating influence. If he does, and a manifestly disadvantageous transaction is proved, 'there would then be room' for a court to presume that it resulted from the exercise of undue influence.

Generations of equity lawyers have conventionally described this situation as one in which a presumption of undue influence arises. This use of the term 'presumption' is descriptive of a shift in the evidential onus on a question of fact. When a plaintiff succeeds by this route he does so because he has succeeded in establishing a case of undue influence. The court has drawn appropriate inferences of fact upon a balanced consideration of the whole of the evidence at the end of a trial in which the burden of proof rested upon the plaintiff. The use, in the course of the trial, of the forensic tool of a shift in the evidential burden of proof should not be permitted to obscure the overall position. . . . There is a rebuttable evidential presumption of undue influence.

The availability of this forensic tool in cases founded on abuse of influence arising from the parties' relationship has led to this type of case sometimes being labelled 'presumed undue influence'. This is by way of contrast with cases involving actual pressure or the like, which are labelled 'actual undue influence': see *Bank of Credit and Commerce International SA v. Aboody* [1990] I QB 923, 953, and *Royal Bank of Scotland Plc v. Etridge (No. 2)*, [1998] 4 All E.R. 705, 711-712, paras 5-7. This usage can be a little confusing. In many cases where a plaintiff has claimed that the defendant abused the influence he acquired in a relationship of trust and confidence the plaintiff has succeeded by recourse to the rebuttable evidential presumption. But this need not be so. Such a plaintiff may succeed even where this presumption is not available to him; for instance, where the impugned transaction was not one which called for an explanation.

The evidential presumption discussed above is to be distinguished sharply from a different form of presumption which arises in some cases. The law has adopted a sternly protective attitude towards certain types of relationship in which one party acquires influence over another who is vulnerable and dependent and where, moreover, substantial gifts by the influenced or vulnerable person are not normally to be expected. Examples of relationships within this special class are parent and child, guardian and ward, trustee and beneficiary, solicitor and client, and medical adviser and patient. In these cases the law presumes, irrebuttably, that one party had influence over the other. The complainant need not prove he actually reposed trust and confidence in the other party. It is sufficient for him to prove the existence of the type of relationship.

It is now well established that husband and wife is not one of the relationships to which this latter principle applies. . . . The Court of Chancery was not blind to the opportunities of obtaining and unfairly using influence over a wife which a husband often possesses. But there is nothing unusual or strange in a wife, from motives of affection or for other reasons, conferring substantial financial benefits on her husband. Although there is no presumption, the court will nevertheless note, as a matter of fact, the opportunities for abuse which flow from a wife's confidence in her husband. The court will take this into account with all the other evidence in the case. Where there is evidence that a husband has taken unfair advantage of his influence over his wife, or her confidence in him, 'it is not difficult for the wife to establish her title to relief': see *In re Lloyds Bank Ltd, Bomze v. Bomze* [1931] 1 Ch 289, at p. 302, per Maugham J.

Independent advice

Proof that the complainant received advice from a third party before entering into the impugned transaction is one of the matters a court takes into account when weighing all the evidence. The weight, or importance, to be attached to such advice depends on all the circumstances. In the normal course, advice from a solicitor or other outside adviser can be expected to bring home to a complainant a proper understanding of what he or she is about to do. But a person may understand fully the implications of a proposed transaction, for instance, a substantial gift, and yet still be acting under the undue influence of another. Proof of outside advice does not, of itself, necessarily show that the subsequent completion of the transaction was free from the exercise of undue influence. Whether it will be proper to infer that outside advice had an emancipating effect, so that the transaction was not brought about by the exercise of undue influence, is a question of fact to be decided having regard to all the evidence in the case.

Manifest disadvantage

As already noted, there are two prerequisites to the evidential shift in the burden of proof from the complainant to the other party. First, that the complainant reposed trust and confidence in the other party, or the other party acquired ascendancy over the complainant. Second, that the transaction is not readily explicable by the relationship of the parties.

Lindley L.J. summarised this second prerequisite in the leading authority of *Allcard v. Skinner* [*supra*], where the donor parted with almost all her property. Lindley LJ pointed out that where a gift of a small amount is made to a person standing in a confidential relationship to the donor, some proof of the exercise of the influence of the donee must be given. The mere existence of the influence is not enough. He continued, at p. 185:

> But if the gift is so large as not to be reasonably accounted for on the ground of friendship, relationship, charity, or other ordinary motives on which ordinary men act, the burden is upon the donee to support the gift.

In *Bank of Montreal v. Stuart* [1911] AC 120, 137 Lord Macnaghten used the phrase 'immoderate and irrational' to describe this concept.

The need for this second prerequisite has recently been questioned: see Nourse L.J. in *Barclays Bank Plc v. Coleman* [2001] QB, 20, 30-32, one of the cases under appeal before your Lordships' House. Mr Sher Q.C. invited your Lordships to depart from the decision of the House on this point in *National Westminster Bank Plc v Morgan* [*supra*].

My Lords, this is not an invitation I would accept. The second prerequisite, as expressed by Lindley L.J., is good sense. It is a necessary limitation upon the width of the first prerequisite. It would be absurd for the law to presume that every gift by a child to a parent, or every transaction between a client and his solicitor or between a patient and his doctor, was brought about by undue influence unless the contrary is affirmatively proved. Such a presumption would be too far-reaching. The law would out of touch with everyday life if the presumption were to apply to every Christmas or birthday gift by a child to a parent, or to an agreement whereby a client or patient agrees to be responsible for the reasonable fees of his legal or medical adviser. The law would be rightly open to ridicule, for transactions such as these are unexceptionable. They do not suggest that something may be amiss. So something more is needed before the law reverses the burden of proof, something which calls for an explanation. When that something more is present, the greater the disadvantage to the vulnerable person, the more cogent must be the explanation before the presumption will be regarded as rebutted.

This was the approach adopted by Lord Scarman in *National Westminster Bank Plc v. Morgan* [*supra* at], 703-707. He cited Lindley L.J.'s observations in *Allcard v. Skinner*, [*supra*, at 185]. He noted that whatever the legal character of the transaction, it must constitute a disadvantage sufficiently serious to require evidence to rebut the presumption that in the circumstances of the parties' relationship, it was procured by the exercise of undue influence. Lord Scarman concluded, at p. 704:

The Court of Appeal erred in law in holding that the presumption of undue influence can arise from the evidence of the relationship of the parties without also evidence that the transaction itself was wrongful in that it constituted an advantage taken of the person subjected to the influence which, failing proof to the contrary, was explicable only on the basis that undue influence had been exercised to procure it. (Emphasis added)

Lord Scarman attached the label 'manifest disadvantage' to this second ingredient necessary to raise the presumption. This label has been causing difficulty. It may be apt enough when applied to straightforward transactions such as a substantial gift or a sale at an undervalue. But experience has now shown that this expression can give rise to misunderstanding. The label is being understood and applied in a way which does not accord with the meaning intended by Lord Scarman, its originator.

The problem has arisen in the context of wives guaranteeing payment of their husband's business debts. In recent years judge after judge has grappled with the baffling question whether a wife's guarantee of her husband's bank overdraft, together with a charge on her share of the matrimonial home, was a transaction manifestly to her disadvantage.

In a narrow sense, such a transaction plainly ('manifestly') is disadvantageous to the wife. She undertakes a serious financial obligation, and in return she personally receives nothing. But that would be to take an unrealistically blinkered view of such a transaction. Unlike the relationship of solicitor and client or medical adviser and patient, in the case of husband and wife there are inherent reasons why such a transaction may well be for her benefit. Ordinarily, the fortunes of husband and wife are bound up together. If the husband's business is the source of the family income, the wife has a lively interest in doing what she can to support the business. A wife's affection and self-interest run hand-in-hand in inclining her to join with her husband in charging the matrimonial home, usually a jointly-owned asset, to obtain the financial facilities needed by the business. The finance may be needed to start a new business, or expand a promising business, or rescue an ailing business.

Which, then, is the correct approach to adopt in deciding whether a transaction is disadvantageous to the wife: the narrow approach, or the wider approach? The answer is neither. The answer lies in discarding a label which gives rise to this sort of ambiguity. The better approach is to adhere more directly to the test outlined by Lindley L.J. in *Allcard v. Skinner,* and adopted by Lord Scarman in *National Westminster Bank Plc v. Morgan* in the passages I have cited.

I return to husband and wife cases. I do not think that, in the ordinary course, a guarantee of the character I have mentioned is to be regarded as a transaction which, failing proof to the contrary, is explicable only on the basis that it has been procured by the exercise of undue influence by the husband. Wives frequently enter into such transactions. There are good and sufficient reasons why they are willing to do so, despite the risks involved for them and their families. They may be enthusiastic. They may not. They may be less optimistic than their husbands about the prospects of the husbands' businesses. They may be anxious, perhaps exceedingly so. But this is a far cry from saying that such transactions as a class are to be regarded as prima facie evidence of the exercise of undue influence by husbands.

I have emphasised the phrase 'in the ordinary course'. There will be cases where a wife's signature of a guarantee or a charge of her share in the matrimonial home does call for explanation. Nothing I have said above is directed at such a case.

.....

I add a cautionary note . . . It concerns the general approach to be adopted by a court when considering whether a wife's guarantee of her husband's bank overdraft was procured by her husband's undue influence. Undue influence has a connotation of impropriety. In the eye of the law, undue influence means that influence has been misused. Statements or conduct by a husband which do not pass beyond the bounds of what may be expected of a reasonable husband in the circumstances should not, without more, be castigated as undue influence. Similarly, when a husband is forecasting the future of his business, and expressing his hopes or fears, a degree of hyperbole may be only natural. Courts should not too readily treat such exaggerations as misstatements.

Inaccurate explanations of a proposed transaction are a different matter. So are cases where a husband, in whom a wife has reposed trust and confidence for the management of their financial affairs, prefers his interests to hers and makes a choice for both of them on that footing. Such a husband abuses the influence he has. He fails to discharge the obligation of candour and fairness he owes a wife who is looking to him to make the major financial decisions.

[Lord Nicholls then discussed when a bank is put on inquiry, the steps it should take and the content of advice to be given. He continued as follows.]

A wider principle

Before turning to the particular cases I must make a general comment on the [*Barclays Bank Plc v.*] *O'Brien* [*supra*] principle. . . . the decision . . . has to be seen as the progenitor of a wider principle . . . This calls for explanation. In the *O'Brien* case the House was concerned with formulating a fair and practical solution to problems occurring when a creditor obtains a security from a guarantor whose sexual relationship with the debtor gives rise to a heightened risk of undue influence. But the law does not regard sexual relationships as standing in some special category of their own so far as undue influence is concerned. Sexual relationships are no more than one type of relationship in which an individual may acquire influence over another individual. The *O'Brien* decision cannot sensibly be regarded as confined to sexual relationships, although these are likely to be its main field of application at present. What is appropriate for sexual relationships ought, in principle, to be appropriate also for other relationships where trust and confidence are likely to exist.

The courts have already recognised this. Further application, or development, of the *O'Brien* principle has already taken place. In *Credit Lyonnais Bank Nederland NV v. Burch* [1997] 1 All E.R. 144 the same principle was applied where the relationship was employer and employee. Miss Burch was a junior employee in a company. She was neither a shareholder nor a director. She provided security to the bank for the company's overdraft. She entered into a guarantee of unlimited amount, and gave the bank a second charge over her flat. Nourse L.J., at p 146, said the relationship 'may broadly be said to fall under [*O'Brien*]'. The Court of Appeal held that the bank was put on inquiry. It knew the facts from which the existence of a relationship of trust and confidence between Miss Burch and Mr Pelosi, the owner of the company, could be inferred.

The crucially important question raised by this wider application of the *O'Brien* principle concerns the circumstances which will put a bank on inquiry. A bank is put on inquiry whenever a wife stands as surety for her husband's debts. It is sufficient that the bank knows of the husband-wife relationship. That bare fact is enough. The bank must then take reasonable steps to bring home to the wife the risks involved. What, then, of other relationships where there is an increased risk of undue influence, such as parent and child? Is it enough that the bank knows of the relationship? For reasons already discussed in relation to husbands and wives, a bank cannot be expected to probe the emotional relationship between two individuals, whoever they may be. Nor is it desirable that a bank should attempt this. Take the case where a father puts forward his daughter as a surety for his business overdraft. A bank should not be called upon to evaluate highly personal matters such as the degree of trust and confidence existing between the father and his daughter, with the bank put on inquiry in one case and not in another. As with wives, so with daughters, whether a bank is put on inquiry should not depend on the degree of trust and confidence the particular daughter places in her father in relation to financial matters. Moreover, as with wives, so with other relationships, the test of what puts a bank on inquiry should be simple, clear and easy to apply in widely varying circumstances. This suggests that, in the case of a father and daughter, knowledge by the bank of the relationship of father and daughter should suffice to put the bank on inquiry. When the bank knows of the relationship, it must then take reasonable steps to ensure the daughter knows what she is letting herself into.

The relationship of parent and child is one of the relationships where the law irrebuttably presumes the existence of trust and confidence. Rightly, this has already been rejected as the boundary of the *O'Brien* principle. *O'Brien* was a husband-wife case. The responsibilities of creditors were enunciated in a case where the law makes no presumption of the existence of trust and confidence.

But the law cannot stop at this point, with banks on inquiry only in cases where the debtor and guarantor have a sexual relationship or the relationship is one where the law presumes the existence of trust and confidence. That would be an arbitrary boundary, and the law has already moved beyond this, in the decision in *Burch* [*supra*]. As noted earlier, the reality of life is that relationships in which undue influence can be exercised are infinitely various. They cannot be exhaustively defined. Nor is it possible to produce a comprehensive list of relationships where there is a substantial risk of the exercise of undue influence, all others being excluded from the ambit of the *O'Brien* principle. Human affairs do not lend themselves to categorisations of this sort. The older generation of a family may exercise undue influence over a younger member, as in parent-child cases. . . .

Sometimes it is the other way round, as with a nephew and his elderly aunt. . . . An employer may take advantage of his employee, as in . . . *Burch*. . . . But it may be the other way round, with an employee taking advantage of her employer, as happened with [a] secretary-companion and her elderly employer. . . . The list could go on.

These considerations point forcibly to the conclusion that there is no rational cut-off point, with certain types of relationship being susceptible to the *O'Brien* principle and others not. Further, if a bank is not to be required to evaluate the extent to which its customer has influence over a proposed guarantor, the only practical way forward is to regard banks as 'put on inquiry' in every case where the relationship between the surety and the debtor is non-commercial. The creditor must always take reasonable steps to bring home to the individual guarantor the risks he is running by standing as surety. As a measure of protection, this is valuable. But, in all conscience, it is a modest burden for banks and other lenders. It is no more than is reasonably to be expected of a creditor who is taking a guarantee from an individual. If the bank or other creditor does not take these steps, it is deemed to have notice of any claim the guarantor may have that the transaction was procured by undue influence or misrepresentation on the part of the debtor.

Different considerations apply where the relationship between the debtor and guarantor is commercial, as where a guarantor is being paid a fee, or a company is guaranteeing the debts of another company in the same group. Those engaged in business can be regarded as capable of looking after themselves and understanding the risks involved in the giving of guarantees.

By the decisions of this House in *O'Brien* and the Court of Appeal in . . . *Burch* . . . English law has taken its first strides in the development of some such general principle. It is a workable principle. It is also simple, coherent and eminently desirable. I venture to think this is the way the law is moving, and should continue to move. Equity, it is said, is not past the age of child-bearing. In the present context the equitable concept of being 'put on inquiry' is the parent of a principle of general application, a principle which imposes no more than a modest obligation on banks and other creditors. The existence of this obligation in all non-commercial cases does not go beyond the reasonable requirements of the present times. In future, banks and other creditors should regulate their affairs accordingly.

[Discussion of the various appeals is omitted.]

QUESTIONS

1. What differences, if any, are there between the *Geffen* and *Etridge* judgments?

2. Is there a sound policy basis for differentiating between "commercial" and other relationships when addressing issues of undue influence?

4.   Unconscionability

It is unclear to what extent the law allows a person to avoid contractual obligations on the ground that the bargain was an unfair one. The traditional and narrower view of unconscionability is, for the most part, uncontroversial. The difficulty exists in relation to the wider view that contracts may be avoided if there is unequal bargaining power or if community expectations are offended.

(a)   THE TRADITIONAL DOCTRINE

Canadian law adopted an unconscionability excuse, of narrow scope, at an early date. The judges initially found their authority in Sir Edward Sullivan's classic formulation of this equitable jurisdiction in *Slator v. Nolan* (1876), Ir. R. 11 Eq. 367 at 386 (Rolls Court):

> I take the law of the Court to be, that if two persons, no matter whether a confidential relationship exists between them or not, stand in such a relation to each other that one can take an undue advantage of the other, whether by reason of distress, or recklessness, or wildness, or want of care, and when the facts shew that one party has taken undue advantage of the other by reason of the circumstances I have mentioned, a transaction resting upon such unconscionable dealing will not be allowed to stand; and there are several cases which shew, even where no confidential relationship exists, that, where parties were not on equal terms, the party who gets a benefit cannot hold it without proving that everything has been right and fair and reasonable on his part.

Our courts determined that this excuse was available where two elements were present: (1) an improvident bargain and (2) an inequality in the positions of the parties.

MORRISON v. COAST FINANCE LTD.

(1965), 54 W.W.R. 257, 55 D.L.R. (2d) 710 (B.C. C.A.)

DAVEY J.A. The appellant, Morrison, an old woman 79 years of age, and a widow of meagre means, was persuaded by two men, Lowe and Kitely, to borrow $4,200 from the respondent, Coast Finance Ltd., on a first mortgage on her home for that amount and interest to maturity and to lend the proceeds to them so that Lowe could repay $915 that he owed the finance company, and he and Kitely could pay the other respondent company $2,302 for two automobiles they were buying from it for resale. The proceeds of the loan were applied accordingly and the balance was repaid at once to the finance company and automobile company, respectively, by way of prepayment of monthly instalments, insurance premiums, and costs. The mortgage was to be repaid at the rate of $300 a month, which was to be secured from payments to be made by Lowe at the finance company's office on her account by way of repayment of the money lent to him and Kitely. She had no other means of repaying the money, and the house was her only substantial asset. She had no independent advice, although the evidence shows she wanted and asked for help. Lowe and Kitely failed to pay the appellant. She commenced action to have the mortgage set aside as having been procured by undue influence and as an unconscionable bargain made between persons in an unequal position. She did not join Lowe and Kitely as defendants to the action.

The learned trial judge dismissed the action on the grounds that the relationship between the parties was not such as to create a presumption of undue influence, and that none had been proven; that there was nothing in the terms of the mortgage to make it an unconscionable transaction. In my respectful opinion, the learned trial judge took too narrow a view of the appellant's case on the second ground.

Appellant's principal submission before us on this second ground was that, not only the mortgage, but the whole transaction was unconscionable; that it was unconscionable for Lowe and Kitely and the two companies to have the appellant mortgage her home in order to secure the money to lend to Lowe and Kitely to enable them to pay off the finance company and buy the two cars from the automobile company. . . .

A plea of undue influence attacks the sufficiency of consent; a plea that a bargain is unconscionable invokes relief against an unfair advantage gained by an unconscientious use of power by a stronger party against a weaker. On such a claim the material ingredients are proof of inequality in the position of the parties arising out of the ignorance, need or distress of the weaker, which left him in the power of the stronger, and proof of substantial unfairness of the bargain obtained by the stronger. On proof of those circumstances, it creates a presumption of fraud which the stronger must repel by proving that the bargain was fair, just and reasonable: *Aylesford (Earl) v. Morris* (1873), 8 Ch. App. 484, 42 L.J. Ch. 546, *per* Lord Selborne at p. 491, or perhaps by showing that no advantage was taken: See *Harrison v. Guest* (1855), 6 De G.M. & G. 424, at 438, affirmed (1860), 8 H.L. Cas. 481, at 492, 493, 11 E.R. 517. In *Fry v. Lane; Whittet v. Bush* (1889), 40 Ch. D. 312, 58 L.J. Ch. 113, Kay, J. accurately stated the modern scope and application of the principle, and discussed the earlier authorities upon which it rests. He said at p. 322:

> The result of the decisions is that where a purchase is made from a poor and ignorant man at a considerable undervalue, the vendor having no independent advice, a Court of Equity will set aside the transaction.
> This will be done even in the case of property in possession, and *a fortiori* if the interest be reversionary.
> The circumstances of poverty and ignorance of the vendor, and absence of independent advice, throw upon the purchaser, when the transaction is impeached, the onus of proving, in Lord Selborne's words, that the purchase was 'fair, just, and reasonable.'

The finance company was engaged in the business of financing automobile purchases and lending money on mortgages. The other respondent company was an automobile dealer. They shared adjoining offices, employed the same solicitor, and had a common office manager, one Crawford, who in the final stages of this transaction acted for both companies. The president, director, and owner of half the shares of the finance company was a director of the automobile company, and with his wife controlled it. The finance company financed most of the automobile company's paper.

There can be no doubt about the inequality in the position of the appellant on one side and the respondent companies and Lowe and Kitely on the other. The question is whether the transaction was so unfair that it creates a presumption of overreaching by the respondents.

The learned trial judge approached this question as if it were a simple case of the appellant borrowing money from the finance company for her own purposes—that is to say, to lend it to Lowe and Kitely. Accordingly, he looked to see if the terms of the mortgage were unconscionable. If that were the true scope of the inquiry, I would agree with his conclusion, for although the rate of interest is high and the mortgage does not state the effective rate of interest required by the *Interest Act*, RSC, 1952, ch. 156, sec. 6, the rate of interest is not so high as to be exorbitant for a loan up to 100 per cent of the value of the security, as this was.

But this was not a simple loan of that kind. It was a loan to the appellant to advance the interests of the companies as well as Lowe and Kitely by providing her with money to lend to Lowe and Kitely to enable them to carry out their arrangements with the companies. Crawford made certain that the proceeds of the loan reached the two respondent companies. The appellant, Lowe and Kitely did not retain one cent of the money advanced, although the two men got delivery of the two automobiles they bought with the money.

The extreme folly of this old woman mortgaging her home in order to borrow money which she could not repay out of her own resources, for the purpose of lending it to the two men, who were comparative strangers, is self evident. It would have been bad enough if there had been any prospect of profit, but there was no expectation of reward and no real security. The amount to be paid back to her was exactly the amount of her mortgage to the finance company. The respondent companies knew the essential facts, and undertook the preparation of the documents for the transaction. For them to take advantage of her obvious ignorance and inexperience in order to further their respective businesses raises a presumption of fraud within the above authorities. The distinction between the case which the learned trial judge considered, and that which arises on the evidence was neatly put by appellant's counsel. He said it would not be wrong for a bank to lend money to an old and ignorant person, upon usual banking terms, for his own purposes, but quite wrong to lend him money on those terms so that he might lend it to an impecunious debtor from whom the bank intended to recover it in payment of a bad debt.

There is supporting evidence of gross overreaching by the respondent companies. They received the application for the loan, not from the appellant, but from Lowe or Kitely, who, with them, were to benefit by it. Without having seen the appellant, Crawford obtained a valuation of her home and instructed the companies' solicitor to prepare the mortgage. He first met her when she came to the companies' office with Lowe, Kitely and Lowe's friend, Ivy Patton, just before signing the mortgage. She was alone with persons expecting to benefit by her folly. He took them to the respondents' solicitor to sign the papers, where he must have heard the appellant say to Lowe, when she learned the amount of the mortgage, "Frank, that is more than I agreed to lend you." He must have heard the appellant ask the solicitor, "Should I sign this?" showing that she felt the need of advice, and the solicitor inform her that he could not advise her without knowing more of her arrangements with her friends. Crawford does not admit hearing these things, but he does not deny that he did so, and he must have heard them since the solicitor says Crawford was within three feet of the appellant at the counter.

After the mortgage had been signed, Crawford escorted the party back to his office, where he had a cheque for the proceeds of the mortgage made out to the appellant and had her endorse and hand it to Lowe or Kitely; then he secured it from them, and it was deposited to the account of the automobile company, out of which Lowe's debt of $915 to the finance company was paid. This money was thereby disbursed and distributed the day before the mortgage was registered, a course so unusual that it excites suspicion. Significant also is the fact that, either late that day or the next, Crawford drew a promissory note from Lowe to the appellant for the amount of the mortgage and had Lowe sign it. At the same time he drew a conditional-sales agreement between Lowe and Kitely and the auto-mobile company for the two cars they had bought, and caused the automobile company to assign its vendor's interest to the appellant, notwithstanding Lowe and Kitely had earlier paid the purchase price in full from the proceeds of the loan. The companies were turning over to this inexperienced, unprotected old woman, as the sole security for a loan she was making to advance the interests of Lowe and Kitely and themselves, a security of questionable value. I cannot believe that the law is so deficient that it cannot reach and remedy such a gross abuse of overwhelming inequality between the parties.

Probably the whole transaction ought to be set aside, but that cannot be done as Lowe and Kitely are not before us, and the automobiles sold to them are likely worthless and irrecoverable. That has troubled me. On reflection, I have concluded that it will be sufficient to set aside the mortgage, without requiring the appellant to repay the money, since, as was intended, that part which was not immediately repaid to or retained by the finance company was immediately returned on other accounts to the companies, who were acting in concert. That will allow the sale of the automobiles and the payment of Lowe's debt to stand. The automobile company loses nothing and justice will be done to the finance company by requiring the appellant as a condition of relief to transfer to it Lowe's promissory note and the conditional-sales agreement that the companies secured for her.

I should add that the companies called only their solicitor and his student-at-law, and did not call Crawford or any other officer, and made no attempt to prove that the whole transaction was fair, just and reasonable.

In view of the tenor of this judgment and the criticism of the companies, I should add that the criticism does not extend to their solicitor or his student. The evidence does not indicate that the solicitor knew that the money the appellant was borrowing was in the main to be at once returned to the companies on transactions between them and Lowe and Kitely. So far as he knew this was a simple routine loan by the finance company. The facts known by the two com-panies and their participation in the proceeds of the mortgage made it their duty to see that the appellant received independent advice, but the knowledge possessed by the solicitor was not sufficient to impose that duty upon him, and he is not to be criticized for not doing so. But I think it would have been better if he had told her to consult another solicitor instead of telling her he could not advise her.

[Bull J.A. delivered a brief judgment agreeing with Davey J.A. Sheppard J.A. found a breach of trust obligations. Appeal allowed.]

MARSHALL v. CAN. PERMANENT TRUST CO.

(1968), 69 D.L.R. (2d) 260 (Alta. S.C.)

KIRBY J. This is an action for specific performance of an agreement for sale of land.

On January 30, 1967, the plaintiff offered to purchase the S.E. 1/4 of section 27 and the N.W. 1/4 of section 26, both in township 38, range 14, west of the 4th meridian, from the defendant for the sum of $7,000 cash, payable immediately upon execution of a transfer by the vendor. The offer was accepted by the owner of these lands, John A. Walsh, on the same date. Both the offer and acceptance are in writing. Cash in the sum of $100 was paid by the purchaser to the vendor. At the time the document was executed, Walsh was a patient at Bow View Rest Home, Calgary.

The plaintiff, in relating the circumstances under which the transaction was made, testified that having tried without success to purchase farm lands from Walsh's brother in the same general area, and on hearing that John Walsh might sell his half-section of land, he went to see him at the rest home and asked him if he wanted to sell his farm near Castor. He stated that Walsh said that he did wish to sell for cash, and felt that he should get between $7,000 and $8,000; that Walsh pointed out that the land was under a lease; that he offered $7,000 cash and would take over the lease. He stated that through an employee of the rest home he was put in touch with Canada Permanent Mortgage Company, who in turn referred him to a solicitor who drew up the offer to purchase and acceptance. The solicitor, he said, showed him a copy of the lease. He related that he returned to the home on Monday, January 30th, with the offer to purchase, which was signed by him and Walsh in the presence of a witness—a member of the staff, and gave him a cheque for $100, which Walsh signed and instructed him to give to his solicitor for deposit in the main branch of the Bank of Montreal, which he did. On February 22nd, he received a letter from a firm of solicitors, informing him that they were acting in this matter, did not intend to deliver a transfer, and were in the process of applying for appointment of a committee for Walsh.

On February 24th, agents for the solicitor for the plaintiff sent a prepared transfer of the lands from Walsh to the plaintiff, together with a certified cheque for $7,000, to the solicitors for Walsh. On March 11th, the cheque was returned with a letter declining to deliver a transfer of the lands in question.

On March 30th, Canada Permanent Trust Company was appointed a committee for the estate of John A. Walsh, pursuant to the provisions of the *Mentally Incapacitated Persons Act*, 1955 (Alta.), c. 3.

The defendant seeks a declaration of rescission of the memorandum of agreement on the grounds that the consideration which the plaintiff proposed to pay to Walsh for the lands in question, was grossly inadequate, that the agreement entered into between the plaintiff and Walsh was not fair and reasonable, and that the plaintiff took advantage of Walsh by reason of the inequality of their positions. In the alternative to specific performance the plaintiff claims damages.

Simply stated, the ground on which the defendant seeks to have the agreement rescinded is that the transaction was unconscionable. In *Knupp v. Bell* (1966), 58 D.L.R. (2d) 466, affirmed 67 D.L.R. (3d) 256 (Sask. C.A.), in considering the equitable jurisdiction of the Court to set aside unconscionable transactions, MacPherson J. (Saskatchewan Court of Queen's Bench), refers to an article by Crawford [(1966), 44 Can. Bar Rev. 143], which he accepts as a fair statement of the law in this matter. The author says at p. 143:

> The jurisdiction of equity to set aside bargains contracted by persons under [undue] influence is well known. But what is referred to here is something distinct from that. It is also technically distinct from the simple refusal of the courts to grant specific performance where the contract has been obtained by sharp practice. In the cases now under discussion the courts intervene to rescind the contract whenever it appears that one of the parties was incapable of adequately protecting his interests and the other has made some immoderate gain at his expense. If the bargain is fair the fact that the parties were not equally vigilant of their interest is immaterial. Likewise if one was not preyed upon by the other, an improvident or even grossly inadequate consideration is no ground upon which to set aside a contract freely entered into. It is the combination of inequality and improvidence which alone may invoke this jurisdiction. Then the onus is placed upon the party seeking to uphold the contract to show that his conduct throughout was scrupulously considerate of the other's interests.

Applying this law, the learned Justice held that where a senile woman of no business experience and who was very easily led was induced to sell her lands to a neighbour at the grossly inadequate price of $35 per acre without taking independent advice from competent members of her family, no binding obligation was created. Hence, no action for specific performance would lie to enforce the contract.

[Kirby J. quoted the principle from *Slator v. Nolan, supra,* and concluded that the authorities established that] . . . if the parties met under such circumstances as to give the stronger party dominion over the weaker, then the principle is applied of requiring the one who gets the benefit to prove that the transaction was fair, just and reasonable.

[In *Waters v. Donnelly* (1884), 9 O.R. 391, these principles were applied and] the Court affirmed a decision rescinding an agreement for the exchange of land and chattels which had been held to be improvident, the plaintiff having been found to be ignorant, wanting skill in business, and comparatively an imbecile of intellect, and the transaction, one into which he would not have entered had he been properly advised and protected.

On the basis of these principles, in this case, the plaintiff's claim for specific performance must fail, and the defendant is entitled to rescission, if it is established:

(1) That Walsh was incapable of protecting his interests;

(2) That it was an improvident transaction for Walsh.

With respect to (1), it is not material whether Marshall was aware of Walsh's incapacity; with respect to (2), the onus rests with the plaintiff to show that the price given for the land corresponded to its fair value.

Was Walsh incapable of protecting his interests?

Marshall, 52 years of age, described himself as a farmer, merchant, auctioneer. It was quite evident that he was an alert, intelligent businessman.

The rest home records indicate Walsh to have been 68 years of age at the time of his admission to the home on June 14, 1966. Dr. Mortis, the house physician for the rest home, referring to the medical records of the home with respect to Walsh, testified that the symptoms reflected in these records were typical of brain damage due to hardening of the arteries; that Walsh had been from the time of his admission, given different forms of medication, some, sedative in nature; that Walsh had a minor stroke on December 14, 1966, and that following such a stroke, ability to think, to rationalize, to speak, gets progressively worse. He expressed the opinion that after the stroke Walsh was definitely not capable of transacting business, and that while it is not surprising that he could read a document, he could not relate to the past or future.

On the basis of this medical evidence, I am satisfied, and find, that Walsh was incapable of protecting his interests at the time the memorandum of agreement was entered into.

Was it an improvident transaction for Walsh? . . .

The evidence of Hunt [a real estate agent] as to the values of comparable land in the same general area in 1967 must be taken as more realistic. . . . The offer made by Dunkle to Walsh in 1967 for this half-section is in line with Hunt's valuation of this land at $50 per acre. On the basis of this evidence I am satisfied, and find, that the price agreed upon by Walsh was considerably less than the actual value of this land, and it therefore was an improvident transaction for him.

By virtue of the authorities cited above, the defendant is entitled to rescission of the agreement, and it is ordered accordingly. . . . The plaintiff has not established that he has suffered, or is entitled to any damage by reason of the non-performance of the agreement.

There was nothing in the conduct of Walsh on the two occasions when Marshall visited him in the rest home, and consummated this transaction, as related by him in his evidence, to suggest that Walsh was suffering from mental incapacity. . . .

For this reason there will be no costs.

QUESTIONS

1. What is the nature of the burden on the other party once it has been shown that there is both inequality and improvidence? Is the onus a procedural one of showing that the contract was fairly entered into or a substantive one of showing that the contract was "fair"? Are there conflicting descriptions of the onus in the *Morrison* case? The *Marshall* case? If the onus is a substantive one, how is it possible to satisfy that onus if the first party has already established that the transaction is an improvident one?

2. Is it only at the time of making the contract that the unconscionability question is relevant? What if a contractual provision in a long term contract becomes unconscionable with the passage of time? May it then be declared unenforceable?

(b) A WIDER VIEW

The essence of the traditional doctrine of unconscionability is that no person should be allowed to take advantage of the severe physical or situational disadvantage of another. Are there other compelling, albeit less severe, circumstances where relief should be forthcoming? Consider the scope of the principle in each of the next two cases.

LLOYDS BANK v. BUNDY

[1975] Q.B. 326, [1974] 3 All E.R. 757 (C.A.)

LORD DENNING M.R. Broadchalke is one of the most pleasing villages in England. Old Herbert Bundy, the defendant, was a farmer there. His home was at Yew Tree Farm. It went back for 300 years. His family had been there for generations. It was his only asset. But he did a very foolish thing. He mortgaged it to the bank. Up to the very hilt. Not to borrow money for himself, but for the sake of his son. Now the bank have come down on him. They have foreclosed. They want to get him out of Yew Tree Farm and to sell it. They have brought this action against him for possession. Going out means ruin for him. He was granted legal aid. His lawyers put in a defence. They said that, when he executed the charge to the bank he did not know what he was doing: or at any rate the circumstances were such that he ought not to be bound by it. At the trial his plight was plain. The judge was sorry for him. He said he was a "poor old gentleman." He was so obviously incapacitated that the judge admitted his proof in evidence. He had a heart attack in the witness-box. Yet the judge felt he could do nothing for him. There is nothing, he said, "which takes this out of the vast range of commercial transactions." He ordered Herbert Bundy to give up possession of Yew Tree Farm to the bank. Now there is an appeal to this court. The ground is that the circumstances were so exceptional that Herbert Bundy should not be held bound.

The events before December 1969

Herbert Bundy had only one son, Michael Bundy. He had great faith in him. They were both customers of Lloyds Bank Ltd., the plaintiff, at the Salisbury branch. They had been customers for many years. The son formed a company called M.J.B. Plant Hire Ltd. It hired out earth-moving machinery and so forth. The company banked at Lloyds, too, at the same branch.

In 1961 the son's company was in difficulties. The father on September 19, 1966, guaranteed the company's overdraft for £1,500 and charged Yew Tree Farm to the bank to secure the £1,500. Afterwards the son's company got further into difficulties. The overdraft ran into thousands. In May 1969 the assistant bank manager, Mr. Bennett, told the son the bank must have further security. The son said his father would give it. So Mr. Bennett and the son went together to see the father. Mr. Bennett produced the papers. He suggested that the father should sign a further guarantee for £5,000 and to execute a further charge for £6,000. The father said that he would help his son as far as he possibly could. Mr. Bennett did not ask the father to sign the papers there and then. He left them with the father so that he could consider them overnight and take advice on them. The father showed them to his solicitor, Mr. Trethowan, who lived in the same village. The solicitor told the father that £5,000 was the utmost that he could sink in his son's affairs. The house was worth about £10,000 and this was half his assets. On that advice the father on May 27, 1969, did execute the further guarantee and the charge, and Mr. Bennett witnessed it. So at the end of May 1969 the father had charged the house to secure £7,500.

The events of December 1969

During the next six months the affairs of the son and his company went from bad to worse. The bank had granted the son's company an overdraft up to a limit of £10,000, but this was not enough to meet the outgoings. The son's company drew cheques which the bank returned unpaid. The bank were anxious. By this time Mr. Bennett had left to go to another branch. He was succeeded by a new assistant manager, Mr. Head. In November 1969 Mr. Head saw the son and told him that the account was unsatisfactory and that he considered that the company might have to cease operations. The son suggested that the difficulty was only temporary and that his father would be prepared to provide further money if necessary.

On December 17, 1969, there came the occasion which, in the judge's words, was "important and disastrous" for the father. The son took Mr. Head to see his father. Mr. Head had never met the father before. This was his first visit. He went prepared. He took with him a form of guarantee and a form of charge filled in with the father's name ready for signature. There was a family gathering. The father and mother were there. The son and the son's wife. Mr. Head said that the bank had given serious thought as to whether they could continue to support the son's company. But that the bank were prepared to do so in this way: (i) the bank would continue to allow the company to draw money on overdraft up to the existing level of £10,000, but the bank would require the company to pay 10 per cent of its incomings into a separate account. So that 10 per cent would not go to reduce the overdraft. Mr. Head said that this would have the effect "of reducing the level of borrowing." In other words, the bank was cutting down the overdraft. (ii) The bank would require the father to give a guarantee of the company's account in a sum of £11,000, and to give the bank a further charge on the house of £3,500, so as to bring the total charge to £11,000. The house was only worth about £10,000, so this charge for £11,000 would sweep up all that the father had.

On hearing the proposal, the father said that Michael was his only son and that he was 100 per cent behind him. Mr. Head produced the forms that had already been filled in. The father signed them and Mr. Head witnessed them there and then. On this occasion, Mr. Head, unlike Mr. Bennett, did not leave the forms with the father: nor did the father have any independent advice.

It is important to notice the state of mind of Mr. Head and of the father. Mr. Head said in evidence:

> Defendant asked me what in my opinion the company was doing wrong and company's position. I told him. I did not explain the company's affairs very fully as I had only just taken

over the account . . . Michael said that company had a number of bad debts. I was not entirely satisfied with this. I thought the trouble was more deep seated . . . It did not occur to me that there was any conflict of interest. I thought there was no conflict of interest. I would think the defendant relied on me implicitly to advise him about the transaction as bank manager . . . I knew he had no other assets except Yew Tree Cottage.

The father said in evidence:

I always thought Head was genuine. I have always trusted him . . . No discussion how business was doing that I can remember. I simply sat back and did what they said.

The solicitor, Mr. Trethowan, said of the father:

He is straightforward. Agrees with anyone . . . I doubt if he understood all that Head explained to him.

So the father signed the papers. Mr. Head witnessed them and took them away. The father had charged the whole of his remaining asset, leaving himself with nothing. The son and his company gained a respite. But only for a short time. Five months later, in May 1970, a receiving order was made against the son. Thereupon the bank stopped all overdraft facilities for the company. It ceased to trade. The father's solicitor, Mr. Trethowan, at once went to see Mr. Head. He said he was concerned that the father had signed the guarantee.

In due course the bank insisted on the sale of the house. In December 1971 they agreed to sell it for £9,500 with vacant possession. The family were very disappointed with this figure. It was, they said, worth much more. Estate agents were called to say so. But the judge held it was a valid sale and that the bank could take all the proceeds. The sale has not been completed because Herbert Bundy is still in possession. The bank have brought these proceedings to evict Herbert Bundy.

The general rule

Now let me say at once that in the vast majority of cases a customer who signs a bank guarantee or a charge cannot get out of it. No bargain will be upset which is the result of the ordinary interplay of forces. There are many hard cases which are caught by this rule. Take the case of a poor man who is homeless. He agrees to pay a high rent to a landlord just to get a roof over his head. The common law will not interfere. It is left to Parliament. Next take the case of a borrower in urgent need of money. He borrows it from the bank at high interest and it is guaranteed by a friend. The guarantor gives his bond and gets nothing in return. The common law will not interfere. Parliament has intervened to prevent moneylenders charging excessive interest. But it has never interfered with banks.

Yet there are exceptions to this general rule. There are cases in our books in which the courts will set aside a contract, or a transfer of property, when the parties have not met on equal terms—when the one is so strong in bargaining power and the other so weak—that, as a matter of common fairness, it is not right that the strong should be allowed to push the weak to the wall. Hitherto those exceptional cases have been treated each as a separate category in itself. But I think the time has come when we should seek to find a principle to unite them. I put on one side contracts or transactions which are voidable for fraud or misrepresentation or mistake. All those are governed by settled principles. I go only to those where there has been inequality of bargaining power, such as to merit the intervention of the court.

The categories

The first category is that of "duress of goods." A typical case is when a man is in a strong bargaining position by being in possession of the goods of another by virtue of a legal right, such as by way of pawn or pledge or taken in distress. The owner is in a weak position because he is in urgent need of the goods. The stronger demands of the weaker more than is justly due: and he pays it in order to get the goods. Such a transaction is voidable. He can recover the excess. . . . To which may be added the cases of "colore officii," where a man is in a strong bargaining position by virtue of his official position or public profession. He relied upon it so as to gain from the weaker—who is urgently in need—more than is justly due. . . . In such cases the stronger may make his claim in good faith honestly believing that he is entitled to make his demand. He may not be guilty of any fraud or misrepresentation. The inequality of bargaining power—the strength of the one versus the urgent need of the other—renders the transaction voidable and the money paid to be recovered back. . . .

The second category is that of the "unconscionable transaction." A man is so placed as to be in need of special care and protection and yet his weakness is exploited by another far stronger than himself so as to get his property at a gross undervalue. The typical case is that of the "expectant heir." But it applies to all cases where a man comes into property, or is expected to come into it—and then being in urgent need—another gives him ready cash for it, greatly below its true worth, and so gets the property transferred to him. . . .

This second category is said to extend to all cases where an unfair advantage has been gained by an unconscientious use of power by a stronger party against a weaker: . . . The third category is that of "undue influence" usually so called. These are divided into two classes as stated by Cotton L.J. in *Allcard v. Skinner* (1887), 36 Ch. D. 145 at 171 (C.A.). The first are those where the stronger has been guilty of some fraud or wrongful act—expressly so as to gain some gift or advantage from the weaker. The second are those where the stronger has not been guilty of any wrongful act, but has, through the relationship which existed between him and the weaker, gained some gift or advantage for himself. Sometimes the relationship is such as to raise a presumption of undue influence, such as parent over child, solicitor over client, doctor over patient, spiritual adviser over follower. At other times a relationship of confidence must be proved to exist. But to all of them the general principle obtains which was stated by Lord Chelmsford L.C. in *Tate v. Williamson* (1866), 2 Ch. App. 55 at 61 (L.C.):

> Wherever two persons stand in such a relation that, while it continues, confidence is necessarily reposed by one, and the influence which naturally grows out of that confidence is possessed by the other, and this confidence is abused, or the influence is exerted to obtain an advantage at the expense of the confiding party, the person so availing himself of his position will not be permitted to retain the advantage, although the transaction could not have been impeached if no such confidential relation had existed.

. . . The fourth category is that of "undue pressure." The most apposite of that is *Williams v. Bayley* (1866), L.R. 1 H.L. 200, where a son forged his father's name to a promissory note and, by means of it, raised money from the bank of which they were both customers. The bank said to the father, in effect: "Take your choice—give us security for your son's debt. If you do take that on yourself, then it will all go smoothly: if you do not, we shall be bound to exercise pressure." Thereupon the father charged his property to the bank with payment of the note. The House of Lords held that the charge was invalid because of undue pressure exerted by the bank. . . .

Other instances of undue pressure are where one party stipulates for an unfair advantage to which the other has no option but to submit. As where an employer—the stronger party—has employed a builder—the weaker party—to do work for him. When the builder asked for payment of sums properly due (so as to pay his workmen) the employer refused to pay unless he was given some added advantage. Stuart V.-C. said:

> Where an agreement, hard and inequitable in itself, has been exacted under circumstances of pressure on the part of the person who exacts it, this court will set it aside.

See *D. & C. Builders Ltd. v. Rees*, [*supra*, Chapter 4, section 5(b)].

The fifth category is that of salvage agreements. When a vessel is in danger of sinking and seeks help, the rescuer is in a strong bargaining position. The vessel in distress is in urgent need. The parties cannot be truly said to be on equal terms. . . .

The general principles

Gathering all together, I would suggest that through all these instances there runs a single thread. They rest on "inequality of bargaining power." By virtue of it, the English law gives relief to one who, without independent advice, enters into a contract upon terms which are very unfair or transfers property for a consideration which is grossly inadequate, when his bargaining power is grievously impaired by reason of his own needs or desires, or by his own ignorance or infirmity, coupled with undue influences or pressures brought to bear on him by or for the benefit of the other. When I use the word "undue" I do not mean to suggest that the principle depends on proof of any wrongdoing. The one who stipulates for an unfair advantage may be moved solely by his own self-interest, unconscious of the distress he is bringing to the other. I have also avoided any reference to the will of the one being "dominated" or "overcome" by the other. One who is in extreme need may knowingly consent to a most improvident bargain, solely to relieve the straits in which he finds himself. Again, I do not mean to suggest that every transaction is saved by independent advice. But the absence of it may be fatal. With these explanations, I hope this principle will be found to reconcile the cases. Applying it to the present case, I would notice these points:

(1) The consideration moving from the bank was grossly inadequate. The son's company was in serious difficulty. The overdraft was at its limit of £10,000. The bank considered that its existing security was insufficient. In order to get

further security, it asked the father to charge the house—his sole asset—to the uttermost. It was worth £10,000. The charge was for £11,000. That was for the benefit of the bank. But not at all for the benefit of the father, or indeed for the company. The bank did not promise to continue the overdraft or to increase it. On the contrary, it required the overdraft to be reduced. All that the company gained was a short respite from impending doom.

(2) The relationship between the bank and the father was one of trust and confidence. The bank knew that the father relied on it implicitly to advise him about the transaction. The father trusted the bank. This gave the bank much influence on the father. Yet the bank failed in that trust. It allowed the father to charge the house to his ruin.

(3) The relationship between the father and the son was one where the father's natural affection had much influence on him. He would naturally desire to accede to his son's request. He trusted his son.

(4) There was a conflict of interest between the bank and the father. Yet the bank did not realise it. Nor did it suggest that the father should get independent advice. If the father had gone to his solicitor—or to any man of business—there is no doubt that any one of them would say:

> You must not enter into this transaction. You are giving up your house, your sole remaining asset, for no benefit to you. The company is in such a parlous state that you must not do it.

These considerations seem to me to bring this case within the principles I have stated. But, in case that principle is wrong, I would also say that the case falls within the category of undue influence of the second class stated by Cotton L.J. in *Allcard v. Skinner* [*supra*]. I have no doubt that the assistant bank manager acted in the utmost good faith and was straightforward and genuine. Indeed the father said so. But beyond doubt he was acting in the interests of the bank—to get further added security for a bad debt. There was such a relationship of trust and confidence between them that the bank ought not to have swept up his sole remaining asset into its hands—for nothing—without his having independent advice. I would therefore allow this appeal.

[Cairns L.J. and Sir Eric Sachs agreed, but on the ground of breach of fiduciary duty. Appeal allowed.]

NOTES

1. In a "Note" (1975), 38 Mod. L.R. 463 at 466, Carr comments on this case:

> The decision is a tantalising one. It hints at great things, yet in the end it can be explained on rather narrow grounds. But it would be a mistake to write the case off so easily. The main point of interest is Lord Denning's attempt to do for the various species of undue influence and duress what Lord Atkin did for the various categories of negligence in *Donoghue v. Stevenson*. If we accept, with Lord Denning, that the guiding principle is to afford protection where there is inequality of bargaining power, we may be witnessing the spawning of a benevolent giant.

Slayton, "The Unequal Bargain Doctrine: Lord Denning in *Lloyds Bank v. Bundy*" (1976), 22 McGill L.J. 94, at 106, also saw the principle as one of wide scope:

In my opinion, under the unequal bargain doctrine as set forth by Lord Denning (1) no confidential relationship or duty of fiduciary care is necessary, and (2) undue influence need not be proved as a fact, but will be presumed when bargaining power is impaired and the terms are very unfair or consideration grossly inadequate. If this is so, then clearly a new doctrine of momentous scope has been introduced into the law of contract.

2. The House of Lords took a broad "fairness" approach in *A. Schroeder Music Publishing Co. v. Macaulay*, discussed *supra*, Chapter 8, section 3(b). The plaintiff was a songwriter. The defendants contracted for his exclusive songwriting services for five years with a possible renewal. In return, he was to receive royalty payments on whatever songs the defendants published. The House of Lords set the contract aside as being in restraint of trade. It also found that the contract was unfair, in part because the defendant had no obligation to publish any songs and the plaintiff had no right to terminate the contract.

The decision attracted heavy criticism from Trebilcock, "The Doctrine of Inequality of Bargaining Power: Post Benthamite Economics in the House of Lords" (1976), 26 U.T.L.J. 350. Trebilcock concluded, at 384, that "to attempt comprehensive wage rate regulation and control over employment of factors by judicial fiat in an industry like the music publishing industry, with many firms and substantial product differentiation, would make the acknowledged problems of public-utility regulation look easy. But anything short of this is like squeezing putty."

HARRY v. KREUTZIGER
(1978), 9 B.C.L.R. 166, 95 D.L.R. (3d) 231 (C.A.)

MCINTYRE J.A. The appellant sued to have the court set aside the sale to the respondent of his 6-ton fishing boat, the "Glenda Marion". . . . At trial, the action was dismissed [reported 3 B.C.L.R. 348]. This appeal was taken, and before this court the appellant confined his claim to that of unconscionable bargain.

The appellant is an Indian who lives in Powell River, British Columbia. He is married, with six children, aged from 6 to 19. He suffers from a congenital hearing defect, but is by no means totally deaf. He has grade 5 education, and according to the trial judge is a mild, inarticulate, retiring person, and it would appear from the evidence that he is not widely experienced in business matters. He is a commercial fisherman and a logger. . . .

[McIntyre J.A. explained that the boat itself was of little value, but that it was highly marketable because of the salmon fishing licence attached to it. The buyer approached the appellant with a view to buying the boat and gave him a cheque in the amount of $2,000.]

The appellant took the cheque and said he would consider the matter and give the respondent his decision the next day.

The appellant decided against the sale overnight, after discussions with his brother, and gave the cheque to his brother to return to the respondent. He said he adopted this course because he did not wish to face the respondent. The cheque was returned the next day, but after receipt the respondent went to the appellant's home and slipped the cheque under his door. A further meeting took place on 20th November 1973, when the respondent gave further assurances to the appellant that he would be able to get a licence for a new boat. The cheque was handed back and forth several times, the respondent returning it to the appellant after each refusal to sell. Finally it was agreed that the boat would be sold for $4,500. . . .

[In fact, to the buyer's knowledge the boat was worth $16,000 because of the fishing licence. Later, the buyer unilaterally reduced the purchase price by $570 because he had been required to pay back licence fees in this amount in order to use the licence. After the sale, the appellant's application to the Indian Fishermen's Assistance Programme for help in purchasing a new boat was denied, partly on the ground that the appellant had left the fishing industry when he sold his boat. McIntyre J.A. continued as follows.]

The question for decision is: Did he enter into this bargain under such circumstances that the court will exercise its equitable jurisdiction to rescind the contract and return the parties to their original positions? . . .

The principles upon which a court will interfere with a concluded transaction and nullify it upon the ground that it is unconscionable have found frequent expression. An early Canadian case is *Waters v. Donnelly* (1884), 9 O.R. 391. The leading pronouncement on the subject in British Columbia is to be found in *Morrison v. Coast Finance Ltd.* [*supra*] . . .

From these authorities, this rule emerges. Where a claim is made that a bargain is unconscionable, it must be shown for success that there was inequality in the position of the parties due to the ignorance, need or distress of the weaker, which would leave him in the power of the stronger, coupled with proof of substantial unfairness in the bargain. When this has been shown a presumption of fraud is raised, and the stronger must show, in order to preserve his bargain, that it was fair and reasonable.

Like many principles of law, it is much easier to state than to apply in any given case. In the cases cited . . . the facts were such that the application of the remedy was clearly required. In the case at bar the facts do not speak as clearly. Nonetheless, I am of the view that this appeal should succeed and the contract be rescinded. The appellant, by education, physical infirmity and economic circumstances, was clearly not the equal of the respondent. The evidence supports the conclusion that the appellant wanted to continue fishing and wanted to retain his licence or tonnage. It shows as well that the respondent proceeded aggressively with full knowledge of the value of the licence. He expressed regret at one stage that he had not acquired three or four more licences, they were so valuable. The appellant did not wish to sell, and resisted for a time by returning the cheque and delaying a decision. The arbitrary withholding of $570 by the respondent is illustrative of his attitude to the appellant. Despite the fact that the trial judge found that the appellant had not shown that he entered the contract on the basis of representations made by the defendant, I cannot but conclude that the appellant was anxious to preserve his licence, and that he was assured falsely or recklessly by the respondent that he would have no difficulty getting another licence if he sold the "Glenda Marion" to the respondent. In this respect, he was given assurances on a subject of prime importance by the respondent, who admitted he knew little or nothing of the matter. The respondent also knew that the preservation of his licence was a vital consideration to the appellant. The respondent sought out the appellant and in his dealings would not take no for an answer. He persuaded the appellant to enter a bargain after, by his own admission, making assurances which were untrue regarding the chance of the appellant to get a licence. He thereby procured an asset worth $16,000 for $4,500, which he later chose to reduce by $570. The position taken by the appellant's counsel was that the appellant's ignorance, coupled with pressures exerted upon him by the respondent, caused the inequality of the bargaining position. In my view, the improvidence of the bargain is shown. On the whole of the evidence, it is also my view that the appellant was so dominated and overborne by the respondent that he was, in the sense of that term used by Davey J.A. in the *Morrison* case, *supra*, within the power of the respondent in these dealings. . . .

I would allow the appeal and direct that the contract be rescinded; that the respondent deliver the "Glenda Marion" to the appellant upon payment by the appellant to the respondent of the sum of $3,930.

LAMBERT J.A. . . . I do not disagree that the principle, as stated by Davey J.A. and by McIntyre J.A., is appropriate to apply in this case as an aid in the determination of whether this is a case where rescission should be granted, though I am not satisfied that the principle, so stated, exhausts all cases where rescission might be ordered under the rubric of unconscionable bargain.

I agree wholeheartedly with McIntyre J.A. when he says that it is easier to state the principle than to apply it in a given case. Indeed, to my mind the principle is only of the most general guidance. It is not a principle of the type which can be applied to facts to produce, by a logical process, a clear conclusion. To think of it as such a principle is to obscure the real process of consideration and judgment that leads to a decision in this kind of case.

I consider that the judgment of the English Court of Appeal in *Lloyd's Bank Ltd. v. Bundy* [*supra*] is subject to the same limitation. In that case, Lord Denning M.R. analyzed five types of unconscionable bargain and synthesized them into one general principle. He called the five types: duress of goods, unconscionable transactions, undue influence, undue pressure and salvage agreements. [Lord Denning's statement of the general principle in *Lloyds Bank, supra*] was clearly not intended as a touchstone, since the liberal employment of adjectives makes it too flexible for that purpose, but rather as a demonstration that the categories of grounds for rescission are interrelated and based on a common foundation, so that cases of one of the five types may provide guidance on another of the types. Accordingly, again, the statement of principle has been of only the most general assistance to me in reaching my decision on the facts of this case.

In my opinion, questions as to whether use of power was unconscionable, an advantage was unfair or very unfair, a consideration was grossly inadequate, or bargaining power was grievously impaired, to select words from both statements of principle, the *Morrison* case and the *Bundy* case, are really aspects of one single question. That single question is whether the transaction, seen as a whole, is sufficiently divergent from community standards of commercial morality that it should be rescinded. To my mind, the framing of the question in that way prevents the real issue from being obscured by an isolated consideration of a number of separate questions; as, for example, a consideration of whether the consideration was grossly inadequate, rather than merely inadequate, separate from the consideration of whether bargaining power was grievously impaired, or

merely badly impaired. Such separate consideration of separate questions produced by the application of a synthetic rule tends to obscure rather than aid the
process of decision.

The single question of whether the transaction, seen as a whole, is sufficiently
divergent from community standards of commercial morality that it should be
rescinded must be answered by an examination of the decided cases and a consideration, from those cases, of the fact patterns that require that the bargain be
rescinded and those that do not. In that examination, Canadian cases are more
relevant than those from other lands, where different standards of commercial
morality may apply, and recent cases are more germane than those from earlier
times when standards were in some respects rougher and in other respects more
fastidious. In my opinion, it is also appropriate to seek guidance as to community
standards of commercial morality from legislation that embodies those standards
in law. I have therefore particularly considered the facts and decisions in *Morrison
v. Coast Finance Ltd., supra*; *Knupp v. Bell* (1966) 58 D.L.R. (2d) 466, affirmed
67 D.L.R. (2d) 256 (Sask. C.A.); *Miller v. Lavoie* (1966), 63 W.W.R. 359, 60
D.L.R. (2d) 495 (B.C.); *Marshall v. Can. Permanent Trust Co.* [*supra*]; *Gladu v.
Edmonton Land Co.* (1914), 8 Alta. L.R. 80, 7 W.W.R. 279, 19 D.L.R. 688; and
Hnatuk v. Chretien (1960), 31 W.W.R. 130 (B.C.); and I have considered the
provisions of the Trade Practices Act, 1974 (B.C.), c. 96, and the Consumer
Protection Act, 1977 (B.C.), c. 6.

I have applied the standards derived from those authorities to the facts in
this case, which are that the respondent purchased for $4,500 a boat that he knew
to be worth $16,000 from the appellant, whom he knew to be partially deaf, easily
intimidated and ill-advised, by a process of harassment. In my opinion, the whole
circumstances of the bargain reveal such a marked departure from community
standards of commercial morality that the contract of purchase and sale should
be rescinded.

I do not believe that the process of reasoning that I have adopted is in any
way different from the process of reasoning adopted by McIntyre J.A. in this case
or by Davey J.A. in the *Morrison* case, supra.

I would allow the appeal and make the order proposed by McIntyre J.A.

[Craig J.A. agreed with both McIntyre J.A. and Lambert J.A. Appeal allowed.]

(c)　THE SCOPE OF THE PRINCIPLE

Many decisions on unconscionability have been rendered since *Harry v.
Kreutziger* was decided. There is a continuing controversy over the test for
obtaining relief on this basis. Gibbs, J.A., dissenting in *Smyth v. Szep*, [1992] 2
W.W.R. 673 (B.C.C.A.), leave to appeal to S.C.C. refused [1992] 6 W.W.R. lviii,
expressed his concern with the Lambert J.A. approach as follows, at 693:

> Lambert J.A. . . . . propounded the commercial morality test on the footing of a compression
> of the statements of principle from *Morrison v. Coast Finance* and *Lloyds Bank Ltd. v. Bundy*,
> . . . into a single question. At p. 177 [B.C.L.R.] he said:

>   That single question is whether the transaction, seen as a whole, is sufficiently divergent
>   from community standards of commercial morality that it should be rescinded.
>
>   It is not apparent that Lambert J.A. intended to substitute a commercial morality test for
>   the *Morrison v. Coast Finance* tests. He seems to have been of the view that it would be
>   employed as a kind of legal shorthand expression encompassing within it all of the *Morrison
>   v. Coast Finance* and *Lloyds Bank Ltd. v. Bundy* tests. But, unfortunately, it appears to have
>   grown in stature into an assumed separate, stand alone test of universal application. Undesirable
>   considerations of a morally subjective nature have thereby been introduced into what had
>   previously been a purely fact-finding exercise to ascertain whether the *Morrison v. Coast
>   Finance* tests had been met.
>
>   There may be cases where a single test of community standards of commercial morality
>   is appropriate, if there is evidence of what the community is and what the generally acceptable
>   standard of morality is in that community, but it is a test to be applied with great care and great
>   caution. The risk is that a trial judge may be induced by its apparent simplicity into introducing
>   his subjective view of the morality of the case as a substitute for the *Morrison v. Coast Finance*
>   factual tests.

The Supreme Court of Canada, for its part, has not closely examined the
notion of unconscionability. Although the court has utilized the doctrine (*e.g.*,
Hunter Engineering Co. v. Syncrude Canada Ltd., *supra*, Chapter 8, section
3(d)(v); *Norberg v. Wynrib*, [1992] 2 S.C.R. 226), it has yet to explore in any
depth the essential nature and scope of this jurisdiction. See, in this respect,
Flannigan, "Hunter Engineering: The Judicial Regulation of Exculpatory
Clauses" (1990), 69 Can. Bar Rev. 514, at 529-36. As for the proper test, it appears
that the *Morrison* test has been widely accepted. Some judges, however, continue
to utilize the "community standards" approach, in various ways, in their analyses.
See *Ellis v. Friedland*, [2001] 2 W.W.R. 130 (Alta. Q.B.); *Canadian Imperial
Bank of Commerce v. Ohlson*, [1997] A.J. No. 1185 (C.A.); *Kassian v. Hill*,
[2002] A.J. No. 209 (C.A.); *Eager v. Blackburn*, [2002] N.S.J. No. 147 (C.A.). It
appears the uncertainty regarding the test(s) will remain until the Supreme Court
revisits the matter and fashions a definitive analysis.

In declaring that transactions are to be evaluated against "community standards of commercial morality", Lambert J.A. arguably merely expressed the
original motivation for both the traditional Canadian doctrine of unconscionability
and Lord Denning's general principle. At the same time, however, the "community standards" test would appear to allow for relief in cases where relief would
have been difficult to justify under the traditional approach. Subsequent cases
illustrate that this has happened. In particular, contracts between business people
have been set aside because of commercial pressure. These latter decisions are
hard to reconcile with the reasoning of the Privy Council in *Pao On*, *supra*, in
relation to the doctrine of duress.

The issue, at this point, is the proper scope of the doctrine. The traditional
doctrine of unconscionability was arguably only narrower because it was used
sparingly and in very compelling circumstances. Is there a demonstrated need for
a wider or more open relief on this basis?

The issue is addressed in the following extract.

TIPLADY, THE JUDICIAL CONTROL OF CONTRACTUAL UNFAIRNESS

(1983), 46 Mod. L.R. 601, at 601-18

[Justice] or fairness, and certainty, are often assumed to be opposed values in contract law. And it is often claimed that there is an underlying conflict between the judicial instinct for justice and the traditional—or, at least, Benthamite—perception of a judge's function in adjudicating contract cases. The tension which these apparent oppositions create is reflected, we are told, in the overstrained way courts have applied supposedly value-free rules—of offer and acceptance, for example, or the incorporation and construction of terms—in order, covertly, to achieve a just result. Further distortion is added by the fact that this method makes it impossible to articulate the true reasons for decision. Judgment is given in terms of a misapplied procedure. The unsuccessful litigant is told that his objective—to exclude or limit liability, for example—*can* be achieved, but that he has simply failed to reach it on this occasion. The implicit invitation is to go away and try again, when in fact the court's true purpose is a substantive, distributional one: to prevent that particular thing from being done at all.

How much better—the argument proceeds—to abandon the pretext of neutrality, to emerge from the closet of outmoded techniques and redundant philosophies, and to declare oneself as the instrument for alleviating oppression, redressing bargaining imbalance, cancelling unfair advantages, and generally overseeing and ensuring probity and fair dealing of both a procedural and substantive kind? If, after all, this is what courts *do* or should be able to do, let us say so openly, and recognize for what they are the means by which they are to do it.

.....

It is my contention that the suppositions which have led to this new approach are fallacious; that, far from being opposed, justice and certainty are close approximations or harmonious objectives; that traditional methods of adjudication already incorporate to a sufficient degree the end of justice (or omit to do so for good reason) and that the rejection of these methods is therefore essentially misguided and itself a source of potential injustice. . . .

Undoubtedly the most radical development of the English law of contract towards an overtly justice-based general principle is the doctrine of inequality of bargaining power. This made its most celebrated appearance in the judgment of Lord Denning M.R. in *Lloyds Bank Ltd. v. Bundy*. . . .

A principle of this quality is a subliminal evocation of the instinct for justice. Like the American doctrine of unconscionability, it is, at the least, "an emotionally satisfying incantation."

.....

Is it in fact anything more than a slogan for unstructured distributive justice? The doctrine invites comparison between the particular situation and some benchmark or norm of "common fairness"; but the factors of comparison are not identified. . . .

The doctrine of inequality of bargaining power does not assist us to distinguish legitimate forms of advantage-taking from illegitimate. Its appearance of content is apochryphal [sic], since only in some cases is advice relevant, only in some is the disparity of terms relevant, and only in some is the positive use of influence or pressure of any importance. An appeal to common justice carries the seductive implication that we all intuitively understand what it is. As a legal principle, however, an appeal to instinct is a poor substitute for the clear articulation of rational standards.

.....

The validity of unconscionability, inequality of bargaining power and related equitable doctrines of more or less specificity is based upon the single proposition that traditional methods of adjudication, when applied to issues of fairness, are essentially dishonest. Given the obsolescent philosophical postulates from which they emanate, they must inevitably cause judges to dissemble the true reason for decision. The reciprocal of this proposition is that only a full break from these traditional methods can restore judicial integrity and re-establish sound doctrine. If the price of this achievement is a period of uncertainty, then it must be paid.

I doubt the wisdom and the necessity of these assumptions. Justice or fairness, though self-evident influences in the formulation and application of contractual principles, are not in themselves instruments of contract law. Nor can they be converted into doctrine under any synonym. They are, rather, descriptions of the way in which lawyers handle the instruments of the law. There is a danger that, once seen as ends in themselves, judges will begin to make choices which they are ill-equipped to make. There is a danger that, though they know the word to start the sorcerer's broom, they will be unable to control it, or to estimate just how clean a sweep it will eventually make.

[Footnotes omitted.]

NOTE

The propriety of a broad general doctrine of unconscionability, in Tiplady's view, is far from self-evident. In the period 1974-85 there was movement in the direction of an expanded doctrine of unconscionability. But in 1985, in what must be considered a direct attack on this idea, the House of Lords emphatically rejected Lord Denning's "inequality of bargaining power" principle. In *Nat. Westminster Bank v. Morgan, supra*, it will be recalled, the House of Lords was dealing with a claim of undue influence. But in the course of his judgment, Lord Scarman, at 830, took the opportunity to deny the existence and utility of the principle put forward by Lord Denning in *Lloyds Bank Ltd. v. Bundy*:

> Lord Denning MR believed that the doctrine of undue influence could be subsumed under a general principle that English courts will grant relief where there has been 'inequality of bargaining power'. He deliberately avoided reference to the will of one party being dominated or overcome by another. The majority of the court did not follow him; they based their decision on the orthodox view of the doctrine as expounded in *Allcard v. Skinner* (1887) 36 Ch D 145. This opinion of Lord Denning MR, therefore, was not the ground of the court's decision, which has to be found in the view of the majority, for whom Sir Eric Sachs delivered the leading judgment.
>
> Nor has counsel for the wife sought to rely on Lord Denning MR's general principle; and, in my view, he was right not to do so. The doctrine of undue influence has been sufficiently

developed not to need the support of a principle which by its formulation in the language of the law of contract is not appropriate to cover transactions of gift where there is no bargain. The fact of an unequal bargain will, of course, be a relevant feature in some cases of undue influence. But it can never become an appropriate basis of principle of an equitable doctrine which is concerned with transactions 'not to be reasonably accounted for on the ground of friendship, relationship, charity, or other ordinary motives on which ordinary men act . . .' (see *Allcard v. Skinner* [*supra*] at 185, per Lindley L.J.). And even in the field of contract I question whether there is any need in the modern law to erect a general principle of relief against inequality of bargaining power. Parliament has undertaken the task (and it is essentially a legislative task) of enacting such restrictions on freedom of contract as are in its judgment necessary to relieve against the mischief: for example, the hire-purchase and consumer protection legislation, of which the Supply of Goods (Implied Terms) Act 1973, the Consumer Credit Act 1974, the Consumer Safety Act 1978, the Supply of Goods and Services Act 1982 and the Insurance Companies Act 1982 are examples. I doubt whether the courts should assume the burden of formulating further restrictions.

Each of the other four law lords adopted Lord Scarman's reasons without qualification. What impact might you expect Lord Scarman's speech to have on Canadian judges? Are you convinced one way or the other?

(d)   UNCONSCIONABILITY LEGISLATION

There are some statutes in Canada which utilize the unconscionability standard. This legislation is of a specific nature, dealing with particular transactions (*e.g.*, money-lending) or particular classes of transactions (*e.g.*, consumer transactions). Set out below is an extract from the Unconscionable Transactions Relief Act of Nova Scotia.

UNCONSCIONABLE TRANSACTIONS RELIEF ACT

R.S.N.S. 1989, c. 481, ss. 3, 4

[This Act is representative of statutory enactments in other provinces.]

3.   Where, in respect of money lent, the court finds that, having regard to the risk and to all the circumstances, the cost of the loan is excessive and that the transaction is harsh and unconscionable, the court may

(a)   re-open the transaction and take an account between the creditor and the debtor;

(b)   notwithstanding any statement or settlement of account or any agreement purporting to close previous dealings and create a new obligation, re-open any account already taken and relieve the debtor from payment of any sum in excess of the sum adjudged by the court to be fairly due in respect of the principal and the cost of the loan;

(c)   order the creditor to repay any such excess if the same has been paid or allowed on account by the debtor;

(d)   set aside either wholly or in part, or revise or alter any security given or agreement made in respect of the money lent and, if the creditor has parted with security, order him to indemnify the debtor.

4.   The powers conferred by Section 3 may be exercised

(a) in an action or proceeding by a creditor for the recovery of money lent;

(b) in an action or proceeding by the debtor, notwithstanding any provision or agreement to the contrary and notwithstanding that the time for repayment of the loan or any instalment thereof has not arrived;

(c) in an action or proceeding in which the amount due or to become due in respect of money lent is in question.

NOTES and QUESTION

1. Trade practice legislation, which was considered in Chapter 7, sections 4 and 6(b), also deals directly with elements of unconscionability.

2. The foregoing legislation is expressly limited in scope. What is your view of a generalized statutory unconscionability doctrine? A general provision on unconscionability is found in the United States Commercial Code, s. 2-302:

(1) If the court as a matter of law finds the contract or any clause of the contract to have been unconscionable at the time it was made the court may refuse to enforce the contract, or it may enforce the remainder of the contract without the unconscionable clause, or it may so limit the application of any unconscionable clause as to avoid any unconscionable result.

(2) When it is claimed or appears to the court that the contract or any clause thereof may be unconscionable the parties shall be afforded a reasonable opportunity to present evidence as to its commercial setting, purpose and effect to aid the court in making the determination.

The comment to the section states:

This section is intended to allow the court to pass directly on the unconscionability of the contract or particular clause therein and to make a conclusion of law as to its unconscionability. The basic test is whether, in the light of the general commercial background and the commercial needs of the particular trade or case, the clauses involved are so one-sided as to be unconscionable under the circumstances existing at the time of the making of the contract. Subsection (2) makes it clear that it is proper for the court to hear evidence upon these questions. The principle is one of the prevention of oppression and unfair surprise . . . and not of disturbance of allocation of risks because of superior bargaining power.

3. The O.L.R.C. has proposed a generalized unconscionability standard. Consider the recommendations of the Commission in its *Report on Amendment of the Law of Contract* (1987), at 136-38. Do the factors listed in the fourth recommendation substantially replicate existing contractual doctrine?

Recommendations

The Commission makes the following recommendations:

1. Legislation should be enacted expressly conferring on the courts power to grant relief from contracts and contractual provisions that are unconscionable.

2. The proposed legislation should not distinguish between procedural and substantive unconscionability.

3. The proposed legislation should include a non-exclusive list of decisional criteria to guide the courts in determining questions of unconscionability (See *infra*, Recommendation 4).

4. In determining whether a contract or part thereof is unconscionable in the circumstances relating to the contract at the time it was made, the court may have regard, among other factors, to evidence of:

(a) the degree to which one party has taken advantage of the inability of the other party reasonably to protect his or her interests because of his or her physical or mental infirmity, illiteracy, inability to understand the language of an agreement, lack of education, lack of business knowledge or experience, financial distress, or because of the existence of a relationship of trust or dependence or similar factors;

(b) the existence of terms in the contract that are not reasonably necessary for the protection of the interests of any party to the contract;

(c) the degree to which the contract requires a party to waive rights to which he or she would otherwise be entitled;

(d) gross disparity between the considerations given by the parties to the contract and the considerations that would normally be given by parties to a similar contract in similar circumstances;

(e) knowledge by one party, when entering into the contract, that the other party will be substantially deprived of the benefit or benefits reasonably anticipated by that other party under the contract;

(f) the degree to which the natural effect of the transaction, or any party's conduct prior to, or at the time of, the transaction, is to cause or aid in causing another party to misunderstand the true nature of the transaction and his or her rights and duties thereunder;

(g) whether the complaining party had independent advice before or at the time of the transaction or should reasonably have acted to secure such advice for the protection of the party's interest;

(h) the bargaining strength of the parties relative to each other, taking into account the availability of reasonable alternative sources of supply or demand;

(i) whether the party seeking relief knew or ought reasonably to have known of the existence and extent of the term or terms alleged to be unconscionable;

(j) in the case of a provision that purports to exclude or limit a liability that would otherwise attach to the party seeking to rely on it, which party is better able to guard against loss or damages;

(k) the setting, purpose and effect of the contract, and the manner in which it was formed, including whether the contract is on written standard terms of business; and

(l) the conduct of the parties in relation to similar contracts or courses of dealing to which any of them has been a party.

5. The proposed legislation should expressly authorize the court to raise the issue of unconscionability of its own motion.

6. The proposed provisions on unconscionability should apply to all types of contracts.

7. The term "contract" in the proposed provisions on unconscionability should be defined to include any enforceable promise.

8. The proposed legislation should incorporate a provision, similar to section 5.2(1) of the proposed *Sale of Goods Act*, with the necessary modifications. Accordingly, the court should be able, in the case of an unconscionable contract to

(a) refuse to enforce the contract or rescind it on such terms as may be just;

(b) enforce the remainder of the contract without the unconscionable part; or

(c) so limit the application of any unconscionable part or revise or alter the contract as to avoid any unconscionable result.

9. The courts should be empowered, at the behest of the Attorney General or other prescribed Minister, to issue injunctions against conduct leading to unconscionability, either in the formation of or in the execution of contracts.

10. A provision, similar to section 5.2(5) of the proposed *Sale of Goods Act*, preventing a party from excluding liability or waiving rights under the provisions dealing with unconscionability, should be included in the proposed legislation.

5.   Incapacity

For some time there were several classes of persons who lacked full capacity to make a binding contract. Legislation has ended the incapacity for a number of these classes, for example, married women and corporations. The most important remaining categories are infants and persons with mental disabilities. In many instances they will not be bound to perform their contracts. In the case of contracts for necessities, however, even these persons were liable under the common law. This specific capacity has also been codified in many jurisdictions, *e.g.*, section 4 of the Sale of Goods Act, R.S.A. 2000, c. S-2.

(a)   INFANCY

The O.L.R.C. has described the various categories of minors' contracts.

ONTARIO LAW REFORM COMMISSION, REPORT ON AMENDMENT OF THE LAW OF CONTRACT

(1987), at 178-80

(ii)   *Void Contracts*

In Ontario, the common law determines whether a contract made by a minor will be treated as void *ab initio*. Unfortunately, there does not seem to be any settled definition of the kind of contract that attracts this consequence. Judges have expressed themselves in different language at different times. To Ferguson J., in *Butterfield v. Sibbitt* [[1950] O.R. 504 at 509 (H.C.)], "[a]ll contracts entered into by an infant must be for his benefit, otherwise they are void". A narrower view of the category of void minors' contracts was expressed by Laidlaw J.A. in *McBride v. Appleton* [[1946] O.R. 17 at 30 (C.A.)]: for a minor's contract to be void, not merely voidable, it must be "as a whole . . . so much to the detriment of . . . the infant, as to render it unfair that he should be bound by it". In *Re Staruch* [[1955] 5 D.L.R. 807 at 809 (Ont. H.C.)], prejudice to the infant was advanced as the criterion of voidness.

In determining when a contract is so unfair, prejudicial, or not beneficial, that it goes beyond being voidable and becomes void, the language of the judges, while intended to be helpful, leaves much to be desired.

(iii)   *Contracts Not Binding on the Minor Unless Ratified After Attaining Majority*

This category appears to comprise all minors' contracts that do not fit into any of the other categories. Contracts that fall into this category do not bind the minor during minority, or after attaining majority unless ratified by the minor after majority.

However, Canadian judges have not been consistent in distinguishing between contracts that are binding on a minor unless repudiated, and those in the category now under discussion. It has sometimes been implied, for example, that all contracts that are neither void nor valid without qualification are subject to repudiation by the minor. On other occasions, judges have asked whether the contract has been ratified, even though the contract could properly have been characterized as one that was valid unless repudiated. In other words, Canadian judges have sometimes tended to confuse both classes of so-called voidable contracts.

Further complexity arises from the requirement of ratification. At common law there seem to have been no special rules governing ratification, provided the minor, on attaining majority, demonstrated an intention to adopt and approve the contract made during minority . . .

(iv) Contracts Binding on the Minor Unless Repudiated

Contracts in this category bind the minor unless he or she takes appropriate steps to repudiate during minority or within a reasonable time after attaining majority. Commentators appear to agree that this category comprehends the following: contracts concerning land; share contracts; partnership agreements; and marriage settlements.

(v) Valid Contracts

There are two types of contracts that may be legally binding on the minor as soon as they are made and that cannot be repudiated by the minor, whether before or after majority. These are, first contracts for necessaries and, secondly, contracts of employment or service.

[Footnotes omitted.]

NOTES

1. The O.L.R.C., *Report on Amendment of the Law of Contract* (1987), concluded, at 202, that "the current law is complex, replete with anomalies, and difficult to apply. Results are uncertain, and the interests of fairness are not adequately served, particularly as regards compensation and restitution under an unenforceable contract." The Commission as a general principle recommends that

> . . . minor's contracts should not be enforceable against them. However, it does not follow that these contracts should not be enforceable against adult parties. None of the policy goals require such reciprocity, and it would be strange if a minor, the person whom we are trying to protect, could not exercise such contractual rights as would be available to an adult.
>
> Accordingly, we recommend that while minors' contracts should not be enforceable against them, minors should have the right to enforce their contracts, subject to the provisions recommended below and to the provisions of other legislation.

The Commission sets out its detailed recommendations at 203-213 of its Report.

Other law reform commissions have found the law of minors' contracts equally unsatisfactory and have recommended major changes in the law. Many of the recommendations of the *Report on Minors' Contracts* (1976) of the B.C. Law Reform Commission have been implemented by the Law Reform Amendment Act, S.B.C. 1985, c. 10. In contrast, no legislative action has been taken on the *Report on Minors' Contracts* (1975) of the Alberta Institute of Law Research and Reform.

2. For a discussion of the common law of minors' contracts, see Percy, "The Present Law of Infants' Contracts" (1975), 53 Can. Bar Rev. 1.

(b)   MENTAL INCOMPETENCE

HART v. O'CONNOR

[1985] A.C. 1000, 2 All E.R. 880 (P.C.)

Hart purchased land from O'Connor. Hart did not know at the time that O'Connor did not have sufficient mental capacity to enable him to enter into such a contract. An action was commenced seeking a declaration that the agreement should be rescinded for want of mental capacity on the part of O'Connor, unfairness and unconscionability.

LORD BRIGHTMAN . . . [The trial judge] first considered the vendor's capacity to contract, and found on a balance of probabilities that the vendor did not have contractual ability to enter into the agreement, and would not have had a proper understanding of the matters for decision even if (contrary to the judge's view) they had been adequately explained to him. He then considered the circumstances in which a contract made by a person who lacked mental capacity was liable to be set aside. The traditional view in English law was that it must be proved that the other contracting party knew of or ought to have appreciated such incapacity. Otherwise the contract stood, assuming it was not voidable on equitable principles as an unconscionable bargain. But in *Archer v. Cutler* [1980] 1 N.Z.L.R. 386 it had been decided that a contract made by a person of insufficient mental capacity was voidable at his option not only if the other party knew of or ought to have appreciated his unsoundness of mind, but also if the contract "was unfair to the person of unsound mind." *Archer v. Cutler*, to which their Lordships will have to refer . . . later, was accepted by both sides and by the judge as a correct statement of the law, and there was no argument upon it; in a court of first instance this was almost inevitable.

. . . . .

In short, the [trial] judge found that the terms of the agreement were "unfair" viewed against the background of the absence of any effective advice for the vendor and the unequal bargaining positions of the contracting parties. Therefore, founding upon *Archer v. Cutler*, the judge held that the agreement was not enforceable (at law) against the party of unsound mind though his impairment was not apparent.

This conclusion would have led to the rescission of the agreement but for the defence of laches raised by the defendant. The judge decided with reluctance that this defence was made out, and consequently he gave judgment in favour of the defendant with costs. . . .

[The Court of Appeal reversed the trial judge on the finding of laches and this decision was not contested before the Privy Council. Nor did the defendant challenge the finding that the vendor lacked the requisite contractual capacity.]

[The] issues raised by the parties on this appeal are as follows: (A) Whether *Archer v. Cutler* . . . was rightly decided; that is to say, whether a contract by a person of unsound mind, whose incapacity is unknown to the other contracting party, can be avoided (at law) on the ground that it is "unfair" to the party lacking capacity (or those whom he represents), there being no imputations against the conduct of the other contracting party. (B) If *Archer v. Cutler* was rightly decided, whether the High Court and the Court of Appeal were correct in finding that the sale agreement was "unfair" to the vendor. (C) If *Archer v. Cutler* was wrongly decided, whether the plaintiffs were entitled to have the contract set aside (in equity) as an "unconscionable bargain" notwithstanding the complete innocence of the defendant. (D) If *Archer v. Cutler* was rightly decided, and the courts below correctly found that the sale agreement was "unfair," whether the sale agreement would escape rescission because it was impossible to achieve restitutio in integrum.

. . . [T]heir Lordships invited counsel to confine their submissions to issues (A) and (C), leaving issues (B) and (D) for subsequent argument if necessary.

Their Lordships turn first to a consideration of *Archer v. Cutler*. . . . Their Lordships attach importance to three factors. First, this decision was accepted by both sides as correct when the case was argued at first instance. Secondly, the Court of Appeal in a strong judgment affirmed without hesitation that the law there set out was the law of New Zealand. Thirdly the Court of Appeal, when they gave judgment on the compensation appeal, underlined their previous statement of the law in the following important passage [1984] 1 N.Z.L.R. 754, 755:

> In that case [*Archer v. Cutler*] it was held that there were no considerations of policy or principle precluding the court from holding that a contract entered into by a person of unsound mind is voidable at his option if it is proved either that the other party knew of his unsoundness of mind or, whether or not he had that knowledge, the bargain was unfair. On the basis that this principle should be adopted for New Zealand this court expressly approved *Archer v. Cutler*. In the result it made a declaration that the agreement for sale and purchase was rescinded.

If *Archer v. Cutler* is properly to be regarded as a decision based on considerations peculiar to New Zealand, it is highly improbable that their Lordships would think it right to impose their own interpretation of the law, thereby contradicting the unanimous conclusions of the High Court and the Court of Appeal of New Zealand on a matter of local significance. If however the principle of *Archer v. Cutler*, if it be correct, must be regarded as having general application throughout all jurisdictions based on the common law, because it does not depend on local considerations, their Lordships could not properly treat the unanimous view of the courts of New Zealand as being necessarily decisive. In their Lordships' opinion the latter is the correct view of the decision.

. . . . .

If a contract is stigmatised as "unfair", it may be unfair in one of two ways. It may be unfair by reason of the unfair manner in which it was brought into existence; a contract induced by undue influence is unfair in this sense. It will be convenient to call this "procedural unfairness." It may also, in some contexts, be described (accurately or inaccurately) as "unfair" by reason of the fact that the terms of the contract are more favourable to one party than to the other. In order to distinguish this "unfairness" from procedural unfairness, it will be convenient to call it "contractual imbalance." The two concepts may overlap. Contractual imbalance may be so extreme as to raise a presumption of procedural unfairness, such as undue influence or some other form of victimisation. Equity will relieve a party from a contract which he has been induced to make as a result of victimisation. Equity will not relieve a party from a contract on the ground only that there is contractual imbalance not amounting to unconscionable dealing. Of the three indicia of unfairness relied upon by the judge in *Archer v. Cutler* (assuming unfairness to have existed) the first was contractual imbalance and the second and third were procedural unfairness.

The judgment in *Archer v. Cutler* . . . contains, if their Lordships may be permitted to say so, a most scholarly and erudite review by the judge of the textbook authorities and reported cases on the avoidance of a contract made by a person of unsound mind. For present purposes the key passages in the judgment are, at p. 400:

> From these authorities, it would seem that the English law on the subject is ill-defined. The case of *Imperial Loan Co. Ltd. v. Stone* [1892] 1 Q.B. 599 widely accepted as being a statement of the law on avoidance of contracts made with persons of unsound mind would, save in the judgment of Lopes L.J., seem to regard unfairness of the contract as being of no moment. Proof of unsoundness of mind and the other party's knowledge of that unsoundness alone will avoid the contract. But the passage cited from the judgment of Lopes L.J. and the dicta of Pollock C.B. in *Molton v. Camroux* (1848) 2 Exch. 487, of Patteson J. on appeal in the same case, of Sir Ernest Pollock M.R. in *York Glass Co. Ltd. v. Jubb* (1924) 131 L.T. 559 and of Sargant L.J. in the same case would suggest that proof of unfairness of a bargain entered into by a person of unsound mind, even though the unsoundness be not known to the other party, will suffice to avoid it.

And, at p. 401:

> I find nothing in policy or principle to prevent me from holding that a contract entered into by a person of unsound mind is voidable at his option if it is proved either that the other party knew of his unsoundness of mind or, whether or not he had that knowledge, the contract was unfair to the person of unsound mind.

Their Lordships apprehend that in these passages the judge is dealing indifferently with procedural unfairness and contractual imbalance, either of which, or both of which in combination, may enable the contract to be avoided against a contracting party ignorant of the mental incapacity of the other.

The original rule at law, and still the rule in Scotland, was that a contract with a person of unsound mind was void, because there could be no consensus ad idem. This was later qualified by a rule that a person could not plead his own unsoundness of mind in order to avoid a contract he had made. This in turn gave way to a further rule that such a plea was permissible if it could be shown that the other contracting party knew of the insanity.

Their Lordships turn to the three cases mentioned in the first citation from *Archer v. Cutler*. . . . [The three cases were reviewed and then Lord Brightman continued.]

In the opinion of their Lordships it is perfectly plain that historically a court of equity did not restrain a suit at law on the ground of "unfairness" unless the conscience of the plaintiff was in some way affected. This might be because of actual fraud (which the courts of common law would equally have remedied) or constructive fraud, i.e. conduct which falls below the standards demanded by equity, traditionally considered under its more common manifestations of undue influence, abuse of confidence, unconscionable bargains and frauds on a power. (cf. *Snell's Principles of Equity*, 27th ed. (1973), pp. 545 et seq.) An unconscionable bargain in this context would be a bargain of an improvident character made by a poor or ignorant person acting without independent advice which cannot be shown to be a fair and reasonable transaction. "Fraud" in its equitable context does not mean, or is not confined to, deceit; "it means an unconscientious use of the power arising out of these circumstances and conditions" of the contracting parties; *Earl of Aylesford v. Morris* (1873) L.R. 8 Ch. App. 484, 491. It is victimisation, which can consist either of the active extortion of a benefit or the passive acceptance of a benefit in unconscionable circumstances.

Their Lordships have not been referred to any authority that a court of equity would restrain a suit at law where there was no victimisation, no taking advantage of another's weakness, and the sole allegation was contractual imbalance with no undertones of constructive fraud. It seems to their Lordships quite illogical to suppose that the courts of common law would have held that a person of unsound mind, whose affliction was not apparent, was nevertheless free of his bargain if a contractual imbalance could be demonstrated which would have been of no avail to him in equity. Nor do their Lordships see a sufficient foundation in the authorities brought to their attention to support any such proposition. . . .

In the opinion of their Lordships, to accept the proposition enunciated in *Archer v. Cutler* that a contract with a person ostensibly sane but actually of unsound mind can be set aside because it is "unfair" to the person of unsound mind in the sense of contractual imbalance, is unsupported by authority, is illogical and would distinguish the law of New Zealand from the law of Australia . . . for no good reason, as well as from the law of England from which the law of Australia and New Zealand and other "common law" countries has stemmed. In so saying their Lordships differ with profound respect from the contrary view so strongly expressed by the New Zealand courts.

To sum the matter up, in the opinion of their Lordships, the validity of a contract entered into by a lunatic who is ostensibly sane is to be judged by the same standards as a contract by a person of sound mind, and is not voidable by the lunatic or his representatives by reason of "unfairness" unless such unfairness amounts to equitable fraud which would have enabled the complaining party to avoid the contract even if he had been sane.

Their Lordships turn finally to issue (C), whether the plaintiffs are entitled to have the contract set aside as an "unconscionable bargain." This issue must also be answered in the negative, because the defendant was guilty of no unconscionable conduct. Indeed, as is conceded, he acted with complete innocence throughout. He was unaware of the vendor's unsoundness of mind. The vendor was ostensibly advised by his own solicitor. The defendant had no means of knowing or cause to suspect that the vendor was not in receipt of and acting in accordance with the most full and careful advice. The terms of the bargain were the terms proposed by the vendor's solicitor, not terms imposed by the defendant or his solicitor. There was no equitable fraud, no victimisation, no taking advantage, no overreaching or other description of unconscionable doings which might have justified the intervention of equity to restrain an action by the defendant at law. The plaintiffs have in the opinion of their Lordships failed to make out any case for denying to the defendant the benefit of a bargain which was struck with complete propriety on his side.

For these reasons their Lordships have tendered to Her Majesty their humble advice that the appeal should be allowed. . . .

NOTES and QUESTION

1. For a discussion of the degree of mental incapacity that is required to avoid a contract, see *Bank of N.S. v. Kelly* (1973), 41 D.L.R. (3d) 273 (P.E.I.S.C.).

2. There was a limited measure of judicial support in Canada for the *Archer v. Cutler* position that the Privy Council rejected in *Hart v. O'Connor*. Subsequently, a number of Canadian courts have adopted *Hart v. O'Connor*. See *Cameron v. Dorcic* (1987), 80 N.S.R. (2d) 152 (T.D.), affirmed (1988), 83 N.S.R. (2d) 85 (C.A.); *Halifax West Aquinas Credit Union Ltd. v. Owens* (1989), 91 N.S.R. (2d) 256 (T.D.); *Permaform Plastics Ltd. v. London & Midland General Insurance Co.*, [1996] 7 W.W.R. 457 (Man. C.A.). See Robertson, *Mental Disability and the Law in Canada*, 2nd ed. (1994), Chapter 8.

3. What is the difference between judicial intervention in a contract on the ground of mental incapacity and intervention on the ground of unconscionability after *Hart v. O'Connor*?

Chapter 13

ILLEGALITY AND PUBLIC POLICY

1.   Introduction

One of the most significant policies reflected in the law of contract is that of freedom of contract. This is a convenient way of expressing the notion that the law should leave individuals free to exercise their own judgment about what agreements are in their best interests. Once they have exercised that judgment and entered into agreements, those agreements should be enforced. This promotes individual freedom and security of expectations. Collins, in *The Law of Contract*, 4th ed. (2003), at 6, in his discussion of the classical law of contract, states that the "latent social ideal of the nineteenth-century law of contract embodies a libertarian state, in which the law maximizes the liberty of individual citizens, encourages self-reliance, and adopts an avowedly neutral stance with regard to permissible patterns of social life."

It is clear however that other public policies are sometimes treated by courts and by legislators as being more significant than freedom of contract. Thus contracts are sometimes said to be illegal or contrary to public policy on various grounds. These grounds, and the effects of such determinations, form the subject-matter of this chapter, which can be seen as straddling the borderline between the "private" and "public" realms. As quoted by Bastarache J., in dissent in *Continental Bank of Canada v. R.*, [1998] 2 S.C.R. 298, at para. 91: "[O]ne way of conceptualizing this area might be to focus on the instances where public or communitarian concerns override the contracting parties' interests in ordering their private affairs as they choose. . . . This approach is well-expressed in the early case of *Maddox v. Fuller* (1937), 173 So. 12 at 16: "The true test . . . is whether the public interest is injuriously affected in such substantial manner that private rights and interests should yield to those of the public." Viewed in this way, this chapter would illustrate the exceptional, perhaps aberrational, instances where the law drops its guise of a neutral agency for the enforcement of freely-chosen commitments.

On the other hand, it is possible to see the enforcement of certain contracts as reflecting public policy concerns just as much as the non-enforcement of other contracts. (See *Continental Bank of Canada, supra*, at para. 92.) Thus the legal protection of "private rights and interests" could be seen as falling on the "public" side of the public/private dichotomy and contrasted with the hands-off approach taken toward certain domestic agreements discussed in Chapter 4, section 6, Intention to Create Legal Relations. There are various reasons why judges and legislators might wish to enforce or not enforce certain commitments. An examination of these reasons will reveal assumptions about the role of contract law and the organization of society. For instance, should "plea bargains" between the Crown and accused persons be enforceable contracts? In *R. v. Pawliuk* (2001), 151 C.C.C. (3d) 155 (B.C. C.A.), the majority stated at para. 52 that "the formation of the agreement is in many ways analogous to the formation of a contract. Once a plea agreement is reached and the accused has fulfilled part of the bargain, it is improper for the Crown to renege on the agreement. This is so for public policy reasons, primarily because withdrawal from the agreement after the accused has given some consideration in exchange for it may in some cases prejudice the ability of the accused to make full answer and defence."

Consider the assumptions, both stated and implicit, that are revealed in the following materials. In particular, you might wish to consider the "public" values revealed in the enforcement of contracts falling *outside* the recognized heads of public policy, such as contracts for the sale of weapons.

There are various sources of public policy, both legislative and judicial. The Law Reform Commission of British Columbia, in its *Report on Illegal Transactions* (1983), stated at 9:

> The "public policy" in issue may be expressed in a statute, or it may be synthesized from common law cases. Whatever the source of the illegality pleaded, the court has to balance the policy allegedly infringed with the general policy of the law favouring freedom of action in order to determine if the transaction is one which ought to be enforced, or in respect of which relief should be given.

A vast range of public policies can be found in statutory form. Some contracts are expressly prohibited, while others may be impliedly forbidden. Here judges have considerable power to decide whether the policy of the statute requires that the contract be classified as illegal. Examples and discussion of the judicial approach to statutory policies can be found in *Still v. Minister of National Revenue*, in section 3 of this chapter.

The common law has developed its own heads of public policy. Restraint of trade is the most significant in terms of litigation. Other examples are contracts that interfere with the administration of justice, such as agreements to oust the jurisdiction of the courts, and contracts which are prejudicial to family life, such as marriage brokerage agreements. At common law, contracts to commit crimes or torts are illegal, as are contracts injurious to public life, for instance, the sale of public offices, or interference with the legislative process.

In *Continental Bank of Canada, supra*, McLachlin C.J. for the majority, at paras 115-116, quoted from an earlier edition of this casebook:

> A word of warning is necessary with respect to terminology. It will be evident already that the expressions "illegal" and "contrary to public policy" are used somewhat loosely and interchangeably. The approach of the British Columbia Law Reform Commission may be helpful. After recognizing **that the word "illegal" is not always entirely appropriate**, the Commission stated in its Report on Illegal Transactions (1983), at 2:
>
>> The term "illegal" is used as a convenient shorthand expression, signifying that the transaction so designated is one which a court will decline to enforce on the ground that it infringes some public policy, or the terms or object of an enactment. [Emphasis added.]

The fact that the court determines that a contract is void or unenforceable for public policy reasons under the doctrine of illegality does not render either the contract itself or the subject of the contract unlawful. As noted by G. H. Treitel in The Law of Contract (9th ed. 1995), at p. 399: "Such contracts are often called 'illegal.' It is sometimes said that they are only 'void' or 'unenforceable'; but these statements only emphasise that **no specific legal wrong is involved**. So long as this point is borne in mind, no harm is done by using the traditional terminology in which these contracts are 'illegal.'" (Emphasis added.)

Further difficulty arises from the fact that some courts and academic commentators decline to use the term "illegal" where some remedy is available. Thus Cheshire, Fifoot and Furmston's *Law of Contract*, 14th ed. (2001), draws a distinction between contracts which are illegal at common law on grounds of public policy (such as a contract to commit a crime) and contracts which are merely void (such as contracts in restraint of trade). Since the latter are not so reprehensible, the classification may have significance with respect to recovery of money paid under the contract or with respect to severance of objectionable terms.

It is difficult to know to what extent such a distinction exists in Canadian law, but the cases do reveal attempts at gradations of offensiveness with remedial implications. An example can be found in *Chambers v. Pennyfarthing Dev. Corp.* (1985), 20 D.L.R. (4th) 488 (B.C. C.A.). Here the court drew a distinction between contracts which are illegal and those which are merely unenforceable. Since the contract in question was merely unenforceable, money paid under it could be recovered. Such issues are dealt with in section 3 of this chapter, Effects of Illegality.

In the section which follows, attention is drawn to examples of both legislative and judicial heads of public policy. These have been chosen with a view to illustrating the broad range of public policy concerns. In the cases, the people concerned are revealed as attempting to contract with respect to economic, sexual, reproductive, and health issues.

2.   Contracts Contrary to Public Policy at Common Law

(a)   RESTRAINT OF TRADE

J.G. COLLINS INS. AGENCIES LTD. v. ELSLEY

[1978] 2 S.C.R. 916

DICKSON J. [delivering the judgment of the court] The question for decision in this case is whether a restrictive covenant contained in a certain contract of employment, to which I will shortly refer, is valid.

The facts are, to all intents, undisputed. On April 24, 1956, an agreement was entered into for the purchase by the Collins company of the general insurance business of a competitor, D.C. Elsley Limited. The price was $46,137. The life insurance business and the real estate business conducted by the Elsley company were not included. The agreement contained a covenant on the part of the vendor that it would not, for a period of ten years, carry on or be engaged in the business of a general insurance agency within the City of Niagara Falls, the Township of Stamford and the Village of Chippewa, all in the County of Welland, and that the vendor would pay the purchaser $1,000 for each and every breach. The parties entered into a further agreement on May 1, 1956, whereby Elsley was employed as interim manager of the combined general insurance businesses, now owned by Collins, upon terms which included a restrictive covenant almost identical with that contained in the purchase agreement of April 24, 1956.

The interim management agreement was short-lived. It was replaced by an agreement of May 30, 1956, by which Elsley undertook to serve as manager of the Collins company's general insurance business in the greater Niagara Falls area, devoting all necessary time and attention to such employment, subject to the proviso that he might supervise the Elsley company in its real estate and life insurance business. The agreement commenced June 1, 1956, and was stated to continue in force from year to year until terminated by either party upon three months notice. As things developed, it continued until May, 1973.

Clause 3 of the management agreement contains the covenant which gave rise to the present proceedings. It reads:

> 3. Subject to the restrictive covenants contained in the Agreement made between the Parties dated May 1, 1956, in consideration of the employment, the Manager shall not, while in the employ of the Company or of its successors and assigns, whether in the capacity in which he is now or in any other capacity, or during the period of five years next after he shall, whether by reason of dismissal, retirement or otherwise, have ceased to be so employed, directly or indirectly, and whether as principal, agent, director of a company, traveller, servant or otherwise, carry on or be engaged or concerned or take part in the business of a general insurance agent within the corporate limits of the City of Niagara Falls, the Township of Stamford and the Village of Chippewa, all in the County of Welland; and in the event of his failing to observe or perform the said agreement, he shall pay to the said Company, its successors or assigns, or other the [sic] person or persons entitled for the time being to the benefit of the said agreement, the sum of One Thousand Dollars ($1,000.00) as and for liquidated damages, and the said Mrs. Elsley, wife of the Manager, by her signature hereto, agrees to observe and be bound by the aforesaid covenant.

The clause differs substantially from the restrictive covenant contained in each of the two earlier agreements. It is for a five-year period after cessation of the employment. It is made subject to the covenant contained in the sale agreement of May 1, 1956, for the purpose, no doubt, of assuring a minimum restrictive period of ten years and a maximum restrictive period of the term of employment plus five years. The sum of $1,000 was to become payable for failure on the part of Elsley to observe or perform the agreement. . . .

. . . Elsley managed the combined general insurance businesses for 17 years, from June 1, 1956, until May 31, 1973, at which time he gave proper notice of termination of employment. During the 17-year period Elsley dealt with the customers of the agency to the almost total exclusion of Collins. To them Elsley was the business, Collins little more than a name. Elsley met the customers, telephoned them frequently, placed their insurance policies and answered their queries. Such were the findings of the trial Judge. People became accustomed to doing business with him on a personal basis and he looked after their insurance needs. He served not only customers of the business he formerly owned, but also Collins' customers.

From 1956 to 1973 the business bore the name "Collins & Elsley Insurance Agencies". During that period, as a convenience, many policy-holders paid their premiums at the office of D.C. Elsley Limited, the real estate office of Elsley, because a large part of the business purchased by Collins from Elsley came from the area in which this office was located. As general manager of the combined businesses, Elsley, of course, had access to all policy-holder records; he was familiar with the nature and extent of coverage and the insurance assets, financial credit, likes and dislikes and idiosyncrasies of each customer, in a recurring and confidential relationship not unlike that of a lawyer/client or doctor/patient. It was only natural that policy-holders would follow him if he made a change.

I

Following termination of his employment with Collins, Elsley commenced his own general insurance business under D.C. Elsley Limited. He took with him two insurance salesmen and an insurance clerk formerly employed by the Collins and Elsley agency. A large number of former clients of the agency transferred their business. Exhibit 10 comprised a list of approximately two hundred former clients who had advised Collins they were transferring their insurance business to Elsley. The only factual dispute in the entire case is as to whether Elsley solicited the business of former clients. He denied having done so. Collins could not say that Elsley himself had solicited former clients, but said that Elsley's employees had done so. When asked as to how many former clients he had had dealings with after leaving the employ of Collins, Elsley replied that he had never "stopped to add them up". There is evidence he advertised for general insurance business and that some advertisements referred to him as being "formerly of Collins and Elsley Insurance Agencies". In the Ontario Court of Appeal, Mr. Justice Evans (with whom Mr. Justice MacKinnon agreed) found that Elsley had actively solicited former clients. Mr. Justice Jessup took a contrary view. Both Courts below considered Collins and Elsley to be successful businessmen, competent and experienced.

At trial, Mr. Justice Stark ordered Elsley restrained until January 1, 1978, from carrying on the business of general insurance agent within the defined area. He also directed a reference to the Local Master to assess the damages of Collins with respect to the business taken from him by Elsley from June 1, 1973, until the date of trial, subject to such damages being restricted to the loss of the agent's share of the premiums from contracts of insurance detailed in ex. 10, to which I have referred [18 C.P.R. (2d) 187].

The majority of the Court of Appeal affirmed the judgment at trial, with one variation [70 D.L.R. (3d) 513, 13 O.R. (2d) 177, 26 C.P.R. (2d) 170]. The Court directed that Collins be compensated for the loss of commission on *all* contracts of general insurance sold by Elsley from June 1, 1973, to the date of the injunction (not limited to the policies set out in ex. 10) after taking into account expenses incurred in securing and servicing the contracts. Mr. Justice Jessup dissented.

The point taken by Mr. Justice Jessup is central to the case. It is this. The restrictive covenant, it is contended, does not merely restrain the solicitation by Elsley of clients of the Collins & Elsley agency, it prevents Elsley engaging at all in the general insurance business in a large area and operates, therefore, to eliminate competition *per se* without regard for the public interest and beyond necessary protection of Collins' interest. The argument, in short, is that the covenant would have been valid if it had precluded Elsley from soliciting clients of his former employer but, drawn in more sweeping terms, it is unenforceable as being in restraint of trade and an interference with individual liberty of action. . . .

II

The principles to be applied in considering restrictive covenants of employment are well-established. They are found in . . . such familiar authorities as the *Nordenfelt* case, *Nordenfelt v. Maxim Nordenfelt Guns & Ammunition Co.*, [1894] A.C. 535. . . . A covenant in restraint of trade is enforceable only if it is reasonable between the parties and with reference to the public interest. As in many of the cases which come before the Courts, competing demands must be weighed. There is an important public interest in discouraging restraints on trade, and maintaining free and open competition unencumbered by the fetters of restrictive covenants. On the other hand, the Courts have been disinclined to restrict the right to contract, particularly when that right has been exercised by knowledgeable persons of equal bargaining power. In assessing the opposing interests the word one finds repeated throughout the cases is the word "reasonable". The test of reasonableness can be applied, however, only in the peculiar circumstances of the particular case. Circumstances are of infinite variety. Other cases may help in enunciating broad general principles but are otherwise of little assistance.

It is important, I think, to resist the inclination to lift a restrictive covenant out of an employment agreement and examine it in a disembodied manner, as if it were some strange scientific specimen under microscopic scrutiny. The validity, or otherwise, of a restrictive covenant can be determined only upon an overall assessment, of the clause, the agreement within which it is found, and all of the surrounding circumstances.

The distinction made in the cases between a restrictive covenant contained in an agreement for the sale of a business and one contained in a contract of employment is well-conceived and responsive to practical considerations. A person seeking to sell his business might find himself with an unsaleable commodity if denied the right to assure the purchaser that he, the vendor, would not later enter into competition. Difficulty lies in definition of the time during which, and the area within which, the non-competitive covenant is to operate, but if these are reasonable, the Courts will normally give effect to the covenant.

A different situation, at least in theory, obtains in the negotiation of a contract of employment where an imbalance of bargaining power may lead to oppression and a denial of the right of the employee to exploit, following termination of employment, in the public interest and in his own interest, knowledge and skills obtained during employment. Again, a distinction is made. Although blanket restraints on freedom to compete are generally held unenforceable, the Courts have recognized and afforded reasonable protection to trade secrets, confidential information, and trade connections of the employer.

The majority of the Court of Appeal considered the present case to be one which did not fit neatly into the category of either sale or employment, being inextricably bound together. . . . In a sense that is true, but I do not think the restrictive covenant of the employment agreement can be fed by the sale agreement. The covenant contained in the sale agreement expired, and its force exhausted, seven years before the restrictive covenant contained in the employment agreement came into operation. The employment agreement was negotiated subsequent to and independent of the sale agreement. The agreement sued upon is the employment agreement. It would be wrong, in my opinion, to test that agreement by the criteria applicable in the case of a vendor/purchaser agreement, or by some hybrid test. The restrictive covenant, if enforceable, must stand up to the more rigorous tests applied in an employer/employee context.

III

The critical question, as I have indicated, is whether the employer, in seeking to protect his trade connection, overreached in the formulation of cl. 3 of the agreement of May 30, 1956.

In assessing the reasonableness of the clause with reference to the interests of the parties, several questions must be asked. First, did Collins have a proprietary interest entitled to protection? The answer to this question must surely be in the affirmative. Shortly before the agreement for the employment of Elsley, Collins had paid Elsley some $46,000 for the general insurance trade connection of Elsley. By the agreement Elsley was placed in control, not only of that trade connection, but also the trade connection which Collins enjoyed prior to that time. Second, were the temporal or spatial features of the clause too broad? Some argument was directed to the Court as to those aspects, but I am in entire agreement with the Courts below that they are not open to successful challenge. The next and crucial question is whether the covenant is unenforceable as being against competition generally, and not limited to proscribing solicitation of clients of the former employer. In a conventional employer/employee situation the clause might well be held invalid for that reason. The fact that it could have been drafted in narrower terms would not have saved it, for as Viscount Haldane, L.C., said in *Mason v. Provident Clothing & Supply Co.* [[1913] A.C. 724], p. 732: ". . . the question is not whether they could have made a valid agreement, but whether the agreement actually made was valid". Whether a restriction is reasonably required for the protection of the covenantee can only be decided by considering the nature of the covenantee's business and the nature and character of the employment. Admittedly, an employer could not have a proprietary interest in people who were not actual or potential customers. Nevertheless, in exceptional cases, of which I think this is one, the nature of the employment may justify a covenant prohibiting an employee not only from soliciting customers, but also from establishing his own business or working for others so as to be likely to appropriate the employer's trade connection through his acquaintance with the employer's customers. This may indeed be the only effective covenant to protect the proprietary interest of the employer. A simple non-solicitation clause would not suffice.

There are cases which uphold the validity of a covenant prohibiting an employee from engaging in a particular type of work within a specified area, and for an acceptable period of time after the termination of his employment: see, e.g., *Fitch v. Dewes*, [1921] 2 A.C. 158; *Marion White Ltd. v. Francis*, [1972] 1 W.L.R. 1423; *P.C.O. Services Ltd. v. Rumleski* (1963), 38 D.L.R. (2d) 390; *Campbell, Imrie and Shankland v. Park*, [1954] 2 D.L.R. 170. In each of these cases the employee was in a position where he acquired a close personal acquaintance with the clients or customers of the business. Such a restrictive covenant was reasonable, in the words of Lord Birkenhead, L.C., in *Fitch v. Dewes* at p. 165, in order that the employee "should not be in a position to use the intimacies and knowledge which he had acquired in the course of his employment in order to create a practice of his own in that same place and by doing so undermine the business and the connection of the [employer]". In the present case, when the clause was drafted it was known that Elsley had, or would acquire, a special and intimate knowledge of the customers of his prospective employer and the means of influence over them.

In the leading case of *Herbert Morris, Ltd. v. Saxelby*, [[1916] 1 A.C. 688], Lord Parker enunciated with clarity the circumstances in which a covenant taken by an employer from an employee or apprentice will be enforceable. He said, p. 709:

> Wherever such covenants have been upheld it has been on the ground, not that the servant or apprentice would, by reason of his employment or training, obtain the skill and knowledge necessary to equip him as a possible competitor in the trade, but that he might obtain such personal knowledge of and influence over the customers of his employer, or such an acquaintance with his employer's trade secrets as would enable him, if competition were allowed, to take advantage of his employer's trade connection or utilize information confidentially obtained.

It is difficult to envisage a factual situation in which an employee would be in a better position than that of Elsley in the present case to obtain "personal knowledge of and influence over the customers of his employer". Later in his speech, Lord Parker made the point that it is of importance: whether "the defendant ever came into personal contact with the plaintiffs' customers". The same point is made in the following passage from Cheshire & Fifoot, *The Law of Contract*, 8th ed., p. 369:

> A restraint is not valid unless the nature of employment is such that customers will either learn to rely upon the skill or judgment of the servant or will deal with him directly and personally to the virtual exclusion of the master, with the result that he will probably gain their custom if he sets up business on his own account.

In the view which I take of this case a covenant against non-solicitation would not have been adequate to protect the proprietary interest entitled to protection. Exhibit 10 is telling support of that view. Elsley testified that he did not solicit former clients; notwithstanding, two hundred clients switched their custom to him. That is a vivid illustration of what Lord Parker had in mind in speaking of the influence of an employee over the customers of his employer. And it is not suggested that Exhibit 10 was a complete list of all those who took action. It was filed as representative only. Collins estimated that Elsley had taken close to one-half of the business on the books when Elsley left. As Salter, J., said in the case of *Putsman v. Taylor*, [1927] 1 K.B. 637 at p. 642, a covenant against solicitation "is difficult to enforce; it is difficult to show breach and difficult to frame an injunction". The difficulty is demonstrated in this case. Does an advertisement which comes to the attention of former clients amount to solicitation? Was there solicitation by Elsley? I need not attempt to answer those questions. The point is that a non-solicitation covenant, in the circumstances here found, would have been meaningless.

Mr. Justice Jessup suggested in his reasons that a simple provision in a non-solicitation agreement would have enabled the plaintiff to examine the defendant's books and records from time to time so that solicitation of clients acquired by the plaintiff could be detected. I do not think any experienced businessman would consent to examination of his books by a competitor, whether a former employer or not. I doubt that clients of the defendant would welcome such intrusion upon their confidential affairs, or permit it if it came to their attention. If the defendant were hired by someone rather than being self-employed, by what right could he open the books of his employer to examination by a former employer? In short, I cannot accept the efficacy of the simple provision Mr. Justice Jessup envisages.

For the foregoing reasons, in my view the impugned covenant is no wider than reasonably required in order to afford adequate protection to Collins.

After the party relying on a restrictive covenant has established its reasonableness as between the parties, the onus of proving that it is contrary to the public interest lies on the party attacking it: *Herbert Morris Ltd. v. Saxelby, supra*. Since in my opinion the respondent has established what is required by him, the matter of the public interest must now be considered.

Unless it can be said that any and every restraint upon competition is bad, I do not think that enforcement of the clause could be considered inimical to the public interest. There were twenty to twenty-two general agents in Niagara Falls according to the evidence as of the date of trial, employing eighty to ninety employees. There was nothing to suggest that the people of Niagara Falls would suffer through the loss, for a limited period, of the services of Elsley in the general insurance business.

I am of opinion that the clause in contention is valid, and enforceable in accordance with its terms. . . .

[Collins had initially obtained an injunction in this action. It ceased to have effect when Elsley died. The portion of the judgment dealing with damages can be found, *infra*, Chapter 14, section 3(e). Appeal dismissed.]

QUESTION

The leading English authority, cited in most Canadian cases, including *J.G. Collins Ins. Agencies Ltd. v. Elsley*, is *Nordenfelt v. Maxim Nordenfelt Guns & Ammunition Co.*, [1894] A.C. 535 (H.L.). The case involved a covenant which restricted the appellant's ability to trade in weapons and ammunition. The House of Lords found the clause to be enforceable. However, the reasoning reveals the absence of any common law head of public policy with respect to trade in weapons. The freedom to so trade was treated like the freedom to trade in other commodities. Consider what heads of public policy you would like to introduce. With respect to *Nordenfelt*, for instance, consideration is currently being given to the use of tort principles to promote responsibility by gun manufacturers. See Eggen and Culhane, "Gun Torts: Defining a Cause of Action for Victims in Suits Against Gun Manufacturers" (2002), 81 North Carolina L.R. 115. For an examination of existing and proposed multinational treaties on the arms trade and the policy reasons for regulating it, see Stoel, "Codes of Conduct on Arms Transfers—The Movement Toward a Multilateral Approach" (2000), 31 Law and Policy in International Business 1285.

TREBILCOCK, THE COMMON LAW OF RESTRAINT OF TRADE

(1986), at 106-119

4.   THE APPLICATION OF THE SECOND BRANCH OF THE NORDENFELT TEST ("THE PUBLIC INTEREST")

In this section the law pertaining to the second or "public interest" branch of the *Nordenfelt* test in the modern era is examined. Very few post-employment covenants have been struck down under this branch and in very few other cases has the second branch been paid serious attention. There are some obvious reasons for this. First, the first branch of the test captures elements of the public interest in seeking to balance the protection of proprietary interests of the employer against the right of the employee (and the community) to continued utilization of his personal skills and to be free of restraints on competition *per se*. Second, to the extent that there is a larger public interest, not captured by the first branch, in avoiding contractual arrangements that reduce consumer welfare by undermining the competitive health of the market in question, however much they may be in the best interests of the contracting parties, this interest will rarely be violated in most standard employment settings where the exclusion of one employee from the market is unlikely to have any significant impact on the number of competitors in that market.

. . . In this context, employment and partnership cases are dealt with together because similar public interest issues are at stake, although typically concerns over inequality of bargaining power between the contracting parties are much less prominent in partnership cases than employment cases. Apart from the medical and analogous professional cases, the sale of an interest in a partnership on dissolution has generally been treated as tantamount to the sale of business goodwill and similar considerations apply to the validity of post-sale restraints.

. . . . .

(b)   THE MEDICAL SERVICES CASES

The cases discussed in this section go beyond the conventional elements of the public interest considered by the doctrine [relating to concern about monopolies]. Most of them involve professional partnerships, and the sorts of ancillary restrictive covenants that have been associated with them for centuries.

They expand the scope of the public interest, and so the second branch of the *Nordenfelt* test, by identifying a public smaller than the general public of professional service consumers as the one whose interests are harmed by the restrictive covenant. This "smaller" public has been defined in two quite distinct ways.

The first line of analysis looks to the availability of adequate quantities of good quality services at reasonable prices from the standpoint of all of the *potential* customers of such services in those areas in which there is judged to be an inadequate supply of such professional services. In these cases, "inadequate" is defined in terms of what are considered to be acceptable levels of service in a particular regional or local market.

The second line of analysis assesses the costs and benefits of the restraint from the standpoint of the *actual* consumers of the services of the particular professional restrained by the restrictive covenant, an even smaller "public" than in the first line of analysis. The interest harmed here is not the adequacy of services, understood as fungible commodities, but rather the privacy and trust of the patients or clients of the restrained party. Dodd ["Contracts Not to Practise Medicine" (1943), 23 B.U.L.R. 305] long ago argued

> the interest of the public in having the seller free to continue his activities is much greater in the case of doctors than of growers. So much of medicine is a matter of understanding the individual patient's physical, mental and moral characteristics rather than professional skill in the abstract that there is a very real loss to the patients of an experienced physician when he retires from practice, even where he sells his practice to one of equal ability.

The particularly personal quality of good medical service, combined with the fact that the service in question pertains to the very fundamental goods of human health and life, make medical partnership cases the leading edge of the tendency to expand the parameters of the "public interest". But the same sort of argument could be applied, albeit perhaps with less force, to legal, accounting, and other sorts of services that require the customer to repose considerable confidential information and trust in the hands of another.

The discussion of recent cases in this context will be divided in terms of the two types of novel definition of the public interest that have been identified. The first type may be called the "regional deprivation" cases, and the second the "patient-client confidentiality" cases.

(i) The "regional deprivation" cases

These cases raise two fundamental questions: (1) if a restrictive covenant in no way reduces the supply or quality of services available to the nation's consumers of those services, considered as a whole, can it still have that effect in certain cities, areas, or regions; and (2) if so, should the restraints be considered unreasonable because they harm this more local public interest?

Despite the ubiquitous, and often very significant, character of regional disparities, this basis for argument was rarely invoked twenty years ago. Since then, it has been invoked with increasing frequency, particularly in the United States, but with little success to date. There are two reasons for the lack of success: first, some courts hold that they are not able to consider novel forms of public interest, and so they refuse to inquire into the empirical claims of regional shortages at all. Second, other courts allow that they may consider the consequences of a restraint for the public affected, but then assert that they can answer this question by the application of *a priori* assumptions. Some recent U.S. decisions illustrate these tendencies.

In *Long v. Huffman* [557 S.W. (2d) 911 (C.A., 1977)] a physician agreed not to practise medicine within a sixty-mile radius of the city in which he had been engaged in a medical partnership, for a period of five years. The Missouri Court of Appeal held that the physician had offered no evidence of a need for more doctors in that city and that the record indicated no such shortage. The court went on, however, to cite with approval the ratio of another case, which held that "the shortage of medical practitioners was pandemic", so that a physician's services were as valuable in one locale as in another.

In *Canfield v. Spear* [254 N.E. (2d) 433 at 435 (Ill. S.C., 1969)], in which a medical partner agreed not to practice within a twenty-five-mile radius of Dockford for a period of three years following the termination of his partnership, Justice House of the Illinois Supreme Court held that

> [i]t cannot be said that the public interest is adversely affected if a physician decides to move from one community to another, nor does it become so if the move results from some agreement made in advance. If a severe shortage exists in any particular place young doctors will tend to move there, thus alleviating the shortage.

In *Field Surgical Associates Ltd. v. Shadab* [376 N.E. (2d) 660 at 664 (Ill. App. I Dist., 1978)], a five-mile, five-year restraint ancillary to a medical partnership agreement was held to entail no injury to the public interest:

> A restraint such as the present one is certainly not injurious to the public at large. Defendant can be equally useful to the public interest by practising his medical specialty in some location other than the prohibited area since the health of individuals living elsewhere in this state is just as important.

In *Marshall v. Irby* [158 S.W. (2d) 693 (Ark. S.C., 1942)] the Supreme Court of Arkansas considered such factors, though it is not clear whether they were decisive. The court found a restrictive covenant, ancillary to a partnership agreement between two dentists, preventing the promisor from practising dentistry within the city in which the partnership was located, for a period of five years, to be void and unenforceable. The court held that the restraint was wider than reasonably necessary to protect the promisee's legitimate interests, but the reason why his interests in his customer connections were not taken to have been harmed was that "the population tributary to Rogers is about ten thousand, and there is only one other dentist practicing that profession in that city, and that there is as much or more dental work than all three dentists can reasonably perform."

More recently, the majority of the Supreme Court of New Jersey explicitly upheld the regional shortage analysis under the public interest branch as the ground for holding a restrictive covenant ancillary to a medical partnership agreement unenforceable. In *Karlin v. Weinberg*, the defendant had signed an agreement by which he was bound not to practise dermatology within a ten-mile radius of the partners' New Jersey office address for a period of five years. The trial judge held that post-employment restraints, when applied to physicians, were *per se* void, but the appellate division reversed that judgment. The Supreme Court affirmed the decision of the appellate court, but the majority also noted that the trial court should consider the effect that enforcement of the covenant would have on the public interest. Significant here is the demand for the services rendered by the employer and the likelihood that those services could be provided by other physicians already practising in the area. If the enforcement of the covenant would result in a shortage of physicians in the area in question, then the court must determine whether this shortage would be alleviated by new physicians establishing practices in the area. [390 A. (2d) 1161 (S.C.N.J., 1978)]

The majority test in *Karlin v. Weinberg* thus affirms the importance of local or regional shortages as an aspect of the public interest reasonableness test. Moreover, it proposed that the means of assessing this dimension of the test is a careful consideration of the factual evidence, rather than recourse to the *a priori* tests advanced by the courts in some of the earlier cases. It appears, then, that the American courts are in a state of some ambivalence on this issue. [While it may] be correct . . . that *Karlin* "is in a distinct minority" on the subject of the public interest test, it may well be that it points to new tendencies in the law.

These issues arose in the Canadian case of *Sherk v. Horwitz* [[1972] 2 O.R. 451 (H.C.), affirmed on other grounds [1973] 1 O.R. 360 (C.A.), leave to appeal refused (1972), 9 C.P.R. (2d) 119n (S.C.C.)]. In that case, the defendant, an obstetrician, agreed to work at a medical clinic in St. Catharines run by eight other physicians. He was to get 60 per cent of his billings and a minimum of $12,000 per annum. Ancillary to the agreement—which could perhaps be described as either an employment or a partnership agreement—was a restrictive covenant to the effect that the defendant would not carry on the practice of any form of medicine or surgery within five miles of St. Catharines' city limits for a period of five years following the termination of the agreement.

The trial judge, Donahue J., explicitly considered whether any public interest more narrowly defined than the public interest "as a whole" ought to be considered in applying the second branch of the doctrine. Donohue J. cited the analysis of Professor Winfeld in support of such consideration: "the interests of the whole public must be taken into account; but it leads in practice to the paradox that in many cases what seems to be in contemplation is the interest of one section only of the public, and a small section at that." Donohue J. found on the evidence of two St. Catharines obstetricians that "there is a definite shortage of obstetricians in St. Catharines; that a proper proportion would be one obstetrician for 10,000 of population and St. Catharines has only seven for a population of 130,000." Donahue J. relied upon the testimony of the former chief of obstetrics at the St. Catharines General Hospital for this "proper proportion" estimate. Donahue J. therefore found the restrictive covenant unreasonable as against the public interest. The Ontario Court of Appeal upheld his decision, but on other grounds.

In a recent Alberta decision, *Baker v. Lintott*, the trial court [(1981), 54 C.P.R. (2d) 200 (Q.B.)] adopted a similar view to Donahue J., holding a restrictive covenant entered into by a member of a medical clinic in the small community of Medicine Hat to be unenforceable as contrary to the public interest. The court held that if the covenant were to be enforced, patients would only have a choice of five family practitioners (treating the clinic as one) and that this tended to a monopoly on the part of the clinic. The trial court also noted that restrictive covenants had been disapproved in a 1950 resolution of the College of Physicians and Surgeons of Alberta. On appeal, the Alberta Court of Appeal [(1982), 70 C.P.R. (2d) 107 (C.A.)] reversed the trial court's decisions, holding that patients enjoyed "sufficient choice".

Adequacy of consumer choice was also treated as a relevant issue in a recent case involving a restrictive covenant ancillary to an employment contract, which was in turn ancillary to a sale of business agreement. In *J.G. Collins Insurance Agencies Ltd. v. Elsley* [*supra*], Dickson J. (as he then was), for the Supreme Court of Canada, implied that regional shortages were a relevant consideration in determining reasonableness in the public interest. . . .

As this was the only factor considered under the heading of the second branch of the reasonableness test in this case, we may infer that Dickson J. and the Supreme Court of Canada considered this to be the dominant consideration in that respect. . . .

A rather less sympathetic view of regional availability considerations was taken by Evershed J. at first instance in *Routh v. Jones* [[1947] 1 All E.R. 179, at 182 affirmed [1947] 1 All E.R. 758 (C.A.)], involving a post-employment restraint on a doctor:

> In considering the efficacy of a covenant such as is here in question, it is true that not only the proper interest of the covenantor, and the covenantee but also the proper interest of the public must be considered. But it is also, in my judgment, true that, if the covenant in question is shown to conform to the proper interests of the covenantor and the covenantee in the light of the general formulation of the law which I have above attempted, then the public interest would equally be served. I say this because in the present case the defendant's evidence was, in fact, directed to showing that there was a dearth of doctors in and around Okehampton, and it was argued that that fact ought at least to have a bearing on the question whether the defendant's covenant should be enforced. In my judgment there is no substance in this argument. If it be true that the inhabitants of this region should have more doctors, it does not follow that they should have the defendant as one of them. If the public interest is invoked, it must not be forgotten that it is very much in the public interest that contracts should be honoured.

(ii) *"Patient/client confidentiality" cases*

The first case of this type to be decided on public interest grounds appears to have been *Green v. Stanton* [(1969), 3 D.L.R. (3d) 358], in which Wooton J. of the B.C. Supreme Court held that the interests of a physician's patients should be taken into account in determining whether a restriction against practising within a ten-mile radius of the office of the physician's former medical partnership was unreasonable as against the public interest. Wooton J. found the restraint unreasonable on this basis. His decision was overturned, however, by the British Columbia Court of Appeal [(1969), 6 D.L.R. (3d) 680]. This reversal caused a political furore in British Columbia, resulting in an amendment by the provincial Legislature to section 94 [now s.100] of the Medical Practitioners Act expressly forbidding the enforcement of restrictive covenants pertaining to members of the medical profession.

Sherk v. Horwitz raised the same issue in the province of Ontario. As noted above, the trial judge considered regional scarcity in his assessment of reasonableness in the public interest. But he also gave a second ground for finding the restrictive covenant unreasonable as contrary to the interests of the public. Donahue J. said

> I do not think that these people [the defendant's patients] should be deprived of his services as they would be bound to be if he were obliged to stay five miles beyond the limits of the City of St. Catharines until 1976. In my view, no answer is to be found in saying that these people, who were formerly treated by the defendant, can easily find another specialist. Choosing a physician or surgeon is not akin to commercial transactions.

Donahue J. did not elaborate on precisely what he considered the difference between the provision of medical services and ordinary commercial transactions to be. He did, however, note that the purpose of the Health Services Insurance Act, passed in 1967, was "to provide the widest medical care for the residents of the Province," and he argued that this implied that "the public are entitled to the widest choice in the selection of their medical practitioners." And he went on to argue that a May 1971 resolution of the Council of the Ontario Medical Association was also relevant to the definition of the public interest in this case. That resolution stated: "RESOLVED that the Ontario Medical Association disapproves the concept of restrictive covenants in the contracts of one physician with another." The Ontario Court of Appeal, without stating whether or not it approved of the two public interest tests employed by the trial judge, dismissed the appeal on a technical issue, and the Supreme Court of Canada refused leave to appeal.

In *Karlin v. Weinberg*, as we saw above, the majority considered that local or regional shortages should be examined by the courts in determining the public interest. The majority then indicated a second element of the public interest test when it noted that the trial court must also examine

> the degree to which enforcement to the covenant would foreclose resort to the services of the "departing" physician by those of his patients who might otherwise desire to seek him out at his new location. If the geographical dimensions of the covenant make it impossible, as a practical matter, for existing patients to continue treatment, then the trial court should consider the advisability of restricting the covenant's geographical scope in light of the number of patients who would be so restricted.

Thus, even the relatively cautious majority decision acknowledged the independent importance of the interests of the actual customers or patients of the promisee, though they were unwilling to go as far as Donahue J. in *Sherk*. The minority, however, took a similar position to that of Donohue J., finding that restrictive covenants in agreements between medical doctors are *per se* invalid as against public policy. Indeed, they might be understood as attempting to supply the sort of rationale that Donahue J. merely alluded to.

Sullivan J., for the minority, sought to ground this position in an analysis of the right to privacy:

> The art of healing the sick and the infirm is affected with a public interest. The restrictive covenant, which the Court is upholding in principle, does violence to the concept of the physician-patient relationship. A person requiring medical treatment and advice goes to the doctor of his or her choice. This is an important consideration because confidence in the doctor, although intangible, is a significant factor in providing effective medical care. Often, diagnosis and treatment require disclosure by the patient of personal and confidential information to the doctor, as well as thorough familiarity with the patient's past medical history. . . .

> The relationship is so personal and so sensitive, and the right of a patient to consult the physician of one's own choice so fundamental, that a restrictive covenant which substantially intrudes on that relationship and interferes with that fundamental right should be held to be contrary to public policy. This benefit does not exist for the benefit of the physician consulted, but rather to protect the patient's right to seek medical treatment from the doctor whom the patient believes is best able to treat him.

In this, the minority followed the majority decision in *Dwyer v. Jung* [336 A. (2d) 498 (N.J. Ch. Div., 1975)], a case in which three lawyers entered into a partnership agreement which included a restrictive covenant providing that upon termination all partners would be restricted from doing business with the clients designated as belonging to another partner for a period of five years. Upon dissolution of the partnership, the plaintiffs had demanded an accounting from the defendant, who then counterclaimed, arguing that the plaintiffs had breached the restrictive covenant. The trial court held that the restrictive covenant was unenforceable as a matter of law, and therefore unreasonable *per se*, because it would violate provision DR2-108(a) of the Disciplinary Rules of the Code of Professional Responsibility of the American Bar Association which specified that

> [a] lawyer shall not be a party to or participate in a partnership or employment agreement with another lawyer that restricts the right of a lawyer to practise law after the termination of a relationship created by the agreement except as may be provided in a *bona fide* retirement plan and then only to the extent reasonably necessary to protect the plan.

Beyond this argument, the court also advanced an argument against enforcement based on the character of lawyer-client relations which was parallel to that advanced by the minority in *Karlin*. The Court held that

> [c]ommercial standards may not be used to evaluate the reasonableness of lawyer restrictive covenants. Strong public policy considerations preclude their applicability. In that sense lawyer restrictions are injurious to the public interest. A client is always entitled to be represented by counsel of his own choosing. . . . The attorney-client relationship is consensual, highly fiduciary on the part of counsel, and he may do nothing which restricts the right of the client to repose confidence in any counsel of his choice. No concept of the practice of law is more deeply rooted.

The majority in *Karlin* endorsed the "sound holding" in *Dwyer*, but went on to distinguish *Karlin* on two grounds. First, it was argued that the restraint in *Dwyer* prevented the lawyers from having any professional dealings with former clients for the specified period, while the restraint in *Karlin* permitted the continuation of doctor-patient relationships provided that the patients were willing to travel the distance to the doctor's new location as specified in the covenant. Second, it was argued that the Constitution gave the courts a unique responsibility for regulating the conduct of attorneys, for which no parallel existed in the case of physicians. The minority, however, argued that there was no "essential difference in principle" between the two cases: both relationships are consensual, highly fiduciary and peculiarly dependent on the patient's or client's trust and confidence in the physician consulted or attorney retained. It should perhaps be noted that between 1976 and 1978, two bills were introduced (though neither had passed at the date of trial) in the New Jersey Assembly which would render restrictive covenants between physicians void and unenforceable.

In contrast to these decisions, patient/client confidentiality concerns have been rejected in some recent decisions concerning both doctors and lawyers. In *Orton v. Melman* [[1981] 1 N.S.W.L.R. 583 at 588 (S.C.)], involving the dissolution of a medical partnership, where a non-competition covenant applied to the outgoing partner, McLelland J. stated that "I do not accept that . . . any independent ground of injury to the public interest based on patients' freedom of choice of doctors has been made out." A year later, McLelland J. took the same position in *Sharah v. Heale* [[1982] 2 N.S.W.L.R. 223 (S.C.)], a case involving a non-competition covenant, operative on dissolution, in a partnership agreement among lawyers. He rejected the view expressed by Lord Denning in *Oswald Dickson Collier & Co. v. Carter-Ruck* [[1984] 2 All E.R. 15 at 18 (C.A.)] that "as the relationship between a solicitor and client is a fiduciary relationship, it would be contrary to public policy that he should be precluded from acting for a client when that client wanted him to act for him". McLelland J. said

> [t]he stated reason for the public policy rule enunciated in *Oswald Hickson Collier & Co. V. Carter-Ruck* is that there is a fiduciary relationship between a solicitor and his client. This is indeed a curious reason, since it is often the position of confidence or influence giving rise to the fiduciary character of the relationship which a solicitor or other professional has with clients of the relevant business that justifies a contractual restraint to protect the legitimate interests of those interested in the goodwill of the business. Does the rule apply, one might ask, to all who may stand in a fiduciary relationship to their clients and in respect of all kinds of relationships recognized as fiduciary for various purposes in law? . . . What of such persons as estate agents or other kinds of agents who are in a fiduciary relationship with their clients?

The Privy Council, in . . . *Deacons v. Bridge* [[1984] 2 All E.R. 19 at 25], involving a non-competition clause operative on resignation from a partnership of lawyers, also rejected Lord Denning's view in *Oswald Dickson Collier & Co. v. Carter-Ruck*, stating

> there is a clear public interest in facilitating the assumption by established solicitors' firms of younger men as partners. It benefits clients by tending to secure continuity in the practice. It also tends to encourage the entry of younger men into the profession. . . . [T]he continuing partners in the plaintiff firm would only feel able to take on new capital partners if they knew that in so doing they would not run the risk that the new partners would acquire a connection with clients of the firm and then depart with that part of the plaintiff's goodwill. Conversely, the new capital partners in the plaintiff firm are required to purchase their share of its goodwill, but they could not reasonably be expected to do that if a retiring partner could freely remove part of the goodwill.

To conclude, while far from unanimously endorsed, some recent Canadian and American cases suggest an increasing recognition of certain interests of the public which are: (a) narrower than the interests of the general public; and (b) derived from principles other than the economic development and equity principles which have conventionally determined the content of the restraint of trade doctrine as a whole, and of the public interest branch of the *Nordenfelt* reasonableness test in particular.

[Footnotes omitted.]

NOTES and QUESTIONS

1. Draupadi qualified as a doctor in India before emigrating to Canada. Five years ago she successfully applied to join a Medical Clinic in Smalltown, in Alberta, where there is no legislation affecting the common law on restraint of trade in medical clinic services contracts. At first she was an employee and then became a partner. The partnership agreement contained the following clause.

> In the event of any Member leaving the Partnership for whatever reason, that Member shall not directly or indirectly practise medicine and/or surgery in any capacity within the limits of Smalltown, or within a radius of 50 kilometres of Smalltown, or within Alberta for a period of two (2) years.

There were difficulties in the partnership and about a year ago, Draupadi agreed to leave. Her departure was amicable, but since then she has begun to practise on her own, within the 50 kilometre radius of Smalltown. Her practice has been quite successful, for a number of reasons. She is willing to perform abortions, which only one other doctor in the area is willing to do. She travels to First Nations communities both inside and outside the radius. Quite a large number of her patients are immigrant women. She stresses the need for a healthy life-style rather than the prescription of drugs. Her success has occurred in spite of the fact that, due to economic decline in what is a beautiful place, there is currently an over-supply of doctors in Smalltown.

Can the Clinic enforce the restraint clause?

2. For cases which could be seen as having a narrower focus, than that described by Trebilcock, on the doctor-patient relationship as an economic commodity, see *Micropublishing Services Canada Ltd. v. Lee*, [1998] O.J. No. 5620 (Gen. Div.) and *Simoni v. Sugarman* (2000), 5 C.P.R. (4th) 221 (Nfld. T.D.).

3. Issues can arise on whether restraint of trade clauses have survived termination of employment. D was employed by W as a designer and fabric cutter of its inflatable cold air advertising balloons. W and a competitor, located in the same city, were the only manufacturers of such balloons in Canada. The employment contract contained the following clause:

"NON COMPETITION & NON SOLICITATION

> 3.01 The Employee expressly covenants and agrees with [W] that the Employee will not, for a period of three (3) years from the date of termination of the Employee's contract with [W], directly or indirectly, solicit, interfere with or endeavor to direct or entice away from [W] any customer or client of [W], or any other person, firm or corporation that has contacted [W], anyone that has had preliminary meetings or has been identified as a potential customer of [W] prior to termination of the Employee's contract with [W].

> 3.02 The Employee expressly covenants and agrees with [W] that the Employee will not, directly or indirectly, for a period of three (3) years from the date of termination of the Employee's contract with [W], act as an consultant, employee, or any other similar role in the sale or production of cold air inflatable advertising systems or any other products offered by [W] across North America.

> 3.03 In the event that any of the above provisions regarding geographical restrictions or duration of time shall be deemed unreasonable or invalid by a court of competent jurisdiction, then the geographical area or duration of time shall be reduced to that area or term the court so determines to be reasonable.

> 3.04 The Employee acknowledges that the foregoing covenants are fair and reasonable in the circumstances and are necessary to protect [W]'s business and economic position in the industry."

W fired D, and then sought an interlocutory injunction, to restrain D from working for a competitor. Do you consider the above clauses to be reasonable? Would they be enforceable if D were dismissed with cause (as argued by W), or wrongfully dismissed, (as argued by D)? You may wish to consider whether the court should grant an interlocutory injunction, discussed in Chapter 14,

4(e), where the issue of just cause has not yet been determined. See *Windship Aviation Ltd. v. deMeulles* (2002), 5 Alta. L.R. (4th) 133 (Q.B.).

4. When drafting contracts it is important to consider in what ways the agreement may be drafted to meet all of the parties' requirements and ensure enforceability. In England, one of the responses by British employers to the unenforceability of restrictive covenants in employment contracts has been the creation of a "garden leave clause". Rather than drafting a clause that simply prevents the employee from working for a competitor, the garden leave clause operates to extend the notice period. The clause requires that the employee provide the employer with an extended period of notice of intent to terminate the employment contract. During the extended notice period the employee is paid but cannot be compelled to work. Thus, the employee is not unreasonably restrained from making a living and the employer is afforded reasonable protection because the employee is still technically an employee and thus cannot work for the competition or cause harm to the employer. Whether similar clauses will catch on and have the same effect in Canada remains to be seen. See Buckley, *Illegality and Public Policy* (2002), at 175 and Lembrich, "Garden Leave: A Possible Solution To The Uncertain Enforceability Of Restrictive Employment Covenants" (2002), 102 Columbia L.R. 2291.

5. A category of restraint of trade cases involves what are often referred to as "solus" agreements between oil companies and gas stations. Such contracts are an example of a broader category of exclusive purchasing agreements in which one party promises to buy all his or her requirements of a certain commodity from the other party. Conversely, exclusive selling contracts involve one party promising to sell all his or her output (*e.g.*, of milk, to a co-operative) to the other party. Such contracts seem to come under the rubric of the doctrine of restraint of trade, although there is no clear answer to the question of which contracts are subject to scrutiny and which are not. In *Esso Petroleum Ltd. v. Harper's Garage (Stourport) Ltd.*, [1967] 1 All E.R. 699 at 714 (H.L.), Lord Morris stated that "[a] workable rule identifying the limits of the doctrine has remained elusive." The test suggested in *Esso* was whether the promise was to give up an existing freedom. Lord Morris went on to say that there is a "clear difference between the case where someone fetters his future by parting with a freedom which he possesses, and the case where someone seeks to claim a greater freedom than that which he possesses". While Trebilcock, *The Common Law of Restraint of Trade*, *supra*, at 309-321, criticizes as "arid legal formalism" the view that the doctrine only applies to the surrender of an existing freedom, support can be found in *Hiebert v. Pacific Petroleums Ltd.* (1980), 109 D.L.R. (3d) 137 (Man. Q.B.). Here the court drew a distinction between acceptance of restraint on property already owned and the acquisition of property subject to a restraint. In the former case, where the owner of a service station agreed to purchase oil products exclusively from an oil company, 5 years rather than 10 was considered reasonable. For an examination of solus agreements in Canada, see also *Stephens v. Gulf Oil Canada Ltd.* (1975), 65 D.L.R. (3d) 193 (Ont. C.A.).

6. There is some overlap between the doctrine of restraint of trade and the doctrine of unconscionability. See the note on *Schroeder Music Publishing Co. v. Macaulay*, *supra*, Chapter 12, section 4(b), note 2 following *Lloyds Bank v. Bundy* and the discussion in Chapter 8, section 3(b).

7. Shopping centre leases have generated considerable restraint of trade litigation. The problem revolves around attempts to limit the number of competitive stores in one shopping centre. For examples, see the following Canadian cases: *F.W. Woolworth Co. v. Hudson's Bay Co.* (1985), 61 N.B.R. (2d) 403 (C.A.); *Kelly, Douglas & Co. v. Marathon Realty Co.* (1985), 6 C.P.R. (3d) 130 (B.C. S.C.); *Bates v. Korn* (1986), 41 Man. R. (2d) 227 (Q.B.). The question has arisen as to whether restraint of trade doctrine applies at all. In *Woolworth*, the landlord had promised Woolco not to lease space to another junior department store. The court held, referring to the need for a proper mix of stores and the absence of inequality of bargaining power, that the clause did not fall in the category of restraint of trade. Reference was made to the test in *Esso*, but it would seem that here the landlord *was* giving up an existing freedom. See generally Shapiro, "Exclusive Rights Clauses in Shopping Centre Leases" (1986), 24 Alta. L.R. 510.

(b) OTHER PUBLIC POLICIES

Without attempting to catalogue all statutory and common law public poli-cies, it is possible to provide a taste of a range of policies, affecting many aspects of our lives about which we may wish to contract. Turning first to the common law, contracts dealing with sexuality illustrate the evolving nature of the law in this area.

What Hugh Collins, in *The Law of Contract*, 4th ed. (2003), at 54, refers to as a "residual moralistic power" to deny enforcement of contracts on the basis of immorality, "lies in wait for the courts to set the limits of the sphere of contracts." With respect to sexual matters in particular, an examination of the 19th century cases reveals some ambivalence about contracts relating to sexuality as well as traces of a paternalistic sensitivity to the vulnerability of women.

On the one hand, *Benyon v. Nettlefold* (1830), 3 Mac. & G. 94, 42 E.R. 196, illustrates the antagonism to commitments for which the real consideration was "prospective illicit cohabitation". On the other, in *Nye v. Mosely* (1826), 6 B. & C. 133, 108 E.R. 402, an annuity promised by John Mosely to his servant Sylvia Nye, for past cohabitation, was enforced. Her counsel had argued that the promise should be enforced as reparation for injury done (an injury that resembles sexual harassment to modern eyes). In *Ayerst v. Jenkins* (1873), L.R. 16 Eq. 275, the Lord Chancellor similarly refused to set aside a settlement where the cohabitation was past. The most famous case is probably *Pearce v. Brooks* (1866), L.R. 1 Ex. 213, in which the plaintiffs unsuccessfully sued for the cost of hire of a carriage to be used for purposes of prostitution. A similar Canadian case is *Dominion Fire Ins. v. Nakata* (1915), 26 D.L.R. 722 (S.C.C.), in which a policy of insurance on a brothel was held to be unenforceable.

There are few modern Canadian cases to reveal the judicial perspective on sexuality. The traditional view was reasserted in *Prokop v. Kohut* (1965), 54 D.L.R. (2d) 717 (B.C. S.C.), where the plaintiff and testator had lived together for 16 years. The plaintiff claimed a share in the estate on the basis of a contract consisting of a commitment to live together as a married couple in exchange for a half interest in the estate. The court simply stated, at 721, that any such contract would be "void as having been made for an illegal consideration and the plaintiff can recover nothing under it". A similar response can be found in the case of *Farrar v. MacPhee* (1970), 13 D.L.R. (3d) 204 (P.E.I. S.C.) reversed on the basis of *quantum meruit* (1971), 19 D.L.R. (3d) 720, in which a woman had lived with a man for 22 years and given birth to seven children. The judge, in rejecting her claim for compensation as being based on an immoral relationship, felt unable, at 212, "to depart from well established principles until authorized by proper legislation." Trainor J. expressed sympathy, at 214, for the "predicament in which the plaintiff finds herself with a family of seven illegitimate children, the majority being still unable to fend for themselves. Yet she acted of her own volition and took over the position in the deceased's home which she knew rightfully belonged to the deceased's wife, who . . . was pushed out of the home on a cold winter's night." However, a different view was taken in *Chrispen v. Topham* (1986), 28

D.L.R. (4th) 754 (Sask. Q.B.), where the court, at 758, equally briefly, dismissed the traditional approach in the following terms:

> In my opinion, it cannot be argued that the [cohabitation] agreement between the plaintiff and the defendant was made for an immoral purpose and, therefore, illegal and unenforceable. Present day social acceptance of common-law living counters that argument.

Cases in the United States have tended to retain a disapproval of contracts involving sexuality while focusing on whether that aspect is severable. For instance, in *Whorton v. Dillingham*, 202 Cal. App. 3d 447, 248 Cal. Rptr. 405 (1988), the court stated at 407:

> Adults who voluntarily live together and engage in sexual relations are competent to contract respecting their earnings and property rights. Such contracts will be enforced "unless expressly and inseparably based upon an illicit consideration of sexual services . . ." (*Marvin v. Marvin* (1976), 557 P.2d 106.) One cannot lawfully contract to pay for the performance of sexual services since such an agreement is in essence a bargain for prostitution. . . .

(Do you agree that a "bargain for prostitution" should be unenforceable, assuming that civil litigation were a realistic possibility?)

However, it seems highly unlikely now that a cohabitation agreement, whatever the sexual identity of the parties, would be found to infringe a public policy about sexual morality. Indeed provincial law may recognize such agreements. See, *e.g.*, the Family Relations Act, R.S.B.C., 1996, c. 128, s. 120.1.

Nevertheless, whatever the evolving law on capacity to marry may be, issues may still arise about policy limitations on contracting about relationships. Some people whose relationships are denied public recognition as marriages, or who do not wish to support the concept of marriage, may turn to the law of contracts to make commitments to each other. Some of the privileges associated with marriage, such as, currently, the spousal testimonial privilege, cannot be created by contract. However contracts can have a role to play, along with powers of attorney, wills, beneficiary designations on insurance and pension plans, and adoption, in providing evidence of the relationship and governing certain matters such as property rights, liability for debts, business interests, bank accounts and shared expenses. Could a couple contract into the personal rights and obligations of marriage, without actually getting married? In *Couture c. Gagnon* (2001), 205 D.L.R. (4th) 680 (Que. C.A.), the Quebec Court of Appeal found enforceable an agreement between cohabitees that provided they would share the value of family assets in the event of separation. The court disagreed with the trial judge, who found that the concept of family assets was reserved for the institution of marriage, holding that common law spouses can privately agree to be bound by the same rules.

A recent Supreme Court of Canada case provides indirect support for the view that same-sex couples can contract into marital obligations, even as it illustrated conflicting views of the implications of this. In *M. v. H.*, [1999] 2 S.C.R. 3, M began a relationship with H in 1982 and lived with her in a house owned by H since 1974. From 1982 to 1992, when the relationship ended, M and H operated an advertising business (with H contributing more than M). They bought a business property (which was later sold) and a vacation property. The business went sour in the late 1980s and H took a job outside the business and mortgaged her house to support herself and M. After the end of the relationship, M sought an order for partition and sale of the house. M later amended her application to include a claim for support pursuant to the provisions of the Family Law Act, R.S.O. c. F.3 (FLA), which involved a constitutional challenge of the Act's definition of "spouse". The court found that the definition of "spouse" in s. 29 of the FLA infringed or denied s. 15(1) of the Charter and that the infringement was not saved under s. 1 of the Charter. The court suspended the declaration that s. 29 was of no force or effect for six months.

The question of whether the law of contract provided an alternative to public support obligations was mentioned in both majority and dissenting judgments. Thus, on the one hand, Iacobucci J. stated for the majority, at paras. 121 and 124:

> In my view, the law of contract is an equally unacceptable alternative to the spousal support scheme under the FLA. The appellant emphasizes that the impugned provisions of the Act do not preclude same-sex partners from contracting for mutual support obligations. However, the voluntary assumption of such obligations is not equivalent to a statutory entitlement to apply for a support order.
>
> . . .
>
> In sum, neither the common law equitable remedies nor the law of contract are adequate substitutes for the FLA's spousal support regime. Indeed, if these remedies were considered satisfactory there would have been no need for the spousal support regime, or its extension to unmarried, opposite-sex couples.

On the other hand, Gonthier J. stated in dissent, at para. 260:

> While the legislature does not force individuals in same-sex relationships to provide support, it also does not prevent them from doing so. Individuals in same-sex relationships are free to formulate contracts which impose support obligations upon themselves, just as the FLA does for some opposite-sex couples. I do not understand how it could be said that individuals in same-sex relationships are rendered "invisible" by non-inclusion in a regime merely because they have the same rights and obligations as all persons other than certain opposite-sex couples, particularly as they can impose equivalent support obligations by way of contract. It is clear that this may result in some additional expenses relating to the contract, but it is difficult to see how this possible expense results in discriminatory non-recognition of the group, and how it results in "severe and localized consequences".

There is a debate about whether lesbians and gay men should turn to the law of contracts. See, for instance, Robson and Valentine, "Lov(h)hers: Lesbians as Intimate Partners and Lesbian Legal Theory" (1990), 63 Temple L.R. 511 at 521-528 (raising concerns about the myths of equality and freedom underlying contract theory but suggesting contracts for legal matters). Ertman, in "Contractual Purgatory for Sexual Marginorities: Not Heaven, But Not Hell Either" (1996), 73:4 Denver U.L.R. 1107 (part of a symposium on "The New Private Law"), challenges the view that contracting is dangerous for people on the margins (both majorities such as women and minorities such as gays and lesbians). She argues that contract offers a space, between public condemnation and public rights, for people to make their own arrangements. Martha Fineman, in "Why Marriage?" (2001), 9 Virginia Journal of Social Policy and the Law 239 goes further, at 263, suggesting that marriage and family law be aborted completely and be replaced by private ordering between sexual affiliates. This change would erode the state's interest in controlling sexual affiliations and thus "[s]ame-sex partners and others . . . would simply be viewed as equivalent forms of privately preferred sexual connection."

The issue of whether there should be any policy limitations on agreements involving an element of sexuality is one that has an obvious constitutional dimension. It raises a broader question about the interaction between the common law and constitutional law. Must common law public policies, and indeed all decisions about whether or not to enforce particular contracts or terms, be consistent with Charter rights and freedoms? In *R.W.D.S.U., Loc. 580 v. Dolphin Delivery* (1986), 33 D.L.R. (4th) 174, the Supreme Court of Canada expressed the view that the Charter applies to the common law only insofar as the common law is the basis of some governmental action. It does not apply in litigation between "private parties". It is nevertheless possible to bring the Charter into the picture by arguing that although a contract may not violate the Charter directly, the Charter, perhaps allied with other legislation, expresses fundamental aspects of Canadian public policy. Some contracts, therefore, may either be enforced or not enforced because a contrary decision would conflict with the fundamental values expressed in the Charter. For a case testing the common law of defamation against Charter values, see *Hill v. Church of Scientology*, [1995] 2 S.C.R. 1130, and generally Hogg, *Constitutional Law of Canada* (1998), at 685-693.

An area which generates current debate about appropriate public policy has to do with reproduction. Various issues are the subject of current debate.

Are contractual agreements (often called surrogacy contracts) in which one party agrees to bear a child for the other contrary to public policy? A famous New Jersey case, *Re Baby M*, 525 A. 2d 1128 (N.J. Super. Ct., 1988), 537 A. 2d 1227 (N.J. S.C.), illustrated judicial ambivalence towards such contracts. M's mother (the infant was named Melissa by the father and designated as M throughout the trial proceedings) had agreed to be artificially inseminated with the father's sperm. At birth she was to turn the child over to the father and relinquish all parental rights in exchange for payment of all medical expenses and a fee. However, when the baby was born her mother would not surrender the infant to the father. At the trial court level it was held that such "surrogate" parentage contracts were largely valid and enforceable, if specific performance was in the child's best interest.

In contrast, on appeal, the court took a different view, although it ultimately granted custody to the father. The court stated, at 1250:

> The surrogacy contract creates, it is based upon, principles that are directly contrary to the objectives of our laws. It guarantees the separation of a child from its mother; it looks to adoption regardless of suitability; it totally ignores the child; it takes the child from the mother regardless of her wishes and her maternal fitness; and it does all of this, it accomplishes all of its goals, through the use of money.

> Beyond that is the potential degradation of some women that may result from this arrangement. In many cases, of course, surrogacy may bring satisfaction, not only to the infertile couple, but to the surrogate mother herself. The fact, however, that many women may not perceive surrogacy negatively but rather see it as an opportunity does not diminish its potential for devastation to other women.

In contrast, the court in *Johnson v. Calvert* (1993), 851 P.2d. 776 (Cal. S.C.) held that gestational surrogacy contracts were not invalid on public policy grounds, stressing the lack of data about adverse effects, choice on the part of the surrogate mother, and the significance of procreation to people who wish to have children of their own genetic stock.

The following extract discusses the broader issue of the right to have children and the grounding of claims of rights to enter reproductive contracts, or to seek reproductive assistance, in contract theory.

SHANNER, THE RIGHT TO PROCREATE: WHEN RIGHTS CLAIMS HAVE GONE WRONG

(1995) 40 McGill L.J. 823 at 847-56

The right of freedom to establish reproductive exchanges may be grounded in several theoretical constructions, and may employ the language of contracts, marketplaces, autonomy, or libertarian theories. All of these theoretical variations are grounded in assumptions of the equal autonomy of moral agents to act, to barter, or to make agreements to achieve their individual goals or preferences. However, frameworks involving contracts, markets, and free exchanges are especially problematic in procreative contexts.

A. Intuitive Limits

Supporters of an exchange model of reproductive assistance envision cases in which autonomous adults agree to cooperate in pursuit of the mutual goal of founding a family. Imagine the following hypothetical scenario: Mr. and Mrs. Smith have tried to initiate a pregnancy for three years without success. Agreeing that raising a loving family together is part of their shared life plan, they seek assistance from trained clinicians to achieve this goal. The clinicians freely chose to practise reproductive medicine to satisfy their own scientific interests, to help other people, and/or to obtain a profit. After the prospective parents and clinicians agree on the contractual terms, which include financial compensation in return for medical services, they embark on the NRT [New Reproductive Technologies] protocol. . . .

Any thoughtful decision to bear children would seem to involve agreements of some sort, as couples may agree to marry in order to establish a nuclear family together, and may decide jointly to stop using contraceptives, or to time intercourse in order to initiate a pregnancy. If making agreements between the two usual reproductive partners is acceptable in the intentional initiation of a family, it seems to follow that contracts with other collaborators or facilitators should be equally acceptable for achieving the same goal in the face of infertility.

On the other hand, we can also imagine cases in which the contracts to create a child established between or among autonomous persons are greatly troubling. Consider, for example, a futuristic "infant supermarket". Mr. and Mrs. Huxley specify the sex, physical features, talents, I.Q., and assorted personality traits they desire their child to have. They then select sperm and ova from the computerized registry at the donor bank. Preimplantation genetic analysis enables the clinicians to dispose of embryos with the wrong sex or with serious genetic flaws, and specific characteristics are inserted with gene replacement techniques. A healthy gestator is selected, and the pregnancy is monitored with several prenatal tests. The contract stipulates that if the infant is born with physical or mental disabilities and falls short of the Huxleys' expectations, they may return the infant to the clinic and demand a refund or replacement.

An "infant supermarket" or "genetic showroom" in which children are custom ordered seems intuitively distressing, but distinctions between acceptable and objectionable reproductive contracts require stronger grounding than intuition. The key difference between these scenarios is that the latter seems to treat the child as an object or product that can be custom designed and returned for a full refund if unsatisfactory, rather than as a developing person in relationships with his or her parents and others.

The critical flaw in contract-based approaches to reproduction is that the contractual model itself does not provide an opportunity to ask whether some matters are by nature unsuitable objects of a contract. The liberty and contractual models fail to explain why we are more bothered by the Huxleys' contract than the Smiths' when both couples and their respective co-contracting parties all acted as fair and equal negotiators. We must consider, therefore, whether our discretion in bargaining over some matters is legitimate only to a certain extent.

In assisted reproduction, the contractual model—taken by itself and unmodified by other moral considerations— creates a slippery slope between the ideal cases of loving, conscientious prospective parents such as the Smiths, and the seemingly acquisitive, emotionally distanced infant consumers represented by the Huxleys. In between lie several types of cases in current and foreseeable medical practice, and the contractual model allows no clear distinctions between the acceptable and troubling variations. If it is appropriate for a couple to retain the services of physicians in the attempt to initiate pregnancies and to conduct prenatal tests to detect abnormalities, arranging for the further services of embryo genetic analysis, sex selection, and gene therapy or enhancement should also be acceptable within the same contractual model. If parents can procure diagnostic services to avoid serious diseases in their offspring, why could they not also procure services to ensure the gender or other traits of their children, for whatever reason? It would be acceptable to use donated sperm, ova, or embryos, and to accept the altruistically motivated service of gestation without payment, if the donations were made freely and without manipulation; it should be equally acceptable for gamete or embryo providers to bargain for payment and fair compensation for their time, risk, and genetic interest and for gestational mothers to charge for the risks and lengthy personal involvement in pregnancy. However, a case of contracted gestation in which the contracting couple agree to pay the gestational mother $10,000 upon the delivery of a healthy child, but will pay nothing in the event of a birth defect or a decision by the gestational mother to keep the baby, seems to be another intuitively objectionable example of treating the child as a commodity. There must be some identifiable difference between the acceptable cases of a couple's agreement to enlarge their family and the impermissible cases of an agreement to buy a child produced according to specifications. Concerns other than the freedom to contract must be at play in defining these notions.

B. The Myth of the Equal Contractors

Most libertarian, contract, or marketplace theories assume the equal status of the contracting parties. The establishment of ethics itself within a libertarian or social contract theory requires free and equal participants who respect the autonomy of their peers, and specific contracts are generally considered unconscionable if one party to the contract has significantly greater power than the other(s). When contracts involve reproductive capacities, however, and especially when they involve reproductive technologies, the ideal of equal parties must be called into question at many levels.

Inequalities between children and parents, between women and men, and between patient and doctors all require attention in the context of reproductive exchanges. Annette Baier ["The Need for More than Justice" (1989) 13 Can. J. Philosophy 41 at 52-53] has articulated the scope and impact of a problem that is usually ignored.

> It is a typical feature of the dominant moral theories and traditions, since Kant, or perhaps since Hobbes, that relationships between equals or those who are deemed equal in some important sense, have been the relations that morality is concerned primarily to regulate. Relationships between those who are clearly unequal in power, such as parents and children, earlier and later generations in relation to one another, states and citizens, doctors and patients, the well and the ill, large states and small state[s], have had to be shunted to the bottom of the agenda, and then dealt with by some sort of 'promotion' of the weaker so that an appearance of virtual equality is achieved. . . . This pretense of an equality that is in fact absent may often lead to desirable protection of the weaker, or more dependent. But it somewhat masks the question of what our moral relationships *are* to those who are our superiors or our inferiors in power. A more realistic acceptance of the fact that we begin as helpless children, [and] that at almost every point of our lives we deal with both the more and the less helpless, . . . might lead us to a more direct approach to questions concerning the design of institutions structuring these relationships between unequals (families, schools, hospitals, armies) and of the morality of our dealings with the more and the less powerful.

1. The Offspring

The most obviously unequal party to any reproductive exchange is the child produced by it, because unconceived children cannot accept or refuse to enter into any contracts regarding their own conception. A child will exist within the relationships of the family structure, and the child's autonomy will come into being in this context. Decisions that so profoundly affect a person's life prospects would normally be at least partly under one's own control, but unconceived children are, of course, simply unable to participate in autonomous negotiations regarding these fundamental life influences.

Because children cannot be equal contractors with adults, their guardians enter into negotiations on their behalf, making the child equal in representation if not in fact. However, transferring the exercise of a right of non-conception to a proxy does not help matters, since at the time of the agreement, there is no one in existence for the proxy to represent. An existing proxy might reasonably represent the future interests of a future child, but those interests are voided if the proxy exercises a right of non-conception on behalf of the future child. In other words, the proxy's authority (the interests of the future child) would be eliminated by the very act of asserting authority to deny conception. Since the child cannot be an equal contracting party—even by proxy—in his or her conception, it appears that the child is better understood to be the object of the reproductive contract made by adults.

2. Women and Men

Even in progressive, egalitarian marriages, women cannot fully overcome systemic and societal oppression. The relative scarcity of female scientists, reproductive physicians, politicians, and policy regulators places women at a distinct disadvantage, both historically and currently, in influencing reproductive policies. Women's incomes are still lower than men's, women's political role is limited, and women do not control the media that so greatly shape our perceptions of "normal" men, women, and families. As Rosalind Petchesky ["Reproductive Freedom: Beyond 'A Woman's Right to Choose'" (1979) 5 J. Women in Culture & Society 661 at 674-75.] observed,

> [t]he critical issue for feminists is not so much the context of women's choices, or even "the right to choose," as it is the social and material conditions under which choices are made. The "right to choose" means very little when women are powerless. . . . [W]omen make their own reproductive choices, but they do not make them just as they please, they do not make them under conditions which they themselves create, but under social conditions and constraints which they, as mere individuals are powerless to change. The fact that individuals themselves do not determine the social framework in which they act does not nullify their choices nor their moral capacity to make them. It only suggests that we have to focus less on the question of "choice" and more on the question of how to transform the social conditions of choosing, working, and reproducing.

Individual men also rarely have the power to change the broad social conditions under which they must make their reproductive decisions. Still, men are dominant in social policy discussions and in the decisions that have shaped the development and use of NRTs. Until women and men share equal influence over social, political, economic, and medical trends—or better, until women achieve the majority voice in reproductive matters that affect their lives more than the lives of men—women will remain unequal parties in medically assisted reproductive decisions.

When women are at a political, economic, or social disadvantage at the outset of the bargaining, it is reasonable to fear that they will be exploited. To be recognized as unequal leaves a woman in a precarious position: she might receive the pity and protection of bargainers in a stronger position, or her needs, like her social standing, might be devalued and dismissed. In a society that values free market forces, the weaker the bargaining position of one of the parties, the greater the danger of exploitation and objectification. Since reproduction involves the sexes differently, special concerns arise for women in reproductive contexts.

. . . . .

a. Gestational Contracts

The objectification of women is clearest in "surrogacy" arrangements, or what should be called "contracted gestational parenting". A preconception adoption agreement is one in which a woman is inseminated on the agreement that she will give her own baby to the father and his social partner. True gestational contracts must involve NRTs for egg or embryo transfer. If one is entering into a contract with the objective of having a child, there seems to be no *prima facie* requirement that a couple's gametes or embryo be transferred to the genetic mother's womb rather than to someone else's for gestation. A rather extreme, but by no means unique, expression of the position I reject is the following from S. Geller ["The Child and/or the Embryo. To Whom Does It Belong?" (1986) 1:8 Human Reproduction 561]:

> It is generally held that the child issued from a surrogate is her child even though she has only carried it, because she delivered it . . . This in my view, is a complete misunderstanding of the problem. The child of the surrogate does not belong to her any more than the child resulting from artificial insemination belongs to the donor, for the genetic contribution is exactly the same in both cases. The child belongs, we believe, to those who have conceived the project of having it: indeed without them this child would never have come to life.

Geller ignores the fact that without the gestating woman's intention, labour, delivery, and literal flesh and blood contributions that transform a microscopic embryo into several pounds of infant, the child would never have come to life. Even when the child is the genetic offspring of the "surrogate", the woman who conceived and bore the child is relegated to the secondary role of the one who "only carried it". In contrast, those who arranged the contract are given moral precedence in claiming the right to raise the child. A woman who carries transferred eggs or embryos would have even less claim to the child than would a sperm donor; her pregnancy would count for nothing. Interestingly, however, parallel arguments are generally not raised in cases of NRTs with donor eggs or embryos, so that the recipient is reduced to "only" a gestating mother. The child, meanwhile, is depicted as an object which "belongs" to one claimant or another on the grounds of one's greater intention in initiating its production.

The "surrogate" mother is usually not described as a pregnant person who has an intimate relationship with the child she carries; she is merely the gestator that produces the contracting couple's baby in their stead, and could as easily be a mechanical womb. Even the word 'surrogate' thus objectifies the woman by focusing on the contracting couple's perspective to the exclusion of the birth mother's and child's points of view. . . .

As the relationship between the mother and child is discounted in a contracted pregnancy, so too is the relationship between a woman and her own body. For a gestational mother to dissociate herself from the phenomenon of her pregnancy, because "it is not her baby" that she carries, is a form of psychological alienation which echoes the philosophical Marxist imagery. The woman is pregnant, however, so certainly it is *her* pregnancy and not someone else's. Pregnancy is the phenomenon of carrying a developing fetus; thus, if it is her pregnancy, the baby she delivers must be her baby, even if she intends someone else to act as the social parent(s), and/or even if she is not genetically related to the child. When a woman either feels or is told that the baby she carries is not her baby because of a contract, she alienates herself from the deeply meaningful experience in which she is involved. When the child is an object, the woman who herself gives rise to the child may come to be seen as an object: the "baby machine" produces goods for herself or for a contracting couple. The fact that the gestational mother and contracting couple may have autonomously entered the agreement does nothing to reduce the alienation and denigration of pregnancy that frequently occurs; indeed, emphasizing the contract tends to intensify these problems.

3. Doctors and Patients

Finally, there is good reason to reject the notion that medical care is properly provided in the context of contract negotiations between doctors and patients. The subject or purpose of such a contract would be medical care—the attempt to promote, maintain, and restore the patient's health—and in this venture it would be inappropriate to employ a typical vision of the contractors as equally self-interested. The Hippocratic tradition specifically *prevents* clinicians from pursuing their own interests by offering unnecessary, unproven, or risky treatments, even if the patient consents to or requests such interventions. The medical relationship is thus far better understood as one based on trust or fiduciary responsibilities than as a contracted service.

Patients need the knowledge that clinicians have; because of this expertise, doctors are permitted to ask deeply personal questions and to perform intimate examinations and procedures that give them more knowledge about individual patients. This personal information creates a knowledge/power nexus that gives the clinician far greater practical and psychological authority to dictate the next step of any medical intervention, to encourage further interventions, and to end unilaterally the provision of medical treatment on the grounds of medical futility. Extreme paternalistic concern for the patient's physical or other interests may prompt the physician to make medical decisions without the patient's full knowledge or consent, and some patients cede decision-making authority to their doctors. Further, infertility patients often have limited options and support available to them outside the clinical setting, and may be suffering intense psychosocial turmoil, a crisis of gender or adult identity, or a profound sense of loss of control. Thus, in establishing the exchange of fees and services in the infertility clinic, the patient has unequal bargaining power with the physician. Even more important than the inclusion of non-exploitative terms in the medical contract is the fact that the patient may not be in position to decline entering the contract at all; the pace of the medical treadmill may be too fast for a patient to get off, and the psychosocial consequences of remaining childless may be too difficult to bear.

Children, women, and patients are thus all disadvantaged against adults, men, and medical practitioners, respectively. That most reproductive specialists are male makes female patients doubly prejudiced with regard to both gender and expertise. The social and psychological forces that transform infertility into a life crisis for many patients also create a subtly coercive context in which decisions about infertility treatments are made. In this light, it is a fiction to suggest that contracts or marketplace exchanges regarding reproductive services, and more specifically reproductive technologies, are made between free and equal parties. It is clear therefore that contract or marketplace language is inadequate to characterize the moral status of claims to reproductive services. Legal constructions of reproductive contracts based on these ethical models are therefore similarly inappropriate.

[Footnotes omitted.]

Attention to the impact on vulnerable groups does not point to a clear answer on what public policy to adopt with respect to reproductive contracts. Are you concerned that enforcement of gestational surrogacy contracts may promote the exploitation of, for instance, Third World women? In *Proceed with Care*, the Final Report of the Royal Commission on New Reproductive Technologies (1993), at 673, the Commission stated that "[p]reconception contracts were of particular concern to many of the groups representing minority women who appeared before the Commission". On the other hand, it was also noted, at 680, that such arrangements might be useful to some women with disabilities. Gay men may also wish to enter into such contracts. For an argument that regulation of surrogacy agreements under an optimal legal framework has the potential to generate mutual gains for all concerned see Trebilcock, *The Limits of Freedom of Contract* (1993), at 48–56. Also, some feminist scholars have recognized that an outright prohibition of surrogacy agreements might simply force the practice underground, where the vulnerable woman would have no recourse to law or legal advice (see Harvison Young, "New Reproductive Technologies In Canada And The United States: Same Problems, Different Discourses" (1998), 12 Temple International & Comparative. L.J. 43, at 62–63).

The Commission, *ibid.*, was strongly of the view that preconception contracts are unacceptable because of the commodification of children and reproduction, the detriment to the autonomy of gestational mothers, and the negative consequences for women and other groups in society. The following recommendations were made, *inter alia*:

> 199. The federal government legislate to prohibit advertising for or acting as an intermediary to bring about the preconception arrangement; and to prohibit receiving payment or any financial or commercial benefit for acting as an intermediary, under threat of criminal sanction. It should also legislate to prohibit making payment for a preconception arrangement, under threat of criminal sanction.
>
> 200. Provinces/territories amend their family law legislation to specify that all preconception agreements, whether or not they involve payment, are unenforceable against the gestational woman.

Art. 541 of the Québec Civil Code states:

Procreation or gestation agreements on behalf of another person are absolutely null.

(Book 2, Family, Title Two, Filiation, Ch. I, Filiation by Blood, s. III Medically Assisted Procreation.)

Contracts relating to reproduction can address issues other than surrogacy. For instance, parties may wish to contract with respect to the donation of sperm with terms relating to, for instance, donor anonymity or the preconception determination of parental rights/obligations. Arguably, a contract for sperm donation, being relatively less intrusive than surrogacy or *in vitro* fertilization, involves less challenging policy issues than an agreement involving other new reproductive technologies (NRT's). However, parties may wish to contract about issues significant to them. The need or desire to establish the sperm donor's anonymity and obligations with respect to the child can be important to both the donor and recipient(s) in a fertility arrangement. Donors may wish to be protected from future claims for support, parental obligations or even challenges to their estate upon their death. The recipients on the other hand may see anonymity as essential to protecting their concept of the family unit, for instance, one consisting of a child with two mothers. A recipient couple may view the potential for the donor to decide to play an active role in the child's life as an unwanted intrusion into their family unit. The potential for such an intrusion is greater in cases where the recipients know the donor than in cases of anonymous donation. This is even more so in the face of the Supreme Court of Canada's decision in *Trociuk v. British Columbia (Attorney General)*, [2003] S.C.J. No. 32, , where it was held that a B.C. law, allowing a mother to unacknowledge the father on their child's birth certificate without reason, was contrary to the Charter equality rights in s. 15. In this situation, the preconception agreement waiving the donor's parental rights may provide the necessary reason for the mother to refuse to acknowledge the father (although this was not specifically discussed by the court).

Whether such agreements should be enforced calls into play various policy considerations that vary depending on who is attacking the agreement and why. In Canada there is virtually no case law directly on the point of whether such an agreement is enforceable. In the United States the case law is in conflict. In *Thomas S. v. Robin Y.*, 618 N.Y.S.2d 356 (U.S. N.Y.A.D. 1st Dept., 1994), leave to appeal dismissed, 631 N.Y.S.2d 611 (U.S. C.A. N.Y., July 26, 1995), the court referred to unspecified public policy considerations as banning enforcement of an oral agreement to waive parental rights. In *Matter of Marriage of Leckie and Voorhies,* 128 Or. App. 289 (1994), the court refused a filiation order on the basis of a written waiver of parental rights. While the circumstances of each case were different, they still make clear the legal uncertainty with respect to such contracts.

The reproductive issues raised above illustrate how analysis of and debate about public policies can shift from the common law to legislation. The Assisted Human Reproduction Act, S.C. 2004, c. 2 will now have an impact on such debates. Principle (f) in s. 2, which refers consistently to "assisted human reproductive technologies" addresses the commodification of reproduction in stating that:

> trade in the reproductive capabilities of women and men and the exploitation of children, women and men for commercial ends raise health and ethical concerns that justify their prohibition. . . .

Section 6 prohibits surrogacy agreements.

> (1) No person shall pay consideration to a female person to be a surrogate mother, offer to pay such consideration or advertise that it will be paid.
>
> (2) No person shall accept consideration for arranging for the services of a surrogate mother, offer to make such an arrangement for consideration or advertise the arranging of such services.

You may wish to consider the pros and cons of the policy reflected in this provision.

With respect to sperm donation, s. 10, dealing with "Controlled Activities", states:

> (3) No person shall, except in accordance with the regulations and a licence, *obtain*, store, transfer, destroy, import or export
>
>> (a) a sperm or ovum, or any part of one, for the purpose of creating an embryo . . . [Emphasis added.]

It seems unlikely that this provision would be interpreted as requiring a person who "obtains" sperm through sexual intercourse to have a licence. As well there is an issue of whether it would apply to "home inseminations" more broadly. On its face, s. 10 looks as if it might apply to private agreements for sperm donation, but the principles which focus on assisted human reproduction may be effective in limiting the operation of the Act to third party assistance. Thus the courts will still be faced with issues of contract enforceability relating to such agreements, issues which are raised in the question below. Interestingly, s. 15 (not yet in force) of the Act forbids licensee disclosure of donors' identity in the absence of donor consent (with exceptions such as administrative and court-ordered purposes).

Under s. 60 of the Act, a person who engages in a prohibited activity is guilty of a hybrid offence and subject to a $500,000 fine and/or 10 years in jail. Section 61 imposes lower maxima for contravening the provisions on controlled activities. Thus the issue of the scope of the Act is significant.

Organ donation provides a further example of legislated public policy. Should human organs be treated as a commodity capable of being bought and sold? The sale of organs is outlawed in many countries. See Takahash, "Tissue and Organ Transfer Regimes: Markets, Ethics and Law Reform" (1994), Law and Economics Working Paper Series (WPS 22), Canadian Law and Economics Association, and Manga, "A Commercial Market for Organs? Why Not" (1987), 1(4) Bioethics 321. However, there is debate over whether compensation for reasonable expenses incurred by the donor should be permitted. In Canada, the sale of organs is provincially regulated. While all provinces make it illegal to buy or sell non-regenerative organs, there are differences. Manitoba allows for the donor to receive compensation for reasonable expenses incurred, so long as the donation is carried out in compliance with the Act (see the Human Tissue Act, C.C.S.M., c. H180, s. 15(4)). In New Brunswick the exchange of consideration for a transplant of tissue that is replaceable by natural process of repair, such as blood or possibly part of a liver, appears to be legal (see the Human Tissue Act, S.N.B. 1992 c. H-12 s. 8). In Ontario the Trillium Gift of Life Network Act, R.S.O. 1990 c. H.20 s. 10 makes any exchange of valuable consideration for human tissue invalid as being contrary to public policy. On the other side of the argument Trebilcock in *The Limits of Freedom of Contract, supra* at 33–38, argues that a futures market in organs and a regulated market in foetal tissue may be more sensible from a public policy perspective than an outright ban.

QUESTION

Siobahan wishes to have a child. She discusses this with her friend John because she admires many of his qualities. John agrees to provide sperm to inseminate Siobahan. They also agree that baby Sheila will never be informed of her genetic father's identity and that John will never be held liable for support payments. In return John agrees never to attempt to assert parental rights to the child. Three years later John decides that his strong desire to be a parent means that he must play a parental role in Sheila's life and he seeks visitation rights. Should the agreement be enforced as a defence to his claim? Consider various scenarios. What if Siobahan is in a lesbian relationship, but separates from her partner who has no support obligation to Sheila? Siobahan is facing financial difficulty. Should the agreement prevent her from seeking support payments from John? (See, *e.g.*, *Alberta (Director, Parentage & Maintenance Act) v. E. (C.)* (1995), 39 Alta. L.R. (3d) 307 (Q.B.)) What if at the age of twelve Sheila demands to know who her genetic father is in order to understand what her roots are? What if Sheila develops leukemia and the most likely bone marrow match is John? (Assume first that John's sperm donation is not governed by the Act discussed above. Then assume both that it is and is an offence. This raises issues of the effects of illegality, addressed in the following section.)

3.   Effects of Illegality

Three issues are dealt with in this section. Are contracts that offend a statute or a common law head of public policy ever enforceable? Can a party ever recover money paid or property passed under the contract? To what extent are courts willing to sever offensive provisions? All three issues require the courts to be sensitive to gradations of offensiveness and the relative innocence of the parties. None is susceptible to any easy line-drawing exercise. As McCamus has pointed out in "Restitutionary Recovery of Benefits Conferred under Contracts in Conflict with Statutory Policy—The New Golden Rule" (1987), 25 Osgoode Hall L.J. 787, at 823:

> It would be surprising if a general rule of broad application could consistently resolve the main difficulties generated by agreements in conflict with public policy. Cases dealing with such varied phenomena as major crime, work done by unlicensed plumbers, Sunday contracts, and lending agreements in which the date of the loan has been carelessly omitted, do, after all, have some material differences. It is obviously necessary to develop a more contextually specific approach to the analysis of these problems.

The following case discusses issues of the consequences of illegality against a background of the evolving law on public policy and the increasing flexibility in the traditional rule that illegal contracts are unenforceable. It illustrates the contextual nature of the analysis required.

STILL v. MINISTER OF NATIONAL REVENUE
(1997), [1998] 1 F.C. 549 (C.A.)

ROBERTSON J.A. . . . The applicant married a Canadian citizen and immigrated to Canada to be with her husband. She applied for permanent resident status and on September 22, 1991 was provided with the following document by immigration officials:

> This will verify that, for the person(s) named hereunder, a recommendation has been sent to the Governor-in-Council for Canada for an exemption pursuant to subsection 114(2) of the *Immigration Act*

> KATHLEEN STILL

> Pending Governor-in-Council approval and provided all other requirements are met, the above-named will be granted permanent resident status in Canada. The above-named is/are hereby eligible to apply for employment and/or student authorizations, as applicable.

The applicant took the above document to mean that she was entitled . . . to work in Canada. From May 9, 1993 to October 1, 1993, she was employed as a housekeeper at Camp Hiawatha in Manitoulin Island, Ontario. On September 23, 1993 she was granted status as a permanent resident, which status embraced the right to work in Canada without a work permit. The applicant was laid off from work on October 1, 1993 and her application for unemployment benefits was denied on the ground that her contract of service was illegal and invalid for the period May 9 to September 23, 1993. The period during which she did work under a valid contract of service, September 23 to October 1, 1993, was not long enough to qualify her for benefits. Ultimately, the applicant appealed to the Tax Court of Canada. . . .

The Tax Court Judge found that the applicant believed in good faith that she was lawfully entitled to work in Canada. He also found that, in the period prior to the date she was declared a permanent resident, the applicant did not qualify for benefits because she was not engaged in insurable employment as contemplated by subsection 3(1) of the *Unemployment Insurance Act*. . . .

Specifically, the Tax Court Judge held that the applicant was not engaged in insurable employment because of a violation of subsection 18(1) of the *Immigration Regulations, 1978* [SOR/78-172 (as am. by SOR/89-80, s. 1)] which states:

> 18.(1) Subject to subsection 19(1) to (2.2), no person, other than a Canadian citizen or permanent resident, shall engage or continue in employment in Canada without a valid and subsisting employment authorization [a work permit].

There is no express penalty for a breach of this particular provision. Section 98 [as am. by S.C. 1992, c. 49, s. 87] of the *Immigration Act* serves as the general penal provision for cases in which no punishment is provided elsewhere in the Act or Regulations. However, it applies only to persons who knowingly contravene the legislation: . . .

4. The Common Law Doctrine of Illegality

Law reform agencies have been quick to conclude that the law of illegality is in an unsatisfactory state. . . . There is a plethora of conflicting decisions and great uncertainty as to the principles which should be guiding the courts. Arguably, so many exceptions have been grafted on to the common law rule that illegal contracts are void *ab initio* that the validity of the rule itself is brought into question. In *Sidmay Ltd. v. Wehttam Investments Ltd.*, [1967] 1 O.R. 508 (C.A.) Laskin J.A. (as he then was) doubted whether a single rationalizing principle could be applied to cases on illegality (at page 534). The treatment accorded the doctrine by scholars reveals the extent to which it is difficult to rationalize the jurisprudence. Each commentator's treatment offers a unique perspective on a complex area of the law: . . . Against this background, I shall attempt to give an overview of those aspects of the doctrine which reasonably bear on the issue at hand.

The doctrine of illegality is divided into two categories: common law illegality and statutory illegality. The former category has its origins in an unreported case said to have been decided in 1725. In *Everet v. Williams*, a highwayman brought an action in equity to obtain an accounting against his partner. Not only was the suit rejected, but the plaintiff's lawyers were allegedly held in contempt of court, fined and committed to Fleet prison pending payment of the fine: see Notes, "The Highwayman's Case (*Everet v. Williams*)" (1893), 9 L.Q. Rev. 197. Invariably, the concept of illegality and its effect on the contractual rights and obligations of parties to an otherwise enforceable agreement is traced to the following passage of Lord Mansfield's reasons in *Holman v. Johnson*, [(1775), 98 E.R. 1120 (K.B.)], at page 1121:

> The principle of public policy is this: ex dole male non oritur actio. No Court will lend its aid to a man who founds his cause of action upon an immoral or an illegal act. If, from the plaintiff's own stating or otherwise, the cause of action appears to arise *ex turpi causa*, or the transgression of a positive law of this country, there the Court says he has no right to be assisted. It is upon that ground the Court goes; not for the sake of the defendant but because they will not lend their aid to such a plaintiff.

As significant as that principle may be to the history and development of the common law of illegality, the factual context in which it was made together with the ultimate outcome, is as revealing as the principle itself. The facts of *Holman* are straightforward. The plaintiff, a resident of Dunkirk (France), sold a quantity of tea to the defendant knowing that it was to be smuggled by the latter into England. The tea was delivered to the defendant in Dunkirk and the plaintiff brought an action in England to recover monies owing. The defendant purchaser resisted the claim on the ground of illegality. Lord Mansfield held that the plaintiff was entitled to recover the price of the goods. He was not guilty of any offence, nor had he breached any statutory laws of England. The plaintiff was free to make a complete contract for the sale of goods in Dunkirk and what the buyer was going to do with the goods was of no concern to that contract. Lord Mansfield noted that had the plaintiff agreed to deliver the tea in England where such goods were prohibited then the defendant would not have been liable for the sale price.

The significance of *Holman* is that it established the general principle (not rule) that contracts can be rendered unenforceable on grounds that they are contrary to public policy. Public policy arguments in contract are rooted in an analysis of moral precepts and so-called criminal acts: that is conduct which is deemed injurious to the public good. In light of subsequent developments in the law, it is of little import that Lord Mansfield did not lay down a rule that any contract tainted with illegality is void *ab initio*. Legal historians have shown that Lord Mansfield was conscious that if his principle was to be of assistance to the just application of the law it should not become inflexible. Unfortunately, subsequent generations of judges would fail to see the wisdom in this adaptable approach. History discloses that the flexibility achieved in contract law in the 18th century was superseded in the 19th and early 20th century. by a doctrinal rigidity which promoted certainty in the law at the expense of other pressing values: . . .

Since *Holman*, the courts have been called upon to examine innumerable transactions which involve so-called immoral or illegal acts. But as this category of illegality is of no concern to the present case, I turn to the concept of statutory illegality. While the refusal of a court to entertain an accounting between high-waymen may seem eminently justified, the refusal to enforce a contract because of a statutory breach has proven to be the more problematic aspect of the illegality doctrine. The fact that the legal maxims embraced by Lord Mansfield were formulated long before the proliferation of diverse regulatory schemes is a factor which, until recently, seems to have been overlooked. Little would be gained from an extensive analysis of the case law in the area of statutory illegality and, thus, the following analysis seeks only to shed some light on where the law has been (the old) and where it appears to be going (the new).

Case law fully supports the understanding that if the making of a contract is expressly or impliedly prohibited by statute then it is illegal and void *ab initio*. Words to the effect that "no contract shall be entered into unless a person is licensed" fit the express category. Less precise language often attracts the allegation that prohibition cannot even be implied. This was the argument advanced in *Cope v. Rowlands* (1836), 150 E.R. 707, a decision still cited today and the one which remains the locus classicus of statutory illegality. Parke B. laid down what he considered to be settled law (at page 710):

> . . . where the contract which the plaintiff seeks to enforce, be it express or implied, is expressly or by implication forbidden by the common or statute law, no court will lend its assistance to give it effect. It is equally clear that a contract is void if prohibited by a statute, though the statute inflicts a penalty only, because such a penalty implies a prohibition.

In *Rowlands*, the plaintiff, an unlicensed broker, sought to recover under a contract for work done. The statute in question merely prohibited a person from acting as broker unless licensed and was silent on the effect of a contract with unlicensed brokers. The argument advanced by the plaintiff was that the statute intended only to impose a penalty for a breach and not to prohibit the contract with the defendant. Parke B. accepted that the statute in question did not expressly prohibit the contract. Hence, the issue turned to whether the prohibition arose by implication. The answer to that question was said to depend on whether the statute was enacted for the purpose of raising revenue through the imposition of licensing fees (in which case no prohibition could be implied) or whether it was passed for the protection of the public by preventing unqualified persons from acting as brokers. It was found that one of the purposes of this section of the statute related to the latter objective and, therefore, the broker was not entitled to succeed. The clause in the statute imposing a penalty "must be taken . . . to imply a prohibition of [unlicensed persons] to act as brokers and consequently to prohibit, by necessary inference, all contracts which such persons make" (at page 711).

According to *Rowlands*, a finding that a contract is impliedly prohibited requires an examination as to the purpose or object underscoring the legislation. To avoid this issue altogether, some statutes have been drafted to actually state, for example, that an unlicensed person cannot maintain an action for services rendered. This is typical of legislation governing the real estate industry: see section 22 of the Ontario *Real Estate and Business Brokers Act* [R.S.O. 1990, c. R.4].

As stated above, case law distinguishes between an express and implied prohibition. In cases where no such express language is found it has not been difficult for courts to imply such a prohibition and rightly so. This is certainly true in regard to contracts that were entered into in breach of section 4 of the *Lords Day Act*, R.S.C. 1970, c. L-13 (since repealed) which provided, *inter alia,* that it was "unlawful" for persons to sell real estate on Sundays. Though that legislation imposed only a penalty for breach, the Supreme Court of Canada readily concluded that contracts entered into on Sunday were illegal and unenforceable: see *Neider v. Carda of Peace River District Limited*, [1972] S.C.R. 678. In response, the law reports are now replete with cases in which courts resorted to various judicial techniques to avoid innocent parties suffering the consequences of a finding of illegality under that legislation. . . . Ultimately the *Lord's Day Act* was held unconstitutional by the Supreme Court see: *R. v. Big M Drug Mart Ltd. et al.*, [1985] 1 S.C.R. 295.

Generally, it is not difficult to make a finding that a contract is either expressly or impliedly prohibited by statute. Nonetheless, there are instances where it is improper to imply such a prohibition. In 1957, Lord Devlin cautioned that: "the courts should be slow to imply the statutory prohibition of contracts and should do so only when the implication is quite clear." This advice was proffered in *St. John Shipping Corpn. v. Rank (Joseph) Ltd.*, [1956] 3 All E.R. 683 (Q.B.), a high point in English law. For the first time a clear distinction is drawn between contracts illegal in their formation and those illegal as performed.

A contract is illegal as to formation when it is prohibited by statute. It is illegal as performed if, though lawful in its formation, it is performed by one of the parties in a manner prohibited by statute. The distinction was of critical significance in *St. John Shipping* because it permitted the plaintiff carrier to recover the full contract price when the defendant resisted payment on the ground that the carrier had overloaded its ship in contravention of the *Merchant Shipping (Safety and Load Line Conventions) Act*, 1932 [(U.K.), 1932, c. 9] even though the goods were delivered safely. The loading restrictions were held to go to the performance of the contract and not its formation. As Professor Waddams has so adroitly remarked (at page 381): "If every statutory illegality, however trivial, in the course of performance of a contract, invalidated the agreement, the result would be an unjust and haphazard allocation of loss without regard to any rational principles."

Despite this welcome development in the law, Lord Devlin reiterates the basic tenets of the illegality doctrine. It is said that if the contract is expressly or impliedly prohibited by statute, the court will not enforce it regardless of whether the parties intended to break the law. That is to say it is immaterial whether the illegal actions were accidental, deliberate, serious or trivial. Above all the argument is that ignorance of the law is not an acceptable reply to a defence of illegality. However, where the statutory prohibition goes to the performance of a contract and not its formation, a party acting in good faith is entitled to relief notwithstanding the statutory breach. In such circumstances a defendant cannot successfully plead his or her own illegality: see *Archbolds (Freightage) Ltd. v. S. Spanglett Ltd.*, [1961] 1 Q.B. 374 (C.A.).

In recognition of the rigidity and oft-times unfair application of the classical illegality doctrine, the courts developed several ways in which a party may be relieved of the consequences of illegality where appropriate. For example, where the doctrine of *ex turpi causa* might otherwise apply, the courts have developed three exceptions to the role that a court will not order the return of property transferred under an illegal contract. These are: (1) where the party claiming for return of property is less at fault; (2) where the claimant "repents" before the illegal contract is performed; and (3) where the claimant has an independent right to recover (for example, a situation where recovery in tort might be possible despite an illegal contract). . . . In situations where a party enters into two related transactions (or makes two promises within an agreement) one of which is illegal and the other legal, courts have been willing to enforce the legal one if convinced that the provisions are "severable". The difficulty with these exceptions to the doctrine arises from the legal manoeuvring that must take place to arrive at what is considered a just result.

Admittedly, the foregoing is but a superficial overview of the law of illegality in its doctrinal form. At this point it is instructive to examine four decisions of the Ontario courts, two of which clearly reflect an antagonism towards the common law doctrine and a refusal to apply blindly its precepts. These two cases, we suggest, represent a departure from the old law, or what can be termed the "classical model" of the illegality doctrine, and the beginnings of the new or "modern approach" to illegality. The first two cases discussed below are representative of the classical model.

In *Kingshott v. Brunskill*, [1953] O.W.N. 133 (C.A.) one farmer sold and delivered his apple crop to another farmer without grading the apples as required by provincial regulations. Both parties expected that the apples would be graded before sale to the public by the second farmer who had the necessary equipment. When a dispute arose as to the quantity of apples actually received, the second farmer successfully resisted payment on the ground of illegality. The first farmer could recover neither the contract price nor the value of the apples. Roach J.A. found that the contract was illegal as the regulations were passed for the protection of the public and could admit of no exceptions. Justice Roach went so far as to suggest that even if the second farmer was the only party with the equipment necessary to grade the apples the legal result would have had to have been the same. The decision has been criticized by the Ontario Law Reform Commission and Professor Waddams. The former regards the result as a penalty totally disproportionate to the offence. The latter on the ground that it was hard to see what public policy was served by the decision: . . .

Kocotis v. D'Angelo, [1958] O.R. 104 (C.A.) is a case in which an electrician with a "Class C" licence (maintenance electrician) was unable to recover for work requiring a "Class A" licence (electrical contractor's licence) under a city by-law. Relying on *Cope v. Rowlands*, Laidlaw J.A. found that there was an implied prohibition and that the plaintiff knowingly breached the by-law intended to protect the public against the mistakes of unqualified persons. In dissent, Schroeder J.A. concluded that the licensing requirement was, in the language of *Rowlands*, intended to protect the revenue and not the public. His advice was that if you want to restrict a person's right to compensation for work performed in deprivation of common law rights clear and unequivocal language should be used. This leads me to the remaining two decisions which, in my view, provide the thread used in weaving the modern approach.

In *Sidmay Ltd. v. Wehttam Investments Ltd.*, *supra*, the plaintiff borrower sought a declaration of invalidity as to certain mortgages given to the defendant, a privately controlled Ontario corporation that had not been registered under the *Mortgage Brokers Registration Act* [R.S.O. 1960, c. 244]. Those who fell within the ambit of that Act were required to register before transacting business in Ontario. In the Court of Appeal the statute was construed (narrowly) so as not to apply to the defendant. (*Sidmay* was affirmed by the Supreme Court of Canada on this ground only: see [1968] S.C.R. 828.)

Kelly J.A. (Wells J.A., concurring) went on to hold that even if he were in error with respect to the interpretation issue, he would not have been prepared to declare the mortgage transaction illegal for two reasons. First, the legislation imposed no penalty on the unregistered corporation, but only its promoters, and there was no reference in it to the effect of a breach on contractual obligations. Second, this view was consistent with the intention of the legislation to protect borrowers, creditors and security holders. To permit the borrower to retain the loaned monies would be to defeat the very purpose for which the registration requirement was legislated in the first place. In the alternative Kelly J.A. indicated that if the mortgage transaction were deemed illegal then the borrower could not seek relief as it was not a person for whose protection the legislation was enacted. Finally, and in the further alternative, he opined that declaratory relief would not be available unless the borrower was willing to repay the loan. In short, Kelly J.A. was not prepared to grant relief to the borrower under any circumstances.

Laskin J.A. (as he then was) reached the same conclusion while framing the issue differently. Assuming that the mortgage transaction was void as between the parties, the true question was whether the borrower could obtain declaratory relief as to the invalidity of the mortgage without being prepared to repay the loan. Laskin J.A. responded "no", for the reason that the borrower was a party to an executed illegal transaction. Finally, he concluded [at page 537] that the facts of the case came within section 601 of the American Law Institute's, *Restatement of the Law of Contracts* which provides "If refusal to enforce or to rescind an illegal bargain would produce a harmful effect on parties for whose protection the law making the bargain illegal exists, enforcement or rescission, whichever is appropriate, is allowed."

The fourth decision is *Royal Bank of Canada v. Grobman et al.*, [(1977), 18 O.R. (2d) 636 (H.C.)], rendered by Krever J. (as he then was) of the Ontario High Court. One of the two issues raised in that case was whether a mortgage taken by the Bank, and which exceeded the 70% loan to value ratio prescribed by the *Bank Act* [R.S.C. 1970, c. B-1], was unenforceable on grounds of illegality. The borrower relied "strongly" on the reasoning of the Supreme Court in *Bank of Toronto v. Perkins* (1883), 8 S.C.R. 603. In that case, and at that time, the Bank Act [*An Act relating to Banks and Banking*, S.C. 1871, c. 5, s. 40] dictated: "The Bank shall not, either direct or indirectly, lend money: . . . upon the . . . hypothecation of any lands". When the plaintiff bank sought to establish its right under the hypothec, the defendant borrower resisted successfully. At page 610 Ritchie C.J. observed: "It would be a curious state of the law if, after the Legislature had prohibited a transaction, parties could enter into it, and, in defiance of the law, compel courts to enforce and give effect to their illegal transactions." Strong J. reiterated the state of the law as it stood at the end of the nineteenth century (at page 613): "Whenever the doing of any act is expressly forbidden by statute, whether on grounds of public policy or otherwise, the English courts hold the act, if done, to be void, though no express words of avoidance are contained in the enactment itself."

In response to the argument based on *Perkins*, Krever J. noted in that case there was an express prohibition against lending on the security of land whereas in *Grobman* the *Bank Act* did not prohibit such lending transactions, but only the amount which could be loaned on the security of land. He went on to suggest that this distinction may be significant in any consideration as to whether Parliament intended to invalidate mortgages given in contravention of the loan to value ratio prescribed by the *Bank Act*.

Without expressly stating as much, Justice Krever's analysis embraces the understanding that if the statutory prohibition goes to the performance of the mortgage contract, and not its formation, the case falls outside the illegality doctrine. Applying *St. John Shipping Corpn. v. Rank (Joseph) Ltd.*, *supra*, it can reasonably be maintained that this was not a case in which the legislature either expressly or impliedly prohibited the giving or taking of a mortgage. However, there is also another valid ground for distinguishing *Bank of Toronto v. Perkins*, *supra*.

I hasten to point out that *Perkins* was on appeal from the Quebec Court of Appeal and that the case was decided on both the ground of illegality at common law and pursuant to Articles 13, 14 and 15 of the *Civil Code of Lower Canada* [1866]. (The Supreme Court appears to have been undecided as to which law was applicable.) Article 13 declared: "No one can by private agreement, validly contravene the laws of public order and good morals." Article 14 went on to state that: "Prohibitive laws import nullity, although such nullity, be not therein expressed." Article 15 of the Code provided that the word "shall" in a statute was to be construed as "imperative". In short, *Perkins* is a case where the Civil Code had the effect of nullifying the hypothec, as did the illegality doctrine (see discussion, *infra*, with respect to the bijuridical nature of the Federal Court).

Justice Krever's decision in *Grobman* is best known for his criticism of the illegality doctrine found at pages 651-652 of his reasons: "As I understand the evolution of the current law of contract, modern judicial thinking has developed in a way that has considerably refined the knee-jerk reflexive reaction to a plea of illegality." He formulated the modern approach in this way (at page 653): "The serious consequences of invalidating the contract, the social utility of those consequences and a determination of the class of persons for whom the prohibition was enacted, are all factors which the Court will weigh."

Justice Krever went on to adopt the reasoning of Laskin J.A. in *Sidmay* and the principle articulated in the *Restatement of the Law of Contracts*, *supra*. In the end, he held that it would be inconsistent with the purpose underlying the existence of the lending restriction to hold the security unenforceable.

At this point, it is proper to ask how it is that the classical model of illegality differs from the modern approach. In my view, the latter approach rejects the understanding that simply because a contract is prohibited by statute it is illegal and, therefore, void *ab initio*. There are alternative ways of expressing this legal conclusion: (1) the contract may be declared illegal but relief is granted under the guise of an exception. Alternatively, (2) the contract is held not to be illegal and therefore enforceable. In either case the legal result is the same. The other distinguishing feature of the modern approach is that enforceability of a contract is dependent upon an assessment of the legislative purpose or objects underlying the statutory prohibition. Under the classical model, the purpose of the statute was only relevant when determining whether the prohibition was for the sole purpose of raising revenue. Today, the purpose and object of a statutory prohibition is relevant when deciding whether the contract is or is not enforceable. Against this background I am in a position to deal with the doctrine of illegality as it applies to the facts of the present case.

5. <u>Analysis</u>

.....

Applying the above doctrinal framework to the facts of this case, the first question is whether it can be said that subsection 18(1) of the *Immigration Regulations, 1978* either expressly or impliedly prohibits persons such as the applicant from entering into and pursuing employment, without a work permit. In my view, the words of that provision leave no doubt that what the applicant did was prohibited by statute: "<u>no person</u>, other than a Canadian citizen or permanent resident, <u>shall engage or continue in employment</u> in Canada" [underlining added]. Even if I were to concede that those words do not evidence an express prohibition, it certainly arises by implication. In reaching this conclusion I am aware of Lord Devlin's caution, in *St. John Shipping Corpn.*, *supra*, not to readily imply a prohibition. But this is certainly not a case where the statutory prohibition goes to the performance of the contract as opposed to its formation.

Under the classical model of the illegality doctrine, the fact that the applicant acted in good faith is an irrelevant consideration. Accordingly, her employment during the period May 9 to September 23, 1993, constituted an illegal contract which was void *ab initio*. Assuming this to be so, the next issue is whether employment under an illegal contract can constitute insurable employment within the meaning of the *Unemployment Insurance Act*. If I accept that the applicant's employment contract was void from the outset then surely that question must be answered in the negative. Nonetheless, I am not prepared to accept the classical model for several reasons.

First, I am of the view that the classical model has long since lost its persuasive force and is no longer being applied consistently. The doctrine is honoured more in its breach than in its observance through the proliferation of so-called judicial "exceptions" to the rule. . . . In my view, decisions such as *Sidmay* and *Grobman* mark a new era in the illegality doctrine while retaining the quintessential feature underlying its existence. That feature is the jurisdiction of the courts to refuse relief to those in breach of a statutory prohibition, the grounds of refusal being on a principled and not arbitrary basis.

The second reason for rejecting the classical model is that it fails to account for the reality that today a finding of illegality is dependent, not only on the purpose underlying the statutory prohibition, but also on the remedy being sought and the consequences which flow from a finding that a contract is unenforceable. It must be remembered that the law of illegality arose out of a live controversy between parties to an allegedly illegal contract. In this case, there is no live controversy between contracting parties and the ramifications of declaring an employment contract illegal are too far-reaching. For example, I might be prepared to speculate that an Ontario court would not hold the applicant's employer liable for breach of contract had it dismissed her after learning that she did not have the required work permit. But am I to assume that the applicant would have no right to unpaid wages earned prior to the dismissal . . .? What if the applicant's employer hired her knowing full well that she had not received a work permit. Would this factor make her claim for unpaid wages more palatable? What if the applicant had been injured on the job? Would an Ontario court conclude that she was not entitled to benefits under the *Workers' Compensation Act* [R.S.O. 1990, c. W.11] of that province? The fact that so many statutes predicate entitlement or eligibility on an existing contract of service is reason enough for any court to decline the invitation to automatically declare any employment contract invalid on grounds of illegality, and more so if the declaration is based on the tenets of the classical doctrine of illegality.

I think it also important to note that the common law of illegality can vary from province to province. There is no seminal jurisprudence on this issue that has yet emanated from the Supreme Court of Canada. Each case turns on its facts within a particular statutory framework. Arguably, this Court should be applying the common law doctrine of illegality as understood and applied in each province. In theory, the legal consequences flowing from a person's failure to obtain a work permit, as required under the *Immigration Act*, could be dependent on the common law of the province in which the employment contract arose. Given the bijuridical nature of the Federal Court, we cannot lose sight of the fact that cases originating from Quebec are to be decided under the illegality provisions found within the *Civil Code of Québec* [S.Q. 1991, c. 64]. Article 13 in force when *Bank of Toronto v. Perkins, supra,* was decided has been recast as Article 9 of the new Civil Code. Article 1413 of that Code provides that: "A contract whose object is prohibited by law or contrary to public order is null": See also Articles 1412 and 1418. . . .

It is true that this Court need only decide the issue of legality in the federal context and nothing we decide with respect to the validity or enforceability of a contract of employment is binding on the provincial courts. Nonetheless, I believe that the Federal Court should strive to promote consistency in decision making with respect to entitlement to unemployment insurance benefits.

Professor Waddams suggests that where a statute prohibits the formation of a contract the courts should be free to decide the consequences (at page 372). I agree. If legislatures do not wish to spell out in detail the contractual consequences flowing from a breach of a statutory prohibition, and are content to impose only a penalty or administrative sanction, then it is entirely within a court's jurisdiction to determine, in effect, whether other sanctions should be imposed. As the doctrine of illegality is not a creature of statute, but of judicial creation, it is incumbent on the present judiciary to ensure that its premises accord with contemporary values. One need only look at the Supreme Court's now infamous decision in *Christie v. The York Corporation*, [1940] S.C.R. 139 to appreciate the significance of this observation. In that case, the classical principles of contract supported the right of a merchant to refuse to accept an offer from a person of colour. Even without human rights legislation, we know that the case would not be decided the same way today.

I also note that, in the law of tort, the effect of wrongdoing on the part of a plaintiff is no longer as severe as it was in the past. . . .

In conclusion, the extent to which the precepts of the common law doctrine of illegality are ill-suited to resolving the issue at hand provides the impetus for this Court to chart a course of analysis which is reflective of both the modern approach and its public law *milieu*. In my opinion, the doctrine of statutory illegality in the federal context is better served by the following principle (not rule): where a contract is expressly or impliedly prohibited by statute, a court may refuse to grant relief to a party when, in all of the circumstances of the case, including regard to the objects and purposes of the statutory prohibition, it would be contrary to public policy, reflected in the relief claimed, to do so.

As the doctrine of illegality rests on the understanding that it would be contrary to public policy to allow a person to maintain an action on a contract prohibited by statute, then it is only appropriate to identify those policy considerations which outweigh the applicant's *prima facie* right to unemployment insurance benefits. Public policy is, of course, a variable concept which is more easily illustrated than defined (e.g. the case of the highwaymen discussed *supra*). In the present case, the public policy dimension manifests itself in two ways. The first is reflected in the strongly held belief that a person should not benefit from his or her own wrong. This is an alternative way of expressing moral disapprobation for wrongful conduct. The second rests in the understanding that relief should not be available to a party if it would have the effect of undermining the purposes or objects of the two federal statutes which are involved in this judicial review application. While on the one hand we have to consider the policy behind the legislation being violated, the *Immigration Act*, we must also consider the policy behind the legislation which gives rise to the benefits that have been denied, the *Unemployment Act*.

The purposes underlying the *Unemployment Insurance Act* are enshrined in the reasons of Wilson J. in *Abrahams v. Attorney General of Canada*, [1983] 1 S.C.R.2. In that case, the Supreme Court considered the interpretation of a section of the *Unemployment Insurance Act*, 1971 [S.C. 1970-71-72, c. 48] providing that a claimant who lost his employment because of a strike was not allowed to claim benefits unless "regularly engaged" in other employment. Wilson J. on behalf of the Court found that it was, "legitimate to ask what the object of the legislature was" in enacting the provision. She concluded that a "liberal" interpretation of the re-entitlement provision would resolve the matter in favour of the claimant and fulfil the overall purpose of the Act to make benefits available to the unemployed.

On the other hand, there are the objectives underlying the restrictions found within the *Immigration Act*. The clearest statement of the purpose underlying the requirement that a person receive a work permit before engaging in employment is found in subsections 20(1) and (3) of the *Immigration Regulations, 1978*. Subsection 20(1) provides that an immigration officer shall not issue a work permit If "in his opinion" the employment of persons such as the applicant: "will adversely affect the employment opportunities for Canadian citizens". Subsection 20(3) goes on to provide that in forming an opinion, the immigration officer is required to consider whether the prospective employer has made reasonable efforts to attract or train Canadian citizens or permanent residents. Consideration must also be given to: "whether the wages and working conditions offered [by the prospective employer] are sufficient to attract and retain in employment Canadian citizens or permanent residents." The latter consideration may be said to be a politically correct way of stating that if Canadians are unwilling to accept poorly paid employment, it can be made available to lawful immigrants.

Using common sense, it can be seriously questioned whether a person who gains employment as a housekeeper would adversely affect the employment opportunities of Canadians. However, I decline to pursue this type of analysis for the reason that it is not for this Court to speculate on whether a work permit would have issued had it been sought by the applicant. To hold otherwise would be tantamount to placing the onus on the Minister to establish in each and every case that a work permit would not have issued. In the end, I recognize that the legislative purpose underlying the requirement of legal immigrants to obtain a work permit is compelling, but non-determinative of the issue at hand. I turn now to the other policy consideration noted earlier, that is, the strongly held belief that a person should not benefit from his or her own wrong.

Moral disapprobation is likely to arise in those cases where a person gains entry to this country through stealth or deception, obtains employment and then seeks unemployment benefits after losing his or her job. Public policy, of course, cannot be equated with public opinion. But there are occasions when community values are rationally supported and not reflective of a "knee-jerk" reaction to a multi-layered problem. While moral disapprobation of employment obtained in flagrant disregard of Canadian laws is not an unreasonable policy consideration, this sentiment should not be permitted to degenerate into the belief that everyone who gains employment in Canada without a work permit should be so judged.

In my view, this is a case in which the *bona fides* of the party seeking relief is of critical significance. Ms. Still is not an illegal immigrant. In concluding that she acted in good faith, the Tax Court Judge took into consideration the government document provided to her. The significant portion [at paragraph 1] reads as follows: "The [applicant] is . . . hereby eligible to apply for employment and/or student authorizations". That document can be said to serve one of two purposes. First, it reinforces the Tax Court Judge's conclusion that the applicant had acted in good faith (in ignorance of the law). Alternatively, it can be said that the document either induced or misled the applicant into believing that she could obtain employment without a work permit. As this argument was not raised before us, I refrain from commenting further.

There is one other factor I believe to be of significance. It is open to ask whether the denial of unemployment benefits is a *de facto* penalty which is disproportionate to the statutory breach. I note that there is no express penalty for the breach in question and that a conviction under the general penal provision could not be obtained because of the requirement that a person knowingly contravene the *Immigration Act*. In effect, the applicant is not subject to any penalty under that legislation because of the statutory breach. If the *Immigration Act* is only concerned with those who knowingly fail to obtain a work permit, why should this Court impose a penalty amounting to thousands of dollars in benefits? The Tax Court Judge expressed concerns about the possible depletion of the unemployment insurance fund by "illegal" workers, however it should be noted in this case that both the claimant and the employer contributed to the fund during the period of "illegal" employment, thus the solvency of the fund was not affected. The Tax Court Judge also concluded that the "social utility" in denying the applicant unemployment benefits lay in the understanding that it would discourage the employment of "non-citizens and non-residents". I take the Tax Court Judge's reasons to mean that the purpose of the requirement to obtain a work permit is to discourage illegal immigrants from undermining the laws of Canada. In response, I simply note that the applicant, Ms. Still, is not an illegal immigrant and that the *Immigration Act* does not seek to discourage her from working in Canada. Rather it encourages her to seek employment for which there are not enough qualified Canadians or employment which Canadians are unwilling to accept. The fabric of many a nation has been woven from the cloth of those who have fallen into the latter category.

Having regard to objects of the *Unemployment Insurance Act*, the fact that the applicant is a legal immigrant to this country and that she acted in good faith, I am not prepared to conclude that she is disentitled to unemployment insurance benefits on the ground of illegality. I recognize that the object of the statutory prohibition is a compelling one, but that in the circumstances of this case the penalty imposed is disproportionate to the breach. Allowing the applicant to claim benefits would not invite people to come to Canada and work illegally. In fact, for a judge to find that an illegal immigrant to Canada acted in good faith would be nothing short of an oxymoron. The payment of unemployment insurance premiums would not by itself guarantee the right to benefits. No one is being given a licence to abuse Canada's social services. In the end, public policy weighs in favour of legal immigrants who have acted in good faith. . . . In conclusion, it is in the public interest, not contrary to public policy, to grant unemployment benefits to the applicant.

Undoubtedly, there will be a few who would prefer to see the classical model of the illegality doctrine applied to the issue at hand. Admittedly, that approach promotes certainty in the law and ease of administration, at least for the Unemployment Insurance Commission. But a uniform approach, while convenient, carries with it the risk of undue rigidity. There are occasions, and this is one, where certainty must give way to flexibility. . . . If I am wrong, it is open to Parliament to amend the legislation.

6. Disposition

In conclusion, I am of the opinion that this judicial review application must be allowed, the decision of the Tax Court of Canada dated September 18, 1996 set aside and the matter referred back to the Tax Court for reconsideration on the basis that the employment held by the applicant for the period May 9 to September 23, 1993 constituted insurable employment within the meaning of the *Unemployment Insurance Act*.

[Strayer and Linden JJ.A. concurred.]

NOTES and QUESTIONS

1. In *Transport North American Express Inc. v. New Solutions Financial Corp.*, [2004] S.C.J. No 9, 235 D.L.R. (4th) 385 (S.C.C.), Arbour J., for the majority, expressly approved, at para. 20, of the "excellent treatment of the doctrine's history" in *Still*.

2. *Still* raises the issues of whether an illegal contract should bar receipt of a benefit. There are various other ways in which issues of the effects of illegality can arise. The most straightforward issue is whether the contract can be enforced in the sense of whether the parties' expectations can be protected. For instance, Buyer and Seller have agreed on the sale of a boat. They have also agreed to state a low, false, price on the receipt so that Buyer may avoid some provincial sales tax. Buyer (or Seller) then refuses to go through with the deal. Should the contract be enforced? See, *e.g.*, *Zimmermann v. Letkeman*, [1978] 1 S.C.R. 1097.

3. A different remedial issue relates to restitution. Suppose Buyer, above, had paid a deposit and then Seller had backed out. Should Buyer be able to recover the deposit? "The general rule at common law is that money paid and other benefits conferred under agreements rendered unenforceable by reason of illegality cannot be recovered in Quasi-contract, or, as we would now say, in a restitutionary claim." McCamus, *supra*, p. 791, at 794. There are some exceptions, such as *locus poenitentiae* (time for repentance). It was pointed out in *Zimmerman*, *supra*, at 1105 that a party to an illegal contract which is still executory can recover what he has paid or transferred to his co-contractor if he repents before the illegal purpose was substantially performed.

Another principle allows recovery where the parties are not *in pari delicto*, that is not equally culpable. An example can be found in *Kiriri Cotton Co. Ltd. v. Dewani*, [1960] A.C. 192 (P.C.), where Lord Denning allowed the recovery of "key money" (an illegal deposit on an apartment) in Uganda. The purpose of rent control was to protect tenants. The court stated, at 205 "Whether it be a rich tenant who pays a premium as a bribe in order to "jump the queue," or a poor tenant who is at his wit's end to find accommodation, neither is so much to blame as the landlord who is using his property rights so as to exploit those in need of a roof over their heads."

4. For a further example of a situation in which the parties were not *in pari delicto* and where the purpose of the legislation was taken into account, see *Re Ont. Securities Comm. and Br. Can. Commodity Options Ltd.* (1979), 93 D.L.R. (3d) 208 (Ont. H.C.). Here the purchaser of securities from an unregistered trader was allowed to recover the price, the court being influenced by the fact that he was a member of the class of persons which the legislation was designed to protect.

5. *Ouston v. Zurowski* (1985), 63 B.C.L.R. 89 (C.A.), contains a useful discussion of the exceptions to the rule of non-recovery under an illegal contract. The plaintiffs had paid $2,200 to the defendants to participate in an illegal pyramid scheme, the defendants promising to repay the money if the scheme did not work out. The defendants knew the scheme was illegal while the plaintiffs did not. Nevertheless they were *in pari delicto* because of their common intention to participate in a scheme which was in fact illegal. The plaintiffs, however, successfully brought themselves within the *locus poenitentiae* principle, Esson J.A., stating at 103:

> What is important is that they abandoned their participation in the scheme before the illegal purpose was carried out in any substantial way, that they entered into it without knowledge of its illegality and were induced to do so by the defendants who had such knowledge.

6. McCamus, *supra*, at p. 791, has argued for a more flexible "golden rule" which would permit recovery in some cases even where the parties are *in pari delicto*, at 810 and 865-67:

> The new golden rule approach to the analysis of restitutionary claims under illegal agreements requires simply that the plaintiff's entitlement to the value of what would otherwise be a windfall for the defendant at his expense be assessed in the light of the purposes and structure of the statutory scheme or rule rendering the underlying transaction unenforceable. The court must consider whether the imposition of the additional sanction of rendering restitutionary relief unavailable is either necessary or so highly desirable for the proper implementation of the statutory policy that the common law's general policy of restoring the value of benefits conferred under ineffective transactions ought to be suppressed. As in *St. John Shipping* [*supra*], it would no doubt be appropriate for a court to consider whether the sanctions imposed in the statutory scheme itself constitute so sufficient a disincentive to unlawful conduct that further sanctions of this kind are not necessary. A court would also consider whether this particular sanction is suited to the crime or misconduct in question. As well, the court would wish to look at such considerations as the relative fault or immorality manifest in the conduct of the parties, the gravity of the offence or conflict with the statutory scheme in question, the extent of the injury to the public interest caused by the particular transaction, and the degree to which the conferral of a substantial windfall on the defendant appears to be unacceptable for these or other reasons.
>
> .....
>
> What has been suggested here is the adoption of a similar analysis for the secondary question of restitutionary liability that arises once it has been determined that the contract is unenforceable. Too often in the past it has been simply assumed that the contractual and restitutionary issues can be collapsed and that if there is a policy basis for refusing to enforce the agreement, so, too, is there a policy justification for refusing restitutionary relief. That this is plainly not so becomes evident when one considers the questions of enforceability and restitutionary relief for what they are—as determinations by the judiciary to impose or withhold additional civil sanctions beyond those sanctions, if any, that have been imposed by the statutory scheme itself. As has been argued, the sanction of unenforceability of the contract is different in important ways from the sanction of not allowing relief in restitution. The policy analysis that would support the imposition of the former would not necessarily support the latter. Indeed, it has been argued that there will be many circumstances, in addition to these now clearly recognized in our law, in which it will be appropriate to hold the agreement unenforceable but still allow a restitutionary claim. The enquiry in each case, then, must be one of determining whether the policies underlying the statutory scheme that renders the agreement unenforceable would also be well-served by the denial of restitutionary relief and then of assessing the desirability of doing so in the light of the general policy of the common law to allow restitutionary recovery of benefits conferred under ineffective transactions. This approach to the analysis of restitutionary claims—here referred to as the new golden rule—has been argued to be manifest in a number of features of our current law on the consequences of illegality and in recent developments in this area. It becomes all the more apparent that this approach is in fact utilized by the judiciary and that, indeed, its use is indispensable if attention is drawn beyond the boundaries of traditional "illegality" to the more general problem of agreements in conflict with statutory authority, of which illegality forms only a part. As has been seen, the case law on *ultra vires* and "informality" reaches different conclusions than the illegality cases, no doubt because a contextual analysis of the golden rule variety suggests that these kinds of statutory schemes, which, at their margins cannot be clearly distinguished from "illegality," do not, as a matter of policy, require the withholding of restitutionary relief.
>
> More explicit recognition of the value of the golden rule approach in the context of the traditional "illegality" cases would, however, facilitate more thoughtful analysis of these issues and a reconsideration of the value of earlier authority. Moreover, explicit adoption of this approach would, it has been argued, relieve the pressure otherwise bearing on the enforceability concept to render agreements enforceable in order to accommodate what are in effect restitutionary objectives. Such a development would also relieve the pressure on the established

exceptions to the *Holman v. Johnson* [*supra*] principle to expand in order to accommodate what are, in reality, meritorious restitutionary claims of *in pari delicto* parties. . . .

It has been argued that a more open use of . . . [the golden rule] analysis would lead to a greater recognition of the availability of restitutionary relief to parties who are, in the traditional sense, *in pari delicto*. Nonetheless, it should be emphasized that it is not part of the thesis here advanced that such relief should invariably, or perhaps even normally, be available to such parties. The appropriateness of granting such relief is a matter to be determined on a case by case basis. What is being suggested is that the golden rule approach will generate consideration of the factors that are material to the determination of whether such a claim should lie. To the extent that this approach is likely to lead, however, to a greater availability of restitutionary claims in this context, this development should be seen as consistent with more general developments occurring in Canadian restitutionary law.

[Footnotes omitted.]

7. The need to distinguish between enforcement and restitutionary claims has been pointed out by critics of *Communities Economic Development Fund v. Canadian Pickles Corp.* (1991), 85 D.L.R. (4th) 88 (S.C.C.). This case did not involve an illegal contract but rather one that was made *ultra vires* the statutory powers of the Development Fund. Nevertheless, similar enforceability arguments can be seen as relevant. The statute (*Communities Economic Development Fund Act*, C.C.S.M., c. C155) authorized the fund to encourage development in remote communities. The fund lent money to a corporation near Winnipeg that was not remote. In an action against the guarantor of the loan (who was also a shareholder, officer, and the director of the corporation) the defence was advanced that the loan was *ultra vires* the fund. The court held that the contract of guarantee was void because the loan itself was *ultra vires* the fund.

The decision has been criticized by Swan, "The 'Void' Contract; *Ultra Vires* and Illegality" (1992), 21 Can. Bus. L.J. 115 as not paying attention to the legislative purpose of the funding limits; the relationship of the penalty to the degree of fault; and, at 118, "the distinction between a claim (whether made explicitly on unjust enrichment for 'money had and received' or *quantum meruit* or not) for what is, in effect, the value of the benefit conferred on the defendant and a claim for damages for the lost opportunity to make a profit".

8. Some contracts, sometimes called "void" rather than "illegal", will only be treated as unenforceable to the extent that they actually offend public policy. Restraint of trade falls into this category, so that offending provisions will be severed, if possible, and the remainder enforced. The issue of whether severance is appropriate also arises where contracts involve the payment of a criminal rate of interest (above 60%, contrary to s. 347 of the Criminal Code). Such contracts can fall along a spectrum from "loan sharking" to good faith commercial transactions between equals.

When is severance possible? Will such a remedy only be granted where words can be deleted without revision of remaining words? Or is "notional severance" possible, for instance with respect to a criminal rate of interest, in effect rewriting the agreement to reduce the effective annual rate of interest. On the one hand, notional severance can be seen as an innovation in the common law which would undermine whatever policy underlies the criminal prohibition. On the other, a posture of remedial flexibility rather than formalism allows the avoidance of unjust enrichment. See *Transport North American Express Inc. v. New Solutions Financial Corp.*, *supra*. Here a majority of the court accepted notional severance as an available remedy with respect to a criminal rate of interest. Four relevant factors were identified, at para. 42.

As outlined above, in [*William E. Thomson Associates Inc. v. Carpenter* (1989), 61 D.L.R. (4th) 1], Blair J.A. identified four considerations relevant to the determination of whether public policy ought to allow an otherwise illegal agreement to be partially enforced rather than being declared void ab initio in the face of illegality in the contract:

1. whether the purpose or policy of s. 347 [of the Criminal Code] would be subverted by severance;

2. whether the parties entered into the agreement for an illegal purpose or with an evil intention;

    3. the relative bargaining position of the parties and their conduct in reaching the agreement;

    4. the potential for the debtor to enjoy an unjustified windfall.

In this case the rate of interest was reduced from 90.9% to the highest legal rate: 60%.

Chapter 14

REMEDIES

1. Introduction

Much of the subject-matter covered in a contracts course deals with the creation of the contractual obligation and the various ways in which that obligation can be broken. Throughout the preceding materials there have been references to the consequences of breach and to some of the remedies that are available to the innocent party following a breach of contract. In this chapter, those remedies will be considered in more detail and various materials are included in order to expose their underlying principles.

The variety of remedies available to the innocent party for breach of contract may be broadly classified as either compensatory (substitutional) or coercive (specific). The compensatory remedy, which provides the normal relief in actions for breach of contract, is the action for damages. Its purpose is to provide monetary compensation for losses suffered by the aggrieved party as the result of the defendant's breach. However, as in many areas of law, arguments constantly arise over the various means by which this compensation can be achieved and over duties that may be imposed upon the innocent party whose interests have been injured by the defendant's default. Recently, another dimension has been added to this debate. Is it appropriate to award damages on the basis of gains achieved by the breaching party, irrespective of whether the innocent party has suffered loss?

Once the money judgment in an action for breach of contract is granted by the court, the plaintiff is of course left to effect the judgment by the best means available, including, if necessary, the seizure of the defendant's assets, though this action is subject to a large number of legislative safeguards which differ in each province. The coercive remedies, in contrast, are directly aimed at holding the parties in breach to their contractual promises, either by requiring performance of the contractual obligations through the decree of specific performance or by prohibiting behaviour contrary to the contractual obligation through an injunction. In the event that the party in breach fails to comply with a coercive remedy, it is enforced by the power of the court to treat the failure as a species of civil contempt. This can involve, in the court's discretion, the imposition of a fine or term of imprisonment.

It is important to appreciate that the materials in this chapter deal with the general principles of contractual remedies. As in many areas of contract law, more specialized rules have been developed in respect of particular types of contracts, especially contracts for the sale of goods and for the sale of land. Some of those rules are discussed in this chapter, but others are left for consideration in discrete courses (such as Land Transactions and Remedies). The application of the general principles to some special types of contracts must therefore be preceded by some careful research.

2.   Damages: The Interests Protected

HOLMES, THE PATH OF THE LAW

(1897), 10 Harv. L. Rev. 457, at 458, 459, 462

A legal duty so-called is nothing but a prediction that if a man does or omits certain things he will be made to suffer in this or that way by the judgment of the court . . . if you want to know the law and nothing else, you must look at it as a bad man, who cares only for the material consequences which such knowledge enables him to predict, not as a good one, who finds his reasons for conduct, whether inside the law or outside of it, in the vaguer sanctions of conscience. . . .

The duty to keep a contract at common law means a prediction that you must pay damages if you do not keep it,—and nothing else. If you commit a tort, you are liable to pay a compensatory sum. If you commit a contract, you are liable to pay a compensatory sum unless the promised event comes to pass, and that is all the difference. But such a mode of looking at the matter stinks in the nostrils of those who think it advantageous to get as much ethics into the law as they can. It was good enough for Lord Coke, however, and here, as in many other cases, I am content to abide with him. In *Bromage v. Genning* [(1616), 81 E.R. 540], a prohibition was sought in the King's Bench against a suit in the marches of Wales for the specific performance of a covenant to grant a lease, and Coke said that it would subvert the intention of the covenantor, since he intends it to be at his election either to lose the damages or to make the lease. Sergeant Harris for the plaintiff confessed that he moved the matter against his conscience, and a prohibition was granted. . . .

POSNER, ECONOMIC ANALYSIS OF LAW

6th ed. (2003), at 119-120

[Holmes' view], though overbroad, contains an important economic insight. In many cases it is uneconomical to induce completion of performance of a contract after it has been broken. I agree to purchase 100,000 widgets custom-ground for use as components in a machine that I manufacture. After I have taken delivery of 10,000, the market for my machine collapses. I promptly notify my supplier that I am terminating the contract, and admit that my termination is a breach. When notified of the termination he has not yet begun the custom grinding of the other 90,000 widgets, but he informs me that he intends to complete his performance under the contract and bill me accordingly. The custom-ground widgets have no use other than in my machine, and a negligible scrap value. To give the supplier a remedy that induced him to complete the contract after the breach would waste resources. The law is alert to this danger and, under the doctrine of mitigation of damages, would not give the supplier damages for any costs he incurred in continuing production after my notice of termination. . . .

Now suppose that the widget contract is broken by the seller rather than the buyer. I really need those 100,000 custom-ground widgets for my machine but the supplier, after producing 50,000, is forced to suspend production because of a mechanical failure. Other suppliers are in a position to supply the remaining widgets that I need but I insist that the original supplier complete his performance of the contract. If the law compels completion (by ordering specific performance, a form of injunction), the supplier will have to make arrangements with other producers to complete his contract with me. Probably it will be more costly for him to procure an alternative supplier than for me to do so directly (after all, I know my own needs best); otherwise he would have done it voluntarily, to minimize his liability for the breach. To compel completion of the contract (or costly negotiations to discharge the promisor) would again result in a waste of resources, and again the law does not compel completion but confines the victim to simple damages.

But what *are* simple contract damages? Usually the objective of giving the promisor an incentive to fulfill his promise unless the result would be an inefficient use of resources (the production of the unwanted widgets in the first example, the roundabout procurement of a substitute supplier in the second) can be achieved by giving the promisee his expected profit on the transaction. If the supplier in the first example receives his expected profit from making 10,000 widgets, he will have no incentive to make the unwanted 90,000. We do not want him to make them; no one wants them. In the second example, if I receive my expected profit from dealing with the original supplier, I become indifferent to whether he completes his performance.

In these examples the breach was committed only to avert a larger loss, but in some cases a party is tempted to break his contract simply because his profit from breach would exceed his profit from completion of the contract. If it would also exceed the expected profit to the other party from completion of the contract, and if damages are limited to the loss of that profit, there will be an incentive to commit a breach. But there should be; it is an efficient breach. Suppose I sign a contract to deliver 100,000 custom-ground widgets at 10¢ apiece to A for use in his boiler factory. After I have delivered 10,000, B comes to me, explains that he desperately needs 25,000 custom-ground widgets at once since otherwise he will be forced to close his pianola factory at great cost, and offers me 15¢ apiece for them. I sell him the widgets and as a result do not complete timely delivery to A, causing him to lose $1,000 in profits. Having obtained an additional profit of $1,250 on the sale to B, I am better off even after reimbursing A for his loss, and B is also better off. The breach is Pareto superior. True, if I had refused to sell to B, he could have gone to A and negotiated an assignment to him of part of A's contract with me. But this would have introduced an additional step, with additional transaction costs—and high ones, because it would be a bilateral-monopoly negotiation. On the other hand, litigation costs would be reduced.

NOTES

1. For a challenge to Posner's view, see Macneil, "Efficient Breaches of Contract: Circles in the Sky" (1982), 68 Va. L. Rev. 947.

2. Although it may be admitted that the normal goal of contractual remedies is to compensate the innocent party for breach, there are several ways in which that goal can be accomplished. The next abstract is from a pioneering work on contract damages and explores the main bases upon which common law courts have sought to fix the compensation to which the innocent party is entitled. It is followed by further materials which illustrate the different purposes served by contract damages and question their interrelationship.

FULLER AND PERDUE, THE RELIANCE INTEREST IN CONTRACT DAMAGES

(1936), 46 Yale L.J. 52, at 52-63

The proposition that legal rules can be understood only with reference to the purposes they serve would today scarcely be regarded as an exciting truth. The notion that law exists as a means to an end has been commonplace for at least half a century. There is, however, no justification for assuming, because this attitude has now achieved respectability, and even triteness, that it enjoys a pervasive application in practice. Certainly there are even today few legal treatises of which it may be said that the author has throughout clearly defined the purposes which his definitions and distinctions serve. We are still all too willing to embrace the conceit that it is possible to manipulate legal concepts without the orientation which comes from the simple inquiry: toward what end is this activity directed? Nietzsche's observation, that the most common stupidity consists in forgetting what one is trying to do, retains a discomforting relevance to legal science.

In no field is this more true than in that of damages. In the assessment of damages the law tends to be conceived, not as purposive ordering of human affairs, but as a kind of juristic mensuration. The language of the decisions sounds in terms not of command but of discovery. We *measure the extent* of the injury; we *determine* whether it was *caused* by the defendant's act; we *ascertain* whether the plaintiff has included the *same item* of damage twice in his complaint. One unfamiliar with the unstated premises which language of this sort conceals might almost be led to suppose that Rochester produces some ingenious instrument by which these calculations are accomplished.

It is, as a matter of fact, clear that the things which the law of damages purports to "measure" and "determine"—the "injuries", "items of damage", "causal connections", etc.—are in considerable part its own creations, and that the process of "measuring" and "determining" them is really a part of the process of creating them. This is obvious when courts work on the periphery of existing doctrine, but it is no less true of fundamental and established principles. For example, one frequently finds the "normal" rule of contract damages (which awards to the promisee the value of the expectancy, "the lost profit") treated as a mere corollary of a more fundamental principle, that the purpose of granting damages is to make "compensation" for injury. Yet in this case we "compensate" the plaintiff by giving him something he never had. This seems on the face of things a queer kind of "compensation". We can, to be sure, make the term "compensation" seem appropriate by saying that the defendant's breach "deprived" the plaintiff of the expectancy. But this is in essence only a metaphorical statement of the effect of the legal rule. In actuality the loss which the plaintiff suffers (deprivation of the expectancy) is not a datum of nature but the reflection of a normative order. It appears as a "loss" only by reference to an unstated *ought*. Consequently, when the law gauges damages by the value of the promised performance it is not merely measuring a quantum, but is seeking an end, however vaguely conceived this end may be.

It is for this reason that it is impossible to separate the law of contract damages from the larger body of motives and policies which constitutes the general law of contracts. It is, unfortunately for the simplicity of our subject, impossible to assume that the purposive and policy-directed element of contract law has been exhausted in the rules which define contract and breach. If this were possible the law of contract damages would indeed be simple, and we would have but one measure of recovery of all contracts. Of course this is not the case. What considerations influence the setting up of different measures of recovery for different kinds of contracts? What factors explain the rather numerous exceptions to the normal rule which measures damages by the value of the expectancy? It is clear that these questions cannot be answered without an inquiry into the reasons which underlie (or may underlie) the enforcement of promises generally.

In our own discussion we shall attempt first an analysis of the purposes which may be pursued in awarding contract damages or in "enforcing" contracts generally; then we shall attempt to inquire to what extent, and under what circumstances, these purposes have found expression in the decisions and doctrinal discussions. As the title suggests, the primary emphasis will be on what we call "the reliance interest" as a possible measure of recovery in suits for breach of contract.

THE PURPOSES PURSUED IN AWARDING CONTRACT DAMAGES

It is convenient to distinguish three principal purposes which may be pursued in awarding contract damages. These purposes, and the situations in which they become appropriate, may be stated briefly as follows:

First, the plaintiff has in reliance on the promise of the defendant conferred some value on the defendant. The defendant fails to perform his promise. The court may force the defendant to disgorge the value he received from the plaintiff. The object here may be termed the prevention of gain by the defaulting promisor at the expense of the promisee; more briefly, the prevention of unjust enrichment. The interest protected may be called the *restitution interest*. For our present purposes it is quite immaterial how the suit in such a case be classified, whether as contractual or quasi-contractual, whether as a suit to enforce the contract or as a suit based upon a rescission of the contract. These questions relate to the superstructure of the law, not to the basic policies with which we are concerned.

Secondly, the plaintiff has in reliance on the promise of the defendant changed his position. For example, the buyer under a contract for the sale of land has incurred expense in the investigation of the seller's title, or has neglected the opportunity to enter other contracts. We may award damages to the plaintiff for the purpose of undoing the harm which his reliance on the defendant's promise has caused him. Our object is to put him in as good a position as he was in before the promise was made. The interest protected in this case may be called the *reliance interest*.

Thirdly, without insisting on reliance by the promisee or enrichment of the promisor, we may seek to give the promisee the value of the expectancy which the promise created. We may in a suit for specific performance actually compel the defendant to render the promised performance to the plaintiff, or, in a suit for damages, we may make the defendant pay the money value of this performance. Here our object is to put the plaintiff in as good a position as he would have occupied had the defendant performed his promise. The interest protected in this case we may call the *expectation interest*.

It will be observed that what we have called the *restitution interest* unites two elements: (1) reliance by the promisee, (2) a resultant gain to the promisor. It may for some purposes be necessary to separate these elements. In some cases a defaulting promisor may after his breach be left with an unjust gain which was not taken from the promisee (a third party furnished the consideration), or which was not the result of reliance by the promisee (the promisor violated a promise not to appropriate the promisee's goods). Even in those cases where the promisor's gain results from the promisee's reliance it may happen that damages will be assessed somewhat differently, depending on whether we take the promisor's gain or the promisee's loss as the standard of measurement. Generally, however, in the cases we shall be discussing, gain by the promisor will be accompanied by a corresponding and, so far as its legal measurement is concerned, identical loss to the promisee, so that for our purposes the most workable classification is one which presupposes in the restitution interest a correlation of promisor's gain and promisee's loss. If, as we shall assume, the gain involved in the restitution interest results from and is identical with the plaintiff's loss through reliance, then the restitution interest is merely a special case of the reliance interest; all of the cases coming under the restitution interest will be covered by the reliance interest, and the reliance interest will be broader than the restitution interest only to the extent that it includes cases where the plaintiff has relied on the defendant's promise without enriching the defendant.

It should not be supposed that the distinction here taken between the reliance and expectation interests coincides with that sometimes taken between "losses caused" (*damnum emergens*) and "gains prevented" (*lucrum cessans*). In the first place, though reliance ordinarily results in "losses" of an affirmative nature (expenditures of labor and money) it is also true that opportunities for gain may be foregone in reliance on a promise. Hence the reliance interest must be interpreted as at least potentially covering "gains prevented" as well as "losses caused". (Whether "gains prevented" through reliance on a promise are properly compensable in damages is a question not here determined. Obviously, certain scruples concerning "causality" and "foreseeability" are suggested. It is enough for our present purpose to note that there is nothing in the definition of the reliance interest itself which would exclude items of this sort from consideration.) On the other hand, it is not possible to make the expectation interest entirely synonymous with "gains prevented". The disappointment of an expectancy often entails losses of a positive character.

It is obvious that the three "interests" we have distinguished do not present equal claims to judicial intervention. It may be assumed that ordinary standards of justice would regard the need for judicial intervention as decreasing in the order in which we have listed the three interests. The "restitution interest," involving a combination of unjust impoverishment with unjust gain, presents the strongest case for relief. If, following Aristotle, we regard the purpose of justice as the maintenance of an equilibrium of goods among members of society, the restitution interest presents twice as strong a claim to judicial intervention as the reliance interest, since if A not only causes B to lose one unit but appropriates that unit to himself, the resulting discrepancy between A and B is not one unit but two.

On the other hand, the promisee who has actually relied on the promise, even though he may not thereby have enriched the promisor, certainly presents a more pressing case for relief than the promisee who merely demands satisfaction for his disappointment in not getting what was promised him. In passing from compensation for change of position to compensation for loss of expectancy we pass, to use Aristotle's terms again, from the realm of corrective justice to that of distributive justice. The law no longer seeks merely to heal a disturbed status quo, but to bring into being a new situation. It ceases to act defensively or restoratively, and assumes a more active role. With the transition, the justification for legal relief loses its self-evident quality. It is as a matter of fact no easy thing to explain why the normal rule of contract recovery should be that which measures damages by the value of the promised performance. Since this "normal rule" throws its shadow across our whole subject it will be necessary to examine the possible reasons for its existence. It may be said parenthetically that the discussion which follows, though directed primarily to the normal measure of recovery where damages are sought, also has relevance to the more general question, why should a promise which has not been relied on ever be enforced at all, whether by a decree of specific performance or by an award of damages?

It should also be said that our discussion of "reasons" does not claim to coincide in all particulars with the actual workings of the judicial mind, certainly not with those of any single judicial mind. It is unfortunately very difficult to discuss the possible reasons for rules of law without unwittingly conveying the impression that these "reasons" are the things which control the daily operations of the judicial process. This has had the consequence, at a time when men stand in dread of being labelled "unrealistic", that we have almost ceased to talk about reasons altogether. Those who find unpalatable the rationalistic flavor of what follows are invited to view what they read not as law but as an excursus into legal philosophy, and to make whatever discount that distinction may seem to them to dictate.

WHY SHOULD THE LAW EVER PROTECT THE EXPECTATION INTEREST?

Perhaps the most obvious answer to this question is one which we may label "psychological". This answer would run something as follows: The breach of a promise arouses in the promisee a sense of injury. This feeling is not confined to cases where the promisee has relied on the promise. Whether or not he has actually changed his position because of the promise, the promisee has formed an attitude of expectancy such that a breach of the promise causes him to feel that he has been "deprived" of something which was "his". Since this sentiment is a relatively uniform one, the law has no occasion to go back of it. It accepts it as a datum and builds its rule about it.

The difficulty with this explanation is that the law does in fact go back of the sense of injury which the breach of a promise engenders. No legal system attempts to invest with juristic sanction all promises. Some rule or combination of rules effects a sifting out for enforcement of those promises deemed important enough to society to justify the law's concern with them. Whatever the principles which control this sifting out process may be, they are not convertible into terms of the degree of resentment which the breach of a particular kind of promise arouses. Therefore, though it may be assumed that the impulse to assuage disappointment is one shared by those who make and influence the law, this impulse can hardly be regarded as the key which solves the whole problem of the protection accorded by the law to the expectation interest.

A second possible explanation for the rule protecting the expectancy may be found in the much-discussed "will theory" of contract law. This theory views the contracting parties as exercising, so to speak, a legislative power, so that the legal enforcement of a contract becomes merely an implementing by the state of a kind of private law already established by the parties. If A has made, in proper form, a promise to pay B one thousand dollars, we compel A to pay this sum simply because the rule or *lex* set up by the parties calls for this payment. . . .

It is not necessary to discuss here the contribution which the will theory is capable of making to a philosophy of contract law. Certainly some borrowings from the theory are discernable in most attempts to rationalize the bases of contract liability. It is enough to note here that while the will theory undoubtedly has some bearing on the problem of contract damages, it cannot be regarded as dictating in all cases a recovery of the expectancy. If a contract represents a kind of private law, it is a law which usually says nothing at all about what shall be done when it is violated. A contract is in this respect like an imperfect statute which provides no penalties, and which leaves it to the courts to find a way to effectuate its purposes. There would, therefore, be no necessary contradiction between the will theory and a rule which limited damages to the reliance interest. Under such a rule the penalty for violating the norm established by the contract would simply consist in being compelled to compensate the other party for detrimental reliance. Of course there may be cases where the parties have so obviously anticipated that a certain form of judicial relief will be given that we can, without stretching things, say that by implication they have "willed" that this relief should be given.

This attitude finds a natural application to promises to pay a definite sum of money. But certainly as to most types of contracts it is vain to expect from the will theory a ready-made solution for the problem of damages.

A third and more promising solution of our difficulty lies in an economic or institutional approach. The essence of a credit economy lies in the fact that it tends to eliminate the distinction between present and future (promised) goods. Expectations of future values become, for purposes of trade, present values. In a society in which credit has become a significant and pervasive institution, it is inevitable that the expectancy created by an enforceable promise should be regarded as a kind of property, and breach of the promise as an injury to that property. In such a society the breach of a promise works an "actual" diminution of the promisee's assets—"actual" in the sense that it would be so appraised according to modes of thought which enter into the very fiber of our economic system. That the promisee had not "used" the property which the promise represents (had not relied on the promise) is as immaterial as the question whether the plaintiff in trespass *quare clausum fregit* was using his property at the time it was encroached upon. The analogy to ordinary forms of property goes further, for even in a suit for trespass the recovery is really for an expectancy, an expectancy of possible future uses. Where the property expectancy is limited (as where the plaintiff has only an estate for years) the recovery is reduced accordingly. Ordinary property differs from a contract right chiefly in the fact that it lies within the power of more persons to work a direct injury to the expectancy it represents. It is generally only the promisor or some one working through or upon him who is able to injure the contract expectancy in a direct enough manner to make expedient legal intervention.

The most obvious objection which can be made to the economic or institutional explanation is that it involves a *petitio principii*. A promise has present value, why? Because the law enforces it. "The expectancy", regarded as a present value, is not the cause of legal intervention but the consequence of it. This objection may be reinforced by a reference to legal history. Promises were enforced long before there was anything corresponding to a general system of "credit", and recovery was from the beginning measured by the value of the promised performance, the "agreed price". It may therefore be argued that the "credit system" when it finally emerged was itself in large part built on the foundations of a juristic development which preceded it.

The view just suggested asserts the primacy of law over economics; it sees law not as the creature but as the creator of social institutions. The shift of emphasis thus implied suggests the possibility of a fourth explanation for the law's protection of the unrelied-on expectancy, which we may call *juristic*. This explanation would seek a justification for the normal rule of recovery in some policy consciously pursued by courts and other lawmakers. It would assume that courts have protected the expectation interest because they have considered it wise to do so, not through a blind acquiescence in habitual ways of thinking and feeling, or through an equally blind deference to the individual will. Approaching the problem from this point of view, we are forced to find not a mere explanation for the

rule in the form of some sentimental, volitional, or institutional datum, but articulate reasons for its existence.

What reasons can be advanced? In the first place, even if our interest were
confined to protecting promisees against an out-of-pocket loss, it would still be
possible to justify the rule granting the value of the expectancy, both as a cure
for, and as a prophylaxis against, losses of this sort.

It is a cure for these losses in the sense that it offers the measure of recovery
most likely to reimburse the plaintiff for the (often very numerous and very
difficult to prove) individual acts and forbearances which make up his total
reliance on the contract. If we take into account "gains prevented" by reliance,
that is, losses involved in foregoing the opportunity to enter other contracts, the
notion that the rule protecting the expectancy is adopted as the most effective
means of compensating for detrimental reliance seems not at all far-fetched.
Physicians with an extensive practice often charge their patients the full office
call fee for broken appointments. Such a charge looks on the face of things like
a claim to the promised fee; it seems to be based on the "expectation interest".
Yet the physician making the charge will quite justifiably regard it as compensation for the loss of the opportunity to gain a similar fee from a different patient.
This foregoing of other opportunities is involved to some extent in entering most
contracts, and the impossibility of subjecting this type of reliance to any kind of
measurement may justify a categorical rule granting the value of the expectancy
as the most effective way of compensating for such losses.

The rule that the plaintiff must after the defendant's breach take steps to
mitigate damages tends to corroborate the suspicion that there lies hidden behind
the protection of the expectancy a concern to compensate the plaintiff for the loss
of the opportunity to enter other contracts. Where after the defendant's breach
the opportunity remains open to the plaintiff to sell his services or goods elsewhere, or to fill his needs from another source, he is bound to embrace that
opportunity. Viewed in this way the rule of "avoidable harms" is a qualification
on the protection accorded the expectancy, since it means that the plaintiff, in
those cases where it is applied, is protected only to the extent that he has in reliance
on the contract foregone other equally advantageous opportunities for accom-
plishing the same end.

But, as we have suggested, the rule measuring damages by the expectancy
may also be regarded as a prophylaxis against the losses resulting from detrimental
reliance. Whatever tends to discourage breach of contract tends to prevent the
losses occasioned through reliance. Since the expectation interest furnished a
more easily administered measure of recovery than the reliance interest, it will in
practice offer a more effective sanction against contract breach. It is therefore
possible to view the rule measuring damages by the expectancy in a quasi-criminal
aspect, its purpose being not so much to compensate the promisee as to penalize
breach of promise by the promisor. The rule enforcing the unrelied-on promise
finds the same justification, on this theory, as an ordinance which fines a man for
driving through a stop-light when no other vehicle is in sight.

In seeking justification for the rule granting the value of the expectancy there
is no need, however, to restrict ourselves by the assumption, hitherto made, that

the rule can only be intended to cure or prevent the losses caused by reliance. A justification can be developed from a less negative point of view. It may be said that there is not only a policy in favor of preventing and undoing the harms resulting from reliance, but also a policy in favor of promoting and facilitating reliance on business agreements. As in the case of the stop-light ordinance we are interested not only in preventing collisions but in speeding traffic. Agreements can accomplish little, either for their makers or for society, unless they are made the basis for action. When business agreements are not only made but are also acted on, the division of labor is facilitated, goods find their way to the places where they are most needed, and economic activity is generally stimulated. These advantages would be threatened by any rule which limited legal protection to the reliance interest. Such a rule would in practice tend to discourage reliance. The difficulties in proving reliance and subjecting it to pecuniary measurement are such that the business man knowing, or sensing, that these obstacles stood in the way of judicial relief would hesitate to rely on a promise in any case where the legal sanction was of significance to him. To encourage reliance we must therefore dispense with its proof. For this reason it has been found wise to make recovery on a promise independent of reliance, both in the sense that in some cases the promise is enforced though not relied on (as in the bilateral business agreement) and the sense that recovery is not limited to the detriment incurred in reliance.

The juristic explanation in its final form is then twofold. It rests the protection accorded the expectancy on (1) the need for curing and preventing the harms occasioned by reliance, and (2) on the need for facilitating reliance on business agreements. From this spelling out of a possible juristic explanation, it is clear that there is no incompatibility between it and the economic or institutional explanation. They view the same phenomenon from two different aspects. The essence of both of them lies in the word "credit". The economic explanation views credit from its institutional side; the juristic explanation views it from its rational side. The economic view sees credit as an accepted way of living; the juristic view invites us to explore the considerations of utility which underlie this way of living, and the part which conscious human direction has played in bringing it into being.

The way in which these two points of view supplement one another becomes clearer when we examine separately the economic implications of the two aspects of the juristic explanation. If we rest the legal argument for measuring damages by the expectancy on the ground that this procedure offers the most satisfactory means of compensating the plaintiff for the loss of other opportunities to contract, it is clear that the force of the argument will depend entirely upon the existing economic environment. It would be most forceful in a hypothetical society in which all values were available on the market and where all markets were "perfect" in the economic sense. In such a society there would be no difference between the reliance interest and the expectation interest. The plaintiff's loss in foregoing to enter another contract would be identical with the expectation value of the contract he did make. The argument that granting the value of the expectancy merely compensates for that loss, loses force to the extent that actual conditions depart from those of such a hypothetical society. These observations make it clear why the development of open markets for goods tends to carry in its wake the view that a contract claim is a kind of property, a conception which—for all the importance he attached to it—MacLeod seemed to regard as the product of a kind of legal miracle. He who by entering one contract passes by the opportunity to accomplish the same end elsewhere will not be inclined to regard contract breach lightly or as a mere matter of private morality. The consciousness of what is foregone reinforces the notion that the contract creates a "right" and that the contract claim is itself a species of property.

If, on the other hand, we found the juristic explanation on the desire to promote reliance on contracts, it is not difficult again to trace a correspondence between the legal view and the actual conditions of economic life. In general our courts and our economic institutions attribute special significance to the same types of promises. The bilateral business agreement is, generally speaking, the only type of informal contract our courts are willing to enforce without proof that reliance has occurred—simply for the sake of facilitating reliance. This is, by no accident, precisely the kind of contract (the "exchange", "bargain", "trade", "deal") which furnishes the indispensable and pervasive framework for the "un-managed" portions of our economic activity.

The inference is therefore justified that the ends of the law of contracts and those of our economic system show an essential correspondence. One may explain this either on the ground that the law (mere superstructure and ideology) reflects inertly the conditions of economic life, or on the ground that economic activity has fitted itself into the rational framework of the law. Neither explanation would be true. In fact we are dealing with a situation in which law and society have interacted. The law measures damages by the expectancy *in part* because society views the expectancy as a present value; society views the expectancy as a present value *in part* because the law (for reasons more or less consciously articulated) gives protection to the expectancy.

[Footnotes omitted.]

(a)   THE EXPECTATION INTEREST

Notwithstanding concerns as to whether it is generally appropriate to respond to claims for damages in contract in terms of the disappointed party's expectation interest, the Canadian courts have long espoused this as the normal entitlement of plaintiffs in breach of contract actions. Though, as we will see below, the courts exercise a considerable degree of control on the extent of damages recoverable under the expectation interest by the use of various limiting principles such as mitigation and remoteness, the general operating principle has been that laid down in 1911 by the Judicial Committee Council of the Privy Council in an appeal from Canada: *Sally Wertheim v. Chicoutimi Pulp Co.*, [1911] A.C. 301. In that advice (at 301), Lord Atkinson stated that the "ruling principle" to be applied in awarding damages for breach of contract was to place plaintiffs in the same position they would have occupied "if the contract had been performed". Indeed, to the extent that the common law historically denied expectation damages for the breach of certain kinds of contract, the clear tendency of most recent Supreme

Court of Canada jurisprudence has been the removal of those "exceptions" and a recognition of the near universality of the expectation interest. Thus, in *A.V.G. Management Science Ltd. v. Barwell Developments Ltd.* (1978), [1979] 2 S.C.R. 43, the Supreme Court removed a long-standing limitation on the availability of expectation damages. Under that limitation, in the absence of fault on the part of the vendor, only reliance, not expectation, losses could be recovered for a failure to complete a contract for the disposition of an interest in land resulting from a defect in title. By 1979, there was no longer any justification for restricting damages based on the difficulty of establishing the accuracy of any title that the vendor purported to convey.

Further examples of the centralizing force of the expectation level of recovery can be seen in *Highway Properties Ltd. v. Kelly, Douglas & Co.*, [1971] S.C.R. 562 and *Keneric Tractor Sales Ltd. v. Langille,* [1987] 2 S.C.R. 440. In these judgments, the Supreme Court of Canada removed traditional limitations on the availability of full expectation damages in, first, leases of real estate and, then, chattel leases. As a consequence, the lessor on termination of a lease for breach by the lessee became entitled not just to rent unpaid at the date of termination but also to claim for the rent for the balance of the term less the actual rental value of the property in question for the unexpired portion of the lease. In delivering the judgment of the Supreme Court of Canada in the latter of these cases, Wilson J. referred to earlier restrictions as an "historical anomaly" (at 452) which could be rectified only by the assessment of damages "on general contract principles" (at 452), those being "that the award should put the plaintiff in the position he would have been in had the defendant fully performed his contractual obligations" (at 456).

On occasion, ingenious attempts have been made to reduce the defendant's damages by examining the position in which the plaintiff would have found itself in the event that the contract had been performed. For example, in *Clydebank Engineering and Shipbuilding Co. v. Yzquierdo-y-Castaneda, Don Jose Ramos,* [1905] A.C. 6 (H.L.), the defendants contracted to supply four "torpedo-boat destroyers" to the Spanish government in 1897-98, by which time the Spanish-American war had commenced. The defendants were late in delivering the destroyers and argued that the plaintiffs had lost little as a result. Earl of Halsbury L.C. commented (at 13):

> Then there comes another argument which, to my mind, is more startling still: the vessel was to be delivered at such and such a time; it was not delivered, but the fleet the Spanish Government had was sent out at such a time and the greater part of it was sunk, and, says the learned counsel, "if we had kept our contract and delivered these vessels they would have shared the fate of the other vessels belonging to the Spanish Government, and therefore in fact you have got your ships now, whereas if we had kept our contract they would have been at the bottom of the Atlantic." My Lords, I confess, after some experience, I do not think I ever heard an argument of that sort before, and I do not think I shall often hear it again. Nothing could be more absurd than such a contention, which, if it were reduced to a compendious form such as one has in a marginal note, would certainly be a striking example of jurisprudence. I think I need say no more to shew how utterly absurd such a contention is. . . .

The court proceeded to find a liquidated damages clause binding.

We will now consider the occasions on which the courts are prepared to award damages on the basis of the other interests identified by Fuller, the reliance and the restitutionary interest. Then, we turn to the various, more general controls that the courts impose on the scope of damages, typically in the context of expectation claims but also, on occasion, claims based on the reliance or restitutionary interest.

(b)   THE RELIANCE INTEREST

Despite the almost universal availability of expectation damages as a matter of principle, damages based on the plaintiff's reliance interest do continue to surface in the jurisprudence. There are a number of reasons for this, the most notable of which is that the plaintiff has not suffered any losses measurable by the expectation level or has been unable to prove or establish expectation losses with the requisite degree of certainty. As a consequence, the damages claim or judgment is confined to restoring the plaintiff to her or his pre-contract position and does not extend to putting the plaintiff in the position that he or she would have occupied had the contract been performed. As we shall also see, there may be occasions on which the plaintiff is seeking reliance recovery because it represents a potentially more lucrative basis of damages than the expectation interest. The first case provides an example of where the plaintiff had difficulties in presenting any kind of evidence in support of expectation losses in a commercial transaction. It also introduces the very important concept of "wasted opportunity" as a possible component of certain kinds of reliance claims.

McRAE v. COMMONWEALTH DISPOSALS COMM.

(1951), 84 C.L.R. 377 (Aust. H.C.)

[The facts of this case are set out, *supra*, Chapter 9, section 3(a). Once it was decided that the Commission was in breach of contract, the issue arose of how the plaintiff should be properly compensated for his losses.]

DIXON and FULLAGAR JJ. The question of damages, which is the remaining question, again presents serious difficulties. It is necessary first to arrive at the appropriate measure of damages. The contract was a contract for the sale of goods, and the measure of damages for non-delivery of goods by a seller is defined in very general terms by s. 55(2) of the Goods Act 1928 as being "the estimated loss directly and naturally resulting in the ordinary course of events from the seller's breach of contract". This states, in substance, the general prima-facie rule of the common law as to the measure of damages for breach of contract. But, if we approach this case as an ordinary case of wrongful non-delivery of goods sold, and attempt to apply the ordinary rules for arriving at the sum to be awarded as damages, we seem to find ourselves at once in insuperable difficulties. There was obviously no market into which the buyers could go to mitigate their loss, and the rule normally applied would require us to arrive at the value of the goods to the buyer at the place where they ought to have been delivered and at the time when they ought to have been delivered. But it is quite impossible to place any value on what the Commission purported to sell. The plaintiffs indeed, on one basis of claim which is asserted in their statement of claim, assessed their damages on the basis of an "average-sized tanker, 8,000-10,000 ton oil tanker, valued at £1,000,000, allowing for the said tanker lying on Jourmand Reef, valued at £250,000", and, for good measure, they added their "estimated value of cargo of oil" at the figure of £50,000. But this, as a basis of damages, seems manifestly absurd. The Commission simply did not contract to deliver a tanker of any particular size or of any particular value or in any particular condition, nor did it contract to deliver any oil.

It was strongly argued for the plaintiffs that mere difficulty in estimating damages did not relieve a tribunal from the responsibility of assessing them as best it could. This is undoubtedly true. In the well-known case of *Chaplin v. Hicks* [*infra*, section 3(a)(i)], Vaughan Williams L.J. said:—"The fact that damages cannot be assessed with certainty does not relieve the wrongdoer of the necessity of paying damages for his breach of contract". That passage, and others from the same case, are quoted by Street C.J. in *Howe v. Teefy* [(1927), 27 S.R.N.S.W. 301 at 305-6 (Aust.)] but the learned Chief Justice himself states the position more fully. He says:—"The question in every case is: has there been any assessable loss resulting from the breach of contract complained of? There may be cases where it would be impossible to say that any assessable loss had resulted from a breach of contract, but, short of that, if a plaintiff has been deprived of something which has a monetary value, a jury is not relieved from the duty of assessing the loss merely because the calculation is a difficult one or because the circumstances do not admit of the damages being assessed with certainty". The present case seems to be more like *Sapwell v. Bass* [[1910] 2 K.B. 486] than *Chaplin v. Hicks*. . . . It does not seem possible to say that "any assessable loss has resulted from" non-delivery as such. In *Chaplin v. Hicks*, if the contract had been performed, the plaintiff would have had a real chance of winning the prize, and it seems proper enough to say that that chance was worth something. It is only in another and quite different sense that it could be said here that, if the contract had been performed, the plaintiffs would have had a chance of making a profit. The broken promise itself in *Chaplin v. Hicks* was, in effect, "to give the plaintiff a chance": here the element of chance lay in the nature of the thing contracted for itself. Here we seem to have something which cannot be assessed. If there were nothing more in this case than a promise to deliver a stranded tanker and a failure to deliver a stranded tanker, the plaintiffs would, of course, be entitled to recover the price paid by them, but beyond that, in our opinion, only nominal damages.

There is, however, more in this case than that, and the truth is that to regard this case as a simple case of breach of contract by non-delivery of goods would be to take an unreal and misleading view of it. The practical substance of the case lies in these three factors—(1) the Commission promised that there was a tanker at or near to the specified place; (2) in reliance on that promise the plaintiffs expended considerable sums of money; (3) there was in fact no tanker at or anywhere near to the specified place. In the waste of their considerable expenditure seems to lie the real and understandable grievance of the plaintiffs, and the ultimate question in the case (apart from any question of quantum) is whether the plaintiffs can recover the amount of this wasted expenditure or any part of it as damages for breach of the Commission's contract that there was a tanker in existence. . . . [The plaintiffs were clearly entitled to] assume that there was a tanker in the locality given. The Commission had not, of course, contracted that she or her cargo was capable of being salved, but it does not follow that the plaintiff's conduct in making preparations for salvage operations was unreasonable, or that the Commission ought not to have contemplated that the course in fact adopted would be adopted in reliance on their promise. It would be wrong, we think, to say that the course which the plaintiffs took was unreasonable, and it seems to us to be the very course which the Commission would naturally expect them to take. . . . So far as the purpose of the expenditure is concerned, the case seems to fall within what is known as the second rule in *Hadley v. Baxendale* [*infra*, section 3(b)(iii)]. A fairly close analogy may be found in a case in which there is a contract for the sale of sheep, and the buyer sends a drover to take delivery. There are no sheep at the point of delivery. Sheep have not risen in price, and the buyer has suffered no loss through non-delivery as such. But he will be entitled to recover the expense which he has incurred in sending the drover to take delivery.

There is, however, still another question. [Counsel for the defendant] not only strongly opposed the view so far expressed, but he also contended that, even if that view were accepted, it still could not be held that the alleged damage flowed from the alleged breach. Let it be supposed, he said in effect, that the plaintiffs acted reasonably in what they did, and let it be supposed that the Commission ought reasonably to have contemplated that they would so act. Still, he said, the plaintiffs are faced with precisely the same difficulty with which they are faced if the case is regarded as a simple and normal case of breach by non-delivery. Suppose there had been a tanker at the place indicated. *Non constat* that the expenditure incurred by the plaintiffs would not have been equally wasted. If the promise that there was a tanker *in situ* had been performed, she might still have been found worthless or not susceptible of profitable salvage operations or of any salvage operations at all. How, then, he asked, can the plaintiffs say that their expenditure was *wasted because* there was no tanker in existence?

The argument is far from being negligible. But it is really, we think, fallacious. If we regard the case as a simple and normal case of breach by non-delivery, the plaintiffs have no starting-point. The burden of proof is on them, and they cannot establish that they have suffered any damage unless they can show that a tanker delivered in performance of the contract would have had some value, and this they cannot show. But when the contract alleged is a contract that there was a tanker in a particular place, and the breach assigned is that there was no tanker there, and the damages claimed are measured by expenditure incurred on the faith of the promise that there was a tanker in that place, the plaintiffs are in a very different position. They have now a starting-point. They can say: (1) this expense was incurred; (2) it was incurred because you promised us that there was a tanker; (3) the fact that there was no tanker made it certain that this expense would be wasted. The plaintiffs have in this way a starting-point. They make a prima-facie case. The fact that the expense was wasted flowed prima-facie from the fact that there was no tanker; and the first fact is damage, and the second fact is breach of contract. The burden is now thrown on the Commission of establishing that, if there had been a tanker, the expense incurred would equally have been wasted. This, of course, the Commission cannot establish. The fact is that the impossibility of assessing damages on the basis of a comparison between what was promised and what was delivered arises not because what was promised was valueless but because it is impossible to value a non-existent thing. It is the breach of contract itself which makes it impossible even to undertake an assessment on that basis. It is not impossible, however, to undertake an assessment on another basis, and, in so far as the Commission's breach of contract itself reduces the possibility of an accurate assessment, it is not for the Commission to complain.

For these reasons we are of opinion that the plaintiffs were entitled to recover damages in this case for breach of contract, and that their damages are to be measured by reference to expenditure incurred and wasted in reliance on the Commission's promise that a tanker existed at the place specified. The only problem now remaining is to quantify those damages. . . .

What actually happened may be summarized as follows. The plaintiffs owned a small steam vessel named the *Gippsland*. This vessel was, at the date of the making of the contract, being refitted in Sydney for trading between Melbourne and King Island. After the making of the contract the plan of refitting seems to have been modified in some respects with a view to making her suitable for salvage work. Certain salvage equipment was purchased and placed on board. A crew was engaged, and Mr. J. E. Johnstone, a shipwright and diver, and an acknowledged expert in salvage work, was also engaged. The ship sailed from Sydney for the supposed locality of the tanker on 28th June 1947. While she was on the voyage north, Mr. Johnstone and a brother of the plaintiffs proceeded together by air to Port Moresby. The ship foundered in the vicinity of Port Moresby on 24th July 1947. Why she took so long to reach this locality from Sydney is not explained, but she appears to have called at Brisbane and other northern ports. No lives were lost when she sank, and the ship's company landed at Port Moresby. Mr. F. E. McRae, one of the plaintiffs, entered into negotiations for the charter of a vessel named the *Betty Joan*, but in the meantime his brother and Mr. Johnstone went to Samarai and there chartered a boat named the *Jessie* for the purpose of looking for the tanker. They found, of course, no tanker, and returned to Port Moresby, where they informed Mr. McRae of the position.

The plaintiffs make their claim on the basis of wasted expenditure under ten heads, several of which it is plainly impossible to support at all. The first claim is under the head of "equipment", and relates to certain equipment purchased for the *Gippsland*. This claim is wholly untenable. Some of the items in it, such as navigating lights and signalling lamps, are ordinary necessities of a ship's equipment, and some were purchased months before the date of the contract. But in any case this was all capital expenditure represented by acquired assets, and it is out of the question to claim it as damages. One would assume, though there is no clear evidence on the matter, that it was covered by insurance.

The second claim is under the head of "reconditioning", and refers to work done on the *Gippsland* herself. Again it is plain that this claim must be wholly disallowed. About one-third of the amount claimed proves to relate to work done long before the date of the contract, but again the whole of it is capital expenditure.

The third claim is of a different character and does not relate to actual expenditure at all. It is made under the head of "loss of revenue", and represents the profit which the *Gippsland* might have been expected to make if she had not been devoted to the futile tanker enterprise. As framed, this claim was based on the profit anticipated as likely to accrue from the use of the vessel under a contract with a company called King Island Scheelite No Liability. . . . [Damages of £500 were allowed in respect of this portion of the plaintiff's claim.

The High Court permitted recovery for other items of expenditure incurred by the plaintiffs, including travel expenses, ships stores consumed before the *Gippsland* foundered, some of Mr. Johnstone's expenses, crew's wages and office expenses. This amount awarded was £3,000, to which was added the £285 purchase price which the plaintiffs had paid to the Commission. McTurnan J. concurred.]

NOTE and QUESTIONS

1. Why were the plaintiffs successful in recovering the revenue which the *Gippsland* might have been expected to earn during the relevant period, but not the expenses of equipping and reconditioning the *Gippsland* for the salvage expedition? For other examples of where the courts have been willing to assume that the plaintiff would have undertaken other lucrative opportunities were it not for entry into the losing contract and have awarded lost opportunity damages on the assumption of the profits that would have been made on those alternative opportunities, see *V.K. Mason Construction Ltd. v. Bank of Nova Scotia*, [1985] 1 S.C.R. 271 and *Esso Petroleum v. Mardon*, [1976] Q.B. 801 (C.A.) (discussed in Chapter 7, section 5 in *Sodd Corp v. N. Tessis* and notes following). As counsel for a plaintiff wanting to set up a claim based on wasted opportunity, how would you go about doing it? What kinds of evidence would you be seeking to adduce before the trial judge?

2. In what circumstances would it be appropriate for the plaintiffs to have recovered some portion of their capital expenditures?

3. An interesting illustration of the application of the reliance measure to calculate the plaintiff's damages occurred in *Anglia Television Ltd. v. Reed*, [1972] 1 Q.B. 60 (C.A.). The plaintiff, intending to produce a film of a play for television, incurred a large number of expenditures in preparation for the production before contracting with the defendant to play the leading role. The defendant repudiated the contract and when the plaintiff was unable to find a suitable alternative actor, it abandoned the production and sued for the expenditures which they had incurred.

The defendant argued that the pre-contractual expenditures ought not to be recoverable, as they were incurred by the plaintiff's own choice and not in reliance on the contract with the defendant. Lord Denning M.R. held that the defendant was liable for damages calculated on this basis, for his breach meant that the plaintiff's expenditures had been wasted.

For a justification of this decision, see Waddams, *The Law of Contracts*, 4th ed. (1999), at para. 714.

BOWLAY LOGGING LTD. v. DOMTAR LTD.

[1982] 6 W.W.R. 528, 37 B.C.L.R. 195, 135 D.L.R. (3d) 179 (C.A.)

SEATON J.A. [delivering the judgment of the court] The appellant contracted with the respondent to log a 10,000 cunit timber sale. The appellant was to cut, skid and load the logs for $15 per cunit. The respondent was to haul the logs but in breach of its contract failed to provide sufficient trucks. In this action for damages for the breach the appellant claimed $124,776.43. It was awarded nominal damages, $250, and this appeal is from that award [[1978] 4 W.W.R. 105, 87 D.L.R. (3d) 325].

In these proceedings the appellant did not ask to be put in the position it would have been in had there been no breach. It asked to be put in the position it would have been in had it never entered into the contract. It says that it incurred expenditures of $232,905, that it was paid $108,128.57 by the respondent, and that it is entitled to recover the difference as expenditures rendered futile by the respondent's breach.

There was a suggestion that the appellant was forced into this position because the job was not profitable and was not going to become profitable. . . . I do not think that an unprofitable venturer that was injured is precluded from recovering damages for breach of contract. If its loss was greater by reason of the breach than it otherwise would have been, the increase in the loss is the amount necessary to put the plaintiff in the position it would have been in had there been no breach. That amount should be recoverable whether or not it can be accurately described as lost profit.

In this case, the appellant offered no evidence of a loss. It simply showed the expenditures it had incurred and the revenue it had received. It then claimed the balance as the loss incurred when it was obliged by the respondent's breach to abandon the project. The respondent does not take issue with the manner in which the appellant formulates its claim. It simply says that the expenditures admittedly incurred were not lost as a result of the breach. It says that no loss was caused by the breach; that the expenditures were rendered futile by the combination of an improvident contract and inefficient execution. The trial judge agreed with that. He said:

> The law of contract compensates a plaintiff for damages resulting from the defendant's breach; it does not compensate a plaintiff for damages resulting from his making a bad bargain. Where it can be seen that the plaintiff would have incurred a loss on the contract as a whole, the expenses he has incurred are losses flowing from entering into the contract, not losses flowing from the defendant's breach. In these circumstances, the true consequence of the defendant's breach is that the plaintiff is released from his obligation to complete the contract or, in other words, he is saved from incurring further losses.

And later:

> The onus is on the defendant. But the onus has been met. The only conclusion that I can reach on the evidence is that if the plaintiff had fully performed the contract its losses would have continued at the rate that the figures show they were running at up to the time the logging operation was closed down.
>
> The case at bar takes the matter farther than any of the cases cited, because here the defendant has shown that the losses the plaintiff would have incurred on full performance exceed the expenditures actually made in part performance. No award for loss of outlay can therefore be made. There is no escaping the logic of this: see Corbin on Contracts (1964), pp. 205-206:
>
>> If, on the other hand, it is provided that full performance would have resulted in a net loss to the plaintiff, the recoverable damages should not include the amount of this loss. *If the amount of his expenditure at the date of breach is less than the expected net*

loss, he should be given judgment for nominal damages only. If the expenditures exceed this loss, he should be given judgment for the excess.

The appellant made a number of attacks on the judgment. Most focus on the calculations that led the trial judge to conclude that the losses would have been incurred by the appellant with or without the respondent's breach.

The appellant argues that the trial judge ought to have taken into account that some of the work was done under circumstances made more difficult by the breach. I think that the judge was justified in rejecting that contention. The evidence does not indicate that the excessive costs were brought about or even significantly contributed to by the breach.

Next it is said that the trial judge ought to have taken from his figures start-up costs and capital costs when he weighed the question whether the loss would have been incurred in any event. The 10,000 cunits in the timber sale at $15 each would have yielded about $150,000 to the appellant if it had completed the job. It spent $232,905 and the respondent was required to pay something over $5,000 to clean up the property and pay Workers' Compensation Board assessments. The work done was worth about $108,000.

The accountant referred to costs prior to the first shipment of logs as start-up costs. There was no evidence of start-up costs that should not have been absorbed, at least substantially, in the first half of the work. I have read the whole of the evidence respecting damages and have concluded that the trial judge did not err when he failed to make an allowance for start-up costs.

Capital costs raise a more difficult question. The appellant claims them as expenditures made on this project but says that they were not an expense on this project and therefore should not be taken into account in the projection of the loss that would have been incurred with or without the breach. The trial judge dealt with this matter on a motion to re-open for further argument. He said this:

> The motion is founded on the contention that in my reasons for judgment I failed to apply properly to the evidence in the case the rule derived from the American authorities, i.e., that the defendant is entitled to offset against the plaintiff's claim for expenses, made in reliance on the contract which has been breached, the loss the plaintiff would have suffered on the contract had there been no breach.
>
> Two complaints are made:
>
> 1. That in calculating the loss that the plaintiff would have suffered on the contract had there been no breach, I included expenses attributable to the breach that would have been incurred had there been no breach; and
>
> 2. That capital expenditures incurred by the plaintiff should not have [been] included in calculating the loss the plaintiff would have suffered had there been no breach.
>
> As to the first contention, I am not persuaded that it had been made out. As to the second contention, it is a fair characterization of the way in which the principle derived from the American authorities was applied. I considered whether it should be applied in that way and I was of the view that it ought to be. Since the principle that the plaintiff relies upon allows such expenses to be claimed as damages, it seems reasonable that the defendant should be allowed to include them in any calculation of the loss the plaintiff would have suffered had there been no breach. In any event, the parties only contracted in the case at bar for the plaintiff to log the timber sale in question. The plaintiff incurred capital expenditures at its peril. I am not persuaded, therefore, that the principle derived from the American authorities was wrongly applied.

There was a modest capital investment. Some equipment was being rented with a provision for purchase, a vehicle was being purchased and some other things were bought outright. There was an element of capital in some payments but that element would be offset, at least in part, by a proper depreciation allowance.

The appellant was prevented from completing this one project which normally would have been finished in the fall. But the respondent's breach did not cause the collapse of the appellant's plans to undertake other logging projects. Those plans were abandoned because of the losses the appellant had incurred—losses that would have been greater had there not been a breach that permitted it to close down the project.

The appellant supported its claim for capital expended with an allegation that it was to have contracts each year. Thus, it said that expenditures made with a view to a series of contracts were rendered futile by the breach of the first contract. The trial judge, rightly in my view, rejected that approach as raising claims that were "too uncertain and remote".

The inquiry is not an accounting process; it is a matter of judgment to be exercised after weighing all of the evidence. I am persuaded that the trial judge reached the right conclusion on the evidence.

The central question in this case is one of fact. The trial judge found that the losses that were being incurred prior to the breach would have continued and that in the end, if there had been no breach, the loss would have been even greater. I take that to be what the trial judge meant when he said:

> . . . here the defendant has shown that the losses the plaintiff would have incurred on full performance exceed the expenditures actually made in part performance.

On the evidence it seems clear that the appellant was losing heavily, not because of the respondent's breach, but because of an improvident contract and grossly inefficient work practices. The appellant's claim that it expended $232,905, partially completing a project that was to yield $150,000, demonstrates the extent to which it was losing money. The result of the breach was to release the appellant from further performance that would have resulted in further losses. In short, no damage was sustained by the appellant as a consequence of the respondent's breach.

The appellant's final argument fell only slightly short of a claim for exemplary damages. The argument is that the respondent breached the contract, took the benefit of the breach, and should not be permitted to escape with impunity. The respondent was penalized by having to absorb some costs that would have been charged to the appellant if the job had been completed, but the appellant has much larger amounts in mind as suitable in the circumstances.

The answer to the final argument is clear. There was not the conduct on which to base a case for exemplary damages, and the appellant suffered no loss as a consequence of the breach on which to found a claim for compensatory damages.

I conclude that the trial judge's award of damages should be upheld and the appeal dismissed.

NOTE and QUESTION

1. Under what circumstances would it be inappropriate to have taken into account capital expenditures incurred by the plaintiff in calculating the loss that the plaintiff would have suffered if there had been no breach? See Baer, "Note" (1979), 3 Can. Bus. L.J. 198.

2. In the trial judgment in *Bowlay Logging* (1978), 87 D.L.R. (3d) 325 (B.C. S.C.) at 333-34, Berger J. summarized the basis for his decision with a quotation from p. 79 of Fuller and Perdue's article, *supra*, section 2:

> We will not in a suit for reimbursement for losses incurred in reliance on a contract knowingly put the plaintiff in a better position than he would have occupied had the contract been fully performed.

If Bowlay Logging had been able to characterize the respondent's failure to provide sufficient logging trucks as negligence, might they have been able to recover their reliance losses in the assumed amount of $125,000 rather than nominal damages?

This possibility can now be contemplated as a result of the decision of the Supreme Court of Canada in *Rainbow Industrial Caterers Ltd. v. Cdn. National Railway Co.*, [1991] 3 S.C.R. 3. In that case, the plaintiff, a food caterer, contracted to supply meals to work crews employed by the defendant railway. The plaintiff's tender was based on the defendant's estimate of the number of meals required. The estimate was approximately 30 per cent too high and by the time the plaintiff terminated the contract, as it was entitled to, it had suffered a loss in excess of $1 million.

In an action that ultimately involved only claims for breach of contract and negligent misrepresentation, the plaintiff was awarded damages representing its entire losses. The award was based on the assumption that, but for the misrepresentation, the plaintiff would not have entered the contract at all. A different award might have been made if, had it not been for the misrepresentation, the plaintiff would still have bid on the contract, but at a higher price.

It was clear that the plaintiff had entered into a bad bargain. Even if the estimate of meals had been correct, the plaintiff would have lost money and, on the authority of *Bowlay Logging*, the plaintiff would have obtained only nominal damages in a contract action.

The majority of the Supreme Court of Canada (McLachlin J. dissenting) found that the plaintiff had discharged its burden of proving damages once it proved that it had entered into the contract because of a negligent misrepresentation and established the loss on the contract. It was then for the defendant to argue that the contract would still have been made if a correct representation had been made. As the defendant had failed to establish this, the plaintiff was entitled to recover all losses, even those that were totally unrelated to the misrepresentation (such as those that arose from the workers' tendency to take too much food). Sopinka J. found that the plaintiff's losses were "causally and directly connected to the contract and the contract is causally connected to the negligent misrepresentation".

In *BG Checo v. B.C. Hydro & Power Authority*, *supra*, Chapter 7, section 5, it was found that the misrepresentation as to the state of the contract site induced the contractor to enter into the contract at a price less than it would have had it known the true facts. It remained to determine how much more the contractor would have bid if it had possessed this information. The majority judgment written by McLachlin J. allowed the contractor to recover the direct costs of clearing the right of way and indirect losses, such as acceleration costs that were incurred when the contractor was required to devote resources to clearing the right of way and to maintain the contract schedule. In McLachlin J.'s opinion, this measure of damages would have been the same if the contractor's action had been framed solely in contract.

See also *Hodgkinson v. Simms*, *infra*, section 3(b)(ii).

SUNSHINE VACATION VILLAS LTD. v. GOVERNOR AND COMPANY OF ADVENTURERS OF ENGLAND TRADING INTO HUDSON'S BAY

(1984), 58 B.C.L.R. 33, 13 D.L.R. (4th) 93 (C.A.)

The plaintiff, Sunshine Vacation, was granted licences to operate travel agencies in six small stores operated by the defendant, the Bay, in the interior of British Columbia in September 1976. The trial judge found that at the same time the Bay had contracted to provide licences to the plaintiff to operate travel agencies in four large Bay stores in the Vancouver and Victoria region in the spring of 1977, when it was planned that the Bay would terminate the agreements with the existing licensee in those stores. In April 1977, the plaintiff discovered that the Bay had renewed the agreements with the existing licensees in the stores in Vancouver and Victoria region.

BY THE COURT . . . Sunshine Vacation was then aware [in April 1977] that the Bay was in breach of its promise to make available the four large outlets. During the next two months, extensive negotiations took place directed towards the possibility of Sunshine Vacation becoming the Bay's exclusive travel agent in Western Canada. In the hope that those negotiations would succeed, Sunshine Vacation carried through with its plans to open an outlet in Cranbrook in June but, by the end of that month, negotiations had broken down. Sunshine Vacation decided in early July that it did not wish to continue doing business with the Bay and advised the latter of its intention to close out the seven outlets then operating and cease business. That intention was carried out with the result that all offices were closed in August 1977.

The damage award [for the Bay's breach of contract] was in the total amount of $275,956.19 plus prejudgment interest. The award was made up of two elements:

Loss of capital $175,956.19
Loss of profit   100,000.00

The Bay submits that the award for loss of capital is wrong in principle, that the circumstances of the case do not support an award under that head and that no loss of profit was proved so that only nominal damages should have been awarded.

The award for the loss of capital is made up of two components. One is the sum of $80,000 invested in the company at the outset by the five shareholders. The second is the increase in the bank line of credit from 2nd April 1977, which was assumed to be the date of breach, to 31st August 1977, by which time all operations had terminated. The loan stood at $19,043.81 on 2nd April and by the end, had risen to $115,000. The trial judge awarded the difference between those two figures ($95,956.19) which he held to be in the same category as the original capital of $80,000.

It should be understood that the reference in this case to "lost capital" is in the sense of unrecovered working capital. It is not an outlay for capital purposes but is rather a measure of the expenses incurred by Sunshine Vacation which, by reason of the breach by the Bay, could not be recovered. They were expenses incurred by Sunshine Villa [*sic*] in part performance of the contract.

In this court, Sunshine Vacation has cross-appealed, seeking an increase in the damages in the amount of $19,043.81. Mr. Nathanson, for the Bay, did not dispute that, if loss of capital is a properly allowable head of damage, the deduction of $19,043.81 was not justified. He accepts that, in the circumstances of this case, the combination of the initial shareholders' investment and the ultimate overdraft balance fairly represents the capital loss. He submits, however, as he did at trial, that loss of capital is not a proper approach to assessing damages. Alternatively, he submits that it is only available as an alternative to loss of profit and that it is wrong in principle to make an award, as here, based upon a mixture of those approaches.

The alternative submission is right. One method of assessment, the return of expenses or loss of capital, approaches the matter by considering what Sunshine Vacation's position would have been had it not entered into the contract. The other, loss of profit, approaches it by considering what the position would have been had the Bay carried out its bargain. The two approaches must be alternatives. McGregor on Damages, 14th ed. (1980), p. 21, para. 24, states that the "normal measure of damages in contract" is:

> If one party makes default in performing his side of the contract, then the basic loss to the other party is the market value of the benefit of which he has been deprived through the breach. Put shortly, the plaintiff is entitled to compensation for the loss of his bargain. That is what may best be called the normal measure of damages in contract.

At p. 25 (para. 31) the author says:

> It is important to notice in all the above cases that not only must the defendant be credited with the amount that the plaintiff has saved by no longer having to perform his side of the bargain, but the plaintiff cannot also recover, in addition to the basic loss which is intended to represent the loss of his bargain, any expenses he has incurred in preparation or in part performance. Such expenses represent part of the price that the plaintiff has to incur to secure his bargain. If he recovers for the loss of his bargain, it would be inconsistent that he should in addition recover for expenses which were necessarily laid out by him for its attainment.

At pp. 32-33 (para. 42) he says:

> Just as expenses rendered futile by the breach may generally be claimed as an alternative to the normal measure of damages, so they may also be claimed as an alternative to recovering for gains prevented by the breach. Again, it is important to realize that such expenses form an alternative and not an additional head of damage, since they represent part of the price that the plaintiff was to incur in order to secure the gain. Sometimes this may have been lost sight of, and a double recovery involving an inconsistency of compensation allowed.

The trial judge, in holding that Sunshine Vacation could recover both lost profits and capital, relied on two cases, one English and one Canadian. He referred first to *Cullinane v. Br. "Rema" Mfg. Co.*, [1954] 1 Q.B. 292, [1953] 3 W.L.R. 923, [1953] 2 All E.R. 1257, a decision of the Court of Appeal of England which supports the law as stated in the passages set out above.

.....

The principal submission of the Bay is that there was no proper basis for making a substantial award for either loss of capital or loss of profits. That submission is based on the contention that the trial Judge should have found that Sunshine Vacation could not have earned a profit, that it was bound to fail, and that only nominal damages should have been awarded.

The authority relied upon in support of that submission is *Bowlay Logging Ltd. v. Domtar Ltd.*, [*supra*] . . . [in which it was] held that the plaintiff could elect to claim its expenses but that, if the owner could show that the plaintiff would have incurred a loss had it completed the contract, nominal damages only should be awarded. . . .

The crucial finding of fact in *Bowlay* is that the amount of the plaintiff's expenditure to the date of breach was less than the net loss which would have been incurred had the contract been completed. The onus of establishing that state of fact rests upon the defendant. It has not been discharged in this case.

To explain that, some reference to the basis of the claim for loss of profit, and the conclusions of the trial judge with respect to it, is necessary. The claim was based on projections as to the profit which Sunshine Vacation would have earned had the Bay kept its bargain and granted Sunshine Vacation a licence for the four [large] stores for three years from 2nd April 1977. The three-year period was chosen because it was a fixed period of the licence agreed to be given by the Bay. The projections put forward by Sunshine Vacation indicated a profit, at the end of that period, of $348,982.

The Bay did not dispute the methodology employed by Sunshine Vacation in calculating loss of profits but challenged the assumptions upon which the calculation was based. It called expert evidence seeking to establish that the factual assumptions made by witnesses for Sunshine Vacation were unrealistic and indicating that, on the basis of what its witnesses said were more realistic assumptions, Sunshine Vacation would have been in a loss position at the end of the three-year period.

The trial judge concluded, on the basis of the conflicting evidence, that the projections of Sunshine Vacation were essentially reliable. . . .

The shortcomings of this aspect of the Bay's case can be illustrated by reference to the facts of *Bowlay Logging*. In that case, the plaintiff had incurred expenditures of over $230,000 in partially completing a contract which, had it been completed, would have produced revenues of $150,000. To the point of termination, it had earned $108,000. Had it been required to complete the contract, its additional expenditures would have exceeded the additional income. So the reality of the situation was that the defendant did the plaintiff a favour by giving it an opportunity to get out of having to complete. On that basis, it was held that nominal damages only should be awarded. The factual situation in the case at bar is entirely different and, as a result, the Bay cannot discharge the onus of establishing that Sunshine Vacation would have suffered a loss.

Sunshine Vacation, on the other hand, has not established that a proper award for loss of profits would have exceeded the amount of the lost capital. That being so, the amount of lost capital is, in all the circumstances of this case, the appropriate amount to award as damages for breach of contract.

That amount represents, in the circumstances of this case, the expenses incurred by Sunshine Vacation and not recovered by it. That approach to assessment is particularly appropriate in this case. The breach was one which went to the root of the contract. After Sunshine Vacation had incurred large expenses in carrying out obligations which were recognized to be the unprofitable portion of the contract, the Bay refused to carry out its promises in relation to the profitable part. Because of the nature of the enterprise and the point at which the breach took place, the assessment of damages for loss of profit is more than usually speculative. In those respects, the case is similar to *Anglia T.V. Ltd. v. Reed*, [1972] 1 Q.B. 60, [1971] 3 W.L.R. 528, [1971] 3 All E.R. 690 (C.A.). . . .

It follows the damage award should be reduced from $275,956.19 to $195,000, being the amount of loss of capital after restoring the amount of $19,043.81 deducted by the trial judge. In all other aspects the appeal and cross-appeal should be dismissed.

[Appeal allowed in part.]

QUESTIONS

1. The British Columbia Court of Appeal accepted that reliance losses are "only available as an alternative to loss of profit and that it is wrong in principle to make an award . . . based upon a mixture of those approaches." Do you agree?

Compare the decision in *Sunnyside Greenhouses Ltd. v. Golden West Seeds Ltd.* (1972), 27 D.L.R. (3d) 434 (Alta. C.A.), affirmed [1973] S.C.R. v, in which the plaintiff was allowed to base part of its claim on wasted expenses and part on lost profits. What principle ought to govern the relationship between the expectation and the reliance measure? See Baer, "Note" (1979), 3 Can. Bus. L.J. 198.

2. Assume that in *Sunshine Vacation*, the plaintiff could have established, with reasonable certainty, that it had lost profits of $100,000 as a result of the defendant's breach and that its reliance loss amounted, as the court found, to $195,000. What influence, if any, might the plaintiff's lost expectancy have on the recovery of reliance losses?

(c)   RESTITUTION

As the extract from Fuller and Purdue's article makes clear, the claims of those seeking no more than restitution when a contract has gone bad are in justice stronger than the claims of those suing for damages on the basis of either expectation or reliance. The defendant has been enriched at the expense of the now impoverished plaintiff and justice demands a return to the previous state of equilibrium between them.

Indeed, throughout this book, we have seen examples of where this is the remedy sought and obtained by the plaintiff. Where moneys are paid under a mistake of fact and, now, also law (*Air Canada v. British Columbia*, [1989] 1 S.C.R. 1161; *Canadian Pacific Airlines v. British Columbia*, [1989] 1 S.C.R. 1133), the appropriate form of relief is the disgorgement of those moneys by the beneficiary of the mistake. In situations such as *Deglman* (Chapter 4, section 8(c)(iii)(E)), where services are rendered on the understanding that they will be paid for, the defendant in appropriate situations will be obliged to pay for those services what they are worth. Indeed, the whole concept of restitution has become the basis of what is generally treated as a separate category of legal obligation, the Law of Restitution or Unjust Enrichment.

Beyond these obvious examples, we do not delve deeply into the details of the Law of Restitution as it operates in the area of contracts that have misfired. We leave that to an upper year course in that subject. However, in the light of recent developments, it has become critical to examine the circumstances under which the courts are now prepared to provide a restitutionary or disgorgement remedy even when the benefit secured by the breaching party has not been at the expense of the innocent party. The foundation judgment of *Attorney-General v. Blake* raises the issues in a stark form.

ATTORNEY-GENERAL v. BLAKE
(Jonathan Cape Ltd. Third Party)

[2001] 1 A.C. 268 (U.K. H.L.)

LORD NICHOLLS OF BIRKENHEAD [delivering a judgment in which the majority concurred] George Blake is a notorious, self-confessed traitor. He was employed as a member of the security and intelligence services for 17 years, from 1944 to 1961. In 1951 he became an agent for the Soviet Union. From then until 1960 he disclosed valuable secret information and documents gained through his employment. On 3 May 1961 he pleaded guilty to five charges of unlawfully communicating information contrary to section 1(1)(*c*) of the Official Secrets Act 1911. He was sentenced to 42 years' imprisonment. This sentence reflected the extreme gravity of the harm brought about by his betrayal of secret information.

In 1966 Blake escaped from Wormwood Scrubs prison and fled to Berlin and then to Moscow. He is still there, a fugitive from justice. In 1989 he wrote his autobiography. Certain parts of the book related to his activities as a secret intelligence officer. By 1989 the information in the book was no longer confidential, nor was its disclosure damaging to the public interest. On 4 May 1989 Blake entered into a publishing contract with Jonathan Cape Ltd. He granted Jonathan Cape an exclusive right to publish the book in this country in return for royalties. Jonathan Cape agreed to pay him advances against royalties: £50,000 on signing the contract, a further £50,000 on delivery of the manuscript, and another £50,000 on publication. Plainly, had Blake not been an infamous spy who had also dramatically escaped from prison, his autobiography would not have commanded payments of this order.

The book, entitled *No Other Choice*, was published on 17 September 1990. Neither the security and intelligence services nor any other branch of the Government were aware of the book until its publication was announced. Blake had not sought any prior authorisation from the Crown to disclose any of the information in the book relating to the Secret Intelligence Service. Jonathan Cape has, apparently, already paid Blake about £60,000 under the publishing agreement. In practice that money is irrecoverable. A further substantial amount, in the region of £90,000, remains payable. These proceedings concern this unpaid money.

On 24 May 1991, the Attorney General commenced an action against Blake, with a view to ensuring he should not enjoy any further financial fruits from his treachery. [Ultimately, the Crown failed in its claim of breach of fiduciary duty as well as in its claim, based on public law, for an injunction. The House of Lords considered another possible basis of liability.]

The private law claim

... On 16 August 1944 Blake signed an Official Secrets Act declaration. This declaration included an undertaking:

> '... I undertake not to divulge any official information gained by me as a result of my employment, either in the press or in book form. I also understand that these provisions apply not only during the period of service but also after employment has ceased.'

This undertaking was contractually binding. Had Blake not signed it he would not have been employed. By submitting his manuscript for publication without first obtaining clearance Blake committed a breach of this undertaking. The Court of Appeal [which found Blake to be in breach of this undertaking, but that the Crown could not establish loss] suggested that the Crown might have a private law claim to 'restitutionary damages for breach of contract', and invited submissions on this issue. The Attorney General decided that the Crown did not wish to advance argument on this point in the Court of Appeal. The Attorney General, however, wished to keep the point open for a higher court. The Court of Appeal expressed the view, necessarily tentative in the circumstances, that the law of contract would be seriously defective if the court were unable to award restitutionary damages for breach of contract. The law is now sufficiently mature to recognise a restitutionary claim for profits made from a breach of contract in appropriate situations. These include cases of 'skimped' performance, and cases where the defendant obtained his profit by doing 'the very thing' he contracted not to do. The present case fell into the latter category: Blake earned his profit by doing the very thing he had promised not to do.

... Prompted by an invitation from your Lordships, the Attorney General advanced an argument that restitutionary principles ought to operate to enable the Crown to recover from Blake his profits arising from his breach of contract. It will be convenient to consider this private law claim first.

This is a subject on which there is a surprising dearth of judicial decision. By way of contrast, over the last 20 years there has been no lack of academic writing. . . . Most writers have favoured the view that in some circumstances the innocent party to a breach of contract should be able to compel the defendant to disgorge the profits he obtained from his breach of contract. However, there is a noticeable absence of any consensus on what are the circumstances in which this remedy should be available. . . . The broad proposition that a wrongdoer should not be allowed to profit from his wrong has an obvious attraction. The corollary is that the person wronged may recover the amount of this profit when he has suffered no financially measurable loss. As Glidewell L.J. observed in *Halifax Building Society v. Thomas* [1996] Ch. 217, 229, the corollary is not so obviously persuasive. In these choppy waters the common law and equity steered different courses. The effects of this are still being felt.

[At this point, Lord Nicholls engaged in a consideration of disgorgement as a remedy in range of situations: for interference with property rights, for breach of trust and fiduciary duty, and in assessing damages under *Lord Cairns' Act*, which is discussed later in this chapter in section 3(d).]

Breach of contract

Against this background I turn to consider the remedies available for breaches of contract. The basic remedy is an award of damages. . . . the rule of the common law is that where a party sustains a loss by reason of a breach of contract, he is, so far as money can do it, to be placed in the same position as if the contract had been performed: . . . Leaving aside the anomalous exception of punitive damages, damages are compensatory. That is axiomatic. It is equally well established that an award of damages, assessed by reference to financial loss, is not always 'adequate' as a remedy for a breach of contract. The law recognises that a party to a contract may have an interest in performance which is not readily measurable in terms of money. On breach the innocent party suffers a loss. He fails to obtain the benefit promised by the other party to the contract. To him the loss may be as important as financially measurable loss, or more so. An award of damages, assessed by reference to financial loss, will not recompense him properly. For him a financially assessed measure of damages is inadequate.

[Reference to injunctions and specific performance omitted, see section 4 of this chapter]

All this is trite law. In practice, these specific remedies go a long way towards providing suitable protection for innocent parties who will suffer loss from breaches of contract which are not adequately remediable by an award of damages. But these remedies are not always available. For instance, confidential information may be published in breach of a non-disclosure agreement before the innocent party has time to apply to the court for urgent relief. Then the breach is irreversible. Further, these specific remedies are discretionary. Contractual obligations vary infinitely. So do the circumstances in which breaches occur, and the circumstances in which remedies are sought. The court may, for instance, decline to grant specific relief on the ground that this would be oppressive.

An instance of this nature occurred in *Wrotham Park Estate Co. Ltd. v. Parkside Homes Ltd.* [1974] 1 W.L.R. 798. For social and economic reasons the court refused to make a mandatory order for the demolition of houses built on land burdened with a restrictive covenant. Instead, Brightman J. made an award of damages under the jurisdiction which originated with Lord Cairns' Act. The existence of the new houses did not diminish the value of the benefited land by one farthing. The judge considered that if the plaintiffs were given a nominal sum, or no sum, justice would manifestly not have been done. He assessed the damages at five per cent of the developer's anticipated profit, this being the amount of money which could reasonably have been demanded for a relaxation of the covenant.

In reaching his conclusion the judge applied by analogy the cases mentioned above concerning the assessment of damages when a defendant has invaded another's property rights but without diminishing the value of the property. I consider he was right to do so. Property rights are superior to contractual rights in that, unlike contractual rights, property rights may survive against an indefinite class of persons. However, it is not easy to see why, as between the parties to a contract, a violation of a party's contractual rights should attract a lesser degree of remedy than a violation of his property rights. As Lionel Smith has pointed out in his article *Disgorgement of the Profits of Contract: Property, Contract and 'Efficient Breach'* 24 Can. B.L.J. 121, it is not clear why it should be any more permissible to expropriate personal rights than it is permissible to expropriate property rights.

[After considering other authority tending not to support the availability of such a claim, Lord Nicholls continued.]

The *Wrotham Park* case, therefore, still shines, rather as a solitary beacon, showing that in contract as well as tort damages are not always narrowly confined to recoupment of financial loss. In a suitable case damages for breach of contract may be measured by the benefit gained by the wrongdoer from the breach. The defendant must make a reasonable payment in respect of the benefit he has gained. In the present case the Crown seeks to go further. The claim is for all the profits of Blake's book which the publisher has not yet paid him. This raises the question whether an account of profits can ever be given as a remedy for breach of contract. The researches of counsel have been unable to discover any case where the court has made such an order on a claim for breach of contract.

[He here considered some breach of contract cases in which the courts may in effect have awarded disgorgement.]

These cases illustrate that circumstances do arise when the just response to a breach of contract is that the wrongdoer should not be permitted to retain any profit from the breach. In these cases the courts have reached the desired result by straining existing concepts. Professor Peter Birks has deplored the 'failure of jurisprudence when the law is forced into this kind of abusive instrumentalism': see (1993) 109 L.Q.R. 518, 520. Some years ago Professor Dawson suggested there is no inherent reason why the technique of equity courts in land contracts should not be more widely employed, not by granting remedies as the by-product of a phantom 'trust' created by the contract, but as an alternative form of money judgment remedy. That well known ailment of lawyers, a hardening of the categories, ought not to be an obstacle: see 'Restitution or Damages' (1959) 20 Ohio L.J. 175.

My conclusion is that there seems to be no reason, in principle, why the court must in all circumstances rule out an account of profits as a remedy for breach of contract. I prefer to avoid the unhappy expression 'restitutionary damages'. Remedies are the law's response to a wrong (or, more precisely, to a cause of action). When, exceptionally, a just response to a breach of contract so requires, the court should be able to grant the discretionary remedy of requiring a defendant to account to the plaintiff for the benefits he has received from his breach of contract. In the same way as a plaintiff's interest in performance of a contract may render it just and equitable for the court to make an order for specific performance or grant an injunction, so the plaintiff's interest in performance may make it just and equitable that the defendant should retain no benefit from his breach of contract.

The state of the authorities encourages me to reach this conclusion, rather than the reverse. The law recognises that damages are not always a sufficient remedy for breach of contract. This is the foundation of the court's jurisdiction to grant the remedies of specific performance and injunction. Even when awarding damages, the law does not adhere slavishly to the concept of compensation for financially measurable loss. When the circumstances require, damages are measured by reference to the benefit obtained by the wrongdoer. This applies to interference with property rights. Recently, the like approach has been adopted to breach of contract. Further, in certain circumstances an account of profits is ordered in preference to an award of damages. Sometimes the injured party is given the choice: either compensatory damages or an account of the wrongdoer's profits. Breach of confidence is an instance of this. If confidential information is wrongfully divulged in breach of a non-disclosure agreement, it would be nothing short of sophistry to say that an account of profits may be ordered in respect of the equitable wrong but not in respect of the breach of contract which governs the relationship between the parties. With the established authorities going thus far, I consider it would be only a modest step for the law to recognise openly that, exceptionally, an account of profits may be the most appropriate remedy for breach of contract. It is not as though this step would contradict some recognised principle applied consistently throughout the law to the grant or withholding of the remedy of an account of profits. No such principle is discernible.

The main argument against the availability of an account of profits as a remedy for breach of contract is that the circumstances where this remedy may be granted will be uncertain. This will have an unsettling effect on commercial contracts where certainty is important. I do not think these fears are well founded. I see no reason why, in practice, the availability of the remedy of an account of profits need disturb settled expectations in the commercial or consumer world. An account of profits will be appropriate only in exceptional circumstances. Normally the remedies of damages, specific performance and injunction, coupled with the characterisation of some contractual obligations as fiduciary, will provide an adequate response to a breach of contract. It will be only in exceptional cases, where those remedies are inadequate, that any question of accounting for profits will arise. No fixed rules can be prescribed. The court will have regard to all the circumstances, including the subject matter of the contract, the purpose of the contractual provision which has been breached, the circumstances in which the breach occurred, the consequences of the breach and the circumstances in which relief is being sought. A useful general guide, although not exhaustive, is whether the plaintiff had a legitimate interest in preventing the defendant's profit-making activity and, hence, in depriving him of his profit.

It would be difficult, and unwise, to attempt to be more specific. In the Court of Appeal Lord Woolf, M.R. suggested there are at least two situations in which justice requires the award of restitutionary damages where compensatory damages would be inadequate: . . . Lord Woolf was not there addressing the question of when an account of profits, in the conventional sense, should be available. But I should add that, so far as an account of profits is concerned, the suggested categorisation would not assist. The first suggested category was the case of 'skimped' performance, where the defendant fails to provide the full extent of services he has contracted to provide. He should be liable to pay back the amount of expenditure he saved by the breach. This is a much discussed problem. But a part refund of the price agreed for services would not fall within the scope of an account of profits as ordinarily understood. Nor does an account of profits seem to be needed in this context. The resolution of the problem of cases of skimped performance, where the plaintiff does not get what was agreed, may best be found elsewhere. If a shopkeeper supplies inferior and cheaper goods than those ordered and paid for, he has to refund the difference in price. That would be the outcome of a claim for damages for breach of contract. That would be so, irrespective of whether the goods in fact served the intended purpose. There must be scope for a similar approach, without any straining of principle, in cases where the defendant provided inferior and cheaper services than those contracted for.

The second suggested category was where the defendant has obtained his profit by doing the very thing he contracted not to do. This category is defined too widely to assist. The category is apt to embrace all express negative obligations. But something more is required than mere breach of such an obligation before an account of profits will be the appropriate remedy.

Lord Woolf . . . also suggested three facts which should not be a sufficient ground for departing from the normal basis on which damages are awarded: the fact that the breach was cynical and deliberate; the fact that the breach enabled the defendant to enter into a more profitable contract elsewhere; and the fact that by entering into a new and more profitable contract the defendant put it out of his power to perform his contract with the plaintiff. I agree that none of these facts would be, by itself, a good reason for ordering an account of profits.

The present case

The present case is exceptional. The context is employment as a member of the security and intelligence services. Secret information is the lifeblood of these services. In the 1950s Blake deliberately committed repeated breaches of his undertaking not to divulge official information gained as a result of his employment. He caused untold and immeasurable damage to the public interest he had committed himself to serve. In 1990 he published his autobiography, a further breach of his express undertaking. By this time the information disclosed was no longer confidential. In the ordinary course of commercial dealings the disclosure of non-confidential information might be regarded as venial. In the present case disclosure was also a criminal offence under the Official Secrets Acts, even though the information was no longer confidential. Section 1 of the Official Secrets Act 1989 draws a distinction in this regard between members of the security and intelligence services and other Crown servants. Under section 1(3) a person who is or has been a Crown servant is guilty of an offence if without lawful authority he makes 'a damaging disclosure' of information relating to security or intelligence. The offence is drawn more widely in the case of a present or past member of the security and intelligence services. Such a person is guilty of an offence if without lawful authority he discloses 'any information' relating to security or intelligence which is or has been in his possession by virtue of his position as a member of those services. This distinction was approved in Parliament after debate when the legislation was being enacted.

. . . When he joined the Secret Intelligence Service Blake expressly agreed in writing that he would not disclose official information, during or after his service, in book form or otherwise. He was employed on that basis. That was the basis on which he acquired official information. The Crown had and has a legitimate interest in preventing Blake profiting from the disclosure of official information, whether classified or not, while a member of the service and thereafter. Neither he, nor any other member of the service, should have a financial incentive to break his undertaking. It is of paramount importance that members of the service should have complete confidence in all their dealings with each other, and that those recruited as informers should have the like confidence. Undermining the willingness of prospective informers to co-operate with the services, or undermining the morale and trust between members of the services when engaged on secret and dangerous operations, would jeopardise the effectiveness of the service. An absolute rule against disclosure, visible to all, makes good sense.

In considering what would be a just response to a breach of Blake's undertaking the court has to take these considerations into account. The undertaking, if not a fiduciary obligation, was closely akin to a fiduciary obligation, where an account of profits is a standard remedy in the event of breach. Had the information which Blake has now disclosed still been confidential, an account of profits would have been ordered, almost as a matter of course. In the special circumstances of the intelligence services, the same conclusion should follow even though the information is no longer confidential. That would be a just response to the breach. I am reinforced in this view by noting that most of the profits from the book derive indirectly from the extremely serious and damaging breaches of the same undertaking committed by Blake in the 1950s. As already mentioned, but for his notoriety as an infamous spy his autobiography would not have commanded royalties of the magnitude Jonathan Cape agreed to pay.

As a footnote I observe that a similar conclusion, requiring the contract-breaker to disgorge his profits, was reached in the majority decision of the United States Supreme Court in *Snepp v. United States* (1980) 444 U.S. 507. The facts were strikingly similar. A former employee of the Central Intelligence Agency, whose conditions of employment included a promise not to divulge any information relating to the agency without pre-publication clearance, published a book about the agency's activities in Vietnam. None of the information was classified, but an agent's violation of his non-disclosure obligation impaired the agency's ability to function properly. The court considered and rejected various forms of relief. The actual damage was not quantifiable, nominal damages were a hollow alternative, and punitive damages after a jury trial would be speculative and unusual. Even if recovered they would bear no relation to either the government's irreparable loss or Snepp's unjust gain. The court considered that a remedy which required Snepp 'to disgorge the benefits of his faithlessness', was swift and sure, tailored to deter those who would place sensitive information at risk and, since the remedy reached only funds attributable to the breach, it could not saddle the former agent with exemplary damages out of all proportion to his gain. In order to achieve this result the court 'imposed' a constructive trust on Snepp's profits.

In this country, affording the plaintiff the remedy of an account of profits is a different means to the same end.

The form of the order

The Attorney General's entitlement to an account of Blake's profits does not, in this case, confer on the Crown any proprietary interest in the debt due to Blake from Jonathan Cape. The Crown is entitled, on the taking of the account, to a money judgment which can then be enforced by attachment of the debt in the usual way. These formal steps may be capable of being short-circuited. Despite the niceties and formalities once associated with taking an account, the amount payable under an account of profits need not be any more elaborately or precisely calculated than damages. But in this case there is a complication. Blake has brought third party proceedings against Jonathan Cape, seeking payment of £90,000 (less tax). In the third party proceedings Jonathan Cape has sought to deduct legal expenses incurred in resisting a defamation claim and in resisting the Crown's claim. Accordingly, the appropriate form of order on this appeal is a declaration that the Attorney General is entitled to be paid a sum equal to whatever amount is due and owing to Blake from Jonathan Cape under the publishing agreement of 4 May 1989. The injunction granted by the Court of Appeal will remain in force until Jonathan Cape duly makes payment to the Attorney General. I would dismiss this appeal

LORD HOBHOUSE OF WOODBOROUGH [dissenting] The principle of compensation is both intellectually sound as the remedy for breach and provides the just answer. The examples discussed in my noble and learned friend's speech do not on the correct analysis disclose the supposed need to extend the boundaries of remedies for breach of contract. The reason why the Crown should not recover damages in the present case derives from the exceptional public law nature of the undertaking which Blake gave. If the relationship had been a commercial one it is probable that by 1989 the undertaking would be regarded as spent or no longer enforcible, but if still enforcible [*sic*] the breach of it would have supported compensatory damages on the 'compulsory purchase' basis. . . .

I must also sound a further note of warning that if some more extensive principle of awarding non-compensatory damages for breach of contract is to be introduced into our commercial law the consequences will be very far reaching and disruptive. I do not believe that such is the intention of your Lordships but if others are tempted to try to extend the decision of the present exceptional case to commercial situations so as to introduce restitutionary rights beyond those presently recognised by the law of restitution, such a step will require very careful consideration before it is acceded to.

My Lords, [counsel] was right to say that the exceptional facts of this case have been critical to its decision. The policy which is being enforced is that which requires Blake to be punished by depriving him of any benefit from anything connected with his past deplorable criminal conduct. Your Lordships consider that this policy can be given effect to without a departure from principle. I must venture to disagree. I would allow the appeal and dismiss the cross-appeal.

[Appeal dismissed]

NOTES and QUESTIONS

1. Who has the better of the argument as to whether such damages should be available as a matter of principle: Lord Nicholls or Lord Hobhouse? Reconsider the extract from Fuller and Perdue. How would they have reacted to the claim in this case? Is their hierarchy in which the restitution interest presents the strongest claim for relief as a matter of abstract justice one that addresses the situation of enrichment of the defendant where there has been no impoverishment of the plaintiff?

2. *Blake* has generated a huge amount of academic commentary. Among the criticisms is that the judgment of Lord Nicholls is situation specific and does not identify any coherent general principles on which future courts can determine whether to allow such claims in other contexts. It has also been criticized from a Posnerian perspective: it discourages efficient breach. See Campbell and Harris, "In Defence of Breach: A Critique of Restitution and the Performance Interest" (2002), 22 Legal Studies 208. Do you agree? For a more supportive opinion, see McCamus, "Disgorgement for Breach of Contract: A Comparative Perspective" (2003), 36 Loyola of Los Angeles Law Review 943.

3. To this point, there has been little discussion of *Blake* in Canadian cases. However, the following statement by Major J. (for the court) in *Bank of America Canada v. Mutual Trust Co.*, [2002] 2 S.C.R. 601, at para. 30, while without any reference to *Blake* is instructive:

> . . . [R]estitution damages can be invoked when a defendant has, as a result of his or her own breach, profited in excess of his or her expected profit had the contract been performed but the plaintiff's loss is less than the defendant's gain. . . . In some but not all cases, the defendant may be required to pay such profits to the plaintiff as restitution damages.

4. In *Amertek Inc. v. Canadian Commercial Corp.* (2003), [2003] O.J. No. 3177 (S.C.J.) O'Driscoll J., citing *Blake*, ordered the government to disgorge $26 million(US) (plus pre-judgment simple interest and $500,000 punitive damages) for breach of a collateral contract which induced the plaintiff to enter into a losing sub-contract. As a consequence of its breach of the collateral contract, the defendant had avoided substantial liabilities to the United States government. Because of a successful proposal to creditors under the *Bankruptcy Act*, most of the plaintiff's damages had been extinguished.

5. There is little Canadian authority on the issue, analogous to that raised in *Bowlay Logging Ltd. v. Domtar Ltd.*, of whether a restitutionary award can rescue the plaintiff from the consequences of a bad bargain. Professor Waddams cites the following example: A promises B $6,000 for the performance of certain work and repudiates the contract after B has done two-thirds of the work. However, the value of B's work at this stage is $7,000. (Waddams, *The Law of Contracts*, 4th ed. (1999), at para. 724). What should B's damages be?

3.   Damages: The Boundaries of Recovery

(a)   CIRCUMSCRIBING THE ZONE OF PROTECTED INTERESTS

(i)   *Loss of a Chance*

CHAPLIN v. HICKS

[1911] 2 K.B. 786 (C.A.)

The defendant, a theatrical manager, announced a competition for aspiring actresses, who were invited to submit photographs for publication in a newspaper. The readers would then take part in a selection process which would result in the nomination of twelve ladies, who would all receive three year contracts from the defendant to work as actresses. The first group of four winners would receive £5 per week for the duration of the contract, the second group £4 per week and the third group £3 per week.

About 6000 entries were received so an alteration in the terms of the competition was announced. A committee selected 300 photographs from the entries and these were to be published in the following way: the United Kingdom would be divided into ten districts, and the photographs of the selected candidates in each district would be submitted to the readers of the newspaper in that district, who were to select by their votes those whom they considered the most beautiful. After the voting was completed the defendant would make an appointment to see the five ladies in each district whose photographs so published obtained the greatest number of votes, and from these fifty the defendant would himself select the twelve who would receive the promised engagements. The plaintiff, one of the entrants, assented to the alteration in the terms of the competition. The fifty photographs were then published in the newspaper, together with a ballot paper on which the reader of the newspaper registered his vote. On January 2, 1909, the poll closed; the plaintiff's name appeared as first in her particular section, and she became one of the fifty eligible for selection by the defendant. On January 4 the defendant's secretary wrote to the plaintiff at her London address asking her to call to see the defendant in London on January 6. The plaintiff was at the time in Dundee and did not receive the letter in time to permit her to keep the appointment. As a result, she was unable to see the defendant, who selected twelve other winners.

The plaintiff sued for the loss of the chance of selection. The jury found that the defendant did not take reasonable steps to give the plaintiff an opportunity of presenting herself for selection and awarded damages of £100. The defendant appealed.

VAUGHAN WILLIAMS L.J. . . . . Then came the point that was more strenuously argued, that the damages were of such a nature as to be impossible of assessment. It was said that the plaintiff's chance of winning a prize turned on such a number of contingencies that it was impossible for any one, even after arriving at the conclusion that the plaintiff had lost her opportunity by the breach, to say that there was any assessable value of that loss. It is said that in a case which involves so many contingencies it is impossible to say what was the plaintiff's pecuniary loss. I am unable to agree with that contention. I agree that the presence of all the contingencies upon which the gaining of the prize might depend makes the calculation not only difficult but incapable of being carried out with certainty or precision. The proposition is that, whenever the contingencies on which the result depends are numerous and difficult to deal with, it is impossible to recover any damages for the loss of the chance or opportunity of winning the prize. In the present case I understand that there were fifty selected competitors, of whom the plaintiff was one, and twelve prizes, so that the average chance of each competitor was about one in four. Then it is said that the questions which might arise in the minds of the judges are so numerous that it is impossible to say that the case is one in which it is possible to apply the doctrine of averages at all.

I do not agree with the contention that, if certainty is impossible of attainment, the damages for a breach of contract are unassessable. . . .

In such a case the jury must do the best they can, and it may be that the amount of their verdict will really be a matter of guesswork. But the fact that damages cannot be assessed with certainty does not relieve the wrong-doer of the necessity of paying damages for his breach of contract. I do not wish to lay down any such rule as that a judge can in every case leave it to the jury to assess damages for a breach of contract. There are cases, no doubt, where the loss is so dependent on the mere unrestricted volition of another that it is impossible to say that there is any assessable loss resulting from the breach. In the present case there is no such difficulty. It is true that no market can be said to exist. None of the fifty competitors could have gone into the market and sold her right; her right was a personal right and incapable of transfer. But a jury might well take the view that such a right, if it could have been transferred, would have been of such a value that every one would recognize that a good price could be obtained for it. My view is that under such circumstances as those in this case the assessment of damages was unquestionably for the jury. The jury came to the conclusion that the taking away from the plaintiff of the opportunity of competition, as one of a body of fifty, when twelve prizes were to be distributed, deprived the plaintiff of something which had a monetary value. I think that they were right and that this appeal fails.

[Fletcher Moulton and Farwell L.JJ. delivered concurring judgments.]

QUESTIONS

1. What factors might legitimately be considered in fixing the award of damages?

2. In the *McRae* case, *supra*, section 2(b), the loss of bargain measure of damages was inapplicable because it was not possible to put a value on what the defendant purported to sell. Would a similar objection have had any effect in *Chaplin v. Hicks*?

3. *Fraser Park South Estates Ltd. v. Lang Michener Lawrence & Shaw* (2001), 84 B.C.L.R. (3d) 65 (C.A.), involved a claim based on the alleged loss of a chance to secure a property at a better price if the plaintiff's lawyer had alerted the plaintiff to the existence of a pollution abatement order on the property. In excusing the law firm defendant from anything but nominal damages for breach of contract, Mackenzie J.A. (delivering the judgment of the majority) said (at para. 80) that the application of *Chaplin v. Hicks*, whether in contract or tort:

> . . . necessarily rests upon a factual foundation of a real and substantial chance that the appellant would have benefited from a better bargain with the vendors but for the respondents' breach of duty . . . In my respectful view, any chance of a loss to the appellant was no more than speculative and a mere speculative chance was insufficient to support any claim for damages beyond nominal damages in contract.

(ii) *Cost of Completion v. Difference in Value*

GROVES v. JOHN WUNDER CO.

(1939), 286 N.W. 235 (Minn. C.A.)

STONE J. [delivering the judgment of the majority] Action for breach of contract. Plaintiff got judgment for a little over $15,000. Sorely disappointed by that sum, he appeals.

In August, 1927, S. J. Groves & Sons Company, a corporation (hereinafter mentioned simply as Groves), owned a tract of 24 acres of Minneapolis suburban real estate. It was served or easily could be reached by railroad trackage. It is zoned as heavy industrial property. But for lack of development of the neighbourhood its principal value thus far may have been in the deposit of sand and gravel which it carried. The Groves company had a plant on the premises for excavating and screening the gravel. Nearby defendant owned and was operating a similar plant.

In August, 1927, Groves and defendant made the involved contract. For the most part it was a lease from Groves, a lessor, to defendant, as lessee; its term seven years. Defendant agreed to remove the sand and gravel and to leave the property "at a uniform grade, substantially the same as the grade now existing at the roadway on said premises, and that in stripping the overburden it will use said overburden for the purpose of maintaining and establishing said grade."

Under the contract defendant got the Groves screening plant. The transfer thereof and the right to remove the sand and gravel made the consideration moving from Groves to defendant, except that defendant incidentally got rid of Groves as a competitor. On defendant's part it paid Groves $105,000. So that from the outset, on Groves' part the contract was executed except for defendant's right to continue using the property for the stated term. (Defendant had a right to renewal which it did not exercise.)

Defendant breached the contract deliberately. It removed from the premises only "the richest and best of the gravel" and wholly failed, according to the findings, "to perform and comply with the terms, conditions, and provisions of said lease with respect to the condition in which the surface of the demised premises was required to be left." Defendant surrendered the premises, not substantially at the grade required by the contract "nor at any uniform grade." Instead, the ground was "broken, rugged, and uneven." Plaintiff sues as assignee and successor in right of Groves.

As the contract was construed below, the finding is that to complete its performance 288,495 cubic yards of overburden would need to be excavated, taken from the premises, and deposited elsewhere. The reasonable cost of doing that was found to be upwards of $60,000. But, if defendant had left the premises at the uniform grade required by the lease, the reasonable value of the property on the determinative date would have been only $12,160. The judgment was for that sum, including interest, thereby nullifying plaintiff's claim that cost of completing the contract rather than difference in value of the land was the measure of damages. The gauge of damage adopted by the decision was the difference between the market value of plaintiff's land in the condition it was when the contract was made and what it would have been if defendant had performed. The one question for us arises upon plaintiff's assertion that he was entitled, not to that difference in value, but to the reasonable cost to him of doing the work called for by the contract which defendant left undone.

1. Defendant's breach of contract was wilful. There was nothing of good faith about it. Hence, that the decision below handsomely rewards bad faith and deliberate breach of contract is obvious. That is not allowable. . . .

2. In reckoning damages for breach of a building or construction contract, the law aims to give the disappointed promisee, so far as money will do it, what he was promised. . . .
Never before, so far as our decisions show, has it ever been suggested that lack of value in the land furnished to the contractor who had bound himself to improve it [allows] any escape from the ordinary consequences of a breach of the contract. . . .

Even in the case of substantial performance in good faith, the resulting defects being remediable, it is error to instruct that the measure of damage is "the difference in value between the house as it was and as it would have been if constructed according to contract." The "correct doctrine" is that the cost of remedying the defect is the "proper" measure of damages. *Snider v. Peters Home Building Co.*, 139 Minn. 413 at 414 and 416 (1918).

Value of the land (as distinguished from the value of the intended product of the contract, which ordinarily will be equivalent to its reasonable cost) is no proper part of any measure of damages for wilful breach of a building contract. The reason is plain.

The summit from which to reckon damages from trespass to real estate is its actual value at the moment. The owner's only right is to be compensated for the deterioration in value caused by the tort. That is all he has lost. But not so if a contract to improve the same land has been breached by the contractor who refuses to do the work, especially where, as here, he has been paid in advance. The summit from which to reckon damages for that wrong is the hypothetical peak of accomplishment (not value) which would have been reached had the work been done as demanded by the contract.

The owner's right to improve his property is not trammeled by its small value. It is his right to erect thereon structures which will reduce its value. If that be the result, it can be of no aid to any contractor who declines performance. As said long ago in *Chamberlain v. Parker*, 45 N.Y. 569 at 572 (1871): "A man may do what he will with his own, . . . and if he chooses to erect a monument to his caprice or folly on his premises, and employs and pays another to do it, it does not lie with a defendant who has been so employed and paid for building it, to say that his own performance would not be beneficial to the plaintiff." To the same effect is Restatement, Contracts, §346, p. 576, Illustrations of Subsection (1), par. 4.

Suppose a contractor were suing the owner for breach of a grading contract such as this. Would any element of value or lack of it, in the land have any relevance in reckoning damages? Of course not. The contractor would be compensated for what he had lost, i.e., his profit. Conversely, in such a case as this, the owner is entitled to compensation for what he has lost, that is, the work or structure which he has been promised, for which he has paid, and of which he has been deprived by the contractor's breach.

To diminish damages recoverable against him in proportion as there is presently small value in the land would favor the faithless contractor. It would also ignore and so defeat plaintiff's right to contract and build for the future. To justify such a course would require more of the prophetic vision than judges possess. This factor is important when the subject matter is trackage property in the margin of such an area of population and industry as that of the Twin Cities. . . .

It is suggested that because of little or no value in his land the owner may be unconscionably enriched by such a reckoning. The answer is that there can be no unconscionable enrichment, no advantage upon which the law will frown, when the result is but to give one party to a contract only what the other has promised; particularly where, as here, the delinquent has had full payment for the promised performance.

3. It is said by the Restatement, Contracts, §346, comment b:

> Sometimes defects in a completed structure cannot be physically remedied without tearing down and rebuilding, at a cost that would be imprudent and unreasonable. The law does not require damages to be measured by a method requiring such economic waste. If no such waste is involved, the cost of remedying the defect is the amount awarded as compensation for failure to render the promised performance.

The "economic waste" declaimed against by the decisions applying that rule has nothing to do with the value in money of the real estate, or even with the product of the contract. The waste avoided is only that which would come from wrecking a physical structure, completed, or nearly so, under the contract. . . . Absent such waste, as it is in this case, the rule of the Restatement, Contracts, §346, is that "the cost of remedying the defect is the amount awarded as compensation for failure to render the promised performance." That means that defendants here are liable to plaintiff for the reasonable cost of doing what defendants promised to do and have wilfully declined to do.

It follows that there must be a new trial.

JULIUS J. OLSON J. [dissenting] As the rule of damages to be applied in any given case has for its purpose compensation, not punishment, we must be ever mindful that, "If the application of a particular rule for measuring damages to given facts results in more than compensation, it is at once apparent that the wrong rule has been adopted." *Crowley v. Burns Boiler & Mfg. Co.* (1907), 110 N.W. 969 at 973.

We have here then a situation where, concededly, if the contract had been performed, plaintiff would have had property worth, in round numbers, no more than $12,000. If he is to be awarded damages in an amount exceeding $60,000 he will be receiving at least 500 per cent more than his property, properly leveled to grade by actual performance, was intrinsically worth when the breach occurred. To so conclude is to give him something far beyond what the parties had in mind or contracted for. There is no showing made, nor any finding suggested, that this property was unique, specially desirable for a particular or personal use, or of special value as to location or future use different from that of other property surrounding it. Under the circumstances here appearing, it seems clear that what the parties contracted for was to put the property in shape for general sale. And the lease contemplates just that, for by the terms thereof defendant agreed "from time to time, as the sand and gravel are removed from the various lots leased, it will surrender said lots to the lessor" if of no further use to defendant "in connection with the purposes for which this lease is made."

The theory upon which plaintiff relies for application of the cost of performance rule must have for its basis cases where the property or the improvement to be made is unique or personal instead of being of the kind ordinarily governed by market values. His action is one at law for damages, not for specific performance. As there was no affirmative showing of any peculiar fitness of this property to a unique or personal use, the rule to be applied is, I think, the one applied by the court. The cases bearing directly upon this phase so hold. Briefly, the rule here applicable is this: Damages recoverable for breach of a contract to construct is the difference between the market value of the property in the condition it was when delivered to and received by plaintiff and what its market value would have been if defendant had fully complied with its terms. . . .

No one doubts that a party may contract for the doing of anything he may choose to have done (assuming what is to be done is not unlawful) "although the thing to be produced had no marketable value." In Restatement, Contracts, §346, pp. 576, 577, Illustrations of Subsection (1), par. 4, the same thought is thus stated: "A contracts to construct a monumental fountain in B's yard for $5,000, but abandons the work after the foundation has been laid and $2800 has been paid by B. The contemplated fountain is so ugly that it would decrease the number of possible buyers of the place. The cost of completing the fountain would be $4000. B can get judgment for $1800, the cost of completion less the part of price unpaid." But that is not what plaintiff's predecessor in interest contracted for. Such a provision might well have been made, but the parties did not. They could undoubtedly have provided for liquidated damages for nonperformance or they might have determined in money what the value of performance was considered to be and thereby have contractually provided a measure for failure of performance.

The opinion also suggests that this property lies in an area where the owner might rightly look for future development, being in a so-called industrial zone, and that as such he should be privileged to so hold it. This he may of course do. But let us assume that on May 1, 1934, condemnation to acquire this area had so far progressed as to leave only the question of price (market value) undetermined; that the area had been graded in strict conformity with the contract but that the actual market value of the premises was only $12,160, as found by the court and acquiesced in by plaintiff, what would the measure of his damages be? Obviously, the limit of his recovery could be no more than the then market value of his property. In that sum he has been paid with interest and costs; and he still has the fee title to the premises, something he would not possess if there had been condemnation. In what manner has plaintiff been hurt beyond the damages awarded? As to him "economic waste" is not apparent. Assume that defendant abandoned the entire project without taking a single yard of gravel therefrom but left the premises as they were when the lease was made, could plaintiff recover damages upon the basis here established? The trouble with the prevailing opinion is that here plaintiff's loss is not made the basis for the amount of his recovery but rather what it would cost the defendant. No case has been decided upon that basis until now.

I think the judgment should be affirmed.

[Holt J. joined in the dissenting judgment.]

NOTES and QUESTION

1. The trial judge expressly found that the land as surrendered to the plaintiff was without any value at all. See Dawson and Harvey, *Contracts and Contract Remedies* (1969), at 2.

2. Should the deliberate nature of the defendant's breach have had any influence on the approach of the majority to the assessment of damages?

3. A well-known decision which contrasts with *Groves v. John Wunder Co.* is *Peevyhouse v. Garland Coal Mining Co.*, 382 P. 2d 109 (Okla. S.C., 1962), in which the owners of a farm leased it for strip-mining. The mining company failed to do the reclamation required under the lease and the owners sought damages. If the mining company had restored the land, the value of the farm would have increased by $300, while the cost of restoration would have been approximately $29,000. On appeal, the owners were held to be entitled to damages of $300. For a discussion of these cases from the standpoint of fairness, see Farnsworth, "Legal Remedies for Breach of Contract" (1970), 70 Columbia L. R. 1145 at 1171. A sharper economic appraisal of *Groves v. John Wunder Co.* is offered in the following extract.

POSNER, ECONOMIC ANALYSIS OF LAW

6th ed. (2003), at 121-122

The court awarded the plaintiff $60,000, reasoning that he was entitled to get the performance he had contracted for and that it was no business of the defendant whether, or how much, his performance would have made the plaintiff's property more valuable. The result is questionable. It was not a case . . . where value and market price were different. The land in question was a commercial parcel, and if the plaintiff had wanted the performance rather than the $60,000 he would have brought an action for specific performance. He did not bring such an action and, even more telling, did not use the money he won from the defendant to level the land. The measure of damages was incorrect from an economic standpoint because, had it been known to the defendant from the start, it would have made him indifferent between breaking his promise to level the land and performing it, whereas efficiency dictated breach; the $60,000 worth of labor and materials that would have been consumed in leveling the land would have brought less than a $12,000 increase in value.

It is true that not enforcing the contract would have given the defendant a windfall. But enforcing the contract gave the plaintiff an equal and opposite windfall: a cushion, which almost certainly the parties had not intended, against the impact of the Depression on land values. Since the plaintiff, as the owner of the land, rather than the defendant, a contractor, would have enjoyed the benefit of any unexpected increase in the value of the land, the parties, if they had thought about the matter, would probably have wanted the plaintiff to bear the burden of any unexpected fall in that value as well.

[Footnotes omitted.]

QUESTION

Would the failure of the plaintiff to seek specific performance be as strong an argument against the adoption of the loss of bargain measure in Canada? *Cf.* the comments of Megarry V.C. in *Tito v. Waddell*, [1977] Ch. 106 at 331-32.

NU-WEST HOMES LTD. v. THUNDERBIRD PETROLEUMS LTD.

(1975), 59 D.L.R. (3d) 292 (Alta. C.A.)

After lengthy negotiations, Nu-West (the respondent) contracted to build a house for Thunderbird, the appellant, for $51,219 in accordance with certain plans and specifications. The respondent began construction in October 1966 and by January 1967 had completed framing, poured the basement floors, finished the roof, installed the windows and siding and "roughed in" the plumbing and electricity.

At this point, the appellants began to complain about serious deviations from the specifications. By January 9th, Nu-West decided that the customer relationship had so deteriorated that no further work should be done on the house until all disputes had been resolved.

The disputes never were resolved. On June 16th, the appellants took possession of the house, had it examined by an architect and two engineers and arranged for its completion by Larwill Construction Ltd. Nu-West then sued the appellants for $16,000 in addition to the sum they had already been paid ($10,600) and the appellants counterclaimed for the cost of rectifying the deficiencies in construction and the difference between the cost of completing the house and the original contract price. At trial, $4,160 was allowed to the appellants on this account and from this judgment they appealed.

It was clear that there were many serious deficiencies in the construction of the house. In particular, there was a hump about 1-1/2 inches in height in one part of the basement floor. This area was jack-hammered out and the operation revealed that the concrete floor and underlying gravel did not match the specifications, that the plenum, which was to conduct heat from the furnace to the ducts, was encased in dirt rather than concrete and contained large quantities of polyethylene, that the duct uncovered was damaged and the other ducts were not watertight or protected against rust or surrounded by concrete. In addition, there were problems with the electric wiring, plumbing, shoddy framing, fireplaces of the wrong size and numerous other defects.

Both the trial judge and the Appellate Division held that these breaches by Nu-West were sufficient to justify Thunderbird's action in treating the contract as terminated and contracting with Larwill to complete construction. After consulting an architect, a structural engineer and a heating engineer, Thunderbird decided to remove the concrete floor in the basement, to re-do the duct work and to demolish and rebuild the fireplaces. This work was done by Larwill at a cost of $16,000. However, the trial judge awarded only $4,238 in respect of this work, as he did not consider demolition of the basement to be necessary under the circumstances. On appeal the question arose of the proper measure of Thunderbird's damages.

MOIR J.A. . . . [The trial judge] went on to say "to demolish the whole of the basement at a relatively high cost because of this, what I consider inconsequential deviation from specifications, is not warranted under the circumstances".

It is not every deviation from the specifications that would justify the removal of the slab. The general law as to the right of the aggrieved party to have the building he contracted for is set out by Mr. Justice Wetmore in *Allen v. Pierce* (1895), 3 Terr. L.R. 319 at pp. 323-24.:

> I will merely repeat that it is not a mere matter of difference between the value of the material supplied and that contracted for, or of the work done and that which ought to have been done, or of the house as it stands and that which ought to have been built under the contract. If these were the standards of damages there would be no point in a man contracting for the best materials; he might as well contract at the start for an inferior quality, because they are cheaper. The owner of the building is, therefore, entitled to recover such damages, or to have such deductions made as will put him in a position to have just the building he contracted for. . . .

It is, of course, obvious that there must be a restriction on such a rule. This restriction is that where the cost of rectification is great in comparison to the nature of the defect, the Court will not force a slavish following of the precise specifications of the contract. This is illustrated in *Jacobs & Youngs Inc. v. Kent* (1921), 129 N.E. 889. In this case, there was an oversight and pipe from a specified manufacturer was not incorporated into the building. The owner attempted to force the contractor to tear large sections of the building down to put in the pipe of the specified manufacturer. Cardozo, J. said at p. 890:

> The courts never say that one who makes a contract fills the measure of his duty by less than full performance. They do say, however, that an omission, both trivial and innocent, will sometimes be atoned for by allowance of the resulting damage, and will not always be the breach of condition to be followed by a forfeiture.

He went on at p. 891 to say:

> It is true that in most cases the cost of replacement is the measure. The owner is entitled to the money which will permit him to complete, unless the cost of completion is grossly and unfairly out of proportion to the good to be attained. When that is true, the measure is the difference in value. Specifications call, let us say, for a foundation built of granite quarried in Vermont. On the completion of the building, the owner learns that through the blunder of a subcontractor part of the foundation has been built of granite of the same quality quarried in New Hampshire. The measure of allowance is not the cost of reconstruction. "There may be omissions of that which could not afterwards be supplied exactly as called for by the contract without taking down the building to its foundations, and at the same time the omission may not affect the value of the building for use or otherwise, except so slightly as to be hardly appreciable." *Handy v. Bliss* (1910), 204 Mass. 513 at 519, 90 N.E. 864.

In my view, one should be careful not to weigh in too fine a set of balances the conduct of the aggrieved party. The wrongdoer is entitled to expect the aggrieved party to act reasonably. He is not entitled to have him act perfectly. In my view the proper test to be applied is that set out by Lord Macmillan in *Banco de Portugal v. Waterlow & Sons Ltd.*, [1932] A.C. 452 at 506 (H.L.), where he states:

> Where the sufferer from a breach of contract finds himself in consequence of that breach placed in a position of embarrassment the measures which he may be driven to adopt in order to extricate himself ought not to be weighed in nice scales at the incidence of the party whose breach of contract has occasioned the difficulty. It is often easy after an emergency has passed to criticize the steps which have been taken to meet it, but such criticism does not come well from those who have themselves created the emergency. The law is satisfied if the party placed in a difficult situation by reason of the breach of a duty owed to him has acted reasonably in the adoption of remedial measures, and he will not be held disentitled to recover the cost of such measures merely because the party in breach can suggest that other measures less burdensome to him might have been taken.

I am fortified in coming to the conclusion that Thunderbird's conduct was reasonable by reason of Thunderbird's conduct in respect of other defects and deficiencies. Thunderbird knew that the reinforcing steel had been omitted from the top of the basement walls but they did not tear down the walls. Thunderbird knew that the joists were too short and improperly braced but they did not jack up the floor or roof and replace them. Thunderbird knew the roof had sagged but they jacked it up and braced it. These actions indicate to me that Thunderbird at this time was acting on the advice of its experts and doing so reasonably.

I look at the defects and deficiencies. In my opinion, they cannot be characterized as "trivial and innocent". I have already said that in my view Thunderbird acted reasonably. It therefore follows that Thunderbird must be allowed the $16,000 paid to Larwill to tear out [and reconstruct] the basement.

[When the total costs of completion were added, the judgment at trial was varied to award Thunderbird damages in excess of $37,000.]

NOTES and QUESTIONS

1. Barbara Boomer has employed Ron Rough, a contractor, to build her house. She has specified an open beam living room ceiling, with the beams to be made of California redwood. In breach of contract, Rough instals beams of B.C. cedar. The difference in wood is barely noticeable, except to an expert, and the cost of replacing them would amount to $15,000. What are Barbara's damages?

If you feel that Barbara is entitled to full loss of bargain damages, can this conclusion be reconciled with Posner's critique of *Groves v. John Wunder Co.*, *supra*? See Harris, Ogus and Phillips, "Contract Remedies and the Consumer Surplus" (1979), 95 L.Q.R. 581, and *Radford v. De Froberville*, [1978] 1 All E.R. 33 (Ch. D.).

An interesting parallel to the pragmatic approach of the Alberta Court of Appeal is to be found in *Ruxley Electronics & Construction Ltd. v. Forsyth*, [1996] 1 A.C. 344 (U.K. H.L.), discussed by Lord Hobhouse in his dissenting judgment in *Blake*. The House of Lords set aside the Court of Appeal's award of cost of completion damages (£21,560) and restored the trial judge's award of a sum representing a loss of amenity (£2,500) in a nine inch deeper, £70,000 swimming pool. In so doing, the House of Lords emphasised that cost of completion and difference in value did not represent the only alternatives in the measurement of damages in such cases. In the circumstances, cost of completion was too high and difference in value under-compensatory; hence the award for loss of amenity or enjoyment. Why would that not have worked in *Nu-West Homes Ltd.*? Consider however another alternative: the costs avoided by the defendant in not performing according to contractual specifications. Would this be consistent with the approach of the majority in *Blake*?

2. In *Strata Corp. NW 1714 v. Winkler* (1988), 45 D.L.R. (4th) 741 (B.C. C.A.), which also involved deficiencies in construction, the plaintiffs argued that the cost of rectification was the general measure of damages. Esson J.A., for the court, accepted that the law of British Columbia was correctly stated by Davey J. in *McGarry v. Richards, Ackroyd & Gall Ltd.*, [1954] 2 D.L.R. 367 (B.C. S.C.). In that case, Davey J. (at 389) considered *Cunningham v. Insinger* and *Cotter v. General Petroleums Ltd.*, both of which are discussed in the following extract, and concluded that:

> These cases establish that the primary measure of damages for non-performance of a contract to build on another's land is the diminution in value resulting from such default. In the case at bar, the work was imperfectly done, but, I can see no difference in principle.
>
> Cases may arise where the damages for the default should be measured by the cost of making good the default. This will be so if the cost of performing the work or making good the defects is less than the diminution in the value of property caused by the default. In such cases, it is the plaintiff's duty to take any reasonable steps to mitigate his damage by doing what is required.

In *Procan Exploration Co. v. Golder Associates (Western Canada) Ltd.* (1991), 48 C.L.R. 86 (B.C. C.A.), the court approved the statement of law in the *Winkler* case in the case of a contract to repair and stated (at 95) that "a factor to be considered is whether the owner intends to carry out the work of reinstatement and if not the proper measure is the diminution in value". In *Farmer Construction Ltd. v. Doncaster Holdings Ltd.* (1990), 46 C.L.R. 80 (B.C. S.C.), an architect committed, in breach of contract, a design defect which caused a membrane on the exterior of the underground portions of a motel to leak. The plaintiff sought as damages $28,500, the cost of repairing the motel. Because of the insolvency of the motel owner, the trial judge was not convinced that the owner intended to carry out the repairs. As the market value of the motel was not affected by the leaking membrane, nominal damages of $10 were awarded. What is the practical effect of the approach of the British Columbia courts in this area?

3. "Farm-out" agreements, such as that considered in *Sunshine Exploration Ltd. v. Dolly Varden Mines Ltd. (N.P.L.)*, [1970] S.C.R. 2, are very common in the oil and gas industry in Canada and the United States. They have given rise to some intractable problems in calculating damages when the operator breaks the covenant to drill or explore; the range of judicial solutions to these problems is canvassed in Sychuk, "Damages for Breach of an Express Drilling Covenant" (1970), 8 Alta. L. Rev. 250.

(iii) *Loss of Enjoyment and Other Intangible Interests*

To this point, our consideration of damages based on the expectations of the disappointed party has been pretty much confined to commercial contracts, ones in which the objective of both parties was to achieve monetary profit or business advantage. Of course, this is not true of all contracts. Frequently, one or sometimes both parties to a contract will be seeking to attain other than financial objectives. While my travel agent has profit as her objective when I purchase a winter holiday in the Caribbean, my principal aims are relaxation and enjoyment. When I agree with a friend to exchange books that we have each read recently and enjoyed, both sides to this transaction have as their objective the achievement of the pleasure that comes from reading a good novel or biography.

Not at all surprisingly, when deals such as this go sour, there is often an uneasy fit between the expectation principle and the computation of the damages necessary to protect the interest recognized by the application of that principle—putting the disappointed party in the position that he or she would have been in had the other party not breached. More specifically, how does or should a court reduce to monetary terms my disappointment when my Caribbean vacation is far removed in terms of what I received than was promised by both my travel agent and the brochure on which I relied? Indeed, should the courts even try? Would it not be better or more satisfactory to recognize these situations as the kinds of case in which expectation damages should cede to damages based on restitution or reliance principles?

In the movie and the book on which it was based, John Jay Osborn's *The Paper Chase* (1971), the opening scene involves the first class in a Harvard Law School Contracts course taught by the fictional Professor Kingsfield. The case which he uses to introduce his students to the Socratic method in its most terrifying form is *Hawkins v. McGee* (1929), 89 N.H. 114; 146 A. 64. Indeed, this is the same case that opens the Contracts Casebook of one of the most famous Harvard Contracts and Jurisprudence Professors, Lon Fuller, the co-author of the article extracted in the opening section of this chapter: Fuller & Eisenberg, *Basic Contract Law*, 3rd ed. (1972) at 1. In *Hawkins v. McGee*, the court is confronted with a contract in which a doctor has guaranteed the successful outcome of plastic surgery on the disfigured hand of a young man. Aside from the question of whether the guarantee should be enforced as a contract, the main dilemma of the case is the determination of how much the plaintiff should receive by way of damages to reflect not just his restitutionary (cost of operation) and reliance losses (the dislocative costs and inconvenience of a wasted operation) but also his disappointment in now having a hand that is even more disfigured than it was previously. Indeed, many of the same issues are raised by a Canadian case in Chapter 2, section 2, *Goldthorpe v. Logan*, [1943] 2 D.L.R. 519 (Ont. C.A.). Consider these issues in the light of one of Lord Denning's more highly publicized judgments in the case that follows.

JARVIS v. SWANS TOURS
[1973] 1 Q.B. 233 (C.A.)

Jarvis, a solicitor, bought a two week holiday package in the Swiss Alps over the Christmas-New Year period. Swans Tours, which sold him the holiday had a brochure in which various assurances were provided. The holiday did not live up to the brochure by a long stretch and, on his return, Jarvis sued the tour company for damages, including the failure of the holiday to meet the expectations generated by the tour company through its brochure and the mental distress and aggravation he experienced both on the holiday and in its wake. He succeeded at trial but only to the extent of half the cost of his holiday. He therefore appealed to the Court of Appeal.

LORD DENNING M.R. . . . Mr. Jarvis read a brochure issued by Swans Tours Ltd. He was much attracted by the description of Mörlialp, Giswil, Central Switzerland. I will not read the whole of it, but just pick out some of the principal attractions:

> House Part Centre with special resident host. . . . Mörlialp is a most wonderful little resort on a sunny plateau . . . Up there you will find yourself in the midst of beautiful alpine scenery, which in winter becomes a wonderland of sun, snow and ice, with a wide variety of fine ski-runs, a skating rink and exhilarating toboggan run . . . Why did we choose the Hotel Krone

... mainly and most of all because of the 'Gemütlichkeit' and friendly welcome you will receive from Herr and Frau Weibel. . . . The Hotel Krone has its own Alphütte Bar which will be open several evenings a week. . . . No doubt you will be in for a great time, when you book this house-party holiday . . . Mr. Weibel, the charming owner, speaks English.

On the same page, in a special yellow box, it was said:

Swans House Party in Mörlialp. All these House Party arrangements are included in the price of your holiday. Welcome party on arrival. Afternoon tea and cake for 7 days. Swiss dinner by candlelight. Fondue party. Yodler evening. Chali farewell party in the 'Alphütte Bar'. Service of representative.

Alongside on the same page there was a special note about ski-packs. "Hire of Skis, Sticks and Boots . . . Ski Tuition . . . 12 days £11.10."

. . . . .

The plaintiff went on the holiday, but he was very disappointed. He was a man of about 35 and he expected to be one of a house party of some 30 or so people. Instead, he found there were only 13 during the first week. In the second week there was no house party at all. He was the only person there. Mr. Weibel could not speak English. So there was Mr. Jarvis, in the second week, in this hotel with no house party at all, and no one could speak English, except himself. He was very disappointed, too, with the ski-ing. It was some distance away at Giswill. There were no ordinary length skis. There were only mini-skis, about 3 ft. long. So he did not get his ski-ing as he wanted to. In the second week he did get some longer skis for a couple of days, but then, because of the boots, his feet got rubbed and he could not continue even with the long skis. So his ski-ing holiday, from his point of view, was pretty well ruined.

There were many other matters, too. They appear trivial when they are set down in writing, but I have no doubt they loomed large in Mr. Jarvis's mind, when coupled with the other disappointments. He did not have the nice Swiss cakes which he was hoping for. The only cakes for tea were potato crisps and little dry nut cakes. The Yodler evening consisted of one man from the locality who came in his working clothes for a little while and sang four or five songs very quickly. The "Alphütte Bar" was an unoccupied annexe which was only open one evening. There was a representative, Mrs. Storr, there during the first week, but she was not there during the second week.

The matter was summed up by the judge:

During the first week he got a holiday in Switzerland which was to some extent inferior . . . and, as to the second week, he got a holiday which was very largely inferior to what he was led to expect.

What is the legal position? I think that the statements in the brochure were representations or warranties. The breaches of them give Mr. Jarvis a right to damages. . . .

The one question in the case is: What is the amount of damages? The judge seems to have taken the difference in value between what he paid for and what he got. He said that he intended to give "the difference between the two values and no other damages" under any other head. He thought that Mr. Jarvis had got half of what he paid for. So the judge gave him half the amount which he had paid, namely, £31.72. Mr. Jarvis appeals to this court. He says the damages ought to have been much more. . . .

What is the right way of assessing damages? It has often been said that on a breach of contract damages cannot be given for mental distress. . . .

I think that those limitations are out of date. In a proper case damages for mental distress can be recovered in contract, just as damages for shock can be recovered in tort. One such case is a contract for a holiday, or any other contract to provide entertainment and enjoyment. If the contracting party breaks his contract, damages can be given for the disappointment, the distress, the upset and frustration caused by the breach. I know that it is difficult to assess in terms of money, but it is no more difficult than the assessment which the courts have to make every day in personal injury cases for loss of amenities. Take the present case. Mr. Jarvis has only a fortnight's holiday in the year. He books it far ahead, and looks forward to it all that time. He ought to be compensated for the loss of it.

A good illustration was given by Edmund Davies L.J. in the course of the argument. He put the case of a man who has taken a ticket for [the opera at] Glyndbourne. It is the only night on which he can get there. He hires a car to take him. The car does not turn up. His damages are not limited to the mere cost of the ticket. He is entitled to general damages for the disappointment he has suffered and the loss of the entertainment which he should have had. Here, Mr. Jarvis's fortnight's winter holiday has been a grave disappointment. It is true that he was conveyed to Switzerland and back and had meals and bed in the hotel. But that is not what he went for. He went to enjoy himself with all the facilities which the defendants said he would have. He is entitled to damages for the lack of those facilities, and for his loss of enjoyment. . . .

I think the judge was in error in taking the sum paid for the holiday £63.45 and halving it. The right measure of damages is to compensate him for the loss of entertainment and enjoyment which he was promised, and which he did not get.

Looking at the matter quite broadly, I think the damages in this case should be the sum of £125. I would allow the appeal, accordingly.

[Edmund Davies and Stephenson L.JJ. delivered concurring judgments. Appeal allowed.]

NOTE and QUESTIONS

1. Edmund Davies and Stephenson L.JJ. concurred, stating at 237:

> When a man has paid for and properly expects an invigorating and amusing holiday and, through no fault of his, returns home dejected because his expectations have been largely unfulfilled, in my judgment it would be quite wrong to say that his disappointment must find no reflection in the damages to be awarded. . . .

2. On what theory would Lord Denning's award of damages increasing the damages from half the cost of the holiday to twice the cost of the holiday be justified? Is there an argument that even this might be under-compensatory?

3. In what other kinds of contracts should damages for loss of enjoyment and mental distress be available? Consider the House of Lords' recognition of a claim for loss of amenity for the breach of a contract involving the depth of a swimming pool in *Ruxley Electronics & Construction Ltd. v.*

Forsyth, supra. This was followed by *Farley v. Skinner,* [2001] 3 W.L.R. 899 (U.K. H.L.) where the House of Lords sustained an award of non-pecuniary damages of £10,000 for physical inconvenience and discomfort where a property surveyor had breached a contract with a client by failing to ascertain that a carriage trade property purchased by the client was directly beneath a flight path to Gatwick Airport. Lord Steyn did, however, describe it, at para. 28, as "at the very top end of what could possibly be regarded as appropriate damages". For Canadian examples, see *Newell v. Canadian Pacific Airlines Ltd.* (1976), 74 D.L.R. (3d) 574 (Ont. Co. Ct.) (mental distress damages being awarded for death of one dog and serious injury to another being transported to Mexico where their owners were vacationing); *Kempling v. Hearthstone Manor Corp.* (1996), 137 D.L.R. (4th) 12 (Alta. C.A.) (damages for disappointment arising from delay in providing occupation of condominium intended for married couple and elderly, frail parent); *Warrington v. Great-West Life Assurance Co.* (1996), 137 D.L.R. (4th) 18 (B.C. C.A.) (mental distress damages awarded for failure of insurance company to meet obligations under disability insurance contract); and, more recently and of much interest to law students: *Sokolsky v. Canada 3000 Airlines Ltd.* (2002), [2002] O.J. No. 3085 (S.C.J.), affirmed (October 3, 2003), [2003] O.J. No. 3920 (Div. Ct.) (*Jarvis* applied in awarding law student who had recently completed the Bar Admission Course twice the cost of the trip reflecting both pecuniary and non-pecuniary loss when advertised package vacation in Cancun proved totally unsatisfactory for the plaintiff and his girlfriend). See also *Wharton v. Tom Harris Chevrolet Oldsmobile Cadillac Ltd.,* [2002] 3 W.W.R. 629 (B.C. C.A.), where the plaintiffs recovered $5,000 non-pecuniary loss for "loss of enjoyment of their luxury vehicle and for inconvenience", the result of a buzzing sound system which, despite numerous efforts at rectification, persisted for two and a half years. The plaintiffs also recovered $2500 for hotel and travel expenses associated with trying to rectify this problem with the Cadillac Eldorado. After a promising start (see *Wilson v. Sooter Studios Ltd.* (1988), 55 D.L.R. (4th) 303 (B.C. C.A.) (wedding photographs) and *Dunn v. Disc Jockey Unlimited Co.* (1978), 87 D.L.R. (3d) 408 (Ont. Dist. Ct.) (disc jockey), those suffering breaches of contract in the context of their wedding and subsequent reception have not been so fortunate recently: see *Baid v. Aliments Rinag Foods Inc.* (2003), [2003] O.J. No. 22153 (S.C.J.) (catering at the reception) and *Olson v. Beaulieu* (2002), [2002] S.J. No. 779 (Prov. Ct.) (wedding dress). How would you deconstruct a body of case law under which aggravated or loss of enjoyment damages are available for temporary deprivation of a luxury motor vehicle but not for breaches of contracts to provide services at weddings? There were also suggestions in some of the jurisprudence that, at least on occasion, the wrongful dismissal of an employee might also represent another occasion on which the courts could award damages for loss of enjoyment and mental distress. As we will see in the next section, that possibility has now been foreclosed by the Supreme Court of Canada. However, it is noteworthy that the Court did so without prejudice to the general line of authority starting with *Jarvis v. Swans Tours.* This is also underscored by *McIsaac v. Sun Life Assurance Co. of Canada* (1999), 173 D.L.R. (4th) 649 (B.C. C.A.), in which *Warrington* was applied notwithstanding the subsequent Supreme Court of Canada jurisprudence on aggravated damages for breach of contract.

4. Does the third party beneficiary rule pose a problem for recovery of the losses of all members of a travelling party when the tickets are purchased by one member of that party on behalf of all of the others? See *Jackson v. Horizon Holidays Ltd.,* [1975] 1 W.L.R. 1468 (C.A.).

(iv) Aggravated and Punitive Damages

VORVIS v. INSURANCE CORP. OF BRITISH COLUMBIA

[1989] 1 S.C.R. 1085, 36 B.C.L.R. (2d) 273, 42 B.L.R. 111, 25 C.C.E.L. 81, [1989] 4 W.W.R. 218, 90 C.L.L.C. 14,035, 58 D.L.R. (4th) 193, 94 N.R. 321

The appellant is a solicitor who was employed by the respondent Insurance Corporation of British Columbia ("I.C.B.C."), in its legal department from 1974 to 1981. He had graduated from law school in 1972 after a successful career as an engineer with DuPont of Canada Ltd. He left DuPont to enter law school rather than accept a transfer to eastern Canada. He was Western District Sales Manager for DuPont at the time. He took up his employment with the respondent as a junior solicitor on 24th September 1973 when the respondent was starting up its business. His work initially was of a routine nature and included the preparation of leases and real estate purchases with a view to the establishment of claim centres and other facilities for the corporation throughout the province. He was promoted from the position of solicitor I to solicitor II on 1st July 1976 and given merit increases in salary in 1978, 1979 and 1980. In January 1981 his employment was abruptly terminated and he was required to vacate his office by 13th February 1981. He was 49 years old at the time. . . . There was no complaint about the quality of the appellant's work or that he failed to meet deadlines required for his assignments nor was it alleged that he did not carry his fair share of the workload. He was simply conscientious to a fault, according to the learned trial judge, and, in the words of Mr. Reid, was prone "to produce a Cadillac when a Ford would do".

Mr. Reid became increasingly dissatisfied with the pace of the appellant's work. By November 1980 he had set up "productivity meetings" each Monday morning in which he reviewed the appellant's work in relation to the number of hours he spent on each project. The trial judge found that these meetings "became an inquisition" and "as the pressure increased the plaintiff became tense, agitated and distressed, finally resorting to medical attention and a tranquillizer".

The appellant was dismissed on 21st January 1981 without any particular precipitating event but simply because, according to the trial judge, he did not fit into Mr. Reid's plans for the department. The trial judge found that the appellant was "an honest, loyal, trustworthy and diligent employee" and was dismissed without cause and without reasonable notice. The respondent offered to pay his salary and certain benefits for an eight-month period if he agreed by 23rd January 1981 to release the corporation from any claim arising out of his employment and its peremptory termination. Since the appellant was not prepared to admit that he was incompetent and that his employer had just cause for his dismissal on account of his incompetence, he refused the offer. He left the respondent's employ on 23rd January 1981 and was paid up to 15th February 1981. He obtained other employment in September 1981 but not as a solicitor.

[This statement of facts is taken from the judgment of Wilson J., extracts of which are set out following the majority judgment.]

McINTYRE J. . . . [T]he trial judge awarded damages for wrongful dismissal . . . In this court, the appellant . . . argued that the court was in error in denying his claim for punitive damages. Damages for mental distress, properly characterized as aggravated damages, were not claimed in this court as a separate head but it was argued that they were included in the general concept of punitive damages. . . .

In his statement of claim, the appellant advanced a claim for mental distress as result of the termination of his contract of employment in these terms:

> The plaintiff makes a claim for mental distress, anxiety, vexation and frustration suffered by the plaintiff as a result of the termination of his contract of employment by the defendant.

Later, in the prayer for relief, in addition to asserting claims for general and special damages for breach of contract, he claimed punitive damages. In pursuit of his claim for mental distress, the appellant argued at trial that the offensive and unjustifiable conduct of Reid, a superior in his employment, was such that it caused great mental distress, anxiety, vexation and frustration as alleged in the pleadings. . . . [The trial judge] refused the general damage claim for aggravated damages for mental distress, and in this he was supported by the Court of Appeal. The trial judge sought to distinguish between damages for mental distress which, as will be explained below, would include cases properly classified as aggravated damages, and punitive or exemplary damages. In respect of punitive damages, he said at p. 735: "If exemplary damages could be awarded in a wrongful dismissal case I would award them here". On his interpretation of *Addis v. Gramophone Co.*, [1909] A.C. 488 (H.L.) . . ., he held that the sole measure of damages for wrongful dismissal was the salary which the plaintiff was entitled to during the period of reasonable notice. Therefore, he awarded neither aggravated nor punitive damages.

Before dealing with the question of punitive damages, it will be well to make clear the distinction between punitive and aggravated damages. . . . The distinction is clearly set out in Waddams, The Law of Damages (1983), at pp. 562-63, para. 979, in these words:

> An exception exists to the general rule that damages are compensatory. This is the case of an award made for the purpose, not of compensating the plaintiff, but of punishing the defendant. Such awards have been called exemplary, vindictive, penal, punitive, aggravated and retributory, but the expressions in common modern use to describe damages going beyond compensatory are exemplary and punitive damages. "Exemplary" was preferred by the House of Lords in *Cassell & Co. Ltd. v. Broome*, but "punitive" has also been used in many Canadian courts including the Supreme Court of Canada in *H.L. Weiss Forwarding Ltd. v. Omnus*. The expression "aggravated damages", though it has sometimes been used interchangeably with punitive or exemplary damages, has more frequently in recent times been contrasted with exemplary damages. In this contrasting sense, aggravated damages describes an award that aims at compensation, but takes full account of the intangible injuries, such as distress and humiliation, that may have been caused by the defendant's insulting behaviour. The expressions vindictive, penal and retributory have dropped out of common use.

Aggravated damages are awarded to compensate for aggravated damage. As explained by Waddams, they take account of intangible injuries and by definition will generally augment damages assessed under the general rules relating to the assessment of damages. Aggravated damages are compensatory in nature and may only be awarded for that purpose. Punitive damages, on the other hand, are punitive in nature and may only be employed in circumstances where the conduct giving the cause for complaint is of such nature that it merits punishment.

The issue which is faced by this court is whether punitive damages may be awarded by the court in an action for breach of contract, based on wrongful dismissal of an employee, and, if so, whether the circumstances of this case would merit such an award. Also, before the court is a similar question with respect to aggravated damages. . . .

There is English authority for the proposition that the *Addis* case will not bar a claim for general damages for mental distress in an action for a breach of contract: see *Jarvis v. Swans Tours Ltd.*, [*supra*]; *Cox v. Philips Indust. Ltd.*, [[1976] 3 A11 E.R. 161 (Q.B.)]; *Heywood v. Wellers (A Firm)*, [1976] Q.B. 446, [1976] 2 W.L.R. 101 . . . (C.A.). These cases stand for the proposition that in some contracts the parties may well have contemplated at the time of the contract that a breach in certain circumstances would cause a plaintiff mental distress.

[W]hile aggravated damages may be awarded in actions for breach of contract in appropriate cases, this is not a case where they should be given. The rule long established in the *Addis* and [other] cases has generally been applied to deny such damages, and the employer/employee relationship (in the absence of collective agreements which involve consideration of the modern labour law régime) has always been one where either party could terminate the contract of employment by due notice, and therefore the only damage which could arise would result from a failure to give such notice.

I would not wish to be taken as saying that aggravated damages could never be awarded in a case of wrongful dismissal, particularly where the acts complained of were also independently actionable, a factor not present here. . . . [Hinkson J.A. in the Court of Appeal quoted] Weatherston J.A. in *Brown v. Waterloo Regional Bd. of Commr. of Police*, [(1983), 150 D.L.R. (3d) 729], p. 736, where, speaking for the court, he said:

> If a course of conduct by one party causes loss or injury to another, but is not actionable, that course of conduct may not be a separate head of damages in a claim in respect of an actionable wrong. Damages, to be recoverable, must flow from an actionable wrong. It is not sufficient that a course of conduct, not in itself actionable, be somehow related to an actionable course of conduct.

Furthermore, while the conduct complained of, that of Reid, was offensive and unjustified, any injury it may have caused the appellant cannot be said to have arisen out of the dismissal itself. The conduct complained of preceded the wrongful dismissal and therefore cannot be said to have aggravated the damage incurred as a result of the dismissal. Accordingly, I would refuse any claim for aggravated damages in respect of the wrongful dismissal.

Punitive damages

Problems arise for the common law wherever the concept of punitive damages is posed. The award of punitive damages requires that (Waddams, p. 563):

> . . . a civil court . . . impose what is in effect a fine for conduct it finds worthy of punishment, and then to remit the fine, not to the State Treasury, but to the individual plaintiff who will, by definition, be over-compensated.

This will be accomplished in the absence of the procedural protections for the defendant—always present in criminal trials where punishment is ordinarily awarded—and upon proof on a balance of probabilities instead of the criminal standard of proof beyond a reasonable doubt. Nevertheless, despite the peculiar nature of punitive damages, it is well settled in law that in appropriate cases they may be awarded: see *Rookes v. Barnard*, [1964] A.C. 1129 (H.L.). But all authorities accept the proposition that an award of punitive damages should always receive the most careful consideration and the discretion to award them should be most cautiously exercised. As has been mentioned earlier, punitive damages are not compensatory in nature. The scope of punitive damages was restricted in *Rookes v. Barnard* and, as noted by Waddams, Lord Devlin in that case retained two categories for their application, namely, abuse of power by government and torts committed for profit. . . . It is fair to say that the courts of the Commonwealth, outside of the United Kingdom, have not, in general, accepted the limitations on the power of the courts to award punitive damages: see Waddams, p. 570, para. 996. I would conclude that the *Rookes v. Barnard* limitation should not apply in Canada. The law of British Columbia, then, accords wider scope for the application of punitive damages than that envisaged in *Rookes v. Barnard*.

When, then, can punitive damages be awarded? It must never be forgotten that when awarded by a judge or a jury, a punishment is imposed upon a person by a court by the operation of the judicial process. What is it that is punished? It surely cannot be merely conduct of which the court disapproves, however strongly the judge may feel. Punishment may not be imposed in a civilized community without a justification in law. The only basis for the imposition of such punishment must be a finding of the commission of an actionable wrong which caused the injury complained of by the plaintiff. This would be consistent with the approach of Weatherston J.A. in *Brown*, supra, and it has found approval in the Restatement (2d) on the Law of Contract in the United States, as noted with approval by Craig J.A., at p. 49 where he referred in the Court of Appeal to §355, which provides:

> Punitive damages are not recoverable for a breach of contract unless the conduct constituting the breach is also a tort for which punitive damages are recoverable.

An example of the application of this principle may be found in the case of *Robitaille v. Vancouver Hockey Club Ltd.*, [1981] 30 B.C.L.R. 286 (C.A.). . . . In that case, the plaintiff, a professional hockey player, suffered severe injury and damage because he was denied proper medical attention, when the defendant was under a duty to provide it, and because he was forced to continue playing and practising until in his weakened condition he suffered serious injury. He was awarded punitive damages in addition to compensatory general damages. The punitive damages were ordered because of the offensive attitude and conduct of the defendants before the final injury occurred, which conduct in refusing medical care and attention, in addition to its abusive nature, was tortious because of its negligent disregard of a duty to provide care. It was, as well, causative of the injury suffered, for the plaintiff, because of the attitude of the defendant, continued to practise and play. These activities caused or materially contributed to his crippling injury: see, as well, *H.L. Weiss Forwarding Ltd. v. Omnus*, [1976] 1 S.C.R. 776 . . . where the award of punitive damages was based on a finding of the tort of conspiracy which led to the breach of the contract of employment.

Turning to the case at bar, it is clear from the judgments below that the appellant's superior, Reid, treated him in a most offensive manner. . . . The question before us now is whether the trial judge was right in concluding that it was not open to him to award the punitive damages. In my view, while it may be very unusual to do so, punitive damages may be awarded in cases of breach of contract. It would seem to me, however, that it will be rare to find a contractual breach which would be appropriate for such an award. In tort cases, claims where a plaintiff asserts injury and damage caused by the defendant, the situation is different. The defendant in such a case is under a legal duty to use care not to injure his neighbour, and the neighbour has in law a right not to be so injured and an additional right to compensation where injury occurs. The injured party is entitled to be made whole. The compensation he is entitled to receive depends upon the nature and extent of his injuries and not upon any private arrangement made with the tortfeasor. In an action based on a breach of contract, the only link between the parties for the purpose of defining their rights and obligations is the contract. Where the defendant has breached the contract, the remedies open to the plaintiff must arise from that contractual relationship, that "private law", which the parties agreed to accept. The injured plaintiff then is not entitled to be made whole; he is entitled to have that which the contract provided for him or compensation for its loss. This distinction will not completely eliminate the award of punitive damages but it will make it very rare in contract cases.

Moreover, punitive damages may only be awarded in respect of conduct which is of such nature as to be deserving of punishment because of its harsh, vindictive, reprehensible and malicious nature. I do not suggest that I have exhausted the adjectives which could describe the conduct capable of characterizing a punitive award, but in any case where such an award is made the conduct must be extreme in its nature and such that by any reasonable standard it is deserving of full condemnation and punishment. This view has found expression in Canadian courts: see *Paragon Properties Ltd. v. Magna Envestments Ltd.* [(1972), 24 D.L.R. (3d) 156 (Alta. C.A.)], where Clement J.A., dissenting on the issue of whether damages should have been awarded but not on the principle governing the award, said at p. 167:

> ... The basis of such an award is actionable injury to the plaintiff done in such a manner that it offends the ordinary standards of morality or decent conduct in the community in such marked degree that censure by way of damages is, in the opinion of the Court, warranted. The object is variously described to include deterrence to other possible wrongdoers, or punishment for maliciousness, or supra-compensatory recognition of unnecessary humiliation or other harm to which the claimant has been subjected by the censurable act. It is the reprehensible conduct of the wrongdoer which attracts the principle, not the legal category of the wrong out of which compensatory damages arise and in relation to which the conduct occurred. To place arbitrary limitations upon its application is to evade the underlying principle and replace it with an uncertain and debatable jurisdiction.

In other cases the same principles have been expressed. . . .

In the case at bar, the plaintiff was entitled to have the salary and benefits agreed upon under the contract of employment while he continued in such employment. Each party had the right to terminate the contract without the consent of the other, and where the employment contract was terminated by the employer, the appellant was entitled to reasonable notice of such termination or payment of salary and benefits for the period of reasonable notice. The termination of the contract on this basis by the employer is not a wrong in law and, where the reasonable notice is given or payment in lieu thereof is made, the plaintiff—subject to a consideration of aggravated damages which have been allowed in some cases but which were denied in this case—is entitled to no further remedy
. . .

It is argued that the conduct of the defendant, that is, the supervisor, Reid, prior to the dismissal was such that it caused mental distress and frustration to the appellant. This conduct, however, was not considered sufficiently offensive, standing alone, to constitute actionable wrong: . . . and in my view was not of such nature as to justify the imposition of an award of punitive damages. I would, accordingly, dismiss the appeal with costs.

WILSON J. [dissenting in part] . . .

Damages for mental suffering

I agree with my colleague, McIntyre J., that in appropriate circumstances aggravated damages for mental suffering may be awarded in breach of contract cases and that they are, in distinction to punitive damages, essentially compensatory. However, I take a somewhat different approach from my colleague as to the test to be applied in determining whether or not to award them.

The trial judge in this case applied the absolute rule set out in *Addis v. Gramophone Co.* and *Peso Silver Mines Ltd. (N.P.L.) v. Cropper* [[1966] S.C.R. 673] to the effect that damages for mental suffering are not available in breach of contract cases because contractual damages must be compensatory, tangible and estimable. They are confined to putting the plaintiff in the financial position he would have been in had he been given reasonable notice. With respect, I think this is no longer the law. The absolute rule has been whittled away by the numerous English and Canadian authorities referred to by my colleague in which damages have been awarded for mental suffering in a variety of different contractual situations. It is my view, however, that what binds all these cases together, their common denominator so to speak, is the notion that the parties should reasonably have foreseen mental suffering as a consequence of a breach of the contract at the time the contract was entered into. That this is the true test appears clearly, I believe, from Lord Denning's judgment in *Jarvis v. Swans Tours Ltd.* and from the Ontario Court of Appeal's judgment in *Brown v. Waterloo Regional Bd. of Commr. of Police*.

In *Jarvis v. Swans Tours Ltd.* Lord Denning allowed compensation for "the disappointment, the distress, the upset and frustration" occasioned by a ruined holiday. He viewed this head of damages as compensatory. He dismissed the argument that such damages were difficult to quantify by asserting the well-known principle that difficulty of assessment should not deter the courts when the plaintiff has a just cause. Finally and most importantly, he held that such damages were properly awardable in contract *provided they conformed to the normal rules for remoteness of damage in contract*. It seems to me that this is the correct approach.

. . . . .

I must respectfully disagree with my colleague's view that conduct advanced in support of a claim for damages for mental suffering must constitute a separate "actionable wrong" from the breach itself. I disagree also that because the conduct complained of preceded the wrongful dismissal, it cannot aggravate the damages resulting from that dismissal. Rather than relying on a characterization of the conduct as an independent wrong, I think the proper approach is to apply the basic principles of contract law relating to remoteness of damage. . . .

It is my view that the established principles of contract law set out in *Hadley v. Baxendale* [*infra*, section 3(b)(iii)] provide the proper test for the recovery of damages for mental suffering. The principles are well-settled and their broad application would appear preferable to decision-making based on a priori and inflexible categories of damages. The issue in assessing damages is not whether the plaintiff got what he bargained for, i.e., pleasure or peace of mind (although this is obviously relevant to whether or not there has been a breach), but whether he should be compensated for damage the defendant should reasonably have anticipated that he would suffer as a consequence of the breach. . . .

[Wilson J. set out the reformulation of the first branch of the rule in *Hadley v. Baxendale* in *The Heron II*, *infra*, section 3(b)(iii) and continued:]

The need for special circumstances under the second branch has been invoked both to allow and to deny recovery. It was used to allow recovery in *Newell v. C.P. Airlines Ltd.* (1976), 74 D.L.R. (3d) 574 (Co. Ct.), and *Heywood v. Wellers (A Firm)* [*supra*]. In the *Newell* case an elderly couple wanted to send their dogs by plane and went to great lengths to check that it was safe, making it abundantly clear in the process that they would be distressed if anything were to happen to their pets. One of the dogs died in transit and, while mental suffering resulting from such an eventuality would not normally be in the reasonable contemplation of the parties, it clearly was so in the special circumstances of this case. In the *Heywood* case lawyers who negligently failed to provide services to protect their client from molestation by securing an injunction were held liable for the mental distress which they were aware would result from their failure to do so. By contrast, recovery was denied in *Cook v. Swinfen*, [1967] 1 W.L.R. 457 (C.A.), because of the absence of special circumstances. In that case a lawyer, Mr. Swinfen, was held not to be liable for the breakdown of the mental health of his client, Mrs. Cook, after he had agreed to pursue divorce proceedings on her behalf and had then negligently failed to do so. After concluding that the client's mental distress was not reasonably foreseeable, Lord Denning M.R. stated at pp. 461-62:

> It was suggested in this case that there were special circumstances in that Mrs. Cook was peculiarly liable to nervous shock. I am afraid she was. The history of her life shows one nervous breakdown after another. If this special circumstance was brought home to Mr. Swinfen, it might enlarge the area of foreseeability so as to make him liable. But it was not pleaded. And when Mr. Moloney put questions to Mr. Swinfen, he did not succeed in showing that special circumstances were brought home to him. All Mr. Swinfen knew was that she was a woman obviously highly strung and worried as any woman would be in the circumstances. But that does not mean that he should foresee that, if he was negligent, she would suffer injury to health.

It remains then to consider whether the circumstances in this case are appropriate for an award of damages for mental suffering under the rule in *Hadley v. Baxendale*. The facts relating to the appellant's age and second career and the humiliating treatment meted out to him both preceding and accompanying his dismissal militate in favour of recovery. On the other hand, he was not employed at I.C.B.C. for a particularly long period of time. It was not suggested that he had security of tenure with the respondent. And he is a member of a profession which restricts entry and therefore keeps the job market reasonably buoyant. . . . There were no special circumstances in this case such as the promise of promotion in order to keep the employee from moving to a competitor. Nor did the employment relationship in this case have the special elements of trust and reliance which characterized the promise of employment security in *Pilon v. Peugeot Canada* [(1980), 114 D.L.R. (3d) 378 (Ont. H.C.)]. I am persuaded therefore that mental suffering would not have been in the reasonable contemplation of the parties at the time the employment contract was entered into as flowing from the appellant's unjust dismissal. I would therefore, like my colleague, deny recovery under this head.

Punitive damages

. . . The availability of punitive damages is clearly another area of the law in which there is considerable uncertainty in the jurisprudence. The once firm prohibition against such awards seems to have fallen by the wayside although some courts continue to proclaim it. It is timely therefore for this court to determine (a) whether punitive damages are available at all in a contractual setting and, if so, (b) under what circumstances. . . .

I do not share my colleague's view that punitive damages can only be awarded when the misconduct is in itself an "actionable wrong". In my view, the correct approach is to assess the conduct in the context of all the circumstances and determine whether it is deserving of punishment because of its shockingly harsh, vindictive, reprehensible or malicious nature. Undoubtedly, some conduct found to be deserving of punishment will constitute an actionable wrong but other conduct might not. I respectfully adopt the following statement made by Clement J.A. in *Paragon Properties Ltd. v. Magna Envestments Ltd.*, *supra*, at 167:

> It is the reprehensible conduct of the wrongdoer which attracts the principle, not the legal category of the wrong out of which compensatory damages arise and in relation to which the conduct occurred. To place arbitrary limitations upon its application is to evade the underlying principle and replace it with an uncertain and debatable jurisdiction.

Nor would I draw the wide divergence that my colleague does between the duties owed to a neighbour under the law of tort and the duties that are breached in contract by the type of flagrant and deliberate misconduct that would merit an award of punitive damages. I agree with the appellant that it would be odd if the law required more from a stranger than from the parties to a contract. The very closeness engendered by some contractual relationships, particularly employer/ employee relationships in which there is frequently a marked disparity of power between the parties, seems to me to give added point to the duty of civilized behaviour.

In my view, the facts of this case disclose reprehensible conduct on the part of the respondent towards a sensitive, dedicated and conscientious employee. The appellant was harassed and humiliated and, so the learned trial judge found, ultimately dismissed for no cause after a sustained period of such treatment. . . .

Anderson J.A. would have allowed the appeal on the punitive damages issue and awarded the appellant punitive damages in the sum of $5,000. The quantum that Anderson J.A. would have awarded is, I believe, a reasonable one and in keeping with the Canadian experience in the award of relatively modest punitive damages. When the purpose of the award is to reflect the court's awareness and condemnation of flagrant wrongdoing and indifference to the legal rights of other people, the award does not need to be excessive. I would allow the appeal on the punitive damages issue in this court in order to give effect to Anderson J.A.'s judgment. I would also award the appellant his costs both here and in the courts below.

[Beetz and Lamer JJ. concurred with McIntyre J. L'Heureux-Dubé J. concurred with Wilson J. Appeal dismissed.]

WALLACE v. UNITED GRAIN GROWERS LTD.

[1997] 3 S.C.R. 701

By the time he had reached the age of 45 in 1972, Wallace had worked for a commercial printing company for twenty-five years. When a rival company, Public Press, a wholly-owned subsidiary of UGG, decided to expand its operations, it lured Wallace away with various inducements including an assurance by the marketing manager of job security until retirement provided he performed to expectations. From 1972 until 1986 when he was dismissed, Wallace was Public Press's top salesperson every year. In firing Wallace, the company purported to have cause, a position that it maintained until the trial of his wrongful dismissal action. After his firing, Wallace was unable to secure similar employment and also needed psychiatric assistance for mental distress caused by his dismissal and the manner in which it had been brought about. At trial, Wallace was unsuccessful for reasons not relevant for current purposes. However, the trial judge contingently assessed damages based on a twenty four month notice period and $15,000 mental distress damages on the basis of both breach of contract and tort. In the Manitoba Court of Appeal, the court reversed the trial judge's finding on liability. However, in so doing, it also overturned the award of aggravated or mental distress damages and reduced the notice period to fifteen months on the basis that here too the trial judge had allowed elements of aggravated or mental distress damages to influence his calculation of the notice period. Wallace obtained leave to appeal to the Supreme Court of Canada and Public Press was also given leave to cross-appeal.

IACOBUCCI J. [delivering the judgment of Lamer C.J. and Sopinka, Gonthier, Cory, and Major JJ.] . . . The Court of Appeal concluded that there was insufficient evidence to support a finding that the actions of UGG constituted a separate actionable wrong either in tort or in contract. I agree with these findings and see no reason to disturb them. I note, however, that in circumstances where the manner of dismissal has caused mental distress but falls short of an independent actionable wrong, the employee is not without recourse. Rather, the trial judge has discretion in these circumstances to extend the period of reasonable notice to which an employee is entitled. Thus, although recovery for mental distress might not be available under a separate head of damages, the possibility of recovery still remains. I will be returning to this point in my discussion of reasonable notice below.

D. Bad Faith Discharge

The appellant urged this Court to find that he could sue UGG either in contract or in tort for "bad faith discharge". With respect to the action in contract, he submitted that the Court should imply into the employment contract a term that the employee would not be fired except for cause or legitimate business reasons. I cannot accede to this submission. The law has long recognized the mutual right of both employers and employees to terminate an employment contract at any time provided there are no express provisions to the contrary. In *Farber v. Royal Trust Co.*, [1997] 1 S.C.R. 846, Gonthier J., speaking for the Court, summarized the general contractual principles applicable to contracts of employment as follows, at p. 858:

> In the context of an indeterminate employment contract, one party can resiliate the contract unilaterally. The resiliation is considered a dismissal if it originates with the employer and a resignation if it originates with the employee. If an employer dismisses an employee without cause, the employer must give the employee reasonable notice that the contract is about to be terminated or compensation in lieu thereof.

A requirement of "good faith" reasons for dismissal would, in effect, contravene these principles and deprive employers of the ability to determine the composition of their workforce. In the context of the accepted theories on the employment relationship, such a law would, in my opinion, be overly intrusive and inconsistent with established principles of employment law, and more appropriately, should be left to legislative enactment rather than judicial pronouncement.

I must also reject the appellant's claim that he can sue in tort for breach of a good faith and fair dealing obligation with regard to dismissals. The Court of Appeal noted the absence of persuasive authority on this point and concluded that such a tort has not yet been recognized by Canadian courts. I agree with these findings. To create such a tort in this case would therefore constitute a radical shift in the law, again a step better left to be taken by the legislatures.

For these reasons I conclude that the appellant is unable to sue in either tort or contract for "bad faith discharge". However, I will be returning to the subject of good faith and fair dealing in my discussion of reasonable notice below.

E. Punitive Damages

Punitive damages are an exception to the general rule that damages are meant to compensate the plaintiff. The purpose of such an award is the punishment of the defendant: S. M. Waddams, *The Law of Damages* (3rd ed. 1997), at p. 483. The appellant argued that the trial judge and the Court of Appeal erred in refusing to award punitive damages. I do not agree. Relying on *Vorvis, supra*, Lockwood J. found that UGG did not engage in sufficiently "harsh, vindictive, reprehensible and malicious" conduct to merit condemnation by such an award. He also noted the absence of an actionable wrong. The Court of Appeal concurred. Again, there is no reason to interfere with these findings. Consequently, I agree with the courts below that there is no foundation for an award of punitive damages.

F. Reasonable Notice

.....

In determining what constitutes reasonable notice of termination, the courts have generally applied the principles articulated by McRuer C.J.H.C. in *Bardal v. Globe & Mail Ltd.* (1960), 24 D.L.R. (2d) 140 (Ont. H.C.), at p. 145:

> There can be no catalogue laid down as to what is reasonable notice in particular classes of cases. The reasonableness of the notice must be decided with reference to each particular case, having regard to the character of the employment, the length of service of the servant, the age of the servant and the availability of similar employment, having regard to the experience, training and qualifications of the servant.

This Court adopted the foregoing list of factors in *Machtinger v. HOJ Industries Ltd.*, [1992] 1 S.C.R. 986, at p. 998. Applying these factors in the instant case, I concur with the trial judge's finding that in light of the appellant's advanced age, his 14-year tenure as the company's top salesman and his limited prospects for re-employment, a lengthy period of notice is warranted. I note, however, that *Bardal, supra*, does not state, nor has it been interpreted to imply, that the factors it enumerated were exhaustive. . . . Canadian courts have added several additional factors to the *Bardal* list. The application of these factors to the assessment of a dismissed employee's notice period will depend upon the particular circumstances of the case.

One such factor that has often been considered is whether the dismissed employee had been induced to leave previous secure employment: see e.g. *Jackson v. Makeup Lab Inc.* (1989), 27 C.C.E.L. 317 (Ont. H.C.); *Murphy v. Rolland Inc.* (1991), 39 C.C.E.L. 86 (Ont. Ct. (Gen. Div.)); *Craig v. Interland Window Mfg. Ltd.* (1993), 47 C.C.E.L. 57 (B.C. S.C.). According to one authority, many courts have sought to compensate the reliance and expectation interests of terminated employees by increasing the period of reasonable notice where the employer has induced the employee to "quit a secure, well-paying job . . . on the strength of promises of career advancement and greater responsibility, security and compensation with the new organization" (I. Christie et al., [*Employment Law in Canada*, 2nd ed. (1993)] at p. 623).

Several cases have specifically examined the presence of a promise of job security: see e.g. *Makhija v. Lakefield Research* (1983), 14 C.C.E.L. 131 (Ont. H.C.), affirmed by the Ontario Court of Appeal (1986), 14 C.C.E.L. xxxi; *Mutch v. Norman Wade Co.* (1987), 17 B.C.L.R. (2d) 185 (S.C.). In particular, I note that the British Columbia Court of Appeal recently adopted this approach in *Robertson v. Weavexx Corp.* (1997), 25 C.C.E.L. (2d) 264. The facts of this case were very similar to those currently before this Court. Writing for the court, Goldie J.A. stated at pp. 271-72:

> Also part of the inducement to the respondent in making the move he did was, no doubt, the discussions as to long term employment. . . . As I have concluded, those discussions lacked contractual force in terms of the respondent's assertion of a fixed term contract but nevertheless, they were and are, in my opinion, significant on the issue of reasonable notice.

In my opinion, such inducements are properly included among the considerations which tend to lengthen the amount of notice required. I concur with the comments of Christie et al., *supra*, and recognize that there is a need to safeguard the employee's reliance and expectation interests in inducement situations. I note, however, that not all inducements will carry equal weight when determining the appropriate period of notice. The significance of the inducement in question will vary with the circumstances of the particular case and its effect, if any, on the notice period is a matter best left to the discretion of the trial judge.

In the instant case, the trial judge found that UGG went to great lengths to relieve Wallace's fears about jeopardizing his existing secure employment and to entice him into joining their company. At p. 172 the trial judge stated:

> The [respondent] wanted a man with the skills of the [appellant] and to get him was prepared to accommodate his demands. . . . I have found that there was no fixed-term contract. However, there was, in the assurance given to him, a *guarantee of security*, provided he gave the [respondent] no cause to dismiss him. [Emphasis added.]

In addition to the promise that he could continue to work for the company until retirement, UGG also offered several assurances with respect to fair treatment. Further, despite the fact that the company only had salary arrangements with their existing employees, they assured Wallace that they would implement a commission basis for him. Although the trial judge did not make specific reference to the inducement factor in his analysis of reasonable notice, I believe that, in the circumstances of this case, these inducements, in particular the guarantee of job security, are factors which support his decision to award damages at the high end of the scale.

The appellant urged this Court to recognize the ability of a dismissed employee to sue in contract or alternatively in tort for "bad faith discharge". Although I have rejected both as avenues for recovery, by no means do I condone the behaviour of employers who subject employees to callous and insensitive treatment in their dismissal, showing no regard for their welfare. Rather, I believe that such bad faith conduct in the manner of dismissal is another factor that is properly compensated for by an addition to the notice period.

[Iacobucci J. here identified authorities which had rejected] extending the notice period to account for manner of dismissal. Generally speaking, these cases have found that claims relating to the manner in which the discharge took place are not properly considered in an action for damages for breach of contract. Rather, it is said, damages are limited to injuries that flow from the breach itself, which in the employment context is the failure to give reasonable notice. The manner of dismissal was found not to affect these damages.

Although these decisions are grounded in general principles of contract law, I believe, with respect, that they have all failed to take into account the unique characteristics of the particular type of contract with which they were concerned, namely, a contract of employment. Similarly, there was not an appropriate recognition of the special relationship which these contracts govern. In my view, both are relevant considerations.

The contract of employment has many characteristics that set it apart from the ordinary commercial contract. Some of the views on this subject that have already been approved of in previous decisions of this Court (see e.g. *Machtinger*, *supra*) bear repeating. As K. Swinton noted in "Contract Law and the Employment Relationship: The Proper Forum for Reform", in B. J. Reiter and J. Swan, eds., *Studies in Contract Law* (1980), 357, at p. 363:

> ... the terms of the employment contract rarely result from an exercise of free bargaining power in the way that the paradigm commercial exchange between two traders does. Individual employees on the whole lack both the bargaining power and the information necessary to achieve more favourable contract provisions than those offered by the employer, particularly with regard to tenure.

This power imbalance is not limited to the employment contract itself. Rather, it informs virtually all facets of the employment relationship. In *Slaight Communications Inc. v. Davidson*, [1989] 1 S.C.R. 1038, Dickson C.J., writing for the majority of the Court, had occasion to comment on the nature of this relationship. At pp. 1051-52 he quoted with approval from P. Davies and M. Freedland, *Kahn-Freund's Labour and the Law* (3rd ed. 1983), at p. 18:

> [T]he relation between an employer and an isolated employee or worker is typically a relation between a bearer of power and one who is not a bearer of power. In its inception it is an act of submission, in its operation it is a condition of subordination. . . .

This unequal balance of power led the majority of the Court in *Slaight Communications*, *supra*, to describe employees as a vulnerable group in society: see p. 1051. The vulnerability of employees is underscored by the level of importance which our society attaches to employment. As Dickson C.J. noted in *Reference Re Public Service Employee Relations Act (Alta.)*, [1987] 1 S.C.R. 313, at p. 368:

> Work is one of the most fundamental aspects in a person's life, providing the individual with a means of financial support and, as importantly, a contributory role in society. A person's employment is an essential component of his or her sense of identity, self-worth and emotional well-being.

Thus, for most people, work is one of the defining features of their lives. Accordingly, any change in a person's employment status is bound to have far-reaching repercussions. In "Aggravated Damages and the Employment Contract", [(1991), 55 Sask. L. Rev. 345] Schai noted at p. 346 that, "[w]hen this change is involuntary, the extent of our 'personal dislocation' is even greater."

The point at which the employment relationship ruptures is the time when the employee is most vulnerable and hence, most in need of protection. In recognition of this need, the law ought to encourage conduct that minimizes the damage and dislocation (both economic and personal) that result from dismissal. In *Machtinger*, *supra*, it was noted that the manner in which employment can be terminated is equally important to an individual's identity as the work itself (at p. 1002). By way of expanding upon this statement, I note that the loss of one's job is always a traumatic event. However, when termination is accompanied by acts of bad faith in the manner of discharge, the results can be especially devastating. In my opinion, to ensure that employees receive adequate protection, employers ought to be held to an obligation of good faith and fair dealing in the manner of dismissal, the breach of which will be compensated for by adding to the length of the notice period.

This approach finds support in the words of my colleague, Gonthier J., in *Farber, supra.* Writing for a unanimous Court he stated at p. 859:

> . . . for the employment contract to be resiliated, it is not necessary for the employer to have intended to force the employee to leave his or her employment or to have been acting in bad faith when making substantial changes to the contract's essential terms. However, if the employer was acting in bad faith, this would have an impact on the damages awarded to the employee.

[At this juncture, Iacobucci J. listed a number of Canadian authorities in which the manner of dismissal was reflected in the notice period.]

The obligation of good faith and fair dealing is incapable of precise definition. However, at a minimum, I believe that in the course of dismissal employers ought to be candid, reasonable, honest and forthright with their employees and should refrain from engaging in conduct that is unfair or is in bad faith by being, for example, untruthful, misleading or unduly insensitive. [He here outlined the facts of the authorities previously listed.]

I note that, depending upon the circumstances of the individual case, not all acts of bad faith or unfair dealing will be equally injurious and thus, the amount by which the notice period is extended will vary. Furthermore, I do not intend to advocate anything akin to an automatic claim for damages under this heading in every case of dismissal. In each case, the trial judge must examine the nature of the bad faith conduct and its impact in the circumstances.

The Court of Appeal in the instant case recognized the relevance of manner of dismissal in the determination of the appropriate period of reasonable notice. However, . . . the court found that this factor could only be considered "where it impacts on the future employment prospects of the dismissed employee" [(1995), 102 Man.R. (2d) 161] (p. 180). With respect, I believe that this is an overly restrictive view. In my opinion, the law must recognize a more expansive list of injuries which may flow from unfair treatment or bad faith in the manner of dismissal.

It has long been accepted that a dismissed employee is not entitled to compensation for injuries flowing from the fact of the dismissal itself: see e.g. *Addis, supra.* Thus, although the loss of a job is very often the cause of injured feelings and emotional upset, the law does not recognize these as compensable losses. However, where an employee can establish that an employer engaged in bad faith conduct or unfair dealing in the course of dismissal, injuries such as humiliation, embarrassment and damage to one's sense of self-worth and self-esteem might all be worthy of compensation depending upon the circumstances of the case. In these situations, compensation does not flow from the fact of dismissal itself, but rather from the manner in which the dismissal was effected by the employer.

Often the intangible injuries caused by bad faith conduct or unfair dealing on dismissal will lead to difficulties in finding alternative employment, a tangible loss which the Court of Appeal rightly recognized as warranting an addition to the notice period. It is likely that the more unfair or in bad faith the manner of dismissal is the more this will have an effect on the ability of the dismissed employee to find new employment. However, in my view the intangible injuries are sufficient to merit compensation in and of themselves. I recognize that bad faith conduct which affects employment prospects may be worthy of considerably more compensation than that which does not, but in both cases damage has resulted that should be compensable.

The availability of compensation for these types of injuries has been recognized in other areas of the law. In *McCarey v. Associated Newspapers Ltd. (No.2)*, [1965] 2 Q.B. 86 (C.A.), Pearson L.J. examined the scope of recovery in an action for libel. At pp. 104-5 he stated:

> Compensatory damages, in a case in which they are at large, may include several different kinds of compensation to the injured plaintiff. They may include not only actual pecuniary loss and anticipated pecuniary loss or any social disadvantages which result, or may be thought likely to result, from the wrong which has been done. They may also include the natural injury to his feelings—the natural grief and distress which he may have felt at having been spoken of in defamatory terms, and if there has been any kind of high-handed, oppressive, insulting or contumelious behaviour by the defendant which increases the mental pain and suffering caused by the defamation and may constitute injury to the plaintiff's pride and self-confidence, those are proper elements to be taken into account in a case where the damages are at large.
>
> .....

In my view, there is no valid reason why the scope of compensable injuries in defamation situations should not be equally recognized in the context of wrongful dismissal from employment. The law should be mindful of the acute vulnerability of terminated employees and ensure their protection by encouraging proper conduct and preventing all injurious losses which might flow from acts of bad faith or unfair dealing on dismissal, both tangible and intangible. I note that there may be those who would say that this approach imposes an onerous obligation on employers. I would respond simply by saying that I fail to see how it can be onerous to treat people fairly, reasonably, and decently at a time of trauma and despair. In my view, the reasonable person would expect such treatment. So should the law.

In the case before this Court, the trial judge documented several examples of bad faith conduct on the part of UGG. He noted the abrupt manner in which Wallace was dismissed despite having received compliments on his work from his superiors only days before. He found that UGG made a conscious decision to "play hardball" with Wallace and maintained unfounded allegations of cause until the day the trial began. Further, as a result of UGG's persistence in maintaining these allegations, "[w]ord got around, and it was rumoured in the trade that he had been involved in some wrongdoing" [(1993), 87 Man.R. (2d) 161] (p. 173). Finally, he found that the dismissal and subsequent events were largely responsible for causing Wallace's depression. Having considered the *Bardal* list of factors, he stated at p. 170:

> Taking [these] factors into account, and particularly the fact that the peremptory dismissal and the subsequent actions of the defendant made other employment in his field virtually unavailable, I conclude that an award at the top of the scale in such cases is warranted.

I agree with the trial judge's conclusion that the actions of UGG seriously diminished Wallace's prospects of finding similar employment. In light of this fact, and the other circumstances of this case, I am not persuaded that the trial judge erred in awarding the equivalent of 24 months' salary in lieu of notice. It may be that such an award is at the high end of the scale; however, taking into account all of the relevant factors, this award is not unreasonable and accordingly, I can see no reason to interfere. Therefore, for the reasons above, I would restore the order of the trial judge with respect to the appropriate period of reasonable notice and allow the appeal on this ground.

.....

I would dismiss the cross-appeal with costs and allow the appeal in part with costs here and in the courts below. I would set aside the judgment of the Manitoba Court of Appeal and restore the trial judge's award of 24 months' salary in lieu of notice. As explained above, the other aspects of the appellant's claim are rejected.

McLACHLIN J. [delivering the reasons of La Forest and L'Heureux-Dubé JJ. for dissenting in part]. . . . My colleague, Iacobucci J., holds that the manner of dismissal may be considered generally in defining the notice period for wrongful dismissal. An alternative view is that the manner of dismissal should only be considered in defining the notice period where the manner of dismissal impacts on the difficulty of finding replacement employment, and that absent this connection, damages for the manner of termination must be based on some other cause of action.

I prefer the second approach for the following reasons. First, this solution seems to me more consistent with the nature of the action for wrongful dismissal. Second, this approach, unlike the alternative, honours the principle that damages must be grounded in a cause of action. Third, this approach seems to me more consistent with the authorities, notably *Vorvis v. Insurance Corporation of British Columbia*, [*supra*], *per* McIntyre J. Fourth, this approach will better aid certainty and predictability in the law governing damages for termination of employment. Finally, there are other equally effective ways to remedy wrongs related to the manner of dismissal which do not affect the prospect of finding replacement work.

1. *Consistency with the Nature of the Action for Wrongful Dismissal*

As already stated, the action for wrongful dismissal is an action for breach of an implied term in the contract of employment to give reasonable notice of termination. Reasonable notice, in turn, represents the time that may reasonably be required to find replacement employment. It follows that only factors relevant to the prospects of re-employment should be considered in determining the notice period. To include other factors is to consider matters unrelated to the breach of contract for which damages are ostensibly being awarded.

.....

5. *The Availability of Other Remedies*

It is argued that employer misconduct in the manner of dismissal not affecting prospects of re-employment must be taken into account in calculating the notice period in order to avoid injustice and provide an adequate remedy to the employee in a case such as this. The answer to this argument is that the law affords other remedies for employer misconduct in these circumstances.

The law of tort and contract recognizes a number of independent causes of action for misconduct in dismissing an employee. If the employer defames the employee or wilfully inflicts mental distress, the employee can sue in tort. If the employer has lured the employee from a secure position with promises of better terms, the employee may be able to sue in tort for negligent misrepresentation or for breach of an express contractual term. Finally, unfair treatment at the time of dismissal may give rise to an action for breach of an implied term in the contract of employment.

The law has now developed to the point that to these traditional actions may now be added another: breach of an implied contractual term to act in good faith in dismissing an employee. I agree with Iacobucci J. that an employer must act in good faith and in fair dealing when dismissing employees, and more particularly that "employers ought to be candid, reasonable, honest and forthright with their employees and should refrain from engaging in conduct that is unfair or is in bad faith by being, for example, untruthful, misleading or unduly insensitive". I also agree that this obligation does not extend to prohibiting employers from dismissing employees without "good faith" reasons; such an extension of employment law would be "overly intrusive and inconsistent with established principles of employment law". Both employer and employee remain free to terminate the contract of employment without cause. This is not inconsistent with the duty of good faith. While some courts have recognized employer obligations of good faith outside of the dismissal context . . ., this case does not require us to go beyond the context of dismissal.

I differ from my colleague, however, in that I see no reason why the expectation of good faith in dismissing employees that he accepts should not be viewed as an implied term of the contract of employment. To assert the duty of good faith in dismissing employees as a proposition of law, as does my colleague, is tantamount to saying that it is an obligation implied by law into the contractual relationship between employer and employee. In other words, it is an implied term of the contract.

Implication of this term meets the test set out by this Court in *Canadian Pacific Hotels Ltd. v. Bank of Montreal*, [1987] 1 S.C.R. 711. Le Dain J., for the majority, held that terms may be implied on the basis of custom or usage, presumed intention, and as legal incidents of a particular class or kind of contract, the nature and content of which have to be largely determined by implication. Whereas the implication of a term based on presumed intention must be necessary "to give business efficacy to a contract or as otherwise meeting the 'officious bystander' test as a term which the parties would say, if questioned, that they had obviously assumed" (p. 775), the implication of a term as legal incident need only be necessary in the sense that it is required by the nature of the contract rather than the presumed intentions of the particular parties.

This is the type of implication that is involved in the proposed obligation of good faith. As Iacobucci J. points out, employment contracts have characteristics quite distinct from other types of contracts as a result of the often unequal bargaining power typically involved in the relationship. This results in employee vulnerability—a vulnerability that is especially acute at the time of dismissal. The nature of the relationship thereby necessitates some measure of protection for the vulnerable party. Requiring employers to treat their employees with good faith at the time of dismissal provides this special measure of protection. It follows that an implied term is necessary in the sense required to justify implication of a contractual term by law.

[On the facts, McLachlin J. concluded that the employer had engaged in bad faith discharge and that the appropriate disposition of the case was to both restore the trial judge's contingent award of damages based on 24 months' notice and to maintain the additional award of $15,000 damages for bad faith discharge.]

NOTES and QUESTIONS

1. How might this case have been useful to Vorvis in formulating his cause of action against his former employer?

2. Obviously, both the majority and the dissent are sympathetic to providing additional compensation to employees who are dismissed in a harsh and humiliating manner. Which approach do you prefer, or might it have been better had the Court reevaluated its position from *Vorvis* that, absent an independent actionable wrong, neither aggravated nor punitive damages are available in a wrongful dismissal action? Indeed, as exemplified by one of the very first of now over 500 judicial considerations of *Wallace*, there is a serious question as to whether the judgment amounts to an extensive opening of a wide back door to what is in effect the award of aggravated damages in wrongful dismissal cases. In *Cassady v. Wyeth-Ayerst Canada Inc.* (1998), 163 D.L.R. (4th) 1 (B.C. C.A.), the court set aside an award of $10,000 for the independent wrong of "negligent infliction of mental distress" in a wrongful dismissal case; such an award was precluded by *Wallace*. However, on the strength of *Wallace*, the court added an award of $10,000 to reflect the circumstances attending the plaintiff's dismissal.

3. Consider also the following post-*Wallace* example: The plaintiff worked for an insurance company as an office manager having been promoted on a number of occasions in her nine years with the company. She was constructively dismissed (*i.e.* demoted) on the basis of concerns (*inter alia*) about possible fraud, her alleged incompetence, disobedience and alcohol and drug dependency, and the character of the person with whom she was having a relationship. Not only did the trial judge find that these concerns were either without foundation or did not justify her constructive dismissal but that the fact they had given rise to her leaving the company also amounted to the "kiss of death" in an industry where fidelity and honesty were paramount. The judge therefore characterized the dismissal as a bad faith one and extended the normal notice period from six months to the date of trial, some 42 months. However, on appeal the notice period was reduced to 12 months with even, Finch J.A., the dissenting judge (who would have awarded 24 months *Wallace* damages) describing, at para. 57, the first instance total award of 42 months as "so far outside the appropriate range, as established in *Wallace*, as to be "plainly wrong" or "a palpable error"." See *Clendenning v. Lowndes Lambert (B.C.) Ltd.* (1998), 41 C.C.E.L. (2d) 58 (B.C. S.C.), varied (2000), 193 D.L.R. (4th) 610 (B.C. C.A.). How would Iacobucci J. and McLachlin C.J. have dealt with a case like this? For other useful higher court considerations of the *Wallace* factor, see *McKinley v. BC Tel*, [2001] 2 S.C.R. 161; *Marshall v. Watson Wyatt & Co.* (2002), 57 O.R. (3d) 813 (C.A.); *Gismondi v. Toronto (City)* (2003), 226 D.L.R. (4th) 334.

4. Subsequently, in a judgment that received a great deal of publicity, the Supreme Court of Canada restored a trial judgment award of $1 million punitive damages for breach of a contract of insurance. In so doing, the court clarified somewhat the concept of what constitutes an independent

actionable wrong for the purposes of crossing the threshold to a punitive damages claim in breach of contract actions.

WHITEN v. PILOT INSURANCE CO.

[2002] 1 S.C.R. 595

BINNIE J. [delivering the judgment of the majority]: . . . The appellant, Daphne Whiten, bought her home in Haliburton County, Ontario, in 1985. Just after midnight on January 18, 1994, when she and her husband Keith were getting ready to go to bed, they discovered a fire in the addition to their house. They and their daughter, who had been upstairs, fled the house wearing only their night clothes. It was minus 18 degrees Celsius. Mr. Whiten gave his slippers to his daughter to go for help and suffered serious frostbite to his feet for which he was hospitalized. He was thereafter confined to a wheelchair for a period of time. The fire totally destroyed the Whitens' home and its contents, including their few valuable antiques and many items of sentimental value and their three cats.

The appellant was able to rent a small winterized cottage nearby for $650 per month. Pilot made a single $5,000 payment for living expenses and covered the rent for a couple of months or so, then cut off the rent without telling the family, and thereafter pursued a hostile and confrontational policy which the jury must have concluded was calculated to force the appellant (whose family was in very poor financial shape) to settle her claim at substantially less than its fair value. The allegation that the family had torched its own home was contradicted by the local fire chief, the respondent's own expert investigator, and its initial expert, all of whom said there was no evidence whatsoever of arson. The respondent's position, based on wishful thinking, was wholly discredited at trial. Pilot's appellate counsel conceded here and in the Ontario Court of Appeal that there was no air of reality to the allegation of arson.

. . . . .

(1) Punitive Damages for Breach of Contract

This, as noted, is a breach of contract case. In *Vorvis, supra*, this Court held that punitive damages are recoverable in such cases provided the defendant's conduct said to give rise to the claim is itself "an actionable wrong" . . . The scope to be given this expression is the threshold question in this case, i.e., is a breach of an insurer's duty to act in good faith an actionable wrong independent of the loss claim under the fire insurance policy? *Vorvis* itself was a case about the employer's breach of an employment contract. This is how McIntyre J. framed the rule at pp. 1105-6 [cites are to S.C.R.]:

> When then can punitive damages be awarded? It must never be forgotten that when awarded by a judge or jury, a punishment is imposed upon a person by a Court by the operation of the judicial process. What is it that is punished? It surely cannot be merely conduct of which the Court disapproves, however strongly the judge may feel. Punishment may not be imposed in a civilized community without a justification in law. *The only basis for the imposition of such punishment must be a finding of the commission of an actionable wrong which caused the injury complained of by the plaintiff.* [Emphasis added.]

This view, McIntyre J. said (at p. 1106), "has found approval in the *Restatement on the Law of Contracts 2d* in the United States", which reads as follows:

> Punitive damages are not recoverable for a breach of contract unless the conduct constituting the breach is also a *tort* for which punitive damages are recoverable. [Emphasis added.]

Applying these principles in *Vorvis*, McIntyre J. stated, at p. 1109:

> Each party had the right to terminate the contract without the consent of the other, and where the employment contract was terminated by the employer, the appellant was entitled to reasonable notice of such termination or payment of salary and benefits for the period of reasonable notice. The termination of the contract on this basis by the employer is not *a wrong in law* and, where the reasonable notice is given or payment in lieu thereof is made, the plaintiff—subject to a consideration of aggravated damages which have been allowed in some cases but which were denied in this case—is entitled to no further remedy. . . . [Emphasis added.]

Wilson J., with whom L'Heureux-Dubé J. concurred, dissented. She did not agree "that punitive damages can only be awarded when the misconduct is in itself an 'actionable wrong'". She stated, at p. 1130:

> In my view, the correct approach is to assess the conduct in the context of all the circumstances and determine whether it is deserving of punishment because of its shockingly harsh, vindictive, reprehensible or malicious nature. Undoubtedly some conduct found to be deserving of punishment will constitute an actionable wrong but other conduct might not.

In the case at bar, Pilot acknowledges that an insurer is under a duty of good faith and fair dealing. Pilot says that this is a contractual duty. *Vorvis*, it says, requires a tort. However, in my view, a breach of the contractual duty of good faith is independent of and in addition to the breach of contractual duty to pay the loss. It constitutes an "actionable wrong" within the *Vorvis* rule, which does not require an independent tort. I say this for several reasons.

First, McIntyre J. chose to use the expression "actionable wrong" instead of "tort" even though he had just reproduced an extract from the *Restatement* which *does* use the word tort. It cannot be an accident that McIntyre J. chose to employ a much broader expression when formulating the Canadian test.

Second, in *Royal Bank of Canada v. W. Got & Associates Electric Ltd.*, [1999] 3 S.C.R. 408, at para. 26, this Court, referring to McIntyre J.'s holding in *Vorvis*, said "the circumstances that would justify punitive damages for breach of contract *in the absence* of actions also constituting *a tort* are rare" (emphasis added). Rare they may be, but the clear message is that such cases do exist. The Court has thus confirmed that punitive damages can be awarded in the absence of an accompanying tort.

Third, the requirement of an independent tort would unnecessarily complicate the pleadings, without in most cases adding anything of substance. *Central Trust Co. v. Rafuse*, [1986] 2 S.C.R. 147 held that a common law duty of care sufficient to found an action in tort can arise within a contractual relationship, and in that case proceeded with the analysis in tort instead of contract to deprive an allegedly negligent solicitor of the benefit of a limitation defence. To require a plaintiff to formulate a tort in a case such as the present is pure formalism. An independent actionable wrong is required, but it can be found in breach of a distinct and separate contractual provision or other duty such as a fiduciary obligation.

I should add that insurance companies have also asserted claims for punitive damages against their insured for breach of the mutual "good faith" obligation in insurance contracts. In *Andrusiw v. Aetna Life Insurance Co. of Canada*, [2001] A.J. No. 789 (Q.B.) (QL), the court awarded $20,000 in punitive damages against an Aetna policy holder in addition to an order for the repayment of $260,000 in disability payments. The insurance company was not required to identify a separate tort to ground its claim for punitive damages. In that case it was the misconduct of the policy holder, not the insurance company, that was seen as such a marked departure from ordinary standards of decent behaviour as to invite the censure of punitive damages, *per* Murray J. at paras. 84-88.

[Binnie J., by reference to the egregious facts, then went on to spell out the factors which justified a restoration of the jury's award of $1 million punitive damages.]

NOTES

1. It is worth contrasting the outcome in *Whiten* with that in another judgment delivered the same day, *Performance Industries Inc. v. Sylvan Lake Golf & Tennis Club Ltd.*, *supra*, Chapter 9, section 5. Despite a finding of fraud such as to justify rectification of a contract for the purchase of land for development, the Court refused to restore a first instance award of punitive damages of $200,000, holding that the compensatory damages were sufficient to achieve the objectives of retribution, deterrence and denunciation. It is also the case that, where there has been an award of aggravated damages, there will be less justification in many instances for a further addition of punitive damages: see *e.g.*, *Fowler v. Maritime Life Assurance Co.* (2002), [2002] N.J. No. 217 (T.D.), another insurance case where there was a bad faith failure to meet the insurer's obligations under the policy but where, unlike *Whiten*, there was a claim for and award of aggravated damage.

2. Binnie J. makes it clear that the requirement of an independent legal wrong for the purposes of punitive damages can be satisfied by the breach of a separate contractual obligation and does not necessarily require proof of a tort, breach of fiduciary or some other different category of legal wrong. In this instance, the wrong identified was breach of a contractual obligation of good faith. Why was the Court prepared to see this as a component of the contract in this instance when it was not prepared to find a contractual requirement of good faith dismissal in *Wallace*? In what other circumstances do you envisage the courts finding an independent requirement of good faith performance? What other contractual obligations might qualify as separate for these purposes?

(b)   CERTAINTY, CAUSATION AND REMOTENESS

Among the most prominent limitations on the scope of expectation damages are those provided by the principles of certainty, causation and remoteness. Indeed, all three also have a role to play in claims based on the plaintiff's reliance interest. Stated more specifically, the three principles mean: (i) that plaintiffs must prove with a sufficient degree of certainty that they would have made profits in the amounts claimed if the defendant had performed; (ii) that that loss was in fact caused by the defendant's breach; and (iii) that it was sufficiently within the range of the defendant's contemplation at the time of entry into the contract.

(i)   *Certainty*

In both the case law and the academic literature, greatest emphasis is placed on the third of these principles. However, that is not to say that the other two do not amount to significant limiting or controlling devices. Thus, we have seen already how in *McRae v. Commonwealth Disposals Commission* and *Anglia T.V. v. Reid, supra*, the plaintiffs' inability to establish on a balance of probabilities that the contracts in question were money-making ones led to a foregoing of any claim based on expectation and, instead, the making of a reliance-based claim. It is also worth remembering that in so far as a reliance claim, as in *McRae*, contains a wasted opportunity component, the plaintiff will also have to establish with a reasonable degree of certainty that there were other available profit-making opportunities that he or she would have taken were it not for entry into the contract with the defendant.

The courts have, however, compromised the purity of the certainty principle in certain respects. This compromise is, of course, evident in cases such as *Chaplin v. Hicks, supra*, where a claim for the loss of a chance to make profits was recognized by the court. Also, in loss of profits claims, the courts are frequently forgiving of plaintiffs who are unable to establish a precise quantum. To quote Waddams: "The onus of proving a loss is on the plaintiff, but it has often been said that if the plaintiff proves some loss, the difficulty in estimating the precise amount is no impediment to an award. The court will estimate the loss, even if such estimation is a matter of 'guess work'." Waddams, *The Law of Contracts*, 4th ed. (1999) at para. 731.

(ii) *Causation*

While not as frequently as in tort claims, issues of causation also arise in the context of damages claims for breach of contract. This section commences with a prominent case in which the Supreme Court of Canada split on the principles to be applied in a case involving a reliance claim. While the primary focus of the majority judgment in this case is on remedies for breach of fiduciary duties, a topic beyond the scope of this course, (although linked to the recurring theme of good faith), the majority also make it clear that, in their view, the result would have been the same had the claim been founded simply in breach of contract. When reading the case, reflect on the validity of this approach and, in particular, on whether or not there should be limits on a plaintiff's entitlement to be restored to her or his pre-contract position under a reliance-based damages claim.

HODGKINSON v. SIMMS

[1994] 3 S.C.R. 377

Hodgkinson was a stock broker with little experience in tax planning. He sought assistance from Simms, a specialist in tax sheltering generally and real estate tax shelter investments in particular. As a result, Hodgkinson purchased four MURBs, a form of income tax sheltered property. While he paid a fair market price for these properties, he lost heavily on his investment when the bottom fell out of the MURB market. Hodgkinson also learned that Simms had been acting for the developers of the MURBs at the time of the sale and had received a commission on the sale as well as his fee from Hodgkinson. As a consequence, Hodgkinson commenced a cause of action against Simms alleging breach of contract, breach of fiduciary duty and negligence. At trial, the judge dismissed the action in negligence and it was thereafter abandoned. However, Hodgkinson was successful in his cause of action for both breach of contract and breach of fiduciary duty with the trial judge accepting Hodgkinson's testimony that he would have never purchased these particular MURBs had he been aware at the time of Simms' involvement with the developers. Damages were assessed on the basis of the losses suffered by Hodgkinson (including associated expenses) but less the tax benefits that he had secured as a consequence of the transactions. On appeal, the British Columbia Court of Appeal reversed the trial judge on the finding of breach of fiduciary duty and varied the damage award by reducing it to the amount of commission that Simms had been paid on the transactions involving Hodgkinson. Hodgkinson appealed.

LA FOREST J. [delivering the judgment of L'Heureux-Dubé, and Gonthier JJ. After restoring the judgment of the trial judge that Simms had both breached his contract with Hodgkinson and his duties as a fiduciary, La Forest J. moved to the issue of damages.]

I turn now to the principles that bear on the calculation of damages in this case. It is well established that the proper approach to damages for breach of a fiduciary duty is restitutionary. On this approach, the appellant is entitled to be put in as good a position as he would have been in had the breach not occurred. On the facts here, this means that the appellant is entitled to be restored to the position he was in before the transaction. The trial judge adopted this restitutionary approach and fixed damages at an amount equal to the return of capital, as well as all consequential losses, minus the amount the appellant saved on income tax due to the investments.

The respondent advanced two arguments against the trial judge's assessment of damages for breach of fiduciary duty. Both raise the issue of causation, and I will address these submissions as they were argued.

The respondent first submitted that given the appellant's stated desire to shelter as much of his income as possible from taxation, and his practice of buying a wide variety of tax shelters, the appellant would still have invested in real-estate tax shelters had he known the true facts. The main difficulty with this submission is that it flies in the face of the facts found by the trial judge. The materiality of the non-disclosure in inducing the appellant to change his position was a live issue at trial which the judge resolved in the appellant's favour, a finding accepted by the Court of Appeal. For reasons given earlier, I agree with this finding.

What is more, the submission runs up against the long-standing equitable principle that where the plaintiff has made out a case of non-disclosure and the loss occasioned thereby is established, the onus is on the defendant to prove that the innocent victim would have suffered the same loss regardless of the breach; see *London Loan & Savings Co. v. Brickenden*, [1934] 2 W.W.R. 545 (P.C.), at pp. 550-51; see also *Huff v. Price*, [(1990), 51 B.C.L.R. (2d) 282] at pp. 319-20; *Commerce Capital Trust Co. v. Berk* (1989), 57 D.L.R. (4th) 759 (Ont. C.A.), at pp. 763-64. This Court recently affirmed the same principle with respect to damages at common law in the context of negligent misrepresentation; see *Rainbow Industrial Caterers Ltd. v. Canadian National Railway Co.*, [1991] 3 S.C.R.

3, at pp. 14-17. I will return to the common law cases in greater detail later; it suffices now to say that courts exercising both common law and equitable jurisdiction have approached this issue in the same manner. In *Rainbow*, Sopinka J., on behalf of a 6-1 majority of this Court, had this to say, at pp. 15-16:

> The plaintiff is the innocent victim of a misrepresentation which has induced a change of position. It is just that the plaintiff should be entitled to say "but for the tortious conduct of the defendant, I would not have changed my position". A tortfeasor who says, "Yes, but you would have assumed a position other than the *status quo ante*", and thereby asks a court to find a transaction whose terms are hypothetical and speculative, should bear the burden of displacing the plaintiff's assertion of the *status quo ante*.

Further, mere "speculation" on the part of the defendant will not suffice; see *ibid.*, at p. 15; *Commerce Capital, supra*, at p. 764. In the present case the respondent has adduced no concrete evidence to "displac[e] the plaintiff's assertion of the *status quo ante*", and this submission must, therefore, be dismissed.

The respondent also argued that even assuming the appellant would not have invested had proper disclosure been made, the non-disclosure was not the proximate cause of the appellant's loss. Rather, he continued, the appellant's loss was caused by the general economic recession that hit the British Columbia real estate market in the early 1980s. The respondent submits that it is grossly unjust to hold him accountable for losses that, he maintains, have no causal relation to the breach of fiduciary duty he perpetrated on the appellant.

I observe that a similar argument was put forward and rejected in [*Burns v. Kelly Peters & Associates Ltd.* (1987), 16 B.C.L.R. (2d) 1 (C.A.)]. . . .

The similarity between *Kelly Peters* and the present case is striking. Both the defendant in *Kelly Peters* and the respondent here induced parties into investments they would not otherwise have made by deliberately concealing their own financial interest. These respective investors were thereby exposed to *all* the risks, i.e., including the general market risks, of these investments. On the finding of facts, these investors would not have been exposed to *any* of the risks associated with these investments had it not been for their respective fiduciary's desire to secure an improper personal gain. In short, in each case it was the particular fiduciary breach that initiated the chain of events leading to the investor's loss. As such it is right and just that the breaching party account for this loss in full.

Contrary to the respondent's submission, this result is not affected by the *ratio* of this Court's decision in *Canson Enterprises*, [*v. Boughton & Co.*, [1991] 3 S.C.R. 534]. *Canson* held that a court exercising equitable jurisdiction is not precluded from considering the principles of remoteness, causation, and intervening act where necessary to reach a just and fair result. *Canson* does not, however, signal a retreat from the principle of full restitution; rather it recognizes the fact that a breach of a fiduciary duty can take a variety of forms, and as such a variety of remedial considerations may be appropriate; see also *McInerney v. MacDonald*, [[1992] 2 S.C.R. 138] at p. 149. Writing extra-judicially, Huband J.A. of the Manitoba Court of Appeal recently remarked upon this idea, in "Remedies and Restitution for Breach of Fiduciary Duties" in *The 1993 Isaac Pitblado Lectures, supra*, pp. 21-32, at p. 31:

> A breach of a fiduciary duty can take many forms. It might be tantamount to deceit and theft, while on the other hand it may be no more than an innocent and honest bit of bad advice, or a failure to give a timely warning.

Canson is an example of the latter type of fiduciary breach, mentioned by Huband J.A. There, the defendant solicitor failed to warn the plaintiff, his client, that the vendors and other third parties were pocketing a secret profit from a "flip" of the subject real estate such that the property was overpriced. . . . In this situation, the principle of full restitution should not entitle a plaintiff to greater compensation than he or she would otherwise be entitled to at common law, wherein the limiting principles of intervening act would come into play.

Put another way, equity is not so rigid as to be susceptible to being used as a vehicle for punishing defendants with harsh damage awards out of all proportion to their actual behaviour. On the contrary, where the common law has developed a measured and just principle in response to a particular kind of wrong, equity is flexible enough to borrow from the common law. As I noted in *Canson*, at pp. 587-88, this approach is in accordance with the fusion of law and equity that occurred near the turn of the century under the auspices of the old *Judicature Acts*; . . . Thus, properly understood *Canson* stands for the proposition that courts should strive to treat similar wrongs similarly, regardless of the particular cause or causes of action that may have been pleaded. As I stated in *Canson*, at p. 581:

> . . . barring different policy considerations underlying one action or the other, I see no reason why the same basic claim, whether framed in terms of a common law action or an equitable remedy, should give rise to different levels of redress.

In other words, the courts should look to the harm suffered from the breach of the given duty, and apply the appropriate remedy.

Returning to the facts of the present case, one immediately notices significant differences from the wrong committed by the defendant in *Canson* as compared to the character of the fiduciary breach perpetrated by the respondent. In *Canson* there was no particular nexus between the wrong complained of and the fiduciary relationship; this was underlined, at p. 577, by my colleague, McLachlin J., who followed a purely equitable route. Rather, the fiduciary relationship there arose by operation of law, and was in many ways incidental to the particular wrong. Further, the loss was caused by the wrongful act of a third party that was unrelated to the fiduciary breach. In the present case the duty the respondent breached was directly related to the risk that materialized and in fact caused the appellant's loss. The respondent had been retained specifically to seek out and make independent recommendations of suitable investments for the appellant. This agreement gave the respondent a kind of influence or discretion over the appellant in that, as the trial judge found, he effectively chose the risks to which the appellant would be exposed based on investments which in his expert opinion coincided with the appellant's overall investment objectives. In *Canson* the defendant solicitor did not advise on, choose, or exercise any control over the plaintiff's decision to invest in the impugned real estate; in short, he did not exercise any control over the risks that eventually materialized into a loss for the plaintiff.

Indeed, courts have treated common law claims of the same nature as the wrong complained of in the present case in much the same way as claims in equity. I earlier referred to *Rainbow Industrial Caterers*. The plaintiff there had contracted to cater lunches to CN employees at a certain price per meal. The price was based on the estimated number of lunches the defendant would require over the period covered by the contract. This estimate was negligently misstated, and the plaintiff suffered a significant loss. The Court was satisfied that but for the misrepresentation, the plaintiff would not have entered into the contract. The defendant, however, alleged that much of the loss was not caused by the misrepresentation but rather by certain conduct of CN employees, e.g., taking too much food. This argument was rejected by the Court in the following terms, at p. 17:

> ... CN bore the burden of proving that Rainbow would have bid even if the estimate had been accurate. That was not proved, and so it is taken as a fact that Rainbow would *not* have contracted had the estimate been accurate. The conduct referred to in para. 49 [i.e. the conduct of the CN employees] would not have occurred if there had been no contract, and therefore the loss caused thereby, like all other losses in the proper execution of the contract by Rainbow, is directly related to the negligent misrepresentation. [Emphasis in original.]

Thus, where a party can show that but for the relevant breach it would not have entered into a given contract, that party is freed from the burden or benefit of the rest of the bargain; see also *BG Checo International Ltd. v. British Columbia Hydro and Power Authority*, [*supra* Chapter 7, section 5], at pp. 40-41 (*per* La Forest and McLachlin JJ.). In short, the wronged party is entitled to be restored to the pre-transaction *status quo*.

.....

The respondent points to a number of cases in which courts have refused to compensate plaintiffs for losses suffered owing to general market fluctuations despite the existence of "but for" causation; *Waddell v. Blockey* (1879), 4 Q.B.D. 678 (C.A); . . .

[La Forest J. here considered the older case law and *Waddell* in particular. He noted that not only was *Waddell* decided at a time when the concept of fiduciary duty was inchoate in English law but also that there was subsequent conflicting British Columbia Court of Appeal authority.]

From a policy perspective it is simply unjust to place the risk of market fluctuations on a plaintiff who would not have entered into a given transaction but for the defendant's wrongful conduct. I observe that in *Waddell*, *supra*, Bramwell L.J. conceded, at p. 680, that if *restitutio in integrum* had been possible, the plaintiff could probably have recovered in full. Indeed counsel for the appellant argued that the proper approach to damages in this case was the monetary equivalent of a rescissionary remedy. I agree. In my view the appellant should not suffer from the fact that he did not discover the breach until such time as the market had already taken its toll on his investments. This principle, which I take to be a basic principle of fairness, is in fact reflected in the common law of mitigation, itself rooted in causation; see S. M. Waddams, *The Law of Contracts* (3rd ed. 1993), at p. 515. In *Asamera Oil Corp. v. Sea Oil & General Corp.*, [1979] 1 S.C.R. 633, this Court held that in an action for breach of the duty to return shares under a contract of bailment, the obligation imposed on the plaintiff to mitigate by purchasing like shares on the open market did not commence until such time as the plaintiff learned of the breach or within a reasonable time thereafter.

There is a broader justification for upholding the trial judge's award of damages in cases such as the present, namely the need to put special pressure on those in positions of trust and power over others in situations of vulnerability. This justification is evident in American caselaw, which makes a distinction between simple fraud related to the price of a security and fraudulent inducements by brokers and others in the investment business in positions of influence. In the case at bar, as in *Kelly Peters* and the American cases cited by the appellant, the wrong complained of goes to the heart of the duty of loyalty that lies at the core of the fiduciary principle. In redressing a wrong of this nature, I have no difficulty in resorting to a measure of damages that places the exigencies of the market-place on the respondent. Such a result is in accordance with the principle that a defaulting fiduciary has an obligation to effect restitution *in specie* or its monetary equivalent. . . . I see no reason to derogate from this principle; on the contrary, the behaviour of the respondent seems to be precisely the type of behaviour that calls for strict legal censure. Mark Ellis puts the matter in the following way in *Fiduciary Duties in Canada*, [1988] at p. 20-2:

> . . . the relief seeks primarily to protect a party owed a duty of utmost good faith from deleterious actions by the party owing the fiduciary duty. The vehicles by which the Court may enforce that duty are diverse and powerful, but are premised upon the same desire: to strictly and jealously guard against breach and to redress that breach by maintenance of the pre-default status quo, where possible.

The remedy of disgorgement, adopted in effect if not in name by the Court of Appeal, is simply insufficient to guard against the type of abusive behaviour engaged in by the respondent in this case. The law of fiduciary duties has always contained within it an element of deterrence. This can be seen as early as *Keech* [*v. Sandford* (1726), Sel. Cas. T. King 61; 25 E.R. 223]. . . . In this way the law is able to monitor a given relationship society views as socially useful while avoiding the necessity of formal regulation that may tend to hamper its social utility. Like-minded fiduciaries in the position of the respondent would not be deterred from abusing their power by a remedy that simply requires them, if discovered, to disgorge their secret profit, with the beneficiary bearing all the market risk. If anything, this would encourage people in his position to in effect gamble with other people's money, knowing that if they are discovered they will be no worse off than when they started. As a result, the social benefits of fiduciary relationships, particularly in the field of independent professional advisors, would be greatly diminished.

In view of my finding that there existed a fiduciary duty between the parties, it is not in strictness necessary to consider damages for breach of contract. However, in my view, on the facts of this case, damages in contract follow the principles stated in connection with the equitable breach. The contract between the parties was for *independent* professional advice. While it is true that the appellant got what he paid for from the developers, he did not get the services he paid for from the respondent. The relevant contractual duty breached by the respondent is of precisely the same nature as the equitable duty considered in the fiduciary analysis, namely the duty to make full disclosure of any material conflict of interest. This was, in short, a contract which provided for the performance of obligations characterized in equity as fiduciary.

Further, it remains the case under the contractual analysis that but for the non-disclosure, the contract with the developers for the MURBs would not have been entered into. The trial judge found as a fact that it was reasonably foreseeable that if the appellant had known of the respondent's affiliation with the developers, he would not have invested. This finding is fully reflected in the evidence I have earlier set forth. Put another way, it was foreseeable that if the contract was breached the appellant would be exposed to market risks (i.e., in connection with the four MURBs) to which he would not otherwise have been exposed. Further, it is well established that damages must be foreseeable as to kind, but not extent; as such any distinction based on the unforeseeability of the *extent* of the market fluctuations must be dismissed; see *H. Parsons (Livestock) Ltd. v. Uttley Ingham & Co.*, [1978] Q.B. 791, at p. 813; *Asamera, supra*, at p. 655. See also S. M. Waddams, *The Law of Damages* (2nd ed. 1991), at paras. 14.280 and 14.290.

The Court of Appeal's approach to contractual damages is puzzling in that it seemed to accept the finding that if the contractual duty had not been breached the investments would not have been made, yet it proceeded to award damages in proportion to the amounts paid by the developer to the defendant. It is clear, however, that there would have been no such fees had the investments not been made. In short, I am unable to follow the Court of Appeal's reasoning on the issue of damages for breach of contract, and I would restore the award of damages made by the trial judge.

SOPINKA and McLACHLIN JJ. [dissenting, Major J. concurring]

(a) *Causation*

The appellant in this case does not allege that the losses which he incurred were caused directly by the respondent's breach of contract. Instead, he claims that "but for" the respondent's breach of the first contract, the appellant would not have entered into subsequent investment contracts which, due to an economic downturn, were significantly devalued. A literal application of the "but for" approach to causation has been rejected in British, Canadian and American case law, in the context of both equitable and common law claims.

In *Waddell v. Blockey* [*supra*], a case involving an action for fraudulent misrepresentation, the Queen's Bench Division ordered damages in the amount of the difference between the price paid by the individual represented by the plaintiff and the fair market value of the item sold. Although the rupee paper would not have been purchased had the defendant made full disclosure of the fact that he owned the paper which he sold to the purchaser, the defendant was not held liable for the resulting losses sustained by the purchaser due to devaluation of the item. Thesiger L.J. reasoned as follows in this regard at pp. 682 and 684:

> There is [in this case] no natural or proximate connection between the wrong done and the damage suffered.

.....

> But the present case is complicated by the circumstance of the defendant's fiduciary position in the matter of the purchase, and by the fact that the fraud did not touch the value of the article sold. . . . *It would seem, however, strange if under such circumstances a plaintiff who has got the article he bargained for, upon whom no fraud as regards its value has been practised, could, after the article has been depreciated and resold at a loss owing to a cause totally unconnected with the fraud, claim to recover all the loss which he has thereby sustained. I cannot see upon what principle such a claim could be based.* [Emphasis added.]

Similarly, in *Canson Enterprises Ltd. v. Boughton & Co.*, [*supra*], at p. 580, this Court recognized that the results of supervening events beyond the control of the defendant are not justly visited upon him/her in assessing damages, even in the context of the breach of an equitable duty.

[At this point, Sopinka and McLachlin JJ. considered U.S. authority.]

. . . While we would not wish to be taken as agreeing with this particular [U.S.] approach to damages in a situation where a material misrepresentation resulted in a loss to an investor, we do agree with the application of the principle in situations where the representation itself is not causally connected to the devaluation. In such situations, where the losses incurred by a plaintiff are related to the contractual breach of the defendant merely on a "but for" basis, it would be unduly harsh to impose liability for all of the losses upon the defendant, especially where the direct cause of the loss is outside of the defendant's control.

C. *Application to the Case at Bar*

In assessing the damages for respondent's breach of contract it is necessary to ask whether the loss sustained by the appellant arose naturally from a breach thereof *or* whether at the time of contracting the parties could reasonably have contemplated the loss flowing from the breach of the duty to disclose. In the event that either criterion is satisfied, the respondent should be held liable for that loss. Finally, the damage assessment as a whole must represent a fair resolution on the facts of this case.

(a)   Causation

In our view, it cannot be concluded that the devaluation of the appellant's investments arose naturally from the respondent's breach of contract. The loss in value was caused by an economic downturn which did not reflect any inadequacy in the advice provided by the respondent. We would reject application of the "but for" approach to causation in circumstances where the loss resulted from forces beyond the control of the respondent who, the trial judge determined, had provided otherwise sound investment advice. . . .

[At this juncture, the minority also held that the losses suffered by Hodgkinson did not come with the range of foreseeable harm for which damages could be awarded for breach of contract.]

Moreover, the fact that the breach of the duty to disclose was a continuing one does not affect our conclusion in this regard. The factual finding was that the investments were sound ones, but for the economic downturn, and there is no evidence to indicate that, had the respondent disclosed his conflicting interests prior in time to the economic downturn, the appellant would have sold his interest in the investments. In fact, it would be unreasonable to infer that he would have done so, given that the investments were sound ones.

In situations involving breach of a duty to disclose, courts have consistently recognized the right of plaintiffs to compensation for losses equivalent to the difference between the price which they paid for a particular investment and the actual value of the investment purchased: *Waddell, supra,* and *Canson, supra.* In the case at bar, the trial judge concluded that there was no evidence to indicate that the appellant had paid anything more than the fair market value for the investments which he made. Therefore, it would appear that no damages should have been assessed. However, McEachern C.J. in the Court of Appeal concluded, at p. 280, that "the law so dislikes a failure of disclosure of material facts that it assumes the value of the investment was less than the amount paid, at least to the extent of the amounts paid by the developer to the defendant." There was no cross-appeal from the judgment of the Court of Appeal. In these circumstances we are not entitled to reduce the award of damages made by the Court of Appeal.

[Iacobucci J. delivered a judgment in which he concurred in the reasoning of La Forest J. thereby creating a majority. Appeal allowed.]

NOTES and QUESTIONS

1. Who has the better of the argument on causation: the majority or the minority? To what extent is the majority's position on this issue influenced by the fact that the wrong is characterized as both a breach of contract and a breach of fiduciary duty?

2. For a critical evaluation of the remedial aspects of *Hodgkinson v. Simms*, see McCamus, "Prometheus Unbound: Fiduciary Duties in the Supreme Court of Canada" (1997), 28 Can. Bus. L.J. 107 at 128-40.

3. In *Esso Petroleum v. Mardon,* (*supra* Chapter 7, section 5 in *Sodd Corp v. N. Tessis* and notes following) the defendant had induced the plaintiff to lease a service station on the basis of negligently prepared estimates of the likely level of sales of gas—it had failed to take account of the fact that contrary to original plans, the service station would not face the street. The Court of Appeal held that the plaintiff was entitled to be restored to his pre-contract position as a result of this negligence. It gave rise to a cause of action in negligent misstatement but could just as easily have been founded in an action for breach of warranty. This involved compensating the plaintiff for the losses sustained on the operation until he was closed down as well as a further amount for foregone opportunities. Would or should the result be the same if, subsequent to the leasing of the service station, the plaintiff's losses were increased further by a municipal rerouting of traffic away from the street on which the service station was located? Would the answer be different depending on whether the plaintiff was claiming damages based on his expectation or his reliance interest?

(iii) *Remoteness*

Clearly in contracts, a claim for damages can give rise to the same issues of remoteness that arise in torts. In *B.C. Saw-Mill Co. v. Nettleship* (1868), L.R. 3 C.P. 499 at 508, Willes J. described a very early example of a startling application of rules of remoteness in contracts. He describes a case in which "a man going to be married to an heiress, his horse having cast a shoe on the journey, employed a blacksmith to replace it, who did the work so unskillfully that the horse was lamed, and the rider not arriving in time, the lady married another, and the blacksmith was held liable for the loss of the marriage."

Remoteness involves issues both of principle and policy. In principle, courts are concerned with the fundamental problem of whether the defendant caused the loss which occurred, but at the same time they deal with the general policy question of whether the defendant ought to be burdened with the payment of damages of the type claimed. Just as in torts, these fundamental issues are inevitably somewhat obscured by verbal formulae, which the courts have adopted in an effort to justify or rationalize their actions in particular cases. It will be immediately appreciated that the verbal tests propounded by courts do not, of course, solve in litmus fashion future cases and that, in this area of law in particular, Holmes' axiom "general propositions do not decide concrete cases" must be borne in mind. Nevertheless, it is important to be familiar with the tests which courts have used to describe their actions, because they present the tools with which remoteness problems are approached from day to day. Further, their application provides valuable practical information on where courts have in the past drawn the line of liability for damages resulting from a breach of contract and on the type of factors that they have found important in that task.

HADLEY v. BAXENDALE

(1854), 9 Exch. 341, 156 E.R. 145

At the trial before Crompton, J., at the last Gloucester Assizes, it appeared that the plaintiffs carried on an extensive business as millers at Gloucester; and that, on the 11th of May, their mill was stopped by a breakage of the crank shaft by which the mill was worked. The steam engine was manufactured by Messrs. Joyce & Co., the engineers, at Greenwich, and it became necessary to send the shaft as a pattern for a new one to Greenwich. The fracture was discovered on the 12th, and on the 13th the plaintiffs sent one of their servants to the office of the defendants, who are the well-known carriers trading under the name of Pickford & Co., for the purpose of having the shaft carried to Greenwich. The plaintiffs' servant told the clerk that the mill was stopped, and that the shaft must be sent immediately; and in answer to the inquiry when the shaft would be taken, the answer was, that if it was sent up by twelve o'clock any day, it would be delivered at Greenwich on the following day. On the following day the shaft was taken by the defendants, before noon, for the purpose of being conveyed to Greenwich, and the sum of 2l. 4s. was paid for its carriage for the whole distance; at the same time the defendants' clerk was told that a special entry, if required, should be made to hasten its delivery. The delivery of the shaft at Greenwich was delayed by some neglect; and the consequence was, that the plaintiffs did not receive the new shaft for several days after they would otherwise have done, and the working of their mill was thereby delayed, and they thereby lost the profits they would otherwise have received.

On the part of the defendants, it was objected that these damages were too remote, and that the defendants were not liable with respect to them.

[The plaintiffs claimed £300 in lost profits. At trial the jury found the defendants liable in total for the amount of £50. The defendants sought a new trial on the ground that the jury had been misdirected.]

ALDERSON B. [delivering the judgment of the court] We think that there ought to be a new trial in this case, but, in so doing, we deem it to be expedient and necessary to state explicitly the rule which the Judge, at the next trial, ought, in our opinion, to direct the jury to be governed by when they estimate the damages. . . .

Now we think the proper rule in such a case as the present is this: Where two parties have made a contract which one of them has broken, the damages which the other party ought to receive in respect of such breach of contract should be such as may fairly and reasonably be considered either arising naturally, i.e., according to the usual course of things, from such breach of contract itself, or such as may reasonably be supposed to have been in the contemplation of both parties, at the time they made the contract, as the probable result of the breach of it. Now, if the special circumstances under which the contract was actually made were communicated by the plaintiffs to the defendants, and thus known to both parties, the damages resulting from the breach of such a contract, which they would reasonably contemplate, would be the amount of injury which would ordinarily follow from a breach of contract under these special circumstances so known and communicated. But, on the other hand, if these special circumstances were wholly unknown to the party breaking the contract, he, at the most, could only be supposed to have had in his contemplation the amount of injury which would arise generally, and in the great multitude of cases not affected by any special circumstances, from such a breach of contract. For, had the special circumstances been known, the parties might have specially provided for the breach of contract by special terms as to the damages in that case; and of this advantage it would be very unjust to deprive them. Now the above principles are those by which we think the jury ought to be guided in estimating the damages arising out of any breach of contract . . .

Now, in the present case, if we are to apply the principles above laid down, we find that the only circumstances here communicated by the plaintiffs to the defendants at the time the contract was made, were, that the article to be carried was the broken shaft of a mill, and that the plaintiffs were the millers of that mill. But how do these circumstances shew reasonably that the profits of the mill must be stopped by an unreasonable delay in the delivery of the broken shaft by the carrier to the third person? Suppose the plaintiffs had another shaft in their possession put up or putting up at the time, and that they only wished to send back the broken shaft to the engineer who made it; it is clear that this would be quite consistent with the above circumstances, and yet the unreasonable delay in the delivery would have no effect upon the intermediate profits of the mill. Or, again, suppose that, at the time of the delivery to the carrier, the machinery of the mill had been in other respects defective, then, also, the same results would follow. Here it is true that the shaft was actually sent back to serve as a model for a new one, and that the want of a new one was the only cause of the stoppage of the mill, and that the loss of profits really arose from not sending down the new shaft in proper time, and that this arose from the delay in delivering the broken one to serve as a model. But it is obvious that, in the great multitude of cases of millers sending off broken shafts to third persons by a carrier under ordinary circumstances, such consequences would not, in all probability, have occurred; and these special circumstances were here never communicated by the plaintiffs to the defendants. It follows, therefore, that the loss of profits here cannot reasonably be considered such a consequence of the breach of contract as could have been fairly and reasonably contemplated by both the parties when they made this contract. For such loss would neither have flowed naturally from the breach of this contract in the great multitude of such cases occurring under ordinary circumstances, nor were the special circumstances, which, perhaps, would have made it a reasonable and natural consequence of such breach of contract, communicated to or known by the defendants. The Judge ought, therefore, to have told the jury, that, upon the facts then before them, they ought not to take the loss of profits into consideration at all in estimating the damages. There must therefore be a new trial in this case.

NOTE

At first sight there appears to be a contradiction between the fact appearing in the headnote that the plaintiff's servant told the clerk that the mill was stopped, and Baron Alderson's assumption that the defendants had no notice of this circumstance. In the *Victoria Laundry* case, *infra*, Asquith L.J. commented (at 537) that if the court had accepted this fact as established it must "have decided the case the other way round". However, in Danzig, "Hadley v. Baxendale: As Study of the Industrialization of the Law" (1975), 4 J. Leg. Stud. 249 at 262-63, it is suggested that the court may have accepted the argument of defence counsel that under the prevailing law of agency notice to the clerk did not constitute notice to the principal. This article also offers an interesting discussion of the historical context of *Hadley v. Baxendale*.

VICTORIA LAUNDRY (WINDSOR) LTD. v. NEWMAN INDUST. LTD.

[1949] 2 K.B. 528, [1949] 1 All E.R. 997 (C.A.)

The plaintiffs wished to expand their laundry and agreed to purchase a large boiler owned by the defendants for £2,150. The defendants knew that the plaintiffs were launderers and dyers and that they required the boiler for use in their business. The plaintiffs agreed to take delivery on 5th June 1946, but the boiler was damaged while it was being dismantled on the defendants' premises. Repairs to the boiler caused a lengthy delay and it was not delivered until 8th November 1946. The plaintiffs sued, *inter alia*, for loss of business profits for the period from 5th June to 8th November 1946. A trial, Streatfield J. awarded £110 under certain minor heads of damage, but refused to allow anything for loss of profits, on the grounds that such a loss was too remote.

ASQUITH L.J. [delivering the judgment of the court] . . . Evidence was led for the plaintiffs with the object of establishing that if the boiler had been punctually delivered, then, during the twenty odd weeks between then and the time of actual delivery, (1) they could have taken on a very large number of new customers in the course of their laundry business, the demand for laundry services at that time being insatiable—they did in fact take on extra staff in the expectation of its delivery—and (2) that they could and would have accepted a number of highly lucrative dyeing contracts for the Ministry of Supply. In the statement of claim, para. 10, the loss of profits under the first of these heads was quantified at £16 a week and under the second at £262 a week. . . .

The authorities on recovery of loss of profits as a head of damage are not easy to reconcile. At one end of the scale stand cases where there has been non-delivery or delayed delivery of what is on the face of it obviously a profit-earning chattel; for instance, a merchant or passenger ship; or some essential part of such a ship; for instance, a propeller, or engines. In such cases loss of profit has rarely been refused. A second and intermediate class of case in which loss of profit has often been awarded is where ordinary mercantile goods have been sold to a merchant with knowledge by the vendor that the purchaser wanted them for resale, at all events, where there was no market in which the purchaser could buy similar goods against the contract on the seller's default. At the other end of the scale are cases where the defendant is not a vendor of the goods, but a carrier, see, for instance, *Hadley v. Baxendale*.

In such cases the courts have been slow to allow loss of profit as an item of damage. This was not, it would seem, because a different principle applies in such cases, but because the application of the same principle leads to different results. A carrier commonly knows less than a seller about the purposes for which the buyer or consignee needs the goods, or about other "special circumstances" which may cause exceptional loss if due delivery is withheld. . . .

[Asquith L.J. considered *Hadley v. Baxendale* and *B.C. Saw-Mill v. Nettle-ship* and continued:]

Cory v. Thames Ironworks Company [(1868), L.R. 3 Q.B. 181]—a case strongly relied on by the plaintiffs—presented the peculiarity that the parties contemplated respectively different profit-making uses of the chattel sold by the defendant to the plaintiff. It was the hull of a boom derrick, and was delivered late. The plaintiffs were coal merchants, and the obvious use, and that to which the defendants believed it was be put, was that of a coal store. The plaintiffs, on the other hand, the buyers, in fact intended to use it for transhipping coals from colliers to barges, a quite unprecedented use for a chattel of this kind, one quite unsuspected by the sellers and one calculated to yield much higher profits. The case accordingly decides, inter alia, what is the measure of damage recoverable when the parties are not ad idem in their contemplation of the use for which the article is needed. It was decided that in such a case no loss was recoverable beyond what would have resulted if the intended use had been that reasonably within the contemplation of the defendants, which in that case was the "obvious" use. This special complicating factor, the divergence between the knowledge and contemplation of the parties respectively, has somewhat obscured the general importance of the decision, which is in effect that the facts of the case brought it within the first rule of *Hadley v. Baxendale* and enabled the plaintiff to recover loss of such profits as would have arisen from the normal and obvious use of the article. The "natural consequence," said Blackburn J., of not delivering the derrick was that

£420 representing those normal profits was lost. Cockburn C.J., interposing during the argument, made the significant observation: "No doubt in order to recover damage arising from a special purpose the buyer must have communicated the special purpose to the seller; but there is one thing which must always be in the knowledge of both parties, which is that the thing is bought for the purpose of being in some way or other profitably applied." This observation is apposite to the present case.

What propositions applicable to the present case emerge from the authorities as a whole, including those analysed above? We think they include the following:—

(1) It is well settled that the governing purpose of damages is to put the party whose rights have been violated in the same position, so far as money can do so, as if his rights had been observed . . . This purpose, if relentlessly pursued, would provide him with a complete indemnity for all loss de facto resulting from a particular breach, however improbable, however unpredictable. This, in contract at least, is recognized as too harsh a rule. Hence,

(2) In cases of breach of contract the aggrieved party is only entitled to recover such part of the loss actually resulting as was at the time of the contract reasonably foreseeable as liable to result from the breach.

(3) What was at that time reasonably so foreseeable depends on the knowledge then possessed by the parties or, at all events, by the party who later commits the breach.

(4) For this purpose, knowledge "possessed" is of two kinds; one imputed, the other actual. Everyone, as a reasonable person, is taken to know the "ordinary course of things" and consequently what loss is liable to result from a breach of contract in that ordinary course. This is the subject matter of the "first rule" in *Hadley v. Baxendale*. But to this knowledge, which a contract-breaker is assumed to possess whether he actually possesses it or not, there may have to be added in a particular case knowledge which he actually possesses, of special circumstances outside the "ordinary course of things," of such a kind that a breach in those special circumstances would be liable to cause more loss. Such a case attracts the operation of the "second rule" so as to make additional loss also recoverable.

(5) In order to make the contract-breaker liable under either rule it is not necessary that he should actually have asked himself what loss is liable to result from a breach. As has often been pointed out, parties at the time of contracting contemplate not the breach of the contract, but its performance. It suffices that, if he had considered the question, he would as a reasonable man have concluded that the loss in question was liable to result.

(6) Nor, finally, to make a particular loss recoverable, need it be proved that upon a given state of knowledge the defendant could, as a reasonable man, foresee that a breach must necessarily result in that loss. It is enough if he could foresee it was likely so to result. It is indeed enough, to borrow from the language of Lord du Parcq in *Monarch S.S. Co. v. A/B Karlshamns Oljefabriker*, [1949] A.C. 196, if the loss (or some factor without which it would not have occurred) is a "serious

possibility" or a "real danger." For short, we have used the word "liable" to result. Possibly the colloquialism "on the cards" indicates the shade of meaning with some approach to accuracy.

If these, indeed, are the principles applicable, what is the effect of their application to the facts of this case? . . . The defendants were an engineering company supplying a boiler to a laundry. We reject the submission for the defendants that an engineering company knows no more than the plain man about boilers or the purposes to which they are commonly put by different classes of purchasers, including laundries. The defendant company were not, it is true, manufacturers of this boiler or dealers in boilers, but they gave a highly technical and comprehensive description of this boiler to the plaintiffs by letter of January 19, 1946, and offered both to dismantle the boiler at Harpenden and to re-erect it on the plaintiffs' premises. Of the uses or purposes to which boilers are put, they would clearly know more than the uninstructed layman. Again, they knew they were supplying the boiler to a company carrying on the business of laundrymen and dyers, for use in that business. The obvious use of a boiler, in such a business, is surely to boil water for the purpose of washing or dyeing. A laundry might conceivably buy a boiler for some other purpose; for instance, to work radiators or warm bath water for the comfort of its employees or directors, or to use for research, or to exhibit in a museum. All these purposes are possible, but the first is the obvious purpose which, in the case of a laundry, leaps to the average eye. If the purpose then be to wash or dye, why does the company want to wash or dye, unless for purposes of business advantage, in which term we, for the purposes of the rest of this judgment, include maintenance or increase of profit, or reduction of loss? . . .

The answer to the reasoning [of Streatfield J.] has largely been anticipated in what has been said above, but we would wish to add: First, that the learned judge appears to infer that because certain "special circumstances" were, in his view, not "drawn to the notice of" the defendants and therefore, in his view, the operation of the "second rule" was excluded, ergo nothing in respect of loss of business can be recovered under the "first rule." This inference is, in our view, no more justified in the present case that it was in the case of *Cory v. Thames Ironworks Company*. Secondly, that while it is not wholly clear what were the "special circumstances" on the non-communication of which the learned judge relied, it would seem that they were, or included, the following:—(*a*) the "circumstance" that delay in delivering the boiler was going to lead "necessarily" to loss of profits. But the true criterion is surely not what was bound "necessarily" to result, but what was likely or liable to do so, and we think that it was amply conveyed to the defendants by what was communicated to them (plus what was patent without express communication) that delay in delivery was likely to lead to "loss of business"; (*b*) the "circumstance" that the plaintiffs needed the boiler "to extend their business." It was surely not necessary for the defendants to be specifically informed of this, as a precondition of being liable for loss of business. . . . (*c*) the "circumstance" that the plaintiffs had the assured expectation of special contracts, which they could only fulfil by securing punctual delivery of the boiler.

Here, no doubt, the learned judge had in mind the particularly lucrative dyeing contracts to which the plaintiffs looked forward and which they mention in para. 10 of the statement of claim. We agree that in order that the plaintiffs should recover specifically and as such the profits expected on these contracts, the defendants would have had to know, at the time of their agreement with the plaintiffs, of the prospect and terms of such contracts. We also agree that they did not in fact know these things. It does not, however, follow that the plaintiffs are precluded from recovering some general (and perhaps conjectural) sum for loss of business in respect of dyeing contracts to be reasonably expected, any more than in respect of laundering contracts to be reasonably expected. . . .

We are therefore of opinion that the appeal should be allowed and the issue referred to an official referee as to what damage, if any, is recoverable in addition to the £110 awarded by the learned trial judge. . . .

QUESTION

A laundry orders a boiler from defendant. Unknown to defendant, the laundry intends to use the boiler, not for their ordinary dyeing operations, but to extract a valuable by-product from certain dyes which they use. Defendant delivers the boiler after the date stipulated and is in breach of contract. On what basis should the laundry's damages be calculated? *Cf.*, the example given by Treitel, *The Law of Contract*, 9th ed. (1995), at 874: "A sells B poisonous cattle food. B eats it himself in the course of an unforeseeable nutritional experiment, and dies. Can his executor sue A for the loss of a cow?"

SCYRUP v. ECONOMY TRACTOR PARTS LTD.

(1963), 43 W.W.R. 49, 40 D.L.R. (2d) 1026 (Man. C.A.)

FREEDMAN J.A. This is an appeal by the defendant from a judgment of Maybank, J., holding the defendant liable to the plaintiff for damages for breach of contract arising from the sale [for approximately $1000] of a hydraulic dozer attachment for the plaintiff's D8 caterpillar tractor. . . .

[The damages at trial included an award for lost profits on a contract which the plaintiff held with Supercrete Ltd.]

Prior to the matters in question in this case the plaintiff had entered into a contract, requiring the use of his tractor, with a company known as Supercrete Ltd. It was to make the tractor fit and suitable for the Supercrete job that the plaintiff needed the hydraulic dozer attachment. It is common ground that he purchased this attachment from the defendant. The plaintiff's evidence establishes that he made known to the defendant the fact that the attachment was for a tractor which was to be used by him on a job with Supercrete Ltd. He also made it plain that he needed this equipment in a hurry and that it had to be in good working order.

The attachment was duly sold and delivered by the defendant to the plaintiff. But . . . the equipment did not measure up to the terms of the contract. The plaintiff first discovered that certain parts were missing. Then, after these were replaced, it was found that the hydraulic attachment would not function. Tests showed that the hydraulic pump did not generate sufficient pressure to operate the unit. The plaintiff later received in turn, three replacing pumps, not one of which proved adequate. Finally the plaintiff had to rebuild one of the pumps in order to make the attachment operable.

In consequence of the attachment equipment being defective the caterpillar could not function. For Supercrete Ltd., it was imperative to have a tractor effectively working at its gravel pit. Since the plaintiff's tractor, in the condition it then was, could not do the job, Supercrete cancelled the contract with the plaintiff and hired another tractor from a third party to do the work. The plaintiff's loss of profit, which he would have earned on the Supercrete contract, represents the main item of the damages which he now claims from the defendant. . . .

The guiding principles are clear. It is usual to think of *Hadley v. Baxendale* as enunciating two rules, or, at all events, one rule with two branches. Under the first rule (or branch) damages for breach of contract should be such as arise naturally—that is, according to the usual course of things—from the breach of contract itself, or such as may reasonably be supposed to have been in the contemplation of the parties, at the time they made the contract, as the probable result of its breach. Under the second rule, if there are special circumstances relating to the contract—and these are actually communicated by the plaintiff to the defendant—damages reasonably contemplated would be the amount of injury which would ordinarily follow from a breach of contract under these special circumstances so known and communicated.

The *Victoria Laundry v. Newman* case, in considering the *Hadley v. Baxendale* rules, made it clear that damages for breach of contract should be measured by what was reasonably foreseeable as liable to result from the breach. That in turn would depend on the knowledge possessed by the parties or at all events, by the party who later commits the breach. Knowledge could be either imputed or actual. Imputed knowledge is sufficient to bring into play the first rule; actual knowledge is required for the second.

Reasonable foreseeability is the test under both rules. Indeed it is not always easy to make a rigid division between the two rules, and one writer comments that "the modern restatement of the rule as a totality is a salutary trend": *vide Mayne & McGregor on Damages*, 12th ed., p. 127.

It seems to me that whether we say there is one rule or two, or one rule with two branches, the test of reasonable foreseeability in either case operates here in favour of the plaintiff. For if imputed knowledge under the first rule is sufficient, it is not unrealistic to ascribe to the defendant an awareness that his breach of contract in selling this defective equipment to the plaintiff would in the ordinary course of events result in damages in the form of loss of profits as here sustained. If, on the other hand, actual knowledge of special circumstances attaching to the contract is required, the evidence on the record shows that the defendant had such knowledge.

I would accordingly agree with the learned trial Judge that the defendant is liable as claimed. The amount of the damages had been agreed to, subject to liability being established.

I would therefore dismiss the appeal and affirm the judgment of the Court below, with costs.

MILLER C.J.M. [dissenting] . . . [Having reviewed the evidence] I am of the opinion that the "foreseeability" inferred by the learned trial judge is not supported by the evidence, and that indeed on the evidence it is not supportable in law.

With respect, I feel it is very doubtful that this second-hand machinery should be saddled with a claim for damages for loss of profits unless it was clearly indicated to defendant at the time the equipment was purchased exactly what kind of contract was being entered into by plaintiff, the type of work that was to be done and the magnitude of the operation. All the evidence in this case discloses is that plaintiff wanted the equipment because he had a contract. It might have been a contract of a very minor nature so far as the evidence is concerned; it might have been a contract involving $100 or one involving $100,000; or a contract that would take a week or a month, or two years. In other words, it is doubtful whether the evidence discloses that sufficient information was given defendant to indicate the responsibilities to be assumed by this second-hand equipment. . . .

Counsel for plaintiff argued before us that these damages for loss of profit naturally flow from breach of contract by defendant and therefore come under the first rule in the *Baxendale* case; that these would be in the same category as damages for the repair costs of the defective parts. I am unable to accept this argument. I do not think that damages for loss of profit naturally flow from the defective character of the equipment or that they could have been reasonably foreseen or anticipated by defendant, because, as I have said above, defendant was not given sufficient information regarding the actual contract in which plaintiff was interested to permit it to determine the scope of its liability if the machine did not work satisfactorily. Defendant was not given an opportunity, by full disclosure or communication, to be put in the position where it could reasonably have anticipated damages for loss of profit by plaintiff on this particular contract and had no opportunity to contract itself out of liability if unwilling to be subjected to damages of unascertained magnitude. That being so, I would not allow the judgment against defendant for loss of profits of $1,650 to stand. The damages, $351.14, allowed to plaintiff for the balance of the repair costs is proper because they flow naturally from the breach of contract disclosed in the evidence.

I would therefore allow the appeal . . .

[Guy J.A. concurred with Miller C.J.M., Monnin and Schultz JJ.A. concurred with Freedman J.A.]

NOTE AND QUESTIONS

1. If the defendant knew that the plaintiff intended to put the attachment on a machine which was to be used in a profit-making venture, can the defendant raise the objection that the plaintiff would have made profits at a higher level than the defendant could have anticipated?

2. If your answer to Question 1 is in the negative, why was the plaintiff in *Victoria Laundry* unable to recover for loss of profit on the "highly lucrative dyeing contracts" when it was able to recover its ordinary loss of profits?

3. Is there justification for the concern of Miller C.J.M. that the seller of a used tractor part worth $1,000 should not "be saddled with a claim for damages for loss of profit"? Should courts be concerned with "the extent of the promisor's information and the proportionality between the risk

he is being asked to undertake and the benefit expected"? See Swinton, "Foreseeability: Where Should The Award Of Contract Damages Cease?" in Reiter and Swan (eds.), *Studies in Contract Law* (1980), at 76.

4. Contrast with the *Scyrup* decision the view of the Manitoba Court of Appeal in *Munroe Equip. Sales Ltd. v. Can. Forest Prod. Ltd.* (1961), 29 D.L.R. (2d) 730, in which C.F.P. sought to recover profits that were lost following the breakdown of a second-hand tractor which it leased from Munroe. C.F.P. obtained the tractor to clear roads in order to permit the removal of timber and sought damages when it was unable to remove the timber as planned. The claim for damages included an allowance for the shrinkage of wood that was left behind. Miller C.J.M., for the majority, found that the failure to remove the timber was not a natural consequence of the lessor's breach and that the lessor could not be taken to have virtually ensured the removal of the timber. Are there rational grounds for distinguishing this decision from *Scyrup*? See Swinton, *supra*, at 75-76. It is also noteworthy that between the two judgments, there had been one change in the composition of the Manitoba Court of Appeal and that change represented the critical swing "vote".

5. In *Victoria Laundry*, the Court of Appeal mentioned that the courts have been slow to allow loss of profit as an item of damage in actions against carriers. However, the obvious flexibility of the principles of *Hadley v. Baxendale* allows courts to impose liability when it seems appropriate, even where breaches of contract by carriers result in a loss of profit. For example, in *Cornwall Gravel Co. v. Purolator Courier Ltd.* (1978), 83 D.L.R. (3d) 267 (Ont. H.C.), a courier service picked up a tender from Cornwall Gravel at 6 p.m. on 1st October 1973. The driver who received the envelope from Cornwall Gravel was aware that it contained a tender and assured employees of Cornwall Gravel that it would be delivered in Toronto prior to noon on the following day. In fact, the tender was not delivered until 3:17 p.m. on the following day. As tenders closed at 3 p.m., the tender of Cornwall Gravel was rejected. It was admitted that, if the tender had been delivered in time, Cornwall Gravel would have been awarded the contract and made a profit on of $70,000. In a judgment later affirmed by the Court of Appeal at (1979), 115 D.L.R. (3d) 511, and by the Supreme Court of Canada at [1980] 2 S.C.R. 118, the loss of profit by Cornwall Gravel was found to be within the reasonable contemplation of the courier service.

KOUFOS v. CZARNIKOW (C.) (THE HERON II)

[1969] 1 A.C. 350, [1967] 3 All E.R. 686 (H.L.)

LORD REID My Lords, by charterparty of October 15, 1960, the respondents chartered the appellant's vessel, *Heron II*, to proceed from Constanza, there to load a cargo of 3,000 tons of sugar; and to carry it to Basrah, or, in the charterer's option, to Jeddah. The vessel left Constanza on November 1, 1960. The option was not exercised and the vessel arrived at Basrah on December 2, 1960. The umpire has found that "a reasonably accurate prediction of the length of the voyage was twenty days." But the vessel had in breach of contract made deviations which caused a delay of nine days.

It was the intention of the respondents to sell the sugar "promptly after arrival at Basrah and after inspection by merchants." The appellant did not know this, but he was aware of the fact that there was a market for sugar at Basrah. The sugar was in fact sold at Basrah in lots between December 12 and 22, 1960, but shortly before that time the market price had fallen, partly by reason of the arrival of another cargo of sugar. It was found by the umpire that if there had not been this delay of nine days the sugar would have fetched £32 10s. 0d. per ton. The actual price realised was only £31 2s. 9d. per ton. The respondents claim that they are entitled to recover the difference as damage for breach of contract. The appellant admits that he is liable to pay interest for nine days on the value of the sugar and certain minor expenses but denies that fall in market value can be taken into account in assessing damages in this case. . . .

[McNair J. at trial had held in favour of the appellant. His decision was reversed by a majority of the Court of Appeal.]

It may be well first to set out the knowledge and intention of the parties at the time of making the contract so far as relevant or argued to be relevant. The charterers intended to sell the sugar in the market at Basrah on arrival of the vessel. They could have changed their mind and exercised their option to have the sugar delivered at Jeddah but they did not do so. There is no finding that they had in mind any particular date as the likely date of arrival at Basrah or that they had any knowledge or expectation that in late November or December there would be a rising or a falling market. The shipowner was given no information about these matters by the charterers. He did not know what the charterers intended to do with the sugar. But he knew there was a market in sugar at Basrah, and it appears to me that, if he had thought about the matter, he must have realized that at least it was not unlikely that the sugar would be sold in the market at market price on arrival. And he must be held to have known that in any ordinary market prices are apt to fluctuate from day to day: but he had no reason to suppose it more probable that during the relevant period such fluctuation would be downwards rather than upwards—it was an even chance that the fluctuation would be downwards.

So the question for decision is whether a plaintiff can recover as damages for breach of contract a loss of a kind which the defendant, when he made the contract, ought to have realised was not unlikely to result from a breach of contract causing delay in delivery. I use the words "not unlikely" as denoting a degree of probability considerably less than an even chance but nevertheless not very unusual and easily foreseeable.

For over a century everyone has agreed that remoteness of damage in contract must be determined by applying the rule (or rules) [in *Hadley v. Baxendale*.]. . . .

[Lord Reid then considered the judgment in *Hadley v. Baxendale*. He noted that Alderson B., having found that the loss of profit was caused by the delay, continued:]

> But it is obvious that, in the great multitude of cases of millers sending off broken shafts to third persons by a carrier under ordinary circumstances, such consequences would not, in all probability, have occurred.

Alderson B. clearly did not and could not mean that it was not reasonably foreseeable that delay might stop the resumption of work in the mill. He merely said that in the great multitude—which I take to mean the great majority—of cases this would not happen. He was not distinguishing between results which were foreseeable or unforeseeable, but between results which were likely because they would happen in the great majority of cases, and results which were unlikely because they would only happen in a small minority of cases. He continued [p. 151]:

> It follows, therefore, that the loss of profits here cannot reasonably be considered such a consequence of the breach of contract as could have been fairly and reasonably contemplated by both the parties when they made this contract.

He clearly meant that a result which will happen in the great majority of cases should fairly and reasonably be regarded as having been in the contemplation of the parties, but that a result which, though foreseeable as a substantial possibility, would only happen in a small minority of cases should not be regarded as having been in their contemplation. He was referring to such a result when he continued:

> For such loss would neither have flowed naturally from the breach of this contract in the great multitude of such cases occurring under ordinary circumstances, nor were the special circumstances, which perhaps, would have made it a reasonable and natural consequence of such breach of contract, communicated to or known by the defendants.

I have dealt with the latter part of the judgment before coming to the well known rule because the court were there applying the rule and the language which was used in the latter part appears to me to throw considerable light on the meaning which they must have attached to the rather vague expressions used in the rule itself. The rule is that the damages "should be such as may fairly and reasonably be considered either arising naturally, i.e., according to the usual course of things, from such breach of contract itself, or such as may reasonably be supposed to have been in the contemplation of both parties, at the time they made the contract, as the probable result of the breach of it."

I do not think that it was intended that there were to be two rules or that two different standards or tests were to be applied. The last two passages which I quoted from the end of the judgment applied to the facts before the court which did not include any special circumstances communicated to the defendants; and the line of reasoning there is that because in the great majority of cases loss of profit would not in all probability have occurred, it followed that this could not reasonably be considered as having been fairly and reasonably contemplated by both the parties, for it would not have flowed naturally from the breach in the great majority of cases.

I am satisfied that the court did not intend that every type of damage which was reasonably foreseeable by the parties when the contract was made should either be considered as arising naturally, i.e., in the usual course of things, or be supposed to have been in the contemplation of the parties. Indeed the decision makes it clear that a type of damage which was plainly foreseeable as a real possibility but which would only occur in a small minority of cases cannot be regarded as arising in the usual course of things or be supposed to have been in contemplation of the parties: the parties are not supposed to contemplate as grounds for the recovery of damage any type of loss or damage which on the knowledge available to the defendant would appear to him as only likely to occur in a small minority of cases.

In cases like *Hadley v. Baxendale* or the present case it is not enough that in fact the plaintiff's loss was directly caused by the defendant's breach of contract. It clearly was so caused in both. The crucial question is whether, on the information available to the defendant when the contract was made, he should, or the reasonable man in his position would, have realised that such loss was sufficiently likely to result from the breach of contract to make it proper to hold that the loss flowed naturally from the breach or that loss of that kind should have been within his contemplation.

The modern rule of tort is quite different and it imposes a much wider liability. The defendant will be liable for any type of damage which is reasonably foreseeable as liable to happen even in the most unusual case, unless the risk is so small that a reasonable man would in the whole circumstances feel justified in neglecting it. And there is good reason for the difference. In contract, if one party wishes to protect himself against a risk which to the other party would appear unusual, he can direct the other party's attention to it before the contract is made, and I need not stop to consider in what circumstances the other party will then be held to have accepted responsibility in that event. But in tort there is no opportunity for the injured party to protect himself in that way, and the tortfeasor cannot reasonably complain if he has to pay for some very unusual but nevertheless foreseeable damage which results from his wrongdoing. I have no doubt that today a tortfeasor would be held liable for a type of damage as unlikely as was the stoppage of Hadley's Mill for lack of a crankshaft: to anyone with the knowledge the carrier had that may have seemed unlikely but the chance of it happening would have been seen to be far from negligible. But it does not at all follow that *Hadley v. Baxendale* would today be differently decided. . . .

But then it has been said that the liability of defendants has been further extended by *Victoria Laundry (Windsor) Ltd. v. Newman Industries Ltd.* I do not think so. . . .

[Lord Reid here took issue with some of the language used by Asquith L.J. in *Victoria Laundry* such as "liable to result", "on the cards", "a real danger", and "a serious possibility". He regarded these as expressions which could result in an inappropriate extension of liability for damages for breach of contract. He also denigrated the use of "reasonably foreseeable as likely to result from the breach of contract" as confusing exposure to damages for breach of contract with damages in tort.]

It appears to me that, without relying in any way on the *Victoria Laundry* case, and taking the principle that had already been established, the loss of profit claimed in this case was not too remote to be recoverable as damages. . . .

I would dismiss the appeal.

[Lords Morris, Hodson, Pearce and Upjohn delivered separate judgments dismissing the appeal.]

NOTE and QUESTIONS

1. The other Law Lords were rather less critical of aspects of *Victoria Laundry*, feeling in most cases that it had not modified the principle of *Hadley v. Baxendale*. Lords Morris and Hodson both felt that the phrase "liable to result" expressed the degree of probability required by principles of remoteness in contracts. Lords Upjohn and Pearce felt that the test of remoteness was well described if the damage could be foreseen as a "serious possibility" or a "real danger".

2. In *Asamera Oil Corp. v. Sea Oil & General Corp.* (1978), [1979] 1 S.C.R. 633 at 673, Estey J. commented:

> We therefore approach the matter of the proper appraisal of the damages assessable in the peculiar circumstances of this case on the following basis: that the same principles of remoteness will apply to the claims made whether they sound in tort or contract subject only

to special knowledge, understanding or relationship of the contracting parties or to any terms express or implied of the contractual arrangement relating to damages recoverable on breach.

Do Lord Reid's objections to equating the tests of remoteness in contract and tort have any substance or are they essentially semantic? See also *H. Parsons (Livestock) v. Uttley Ingham & Co.*, [1978] 1 All E.R. 525 (C.A.), and the discussion in Swinton, *supra*, at 87-89, and in Smith, *Liability in Negligence* (1984), at 163-70.

3. Would your view as to the liability of the defendant be affected if it became apparent during the voyage that the market in sugar at Basra was collapsing and, despite that, the captain made no attempt to keep to the original schedule for the voyage? Are there circumstances where the courts should deviate from foreseeability at the time of the contract as the touchstone for the assessment of whether damages are too remote to be recoverable? Recollect that, in her partially dissenting judgment in *Vorvis*, Wilson J., in a relational contract setting, refused to deviate from the general rule in considering whether any mental distress suffered by the plaintiff was too remote to be recoverable. The test was what the employer could have foreseen at the date of entry into the contract, not what was reasonably foreseeable at the date of breach as likely to be the plaintiff's reaction to a harsh and humiliating dismissal. However, in the context of a case in which issues were raised as to the breach by a Bank of a long-standing line of credit arrangement, Adams J. (in what was admittedly *obiter dicta*) stated that, if necessary, he would have probably dealt with the issue of foreseeability for the purposes of breach of contract by reference to the knowledge of the Bank at the date of breach as opposed to its knowledge at the time the line of credit was created initially: *Murano v. Bank of Montreal* (1995), 20 B.L.R. (2d) 61 (Ont. Gen. Div. [Commercial List]). (On appeal, this issue was not reached by the Ontario Court of Appeal: (1998), 163 D.L.R. (4th) 21 (Ont. C.A.)).

4. In *Hamilton v. Open Window Bakery Ltd.* (2003), 2004 SCC 9, Arbour J. (for the court) held that, in cases where a contract might be performed in several ways (such as by the delivery of varying quantities of the goods contracted for or at different dates), the courts should measure damages by reference to the mode which was least profitable to the plaintiff and least burdensome to the defendant. It was not appropriate to deal with the issue by reference to the manner in which it was likely that the defendant would have performed but for the breach. This inappropriately injected tort concepts into a breach of contract action. Do you agree? Does this bring Sopinka J.'s statement in *Asamera* into question?

(c) MITIGATION

ASAMERA OIL CORP. v. SEA OIL & GENERAL CORP.

[1979] 1 S.C.R. 633, [1978] 6 W.W.R. 301, 5 B.L.R. 225, 23 N.R. 181, 12 A.R. 271, 89 D.L.R. (3d) 1

Baud Corporation sought the return of 125,000 shares in Asamera from Brook, the president of Asamera. The shares had been lent to Brook in 1957 under an agreement, the final terms of which required their return to Baud by December 1960. In addition to the claim for the return of the shares, Baud claimed damages in the sum of $6 million.

The actual shares lent to Brook had been sold in 1958.

In 1960, Brook was made subject to an injunction restraining him from selling 125,000 shares in Asamera, though Brook interpreted that as meaning that he must at all times remain in possession of at least 125,000 shares, rather than the identical shares which he had received from Baud.

Baud's action for specific performance of the agreement to return the shares was dismissed, on the grounds that damages were an adequate remedy. The value of the shares fluctuated during the relevant period from 29 cents (1960) to $4.30 (mid-1967), $7.25 (end 1967), $46.50 (1969), and to $22 in 1971.

ESTEY J. [delivering the judgment of the court] . . . The learned trial Judge dismissed Baud's claim in detinue and conversion and assessed damages on the basis that Brook's failure to deliver constituted a breach of contract. The action in substance is a simple case of breach of contract to return 125,000 Asamera shares and, in my view, the claims made and the issues arising in this action should be disposed of on that basis. That being so, we come to the only real issue in this appeal, namely, to what recovery is the appellant Baud in these circumstances entitled and . . . the quantum of damages. . . .

In cases dealing with the measure of damages for non-delivery of goods under contracts for sale, the application over the years of the [well-established principles of common law] has given the law some certainty, and it is now accepted that damages will be recoverable in an amount representing what the purchaser would have had to pay for the goods in the market, less the contract price, at the time of the breach. This rule . . . may be seen as a combination of two principles. The first, as stated earlier, is the right of the plaintiff to recover all of his losses which are reasonably contemplated by the parties as liable to result from the breach. The second is the responsibility imposed on a party who has suffered from a breach of contract to take all reasonable steps to avoid losses flowing from the breach. This responsibility to mitigate was explained by Laskin, C.J.C., in *Red Deer College v. Michaels* (1975), 57 D.L.R. (3d) 386 at 390 (S.C.C.):

> It is of course, for a wronged plaintiff to prove his damages, and there is therefore a burden upon him to establish on a balance of probabilities what his loss is. The parameters of loss are governed by legal principle. The primary rule in breach of contract cases, that a wronged plaintiff is entitled to be put in as good a position as he would have been in if there had been proper performance by the defendant, is subject to the qualification that the defendant cannot be called upon to pay for avoidable losses which would result in an increase in the quantum of damages payable to the plaintiff. The reference in the case law to a "duty" to mitigate should be understood in this sense.

In short, a wronged plaintiff is entitled to recover damages for the losses he has suffered but the extent of those losses may depend on whether he has taken reasonable steps to avoid their unreasonable accumulation.

and later in the judgment at pp. 390-1:

> If it is the defendant's position that the plaintiff could reasonably have avoided some part of the loss claimed, it is for the defendant to carry the burden of that issue, subject to the defendant being content to allow the matter to be disposed of on the trial Judge's assessment of the plaintiff's evidence on avoidable consequences.

Thus, if one were to adopt, without reservation, in the settlement of Baud's damage claims, the rules governing recovery for non-delivery of goods in sales contracts, the *prima facie* measure of damages in the case at bar would be the value of the shares on the date of breach, that is, December 31, 1960. The learned trial Judge found the market price on December 31, 1960 to be 29¢ per share. The value of the 125,000 shares wrongfully retained by Brook, and thus the loss to Baud by reason of its not being in possession of those shares, on that date therefore was $36,250 assuming, for the purposes of discussion only, the market price to be constant throughout the purchase or sale of such a number of shares. To this must be added other expenses which could reasonably be said to be incidental to steps taken to mitigate the damages flowing from the breach. The most obvious of these are brokerage and commission fees which would have been incurred by Baud in purchasing replacement shares. Of greater importance is the inevitable upward pressure the purchase on the open market of such a large number of Asamera shares would exert on the market price. The impact of forced sales or purchases of shares on market prices has been the subject of judicial comment in the past (*vide Crown Reserve Consl. Mines Ltd. v. Mackay*, [1941] 3 D.L.R. 461 (Ont. C.A.)) and must be taken into account in determining the weight to be accorded to mitigation factors in an assessment of damages in circumstances such as exist here. Unhappily, Baud has led no evidence on this problem and one is left to take note of the presence of this factor without being able precisely to quantify it. This point requires more detailed discussion at a later stage.

Assuming for the moment that the breach of contract occurred on December 31, 1960, and that the appellant's right to damages came into being at that time and assuming that it should then have acted to forestall the accumulation of avoidable losses, what action did the law then require of the appellant by way of mitigation of damages? A plaintiff need not take all possible steps to reduce his loss and, accordingly, it is necessary to examine some of the special circumstances here present. The appellant argues that there exist in this case clear circumstances which render the duty to purchase 125,000 Asamera shares an unreasonable one. The first of these has its foundations in the established principle that a plaintiff need not put his money to an unreasonable risk including a risk not present in the initial transaction in endeavouring to mitigate his losses. This principle was demonstrated in *Lesters Leather & Skin Co. v. Home & Overseas Brokers* (1948), 64 T.L.R. 569 (C.A.), and in *Jewelowski v. Propp*, [1944] 1 K.B. 510, as well as in *Pilkington v. Wood*, [1953] Ch. 770. The appellant here was placed in the unusual position where mitigative action would require that it purchase as replacement property, shares of a company engaged in a speculative undertaking under the effective control and under the promotional management of a person in breach of contract, the respondent, Brook, who thereafter was in an adversarial position in relation to the appellant.

On the evidence adduced at trial, the market value of shares in Asamera had fallen from $3 shortly before the dates on which Baud first loaned the two blocs of shares to Brook, to between $1.62 and $1.87 in November, 1958, and to 29¢ per share on December 31, 1960. Evidence of share values after that date indicates only that there was a relatively small recovery in value to about $1.21 a share by March, 1965, when the fortunes of the company improved. The appellant argues that it could not have been expected in December, 1960, to purchase shares in mitigation of its losses where the value of these shares had fallen as rapidly as is indicated in the evidence.

A more important circumstance which might render unreasonable any requirement that Baud purchase shares in the market was the existence of the aforementioned injunction issued on July 27, 1960, restraining the respondent from selling 125,000 Asamera shares. The appellant contends that it is inconceivable that the law should require a party, who has suffered a misappropriation of his property and who has requested and been afforded the considerable protection of an injunction granted by a Court of Equity, to ignore the force and effect of that injunction and to go out and acquire the same number of shares as Brook was required to retain, however the terms of the injunction be construed.

Even if one accepts that submission, it must be acknowledged that the right of Baud to rely on the injunction as a shield against an obligation to minimize its losses is not absolute. In the first place, Baud was informed by Brook in his pleadings of July 6, 1967, that shares which were subject to the injunction had been sold. As of that date the shares were selling at $4.30 to $4.35 and had been rising in value since April, 1965, and at a median price of $4.33 would have cost Baud $541,250. Accordingly, at least by July, 1967, it could not be said that Baud would reasonably be discouraged from replacing the 125,000 shares in the open market because of the low price of an inactive company, nor could it be said that thereafter it could reasonably refrain from prosecuting its claim for damages because of the order enjoining the disposition of the shares by Brook. It remains the case, however, that the market value for such speculative shares as those of an oil-exploration company was subject to wide price fluctuations sometimes inspired by management which itself held, as did Brook, a considerable number of shares.

The learned trial Judge referred to a number of English authorities in support of the proposition that in the case of a loan of shares a plaintiff need not mitigate his losses either by purchasing shares on the market or even by bringing a suit for recovery of damages within a reasonable time. The result under these authorities where the market value of the shares has risen or fallen between breach and trial, has been an award of damages representing the value of the shares at the time of the breach or of the trial at the election of the plaintiff. . . . These authorities raise no responsibility in the plaintiff to mitigate his losses: *Shepherd v. Johnson* (1802), 2 East 211, *per* Grose, J., at p. 211. The application of the principle developed in these early cases would produce damages calculated at the end of the trial or perhaps at the highest point prior to that date. The trial proceeded intermittently from June, 1969, to December, 1971, and final judgment was pronounced in May, 1972. The latter price would be about $21 a share and the highest price attained was about $46.50 per share, allowing recovery of approximately $2,625,000 and $5,812,500 respectively.

A proper analysis of these cases is made difficult by reason of their antiquity, and after serious consideration, I have concluded that they ought not to be followed by this Court. In the first place, they were decided long before modern principles of contractual remedies had been developed. Secondly, they are not in accord with recent decisions of this Court. Thirdly, they ignore the all-important and overriding considerations which have led to the judicial recognition of the desirability and indeed the necessity that a plaintiff mitigate his losses arising on a breach of contract. There is a fourth consideration. This old principle produces an arbitrary, albeit a readily ascertainable result because it lacks the flexibility needed to take into account the infinite range of possible circumstances in which the parties may find themselves at the time of the breach and before a trial can in practice take place. The pace of the market place and the complexities of business have changed radically since this rule or principle was developed in the early 19th century. . . .

The cases which establish the exceedingly technical rules relating to recovery of damages for the non-return of shares turn on the theory that only where a breach of contract gives rise to an asset in the hands of the plaintiff will the law require him to mitigate his losses by employing that asset in a reasonable manner. Thus if an employer wrongfully dismisses an employee the breach results in the employee obtaining an asset, an ability to work for another employer, or at least the opportunity to offer his services to that end, which he did not enjoy prior to the dismissal. This is no more than a philosophical explanation of the simple test of fairness and reasonableness in establishing the presence and extent of the burden to mitigate in varying circumstances.

This approach was adopted by Rand, J., in *Karas v. Rowlett*, [1944] S.C.R. 1 at 8, where he said, in a case of fraud resulting in a loss of profits:

> . . . by the default or wrong there is released a capacity to work or to earn. That capacity becomes an asset in the hands of the injured party, and he is held to a reasonable employment of it in the course of events flowing from the breach.

An analogous situation arises in the breach of a contract for the sale of goods where on the failure of a supplier to deliver goods, the purchaser because he is relieved of the obligation to pay, has an asset (the financial resource represented by the sums previously committed to the purchase) of which he did not have the free use prior to the breach. This is not the situation of Baud, who might in mitigation of the damage suffered on the non-return of its shares of Asamera, be called upon to lay out substantial assets to replace the shares retained by Brook. Because there is no evidence of lack of funds for these purposes we need not be concerned with the relevance of the judgment in *Liesbosch, Dredger v. Edison S.S.* [1933] A.C. 449 (H.L.). There is of course no asset created by the breach of the contract to return shares and if that theory be the law and the creation of an asset be a necessary prerequisite of a duty to mitigate, no such duty arose in the case at hand.

It follows that a contrary result should arise where damages are recoverable for a breach of contract by a vendor on a *sale of shares*. There the breach would normally allow a buyer the use of his funds formerly committed to the purchase and consequently damages should be calculated on the basis that he ought to have taken steps to avoid his losses by the purchase of shares on the market at the time of the breach. This, in fact, appears to be the law at present . . .

A different consideration arises where the plaintiff-buyer has prepaid the contract price and has not received delivery. As in the case of non-return of shares, the breach does not give rise to any asset in the hands of the plaintiff since he has already parted with his funds, and on that basis some Courts have held that the injured party need not purchase like goods in the market . . . In *Peebles v. Pfeifer*, [1918] 2 W.W.R. 877 (Sask. K.B.), Bigelow, J., held that a purchaser of wheat who had paid for delivery was entitled to recover the market price of the wheat not at the time of breach when the price was 76¢ a bushel but at the time of trial when the price was $1.68. . . .

In *Hoefle v. Bongard & Co.*, [1945] S.C.R. 360, this Court had to contend with facts which bear a remarkable similarity to the facts in the case at bar. Rand, J., adopted the English test and denied a duty to mitigate after a breach involving the non-return of shares. . . .

The creation of an "asset" on a breach of contract cannot be an invariable prerequisite to the operation of the principle that a party injured by a breach of contract must respond in mitigation to avoid an unconscionable accumulation of losses. Nor should the absence of such an "asset" invariably exonerate a plaintiff from taking mitigative action. The presence or absence of such an "asset" is but one of many factors which bear on the task of determining in a particular case what is or is not reasonable on the part of the injured party in all the circumstances. The decisions which purport to allow recovery on the basis of the increased value of the *res* of the action between the date of breach and the end of trial have been denied authority by the learned editors of Halsbury's Laws of England, 3rd ed., vol. 34, p. 155. After noting the old cases, some of which are reviewed above, the editors conclude that "the measure [of damages] must vary accordingly to the facts" [footnote (*o*)].

In short, it would appear that the principles of mitigation in respect of contracts for the sale of goods generally may not be applied without reservation to the determination of the duty to mitigate arising in respect of contracts for the sale of shares and, in any case, differ fundamentally from the case of a breach of a contract for the return of shares. It is inappropriate in my view simply to extend the old principles applied in the detinue and conversion authorities to the non-return of shares with the result that a party whose property has not been returned to him could sit by and await an opportune moment to institute legal proceedings, all the while imposing on a defendant the substantial risk of market fluctuations between breach and trial which might very well drive him into bankruptcy. Damages which could have been avoided by the taking of reasonable steps in all the circumstances should not and, indeed, in the interests of commercial enter-prise, must not be thrown onto the shoulders of a defendant by an arbitrary although nearly universal rule for the recovery of damages on breach of the contract for redelivery of property.

We start of course with the fundamental principle of mitigation authorita-tively stated by Viscount Haldane, L.C., in *British Westinghouse Electric & Mfg. Co., Ltd. v. Underground Electric R. Co. of London, Ltd.*, [1912] A.C. 673 at p. 689:

> The fundamental basis is thus compensation for pecuniary loss naturally flowing from the breach; but this first principle is qualified by a second, which imposes on a plaintiff the duty of taking all reasonable steps to mitigate the loss consequent on the breach, and debars him from claiming any part of the damage which is due to his neglect to take such steps. In the words of James L.J. in *Dunkirk Colliery Co. v. Lever* (1898), 9 Ch. D. 20, at p. 25, "The person who has broken the contract is not to be exposed to additional cost by reason of the plaintiffs not doing what they ought to have done as reasonable men, and the plaintiffs not being under any obligation to do anything otherwise than in the ordinary course of business."

> As James L.J. indicates, this second principle does not impose on the plaintiff an obligation
> to take any step which a reasonable and prudent man would not ordinarily take in the course
> of his business. But when in the course of his business he has taken action arising out of the
> transaction, which action has diminished his loss, the effect in actual diminution of the loss he
> has suffered may be taken into account even though there was no duty on him to act.

.....

There may, as already discussed, be instances where mitigation will not require a plaintiff to incur the significant risk and expense of purchasing replacement property, but in any case the plaintiff must crystallize his claim either by replacement acquisition or in some circumstances by prompt litigation expeditiously prosecuted which will enable the Court to establish the damage with reference to the mitigative measures imposed by law. The failure of the appellant either to mitigate or litigate promptly makes difficult the task of applying these principles to the circumstances of this case.

In the light of the enormous hardships sometimes occasioned by the application of the old doctrine of damage assessment, and in view of the massive distortion which may follow when the principles of mitigation are, as in the older authorities, made inapplicable to non-delivery of shares, I have come to the conclusion that the authorities cited from the early 1800's, principally from the Courts of England, which in effect allow recovery of "avoidable losses" ought not to be followed. Rather the lead furnished by *R. v. Arnold* [[1971] S.C.R. 209] should be taken. Subject always to the precise circumstances of each case, this will impose on the injured party the obligation to purchase like shares in the market on the date of breach (or knowledge thereof in the plaintiff) or, more frequently, within a period thereafter which is reasonable in all the circumstances. The implementation of this principle must take cognizance of the realities of market operations, including the nature of the shares in question, the strength of the market when called upon to digest large orders to buy or sell, the number of shares qualified for public trading, the recent volatility of the price, the recent volume of trading, the general state of the market at the time, the susceptibility of the price of the shares to the current operation of the corporation and similar considerations. . . .

It is contended by the appellant, Baud, however, that the peculiar circumstances of this case rendered the purchase of highly speculative shares in a company controlled by its adversary unreasonable in all of the circumstances, particularly the injunction obtained by the appellant restraining the sale of 125,000 Asamera shares held by Brook. None the less, it remains the case that at least some of the losses claimed by the appellant could have been avoided by the taking of other reasonable steps. The most obvious of these would have been to move with reasonable speed to institute and proceed with legal action in an effort to recover the shares and, if that was not possible, then to recover damages. It is, of course, exceedingly difficult to establish in this Court the precise point in time at which the trial in this action would have been held had the appellant moved with reasonable dispatch. The case has slowly wended its way thorough interlocutory stages and eventually reached trial which in turn was spread over one and one-half years. The litigation has been in the Courts now some 18 years having commenced in July, 1960.

There are numerous explanations given by the appellant and indeed not seriously disputed in this Court by the respondent for these protracted proceedings. At one stage, for example, Brook asked Baud some time prior to 1966 to "abstain from following up the lawsuit". Baud, on the other hand, expressed no desire for very practical reasons either to press its suit until the end of 1966, when Asamera finally managed to produce its first oil in Sumatra "and the shares began to slowly get up in value" and, as the appellant put it, "we had to renew the case against him". In my view the law required more of Baud. It placed upon Baud the duty in the sense referred to in *Red Deer College v. Michaels* (1975), 57 D.L.R. (3d) 386, to mitigate its losses by acquiring shares in a company known by Baud to be far from financially sound. It might therefore be said that Baud would have hung back from any action (either the purchase of shares or the pressing of its claims in Court) until Asamera struck oil, whether or not Brook had requested it to do so. . . .

The appellant bases its contention that it has no obligation to purchase shares in the market in part on the ground that it ought to be allowed to seek specific performance of the contract to return the shares, and while relying on an injunction restraining their disposition it need not have any concern with losses occasioned by its inaction. Counsel for the appellant did not refer this Court to any cases in which the principle of mitigation has interacted and conflicted with recovery by way of specific performance, and such authority as I have been able to discover supports the common sense view that the principle of mitigation should, unless there is a substantial and legitimate interest represented by specific performance, prevail in such a case. . . .

On principle it is clear that a plaintiff may not merely by instituting proceedings in which a request is made for specific performance and/or damages, thereby shield himself and block the Court from taking into account the accumulation of losses which the plaintiff by acting with reasonable promptness in processing his claim could have avoided. Similarly, the bare institution of judicial process in circumstances where a reasonable response by the injured plaintiff would include mitigative replacement of property, will not entitle the plaintiff to the relief which would be achieved by such replacement purchase and prompt prosecution of the claim. Before a plaintiff can rely on a claim to specific performance so as to insulate himself from the consequences of failing to procure alternate property in mitigation of his losses, some fair, real and substantial justification for his claim to performance must be found. Otherwise its effect will be to cast upon the defendant all the risk of aggravated loss by reason of delay in bringing the issue to trial. The appellant in this case contends that it ought to be allowed to rely on its claim for specific performance and the injunction issued in support of it, and thus recover avoidable losses. After serious consideration, I have concluded that this argument must fail . . .

Having regard to the complex issues raised in all three actions (and the period devoted to this litigation must take into account more than the simple action for the recovery of shares loaned to Brook) and taking into account the other circumstances mentioned, it would be unreasonable to hold the appellant to any timetable which contemplated the trial of these many issues prior to the end of 1966 or early 1967. If litigation may represent an alternative to the investment by a plaintiff of substantial funds to avoid the accumulation of losses, the Courts cannot apply in the computation of damages a principle recognizing some relevance of the fluctuating value of the *res* of the contract between breach and trial and not at the same time maintain a strict surveillance on the assiduity of a plaintiff in bringing his claim to judgment.

[Accordingly, given the time necessary to organize finances and to plan carefully the acquisition of 125,000 shares, damages were fixed on the basis of an adjusted median price of Asamera shares from late 1966 to mid-1967. The share price thus selected was $6.50 and it gave rise to a damage award of $812,500.]

NOTE and QUESTIONS

1. What notions underlie the so-called "duty to mitigate" damages?

2. Assume that in the *Asamera* case the plaintiff had mitigated by buying shares at $6.50 in 1967. However, shares in the company plummet and are worth only 5¢ each by the time of the trial. What damages should the plaintiff receive?

3. What would have been the result in the *Asamera* case if in 1967 the plaintiff had been entirely unable to mitigate by buying shares on the market because he was then impoverished? See Reiter and Sharpe, "*Wroth v. Tyler*: Must Equity Remedy Contract Damages?" (1979), 3 Can. Bus. L.J. 146 at 151-54; *Freedhoff v. Pomalift Indust. Ltd.* (1971), 19 D.L.R. (3d) 153 (Ont. C.A.); *Burns v. M.A.N. Automotive (Aust.) Pty. Ltd.* (1986), 161 C.L.R. 653 (Aust. H.C.).

4. For an exhaustive analysis of the *Asamera* case, see Waddams, "Damages for Failure to Return Shares" (1979), 3 Can. Bus. L.J. 398.

5. Client agreed to purchase a number of parcels of land from Vendor under an interim agreement. Client retained Solicitor to represent his interest in the sale. Owing to Solicitor's carelessness in searching the title to the parcels of land and checking the searches against the property described in the interim agreement, Client failed to obtain all the land to which he was entitled under the terms of the agreement.

Accordingly, Client sued Solicitor for failing to use reasonable care in the transaction. Solicitor, however, while acknowledging his own carelessness, feels that the real villain of the piece is Vendor, who failed to convey good title in accordance with her contractual obligation.

    (a) How might Solicitor frame an argument in contract to give effect to this objection? See *Pilkington v. Wood*, [1953] Ch. 770.

    (b) How might Solicitor's argument be changed by the availability of tort actions in contractual settings? See *Silliman Const. (Alta.) Ltd. v. Johnson, Ming & Co.* (1984), 31 Alta. L.R. (2d) 284 (C.A.).

6. Although a dismissed employee is under an obligation to mitigate, would it make any difference if the employee's salary were "guaranteed" for the term of the agreement? See *Neilson v. Vancouver Hockey Club Ltd.* (1986), 29 D.L.R. (4th) 551 (B.C. S.C.) (holding the plaintiff entitled to his salary for the balance of the term), reversed (1988), 51 D.L.R. (4th) 40 (B.C. C.A.) (insisting that there was a duty to mitigate even where there was a guaranteed salary).

WHITE AND CARTER (COUNCILS) LTD. v. McGREGOR
[1962] A.C. 413, [1961] 3 All E.R. 1178 (H.L.)

LORD REID My Lords, the pursuers [plaintiffs] supply to local authorities litter bins which are placed in the streets. They are allowed to attach to these receptacles plates carrying advertisements, and they make their profit from payments made to them by the advertisers. The defender carried on a garage in Clydebank and in 1954 he made an agreement with the pursuers under which they displayed advertisements of his business on a number of these bins. In June, 1957, his sales manager made a further contract with the pursuers for the display of these advertisements for a further period of three years. The sales manager had been given no specific authority to make this contract and when the defender heard of it later on the same day he at once wrote to the pursuers to cancel the contract. The pursuers refused to accept this cancellation. They prepared the necessary plates for attachment to the bins and exhibited them on the bins from November 2, 1957, onwards.

The defender refused to pay any sums due under the contract and the pursuers raised the present action in the Sheriff Court craving payment of £196 4s. the full sum due under the contract for the period of three years. . . .

[The pursuers' claim was dismissed at trial and on appeal.]

The case for the defender (now the respondent) is that, as he repudiated the contract before anything had been done under it, the appellants were not entitled to go on and carry out the contract and sue for the contract price: he maintains that in the circumstances the appellants' only remedy was damages, and that, as they do not sue for damages, this action was rightly dismissed.

The contract was for the display of advertisements for a period of 156 weeks from the date when the display began. This date was not specified but admittedly the display began on November 2, 1957, which seems to have been the date when the former contract came to an end. The payment stipulated was 2s. per week per plate together with 5s. per annum per plate both payable annually in advance, the first payment being due seven days after the first display. The reason why the appellants sued for the whole sum due for the three years is to be found in clause 8 of the conditions: "In the event of an instalment or part thereof being due for payment, and remaining unpaid for a period of four weeks or in the event of the advertiser being in any way in breach of this contract then the whole amount due for the 156 weeks or such part of the said 156 weeks as the advertiser shall not yet have paid shall immediately become due and payable."

A question was debated whether this clause provides a penalty or liquidated damages, but on the view which I take of the case it need not be pursued. The clause merely provides for acceleration of payment of the stipulated price if the advertiser fails to pay an instalment timeously. As the respondent maintained that he was not bound by the contract he did not pay the first instalment within the time allowed. Accordingly, if the appellants were entitled to carry out their part of the contract notwithstanding the respondent's repudiation, it was hardly disputed that this clause entitled them to sue immediately for the whole price and not merely the first instalment.

The general rule cannot be in doubt. It was settled in Scotland at least as early as 1848 and it has been authoritatively stated time and again in both Scotland and England. If one party to a contract repudiates it in the sense of making it clear to the other party that he refuses or will refuse to carry out his part of the contract, the other party, the innocent party, has an option. He may accept that repudiation and sue for damages for breach of contract, whether or not the time for performance has come; or he may if he chooses disregard or refuse to accept it and then the contract remains in full effect. . . .

I need not refer to the numerous authorities. They are not disputed by the respondent but he points out that in all of them the party who refused to accept the repudiation had no active duties under the contract. The innocent party's option is generally said to be to *wait* until the date of performance and then to claim damages estimated as at that date. There is no case in which it is said that he may, in face of the repudiation, go on and incur useless expense in performing the contract and then claim the contract price. The option, it is argued, is merely as to the date as at which damages are to be assessed.

Developing this argument, the respondent points out that in most cases the innocent party cannot complete the contract himself without the other party doing, allowing or accepting something, and that it is purely fortuitous that the appellants can do so in this case. In most cases by refusing co-operation the party in breach can compel the innocent party to restrict his claim to damages. Then it was said that, even where the innocent party can complete the contract without such co-operation, it is against the public interest that he should be allowed to do so. An example was developed in argument. A company might engage an expert to go abroad and prepare an elaborate report and then repudiate the contract before anything was done. To allow such an expert then to waste thousands of pounds in preparing the report cannot be right if a much smaller sum of damages would give him full compensation for his loss. It would merely enable the expert to extort a settlement giving him far more than reasonable compensation.

The respondent founds on the decision of the First Division in *Langford Co. v. Dutch* [[1952] S.C. 15]. There an advertising contractor agreed to exhibit a film for a year. Four days after this agreement was made the advertiser repudiated it but, as in the present case, the contractor refused to accept the repudiation and proceeded to exhibit the film and sue for the contract price. The Sheriff-Substitute dismissed the action as irrelevant and his decision was affirmed on appeal. . . .

Langford & Co. Ltd. v. Dutch is indistinguishable from the present case. . . . We must now decide whether that case was rightly decided. In my judgment it was not. It could only be supported on one or other of two grounds. It might be said that, because in most cases the circumstances are such that an innocent party is unable to complete the contract and earn the contract price without the assent or co-operation of the other party, therefore in cases where he can do so he should not be allowed to do so. I can see no justification for that.

The other ground would be that there is some general equitable principle or element of public policy which requires this limitation of the contractual rights of the innocent party. It may well be that, if it can be shown that a person has no legitimate interest, financial or otherwise, in performing the contract rather than claiming damages, he ought not to be allowed to saddle the other party with an additional burden with no benefit to himself. If a party has no interest to enforce a stipulation, he cannot in general enforce it: so it might be said that, if a party has no interest to insist on a particular remedy, he ought not to be allowed to insist on it. And, just as a party is not allowed to enforce a penalty, so he ought not to be allowed to penalise the other party by taking one course when another is equally advantageous to him. If I may revert to the example which I gave of a company engaging an expert to prepare an elaborate report and then repudiating before anything was done, it might be that the company could show that the expert had no substantial or legitimate interest in carrying out the work rather than accepting damages: I would think that the de minimis principle would apply in determining whether his interest was substantial, and that he might have a legitimate interest other than an immediate financial interest. But if the expert had no such interest then that might be regarded as a proper case of the exercise of the general equitable jurisdiction of the court. But that is not this case. Here the respondent did not set out to prove that the appellants had no legitimate interest in completing the contract and claiming the contract price rather than claiming damages; there is nothing in the findings of fact to support such a case, and it seems improbable that any such case could have been proved. It is, in my judgment, impossible to say that the appellants should be deprived of their right to claim the contract price merely because the benefit to them, as against claiming damages and re-letting their advertising space, might be small in comparison with the loss to the respondent: that is the most that could be said in favour of the respondent. Parliament has on many occasions relieved parties from certain kinds of improvident or oppressive contracts, but the common law can only do that in very limited circumstances. Accordingly, I am unable to avoid the conclusion that this appeal must be allowed and the case remitted so that decree can be pronounced as craved in the initial writ.

[Lord Hodson made a separate speech, with which Lord Tucker agreed, allowing the appeal. Lords Keith and Morton dissented.]

NOTES and QUESTION

1. What "substantial and legitimate interest" did the pursuers have in "carrying out the work rather than accepting damages"?

2. In *Finelli v. Dee* (1968), 67 D.L.R. (2d) 393 (Ont. C.A.), the plaintiffs entered into a contract for the paving of the driveway of the defendants' home for a fixed price. Before any performance was contemplated, the defendants telephoned the plaintiffs and purported to cancel the contract. Some time later, when the defendants were away from home, the plaintiffs carried out their contract and the defendants were confronted with a new driveway upon their return.

On the assumption that the defendants' cancellation amounted to a repudiation, Laskin J.A. found that the case was not covered by the *White and Carter* principle. In this case, the plaintiffs were unable to carry out the work without the defendants' co-operation, because it required entry to the defendants' land and a prior intimation that the plaintiffs proposed to perform the work. In any event, Laskin J.A. professed that he was attracted by the reasoning of the dissenting members of the court in *White and Carter*. He commented (at 395) that "Repudiation is not something that calls for acceptance when there is no question of rescission, but merely excuses the innocent party from performance and leaves him free to sue for damages."

3. In the *Asamera* case, *supra*, Estey J. also suggests some reluctance to follow the principle of *White and Carter (Councils) Ltd. v. McGregor* by commenting that the plaintiff in such a case will ordinarily be required to mitigate. See [1979] 1 S.C.R. 633 at 668-69. The reversal of the *White and Carter (Councils) Ltd.* principle is advocated by the O.L.R.C., *Report on Sale of Goods* (1979), vol. II, at 532-41. In *Attica Sea Carriers Corp. v. Ferrostaal-Poseidon Bulk Reederei G.m.b.H.*, [1976] 1 Lloyd's Rep. 250 (C.A.), Lord Denning suggested that the English Court of Appeal would follow the principle only in a precisely similar case. Lord Denning continued to say (at 255) that the principle "has no application whatever in a case where the plaintiff ought, in all reason, to accept the repudiation and sue for damages—provided that damages would provide an adequate remedy for any loss suffered."

(d)   TIME OF MEASUREMENT OF DAMAGES

SEMELHAGO v. PARAMADEVAN

[1996] 2 S.C.R. 415

SOPINKA J. [delivering the judgment of Gonthier, Cory, McLachlin, Iacobucci and Major JJ.] In August 1986, the respondent purchaser agreed to buy a house under construction in the Toronto area from the appellant vendor Sinnadurai Paramadevan for $205,000, with a closing date of October 31, 1986. To finance the purchase, the respondent was going to pay $75,000 cash, plus $130,000 which he was going to raise by mortgaging his current house. The respondent negotiated a six-month open mortgage, so that he could close the deal on the new house and then sell his old one at an appropriate time in the six months following closing. Before the closing date, the appellant vendor reneged and in December 1986 title to the house was taken by the appellant Blossom Paramadevan. The respondent remained in his old house, which was worth $190,000 in the fall of 1986, and $300,000 at the time of the trial.

The respondent sued the appellants for specific performance or damages in lieu. . . . At the time of trial, the market value of the property was $325,000. The respondent elected to take damages rather than specific performance and . . . the Ontario Court (General Division) awarded him $120,000, that being the difference between the purchase price he had agreed to pay and the value of the property at the time of trial. The appellants appealed . . . on the ground that the assessment was a "windfall" because the respondent was benefiting not only from the increase in the value of the new house, but also from the gain in the value of the old house. The respondent cross-appealed against the disallowance of legal and appraisal fees. The Court of Appeal allowed the appeal, [deducting from the amount awarded at trial the carrying costs of the $130,000 mortgage for six months, notional interest earned on the $75,000, and legal costs on closing] and the cross-appeal.

. . . . .

III. *Issue*

What principles apply to the assessment of damages in lieu of specific performance and, further, how do those principles apply to the facts of this case?

IV. *Analysis*

The trial judge expressed reservations about the propriety of an award of specific performance in this case. While I share those reservations and will return to the question as to the circumstances under which specific performance is an appropriate remedy, this appeal should be disposed of on the basis that specific performance was appropriate. The case was dealt with by the parties in both courts below and in this Court on the assumption that specific performance was an appropriate remedy.

A party who is entitled to specific performance is entitled to elect damages in lieu thereof. The jurisdiction to award damages in lieu of specific performance was conferred on the Court of Chancery by *The Chancery Amendment Act, 1858* (U.K.), 21 & 22 Vict., c. 27 (known as *Lord Cairns' Act*). Although the Act was repealed, in *Leeds Industrial Co-operative Society, Ltd. v. Slack*, [1924] A.C. 851, the House of Lords established that the jurisdiction to award damages in lieu of specific performance was maintained. This jurisdiction exists as part of the law of Ontario by virtue of the *Courts of Justice Act*, R.S.O. 1990, c. C.43, s. 99, which provides:

> **99.** A court that has jurisdiction to grant an injunction or order specific performance may award damages in addition to, or in substitution for, the injunction or specific performance.

Lord Cairns' Act permits damages to be awarded in some circumstances in which no claim for damages could be entertained at common law. See *Leeds*, *supra*, and *Wroth v. Tyler*, [1974] 1 Ch. 30, at p. 57. In cases in which damages could also be claimed at common law, the principles generally applicable are those of the common law. In *Johnson v. Agnew*, [1980] A.C. 367, at pp. 400-401, Lord Wilberforce stated that:

> (2) The general principle for the assessment of damages is compensatory, i.e., that the innocent party is to be placed, so far as money can do so, in the same position as if the contract had been performed. Where the contract is one of sale, this principle normally leads to assessment of damages as at the date of the breach—a principle recognised and embodied in section 51 of the Sale of Goods Act 1893. But this is not an absolute rule: if to follow it would give rise to injustice, the court has power to fix such other date as may be appropriate in the circumstances.

The rationale for assessing the damages at the date of breach in the case of breach of contract for the sale of goods is that if the innocent purchaser is compensated on the basis of the value of the goods as of the date of breach, the purchaser can turn around and purchase identical or equivalent goods. The purchaser is therefore placed in the same financial situation as if the contract had been kept.

Different considerations apply where the thing which is to be purchased is unique. Although some chattels such as rare paintings fall into this category, the concept of uniqueness has traditionally been peculiarly applicable to agreements for the purchase of real estate. Under the common law every piece of real estate was generally considered to be unique. Blackacre had no readily available equivalent. Accordingly, damages were an inadequate remedy and the innocent purchaser was generally entitled to specific performance. Given the flexibility of the rule at common law as to the date for the assessment of damages, it would not be appropriate to insist on applying the date of breach as the assessment date when the purchaser of a unique asset has a legitimate claim to specific performance and elects to take damages instead (see *Wroth v. Tyler*; *Johnson v. Agnew*; and *Mavretic v. Bowman*, [1993] 4 W.W.R. 329). The rationale that the innocent purchaser is fully compensated, if provided with the amount of money that would purchase an asset of the same value on the date of the breach, no longer applies. This disposition would not be a substitute for an order of specific performance. The order for specific performance may issue many months or even years after the breach. The value of the asset may have changed.

Moreover, the claim for specific performance revives the contract to the extent that the defendant who has failed to perform can avoid a breach if at any time up to the date of judgment, performance is tendered. In cases such as the one at bar, where the vendor reneges in anticipation of performance, the innocent party has two options. He or she may accept the repudiation and treat the agreement as being at an end. In that event, both parties are relieved from performing any outstanding obligations and the injured party may commence an action for damages. Alternatively, the injured party may decline to accept the repudiation and continue to insist on performance. In that case, the contract continues in force and neither party is relieved of their obligations under the agreement. As is elaborated in *McGregor on Damages* (13th ed. 1972), at p. 149:

> Where a party to a contract repudiates it, the other party has an option to accept or not to accept the repudiation. If he does not accept it there is still no breach of contract, and the contract subsists for the benefit of both parties and no need to mitigate arises. On the other hand, if the repudiation is accepted this results in an anticipatory breach of contract in respect of which suit can be brought at once for damages. . . .

Thus, the claim for specific performance can be seen as reviving the contract to the extent that the defendant who has failed to perform can avoid a breach if, at any time up to the date of judgment, performance is tendered. In this way, a claim for specific performance has the effect of postponing the date of breach.

For all of these reasons, it is not inconsistent with the rules of the common law to assess damages as of the date of trial. It must be remembered that the rules of the common law did not contemplate awarding damages as a substitute for specific performance. The rules of the common law must be applied in light of the statutory imperative contained in s. 99 of the *Courts of Justice Act*. The damages that are awarded must be a true substitute for specific performance. This point is forcefully made by Megarry J. in *Wroth v. Tyler*. In that case, the purchaser had contracted for the purchase of a house for £6,000. The vendor defaulted. On the closing date, the property was worth £7,500. As of the date of trial the property was worth £11,500. In assessing damages as of the date of trial, Megarry J. stated, at p. 58:

> On the wording of the section, the power "to award damages to the party injured, . . . in substitution for such . . . specific performance," at least envisages that the damages awarded will in fact constitute a true substitute for specific performance. Furthermore, the section is speaking of the time when the court is making its decision to award damages in substitution for specific performance, so that it is at that moment that the damages must be a substitute. The fact that a different amount of damages would have been a substitute if the order had been

made at the time of the breach must surely be irrelevant. In the case before me, I cannot see how £1,500 damages would constitute any true substitute for a decree of specific performance of the contract to convey land which at the time of the decree is worth £5,500 more than the contract price.

At p. 59 Megarry J. added:

Yet on principle I would say simply that damages "in substitution" for specific performance must be a substitute, *giving as nearly as may be what specific performance would have given.* [Emphasis added.]

This was also the basis upon which [*306793 Ontario Ltd. in Trust v. Rimes* (1979), 25 O.R. (2d) 79 (C.A.)] was decided. . . . The reasons for judgment of MacKinnon A.C.J.O. cite *Wroth v. Tyler* with approval, pointing out that that case was not overruled by *Johnson v. Agnew, supra.* I agree with that observation. In *Johnson v. Agnew*, Lord Wilberforce, speaking for the House of Lords, concluded that in view of the flexibility of the common law rule with respect to the date for the assessment of damages to which I have referred, the view taken by Megarry J. in *Wroth v. Tyler* was consistent with the common law.

I therefore conclude that, in the circumstances of this case, the appropriate date for the assessment of damages is the date of trial as found by the trial judge. Technically speaking, the date of assessment should be the date of judgment. That is the date upon which specific performance is ordered. For practical purposes, however, the evidence that is adduced which is relevant to enable damages to be assessed will be as of the date of trial. It is not usually possible to predict the date of judgment when the evidence is given.

The difference between the contract price and the value "given close to trial" as found by the trial judge is $120,000. I would not deduct from this amount the increase in value of the respondent's residence which he retained when the deal did not close. If the respondent had received a decree of specific performance, he would have had the property contracted for and retained the amount of the rise in value of his own property. Damages are to be substituted for the decree of specific performance. I see no basis for deductions that are not related to the value of the property which was the subject of the contract. To make such deductions would depart from the principle that damages are to be a true equivalent of specific performance.

This approach may appear to be overly generous to the respondent in this case and other like cases and may be seen as a windfall. In my opinion, this criticism is valid if the property agreed to be purchased is not unique. While at one time the common law regarded every piece of real estate to be unique, with the progress of modern real estate development this is no longer the case. Residential, business and industrial properties are all mass produced much in the same way as other consumer products. If a deal falls through for one property, another is frequently, though not always, readily available.

It is no longer appropriate, therefore, to maintain a distinction in the approach to specific performance as between realty and personalty. It cannot be assumed that damages for breach of contract for the purchase and sale of real estate will be an inadequate remedy in all cases. The common law recognized that the distinction might not be valid when the land had no peculiar or special value. In *Adderley v. Dixon* (1824), 1 Sim. & St. 607, 57 E.R. 239, Sir John Leach, V.C., stated (at p. 240):

> Courts of Equity decree the specific performance of contracts, not upon any distinction between realty and personalty, but because damages at law may not, in the particular case, afford a complete remedy. Thus a Court of Equity decrees performance of a contract for land, not because of the real nature of the land, but because damages at law, which must be calculated upon the general money value of land, may not be a complete remedy to the purchaser, to whom the land may have a peculiar and special value.

Courts have tended, however, to simply treat all real estate as being unique and to decree specific performance unless there was some other reason for refusing equitable relief. See *Roberto v. Bumb*, [1943] O.R. 299 (C.A.), at p. 311; *Kloepfer Wholesale Hardware and Automotive Co. v. Roy*, [1952] 2 S.C.R. 465; *Nepean Carleton Developments Ltd. v. Hope*, [1978] 1 S.C.R. 427, at p. 438. Some courts, however, have begun to question the assumption that damages will afford an inadequate remedy for breach of contract for the purchase of land. In *Chaulk v. Fairview Construction Ltd.* (1977), 14 Nfld. & P.E.I.R. 13, the Newfoundland Court of Appeal (*per* Gushue J.A.), after quoting the above passage from *Adderley v. Dixon*, stated, at p. 21:

> The question here is whether damages would have afforded Chaulk an adequate remedy, and I have no doubt that they could, and would, have. There was nothing whatever unique or irreplaceable about the houses and lots bargained for. They were merely subdivision lots with houses, all of the same general design, built on them, which the respondent was purchasing for investment or re-sale purposes only. He had sold the first two almost immediately at a profit, and intended to do the same with the remainder. It would be quite different if we were dealing with a house or houses which were of a particular architectural design, or were situated in a particularly desirable location, but this was certainly not the case.

Specific performance should, therefore, not be granted as a matter of course absent evidence that the property is unique to the extent that its substitute would not be readily available. The guideline proposed by Estey J. in *Asamera Oil Corp. v. Seal Oil & General Corp.*, [*supra*, section 3(c)], with respect to contracts involving chattels is equally applicable to real property. At p. 668, Estey J. stated:

> Before a plaintiff can rely on a claim to specific performance so as to insulate himself from the consequences of failing to procure alternate property in mitigation of his losses, some fair, real and substantial justification for his claim to performance must be found.

                                         .....

The trial judge was of the view in this case that the property was not unique. She stated that, "It was a building lot under construction which would be inter-changeable in all likelihood with any number of others." Notwithstanding this observation, she felt constrained by authority to find that specific performance was an appropriate remedy. While I would be inclined to agree with the trial judge as to the inappropriateness of an order for specific performance, both parties were content to present the case on the basis that the respondent was entitled to specific performance. The case was dealt with on this basis by the Court of Appeal. In the circumstances, this Court should abide by the manner in which the case has been presented by the parties and decided in the courts below. In future cases, under similar circumstances, a trial judge will not be constrained to find that specific performance is an appropriate remedy.

This takes me to the deductions made by the Court of Appeal. While I have some reservations about the propriety of these deductions, there was no cross-appeal by the respondent with respect to the award of damages. No argument was presented with respect to these deductions. My reservations relate to the basis upon which the Court of Appeal distinguished *Rimes*. In this regard, the Court stated (at p. 481):

> Those are not the facts of the case now before the court. In this case, the purchaser is not a shell and the trial judge found that the evidence established what probably would have happened had the transaction closed.

On my reading of the reasons of MacKinnon A.C.J.O. in *Rimes*, the principal reason for deciding not to deduct the carrying charges was that to do so would be inconsistent with adopting the date of trial as the assessment date. I am not convinced that there is an inconsistency but would prefer not to express any further opinion on the question inasmuch as there is no cross-appeal and these matters are not in issue here.

The Court of Appeal added out-of-pocket expenses of $673.75 for legal fees and $250 for appraisal fees, amounts which were apparently inadvertently omitted from the judgment at trial. There was no dispute about these items.

Disposition

In the result, the appeal is dismissed with costs.

NOTES and QUESTIONS

1. La Forest J. delivered a concurring judgment confined to the facts of this case and demurring on the issue of the general principles governing the availability of specific performance and the interpretation of the modern successors of Lord Cairns' Act.

2. Do you agree with the conclusion that no account should be taken of the fact that the plaintiff had offset most of the increase in value in the property by the rise in value of his own house that he had retained in the meantime? To what extent, if at all, is your view affected by the question of whether the plaintiff had sufficient financial elasticity to have both purchased the house which was the subject of the dispute and retained his existing house? Does the fact that he was intending to sell his existing house and move into the house that was the subject of the dispute have any relevance to this matter?

3. The Court of Appeal did allow deductions for certain other items that the plaintiff may have saved or gained as a consequence of the defendant not closing the deal—the payments on the bridging mortgage that he was going to take out on his existing house and interest on the money that he was going to use as a down payment. The Supreme Court was obviously sceptical about this but did not need to express a definitive opinion as there had been no cross-appeal from that aspect of the Court of Appeal's judgment. Do you share the Supreme Court's scepticism as to the appropriateness of these deductions?

4. The Sopinka judgment is very obviously predicated on the assumptions under which both sides were operating, namely, that this was a case in which the plaintiff had properly commenced and maintained until trial an action for specific performance. Without a legitimate interest in pursuing specific performance, the plaintiff would never have recovered damages based on the value of the property at the date of the trial. Rather, in terms of *Asamera Oil*, he would have come within the principles of mitigation and could have claimed no more, at least under this head, than the difference

between the purchase price and the market price of a true substitute at the point at which he should reasonably have acquired such a substitute. Sopinka J. also indicates very clearly that he thinks the defendant erred in making the concession that he did and that this was not a case in which it was legitimate for the plaintiff to have commenced and pursued an action for specific performance right up until the trial date. Is this because the plaintiff's abandonment of the specific performance claim at the time of trial indicated that he was more interested in money than in the house or because Sopinka J. was out of sympathy with the historic rules governing the availability of specific performance of contracts involving an interest in land? To the extent that it was the latter, under what circumstances would you advise a client that it was still not a risky undertaking to seek specific performance of a contract involving an interest in land? Given that this part of the judgment was unnecessary for the disposition of this case, was La Forest J.'s refusal to be drawn into this debate a more appropriate posture?

5. For commentary on *Semelhago*, see De Silva, "The Supreme Court of Canada's Lost Opportunity: *Semelhago v. Paramadevan*" (1998), 23 Queen's L.J. 475 and Siebrasse, "Damages in Lieu of Specific Performance" (1997), 76 Can. Bar Rev. 551. We also return under the heading "Equitable Remedies" to the issue of the availability of specific performance for contracts for the sale of land.

6. Another instance where fluctuations in value between the date of the breach and the date of the trial matter is found in the case of currency. Assume a Canadian company enters into a contract with an American company for the purchase of a piece of machinery to be manufactured in the United States, the price for which is stated in American dollars. Assume also that at the time of the contract, the Canadian and American dollars are at par, that when the machinery is delivered the Canadian dollar is worth 90 cents U.S., and that at the date of the trial in Canada of an action for non-payment, the Canadian dollar is worth 85 cents U.S. What should be the amount recovered by the U.S. company if it is successful in its action? Given that the proper law of the contract is that of the U.S. and that the currency of account and payment is that of the U.S., the answer provided by the House of Lords in *Miliangos v. George Frank (Textiles) Ltd.*, [1976] A.C. 443 (H.L.) is none of these. Rather, provided the claim is made for judgment in the foreign currency, the date of conversion should be the date on which the payment of any judgment is made by the defendant. Previously, the English courts had used a date of breach conversion date. What justifications are there for this new position? As yet, there is no clear Canadian support for the *Miliangos* position with most Canadian courts seeing the date of payment rule precluded by the terms of s. 12 of the Currency Act, R.S.C. 1985, c. C-52. It provides that any reference to money in legal proceedings "shall be stated in the currency of Canada". This has been interpreted as requiring the conversion date of a foreign currency obligation to be no later than the date of judgment: see *Batavia Times Publishing Co. v. Davis* (1978), 20 O.R. (2d) 437 (H.C.). Indeed, some courts have continued to establish the conversion rate at an earlier date: *Clinton v. Ford* (1982), 37 O.R. (2d) 448 (C.A.) (date of issuance of statement of claim); *Stevenson Estate v. Siewert* (2000), 191 D.L.R. (4th) 151 (Alta. C.A.), using the date of the wrong in a tort action and justifying it on the basis that to use the date of judgment would have produced a windfall given a ten year period of appreciation in the value of the U.S. dollar. In Ontario, however, the situation is now seemingly covered by s. 121 of the Courts of Justice Act, R.S.O. 1990, c. C.43. This makes provision for the conversion date of an order to enforce an obligation in a foreign currency as "the close of business on the first day on which the bank quotes a Canadian dollar rate for purchase of the foreign currency before the day payment of the obligation is received by the creditor". However, ss. 3 does confer a discretion on the court to establish some other conversion date to prevent inequity. *Quaere* the relationship between this provision and s. 12 of the Currency Act. See also the Foreign Money Claims Act, R.S.B.C. 1996, c.155, s.1(2):

> The conversion date is the last day, before the day on which the payment under the order is made by the judgment debtor to the judgment creditor, that the bank . . . quotes a Canadian dollar equivalent to the other currency.

For a discussion of the competing positions (including the date of breach rule), see Waddams, *The Law of Damages*, 3rd ed. (1997) at paras. 7.80-7.330.

(e) LIQUIDATED DAMAGES, DEPOSITS AND FORFEITURES

SHATILLA v. FEINSTEIN

16 Sask. L.R. 454, [1923] 1 W.W.R. 1474, [1923] 3 D.L.R. 1035 (C.A.)

Until 16th April 1920, the defendant and his brother carried on a business in wholesale dry goods in Saskatoon under the name of Bertrams Ltd. On that date, the defendant and his brother sold their business to the plaintiff. One of the terms of the sale was that the defendant and his brother agreed that:

> they will not, either alone, or jointly, or in partnership with, or directly or indirectly, either as principal or agent, or as director or manager of a company, or for any other person or persons, or as a servant in any capacity, or otherwise howsoever carry on or be engaged or concerned or take part in or be in any wise interested in, or assist any other person or persons to carry on, the business of wholesale drygoods, men's furnishings, or small wares, merchants, or jobbers in drygoods, men's furnishings or small wares, within the corporate limits of the city of Saskatoon, in the Province of Saskatchewan, for a period of 5 years from the date thereof, and in case of any breach of this covenant they shall pay to the parties of the second part the sum of ten thousand (10,000) dollars to be recoverable on each and every such breach as liquidated damages, and not as a penalty.

In April 1921, the defendant purchased shares in Harley Henry Ltd. in the amount of $25,000 and became a director of that company. In May 1921, Harley Henry Ltd. entered into the business of "wholesale merchants of woollen and cotton mitts, gloves, men's socks, and ladies' and men's leather coats." In October 1921 the defendant and Harley Henry Ltd. entered into the business of wholesale merchants of hosiery.

The trial judge found that the term "dry goods" in the covenant executed by the defendant included hosiery and that the term "men's furnishings" included gloves and mitts. It also appeared that the defendant had ceased to participate in Harley Henry Ltd.

MARTIN J.A. . . . The main question to be determined is, whether or not the sum fixed by the covenant is a penalty, or whether it is recoverable by way of liquidated damages. When the damages which may arise out of the breach of a contract are in their nature uncertain, the law permits the parties to agree beforehand as to the amount to be paid in case of breach. Whether such an agreement has been made by the parties or not, or whether the sum agreed upon is a penalty, must depend upon the circumstances of each case. If the sum fixed is in excess of any actual damage which can possibly arise from the breach of the contract, the sum fixed as damage is not considered to be a *bona fide* pre-estimate of the damage. The same principle is applied when the payment of a larger sum is stipulated in the event of the breach of a covenant to pay a smaller sum. In the case of a contract containing a single stipulation which, if broken at all, can be broken once only—such as a covenant not to reveal a trade secret—when the parties have agreed to the amount which shall be paid in case of breach and referred to such sum as liquidated damages, there would appear to be no reason, on the authorities, why the Court should not treat such a sum as liquidated damages. If, however, the covenant is one which is capable of being broken more than once, such as an agreement not to solicit the customers of a firm, or an agreement not to sell certain specified articles below a certain price, the question is a more difficult one. In such a case, however, the damage in the case of each breach is of the same kind, and the fact that such damage may vary in amount for each breach has not been held by the Courts to raise a presumption that the sum agreed upon is a penalty, particularly where the parties have agreed to the sum as liquidated damages. This, I think, is a fair deduction from the decision in the House of Lords in *Dunlop Pneumatic Tyre Co. v. New Garage and Motor Co.*, [1915] A.C. 79.

In cases, however, where it is agreed to pay a fixed sum on the breach of a number of stipulations of various degrees of importance, a presumption is said to be raised against the sum so fixed being treated as liquidated damages, even though the parties have referred to it as such; that is, there is a presumption against the parties having pre-estimated the damages. The damage likely to accrue from breaches of various kinds in such a case is different in kind and amount, and a separate estimate in the case of each breach would be necessary. Such a presumption may, however, be rebutted if it is shown on the face of the agreement, or on the evidence, that the parties have taken into consideration the different amounts of damages that might occur, and had actually arrived at an amount which was considered proper under all the circumstances. Even then, however, the amount fixed must not be extravagant or unreasonable.

In *Elphinstone v. Monkland Iron & Coal Co.* (1886), 11 App. Cas. 332 (H.L.), the facts were that the lessees of land had been granted the privilege of placing slag from blast furnaces on land let to them, and covenanted to restore the land at a certain date. Provision was made that failing performance the lessees should pay the lessors "at the rate of £100 per Imperial acre for all ground not so restored, together with legal interest thereon, from and after the date when the operations should have been completed until paid." It was held that the sum, although it was described in one part of the agreement as "the penalty therein stipulated," was not a penalty but estimated or stipulated damages. Lord Watson, at pp. 342-3, said:—

"When a single lump sum is made payable by way of compensation, on the occurrence of one or more or all of several events, some of which may occasion serious and others but trifling damage, the presumption is that the parties intended the sum to be penal, and subject to modification. The payments stipulated in article 12 are not of that character; they are made proportionate to the extent to which the respondent company may fail to implement their obligations, and they are to bear interest from the date of the failure. I can find neither principle nor authority for holding that payments so adjusted by the contracting parties with reference to the actual amount of damage ought to be regarded as penalties." . . .

In *Clydebank Eng. & Shipbldg. Co. v. Izquierdo-y-Castaneda, Don Jose Ramos*, [1905] A.C. 6 (H.L.), the shipbuilding company contracted for the construction of four vessels of war for the Spanish Government, each of which was to be completed at a certain date. In the event of a non-completion they were to pay £500 for each ship for every week's delay. The contract entered into contained the following clause:—"The contractors undertake that the said vessel shall be finished, complete and ready for sea, the first vessels in six and three-quarter months, and the second in seven and three-quarter months from signing of this contract and accompanying specifications and plans." And also:—"The penalty for later delivery shall be at the rate of £500 per week for each vessel not delivered by the contractors in contract time."

It appeared from the evidence that the sum to be paid on breach of delivery was suggested by the contracting company itself, and this fact must have had some influence on the decision of the Court. It was held that the sum stipulated was liquidated damage, and not a penalty. Lord Halsbury, L.C., at p. 10 said:—

> It is impossible to lay down any abstract rule as to what it may or it may not be extravagant or unconscionable to insist upon without reference to the particular facts and circumstances which are established in the individual case.

At p. 13 he says:—"It seems to me, when one looks to see what was the nature of the transaction in this case, it is hopeless to contend that the parties only intended this as some thing *in terrorem*. Both parties recognized the fact of the importance of time; it is a case in which time is of the essence of the contract, and so regarded by both parties; and the particular sum fixed upon as being the agreed amount of damages was suggested by the defendants themselves; and to say that that can be unconscionable, or something which the parties ought not to insist upon, that it was a mere holding out something *in terrorem*, after looking at the correspondence between the parties, is to my mind, not a very plausible suggestion." . . .

In *Pub. Works Commr. v. Hills*, [1906] A.C. 368 (P.C.), Lord Dunedin in discussing the decision in the *Clydebank* case says, that the general principle to be deduced from the decision seems to be this: that the criterion of whether a sum, be it called penalty or damages, is truly liquidated damages, and as such not to be interfered with by the Court, is to be founded on whether the sum stipulated for can or cannot be regarded as "a genuine pre-estimate of the creditor's probable or possible interest in the due performance of the principal obligation." He further states that the *indicia* of this question will vary according to the circumstances; on the one hand, the enormous disparity of the sum to any conceivable loss will point one way, while the fact of the payment being in terms proportionate to the loss will point the other way. The circumstances as a whole, however, must be taken into consideration, and must be viewed as at the time when the bargain was made. . . .

The covenant in the present case covers a number of matters which would constitute breach of it. It provides that the defendant shall not "carry on or be engaged in or take part in or be in any way interested in the business of wholesale drygoods, etc." This, the main portion of the covenant, is further described by words preceding it: "directly or indirectly, either as principal or agent or as director or manager of a company, or as a servant in any capacity." There could be many breaches of this covenant, some of which would be very important, others of a less important and even trivial character. For instance, if the defendant had engaged as a clerk with some one carrying on a similar business, or if he purchased a small amount of stock in a similar business, it could scarcely be said that such action would cause serious damages to the plaintiffs, not that it would constitute an important breach of the agreement; certainly it would seem "extravagant and unconscionable" that for either one of such breaches he should pay damages amounting to $10,000. On the other hand, if he actually went into business in partnership with some one or carried on a competing business on his own account, or became manager of a company carrying on a similar business, or purchased a large interest in a similar concern carrying on business as a company and became a director of such company, such breaches would be of an important character and might conceivably cause serious damage to the plaintiffs. I think the law as laid down by Lord Watson in the *Elphinstone* case, *supra*, is applicable to the facts of this case, and that it must be held that covenant provides a penalty which the Court will not enforce. The covenant provides for the payment of a lump sum upon the occurrence of any one of a number of things differing in importance, and some of them trivial in character, and where a sum is stipulated to be paid as liquidated damages, and is payable not on the happening of a single event but on one or more of a number of events, some of which might result in inconsiderable damage, the Court may decline to construe the words "liquidated damages" according to their ordinary meaning and may treat such a sum as a penalty. Lord Dunedin, in the *Dunlop* case, [*supra*] at p. 89, considers that if there are various breaches to which an indiscriminate sum is applied, "then the strength of the chain must be taken to be its weakest link," and if it can be seen clearly that the loss in one particular breach could never amount to the sum stated, then the conclusion that the sum is a penalty may be reached. I think this statement of the law is peculiarly applicable to the facts of the present case. . . .

The appeal should be dismissed with costs.

QUESTIONS

1. Why would parties wish to include a stipulated damages clause in a contract? Why did the parties in *Shatilla v. Feinstein* wish to do so? Should these reasons have been considered acceptable by the court?

2. Would it be possible to identify a smaller sub-set of *in terrorem* cases than that identified by the tests articulated in *Shatilla v. Feinstein*?

3. How could the drafting of the clause in this case be improved?

4. Would the court's analysis of the covenant make more sense in the context of an employment contract in which liquidated damages were stipulated for breach of a covenant that an employee would not compete with his employer after the termination of employment?

5. Why is it essential to the rationale of the principles evidenced in *Shatilla* that the estimate of damages occur at the time of formation of the agreement? If there has been a genuine pre-estimate of loss, should it make any difference if, in the event, actual damages are significantly less or more than the stipulated amount?

H.F. CLARKE LTD. v. THERMIDAIRE CORP.

[1976] 1 S.C.R. 319

LASKIN C.J.C. . . . The contract which is the subject of this litigation was dated January 14, 1966, and as amended shortly thereafter, it constituted the appellant, as from January 1, 1966, the exclusive distributor of the respondent's products (as defined) in a specified area of Canada, embracing the larger part of Canada from Ontario to the west coast and including the Northwest Territories and part of Quebec but excluding the eastern part of Quebec and the four Atlantic Provinces. This contract replaced an earlier one under which the two covenants against competition, one respecting competition during the currency of the contract, and the second respecting competition during the three-year period after termination or cancellation of the contract showed one marked variation from the successor covenants. Article 7 of the first contract of January 20, 1964, provided as follows:

> 7. *Sale of Competitive Products*
>
> Distributor undertakes and agrees that during the currency of this Agreement and for a period of three (3) years after the termination hereof, as herein provided, neither it nor any company affiliated or associated with it shall sell competitive products in the Territory.

In the contract out of which this litigation arises, the references to the three-year period and to the territory were left out, and the paragraph, numbered 7 as before, was in these words:

> 7. *Sale of Competitive Products*
>
> Clarke undertakes and agrees that during the currency of this Agreement, neither it nor any company associated or affiliated with it shall manufacture, sell, cause to be manufactured or sold, products competitive to Thermidaire products.

Neither art. 14 of the first contract nor its successor art. 15 of the second contract, in restraining competition for three years after termination or cancellation made any reference to its operation in the territory of the distributorship. The two articles were substantially the same in their relevant particulars, and it is enough to reproduce the one that is in issue here. It reads as follows:

> 15. *Termination of Agreement by Clarke*: In the event of the termination or cancellation of this Agreement by, or caused by, Clarke, either by reason of its non-renewal by Clarke or by reason of any default on the part of Clarke or by reason of any violation or non-fulfilment of the conditions of this contract by Clarke and not remedied by Clarke as laid down in Section 12, including the grounds for termination specified in paragraph 19 hereof, Clarke further undertakes and agrees that neither it nor any company affiliated or associated with it will produce, sell or cause to be produced or sold, directly or indirectly, products competitive with Thermidaire Products for a period of three (3) years after the date of termination or cancellation. In the event of breach by Clarke of this covenant pertaining to competitive products, Clarke shall pay to Thermidaire by way of liquidated damages an amount equal to the gross trading profit realized through the sale of such competitive products. . . .

I need not embark here on any discussion of whether the two covenants, . . . as limited by construction to operation only in the distributorship territory, are invalid as in the unreasonable restraint of trade. Both the trial Judge and the Court of Appeal found them to be reasonable *inter partes* and consonant with the public interest, and this conclusion was not questioned by the appellant. . . .

This brings me to . . . the main point in the appeal. The trial Judge found, and the Court of Appeal confirmed, that the appellant Clarke had broken the contract during its currency by selling competitive products other than those of the respondent and that it had also broken the covenant against post-contract competition. These findings, and as well a finding that the respondent was entitled to terminate the contract before it had run its five-year period, were not contested in this Court by the appellant.

At the time the parties hereto commenced their business relationship the appellant was in the business of selling boilers in western Canada. The respondent from 1958 on concentrated on the manufacture and sale of water treatment products; and in agreeing to give the appellant the exclusive distributorship of its products in the defined territory it necessarily excluded itself from sales therein and thus depended on the appellant to keep its name and its reputation before the public in the territory. The appellant was not only precluded by the contract between the parties from selling products in the territory competitive to those of the respondent but was also subject to other supporting contractual obligations, such as being required to give the respondent upon request its list of customers, and various provisions respecting advertising and packaging.

It was the appellant which initiated suit, claiming damages for wrongful termination of the contract on January 19, 1967, by the respondent and the latter counterclaimed for damages under the covenants against competition. The action was brought on March 9, 1967, the statement of claim was delivered on April 10, 1967 and the defence and counterclaim on April 25, 1967. The appellant discontinued its action on April 29, 1968, and the trial of the counterclaim began on September 19, 1971, well after the expiry of the three-year period within which the post-contract covenant against competition was effective. The respondent did not seek an interim or interlocutory injunction, which it might have done promptly and thus avoided the running of some of the damages which it claimed in its suit. Its explanation, which is far from satisfactory, was that there was a serious question whether there was a breach of the agreement by the appellant and, even if there was a breach, whether it was not remedied. The prayer for relief in the counterclaim did ask for an injunction but, of course, by the time the action came on for trial there was no longer any basis for one. None the less, it was obvious from the record that the appellant continued to sell competitive products other than those of the respondent after the contract was terminated and thus put itself at the risk, which indeed materialized, of being called to account under the formula for post-contract damages. Notwithstanding this, no interlocutory injunction was sought by the respondent.

No question arises here as to the entitlement of the respondent to damages for breach of the covenant against competition during the currency of the contract (the covenant in this respect being enforceable), such damages being the loss suffered by the respondent by reason of sales by the appellant of products competitive with those of the respondent and not purchased from the respondent. The formula for assessing damages for breach of art. 15, the post-contract covenant, was however attacked as constituting a penalty rather than a measure of liquidated damages. It was accepted by counsel . . . that the damages under the prescribed formula, namely, the gross trading profit realized by the covenantor on the sale of competitive products, would be about $200,000. . . . To support its contention of the extravagance of the formula as a measure of liquidated damages, counsel for the appellant noted (although not accepting the sum as properly based) that the respondent had, in the alternative, claimed some $92,000 as the amount of its actual loss of net profit over the three-year post-contract period.

The trial Judge concluded that the formula of gross trading profit as the measure of liquidated damages was a business-like and reasonable one, but this conclusion was associated with an apparent belief that the damages according to this formula would be small. The Court of Appeal accepted, as did counsel, that they would reach $200,000, but it held none the less that the formula, in the circumstances, was "one designed for the determination of liquidated damages in the truest sense and . . . therefore enforceable". . . .

I think it important to appreciate that we are dealing here with a not very usual case (so far as reported decisions go) where the pre-estimate of damages was not a fixed sum (as was the situation in the leading English case of *Dunlop Pneumatic Tyre Co. v. New Garage & Motor Co.*, [1915] A.C. 79) but was based upon a formula which when applied necessarily yielded a result far in excess of loss of net profits. Gross trading profit, in the words of the trial Judge, "means the difference between the net selling prices of the goods and their laid down cost", the laid down cost being the seller's invoice price plus transportation charges to put the goods on the purchaser's shelves. In the words of the Court of Appeal, "the term 'gross trading profit' is profit after cost of sales but before costs customarily deducted to determine net profit".

The contract in this case was lawfully terminated by the respondent on January 19, 1967 and the three-year post-contract covenant against competition ran from that date. . . .

I take the judgment of the Ontario Court of Appeal to be based on the fact that the parties had fixed the formula of gross trading profit after a mutual consideration of the difficulty of establishing compensation for a probably substantial loss, having regard to the factors to be considered, if there was a breach of the post-contract covenant not to compete. The extent of the loss, by reason of the formula, would vary directly with the length of time, up to the three-year limit over which the breach would continue. In his reasons in the Court of Appeal, Brooke, J.A., assessed the matter as follows [33 D.L.R. (3d) 13 at 25-6]:

> The disproportion of gross trading profit and net profit and the financial position of Thermidaire were known by the parties when this agreement was struck. No doubt net profit was considered inappropriate as a measure of damage or loss since its application would involve charging all the costs of advertising, promotion and administration used to put down Thermidaire in a prohibited competitive venture. As to the true object of the provision, Mr. Deeks stated that the formula was used because of serious difficulties involved in calculating not only simple loss of profit through the prohibited competition, but also the loss of things of value, of real value, which the parties well understood. This included such matters as the loss of the past value of previous years of advertising by Clarke of the Thermidaire products, the loss of present and future worth of advertising by Thermidaire by reason of Clarke's active competition and, of course, the loss of the value of product identification, product integrity and the loss of customers and, of importance, the name and reputation of the product in the market-place. If the effect in terms of loss of present and future sales because of adverse advertising and competitive sales suffered by the company which had placed its entire reliance upon the conduct of its exclusive agent was properly a part of the parties' consideration, perhaps the difficulty encountered by the witness Anderson in his attempt to establish the loss limited to Thermidaire's net profit reflects the difficulties which the parties foresaw in any

effort to assess the real loss which would be sustained by Thermidaire in the event of a breach. It is clear to me that the learned trial Judge accepted the evidence of Mr. Deeks as worthy of belief and entirely reasonable in these circumstances.

Does the formula represent a genuine attempt by the parties to pre-estimate the loss as best they could within their special knowledge of the circumstances? It is true that the amount that may eventually be assessed may be large, but this was foreseeable when the contract was entered upon. Equally clear was the fact that the loss in terms of both profits and value, as above-mentioned, would also be large. Indeed, the longer the competition was carried on within the prohibited period the greater would be the loss, and the more successful the competition, the greater was the probability that Thermidaire would suffer substantial and permanent damage in the light of the various factors above-mentioned. Losses such as loss of product identification, loss of benefits of advertising through the operations of its exclusive agent throughout a large territory are among the imponderables for the appraisal which this clause was intended to provide. To have fixed a lump sum as a measure of Thermidaire's damages would have been a haphazard measure at best and, in all the circumstances, the employment of a formula geared to sales of competitive products during the prohibited period was adopted by two keen business firms as the best method of determining the loss resulting from a breach of the covenant—a covenant into which they entered with their eyes open.

When is the amount of recovery in such circumstances extravagant as opposed to actual probable loss? The fact that the estimated loss of net profit, $92,000, is something a little less than half of the possible recovery of $200,000 in circumstances like these is not by itself proof of extravagance. The figures may be large, but I am not persuaded that they are unrealistic or extravagant. The parties knew and appreciated these factors and chose this method to establish compensation for a loss, the amount of which was difficult to determine and, no doubt, very costly to establish. I am convinced that they agreed upon a method which they both regarded as one which would lead to a fair and just determination of Thermidaire's damages and losses in the event of a breach of the covenant.

If all that was involved in determining whether the parties had agreed on a measure of liquidated damages or on a penalty was the intention of those parties, there could be no quarrel with the result reached at trial and on appeal. Indeed, if that was the case it is difficult to conceive how any penalty conclusion could ever be reached when businessmen or business corporations, with relatively equal bargaining power, entered into a contract which provided for payment of a fixed sum or for payment pursuant to a formula for determining damages, in case of a breach of specified covenants, including a covenant not to compete. The law has not, however, developed in this way in common law jurisdictions; and the power to relieve against what a Court may decide is a penalty is a recognized head of equity jurisdiction. Of course, the Court will begin by construing the contract in which the parties have objectively manifested their intentions, and will consider the surrounding circumstances so far as they can illuminate the contract and thus aid in its construction. It seems to me, however, that if, in the face of the parties' assertion in their contract that they were fixing liquidated damages, the Court concluded that a penalty was provided, it would be patently absurd to say that the Court was giving effect to the real intention of the parties when the Court's conclusion was in disregard of that intention as expressed by the parties.

What the Court does in this class of case, as it does in other contract situations, is to refuse to enforce a promise in strict conformity with its terms. The Court exercises a dispensing power (which is unknown to the civil law of Quebec) because the parties' intentions, directed at the time to the performance of their contract, will not alone be allowed to determine how the prescribed sum or the loss formula will be characterized. The primary concern in breach of contract cases (as it is in tort cases, albeit in a different context) is compensation, and judicial interference with the enforcement of what the Courts regard as penalty clauses is simply a manifestation of a concern for fairness and reasonableness, rising above contractual stipulation, whenever the parties seek to remove from the Courts their ordinary authority to determine not only whether there has been a breach but what damages may be recovered as a result thereof.

The Courts may be quite content to have the parties fix the damages in advance and relieve the Courts of this burden in cases where the nature of the obligation upon the breach of which damages will arise, the losses that may reasonably be expected to flow from a breach and their unsusceptibility to ready determination upon the occurrence of a breach provide a base upon which a pre-estimation may be made. But this is only the lesser half of the problem. The interference of the Courts does not follow because they conclude that no attempt should have been made to predetermine the damages or their measure. It is always open to the parties to make the predetermination, but it must yield to judicial appraisal of its reasonableness in the circumstances. This becomes a difficult question of judgment, especially in a case like the present one involving a covenant not to compete which engages the reputation and the vicarious presence of the covenantee in the territorial area of the covenant as well as the products which are the subject of the covenant.

In the present case the formula of gross trading profit was not defined, but in the general understanding of the term as adopted by the Courts below it departs markedly from any reasonable approach to recoverable loss or actual loss since all the elements of costs and expenses which would be taken into account to arrive at net profit are excluded from consideration. It is of considerable significance on this aspect of the matter to note how the respondent, in putting its best foot forward to show its actual loss, made up its estimated loss of net profits of $92,017, which is less than half of the sum, in fact about 40%, which would be its recoverable damages under the contract formula of gross trading profits. . . .

I think it well to emphasize that the estimated actual loss of $92,017 and the estimated loss of gross trading profits of $239,449.05 are sums which relate to the entire three-year post-contract period during which the covenant not to compete was operative. Had the Court been called upon to deal with the question of liquidated damages or penalty at or shortly after the time that the contract was lawfully terminated neither the actual loss nor the gross trading profits would have been in any substantial figure, a result that would be fortified, and indeed secured, if an interlocutory injunction had been sought and granted. No such injunction was, however, even sought, and hence the continuation of the breach to the end of the post-contract covenant period yielded the high figures to which reference has been made.

Had a single sum been fixed as a pre-estimate in the amount of $200,000, it is impossible to think that the Court would not have concluded that an *in terrorem* penalty had been fixed at the time of the contract. Moreover, to regard that sum as being equally claimable for a breach that lasted for a short time as well as for a breach which continued over the entire covenant period would be an unreasonable conclusion. The question that arises here however is whether the same appreciation should prevail in a case where the quantum of damages, actually suffered or claimable, depends on the length of time over which the covenantor continues to be in breach of its covenant.

Should the respondent here be faulted then because it did not seek an interim injunction when it filed its counterclaim on April 25, 1967, some three months after it terminated the contract, or because it did not thereafter seek an interlocutory injunction until trial through which to stanch the flow of damages measured by gross trading profits? There is no doubt that a covenantee cannot have both an injunction during the covenant period and damages based on a breach of covenant for the entire period where they are based on a formula. There is case law holding that where a fixed sum is stipulated as the liquidated damages upon a breach, the covenantee cannot have both the damages and an injunction but must elect between the two remedies: see *Gen. Accident Assur. Corp. v. Noel*, [1902] 1 K.B. 377; *Wirth & Hamid Fair Booking Inc. v. Wirth* (1934), 192 N.E. 297. I do not however read these cases as excluding damages for past loss by reason of the breach, but only as precluding recovery of the liquidated amount referable to breach in the future which that amount was designed to cover and against which an injunction has been granted. By not seeking an interim or interlocutory injunction, the respondent gives some support to the proposition that it was more profitable to it to let the default of the appellant continue. On the other hand, the appellant accepted the risk of being held liable for gross trading profits by continuing to be in breach for the entire post-contract period of the covenant's operation.

In this state of affairs, I think the proper course is to look at the situation (as in fact it was at the time of the trial) as one where each party was content to have the issue of liquidated damages or penalty determined according to the consequences of a breach over the entire period of the covenant. The appellant cannot, of course, escape liability for at least the damages which a Court would fix if called upon to do so. Should it be so called upon in this case by a holding that to allow recovery of gross trading profits would be to impose a penalty and not give compensation in a situation where calculation of damages is difficult and incapable of precise determination? I would answer this question (and I do it after anxious consideration) in the affirmative.

I do not ignore a factor or factors in connection with breach of a covenant not to compete that are not as easily measured in dollars as are gross trading profits and net profits but which none the less have a value. . . . When regard is had, on the one hand, to the market situation with which the respondent had to contend before the appellant became its distributor, and, on the other hand, to the position of the distributor as itself an already known firm in that market, the respondent is undoubtedly entitled to an allowance for what it has termed loss of product identification and goodwill and for depreciation of its customer and trade relations during the three- year period of unlawful competition by the appellant. This allowance cannot, however, be assessed on the basis that ignores completely the existence of the appellant. Whatever it may turn out to be, as related to and as in addition to the estimated net profit loss of $92,017, in my opinion it cannot, because of the difficulty of putting a figure on it, lend the necessary support to make the gross trading profits of $239,449.05 an acceptable measure of liquidated damages.

I regard the exaction of gross trading profits as a penalty in this case because it is, in my opinion, a grossly excessive and punitive response to the problem to which it was addressed; and the fact that the appellant subscribed to it, and may have been foolish to do so, does not mean that it should be left to rue its unwisdom. *Snell's Principles of Equity*, 27th ed. (1973), at p. 535 states the applicable doctrine as follows:

> The sum will be held to be a penalty if it is extravagant and unconscionable in amount in comparison with the greatest loss that could conceivably be proved to have followed from the breach . . .

I do not think that it loses its force in cases where there is difficulty of exact calculation or pre-estimation when the stipulation for liquidated damages, as in this case, is disproportionate and unreasonable when compared with the damages sustained or which would be recoverable through an action in the Courts for breach of the covenant in question: see 25 Corp. Jur. Sec., §108, pp. 1051 *et seq*. The fact that the highest amount put forward by the respondent as its actual loss was $92,017 is plainly indicative of the disproportion that resides in the exaction of gross trading profits of $239,449.05.

I would characterize the exaction of gross trading profits for a three-year period as a penalty and not as giving rise to a sum claimable as compensation by way of liquidated damages. . . .

In the result, I would allow the appeal on what I have called the main issue, set aside the judgments below and in their place I would direct judgment for the respondent for damages for breach of the covenants not to compete with a reference to the Master at Toronto, Ontario, to ascertain the damages. . . .

[Judson and Spence JJ. concurred with Laskin C.J.C.; Martland and Dickson JJ. dissented and indicated that they were in agreement with the reasons of the Court of Appeal for Ontario.]

NOTES and QUESTIONS

1. Has the Supreme Court of Canada altered the law relating to liquidated damages as you had come to understand it? As the Ontario Court of Appeal had understood it?

2. As the judgment of Laskin C.J.C. emphasizes, the respondent had legitimate business interests to protect when it entered the distributorship arrangement. In the light of the decision in the case, how would you advise the respondent to achieve that protection in the future?

3. For an economic view of the legal debate in the *Thermidaire* case, see Goetz and Scott, "Liquidated Damages, Penalties and the Just Compensation Principle: Some Notes on an Enforcement Model and a Theory of Efficient Breach" (1977), 77 Columbia L. Rev. 554.

4. A common form of remedial provision that is sometimes classified as a penalty is one that accelerates instalment payments in the event of a failure to pay one or more instalments on time. However, note the sympathetic treatment of such clauses in *32262 B.C. Ltd. v. See-Rite Optical Ltd.*, [1998] 9 W.W.R. 442 (Alta. C.A.). This involved a demand for the accelerated payment of 70 monthly payments on a sign that See-Rite had rented and then returned after failing to give notice that it was not renewing its contract with the sign supplier. Despite the fact that the amount being sued for was pure profit, the initial costs having been recovered under the original renting, the court,

reversing the first instance judge, allowed the claim. Accelerated payment clauses in chattel leases of this kind were normally not penalties even where the chattel which was the subject of the lease has been recovered by the lessor. However, it was noteworthy that the sign in this case had no residual value.

5. Before proceeding to the next case, you should re-read *Howe v. Smith, supra*, Chapter 7, section 8.

J.G. COLLINS INSURANCE AGENCIES LTD. v. ELSLEY

[1978] 2 S.C.R. 916

The facts of this case and the discussion of the enforceability of a restrictive covenant in a contract of employment are set out *supra*, Chapter 13, section 2(a). The Supreme Court found the restrictive covenant binding and went on to consider the enforceability of a clause which stated that the defendant "in the event of his failing to observe or perform" the agreement would pay to the plaintiff "the sum of $1000 as and for liquidated damages".

DICKSON J. [delivering the judgment of the court] The matter of the right of a plaintiff to recover legal damages for actual loss sustained where a lesser stipulated amount is mentioned was considered in the House of Lords decision in *Cellulose Acetate Silk Co. v. Widnes Foundry (1925) Ltd.*, [1933] A.C. 20. The amount stipulated was £20 for each week of delay in the erection of an acetone recovery plant. The contractors were 30 weeks late. The actual loss suffered was £5,850. The case is of interest in two respects. First, the recovery was limited to £600, the agreed damages. Second, Lord Atkin, delivering judgment, said that he found it unnecessary to consider what would be the position if the stipulated £20 per week were a penalty, adding, p. 26:

> It was argued by the appellants that if this were a penalty they would have an option either to sue for the penalty or for damages for breach of the promise as to time of delivery. I desire to leave open the question whether, where a penalty is plainly less in amount than the prospective damages, there is any legal objection to suing on it, or in a suitable case ignoring it and suing for damages.

There is authority indicating that a penalty clause is ineffective even where it is less than the actual loss suffered (see 12 Hals., 4th ed., para. 118, p. 422, and the authorities cited therein). The result would be that actual damages could be recovered which exceeded the amount stipulated as a penalty. To that extent, the proposition appears to me to be contrary to principle and productive of injustice. The foundation of relief in equity against penalties is expressed in Story, *Equity Jurisprudence*, 14th ed. at s. 1728, as follows:

> Where a penalty or forfeiture is designed merely as a security to enforce the principal obligation, it is as much against conscience to allow any party to pervert it to a different and oppressive purpose as it would be to allow him to substitute another for the principal obligation.

The operation of this relief in the face of contrary agreement by the party is also explained in this section:

> If it be said that it is his own folly to have made such a stipulation, it may equally well be said that the folly of one man cannot authorize gross oppression on the other side.

It is now evident that the power to strike down a penalty clause is a blatant interference with freedom of contract and is designed for the sole purpose of providing relief against oppression for the party having to pay the stipulated sum. It has no place where there is no oppression. If the actual loss turns out to exceed the penalty, the normal rules of enforcement of contract should apply to allow recovery of only the agreed sum. The party imposing the penalty should not be able to obtain the benefit of whatever intimidating force the penalty clause may have in inducing performance, and then ignore the clause when it turns out to be to his advantage to do so. A penalty clause should function as a limitation on the damages recoverable, while still being ineffective to increase damages above the actual loss sustained when such loss is less than the stipulated amount. As expressed by Lord Ellenborough in *Wilbeam v. Ashton* (1807), 1 Camp. 78, 170 E.R. 883: " . . . beyond the penalty you shall not go; within it, you are to give the party any compensation which he can prove himself entitled to". Of course, if an agreed sum is a valid liquidated damages clause, the plaintiff is entitled at law to recover this sum regardless of the actual loss sustained.

In the context of the present discussion of the measure of damages, the result is that an agreed sum payable on breach represents the maximum amount recoverable whether the sum is a penalty or a valid liquidated damages clause. . . .

[Accordingly, the plaintiff was found to be entitled to an injunction and to such damages as he could prove to date of trial, not exceeding $1000.]

QUESTIONS

1. How does the approach of Dickson J. differ from that of the majority in *H.F. Clarke Ltd. v. Thermidaire Corp*?

2. Was the liquidated damages clause intended to be oppressive? Should we assume it to be so? Did Dickson J. make this assumption?

3. Has Dickson J. identified the only conceivable rationale for the penalty rule? Could another rationale be articulated which would be consistent with recovery of actual damages?

4. The real estate market in Sudbury is falling. A is having difficulty selling his modest bungalow. B is willing to pay $100,000 for it but cannot afford a large deposit. A agrees to accept a $100 deposit and inserts this amount in the appropriate place in the standard form agreement which contains the following provision:

> It is understood that time shall be of the essence hereof, and unless the balance of the cash payment is paid and a formal agreement entered into within the time mentioned to pay the balance, the owner may (at his option) cancel this agreement, and in such event the amount paid by the purchaser shall be absolutely forfeited to the owner as liquidated damages.

The market value falls to $60,000. B refuses to pay the outstanding balance of the purchase price. What are A's damages?

See, generally, *Gisvold v. Hill* (1963), 37 D.L.R. (2d) 606 (B.C. S.C.); *Lozcal Hldg. Ltd. v. Brassos Dev. Ltd.* (1980), 111 D.L.R. (3d) 598 (Alta. C.A.); *Raymer v. Stratton Woods Holdings Ltd.* (1988), 51 D.L.R. (4th) 145 (Ont. C.A.).

5. Irrespective of whether it is a fair reading of Dickson J.'s judgment in *Elsley*, there is now a significant body of Canadian case law supporting the proposition that penalty clauses are enforceable provided they are not oppressive: *Fern Investments Ltd. v. Golden Nugget Restaurant (1987) Ltd.* (1994), 19 Alta. L.R. (3d) 442 (C.A.); *Lee v. OCCO Developments Ltd.* (1996), 181 N.B.R. (2d) 241

(C.A.) (*per* Bastarache J.A., as he then was); *MTK Auto West Ltd. v. Allen* (2003), [2003] B.C.J. No. 2430, 2003 CarswellBC 2589 (S.C. [In Chambers]); *iTV Games Inc., Re* (2002), 21 B.L.R. (3d) 258 (B.C. C.A. [In Chambers]); *McNamara Construction Co. v. Newfoundland Transshipment Ltd.* (2002), 213 Nfld. & P.E.I.R. 1 (Nfld. T.D.).

STOCKLOSER v. JOHNSON

[1954] 1 Q.B. 476, [1954] 1 All E.R. 630 (C.A.)

The defendant owned a plant and machinery which was located in two quarries and which he rented to two separate companies. In 1950, he sold the plant and machinery in both quarries, together with the benefit of the rental agreements, to the plaintiff for a total price of £22,000. The purchase price was payable by an initial instalment of £4,000, to be followed by periodic instalment payments until the entire price was paid. It was a term of the contract that the defendant remained owner of the plant and machinery until the entire purchase price was paid. The contract further provided that if the purchaser defaulted in payment, the vendor was entitled to terminate the contract and that all payments made by the purchaser to the vendor would be forfeited to the vendor. In December, 1951, the plaintiff failed to make the necessary payment of instalments and in February, 1952, the defendant terminated the contract. The plaintiff sought to recover from the defendant the instalments that had been paid before the termination of the contract.

DENNING L.J. . . . . There was acute contest as to the proper legal principles to apply in this case. On the one hand, counsel for the plaintiff urged us to hold that the buyer was entitled to recover the instalments at law. He said that the forfeiture clause should be ignored because it was of a penal character, and, once it was ignored, it meant that the buyer was left with a simple right to repayment of his money . . . subject only to a cross-claim for damages. In asking us to ignore the forfeiture clause, counsel relied on the familiar tests which are used to distinguish between penalties and liquidated damages. . . . There is, I think, a plain distinction between penalty cases, strictly so called, and cases like the present. It is this. When one party seeks to exact a penalty from the other, he is seeking to exact payment of an extravagant sum either by action at law or by appropriating to himself moneys belonging to the other party. The claimant invariably relies, like Shylock, on the letter of the contract to support his demand, but the courts decline to give him their aid because they will not assist him in an act of oppression.

In the present case, however, the defendant is not seeking to exact a penalty. He only wants to keep money which already belongs to him. The money was handed to him in part payment of the purchase price and, as soon as it was paid, it belonged to him absolutely. He did not obtain it by extortion or oppression or anything of that sort, and there is an express clause—a forfeiture clause, if you please—permitting him to keep it. It is not the case of a seller seeking to enforce a penalty, but a buyer seeking restitution of money paid. If the buyer, the plaintiff, is to recover it, he must, I think, have recourse to somewhat different principles from those applicable to penalties, strictly so called. On the other hand, counsel for the defendant urged us to hold that the plaintiff could only recover the money if he was able and willing to perform the contract and for this purpose he ought to pay or offer to pay the instalments which were in arrear and be willing to pay the future instalments as they became due. . . . I think that this contention goes too far in the opposite direction. If the plaintiff was seeking to re-establish the contract, he would, of course, have to pay up the arrears and to show himself willing to perform the contract in the future, just as a lessee, who has suffered a forfeiture, has to do when he seeks to re-establish the lease. So, also, if the plaintiff were seeking specific performance, he would have to show himself able and willing to perform his part. But the plaintiff's object here is not to re-establish the contract. It is to get his money back: and to do this, I do not think it is necessary for him to go so far as to show he is ready and willing to perform the contract.

I reject, therefore, the arguments of counsel at each extreme. It seems to me that the cases show the law to be this. (i) When there is no forfeiture clause, if money is handed over in part payment of the purchase price, and then the buyer makes default as to the balance, then, so long as the seller keeps the contract open and available for performance, the buyer cannot recover the money, but once the seller rescinds the contract or treats it as at an end owing to the buyer's default, then the buyer is entitled to recover his money by action at law, subject to a cross-claim by the seller for damages . . . (ii) But when there is a forfeiture clause or the money is expressly paid as a deposit (which is equivalent to a forfeiture clause), then the buyer who is in default cannot recover the money at law at all. He may, however, have a remedy in equity, for, despite the express stipulation in the contract, equity can relieve the buyer from forfeiture of the money and order the seller to repay it on such terms as the court thinks fit. . . .

The difficulty is to know what are the circumstances which give rise to this equity. . . . Two things are necessary: first, the forfeiture clause must be of a penal nature, in the sense that the sum forfeited must be out of all proportion to the damage; and, secondly, it must be unconscionable for the seller to retain the money. Inasmuch as the only case in which this jurisdiction has been exercised is *Steedman v. Drinkle* [(1915), 25 D.L.R. 420], I have examined the record and would draw attention to the circumstances of that case. The agreement was, in effect, a hire-purchase agreement of land. The purchase money was payable by instalments over six years, completion to be at the end of the six years, and meanwhile the purchasers were to be let into possession of the land as tenants, with the instalments ranking as rent. In case of default the vendor was at liberty to cancel the contract and retain the payments that had been made. The purchasers paid the first instalment and went into possession, but they failed to pay the second instalment which was due at the end of the first year. The value of the land had risen greatly during that year and the vendor seized on the purchaser's default as giving him the opportunity to rescind the contract. Without previous warning, the vendor gave notice of cancelling the contract. The purchasers at once tendered the amount due, but the vendor refused to accept it. The purchasers issued a writ for specific performance and meanwhile remained in possession of the land, taking the crops off it. They failed to get specific performance in the first court, then succeeded in the Court of Appeal [the Supreme Court of Saskatchewan en banc], but failed again in the Privy Council on the ground that time was expressly of the essence of the contract. Nevertheless, the Privy Council relieved the purchasers from forfeiture of the sums already paid. The purchasers would, no doubt, have to give credit for the crops they had taken from the land during the three years or more that they had been in possession, but, subject to that credit, they would get their money back. . . .

The basis of the decision in *Steedman v. Drinkle* was, I think, that the vendor had somewhat sharply exercised his right to rescind the contract and re-take the land, and it was unconscionable for him also to forfeit the sums already paid. Equity could not specifically enforce the contract, but it could and would relieve against the forfeiture.

In the course of the argument before us Somervell, L.J., put an illustration which shows the necessity for this equity even though the buyer is not ready and willing to perform the contract. Suppose a buyer has agreed to buy a necklace by instalments, and the contract provides that, on default in payment of any one instalment, the seller is entitled to rescind the contract and forfeit the instalments already paid. The buyer pays ninety per cent of the price but fails to pay the last instalment. He is not able to perform the contract because he simply cannot find the money. The seller thereupon rescinds the contract, retakes the necklace, and re-sells it at a higher price. Surely equity will relieve the buyer against forfeiture of the money on such terms as may be just. Again, suppose that a vendor of property, in lieu of the usual ten per cent deposit, stipulates for an initial payment of fifty per cent of the price as a deposit and a part payment, and later, when the purchaser fails to complete, the vendor re-sells the property at a profit and, in addition, claims to forfeit the fifty per cent deposit. Surely the court will relieve against the forfeiture. The vendor cannot forestall this equity by describing an extravagant sum as a deposit, any more than he can recover a penalty by calling it liquidated damages. These illustrations convince me that in a proper case there is an equity of restitution which a party in default does not lose simply because he is not able and willing to perform the contract. Nay, that is the very reason why he needs the equity. The equity operates, not because of the plaintiff's default, but because it is, in the particular case, unconscionable for the seller to retain the money. In short, he ought not unjustly to enrich himself at the plaintiff's expense. This equity of restitution is to be tested, I think, not at the time of the contract, but by the conditions existing when it is invoked. Suppose, for instance, that in the instance of the necklace, the first instalment was only five per cent of the price and the buyer made default on the second instalment. There would be no equity by which he could ask for the first instalment to be repaid to him any more than he could claim repayment of a deposit. But it is very different after ninety per cent has been paid . . .

Applying these principles to the present case, even if one regards the forfeiture clause as of a penal nature—as the judge did and I am prepared to do—nevertheless I do not think it was unconscionable for the defendant to retain the money. The plaintiff seems to have gambled on the royalties being higher than they were. He thought they would go a long way to enable him to pay the instalments, but owing to bad weather they turned out to be smaller than he hoped and he could not find the additional amount necessary to pay the instalments. The judge summarised the position neatly when he said that the plaintiff

> is in the position of a gambler who has lost his stake and is now saying that it is for the court of equity to get it back for him.

He said:

> If it is a question of what is unconscionable, or, to use a word with a less legal flavour, unfair, I can see nothing whatever unfair in the defendant retaining the money.

With that finding of the judge I entirely agree and think that it disposes of the plaintiff's claim to restitution. . . .

[Separate opinions concurring in the result were delivered by Somervell and Romer L.JJ.]

NOTES and QUESTIONS

1. What remedy does Denning L.J. envisage where the purchaser defaults after having paid 90 per cent of the price of the necklace?

Compare the comment of Romer L.J., concurring in the result but not the reasoning of Denning L.J. ([1954] 1 Q.B. 476 at 501-02):

> It would certainly seem hard that the purchaser should lose both the necklace and all previous instalments owing to his inability to pay the last one. But that is the bargain into which the purchaser freely entered and the risk which he voluntarily accepted. The court would, doubtless, as I have already indicated, give him further time to find the money if he could establish some probability of his being able to do so, but I do not know why it should intervene further; nor would it be easy to determine at what point in his failure to pay the agreed instalments the suggested equity would arise. In any event, I venture to suggest that it is extremely unlikely that such a case would occur in practice, for a purchaser who had paid, say, nine-tenths of the agreed price for the necklace would have little difficulty in borrowing the remaining one-tenth on the security of his interest therein.

For a Canadian endorsement of the Denning approach, see the judgment of Ritchie J. in *Dimensional Investments Ltd. v. R.* (1967), [1968] S.C.R. 3. See also *Digger Excavating (1983) Ltd. v. Bowlen* (2001), 97 Alta. L.R. (3d) 41 (C.A.), where the principles of *Stockloser* were applied to a forfeiture of deposit case.

2. What can you learn about structuring sales transactions from the approaches that courts have traditionally taken to deposits and penalty clauses?

In *Damon v. Hapag-Lloyd*, [1983] 3 All E.R. 510, affirmed [1985] 1 All E.R. 475 (C.A.), the buyers agreed to buy three ships for $2,365,000 and to pay a deposit of 10 per cent. Upon repudiation by the buyer, the seller resold the ships for a loss of $70,000 and sued the buyer for the unpaid deposit of $236,500. Despite the disparity between the amount of the deposit and the actual loss, the court found that the seller was entitled to recover the deposit, because the right to receive the deposit had accrued before the buyer's repudiation.

What might have been the result if there had been no provision in the contract for a deposit, but merely a term which stated that upon breach the seller was entitled to recover from the buyer $236,500 by way of liquidated damages?

Is there a justification for the traditional distinction between liquidated damages clauses and deposits?

3. There are other forms of remedy stipulation besides liquidated damages, accelerated payment and forfeiture clauses. However, here too, there are potential problems with their recognition by the courts. Thus, for example, in *Tritav Holdings Ltd. v. National Bank Ltd.* (1996), 47 C.P.C. (3d) 91 (Ont. Gen. Div.), the court refused to recognize a clause in a lease prescribing specific performance as being available to force a key or anchor tenant to honour a "stay open" clause in a lease of business premises in a shopping centre. The actual specification of the remedy could not overcome the

unwillingness of the common law courts to provide specific relief in such cases. (See further under Specific Performance.)

4. Equitable Remedies

(a) SPECIFIC PERFORMANCE

Unlike the situation in many civil law jurisdictions, the availability of specific as opposed to substitutional relief is very restricted at common law. Thus, only in situations where substitutional relief (damages) does not protect sufficiently a plaintiff's interest in a contract will specific performance or injunctive relief be available. Moreover, even then, the courts possess quite broad discretionary powers to deny these forms of equitable relief for reasons generally having to do with the conduct of the plaintiff. (These discretionary considerations are detailed more fully below.)

Part of the explanation for this position is found in the historical origins of the remedies of specific performance and injunction. They are equitable in nature and represented a typical Court of Chancery response to situations where the common law was not providing sufficient protection to the rights of citizens. Equity came in to fill the gaps of the common law. However, as was generally the case, equity's intervention was not available when it was not needed and, therefore, in any case where the Court of Chancery believed that damages at common law would compensate a plaintiff adequately, specific performance and injunctive relief were not awarded. Moreover, to the extent that there were market substitutes available for most goods and services that were traded by way of contract, the normal response to the breach of such contracts was that, as replacements were available, damages reflecting any higher price that had to be paid along with added transactional costs were generally seen as a perfectly adequate remedy in such instances.

Indeed, it is argued by many that the preference for damages over specific relief is explicable not simply in terms of the history of common law and equity but also by considerations of economic efficiency as reflected more generally in the mitigation principle. Given the delays inherent in going to court and securing specific relief, economically rational persons when confronted with a contract breach will generally be acting far more sensibly if they go immediately into the substitute market rather than suing for specific performance. Such a course of action will also cause less disruption to the person in breach. Thereafter, any dislocation of the contractual expectations of the plaintiff can be adjusted by an appropriate award of damages. There is much that is sensible in this argument. However, assuming that most contractual parties will generally act in an economically rational way, there is a question as to whether there should be a presumption in favour of an award of specific performance to those who actually seek it. Surely, it will be a rare instance indeed that someone will go against her or his economic self-interest and sue for specific performance when damages are an adequate form of compensation?

The courts have also always been reluctant to award specific performance or an injunction where there will be difficulty in determining whether the order of the court has been obeyed. Where contractual performance depends upon the exercise of personal talents (such as performing in a play), questions can easily arise as to whether a person subject to an equitable decree has given of her or his best. The courts are unwilling to become engaged in such problematic assessments in the context of subsequent enforcement proceedings. Similarly, if a decree cannot be formulated with a reasonable degree of precision, the courts may later be called upon to make difficult judgments in the context of enforcement proceedings such as in the case of a building contract where there are significant gaps in the original contractual specifications.

This concept of "difficulty of supervision" also feeds into a final justification for the courts' reluctance to award specific and injunctive relief. This springs from the nature of equitable decrees. As opposed to common law remedies which operate *in rem* (on the goods and possessions of the defendant), equitable decrees operate *in personam* (on the person). This means that disobedience to an equitable decree will expose a defendant to the possibility of citation for civil contempt of court with its attendant risk of incarceration until such time as the contempt is "purged". Often, the courts are reluctant to give remedies where such a possibility exists and this is particularly so in situations where questions may arise as to whether or not the decree actually has been disobeyed. In contrast, those not paying damages stand exposed only to judgment debt proceedings where the ultimate sanction is seizure and sale of the judgment debtor's goods and possessions in order to satisfy the judgment debt. While it is highly questionable whether these differences are really of practical significance today, it is commonly asserted that they do provide further explanation for the courts' preference for common law over equitable relief.

The one domain, however, where historically equitable relief was generally regarded as available almost as of right was with respect to contracts involving an estate or interest in land. While there were generally always market substitutes for goods and services, equity traditionally regarded each piece of land as unique and as generating a claim for specific performance whenever a failure to complete a land transaction occurred. Indeed, fueled in part by principles of mutuality, in part by the immediate passing of a form of equitable title at the conclusion of any agreement of purchase and sale, and in part by the fact that on occasion damages would not be adequate remedy even to vendors, vendors of land generally had as strong a case for specific performance as purchasers: *Kloepfer Wholesale Hardware & Automotive Co. v. Roy*, [1952] 2 S.C.R. 465.

However, as we have seen already in the context of *Semelhago*, with the increasing commodification of interests in land ("cookie cutter" apartment buildings, factories in industrial parks, and shops in strip malls), judicial attitudes towards the availability of specific performance of contracts trading such interests have begun to change dramatically. Thus, while it might be argued that Sopinka J.'s reflections on the need to reassess the automatic availability of specific performance of contracts for the sale of interest land were no more than *obiter dicta*, they have been picked up and applied in a significant number of cases. An inquiry into whether the particular property is unique has now become standard in such cases. Indeed, some courts now insist that the plaintiff bears the onus of establishing uniqueness: *11 Suntract Holdings Ltd. v. Chassis Service & Hydraulics Ltd.* (1997), 36 O.R. (3d) 328 (Gen. Div.).

JOHN E. DODGE HOLDINGS LTD. v. 805062 ONTARIO LTD.

(2003), 63 O.R. (3d) 304 (C.A.)

This case involved a conditional contract for the purchase and sale of 4.12 acres of serviced but undeveloped land near Canada's Wonderland. The purchaser was a hotel builder and manager. It was held at first instance that this was an appropriate case for an order of specific performance in accordance with the *Semelhago* principles. The vendor appealed on this and other grounds.

WEILER J.A. [delivering the judgment of the court.] In *Semelhago* v. *Paramadevan* [*supra*] at para. 22, Sopinka J. observed that specific performance will only be granted if the plaintiff can demonstrate that the subject property is unique in the sense that, "its substitute would not be readily available". Although Sopinka J. did not elaborate further on this definition, in *1252668 Ontario Inc.* v. *Wyndham Street Investments Inc.,* [1999] O.J. No. 3188 at para. 23, Justice Lamek stated that he:

> [does] not consider that the plaintiff has to demonstrate that the Premises are unique in a strict dictionary sense that they are entirely different from any other piece of property. It is enough, in my view, for the plaintiff to demonstrate that the Premises have a quality that makes them especially suitable for the proposed use and that they cannot be reasonably duplicated elsewhere.

I agree that in order to establish that a property is unique the person seeking the remedy of specific performance must show that the property in question has a quality that cannot be readily duplicated elsewhere. This quality should relate to the proposed use of the property and be a quality that makes it particularly suitable for the purpose for which it was intended. . . .

The time when a determination is to be made as to whether a property is unique is the date when an actionable act takes place and the wronged party must decide whether to keep the agreement alive by seeking specific performance or accept the breach and sue for damages: *Greenforco Holding Corp. v. Yonge-Merton Developments Ltd.,* [1999] O.J. No. 3232. at para. 76. It may also be that in certain cases the date chosen for determining the issue of whether specific performance is appropriate is a later date but the date will not, in any event, occur before the breach has taken place.

In oral submissions Magna submits that this date is March 6, 2000. On that date, Magna sent Dodge a fax which stated in part:

> To date, the attempts to eliminate the construction and dedication of Caldari Road have been unsuccessful. In light of the foregoing, this should cause no surprise However, it may cause a concern to the Purchaser because if the City continues to insist on the construction and dedication of the Additional Road as a condition of severance, Magna is not prepared to accept such a condition. This is why we have formally advised you of our concern that the transaction may be in jeopardy, as we are not prepared to accept such a condition, . . .
>
> There are many comparable sites in the immediate vicinity of the subject property available for sale at this time, and we invite you to explore this as a means for avoiding any losses you

may incur by reason of the City's delay or a failure to grant the severance required under the Planning Act.

Magna submits that following receipt of this letter Dodge was obliged to consider alternatives as part of its duty to mitigate its losses and that Dodge refused to do so. Dodge was only obliged to consider alternatives if it was not entitled to specific performance: see *Asamera Oil Corp. v. Sea Oil & General Corp., [supra]* at 668. Magna also submits that the date of this letter is the date of the actionable wrong. However, on April 28, 2000 Magna faxed a letter to Dodge indicating that it was appealing the decision of the Committee of Adjustment to the OMB. In light of this, the letter of March 6, 2000 cannot be taken as notice by Magna that the Agreement was terminated. The date of the actionable wrong was May 11, 2000, when Magna notified Dodge it would not appeal the decision of the Committee of Adjustment to the OMB but was terminating the Agreement instead.

The question then becomes whether the property was unique on the date of the actionable wrong. Magna contends that the trial judge erred in finding that the property was unique. It submits that other comparable commercial properties were available and, in particular, a property owned by a group of persons including Mr. Sorbara (the Sorbara property) and another at the Vaughan Mills Mall. At the date of the actionable wrong, May 11, 2000, the Sorbara property had been sold. The trial judge found that although the comparables from Magna's expert permitted a hotel to be built, none of them were in as close proximity to Canada's Wonderland or the Vaughan Mills Centre, a planned $250 million retail mall to be located directly west of the site. At para. 69 of her reasons she found:

> The Magna site offers superior access, visibility, traffic patterns and location to each of the other sites that were under consideration. It also has a C7 commercial zoning designation that is more favourable for ancillary uses such as banquet halls and eating establishments. This was significant for Dodge as the hotel concept it was considering at the time of the contract and later pursued was for a Hilton Garden Inn. This concept does not require full restaurant facilities in the hotel. The ability to have an unrestricted, independent dining facility on the land to accommodate hotel guests, but also to serve patrons in the area, was another distinguishing feature of this site. None of the other sites offered this combination of attractive features at a comparable price.

The appellant has not shown that the trial judge misapprehended the evidence or committed any overriding and palpable error in her findings. The trial judge did not err in her conclusion that this particular piece of commercial real estate was unique.

Finally, Magna also submits that a court cannot simply give Dodge the remedy that it seeks, namely an order for specific performance of the Agreement, because the court will have to go further than ordering a transfer of the property in issue from Magna to Dodge. Clause (j) of Schedule A to the Agreement contains a restrictive covenant. It states:

> The Purchaser consents to the Vendor including a restrictive covenant in the transfer deed or separate document whereby the Purchaser on its own behalf and on behalf of future occupiers and owners of the Property will not object to the use of the Vendor's property adjacent to the Property for the purposes of an industrial paint and plastics and/or manufacturing business.

Magna submits that the parties will be unable to agree on the terms of the restrictive covenant and the court will undoubtedly have to intervene again. Such an intervention, it submits, is more akin to contract redrafting than judicial supervision. I do not agree. Clause (j) does not say that the parties will negotiate a restrictive covenant, but instead contains the language of the restrictive covenant within it. The existence of clause (j) does not make the remedy of specific performance impractical or unfair.

[Appeal dismissed.]

NOTES and QUESTIONS

1. In contrast, where commercial and other land is purchased for development and resale, the trend in the case law is to deny specific performance. See *e.g.*, *Monson v. West Barrhaven Development Inc.*, [2000] O.J. No. 5209 (S.C.J.). However, there have been *obiter dicta* to the effect that, among the considerations that might lead to an order of specific performance in cases such as this is that of whether the calculation of damages would be "extremely difficult": *Neighbourhoods of Cornell Inc. v. 14401066 Ontario Inc.*, [2003] O.J. No. 2919 (S.C.J.), at para. 112 [O.J. No.] (*per* Speigel J.). In the context of residential property, the courts seem to have been looking for something about the property that makes it particularly desirable, a consideration that to this point has been favouring the wealthy: see *e.g.*, *Cormack v. Harwardt*, [1998] B.C.J. No. 2684 (S.C.) (large rural property suitable for raising and riding horses); *Hoover v. Mark Minor Homes Ltd.* (1998), 75 O.T.C. 165 (Gen. Div.) (rare property with trees and a pond though, interestingly, in this instance, it was the vendor who secured the order of specific performance).

2. Why do courts ordinarily award the decree of specific performance only when damages are inadequate? See Sharpe, *Injunctions and Specific Performance*, 2nd ed. (1992), at paras. 1.60–1.250. For an argument for the wider use of specific performance, see Schwartz, "The Case for Specific Performance" (1979), 89 Yale L.J. 271. For a historical view, see Berryman, "The Specific Performance Damages Continuum: An Historical Perspective" (1985), 17 Ottawa L. Rev. 295.

3. All Canadian Sale of Goods Acts provide that purchasers of "specific or ascertained goods" may seek specific performance of such contracts. However, the courts have never interpreted this provision, from the original English legislation, as extending their jurisdiction over the award of specific relief in goods contracts. Rather, the courts have treated the statement in the section that specific performance "may" be ordered as preserving the discretionary nature of such relief and, in particular, its general unavailability when damages are an adequate remedy. See, generally, Treitel, "Specific Performance in the Sale of Goods", [1966] J. Bus. L. 211. It should also be noted that, while there is some considerable uncertainty over the meaning of "specific or ascertained goods" for the purposes of the section, this does not necessarily mean that the section precludes the awarding of specific performance whenever the goods in question are not "specific or ascertained". That jurisdiction almost certainly continues to exist outside the Act. Thus, in *Sky Petroleum v. V.I.P. Petroleum*, [1974] 1 All E.R. 954 (Ch.), Goulding J. acknowledged the capacity of the courts to award specific relief of contracts for goods which were not specific or ascertained in granting an interlocutory injunction restraining the defendant from breaching its oil supply contract with the plaintiff. In this case, damages were not an adequate remedy as substitute long-term supply contracts for oil were not available during the Middle East Oil crisis. For a similar Canadian case, see *Marquest Indust. Ltd. v. Willows Poultry Farms Ltd.* (1967), 63 D.L.R. (2d) 753 (B.C. S.C.), reversed on other grounds 1 D.L.R. (3d) 513 (B.C. C.A.), where specific performance of a suddenly valuable commodity (chicken offal) was ordered at trial.

4. (a) Suppose A contracts to purchase "the Potato-Eaters" by Vincent Van Gogh from B for $30 million. Further assume that, although the masterpiece is unique, the purchaser simply intends to resell the picture in order to make a quick profit. Should the purchaser succeed in a suit for specific performance if the vendor refused to deliver "the Potato-

Eaters"? Does your answer depend on whether the vendor knew or should reasonably have known that the opportunity to take a quick profit was available to the purchaser?

(b) P contracts to purchase fifty pounds of grass-seed from D, with delivery due in two weeks time. At the date of delivery, the market price is $10 per pound, but D fails to deliver. A year later, the market price is $15 per pound. Should P claim specific performance (if it is available), or damages at common law? See the materials on the duty to mitigate, *supra*, section 3(c). Suppose D was in financial difficulties, with a host of unsecured creditors about to force D into bankruptcy. Would P gain any advantage by pursuing specific performance rather than damages?

5. In *Beswick v. Beswick*, [1968] A.C. 58 (H.L.), *supra*, Chapter 5, section 3(b), the following problem was discussed. Suppose A has a contract with B whereby B agrees to pay $2,000 to C, but refuses to do so. What damages could A recover in an action against B at common law? Is this a situation where specific performance is an appropriate remedy? In *Beswick v. Beswick* did the plaintiff suffer any loss *at all* for which an action for damages at common law could have been maintained? If specific performance is available where damages at law are inadequate to compensate for the loss, does it follow that specific performance is available where the plaintiff has suffered no legally recoverable loss? If the plaintiff were limited to nominal damages, wouldn't the defendant be unjustly enriched? Should it matter that the third party beneficiary cannot directly recover in these situations? For a detailed discussion of the availability of specific performance for the benefit of third parties, see Martin (ed.), *Hanbury and Maudsley's Modern Equity*, 13th ed. (1989), at 689-93; see also *Waugh v. Slavik* (1975), 62 D.L.R. (3d) 577 (B.C. S.C.).

6. Sale of Shares: Where shares are easily obtained in the market, and are of the same value to the plaintiff as those he has contracted to purchase from the defendant, specific performance will generally be refused. See the *Asamera* case, *supra*. Suppose, however, that A has a contract to purchase shares from D. Co. which D. Co. refuses to perform because A's rival, B, now controls the company. The shares are available in the market, but only from A's ally. If A obtains specific performance, he can regain control of the company. Should specific performance be decreed? See *Dobell v. Cowichan Copper Co.* (1967), 65 D.L.R. (2d) 440 (B.C. S.C.), where Seaton J. granted an interlocutory injunction restraining the issue of the shares to anyone other than the plaintiff. For a more detailed analysis of the availability of specific performance in the context of contracts for the sale of shares, see Note, "Specific Performance on Contracts for a Controlling Interest in a Corporation" (1935), 49 Harv. L.R. 122, and Neef, "Equity-Specific Performance—Recent Trends in the Specific Enforcement of Contracts to Sell Securities" (1953), 51 Mich. L.R. 408.

Under the Ontario Business Corporations Act, R.S.O. 1990, c. B.16, s. 80(3), "The right to reclaim possession of a security may be specifically enforced, its transfer may be restrained and the security may be impounded pending litigation."

See also s. 80(1) and s. 80(2). The same provisions are found in s. 72 of the Canada Business Corporations Act, R.S.C. 1985, c. C-44, s. 71 of the Alberta Business Corporations Act, R.S.A. 2000, c. B-9, and s. 68 of both Manitoba's Corporations Act, C.C.S.M., c. C225, and the Saskatchewan Business Corporations Act, R.S.S. 1978, c. B-10. Do these provisions change the law in any way?

7. Contracts for Personal Service: Where a defendant has contracted to perform a particular service requiring personal skill and then refuses to comply with the contractual obligation, the plaintiff will usually prefer to have the contract specifically performed rather than to collect damages, since the personal service might well be unique or especially prized. In these cases, damages do not appear to be adequate. However, courts of equity decided not to enforce contracts of personal service notwithstanding the inadequacy of monetary awards. First, any attempt at decreeing specific performance could well be a prelude to subsequent applications to determine whether there has been a proper performance of the personal obligation in question. Second, and more important, it is thought improper as a matter of public policy to compel persons to maintain certain personal relationships against their wills, although they had earlier agreed to do so. In *Lumley v. Wagner* (1852), 42 E.R. 687, Lord St. Leonards L.C. refused to decree specific performance of a contractual obligation of the defendant to sing in the plaintiff's theatre for a stipulated period, although the defendant was enjoined from singing elsewhere. In *Emerald Resources Ltd. v. Sterling Oil Properties Management*

Ltd. (1969), 3 D.L.R. (3d) 630 (Alta. C.A.), affirmed 15 D.L.R. (3d) 256 (S.C.C.), one reason given for refusing to order specific performance of a contract to pay royalties was that the plaintiff had agreed to work for the defendant in consideration of the royalty payments. See also *Dowsley v. Br. Can. Trust Co.*, [1933] S.C.R. 115. The courts have the means of enforcing compliance with a monetary award; could not the same be said regarding obligations to perform personal services? Where the contract in question requires the defendant to render an artistic performance, the threat of committal is not a satisfactory method of securing compliance, for how is the quality of the performance to be evaluated? In *C.H. Giles & Co. Ltd. v. Morris*, [1972] 1 All E.R. 960, Megarry J. adverted to this problem and stated (at 970):

> [N]ot all contracts of personal service or for the continuous performance of services are as dependent as this on matters of opinion and judgment. . . . I do not think that . . . as soon as any element of personal service or continuous services can be discerned in a contract the court will, without more, refuse specific performance.

The Court of Appeal approved this view in *Price v. Strange*, [1978] Ch. 337.

Related to the difficulty of quality control in contracts for personal service is the proposition that courts will not specifically enforce contracts requiring continuous successive acts because this would require constant supervision. Thus in *Ryan v. Mutual Tontine Westminster Chambers Assn.*, [1893] 1 Ch. 116 (C.A.), it was held that an undertaking in a lease to provide a porter "constantly in attendance" to perform various services could not be specifically enforced, since specific enforcement would require continuous supervision. Treitel questions whether this "difficulty" of supervision is really a severe problem, and cites several examples where courts have appointed individuals to administer or supervise other matters. See *The Law of Contract*, 9th ed. (1995), at 930-31. Another criticism of the "supervision" requirement is that insofar as it concerns contracts for personal service, the time has long since passed when employer-employee contracts brought the individuals concerned into a direct personal relationship.

Modern Canadian labour legislation providing for reinstatement as a remedy available to arbitrators and adjudicators suggests that, at least in the case of suits by employees, the common law position may be somewhat outmoded. See *e.g.*, *National Ballet of Canada v. Glasco* (2000), 186 D.L.R. (4th) 347 (S.C.J.), in which Swinton J. refused to interfere with an arbitral award obliging the National Ballet to continue to employ Ms. Glasco as a dancer pending the resolution of a civil action in which she was alleging, *inter alia*, wrongful dismissal. In rendering judgment, Swinton J. stated, at para. 50:

> While it is unusual for a court to order specific performance of an employment contract or a contract of personal service, there is no absolute rule against this, and the appellant conceded this.

A major reason for the refusal to order specific performance of contracts for personal service or skill is that the contractual requirements may not be sufficiently well-defined. As the penalty for disobedience to a decree of specific performance is severe, the courts have taken the position that before the defendant can be held responsible for a failure to perform as specified, the specifications must have been spelled out very clearly. In *Tanenbaum v. W.J. Bell Paper Co.* (1956), 4 D.L.R. (2d) 177 (Ont. H.C.), some exceptions to the general rule that specific performance of building contracts will not be decreed were established. Where damages would not adequately compensate the plaintiff, specific performance will be ordered if the specifications are defined by the contract with a sufficient degree of certainty and the labour is to be performed on the builder's land, obtained pursuant to the contract. The reason for this last requirement is that mere damages would not allow the plaintiff to obtain substitute performance, because (s)he would have to trespass in order to continue performance. However it is difficult to understand why the defendant must obtain the land by the contract. In *Tanenbaum*, this issue was not settled, although Farwell J. had held in *Carpenters Estates Ltd. v. Davies*, [1940] Ch. 160, that a possessory interest would suffice, provided that the other criteria were met.

8. Contracts to Keep Open a Business or Provide a Service: Recently, there have been a number of instances where plaintiffs have tried to secure orders compelling defendants to live up to obligations to keep a business operating. Generally, this is done by way of application for a mandatory injunction

rather than specific performance. Typically, these attempts happen when a key or anchor tenant is threatening to abandon a lease in a shopping complex or mall in breach of a clause in its lease obliging it to stay in business there throughout the term of the lease. In common law jurisdictions, such applications have universally been unsuccessful: see *e.g., S.B.I. Management Ltd. v. Wabush (Carol) Co-op Society Ltd.* (1985), 51 Nfld. & P.E.I.R. 257 (Nfld. T.D.); *Toulon Development Corporation v. Loblaws* (1995), 161 N.B.R. (2d) 313 (Q.B.); and *Co-operative Insurance Society Ltd. v. Argyll Stores (Holdings) Ltd.,* [1997] 2 W.L.R. 898 (U.K. H.L.). Indeed, as noted already, the situation of such a plaintiff has not been improved by the presence of a remedy stipulation clause in the lease: *Tritav Holdings Ltd. v. National Bank of Canada* (1996), 47 C.P.C. (3d) 91 (Ont. Gen. Div.). In this domain, difficulty in the formulation of a sufficiently precise decree and the attendant potential for subsequent enforcement proceedings loom as the major obstacles to the securing of relief. It is, however, noteworthy, that precedents for the issue of such relief do exist in civil and Roman-Dutch law jurisdictions: see, for example, *Retail Parks Investments Ltd. v. Royal Bank of Scotland,* [1996] S.L.T. 669 (Extra Division of Inner Court of Session) and *Propriétés Cité Concordia Ltée v. Royal Bank,* [1983] R.D.J. 524 (Que. C.A.).

(b) DEFENCES TO ACTIONS FOR SPECIFIC PERFORMANCE

(i) *Mutuality of Remedy*

Because specific performance is an equitable remedy, courts exercising equitable jurisdiction have attempted to develop an even-handed attitude towards those who seek it. This attitude is manifested by the proposition that the remedy is available to those against whom it would be available if they were in breach, and its corollary, that it is not available to those against whom it would be unavailable if they were in breach. For example, in *Gretzky v. Ont. Minor Hockey Assn.* (1975), 64 D.L.R. (3d) 467 (Ont. H.C.), Southey J. refused an application for an injunction by infant hockey players in which they were seeking to restrain the defendant from preventing them playing in a particular league. He stated, at 469, that:

> If there are contracts between the boys and the associations, they are voidable because of the ages of the boys and are not enforceable against the boys. There is no mutuality of rights and obligations as between the boys and the associations and I do not think that the court should grant an interim [*sic*] injunction, which is an equitable relief, to enforce a contract at the suit of a party who can avoid the contract.

The doctrine of mutuality is not free from controversy, as significant differences of opinion exist regarding its scope, rationale and application. Reference should be made to Fry, *Specific Performance,* 6th ed. (1921), at 219-28; and Ames, "Mutuality in Specific Performance" (1903), 3 Columbia L.R. 1 (reprinted in Ames, *Lectures on Legal History*); Cook, "The Present Status of the 'Lack of Mutuality' Rule" (1927), 36 Yale L.J. 897. See *Price v. Strange, supra,* where Goff and Buckley L.JJ. (Scarman L.J. concurring) thought that Sir Edward Fry's traditional view was incorrect.

It should also be observed that the doctrine of mutuality is responsible for the vendor's right to compel specific performance of a contract for the sale of land despite the fact that damages will usually be adequate compensation.

(ii) *Misrepresentation and Mistake*

Aside from circumstances which operate to vitiate the contract, and which necessarily establish defences to suits for specific performance, there are situations where courts will not rescind the contract, but will refuse to allow the plaintiff to compel performance, thus restricting the remedy to one of damages. For example, the requirements of misrepresentation as a defence differ from those of actionable misrepresentation. See *Redican v. Nesbitt*, [1924] S.C.R. 135; *Whitney v. MacLean*, [1932] 1 W.W.R. 417 (Alta. C.A.). Suppose that the plaintiff's misrepresentation was actionable by the defendant (in a suit for rescission) but the defendant has decided not to bring an action. Can the plaintiff obtain specific performance? See *Shaw v. Masson*, [1923] S.C.R. 187. If the defendant decides not to seek rescission, why should the plaintiff be precluded from specifically enforcing the contract?

Specific performance has also been refused in the case of a mistake that was not sufficiently serious to impair the validity of the contract, at least where there is an element of fault on the part of the plaintiff.

(iii) *Conduct of the Plaintiff*

A well-established maxim of equity is that "he who seeks equity must do equity", which is closely related, if not identical to, the maxim "he who comes to equity must come with clean hands". These maxims are illustrated by the equitable doctrines of laches and acquiescence which operate when the courts exercise their discretion in considering whether to decree any form of equitable relief. See *Bark Fong v. Cooper* (1913), 49 S.C.R. 14; *Mathews v. McVeigh*, [1954] 2 D.L.R. 338 (Ont. C.A.); *Orsi v. Morning* (1971), 20 D.L.R. (3d) 25 (Ont. C.A.). See also the discussion in *Kupchak v. Dayson Holdings Ltd.*, *supra*, Chapter 7, section 2. Where the plaintiff is in breach, the remedy will be refused.

(iv) *Hardship*

Where a decree of specific performance would cause severe and unnecessary hardship to the parties, or perhaps to a third party, specific performance may be refused, leaving the plaintiff to the remedy in damages. Before the defence will affect the exercise of the court's discretion, however, the circumstances giving rise to hardship must exist at the time the contract was formed, unless the plaintiff's conduct has caused a change in circumstances resulting in hardship. See *Stewart v. Ambrosina* (1975), 63 D.L.R. (3d) 595 (Ont. H.C.), affirmed 78 D.L.R. (3d) 125 (Ont. C.A.), although a more lenient view was taken in *Patel v. Ali*, [1984] Ch. 283. Hardship caused by inadequacy of consideration standing alone is not sufficient.

(v)   *Other Equitable Defences*

There are a number of other grounds which can influence the exercise of equitable jurisdiction in determining whether to grant the specific relief requested. For an excellent discussion of these grounds and the equitable defences generally, see Sharpe, *Injunctions and Specific Performance*, 2nd ed. (1992), c. 10.

(c) INJUNCTIONS

An injunction is an order of the court forbidding the defendant from doing something or requiring the defendant to do a particular act. In the former case it is a prohibitory injunction, in the latter the injunction is described as mandatory.

Before the enactment of the Judicature Acts, courts of law possessed a restricted right to grant injunctions, because the injunction was principally an equitable remedy, exercised by courts of equity. The Judicature Acts attempted to fuse the administration of the two systems and gave the "fused" court the jurisdiction to dispense both damages at law and equitable relief, including the injunction. The terms of provincial Judicature Acts and equivalent legislation appear to confer wide powers to award injunctions and other equitable remedies, but the weight of precedent consisting of cases decided before and after the Judicature Acts have restricted the scope of the power to a considerable degree, so the current availability of the injunction approximates its availability before "fusion".

Aside from the "mandatory/prohibitory" dichotomy, there are several types of injunctions that are defined with reference to their duration. An interim injunction is usually obtained *ex parte*, and lasts for a very short specified period (*e.g.*, 7 days) in order to enable the parties to prepare for a more thorough hearing of the matter. Because it is frequently obtained in the defendant's absence, the plaintiff will only succeed where the existence of an emergency can be demonstrated. The interlocutory injunction is usually obtained after the issue of the writ, and will last until trial or final disposition of the matter. Both the interim and the interlocutory injunctions are extraordinary remedies and their purpose is not so much to provide the courts with an opportunity of deciding the issues on the merits, but rather to prevent any irreparable or uncompensable injury from accruing before the dispute is finally resolved. A perpetual injunction is granted to the successful plaintiff at trial and is perpetual only in the sense that it finalizes the adjudication. In some circumstances it is also possible to obtain a *quia timet* injunction where the threat of serious damage is so great that an injunction will issue although no injury has actually been sustained.

(d) CONTRACTS OF PERSONAL SERVICE

Injunctive relief is not limited to the enforcement of contracts, as it is also available, for example, to restrain nuisances and other torts. However, we need not investigate its availability in contexts other than its use as a contractual remedy. We have already seen that courts will not generally decree specific performance in the case of contracts for personal service. Can a plaintiff obtain an injunction to enforce a contractual obligation when specific performance would not be ordered?

WARNER BROS. PICTURES INC. v. NELSON
[1937] 1 K.B. 209, [1936] 3 All E.R. 160

BRANSON J. The facts of this case are few and simple. The plaintiffs are a firm of film producers in the United States of America. In 1931 the defendant, then not well known as a film actress, entered into a contract with the plaintiffs. Before the expiration of that contract the present contract was entered into between the parties. Under it the defendant received a considerably enhanced salary, the other conditions being substantially the same. The contract was for fifty-two weeks and contains options to the plaintiffs to extend it for further periods of fifty-two weeks at ever-increasing amounts of salary to the defendant. No question of construction arises upon the contract, and it is not necessary to refer to it in any great detail; but in view of some of the contentions raised it is desirable to call attention quite generally to some of the provisions contained in it. It is a stringent contract, under which the defendant agrees "to render her exclusive services as a motion picture and/or legitimate stage actress" to the plaintiffs, and agrees to perform solely and exclusively for them. She also agrees, by way of negative stipulation, that "she will not, during such time"—that is to say, during the term of the contract—

> render any services for or in any other phonographic, stage or motion picture production or productions or business of any other person . . . or engage in any other occupation without the written consent of the producer being first had and obtained.

With regard to the term of the contract there is a further clause, clause 23, under which, if the defendant fails, refuses or neglects to perform her services under the contract, the plaintiffs have

> the right to extend the term of this agreement and all of its provisions for a period equivalent to the period during which such failure, refusal or neglect shall be continued.

In June of this year the defendant, for no discoverable reason except that she wanted more money, declined to be further bound by the agreement, left the United States and, in September, entered into an agreement in this country with a third person. This was a breach of contract on her part, and the plaintiffs on September 9 commenced this action claiming a declaration that the contract was valid and binding, an injunction to restrain the defendant from acting in breach of it, and damages. The defence alleged that the plaintiffs had committed breaches of the contract which entitled the defendant to treat it as at an end; but at the trial this contention was abandoned and the defendant admitted that the plaintiffs had not broken the contract and that she had; but it was contended on her behalf that no injunction could as a matter of law be granted in the circumstances of the case.

At the outset of the considerations of law which arise stands the question, not raised by the pleadings but urged for the defendant in argument, that this contract is unlawful as being in restraint of trade. The ground for this contention was that the contract compelled the defendant to serve the plaintiffs exclusively, and might in certain circumstances endure for the whole of her natural life. No authority was cited to me in support of the proposition that such a contract is illegal, and I see no reason for so holding. Where, as in the present contract, the covenants are all concerned with what is to happen whilst the defendant is employed by the plaintiffs and not thereafter, there is no room for the application of the doctrine of restraint of trade. . . .

I turn then to the consideration of the law applicable to this case on the basis that the contract is a valid and enforceable one. It is conceded that our Courts will not enforce a positive covenant of personal service; and specific performance of the positive covenants by the defendant to serve the plaintiffs is not asked in the present case. The practice of the Court of Chancery in relation to the enforcement of negative covenants is stated on the highest authority by Lord Cairns in the House of Lords in *Doherty v. Allman* [(1878), 3 App. Cas. 709 at 719 (H.L.)]. His Lordship says:

> My Lords, if there had been a negative covenant, I apprehend, according to well-settled practice, a Court of Equity would have had no discretion to exercise. If parties, for valuable consideration, with their eyes open, contract that a particular thing shall not be done, all that a Court of Equity has to do is to say, by way of injunction, that which the parties have already said by way of covenant, that the thing shall not be done; and in such case the injunction does nothing more than give the sanction of the process of the Court to that which already is the contract between the parties. It is not than a question of the balance of convenience or inconvenience, or of the amount of damage or injury—it is the specific performance, by the Court, of that negative bargain which the parties have made, with their eyes open, between themselves.

That was not a case of a contract of personal service; but the same principle had already been applied to such a contract by Lord St. Leonards in *Lumley v. Wagner* [(1852), 42 E.R. 687]. The Lord Chancellor used the following language:

> Wherever this Court has not proper jurisdiction to enforce specific performance, it operates to bind men's consciences, as far as they can be bound, to a true and literal performance of their agreements; and it will not suffer them to depart from their contracts at their pleasure, leaving the party with whom they have contracted to the mere chance of any damages which a jury may give. The exercise of this jurisdiction has, I believe, had a wholesome tendency towards the maintenance of that good faith which exists in this country to a much greater degree perhaps than in any other; and although the jurisdiction is not to be extended, yet a Judge would desert his duty who did not act up to what his predecessors have handed down as the rule for his guidance in the administration of such an equity.

.....

The defendant, having broken her positive undertakings in the contract without any cause or excuse which she was prepared to support in the witness-box, contends that she cannot be enjoined from breaking the negative covenants also. The mere fact that a covenant which the Court would not enforce, if expressed in positive form, is expressed in the negative instead, will not induce the Court to enforce it. . . .

The Court will attend to the substance and not to the form of the covenant. Nor will the Court, true to the principle that specific performance of a contract of personal service will never be ordered, grant an injunction in the case of such a contract to enforce negative covenants if the effect of so doing would be to drive the defendant either to starvation or to specific performance of the positive covenants. . . .

The conclusion to be drawn from the authorities is that, where a contract of personal service contains negative covenants the enforcement of which will not amount either to a decree of specific performance of the positive covenants of the contract or to the giving of a decree under which the defendant must either remain idle or perform those positive covenants, the Court will enforce those negative covenants; but this is subject to further consideration. An injunction is a discretionary remedy, and the Court in granting it may limit it to what the Court considers reasonable in all the circumstances of the case.

This appears from the judgment of the Court of Appeal in *Robinson (William) & Co. Ltd. v. Heuer* [[1898] 2 Ch. 451]. The particular covenant in that case is set out at p. 452 and provides that "Heuer shall not during this engagement, without the previous consent in writing of the said W. Robinson & Co. Ltd.," and so forth, "carry on or be engaged either directly or indirectly, as principal, agent, servant, or otherwise, in any trade, business, or calling, either relating to goods of any description sold or manufactured by the said W. Robinson & Co. Ltd. . . . or in any other business whatsoever." There are passages in the judgment of Lindley M.R. which bear so closely on several aspects of the present case that I shall refer to them. He begins his judgment by saying that the result at which he is arriving is that justice requires that some injunction should be granted. He goes on to say:

> This defendant is avowedly breaking the agreement, and the question is whether he should be at liberty to do so.

There was a question raised whether that agreement was or was not illegal, and as to that the Master of the Rolls says:

> There is no authority whatever to shew that this is an illegal agreement—that is to say, that it is unreasonable, and goes further than is reasonably necessary for the protection of the plaintiffs. It is confined to the period of the engagement, and means simply this—'So long as you are in our employ you shall not work for anybody else or engage in any other business.' There is nothing unreasonable in that at all.

That seems to me to apply very precisely to the present case. The Master of the Rolls continues:

> When, however, you come to talk about an injunction to enforce it, there is great difficulty. The real difficulty, which has always to be borne in mind when you talk about specific performance of or injunctions to enforce agreements involving personal service is this—that this Court never will enforce an agreement by which one person undertakes to be the servant of another, and if this agreement were enforced in its terms, it would compel this gentleman personally to serve the plaintiffs for the period of ten years. That the Court never does. Therefore an injunction in these terms cannot be granted, although the agreement to serve the plaintiffs and give his whole care, time, and attention to their business, and not to engage in any other business during his engagement, is valid in point of law. But the plaintiffs do not ask for an injunction in the terms of that agreement.

Before parting with that case, I should say that the Court there proceeded to sever the covenants and to grant an injunction, not to restrain the defendant from carrying on any other business whatsoever, but framed so as to give what was felt to be a reasonable protection to the plaintiffs and no more. The plaintiffs waived an option which they possessed to extend the period of service for an extra five years, and the injunction then was granted for the remaining period of unextended time. . . .

The case before me is, therefore, one in which it would be proper to grant an injunction unless to do so would in the circumstances be tantamount to ordering the defendant to perform her contract or remain idle or unless damages would be the more appropriate remedy.

With regard to the first of these considerations, it would, of course, be impossible to grant an injunction covering all the negative covenants in the contract. That would, indeed, force the defendant to perform her contract or remain idle; but his objection is removed by the restricted form in which the injunction is sought. It is confined to forbidding the defendant, without the consent of the plaintiffs, to render any services for or in any motion picture or stage production for any one other than the plaintiffs.

It was also urged that the difference between what the defendant can earn as a film artiste and what she might expect to earn by any other form of activity is so great that she will in effect be driven to perform her contract. That is not the criterion adopted in any of the decided cases. The defendant is stated to be a person of intelligence, capacity and means, and no evidence was adduced to show that, if enjoined from doing the specified acts otherwise than for the plaintiffs, she will not be able to employ herself both usefully and remuneratively in other spheres of activity, though not as remuneratively as in her special line. She will not be driven, although she may be tempted, to perform the contract, and the fact that she may be so tempted is no objection to the grant of an injunction. This appears from the judgment of Lord St. Leonards in *Lumley v. Wagner* [*supra*], where he used the following language:

> It was objected that the operation of the injunction in the present case was mischievous, excluding the defendant J. Wagner from performing at any other theatre while this Court had no power to compel her to perform at Her Majesty's Theatre. It is true, that I have not the means of compelling her to sing, but she has no cause of complaint, if I compel her to abstain from the commission of an act which she has bound herself not to do, and thus possibly cause her to fulfil her engagement. The jurisdiction which I now exercise is wholly within the power of the Court, and being of opinion that it is a proper case for interfering, I shall leave nothing unsatisfied by the judgment I pronounce. The effect too of the injunction, in restraining J. Wagner from singing elsewhere may, in the event—that is a different matter—of an action being brought against her by the plaintiff, prevent any such amount of vindictive damages being given against her as a jury might probably be inclined to give if she had carried her talents and exercised them at the rival theatre: the injunction may also, as I have said, tend to the fulfilment of her engagement; though, in continuing the injunction, I disclaim doing indirectly what I cannot do directly.

With regard to the question whether damages is not the more appropriate remedy, I have the uncontradicted evidence of the plaintiffs as to the difficulty of estimating the damages which they may suffer from the breach by the defendant of her contract. I think it is not inappropriate to refer to the fact that, in the contract between the parties, in clause 22, there is a formal admission by the defendant that her services, being "of a special, unique, extraordinary and intellectual character" gives them a particular value "the loss of which cannot be reasonably or adequately compensated in damages" and that a breach may "cost the producer great and irreparable injury and damage," and the artiste expressly agrees that the producer shall be entitled to the remedy of injunction. Of course, parties cannot contract themselves out of the law; but it assists, at all events, on the question of evidence as to the applicability of an injunction in the present case, to find the parties formally recognizing that in cases of this kind injunction is a more appropriate remedy than damages.

Furthermore, in the case of *Grimston v. Cuningham*, [[1894] 1 Q.B. 125 (D.C.)] which was also a case in which a theatrical manager was attempting to enforce against an actor a negative stipulation against going elsewhere, Wills J. granted an injunction, and used the following language:

> This is an agreement of a kind which is pre-eminently subject to the interference of the Court by injunction, for in cases of this nature it very often happens that the injury suffered in consequence of the breach of the agreement would be out of all proportion to any pecuniary damages which could be proved or assessed by a jury. The circumstance affords a strong reason in favour of exercising the discretion of the Court by granting an injunction.

I think that that applies to the present case also, and that an injunction should be granted in regard to the specified services.

Then comes the question as to the period for which the injunction should operate. The period of the contract, now that the plaintiffs have undertaken not as from October 16, 1936, to exercise the rights of suspension conferred upon them by clause 23 thereof, will, if they exercise their options to prolong it, extend to about May, 1942. . . . The Court should make the period such as to give reasonable protection and no more to the plaintiffs against the ill effects to them of the defendant's breach of contract. The evidence as to that was perhaps necessarily somewhat vague. The main difficulty that the plaintiffs apprehend is that the defendant might appear in other films whilst the films already made by them and not yet shown are in the market for sale or hire and thus depreciate their value. I think that if the injunction is in force during the continuance of the contract or for three years from now, whichever period is the shorter, that will substantially meet the case.

The other matter is as to the area within which the injunction is to operate. The contract is not an English contract and the parties are not British subjects. In my opinion all that properly concerns this Court is to prevent the defendant from committing the prohibited acts within the jurisdiction of this Court, and the injunction will be limited accordingly.

NOTE and QUESTIONS

1. Branson J. stated that it would "be impossible to grant an injunction covering all the negative covenants in the contract . . . but this objection is removed by the restricted form in which the injunction is sought". Why was the plaintiff able to disregard some of the negative covenants in the contract and thereby enforce a different contract than the one originally created? The terms of the injunction awarded forbade the defendant ". . . to render any service for or in any motion picture or stage production for any one other than the plaintiffs". Suppose that Mrs. Nelson was employed by a rival film producer as a script writer. Would she be in breach of the injunction? If so, was the injunction granted too broad?

2. Mrs. Nelson's stage name was Bette Davis. Do you think that the injunction merely "tempted" her to perform the contract, or "drove" her to perform it?

In *Warren v. Mendy*, [1989] 1 W.L.R. 853 (C.A.), where a boxing manager sought an injunction to restrain a "talented young boxer" from acting in breach of the management agreement, Nourse J.A. commented on the judgment of Branson J. in the *Warner Bros.* case (at 865):

> . . . that judge's view that Miss Bette Davis might employ herself both usefully and remuneratively in other spheres of activity for a period of up to three years appears to have been extraordinarily unrealistic. It could hardly have been thought to be a real possibility that an

actress of her then youth and soaring talent would be able to forego screen and stage for such a period.

In *Warren v. Mendy*, the court re-cast the test for the award of the injunction (at 867) as follows:

> . . . [T]he court ought not to enforce the performance of the negative obligations if their enforcement will effectively compel the servant to perform his positive obligations under the contract. Compulsion is a question to be decided on the facts of each case, with a realistic regard for the probable reaction of an injunction on the psychological and material, and sometimes the physical, need of the servant to maintain the skill or talent. The longer the term for which an injunction is sought, the more readily will compulsion be inferred. Compulsion may be inferred where the injunction is sought not against the servant but against a third party if either the third party is the only other available master or if it is likely that the master will seek relief against anyone who attempts to replace him. An injunction will less readily be granted where there are obligations of mutual trust and confidence, more especially where the servant's trust in the master may have been betrayed or his confidence in him has genuinely gone.

3. In *Detroit Football Co. v. Dublinski*, [1956] O.R. 744, the plaintiff had originally applied for an injunction preventing Dublinski from playing football with the Toronto Argonauts. McRuer C.J.H.C. initially refused the application and distinguished *Warner Brothers Pictures Inc. v. Nelson* on the basis (*inter alia*) that the plaintiff and the Toronto Argonauts played in different competitions for different audiences, so that Dublinski's proposed contract with the Canadian team would not result in any loss or injury beyond that which would occur if he remained idle. On appeal, the Ontario Court of Appeal awarded damages based *inter alia* on the difference between Dublinski's salary and the cost of acquiring and paying for his replacement. At that stage the award of an injunction was no longer in issue, as Dublinski's contract with the plaintiff had expired. See [1957] O.R. 58 (C.A.). In *Kapp v. B.C. Lions Football Club* (1967), 61 W.W.R. 31 (B.C. S.C.), Dryer J. refused an application for an injunction preventing the defendant from suspending the plaintiff pursuant to their contract and replacing his name on the list of suspended players of the C.F.L. To grant the application would have been tantamount to specific performance of the contract and there was a distinction to be drawn between the enforcement of a contract for personal services and the enjoining of a negative covenant. This same point emerges from *Yashin v. National Hockey League* (2000), 192 D.L.R. (4th) 747 (Ont. S.C.J.), where Cunningham J. stated (in what was admittedly *obiter dicta*) that while the Ottawa Senators and the League could not force Yashin to play ice hockey for the Senators, there was no basis on which Yashin could insist on being entitled to play for another team in the League during the final year of a contract under which he was meant to be playing for the Senators. Where the employer is part of a monopoly, there is nothing wrong with a contract that in effect requires performance or non-participation unless it is possible to mount a successful restraint of trade argument.

(e)   INTERIM AND INTERLOCUTORY INJUNCTIONS

We have already observed that it is possible to obtain injunctive relief before trial. An interim or interlocutory injunction is therefore a very potent weapon in the hands of a plaintiff who attempts to restrain the defendant's activities immediately, rather than wait until trial. Because pre-trial relief is an extraordinary measure, courts are loath to grant interim or interlocutory injunctions notwithstanding the very wide language of the Judicature Acts and equivalent legislation. In Alberta, for example, s. 13(2) of the Judicature Act, R.S.A. 2000, c. J-2, provides (in part) as follows:

> [An] injunction may be granted . . . by an interlocutory order of the Court in all cases in which it appears to the Court to be just or convenient that the order should be made, and the order may be made either unconditionally or on any terms and conditions the court thinks just. . . .

Similarly worded sections are found in the equivalent legislation of the other common law provinces, although Manitoba has a unique provision limiting the use of injunctions which would have the effect of denying freedom of speech or enforcing contracts of personal service (Court of Queen's Bench Act, C.C.S.M., c. C280, ss. 57(1) and 56(1).)

ZIPPER TRANSPORTATION SERVICES LTD. v. KORSTROM

(1997), 122 Man. R. (2d) 139 (Q.B.)

NURGITZ J. The plaintiff makes application for an interlocutory injunction to enforce a non-competition clause contained in an agreement between the plaintiff and the personal defendant David W. Korstrom.

The agreement bearing date June 29, 1989 provides for the defendant Korstrom to be an independent contractor of the plaintiff in supplying courier, messenger, cartage and delivery services for various customers of the plaintiff.

In July of 1996 the defendant Korstrom began to service the account of Piston Ring Service, a longtime customer of the plaintiff.

On August 5, 1997 the defendant Korstrom gave notice that he was terminating the "independent contractor agreement" and the following day Piston Ring provided notice to the plaintiff that its services would no longer be required. There is no dispute but that the defendant Korstrom, either in his personal capacity or by means of a corporate entity 3663931 Manitoba Ltd., is now providing the courier, messenger, cartage and delivery service to Piston Ring.

The plaintiff relies upon paragraph 11.02 of the agreement:

The Driver:

(a) for a period of twelve (12) months after the termination of this agreement, (for any reason whatsoever) shall not either individually or in partnership or in conjunction with any persons, firm, partnership, association, syndicate, company, or corporation as employee, principal, agent, shareholder or in any manner whatsoever, carry on or be engaged in or be concerned with or interested in, or advise, lend money to, guarantee the debts or obligations of or permit his name or any part thereof to be used or employed by any person or persons, firm, partnership, association, syndicate, company or corporation engaged in any courier, messenger, delivery or cartage business which services customers and accounts in the City of Winnipeg, in the Province of Manitoba, which is the same or similar to the business carried on by the company;

or

(b) shall within 5 business days of the termination of this Agreement (for any reason whatsoever) pay the Company the sum of THIRTY THOUSAND ($30,000.00) DOLLARS.

(c) if the Driver does not within 5 business days of termination of this Agreement pay the Company the amount set out in subparagraph 11.02(b), he shall be bound to carry out his obligations pursuant to subparagraph 11.02 (a) hereof.

The defendant did not pay the sum of $30,000 pursuant to paragraph 11.02(b) and at issue is only the question of the enforceability of 11.02(a).

The plaintiff relies on *Miller v. Toews*, [1991] 2 W.W.R. 604 (C.A.), a case involving sale of a restaurant business, the sales agreement containing a covenant not to compete where Twaddle, J.A. said:

In cases of this kind, there is less need for a judge to concern himself with proof of irreparable harm or to weigh the balance of convenience nicely. The point was put in unambiguous terms of Megarry, J. (as he then was), in *Hampstead v. Diomedous*, [1968] 3 All E.R. 545, when he said (at p. 550):

> "Where there is a plain and uncontested breach of a clear covenant not to do a particular thing, and the covenantor promptly begins to do what he has promised not to do, then in the absence of special circumstances it seems to me that the sooner he is compelled to keep his promise the better . . . I see no reason for allowing a covenantor who stands in clear breach of an express prohibition to have a holiday from the enforcement of his obligation until the trial. It may be that there is no direct authority on this point; certainly none has been cited. If so, it is high time that there be such authority; and now there is."

In *Elsley v. J.G. Collins Insurance Agencies Limited,* [*supra*] Dickson, J. (as he then was) dealt with principles to be applied in considering restrictive covenants especially where it was a relationship of employer/employee. . . . [See Chapter 13, section 2(a).]

Applying the test as set out in *Elsley v. J. G. Collins Insurance Agencies Limited*, I find that the covenant as contained in paragraph 11.02 of the agreement of June 29, 1989 is reasonable and understandably the kind of covenant that would be required in order to afford protection to the plaintiff. The reasonableness having been established, I find that it is not contrary to the public interest to enforce this covenant and accordingly that the clause in question is valid and enforceable. Accordingly, the plaintiff will have its injunctive relief.

The plaintiff will have its costs.

[Korstrom appealed to the Manitoba Court of Appeal.]

ZIPPER TRANSPORTATION SERVICES LTD. v. KORSTROM

(1998), 126 Man. R. (2d) 126 (C.A.)

LYON J.A. [delivering the judgment of the court] . . . Counsel [for Korstrom] argues that this is essentially an employer-employee contract with the employee being in an unequal bargaining position to the employer. She submits that the motions court judge erred

(1) in finding that the restrictive covenant was reasonable; and

(2) in not considering either irreparable harm or balance of convenience.

On the first point, she argues that the restrictive covenant should be confined to Zipper's own clients. As it stands, it effectively prohibits Korstrom from working for any company in the same or similar business to Zipper's in Winnipeg. The clause, she states, is not severable and cannot be read down and must fail because of its excessive reach.

As for the test of balance of convenience, there is no evidence at this stage that Zipper will regain the Piston Ring runs now operated by Korstrom. Therefore, if the injunction is upheld, no benefit will accrue to Zipper by regaining the Piston Ring runs. Indeed, if the injunction is upheld, it is possible that neither party may enjoy Piston Ring's business and both could lose. Accordingly, she submits the injunction, while causing major economic harm to Korstrom, confers no benefit on Zipper.

Zipper's submission

Counsel for Zipper contends that the trial judge did consider balance of convenience and irreparable harm, relying on *Miller v. Toews* (1990), 70 Man. R. (2d) 4 (C.A.). Korstrom, he states, cannot tip the balance of convenience in his favour by his own breach of the covenant. He concedes, however, that if Korstrom had paid the $30,000 within five days as required by the covenant, this action would not have been brought. He described Korstrom's conduct as a flagrant breach for which the defendant should not be granted a "holiday" by the Court.

Decision

In *Apotex Fermentation Inc. et al v. Novopharm Ltd. et al.* (1994), 95 Man. R. (2d) 241 (C.A.), this Court endorsed the proposition that (at p. 244):

> ... the three requirements which are usually necessary to support injunctive relief are to be considered, not as separate hurdles but as interrelated considerations. The approach which will normally be taken by the court in considering an interlocutory injunction is well set forth in R.J. Sharpe, *Injunctions and Specific Performance* (2nd ed. 1992) at pp. 2, 32, 34:
>
> > The terms "irreparable harm", "status quo" and "balance of convenience" do not have a precise meaning. They are more properly seen as guides which take colour and definition in the circumstances of each case. More importantly, they ought not to be seen as separate, water-tight categories. These factors relate to each other, and strength on one part of the test ought to be permitted to compensate for weakness on another. It is not clear that the *Cyanamid*, [[1975] A.C. 396] approach allows for this and the decision suggests a misleading mechanical approach. The Manitoba Court of Appeal has quite properly held that "it is not necessary . . . to follow the consecutive steps set out in the *American Cyanamid* judgment in an inflexible way; nor is it necessary to treat the relative strength of each party's case only as a last step in the process."
> >
> > .....
> >
> > The checklist of factors which the courts have developed—relative strength of the case, irreparable harm and balance of convenience—should not be employed as a series of independent hurdles. They should be seen in the nature of evidence relevant to the central issue of assessing the relative risks of harm to the parties from granting or withholding interlocutory relief."

[The court doubted the reasonableness of the covenant but found it unnecessary to rule on that question.]

It is trite law that if the damages suffered by the employer are ascertainable and monetarily compensable, no injunction should lie. In this case, the evidence thus far would seem to indicate that the records of both parties would enable the court, at trial, to determine with some precision the quantification of any damages caused to Zipper. This finding is underlined by the admission of Zipper that had Korstrom paid $30,000 (presumably as liquidated damages or penalty), Zipper would not have initiated this action.

It therefore follows that there is no irreparable harm resulting to Zipper if the injunctive relief is denied. In *RJR-MacDonald Inc. v. Canada (Attorney General)*, [1994] 1 S.C.R. 311, the Supreme Court stated as follows, at pp. 334:

> *Metropolitan Stores* [[1987] 1 S.C.R. 110] adopted a three-stage test for courts to apply when considering an application for either a stay or an interlocutory injunction. First, a preliminary assessment must be made of the merits of the case to ensure that there is a serious question to

be tried. Secondly, it must be determined whether the applicant would suffer irreparable harm if the application were refused. Finally, an assessment must be made as to which of the parties would suffer greater harm from the granting or refusal of the remedy pending a decision on the merits. It may be helpful to consider each aspect of the test and then apply it to the facts presented in these cases.

And at pp. 340-41:

Beetz J. determined in *Metropolitan Stores*, at p. 128, that "[t]he second test consists in deciding whether the litigant who seeks the interlocutory injunction would, unless the injunction is granted, suffer irreparable harm". The harm which might be suffered by the respondent, should the relief sought be granted, has been considered by some courts at this stage. We are of the opinion that this is more appropriately dealt with in the third part of the analysis. Any alleged harm to the public interest should also be considered at that stage.

.....

"Irreparable" refers to the nature of the harm suffered rather than its magnitude. It is harm which either cannot be quantified in monetary terms or which cannot be cured, usually because one party cannot collect damages from the other. Examples of the former include instances where one party will be put out of business by the court's decision (*R.L. Crain Inc. v. Hendry* (1988), 48 D.L.R. (4th) 228 (Sask. Q.B.)); where one party will suffer permanent market loss or irrevocable damage to its business reputation (*American Cyanamid, supra*); or where a permanent loss of natural resources will be the result when a challenged activity is not enjoined (*MacMillan Bloedel Ltd. v. Mullin*, [1985] 3 W.W.R. 577 (B.C. C.A.)). The fact that one party may be impecunious does not automatically determine the application in favour of the other party who will not ultimately be able to collect damages, although it may be a relevant consideration (*Hubbard v. Pitt*, [1976] Q.B. 142 (C.A.)).

And at p. 342:

The third test to be applied in an application for interlocutory relief was described by Beetz J. in *Metropolitan Stores* at p. 129 as: "a determination of which of the two parties will suffer the greater harm from the granting or refusal of an interlocutory injunction, pending a decision on the merits". In light of the relatively low threshold of the first test and the difficulties in applying the test of irreparable harm in Charter cases, many interlocutory proceedings will be determined at this stage.

I am not satisfied that the motions court judge took into consideration the tests of irreparable harm and balance of convenience. It seems evident at this stage of the proceedings that no irreparable harm will be caused to Zipper before trial if injunctive relief is denied. By contrast, if the injunction is upheld, Korstrom will effectively be prohibited from making a living in the courier or trucking business in the city of Winnipeg and will suffer markedly greater harm. Ironically, the injunction, by denying him employment in his chosen trade, could further result in his being without funds to pay any damages which might be awarded against him at the eventual trial. Beggaring Korstrom serves no interest, save revenge. Accordingly, applying the third test, the balance of convenience favours the refusal to grant injunctive relief.

As previously indicated, it is in the interest of both parties to bring this matter to trial as quickly as possible to settle all outstanding issues.

Accordingly, I would allow the appeal and set aside the injunctive order against Korstrom, with costs to the appellant.

[Helper and Monnin JJ.A. concurred.]

NOTE and QUESTIONS

1. How would you assess the difference in approach between the judgment at first instance and that on appeal? Is the Court of Appeal concerned with the breadth of the restrictive covenant and its impact on the defendant? Would the plaintiff have been better advised (as in *Warner Bros. v. Nelson*) to have framed its application for interlocutory relief more narrowly? What role do the merits of the claim for a permanent injunction play in the availability of interlocutory relief in each judgment? If not here, under what circumstances might a restraining order of this kind be issued? The motions court judge seems particularly concerned with not allowing a former "employee" to breach his contract by using to his profit the trade connection he initially secured through his relationship with the plaintiff. That seems a laudable concern but it ultimately does not carry the day in the Court of Appeal. Why not? When might it?

2. On this topic generally, see Berryman, *The Law of Equitable* Remedies (2000), Chapter 2. For a very useful and stimulating theoretical perspective, see Hammond, "Interlocutory Injunctions: Time for a New Model" (1980), 30 U.T.L.J. 241.

3. For a recent example of where the Supreme Court endorsed a deviation from the test of a "serious case to be tried" in favour of a more searching "strong cause" threshold requirement, see *Z.I. Pompey Industrie v. ECU-Line N.V.* (2003), 224 D.L.R. (4th) 577 (S.C.C.). The context was a forum selection clause in a bill of lading, and the Court held that to too readily award interlocutory injunctions against the operation of such clauses would in effect write them out of contracts thereby creating commercial uncertainty.